CHAPTER 3

Fasteners, Gaskets, Sealants, and Bearings

INTRODUCTION   The automobile is a complex combination of many parts. These parts are held together by fasteners such as screws, bolts, and rivets. When parts are placed together near or around oil, different gaskets, sealants, and seals are used to keep the oil from leaking. Also, many vehicle parts move next to stationary parts. Bearings must be used to reduce friction between these parts. The purpose of this chapter is to examine the many types of fasteners, gaskets, sealants, seals, and bearings used on the automobile.

OBJECTIVES   After reading this chapter, you should be able to:

- Identify the different types of bolts, washers splines, keyways, snap rings, and screws used on the automobile.

- Determine how to select torque specifications for different size bolts.

- Examine the purposes and styles of different types of gaskets.

- Define the purposes of and the types of seals, sealants, and gaskets that are used on the automobile.

- Define the parts of a bearing.

- Identify the types of bearings used on the automobile, including ball, roller, and thrust bearings.

- Identify various service and diagnostic procedures used when working with fasteners, gaskets, seals, and bearings.

 SAFETY CHECKLIST

When working with fasteners, gaskets, sealants, and bearings there are several important safety checks to remember.

✔ Always wear safety glasses around the shop.
✔ Always pull the wrench toward you rather than push it away from you.
✔ Tighten bolts and nuts only to their torque specification.

✔ Always use tools that are in good condition.
✔ Make sure that all tools used in the shop are clean and free of grease.
✔ Be careful not to cut your hand on the sharp edges of the engine.
✔ Be careful not to inhale fumes or odors from chemical gaskets.

3.1 FASTENERS

Fasteners are those objects that secure or hold together parts of the automobile. Examples include bolts, nuts, washers, snap rings, splines, keyways, rivets, and setscrews. Actually, there are many types of fasteners. In this chapter certain fasteners will be defined. Their applications will also be illustrated.

Threaded Fasteners

One of the most popular types of fastener is the *threaded fastener*. Threaded fasteners include bolts, nuts, screws, and similar items that allow the technician to install or remove parts easily. Examples of threaded fasteners are shown in *Figure 3–1*.

Types of Threaded Fasteners

Figure 3–2 shows a few of the more common types of fasteners used on the automobile. These include bolts, studs, setscrews, cap screws, machine screws, and self-tapping screws.

Bolts have a head on one end and threads on the other. Their length is measured from the bottom surface of the head to the end of the threads. Most automotive bolts have a hexagon head.

Studs are rods with threads on both ends. They are used where bolts are not suitable. For example, studs are used on parts that must be removed frequently for service, such as the exhaust manifold. One end of the stud is screwed into a threaded or tapped hole in the exhaust manifold. The other end of the stud passes through the flange on the exhaust pipe. A nut is then used on the projecting end of the stud to hold the parts together.

Setscrews are used to prevent rotary motion between two parts such as a pulley and shaft. Setscrews are either headless or have a square head. As shown in Figure 3–2, they are available with a variety of points.

Cap screws pass through a clearance hole in one member of a part. They then screw into a threaded or tapped hole in another part.

Machine screws are similar to cap screws, but they have a flat point. The threads on a machine screw run the entire length of the stem or shank. Several types of heads are used, including the round, flat, fillister, Torx, and oval heads.

Self-tapping screws are used to fasten sheet-metal parts or to join light metal, wood, or plastic together. These screws form their own threads in the material as they are turned. They are available with different head shapes and points.

Torx head bolts are also used throughout the automotive industry. A star-shaped wrench or screwdriver tip is used to loosen and tighten the bolts.

Bolt Identification

To identify the type of threads on a bolt, bolt terminology must be defined. The bolt has several parts, as shown in *Figure 3–3*. The *head* is used to *torque* or tighten the bolt.

FIGURE 3–1. Many types of threaded fasteners are used on the automobile. Bolts, nuts, and screws are all threaded fasteners.

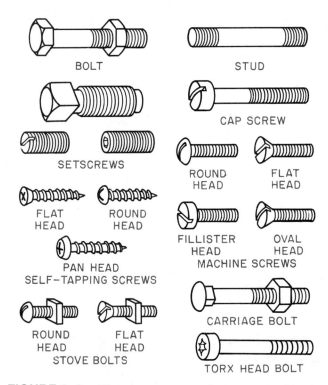

FIGURE 3–2. These are common fasteners used in the automotive industry.

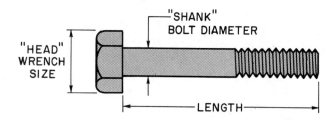

FIGURE 3–3. Bolts are identified by defining the head size, the shank size, the number of threads per inch, and the length. Tensile strength markings are also indicated by the number of lines on the head of the bolt.

CHAPTER 2

Safety in the Automotive Shop

INTRODUCTION Most of the service and maintenance work done on the automobile is completed in the automotive shop. Because of the complexity of the automobile, many tools, instruments, and machines are used for service. In addition, there are many people in the service area. Complex tools, machines, and instruments, coupled with many people, make the automotive shop a likely place for accidents to happen. In addition, the automobile has very explosive and flammable fuel that can be dangerous. Safety in the automobile shop has become a very important aspect in the total study of automotive technology.

Safety has become such an important part of our society and industry that the federal government established the Occupational Safety and Health Act of 1970. This act is known as OSHA. This act makes safety and health on the job a matter of law for four million American businesses. It also applies to automotive service shops.

OSHA provides several things. It establishes standards and regulations for safety. It improves unsafe and unhealthful working conditions. It also assists in establishing plans for safe working conditions.

OBJECTIVES After reading this chapter, you should be able to:

- Define and illustrate common safety equipment used in the automobile service area.

- List various safety rules used in any automobile service area.

- Define OSHA.

- Develop certain safety attitudes concerning safety in the automobile service area.

- List the possible danger areas for common chemicals and accidents in the automobile service area.

2.1 SAFETY IN THE WORKPLACE

Types of Hazards

Since the 1970s, a great deal of research has been done on the various environmental factors related to safety in the workplace. These factors can cause sickness, impaired health, significant discomfort to workers, and even death in some cases. These environmental hazards can be classified as chemical, physical, ergonomic, and biological. Within the automotive area, chemical, physical, and ergonomic factors are the ones most often found.

Chemical hazards arise from high concentrations of airborne mists, vapors, gases, or solids in the form of dust or fumes. Chemically hazardous substances include cleaning solvents, gasoline, asbestos, and antifreeze.

Physical hazards arise from excessive levels of noise, vibration, temperature, and pressure and also include cutting and crushing hazards. Examples include stamping, grinding, exhaust heat, coolant-system pressures, and electrical shock.

Ergonomic hazards are defined as conditions that relate to one's physical body or to motion. (The field of ergonomics is defined as the study of human characteristics for the appropriate design of the living and working environment.) Ergonomic hazards include poorly designed tools or work areas, improper lifting or reaching, poor lighting, and so on.

Occupational Safety and Health Act

About one of every four workers today is exposed to known health and safety hazards on the job. Thus, a need exists for a program to monitor, control, and educate the workforce about safety. In 1970, the Occupational Safety and Health

Act (*OSHA*) was enacted by the federal government. OSHA was designed to

assure safe and healthful working conditions for working men and women; by authorizing enforcement of the standards developed under the Act; by assisting and encouraging the States in their efforts to assure safe and healthful working conditions by providing research, information, education, and training in the field of occupational safety and health.

Safety standards have been established that will be consistent across the country. It is the employers' responsibility to provide a place of employment that is free from all recognized hazards and that will be inspected by government agents knowledgeable in the law of working conditions.

Because of the nature of the automotive industry, especially in the area of automotive service and repair, all safety and health issues have been established and are now controlled by OSHA.

2.2 SAFETY EQUIPMENT

To have safe working habits in the automotive shop, it is important to know the safety equipment. Several important types of safety equipment are used. Some examples of safety equipment are safety glasses, fire extinguishers, airtight containers, gasoline containers, gloves, first-aid boxes, and ear protectors.

Safety Glasses

One of the most important aspects of safety is to have all shop personnel wear *safety glasses*. Many service technicians have been permanently blinded because they thought safety glasses were not important.

There are many types of safety glasses. An important rule to remember is that all safety glasses should have safety glass and some sort of side protection. *Figure 2–1* illustrates several types of approved safety glasses. In some cases, the entire face may need to be protected. *Figure 2–2* shows a full face shield. This type of shield may be needed when grinding or cleaning carbon from valves.

When purchasing safety glasses, always remember to buy a pair that feels comfortable. If the glasses are not comfortable, people have a tendency to either remove them or wear them on the top of the head. Both situations leave the eyes totally unprotected.

Eyewash Fountains

Various types of damage can be done to the eyes within the automotive shop. Some of the more common eye hazards include:

1. A blow from a blunt or sharp object

2. Foreign bodies in the eye

3. Thermal burns of the eye

FIGURE 2–1. Many types of safety glasses are approved for use in industry. Select a pair that has safety glass and side protectors and is comfortable so you can keep it on without discomfort. Certain models of safety glasses have vents to reduce fogging. *(Courtesy of Sellstrom Manufacturing)*

sanitary or storm sewer facilities. All solvents, liquids, fuels, and the like should be disposed of by being delivered to a waste-liquids collection agency. Check your school, city, or state rules and ordinances for the correct location.

Material Safety Data Sheets (MSDS)

People involved with safety in the automotive shop (especially those who order the chemicals) must be able to recognize the many chemicals that are used as raw materials in the automotive industry. Today, this information can be obtained from the Material Safety Data Sheet *(MSDS)*. The information on the MSDS comes from the Department of Labor. The MSDS is a summary of important health and safety information on any chemical. It includes any hazardous ingredients, physical/chemical properties, fire/explosion hazard data, reactivity data, health hazards, control measures, and precautions for use.

Electrical Safety

Within the automotive shop there are many electrical hazards. These would be classified as physical hazards. Often electrical tools are used for grinding, drilling, honing, and so on. When using these tools, there is always a possibility of serious shock or electrocution. Poor insulation or defective wiring in tools or frayed electrical cords can cause electrical shock. The severity of the electrical shock is related to the amount and length of the electrical current the victim receives. To reduce the risk of electrical shock from power tools, the following should be considered:

1. Use three-prong grounded plugs or double-insulated equipment. Never cut the grounded prong if the outlet has only two prongs. If an adaptor must be used, the pigtail wire (usually green) should be attached to the screw holding the faceplate of the wall socket.

2. Make sure all of the wires to the power tools are not frayed and are in good condition. Buy tools that have the double insulation around the wires.

3. Make sure there is a ground fault circuit protector. This device operates on the current flowing through a person's body during an accidental line to ground fault. It is attached to the panel circuit breaker or is an integral part of the electrical outlet. This fast-acting circuit breaker will rapidly stop current flow to the tool, and the operator will receive only a modest electrical shock.

4. If an electrical tool, such as a drill or hand grinder seems to be shorting out (you might hear electricity arcing inside the tool housing or receive a shock), shut the tool off immediately. Have an electrician check the tool for shorting or grounding.

Other Rules to Follow

The following list of rules should always be observed when working in an automotive service area.

1. Make sure all hand tools are in good condition. Using a damaged hand tool or the incorrect tool for the job may result in a severe hand injury.

2. When lifting a car by using an air or hydraulic jack, always make sure the jack is centered. When the vehicle is raised, always use safety *jack stands* under the car. Never go under a car without safety jack stands in place. A set of safety jack stands is shown in ***Figure 2–16***.

3. Never wear jewelry such as rings, bracelets, necklaces, or watches when working on a car. In addition, if your hair is long, always tie it back. These items can easily catch on moving parts or cause an electrical short and cause serious injury.

4. Never use compressed air to remove dirt from your clothing or you may get dirt in your eyes. Also, never spin bearings with compressed air. If the bearing is damaged, one of the steel balls may come loose and cause serious injury. Damage to the bearing may also result.

5. Always be careful where welding sparks are falling. Sparks can cause a fire or explosion if dropped on flammable materials.

6. When using any machines, such as hydraulic presses, hoists, drill presses, or special equipment, make absolutely certain that all operational procedures are studied

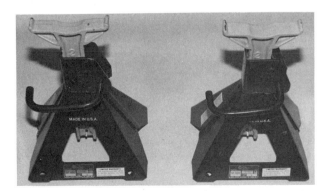

FIGURE 2–16. Always support the raised vehicle with safety jack stands. Never work under a vehicle without the proper safety jack stands in place under the vehicle.

Carbon Monoxide

It is important to be familiar with *carbon monoxide* when working with the automobile. Carbon monoxide is always given off from the exhaust of running engines. Most new cars have exhaust emission controls. However, poorly running new cars and most older cars give off carbon monoxide. The gas is odorless and colorless. You may not even be aware that it is there. If taken in through normal breathing, carbon monoxide can cause death. The presence of carbon monoxide in a person can be noticed by the following symptoms:

1. Headaches

2. Nausea

3. Ringing in the ears

4. Tiredness

5. Fluttering heart

If any of these symptoms appear, it is very important to get fresh air immediately.

To eliminate the possibility of carbon monoxide poisoning, always have good ventilation and make sure the engine is properly exhausted in the shop. Carbon monoxide is eliminated by using the proper exhaust systems as shown in *Figure 2–15*.

Carbon Monoxide Monitors

Carbon monoxide is easy to detect in an automotive repair shop by use of various monitors. Some are able to read direct amounts of carbon monoxide in the air, while others have audible alarms that alert the user when the danger level is reached. Most of these monitors are small and easy to hold in one's hand.

Asbestos

One chemical often found in automotive shops is asbestos. *Asbestos* is a term used to describe a number of naturally occurring, fibrous materials. Asbestos fibers are commonly found in various types of brake pads, in clutches, and in other similar materials. (Always clean all brake and clutch dust and powder using an approved vacuum container to limit asbestos into the lungs.) Asbestos has also been used extensively as a building material and as an insulator.

Asbestos has been shown to be associated with the development of a variety of diseases that can cause cancer. One of the most common types is called mesothelioma, or asbestos-caused cancer. This disease and others, such as asbestosis, causes cancer of the lungs. The asbestos fibers cause a scarring of the lungs. Also, asbestos inhaled into the lungs can cause increased injury to the lining of the lung's air passages. The effects of asbestos may not appear immediately, but may take a month to 45 years after exposure to cause damage. There seems to be no recovery from asbestos damage. In some cases, persons who were exposed to asbestos for only a few days have been afflicted.

Disposal of Solvents

Many laws and ordinances strictly prohibit pouring chemical solvents into sinks or floor drains that connect with

FIGURE 2–15. Always use the proper exhaust piping when running a vehicle in the shop. Also, remember to turn on the fan to remove exhaust from the vehicle. *Reminder:* Carbon monoxide is a colorless, odorless gas that can cause death.

A socket fits over the head, which enables the bolts to be tightened. Common USC (U.S. Customary) and metric sizes for bolt heads include those shown in *Figure 3–4*. The sizes are given in fractions of an inch and in millimeters (metric). Some of the USC and metric sockets are very close in size. It is important not to use metric sizes for USC bolts or USC sizes for metric bolts. The bolt heads may be damaged.

The second part of the bolt is called the *shank*. The shank is the distance between the bolt head and the thread. The shank is illustrated in Figure 3–3. Bolts are identified by the shank size or the outer diameter of the threads. Common bolt shank or diameter sizes include 1/4, 5/16, 3/8, 7/16, 1/2, 9/16, and 5/8 inches in diameter.

Another way of identifying the size of a bolt is by the number of *threads per inch* as shown in *Figure 3–5*. This number can be determined by using a ruler and counting the number of threads per inch for each bolt.

The number of threads per inch can also be measured by a *screw-pitch gauge*, *Figure 3–6*. The tool consists of numerous blades with thread-shaped teeth on one edge. The blades are inserted over the thread until one that fits the thread exactly is found. The number stamped on the blade

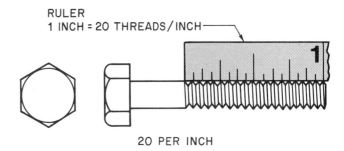

FIGURE 3–5. Threads on bolts can be measured by using a ruler and counting the number of threads per inch.

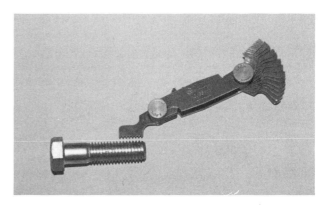

FIGURE 3–6. A screw-pitch gauge is used to determine the exact number of threads per inch.

that matches the thread indicates the number of threads per inch of the bolt.

The size of a bolt can also be expressed in terms of its length. A ruler is used to measure the length from the end of the bolt to the bottom surface of the head. Bolts are commonly manufactured in lengths with 1/2-inch increments or sizes.

Figure 3–7 shows how the identifying features of a bolt are combined to specify a bolt size. For example, a bolt identified as 3/8 × 16 × 1 1/2 has a shank diameter of 3/8 inch; there are 16 threads per inch; and the bolt is 1 1/2 inches long.

Bolts can have different numbers of threads per inch and still have the same shank size. For example, a 3/8-inch bolt

COMMON ENGLISH (U.S. CUSTOMARY) HEAD SIZES	COMMON METRIC HEAD SIZES
WRENCH SIZE	WRENCH SIZE
3/8"	9 mm
7/16"	10 mm
1/2"	11 mm
9/16"	12 mm
5/8"	13 mm
11/16"	14 mm
3/4"	15 mm
13/16"	16 mm
7/8"	17 mm
15/16"	18 mm
1"	19 mm
1 1/16"	20 mm
1 1/8"	21 mm
1 3/16"	22 mm
1 1/4"	23 mm
1 5/16"	24 mm
1 3/8"	26 mm
1 7/16"	27 mm
1 1/2"	29 mm
	30 mm
	32 mm

FIGURE 3–4. There are many standard bolt head sizes. Both USC and metric sizes are shown.

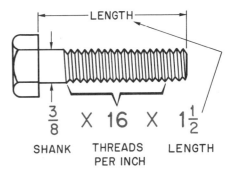

FIGURE 3–7. When a bolt is identified, the shank size, the number of threads per inch, and the length are all used to determine its size.

SAE GRADE MARKINGS	⬡	⬡	⬡	⬡	⬡
DEFINITION	No lines — unmarked indeterminate quality SAE Grades 0-1-2	3 Lines — common commercial quality Automotive & AN Bolts SAE Grade 5	4 Lines — medium commercial quality Automotive & AN Bolts SAE Grade 6	5 Lines — rarely used SAE Grade 7	6 Lines — best commercial quality N.A.S. & Aircraft Screws SAE Grade 8
MATERIAL	Low Carbon Steel	Med. Carbon Steel Tempered	Med. Carbon Steel Quenched & Tempered	Med. Carbon Alloy Steel	Med. Carbon Alloy Steel Quenched & Tempered
TENSILE STRENGTH	65,000 psi	120,000 psi	140,000 psi	140,000 psi	150,000 psi

FIGURE 3–8. Bolts are identified by hardness. The more lines shown on the head of the bolt, the stronger the bolt.

can have either 16 or 24 threads per inch. The greater the number of threads per inch, the finer the thread. The finer the thread, the greater its holding ability.

Unified and American National Thread Sizes

Threads can also be identified by referring to them as either coarse threads or fine threads. Coarse threads identified as *NC* or *UNC* (National Coarse or Unified National Coarse) are used for general-purpose work. They are very adaptable for cast iron and soft metals where rapid assembly or disassembly is required. Fine threads identified as *NF* or *UNF* (National Fine or Unified National Fine) are used where greater resistance to vibration is required. NF threads are also used where greater strength or holding force is necessary.

Bolt Hardness and Strength

Bolts are made from different metals having various degrees of hardness. Softer metal or harder metal can be used to manufacture the bolts. Under certain conditions, the standard hardness used in a particular situation is not sufficient. Therefore, bolts are made with different hardnesses and strengths for use in different situations. Bolts are marked with lines on the top of the head to identify *bolt hardness* as shown in *Figure 3–8*. The number of lines on the head of the bolt is related to the *tensile strength*. As the number of lines increases, so does the tensile strength. Tensile strength is the amount of pressure per square inch the bolt can withstand before breaking when being pulled apart. The harder or stronger the bolt, the greater the tensile strength.

Prevailing Torque Fasteners

A *prevailing torque nut* is designed to develop an interference between the nut and bolt threads. This interference is most often accomplished by distorting the top of an all-metal nut or by using a nylon patch in the middle of the threads. A nylon insert may also be used as a method of interference between the nut threads and the threads of the tapped hole. *Figure 3–9* shows examples of various prevailing torque fasteners used on automobiles.

Metric Threads

Metric threads are being used increasingly on all cars manufactured in the United States. This means that metric bolts will also be used more often. Many vehicles have transmissions and other automotive components made in metric sizes. Because metric threads and fasteners are being used more often, it is important that they not be mixed with bolts that have standard threads.

For metric bolts, the shank and length are measured in millimeters. In addition, to determine the type of thread used,

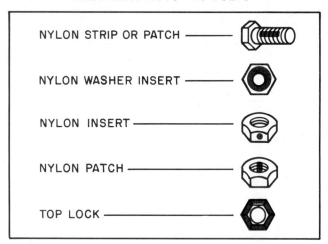

PREVAILING NUTS AND BOLTS

NYLON STRIP OR PATCH

NYLON WASHER INSERT

NYLON INSERT

NYLON PATCH

TOP LOCK

FIGURE 3–9.   These are examples of various prevailing threaded fasteners.

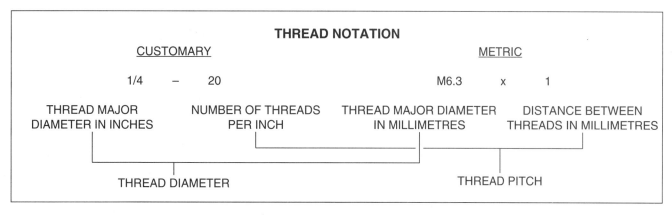

FIGURE 3–10. Customary and metric thread notation.

the distance between threads is measured in millimeters. Thus, the bolts are considerably different from inch or USC sizes. *Figure 3–10* shows an example of the difference between the USC and metric thread pitch.

The hardness or strength of metric bolts is indicated by using a *property class* number stamped on the head of the bolt as shown in *Figure 3–11*.

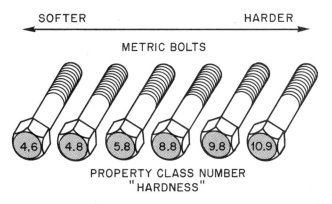

FIGURE 3–11. Metric bolts are rated in hardness by using the property class number.

Determining Torque on Customary Bolts

All bolts and nuts used on the automobile should be torqued or tightened to specifications. Many repair manuals list all common torque specifications. A torque wrench is used to measure the tightening force. These specifications are known as *standard bolt and nut torque specifications* shown in *Figure 3–12*. The correct torque in pound-inches and/or pound-feet should always be followed when tightening bolts and nuts. If the bolt is tightened to a value less than that given by the specification, the bolt may vibrate loose. The bolt can also be tightened too much. This may cause the threads to strip or the bolt to break. In either case, damage to other automobile parts can result. Always torque all bolts and nuts to the manufacturer's specifications. If there are no specifications listed, use the torque specifications shown in Figure 3–12.

Torque-to-Yield Bolts

Manufacturers also use bolts that are called *torque-to-yield bolts*. Torque-to-yield bolts are those that have been tightened at the manufacturer to a preset yield or stretch point. Often these torque-to-yield bolts are used on main or

STANDARD BOLT AND NUT TORQUE SPECIFICATIONS								
SIZE NUT OR BOLT		TORQUE (lb-ft)	SIZE NUT OR BOLT		TORQUE (lb-ft)	SIZE NUT OR BOLT		TORQUE (lb-ft)
SHANK SIZE	THREADS PER INCH		SHANK SIZE	THREADS PER INCH		SHANK SIZE	THREADS PER INCH	
1/4	– 20	7–9	7/16	– 20	57–61	3/4	– 10	240–250
1/4	– 28	8–10	1/2	– 13	71–75	3/4	– 16	290–300
5/16	– 18	13–17	1/2	– 20	83–93	7/8	– 9	410–420
5/16	– 24	15–19	9/16	– 12	90–100	7/8	– 14	475–485
3/8	– 16	30–35	9/16	– 18	107–117	1	– 8	580–590
3/8	– 24	35–39	5/8	– 11	137–147	1	– 14	685–695
7/16	– 14	46–50	5/8	– 18	168–178			

FIGURE 3–12. All bolts and nuts have a standard bolt and nut torque specification. All bolts and nuts should be properly torqued unless stated differently in the maintenance manual.

connecting rod bearings. Usually the automotive manufacturer recommends that these bolts be replaced with new ones or torqued by using a torque angle meter. A torque angle meter measures the amount of twisting on the bolt by measuring the number of degrees of turning.

Determining Torque on Metric Bolts

Metric bolts and nuts are torqued in newton-meters (N·m). For reference and a comparison between newton-meters and pound-inches or pound-feet use the following:

Multiply	By	To Get
pound-inches	0.112 98	newton-meters
pound-feet	1.355 8	newton-meters

Figure 3–13 shows the standard metric torque readings in newton-meters for various sizes of bolts. In addition, note that prevailing torque fasteners also have a set of standard torque specifications. It is important to always torque bolts and nuts to the manufacturer's specifications. If no specifications are listed, then you can use the torque specifications shown in Figure 3–13.

Nuts

Many types and styles of nuts are used on the automobile. **Figure 3–14** illustrates some common types of nuts. The most common type is called the hex style.

Hex nuts are classified as regular or heavy. They are used on all high-quality work. These nuts are easy to tighten with wrenches in close or tight places.

Slotted hexagon nuts, also called castellated nuts, are used where there is danger of the nuts coming off. For example, vibration may cause the nuts to loosen. A cotter pin is used to lock the nut in place.

Jam hexagon nuts are thinner than regular nuts. They are used where height is restricted or as a means of locking the working nut in place.

Square nuts are regular or heavy unfinished nuts. They are used with square-head bolts in rough assembly work such as assembly of body parts.

Lock nuts have a self-contained locking feature to prevent back-off rotation. They are designed with under-sized threads and plastic or fiber inserts. This design acts as a gripping force.

Free-running seating lock nuts are applied over hexagon nuts. These nuts have a concave surface that flattens when it contacts the top of the hexagon nut. This causes the threads to deflect. The nut binds on the bolt and prevents it from coming loose.

Spring nuts are made of thin spring metal. They are designed with formed prongs as shown in Figure 3–14. Spring nuts are used in sheet-metal construction where high torque is not required.

Crown nuts are used where the ends of the external threaded part must be concealed or hidden or where the nut must be attractive.

Wing nuts have two arms (or projections) to aid hand tightening and loosening. Typically, these nuts are tightened and loosened frequently. High torque is not a consideration.

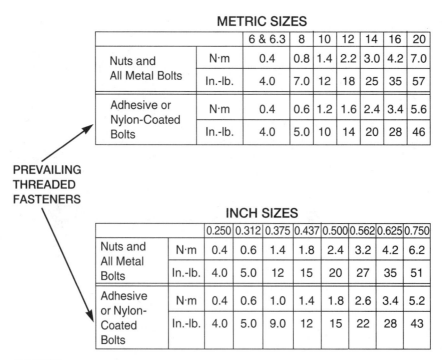

METRIC SIZES

		6 & 6.3	8	10	12	14	16	20
Nuts and All Metal Bolts	N·m	0.4	0.8	1.4	2.2	3.0	4.2	7.0
	In.-lb.	4.0	7.0	12	18	25	35	57
Adhesive or Nylon-Coated Bolts	N·m	0.4	0.6	1.2	1.6	2.4	3.4	5.6
	In.-lb.	4.0	5.0	10	14	20	28	46

PREVAILING THREADED FASTENERS

INCH SIZES

		0.250	0.312	0.375	0.437	0.500	0.562	0.625	0.750
Nuts and All Metal Bolts	N·m	0.4	0.6	1.4	1.8	2.4	3.2	4.2	6.2
	In.-lb.	4.0	5.0	12	15	20	27	35	51
Adhesive or Nylon-Coated Bolts	N·m	0.4	0.6	1.0	1.4	1.8	2.6	3.4	5.2
	In.-lb.	4.0	5.0	9.0	12	15	22	28	43

FIGURE 3–13. These charts show torque specifications for English, metric, and prevailing threaded bolts.

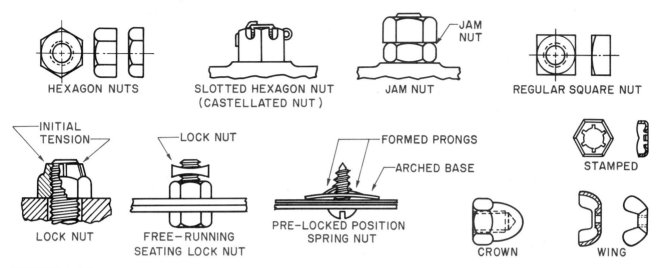

FIGURE 3–14. Many styles of nuts are used on the automobile. Each style has a specific purpose and application.

Washers

Most washers are placed on bolts to lock the bolt and keep it from coming loose. Several types of washers are used for locking bolts in place as shown in *Figure 3–15*. Washers are also used for other reasons. For example, copper washers are used to aid in sealing the bolt to a structure. These are called *compression washers*. They may help reduce oil leakage when the threads of the bolt are in or near oil. Certain cars use copper washers on oil pans to eliminate leakage. Flat washers are also used to help spread out the load of tightening the nut to prevent the nut from digging into the material when it is tightened.

Snap Rings

Snap rings are used to prevent gears and pulleys from sliding off the shaft. There are two types of snap ring: the external and internal snap ring. *Figure 3–16* illustrates snap ring pliers being used to install a snap ring.

Splines

Splines are defined as external or internal teeth cut in a shaft. When a shaft must be inserted into a gear, pulley, or other part, and the part must be able to move on the shaft, a spline will be used. The output shaft on the transmission has an external spline. The end of the drive shaft connected to the transmission has an internal spline. This allows the

PLAIN   SPRING LOCK   EXTERNAL TOOTH LOCK   INTERNAL

FIGURE 3–15. Washers are typically used to lock the bolts to the structure to keep them from coming loose and to prevent damage to softer metal parts.

FIGURE 3–16. Snap rings can be external or internal types. They are used to keep gears and pulleys on the shaft.

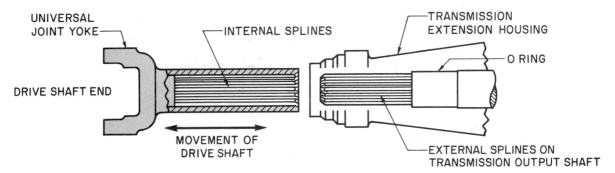

FIGURE 3–17. Splines, both external and internal, are used to lock rotating shafts together while allowing slide (axial) movement between shafts.

drive shaft to move along the axis when the rear wheels go over a bump in the road. See *Figure 3–17*.

Keyways

Keyways are used to lock parts together by fitting a key between a slot on the shaft and a pulley. *Figure 3–18* shows a keyway application. Keyways are used to lock the front drive pulley on the engine to the engine crankshaft. The only difference between a keyway and a spline is that, on a spline, the hub or pulley can move parallel or axially along the shaft.

Helicoils

A common problem is threads stripping inside an engine block, cylinder head, or other structure. This problem is usually caused by too high a torque or by threading the bolt into the hole incorrectly. Rather than replacing the block or cylinder head, the threads can be replaced by the use of threaded inserts or *helicoils*. *Figure 3–19* illustrates a helicoil.

The procedure for replacing damaged threads as shown in *Figure 3–20* is as follows: (1) the damaged threads are drilled out to a specific size depending on the helicoil size; (2) the hole is tapped, using the outside diameter of the helicoil; (3) the helicoil is threaded into the new, larger threads. The inside of the helicoil provides the new threads for the bolt. There are many sizes of helicoils. The tap, drill sizes, and necessary tools are all included in the helicoil kit.

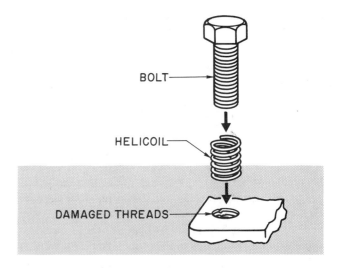

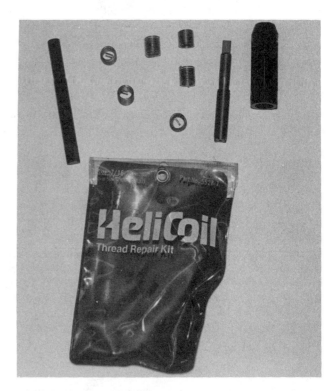

FIGURE 3–19. Helicoils are used to replace damaged internal threads in engine blocks, cylinder heads, and other structures.

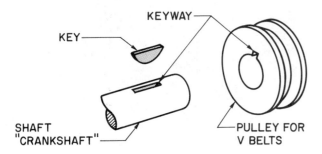

FIGURE 3–18. Keyways are used to hold parts to shafts so that the part and shaft rotate as one unit.

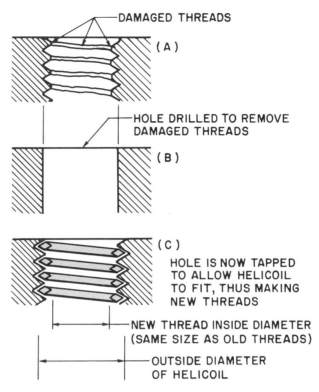

FIGURE 3–20. To replace (A) damaged threads, (B) drill out old thread, (C) tap new threads, and install helicoil.

CAR CLINIC

PROBLEM: Leaky Bolts Sealed with Teflon Tape

A vehicle was recently overhauled. However, there are several leaks coming from the oil pan. Why are there leaks, and how can they be eliminated?

SOLUTION:

Often oil will leak around the threads of a bolt, especially if the bolt threads come into contact with a cavity that has oil in it, as oil pan bolts often do. Many manufacturers (especially of foreign cars) allow the bolt to come into contact with the crankcase area. To eliminate the bolt from leaking oil around the threads, always wrap the bolt threads with Teflon tape. This method will seal the bolt and stop all oil leakage around the bolt threads.

3.2 GASKETS, SEALS, AND SEALANTS

Purpose of Gaskets

Gaskets are used on the automobile to prevent leakage of gases, liquids, or greases between two parts bolted together. Examples of gaskets are shown in *Figure 3–21*. Gaskets are placed between two mating machined surfaces. Bolts or fasteners are then tightened according to standard specifications. Gaskets are used between the cylinder head and the engine block or between the water pump housing and the engine.

Gaskets are designed for a particular job. For this reason, gaskets are made from different materials. Some of the more common materials used are cork, synthetic rubber, steel, copper, and asbestos.

Compression Gaskets

Compression gaskets are designed to be squeezed during tightening, *Figure 3–22*. Tightening a compression gasket seals the parts to contain high-pressure gases. Compression gaskets are used most often for head gaskets. As the cylinder head is torqued to specifications, the head gasket is squeezed and forms a good seal for high compression during combustion. Some spark plugs also use compression gaskets as washers to seal in the high-compression gases from compression and combustion.

Seals

There are many uses for *seals* in the automobile. Seals are devices placed on rotating shafts to prevent oil, gases, and other fluids from escaping. For example, seals are used on the front and back axles, crankshafts, water pump shafts, and many other locations throughout the vehicle.

Seals are designed to withstand high pressures and to seal fluids in the engine. Seals are made of felt, synthetics, rubber,

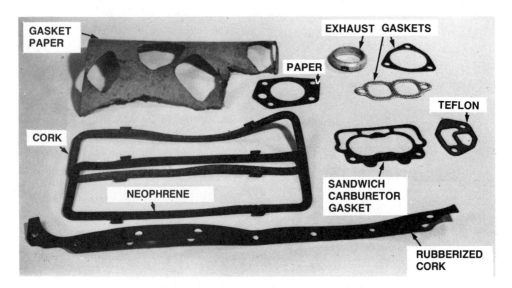

FIGURE 3–21. Many gaskets are used on the automobile engine to seal parts that are bolted together. Gaskets keep oil, grease, and gases from escaping and dirt from entering the engine. *(Courtesy of Gilles,* Engine Mechanics Diagnosis and Repair, *Delmar Publishers Inc.)*

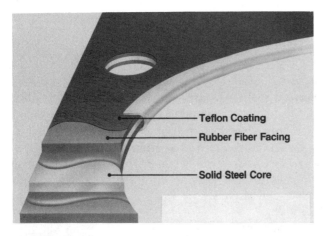

FIGURE 3–22. Compression gaskets are used to seal high pressures produced from the cylinder during the compression and power strokes. *(Courtesy of Fel-Pro Incorporated)*

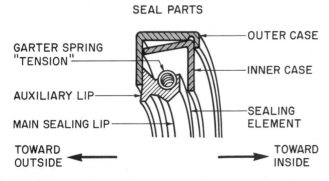

FIGURE 3–23. Seals must be placed so that the main sealing lip points toward the liquid, gas, or pressure being contained.

fiber, or leather. The parts of the common seal are shown in *Figure 3–23*.

The outer case is usually pressed into the housing that contains the stationary part. The inner case holds the parts of the seal. Seals are sometimes designed with one or two lips. The lips are pressed against the rotating part. This pressure causes the sealing action. Springs may be added to the lip tension so that higher pressures can be contained.

Seals should always be installed according to the manufacturer's specifications. In general, the sealing lip should always be placed toward the fluid or pressure being contained.

Sealants

Several sealants can be used in the automotive industry. *Sealants* are similar to a thick liquid that hardens after being placed on the metal. Some sealants are called form-in-place gaskets. Certain sealants are used to seal between metal surfaces. There are many brands of seals available, made from many materials. Silicon is one of the most popular sealant materials. Use sealants only where the manufacturer recommends them. If not recommended, use the correct gasket for the parts to be sealed.

Chemical Gaskets

Several chemical gaskets are currently used in the automotive shop. See *Figure 3–24*. These chemical gaskets, also called form-in-place gaskets or sealants are typically categorized into two types:

- those that harden in the presence of oxygen, or air and

- those that harden in the absence of oxygen, or air, also called anaerobic.

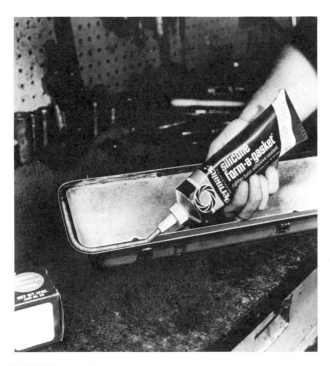

FIGURE 3–24.   Silicon and RTV sealants are considered chemical gaskets. *(Courtesy of the Loctite Corporation Automotive and Consumer Group)*

One type of sealant that hardens in the presence of oxygen is a silicon gasket called an *RTV* (room temperature vulcanizing) *sealant*. RTV sealants dry or cure from the moisture and oxygen in the air. This type of chemical gasket is clear in color; however, sometimes a dye is added to make it black, red, orange, blue, or some other color. This type of silicon gasket is used to form a rubberlike gasket on engine parts that have thin flexible flanges (such as a valve cover). See *Figure 3–25*. Generally, RTV sealants have a shelf life of about a year. After that time the sealant will not cure properly. Certain types of RTV sealants are not compatible with the oxygen sensor used on automobiles. Always check the container. It should say "O2 Sensor Safe."

RTV sealant is normally applied in a continuous bead about 1/8 in. in diameter. Make sure to go around all bolt holes and to torque within 10 minutes after application. Also make sure that the RTV sealant is wet at the time the parts are mated.

The second type of chemical gasket is called the *anaerobic sealant*. This sealant cures to a plasticlike substance in the absence of air. Generally it is applied to very smooth, mating parts. For example, this sealant can be used between a water pump and the engine block. It will cure easily when the two parts are torqued to specifications. Generally, a 1/16 in. diameter bead is placed on the mating surface for correct sealing.

Gasket Sealants

Several types of gasket sealants are also on the market. A *gasket sealant* is a chemical (usually a black, thick liquid) placed on the gasket to (1) help paper and cork gaskets seal better or (2) position gaskets during installation.

Antiseize Lubricants

Often bolts in various engine applications can become "cold-welded" together, because the bolt and internal threads are continuously exposed to heating and cooling. Once the bolts have cold-welded it is almost impossible to remove them. To eliminate this action, antiseize lubricants are placed on the bolt threads before installation. Antiseize lubricants are most often used on bolts and nuts that are attached to the exhaust system.

Locking Thread Sealants

Locking thread sealants are used on various engine bolts to keep the bolts from loosening. In this case an anaerobic chemical sealant is used. This sealant, when placed on bolt threads, acts as a glue to keep the bolt from coming loose. Typically, two types are used: (1) a blue locking thread sealant is used when the parts may need to be disassembled at a later date (2) a red locking thread sealant is used when the parts will not need to be disassembled at a later date.

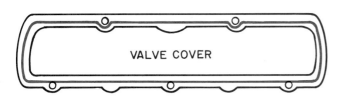

FIGURE 3–25.   Apply a 1/4" bead of RTV sealant on the valve cover as shown.

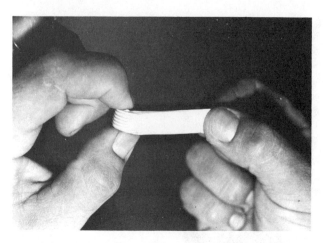

FIGURE 3–26. Teflon tape can be used to seal fluids from seeping past threads. *(Courtesy of Gilles,* Engine Mechanics Diagnosis and Repair, *Delmar Publishers Inc.)*

Teflon Tape Sealant

Various bolts come in contact with a liquid such as oil or antifreeze. These bolts must be sealed to stop the liquid from seeping past the threads. They are usually sealed with Teflon tape as shown in *Figure 3–26*. Generally, the Teflon tape is stretched around the threaded part of the bolt before installation.

Static and Dynamic Seals

Seals are classified as either static or dynamic. O rings are examples of static seals. An *O ring* is placed between two

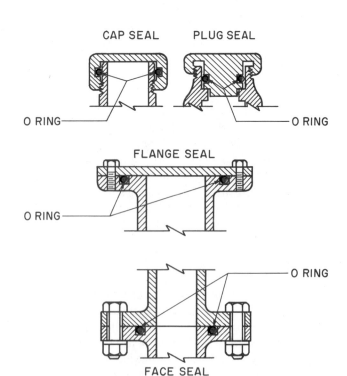

FIGURE 3–27. O rings are considered static seals. Static seals are placed between two stationary parts to eliminate leakage. *(Courtesy of Federal-Mogul Corporation)*

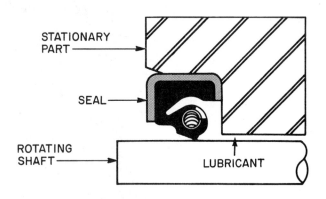

FIGURE 3–28. Dynamic seals are used to seal fluids where one part is stationary and one part is rotating. *(Courtesy of CR Industries)*

stationary parts where a fluid passes between the parts. The O rings shown in *Figure 3–27* keep the fluid from leaking out of the two stationary objects.

Dynamic seals provide sealing between a stationary part and a rotating part. A dynamic seal is shown in *Figure 3–28*. In this case, the fluid is contained by the seals. Note that the lip rides directly on the rotating shaft.

Labyrinth Seals

Labyrinth seals are used on high-speed shafts or where the lips of the seal can cause excessive wear on the shaft. A labyrinth seal is shown in *Figure 3–29*. As liquid is moved toward the sealing area, it contacts the first labyrinth. Centrifugal force causes the fluid to spin outward into the upper groove. If the pressure is great enough to push the fluid farther, the next labyrinth seal will also produce a sealing effect. Because of centrifugal forces, the fluid has difficulty going toward the center of the shaft. This action keeps the fluid from leaking out of the area. The labyrinth seals will not work if a fluid touches the seal directly when the shaft is not rotating. There is no contact of the seal to the shaft;

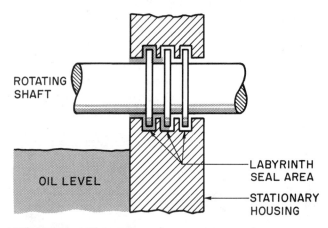

FIGURE 3–29. Labyrinth seals use centrifugal force to spin the fluid outward. Because of this action, the fluid cannot pass through to the outside.

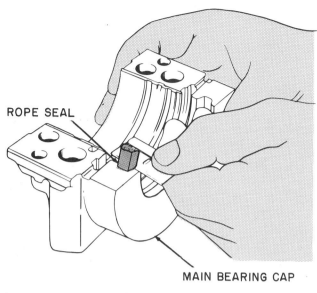

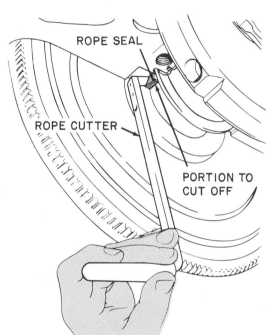

FIGURE 3–30. After the seal has been lightly pounded into the groove, the seal is cut flush with the block or main bearing cap. *(Courtesy of Oldsmobile, Division of General Motors)*

therefore, oil will leak out. Certain foreign car manufacturers use labyrinth seals on the crankshaft to seal oil in the crankcase area. In this case, the seal will not wear on the metal, eliminating possible damage to this area of the crankshaft.

Rope Seals

Another type of seal (often used on the crankshaft) is called the *rope seal*. This seal is made of two separate parts. One part fits into a groove in the block, and one part fits into a groove in the rear main bearing cap. Rope seals look much like a thin, flexible rope. They are installed by first soaking the seal in oil for several minutes and then lightly pounding it into the grooves using a special tool. Once installed and trimmed to the correct length (see *Figure 3–30*) the rope seal takes a more precise shape when the main bearing cap is torqued to its specification.

One advantage of using rope seals is that they can be replaced without removing the crankshaft. With a set of special tools, the old seal can be removed and a new seal installed. See *Figure 3–31*.

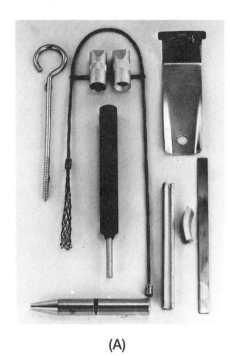

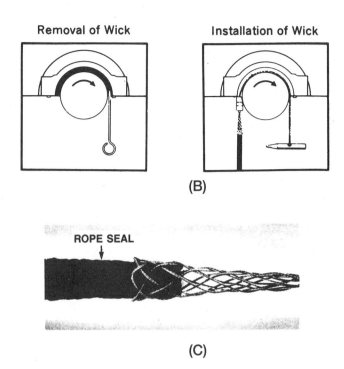

Removal of Wick   Installation of Wick

(B)

ROPE SEAL

(A)   (C)

FIGURE 3–31.   (A) A tool kit for replacing rope seals. (B) Removal and installation of rope seals with crankshaft in engine. (C) Rope seal. *(Courtesy of K.D. Tools)*

CAR CLINIC

PROBLEM: Bad O Ring Causes Vehicle to Smoke

A Honda engine has heavy smoking immediately after startup. The smoke lasts about 10 minutes. The rings and valves have been checked and seem OK. What could be the problem?

SOLUTION:

This smoking is a common problem in engines that have precombustion chambers. There is a rubber O ring that seals the chamber where the auxiliary intake valves are located. The O rings have been known to harden over time. The hardened O rings do not seal very well, and oil can seep into the combustion chambers. The problem goes away when the engine heats up and the parts expand enough to make a good seal. The solution is to replace the rubber O rings.

3.3   BEARINGS

Purpose of Bearings

Bearings are used in the automobile to reduce friction between moving parts and stationary parts. A secondary purpose is to remove the heat produced by unavoidable friction. There are two types of bearings: *friction bearings* and *anti-*

friction bearings. Friction bearings have no rotating or moving parts, whereas antifriction bearings use small rollers or steel balls to reduce friction. The two types are shown in *Figure 3–32*. With friction bearings, rotating or moving parts slide on the stationary part. Antifriction bearings contain balls or rollers to support the rotating part.

Friction Bearings

Friction bearings will produce more heat and frictional losses in the engine than other types of bearings. However, this type of bearing usually requires less maintenance and can be replaced easily. When friction bearings are used, the load of the moving part is supported by a layer of oil between the load and the stationary part. The oil molecules act like small ball bearings.

There are two types of friction bearings, *Figure 3–33*. One type is a two-piece bearing that is used on the crankshaft of most gasoline engines. The second type is a one-piece bearing. It is commonly known as a *bushing*.

Bushings are held in place by pressing them into the block or stationary part. In an automobile, bushings are used on the camshaft, some generator and alternator shafts, the starter armature shaft, and the distributor shaft.

Friction Bearing Design

Friction bearings have a strong back or shell, generally made of steel, *Figure 3–34*. A thin intermediate layer of copper-lead is added to the shell. On top of this is an anti-friction material called Babbitt. *Babbitt* is composed mostly of tin or lead, occasionally silver, or it may be an aluminum alloy. This material may be only 1/1000 of an inch thick.

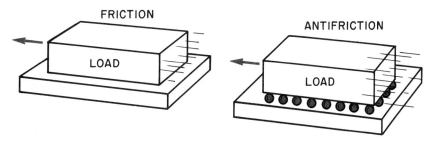

FIGURE 3–32. There are two types of bearings. Friction bearings have oil between the moving and stationary parts. Antifriction bearings have balls or rollers between the moving and stationary parts.

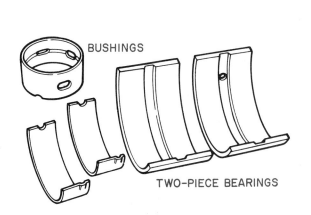

FIGURE 3–33. Bushings are designed as one piece, while bearings are designed with two pieces. *(Courtesy of Federal-Mogul Corporation)*

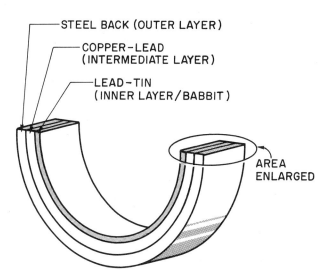

FIGURE 3–34. Friction bearings are made of many materials. The more common materials are shown.

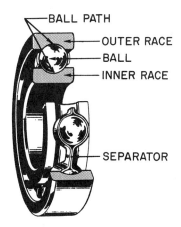

FIGURE 3–35. Parts of a standard ball bearing. *(Courtesy of CR Industries)*

Antifriction Bearings

Antifriction bearings are used where a greater load is placed on the rotating shaft. *Figure 3–35* illustrates the parts of the common ball bearing.

Antifriction bearings rely on rolling friction for operation. This type of friction offers less resistance to rotation, resulting in less frictional loss.

There are many designs for antifriction bearings. *Figure 3–36* illustrates both ball and roller bearing types. In reference to Figure 3–36, a radial load is a load perpendicular to the axis of the shaft. An *axial load* is a load parallel to the axis of the shaft. An axial load may also be called a *thrust load*. *Thrust bearings* are designed to reduce friction on the rotating shaft when thrust forces are produced parallel to the axis of the shaft. See *Figure 3–37*.

1. BALL BEARINGS:
ECONOMICAL, WIDELY USED

2. ROLLER BEARINGS:
FOR SHOCK, HEAVY LOAD

SINGLE ROW RADIAL
FOR RADIAL LOADS.

CYLINDRICAL
FOR RELATIVELY HIGH SPEEDS.

SINGLE ROW ANGULAR CONTACT
FOR RADIAL AND AXIAL LOADS.

NEEDLE
FOR LOW SPEEDS,
INTERMITTENT LOADS.

AXIAL THRUST
FOR AXIAL LOADS.

TAPERED
FOR HEAVY AXIAL LOADING.

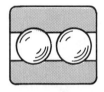
DOUBLE ROW
FOR HEAVIER RADIAL LOADS.

SPHERICAL
FOR THRUST LOADS AND LARGE
AMOUNTS OF ANGULAR
MISALIGNMENT.

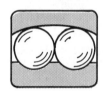
SELF-ALIGNING
FOR RADIAL AND AXIAL LOADS,
LARGE AMOUNTS OF ANGULAR
MISALIGNMENT.

SPHERICAL THRUST
TO MAINTAIN ALIGNMENT UNDER
HIGH THRUST LOADS AND
HIGH SPEEDS.

FIGURE 3–36.   Both ball and roller bearings are considered antifriction. Many styles and types are used in the automobile.

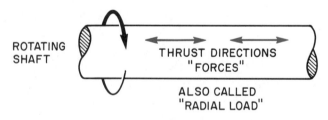

FIGURE 3–37.   Thrust is produced when there is a pressure or load that is parallel to the axis of the rotating shaft.

Sealed Bearings

At times bearings are used in applications where the bearings must seal as well as reduce friction. Sealed bearings not only reduce friction but also keep dust, dirt, or other debris away from the internal parts of the bearing. *Figure 3–38* shows a type of sealed bearing in which the seal is housed within the bearing. A plate on the outside of the bearing keeps out dirt. The seal has four spots that seal. The seal also uses a labyrinth to keep oil in the bearing and dirt out of the bearing.

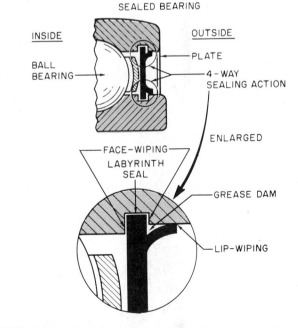

FIGURE 3–38.   Seals are also used in bearings to keep dirt out and lubrication in. In this case, a labyrinth seal design is used.

Problems, Diagnosis and Service

⏵ ⏹ SAFETY PRECAUTIONS ⏹ ◁

1. When tightening bolts and nuts, make sure the wrench is always placed solidly on them. If the wrench slips off the bolt when you are tightening it, your knuckles and fingers may be injured.
2. Always wear safety glasses when tightening or loosening bolts and nuts, especially when using air tools.
3. When using pullers, remember that you are applying very high forces and pressures on the bolts, nuts, and equipment. Always be sure the pullers are securely fastened before beginning.
4. Never use an air gun with high pressure to dry off a spin roller or ball bearings. The roller or ball bearings may fly out under the high speed and injure you.
5. Make sure to immediately clean up any grease spilled on the floor so that you won't slip and injure yourself.
6. Tighten bolts and nuts only to their specified torque. If the bolt breaks, the wrench may slip and injure your hands.
7. When tightening cap and machine screws, always use a screwdriver that is in good condition so it won't slip off the head of the screw.
8. Make sure all tools used in the shop are clean and free of grease.
9. When removing or installing snap rings, always be sure the snap ring pliers have a solid hold on the snap ring. The snap ring may slip off and injure your face or eyes.
10. When placing gaskets on various engine parts, be careful not to cut your hand on the sharp edges of of the sealing surface where the gasket is being placed.

PROBLEM: Bad Bearings

Many types of roller and ball bearings are used in the automobile. For example, the front and rear wheels use bearings. These bearings will often begin to make a soft rumbling noise when they get bad.

DIAGNOSIS

If a bearing is thought to be bad several checks can be made. These include:

1. Remove all weight and load from the bearing in question.
2. Slowly rotate the wheel or other component that is supported by the bearing.

3. Check to see if there is a rough feeling, coarse sound, or slight vibration as the component is rotated on the bearing. If these conditions are found, the bearing most likely damaged. If the bearing is good there should be absolutely no rough feeling, coarse sound, or any vibration as the component is turned on the rotating shaft.
4. Most bearings are protected from dirt by various types of seals. Seals generally harden with age. Under normal conditions, however, seals should not harden and should remain flexible. A seal can harden because of excessive temperatures near it. Always investigate if it is suspected that excessive temperature caused the seal to harden.

SERVICE

Service on bearings can be of several types. If the bearing is determined to be bad or damaged, it must be replaced. Always check the condition of the seals that protect the bearings as well. Make sure the replacement bearing and seal are exact replacements. Other service checks on roller and ball bearings and seals include:

1. Roller and ball bearings should be repacked with grease at regular intervals. Repacking of bearings usually includes the following procedure:
   a. Clean the bearing thoroughly with solvent.
   b. Dry the bearing completely.
   c. Force grease into the bearing by placing a sufficient amount of grease in one hand. With the bearing in the other hand, force the grease into the bearing. Make sure the grease has completely surrounded the balls or rollers and comes out the other side.
   d. Repeat the previous step on the opposite side of the bearing.

2. *Brinelling*, small dents in the bearing race, can be caused by improper bearing installation, such as impacts on the outer race. Brinelling will normally cause severe bearing damage.

3. Contamination of bearings usually shows up as small scratches, pitting, and scoring along the raceway. To prevent contamination, always keep all parts of the bearing free of dirt, dust, and other particles.

4. Misalignment is another cause of bearing failure. When the balls or rollers of a bearing are running from one side of the race to the other, one race may be misaligned. Misalignment causes uneven load distribution, which causes excess friction and heat buildup. In this case, the bearing was probably installed incorrectly. To prevent misalignment, always follow the manufacturer's recommended procedure for installation.

5. When installing bearings or bushings, always keep the parts well lubricated during assembly and keep them free of all dirt.

6. Some bearings may have the inside race pressed onto the center shaft. If this is the case, always use a hydraulic press and follow the manufacturer's recommendations when removing and installing the bearings.

7. When installing seals, make sure the seal is not cocked or installed at an angle. A cocked seal may leak oil readily and cause dirt to get into the bearings. When a seal has been cocked or replaced incorrectly, it must be removed and replaced with a new seal. Seal installation must be done with the proper tools to avoid damaging the metal that supports the seal.

8. Always place a seal on a rotating shaft so the lip of the seal is toward the fluid being contained or toward the dirt that is being held back.

PROBLEM: Broken, Loose, or Stripped Bolts

Many types of bolts and nuts are used to fasten components together on the automobile engine. Problems often occur in which the bolts either break, become loose, or are stripped.

DIAGNOSIS

When automotive fasteners become broken, loose, or are damaged, check for the following:

1. Make sure the damaged fastener is the correct one recommended by the manufacturer.

2. Make sure the bolt or nut was tightened to the correct torque specification.

3. Make sure the correct size lock washer is being used.

4. Make sure the length of the bolt is correct. It may be too short for the component being secured or too long for the hole.

5. Look for signs of wear, vibration, or damage near and around the component being checked.

SERVICE

Various service tips are important when working with automotive fasteners. Some include:

1. Always use the standard bolt and nut torque specifications when tightening bolts and nuts.

2. When replacing bolts that are stripped or broken, always use a bolt having the same hardness.

3. Never mix metric and USC threads.

4. Never use a USC wrench with a metric bolt or nut.

5. Always determine the torque of the bolt by the number of threads per inch or per millimeter and the shank size

of the bolt. Never use the head size of the bolt to determine the torque specification.

6. Never use an NC bolt in place of an NF bolt of the same shank size.

7. Always use a lock washer on bolts that may vibrate loose. Make sure the lock washer is the correct size and type recommended by the manufacturer.

8. When removing parts that use a keyway, always store the key in a safe place.

9. Use a helicoil to replace damaged threads.

10. When a bolt breaks use the following procedure to remove the part of the bolt still in the hole:

   a. Soak the bolt in penetrating oil.

   b. Try to remove the broken bolt using a needle nose pliers or vise-grip pliers. These tools can be used only if part of the bolt is sticking out of the hole.

   c. If the bolt is too tight or not enough of the bolt is sticking out of the hole, carefully use a small center punch and a hammer, tapping the bolt on the side, to try to remove the bolt. *Figure 3–39* shows a broken bolt being removed by this method.

   d. If the center punch cannot remove the bolt, use a screw extractor as shown in *Figure 3–40*. First drill a hole in the center of the broken bolt. Carefully tap the correct size screw extractor into the hole. Using a socket and ratchet or equivalent wrench unscrew the extractor and broken bolt as one piece. Now remove the screw extractor from the broken bolt, using a vise-grip pliers or other suitable gripping device.

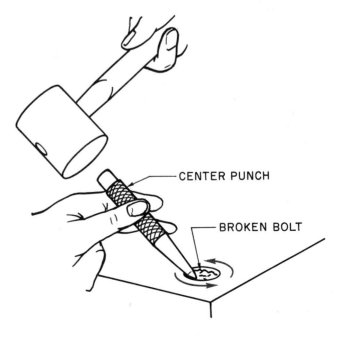

CENTER PUNCH

BROKEN BOLT

FIGURE 3–39.   At times a broken bolt can be removed by using a center punch to loosen the bolt.

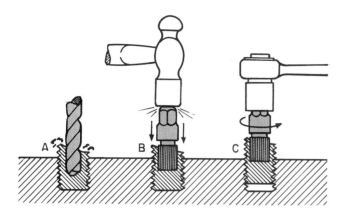

FIGURE 3–40. If a broken bolt cannot be removed easily a screw extractor may be used. *(Courtesy of Lisle Tools)*

e. As a last resort for real problem bolts, it is possible to weld a metal tag to a broken bolt and then use a pliers on the metal tag to remove the bolt.

PROBLEM: Leaky Gaskets and Seals

Over the life of an engine, many of the gaskets and seals either break, shrink, or become brittle. If this happens, oil or other fluids will most likely leak from the engine. Components that most often produce leaks include valve covers, fuel pumps, water pumps, timing chain covers, and oil pans.

DIAGNOSIS

Many times it is difficult to locate the component or part that is leaking. To determine the location of the oil leak:

1. check for spots where the oil has washed dirt away;

2. check for gaskets that have become brittle;

3. check for bolts that are loose, causing the gasket to lose its seal;

4. remember that as the oil is leaking, it is blown backward by the air as the vehicle moves down the road.

SERVICE

When servicing an engine that has an oil leak or that needs new gaskets or seals, keep the following suggestions in mind:

1. When leaks occur near covers such as valve and timing chain covers, always check the covers for bent sides and flanges. If the flanges are bent slightly, an oil leak may occur that may not be sealed by the gasket. Bend or straighten the cover to eliminate the leak.

2. Sometimes when gaskets are being installed, they slip out of place. To help keep the gasket in place during installation, use a thick grease or gasket sealant. Also, the gasket can be tied in place using a very thin wire that can easily be removed. Another technique for keeping a gasket in place during installation is shown in *Figure 3–41*. Use small wires or cut-down paper clips to hold the bolts in place. The gasket is held in place with the bolts.

3. Remember that new gaskets must seal on smooth surfaces. Always scrape the machined surfaces and flanges clean of all old gasket materials, gasket sealants, and dirt. Any old gasket parts left on the surfaces may cause the new gasket to leak.

4. Oil leaks can also occur from seals that are working on rotating shafts. For example, seals are used on rotating shafts in transmissions, rear drive shafts, and drive shafts. When a leak is observed, make sure the shaft is not damaged where the seal rides on the metal surface. At times, this area may wear so that even a new seal may not stop an oil leak. Replacing the shaft may be necessary. However, in certain applications, sleeves may be purchased for the shaft. These sleeves are placed on the shaft to provide a new surface for the seal lip to ride on.

5. Never use a compression type gasket twice. Always use a new one to replace compression type gaskets.

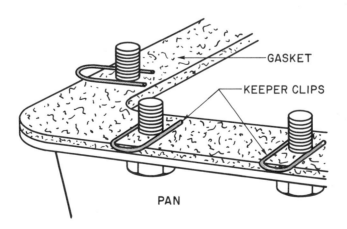

FIGURE 3–41. Gaskets can be held in place by using small paper clips cut to hold the bolts of the cover in place. The oil pan, gasket, and bolts are shown here.

Linkage to
Automotive Manufacturing

SEALANTS APPLIED BY ROBOTS

Various types of sealants are used throughout the automobile. In these photos robots are applying sealants to the trunk area of a vehicle and to the windows. Robots perform many jobs in the production of an automobile. The robots that apply sealants must be extremely accurate, and must repeat the procedure many times. They are programmed to apply the sealants between the body and the parts before installation. *(Courtesy of GMF Robotics Corporation and Chrysler Corporation)*

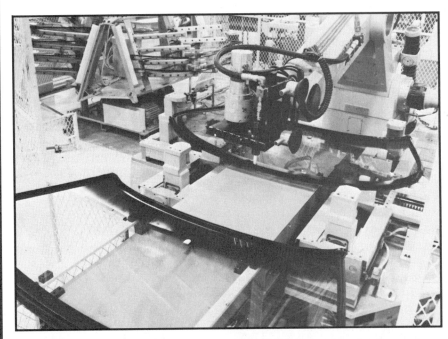

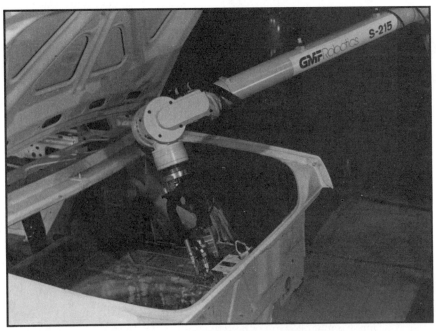

SERVICE MANUAL CONNECTION

Fasteners, gaskets, sealants, and bearings all are mentioned in many of the service manuals. However, one of the most mentioned is fasteners and their torque specifications. Although each size bolt and nut has a standard torque, manufacturers list specific torque readings in the service manuals. To identify the torque specifications for your engine, you will need to know the VIN (vehicle identification number) of the vehicle, the type and year of the vehicle, and the type of engine. Although they may be titled differently, some of the more common torque specifications (not all) found in service manuals are listed below. Today, most torque specifications are given in metric newton-meters (N·m) or customary pound-feet (lb-ft). Note that these specifications are typical examples. Each vehicle and engine will have different specifications.

Application	N·m	Lb-ft
Connecting rod nuts	57	42
Exhaust manifold to cylinder head bolts	34	25
Exhaust system pipes to manifold	34	25
Flywheel to converter	63	46
Flywheel to crankshaft	81	60
Front cover to cylinder block	47	35
Injection pump attaching bolts	34	25
Injection pump fuel inlet line	30	22
Oil pan bolts	14	10
Water pump to front cover bolts	18	13

CAR CLINIC

PROBLEM: Correct Use of RTV Sealants

A valve cover gasket was recently replaced with an RTV sealant. Shortly after, the oxygen sensor had to be replaced. What is the problem?

SOLUTION:

Some types of RTV silicon sealants may emit vapors when curing. These vapors can damage the oxygen sensor. When using RTV sealants, read the package or tube to make sure the sealant will not damage various components in the engine.

SUMMARY

This chapter showed the many types of fasteners, gaskets, sealants, and seals used on the automobile. Threaded fasteners such as bolts, nuts, and a variety of screws are used in many locations on the automobile. Bolts are identified by the shank size, hardness, number of threads per inch, and whether the threads are coarse or fine. This information is used as the basis for selecting the proper torque values as listed on the *Standard Bolt and Nut Torque Specifications* chart.

In addition to these fasteners, many types of lock washers, snap rings, splines, and keyways are also used on the automobile. Snap rings, splines, and keyways are used to hold parts to rotating shafts.

When threads are damaged by incorrect tightening or incorrect threading of the bolt into the hole, helicoils can be used. Helicoils provide new threads for the bolts.

Gaskets and seals are used on the engine, differentials, and axles. The purpose of gaskets and seals is to seal gases, oil, greases, and other fluids in the vehicle. This is especially important when oil is near or in contact with a rotating shaft. Compression gaskets are used when high-pressure gases such as those produced by combustion must be contained. Both static and dynamic seals are used. Labyrinth seals are used when the lips of the seal could cause wear on the shaft.

Whenever a rotating shaft is to be supported in a stationary part, a bearing is used. There are two types of bearings: friction and antifriction. Friction bearings have oil between the rotating shaft and the stationary part. Two types of friction bearings are commonly used. One-piece bearings, also called bushings, are used for camshafts, alternator and generator shafts, and similar applications. Split, or two-piece, bearings are used primarily on crankshafts.

Antifriction bearings use rollers or balls between the stationary part and the rotating shaft. There are many types of antifriction bearings. Many are designed to absorb thrust or axial loads.

Some bearings are also sealed. Sealed bearings are used when a seal and a bearing are needed together. Sealed bearings are used on rear axles, on wheel bearings, and in other applications where oil or grease is in direct contact with the bearing.

Several service and diagnostic procedures should be followed when using fasteners, gaskets, and bearings. Important areas include using correct bolts and nuts, making sure bearings are maintained and serviced properly, and installing gaskets, bearings, and fasteners correctly.

TERMS TO KNOW

Can you explain each of the following terms? Review the chapter until you can use each term correctly.

Threaded fasteners	Screw-pitch gauge
Head	National Coarse (NC)
Torque	National Fine (NF)
Shank	Bolt hardness
Threads per inch	Tensile strength

(continued)

Prevailing torque nuts
Metric threads
Property class
Standard bolt and nut
   torque specifications
Torque-to-yield bolts
Compression washer
Snap ring
Spline
Keyway
Helicoil
Gasket
Seal
Sealants
RTV sealants

Anaerobic sealants
Gasket sealant
O ring
Labyrinth seal
Rope seals
Bearing
Friction bearing
Antifriction bearing
Bushing
Babbitt
Axial load
Thrust load
Thrust bearing
Brinnelling

REVIEW QUESTIONS

Multiple Choice

1. Which of the following are used to keep a gear on a shaft?
   a. Washers
   b. Snap rings
   c. Gaskets
   d. Sealants
   e. Bearings

2. Which of the following is used to seal liquid flowing through two stationary parts?
   a. Labyrinth seal
   b. Dynamic seal
   c. O rings
   d. All of the above
   e. None of the above

3. In order to replace threads, a _____ is commonly used.
   a. Helicoil
   b. Stud
   c. Snap ring
   d. Sealant
   e. Bearing

4. Another word for axial load is _____.
   a. Force
   b. Thrust
   c. Bushing
   d. End forces
   e. Expansion force

5. A gasket used to seal high-pressure gases is called a:
   a. Compression gasket
   b. Thrust gasket
   c. Labyrinth gasket
   d. Sealant
   e. Bearing

6. Torque for bolts should always be determined by the:
   a. Socket size of the bolt
   b. Length of the bolt
   c. Shank size of the bolt
   d. All of the above
   e. None of the above

7. The greater the number of lines on the bolt head, the:
   a. Softer the bolt
   b. More threads per inch on the bolt
   c. Harder the bolt
   d. Easier it is to turn
   e. Harder it is to turn

8. Which bolt has the greatest ability to hold two objects together?
   a. An NC bolt
   b. An NF bolt
   c. A UNC bolt
   d. All of the above
   e. None of the above

9. The lip of a dynamic seal should always be pointed toward the:
   a. Outside or dirty area
   b. Fluid to be contained
   c. Stationary part
   d. Air
   e. None of the above

10. Which of the following allows two shafts to be locked together yet able to slide axially?
    a. Keyways
    b. Splines
    c. Helicoils
    d. Bearings
    e. None of the above

11. A compression gasket should be used:
    a. Only once
    b. After the gasket has been compressed
    c. To seal oil and low pressures
    d. To seal air only
    e. None of the above

12. Which of the following are used to prevent motion between two rotating parts?
    a. Setscrews
    b. Snap rings
    c. Machine screws
    d. Bearings
    e. Sealants

13. Which of the following are used to join light metal or plastic?
    a. Self-tapping screws
    b. Splines
    c. Setscrews
    d. Bearing seals
    e. Compression gaskets

14. Helicoils are used to:
    a. Replace external threads
    b. Replace internal threads
    c. Lock two shafts together
    d. Seal surfaces together
    e. Tighten bolts correctly

15. A bolt identified as $3/8 \times 16 \times 1\ 1/2$ means:
    a. 3/8-inch shank size
    b. 16 millimeters long
    c. 1 1/2-inch socket size
    d. All of the above
    e. None of the above

16. Which type of bearing uses a set of rollers or balls between the moving and stationary parts?
    a. Antifriction
    b. Friction
    c. Bushing
    d. Compression bearings
    e. None of the above

17. Which type of bearing produces the most heat and frictional losses in the engine?
    a. Antifriction
    b. Friction
    c. Radial
    d. Roller
    e. Ball bearing

18. Which type of bearing is used on camshafts, crankshafts, and alternator shafts?
    a. Antifriction bearings
    b. Bushings
    c. Thrust roller bearings
    d. Sealed ball bearings
    e. None of the above

The following questions are similar in format to ASE (Automotive Service Excellence) test questions.

19. Technician A says that O rings are used to form a compression gasket for high pressures. Technician B says that O rings are used to improve the accuracy of torquing a bolt. Who is right?
    a. A only   c. Both A and B
    b. B only   d. Neither A nor B

20. A bolt is identified as $3/8 \times 16 \times 1\ 1/2$. Technician A says the bolt has 16 threads per inch. Technician B says the bolt is 3/8 inch in shank size. Who is right?
    a. A only   c. Both A and B
    b. B only   d. Neither A nor B

21. Technician A says the tensile strength of a bolt is identified by the type of chrome on the bolt. Technician B says the tensile strength of a bolt is identified by the number of lines on the top of the bolt. Who is right?
    a. A only   c. Both A and B
    b. B only   d. Neither A nor B

22. Technician A says that metric bolts have the same torque as English or customary bolts. Technician B says that metric bolts are not used at all today on automobiles. Who is right?
    a. A only   c. Both A and B
    b. B only   d. Neither A nor B

23. Technician A says that RTV sealants should be used in the presence of air, or oxygen. Technician B says that RTV sealants should not be used on automotive engines. Who is right?
    a. A only   c. Both A and B
    b. B only   d. Neither A nor B

24. Technician A says that prevailing thread fasteners have an interference fit with the mating threads. Technician B says that prevailing thread fasteners use nylon inserted into the threads to prevent the fasteners from coming loose. Who is right?
    a. A only   c. Both A and B
    b. B only   d. Neither A nor B

Essay

25. Describe how the torque is determined on a bolt.
26. Describe the difference between a spline and a snap ring.
27. What is the purpose of a helicoil?
28. What is the difference between friction and antifriction bearings?
29. In which direction should the lip of a seal be positioned? Why?

Short Answer

30. A nut that has an interference fit between the nut and bolt threads is called a _____ fastener.
31. Metric bolts are torqued in the unit called _____.
32. A form-in-place gasket is categorized as a _____ type of gasket.
33. When various bolts come into contact with oil or antifreeze, it is a good idea to use _____ to seal the threads.
34. Most bearings are protected from dirt by using _____.

CHAPTER 4

Measuring Instruments and Common Hand Tools

INTRODUCTION   In the automotive shop, it is necessary to use many tools. In most shops, each service technician has his or her own set of tools. The tool set may include several hundred tools used to work on the automobile.

Tools are used to make service easier for the mechanic. They are used for pulling parts off of shafts, tightening bolts and nuts to correct specifications, measuring various distances and clearances, and lifting heavy objects. These tools maximize the technician's effort by multiplying forces. Today's automotive service technician should be familiar with the use of many tools. Proper tool selection will improve both the quality and quantity of the service done on the automobile.

The purpose of this chapter is to introduce the common tools used on the automobile. Because so many tools are now available, only identification of these tools will be presented.

OBJECTIVES   After reading this chapter, you should be able to:

- Compare the USC and metric systems of measurement.

- Identify common hand tools used in the shop, including hammers, pliers, screwdrivers, wrenches, taps and dies, chisels and punches, screw extractors, and sockets.

- Analyze the common measuring tools, including micrometers, vernier calipers, feeler gauges, torque wrenches, dial

indicators, and pressure and vacuum gauges.

- Analyze power and pressing tools such as pulleys, bushing/bearing/seal installers, hydraulic tools, and impact wrenches.

- Define the use of various electrical testing tools including multimeters, test lights, tachometers, dwell/tach meters, timing lights, electronic engine analyzers, and scanners.

✔ SAFETY CHECKLIST ✔

When working with measuring instruments and tools in the automotive shop keep in mind these important safety suggestions.

✔ Always select the right size wrench for the bolt or nut. If the wrench is too large it may slip off the bolt during heavy torque, possibly injuring your hands.

✔ Make sure all tools used in the automotive shop are clean and free of grease and oil.

✔ Return all tools to their designated tool box or location on the wall after each use. Tools left on the vehicle may fall into moving parts of the engine. They could then fly out and cause injury.

Continued

SAFETY CHECKLIST Continued

✔ Make sure screwdriver tips are not worn away. During high-torque applications, the screwdriver may slip off the screw and cause injury.

✔ When working with any tools in the shop, always wear approved safety glasses.

✔ Occasionally, a tap for cutting internal threads may break. Be careful not to touch the edges of the broken tap, as they are extremely sharp.

✔ If you are not familiar with the correct use of any tool, always check with the instructor. Never use a tool that you don't know how to use correctly.

✔ When using torque wrenches, always pull the wrench toward your body. With this technique, you get the maximum leverage and greatest safety margin.

✔ While you are using pressure and vacuum gauges the engine may need to be running. Always be careful where you place the gauges, and make sure the gauge connections and piping and tubing to the engine are away from moving parts.

✔ Pullers create extremely high pressures. Always make sure the pullers are correctly installed for maximum safety.

✔ Always use the correct puller to match the component or part being removed.

✔ When installing bearings using a bearing and seal driver set, be careful not to pinch the edges of your hand and fingers during installation.

✔ Hydraulic presses produce extremely high pressures. Always have the parts supported securely on the hydraulic press before removing bearings, gears, and so on.

✔ When using any electrical test equipment, make sure the wires are not touching any moving parts such as fan blades, alternators, air compressors, water pumps, or timing belts.

✔ When using any power tool, make sure the electrical cord is correctly grounded and there are no torn or frayed cords or exposed electrical wires.

4.1 MEASURING SYSTEMS

The United States is now committed to using two measuring systems. These are called the United States Customary system, known as *USC*, and the *metric system*. In the past, all parts, tools, and measuring instruments made in the United States were designed using the USC measurements. However, the United States has been increasingly using the metric system. Manufacturers are slowly converting to the metric system, because many foreign countries use the metric system. Many American automobile manufacturers now design certain components in metric sizes. Because of these changes, it is important to study both measurement systems.

USC Measurements

The measuring system used most often in the United States is called the U.S. Customary system (USC). This system measures length, volume, and mass as shown in *Figure 4–1*.

Tools in the automobile industry use many length measurements. For example, wrench and socket sizes typically increase in 1/64-, 1/32-, 1/16-, and 1/8-inch sizes, *Figure 4–2*. In addition, many small measurements and clearances are listed in 1/1,000 of an inch. This can be shown in decimal form as 0.001 inch.

Metric System

When you are familiar with it, the metric system is much easier to use than the USC measurements, because all of the

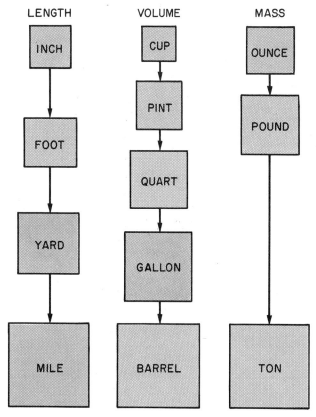

FIGURE 4–1. The USC measurements are shown. Length, volume, and mass all have specific units for measurement.

COMMON WRENCH SIZES USC	COMMON WRENCH SIZES METRIC
1/4"	9 mm
5/16"	10 mm
3/8"	11 mm
7/16"	12 mm
1/2"	13 mm
	14 mm
9/16"	15 mm
5/8"	16 mm
11/16"	17 mm
3/4"	18 mm
13/16"	19 mm
	20 mm
7/8"	21 mm
15/16"	22 mm
1"	

FIGURE 4–2.   Many length measurements are taken on the automobile. The USC system and the metric system use these common sizes.

units use a *base of 10*. This means that all units are multiples of 10. This is not true with USC measurements. The foot has a base of 12 (12 inches in a foot), the yard has a base of 3 (3 feet in a yard), the pound has a base of 16, (16 ounces in a pound), and so on. Figure 4–2 shows common metric wrench sizes.

Measuring Length in Meters

The base unit in the metric system is the *meter*. The distance of a meter is defined as the length equal to 1,650,763.73 wavelengths of krypton in a vacuum. This distance is always constant and can easily be duplicated under laboratory conditions. In relation to the USC measurement, 1 meter is equal to 39.37 inches.

Metric Prefixes

Instead of using such phrases as 1/16 of an inch, the metric system uses a set of *prefixes*. These prefixes are shown in *Figure 4–3*. For example, the prefix *kilo* means 1,000. If a distance is measured as 1,000 meters, it can also be called a

SOME COMMON PREFIXES			
NAME	SYMBOL	MEANING	MULTIPLIER
mega	M	one million	1 000 000
kilo	k	one thousand	1 000
hecto	h	one hundred	100
deca	da	ten	10
deci	d	one tenth of a	0.1
centi	c	one hundredth of a	0.01
milli	m	one thousandth of a	0.001
micro	μ	one millionth of a	0.000 001

FIGURE 4–3.   The metric system uses these prefixes to aid in defining measurements.

kilometer. In terms of small distances, the prefix *milli* means one-thousandth of a unit. If the unit is the meter, one millimeter is equal to 1/1,000 of a meter. Each small increment on a meter stick, as shown in **Figure 4–4**, is a measure of one millimeter. One thousand millimeters make up one complete meter. A decimeter is 1/10 of a meter, while a centimeter is 1/100 of a meter.

Measuring Volume

In the metric system, volume is measured by the *liter*. One-tenth of a meter is called a decimeter. This is about the width of a person's fist. If a cube is made with each edge one decimeter long, the cube will have a volume of one cubic decimeter. A cubic decimeter is equal to a liter. See **Figure 4–5**. Note also that the length of one decimeter is equal to 10 centimeters. If one centimeter is cubed, the unit is called a *cubic centimeter*. Both liters and cubic centimeters are used to measure the volume of an engine.

Measuring Mass

The unit used to measure mass in the metric system is called the *gram*. Kilogram is often used because the gram is so small. If one cubic centimeter is filled with water, the mass is one gram. If a liter, 1,000 cubic centimeters, is filled with water, the mass is 1,000 grams, or 1 kilogram.

Other Metric Units

Other units are used in the metric system. **Figure 4–6** illustrates a listing of common metric units. The quantity, the unit, and the common symbols are shown. The automotive technician should become familiar with these units.

Conversion between USC and Metric Systems

At times it may be necessary to convert from USC units to metric system units or from metric system units to USC units. If this is necessary, the chart shown in **Figure 4–7** gives some of the more common *conversion factors*. Slide rules and calculators can be used for conversion.

4.2 COMMON HAND TOOLS

There are many types of tools used by the automotive service technician. Hand tools are designed to make the technician's work much easier. They receive energy from the technician's hand and transform that energy into productive work. Hand tools multiply forces to accomplish work. A person cannot loosen a bolt by hand. However, the bolt can be loosened easily by using the correct wrench. Tools accomplish this work in two ways: (1) by multiplying forces, as in prying a heavy object with a bar, and (2) by concentrating applied force into a small area, as in using a wrench.

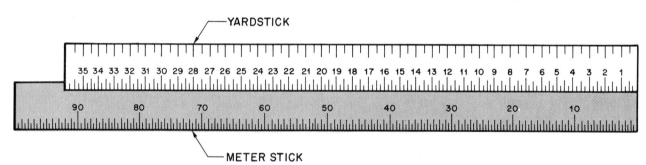

FIGURE 4–4. A meter stick is composed of 1,000 small increments. Each increment is called one millimeter.

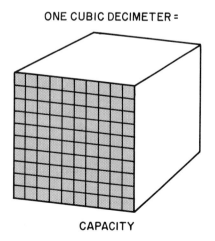

ONE CUBIC DECIMETER =

CAPACITY

FIGURE 4–5. A cubic decimeter, also called a liter, is a volume measurement in the metric system. Engines are sized by indicating the number of ccs (cubic centimeters), or liters.

QUANTITY	UNIT	SYMBOL
Length	millimeter *(one thousandth of a meter)* meter kilometer *(one thousand meters)*	mm m km
Area	square meter hectare *(ten thousand square meters)*	m² ha
Volume	cubic centimeter cubic meter milliliter *(one thousandth of a liter)* liter *(one thousandth of a cubic meter)*	cm³ m³ ml l
Mass	gram *(one thousandth of a kilogram)* kilogram ton *(one thousand kilograms)*	g kg t
Time	second minute, hour, day, month, year	s min, h, d, mo, yr
Speed	meter per second kilometer per hour	m/s km/h
Power	watt kilowatt *(one thousand watts)*	W kW
Energy	joule kilowatt-hour	J kW•h
Electric potential difference	volt	V
Electrical current	ampere	A
Electrical resistance	ohm	Ω
Frequency	hertz	Hz
Temperature	degree Celsius	°C

FIGURE 4–6. Many units are used in the metric system. Note that each has a symbol to represent the unit.

Wrenches

Many types of wrenches are used. Wrenches are used to turn threaded fasteners with primarily hexagonal heads. Three types of wrenches are commonly used. They are the open end, box, and combination wrenches. ***Figure 4–8*** illustrates the differences between these wrenches. The box end wrench is closed, the open end wrench is open, and the combination wrench has a box and an open end. ***Figure 4–9*** illustrates many of the different sizes of combination, open end, and box end wrenches available today. Wrench sets such as these can be purchased in both English (USC) and metric sizes.

Other styles of wrenches are used on the automobile as well. The adjustable wrench is used when certain size wrenches are not available. This wrench is able to fit bolts and nuts of different sizes by adjusting the size of the jaws. Adjustable wrenches come in different lengths and sizes. See ***Figure 4–10***.

Hammers

The automotive shop is not complete unless there are hammers available for various service jobs. There are several types of hammers used in the shop. Using a hammer correctly, matched to the job in style, size, and weight, helps get the work done faster and safer. The common types of hammers include the ball peen, plastic tip, rubber tip, and bronze tip hammers. See ***Figure 4–11***.

UNIT	CONVERSION FACTOR
Length	1 inch = 25.4 mm 1 foot = 30.48 cm 1 yard = 0.9144 m 1 mile = 1.609 344 km
Area	1 square inch = 6.4516 cm^2 1 square foot = 9.290 304 dm^2 1 square yard = 0.836 127 4 m^2 1 acre = 0.404 685 6 ha 1 square mile = 2.589 988 km^2
Volume	1 cubic inch = 16.387 064 cm^3 1 cubic foot = 28.316 85 dm^3 (or liters) 1 cubic yard = 0.764 555 m^3 1 fluid ounce = 28.413 062 cm^3 1 gallon = 4.546 090 dm^3 (or liters)
Mass	1 ounce (avoirdupois) = 28.349 523 g 1 pound (avoirdupois) = 0.453 592 37 kg 1 ton (short, 2,000 lb) = 907.184 74 kg
Temperature	(5/9) × (number of degrees Fahrenheit – 32) = number of degrees Celsius
Speed	1 mile per hour = 0.447 04 m/s = 1.609 344 km/h
Force	1 pound-force = 4.448 222 N 1 kilogram-force = 9.806 65 N
Pressure	1 pound-force per square inch (psi) = 6.894 757 kPa (kilopascal) 1 inch of mercury (0˚C) = 3.386 39 kPa 1 mm of mercury (0˚C) = 133.322 Pa 1 standard atmosphere (atm) = 101.325 kPa
Energy, Work	1 British thermal unit (Btu) = 1055.06 J 1 foot-pound force = 1.355 818 J 1 calorie (international) = 4.1868 J 1 kilowatt-hour (kW•h) = 3.6 MJ
Power	1 horsepower (550 ft-lb/s) = 745.6999 W 1 horsepower (electric) = 746 W

FIGURE 4–7. Some of the more common conversion factors are listed. Calculators can be used if conversion is necessary.

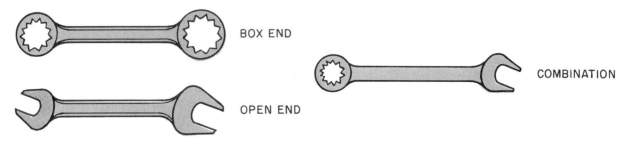

FIGURE 4–8. The three most common types of wrenches are the box end, open end, and combination wrenches.

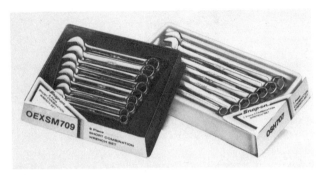

FIGURE 4–9. Wrenches come in many sizes. Tool manufacturers will sell different sets of tools. *(Courtesy of Snap-On Tools Corporation)*

FIGURE 4–10. Adjustable wrenches are used for a variety of service jobs. Always make sure the wrench is adjusted as tightly as possible or the bolt head may be damaged. *(Courtesy of Snap-On Tools Corporation)*

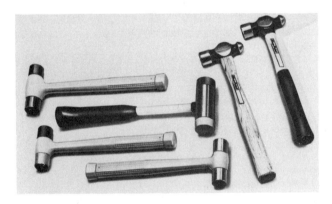

FIGURE 4–11. Many types of hammers are used in the automotive shop. The softer hammers with rubber tips should be used on material that may damage easily. *(Courtesy of Snap-On Tools Corporation)*

Socket Sets and Drives

Socket sets, drives, and extensions are used to tighten and loosen bolts and nuts. They are usually faster than open or box end wrenches. Socket sets can also loosen bolts and nuts that standard wrenches cannot get at. Socket sets include various sizes of sockets, drives, extensions, and ratchets. They

are identified by the drive size. The *drive* on a socket set is the square area that connects the ratchet to the socket. The most common drive sizes are 1/4, 3/8, and 1/2 inch.

Socket Points

The sockets can be purchased with different *socket points*. Either 6-point, 8-point, or 12-point styles are available. See *Figure 4–12*. If a bolt is positioned so that only a small amount of rotation is available with the ratchet, then a 12-point socket should be used. Twelve-point sockets can be repositioned every 30 degrees. Eight-point sockets can be repositioned every 45 degrees, and 6-point sockets can be repositioned every 60 degrees. In addition to these uses, 4-point and 8-point sockets are typically used for square nuts. Six-point and twelve-point sockets are used for hex nuts. *Figure 4–13* illustrates a standard socket set showing the sockets, drives and extensions, ratchets, and other accessories.

Types of Sockets

Sockets are also designed as *deep length*, swivel or universal, and standard. Deep length sockets are used for nuts that are on long studs. Swivel or universal sockets are used for nuts and bolts that cannot be loosened with the ratchet directly above the bolts. In this case, the ratchet and

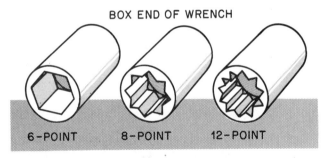

FIGURE 4–12. Sockets can be identified by stating the number of points in the socket. Twelve-point sockets are used for applications where the degree of rotation is restricted.

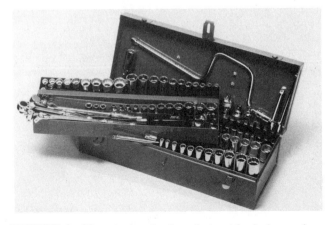

FIGURE 4–13. A standard socket set includes various sockets, ratchets, drives, and extensions and several accessories. *(Courtesy of Snap-On Tools Corporation)*

FIGURE 4–14.   Three types of sockets are commonly used in the automotive shop: deep length, swivel or universal, and standard sockets. *(Courtesy of Snap-On Tools Corporation)*

extensions can be rotated from an angle. Standard sockets are used in most applications that simply require tightening and loosening without any restrictions. ***Figure 4–14*** illustrates the three types of sockets that are commonly used. These sockets can be identified by their chrome covering.

Impact Sockets

In addition to the standard socket sets, there are also heavy-duty sockets used on impact wrenches or wrenches powered by electricity or air. These sockets can be identified by their black color. These sockets should be used where heavy-duty work is required, such as removing nuts from a wheel and rim. ***Figure 4–15*** shows a set of impact sockets with 6-point style.

Screwdrivers

Screwdrivers come in a variety of sizes and shapes. Screwdrivers are identified by the type of tip they have. The two most common types of screwdriver tips are the slotted tip and the Phillips tip. These are shown in ***Figure 4–16***. Always make sure the tip of the screwdriver fits the screw head correctly.

Other tips are also designed on screwdrivers. There are several special screwdrivers that are also used on the automobile. These include the Torx (star) tip, magnetic tip, offset tip, Reed and Prince tip (similar to the Phillips tip), and flexible shaft screwdriver.

FIGURE 4–15.   Impact sockets are used where high torque is required. These sockets are made with the 6-point style. They are stronger and capable of more torque than ordinary sockets. Standard sockets may break easily under these conditions. *(Courtesy of Snap-On Tools Corporation)*

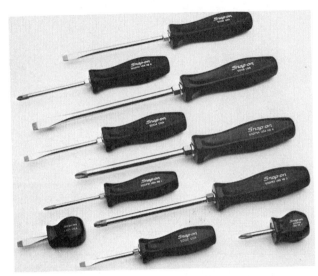

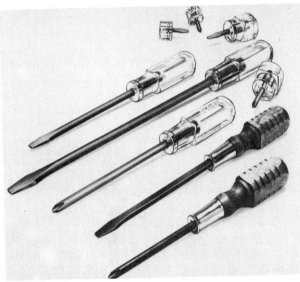

FIGURE 4–16.   Of the many types of screwdriver tips, the slotted and the Phillips tip are the most common. *(Courtesy of Snap-On Tools Corporation)*

Pliers

Pliers are used to grip objects of various sizes and shapes and for cutting. Because of the many uses of pliers, there are many styles. *Figure 4–17* illustrates the pliers commonly used in the automotive shop. Pliers should not be used in place of a wrench. The pliers and the head of the bolt or nut may be damaged.

The different types of pliers give the mechanic a variety of options. Some pliers are used for gripping, some for electrical work, some for cutting, and some for special purposes.

The following types of pliers are commonly used in the automotive shop: *Slip-joint* pliers are used for common gripping applications. Slip-joint pliers have a joint to allow for two different sizes. *Needle nose* pliers have long, slim jaws used for holding small objects such as pins and electrical components. *Adjustable joint* pliers have an adjustable jaw that interlocks in several positions. These pliers have the

ability to grip large or small objects depending upon where the jaw is locked. *Cutter* pliers enable the mechanic to cut wire and other small objects. *Electrical service* pliers have a wire cutter, stripper, and clamping device built into one plier. *Retaining ring* pliers are designed to install and remove either internal or external retaining rings. *Vise-grip* pliers are used to grip and hold an object in place. The vise-grip pliers use a locking mechanism to hold the object so the technician's hands are free. *Wire-stripping* pliers are used to strip the insulation from electrical wires so that proper electrical connections can be made.

Taps and Dies

Threads can be either internal or external. Internal threads are cut with a tap. External threads are formed or cut with a die. *Figure 4–18* shows a complete tap and die set for use in the automotive shop.

A *tap* is a hardened piece of steel with threads on the outside. There are three types of taps. The *taper tap* has a long taper. It is used to cut threads completely through open

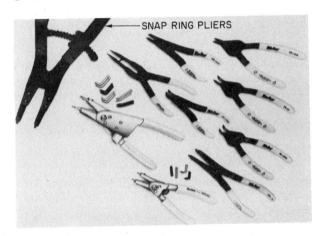

SNAP RING PLIERS

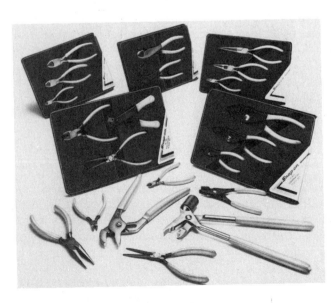

FIGURE 4–17.   Many types of pliers are used in the automotive shop today. Always use the correct pliers for the service required. *(Courtesy of Snap-On Tools Corporation)*

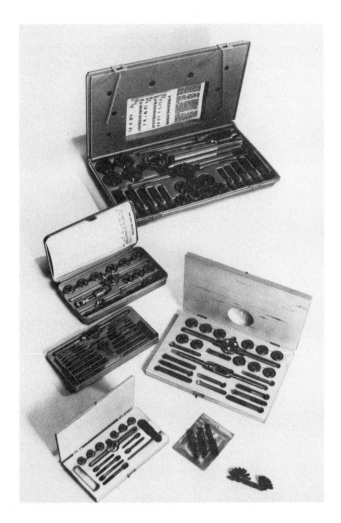

FIGURE 4–18. Taps are used to cut internal threads such as in a block. Dies are used to form external threads such as on a bolt. *(Courtesy of Snap-On Tools Corporation)*

holes. It is also used to start threads in blind and partly closed holes.

The *plug tap* has a shorter taper and is used after the taper tap to provide fuller threads in blind holes.

The *bottoming tap* is used after the taper and plug taps. It is used to cut a full thread to the very bottom of the hole.

A *threading die* is a round, hardened-steel block with a hole containing threads. The threads are slightly tapered on one side to make it easier to start the cutting.

Chisels and Punches

Chisels and punches are used in the automotive shop for a variety of jobs, from punching pins through an object to removing a bearing. A good set of punches and chisels should always be available for the technician to use. *Figure 4–19* shows a complete set of chisels and punches.

Screw Extractor

There are many occasions where bolts are broken off. A broken bolt that is not made of hardened steel may be

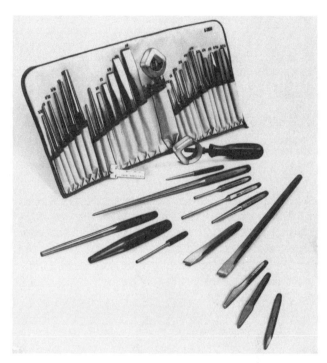

FIGURE 4–19. A quality set of chisels and punches should be available for use in all automotive shops. *(Courtesy of Snap-On Tools Corporation)*

removed from a hole with a screw extractor. See *Figure 4–20*. First a hole must be drilled into the broken bolt. Then the correct size screw extractor is placed into the hole. The screw extractor is then turned counterclockwise with a tap wrench. The screw extractor acts much like a corkscrew to remove the broken bolt.

Many other hand tools are used in the automotive shop. Some of these tools include hex head (Allen) wrenches, pipe wrenches, ratchet box wrenches, prybars, and crowfoot wrenches. All of these hand tools make the automotive technician's job much easier and safer.

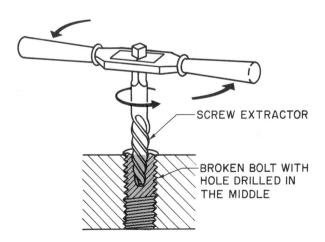

SCREW EXTRACTOR

BROKEN BOLT WITH HOLE DRILLED IN THE MIDDLE

FIGURE 4–20. A screw extractor can be used to remove broken bolts from inside an object.

CAR CLINIC

PROBLEM: Buying the Correct Type of Sockets for the Job

A service technician seems to always be breaking sockets. The sockets either strip in the middle or crack along the sides. What is the problem?

SOLUTION:

Sockets are identified as either 6-, 8-, or 12-point sockets. When an 8- or 12-point socket is used on a high-torque application, it might break. For high-impact or high-torque applications, the 6-point socket should always be used. To solve this problem, make sure that only 6-point sockets or high-impact sockets are used for high-torque or high-impact applications.

4.3   MEASURING TOOLS

When servicing an automobile, certain dimensions, specifications, and clearances must be measured. These may include torque specifications and various clearances. Measuring tools aid the automotive technician in checking these specifications and clearances.

Torque Wrenches

Torque wrenches are used to tighten bolts and nuts to their correct torque specification. Torque specifications were given in Chapter 3, as part of threaded fasteners. Torque wrenches are used to control the amount of tension on a bolt by measuring the amount of twist (torque) developed while tightening the bolt. Torque wrenches are designed to match sockets using 1/4-, 3/8-, and 1/2-inch drives. Other drives are also available but are not as common. They include 3/4-, 1-, and 1 1/2-inch drives for heavy-duty service. Torque wrenches typically have a dial or scale that indicates the amount of torque in pound-inches (lb-in.) or in pound-feet (lb-ft). *Figure 4–21* shows torque wrenches used in the automotive shop.

Types of Torque Wrenches

A common type of torque wrench is called the *adjustable click* type. A specified torque value is adjusted on the torque wrench. When that torque level is reached, the wrench clicks so the operator knows the correct value of torque has been reached.

The *dial* torque wrench has a dial on top so that as the torque is being applied to the bolt an exact reading can be obtained immediately. *Figure 4–22* shows one type of dial used on this type of torque wrench.

T handle torque wrenches are used with standard ratchet wrenches. A dial is also used to indicate the exact amount of

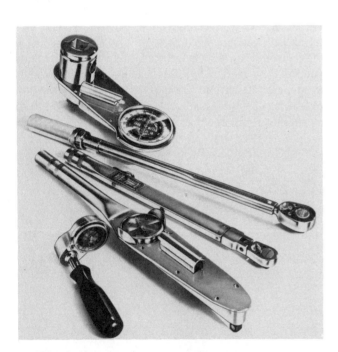

FIGURE 4–21.   Torque wrenches are used to tighten bolts and nuts. Several types are available, including dial, adjustable click, and torque drives. *(Courtesy of Snap-On Tools Corporation)*

FIGURE 4–22.   Several types of dials are used on torque wrenches. Some read in meter-kilograms, some in foot-pounds, and some, like the one shown here, read both.

torque being applied. A socket is placed on the bottom of the torque wrench, while the ratchet is placed on top.

The *torque driver* is used for small torque specifications, where a screwdriver or nut driver would normally be used.

The *deflecting beam* torque wrench uses a deflecting rod in the center of the wrench to measure the exact value of torque applied to the bolt or nut. *Figure 4–23* shows a deflecting beam torque wrench.

FIGURE 4–23. Another kind of torque wrench is called the deflecting beam torque wrench. As the bolt is tightened, the pointer reads the correct torque on the scale.

Micrometers

Micrometers are made to measure very small, accurate clearances. A micrometer is capable of measuring length in 0.001 of an inch. There are several types of micrometers. *Outside micrometers* measure outside dimensions such as shaft diameters, bearing thickness, and shim thickness. *Inside micrometers* are designed to measure internal dimensions such as engine cylinders and small holes. Inside diameters can also be measured with telescoping gauges. These gauges are used to measure the inside diameter of a bore. They are then measured with an outside micrometer for exact bore diameters.

Micrometers come in many sizes, *Figure 4–24*. Common sizes include 0"–1", 1"–2", 2"–3", 3"–4", and 4"–5". In some cases, the micrometer set may include several adapters and extensions.

Parts of a Micrometer

Figure 4–25 shows the basic parts of the micrometer. In this case, an outside micrometer is used.

All outside micrometers are the same except for the frame. When larger dimensions are used, the frame is made larger to fit larger dimensions.

Reading a Micrometer

There are three steps to reading a micrometer. First, using the ratchet, slowly and gently turn the thimble until there is no clearance between the object being measured and the spindle and frame. At this point, note the highest figure on the barrel that is uncovered by the thimble. This number is the first figure to the right of the decimal point. For example, this number would be 0.200 on the micrometer shown in *Figure 4–26*.

Second, note the whole number of graduations between the 0.200 mark and the thimble. In the case shown in Figure 4–26, there is one complete division after the 0.200 mark. Each of these graduations represents 0.025 of an inch.

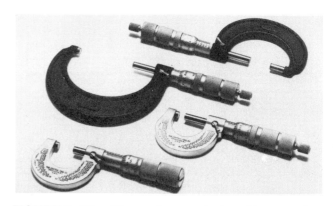

FIGURE 4–24. Micrometers are designed in many sizes to match many types of measurements. *(Courtesy of Snap-On Tools Corporation)*

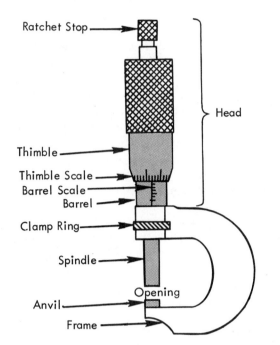

FIGURE 4–25. The outside micrometer has several parts. The object to be measured is placed between the anvil and the spindle. The measurement is taken on the barrel and thimble.

READING A STANDARD MICROMETER
Barrel Scale

Large Divisions 0.100" each
Small Divisions 0.025" each

Thimble Scale
0.001 Divisions
from 0.000 to 0.025

3 steps to read, add together: Example Above:

1. Large barrel divisions ------- X 0.100 = 0.200"
2. Small barrel divisions ------- X 0.025 = 0.025"
3. Thimble divisions _____ X 0.001 = 0.016"
          Reading ----------------- 0.241"

FIGURE 4–26. A micrometer is read by simply totaling the number of whole divisions on the barrel scale and adding the thousandths from the thimble scale.

Therefore, add 0.025 to the 0.200 found in step one. This sum equals 0.225 of an inch.

Third, read the thimble opposite the index on the barrel. The graduations on the thimble represent 0.001 inch. In this case, add 0.016 of an inch to the reading in the first and second steps. The total reading shown in Figure 4–26 is 0.241 of an inch. Note that if the micrometer were a 2–3 inch micrometer, the reading would be 2.241 inches. When using the metric micrometer, the procedure is the same except the

graduations represent different values. *Figure 4–27* shows what each graduation represents.

Other styles and types of micrometers read the same as the outside type of micrometer. The only difference is the method the micrometer fits on the object to be measured.

Vernier Caliper

The *vernier caliper* is a useful tool for measuring various dimensions on the automobile engine. The vernier caliper

READING METRIC MICROMETERS

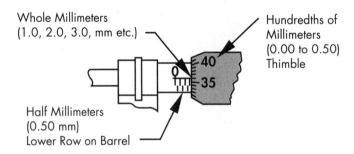

Whole Millimeters
(1.0, 2.0, 3.0, mm etc.)

Hundredths of Millimeters
(0.00 to 0.50)
Thimble

Half Millimeters
(0.50 mm)
Lower Row on Barrel

Example:
Whole mm lines visible on barrel	3	= 3.00 mm
Additional half mm line (lower) visible on barrel	1	= 0.50 mm
Lines on thimble that have passed long line on barrel	36	= 0.36 mm
Reading of measurement	Total	= 3.86 mm

FIGURE 4–27. The metric micrometer is read the same way as the standard micrometer. The graduations now read in millimeters rather than inches.

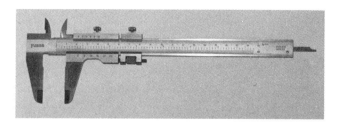

FIGURE 4–28.   A vernier caliper is a useful tool for the automotive service technician. Clearances, both inside and outside, can be measured to 0.001 of an inch.

measures length to 0.001 of an inch. A vernier caliper can measure inside or outside and in some cases depth measurements. See *Figure 4–28*. Vernier calipers can also be used to measure the inside diameter along with the telescoping gauges.

Reading a Vernier Caliper

There are several steps to reading a vernier caliper. Referring to *Figure 4–29*, the steps are as follows:

1. Read the number of whole inches on the main scale, left of the index zero on the vernier scale. In this case the reading is 1.000.

2. Read the number of major divisions on the main scale that also lie to the left of the index zero on the *vernier scale*. Each major division on the main scale is 0.100 of an inch. In this case there are five major divisions, so the reading is 0.500 of an inch. This reading is now added to the first reading for a total of 1.500 inches.

3. Read the number of minor divisions on the main scale between the number found in step 2 (5, or 0.500 inch) and the index zero on the vernier scale. In this case there are three minor divisions. Each minor division equals 0.025 of an inch. Add this number (three minor divisions,

or 0.075 of an inch) to the reading in step 2. The total so far is 1.575 inches.

4. Look at the vernier scale. Identify the lines or divisions that most perfectly coincide with any graduation on the main scale. Each of these divisions on the vernier scale represents 0.001 inch. In this example, there are seven divisions from the index zero, so the reading would be 0.007 inch. This reading is then added to the result in step 3. The total reading is 1.582 inches. Once a vernier caliper scale is mastered, readings can be taken with ease and accuracy.

Feeler Gauges

Feeler gauges are used to help check or adjust clearances to a specific measurement. They are made of thin metal blades or wires, each of which is designed to be a different thickness in thousandths of an inch. The set of feeler gauges shown in *Figure 4–30* ranges in thickness from 0.0015 to 0.025 of an inch. When an adjustment is needed, such as the clearances between valves and rocker arms, the correct gauge is placed between the two objects. The clearance is adjusted so that a small amount of drag can be felt when pulling the feeler gauge out of the area of adjustment.

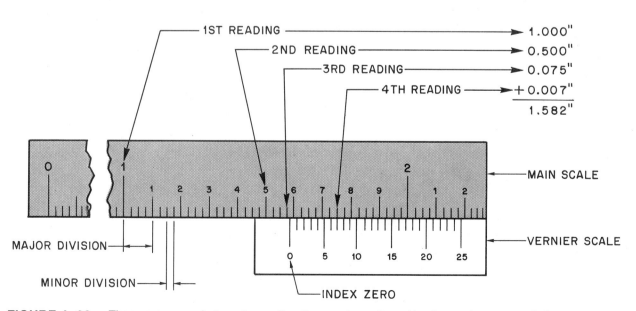

FIGURE 4–29.   There are several steps to reading the vernier caliper. Vernier scales are much the same as a micrometer, except the readings are spread out on the vernier scale.

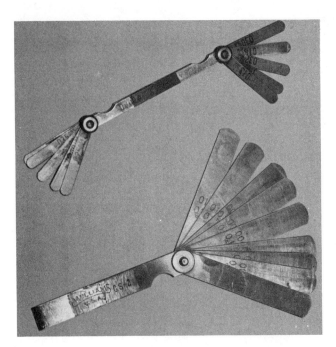

FIGURE 4–30.   Feeler gauges are used to check or adjust clearances to a specific dimension. *(Courtesy of Snap-On Tools Corporation)*

Figure 4–31 shows various types and sizes of feeler gauges used on the automobile engine. Note that some of the feeler gauges are long, while others are short. The length of the gauge that should be used depends on the measurement being taken. Certain feeler gauges are made of nonmetallic metal such as brass. These feeler gauges are used to measure clearances on magnetic pickup coils on electronic ignition systems. In addition, several wire feeler gauges (called wire gap gauges) are shown. Wire gap gauges are used mostly for setting spark plug clearances. Note that some feeler gauge sets include both the feeler gauges and the wire gap gauges.

Dial Indicators

Figure 4–32 shows a *dial indicator* set. A dial indicator is a measurement tool used to determine clearances between two objects. For example, gear backlash (the clearances between the teeth on two gears in mesh) may have to be measured. Dial indicators are also used to check ball joints, tie rods, cam and valve guide wear, crankshaft end play, and disc brake runout. Dial indicators measure clearances in 0.001 of an inch.

When using the dial indicator for checking end play of a shaft, position the dial indicator on the end of the shaft, by using the adapters in the set. When positioned correctly, set the indicator dial at zero. Proceed to move the shaft back and forth axially. See *Figure 4–33*. While moving this shaft, read the clearance in 0.001 of an inch.

FIGURE 4–32.   Dial indicators are used to measure small clearances such as crankshaft end play and flywheel runout. *(Courtesy of Snap-On Tools Corporation)*

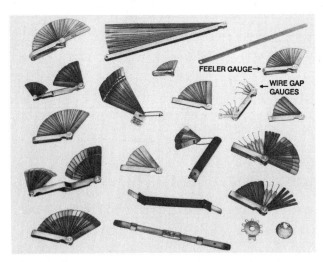

FIGURE 4–31.   Various feeler and wire gap gauges are used on the automobile. *(Courtesy of Snap-On Tools Corporation)*

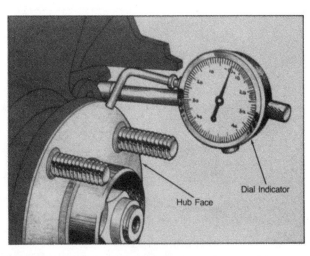

Dial Indicator

Hub Face

FIGURE 4–33.   A dial indicator can read runout. The movement shown on the dial indicator is in 0.001-inch increments. *(Courtesy of Motor Magazine)*

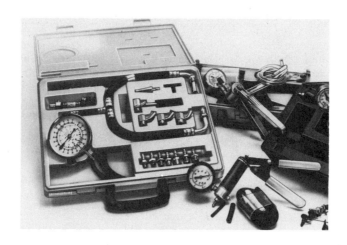

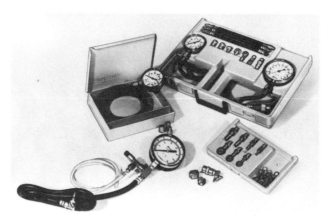

FIGURE 4–34. Pressure and vacuum gauges are used to test the automobile during service. *(Courtesy of Snap-On Tools Corporation)*

Vacuum and Pressure Gauges

Vacuum and *pressure gauges* are used to help troubleshoot, or, when necessary, to check various pressures and vacuum on the engine. *Figure 4–34* illustrates a complete set of pressure and vacuum gauges. The more common gauges include the engine oil pressure gauge, transmission oil pressure gauge, engine vacuum gauge, fuel pump pressure gauge, fuel injection pressure gauge, the vacuum pump gauge, and the engine compression gauge. Service and diagnosis using vacuum and pressure gauges are shown in many of the following chapters.

4.4 POWER AND PRESSING TOOLS

The automotive service technician uses power and pressing tools in the shop. These make the heavy jobs that must be done on the automobile much easier, safer, and quicker. These tools include pullers, presses, impact wrenches, and bushing, bearing, and seal installers.

Pullers

Pullers are used to accomplish three types of action. These actions are pulling an object off of a shaft, pulling an object

---

CAR CLINIC

PROBLEM: Correct Use of Feeler Gauge

A service technician seems to be getting different readings when using a feeler gauge on a set of contact points. What is a good method to make sure a feeler gauge is used correctly?

SOLUTION:

A feeler gauge uses the technician's "feel" to get the correct reading. Often it is difficult to get an accurate reading using a feeler gauge. To increase accuracy when using a feeler gauge, slip the gauge into the clearance being checked. Now twist or tilt the feeler gauge from one side to the other. If there is movement, the clearance is still too high. Each time you use the feeler gauge, remember to twist or tilt the gauge from side to side to get an accurate reading.

out of a hole, and pulling a shaft out of an object. These are illustrated in *Figure 4–35*.

The first example represents pulling a gear, wheel, or bearing, off of a shaft. The second example represents removing bearing cups, retainers, or seals from holes. The third action represents gripping a shaft and bracing against the housing to remove the shaft.

The pullers shown in *Figure 4–36* illustrate how pullers are designed for these uses. The jaw-type puller is used to pull a gear off a shaft. The internal puller is used to remove bearing cups and seals. The push-puller is used to pull a shaft out of a stationary housing.

Because there are so many types, styles, and sizes of seals, pulleys, and shafts, pullers must be designed to fit many applications. *Figure 4–37* illustrates a set of gear and bearing pullers that are commonly used on the automobile.

Bushing, Bearing, and Seal Installers

Installing bushings, bearings, and seals can be a very difficult job. During installation, these components must be aligned correctly. Even pressure must be applied as the component is installed. *Bushing installers* are used to perform this job. *Figure 4–38* shows a bushing, bearing, and seal driver set. These sets include discs and handles to provide a pilot. There are several spacers and drivers to help apply an even force on the part being installed. *Figure 4–39* shows a three-step process for installation. Discs range in size from 1/2 inch through 4 1/2 inches in diameter.

Hydraulic Presses

There are many times when working on automotive parts that pressing is required. For example, presses are used to work on rear axle bearings and piston pins, to press out studs, to straighten parts, and to press in bearings. These jobs are typically done with a hydraulic press. These presses are

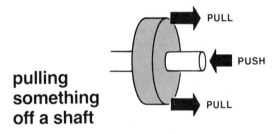

pulling something off a shaft

Removing a gear, bearing, wheel, pulley, etc., to replace it or get at another part.

pulling something out of a hole

Internal bearing cups, retainers or oil seals are usually press-fitted and are difficult to remove.

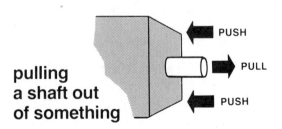

pulling a shaft out of something

A transmission shaft or pinion shaft is often hard to remove from a bore or housing.

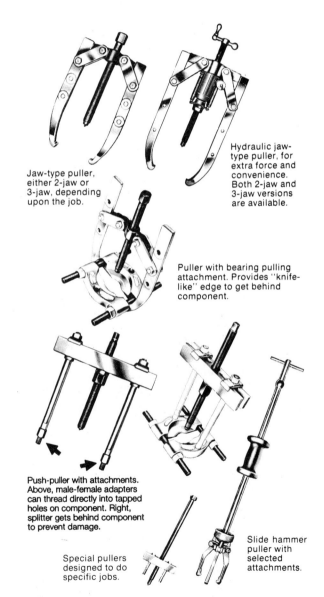

Jaw-type puller, either 2-jaw or 3-jaw, depending upon the job.

Hydraulic jaw-type puller, for extra force and convenience. Both 2-jaw and 3-jaw versions are available.

Puller with bearing pulling attachment. Provides "knife-like" edge to get behind component.

Push-puller with attachments. Above, male-female adapters can thread directly into tapped holes on component. Right, splitter gets behind component to prevent damage.

Special pullers designed to do specific jobs.

Slide hammer puller with selected attachments.

FIGURE 4–35. Pullers are used for many problems in the automotive shop. Pullers are designed for all three actions shown. *(Courtesy of Owatonna Tool Company, Division of Sealed Power Corporation)*

FIGURE 4–36. The different types of pullers are used to accomplish the necessary forces to pull gears, remove seals, and pull shafts from housings. *(Courtesy of Owatonna Tool Company, Division of Sealed Power Corporation)*

capable of producing 50 tons or more of pressure on a part. *Figure 4–40* is an example of a typical hydraulic press.

Impact Wrenches

An *impact wrench* is a powered wrench. It can be operated by using either compressed air (called pneumatic) or electrical power. The wrench works using the principle of impact rotation. Impact rotation is a pounding or impact force to aid in loosening or tightening nuts or bolts. Impact wrenches speed up the process of tightening or loosening bolts and nuts.

1. Select the proper-size components

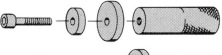

2. Assemble your driver tool

3. Perform the job easily

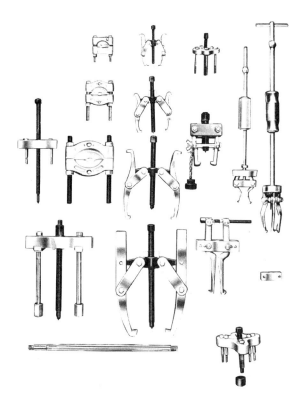

FIGURE 4–37.   Many types of pullers are used on the automobile, because there is a wide variety of pulling jobs. *(Courtesy of Owatonna Tool Company, Division of Sealed Power Corporation)*

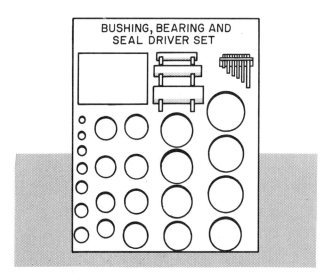

FIGURE 4–38.   A bushing, bearing, and seal driver set is used to correctly install these components. Correct alignment and even distribution of force are provided by these tools. *(Courtesy of Owatonna Tool Company, Division of Sealed Power Corporation)*

FIGURE 4–39.   Three-step process in using the driver set: (1) select proper size, (2) assemble driver tool, and (3) perform the installation. *(Courtesy of Owatonna Tool Company, Division of Sealed Power Corporation)*

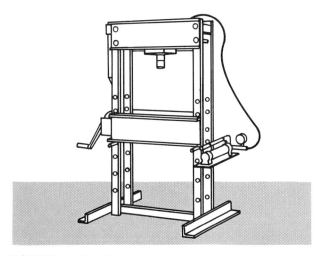

FIGURE 4–40.   Hydraulic presses are used for a variety of pressing jobs. These may include work on piston pins, axle bearings, and other heavy pressing applications. *(Courtesy of Owatonna Tool Company, Division of Sealed Power Corporation)*

Figure 4–41 shows an air-type impact wrench. The drive can have 3/8-, 1/2-, 3/4-, or 1-inch ends. An internal valve regulates the power output. Also, both forward and reverse directions are selected easily.

4.5 ELECTRICAL TESTING TOOLS

Many electrical tools are used to service electronic engine controls. Electrical tools are used mostly for diagnosing various problems in the electrical systems. These tools make the diagnosing job easier and faster. Some of the more common electrical tools include voltmeters, ohmmeters, ammeters, test lights, tachometers, dwell/tach meters, timing lights, electronic engine analyzers and computers, and scanners.

Volt-Ohm-Ammeter

One of the most useful tools today is the *volt-ohm-ammeter*. This testing instrument, also called the multimeter, shown in *Figure 4–42*, can be used to test a variety of components, especially on electronically controlled engines. Depending upon the manufacturer, year and make of the multimeter, various styles can be purchased. Today, the most common type of multimeter has a digital reading. Generally, this meter is used to measure such values as:

1. voltage drop across an electrical component or circuit;

2. internal resistance of any electrical component or circuit;

3. current, or amperage, flowing through small electrical components;

4. grounded circuits;

5. open circuits; and

6. high-resistance circuits.

Test Light

A *test light* as shown in *Figure 4–43* is a very simple testing instrument used to test if there is electricity at certain

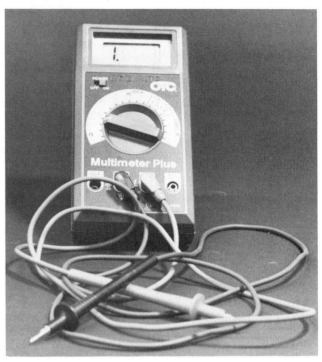

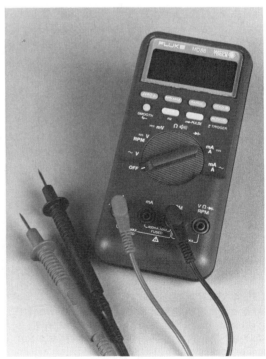

FIGURE 4–41. Impact wrenches are used to produce impact forces during rotation. They are easy to use and can speed up the process of loosening and tightening bolts and nuts. *(Courtesy of Ingersoll-Rand Power Tool Division)*

FIGURE 4–42. Multimeters are often used in the automotive shop for testing various circuits for voltage, amperage, and/or resistance. *(Courtesy of Santini,* Automotive Electricity and Electronics, *Delmar Publishers Inc.)*

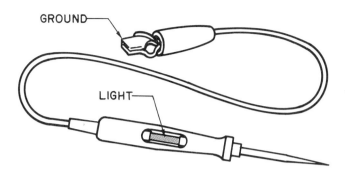

FIGURE 4–43. This test light is able to determine if a circuit has voltage at a specific point. When correctly connected, the test light in the center handle will light, showing that a voltage is present.

points in electrical circuits. Typically, one end of the test light is grounded. The other end of the test light has a sharp, pointed terminal. This pointed terminal can be inserted through wire insulation to touch the electrical wire. The two terminals are connected to a filament or bulb inside the test light. The test light will light if there is voltage available where the pointed terminal is touching. In troubleshooting electrical circuits, the test light can be helpful in finding the problem. The test light is not recommended, however, for troubleshooting electronic computerized circuits and controls.

Tachometer

Tachometers are used to determine the speed, in revolutions per minute (RPM), at which the engine is operating. Most tachometers are part of other electrical analysis equipment used on automotive engines. Electrical tachometers generally measure the firing pulses sent to the spark plugs by the distributor. Other tachometers use a photoelectric or magnetic pickup.

Dwell/Tach Meters

Older engines often used a *dwell/tach meter*. These meters are able to measure the dwell setting on engines that have conventional ignition systems. In addition, the meters are

able to measure the RPM of the engine and the resistance of the ignition points.

Timing Light

The *timing light* shown in **Figure 4–44** is used to determine the exact timing in degrees rotation of the crankshaft. Timing lights are similar to strobe lights that are able to flash off and on rapidly. They sense exactly when cylinder 1 is firing. The firing of the cylinder creates a signal that is amplified enough to operate a light. The pulsing light is then used to monitor the exact timing of the engine ignition system.

Electronic Engine Analyzer

As automotive engines become more electronically controlled, electronic testing tools must also be improved. ***Figure 4–45*** shows an electronic engine analyzer. This testing

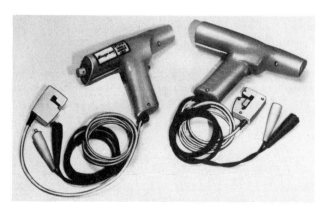

FIGURE 4–44. A timing light is used to determine the exact timing of the spark on the ignition system. *(Courtesy of Snap-On Tools Corporation)*

FIGURE 4–45. Today's engines require sophisticated electronic engine analyzers to help solve many engine problems. *(Courtesy of Sun® Electric Corporation)*

instrument is capable of taking many readings on an engine. Depending on the type, most electronic engine analyzers are capable of reading such items as:

1. RPM of engine;

2. firing sequence;

3. voltage (kV) of each spark plug, under no load and load conditions;

4. spark duration;

5. oscilloscope patterns on the electronic ignition systems;

6. cranking voltages-current-resistances;

7. timing;

8. charging system output;

9. comparative cylinder compression;

10. dwell (if conventional ignition);

11. intake manifold vacuum; and

12. exhaust characteristics (carbon monoxide, hydrocarbons, and oxygen).

In addition, many newer electronic engine analyzers are now connected directly to computers to help the automotive technician troubleshoot the engine. Computer programs direct the technician through a series of tests to determine the exact failure on the engine.

Scanners

Various tool manufacturers produce and sell *scanners* to help automotive technicians troubleshoot the electronic systems. Scanners are small hand-held diagnostic instruments that guide the automotive technician through a series of diagnostic steps and checks to find faulty components or sensors. The technician will typically input data into the scanner such as the vehicle's VIN, make, model, year, and type of engine. The scanner then will read out trouble codes that may have been stored in the engine's on-board computer when some electronic component has failed. The scanner is also able to provide a reading of the information that the car's computer is receiving from its various input devices. The scanner can also provide information concerning the outputs that the computer is controlling. After the scanner gives an indication of a faulty part, the digital multimeter is typically used to perform the pinpoint diagnosis before the faulty part is replaced. *Figure 4–46* shows a typical hand-held diagnostic scanner.

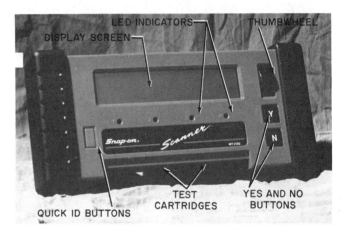

FIGURE 4–46. The electronic scanner is an excellent test instrument to help find problems in many electronic circuits. (*Courtesy of Snap-On Tools Corporation*)

SERVICE MANUAL CONNECTION

Special Tools

Many common tools are required in the automotive shop, and, because of the complexity of vehicles and engines today, many special tools may also be required. These special tools are usually listed at the end of each section in the manufacturer service manuals. The tools are then mentioned in the individual procedures for performing certain tasks on the automobile. At times these special tools can be used only on one make of vehicle. Each special tool is usually referenced by a number. An example of a set of special tools for the brake systems manufactured by Oldsmobile is shown in *Figure 4–47*.

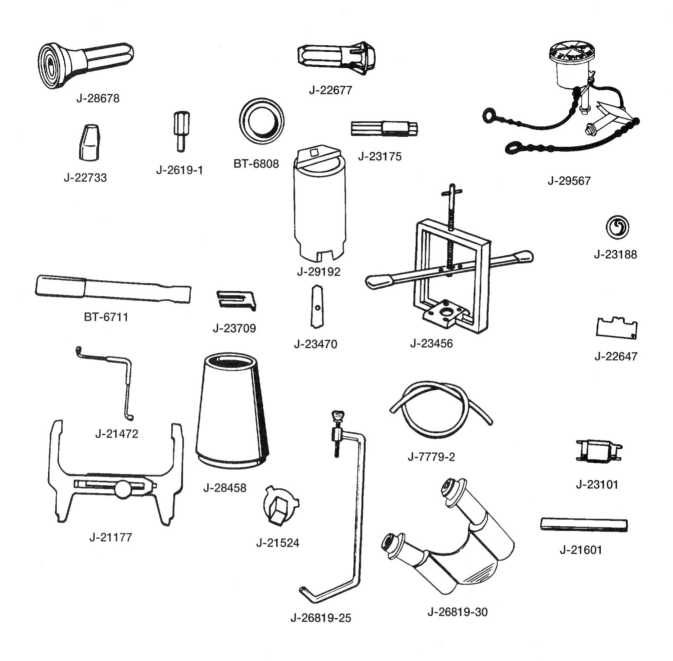

J-2619-1	HEX ADAPTER	
J-7779-2	BRAKE BLEEDER HOSE	
BT-6711	PISTON DISENGAGING TOOL	
BT-6808	SEAL INSTALLER	
J-21177	DRUM AND SHOE GAGE	
J-21472	BLEEDER WRENCH	
J-21524	VACUUM PISTON AND SUPPORT REMOVER AND INSTALLER	
J-21601	VALVE RETAINER INSTALLER	
J-22647	PUSH ROD ADJUSTING GAGE	
J-22677	SEAL INSTALLER	
J-22733	SEAL PROTECTOR	
J-29567	BLEEDER ADAPTER	

J-23101	DIAPHRAGM PLATE SEPARATOR
J-23175	CONTROL VALVE INSTALLER
J-23188	BEARING SEAL PROTECTOR
J-23456	TANDEM DIAPHRAGM SEPARATING TOOL
J-23470	REACTION PISTON GAGE
J-23709	METERING VALVE DEPRESSOR
J-26819-25	BRAKE BLEEDER CLAMP
J-26819-30	BRAKE BLEEDER ADAPTER EXTENSION
J-28458	POWER PISTON SEAL PROTECTOR
J-28678	REAR DUST BOOT SEAL INSTALLER
J-29192	MOUNTING BRACKET NUT SOCKET

FIGURE 4–47. Many special tools are recommended by each manufacturer to service vehicles. (*Courtesy of Oldsmobile Division of General Motors*)

TECHNICIAN'S TOOL SET AND SPECIAL TOOLS

A service technician needs a wide variety of tools. A high-quality set of tools will help the technician to diagnose problems and to service the automobile accurately and completely. As the automobile becomes more and more sophisticated, many special tools are needed to service it. These photos show an assortment of pullers, special mirrors, and instruments that aid in servicing the automobile. *(Courtesy of Snap-On Tools Corporation and Owatonna Tool Company)*

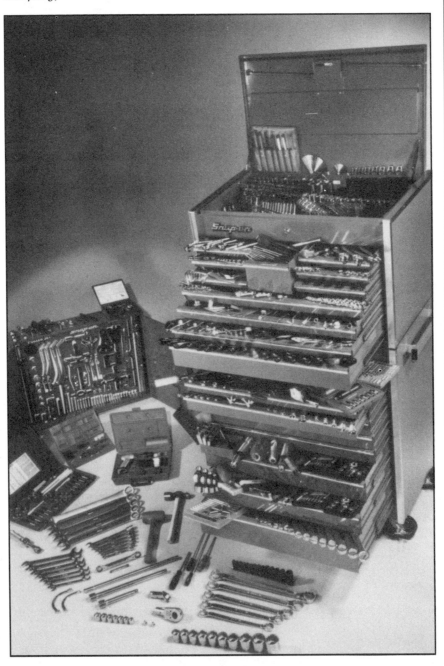

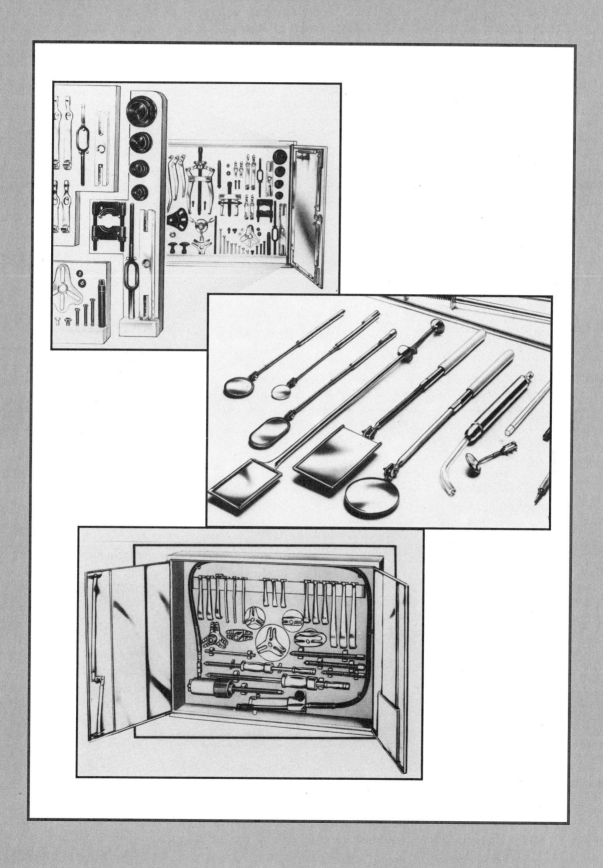

SUMMARY

This chapter introduced common hand tools and measuring tools that are used on the automobile. In order to study these tools, a sound knowledge is needed in measuring systems.

There are two types of measuring systems. They are the USC, or English system, and the metric system. USC measurements use feet, inches, miles, and so on to represent length measurements. Volume is measured by quarts, pints, and so on. Mass is measured by pounds, ounces, and so forth. This system uses several bases such as 12, 3, and 64.

The metric system is based on one unit of length called the meter. All other units of length are derived from the meter, using a base of 10. That is, one meter has 10 decimeters, 100 centimeters, and 1,000 millimeters. Both the USC measuring units and metric system measurements will be used where appropriate in this book.

Once the basic measurement system is known, the tools used in the automotive shop can be explained. Two types of tools were defined in this chapter. These are common hand tools and measuring tools.

Common hand tools include wrenches, hammers, socket sets and drives, screwdrivers, pliers, taps and dies, chisels and punches, and screw extractors.

Wrenches come in three common styles. They are the open end, box end, and combination wrench. Adjustable wrenches are also used in the automotive shop.

There are several types of hammers used in the automotive shop. The most common is called the ball peen hammer. Other styles that have rubber, plastic, and bronze tips are used. These should be used where damage may occur on the material being hammered.

There are several types of sockets, drives, and extensions. Swivel, deep length, and impact are all used in the automotive shop. The sockets are designed to have a certain number of points in the socket. Common point numbers include 6, 8, and 12. When a bolt is positioned so that only a small amount of ratchet rotation is possible, use the 12-point socket. It can be repositioned every 30 degrees.

Screwdrivers are an important tool for the automotive technician. Screwdrivers are identified by the type of tip they have. Common tip styles include the slotted and Phillips tip. Other tips include Torx, magnetic, offset, and Reed and Prince.

Pliers are designed in a variety of styles and types. Pliers are used for cutting and gripping various objects. Common types include slip-joint, needle nose, cutter, electrical service, and retaining ring pliers.

Measuring tools are used to measure various lengths, to torque bolts, to adjust clearances, and to check pressures and vacuums. These tools are micrometers, torque wrenches, vernier calipers, feeler gauges, dial indicators, and pressure and vacuum gauges.

Micrometers are used to measure clearances up to 0.001 of an inch. Micrometers come in any size. Common sizes are 1–2, 2–3, and 3–4 inch micrometers. Measurements are taken by reading a series of numbers on the barrel of the micrometer.

Torque wrenches are used to tighten bolts and nuts to their correct torque specification. They usually read torque in inch-pounds or in foot-pounds. One common type of torque wrench uses a dial to indicate the exact torque being applied to a bolt.

Vernier calipers measure clearances up to 0.001 of an inch. Vernier calipers are read by using a vernier scale placed on the instrument.

Feeler gauges are used to help check and adjust small clearances in a range from 0.0015 to 0.080 of an inch. Clearances such as spark plugs, points, and valves can all be adjusted by using feeler gauges.

Dial indicators are used to measure clearances between two objects. When a feeler gauge cannot be inserted between two objects, a dial indicator may be used. An example might be the clearance between two gears or the crankshaft end play. Dial indicators can also read in 0.001 of an inch.

Vacuum and pressure gauges are used when troubleshooting a vehicle or when certain vacuum and pressure readings must be checked. Common gauges include engine oil pressure, transmission oil pressure, engine vacuum, fuel pump pressure, and fuel injection pressure.

Certain tools are identified as power and pressing tools. These are pullers, bushing, bearing, and seal installers, hydraulic presses, and impact wrenches.

Pullers are used to remove gears, bearings, and seals in a variety of sizes and styles. Bushing, bearing, and seal installers are used to provide correct alignment and force when installing these components. Hydraulic presses are used to press bearings on shafts, remove studs, and straighten objects. Impact wrenches are used to produce an impact force during rotation when loosening or tightening nuts and bolts.

The tools mentioned in this chapter are a small portion of the many tools used by the automotive service technician. Many variations of these tools are also available. A solid foundation in the types, styles, and uses of tools will make the service technician more productive and safe in the workplace.

Various electrical tools are also used by the service technician to aid in diagnosis and troubleshooting. One of the most popular is the volt-ohm-ammeter, also called a multimeter. Other important electrical diagnostic instruments include the dwell/tach meters, timing lights, electronic engine analyzers, and scanners. The scanner is used to help the service technician identify various trouble codes in the onboard computer.

TERMS TO KNOW

Can you explain each of the following terms? Review the chapter until you can use each term correctly.

USC measurements	Cubic centimeter
Metric system	Gram
Base 10	Conversion factor
Prefix	Drive
Liter	Socket point

(continued)

Deep length (well) socket

Impact socket

Pliers

Torque wrench

Micrometer

Vernier caliper

Vernier scale

Feeler gauge

Dial indicator

Vacuum gauge

Pressure gauge

Puller

Bushing installer

Impact wrench

Volt-ohm-ammeter

Test light

Tachometer

Timing light

Electronic engine analyzer

Scanners

REVIEW QUESTIONS

Multiple Choice

1. Which of the following systems of measurement uses the base of 10?
   a. The USC
   b. The metric system
   c. The English system
   d. The SSC system
   e. The OSC system

2. What is the basic unit of length in the metric system?
   a. The foot
   b. The meter
   c. The cubic centimeter
   d. The liter
   e. The inch

3. What type of wrench has the end closed off rather than open?
   a. Open end
   b. Adjustable
   c. Box end
   d. Closed end
   e. None of the above

4. When there is only a small amount of room for ratchet rotation which type of socket should be used?
   a. 6-point
   b. 8-point
   c. 12-point
   d. 24-point
   e. 36-point

5. Which type of socket should be used for high torque when using a power wrench?
   a. Impact socket
   b. Standard socket
   c. Deep length socket
   d. Chrome socket
   e. None of the above

6. A _____ is used to cut external threads on a shaft.
   a. Tap
   b. Die
   c. Chisel
   d. Wrench
   e. Socket

7. Which measurement tool is used to tighten bolts to correct specifications?
   a. Dial indicator
   b. Adjustable wrench
   c. Torque wrench
   d. Pressure gauge
   e. Vacuum gauge

8. Which measurement tool can accurately measure 0.001 of an inch?
   a. Vernier caliper
   b. Vacuum gauge
   c. Pressure gauge
   d. Micrometer
   e. A and D

9. Which of the following tools should be used to adjust or measure small clearances of 0.001 of an inch?
   a. Feeler gauge
   b. Torque wrench
   c. Micrometer
   d. Pressure gauge
   e. Vacuum gauge

10. Which measuring tool has a scale in which two graduations or lines are lined up with each other to obtain the reading?
    a. Micrometer
    b. Vernier caliper
    c. Feeler gauge
    d. Torque wrench
    e. None of the above

11. Which of the following tools would be used to install a bearing on a shaft with a press fit?
    a. Bearing puller
    b. Hydraulic press
    c. Impact wrench
    d. Torque wrench
    e. None of the above

12. Which of the following tools would be used to remove a gear from a shaft?
    a. Puller
    b. Hydraulic press
    c. Impact wrench
    d. Torque wrench
    e. All of the above

13. Which of the following are controls that can be adjusted on the impact wrench?
    a. Power or force
    b. Forward or reverse
    c. Angle of operation
    d. A and B
    e. All of the above

14. When using a bearing or bushing installer, it is important to:
    a. Apply the correct distribution of forces
    b. Make sure the bushing is not aligned
    c. Never use a driver or spacer
    d. Apply oil to the surface
    e. None of the above

15. Which type of tap is used to start threads?
    a. Plug tap
    b. Taper tap
    c. Bottoming tap
    d. Top tap
    e. All of the above

16. When a bolt is broken off and is still partly in the hole, which tool should be used?
    a. Tap and die
    b. Impact wrench
    c. Screw extractor
    d. Torque adapter
    e. Vacuum adapter

17. Which of the following wrenches uses a long pointer that points to a scale as the bolt is tightened?
    a. Deflecting beam torque wrench
    b. Dial torque wrench
    c. Dial indicator
    d. Vernier caliper
    e. Micrometer

18. Which prefix represents the number 1,000?
    a. Milli
    b. Centi
    c. Deci
    d. Kilo
    e. None of the above

19. Which of the following prefixes represents the number 1/1,000?
    a. Milli
    b. Centi
    c. Deci
    d. Kilo
    e. Mega

20. When one foot is divided into 12 inches, a base of _____ is used.
    a. 12
    b. 10
    c. 1/12
    d. 120
    e. 15

The following questions are similar in format to ASE (Automotive Service Excellence) test questions.

21. Technician A says that a feeler gauge can be used to measure small clearances of 0.001 of an inch. Technician B says that a micrometer can be used to measure clearances with an accuracy of 0.001 of an inch. Who is right?
    a. A only   c. Both A and B
    b. B only   d. Neither A nor B

22. Technician A says a tap is used to cut internal threads. Technician B says a die is used to cut internal threads. Who is right?
    a. A only   c. Both A and B
    b. B only   d. Neither A nor B

23. Technician A says the metric system uses a base of 12. Technician B says the USC system uses a base of 10. Who is right?
    a. A only   c. Both A and B
    b. B only   d. Neither A nor B

24. Technician A says that the vernier scale on the vernier caliper can read inches. Technician B says that the vernier scale on the vernier caliper can read in 0.001 inches. Who is right?
    a. A only   c. Both A and B
    b. B only   d. Neither A nor B

25. Technician A says that a nonmetallic feeler gauge should be used to measure clearances between the pickup coil and reluctor on electronic ignition engines. Technician B says that a nonmetallic feeler gauge cannot be purchased. Who is right?
    a. A only   c. Both A and B
    b. B only   d. Neither A nor B

26. Technician B says that a multimeter can check only voltages. Technician B says that a multimeter can check amperage. Who is right?
    a. A only   c. Both A and B
    b. B only   d. Neither A nor B

27. Technician A says that most tachometers measure the firing pulses sent to the spark plugs. Technician B says that most tachometers measure battery voltages. Who is right?
    a. A only   c. Both A and B
    b. B only   d. Neither A nor B

28. Technician A says that scanners are hand-held diagnostic instruments. Technician B says that scanners are able to identify trouble codes stored in the engine computer. Who is correct?
    a. A only   c. Both A and B
    b. B only   d. Neither A nor B

Essay

29. Describe the relationship between a liter and a cubic centimeter.

30. What is the difference between 6-, 8-, and 12-point sockets?

31. Describe the different types of taps used to cut threads.

32. What is the difference between a vernier caliper and a micrometer?

33. Which type of measuring tool would be used to measure small clearances such as valve clearances?

Short Answer

34. When checking clearances on magnetic pickup coils on electronic ignition systems, always use a _____ type feeler gauge.

35. The _____ is used to check if electricity is found at different parts of an electrical circuit.

36. To check the exact timing of an engine, a _____ is used.

37. Electrical and computer circuits can easily be checked using a hand-held _____.

38. To check the RPM of an engine the service technician uses a _____.

CHAPTER 5

Manuals and Specifications

INTRODUCTION   When an automobile is brought to the service shop for repair, it is the service technician's responsibility to repair the vehicle. The automotive technician must have many specifications and service procedures available. The technical data are different for each automobile. This information pertains to new and old vehicles, many manufacturers, both foreign and American, and many assorted problems. It is impossible for any person to remember all of this technical information.

The service manuals available to the automotive technician become one of the most important tools used. It is important to know what is available, how to locate information, what this information means, and how to use specifications correctly. This chapter is designed to address these areas.

OBJECTIVES   After reading this chapter, you should be able to:

- List the different types of information in service manuals.

- List different types of specifications.

- Recognize where technical data can be obtained.

- Identify how to locate and identify the VIN.

- State the common publishers of service data.

- Define the use of service bulletins.

- Identify computer information systems used by automotive service technicians.

5.1   SERVICE MANUALS

Service manuals for automobiles include technical data, procedures, and service descriptions. This information is needed to troubleshoot and diagnose, service, and repair components on the automobile. It includes anything from a description of how to remove a part, to finding the problem, to determining the exact measurement for a clearance.

Typically, maintenance or service manuals do not include much information on theory or operational characteristics. They are designed and written to help the service technician service the vehicle. The best procedure and method of service are shown. In addition, special factory tools and their part numbers are shown in some service manuals.

VIN (Vehicle Identification Number)

The official vehicle identification number is needed to identify the exact type of vehicle being worked on. The VIN is also used for title and registration purposes. It is normally stamped on a metal tab that is fastened to the instrument panel close to the windshield. The VIN can be seen from the

driver's side of the car and is visible from outside the vehicle. See *Figure 5–1*. Each manufacturer has assigned a VIN to each vehicle manufactured. However, each VIN number represents different data. Depending upon the manufacturer, the following information can (in most cases) be determined by reading the VIN number:

1. The country in which the vehicle was manufactured or world manufacturer

2. The corporation and division

3. Model or series of the vehicle

4. Model year

5. Body style

6. Check digit

7. Engine type

8. Factory or plant code

9. Vehicle serial number

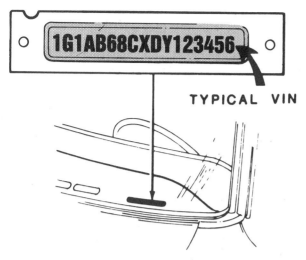

FIGURE 5–1. The VIN can be found on the driver's side of the dashboard, read through the window from outside. *(Courtesy of Chevrolet Division of General Motors)*

Each vehicle service manual has a section in the front identifying the VIN and describing exactly what information it contains. For example, *Figures 5–2* and *5–3* show two typical VIN numbers and what each digit and number means.

Other Vehicle Numbers

Other numbers are also stamped on the vehicle to help the automotive technician identify other information. For example, various numbers are located on the vehicle to identify:

1. Engine type

2. Transmission type

3. Axle/differential ratio

4. Tire information

5. Emission control information

6. Final drive assembly

7. Paint color codes

Each manufacturer has a different system to identify these components. In addition, these numbers may be found in different locations on the vehicle. The exact location of each number can be found in the front of all service manuals for each vehicle. *Figure 5–4* shows one manufacturer's method of showing the vehicle numbers and their locations.

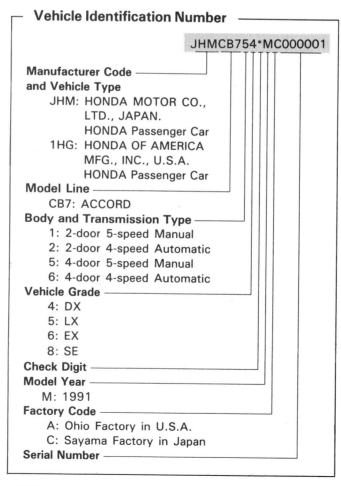

FIGURE 5–2. The VIN can provide various types of information about the vehicle. *(Courtesy of Honda Motor Company, LTD)*

PASSENGER CAR
VEHICLE IDENTIFICATION NUMBER

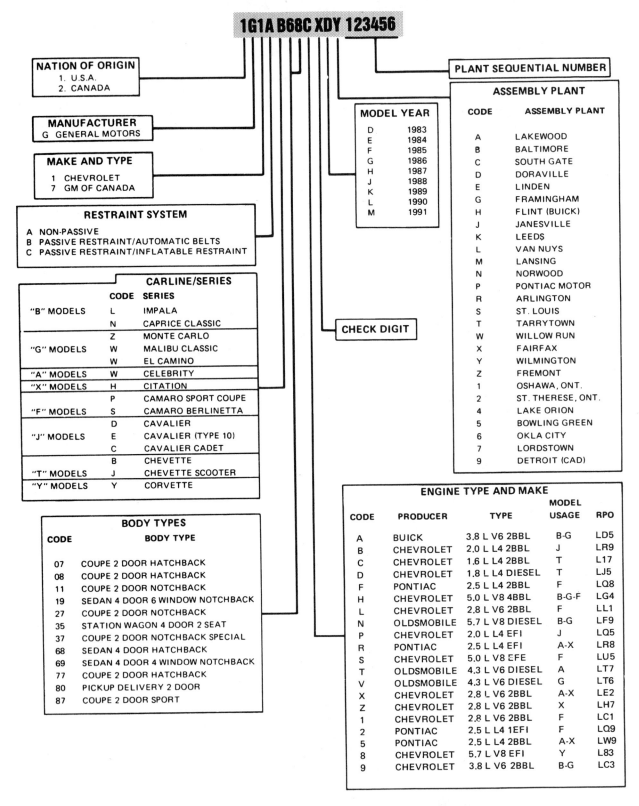

1G1A B68C XDY 123456

NATION OF ORIGIN
1. U.S.A.
2. CANADA

MANUFACTURER
G GENERAL MOTORS

MAKE AND TYPE
1 CHEVROLET
7 GM OF CANADA

RESTRAINT SYSTEM
A NON-PASSIVE
B PASSIVE RESTRAINT/AUTOMATIC BELTS
C PASSIVE RESTRAINT/INFLATABLE RESTRAINT

CARLINE/SERIES

	CODE	SERIES
"B" MODELS	L	IMPALA
	N	CAPRICE CLASSIC
	Z	MONTE CARLO
"G" MODELS	W	MALIBU CLASSIC
	W	EL CAMINO
"A" MODELS	W	CELEBRITY
"X" MODELS	H	CITATION
	P	CAMARO SPORT COUPE
"F" MODELS	S	CAMARO BERLINETTA
	D	CAVALIER
"J" MODELS	E	CAVALIER (TYPE 10)
	C	CAVALIER CADET
	B	CHEVETTE
"T" MODELS	J	CHEVETTE SCOOTER
"Y" MODELS	Y	CORVETTE

BODY TYPES

CODE	BODY TYPE
07	COUPE 2 DOOR HATCHBACK
08	COUPE 2 DOOR HATCHBACK
11	COUPE 2 DOOR NOTCHBACK
19	SEDAN 4 DOOR 6 WINDOW NOTCHBACK
27	COUPE 2 DOOR NOTCHBACK
35	STATION WAGON 4 DOOR 2 SEAT
37	COUPE 2 DOOR NOTCHBACK SPECIAL
68	SEDAN 4 DOOR HATCHBACK
69	SEDAN 4 DOOR 4 WINDOW NOTCHBACK
77	COUPE 2 DOOR HATCHBACK
80	PICKUP DELIVERY 2 DOOR
87	COUPE 2 DOOR SPORT

MODEL YEAR

D	1983
E	1984
F	1985
G	1986
H	1987
J	1988
K	1989
L	1990
M	1991

CHECK DIGIT

PLANT SEQUENTIAL NUMBER

ASSEMBLY PLANT

CODE	ASSEMBLY PLANT
A	LAKEWOOD
B	BALTIMORE
C	SOUTH GATE
D	DORAVILLE
E	LINDEN
G	FRAMINGHAM
H	FLINT (BUICK)
J	JANESVILLE
K	LEEDS
L	VAN NUYS
M	LANSING
N	NORWOOD
P	PONTIAC MOTOR
R	ARLINGTON
S	ST. LOUIS
T	TARRYTOWN
W	WILLOW RUN
X	FAIRFAX
Y	WILMINGTON
Z	FREMONT
1	OSHAWA, ONT.
2	ST. THERESE, ONT.
4	LAKE ORION
5	BOWLING GREEN
6	OKLA CITY
7	LORDSTOWN
9	DETROIT (CAD)

ENGINE TYPE AND MAKE

CODE	PRODUCER	TYPE	MODEL USAGE	RPO
A	BUICK	3.8 L V6 2BBL	B-G	LD5
B	CHEVROLET	2.0 L L4 2BBL	J	LR9
C	CHEVROLET	1.6 L L4 2BBL	T	L17
D	CHEVROLET	1.8 L L4 DIESEL	T	LJ5
F	PONTIAC	2.5 L L4 2BBL	F	LQ8
H	CHEVROLET	5.0 L V8 4BBL	B-G-F	LG4
L	CHEVROLET	2.8 L V6 2BBL	F	LL1
N	OLDSMOBILE	5.7 L V8 DIESEL	B-G	LF9
P	CHEVROLET	2.0 L L4 EFI	J	LQ5
R	PONTIAC	2.5 L L4 EFI	A-X	LR8
S	CHEVROLET	5.0 L V8 EFE	F	LU5
T	OLDSMOBILE	4.3 L V6 DIESEL	A	LT7
V	OLDSMOBILE	4.3 L V6 DIESEL	G	LT6
X	CHEVROLET	2.8 L V6 2BBL	A-X	LE2
Z	CHEVROLET	2.8 L V6 2BBL	X	LH7
1	CHEVROLET	2.8 L V6 2BBL	F	LC1
2	PONTIAC	2.5 L L4 1EFI	F	LQ9
5	PONTIAC	2.5 L L4 2BBL	A-X	LW9
8	CHEVROLET	5.7 L V8 EFI	Y	L83
9	CHEVROLET	3.8 L V6 2BBL	B-G	LC3

FIGURE 5–3. This VIN shows the variation in information for a specific manufacturer. *(Courtesy of Chevrolet Division of General Motors)*

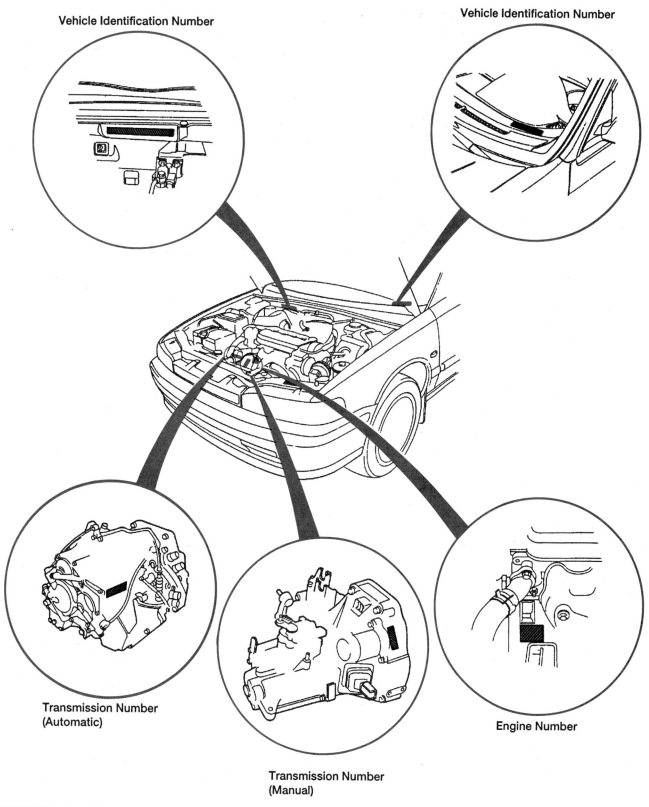

Vehicle Identification Number

Vehicle Identification Number

Transmission Number
(Automatic)

Transmission Number
(Manual)

Engine Number

FIGURE 5–4. Other components on the vehicle can also be identified by numbers. *(Courtesy of Honda Motor Company, LTD)*

Diagnosing Information

Because the automobile is so complex, service manuals include information to aid the technician in *diagnosing* and *troubleshooting* the vehicle. Diagnosing or troubleshooting is defined as identifying a problem, finding a cause, and correcting the problem. Diagnosis is one of the most important skills that the technician must have.

Figure 5–5 illustrates an example of a fuel system diagnostic sheet. Three things are given. The technician must first identify the condition, then select a possible cause. When the cause has been identified, the correction is then provided. There are usually several causes for a particular condition. This gives the mechanic the option of using experience when diagnosing a problem. This diagnostic guide is very easy to read. This guide also is especially helpful for identifying major problem areas on a vehicle.

A second method used to help diagnose a problem in a vehicle is shown in *Figure 5–6*. Here a flowchart is shown. The mechanic follows through each level, taking various readings and measurements. On the basis of the results, the technician follows the flowchart until an incorrect reading is obtained. Finally, a suggested repair helps solve the problem. This format has more detailed explanations than the diagnostic sheet, especially for more complex technical systems. It is very important not to skip any procedures when using this method of diagnosis.

Procedure Information

The correct *service procedure* should always be followed when servicing an automobile. Suggested procedures are shown in the service manual to aid the technician. These procedures are used to speed up the technician's work and to make the job easier and safer. An example of a set of procedures is shown in *Figure 5–7*. This procedure shows how to remove and replace the cylinder head on a particular vehicle. As indicated earlier, very little theory is given.

Specifications

Specifications are included as part of the service manual. Specifications are technical data, numbers, clearances, and measurements used to diagnose and adjust automobile components. Specifications can be referred to as specs. They are usually considered precise measurements under standard conditions. Most specifications can be measured with the measuring tools described in Chapter 4. Specifications are

---

FUEL SYSTEM DIAGNOSIS

The following diagnostic procedures are for fuel system problems and their effects on vehicle performance. Other systems of the vehicle can also cause similar problems and should be checked when listed on the chart. The problem areas described are:

1. Engine cranks normally. Will not start.
2. Engine starts and stalls.
3. Engine starts hard.
4. Engine idles abnormally and/or stalls.
5. Inconsistent engine idle speeds.
6. Engine diesels (after-run) when shut off.
7. Engine hesitates on acceleration.
8. Engine has less than normal power at low speeds.
9. Engine has less than normal power on heavy acceleration or at high speed.
10. Engine surges.
11. Poor gas mileage.

CONDITION	POSSIBLE CAUSE	CORRECTION
Engine Cranks Normally — Will Not Start	Improper starting procedure used.	Check with the customer to determine if proper starting procedure is used, as outlined in the Owner's Manual.
	Choke valve not operating properly.	Check the choke valve and/or linkage as necessary. Replace parts if defective. If caused by foreign material and gum, clean with suitable non-oil-base solvent.
	No fuel in carburetor.	• Perform fuel pump flow test. • Inspect fuel inlet filter. If plugged, replace. • If fuel filter is okay, remove air horn and check for a bind in the float mechanism.

FIGURE 5–5. Service manuals provide information about troubleshooting and diagnosing technical problems. The procedure to be followed is: identify the problem (condition), select a possible cause, and then correct the problem (remedy).

FLOW DIAGRAM

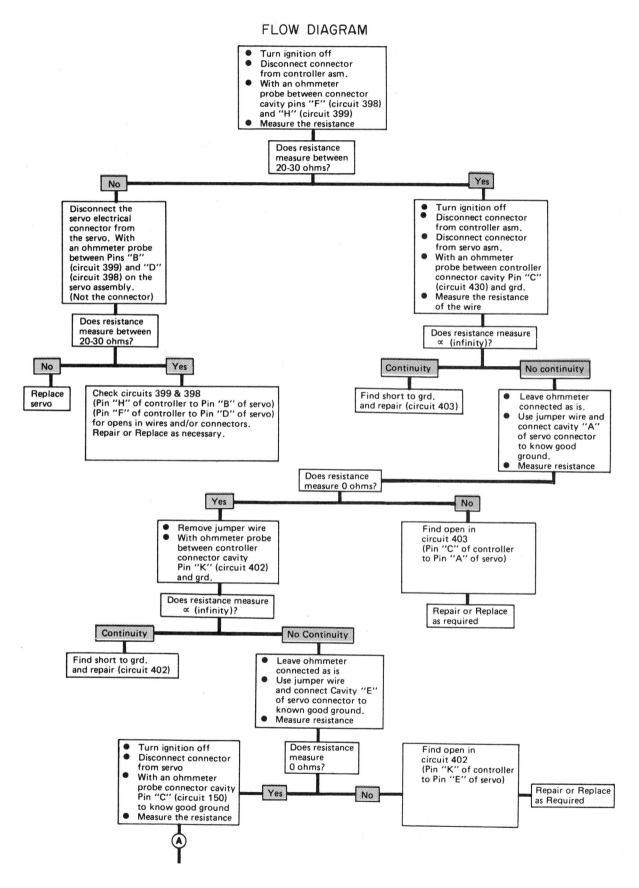

FIGURE 5–6.   This flow diagram presents a detailed system for troubleshooting complex technical systems. Measurements are taken. On the basis of the result of each step, the service technician makes a decision as to what to do next. *(Courtesy of Motor Publications, Auto Repair Manual)*

CYLINDER HEAD
REPLACE

4-151

1. Raise and support front of vehicle, then drain cooling system and disconnect exhaust pipe from exhaust manifold.
2. Lower vehicle and remove oil dipstick tube and air cleaner.
3. Disconnect wire connectors and vacuum hoses from carburetor or TBI unit.
4. Remove EGR valve base plate from intake manifold, if applicable.
5. Disconnect heater hose from intake manifold, then remove AIR system discharge tube attaching bolt from intake manifold.
6. Remove ignition coil lower attaching bolt, then disconnect wiring from coil.
7. Disconnect all wiring from cylinder head and intake manifold, then remove engine upper support attaching bolt from engine strut.
8. Remove A/C compressor and position aside with refrigerant lines attached.
9. Remove alternator drive belt, then remove AIR pump bracket bolt from engine block, if equipped.
10. Disconnect throttle and throttle valve cables from throttle lever and intake manifold.
11. Disconnect upper radiator hose from cylinder head, then disconnect AIR hose from tube assembly, if equipped.
12. Remove rocker arm cover, then remove rocker arms and push rods.
13. Remove cylinder head attaching bolts, then lift cylinder head and intake and exhaust manifolds as an assembly from cylinder block.
14. Reverse procedure to install. Coat heads and threads of cylinder bolts with a suitable sealing compound, then install bolts finger tight. Tighten cylinder head bolts in sequence shown in **Fig. 5**. Tighten intake manifold bolts in sequence shown in **Fig. 6**, if necessary.

FIGURE 5–7. The correct procedures are written in service manuals. This information will aid the technician in performing service in a timely and safe manner. *(Courtesy of Motor Publications, Auto Repair Manual)*

supplied by the automotive manufacturer. Examples of selected specifications include valve clearance, spark plug gaps, tire pressure, number of quarts of oil, ignition timing, and size of engine. There are many other specifications as well.

Specifications are not necessarily the law. They should be used as guides to show the technician how the automobile was set up when it was manufactured. A technician working on a new car should follow the factory specifications as closely as possible. However, when an automobile gets older, some specifications may not be exactly right for best operation. In this case, the manufacturer's specifications must be considered with the technician's experience. This may result in a departure from the factory's specifications. However, it is important to stay as close to the original specifications as possible. In addition, many mechanics subscribe to magazines that feature technical updates on older vehicles.

Types of Specifications

Many types of specifications are needed in the automotive shop. Many of the specifications require the automotive technician to obtain certain information from the vehicle identification number (VIN). This information can then be used to help identify other types of specifications needed. The following is a list of common specifications found in many service manuals. Depending on the exact service manual, the publisher may or may not list the specifications using the categories shown.

1. *General Engine Specifications:* These specifications identify the size and style of the engine. They include cubic-inch displacement, engine codes, fuel system settings, bore and stroke, horsepower, torque, compression ratio, and normal oil pressure. See *Figure 5–8*. Each publisher may include different data in this section. For example, engine numbers, firing order, and number of cylinders may also be included.

2. *Tune-up Specifications:* These specifications help identify adjustments necessary for a tune-up on the vehicle. These include spark plug gap, firing order, degrees of ignition timing, fuel system settings, and fuel pump pressure. *Figure 5–9* shows a set of tune-up specifications. Publishers may include different data for tune-up. Certain tune-up information is also printed on a decal affixed in the engine compartment. See *Figure 5–10*.

3. *Capacity Specifications:* These specifications include measurements needed to identify the capacity of different fluids on the vehicle. These include cooling capacity, number of quarts of oil, fuel tank size, transmission transaxle capacity, and rear axle capacity. *Figure 5–11* shows a standard list of capacity specifications.

4. *Overhaul and Maintenance Specifications:* These include specifications used to aid the technician in servicing the

vehicle. They include distributor advance at different speeds, valve seat angles, valve stem clearances, piston measurements, ring end gaps, bearing clearances, shaft end play, and many more. *Figure 5–12* shows common specifications for cylinder block, pistons, pins, and rings. These specifications help the technician determine how much wear has occurred. The mechanic is then able to decide whether or not to replace the component in question. Usually maximum or minimum clearances are given for this purpose. In some cases, specifications are also given for a new vehicle or a used vehicle.

5. *Operational Specifications:* These specifications tell how the vehicle is to operate, what type of oil to use, and so on. Some of them are found in the owner's manual. For example, *Figure 5–13* shows the break-in speed limit taken from an owner's manual. Some specifications are found in magazines and other technical literature. For example, *Figure 5–14* shows a performance comparison with several vehicles. Other specifications include tire inflation, type of gasoline to use, tire size, and general information for the operator of the vehicle.

6. *Torque Specifications:* It was mentioned in an earlier chapter that it is important to torque each bolt or nut correctly when replacing or installing a component on the automobile. Torque specifications are used for this purpose. *Figure 5–15* shows an example of several torque specifications on a particular manufacturer's engine. These torque specifications should be used in place of any standard bolt and nut torque specifications.

Specifications
GENERAL ENGINE SPECIFICATIONS

Year	Engine CID/Liter	VIN Code①	Fuel System	Bore & Stroke	Compression Ratio	Net Brake H.P. @ RPM②	Maximum Torque	Normal Oil Pressure Psi.
1989	4.3L/V6-262	Z	TBI	4.00 x 3.48	9.3	145 @ 4200	225 @ 2000	③
	5.0L/V8-305	E	TBI	3.74 x 3.48	9.3	170 @ 4000	255 @ 2400	③
	5.0L/V8-307	Y	4 Bbl.	3.800 x 3.385	8.0	140 @ 3200	255 @ 2000	30④
1990	4.3L/V6-262	Z	TBI	4.00 x 3.48	9.3	145 @ 4200	225 @ 2000	③
	5.0L/V8-305	E	TBI	3.74 x 3.48	9.3	170 @ 4400	255 @ 2400	③
	5.0L/V8-307	Y	4 Bbl.	3.800 x 3.385	8.0	140 @ 3200	255 @ 2000	30④
	5.7L/V8-350	7	TBI	4.00 x 3.48	9.3	175 @ 4200	295 @ 2000	③
1991	5.0L/V8-305	E	TBI	3.74 x 3.48	9.3	170 @ 4200	255 @ 2400	③
	5.7L/V8-350	7	TBI	4.00 x 3.48	9.8	185 @ 3800	300 @ 2400	③
1992	4.3L/V6-262	Z	TBI	4.00 x 3.48	9.3	145 @ 4200	225 @ 2000	③
	5.0L/V8-305	E	TBI	3.74 x 3.48	9.3	170 @ 4200	255 @ 2400	③
	5.7L/V8-350	7	TBI	4.00 x 3.48	9.8	185 @ 3800	300 @ 2400	③

TBI—Throttle Body Fuel Injection.
4 Bbl.—4 barrel carburetor.
①—The eighth digit of the VIN denotes engine code.

②—Ratings are net, as installed in vehicle.
③—Minimum with engine hot, 6 psi. @ 1000 RPM; 18 psi. @ 2000 RPM; 24

psi. @ 4000 RPM.
④—Minimum with engine hot @ 1500 RPM.

FIGURE 5–8. One type of specification is called "General Engine Specifications." It gives information about the engine to help the technician identify the exact type of engine in a vehicle. *(Courtesy of Motor Publications, Auto Repair Manual)*

TUNE UP SPECIFICATIONS

Year & Engine/VIN Code ①	Spark Plug Gap	Ignition Timing			Curb Idle Speed ④	Fast Idle Speed ④	Fuel Pump Pressure Psi.
		Firing Order Fig. ②	Degrees BTDC ③	Mark Fig.			
1989							
4.3L/V6-262/Z	.035	E	TDC⑤	B	⑥	⑥	9–13⑦
5.0L/V8-305/E	.035	A	6⑤	B	⑥	⑥	9–13⑦
5.0L/V8-307/Y	.060	C	20⑫	D	⑥	550D⑨	⑪
5.7L/V8-350/7	.035	A	6⑤	B	⑥	⑥	9–13⑦
1990							
4.3L/V6-262/Z	.035	E	TDC⑤	B	⑥	⑥	9–13⑦
5.0L/V8-305/E	.035	A	6⑤	B	⑥	⑥	9–13⑦
5.0L/V8-307/Y	.060	C	20⑫	D	⑧	550D⑨	⑪
5.7L/V8-350/7	.035	A	6⑤	B	⑥	⑥	9–13⑦
1991							
5.0L/V8-305/E	.035	A	TDC⑧	B	⑥	⑥	9–13⑦
5.7L/V8-350/7	.035	A	⑩	B	⑥	⑥	9–13⑦
1992							
4.3L/V6-262/Z	.035	E	TDC⑤	B	⑥	⑥	9–13⑦
5.0L/V8-305/E	.035	A	TDC⑧	B	⑥	⑥	9–13⑦
5.7L/V8-350/7	.035	A	⑩	B	⑥	⑥	9–13⑦

① —The eighth digit of the VIN denotes engine code.

② —Before removing wires from distributor cap, determine location of No. 1 wire in cap, as distributor position may have been altered from that shown at the end of this chart.

③ —BTDC: Before Top Dead Center.

④ —D: Drive. When adjusting idle speed set parking brake & block drive wheels.

⑤ —Disconnect set timing by-pass connector (tan/black wire) when adjusting ignition timing. The timing by-pass connector breaks out of the engine wiring harness on the righthand side of the engine compartment. After completing adjustment, reconnect set timing connector. With engine off, clear trouble code from ECM memory by removing battery voltage to the ECM for 30 seconds.

⑥ —Idle speed is controlled by IAC (Idle Air Control) or ILC (Idle Load Compensator).

⑦ —Wrap shop towel around fuel hose to steel line connection in engine compartment to prevent fuel spillage. Disconnect hose from steel line & install suitable fuel pressure gauge between hose & line. Ensure gauge connections are tight, then start engine & check fuel pressure readings.

⑧ —Disconnect EST bypass electrical connector when checking ignition timing. The bypass connector is located on the AIR control valve tube. After completing adjustment, reconnect EST bypass electrical connector.

⑨ —On low step of fast idle cam.

⑩ —Computer controlled, no adjustment.

⑪ —Mechanical fuel pump pressure, 5.5–6.5 psi, electric pump

⑫ —At 1100 RPM with jumper wire connected between ALCL connector terminals A & B. The ALCL connector is located under the instrument panel to the right of the steering column. After completing adjustment, disconnect jumper wire from between terminals A & B. With engine Off, clear trouble code from Electronic Control Module (ECM) by removing battery voltage from ECM for 30 seconds.

FIGURE 5–9. Tune-up specifications are used to help the service technician tune up the vehicle. Only those specifications for tune-up are shown. *(Courtesy of Motor Publications, Auto Repair Manual)*

FIGURE 5–10. Some tune-up specifications are located on a decal, which is affixed to the engine compartment.

COOLING SYSTEM & CAPACITY DATA

Engine & VIN Code	Cooling Capacity, Qts.	Radiator Cap Relief Pressure, Psi.	Thermo. Opening Temp.	Fuel Tank Gals.	Engine Refill Qts.	Transmission Oil			Rear Axle Oil Pts.
						Man. Trans. Pts.	Auto. Trans. Qts. ①		
1989–90									
3.8L/V6-232 (4)	11.6	16	197	18.8	4②	—	12.3③		④
3.8L/V6-232 SC (C, R)	12	16	197	18.8	4②	6.3③	12.3③		⑤
5.0L/V8-302 (F)	14.1	16	197	18	4②⑥	—	12.3③		⑦
1991									
3.8L/V6-232 (4)	11.8	16	196	19	4.5⑧	—	12.3③		3.1
3.8L/V6-232 SC (C, R)	11.8	16	197	19	4.5⑧	6.3③	12.3③		3.4
5.0L/V8-302 (F) ⑨	14.4	16	192	18	4②⑥	—	12.3③		3.8
5.0L/V8-302 HO (T) ⑩	14.1	16	195	19	4②⑥	—	12.3③		3.4
1992									
3.8L/V6-232 (4, C, R)	12.5	16	197	18	4.5⑧	6.3	12.3③		3.1⑪
4.6L/V8-281 (F)	13.6	14–18	195	20	5.0	—	12.3③		3.8
5.0L/V8-302 HO (T)	14.1	14–18	192–197	18	4.0②	—	12.3③		3.35

①—Approximate, make final check with dipstick.
②—Add 1 qt. with filter change.
③—Use Mercon type transmission fluid.
④—Conventional axle, 3 pts. Traction-Lok axle, 2.75 pts. plus 4 oz. of friction modifier meeting Ford Motor Co. specification EST-M2C118-A.
⑤—Models w/7.5 inch ring gear, conventional axle, 3 pts.; Traction-Lok axle, 2.75 pts. plus 4 oz. of friction modifier meeting Ford Motor Co. specification EST-M2C118-A. Models w/8.8 inch ring gear, conventional axle, 3.5 pts.; traction-Lok axle, 3.75 pts. plus 4 oz. of friction modifier meeting Ford Motor Co. specification EST-M2C118-A.
⑥—Equipped with dual sump oil pan. Remove both drain plugs to fully drain oil. One drain plug is located at front of oil pan. Second drain plug is located at left hand bottom of oil pan.
⑦—Conventional axle, 4 pts. Traction-Lok axle, 3.75 pts. plus 4 oz. of friction modifier meeting Ford Motor Co. specification EST-M2C118-A.
⑧—Add ½ qt. with filter change.
⑨—Crown Victoria & Grand Marquis.
⑩—Cougar & Thunderbird.
⑪—On Super Charged Engines, 3.50 Pts.

FIGURE 5–11. Capacity specifications tell the technician how much fluid is required in such components as the fuel tank, cooling system, engine, and transmission. *(Courtesy of Motor Publications, Auto Repair Manual)*

Procedure for Finding Specifications

There are many procedures for identifying and locating specifications in the service manuals. Use the following general procedure when locating such information:

1. Identify the type, model, and year of the vehicle. Say for example engine rebuilding specifications are needed for a 1991 Oldsmobile 88.

2. Locate the VIN on the vehicle for reference.

3. Select the appropriate year of the service manual.

4. Refer to the first table of contents in the manual on the inside cover. Locate Oldsmobile 88 and the page number that covers this type of vehicle.

5. Turn to that page and read the index of service operations.

6. Look for the engine rebuilding specifications page number and turn to that page.

7. Engine rebuilding specifications are shown in various tables in this section.

8. Often these specifications will be listed according to the size and configuration of the engine. If you are unsure of this information, use the VIN to identify size and con-

CAR CLINIC

PROBLEM: Using the VIN

When looking up specifications in many service and maintenance manuals, you need to know the VIN. What is the VIN, and where is it located?

SOLUTION:

The VIN is the vehicle identification number. In the specifications for a particular vehicle, publishers of service manuals use the VIN to identify the exact type of vehicle. In most cases, the VIN is located on the driver's side of the vehicle on the front of the dashboard. It can be read from outside the vehicle looking at where the windshield and dashboard meet. This number is used to identify various components on the vehicle such as model, body and transmission type, year manufactured, serial number, and so on. When looking up any specification for your vehicle always have the VIN available and ready for reference.

PISTONS, PINS, & RINGS

Engine Liter/ CID	Year	Piston Diameter (Std.)	Piston Clearance	Piston Pin Diameter	Pin To Piston Clearance	Piston End Ring Gap ①		Piston Ring Side Clearance	
						Comp.	Oil	Comp.	Oil
1.3L/4-80.8	1989-91	2.793-2.794	.006	.7864-.7866	.0-.0010	.006	.008	.001-.003	—
1.6L/4-97	1991	3.0690-3.0698	.0010-.0026	.7869-.7871	.0004-.0012	⑬	.008	.0012-.0026	.0012-.0026
1.8L/4-112	1991	3.2659-3.2667	.0015-.0020	.7869-.7871	.0002-.0005	.006-.012	.008	.0012-.0028	—
1.9L/4-116	1989-91	②	.0016-.0024	.8119-.8124	.0003-.0005	.010	.016	⑪	—
2.2L/4-133	1989-91	3.3836-3.3844	.0014-.0030	.8651-.8654	—	⑬	⑭	.001-.003	—
2.3L/4-140③	1989-91	④	.0030-.0038	.9118-.9124	.0003-.0005	.010	.015	.002-.004	—
2.3L/4-140⑤	1989-91	⑥	.0012-.0022	.9119-.9124	.0002-.0005	.008	.015	.002-.004	—
2.5L/4-153	1989-91	⑥	.0013-.0021	.9119-.9124	.0002-.0005	.008	.015	.002-.004	—
2.9L/V6-177	1989-91	⑫	.0011-.0019	.9446-.9450	.0003-.0006	.015	.015	.0020-.0033	—
3.0L/V6-182	1989-91	⑦	.0014-.0022	.9119-.9124	.0002-.0005	.010	.010	.0012-.0031	—
3.0L/V6-182⑮	1989-91	3.5023-3.5035	.0012-.0020	.8267-.8271	.00004	.012	.008	⑯	.0024-.0059
3.8L/V6-232	1989-90	⑧	⑰	.9119-.9124		⑱	⑲	.0016-.0034	—
3.8L/V6-232	1991	⑧	⑳	.9119-.9124	.0002-.0005	.010	.015	.0016-.0034	—
4.6L/V8-281	1991	㉑	.0008-.0018	.8659-.8661	.0002-.0039	.009	.010	㉒	㉓
5.0L/V8-302	1989-91	⑩	⑨	.9119-.9124	.0002-.0004	.010	.015	.002-.004	—
5.8L/V8-351	1989-91	㉔	.0018-.0026	.9119-.9124	.0003-.0005	.010	.015	.002-.004	—

① —Minimum.
② —Coded red, 3.224-3.225 inch; coded blue, 3.225-3.226 inch.
③ —Overhead cam (OHC) engine.
④ —Coded red, 3.7764-3.7770 inch; coded blue, 3.7776-3.7782 inch.
⑤ —High swirl combustion (HSC) engine.
⑥ —Coded red, 3.6783-3.6789 inch; coded blue, 3.6795-3.6801 inch; coded yellow, 3.6807-3.6811 inch.
⑦ —Coded red, 3.5024-3.5031 inch; coded blue, 3.5035-3.5041 inch; coded yellow, 3.5045-3.5051 inch.
⑧ —Coded red, 3.8095-3.8101 inch; coded blue, 3.8107-3.8113 inch; coded yellow, 3.8119-3.8125 inch.
⑨ —Except V8-302 HO engine, .0014 to .0022 inch; V8-302 HO engine, .0030-.0038 inch.
⑩ —Except V8-302 HO engine, coded red, 3.9989-3.9995 inch; coded blue, 4.0001-4.0007 inch; coded yellow, 4.0013-4.0019 inch. V8-302 HO engine, coded red, 3.9972-3.9980 inch; coded blue, 3.9984-3.9992 inch; coded yellow, 3.9996-4.0004 inch.
⑪ —First ring, .0015-.0032 inch; second ring, .0015-.0035 inch.
⑫ —Coded red, 3.6605-3.6615 inch.
⑬ —First ring, .008 inch; second ring, .006 inch.
⑭ —Turbo, .006 inch; non-turbo, .012 inch.
⑮ —Super High Output (SHO) engine.
⑯ —First ring, .0008-.0024 inch; second ring, .0006-.0022 inch.
⑰ —EFI, .0014-.0032 inch; SC, .0035-.0040 inch.
⑱ —EFI, .0002-.0005 inch; SC, .0003-.0006 inch.
⑲ —First ring, .011 inch; second ring, .009 inch.
⑳ —EFI, .0014-.0032 inch; SC, .0040-.0045 inch.
㉑ —Coded red, 3.5498-3.5503 inch; coded blue, 3.5503-3.5509 inch; coded yellow, 3.5509-3.5514 inch.
㉒ —First ring, .002-.004 inch; second ring, .001-.003 inch.
㉓ —Maximum .0006 inch.
㉔ —Coded red, 3.9978-3.9984 inch; coded blue, 3.9990-3.9996 inch; coded yellow, 4.0002-4.0008 inch.

FIGURE 5–12.   Overhaul and maintenance specifications tell the technician the exact measurements of the internal parts of the engine. *(Courtesy of Motor Publications, Auto Repair Manual)*

BREAK-IN SPEED LIMIT MPH (KM/H)						
		1ST	2ND	3RD	4TH	5TH
MANUAL TRANSAXLE	4-speed	0 to 22 (0 to 35)	12 to 37 (20 to 60)	20 to 55 (30 to 90)	25 to 75 (40 to 120)	
	5-speed	0 to 22 (0 to 35)	10 to 37 (15 to 60)	15 to 53 (25 to 85)	22 to 68 (35 to 110)	28 to 80 (45 to 130)
AUTOMATIC TRANSAXLE		"1" Low		"2" Second		"D" Drive
		0 to 30 (0 to 50)		0 to 53 (0 to 85)		0 to 75 (0 to 120)

FIGURE 5–13.   Operational specifications show how the vehicle operates. In this case, the specifications are showing the break-in speed limit for operating the vehicle. *(Courtesy of Nissan Motor Corporation in USA)*

	MPG (CITY DRIVING)	ACCELERA-TION 0–60 MPH (SEC.)	BRAKES 60–0 MPH (HOT) (FT.)	HANDLING (MPH)	MANEUVER-ABILITY (MPH)	NOISE @ 60 MPH (dBA)
Chevrolet Camaro	16	10.5	192	61.9	27.7	71
Toyota in-line 6	21	11	172	66.5	28.5	71
Chevrolet Corvette V8	14	8.4	184	59.5	27.6+	74
Datsun turbo in-line 6	21	9.8	148	65+	27.6+	73
Mazda RX7 rotary	21	11.8	209	65+	27.6+	75
Porsche 924 turbo in-line 4	20	9.5	150	65+	27.6	74

FIGURE 5–14. Certain operational specifications compare vehicles on acceleration, miles per gallon, and so on.

Engine Tightening Specifications

Torque specifications are for clean & lightly lubricated threads only. Dry or dirty threads increase friction which prevents accurate measurement of tightness.

Engine MODEL/V.I.N	Spark Plugs Ft. Lbs.	Cylinder Head Bolts Ft. Lbs.	Intake Manifold Ft. Lbs.	Exhaust Manifold Ft. Lbs.	Rocker Arm Shaft Bracket Ft. Lbs.	Rocker Arm Cover Ft. Lbs.	Connecting Rod Cap Bolts Ft. Lbs.	Main Bearing Cap Bolts Ft. Lbs.	Flywheel To Crankshaft Ft. Lbs.	Vibration Damper Or Pulley Ft. Lbs.
4-150/U	27	85②	23	23	19③	28①	33	80	⑤	90④
4-151/B	11	92	37	37	20③	7	30	65	66	160
4-151/B	11	92	26	37	20③	7	30	65	66	162
6-258/C	11	85	23	23	19③	28①	33	65	105	80④
6-258/C	11	85②	23	23	19③	28①	33	80	105	80

① —In Lbs.
② —Coat under side of cylinder head bolt heads & threads with a suitabile sealing coumpound.
③ —Rocker Arm Cap Screw.
④ —Lubricate bolt threads lightly before assembly.
⑤ —Torque bolts to 50 Ft. Lbs., then tighten bolts an additional 60 degrees.

FIGURE 5–15. Torque specifications are used to help the technician determine the exact torque for certain bolts and nuts. *(Courtesy of Motor Publications, Auto Repair Manual)*

figuration. VIN information can be found by referring to the first table of contents.

9. Also, pay close attention to the footnotes identified by numbers such as 1, 2, 3, 4, 5. These footnotes give valuable information to the service technician concerning specific engine styles.

5.2 SOURCES OF INFORMATION

There are many sources from which specifications, service procedures, and troubleshooting information can be obtained. Both *independent publishers* and automotive manufacturers write service manuals. Parts manufacturers also distribute booklets with specifications and procedures, so their parts will be installed correctly.

Independent Publishers

One of the more popular service and repair manuals is a series published by The Hearst Corporation. These are referred to as *Motor* manuals. See *Figure 5–16*. In these Motor manuals, all specifications, service procedures, and troubleshoot-

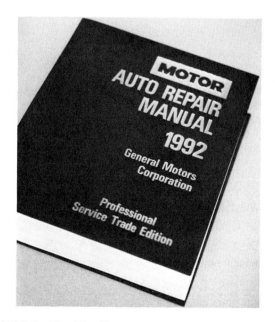

FIGURE 5–16. The Motor manuals are among the most commonly used manuals in the automotive shop. *(Courtesy of Motor Publications, Auto Repair Manual)*

ing guides are printed. They are easy to read, and illustrate the service procedures clearly. These manuals usually include information about cars for the past seven years.

Figure 5–17 shows a typical contents for one of the Motor auto repair manuals. There are several sections. A troubleshooting section gives various tips on how to diagnose the major systems of the vehicle. Then there is an extensive section (vehicle information) on each of the major cars being produced. In each car section, there is also general service information that is common to a particular vehicle. Common service topics include alternator service, disc brakes, power brakes, transmissions, steering columns, and universal joints. This section is very helpful in finding specific service information, tests to make in each area, and general disassembly and reassembly procedures. In addition there are also several other sections on specifications and special service tools.

Each of the vehicle sections also includes extensive information about specifications. Typical specifications in each section include:

1. Engine identification code
2. General engine specifications
3. Tune-up specifications
4. Valve specifications
5. Distributor specifications
6. Alternator specifications
7. Pistons, pins, rings, crankshaft, and bearing specifications
8. Engine tightening specifications
9. Wheel alignment specifications
10. Starting motor specifications
11. Cooling system and capacity data
12. Drive axle specifications

Motor also publishes a series of manuals that can be used on special parts of the vehicle. *Figure 5–18* illustrates the variety of service manuals published by Motor. They include emission controls, automatic transmissions, air conditioners, heaters, and so on. These manuals are extremely helpful for service and diagnosis of special systems. For example, *Figure 5–19* shows the contents for the Motor *Emission Control Manual.* This manual includes all service information, specifications, and diagnosis procedures for the many emission controls that are and have been used on vehicles to date. The information is subdivided by Domestic Cars, Domestic Trucks, and Imports. Motor has a complete line of foreign car manuals as well.

Motor also publishes a monthly magazine entitled *Motor.* This magazine includes information about new automotive products, various special service and diagnosis information, special tools, and various interesting articles about performance and testing of vehicles. See *Figure 5–20.*

Chilton Auto Repair Manuals, Figure 5–21, are also a common source of technical information for automobile service shops. Auto manufacturers now produce automobiles in major lines, or "families." Internally, different models from a single manufacturer are quite similar. They share common systems and components. When dealing with large numbers of automobiles and components, it is easier sometimes to locate information about a technical system. Chilton manuals, for example, have a section on fuel systems and carburetor systems. This information would be the same for one family of vehicles. Chilton manuals carry service information over a seven-year period.

Mitchell Manuals approach the service information from a repair, rather than a particular vehicle manufacturer. There are volumes for each area of repair. The three main volumes include tune-up, mechanical, and transmission. Other man-

TABLE OF CONTENTS

This edition of the MOTOR Auto Repair Manual, Vol. 1, covers specifications and service procedures on 1988-91 General Motors Corporation models available at time of publication. For service information on Chrysler Motors and Ford Motor Company models, refer to the MOTOR Auto Repair Manual, Vol. 2.

Data reported in this manual is subject to change. To report current additions or revisions between editions of this manual, a "Manual Update" page is published every month for your guidance in MOTOR magazine.

FIGURE 5–17. The Motor auto repair manuals have complete sections on vehicle information, specifications, special tools, and troubleshooting. *(Courtesy of Motor Publications, Auto Repair Manual)*

MOTOR MANUALS

FIGURE 5–18. Motor auto repair manuals provide a complete listing of repairs, specifications, and troubleshooting for all American and foreign vehicles. *(Courtesy of Motor Publications)*

uals are available, including wiring diagrams, alternators, starters, air conditioning, and emission controls. Within each section or volume, vehicles are listed with corresponding specifications and necessary information. A set of Mitchell manuals is shown in *Figure 5–22*.

Another publisher that prints service manuals is *Haynes Publishing Group*. These manuals, as shown in *Figure 5–23*, can be purchased at parts stores. Manuals are written to cover specifications, procedures, and troubleshooting for a specific family of vehicles. Manuals are also written for older imported vehicles. These manuals may include more than just service procedures and specifications. They may also include principles of operation and theory.

Manufacturer's Service Manuals

The automotive manufacturers also provide service manuals for their dealerships. *Manufacturer's service manuals* include principles of operation and some theory. These service manuals are written for one family or type of vehicle. *Figure 5–24* shows a set of a service manuals from the manufacturer. Manuals are also available for a particular year and model of vehicle. Common manuals are:

1. Chassis service manual

2. Body manual

3. Electrical troubleshooting manual

TABLE OF CONTENTS

This edition covers specifications and service procedures on 1991 models available at time of publication. Data reported in this manual is subject to change. To report current additions or revisions between editions of this manual, a "Manual Update" page is published every month for your guidance in MOTOR magazine.

FIGURE 5–19. The Motor *Emission Control Manual* has extensive information about emission controls for domestic cars, domestic trucks, and imports. *(Courtesy of Motor Publications, Emission Control Manual)*

4. Owner's manual

5. Wiring diagram manual

6. Do-it-yourself service guide

These manuals can be obtained by writing to the manufacturer of the vehicle. Also, the owner's manual, which is usually kept in the vehicle, may have an address to write to for specific manuals.

Service Bulletins

There are numerous technical changes on specific vehicles each year. Therefore, the service manuals from the manufac-

FIGURE 5–20. Motor publishes a monthly magazine entitled *Motor* that has new product information, service and diagnosis procedures, new tools, and vehicle tests. *(Courtesy of Motor Publications)*

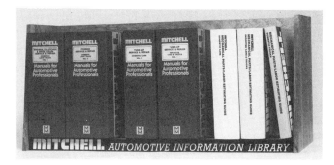

FIGURE 5–22. Mitchell manuals are another source of comprehensive technical information on the automobile. The volumes of the manual include tune-up, mechanical, and diagnosis. *(Courtesy of Mitchell)*

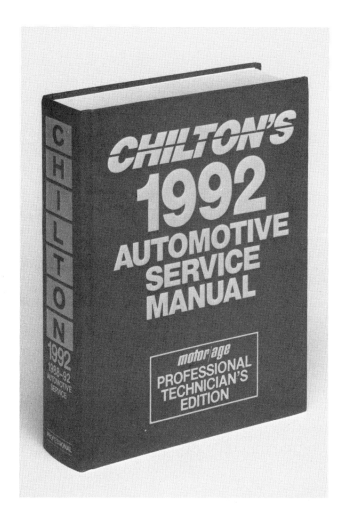

FIGURE 5–21. Chilton automotive service manuals offer a variety of technical data for automobiles. Each vehicle section is subdivided into technical systems such as brakes, engine, suspension, and so on. *(Courtesy of Chilton Book Company)*

FIGURE 5–23. Haynes Publishing Group provides specialized manuals on certain types of older vehicles. They can be purchased in most automotive parts stores.

turer must be updated. Updates are published using *service bulletins*. Service bulletins, shown in ***Figure 5–25***, have changes in specifications and/or repair procedures during the model year. These changes do not appear in the service manual until the next year. The car manufacturer provides these bulletins to the dealers and repair facilities on a regular basis.

Owner's Manuals

Each new vehicle that is manufactured has an Owner's Manual or Owner's Guide available to the car buyer. This manual contains only general information about the vehicle.

SERVICE AND TRAINING CENTERS

Various types of service and training centers are available for the customer and the service technician. The automotive service technician must have a great deal of information. To help improve the technician's level of competence, many companies have technical training centers. These training centers teach the service technician specific, up-to-date technical information about automobiles. In addition there are many service centers available for the automotive customer. Service centers are the link between the customer and the manufacturer of the automobile and its parts. Service centers are available to provide technical advice and to help customers with warranty problems. In addition, these service centers are designed to make the customer comfortable and to develop attractive product display areas. *(Courtesy of the Firestone Tire and Rubber Company)*

Service and Education

FIGURE 5–24.   Service manuals can also be obtained directly from the manufacturer. These manuals usually cover a specific family of vehicles or a particular vehicle.

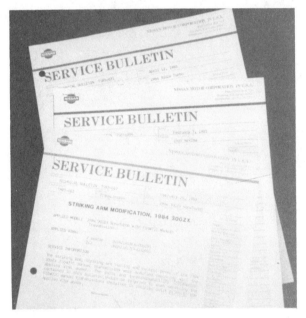

FIGURE 5–25.   Service bulletins provide updated information and changes not included in the service manuals.

For example, the following areas are generally found in most of the owner's manuals:

■ Vehicle instrumentation
■ Getting to know the vehicle
■ Starting and operating the vehicle
■ Specifications and capacities (basic)
■ Servicing the vehicle (basic)
■ Customer assistance
■ Trailer towing

Computerized Information Systems

The need for automotive service and diagnostic information is steadily increasing. Computers are available to provide this information. Recently several computerized networks have been developed to provide additional service and diagnostic information to automotive dealers, technicians, and service shops.

One such network is called the *Service Bay Diagnosis System*. This system has a computerized network connected to the manufacturer in Detroit, Michigan. Specifically, when a service or diagnostic question needs to be answered, the vehicle serial number can be entered into the computer network. Through a series of computer prompts, various system codes can be entered. On the basis of this information, the computer tells the service technician what the problem is, if it is correctable, and helps to do a service bulletin search if a past service bulletin can help solve the problem.

Another system that is now available is called *OASIS*. OASIS stands for On-Line Automotive Service Information System. This system is also capable of communicating with the vehicle manufacturer (through a computer network) to help answer most diagnostic and service questions. This information is extremely important especially when working on the newer computerized/electronic engines. Again, the system works by inserting the serial number of the vehicle and various codes to identify the problem. This system is more sophisticated than the Service Bay Diagnosis System, and, in some cases, the computer tells the service technician exactly what to replace and the repair procedures, on the basis of inputs given to the computer.

A third system often used in automotive service facilities is called the *AllData* Electronic Retrieval system. AllData is a system that incorporates all of selected manufacturers' service manuals and all service bulletins published by each of those manufacturers. This information is contained in a single computer information terminal available to the service technician. AllData has several data bases in its CD-ROM system. A CD-ROM system uses discs like those in a CD audio player to store the data. The data on these discs includes service and repair procedures, parts numbers, wiring diagrams, vacuum hose routings, flat rate information, and the latest TSB, or technical service bulletins. *Figure 5–26* shows an example of the AllData electronic data retrieval system.

FIGURE 5–26.   This system, called AllData Electronic Retrieval, consists of 200,000 pages of data stored on CDs for automotive service and diagnosis. *(Courtesy of Motor Publications, Auto Repair Manual)*

**PROBLEM: Break-in Procedure —
Follow the Manufacturer's
Recommendation**

A customer has been told several methods used to
break in a new engine. The driver is keeping the engine
at a constant 55 mph as much as possible. Also, it was
suggested that the oil be changed after the first 500 miles.
What is the best procedure for breaking in an engine?

SOLUTION:

The best method is to follow the manufacturer's recommendation. This usually includes driving moderately
between 50 and 60 miles per hour for about 2,000 miles
under normal loads. Use the manufacturer's break-in oil.
The oil is designed to aid the engine parts in wearing in
to the mating surfaces. Also, the engine needs about 50–60
cycles of from cold to hot to help wear in the parts.
Change the break-in oil according to the owner's manual
for new cars.

SUMMARY

Manuals and specifications are important tools for working
on the automobile. This chapter introduced manuals and
specifications that are used by the service technician.

Service manuals include diagnosis information, troubleshooting, and procedure information. There are also many
vehicle specifications in service manuals. These include
general engine specifications, tune-up specifications, and
capacity and overhaul specifications. The car owner may also
need operational specifications to determine how the vehicle
operates. Service manuals also include torque specifications.
These tell exactly the torque and horsepower the engine can
produce under certain conditions and RPM.

There are many sources of information to obtain specifications. Motor's manuals provide many service and troubleshooting procedures. They are easy to read and are illustrated
well. Chilton Automotive Service Manuals also provide a
source for technical information. These service manuals break
information into technical systems within all vehicles. Mitchell Manuals have several volumes, which include tune-up,
mechanical, and transmission information. Haynes Publishing Group has manuals that cover specifications, procedures,
and troubleshooting for a specific type of car. Many manuals
are available for foreign vehicles.

Manufacturers provide their own service manuals for each
family of vehicles produced. They also provide service bulletins
to update the technicians who work on the vehicles in a
dealership.

TERMS TO KNOW

Can you explain each of the following terms? Review the
chapter until you can use each term correctly.

Service manual
VIN
Diagnosis
Troubleshooting
Service procedures
Specifications
General engine
  specifications
Tune-up specifications
Capacity specifications
Overhaul and maintenance
  specifications

Operational specifications
Torque specifications
Independent publishers
Manufacturer's service
  manuals
Service bulletins
Service Bay Diagnosis
  System
OASIS
AllData

 REVIEW QUESTIONS

Multiple Choice

1. Which of the following information is not included in a
   service manual?
   a. Specifications
   b. Sales and promotion information
   c. Disassembly procedures
   d. Detailed theoretical information
   e. Vehicle colors and styling

2. Which of the following information can be shown in a
   service manual using a flow diagram form?
   a. Specifications
   b. Troubleshooting and diagnostic information
   c. Overhaul information
   d. Special tools
   e. Types of vehicles

3. Which of the following information is usually shown as
   measurements, clearances, and numbers?
   a. Procedure information
   b. Troubleshooting information
   c. Specification information
   d. Overhaul procedures
   e. Special tools

4. Specifications that include spark plug gap, ignition
   timing, and carburetor adjustments are called:
   a. Tune-up specifications
   b. Capacity specifications
   c. Overhaul and maintenance specifications
   d. Procedure specifications
   e. None of the above

5. Specifications that show bearing clearances, shaft end play, and ring gaps are called:
   a. Tune-up specifications
   b. General engine specifications
   c. Overhaul and maintenance specifications
   d. Capacity specifications
   e. Troubleshooting specifications

6. Torque specifications are identified as:
   a. Torque on nuts and bolts
   b. Engine torque at certain speeds
   c. Torque applied to the crankshaft during operation
   d. Torque applied to the generator
   e. Torque applied on turns

7. Motor manuals are published by:
   a. The manufacturer of the automobile
   b. An independent publisher
   c. Dealerships
   d. Mechanics
   e. Universities

8. Which is not a common title of a service manual provided by a publisher?
   a. Emission Control Manual
   b. Chassis Service Manual
   c. Wiring Diagram Manual
   d. Water Pump Manual
   e. Fasteners Manual

9. Approximately how many years do the Chilton and Motor manuals cover?
   a. 3 years   d. 18 years
   b. 7 years   e. None of the above
   c. 15 years

10. Which of the following types of technical information is sent to the service dealers for updates on the service manuals?
    a. Service bulletins   d. Technique bulletins
    b. Update bulletins   e. Sales bulletins
    c. New data bulletins

The following questions are similar in format to ASE (Automotive Service Excellence) test questions.

11. When repairing an engine, Technician A says overhaul procedures can be found in the service manual. Technician B says overhaul procedures can be found in the sales literature. Who is right?
    a. A only   c. Both A and B
    b. B only   d. Neither A nor B

12. Technician A says that plug gaps, clearances, and torque on bolts cannot be found in a service manual. Technician B says that plug gaps, clearances, and torque on bolts can be found in a service manual. Who is right?
    a. A only   c. Both A and B
    b. B only   d. Neither A nor B

13. Technician A says that diagnosis information can be found in the service manuals. Technician B says that diagnosis information can be found only in literature obtained from the manufacturer. Who is right?
    a. A only   c. Both A and B
    b. B only   d. Neither A nor B

14. Technician A says that the VIN does not include any information about the engine in the vehicle. Technician B says that the VIN does not include the vehicle serial number. Who is right?
    a. A only   c. Both A and B
    b. B only   d. Neither A nor B

15. When looking for the VIN on the vehicle, Technician A says it can be found on the dashboard on the driver's side. Technician B says it can be found in the owner's manual. Who is right?
    a. A only   c. Both A and B
    b. B only   d. Neither A nor B

16. Technician A says that there are numbers placed on the vehicle to identify the type of transmission. Technician B says there are numbers placed on the vehicle to identify axle and differential ratios. Who is right?
    a. A only   c. Both A and B
    b. B only   d. Neither A nor B

Essay

17. What are examples of capacity specifications in the service manuals?

18. What is the purpose of service bulletins?

19. What are the major service manual names?

20. What is the purpose of having diagnosis sheets?

21. What type of specifications might be found in the "general engine specifications"?

Short Answer

22. The number that gives the service technician information about model, year, body style, and so on of the vehicle is called the _____.

23. The _____ provides general information about the vehicle such as vehicle instrumentation, servicing times, and trailer towing.

24. In order to make the service technician's job easier, several new _____ network systems are being used to provide service, diagnostic, and parts information.

25. The VIN is generally located on the _____ part of the vehicle.

26. To identify the exact information represented by the VIN, the service technician can look in the _____.

FUNDAMENTALS OF AUTOMOTIVE ENGINES

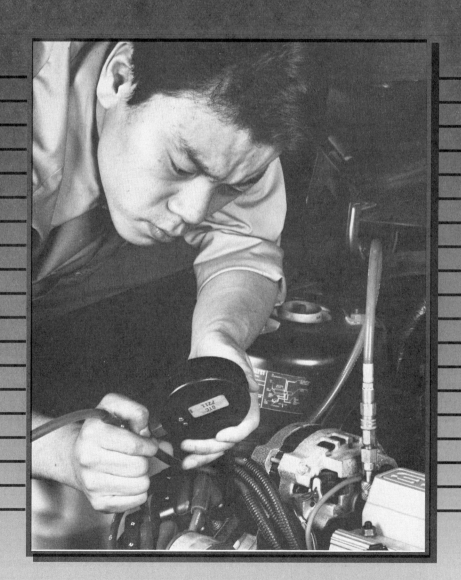

CHAPTER 6

Engine Principles

INTRODUCTION   The component in an automobile that powers the vehicle is called the engine. The engine is a device that is constructed to do one major thing. It converts energy in fuel into power so the vehicle can be moved. This chapter is designed to introduce you to the principles of engine design.

OBJECTIVES   After reading this chapter, you should be able to:

- Define how energy is converted in the automobile.

- Classify engines according to their design.

- Determine how to identify engines.

- Analyze the major components needed to make an engine run.

- Specify the requirements for combustion.

- Compare the strokes of a four-stroke cycle engine.

- Compare gasoline with diesel engine principles.

- Analyze the operation of the Wankel engine.

- Identify the operation of the two-cycle engine.

6.1   ENERGY CONVERSION

Energy Defined

The engine in an automobile is designed to accomplish one thing: to convert *energy* from one form to another. Energy is defined as the ability to do work. There is energy within the fuel that is put into the engine. The engine takes the energy from the fuel and converts it into a form of power. The power is used to propel the vehicle.

Power Defined

Power is defined as a measure of the work being done. Power is the final output of the engine after it has converted the energy in the fuel into work. A more common term used today is horsepower. Horsepower is a measure of the work being done by the engine.

Forms of Energy

Energy can take on one of six forms. Referring to *Figure 6–1*, they include chemical, electrical, mechanical, thermal, radiant, and nuclear forms of energy. The automobile uses all of the preceding energy forms except nuclear energy.

1. *Chemical energy* is defined as energy contained in mole-

cules of different atoms. Examples of chemical energy are gasoline, diesel fuel, coal, wood, chemicals inside a battery, and food.

2. *Electrical energy* is defined as the ability to move elec-

FORMS OF ENERGY	
ELECTRICAL	THERMAL
CHEMICAL	RADIANT
NUCLEAR	MECHANICAL

FIGURE 6–1.   There are six forms of energy, including chemical, electrical, mechanical, thermal, radiant, and nuclear. All of these forms of energy are used on the automobile except the nuclear form. *(Courtesy of DCA Educational Products)*

trons within a wire. Electrical energy uses voltage, wattage, resistance, and so on for operation. Many of the components on a car, including the radio, horn, lights, and starter, utilize electrical energy.

3. *Mechanical energy* is defined as the ability to physically move objects. Examples include water falling over a dam, the ability to move a vehicle forward, and gravity. The starter motor on a car takes electrical energy and converts it into mechanical energy to start the engine.

4. *Thermal energy* is defined as heat. This form of energy is released when fuel burns. The radiator removes excess thermal energy from the engine. The combustion of fuel produces thermal energy.

5. *Radiant energy* is defined as light energy. It is measured by frequencies. Examples of radiant energy include the energy coming to the earth from the sun, the energy from a light bulb, and the energy from anything that glows.

6. *Nuclear energy* is defined as the energy within atoms when they are split apart or combined. Uranium, the fuel used in a nuclear power plant, has nuclear energy internally. Nuclear energy is not used in the automobile.

Energy Conversion

Energy conversion is defined as changing one form of energy to another. Energy usually does not come in the right form. Therefore, it must be converted to a form we can use. For example, the vehicle uses mechanical energy to go forward, electrical energy for the radio, and radiant energy from the light bulbs. Gasoline or diesel fuel is the main source of energy on the vehicle. It is in the form of chemical energy. The engine is designed to convert the chemical energy into the correct forms of energy needed.

Chemical to Thermal Conversion

When any fuel is burned, it changes the energy from chemical (fuel) to thermal (heat). See *Figure 6–2*. This process happens when the fuel burns in an engine. However, thermal energy is not really needed. Mechanical energy is what is needed from the engine.

Thermal to Mechanical Conversion

Once the thermal energy is produced by burning the fuel, the thermal energy causes rapid expansion of the gases within the engine. This rapid expansion is called mechanical energy. The combustion process on any engine converts chemical to thermal, and thermal to mechanical energy. This mechanical energy is then used to help propel the vehicle.

Mechanical to Electrical Conversion

The alternator or generator, *Figure 6–3*, is designed to convert some of the mechanical energy into electrical energy. The electrical energy is used to operate the radio, start the car, provide ignition, and operate other electrical appliances on the vehicle. The storage battery is used to store any excess electrical energy, especially if needed when the car is not running.

Electrical to Mechanical Conversion

The starter motor, *Figure 6–4*, is designed to convert electrical energy into mechanical energy to start the vehicle. This device is called a motor. All motors, including windshield wiper motors, heater fans, and starters, convert electrical energy to mechanical energy.

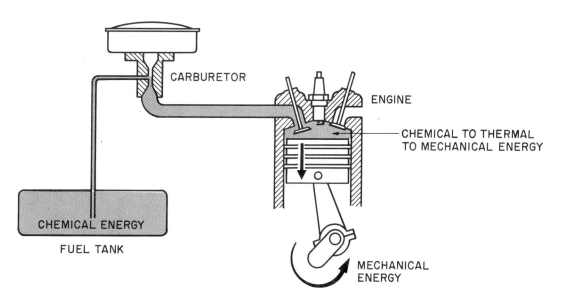

FIGURE 6–2. The internal combustion engine converts chemical energy in the fuel into thermal energy in the combustion area. The thermal energy is then converted into mechanical energy by the piston and crankshaft.

FIGURE 6–3. The alternator on a car engine is used to convert mechanical energy into electrical energy.

FIGURE 6–4. The starter motor on a car engine is used to convert electrical energy into the mechanical energy required to start the engine.

Electrical to Radiant Conversion

Electrical to radiant conversion occurs when light bulbs are used. The energy coming out of a light bulb is radiant energy. Electrical energy is used to operate a light bulb. A light bulb, then, converts electrical energy to radiant energy.

6.2 ENGINE CLASSIFICATIONS

Engines can be classified several ways. These include (1) by the location of the combustion, (2) by the type of combustion, and (3) by the type of internal motion.

Internal Combustion Engines

Engines can be classified by defining the location of combustion. *Combustion* is defined as ignition of the exact amount of fuel mixed with the correct amount of air inside an engine.

In an *internal combustion* engine (ICE), the combustion occurs within the engine. The combustion process occurs directly on the parts that must be moved to produce mechanical energy. The fuel is burned within the engine. See **Figure 6–5**. A gasoline engine is an internal combustion engine. Small lawn mower engines, snowmobile engines, and motorcycle engines are also internal combustion engines.

External Combustion Engines

In an *external combustion* engine, the combustion is removed from the parts that must be moved. See **Figure 6–6**. For example, the boiler in a steam engine is external. It is not touching the piston. Actually, the thermal energy in an external combustion engine heats another fluid. In this case, it is water. Water, converted to steam, pushes against the piston.

There has been some research to determine if an external combustion engine could work in an automobile application. So far, this type of engine has not proven successful in the automobile market.

Intermittent Combustion Engines

The second classification is by the type of combustion. *Intermittent combustion* means that the combustion within the engine starts and stops. A standard gasoline engine has an intermittent combustion design. The combustion starts and stops many times during operation. Diesel engines are called intermittent combustion engines as well. Diesel engines have been used by several automobile manufacturers in the past years in the automobile.

Continuous Combustion Engines

A *continuous combustion* engine has combustion that continues all of the time. The combustion does not stop. It keeps burning continuously. A blow torch is an example of continuous combustion. See **Figure 6–7**. Engines that use continuous combustion include turbine engines, rocket

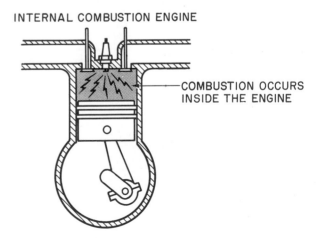

INTERNAL COMBUSTION ENGINE

COMBUSTION OCCURS INSIDE THE ENGINE

FIGURE 6–5. In an internal combustion engine, the combustion of gases occurs inside the engine, touching the moving parts.

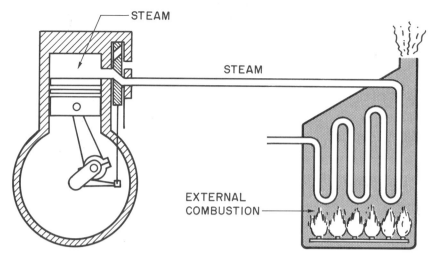

FIGURE 6–6. An external combustion engine has the combustion area removed from the pistons.

engines, Stirling engines, and jet engines. Research has shown that turbines could be used in the automobile, but they are very costly for this purpose.

Reciprocating Engines

The third classification is by the type of internal motion. In a *reciprocating engine*, the motion produced from the energy within the fuel moves parts up and down. The motion reciprocates, or moves back and forth. Gasoline and diesel engines are reciprocating engines. In this case, the power from the air and fuel burning starts the piston moving. The piston starts, then stops, then starts, then stops, and so on. In this engine, the reciprocating motion must then be changed to rotary motion. A crankshaft is designed to change this motion. Refer to *Figure 6–8*.

Rotary Engines

In a *rotary engine*, the parts that are moving rotate continuously. For example, a turbine and a Wankel engine are considered rotary engines. The mechanical movement of the parts takes the shape of a circle. Referring to Figure 6–8, the crankshaft is also an example of rotary motion.

Other Classification Methods

Engines can also be classified by the following methods:

1. *By stroke* — There are two- and four-stroke engines.

2. *By cooling systems* — There are liquid-cooled and air-cooled engines.

3. *By fuel systems* — There are gasoline-fueled and diesel-fueled engines.

4. *By ignition systems* — There are spark-ignition and compression-ignition engines.

All of these methods of classifying engines can be combined with those previously mentioned.

Classification of Engines Used in Automobiles

The automobile uses engines with several of the classifications just listed. The gasoline and diesel engines used in

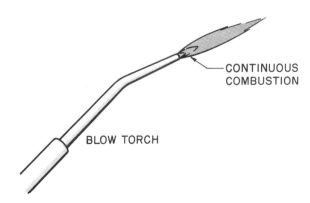

FIGURE 6–7. An example of continuous combustion is a blow torch. The combustion is continuous, not intermittent. Turbine engines have a continuous combustion process.

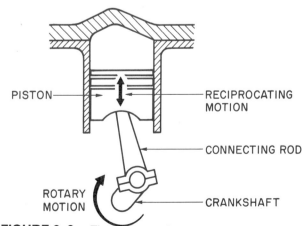

FIGURE 6–8. The reciprocating motion means the parts are moving up and down. Gasoline and diesel engines are considered reciprocating engines.

cars are considered internal combustion, intermittent combustion, reciprocating engine designs. If the rotary (Wankel) engine is used, it is considered an internal combustion, intermittent combustion, rotary design. Many alternative designs have been tested for use in the automobile. The gasoline, diesel, and rotary (Wankel) engines are the ones used today. The gasoline engine is still the most popular form used. The gasoline engine is considered a four-cycle, spark-ignition engine. It can be either liquid-cooled or air-cooled.

6.3 BASIC ENGINE TERMINOLOGY

To understand the principles of automobile engines, certain parts must be defined. These parts are considered the major components of the engine. They include the cylinder block, cylinders, pistons, connecting rods and crankshaft, cylinder head, combustion chamber, valves, camshaft, flywheel, and carburetor.

Cylinder Block

The *cylinder block* is defined as the foundation of the engine. See *Figure 6–9*. The cylinder block is most often made of cast iron or aluminum. All other components of the engine are attached to the cylinder block. The cylinder block has several internal passageways to let cooling fluid circulate around the block. It also has several large holes machined into the block where the combustion occurs.

Cylinders

The *cylinders* are defined as internal holes in the cylinder block. See Figure 6–9. These holes are used for combustion. The holes tell the number of cylinders used on an engine. For example, on small gasoline engines, such as lawn mowers, there is one cylinder. Automobiles usually use four, six, or eight cylinders. Some engines used on heavy equipment have as many as 24 cylinders.

Pistons

Pistons are defined as the round object that slides up and down in a cylinder. Refer to *Figure 6–10*. There is one piston for each cylinder. Pistons are made of light material such as high-quality aluminum that can withstand high temperatures. If fuel and air ignite to cause expansion above the piston, this expansion will force the piston downward. The motion converts the energy in the fuel into mechanical energy (piston moving downward). The piston must also have seals or rings on it. These seals stop any combustion from passing by the piston.

Connecting Rod and Crankshaft

Attached to the bottom of the piston is the *connecting rod*. This is shown in *Figure 6–11*. Its main purpose is to attach the piston to a device known as the *crankshaft*. The crankshaft is used to change the reciprocating motion of the piston and connecting rod to rotary motion. Rotary motion

FIGURE 6–9. The cylinder block is the foundation of the engine. All other parts are attached to the cylinder block. *(Courtesy of Peugeot Motors of America, Inc.)*

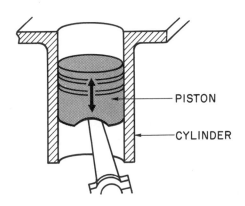

FIGURE 6–10. The piston slides up and down inside the cylinder.

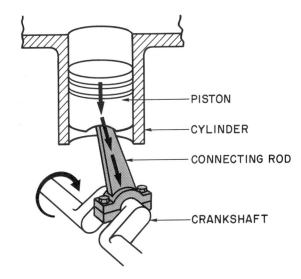

FIGURE 6–11. The connecting rod is attached to the bottom of the piston. The crankshaft changes reciprocating motion to rotary motion.

FIGURE 6–12. A piston, connecting rod, and crankshaft for a four-cylinder engine. All parts are connected to change reciprocating motion to rotary motion. *(Courtesy of Peugeot Motors of America, Inc.)*

is used as the output power of the engine. The piston, connecting rod, and crankshaft parts are shown in Figure *6–12*.

Cylinder Head

The *cylinder head* is the part that fits over the top of the cylinder block. See *Figure 6–13*. It usually houses the ports and valves that allow fuel and air to enter into the cylinder. The spark plug is also attached to the cylinder head. The cylinder head is made of cast iron or aluminum. When it is bolted to the cylinder block, it seals the cylinders so that air and fuel can be controlled in and out of the cylinder.

Combustion Chamber

The *combustion chamber* is where the combustion takes place inside the cylinder. When the cylinder head has been attached, the area inside of the cylinder head and block is called the combustion chamber. On some engines, the combustion chamber is located inside the head. Other engines have the combustion chamber located inside the top of the piston. This is true on most diesel engines.

Valves

Valves are placed inside the cylinder head to allow air and fuel to enter and leave the combustion area. The valves are designed as shown in *Figure 6–14*. Valves must be designed so that when they are closed, the port is sealed perfectly. They must also be designed so that they can be opened exactly at the right time. These valves are opened by using a camshaft and are closed by using springs. There is an intake valve to allow fuel and air to enter the cylinder. There is an exhaust valve to allow the burned gases to escape the cylinder.

Valve and Cylinder Head Arrangements

In the past, engines had two valves in each cylinder, one for the exhaust and one for the intake. There are other arrangements as well. Several arrangements that are currently being used are:

1. Twelve-valve engines usually have three valves in each cylinder and four cylinders. They are called three-valve engines. Generally, each cylinder has two intake valves and one exhaust valve. Other three-valve arrangements are also possible, depending upon the manufacturer. An in-line six-cylinder engine with two valves for each cylinder would also be a 12-valve engine.

2. Sixteen-valve engines have four valves for each cylinder and four cylinders. They are called four-valve engines. Generally, each cylinder has two intake and two exhaust valves. The purpose of having so many valves is to allow more air and fuel to enter smaller-sized engines, thus producing more power. A V-8 engine with two valves for each cylinder would also be a 16-valve engine.

3. Twenty-four-valve engines have four valves in each cylinder and six cylinders. Each cylinder has two intake and two exhaust valves.

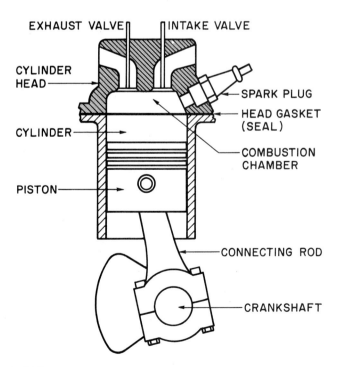

FIGURE 6–13. A cylinder head seals the top of the engine. It houses the intake and exhaust ports, valves, and the spark plug. The combustion chamber is located in the head area. The valves for intake and exhaust are shown.

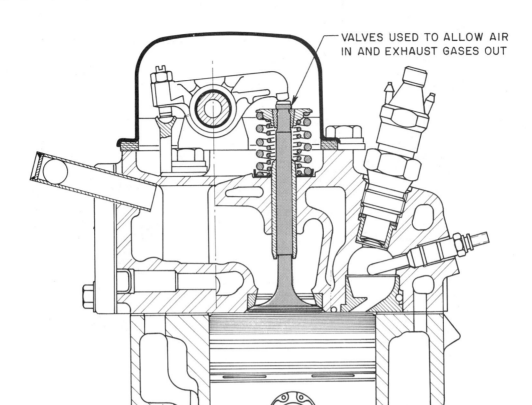

FIGURE 6–14. Valves open and close the ports in the combustion chamber to allow intake and exhaust gases to enter and leave the engine. *(Courtesy of Peugeot Motors of America, Inc.)*

Camshaft

The *camshaft* is used to open and close the valves at the correct time. Cam lobes, or slightly raised areas, are machined on the camshaft to open the valves so that air and fuel can enter the cylinder. The valves are then closed by springs on each valve. The camshaft is driven by the crankshaft. Refer to *Figure 6–15*. The camshaft must be timed to the crankshaft so that the valves will open and close in correct time with the position of the piston. There is one lobe placed on the camshaft for each valve that must be opened and closed. The camshaft can also be placed or mounted directly on top of the cylinder head. This design is called an overhead camshaft (OHC).

The overhead camshaft has several advantages. These include (1) fewer moving parts, (2) more-precise valve operation, (3) higher RPM range, and (4) less frictional horsepower. Often only a single overhead camshaft is used for each bank of cylinders. This arrangement is referred to as an SOHC (single overhead camshaft) engine. When more valves (three or four) are used on each cylinder, then two camshafts may be needed. This arrangement is referred to as a DOHC (dual overhead camshaft) engine.

Flywheel

The *flywheel* is located on the end of the crankshaft. It is designed to act as a weight to keep the crankshaft rotating once power has been applied to the piston. The flywheel is usually heavy. It smooths out any intermittent motion from the power pulses. See *Figure 6–16*.

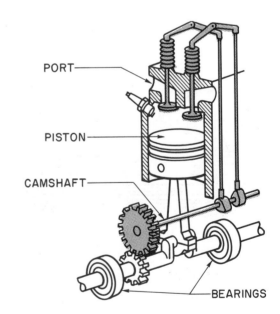

FIGURE 6–15. The camshaft opens and closes the valves at the correct time. The camshaft is driven by the two gears on the cam and crankshaft.

Carburetor

The *carburetor* is placed on the engine to mix the air and fuel in the correct proportion. This is called the fuel induction system. On many cars, fuel induction can also be done by

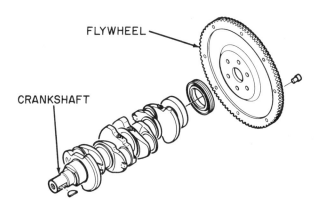

FIGURE 6–16. The flywheel is a heavy weight on the end of the crankshaft. It smooths out any power pulses and helps return the piston to the top of the cylinder. *(Courtesy of Federal-Mogul Corporation)*

fuel injection. Air and fuel must be mixed correctly for the engine to operate efficiently. The carburetor's or fuel injector's job is to mix the air and fuel during cold weather, warm weather, high altitudes, high humidity, and low-speed and high-speed conditions and acceleration.

CAR CLINIC

PROBLEM: Sixteen- and Twenty-four-Valve Engines

Many manufacturers are designing engines using 16 valves or 24 valves. What is the importance of using more valves in an engine?

SOLUTION:

A four-cylinder engine may use four valves for each cylinder, making up the 16 valves. A six-cylinder engine may use four valves for each cylinder, making up the 24 valves. More valves are being used in engines for two reasons. One is to get more air and fuel into smaller engines. Another method would be to make the valves bigger. But if the valves were simply made bigger, they would be heavier and not able to move as fast. In that case, the engine could not run at as high an RPM. Thus efficiency would drop. The use of several smaller valves allows the same amount of air and fuel to enter and exhaust, and the smaller valves do not limit the rpm as do larger valves.

6.4 COMBUSTION REQUIREMENTS

Air, Fuel, and Ignition

The internal combustion engine has certain requirements for efficient operation. Any engine requires three things for

its operation. There must be sufficient air for combustion, correct amounts of fuel mixed with the air, and some type of ignition to start combustion. When these three ingredients are present, *Figure 6–17*, combustion will take place. This combustion will change chemical energy in the fuel to thermal energy. The thermal energy will then cause rapid expansion of gases. This expansion pushes the piston downward. The downward force on the piston makes the crankshaft rotate. This rotary power can be used for pushing the vehicle forward. If any one of these three ingredients is missing, the engine will not run.

Timing

Timing is defined as the process of identifying when the air, fuel, and ignition combine to make combustion occur. This is done in relationship to the position of the piston and crankshaft. For the engine to operate efficiently, the air and fuel mixture must enter the cylinder at the correct time. This means that the intake valve must be opened and closed at the correct time. The exhaust valve must also be opened and closed at the correct time.

The ignition must also be timed. Ignition of the air and fuel must occur at a precise time. The timing of the ignition changes with speed and load. When the intake and exhaust valves are correctly timed and the ignition occurs at the correct time, maximum power will be obtained in converting chemical energy into mechanical energy.

Air-Fuel Ratio

Air-fuel ratio is defined as the ratio of air to fuel mixed by the carburetor. The term *air-fuel ratio* is often called the *stoichiometric ratio*. The air and fuel must be thoroughly mixed. Each molecule of fuel must have enough air surrounding it to be completely burned. If the two are not mixed in the correct ratio, engine efficiency will drop, and exhaust emission levels will increase.

The standard air-fuel ratio should be near 15 parts of air to 1 part of fuel. This measurement is calculated by weight. Actually, the most efficient ratio is stated as 14.7:1. For every pound of fuel used, 14.7 pounds of air would be needed, *Figure 6–18*. In terms of size, this is equal to burning 1 gallon of fuel to 9,000 gallons of air. Although 14.7:1 is the

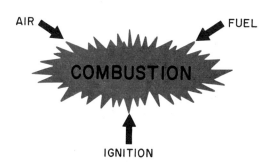

FIGURE 6–17. Three things are needed for combustion: air, fuel, and ignition. If one ingredient is missing, combustion will not happen.

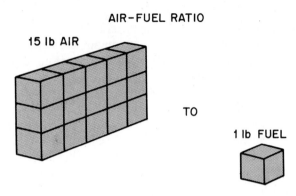

FIGURE 6–18. The air-fuel ratio should be as close as possible to 14.7 parts of air to 1 part of fuel. This ratio is measured by the weight of the air and fuel.

most efficient air-fuel (stoichiometric) ratio, there are times when this ratio is not effective. For example, more fuel is needed during starting and acceleration of the vehicle.

Rich and Lean Mixtures

A low ratio of around 12:1 suggests a *rich mixture* of fuel. A mixture of 17:1 suggests a *lean mixture*. See *Figure 6–19*. Generally, rich mixtures are less efficient during combustion. The rich mixture is used during cold weather and starting conditions. The lean mixture burns hotter than a rich mixture. Normally, the fuel acts as a coolant in the combustion process. With less fuel to cool, the combustion process gets hotter. This condition can cause severe damage to the pistons and valves if not corrected.

Much has been done to control the air-fuel ratio to exact requirements. New carburetors are able to keep the mixture under better control with the use of computers and special

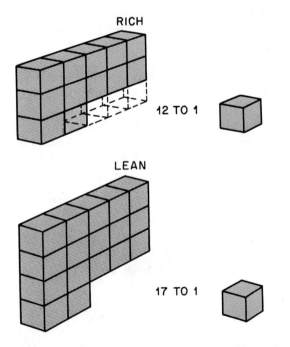

FIGURE 6–19. A rich mixture has a ratio of less air to 1 part of fuel (12 to 1). A lean mixture has more air per 1 part of fuel (17 to 1).

types of fuel injection. By controlling air-fuel mixtures accurately, fuel mileage can be increased well into the 40–50 miles per gallon range for smaller engines.

TDC and BDC

TDC stands for top dead center. *BDC* stands for bottom dead center. TDC indicates the position of the piston when it is located at the top of its motion. When the piston is at the bottom of its travel, it is at bottom dead center (BDC). These two terms are used to help identify the position of the piston during some of the timing processes. See *Figure 6–20*.

Bore and Stroke

The *bore* and *stroke* of an engine help identify its size. The bore of the engine is defined as the diameter of the cylinder. See *Figure 6–21*. The stroke of the engine is a measurement of the distance the piston travels from the top to the bottom of its movement. It is the distance from TDC to BDC.

The stroke is determined by the design of the crankshaft. The distance from the center of the crankshaft to the center of the crankpin is called the *throw*. See *Figure 6–22*. If multiplied by 2, this dimension will be the same distance as

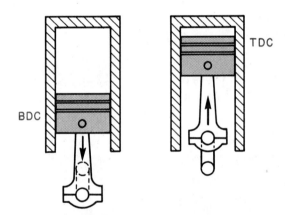

FIGURE 6–20. TDC means top dead center and is the highest point in the piston's travel. BDC means bottom dead center and is the lowest point in the piston's travel.

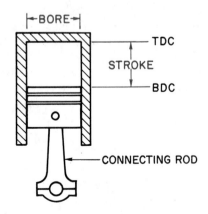

FIGURE 6–21. The bore and stroke of the engine help determine the size of the engine. Bore is the diameter of the cylinder, and stroke is the distance from TDC to BDC.

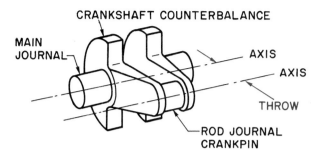

FIGURE 6–22. The distance from the center of the crankshaft to the center of the crankpin is called the throw. When this distance is multiplied by 2, the result is the stroke.

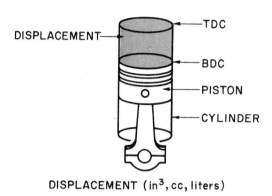

DISPLACEMENT (in³, cc, liters)

FIGURE 6–23. Cubic-inch displacement is the volume of the cylinder from BDC to TDC. It is also stated in cubic centimeters or in liters.

the stroke. If the stroke is changed on the engine, the crankshaft will have a different length throw.

Engine Displacement

Engine *displacement* is defined as the volume of air in all of the cylinders of an engine. Each cylinder has a certain displacement. It can be determined by using the following formula:

$$\text{displacement} = 0.785 \times \text{bore}^2 \times \text{stroke}$$

This formula will tell the exact displacement of one piston from top dead center to bottom dead center. See *Figure 6–23*. If there is more than one cylinder, the total displacement would be multiplied by the number of cylinders.

From this information, and using this formula, what is the displacement of an engine that has six cylinders, a bore of 3.5 inches, and a stroke of 3.70 inches?

Solution: displacement = $0.785 \times 3.5^2 \times 3.7 \times 6$
displacement = 213.4 cubic inches

This formula calculates displacement in cubic inches. Today, however, many engines are sized by cubic centimeters (cc or cm³) and by liters. For example, today's engines are identified as 2.5 liters, 850 cc, and so on. The conversion from cubic inches to cubic centimeters to liters is:

1 cubic inch = 16.387 cc
1,000 cc = 1 liter

The same formula is used to calculate the displacement in metric units. In this case, the bore and stroke are measured in centimeters.

Compression Ratio

During engine operation, the air and fuel mixture must be compressed. This will be covered in the discussion of the four-cycle principle following this section. This compression helps squeeze and mix the air and fuel molecules for better combustion. Actually, the more the air and fuel are compressed, the better will be the efficiency of the engine.

Compression ratio is a measure of how much the air and fuel have been compressed. Compression ratio is defined as the ratio of the volume in the cylinder above the piston when the piston is at BDC to the volume in the cylinder above the piston when the piston is at TDC. The compression ratio is shown in *Figure 6–24*. The formula for calculating compression ratio is:

$$\text{compression ratio} = \frac{\text{volume above the piston at BDC}}{\text{volume above the piston at TDC}}$$

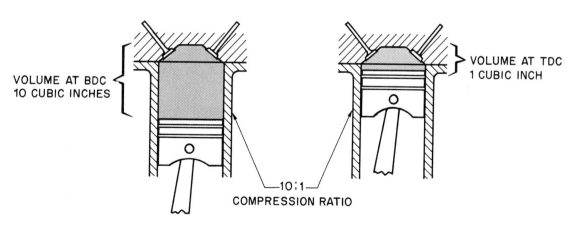

FIGURE 6–24. Compression ratio is the ratio of the volume above the piston at BDC to the volume above the piston at TDC.

In many engines, at TDC, the top of the piston is even or level with the top of the cylinder block. The combustion chamber volume is in the cavity in the cylinder head above the piston. This volume is modified slightly by the shape of the top of the piston. The combustion chamber volume must be added to each volume stated in the formula to give accurate results.

With this information, calculate the compression ratio if piston displacement is 45 cubic inches, and combustion chamber volume is 5.5 cubic inches.

$$\text{compression ratio} = \frac{45 + 5.5}{5.5}$$

$$\text{compression ratio} = 9.1 \text{ to } 1$$

Common compression ratios are anywhere from 8 to 1 on low-compression engines to 25 to 1 on diesel engines.

BMEP

BMEP stands for the term *brake mean effective pressure*. This is a theoretical term used to indicate how much pressure is applied to the top of the piston from TDC to BDC. It is measured in pounds per square inch. This term becomes very useful when analyzing the results of different fuels used in engines. For example, if diesel fuel is used in an engine, more BMEP will be produced and there will be more output power than if gasoline fuel were used. Also, as different injection systems, combustion designs, and new ignition systems are added, the BMEP of the engine is affected.

Engine Efficiency

The term *efficiency* can be used to indicate the quality of different machines. Efficiency can also pertain to engines. Engine efficiency is a measure of the relationship between the amount of energy put into the engine and the amount of energy available out of the engine. The many types of efficiency will be discussed in a later chapter. For understanding basic engine principles, efficiency is defined as:

$$\text{efficiency} = \frac{\text{output energy}}{\text{input energy}} \times 100$$

For example, if there were 100 units of energy put into the engine, and 28 units came back out, the efficiency would be equal to 28%. Efficiency will be discussed later in this chapter.

Engine Identification

Depending on the engine and the manufacturer, various styles and types of engines are found in automobiles. They are identified by stating the number of valves, the camshaft arrangements, and the displacement of the engine. For example, the following engine identification styles are used.

1. Twin-cams (two camshafts)

2. 3.0 LV6 24-valve engine (3.0 liter, V-6, 24 valves)

3. DOHC 16-valve, 660 cc, L4 engine (dual overhead cam-

shaft, with four valves per cylinder, 660 ccs displacement, and four in-line cylinders)

4. 2.2-L DOHC 16-valve turbo engine (2.2 liter, dual overhead camshafts, four valves per cylinder, turbocharged engine)

5. 4.6-L SOHC V-8 engine (4.6 liter, single overhead camshaft for each side of the V-8 configuration)

6.5 FOUR-STROKE ENGINE DESIGN

Automotive vehicles use *four-stroke engines*. A four-stroke engine is sometimes referred to as a four-cycle engine. The terms *stroke* and *cycle* are often interchanged. Interchanging these terms causes some confusion. A stroke is defined as the movement of the piston from top dead center to bottom dead center. A cycle is defined as the events that occur in 360 degrees of crankshaft rotation. A four-stroke engine has a very distinct operation. These four strokes are titled intake, compression, power, and exhaust. In this section, the four-stroke gasoline engine will be explained.

Intake Stroke

Refer to *Figure 6–25*. To start, the location of the piston is near TDC. Note that the intake valve is open. As the piston is cranked downward (called the intake stroke), air and fuel are drawn into the cylinder. This occurs because as the piston moves down, a vacuum is created. When any object is

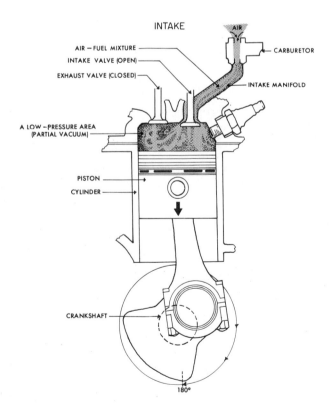

FIGURE 6–25. During the intake stroke, the piston moves down, bringing in fresh air and fuel. The intake valve is open until BDC. *(Courtesy of Breton Publishers)*

removed from an area, a vacuum is created. This vacuum (lower than atmospheric pressure) draws fresh air and fuel into the cylinder. It can also be said that the atmospheric pressure pushes the air and fuel into the cylinder.

The air is first drawn through the carburetor. Here the air is mixed with the fuel at the correct air-fuel ratio (14.7:1). When the piston gets to BDC, the intake valve starts to close. With the valve closed, the air and fuel mixture is trapped in the cylinder area.

Compression Stroke

The piston now travels from BDC to TDC with air and fuel in the cylinder. This action is called the compression stroke. See *Figure 6–26*. The compression stroke takes the air-fuel mixture and compresses it according to the compression ratio of the engine. This compression causes the air and fuel to be mixed very effectively. Actually, the higher the compression ratio, the greater the mixing of air and fuel. This leads to improved engine efficiency.

It is very important that there be no leaks for the compression gases to escape. Leaks may occur in the valves, the gasket between the head and cylinder block, and past the rings on the piston. Note that at the end of the compression stroke, the crankshaft has revolved 360 degrees or one revolution.

During the compression stroke, the air and fuel mixture is actually heated from the action of compression. It is like using an air pump to pump up a tire. As the air at the bottom of the pump is compressed, the air gets hotter. If the com-

pression ratio is too high, temperatures within the combustion chamber may ignite the fuel. This process is referred to as preignition and can cause pinging. This means that the explosion in the combustion chamber started before the piston got to TDC.

It would be very helpful if compression ratios were increased. However, as long as air and fuel are being compressed, the compression ratios must be low so the air and fuel don't preignite. Engines with higher compression ratios will be discussed in the diesel section of this chapter.

Power Stroke

During the power stroke, *Figure 6–27*, both the intake and exhaust valves remain closed. When the piston is coming up on the compression stroke, spark will occur very near TDC. At this point, air, fuel, and ignition are present. This combination causes the air and fuel mixture to burn rapidly. As it burns, the expanding gases push down on the top of the piston. This pressure pushes the piston downward through the power stroke. This is also when BMEP is created.

Again, it is very important for the entire combustion chamber to be sealed without any leaks. Leaks may allow some of the energy in the fuel to escape. This reduces the amount of power pushing down on the piston.

Exhaust Stroke

The last stroke in the four-stroke design is called the exhaust stroke. The exhaust stroke, *Figure 6–28*, starts when

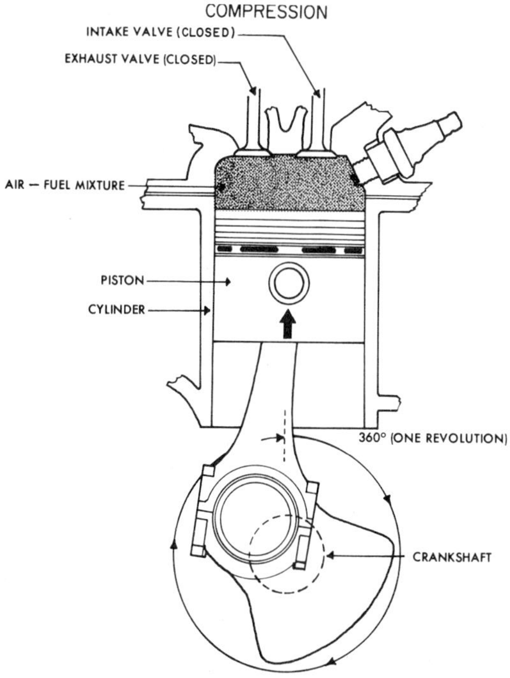

FIGURE 6–26. During the compression stroke, the piston moves from BDC to TDC. This action compresses the air and fuel in the cylinder. *(Courtesy of Breton Publishers)*

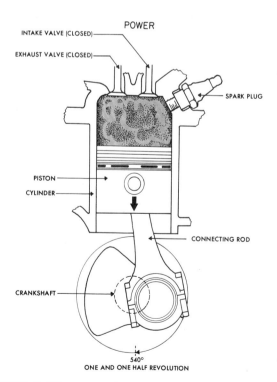

FIGURE 6–27. During the power stroke ignition occurs slightly before TDC. The combustion pushes the piston downward through the power stroke. *(Courtesy of Breton Publishers)*

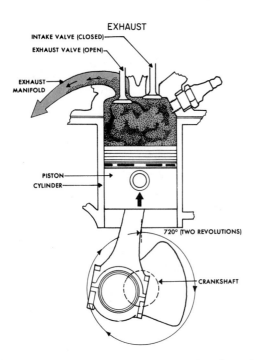

FIGURE 6–28. During the exhaust stroke, the exhaust valve opens. The upward motion of the piston pushes the exhaust gases out of the engine. *(Courtesy of Breton Publishers)*

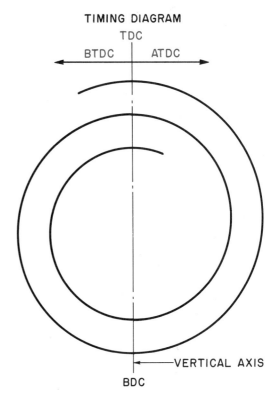

FIGURE 6–29. A timing diagram helps to identify when all of the four stroke events occur. The 360 degrees rotation represents the revolutions of the crankshaft. BTDC stands for before top dead center, and ATDC stands for after top dead center.

the piston starts moving upward again. The crankshaft will continue to rotate because of the flywheel weight. At the beginning of the exhaust stroke, the exhaust valve opens. As the piston travels upward, it pushes the burned or spent gases out of the cylinder into the atmosphere.

Near the top of the exhaust stroke, the exhaust valve starts to close. At this point, the intake valve is already starting to open for the next intake stroke. It is important to note that the crankshaft has revolved two revolutions at this point. Only one power stroke has occurred. If the engine is running at 4,000 RPM (revolutions per minute), then there are 2,000 power pulses for each cylinder per minute.

Timing Diagrams

A *timing diagram* is a method used to identify time in which all of the four stroke events occur. A timing diagram is shown in *Figure 6–29*. The diagram is set on a vertical and horizontal axis. There are 360 degrees around the axis. On the circle, events of the four-stroke engine can be graphed. One way to look at the diagram is to think of these events in terms of the position of the crankshaft and 360 degrees rotation. For example, at the top of the diagram, the piston would be located exactly at TDC. Any event that happens before TDC is referred to as BTDC (before top dead center). Any event that happens after top dead center is called ATDC (after top dead center). The mark at the bottom of the graph would illustrate the position of the piston at BDC. Two circles are shown to represent two complete revolutions of the crankshaft. During the four strokes of operation, the crankshaft revolves two complete revolutions, or 720 degrees of rotation.

Four-Stroke Timing Diagram

Referring to *Figure 6–30*, follow through the four-stroke design on the timing diagram. Note that these events and degrees may vary with each engine and manufacturer. The cycle starts with the intake valve opening slightly before TDC. It should be fully open at TDC. It takes this many degrees of crankshaft rotation to open the intake valve completely.

As the piston travels downward on the intake stroke, the intake valve starts to close shortly before BDC. It is fully closed slightly after BDC. At this point, the intake stroke is completed.

The compression stroke starts when the intake valve is fully closed. The piston travels upward, compressing the air and fuel mixture. As the piston is traveling upward, the air-fuel mixture is being mixed by the compression of gases. Also, the temperature is rising inside the combustion chamber. About 12 degrees before TDC, ignition from a spark plug occurs. The point of ignition is several degrees before TDC. It takes about 12 degrees for the explosion or expansion to actually build up to a maximum. At TDC the expansion is at a maximum point. Now the piston is ready to be pushed downward.

If the timing of the ignition were sooner, or more degrees before TDC, then the explosion would occur too soon. This would then reduce the BMEP during the power stroke. If the

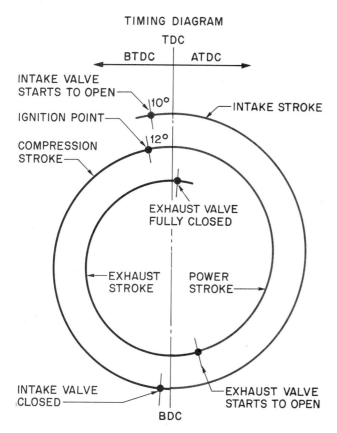

FIGURE 6–30. The timing diagram shows the events of the four-stroke engine. Intake, compression, power, and exhaust are plotted on the diagram.

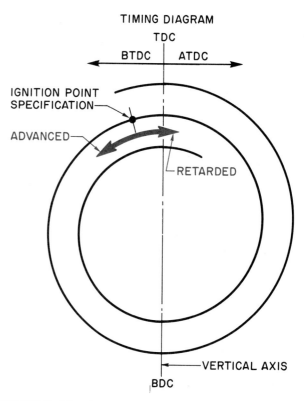

FIGURE 6–31. If the ignition timing moves farther before TDC, the engine is advanced. If the ingition timing moves toward TDC or after, the ignition is retarded.

timing of the ignition were too late, or after TDC, then the BMEP would also be less. It is important that maximum power from the explosion of gases occurs just when the piston is at TDC.

The power stroke starts when the piston starts downward. In this case, the power stroke is shown on the inside circle of the timing diagram. As the explosion occurs, the gases expand very rapidly. This expansion causes the piston to be forced down. This action produces the power for the engine.

Near BDC, at the end of the power stroke, the exhaust valve starts to open. By the time the piston gets to BDC, the exhaust valve is fully open. As the crankshaft continues to turn, the piston travels upward. This action forces the burned gases out of the exhaust valve into the atmosphere. The exhaust valve is fully closed a few degrees after TDC. The time during which both the intake valve and the exhaust valve are open (near TDC) is called valve overlap.

Advance and Retarded Timing

The only part of the timing on the gasoline engine that is adjustable is the timing of the ignition. If the ignition time is moved or adjusted more BTDC, the condition is called advance timing. If the ignition time is moved or adjusted toward or after TDC (ATDC), the condition is called retarded timing. See *Figure 6–31*.

6.6 DIESEL ENGINE PRINCIPLES

The *diesel engine* is much the same as the gasoline engine in many of its principles. It is considered a four-stroke engine. The diesel engine is considered an internal combustion engine. It is also considered a compression ignition rather than a spark ignition engine.

Diesel Compression Ratio

One major difference between a diesel engine and a gasoline engine is that the diesel engine has a very high compression ratio. Compression ratios from 20 to 1 up to 25 to 1 are very common. This high compression ratio means that any fuel that is in the cylinder during compression will be ignited. Therefore, only air is brought into the cylinder during the intake stroke. No carburetor is needed to mix the air and fuel. Fuel is injected in a diesel engine. With high compression ratios, temperatures inside the combustion chamber may be as high as 1,000 degrees Fahrenheit. This temperature would be high enough to ignite most fuels. Because the fuel is ignited by the high temperatures produced by compression, the diesel engine is called a compression ignition engine.

Fuel Injection

At, or slightly before, TDC, a fuel injector injects fuel into the combustion chamber on diesel engines. This design is

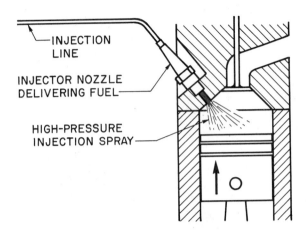

FIGURE 6–32. In a diesel engine, air and fuel are mixed near TDC. Fuel is injected into the combustion chamber under high pressure. The heat of compression then ignites the air and fuel mixture.

called *fuel injection*. A fuel injector is a device that pressurizes fuel near 20,000 psi. This fuel is injected into the combustion chamber. See *Figure 6–32*. At this point, all three ingredients are there to produce combustion. The power and exhaust strokes are the same as in the gasoline engine.

Comparison of Diesel and Gasoline Engines

Figure 6–33 shows common comparisons between the diesel and gasoline four-stroke engines.

1. The intake on the gasoline engine is an air-fuel mixture. The diesel engine has only air during the intake stroke.

2. The compression pressures on the gasoline engine are lower, because the compression ratios are lower. The compression temperatures on the gasoline engine are also lower.

3. The air and fuel mixing point on the gasoline engine is at the carburetor. The mixing point on the diesel engine is near TDC or slightly BTDC.

4. Combustion is caused by a spark plug on the gasoline engine. The diesel engine uses compression ignition.

5. The power stroke on the gasoline engine produces around 460 psi. On the diesel engine, the power stroke produces near 1,200 psi. There is more energy in diesel fuel than in gasoline.

6. The exhaust temperature of the gasoline engine is much higher than that of the diesel engine, because some of the fuel is still burning when it is being exhausted. There is also a higher percentage of carbon monoxide in gasoline exhaust.

7. The efficiency of the diesel engine is about 10% higher than that of the gasoline engine. The compression ratios are higher in the diesel engine, so there is more energy in a gallon of diesel fuel than in a gallon of gasoline.

6.7 ROTARY DESIGN (WANKEL)

In the late 1960s, several new engine designs were introduced into the automotive market. One such engine is called the *rotary engine*. The rotary design has been in existence for some time. Lately there has been a renewed interest in

COMPARISON OF GASOLINE AND DIESEL ENGINES		
	GASOLINE	**DIESEL**
Intake	Air-Fuel	Air
Compression	8–10 to 1 130 psi 545°F	16–20 to 1 400–600 psi 1,000°F
Air-Fuel Mixing Point	Carburetor or Before Intake Valve With Fuel Injection	Near Top Dead Center By Injection
Combustion	Spark Ignition	Compression Ignition
Power	464 psi	1,200 psi
Exhaust	1,300°–1,800°F CO = 3%	700°–900°F CO = 0.5%
Efficiency	22–28%	32–38%

FIGURE 6–33. There are several differences between a gasoline engine and a diesel engine. Differences are in the intake, compression, air-fuel mixing point, combustion, power, exhaust, and efficiency.

developing the rotary engine for automotive applications. In this converter, a rotor, instead of a piston, is used to convert chemical energy into mechanical energy. The engine is an intermittent combustion, spark ignition, rotary design (not reciprocating).

Rotary Cycle Operation

Refer to *Figure 6–34*. This is called position 1. It corresponds to the intake stroke. The upper port is called the intake port. The lower port is called the exhaust port. There are no valves. The position of the center rotor opens and closes the ports much as a valve would. The rotor moves inside an elongated circle. Because of the shape of the housing, certain areas are enlarged or compressed during rotation. As the rotor is turned, an internal gear causes the center shaft to rotate. This rotation is the output power.

When the leading edge of the rotor face sweeps past the inlet port, the intake cycle begins. Gasoline and air (14.7:1 air-fuel ratio) are drawn into the enlarging area. They continue to be drawn in until the trailing edge passes the intake port.

As the rotor continues to rotate, the enlarged area is now being compressed. This is called position 2. It corresponds to the compression stroke. See *Figure 6–35*. The compression ratio is very close to that of a standard gasoline engine, because air and fuel are being mixed.

When the rotor travels to position 3 (the power stroke), *Figure 6–36*, the air and fuel are completely compressed. At this point, ignition occurs from two spark plugs. There are two spark plugs for better ignition. On some newly engineered rotary engines, three spark plugs are being used to improve combustion. All three ingredients are now available for correct combustion. The air and fuel ignite rapidly. Combustion causes expansion of gases. This expansion pushes the rotor face downward, causing the rotor to receive a power pulse.

Figure 6–37 illustrates position 4 (the exhaust stroke). As the rotor continues to travel or rotate, the leading edge uncovers the exhaust port. The rotor's movement within the housing causes the exhaust gases to be forced out of the engine.

So far, only one side of the rotor has been analyzed. Note that while intake is occurring in position 1, compression is occurring on another face of the rotor, and exhaust is occurring on the third side of the rotor. In this engine there are three power pulses for each rotation of the rotor.

The rest of the rotary engine uses many of the same com-

POSITION 1

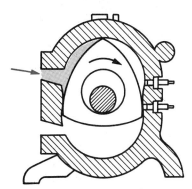

FIGURE 6–34. Intake on the rotary engine is produced when, in the shaded area, the leading edge of the rotor passes the intake port and leaves an opening that allows gas and air to enter.

POSITION 3

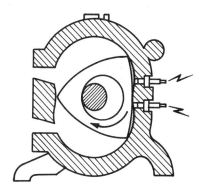

FIGURE 6–36. During the power stroke on the rotary engine, the expansion of gases causes pressure against the rotor face. This pressure causes the rotor to continue turning.

POSITION 2

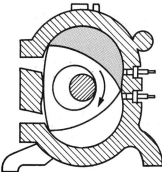

FIGURE 6–35. As the rotor continues to turn, the air and fuel are compressed to a standard compression ratio.

POSITION 4

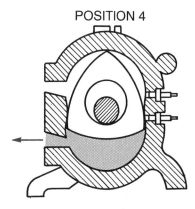

FIGURE 6–37. As the rotor continues to rotate, the leading edge uncovers an exhaust port. Exhaust gases are then forced out of the chamber.

ponents as the standard gasoline engine. The carburetor or fuel injection system is the same. The starter, alternator, and external components are the same. A complete rotary engine is shown in *Figure 6–38*.

6.8   TWO-STROKE ENGINE DESIGN

In recent years most automotive manufacturers have been considering the use of another type of engine design for automobiles. This design is called the *two-stroke engine*. Two-stroke engines are commonly used on smaller power applications such as outboard motors, snowmobiles, and chain saws. Because it is simple and light, it is being considered for automotive uses.

Two-Stroke Engine Operation

Figure 6–39 shows an example of a two-stroke engine

operation. Note that many of the engine parts are the same as for the four-stroke engine. One difference is that the cylinder does not use the standard type of valves to allow air and fuel to enter the engine. In order to follow the operation, consider the events both above and below the piston. As the piston in Figure 6–39 (A) moves upward, compression is produced above it. A vacuum is created in the crankcase area below the piston. The vacuum brings in a fresh charge of air and fuel past a reed valve. Note that oil must be added to the air-fuel mixture at this point, because there is no oil in the crankcase as with four-stroke engines. The oil in the fuel acts as the lubricant. Oil can also be injected into the crankcase to obtain lubrication. Normally, an oil-gas ratio of from 20:1 to 50:1 or higher is used.

As the piston continues upward on the compression stroke, eventually a spark, and thus combustion occurs, Figure 6–39 (B). The combustion pushes the piston downward. As the

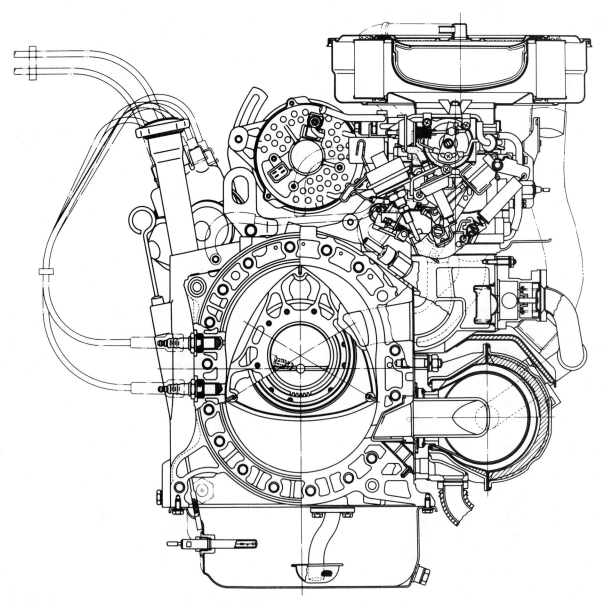

FIGURE 6–38.   The rotary engine uses many of the same components as the gasoline reciprocating engine. This is a cross-cut section showing many internal parts. *(Courtesy of Mazda Motor Corporation)*

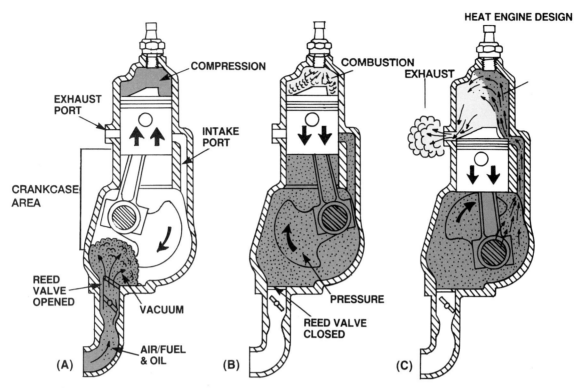

FIGURE 6–39. The two-stroke engine uses the pressure and vacuum created below the piston to draw a fresh charge of air, fuel, and oil to be used in the combustion chamber. *(Courtesy of DCA Educational Products)*

piston moves farther down, high pressure is created in the crankcase area. The reed valve is forced closed by the pressure, sealing the crankcase area. When the piston gets low enough in its stroke, it eventually opens both the intake and exhaust ports, Figure 6–39 (C). Ports are simply holes cut into the cylinder to allow air and fuel to enter and exhaust to escape.

When the ports are open, the crankcase pressure forces a mass of air, fuel, and oil mixture into the combustion chamber. This mass also helps to remove any exhaust gases by way of the exhaust port. As the piston starts upward, the ports are closed. Compression and power continue above the piston, while suction and a small pressure continue below the piston.

Two-Stroke Timing Diagram

A timing diagram can be used to illustrate the two-stroke engine. Remember, the vertical axis represents the TDC and BDC point on the piston and crankshaft. The events of the two-stroke process can be graphed on the timing diagram, as shown in *Figure 6–40*. Although the two-stroke and four-stroke engine diagrams differ slightly, they show several common points.

1. Timing for combustion occurs slightly before TDC.

2. During the power stroke, the exhaust valve or port opens slightly before the intake valve or port.

3. During the compression stroke, the exhaust valve or port closes slightly after the intake valve or port.

4. When the piston is at the bottom of its travel, both intake and exhaust are occurring.

Advantages and Disadvantages of Two-Stroke Engines

There are several advantages and disadvantages of using the two-stroke engine in automobiles. Two advantages are:

1. Two-stroke engines are generally very responsive because there is a power pulse every revolution. Therefore, it takes less time to get from 500 RPM at idle to say, 4,000 RPM at maximum speed.

2. Two-stroke engines usually weigh less than four-stroke

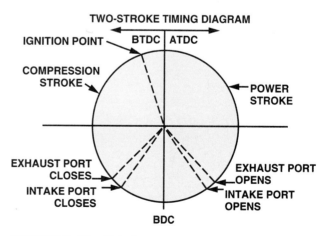

FIGURE 6–40. This timing diagram shows the events that occur during two-stroke engine operation *(Courtesy of Schwaller, Transportation, Energy and Power Technology, Delmar Publishers Inc.)*

engines, because they usually have fewer parts. With a lighter engine, vehicle fuel mileage generally improves.

The disadvantages of two-stroke engines are related to efficiency. They are less efficient than four-stroke engines for several reasons.

1. Poor movement of air and fuel. Air and fuel can enter the cylinder for only a very short period of time. Because less air and fuel can enter the engine, efficiency is reduced.

2. Poor combustion efficiency. The oil in the air-fuel mixture reduces combustion efficiency because of its burning characteristics.

3. Less BMEP. Total force during the power stroke is less because the power stroke is shorter. The power stroke ends when the exhaust port is opened.

Although many problems still exist, engineering efforts are being directed at improving efficiency, combustion, fuel injection, and scavenging (ease of air and exhaust movement).

Loop-Scavenging Two-Stroke Engine

The basic design of the two-stroke engine is continually being improved. *Loop scavenging* is a two-stroke design used to improve the ease with which air and fuel can enter and leave the cylinder. The main difference between loop scavenging and the basic design shown in Figure 6–39 is that the reed valve system is replaced with an intake port located on the bottom of the cylinder. The intake port is opened and closed by the position of the piston skirt (bottom of the piston). Events again occur both above and below the piston. *Figure 6–41* shows the operation of a loop-scavenging two-stroke engine.

The events occur in three phases. In phase 1, the piston moves upward, and the piston skirt opens the intake port in the lower right of the cylinder. The vacuum below the piston draws in fresh fuel, air, and oil for lubrication. During phase 2, the power stroke above the piston is occurring. Below the piston, compression occurs on the air-fuel-oil mixture. During phase 3, the exhaust port and the intake port to the cylinder are opened. This opening causes the air-fuel-oil mixture below the piston to transfer to the combustion chamber. The spent exhaust gases in the cylinder are also exhausted to the atmosphere.

SERVICE MANUAL CONNECTION

The material in this chapter is directly related to information in most service manuals. For example, all engine specifications are listed according to the specific type and size of engine. Generally, service manuals identify engines by various characteristics. For example, number of cylinders, CID (cubic-inch displacement), bore and stroke, and compression ratios are often found in service manuals to identify specific engines. The following is an example of how selected engines can be identified using these characteristics.

Engine (No. of cyl.-CID/liter)	Bore × Stroke (Inches)	Compression Ratio (Ratio to 1)
V8-350/5.7l	4.057 x 3.385	21.6 (diesel)
4-151/2.5l	4.00 x 3.48	9.0
6-225/3.7l	3.40 x 4.12	8.4
V8-302/5.0l	4.00 x 3.00	8.9
6-258/4.23l	3.75 x 3.90	9.2

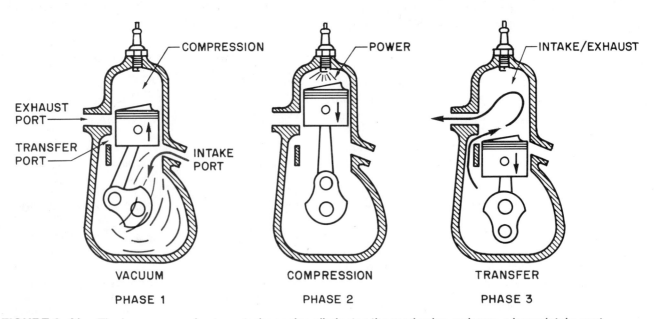

COMPRESSION — POWER — INTAKE/EXHAUST

EXHAUST PORT

TRANSFER PORT

INTAKE PORT

VACUUM
PHASE 1

COMPRESSION
PHASE 2

TRANSFER
PHASE 3

FIGURE 6–41. The loop-scavenging two-stroke engine eliminates the reed valve and uses a lower intake port.

Linkage to Science and Mathematics

CALCULATING ENGINE DISPLACEMENT: ENGLISH AND METRIC

Engine displacement = $0.785 \times$ bore$^2 \times$ stroke $\times$ no. of cylinders
1 cubic inch = 16.387 cc
1000 cc = 1 liter

Determine the total engine displacement of an engine that has the following specifications:

- Cylinder bore of 2.87 inches

- Piston stroke 3.5 inches

- Four-cylinder engine

Find:

Total cubic-inch displacement = _____

Total cubic centimeters = _____

Total liters = _____

CAR CLINIC

PROBLEM: Two-Stroke Engine

Why are the big automotive manufacturers looking into using the two-stroke rather than the four-stroke engine?

SOLUTION:

Most automotive manufacturers have research programs to evaluate and test different types of engines. One type being considered is the two-stroke engine. It is generally a very responsive engine because it has a power pulse on each piston, every revolution. It is able to go from idle to maximum RPM faster than the four-stroke engine. It is also much lighter, because it has fewer parts. With a lighter engine, vehicle fuel mileage generally improves.

On the other hand, research must continue to improve the combustion efficiency and air movement through the cylinder, and ways must be found to increase its BMEP.

SUMMARY

This chapter introduced various engine principles. Many terms were defined and engine principles were introduced.

The engine in the automobile converts energy in the fuel to power for moving the vehicle. In this process, energy takes on several forms, including chemical, electrical, mechanical, thermal, and radiant.

Engines are classified in several ways. Combustion occurs inside the internal combustion engine. In the external combustion engine, combustion is removed from the center of the engine. Intermittent combustion starts and stops. Continuous combustion means the combustion continues all of the time. Reciprocating engines have motion that moves parts up and down. Rotary engines have continuous rotation of parts.

Several terms are helpful in understanding engine principles. The cylinder block is the foundation of the engine. Inside the cylinder block, there are cylinders that pistons fit into. The connecting rod connects the piston to the crankshaft. The cylinder head fits over the top of the engine. The combustion chamber is where combustion of the fuel takes place. The valves open and close ports to let the air and fuel in and out. The camshaft is used to help open and close the valves. The flywheel is a weight that keeps the crankshaft rotating. The carburetor mixes the air and fuel within the engine.

For an engine to work properly, there are certain combustion requirements. There must be the right air and fuel mixture. Normally about 15 parts of air will mix with 1 part of fuel. A lean mixture would have more air or less fuel. A rich mixture would have less air or more fuel. This air-fuel mixture must be ignited at the correct time.

The bore and stroke of the engine help determine the size and power of the engine. Bore is the diameter of the cylinder, while stroke is the distance from TDC to BDC. These are used to determine engine displacement. Compression ratio is a measure of how much the air and fuel mixture has been compressed in the cylinder. BMEP stands for brake mean effective pressure. It is a theoretical term that indicates the amount of pressure applied to the top of a piston. Engine efficiency is a measure of the output power related to the input power. Usually gasoline engines are about 28% efficient.

The automobile engine is called a four-stroke engine. This means that there are intake, compression, power, and exhaust strokes while the engine is operating. The intake stroke brings in fresh air and fuel. The compression stroke compresses the air-fuel mixture. The mixture is ignited, and the power stroke occurs. As the piston comes up again, exhaust gases are pushed out of the engine. This is the exhaust stroke. Timing diagrams are used to help show the events of the four-stroke engine. Both advance and retarded timing can be seen on the timing diagram.

The diesel engine is also being used in some automobiles today. The compression ratio is much higher, near 25:1. Fuel is injected near TDC. No carburetor or spark plug is used. Combustion starts by the heat of compression rather than by using the spark plug.

The rotary engine uses a triangular rotor to cause the intake, compression, power, and exhaust strokes. Air and fuel are mixed in a carburetor, and the compression ratios are about the same as in a gasoline engine.

The two-stroke engine is also being considered as an alternative engine for automobiles. The two-stroke engine is able to produce the intake, compression, power, and exhaust events within one crankshaft revolution. The engine uses a set of ports in the cylinder to allow air and fuel to enter the combustion chamber at the correct time. Several designs are being studied. One such design is called loop scavenging, in which the ports for air and fuel entry are controlled by the position of the piston.

TERMS TO KNOW

Can you explain each of the following terms? Review the chapter until you can use each term correctly.

Energy	Piston
Power	Connecting rod
Combustion	Crankshaft
Internal combustion	Cylinder head
External combustion	Combustion chamber
Intermittent combustion	Valve
Continuous combustion	Camshaft
Reciprocating engine	Flywheel
Rotary engine	Carburetor
Cylinder block	Timing
Cylinder	Air-fuel ratio

(continued)

Rich mixture

Lean mixture

TDC and BDC

Bore

Stroke

Throw

Displacement

Compression ratio

BMEP (brake mean effective pressure)

Efficiency

Four-stroke engine

Timing diagram

Diesel engine

Fuel injection

Two-stroke engine

 REVIEW QUESTIONS

Multiple Choice

1. The ability to do work is defined as _____ .
   a. Power
   b. Energy
   c. Pressure
   d. Force
   e. Work done

2. A measure of the work being done is defined as _____ .
   a. Energy
   b. Power
   c. Thermal Energy
   d. Force
   e. Work started

3. The energy used to start the vehicle is called:
   a. Radiant energy
   b. Mechanical energy
   c. Thermal energy
   d. Electrical energy
   e. Forced energy

4. Which form of energy is defined as the ability to move electrons in a wire?
   a. Thermal
   b. Electrical
   c. Mechanical
   d. Radiant
   e. None of the above

5. Which type of energy does a gasoline engine convert the chemical energy to?
   a. Thermal
   b. Mechanical
   c. Nuclear
   d. A and B
   e. All of the above

6. The gasoline engine is considered which type of engine?
   a. External combustion
   b. Continuous combustion
   c. nternal combustion
   d. Rotary
   e. All of the above

7. Other methods are used to classify engines. Which of the following methods is used to classify engines?
   a. By the cycles
   b. By the ignition system
   c. By the fuel system
   d. All of the above
   e. None of the above

8. The object that is the foundation of the engine and the point to which all other parts are attached is called the:
   a. Piston
   b. Crankshaft
   c. Carburetor
   d. Block
   e. Cylinders

9. The part in the engine that moves up and down in a cylinder is called the:
   a. Piston
   b. Crankshaft
   c. Carburetor
   d. Flywheel
   e. Camshaft

10. Which part of the gasoline engine houses the valves?
    a. Carburetor
    b. Camshaft
    c. Cylinders
    d. Cylinder head
    e. Piston

11. Which object is used to keep the engine turning when the power is not being applied?
    a. Flywheel
    b. Crankshaft
    c. Camshaft
    d. Piston
    e. Connecting rod

12. Which of the following is used to mix the air and fuel?
    a. Starter
    b. Carburetor
    c. Alternator
    d. Cooling fan
    e. Cylinder head

13. What is the best air-fuel ratio for a gasoline engine?
    a. 14.7:1
    b. 18.3:1
    c. 13.2:1
    d. 12.1:3
    e. 20.0:1

14. Which of the following is considered a lean mixture?
    a. 13:1
    b. 10:1
    c. 17:1
    d. 11:1
    e. 12:1

15. The diameter of the cylinder is called the _____.
    a. Stroke
    b. Throw
    c. Bore
    d. Torque
    e. Force

16. Engine displacement can be measured in:
    a. Liters
    b. Cubic inches
    c. Cubic centimeters
    d. All of the above
    e. None of the above

17. When the volume above the piston at BDC is divided by the volume above the piston at TDC, the result is called:
    a. Air-fuel ratio
    b. Compression ratio
    c. Fuel injection
    d. Engine displacement
    e. Rotary displacement

18. The pressure on top of the piston during the power stroke is called:
    a. BMEP
    b. Air pressure
    c. Combustion
    d. Force
    e. All of the above

19. Which of the following is not called one of the strokes on the four-stroke engine?
    a. Intake
    b. Spark
    c. Power
    d. Exhaust
    e. Compression

20. Which of the following events on the four-stroke engine is adjustable?
    a. Ignition time
    b. Exhaust valve opening time
    c. Intake valve opening time
    d. Top dead center
    e. Bottom dead center

21. What is the compression ratio on some diesel engines?
    a. 25:1
    b. 8:1
    c. 10:1
    d. 6:1
    e. 5:1

22. The diesel engine uses _____ to mix the air and fuel correctly.
    a. Fuel injection
    b. Carburetors
    c. Spark plugs
    d. Camshafts
    e. Electric motors

23. The diesel engine ignites the fuel from:
    a. The heat of compression
    b. A spark plug
    c. The fuel injection
    d. The igniter
    e. Exhaust from the first cylinder

24. How many power pulses are there per rotor revolution on the rotary engine?
    a. 1
    b. 2
    c. 3
    d. 4
    e. 5

25. What object opens and closes the ports on the rotary (Wankel) engine?
    a. The valves
    b. The position of the rotor
    c. The carburetor
    d. The spark plug
    e. The camshaft

The following questions are similar in format to ASE (Automotive Service Excellence) test questions.

26. Technician A says that an automobile engine converts chemical energy to thermal energy. Technician B says that an automobile engine converts thermal energy to mechanical energy. Who is right?
    a. A only
    b. B only
    c. Both A and B
    d. Neither A nor B

27. Technician A says the compression ratio on a diesel engine is higher than on a gasoline engine. Technician B says the compression ratio on a diesel engine is lower than on a gasoline engine. Who is right?
    a. A only
    b. B only
    c. Both A and B
    d. Neither A nor B

28. Technician A says the order of strokes on a four-stroke engine is intake, power, compression, and exhaust. Technician B says the order of strokes on a four-stroke engine is intake, compression, power, and exhaust. Who is right?
    a. A only
    b. B only
    c. Both A and B
    d. Neither A nor B

29. Technician A says the gas engine used in a car is called an external combustion engine. Technician B says the gas engine used in a car is called an internal combustion engine. Who is right?
    a. A only
    b. B only
    c. Both A and B
    d. Neither A nor B

30. Technician A says that the two-stroke engine uses a reed valve to control the pressure in the combustion chamber. Technician B says the two-stroke engine uses a reed valve to control the vacuum in the crankcase area. Who is right?
    a. A only
    b. B only
    c. Both A and B
    d. Neither A nor B

31. Technician A says that the two-stroke engine is lighter than a four-stroke engine. Technician B says that the two-stroke engine is more responsive than a four-stroke engine. Who is right?
    a. A only
    b. B only
    c. Both A and B
    d. Neither A nor B

32. Technician A says that engines today can have one valve per cylinder. Technician B says that engines today can have three or even four valves per cylinder. Who is right?
    a. A only
    b. B only
    c. Both A and B
    d. Neither A nor B

33. Technician A says that a DOHC engine has two camshafts operating on each bank of cylinders. Technician B says that a DOHC engine has four valves per cylinder. Who is right?
    a. A only
    b. B only
    c. Both A and B
    d. Neither A nor B

34. When defining the points on a two-stroke diagram, Technician A says the intake ports close about 5 degrees BTDC. Technician B says the exhaust ports close about 5 degrees ATDC. Who is right?
    a. A only
    b. B only
    c. Both A and B
    d. Neither A nor B

Essay

35. Describe how the intake, compression, power, and exhaust strokes occur in a Wankel engine.

36. What is the purpose of using a cylinder head on an engine?

37. Define the term *timing* on an engine.

38. Why is it so important to get the exact air-fuel ratio on an engine?

39. How is engine displacement calculated?

40. Define compression ratio, and describe how it can be increased and decreased.

Short Answer

41. The term *power* is defined as a measure of _____.

42. Engines today can have _____, _____, or _____ valves per cylinder.

43. If the total volume above the piston at BDC is 60 cubic inches, and at TDC it is 5.2 cubic inches, the compression ratio is _____.

44. During starting of an engine, the air-fuel ratio must be _____.

45. The total displacement of an engine that has a bore of 3.1 inches and a stroke of 3.5 inches is _____.

CHAPTER 7

Engine Performance

INTRODUCTION Over the past years, automotive manufacturers have built many sizes and types of engines. These engines differ in the amount of power they can produce. Horsepower, torque, fuel consumption, and efficiency have changed and improved. The purpose of this chapter is to define the many terms used to measure engine performance and operation.

OBJECTIVES After reading this chapter, you should be able to:

- Define the term *horsepower*.
- Compare the different types of horsepower.
- Relate torque to horsepower.
- Identify the effects of frictional losses on vehicle performance.

- Examine the use of dynamometers.
- Analyze performance charts.
- Compare different types of engine efficiency.

7.1 TYPES OF HORSEPOWER

Many types of horsepower are used for automobile engines. When comparing engines, brake horsepower is used. When discussing efficiency, frictional and indicated horsepower are used. When analyzing gasoline mileage, road horsepower is used. These and other horsepower definitions should be analyzed. To do this, the term *work* must first be discussed.

Work

Work is defined as the result of applying a force. This force is created by a source of energy. When the force moves a certain mass a certain distance, work is produced. Work is defined as shown in *Figure 7–1*.

Force is measured in pounds. Distance is measured in feet. When the two units are put together, foot-pounds are measured. Work, then, is measured in foot-pounds (ft-lb). For example, as shown in *Figure 7–2*, if a vehicle were moved 50 feet with a force of 20 pounds, then 1,000 ft-lb of work would be produced.

Torque

Torque is one way to measure work. Torque is defined as twisting force. See *Figure 7–3*. This force is produced in an

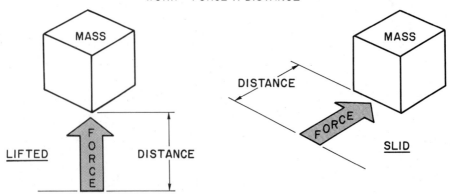

FIGURE 7–1. Work is defined as the result of moving a certain mass a certain distance. It is measured in ft-lb. The movement can be lifting or sliding motion.

130

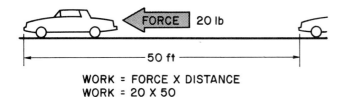

FIGURE 7-2.   When a vehicle is pushed by 20 pounds of force a distance of 50 feet, 1,000 foot-pounds of work are created.

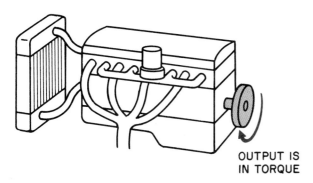

FIGURE 7-3.   Torque is defined as twisting force. The work that an engine produces is measured as torque at the back of the engine. *(Courtesy of DCA Educational Products)*

engine because of the combustion of fuel. Combustion pushes the piston down. The piston causes the crankshaft to rotate, producing torque. This force causes the wheels to rotate.

Torque is actually available at the rear of the engine. Torque is expressed in foot-pounds (energy needed to move a certain number of pounds one foot). An engine is said to have 500 ft-lb of torque at a certain speed. Speed on a gasoline or diesel engine is measured in *RPM*. This term means revolutions per minute. Torque can be measured directly from a rotating shaft by using a dynamometer. Dynamometers will be discussed later in this chapter.

Horsepower Defined

Horsepower (hp) is also a measure of the work being done. It is a unit of work or a measure of work done within a certain time. Horsepower is defined as the *rate* at which work is being done. When anything is measured by a rate, time is considered. Therefore, horsepower is defined as how long it takes to do work.

One horsepower is defined as the amount of work needed to lift 550 pounds one foot in one second. See *Figure 7-4*. If this work is measured per minute (rather than per second), one horsepower is defined as the amount of work needed to lift 33,000 pounds one foot in one minute. These two definitions are the standard way of defining horsepower. It is important to note that the direction of motion when horsepower is applied is in a straight line. However, torque is always related to rotation. See *Figure 7-5*.

Figure 7-6 shows the horsepower and torque specifications from a service manual. Note that both the torque and horsepower are stated at a specific RPM.

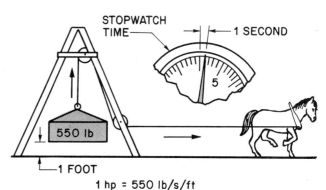

1 hp = 550 lb/s/ft

FIGURE 7-4.   One horsepower is defined as the amount of work required to raise 550 pounds one foot in one second.

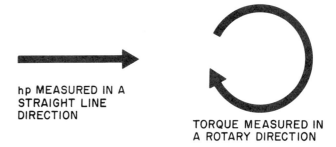

hp MEASURED IN A STRAIGHT LINE DIRECTION

TORQUE MEASURED IN A ROTARY DIRECTION

FIGURE 7-5.   Horsepower is always a measure of work applied in a straight line. Torque is a measure of force in rotary motion.

Brake Horsepower

Brake horsepower (bhp) is defined as the actual horsepower measured at the rear of the engine under normal conditions. It is called brake horsepower because a brake is used to slow down the shaft inside a dynamometer. Brake horsepower is often used to compare engines and their characteristics. Automotive manufacturers use brake horsepower to show differences between engines. For example, a 235 cubic inch engine will produce less bhp than a 350 cubic inch engine. Other factors that may change bhp include type of carburetor, quality of combustion, compression ratio, type of fuel, and air-fuel ratio.

Indicated Horsepower

Indicated horsepower (ihp) is defined as theoretical horsepower. Indicated horsepower has been calculated by the automotive manufacturers. Ihp represents the maximum horsepower available from the engine under ideal or perfect conditions. Ihp is calculated on the basis of engine size, displacement, operational speed, and the pressure developed theoretically in the cylinder. Indicated horsepower will always be more than bhp.

Frictional Horsepower

Frictional horsepower (fhp) is defined as the horsepower used to overcome internal friction. Any time two objects touch each other while moving, friction is produced. Friction

Specifications
GENERAL ENGINE SPECIFICATIONS

Year	Engine Liter/CID①	VIN Code②	Fuel System	Bore & Stroke	Comp. Ratio	Net H.P. @ RPM③	Maximum Torque Ft. Lbs. @ RPM	Normal Oil Pressure Psi.
CHRYSLER								
1989	5.2L/V8-318	P	6280, 2 BBL.④	3.91 X 3.31	9.0	140 @ 3600	265 @ 2000	30–80
DODGE								
1989	5.2L/V8-318⑤	P	6280, 2 BBL.④	3.91 X 3.31	9.0	140 @ 3600	265 @ 2000	30–80
	5.2L/V8-318⑥	S	4 Bbl.⑦	3.91 x 3.31	8.4	175 @ 4000	250 @ 3200	30–80
PLYMOUTH								
1989	5.2L/V8-318⑤	P	6280, 2 BBL.④	3.91 X 3.31	9.0	140 @ 3600	265 @ 2000	30–80
	5.2L/V8-318⑥	S	4 Bbl.⑦	3.91 x 3.31	8.4	175 @ 4000	250 @ 3200	30–80

①—CID-Cubic Inch Displacement.
②—The eighth digit in the VIN denotes engine code.
③—Ratings are net-as installed in vehicle.
④—Holley.
⑤—Except police package.
⑥—Police package.
⑦—Rochester quadrajet.

FIGURE 7–6. Horsepower and torque are usually stated for each engine type in the service manuals. *(Courtesy of Motor Publications, Auto Repair Manual)*

must be overcome with more energy. This happens within an engine. Sources of frictional horsepower include bearings, pistons sliding inside the cylinder, the compression stroke, the generator, fan, water pump, belts, air conditioner, and so on. Refer to *Figure 7–7*.

Other sources of frictional horsepower losses outside the engine include the wind, tire rolling resistance, road conditions, and so on. All of these have a tendency to slow down the engine. They make up the frictional horsepower.

It is advantageous to reduce frictional horsepower as much

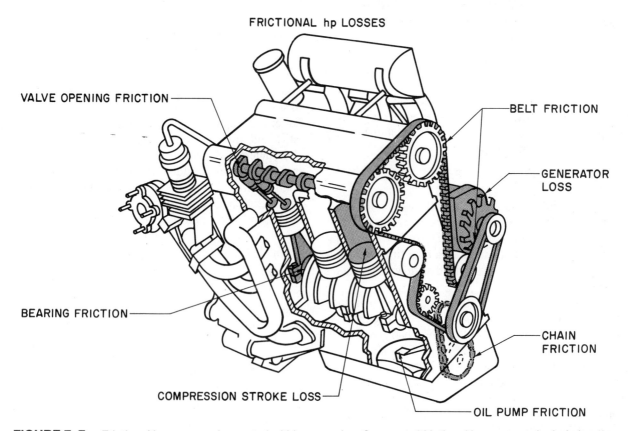

FIGURE 7–7. Frictional horsepower is created within an engine. Sources of frictional horsepower include bearing friction, the compression stroke, belts, generator, valve opening, and so on. *(Courtesy of Peugeot Motors of America)*

as possible. The more frictional horsepower that the engine must overcome, the more energy will be needed to operate the vehicle. This means poorer fuel mileage on the vehicle.

Reducing Frictional Horsepower

Frictional horsepower has been analyzed very carefully in the past few years. Research efforts have found that poor gasoline mileage occurred because of large amounts of frictional horsepower. Considerable changes have been made in the automobile to reduce frictional losses. Some of these changes include:

1. Reducing the rolling resistance on tires. Tires are designed by using computers to reduce the rolling resistance. Radial tires also reduce rolling resistance.

2. Reducing the air drag on a vehicle. Manufacturers have been making vehicles that have less wind resistance. Today, all vehicles have a specified *coefficient of drag.* The coefficient of drag is a measure of how much air is moved as the vehicle moves from one point to another. Generally, the coefficient of drag ranges from 1.00 to 0.00. The lower the number, the less wind resistance the vehicle has to overcome.

3. Running the cooling fan on an electric motor, rather than from the engine. The fan now operates only when needed. Also, some fans turn off and on by using a clutch system.

4. Making the vehicle lighter. On the average, one mile per

gallon (mpg) of fuel is lost for every 400 pounds on the vehicle. To help reduce the weight of the vehicle lighter materials are being used and smaller vehicles are being designed.

5. Changing the undercarriage of the vehicle to reduce air drag on the bottom.

These and other designs have enabled automotive manufacturers to improve gasoline mileage from 12–15 miles per gallon to over 50 miles per gallon on some vehicles.

Road Horsepower

Road horsepower is defined as the horsepower available at the drive wheels of the vehicle. Road horsepower will always be less than bhp. The difference between road horsepower and brake horsepower is the result of frictional horsepower. Frictional horsepower losses are also produced from the friction in the transmission, drive shaft, and rear differential assemblies. See *Figure 7–8*. Road horsepower can be shown as:

Road hp = bhp − fhp through the drive train

7.2 DYNAMOMETERS

Dynamometer Defined

At times it may be necessary to *load* the engine while operating. Loading the engine is the same as pulling a trailer up a steep hill. A *dynamometer* is a device attached to the back

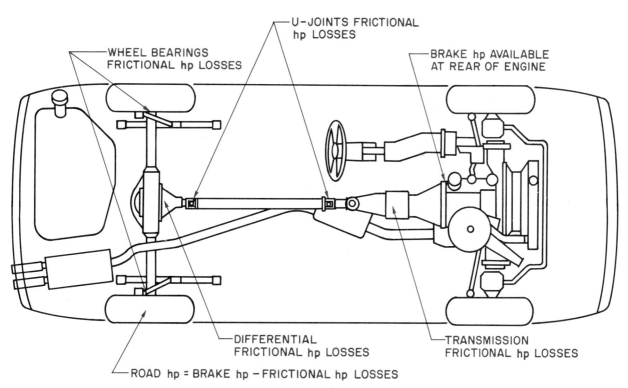

FIGURE 7–8. Road horsepower is defined as the horsepower available at the drive wheels of the vehicle. The frictional horsepower from the drive train is subtracted from the brake horsepower of the engine. The result is road horsepower. *(Courtesy of Mazda Motors of America, Inc.)*

CAR CLINIC

PROBLEM: Reducing Frictional Horsepower

As frictional horsepower increases, fuel consumption will increase. What are some good methods used to reduce frictional horsepower in a typical vehicle?

SOLUTION:

Frictional horsepower can be reduced in several ways. First, keep the windows closed. As the air rushes around the window, frictional horsepower increases. A second way is to use radial tires. There is less rolling resistance with radial tires than with the older four-ply tires. A third way is to make sure the front and rear wheels are aligned to specifications. If the front and rear alignment are out of line, the wheel may have more rolling resistance. The end result is more frictional horsepower. Another method used to reduce frictional horsepower is to reduce the weight in the vehicle. Never carry anything not needed. For example, wood in the back of a pickup truck, sand bags for winter driving, and tools all make the vehicle heavier and thus increase frictional horsepower.

of the engine to absorb the power being created by the engine. When the engine is at idle, it is impossible to determine how much horsepower or torque can be produced. If an engine is run on a dynamometer, it can be loaded down to simulate actual driving conditions. *Figure 7–9* shows a dynamometer attached to the rear of an engine on a stand. The *engine dynamometer* measures brake horsepower and torque at the output of the engine.

Another type of dynamometer can be used to measure road horsepower. It is called a *chassis dynamometer*. A chassis dynamometer measures the horsepower and torque available at the drive wheels of the vehicle. This dynamometer measures road horsepower. *Figure 7–10* shows the layout of a chassis dynamometer. In this case, the tires roll on two rollers. These are called the idle roll and the drive roll. The power absorption unit absorbs the energy. This unit acts as the load on the vehicle. Both speed (RPM) and torque are measured on the scales shown.

Performance Charts

Gasoline and diesel engines have certain operating characteristics. This means that they have different torque, horsepower, and fuel consumption at different RPM. By using a dynamometer, a *performance chart* (also called a characteristic curve) can be developed. *Figure 7–11* shows a standard performance chart. The bottom axis shows the RPM of the engine. The left axis shows the bhp on the engine. The right axis shows the torque being produced on the engine. Also, note that on the bottom right, a fuel consumption scale is included. This indicates the amount of fuel used in pounds per brake horsepower per hour. This unit is sometimes referred to as BSFC, or brake specific fuel consumption.

When the engine is loaded with a dynamometer, a certain maximum torque and horsepower can be produced at a specific RPM. For example, refer to Figure 7–11. Four specific characteristics can be read from the performance chart. Take the specific reading of 2500 RPM. At this speed the engine is capable of producing the following output characteristics:

1. RPM, 2500

2. Torque, 125 foot-pounds

3. Horsepower, 58

4. BSFC, (0.23 lb/bhp/h)

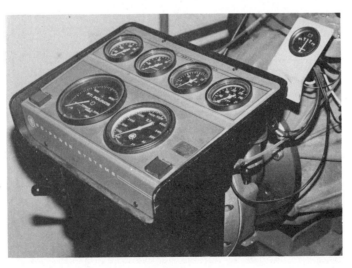

FIGURE 7–9. An engine dynamometer, used to load the engine, can be attached to the rear of the engine.

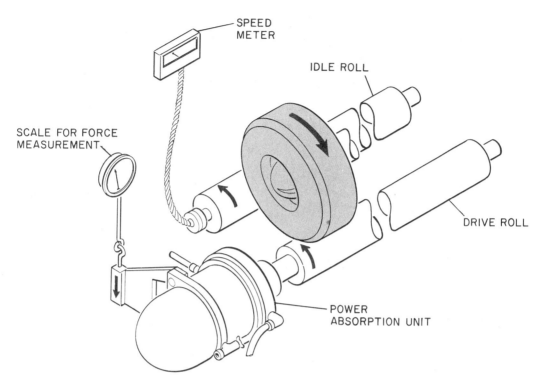

FIGURE 7–10. A chassis dynamometer is used to measure the road horsepower. The tires roll directly on the idle and drive roll. The absorption unit loads the system. *(Courtesy of Clayton Manufacturing Company)*

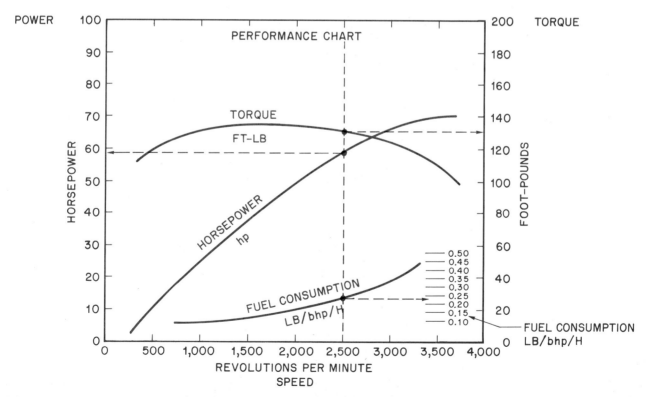

FIGURE 7–11. Performance charts show the amount of horsepower and torque that an engine can produce for a range of RPM. Fuel consumption is also shown and is measured in pounds per brake horsepower per hour. *(Courtesy of DCA Educational Products)*

It should be noted that a dynamometer can measure only the torque being produced at the rear of the engine or at the drive wheels. The dynamometer does not measure horsepower. The following formula is used to obtain horsepower readings so the curve can be made:

$$horsepower = \frac{torque \times RPM}{5{,}252}$$

The number 5,252 is called a constant and is related to the definition of one horsepower (33,000 foot-pounds per minute).

Procedure for Dynamometer Testing

The procedure for dynamometer testing and producing a performance chart varies with the dynamometer manufacturer. However, most engine dynamometers have similar procedures. The following is the general procedure used.

1. Start the engine and run at idle RPM.

2. Increase the load controls to produce maximum load.

3. Using the engine throttle, increase the speed by 100-RPM increments. At each point read the torque in foot-pounds.

4. Continue to increase the RPM until the maximum throttle has been reached.

5. Plot the torque curve using the torque data from each 100-RPM increment.

6. For each 100-RPM increment, calculate the horsepower using the formula previously stated.

7. Plot the horsepower curve with the calculated data for each 100-RPM increment.

7.3   ENGINE EFFICIENCY

The term *efficiency* means many things in the automotive field. Efficiency generally refers to how well a particular job can be done. It is usually expressed as a ratio of input to output. There are, however, other types of efficiency, including mechanical efficiency, volumetric efficiency, and thermal efficiency.

Efficiencies are expressed as percentages. They are always less than 100%. The difference between the efficiency and 100% is the percentage lost during the process.

Mechanical Efficiency

One way to show efficiency is by measuring the mechanical systems of the machine. This method measures how efficient the mechanical systems are in a machine. The machine we are concerned about is the gasoline engine. *Mechanical efficiency* is a relationship between the theoretical (ihp) amount of work required to do a certain job and the actual (bhp) amount of work required to do the job. For example, if a certain car requires 185 actual horsepower and the theoretical horsepower required to do the same amount of work

CAR CLINIC

PROBLEM: Coefficient of Drag

In much of the automotive literature, reference is made to the coefficient of drag. What is the coefficient of drag, and why is it so important?

SOLUTION:

The coefficient of drag is a measure of how much air is moved as the vehicle travels from one point to another at a specific speed. Generally, the coefficient of drag ranges from 1.00 to 0.00. The smaller the number, the less air is moved as the vehicle travels down the road. Today, it is not uncommon to have low coefficient of drag ratings such as 0.33, 0.38, 0.32, and 0.28.

In the calculation for coefficient of drag, many factors are included such as vehicle speed, shape of the vehicle, and smoothness of outer surface of the vehicle. Generally, as the coefficient of drag decreases, the vehicle is able to cut through the air more efficiently. This means less air is moved, and the engine works less for the same speed. The result is that the vehicle will get better fuel mileage than a vehicle with a higher coefficient of drag, assuming, of course, all other factors are equal.

is 205, the mechanical efficiency can be calculated. The formula to calculate mechanical efficiency is:

$$mechanical\ efficiency = \frac{actual\ horsepower}{theoretical\ horsepower} \times 100$$

$$mechanical\ efficiency = \frac{185}{205}$$

$$mechanical\ efficiency = 90\%$$

The losses on any mechanical system are caused primarily by friction. If frictional horsepower can be reduced on an engine, the mechanical efficiency will increase. If frictional horsepower increases on an engine, the mechanical efficiency will decrease.

Volumetric Efficiency

Another way to measure the efficiency of an engine is related to how easily air flows in and out of the engine. As the piston starts down on the intake stroke, air (and fuel) flow into the engine. As the engine increases in revolutions per minute, the intake valves are not open for as long a time. This means that the amount of air per time period may be less. Volumetric efficiency measures this condition. The formula for measuring volumetric efficiency is:

$$volumetric\ efficiency = \frac{actual\ air\ used}{maximum\ air\ possible} \times 100$$

For example, at a certain engine speed, 40 cubic inches of air-fuel mixture enter the cylinders. However, to completely fill the cylinder, 55 cubic inches should enter. Using these two numbers:

$$\text{volumetric efficiency} = \frac{40}{55} \times 100$$

$$\text{volumetric efficiency} = 90\%$$

One way to improve the volumetric efficiency is to improve the scavenging of the cylinder. This means to improve the ease at which air and fuel can enter the engine. Over a period of time the valves may have a buildup of carbon deposits, as shown in *Figure 7–12*. It is obvious that this condition will reduce the volumetric efficiency of the engine.

Other factors that will affect volumetric efficiency are:

1. Exhaust restriction

2. Air cleaner restrictions

3. Carbon deposits on cylinders and valves

4. Shape and design of valves

5. Amount of restriction in the intake and exhaust ports by curves. Ports can be polished to reduce friction.

Thermal Efficiency

A more specific form of efficiency is called *thermal efficiency*. Thermal efficiency tells how effectively an engine converts the heat energy in its fuel into actual power at the output shaft. It takes into account all of the losses on the engine, including thermal losses, mechanical losses, and volumetric losses. For this reason, thermal efficiency is sometimes called overall efficiency. It is the most common form of efficiency used to compare engines.

Thermal efficiency is found by using the following formula:

$$\text{thermal efficiency} = \frac{\text{actual output}}{\text{heat input}}$$

When using this formula, always make sure the units of input and output are the same. The heat input is expressed in Btus. A Btu is an amount of heat needed to raise one pound of water one degree Fahrenheit. A gallon of gasoline has approximately 110,000 Btus.

To get the actual output in the same unit, note that one horsepower is equal to 42.5 Btu/min. Therefore, the formula can be shown as:

$$\text{thermal efficiency} = \frac{\text{bhp} \times 42.5 \text{ Btu/min}}{110,000 \text{ Btu/gal} \times \text{gal per min (gpm)}}$$

Relating this efficiency to a gasoline engine, approximately 25% of the input energy is available at the output. Referring to *Figure 7–13*, the remaining part of the input energy is lost through various ways. The cooling system absorbs a certain percentage of the input energy. The exhaust system carries away a certain amount of energy. Nine percent of the input energy is lost through radiation. When all of these losses are added together, the output energy drops to about 25%.

Different machines have different efficiencies. *Figure 7–14* shows some of the more common machines and their thermal efficiencies. Diesel engines are about 10% more efficient than gasoline engines.

Many things affect efficiency. Some of these factors include the amount of energy in the fuel, the quality of combustion, the amount of frictional loss, and the mechanical quality of the machine. It is important to improve the efficiency of the automobile so that fuel mileage can be increased.

FIGURE 7–12.   Volumetric efficiency of an engine can be reduced by restricting the air flow in and out of the engine. The valve shows a buildup of carbon deposits. This condition would reduce the volumetric efficiency of the engine.

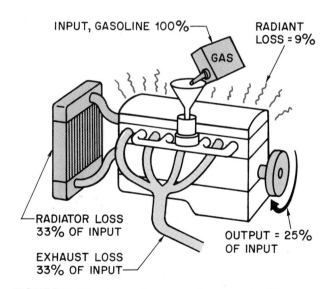

FIGURE 7–13.   A gasoline engine loses much of its energy to other systems. Thirty-three percent of the input energy is lost through the radiator. Thirty-three percent is lost to the exhaust. Nine percent is lost from radiation. Approximately 25% is left for power to the rear wheels. *(Courtesy of DCA Educational Products)*

Engine and vehicle performance can be tested while the car is in the shop. A dynamometer is used to load down the car. The front drive wheels are placed on two rollers that are built into the floor. A turbine is attached, under the floor, to the rollers. The rollers can be slowed down by increasing the amount of liquid the turbine must flow through. This arrangement produces a load on the drive wheels. Performance testing can give the technician important information when troubleshooting an engine.

Engine performance curves are used to illustrate horsepower and torque at different RPM. This performance chart shows the difference between a non-turbocharged and a turbocharged engine. *(Courtesy of Chrysler Corporation)*

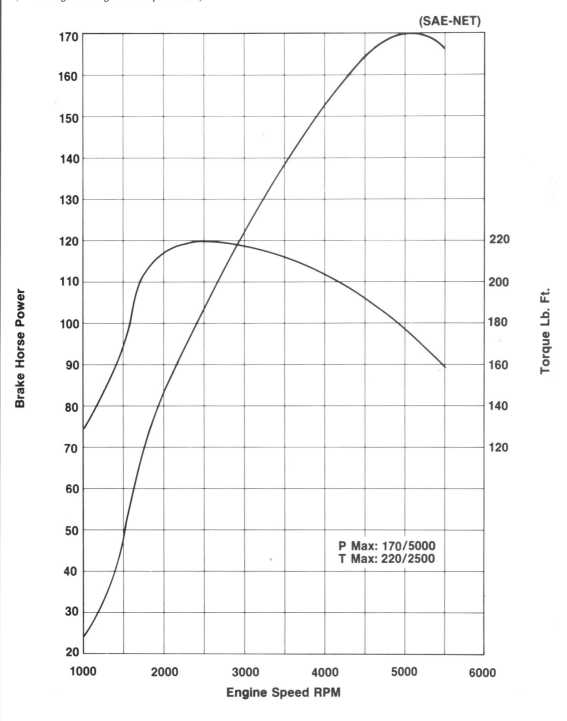

(SAE-NET)

P Max: 170/5000
T Max: 220/2500

Brake Horse Power

Torque Lb. Ft.

Engine Speed RPM

EFFICIENCIES OF DIFFERENT ENGINES	
Gasoline Engine	25–28%
Diesel Engine	35–38%
Aircraft Gas Turbine	33–35%
Liquid Fuel Rocket	46–47%
Rotary Engine	20–22%
Steam Locomotive	10–12%

FIGURE 7–14. All machines have an overall efficiency. Gasoline engines are approximately 25% efficient. Diesel engines are about 35% efficient. Other engine efficiencies are shown for comparison.

SUMMARY

The purpose of this chapter was to introduce engine performance. Horsepower, torque, dynamometers, and engine efficiency are all part of engine performance.

Work is defined as the result of applying a force. It is part of the definition of horsepower. Torque is also a way to measure work. Torque is defined as twisting force. When torque and RPM are used, horsepower can be calculated. Horsepower is a measure of the work being done. It is the rate of work being done.

Several types of horsepower are used to describe engine performance. These include brake horsepower, indicated horsepower, frictional horsepower, and road horsepower. Frictional horsepower can be reduced in several ways. These include reducing rolling resistance and air drag, making the vehicle lighter, and operating small loads such as the cooling fan from electrical sources.

Horsepower and torque are measured on a dynamometer. This is a device that loads the engine so horsepower can be produced. There are two types of dynamometer: the engine dynamometer and the chassis dynamometer.

When an engine is loaded on the dynamometer, a performance chart is made from the data. The dynamometer can measure only torque and RPM. Horsepower has to be calculated for different RPM.

Engine efficiency is also a way to indicate engine measurements. There are several types of efficiency. Mechanical efficiency measures the mechanical systems. It is the relationship between actual horsepower and theoretical horsepower. Volumetric efficiency measures how easily the air flows in and out of the engine. It is the relationship between the actual air used and the maximum air possible. Thermal efficiency measures how well the engine converts heat energy into actual power at the output shaft. It is the relationship between actual power output and heat input.

TERMS TO KNOW

Can you explain each of the following terms? Review the chapter until you can use each term correctly.

Work	Horsepower
Torque	Revolutions per minute (RPM)

Brake horsepower
Indicated horsepower
Frictional horsepower
Coefficient of drag
Road horsepower
Load
Dynamometer

Engine dynamometer
Chassis dynamometer
Performance chart
Efficiency
Mechanical efficiency
Volumetric efficiency
Thermal efficiency

REVIEW QUESTIONS

Multiple Choice

1. When force is multiplied by distance the result is called _____.
   a. Work
   b. RPM
   c. Torque
   d. Distance
   e. Pressure

2. Which of the following work units is measured in a straight line?
   a. Torque
   b. Horsepower
   c. RPM
   d. All of the above
   e. None of the above

3. Which of the following is true about horsepower and torque?
   a. Torque is a measure of rotation; horsepower is measured in a straight line.
   b. Horsepower is measured in time.
   c. Torque is measured in foot-pounds.
   d. All of the above.
   e. None of the above.

4. When 550 pounds are lifted in one _____ a distance of one foot, one horsepower is created.
   a. Second
   b. Minute
   c. Hour
   d. Day
   e. Month

5. Horsepower measured at the rear of the engine is called:
   a. Road horsepower
   b. Brake horsepower
   c. Indicated horsepower
   d. Rear engine horsepower
   e. Frictional horsepower

6. Horsepower measured at the drive wheels of a vehicle is called:
   a. Road horsepower
   b. Brake horsepower
   c. Indicated horsepower
   d. Frictional horsepower
   e. Theoretical horsepower

7. Theoretical horsepower is referred to as:
   a. Road horsepower
   b. Frictional horsepower
   c. Indicated horsepower
   d. Brake horsepower
   e. Torque

8. Horsepower lost because of friction in the engine is called _____ horsepower.
   a. Frictional
   b. Chassis
   c. Indicated
   d. Heat horsepower
   e. All of the above

9. The greater the frictional horsepower, the
   a. Better the gasoline mileage
   b. Better the efficiency
   c. Less the gasoline mileage
   d. More the power available
   e. Better the performance of the vehicle

10. Which chart is not shown on a performance curve?
    a. Brake horsepower
    b. Torque
    c. Frictional horsepower
    d. Fuel consumption
    e. Indicated horsepower

11. How is a load applied to a vehicle to measure road horsepower?
    a. By a chassis dynamometer
    b. By an engine dynamometer
    c. By an RPM gauge
    d. Road horsepower cannot be measured
    e. By a pressure gauge

12. Fuel consumption is measured by what unit?
    a. Lb/ihp/h
    b. Lb/bhp/h
    c. Lb/fhp/h
    d. Gallons per day
    e. Quarts per hour

13. Which efficiency measures the air flow in an engine?
    a. Volumetric
    b. Thermal
    c. Mechanical
    d. Air flow efficiency
    e. Electrical efficiency

14. Which efficiency measures the ratio of actual horsepower to theoretical horsepower?
    a. Thermal
    b. Mechanical
    c. Volumetric
    d. Indicated
    e. Electrical

15. Which of the following could have a negative effect on volumetric efficiency?
    a. An exhaust restriction
    b. A dirty air cleaner
    c. Heavy carbon deposits on the valves
    d. All of the above
    e. None of the above

The following questions are similar in format to ASE (Automotive Service Excellence) test questions.

---

16. Technician A says as frictional horsepower increases fuel consumption decreases. Technician B says as frictional horsepower increases engine efficiency decreases. Who is right?
    a. A only
    b. B only
    c. Both A and B
    d. Neither A nor B

17. Technician A says that if a vehicle has a dirty air cleaner, the volumetric efficiency will decrease. Technician B says that if a vehicle has a dirty air cleaner, the mechanical efficiency will decrease. Who is right?
    a. A only
    b. B only
    c. Both A and B
    d. Neither A nor B

18. Technician A says that torque and horsepower are different terms and have different meanings. Technician B says the two terms are the same. Who is right?
    a. A only
    b. B only
    c. Both A and B
    d. Neither A nor B

19. The actual horsepower is 80, and the theoretical horsepower is 100. Technician A says the mechanical efficiency of the engine is 80%. Technician B says the mechanical efficiency of the engine is 100%. Who is right?
    a. A only
    b. B only
    c. Both A and B
    d. Neither A nor B

20. Technician A says that BSFC is a measure of piston size. Technician B says BSFC is a measure of horsepower. Who is right?
    a. A only
    b. B only
    c. Both A and B
    d. Neither A nor B

21. Technician A says that one horsepower is equal to the amount of work necessary to raise 33,000 pounds one foot in one minute. Technician B says that one horsepower is equal to the amount of work necessary to raise 550 pounds one foot in one second. Who is right?
    a. A only
    b. B only
    c. Both A and B
    d. Neither A nor B

22. Technician A says that as more horsepower is created, torque automatically drops. Technician B says that as more torque is created, horsepower automatically drops. Who is right?
    a. A only
    b. B only
    c. Both A and B
    d. Neither A nor B

23. Technician A says that mechanical efficiency can be calculated by dividing the actual horsepower by the actual air used. Technician B says that mechanical efficiency can be calculated by dividing the actual horsepower by the theoretical horsepower and then multiplying the result by 100. Who is right?
    a. A only
    b. B only
    c. Both A and B
    d. Neither A nor B

Essay

24. Identify several ways in which frictional horsepower can be reduced.

25. What is the formula for calculating horsepower when both torque and RPM are known?

26. What is the difference between mechanical and volumetric efficiency?

27. Define thermal efficiency.

28. Define frictional horsepower.

Short Answer

29. If a vehicle is pushed by 50 pounds of force a total distance of 30 feet, the total foot-pounds of work done equals _____.

30. A measure of how much air is moved as the vehicle goes from one point to another is called the _____ of _____.

31. A dynamometer is producing 80 foot-pounds of torque at 3600 RPM. The horsepower being produced under these conditions is _____.

32. When an engine is producing a BSFC of 24 lb/bhp/h, at 42 hp, the engine is using _____ pounds of fuel each hour.

33. In a dynamometer test, the three readings taken include the _____, _____, and _____.

CHAPTER 8

Types of Engine Design

INTRODUCTION   Gasoline and diesel automobile engines can be designed in different styles, types, and configurations. Some engines may have an overhead cam, while others may have valves in the block. The principles of the engine design remain the same, but the location and configuration change. Some of the shapes the engine can take include in-line or V, slant or opposed, number of cylinders, types of head design, location of valves, and shape of the block. The purpose of this chapter is to investigate different types and styles of engines used in the automobile. Alternative engine types will also be studied.

OBJECTIVES   After reading this chapter, you should be able to:

- Identify the difference between in-line, V, slant, and opposed piston and cylinder arrangement.

- Define the variable displacement engine.

- Define the differences between the 4-, 6-, 8-, and 12-cylinder engines.

- Compare the differences between the L and I head designs.

- Analyze the difference between overhead, in-block, and dual camshaft design engines.

- Compare two-valve and four-valve engines.

- Examine the operation of the stratified charged engine.

- Identify the operation of the Stirling cycle engine.

- Analyze the design and operation of the gas turbine engine.

8.1 CYLINDERS AND ARRANGEMENT

Automobiles use many styles, types, and configurations. *Configuration* means the figure, shape, or form of the engine. One style used is identified by its shape and number of cylinders. Depending upon the vehicle, either an in-line, V, slant, or opposed cylinder arrangement can be used. Common engine designs are the 4-, 6-, 8-, or 12-cylinder engines.

In-Line Engines

Engines can be designed as an *in-line* style. This means the cylinders are all placed in a single row, *Figure 8–1*. There is one crankshaft and one cylinder head for all of the cylinders. The block is a single cast piece with all cylinders located in an upright position.

In-line engine designs have certain advantages and disadvantages. They are easy to manufacture, which brings the cost down somewhat. They are very easy to work on and to perform maintenance on. In-line engines have adequate room under the hood to work on other vehicle parts. However, because the cylinders are positioned vertically, the front of the vehicle must be higher. This affects the *aerodynamic* design of the car. Aerodynamic design refers to the ease with which the car can move through the air. The front of the vehicle cannot be made lower as with other engines. This means that the aerodynamic design of the car cannot be improved easily.

V-Configuration Engines

The *V-configuration* cylinder design has two rows of cylinders. See *Figure 8–2*. These cylinder rows are approximately 90 degrees from each other. This is the angle in most V configurations. However, other angles, ranging from 60 to 90 degrees are used.

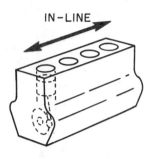

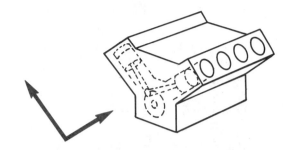

FIGURE 8–1. Engines can be designed using an in-line configuration. This means the cylinders are all in a line and vertical.

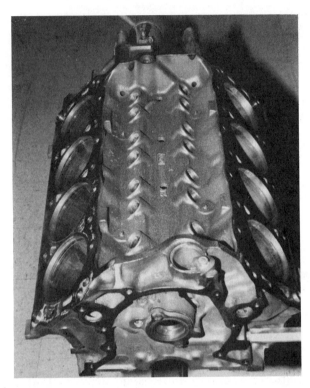

FIGURE 8–2. Engines can be designed in a V configuration. This means two rows of cylinders are in the shape of a V.

This design utilizes one crankshaft that operates the cylinders on both sides. Two connecting rods are attached to each journal on the crankshaft. However, there must be two cylinder heads for this type of engine.

One advantage of using a V configuration is that the engine is not as vertically high as with the in-line configuration. The front of a vehicle can now be made lower. This design improves the outside aerodynamics of the vehicle.

If eight cylinders are needed for power, a V configuration makes the engine much shorter and more compact. Manufacturers used to make in-line eight-cylinder engines. This made the engine rather long. The vehicle was hard to design around this long engine. The long crankshaft also caused more torsional vibrations in the engine.

Slant Cylinder Engines

Another way of arranging the cylinders is in the *slant* configuration. This is shown in *Figure 8–3*. It is much like

an in-line engine except the entire block has been placed at a slant. The slant engine was designed to reduce the distance from the top to the bottom of the engine. Vehicles using the slant engine can be designed more aerodynamically.

Opposed Cylinder Engines

Several manufacturers have designed engines called *opposed cylinder* engines. An example is shown in *Figure 8–4*. Opposed cylinder engines are used in applications where there is very little vertical room for the engine. For this reason, opposed cylinder designs are commonly used on vehicles that have the engine in the rear. The angle between the two cylinders is typically 180 degrees. One crankshaft is used with two cylinder heads. There are two connecting rods attached to each journal on the crankshaft. Several car manufacturers, both foreign and American, have used this type of engine, mostly in smaller vehicles.

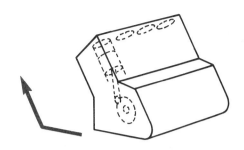

FIGURE 8-3. A slant cylinder configuration reduces the distance from the top of the engine to the bottom of the engine.

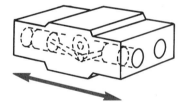

FIGURE 8-4. Opposed cylinder engines are used when there is very little vertical room for the engine. They are used mostly as rear-mounted engines on smaller vehicles.

Radial Cylinder Engines

In a *radial cylinder* engine, ***Figure 8-5***, all of the cylinders are set in a circle. All cylinders point toward the center of the circle. The connecting rods of all pistons work on a single journal of the crankshaft. The journal rotates around the center of the circle. The name *radial* is given because each cylinder is set on a radius of the circle. There is usually an odd number of cylinders. The radial engine occupies very little space. Although this design is used quite often in aircraft engines, it has not been used as an automobile engine.

Number of Cylinders

Automotive engines are designed using a variety of cylinder numbers. The most common are four-, six-, and eight-cylinder engines. The differences are in the horsepower and torque

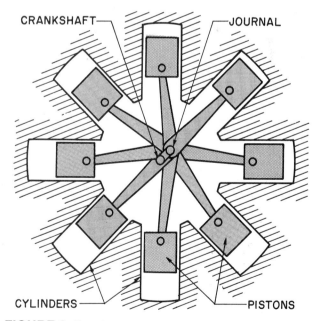

FIGURE 8-5. Gasoline engines can also be designed using a radial configuration. However, these engines are mostly used in the aircraft industry and not in automobiles.

needed for the vehicle. For example, average horsepower and torque figures are shown for several engines in ***Figure 8-6***. The differences are caused by the number of cylinders used on the engine.

Specifications

GENERAL ENGINE SPECIFICATIONS

Year	Engine Liter/CID ①	VIN Code ②	Fuel System	Bore & Stroke	Compression Ratio	Net H.P. @ RPM ③	Maximum Torque Ft. Lbs. @ RPM	Normal Oil Pressure Psi.
1989–90	3.8L/V6-232	4	SEFI	3.80 x 3.40	9.0	140 @ 3800	215 @ 2400	40–60 ④
	3.8L/V6-232 SC ⑤	C, R	SEFI	3.80 x 3.40	8.2	210 @ 4000	315 @ 2600	40–60 ④
	5.0L/V8-302 ⑥	F	SEFI	4.00 x 3.00	8.9	150 @ 3200	270 @ 2000	40–60 ⑦
	5.0L/V8-302 ⑥	F	SEFI	4.00 x 3.00	8.9	160 @ 3400	280 @ 2200	40–60 ⑦
1991	5.0L/V8-302 ⑥	F	SEFI	4.00 x 3.00	8.9	150 @ 3200	270 @ 2000	40–60 ⑦
	5.0L/V8-302 ⑥	F	SEFI	4.00 x 3.00	8.9	160 @ 3400	280 @ 2200	40–60 ⑦
1991–92	3.8L/V6-232	4	SEFI	3.80 x 3.40	9.0	140 @ 3800	215 @ 2400	40–60 ④
	3.8L/V6-232 SC ⑤	C, R	SEFI	3.80 x 3.40	8.2	210 @ 4000	315 @ 2600	40–60 ④
	5.0L/V8-302 HO ⑨	T	SEFI	4.00 x 3.00	9.0	200 @ 4000	275 @ 3000	40–60 ⑦
1992	4.6L/V8-281 ⑥	F	SEFI	3.60 x 3.60	9.0	190 @ 4200	260 @ 3200	40–60 ⑦
	4.6L/V8-281 ⑥	F	SEFI	3.60 x 3.60	9.0	210 @ 4600	270 @ 3400	40–60 ⑦

SEFI—Sequential Multi-Port Electronic Fuel Injection
① —C.I.D.-Cubic Inch Displacement.
② —The eighth digit of VIN denotes engine code.
③ —Ratings are net-as installed in vehicle.
④ —At 2500 RPM with engine at operating temperature.
⑤ —Supercharged engine.
⑥ —Single exhaust.
⑦ —At 2000 RPM with engine at operating temperature.
⑧ —Dual exhaust.
⑨ —Cougar & Thunderbird.

FIGURE 8–6. Automotive engines are primarily designed using 4, 6, and 8 cylinders. The difference in engines is the horsepower and torque available from each engine. *(Courtesy of Motor Publications, Auto Repair Manual)*

An advantage to using fewer cylinders is reduced *fuel consumption*. Over the past few years, automotive manufacturers have made many changes in the engine to reduce fuel consumption. One change is designing engines that have fewer cylinders. With the current concern for a clean environment and improved gasoline mileage, it is difficult to justify designing a vehicle with eight cylinders. The horsepower and torque developed by an eight-cylinder engine are usually well above that needed for most driving applications. Applications that require heavy hauling, such as trailers and boats, may require the additional horsepower and torque of an eight-cylinder engine.

Combining the number and type of cylinders, manufacturers design the following common types of engines:

1. In-line (4- and 6-cylinder engines, most common, as well as 3- and 5-cylinder engines)

2. V configuration (6- and 8-cylinder engines)

3. Slant (4- and 6-cylinder engines)

4. Opposed (4- and 6-cylinder engines)

There are also other common engine configurations, which include:

1. In-line (6- and 8-cylinder engines)

2. V configuration (8- and 12-cylinder engines)

Five-Cylinder and Three-Cylinder Engines

Some five-cylinder and three-cylinder engines have been built for automobiles by both American and foreign manufacturers. Although these engines are not commonly found in the automotive field, they are used.

Variable Displacement Engines

There have been several attempts to build engines that have a variable displacement. One method that has been tried is to start with an eight-cylinder engine then deactivate cylinders to reduce the displacement of the engine. Thus, if high power is needed, all eight cylinders (maximum displacement) would be in operation. If lighter loads are required, then four cylinders could be deactivated, thus running the engine on the remaining four cylinders (minimum displacement). Several manufacturers have produced variable displacement engines. Additional research and testing are required to improve efficiency and please the customer with this approach.

8.2 VALVE AND HEAD ARRANGEMENT

Engines used in the automobile can be designed with different valve and head designs. I- and L-head designs are used. Also, in-block, overhead and dual camshafts are used. In addition, stratified charged engines and jet valves are now becoming popular.

I-Head Design

The *I-head* valve design is the most common arrangement of valves. Referring to *Figure 8–7*, I-head means the valves are directly above the piston (overhead valves). The valves are located in the cylinder head. The design allows easy breathing of the engine. Air and fuel can move easily into

CAR CLINIC

PROBLEM: V-8 and In-Line Four-Cylinder Engines

Years ago, most manufacturers built eight-cylinder engines (V-8). Why is the V-8 engine not manufactured as much any more, and why has the in-line four-cylinder engine become so popular?

SOLUTION:

In the 1960s and early 1970s the V-8 was a very popular engine. However, it was not designed to be very fuel-efficient. After the energy crisis in 1973, the cost of gasoline increased rapidly, and the amount of gasoline available seemed to decline. We could no longer afford to drive cars that get poor fuel mileage, so manufacturers started building smaller vehicles and smaller engines. Today, engines are very fuel-efficient, especially the in-line four-cylinder engines. Cars with smaller engines cost less and make better use of the fuel available to our society.

FIGURE 8–8.   On an I-head design, the valves are located in the head.

and out of the cylinder with little restriction. This process improves the volumetric efficiency of the engine. The I-head is also easy to maintain. For example, if a valve is damaged, it can be replaced easily. Adjusting the valves is easier too.

The valves can be on both sides of the piston, on top, or on one side only. *Figure 8–8* shows an example of a head with an I design. This type of valve arrangement is also called overhead valves, sometimes referred to as OHV. A rather complex mechanical system must be used to open the valves from the camshaft. It includes the *lifters, pushrods, rocker arms,* and valves.

L-Head Design

Another type of valve arrangement is called the *L-head*. See *Figure 8–9*. The valves are located in the block. The inlet and outlet ports are shorter. The head does not have any mechanical valves located within its structure. This head is referred to as a "flat head." Older vehicles, especially from Ford Motor Company, utilized the flat-head design with the valves built within the block. These engines were commonly called the flat-head V-8. They were common in the 1930s, 40s, and 50s. *Figure 8–10* shows the head on this type of engine.

In the L-head design, fewer mechanical parts are needed to operate the valves from the camshaft. Here the rocker arms and pushrods have been eliminated. See *Figure 8–11*.

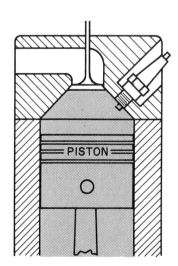

FIGURE 8–7.   An I-head engine has the valves located above the piston in the head. The shape of the engine is an I.

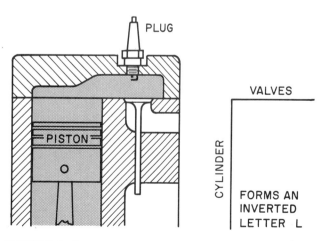

FIGURE 8–9.   L-head engines have the valves located within the block. These engines are commonly called the "flat-head engine."

FIGURE 8–10. The L-head engine uses a flat head.

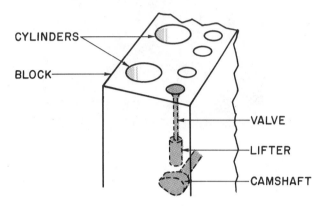

FIGURE 8–11. The L-head engine does not use any pushrods or rocker arms. The valves are located in the block and ride directly above the camshaft.

The valves and lifters are operated directly on top of the camshaft. One disadvantage is that if any damage occurs around the valve port, the block may have to be replaced. It is also more difficult to adjust the valves when they are located in the block.

In-Block Camshaft

Many engines have the camshaft located directly within the block. This type of camshaft can be used on L- and I-head engines. *Figure 8–12* shows where the camshaft is located in this design. An advantage is that the camshaft can be driven directly off of the crankshaft. A standard gear set or a gear and chain arrangement can be used. See *Figure 8–13*.

A disadvantage of in-block camshafts is the linkage needed

FIGURE 8–12. Many engines have the camshaft located directly within the block.

FIGURE 8–13. The camshaft is driven directly from the crankshaft when located within the block. Either gears or a chain drive can be used.

to open and close the valves. This includes the lifters, pushrods, and rocker arms. All of these parts can become worn, causing more chance of failure of the parts. Another disadvantage of this system is that the maximum RPM range of the engine is limited by the valve mechanism. The valves have a tendency to float (not close completely) at higher speeds.

This system must also have some way of accounting for the clearance between all of these parts. There is an adjustment called *valve clearance*. As the engine and parts heat up, the parts expand. If there were no valve clearances, the heated parts would expand and keep the valves open during the compression and power strokes. If this happened, the engine would not run correctly. The valve clearance can be accounted for by using hydraulic lifters or by adjusting the valve clearance. Valve clearance will also be discussed in a later chapter.

Overhead Camshaft

Many manufacturers are now designing engines that have an *overhead camshaft*. The camshaft is placed directly above the valves in the head. This design is used on I-head valve designs. See *Figure 8–14*. One advantage of this design is that the cam operates directly on the valves. There are fewer parts that could wear, causing failure. Also, having fewer valve train parts gives the engine a higher RPM range. In addition, there is less valve clearance needed for expansion as the engine heats up. There is also a more positive opening and closing of the valves. The valve movement, therefore, responds more quickly to the cam shape. This may not be true for in-block camshafts because of the extra linkage. The camshaft is now driven by either a chain or a belt as shown in *Figure 8–15*.

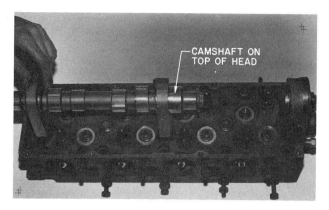

FIGURE 8–14. Engine manufacturers also design overhead camshafts (OHC). The camshaft is mounted on top of the cylinder head.

Dual Camshafts

Some engines use more than one camshaft. This type of engine is called a *dual camshaft* engine. Dual camshaft engines are designed so that one camshaft operates the intake valves, while the second camshaft operates the exhaust valves. Many foreign and domestic automotive companies manufacture engines using the dual overhead camshaft (DOHC) design. *Figure 8–16* shows an example of an engine with dual overhead camshafts.

Four-Valve Engines

Most engines used today have two valves per cylinder. One is for the intake stroke, and one is for the exhaust stroke. There are times when more air and fuel must be brought into the engine. This is done with a *supercharger*. Supercharging means to force more air into the cylinders for more power. Supercharging will be discussed in a later chapter. *Four-valve heads* are used to get more air into the engine. There are two intake and two exhaust valves per cylinder. With the additional valves, more intake air and fuel and exhaust gases can be moved through the engine. Although the cost is somewhat higher, four-valve engines operate with higher volumetric efficiency. *Figure 8–17* shows a four-valve cylinder head.

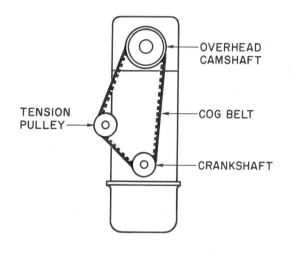

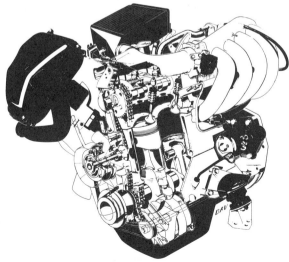

FIGURE 8–15. Overhead camshafts are operated by chains or belts driven from the crankshaft. The chain or cogs on the belt keep the cam and crankshaft in time with each other. *(Courtesy of Peugeot Motors of America, Inc.)*

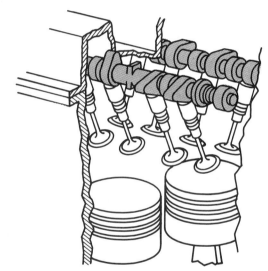

FIGURE 8–16. Today many engines utilize the twin, or dual, overhead camshaft style. Here, both cams are driven by a chain drive or belt drive system from the crankshaft.

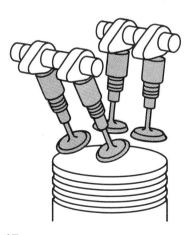

FIGURE 8–17. Four-valve heads are used where additional air and fuel must enter the engine.

Stratified Charged Engine

Certain engines used in the automobile are called stratified charged engines. When the mixture within the combustion chamber is thoroughly mixed, the charge is called homogeneous. When the mixture is not evenly mixed, the charge is said to be *stratified*, or in layers. A *stratified charged engine* has a second, small area for combustion in the cylinder head. See ***Figure 8–18***. There is a spark plug in the chamber. A rich mixture of air and fuel enters the stratified chamber. A lean mixture of air and fuel enters the major combustion chamber. The overall air-fuel mixture is leaner. This is done primarily to reduce pollution from the engine. When the spark plug ignites the rich air-fuel mixture, this burning mixture is used to ignite the lean mixture.

Swirling Air Combustion Chamber

Another method used to improve the combustion efficiency and to make the air-fuel ratio leaner is to swirl part of the

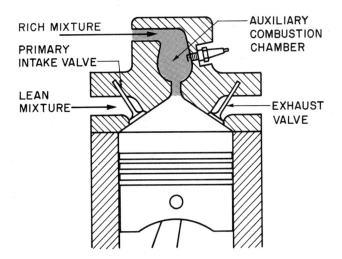

FIGURE 8–18. A stratified charged engine has an auxiliary combustion chamber that ignites the air-fuel mixture. This arrangement allows a leaner mixture to be burned in the regular combustion chamber.

intake mixture around the combustion chamber. One method of swirling is called the *jet valve*, shown in ***Figure 8–19***. The jet valve assembly is a self-contained device that threads into the cylinder head right next to the intake valve. It contains a very small valve, valve spring, valve stem seal, and keepers. The intake rocker arm opens the intake valve and the jet valve simultaneously. In operation, a separate passage inside the intake manifold and cylinder head feeds air into the jet valve. When the valve opens, the air flows through a steel insert that aims it directly at the spark plug. This mechanism creates a swirl effect inside the combustion chamber. The jet valve allows the engine to run leaner and cleaner without suffering from a lean misfire. It has much the same effect as the design of the stratified charged engine.

8.3 ALTERNATIVE ENGINE TYPES

Although gasoline and diesel engines are the most common, engineers and scientists are working on new types of engines. Two engines being studied for possible use in the automobile are the Stirling engine and the gas turbine engine.

Stirling Engine

The *Stirling engine* operates very smoothly with complete combustion and low emission characteristics. Both General Motors and Ford Motor Company have studied Stirling engines. Several designs have been tested. The most popular Stirling engine uses a swash plate design.

There are four cylinders in the swash plate design as shown in ***Figure 8–20***. An external combustion chamber is used. The combustion is considered continuous. The heat from combustion causes the four pistons to be forced downward. Each piston is attached to a *swash plate*. Mechanically, the swash plate is an angular disc attached to the output shaft of the engine. As the pistons are forced downward, the connecting rods move sequentially, pushing the swash plate in a rotary motion. The power pulses must occur in the correct order. Referring to ***Figure 8–21***, as number 1 piston fires, it pushes the swash plate clockwise. Then number 4 piston

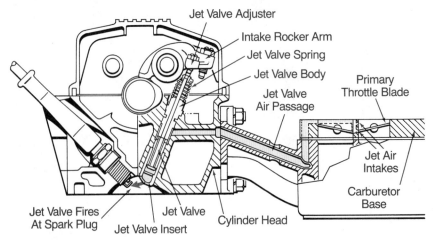

FIGURE 8–19. This jet valve is operated by the intake rocker arm. It is designed to shoot intake air into the spark plug, swirling the already-lean mixture for more efficient combustion. *(Courtesy of Motor Magazine)*

SWASH PLATE

(Side View)

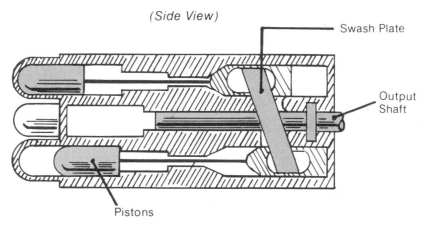

FIGURE 8–20. A Stirling engine uses four pistons, a swash plate, and an external combustion chamber. *(Courtesy of Davis Publications, Inc.)*

must fire, followed by number 3, number 2, and so on. The engine runs smoothly because of the swash plate. The swash plate is doing the same thing as a crankshaft on a conventional internal combustion engine. It changes reciprocating motion to rotary motion.

Stirling Gas Cycle

The Stirling gas cycle is shown in *Figure 8–22*. Thermal energy from any resource, such as coal, oil, or diesel fuel, is

CAR CLINIC

PROBLEM: New Engine Designs

What are some of the newer engine designs that we may see in the future?

SOLUTION:

The engineering departments of the big automotive manufacturers are constantly trying to improve the basic engine. Many new designs will be tested and improved in the future. Some of the more popular designs being researched and tested include:

- Variable piston displacement
- Variable valve timing
- Two-stroke engine design
- Variable compression
- Improved electronic combustion control
- Stirling engine design
- Gas turbine design

(End View)

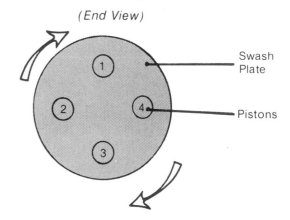

FIGURE 8–21. The swash plate is used to convert the downward motion of the piston to rotary motion needed for pushing a vehicle forward. *(Courtesy of Davis Publications, Inc.)*

applied to the heater. Although they appear to be separate in the diagram, all heaters are connected together. The heat causes the gases to expand above the number 1 piston. The area below the number 1 piston is connected to the cooler near the number 4 piston. This causes the gases below the number 1 cylinder to contract. The difference in pressure across the number 1 cylinder forces the piston downward.

As number 1 piston moves down, the gases below number 1 piston are forced through the cooler, generator, and heater to number 4 piston. As the gases pass through the cooler, they contract. The gases are then heated by the generator and heater. The gases expand and build up pressure above number 4 piston. At the same time, the gases below number 4 piston are near the number 3 cooler. This contracts the gases. Now there is a pressure differential across number 3 piston. This process continues to the number 2 piston, then number 1 piston again. The firing order, then, is number 1, 4, 3, and 2.

The Stirling engine gets four power pulses per revolution against the swash plate. There is also a suction on the bottom of the piston. This design has great potential for higher efficiency. A Stirling engine is shown in *Figure 8–23*.

STIRLING CYCLE

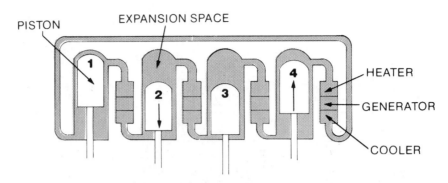

FIGURE 8–22.   The Stirling engine has four pistons. The firing order is 1, 4, 3, 2. For example, as number 1 piston is forced down, the pressure on the underside of the piston helps push down number 4 piston. *(Courtesy of Davis Publications, Inc.)*

Gas Turbine Engine

Another type of engine being studied for use in the automotive market is called the *gas turbine engine*. This engine uses continuous combustion. The combustion is classified as internal. The motion produced by the turbine is considered rotary motion. The gas turbine engine has been tested by several manufacturers since the 1970s. Because of its high cost, however, it still has not been used extensively in the automotive market.

Gas Turbine Cycle

The gas turbine burns diesel fuel. ***Figure 8–24*** is an example of a gas turbine. There is a centrifugal air *compressor*. Rotating at 35,000 RPM, this compressor forces pure air (not air and fuel) into the engine. The heat of compression increases the temperature to about 500 degrees F.

Air passes through the compressor and through a *regenerator*. The regenerator is designed to pick up excess heat from the exhaust. As the exhaust gases flow through the regenerator, the heat is conducted into the metal of the regenerator. The regenerator turns only 18 revolutions per minute so heat can be absorbed easily. As the intake air passes through the regenerator, it picks up this excess heat. The process brings the air temperature up to about 1,200 degrees F.

The air is then sent into the *burner*. This is the combustion chamber. Air and fuel are added to an already-burning flame. Coming out of the burner, the gas is near 2,200 degrees F. This hot gas is sent through the first turbine called the compressor turbine. The temperature of the gases at the first turbine is about 2,200 degrees F. The compressor turbine turns near 35,000 RPM. Its major purpose is to turn the air compressor at that speed.

The remaining energy in the gases from the first turbine enter the second turbine. This is called the power turbine. It

FIGURE 8–23.   This burner-powered version of the Stirling engine runs smoothly on any liquid fuel and produces few pollutants. *(Courtesy of Ford Motor Company)*

GAS TURBINE FLOW DIAGRAM

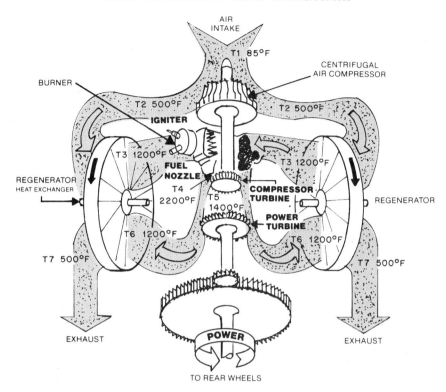

FIGURE 8–24. The gas turbine engine uses a compressor, two turbines, two regenerators, and a continuous combustion process. Efficiency is near 48%. *(Courtesy of Davis Publications, Inc.)*

is connected to the back wheels of the vehicle. The temperature of the gases going into the power turbine is near 1,400 degrees F. This energy turns the power turbine to produce power for the wheels of the vehicle. The gases then pass through the regenerator and out into the atmosphere. The layout of turbine parts is shown in *Figure 8–25.*

The turbine engine has potential for heavy-duty applications in the automobile. It averages about 48% efficiency.

However, the cost of this engine is still well above a comparable gasoline or diesel engine. The advantages include smooth running, multiple fuels, higher efficiency, and no cooling system. The disadvantages include high cost, no dealerships for repair, no parts distribution systems available, and too much power for the average vehicle. Automotive manufacturers, however, are downsizing these engines to be competitive with the gasoline engine.

GAS TURBINE FLOW CHART

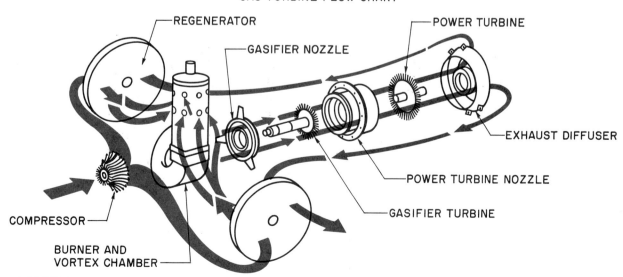

FIGURE 8–25. The gas flow is shown through the turbine parts. *(Courtesy of General Motors Corporation)*

Linkage to Automotive Technology

FIVE-CYLINDER ENGINE

This 2.2-liter, five-cylinder engine produces approximately 10% more horsepower and 9% more torque than the engine it replaced. It has a sophisticated electronic fuel injection system and electronic ignition. *(Courtesy of Volkswagen United States, Inc.)*

SUMMARY

The purpose of this chapter was to introduce various types of engines. There are many types of engines. For example, some have the cylinders in-line or in a row, and some have the cylinders in a V configuration. Common in-line engines have either 4, 6, or 8 cylinders. Common V-type engines are V-6 and V-8 styles. In addition, the cylinders can be arranged in a slant configuration. These are built so they have a low profile. This makes the vehicle lower and better aerodynamically.

Engine manufacturers also build opposed cylinder engines. This engine has the cylinders arranged horizontally. The angle between the two sides is near 180 degrees.

Many additional engine designs are being tested. For example, engines can be designed to have variable displacement. In this case, different cylinders are deactivated or activated to change the total engine displacement.

Another method used to identify engine types is by the valve and head arrangement. I-head engines have the valves located in the cylinder head above the cylinders and pistons. L-head designs have the valves located to the side of the pistons, built in the block.

Camshafts can be located either in the block or overhead and above the valves. Both methods are used in engines today. Some engines have dual camshafts. One camshaft operates the intake valves, and one camshaft operates the exhaust valves.

When more air is needed in the engine, four-valve heads can be used. There are two exhaust valves and two intake valves. Engines that are supercharged may use this design.

The stratified charged engine is becoming very popular. A small combustion chamber has a very rich air-fuel mixture that is ignited by the spark plug. This combustion is used to ignite a lean air-fuel mixture in the main combustion chamber. The result is better fuel mileage.

Other types of engines, including the Stirling engine and the gas turbine engine, are being tested for use in the automobile. The Stirling engine uses a swash plate instead of the crankshaft. Four pistons are used to push the swash plate in a circular motion.

The gas turbine engine uses continuous combustion. Air is forced into the engine by a large compressor. The air is heated by a regenerator and sent to the combustion chamber. Fuel is added, and the hot exhaust gases pass through turbines that rotate. This motion is used to turn the wheels of the vehicle.

TERMS TO KNOW

Can you explain each of the following terms? Review the chapter until you can use each term correctly.

Configuration	Slant
In-line	Opposed cylinder
Aerodynamic	Radial cylinder
V configuration	Fuel consumption
Variable displacement	Stratified
I-head	Stratified charged engine
Lifters	Jet valve
Pushrods	Stirling engine
Rocker arms	Swash plate
L-head	Turbine
Valve clearance	Gas turbine engine
Overhead camshaft	Compressor
Dual camshaft	Regenerator
Four-valve heads	Burner
Supercharger	

REVIEW QUESTIONS

Multiple Choice

1. The _____ engine design has the cylinders in a vertical row.
   a. Slant
   b. In-line
   c. V-configuration
   d. Rotary
   e. Gas turbine

2. What is the approximate angle between the sides of the V on a V-type engine?
   a. 60–90 degrees
   b. 150–160 degrees
   c. 180–190 degrees
   d. 195–205 degrees
   e. 350–360 degrees

3. The slant engine is used because:
   a. The engine has a lower profile
   b. The engine has more power
   c. The engine is easier to manufacture
   d. The engine is lighter
   e. All of the above

4. Which type of engine would be best suited for placement in the rear of the vehicle?
   a. Slant
   b. Opposed
   c. V configuration
   d. In-line
   e. Slant, V configuration

5. One of the biggest differences between four-, six-, and eight-cylinder engines is:
   a. Each has different horsepower and torque
   b. Only six-cylinder engines can be used on small vehicles
   c. Only four cylinders can be used in automobiles
   d. Eight cylinders are lighter and more efficient
   e. Four cylinders have more power

6. Which of the following is the most common valve arrangement today?
   a. L-head
   b. A-head
   c. I-head
   d. P-head
   e. V-head

7. Which type of valve arrangement uses a rocker arm, pushrods, and lifters?
   a. L-head
   b. A-head
   c. I-head
   d. V-head
   e. T-head

8. The reason for having a four-valve engine is:
   a. So more fuel and air can enter the engine
   b. To get better fuel mileage
   c. To reduce the power available on an engine
   d. To heat up the engine more
   e. To cool down the engine more

9. What type of engine uses a small additional combustion chamber with a rich air-fuel mixture?
   a. Stirling engine
   b. Stratified charged engine
   c. Gas turbine
   d. All of the above
   e. None of the above

10. Which engine uses a swash plate?
    a. Gas turbine engine
    b. Stratified charged engine
    c. Stirling engine
    d. All of the above
    e. None of the above

11. How many pistons are used on the Stirling engine?
    a. 4 pistons
    b. 6 pistons
    c. 8 pistons
    d. 10 pistons
    e. 12 pistons

12. The Stirling engine is considered a/an:
    a. Continuous combustion engine
    b. External combustion engine
    c. Multifuel engine
    d. All of the above
    e. None of the above

13. What part on the gas turbine takes the heat of exhaust and puts it into the intake?
    a. Compressor
    b. Turbine
    c. Regenerator
    d. Fuel injector
    e. Exhaust manifold

14. The gas turbine engine is considered a/an:
    a. Continuous combustion engine
    b. Internal combustion engine
    c. Rotary engine
    d. All of the above
    e. None of the above

15. Which device on the gas turbine is used to extract the power from the gases?
    a. Turbine
    b. Compressor
    c. Burner
    d. Fuel injector
    e. Exhaust manifold

The following questions are similar in format to ASE (Automotive Service Excellence) test questions.

16. Technician A says the type of engine most commonly used in vehicles is the in-line type. Technician B says the type of engine most commonly used in vehicles is the opposed type. Who is right?
    a. A only
    b. B only
    c. Both A and B
    d. Neither A nor B

17. Technician A says that a stratified charged engine means the engine also has a turbocharger. Technician B says that a stratified charged engine means the engine has a precombustion chamber for burning more efficiently. Who is right?
    a. A only
    b. B only
    c. Both A and B
    d. Neither A nor B

18. Technician A says that the reason for having a valve clearance is to help lubricate the parts. Technician B says the reason for a valve clearance is to improve the efficiency of the engine. Who is right?
    a. A only
    b. B only
    c. Both A and B
    d. Neither A nor B

19. Technician A says that a stratified charged engine is the same as a four-valve engine. Technician B says that a stratified charged engine means the spark plugs are firing sooner before top dead center. Who is right?
    a. A only
    b. B only
    c. Both A and B
    d. Neither A nor B

20. Technician A says that in-line engines have pistons that are horizontal. Technician B says that an in-line engine can have the cylinders at a slant. Who is correct?
    a. A only
    b. B only
    c. Both A and B
    d. Neither A nor B

21. Technician A says that a variable displacement engine deactivates cylinders to reduce the total displacement. Technician B says that a variable displacement engine reduces the total displacement by changing the piston size. Who is correct?
    a. A only
    b. B only
    c. Both A and B
    d. Neither A nor B

22. Technician A says that the flat-head engine is called the L-head design. Technician B says that the flat-head engine has the valves above the pistons. Who is correct?
    a. A only
    b. B only
    c. Both A and B
    d. Neither A nor B

23. Technician A says that a four-valve engine is designed to improve the volumetric efficiency. Technician B says that a four-valve engine is designed to produce more horsepower. Who is correct?
    a. A only
    b. B only
    c. Both A and B
    d. Neither A nor B

Essay

24. Describe the design and operation of a Stirling engine.

25. What is the purpose of a swash plate?

26. What is the advantage of using an overhead camshaft type engine?

27. Describe the operation of a gas turbine engine.

28. Compare the in-line and V-configuration types of engines.

29. Compare the differences between the I-head and the L-head design of valve arrangements.

Short Answer

30. An engine that has variable displacement is designed so that the _____ can be activated and deactivated.

31. The combustion chamber that has a small jet valve is called the _____.

32. An engine that has an auxiliary combustion chamber to premix the air and fuel is called a _____.

33. Dual camshafts are used on engines that have _____.

34. An advantage of having an engine with fewer cylinders is that there is _____.

CHAPTER 9

Basic Engine Construction

INTRODUCTION   Basic engine construction is a prerequisite when studying the automotive power plant. This section will introduce the basic parts of the engine. The cylinder block, crankshaft, pistons, rods, and camshafts will be discussed.

OBJECTIVES   After reading this chapter, you should be able to:

- Identify the major parts of the cylinder block.

- Recognize the purpose of core plugs.

- Identify cylinder block differences such as aluminum versus cast iron, types of sleeves, and water jackets.

- List the parts of the crankshaft assembly and the purpose of crankshaft grinding.

- Identify the purpose of bearings and caps, oil passageways, vibration dampers, flywheels and thrust surfaces on the crankshaft.

- Identify crankshaft seals and their purpose.

- List the parts of the piston and rod assembly.

- Identify the purpose of oversize pistons and rings.

- State the purpose and operation of the rings, pistons, pins, and bearings.

- Identify the effect of pressures and temperatures on the design of the piston.

- Identify various problems, diagnosis and service tips and procedures on the block, pistons, crankshaft, and bearings.

 SAFETY CHECKLIST

When working with the basic engine components, keep these important safety precautions in mind.
✔ Always wear safety glasses around the shop.
✔ When lifting the block always use the correct engine hoist.
✔ Always use gloves when lifting or moving engine parts.
✔ Make sure that all tools are clean and free of grease.
✔ Always use the correct tools for the job.
✔ When rebuilding an engine, always clean all parts before inspection.

Some of the information in this chapter can help you prepare for the National Institute for Automotive Service Excellence (ASE) certification tests. The test most directly related to this chapter is entitled

ENGINE REPAIR (TEST A1).

The content area that closely parallels this chapter is

ENGINE BLOCK DIAGNOSIS AND REPAIR.

9.1 CYLINDER BLOCK

Block Design

The engine block is the main supporting structure to which all other engine parts are attached. A cylinder block is a large cast iron or aluminum casting. It has two main sections: the cylinder section and the crankcase section. *Figure 9–1* shows a cylinder block for a four-cylinder engine. The cylinder section is designed for the pistons to move up and down during operation. The surfaces are machined to allow the pistons to move with minimum wear and friction.

The *crankcase* section is used to house the crankshaft, oil pump, oil pan, and the oil during operation. Cooling passageways are built within the block. These passageways, also known as water sockets, surround the cylinder. They allow coolant to circulate throughout the cylinder area to keep the engine cool. There is also a drilled passageway within some blocks for the camshaft. Many oil holes are drilled internally so that engine parts can be adequately lubricated. Other holes are also drilled to allow other parts to be attached to the cylinder block.

Block Manufacturing

The first step in building a block is to design a pattern. Sand is then formed around the pattern. When the pattern is removed, sand cores are placed within the cavity. These sand cores will eventually be the cooling passageways and cylinders. Molten metal is poured into the cavity made by the sand. After the metal has cooled, the sand is removed and the cores are broken so they can be removed. This design is called a *cast* block. The metal is usually a gray cast iron with several special metals added to it. The added metals increase the strength and wear characteristics of the block. The extra metals also help to reduce shrinkage and warpage from the heat produced by combustion.

Once the block is cast, and after it has been cooled and cured, surfaces are machined so other parts can be attached to the block. These surfaces include the cylinders, top of the block (deck), camshaft bore, crankshaft bore, and oil pan surfaces. The front and rear of the block and engine mounts are also machined so that parts can be attached and sealed correctly. See *Figure 9–2*.

Certain smaller engines can also be *die cast*. This means that the liquid metal is forced into a metal rather than sand mold. This kind of casting gives smoother surfaces, and more precise shapes can be made. Less machining is needed on this type of block.

Core Plugs

All cylinder blocks use *core plugs*. These are also called freeze or expansion plugs. During the manufacturing process, sand cores are used. These cores are partly broken and dissolved when the hot metal is poured into the mold. However, holes have to be placed in the block to get the sand out of the internal passageways. These are called core holes. The holes are machined, and core plugs are placed into these holes. See *Figure 9–3*.

Core plugs are made of soft metal. At certain times the core plugs can also protect the block from cracking. For example, if there is not enough antifreeze in the coolant during the winter, the coolant may freeze. As the liquid freezes it expands. This expansion may cause the block to crack. However, if the expansion is near a core plug, the plug may pop out and possibly save the block.

Cylinder Sleeves

Some manufacturers use *cylinder sleeves*. Rather than casting the cylinder bores directly into the block, they insert a machined sleeve. *Figure 9–4* shows a sleeve for a cylinder block. Sleeves are inserted after the block has been machined. The purpose of using a sleeve is that if the cylinder is damaged, the sleeve can be removed and replaced rather easily. Blocks that don't have sleeves have to be bored out to

CYLINDER BLOCK

CYLINDERS

REAR

FRONT

FIGURE 9–1. The cylinder block is the main structure of the engine. All other engine parts are attached to the cylinder block. *(Courtesy of Peugeot Motors of America)*

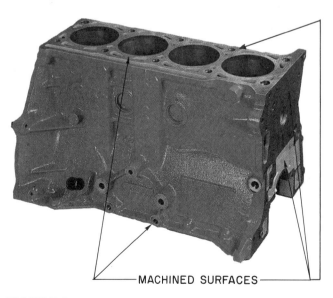

MACHINED SURFACES

FIGURE 9–2. The cylinder block has many machined surfaces to which other parts are bolted. *(Courtesy of Peugeot Motors of America)*

FIGURE 9–3. Freeze or expansion plugs are used to protect the block if the coolant freezes. Rather than cracking the block from expansion, the freeze plugs are popped out.

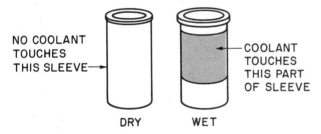

FIGURE 9–4. Cylinder sleeves are used on some engines. The sleeve is inserted into the block after it has been machined. The sleeve acts as the cylinder bore. There are both wet and dry sleeves.

remove any damage. After boring, larger pistons will be needed.

There are two types of sleeves. They are called wet and dry sleeves. The dry sleeve is pressed into a hole in the block. It can be machined quite thin because the sleeve is supported from the top to the bottom by the cast iron block.

The wet sleeve is also pressed into the block. The cooling water touches the center part of the sleeve. This is why it is called a wet sleeve. It must be machined thicker than the dry sleeve because it is supported only on the top and bottom. Seals must be used on the top and bottom of the wet sleeve. Seals are used to keep the cooling water from leaking out of the cooling system. Wet sleeves are used on some larger diesel engines.

Aluminum vs. Cast Iron Blocks

Blocks can be made from either cast iron or aluminum. In the past, most blocks were made of cast iron. Cast iron improved strength and controlled warpage from heat. With the increased concern for improved gasoline mileage, however, car manufacturers are trying to make the vehicle lighter. One way is to reduce the weight of the block. Alumi-

num is used for this purpose. Aluminum is a very light metal. Certain materials are added to the metal before it is poured into the mold. These materials are used to make the aluminum stronger and less likely to warp when heat is applied from combustion. Aluminum blocks must also have a sleeve or steel liner placed in the block. Steel liners are placed in the mold before the metal is poured. After the metal is poured, the steel liner cannot be removed.

Silicon is also added to the aluminum. Through a special process, the silicon is concentrated on the cylinder walls. This process eliminates the need for a steel liner. This design is called silicon-impregnated cylinder walls. One problem with this design is that it requires the use of very high-quality engine oils. Because of owner neglect, this engine does not usually survive its intended service life.

CAR CLINIC

PROBLEM: Engine Vibration

A customer has noticed that the engine seems to have excessive vibration at idle. At higher speeds solid vibration is also felt throughout the vehicle. What could be the problem?

SOLUTION:

The most likely cause of engine vibration as described in this problem is a bad or broken motor mount. This assumes, of course, that the engine itself is operating correctly and that the engine is not missing because of ignition or fuel problems. Make a visual observation of all motor mounts and replace where necessary.

9.2 CRANKSHAFT ASSEMBLY

The crankshaft is designed to change the reciprocating motion of the piston to rotary motion. It is bolted to the bottom of the cylinder block. The crankshaft assembly includes the crankshaft, bearings, flywheel, harmonic balancer, timing gear, and front and rear seals.

Crankshaft Design

The crankshaft is manufactured by either forging or casting. *Forged* steel crankshafts are stronger than cast iron crankshafts, but they cost more. Forging is a process where metal is heated to a certain temperature then stamped or forged into a particular shape. Casting means to heat the metal to its melting point and pour the liquid metal into a form made from sand. Because of the improvements in casting, more crankshafts are being cast today. Cast and forged crankshafts can be identified by the flashing and parting lines. Refer to *Figure 9–5*. Forged crankshafts have a ground-off separation line. Cast crankshafts have a small parting line where the mold came together.

After the crankshaft is cast or forged, it must be *heat treated*. This means the outer surfaces must be made harder so that the crankshaft will not wear on the bearing surfaces. Heat treating is done by heating the outer part of the crankshaft to 1,600–1,800 degrees F. Then the metal is cooled rapidly in oil, water, or brine (salt water). The rapid cooling causes the outer part of the crankshaft (0.060 inch) to be hardened.

The parts of the crankshaft include:

1. Throw — The distance from the centerline of the main journal to the centerline of the connecting rod journal.

2. The main journal — The position on the crankshaft that connects the crankshaft to the block.

3. The connecting rod journal — The position on the crankshaft where the connecting rod is attached.

4. The *counterweights* — Weights are cast or forged into the crankshaft for balance. For each throw, there is a counterweight to balance the motion. Depending on the engine, the counterweight can be a weight or another connecting rod journal.

5. Thrust surfaces — Surfaces machined on the crankshaft to absorb axial motion or thrust. See *Figure 9–6*. Axial motion (back and forth motion on the crankshaft axis) is produced from the general motion of the crankshaft. It is also produced from using timing gears on the crankshaft that have angled teeth. This type of gear is called a helical gear. As the engine increases and decreases in speed, the load on the helical gear moves the crankshaft back and forth on its axis. This motion is absorbed by machining thrust surfaces on the crankshaft and using a thrust bearing.

6. Drive flange — The end of the crankshaft that drives the transmission. A flywheel or flexplate is bolted to the drive flange. The transmission is attached to the flexplate or driven by the flywheel.

7. *Fillets* — Small rounded areas that help strengthen the crankshaft near inside corners. Stress tends to concentrate at sharp corners and drilled passageways. Fillets help reduce this stress. See *Figure 9–7*.

Crankshaft Alignment

When the crankshaft fits into the block, it must be exactly in line with the holes in the block. This is called *alignment*. When the block is bored for the crankshaft main bearing bore, a line boring machine is used. To do this, the main bearing caps are bolted and torqued to the block. The line borer then machines each main bearing area in line with the others. Over a period of time, the block may warp. Warping could cause the alignment to be incorrect. This condition could cause excessive wear on certain parts of the crankshaft.

FIGURE 9–5. Crankshafts can be either forged or cast. Forged crankshafts can be identified by a ground-off separation line, and cast crankshafts have a parting line.

FIGURE 9–6. Thrust surfaces are machined into the crankshaft to absorb axial motion or thrust motion on the crankshaft.

FIGURE 9–7. Fillets are used to strengthen the crankshaft. Fillets are rounded corners where stresses are increased.

Alignment can be checked by using a feeler gauge and a straight-edge bar as shown in *Figure 9–8*.

Crankshaft Vibration

During normal operation, the crankshaft is twisted and turned, producing constant vibration within the crankshaft. For example, when one cylinder is on a compression stroke, that part of the crankshaft tries to slow down. At the same time, other cylinders may have full pressure from the power stroke. This causes the crankshaft to partially twist and snap back during each revolution. This effect is called *torsional vibration*. Additional torsional vibration can be caused from using the wrong flywheel, converter drive plate, or torque converter in the transmission. *Figure 9–9* illustrates the results of too much torsional vibration. Crankshafts typically crack near the connecting rod journal of number 1 cylinder.

Vibration Dampers

Vibration dampers are used to compensate for the torsional vibration. See *Figure 9–10*. The vibration damper is also called a harmonic balancer. It is constructed by using an inertia ring and a rubber ring. The inertia ring is used to help dampen the internal vibrations. The two are bonded together and attached to the front of the crankshaft. As the crankshaft twists back and forth, the inertia ring has a dragging or slowing down effect. As torsional vibrations occur, the rubber and inertia rings absorb the vibration.

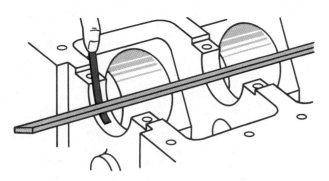

FIGURE 9–8. The block can be checked for correct alignment by using a straight bar and a set of feeler gauges. *(Courtesy of Federal-Mogul Corporation)*

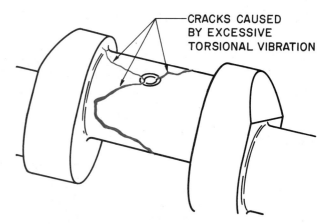

FIGURE 9–9. Torsional vibration within the crankshaft can cause severe cracking.

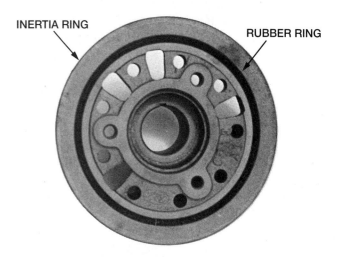

FIGURE 9–10. The vibration damper is used to absorb torsional vibration. It is placed on the front of the engine and includes a rubber ring and an inertia ring.

The weight of the inertia ring is sized to a particular engine. If the wrong vibration damper is used, the crankshaft may be damaged. Incorrect vibration dampers can be identified by observing the timing marks. The timing marks on the vibration damper may not line up correctly with the timing tag on the front of the block.

Bearings and Bearing Caps

The crankshaft is held in place by main bearings and caps. There is usually one more main bearing cap than the number of cylinders. Depending upon the engine, however, there may be fewer main bearing caps than cylinders. The main bearing caps are bolted to the block. *Figure 9–11* shows the main bearing cap and bolts.

When in place, the main bearings hold the crankshaft securely in place to allow for rotation. On some high-performance gas engines and diesel engines, there may be four bolts, rather than two, holding the bearing cap to the block. The extra support is needed because these engines produce more torque and higher loads on the crankshaft.

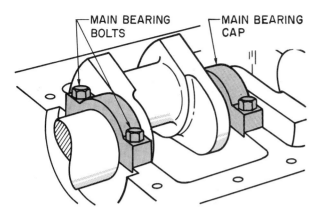

FIGURE 9–11.   Main bearing caps are used to hold the crankshaft in place in the cylinder block. They can be removed by removing the bearing bolts. *(Courtesy of Federal-Mogul Corporation)*

Bearing Design

Insert bearings are placed between the main bearing caps and the crankshaft. As discussed in an earlier chapter, these bearings are designed as two-piece friction-type bearings. Main bearings have what is called spread. They are slightly larger than the housing into which they fit. See *Figure 9–12*. The spread allows them to snap into place. Half the bearing is placed into the block. The other half is placed in the bearing cap.

The main bearings have several parts. All bearings have a steel backing. This provides the strength and support for the bearing. There are also several soft metals used on the bearing surface. Soft metals such as copper-lead, *Babbitt*, aluminum, and tin allow a certain amount of dirt to be embedded into the soft metal. They also help the bearing to form to the shape of the crankshaft journals. *Figure 9–13* shows a common bearing with several metals in its design.

Bearings must be designed to accomplish several things. These include:

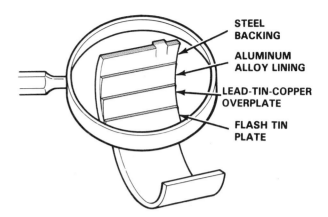

FIGURE 9–13.   Main bearings have a steel backing and several soft metals such as copper, lead, and aluminum. *(Courtesy of Federal-Mogul Corporation)*

1. Load-carrying capacity — The ability to withstand pressure loads from combustion.

2. Fatigue resistance — The ability to withstand constant bending.

3. Embedability — The ability to permit foreign particles to embed or be absorbed into the metal.

4. Conformability — The ability to be shaped to the small variations in shaft alignment. See *Figure 9–14*.

5. Corrosion resistance — The ability to resist the by-products of combustion that are carried to the bearing by the oil.

6. Wear rate — The ability to be strong enough to eliminate excessive wear, but soft enough not to wear the crankshaft journals.

The bearing insert also has a locating lug. See *Figure 9–15*. This lug holds the bearings in place within the block

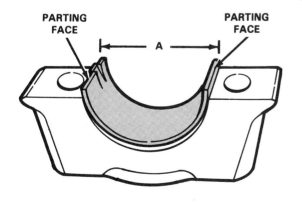

A = FREE SPREAD DIAMETER

FIGURE 9–12.   Spread (dimension A) helps keep the bearing in place in the block and bearing cap. *(Courtesy of Federal-Mogul Corporation)*

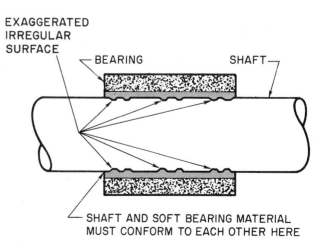

FIGURE 9–14.   Bearings must be able to conform to the shape of the crankshaft. This condition is called conformability. *(Courtesy of Federal-Mogul Corporation)*

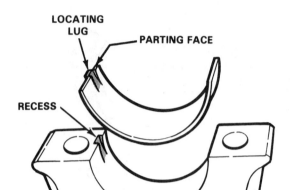

FIGURE 9–15. Bearings have locating lugs. These are used to hold the bearing in place and to keep the bearing from spinning in its bore. *(Courtesy of Federal-Mogul Corporation)*

and cap so that the bearing cannot spin. Oil grooves and holes are also machined into the bearing insert. Oil passes from the center of the crankshaft through the hole in the bearing and circles around the crankshaft in the oil groove. This design provides complete lubrication of the crankshaft journals. See *Figure 9–16*.

There must also be a clearance between the crankshaft journals and the insert bearings. This clearance is called the *main bearing clearance*. Main bearing clearance can be checked using *Plastigage*. Plastigage is a small, thin string of plastic with a predetermined diameter. A short piece of the Plastigage is placed between the crankshaft and the bearing. The bearing and cap are then torqued to their normal specifications. This torquing causes the thin Plastigage to flatten. The resulting width of the Plastigage is a measure of the bearing clearance. The procedure for using Plastigage is shown in the Problems, Diagnosis and Service section of this chapter.

Thrust Bearings

The crankshaft moves back and forth axially (movement parallel to the axis of the crankshaft) during operation. This movement can be created from angled gears on the front of the crankshaft. This *axial motion*, called thrust, could cause the crankshaft to wear heavily on the block. Thrust bearings are used to compensate for this motion. One of the main bearings is designed for thrust absorption. The center bearing in Figure 9–16 is a thrust bearing. The thrust bearing has a thrust face where a machined surface on the crankshaft rubs against it. On most engines, the thrust bearing is the center main bearing. On some engines, however, the thrust bearing is the flange on the rear main bearing. Other engines use separate thrust washers instead of the flanged type. See *Figure 9–17*.

Oil Passageways

For the crankshaft to receive proper lubrication, oil must pass through the crankshaft to the bearings. *Figure 9–18* illustrates the internal passageways drilled for oil. Oil pressure from the lubrication system is fed through the block to each

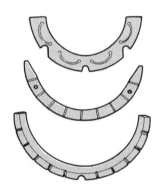

FIGURE 9–17. Separate thrust bearings are used on some older engines. *(Courtesy of Federal-Mogul Corporation)*

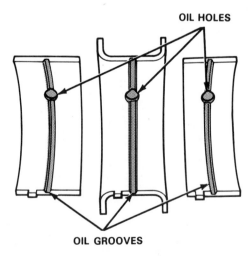

FIGURE 9–16. Oil holes and grooves are used to help lubricate the bearings. *(Courtesy of Federal-Mogul Corporation)*

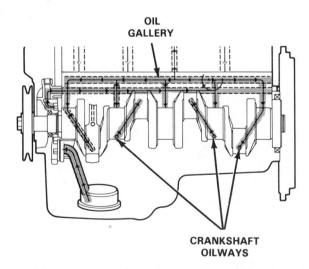

FIGURE 9–18. Oil passageways are drilled into the crankshaft to allow oil to flow from the main bearing to the connecting rod bearing journal. *(Courtesy of Federal-Mogul Corporation)*

main bearing. The oil goes through the bearing insert and into a groove in the bearing. There is a drilled passageway from the main bearing through the crankshaft to the connecting rod bearing. Oil is then fed into the connecting rod bearings, where it eventually leaks out and sprays against the cylinder walls. The oil then drips back to the oil pan.

Bearing Clearance

The clearance between the bearing and the journal is called bearing clearance. This clearance is designed so that just the right amount of oil is allowed to flow through it. See *Figure 9–19*. If the bearings wear, the clearance will increase. This condition may reduce oil pressure. If the connecting rod clearance is larger, more oil may pass through this clearance. With the correct bearing clearance, the amount of oil thrown off from the rotating shaft is minimal. When the clearance is doubled, oil throw-off is five times greater. As the clearance increases, oil throw-off is increased even more. Under these conditions, piston rings are unable to scrape this excessive oil from the cylinder walls. Oil will then enter the combustion chamber and be burned. The clearance between the bearing and the connecting rod journal can be checked using Plastigage as shown in the Problems, Diagnosis and Service section of this chapter.

Crankshaft Seals

A seal is used at the front and rear of the crankshaft to keep the oil in the engine. See *Figure 9–20*. The rear crankshaft seals are placed in the rear main bearing cap and the block. There are several designs. Both lip-type synthetic rubber seals and graphite-impregnated wick or rope-type seals are used on the rear of the crankshaft. Some are a two-piece design, others are a one-piece insert design. One-piece lip-type seals that ride on the vibration damper are used on the front of the engine.

Crankshaft Grinding

At times it may be necessary to grind the crankshaft or main bearing journals or both to a smaller size. Grinding would be necessary if there were excessive wear on the journal surfaces. Crankshafts are ground in special machine shops. When a crankshaft is ground, new bearings will be needed. Main and rod bearings are available in standard sizes and various undersizes, depending upon the manufacturer. Bearings can typically be purchased in 0.001-, 0.002-, 0.010-, 0.020-, 0.030- and 0.040-inch undersizes. However, the exact size is determined by the manufacturer. Often, the amount of undersize is stamped on the back of the bearing.

9.3 PISTON AND ROD ASSEMBLY

The piston and rod assembly is designed to transmit the power from combustion to the crankshaft. There are several parts on this assembly. The piston and rod assembly is shown in *Figure 9–21*. It consists of the following parts:

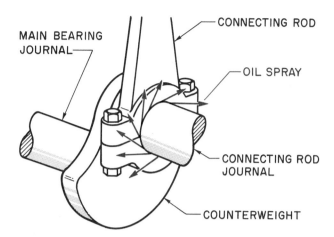

FIGURE 9–19. The bearing clearance determines how much oil will flow past and out of the bearing area. Too much clearance will reduce oil pressure and increase the amount of oil on the cylinder walls.

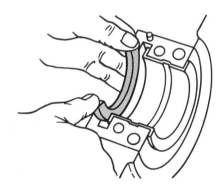

FIGURE 9–20. Seals are installed in the front and rear of the crankshaft to keep oil inside the engine. *(Courtesy of Federal-Mogul Corporation)*

CAR CLINIC

PROBLEM: Core Plugs Leak Coolant

A customer complains that coolant is leaking from the side of the cylinder block. The engine was recently overhauled, and the coolant has been leaking since the engine was rebuilt. What could be the problem?

SOLUTION:

Cylinder block core plugs are usually replaced during an overhaul. Sometimes when new core plugs are installed they are not inserted correctly. If they are inserted at a slight angle, they may leak engine coolant. Also, a sealant should be used during installation. Not using a sealant may also cause the core plugs to leak. To solve the problem, the leaky core plug must be removed and replaced correctly, using the recommended sealant.

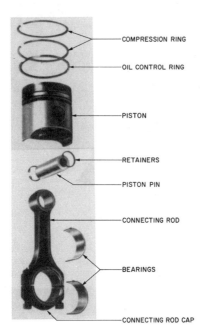

FIGURE 9-21. The piston and rod assembly is used to transmit the power from combustion to the crankshaft. *(Courtesy of Peugeot Motors of America)*

1. Compression rings
2. Oil control rings
3. Piston
4. Piston pin (wrist pin) and lock ring (if used)
5. Connecting rod and bushing
6. Bolts
7. Bearing shells
8. Cap
9. Nuts

When this assembly is placed into the cylinder block, the downward motion from combustion is transmitted to the crankshaft.

Piston Parts

The piston is defined as a hollow aluminum cylinder. See *Figure 9-22*. It is closed on the top and open on the bottom. It fits closely within the engine cylinder or sleeve and is able to move alternately up and down in the cylinder. The piston serves as a carrier for the piston rings.

The parts of the piston are shown in *Figure 9-23*. Each part is defined.

1. Land — That part of the piston above the top ring or between ring grooves. The lands confine and support the piston rings in their grooves.

2. *Heat dam* — A narrow groove cut in the top land of some pistons to reduce heat flow to the top ring groove. This groove fills with carbon during engine operation and reduces heat flow to the top ring. Heat dams are also designed as cast slots in the piston.

FIGURE 9-22. The piston, rings, and piston pins. *(Courtesy of AE Piston Products)*

3. Piston head — The top piston surface against which the combustion gases exert pressure. The piston head may be flat, concave, convex, or of irregular shape.

4. Piston pins (wrist pins or gudgeon pins) — Connections between the upper end of the connecting rod and the piston. They can be (1) anchored to the piston and floating in the connecting rod, (2) anchored to the connecting rod and floating in the piston, or (3) full floating in both connecting rod and piston. Number 3 requires a lock ring to hold the pin in place. Some piston pins and connecting rods are connected together using an interference fit. An *interference fit*, also called a press fit, is one in which the internal diameter of the connecting rod and the external diameter of the piston pin interfere with each other. This means the external diameter is larger than the internal diameter. Thus, the two parts must be pressed together during assembly.

5. Skirt — That part of the piston located between the first ring groove above the wrist pin hole and the bottom of the piston. The skirt forms a bearing area in contact with the cylinder wall and is 90 degrees opposite the piston pin.

6. Thrust face — The portion of the piston skirt that carries the thrust load of the piston against the cylinder wall.

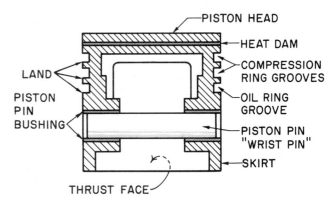

FIGURE 9-23. The piston has many parts. Some of the more important parts are shown.

7. Compression ring groove — A groove cut into the piston around its circumference to hold the compression rings.

8. Oil ring groove — A groove cut into the piston around its circumference. Oil ring grooves are usually wider than compression ring grooves. They generally have holes or slots through the bottom of the groove for oil drainage back to the crankcase area.

9. Piston pin bushing — A bushing fitted between the piston pin and the piston. It acts as a bearing material and is used mostly on cast iron pistons. This bushing can also be located in the small end of the connecting rod assembly. It is usually made of bronze.

Piston Requirements

The piston assembly must be designed to operate under severe conditions. The temperatures produced on top of the piston are very high. This heat causes stress and expansion problems. The piston is moved up and down many times per minute, which produces high pressures and stress. To handle these conditions, most pistons are made of aluminum. Aluminum makes the piston lighter. However, some larger engines, especially certain diesels, may use a cast iron piston. In this case, the RPM would be lower. The lighter pistons can operate much more effectively in today's gasoline engines, which run in excess of 5,000 RPM.

Piston Expansion

When combustion occurs on the top of the piston, some of the heat is transmitted down through the piston body. This causes the piston to expand. If the expansion were too great, the piston might wear the cylinder to a point of damage. To compensate for expansion, older pistons have a split skirt. See *Figure 9–24*. When the piston skirt expands, the slot closes rather than increasing in size.

The T slot, which is also used on older engines, is another method of controlling expansion. In this case the T slot tends to hold back the transfer of heat from the head to the skirt. It also allows for expansion within the slot.

Some pistons use steel rings, which are cast directly into the piston. These steel rings will not expand as much as the aluminum. The steel rings have a tendency to control or minimize expansion.

Cam ground pistons are also used to control the expansion in a gasoline engine. Refer to *Figure 9–25*. The pistons are ground in the shape of a cam or egg. As the piston heats up during operation, it becomes round. The piston is designed

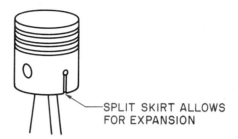

FIGURE 9–24. Piston with a split skirt to allow for expansion when heated.

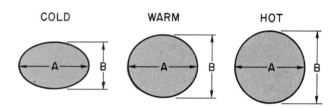

FIGURE 9–25. Cam ground pistons also help control expansion. As the piston heats up, it becomes round. This shape makes the piston fit more accurately in the cylinder bore.

so that maximum expansion takes place on dimension B. Dimension A remains about the same.

Head Shapes

The shape of the piston head varies according to the engine. Head shapes are used to create turbulence and change compression ratios. Generally, small, low-cost engines use the flat top. This head comes so close to the valves on some engines that there must be a recessed area in the piston for the valves. Another type of head is called the raised dome or pop-up head. This type is used to increase the compression ratio. The dished head can also be used to alter the compression ratio. *Figure 9–26* illustrates different types of piston head design. Other types of piston heads are used, but only for special applications.

Piston Skirt

Since the 1970s, it has become important to make the engine as small as possible, yet still powerful. One way to do this is to keep the height of the piston and connecting rod to a minimum. This is done by shortening the connecting rod. A *slipper skirt* is used. Part of the piston skirt is removed so the counterweights won't hit the piston. This design means there can be a smaller distance between the center of the

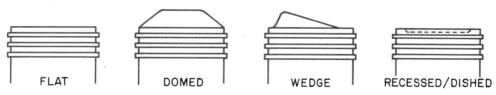

FLAT   DOMED   WEDGE   RECESSED/DISHED

FIGURE 9–26. Pistons are designed with different head shapes. These are the most common types.

crankshaft and the top of the piston. The output power of the engine is not affected because the bore and stroke still remain the same. See *Figure 9–27*.

Skirt Finish

The surface of the skirt is somewhat rough. Small grooves are machined on the skirt so that lubricating oil will be carried in the grooves. See *Figure 9–28*. This helps lubricate the piston skirt as it moves up and down in the cylinder. If the engine overheats, however, the oil will thin out and excessive piston wear may occur. Some pistons have an impregnated silicon surface on the skirt of the piston. Impregnated silicon (silicon particles placed into the external finish of the piston) helps to reduce friction between the skirt and the cylinder wall.

FIGURE 9–27.   A slipper skirt is used to make the connecting rod shorter. This makes the engine smaller and lighter.

FIGURE 9–28.   Small grooves are sometimes placed on the skirt of the piston. These grooves help to keep oil on the walls, improving lubrication.

Piston Rings

There are two types of sealing problems on the piston. Compression pressures must not be allowed to escape past the rings. Escape of compression pressures is defined as *blow-by*. See *Figure 9–29*. If blow-by occurs, there is a loss of power. If there is excessive blow-by, too much oil might be forced off the cylinder walls, causing excessive *scuffing* and wear on the cylinder walls and piston rings.

The rings must also keep the oil below the combustion chamber. If they don't, there may be excessive oil consumption. The moving piston is sealed with compression and oil control rings. The rings are slightly larger than the piston. When installed, they push out against the cylinder walls. Since they contact the cylinder wall, they seal against pressure losses and oil loss. Most engines use two compression rings and one oil control ring. In certain diesel engines, however, more compression rings may be used to seal the higher pressures.

Piston Ring End Gap

When the compression ring is placed in the cylinder, there is a gap at the ends of the ring. See *Figure 9–30*. This gap is referred to as piston ring end gap. The piston ring end gap gets smaller as the ring increases in temperature. If it were

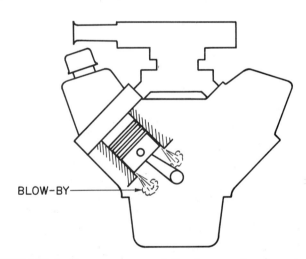

FIGURE 9–29.   Blow-by is defined as combustion gases that escape past the rings and into the crankcase area.

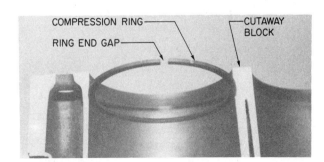

FIGURE 9–30.   Piston ring end gap is the distance between the ends of the compression ring when placed in the cylinder.

too small, the ring would bind in the cylinder and break, causing excessive scoring of the cylinder walls. If the piston ring end gap were too large, excessive blow-by would result. Piston ring end gap should be checked when rebuilding engines. *Figure 9–31* illustrates the measuring of piston ring end gap.

Compression Ring Material

Compression rings are made of cast iron. This material is very brittle and can break easily if bent. However, the brittle material wears very well. Certain heavy-duty engines and some diesel engines use ductile iron as piston ring material. This material is stronger and resists breaking, but the cost of these rings is higher. Some high-quality piston rings have a fused outside layer of chromium or molybdenum. Chromium or molybdenum reduces wear on the rings and cylinder walls. See *Figure 9–32*.

Ring Design

There are several types of compression rings. *Figure 9–33* shows some of the more common rings. The plain or rectangular ring fits flat against the cylinder walls. The taper-faced ring improves scraping ability on the down stroke. Other rings such as the corner-grooved and reverse-beveled rings are designed as *torsional rings*. They have either a chamfer or counterbore machined into the rings.

Torsional rings are also shown in Figure 9–32. Any chamfer or counterbore causes internal stresses in the ring. These stresses cause the ring to twist slightly as shown in *Figure 9–34*. This only happens when the ring is compressed inside the cylinder. Twist is used to form *line contact* sealing on the cylinder wall and the piston ring groove. Line contact

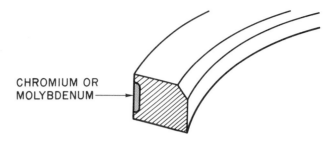

FIGURE 9–32. A chromium or molybdenum layer is placed on some compression rings to improve the wearing characteristics.

improves the sealing and scraping characteristics of the rings. This is also called static tension.

When the ring is in this position, there is no downward pressure on the ring. This happens during the intake, compression, and exhaust strokes of the engine. High pressure is applied to the ring only on the power stroke. On the intake stroke, the twist forces the bottom corner of the ring to act as a scraper against the cylinder walls. This aids in removing any excess oil on the cylinder walls. On the compression stroke, the ring still retains the twist. This allows the ring to glide over any oil still on the cylinder walls rather than carrying it to the combustion chamber.

As the piston rises, compression pressures help flatten the ring for better sealing. On the power stroke, hot gases from the combustion chamber enter the ring groove. The ring is forced out and flat against the cylinder wall. See *Figure 9–35*. Now there is a good seal during the power stroke. This process is also called dynamic sealing. During the exhaust stroke, static conditions are present again. The ring has a twist again. This twist causes the ring to glide again over any oil on the cylinder walls. Both the multiple-groove and radius or barrel-faced ring are designed to produce line contact as well. Better sealing characteristics are the result.

Oil Control Rings

When the engine is operating normally, a great deal of oil is thrown onto the cylinder walls. The connecting rods also splash oil on the walls. Some engines have a hole in the connecting rod to help spray oil directly on the cylinder walls. Oil on the cylinder walls aids lubrication and reduces wear. This oil, however, must be kept out of the combustion chamber.

Oil rings are made to scrape oil from the cylinder walls. They are also used to stop any oil from entering the combustion chamber and to lubricate the walls to prevent excessive wear.

All oil control rings are designed to scrape the oil off the walls on the down stroke. See *Figure 9–36*. After being scraped off the cylinder walls, the oil passes through the center of the ring. It then flows through holes on the piston and back to the crankcase. This scraping process helps remove carbon particles that are in the ring area. The oil flow also helps cool and seal the piston.

Oil control rings are made of two, three, or four parts. These usually include an expander, a top rail, a spacer, and a bottom rail. On some rings, several of these parts may be

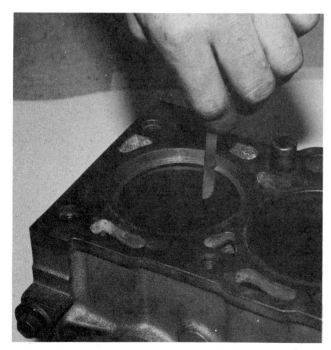

FIGURE 9–31. Piston ring end gap can be checked with a feeler gauge when placed in the cylinder.

COMPRESSION RINGS
POPULAR RING TYPES

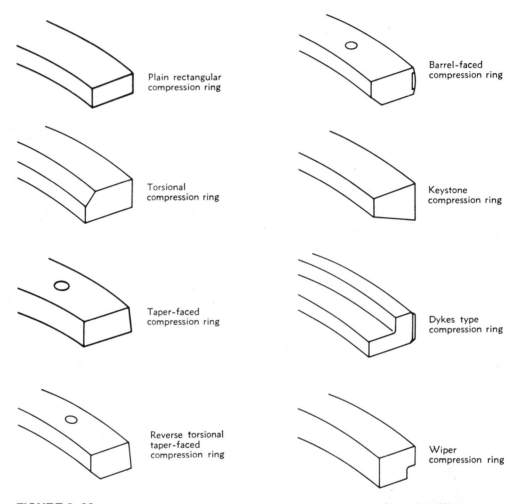

FIGURE 9–33. Compression rings can be designed in several ways. Note the different cross-sectional shapes used. *(Courtesy of Hastings Manufacturing Company)*

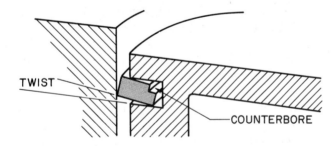

FIGURE 9–34. When a chamfer or counterbore is put on a compression ring, it causes the ring to twist in the groove. Twisting helps to seal the ring to the cylinder bore during operation.

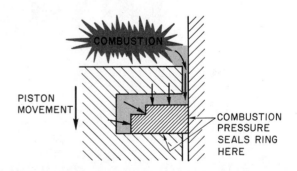

FIGURE 9–35. Pressure from combustion causes the rings to seal against the cylinder wall.

built together in one piece. The expander is used to push the ring out against the cylinder walls. The top and bottom rails are used to scrape the oil off of the cylinder walls. These are sometimes called scraper rings. The spacer is used to keep the two scrapers apart. *Figure 9–37* shows a common type of oil control ring. On certain scraper rings, a chrome-plated section is used to improve wear characteristics. *Figure 9–38* shows several rings used on automobile engines.

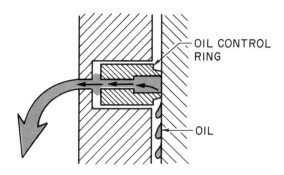

FIGURE 9–36. The oil being scraped off the cylinder wall passes through the ring, through holes in the piston, and back to the crankcase.

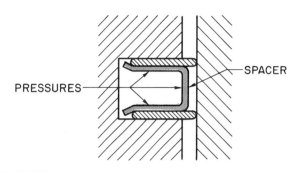

FIGURE 9–37. Oil control rings use a spacer to keep the two scrapers apart.

TYPES OF OIL CONTROL RINGS

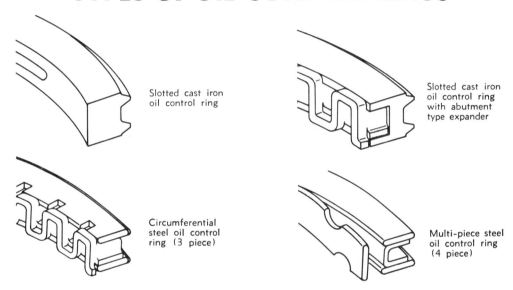

Slotted cast iron oil control ring

Slotted cast iron oil control ring with abutment type expander

Circumferential steel oil control ring (3 piece)

Multi-piece steel oil control ring (4 piece)

FIGURE 9–38. Many styles of oil rings are used on the piston. Each has a special purpose and design. *(Courtesy of Hastings Manufacturing Company)*

Cylinder Wear

The motion of the piston and the position of the rings cause the cylinder to wear unevenly. *Figure 9–39* shows how a typical cylinder wears. The cylinder develops a taper. *Cylinder taper* is produced only where the rings touch the cylinder walls. The greatest amount of wear is near the top of the cylinder. The least amount of wear is near the bottom of the cylinder. This wear produces a ridge in the upper part of the cylinder bore. The ridge must be removed before the pistons are removed during an overhaul. If the ridge is not removed, the pistons will be damaged upon removal. New rings may also be damaged by hitting the bottom of the ridge.

Manufacturer's specifications as listed in maintenance manuals allow only a certain amount of taper on the cylinder walls. Too much taper will affect the piston ring end gap as shown in *Figure 9–40*. Too much end gap, as shown on the top of the cylinder walls, will produce excessive blow-by.

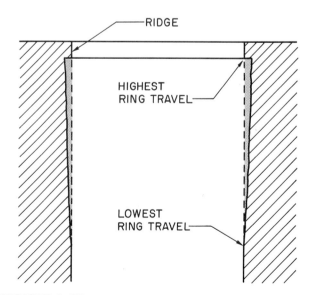

FIGURE 9–39. Over a period of time, the rings on the piston wear the cylinder bore to a tapered shape.

EFFECT OF 0.012 CYLINDER TAPER ON RING
GAP IN FOUR INCH BORE

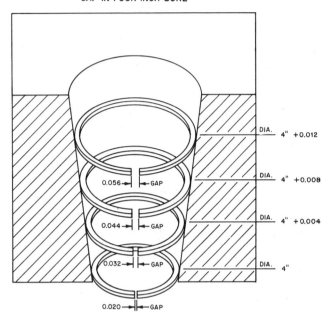

FIGURE 9–40. A tapered cylinder bore can change the ring end gap. This change may cause excessive blow-by. *(Courtesy of Hastings Manufacturing Company)*

Cylinder Deglazing

When new piston rings are placed in the piston, the outside of the ring and the cylinder wall will not have the same shape. This difference is shown in *Figure 9–41*. The ring touches the cylinder only on the high spots of the ring. This causes poor sealing between the ring and cylinder walls.

Because of this condition, the ring and cylinder walls are

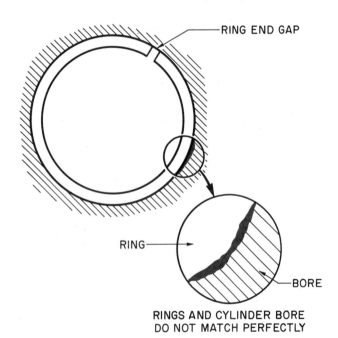

FIGURE 9–41. When new rings are placed in an engine, they are not seated. The shape of the ring is not exactly the same as the shape of the cylinder bore.

designed to have a somewhat rough finish. Then, as the ring and cylinder walls begin to wear, the high spots on the rough surfaces will wear first. The two objects will then take on the same shape. This condition is known as breaking-in, seating-in, or wearing-in an engine. Deglazing is the operation used to make the cylinder rough. See *Figure 9–42*. Deglazing also tends to help retain some oil on the cylinder walls. The extra oil helps to lubricate the new piston rings and aids in the break-in process.

Honing is another process used to improve the cylinder walls. Honing is somewhat different from deglazing. Deglazing is used to roughen up the cylinder walls to remove the glaze, while honing is used to make the cylinder rounder. Honing removes more material than deglazing, although the same size piston can be used. The tool used to hone has stones positioned in a very rigid tool. Usually there are four stones on a hone and only three stones on a deglazer. Note that cylinders can also be bored using a boring tool. In this case, boring removes more material so that larger pistons and rings must be used.

Oversize Pistons and Rings

If the ring end gap is too large, or if there is excessive wear on the cylinder bore, it is necessary to bore the cylinders to a larger size. If this must be done, both standard and oversize pistons and rings are available. The exact oversize ranges vary according to the vehicle make and manufacturer. Common specifications include pistons that have 0.005-, 0.010-, 0.020-, and 0.030-inch oversizes. Common specifications for rings include 0.003-, 0.005-, 0.010-, 0.020-, and 0.030-inch oversizes. Each manufacturer may have different oversize ranges for both pistons and rings.

Piston Pins

Piston pins, also known as wrist pins, are used to attach the piston to the connecting rod. *Figure 9–43* shows a common piston pin made of high-quality steel in the shape of a tube. Piston pins are both strong and lightweight. They are *case-hardened* to provide long-wearing operation. Case-hardened means the outer surface of the piston pin is hardened. The inside is still considered soft metal. Hardening a

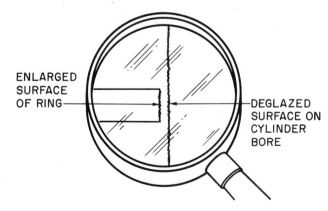

FIGURE 9–42. Deglazing a cylinder will aid in seating rings.

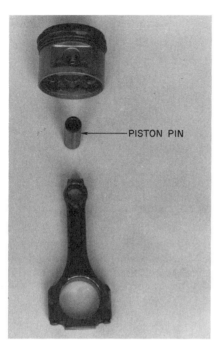

FIGURE 9–43. The piston pin, also called the wrist pin, is used to attach the piston to the connecting rod.

metal makes it very brittle and could cause the piston pin to break easier. The softer metal on the inside prevents the piston pin from cracking.

Piston Thrust Surfaces

As the piston moves up and down in the cylinder, there are *major* and *minor thrust* forces on the side of the piston. Minor thrust force is the pressure placed on the right side of the piston when viewing the piston from the rear of the engine. This is when the engine is turning clockwise. Minor thrust force occurs on the compression stroke.

Major thrust force is the reverse. Major thrust force is the pressure placed on the left side of the piston when viewed from the rear and turning clockwise. See *Figure 9–44*. Major

thrust occurs when the piston is on the power stroke. When the crankshaft crosses over top dead center, the piston shifts from minor to major thrust force. *Piston slap* is produced at this time. This means the piston slaps against the cylinder walls. Excessive piston slap occurs when there is too much clearance between the piston and the cylinder walls. This can cause noise and wear on the piston and cylinder walls. Excessive piston slap can usually be eliminated by replacing the rings or by boring out the cylinder and replacing with oversize piston and rings.

Piston Pin Offset

To eliminate piston slap, the piston pin is located slightly off center. The piston pin is located closer to the minor thrust surface. Because the mechanics of movement have been changed, piston slap is reduced.

Connecting Rod

The connecting rods, shown in *Figure 9–45*, connect the piston to the crankshaft. One end is attached to the piston pin. The other end is attached to the crankshaft rod journal. *Figure 9–46* shows the parts of the connecting rod. These include the connecting rod, the rod cap, two bearing inserts, the connecting rod bolts, and the nuts. Surfaces called *bosses* are forged into the connecting rod to balance it. They are machined until a perfect balance is obtained.

The connecting rod and cap are line bored. The cap is attached to the connecting rod when the inside bore is machined. It is important to keep the connecting rod cap matched to the connecting rod during service. If they are ever mismatched, the bore may be incorrect. This will cause the connecting rod and bearing cap to be misaligned, causing damage or excessive wear on the bearings.

The caps and connecting rods are marked with numbers to keep the caps matched to the connecting rods. See *Figure 9–47*. Always match these numbers when rebuilding an engine. On certain engines, the numbers have been omitted, while on others the same number may appear on the con-

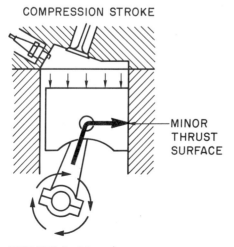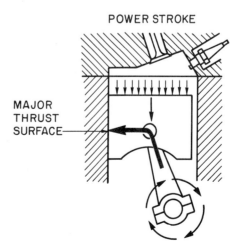

FIGURE 9–44. Major and minor thrust surfaces are built into the piston to absorb piston thrusts.

FIGURE 9–45.   Two connecting rods are shown. *(Courtesy of Masco Industries)*

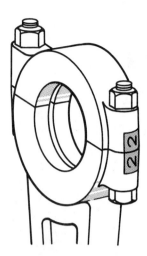

FIGURE 9–47.   Connecting rod caps and connecting rods should always be kept together. Numbers are stamped on them to keep them in order. *(Courtesy of Federal-Mogul Corporation)*

necting rod. A good rule is to always keep the cap matched to the correct connecting rod. Some technicians also use a punch to mark each cap and cylinder rod accordingly. This assures the technician that the cap and connecting rod will be assembled correctly.

Some connecting rods have an oil squirt hole in their lower section. This hole directs oil to the cylinder walls for improved lubrication. Other designs have a squirt hole in the cap mating surface. Some designs have no squirt hole.

Connecting Rod Bearings

The connecting rod bearings are designed the same as the

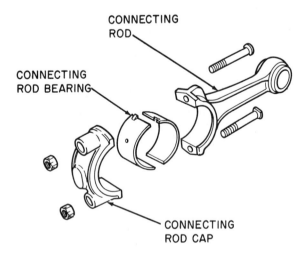

FIGURE 9–46.   The connecting rod assembly includes the connecting rod, the connecting rod bearing cap, two bearing inserts, and the bolts and nuts. *(Courtesy of Federal-Mogul Corporation)*

main bearings. Each bearing is made of two pieces. Small locating lugs are used to locate the bearing in the proper position and to prevent the bearing from spinning in the bore. These lugs fit into a slot machined into the connecting rod cap and connecting rod. As in main bearings, the connecting rods are made of a steel back, copper and lead inside, and a thin coating of pure tin.

CAR CLINIC

PROBLEM: Main Bearing Alignment

An engine was recently rebuilt. However, after about 200 miles, the engine is making loud knocking noises at all speeds. The knock sounds like bad bearings.

SOLUTION:

When an engine is rebuilt, the crankshaft main bearings are replaced. Each main bearing cap must be replaced to its original position. During the manufacturing process, all main bearings are placed on the engine, and the main bearing bore is line bored. This means that the main bearing caps *must* be reinstalled to their original position. They are often marked with a number. If the main bearing caps are not installed to their original position, there is a good possibility that the main bearing will wear quickly. The solution to the problem is to replace the main bearings and make sure the main bearing caps are installed to their correct position.

Problems, Diagnosis and Service

SAFETY PRECAUTIONS

1. Many corners on the engine block may be sharp from being machined. Be careful not to cut your hands when handling the block.
2. The clearances between the crankshaft and the block are very small. When turning the crankshaft during bearing installation, be careful not to get your fingers caught, as injury may result.
3. The engine crankshaft, pistons, and other parts are heavy. Be careful not to drop them on your toes or feet.
4. Always wear safety glasses when working on the internal parts of the engine, especially during deglazing. Parts of the deglazer may break off and fly into your eyes.
5. When taking a compression test, make sure the engine will not start during cranking. High-pressure gases may escape from the cylinder being tested, and you may get a shock from the spark plug wires. Always disconnect the ignition system before cranking.
6. Make sure that all tools are clean and free of grease. Under high torque applications, the tools can become very slippery and slip off the bolt or nut.
7. Many of the bolts and nuts require high torque readings. Always use the correct tools for the job.
8. When removing the vibration damper bolt, make sure the crankshaft can be held tight. Use a small piece of wood or other soft object to hold the crankshaft in place while loosening or tightening the vibration damper bolt.
9. When rebuilding an engine, always clean all parts before inspection. Parts that are dirty may easily slip and be dropped when being moved around.

PROBLEM: Lack of Power, Excessive Oil Consumption, and/or Steady Engine Miss on One Cylinder

Engines, especially those with many miles on them, often lack power. In addition, these engines may also burn oil excessively. One area often identified as the problem is that of bad or worn rings.

DIAGNOSIS

Worn rings can be identified easily by checking the compression pressure within each cylinder and comparing the readings. Each manufacturer suggests maximum variations in cylinder pressure. For example, an engine that has a cylinder variation of more than 20–30% probably needs the piston rings replaced.

SERVICE

A compression test is made to determine the condition of the engine parts that affect cylinder pressure. This test should always be performed as part of a tune-up or whenever there is a complaint about poor engine performance. Also this check should be made when there is excessive oil or fuel consumption. A compression test is a performance comparison between the cylinders, which is then compared with manufacturer specifications. The specifications are listed in many automotive maintenance and service manuals. All conditions during the test should be the same. These include the cranking speed, position of throttle and choke, and the temperature of the engine during the entire test. There are two types of compression test: the dry and wet compression tests. Preparation for both tests includes:

1. The engine must be at normal operating temperature.
2. Check to be sure the battery is fully charged.
3. Check the starter for operation at the same speed.
4. Remove all spark plugs.
   CAUTION: When removing the spark plug wires, pull only on the boot. Pulling on the wires may damage certain types of carbon-impregnated plug wires. This damage may cause the engine to misfire severely.
5. Connect a jumper wire between the high-tension terminal of the coil and ground. This connection will disable the ignition system to prevent high-tension sparking while cranking.
6. Connect a remote starter switch so the engine can be cranked from the engine compartment.

The Dry Compression Test

The dry compression test is performed to get a basic comparison between the cylinders and to determine the overall condition of the compression chamber. The dry compression test is performed as follows:

1. Hold the carburetor linkage and choke wide open.
2. Screw the compression tester into the spark plug hole. Do not use a wrench to tighten the compression tester. See *Figure 9–48*.
   CAUTION: Be careful not to touch the hot exhaust manifold if the engine is at operating temperature.
3. Crank the engine until the compression gauge reaches the highest reading. This should be reached with three or four revolutions of the engine. Write down the highest reading.
   CAUTION: Be careful not to get the remote starter wires or other tools in the fan area.

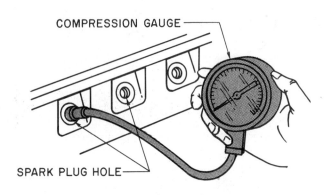

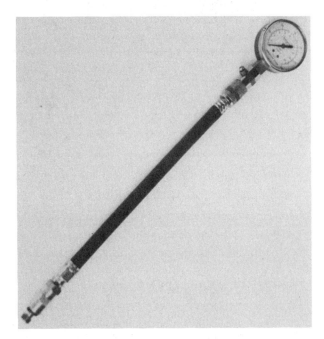

FIGURE 9–48. Both a wet and dry compression test can be made using the compression tester.

4. Repeat this procedure with the same number of revolutions on all cylinders. Be sure to release the compression gauge after each test.

5. Compare the readings of all cylinders.

6. A 20% variation between the cylinder readings is usually satisfactory. If the readings vary more than 20%, the cause should be determined. Refer to the manufacturer's specifications for the exact amount of variation on each cylinder.

The Wet Compression Test

The wet compression test is taken to determine if low readings are caused by compression leakage past the valves, piston rings, head gasket, or other leaks such as a crack or hole in the piston. The procedure for the wet compression test is as follows:

1. Squirt a small amount of oil into each cylinder through the spark plug hole.

2. Now perform the compression test as outlined in the dry

test. The oil should temporarily form an improved seal between the piston and cylinder wall.

3. If the readings are 10 pounds or more higher than during a dry test, compression is probably leaking by the rings.

4. If there is no difference between the wet and dry test, or if the wet test is less than 10 pounds higher, a compression loss is probably caused by compression leaking past the valves.

5. When taking a compression test on new rings, you may not be able to obtain the full compression until the rings are seated.

PROBLEM: Engine Needs Rebuilding

As an engine accumulates miles, many parts eventually wear out or break. Often it is necessary to rebuild an engine and to replace those parts that have excessive wear. In addition, many of the parts that are worn are part of the basic engine block, including the crankshaft, block, pistons, and seals.

DIAGNOSIS

Various signs and conditions help the automotive technician determine if an engine needs a complete overhaul. Some of the more common signs include:

1. Excessive oil consumption

2. Low or uneven compression readings

3. Lack of power and performance

4. Excessive mileage on the vehicle

5. Dirty oil from combustion blow-by

6. Engine missing on one or more cylinders

SERVICE

There are many important service procedures and suggestions for rebuilding an engine.

Cylinder Block

1. Always *deglaze* the cylinder bore when using new piston rings. A deglazing tool is shown in *Figure 9–49.*
   a. With the piston removed from the cylinder, place the deglazer in the cylinder bore.
   b. Place a small amount of cutting oil in the cylinder.
   c. Using a drill attached to the deglazer, rotate slowly, making sure the deglazer does not hit against the crankshaft. If it does hit the crankshaft the deglazer stones may break.

   CAUTION: Keep your fingers away from the spinning deglazer. Also, never spin the deglazer outside of the cylinder; it may separate and be thrown into your body.

FIGURE 9–49. A deglazer is used to roughen up the cylinder walls to aid in break-in when rebuilding an engine. A ridge reamer, which is also shown, is used to remove the small ridge on the top of a cylinder before removing the pistons. *(Courtesy of Snap-On Tools Company)*

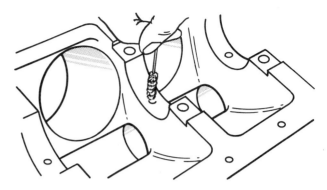

FIGURE 9–50. All oil passages on the crankshaft should be cleaned before installing. *(Courtesy of Federal-Mogul Corporation)*

d. While rotating the deglazer, move it up and down to obtain a cross-hatched pattern in the cylinder bore.

e. Remove the deglazer and clean the bore.

f. Check the bore for any spots on the cylinder bore that were not deglazed evenly.

g. If there are spots that have not been deglazed, deglaze again for a short time. If the spots are too large, however, the cylinder bore may have to be honed. Honing takes more material off than deglazing. Again, make sure the cylinder bore has been completely cleaned after deglazing, using clean rags.

2. Always check the top of the block for *flatness*. Checking the flatness of the block determines if there has been warpage of the block. Warpage can be created from excessive heat. If the block is slightly warped, the head gasket may not seal correctly and will leak. Use the following procedure to check for flatness on the block:

a. Use a long, steel, straight-edged ruler.

b. Place the straight-edge on the top of the block.

c. Using a feeler gauge, check for clearance under the straight-edge. If the space is greater than the specifications listed in the repair manual, the block may have to be machined to produce a flat surface again.

3. Always check the block for small *cracks* between the cylinder walls and the coolant passageways. Excessive heat can cause the block to crack at this point, coolant water can get into the cylinder.

4. When installing core plugs, make sure the plug is inserted evenly. If it is not inserted evenly, there is a good possibility that the core plug will leak engine coolant. Use a small amount of sealant between the block and the plug.

5. Remember to check the oil passageways in the block for foreign matter blocking the holes. See *Figure 9–50.*

CAUTION: Be careful not to cut or scrape your hands on the sharp corners of the block.

Crankshaft and Main Bearings

1. When installing main bearing caps, make sure the caps are placed in the correct order. The caps should be inserted exactly in the same cylinder and position as when disassembled.

2. Always check *bearing clearance* with Plastigage. See *Figure 9–51.* Use the following procedure when using Plastigage:

a. Place a small amount of Plastigage on the bearing journal.

b. Place the bearing and bearing cap on the journal and torque to service manual specifications.

c. Remove the bearing cap and bearing,

d. Measure the width that the Plastigage has been flattened. This measurement can be made using a vernier caliper or the gauge furnished on the Plastigage container.

e. The width of the flattened Plastigage is a measure of the bearing clearance.

3. When installing the crankshaft, use a feeler gauge or dial indicator to check for *crankshaft end play*. See *Figure 9–52.*

a. Place the crankshaft in the block.

CAUTION: The crankshaft is very heavy. Be careful not to pinch your fingers as the crankshaft is being set into the block.

b. Move the crankshaft fully to one end of its end play.

c. Select the correct size feeler gauge to measure the amount of movement axially on the crankshaft.

d. Check the clearance between the thrust bearing (usually the center bearing) and the thrust surfaces on the crankshaft and compare with manufacturer's specifications.

4. Care must always be taken to install the main bearings in the correct position. All oil holes must be correctly lined up with the oil passages in the block assembly for correct installation. Also, the small notches on both bearing segments (used to stop the bearings from spinning) must be installed on the same side.

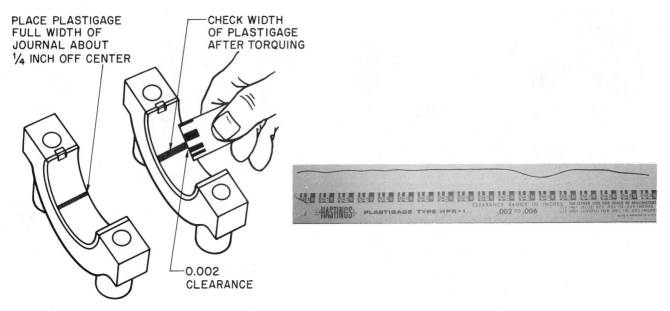

PLACE PLASTIGAGE
FULL WIDTH OF
JOURNAL ABOUT
¼ INCH OFF CENTER

CHECK WIDTH
OF PLASTIGAGE
AFTER TORQUING

0.002
CLEARANCE

FIGURE 9–51. Plastigage is used to check the clearance of the main and connecting rod bearings. As the cap is torqued to specifications, the small plastic strip flattens out. The width of the strip determines the clearance.

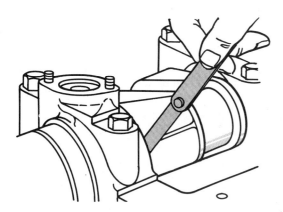

FIGURE 9–52. A feeler gauge can be used to check the crankshaft end play. *(Courtesy of Federal-Mogul Corporation)*

5. When rebuilding the engine, make sure to replace both the front and the rear crankshaft seals. Replacing these seals will ensure that there will be no oil leaks after the engine is running.

6. Whenever any part is installed on the cylinder block, always torque the fasteners to the correct torque specifications. To get accurate readings make sure the bolt and hole threads are clean and free of dirt.

Pistons and Connecting Rods

1. Before removing pistons from the cylinder bore, remove the ridge that has been produced on top of the cylinder with a *ridge reamer.*
   a. A ridge reamer such as the one shown at the top of Figure 9–49 can be used to remove the ridge on top of the cylinder bore.
   b. Bolt the ridge reamer on the block according to the manufacturer's recommendations.

   c. Adjust the ridge reamer to take a very small cut.
   d. After getting the feel of rotating the ridge reamer, adjust it to take a larger cut.
      CAUTION: If the ridge reamer is too hard to turn, too much of a cut is being made. Readjust as necessary.
   e. Be careful that the ridge reamer doesn't produce chatter. This chatter may cause vertical grooves to be cut into the cylinder, possibly damaging the cylinder bore.
   f. Continue removing the ridge until there is no ridge left on the cylinder wall.

2. When pistons are being removed from the cylinder bore, cover the connecting rod bolts with a piece of rubber hose to protect the rod bolt threads and crankshaft journal from being damaged. Using a soft piece of wood, push against the connecting rod to remove the piston from the top of the cylinder block.

3. When pistons are removed, check for cracking between the piston pin and the top of the piston.

4. After the pistons have been removed, always check the piston pin for excessive wear in the piston.

5. When pistons have been removed from the cylinder bore, *check the amount of cylinder taper* on the bore.
   a. Cylinder bore taper can be checked by using a bore gauge.
   b. Taper can also be checked using an inside diameter micrometer.
   c. Take two readings at several points down the cylinder (take one reading, then rotate the gauge 90 degrees and take a second reading).

6. Use a *ring groove cleaner,* **Figure 9–53,** to clean the carbon built up in the ring grooves before installing new

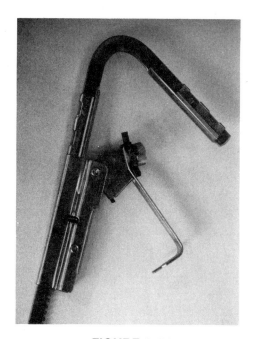 

FIGURE 9–53. The ring groove cleaner is used to remove carbon from the ring grooves.

piston rings. Cleaning the carbon from the ring grooves ensures that the piston rings will be able to move adequately for proper sealing.

a. Select the correct size cutting tool for the ring groove.

b. Place the ring groove cleaner in place with the cutting tool in the ring groove.

c. Rotate the ring groove cleaner until all carbon is removed from the groove.

CAUTION: Always use protective gloves when cleaning the ring grooves as the tool may stick during rotation and injure your hands.

d. Continue cleaning each groove until the carbon has been cleaned from all ring grooves.

e. Clean the piston completely before installing new rings.

7. Always check *piston ring end gap* on new piston compression rings. End gap measurements are typically about 0.004 inch for each inch diameter of the piston.

a. Place the compression ring near the top of the cylinder bore without the piston.

b. Make sure the compression ring is placed evenly in the bore.

c. Using a feeler gauge, measure the gap produced by the ring in the cylinder and compare with the manufacturer's specifications. If the end gap is too large, the cylinder may have to be bored to a larger diameter, thus requiring a different set of pistons and rings.

8. When installing the rings on the pistons, make sure the rings are placed in the correct groove and installed with the correct side up. In addition, the ring end gaps should be correctly positioned. Generally the ring end gaps

should be placed at between 90 and 120 degrees from the other gaps.

CAUTION: Always use a ring expander to expand the rings over the piston, being careful not to break the brittle compression rings.

9. When installing the pistons after they have been removed and cleaned, replace them in the same cylinder and in the correct position. The service manual states the correct position for each piston during installation.

10. Always check the connecting rod bearing clearance with Plastigage. Use the same procedure as with the main bearings.

11. When installing pistons, use a *piston ring compressor*. See *Figure 9–54.*

a. Make sure there is sufficient lubrication on the new rings and cylinder walls before installing the piston into the cylinder.

b. Place the bearings on the connecting rods.

c. Place the connecting rod gently in a vise.

d. Make sure the end gaps of the rings are not aligned together. The end gaps are typically staggered around the piston (90–120 degrees apart).

e. Place a sufficient amount of oil on the piston and rings. Then place the piston ring compressor around the top of the piston and rings.

f. Tighten the ring compressor to compress the rings.

g. Place the assembly in the cylinder bore, making sure the piston and connecting rod are in the correct position.

h. Push the piston down into the bore with a soft rubber hammer until all the rings are inside the cylinder. The ring compressor will relax somewhat when the rings are inside the cylinder.

CAUTION: Do not force the piston into the cylinder.

FIGURE 9–54. The ring compressor is used to compress the rings so the piston can be inserted into the cylinder bore.

There should be little resistance as the piston goes into the cylinder. If the piston is forced into the cylinder bore, the rings may break. If there is resistance, the ring compressor may not be aligned correctly, or it may not have compressed the rings enough. Remove the assembly and start over again.

12. Care must always be taken to install the connecting rod bearings in the correct position. All oil holes must be correctly lined up with the oil passages in the crankshaft for correct installation. Also, the small notches on both bearing segments (used to stop the bearings from spinning) must be installed on the same side.

SUMMARY

The purpose of this chapter was to investigate the design of the basic engine. The basic engine includes the cylinder block, crankshaft, bearings, seals, piston and rod assembly, and the camshaft.

The cylinder block is the basic structure of the engine. All other parts are attached to the cylinder block. It is made with large cylinder holes for the pistons. The lower section contains the crankshaft. There are many drilled passageways for oil to lubricate other parts of the engine.

Cylinder blocks are made by pouring liquid metal into a mold. Special metals are added to the metal to make it stronger and able to withstand more wear. After the block is cast, it is machined so other parts can be attached to it. Core or expansion plugs are installed into the cylinder block. These are used so that if the coolant freezes and expands, the plugs will pop out. This will prevent the block from cracking.

On certain engines, the cylinders are machined so the piston can fit correctly. Other engines use a machined sleeve that is pressed into the block. Both wet and dry sleeves are

SERVICE MANUAL CONNECTION

There are many important specifications to keep in mind when rebuilding an engine. These specifications can be found in most service manuals. To identify the specifications for your engine, you will need to know the VIN (vehicle identification number) of the vehicle, the type and year of the vehicle, and the type of engine. Although they may be titled differently, some of the more common specifications found in service manuals are listed below. Note that these specifications are typical examples. Each vehicle and engine will have different specifications.

Common Specification	Typical Example
Compression test	the lowest cylinder must be within 70% of the highest
Connecting rod cap bolts (torque)	45 ft-lb
Crankshaft end play	0.0035–0.0135 inch
Flywheel to crankshaft (torque)	60 ft-lb
Main bearing cap bolts (torque)	100 ft-lb
Main bearing clearance	0.0005–0.0015 inch
Piston clearance	0.0010–0.0020 inch
Piston ring end gap (compression rings)	0.010 inch
Piston ring end gap (oil)	0.015 inch
Rod bearing clearance	0.0005–0.0026 inch
Vibration damper (torque)	300–310 ft-lb

used. Wet sleeves have coolant touching them. Dry sleeves do not have coolant touching them. Certain aluminum blocks also have sleeves. A steel sleeve is placed into the mold before *(continued)*

Linkage to Future Automotive Technology

Many new engine designs are being tested to improve efficiency. This V-6 engine uses a 90-degree V, rather than the usual 60-degree V. This design makes the engine more compact and lowers the center of gravity. Both features are important for aerodynamics and handling. The crankpins are offset 30 degrees to retain an even firing sequence. *(Courtesy of Peugeot Motors of America)*

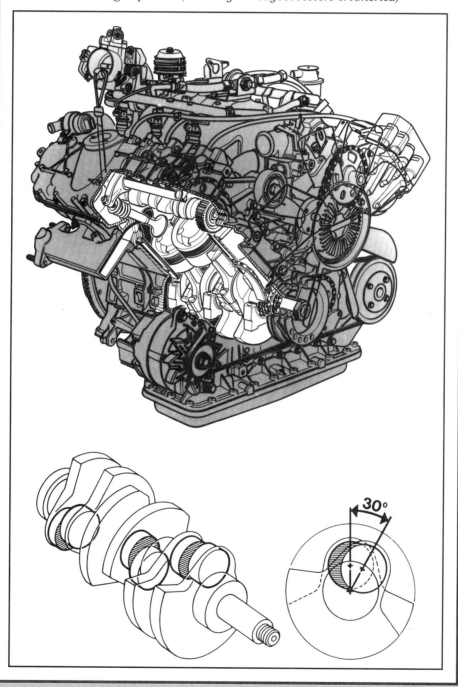

the aluminum is poured. This sleeve, called a liner, cannot be removed.

The crankshaft assembly is used to convert the downward motion of the piston to rotary motion. It includes bearings, the flywheel, vibration damper, timing gears and sprockets, and seals. The crankshaft can either be forged or cast. In addition, the outside surfaces of the bearing journals are hardened steel to prevent excessive wearing. Counterweights are used to balance the crankshaft as it revolves.

Vibration dampers are used to reduce internal vibration in the crankshaft. They are also called harmonic balances. These devices help reduce torsional vibration.

The bearings used on the crankshaft are made of several metals. These metals provide support and strength as well as a good bearing surface for the crankshaft. Bearings must be designed to carry heavy loads, be corrosion resistant, be able to conform to the shape of the crankshaft, and be able to resist fatigue. They also have small locating lugs to keep them from spinning.

Thrust bearings are another part of the crankshaft assembly. They help absorb thrust forces from the crankshaft. The crankshaft has holes drilled from each main bearing journal to the connecting rod journal. These passages feed oil to the connecting rod journal.

It is very important to keep the bearing clearances within the manufacturer's specifications. Too much clearance will reduce oil pressure and increase oil thrown on the cylinder walls.

There are seals on both ends of the crankshaft. These seals are used to keep the oil contained within the engine.

The piston and rod assembly includes compression and oil control rings, the piston, piston pin, connecting rod and bushing, bolts and nuts, and bearing inserts. The piston is made of aluminum. It must be designed to withstand many forces, including pressures on top of the piston, high temperatures, and various thrust forces. Pistons have heat dams to control the flow of heat through the piston. They are designed to allow for expansion as the piston heats up.

Piston rings are used on the piston to help seal the pressures of compression and power. Oil must also be scraped from the cylinder walls. To do this, two compression rings are used, along with one set of oil control rings. There are many types of compression rings. The most common are rings designed to provide a twist when placed in the cylinder bore. This helps to create a seal during engine operation. Rings should also be checked for piston ring end gap. Too little or too large ring end gap may cause damage and poor performance.

During normal operation, the cylinder bore wears in the shape of a taper. The rings wear the cylinder bore into this shape. The taper should be checked to determine if it is within specifications. When new rings are placed on the piston, deglazing is performed to help the rings seat into the cylinder bore.

As the piston moves up and down in the cylinder, thrust forces push the piston from side to side. Piston pins are offset to help reduce the side thrust. Because of this offset, it is important that the piston be replaced in the correct position.

There are many service tips that should be followed when working on an engine. Always follow the manufacturer's recommended procedures when servicing the engine.

TERMS TO KNOW

Can you explain each of the following terms? Review the chapter until you can use each term correctly.

Crankcase	Heat dam
Cast	Interference fit
Die cast	Cam ground pistons
Core plugs	Slipper skirt
Cylinder sleeve	Blow-by
Forged	Scuffing
Heat treated	Line contact
Counterweights	Torsional ring
Fillet	Cylinder taper
Alignment	Case-harden
Torsional vibration	Major thrust
Babbitt	Minor thrust
Main bearing clearance	Piston slap
Plastigage	Bosses
Axial motion	

 REVIEW QUESTIONS

Multiple Choice

1. The part of an engine that is the basic structure to which other parts are bolted is called the:
   a. Crankcase
   b. Crankshaft
   c. Cylinder block
   d. Camshafts
   e. Cylinder head

2. When a cylinder block is cast, the internal passageways have a _____ core.
   a. Metal
   b. Sand
   c. Cast
   d. Plastic
   e. Paper

3. _____ are used to seal up holes (used to remove sand cores during casting) in the block and can protect the block at times from cracking if the coolant freezes.
   a. Core plugs
   b. Metal seals
   c. Rubber seals
   d. Sand plugs
   e. All of the above

4. Which of the following is a type of sleeve or liner used on a cylinder block?
   a. Wet sleeve
   b. Dry sleeve
   c. Cast in liner
   d. All of the above
   e. None of the above

5. Cylinder blocks can be made of:
   a. Cast iron
   b. Brass
   c. Aluminum
   d. Plastic
   e. A and C

6. The device used to change reciprocating motion to rotary motion on the engine is called the:
   a. Crankshaft
   b. Piston
   c. Piston rings
   d. Connecting rod
   e. Cylinder head

7. Thrust surfaces are machined on the crankshaft to:
   a. Absorb rotary thrust
   b. Absorb axial thrust
   c. Help balance the crankshaft
   d. Improve friction
   e. Reduce oil flow

8. Which device is used to reduce torsional vibration?
   a. Crankshaft
   b. Piston rings
   c. Vibration damper
   d. All of the above
   e. None of the above

9. Main bearings are designed for:
   a. Fatigue resistance
   b. Embedability
   c. Conformability
   d. All of the above
   e. None of the above

10. The small lug on the bearing insert is used to:
    a. Keep the bearing from spinning in the bore
    b. Increase lubrication to the bearings
    c. Keep the bearing in balance
    d. Help in manufacturing
    e. None of the above

11. _____ are used to absorb the axial thrust produced on the crankshaft.
    a. Thrust weights
    b. Thrust bearings
    c. Expansion rings
    d. Core plugs
    e. Radial bearings

12. As the amount of main bearing clearance increases, which of the following will happen?
    a. Oil pressure will increase
    b. Oil pressure will decrease
    c. Blow-by will decrease
    d. Blow-by will increase
    e. Compression will increase

13. A/an _____ is used to reduce the heat flow to the top piston ring.
    a. Oil control ring
    b. Heat dam
    c. Piston pin
    d. Compression ring
    e. Cylinder heat sink

14. The part that connects the piston to the connecting rod is called a/an _____.
    a. Compression ring
    b. Heat dam
    c. Wrist pin
    d. Expansion pin
    e. Connecting pin

15. Pistons are designed to have a major and minor _____.
    a. Pressure area
    b. Heat sink
    c. Wear surface
    d. Thrust surface
    e. Speed surface

16. Which of the following are used as a means to control the expansion of the piston (both new and older pistons)?
    a. Cam-shaped pistons
    b. Split or slotted skirt
    c. Oil control ring gap
    d. T slot in piston
    e. A, B, and D of the above

17. As the end gap of the compression rings increases,
    a. Blow-by increases
    b. Power from combustion increases
    c. Oil consumption decreases
    d. Compression ratio increases
    e. All of the above

18. Piston rings that have a chamfer or counterbore cut into them are called:
    a. Oil control rings
    b. Torsional rings
    c. High-pressure rings
    d. Low-pressure rings
    e. Lubrication rings

19. The oil scraped off of the cylinder walls by the oil control rings is:
    a. Sent back to the crankcase through small tubes
    b. Sent back to the crankcase through small holes in the ring groove
    c. Held in the ring groove for further lubrication
    d. Not used again
    e. Sent to the cylinder head

20. The greatest amount of cylinder wear is found:
    a. Near the top of the cylinder bore
    b. In the middle of the cylinder bore
    c. On the bottom of the cylinder bore
    d. On the extreme bottom of the cylinder bore
    e. None of the above

21. To get new piston rings to fit the cylinder bore correctly, it is necessary to:
    a. Bore all cylinders
    b. Deglaze each cylinder
    c. Polish each cylinder
    d. Replace the cylinder each time
    e. Insert a new piston each time

22. Which of the following tools is used to check the clearance between the main bearing and the main bearing journals?
    a. Plastigage
    b. Micrometer
    c. Ruler
    d. Dial indicator
    e. Vernier caliper

The following questions are similar in format to ASE (Automotive Service Excellence) test questions.

23. A piston is removed from the vehicle. After careful inspection, carbon is observed under the rings and in the ring grooves. Technician A says the carbon in the ring grooves should be removed and new rings should be installed. Technician B says the piston can and should be replaced in the cylinder bore without removing the carbon buildup. Who is right?
    a. A only   c. Both A and B
    b. B only   d. Neither A nor B

24. On a compression test, the psi readings on all four cylinders are within 30% of each other. Technician A says all cylinders are OK. Technician B says all are bad. Who is right?
    a. A only   c. Both A and B
    b. B only   d. Neither A nor B

25. After removing the cylinder heads, a small ridge is noticed on the top of the cylinder. Technician A says to leave the ridge there and remove it with a cylinder deglazer after the pistons have been removed. Technician B says to remove the ridge with a ridge reamer before removing the pistons. Who is right?
    a. A only   c. Both A and B
    b. B only   d. Neither A nor B

26. Technician A says it is not OK to exchange vibration dampers from different engines. Technician B says it is OK to exchange vibration dampers from different engines. Who is right?
    a. A only   c. Both A and B
    b. B only   d. Neither A nor B

27. Technician A says that core plugs protect the block from cracking. Technician B says they may pop out if the coolant freezes. Who is correct?
    a. Technician A   c. Both A and B
    b. Technician B   d. Neither A nor B

28. Technician A says that axial motion on the crankshaft is caused from using straight-toothed gears. Technician B says that thrust surfaces are not needed to absorb axial motion on the crankshaft. Who is correct?
    a. Technician A   c. Both A and B
    b. Technician B   d. Neither A nor B

29. Technician A says that Plastigage is used to check valve clearance. Technician B says that Plastigage can be used to check main bearing clearance. Who is correct?
    a. Technician A   c. Both A and B
    b. Technician B   d. Neither A nor B

30. Technician A says that to determine the clearance with Plastigage, measure its length. Technician B says that Plastigage cannot be used to measure connecting rod clearance. Who is correct?
    a. Technician A   c. Both A and B
    b. Technician B   d. Neither A nor B

Essay

31. Explain how a forged crankshaft can be identified.

32. List the parts of the crankshaft.

33. What is torsional vibration?

34. What are some of the characteristics in the design of bearings?

35. What is the purpose of a thrust face on a piston?

36. What would be the result if the piston ring end gap were too small during installation?

Short Answer

37. The crankshaft can be _____ to make the journals a smaller size.

38. When the external diameter of the piston pin interferes with the internal diameter of the connecting rod, it is called an _____ fit.

39. To help reduce friction between the piston skirt and the cylinder wall, some pistons have _____.

40. Three common sizes for oversize pistons include _____, _____, and _____.

41. When completing a cylinder compression, if the cylinder variation is more than _____, the piston rings need to be replaced.

CHAPTER 10

Cylinder Heads and Valves

INTRODUCTION All automotive engines use a cylinder head and a set of valves to operate the engine correctly. The cylinder head acts as a cover or top to the engine. The valves allow the air and fuel to enter and exhaust the engine at the correct time. The components make up the cylinder head and valve mechanism. This chapter is designed to acquaint you with the parts used on the cylinder head and valves.

OBJECTIVES After reading this chapter, you should be able to:

- Identify the purpose of the cylinder head.
- List all parts on the cylinder head.
- Identify the designs used for combustion chambers.
- List the parts of the valve assembly.
- Analyze the purposes of the valve guides, seals, seats, springs, keepers, retainers, and rotators.
- Define the purpose and parts of the camshaft, including the thrust plate and bushings.

- Analyze the design of cam lobes.
- Determine how to time the camshaft to the crankshaft.
- Identify the parts in the valve operating mechanism, including lifters, pushrods, and rocker arms.
- Identify the operation of variable valve timing.
- Analyze several problems, diagnosis and service procedures used on the cylinder head and valve assemblies.

 SAFETY CHECKLIST

When working with cylinder heads and valves there are several important safety checks to know:
✔ Always wear safety glasses around the shop.
✔ When lifting the cylinder head onto a bench, always lift with the legs and keep your back straight.
✔ Always wear protective gloves when lifting or moving cylinder heads.

✔ Make sure that all tools used are clean and free of grease.
✔ Always use the correct torque wrench and specifications when working with cylinder heads.
✔ Make sure all electrical tools are grounded.
✔ Never use electrical tools while standing in wet areas.

Some of the information in this chapter can help you prepare for the National Institute for Automotive Service Excellence (ASE) certification tests. The test most directly related to this chapter is entitled

ENGINE REPAIR (TEST A1).

The content area that closely parallels this chapter is

CYLINDER HEAD AND VALVE TRAIN DIAGNOSIS AND REPAIR.

10.1 CYLINDER HEAD DESIGN

The cylinder head has several purposes. It acts as a cap or seal for the top of the engine. It holds the valves, and it has ports to allow air, fuel, and exhaust to move through the engine. The cylinder head on many engines also contains the combustion chamber for each cylinder or piston. *Figure 10–1* shows a cylinder head for a V-8 engine.

Cylinder Head Manufacturing

Cylinder heads can be made from cast iron or aluminum. Aluminum is used to make the engine lighter, but it transfers heat more rapidly and expands more than cast iron with the addition of heat. This may cause warpage. Both aluminum and cast iron objects are made by pouring hot liquid metal into a sand mold.

The cylinder head must have coolant passages. This means that sand cores also have to be used in the casting process. In addition, passages must be cast for intake and exhaust ports. Figure 10–1 shows some of the ports that are cast into the cylinder head.

After the cylinder head has been cast, it must be machined.

Areas must be machined so that intake and exhaust manifolds can be attached, valves can be seated, spark plugs and injectors can be installed, and a good seal can be provided to the block.

Intake and Exhaust Ports

Intake and exhaust ports must be cast into the cylinder head. These ports are made so the air and fuel can pass through the cylinder head into the combustion chamber. It would be ideal if one port could be used for each valve. Because of space, however, ports are sometimes combined. These ports are called *siamese ports*. See *Figure 10–2*. Siamese ports can be used because each cylinder uses the port at a different time.

Crossflow ports are used on some engines. Crossflow heads have the intake and exhaust ports on the opposite sides.

Coolant Passages

Large openings that allow coolant to pass through the head are cast into the cylinder head. Coolant must circulate throughout the cylinder head so excess heat can be removed. The coolant flows from passages in the cylinder block through the head gasket and into the cylinder head. Depending upon the engine configuration, the coolant then passes back to other parts of the cooling system.

Combustion Chamber

The shape of the combustion chamber affects the operating efficiency of the engine. Two types of combustion chamber designs are commonly used. They are the *wedge-shaped combustion chamber* and the *hemispherical combustion chamber*.

Several terms are used to describe combustion chambers. *Turbulence* is a very rapid movement of gases. When gases move, they make contact with the combustion chamber walls and pistons. Turbulence causes better combustion because the air and fuel are mixed better. *Quenching* is the cooling of gases by pressing them into a thin area. The area in which gases are thinned is called the quench area.

FIGURE 10–1. The cylinder head is used to seal off the top of the engine and to hold valves, allow air and fuel to flow through, and to hold the injector or spark plug.

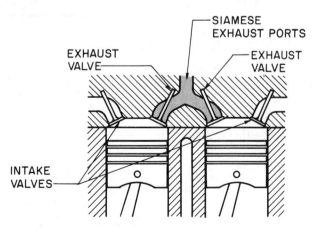

FIGURE 10–2. Siamese ports are used on the cylinder head. This means that two cylinders will feed the same exhaust port.

Wedge Combustion Chamber

The wedge-shaped combustion chamber was used on cars until about 1968. Refer to *Figure 10–3*. As the piston comes up on the compression stroke, the air and fuel mixture is squashed in the quench area. The quench area causes the air and fuel to be mixed thoroughly before combustion. This helps to improve the combustion efficiency of the engine. Spark plugs are positioned to get the greatest advantage for combustion. When the spark occurs, smooth and rapid burning moves from the spark plug outward. The wedge-shaped combustion chamber is also called a turbulence-type combustion chamber. On newer model cars, the quench area has been reduced, which helps reduce exhaust emissions.

Hemispherical Combustion Chamber

The hemispherical combustion chamber gets its name from the chamber shape. *Hemi* is defined as half, and *spherical* means circle. The combustion chamber is shaped like a half-circle. This type of chamber is also called the hemi-head. The valves are located as shown in *Figure 10–4*. One distinct advantage is that larger valves can be used. This improves the volumetric efficiency of the engine.

The hemispherical combustion chamber is considered a nonturbulence-type combustion chamber. Little or no turbulence is produced in this chamber. The air and fuel mixture is compressed evenly on the compression stroke. When flat-top pistons are used, little turbulence can be created. The spark plug is located directly in the center of the valves. Combustion radiates evenly from the spark plug, completely burning the air-fuel mixture.

One of the more important advantages of the hemispherical combustion chamber is that air and fuel can enter the chamber very easily. The wedge combustion chamber restricts the flow of air and fuel to a certain extent. This restriction is called *shrouding*. *Figure 10–5* shows the valve very close to the side of the combustion chamber, which causes the air and fuel to be restricted. Volumetric efficiency is reduced. Hemispherical combustion chambers do not have this restriction. Hemispherical combustion chambers are used on many high-performance applications. This is especially true when large quantities of air and fuel are needed in the cylinder.

Some high-performance engines use a domed piston. This type of piston has a quench area to improve turbulence. See *Figure 10–6*. Several variations of this design are used by different engine manufacturers.

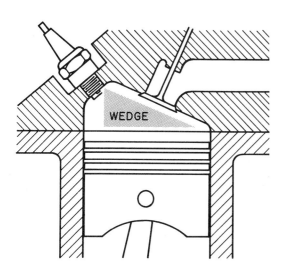

FIGURE 10–3. The wedge combustion chamber is shaped like a wedge to improve the turbulence within the chamber.

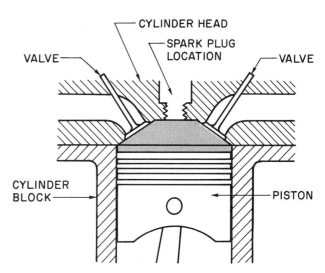

FIGURE 10–4. The hemispherical combustion chamber is shaped like a half-circle. The valves are placed on both sides of the spark plug.

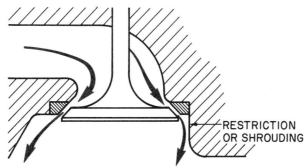

FIGURE 10–5. Shrouding is defined as a restriction in the flow of intake gases caused by the shape of the combustion chamber.

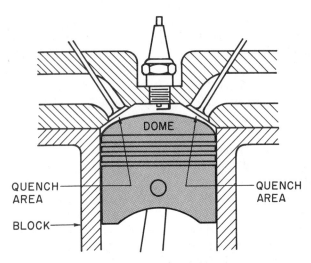

FIGURE 10–6. Certain pistons are dome-shaped on the top. This design improves the efficiency of the hemispherical combustion chamber by producing a quench area.

Diesel Combustion Chamber

Diesel combustion chambers are different from gasoline combustion chambers. Diesel fuel burns differently, so the combustion chamber must be different. Three types of combustion chambers are used in diesel engines: the open combustion chamber, the precombustion chamber, and the turbulence combustion chamber.

The open combustion chamber has the combustion chamber located directly inside the piston. *Figure 10–7* shows the open combustion chamber with diesel fuel being injected directly into the center of the chamber. The shape of the chamber and the quench area produces turbulence.

The *precombustion chamber* shown in *Figure 10–8* is used on both the gas and diesel engines. A smaller, second chamber is connected to the main combustion chamber. On the power stroke, fuel is injected into the small chamber. Combustion is started and then spreads to the main chamber.

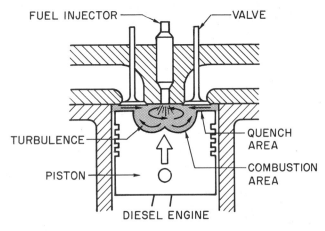

FIGURE 10–7. On certain diesel applications, the open combustion chamber is located directly within the top of the piston. This design has both a quench and a turbulence area.

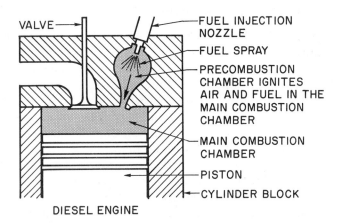

FIGURE 10–8. Precombustion chambers are used to ignite air and fuel in a small prechamber. The combustion in this chamber ignites the air and fuel in the main combustion chamber.

This design allows lower fuel injection pressures and simpler injection systems on the diesel engines. On gas engines, the precombustion chamber has a very rich mixture, but the main chamber can be very lean. The overall effect is a leaner engine, producing better fuel economy.

The turbulence combustion chamber is shown in *Figure 10–9*. The chamber is designed to create an increase in air velocity or turbulence in the combustion chamber. The fuel is injected into the turbulent air and burns more completely.

CAR CLINIC

PROBLEM: Engine Misses on One Cylinder

An engine has developed a steady miss on one cylinder. The engine has 45,000 miles on it. The engine developed the miss suddenly. The spark plugs and wires have been checked and are all OK. What might be a good thing to check?

SOLUTION:

The key is that the engine has developed a steady miss and that it happened suddenly. A common cause of this problem is a broken valve spring. To check which cylinder is missing, run the engine and carefully remove and replace each spark plug wire with the appropriate spark plug wire pliers. Note the cylinder where there is no change in the rpm. This is the cylinder that probably has a broken valve spring. Remove the valve cover and check the condition of the valve spring. Use tools designed to replace the valve spring without removing the cylinder head.

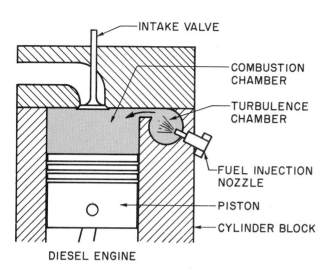

FIGURE 10–9.   The turbulence combustion chamber is used on certain diesel applications to increase turbulence of air and fuel.

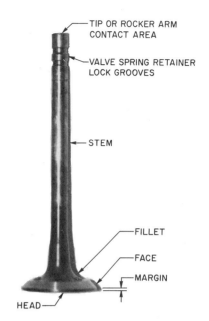

FIGURE 10–10.   The parts of a typical valve.

10.2   VALVE ASSEMBLY

The valves are located within the cylinder head on most engines designed today. There are two valves for each cylinder. One is for the intake and one for the exhaust. Certain high-performance engines, however, use four valves per cylinder.

The valve and associated parts include the valves, valve seats, valve guides, springs, retainers, and seals. The intake valve is usually larger in diameter than the exhaust valve because the intake valve and port handle a slow-moving air-fuel mixture. On the exhaust stroke, the gases move more easily from the pressure of the piston forcing them out. This type of valve is called a *poppet-type valve*. It is usually smaller in diameter than the intake valve.

Valve Parts

The valve has several parts. *Figure 10–10* shows the parts of the valve. The head of the valve is the part that is inside the combustion chamber. It must withstand extremely high temperatures, in the range of 1,300 to 1,500 degrees F.

The valves can be designed with different head shapes. *Figure 10–11* shows some of the shapes used on engines today. The more metal on the head of the valve, the more rigid the valve. Less metal means the valve will be able to conform to the seat more effectively. The valve is said to be elastic. Rigid valves last longer, but they don't seal as well. Elastic valves seat better, but they may not last as long.

The *valve face* is the area that touches and seals the valve to the cylinder head. This is the area that must be machined if the valve is damaged. The valve stem is used to support the valve in the cylinder head. The valve spring retainer lock grooves are used to keep the spring attached to the valve during operation. The valve margin is the distance between the face of the valve and the head. The margin is reduced whenever the valve is machined or ground down. If this margin is too small (see manufacturer's specification), the valve may burn easily. The fillet is the curved area between the stem and the inner edge of the face. The fillet provides extra strength for the valve.

Valve Material

The valve is made of very strong metal with nickel, chromium, and small amounts of manganese and other materials. The metal must be able to transfer heat very rapidly. If heat is not transferred rapidly, the valve will burn and become damaged. Certain valves also use a metallic sodium inside the stem. The sodium becomes a liquid at operating temperature. The liquid sodium then helps to transfer the heat from the stem to the valve guide more rapidly.

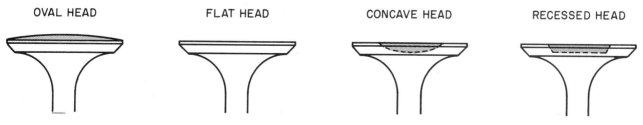

FIGURE 10–11.   Valves are designed with different head shapes for different purposes.

Valve Guides

The *valve guide* is defined as the hole that supports the valve in the cylinder head. It acts as a bushing for the valve stem to slide in. The valve guide is part of the cylinder head. The valve guide helps to support and center the valve so that correct *seating* can be obtained. It also helps to dissipate the heat produced within the combustion chamber through the valve. *Figure 10–12* shows a valve guide and how heat is transferred to the guide and finally to the cylinder head.

The clearance between the valve stem and the guide is very important. Generally, the clearance is between 0.001 and 0.004 inch. If the valve guides are worn and there is greater clearance, several things may happen. The valve may leak air, causing the air-fuel ratio to be altered. Oil may leak past the valve guide, causing high oil consumption. And the valve may not seat evenly, causing the valve seat to wear rapidly.

There are two types of valve guides: integral and insert. *Integral guides* are those that are machined directly into the cylinder head. The guide is part of the cast cylinder head. *Insert guides* are small cast cylinders that are pressed into the cylinder head. When valve guides are worn excessively, insert guides can be removed and replaced with new insert guides. This cannot be done with integral guides without expensive machining.

Valve Seals

Because there is a clearance necessary between the valve stem and the valve guide, oil control methods must be used. Oil deflectors are placed on the valve stem or spring. These deflectors shed oil from the valve stem and prevent oil from collecting on the top of the guide.

Positive guide seals are another means of controlling oil flow. Positive guide seals are small seals that fit snugly around the valve stem. The seal is held to the stem with small springs or clamps. These seals restrict most oil that would normally pass through the valve guide.

Some car manufacturers use *passive seals,* including O rings and umbrella-type valve stem seals. See *Figure 10–13*. These seals are used mostly on new engines. They do not work as well on older engines that have more wear on the valve stem.

Valve Seats

Valve seats are defined as circular surfaces that are machined into the cylinder block or head. The valve face seals or seats against the valve seat, *Figure 10–14*. These seats provide a surface for the intake and exhaust valves to seal for gas leakage. The seats also help to dissipate the heat built up in the valve.

There are two types of valve seats: integral and insert. As with valve guides, the integral type is cast directly as part of the cylinder head. The insert type uses a metal ring as the seat. It is pressed into the cylinder block and ground to the correct angle. The insert type of valve seat is used most often on engines with aluminum cylinder heads. Insert valve seats can be made from cast iron, hardened cast iron, hi-chrome steel, and *stellite* (very hard steel).

Valve seats are ground to a specific angle for correct operation. They are either 30 or 45 degrees. An *interference angle* is becoming very common when grinding valves. An interference angle is obtained by grinding the valve face about one degree less than the valve seat. This is shown in *Figure 10–15*. In this example, the valve is ground to 44 degrees while the seat is ground to 45 degrees. The interference angle tends to cut through any deposits that have been formed on the seat. It also produces a more positive seal. As the engine is run and the valve seats wear, the interference angle is gradually eliminated. The result is good *line contact,* which helps

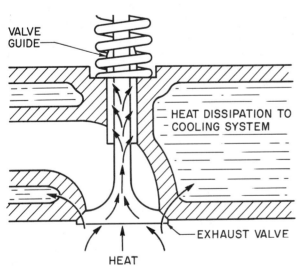

FIGURE 10–12. The valve guide helps to dissipate heat from the valve.

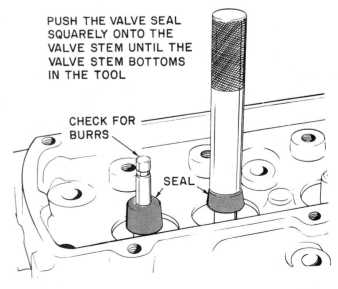

FIGURE 10–13. Valve seals are used to stop oil from going down the valve guide. *(Courtesy of Oldsmobile Chassis Service)*

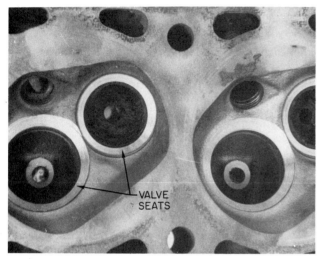

FIGURE 10–14. Valve seats help the valves seal to the cylinder block or head. They are machined into the block or head.

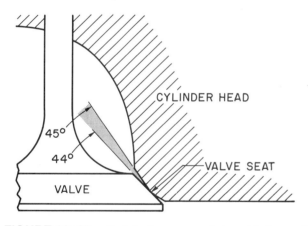

FIGURE 10–15. An interference angle is cut between the valve face angle and the seat angle. This helps the valves to seat to the cylinder head faster.

transmit excess heat away from the valve. The valve seat must be positioned correctly for maximum sealing efficiency. The seat can be repositioned either higher or lower by grinding the top or bottom part or both of the seat. This is done by using a 30-degree or a 60-degree stone or both.

Valve Springs

The valve springs are designed to keep the valves closed when the camshaft is not lifting the valve. The valve springs are held to the valve stem with various types of *keepers*. The spring must be designed to close the valve correctly. If the valve spring is weak, there may be *valve float*. Valve float means the valve stays open slightly longer than it is designed to. This usually happens when the valve springs are weak and the engine is operating at high speeds. *Valve bounce* can also occur if the spring is weak and operated at high speeds. Valve bounce occurs when the valve slams against the seat, causing it to bounce slightly.

Valve springs are made from several types of wire materials. These include carbon wire, chrome vanadium, and chrome silicon. The stress or load temperature and aging qualities determine exactly what type of material is used.

Valve Spring Vibration

During normal operation, valve springs may develop vibration. This vibration is known as *harmonics*. At times, these harmonics cause the spring to function incorrectly. Several designs are used to reduce harmonics. These include using stronger springs, variable *pitch* springs, dual springs, varying the outside diameter of the spring, and placing small vibration dampers inside the springs. *Figure 10–16* shows the variable pitch spring. The end with the closer spacing should always be installed toward the cylinder head. *Figure 10–17* shows a valve spring with a damper spring inserted inside.

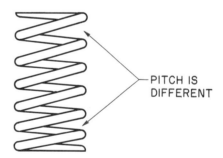

FIGURE 10–16. Variable pitch springs reduce vibration within the spring during operation.

FIGURE 10–17. A damper spring placed inside the valve spring reduces harmonics during spring vibration.

Valve Keepers and Retainers

Keepers and retainers are used to keep the valve spring secured to the valve stem. The retainer acts as a washer and seat for the top of the spring. See *Figure 10–18*. The retainer sits on top of the spring. The valve then passes through the retainer.

Valve keepers are used to hold the retainers to the valve stem. See *Figure 10–19*. Valve keepers are designed as tapered keys or locks. As the spring pressure pushes up on the retainer, the keepers are pinched or wedged into the retainer. This action causes the spring to be firmly attached to the valve during all operation. Several types of keepers are used, but the most common is the split type. The split type is easy to remove yet maintains a positive lock.

Valve Rotators

Valve rotators are used on certain engines. If valves are rotated a small amount each time they are opened, valve life will be extended. This is especially true when using leaded fuels. (The effect of using rotators with unleaded fuels is still being studied.) Rotating the valves:

1. minimizes deposits of carbon on the stem of the valve,

2. keeps the valve face and seat cleaner,

3. prevents valve burning caused by localized hot spots,

4. prevents valve edge distortion,

5. helps to maintain uniform valve head temperatures,

6. helps to maintain even valve stem tip wear,

7. helps to improve lubrication on the valve stem.

There are several types of valve rotators. Most operate on the principle that as the valve is compressed, small balls inside the rotator roll up an *inclined surface*. This action causes the valve to rotate slightly as it is being compressed.

Number of Valves per Cylinder

In the past few years, automotive manufacturers have been experimenting with different numbers of valves per cylinder. In the past, most engines had one intake and one exhaust valve for each cylinder. Then several manufacturers designed engines that had three valves per cylinder. Today, however, many smaller engines have two intake valves and two exhaust valves per cylinder. This design helps to make smaller engines more powerful.

Recently, other designs have also been tested. For example one manufacturer is testing a five-valve cylinder head. This design uses three intake valves and two exhaust valves per cylinder. Five valves are better than two, three, or four valves per cylinder because they provide optimal flow of air and fuel into the cylinders. This flow path in engineering terms is called the *curtain area*. Some engineering reports suggest that there is about a 30% increase in the curtain area efficiency.

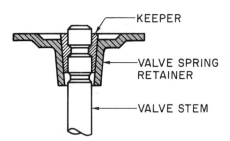

FIGURE 10–18.   The valve is held in place with a valve spring retainer.

FIGURE 10–19.   Valve keepers are used to keep the valve spring and retainer in place.

CAR CLINIC

PROBLEM: Engine Misses When Cold

A vehicle misses very severely when it is cold. The car has about 80,000 miles on it. After the engine warms to operating temperature, the miss disappears. The problem started at about 45,000 miles.

SOLUTION:

Misses such as this are usually caused by a cracked head. When the engine warms up, the crack is sealed and the miss disappears. Give the engine a cylinder leakdown test when it is cold to see if the compression is leaking. Crank the engine at night and look for stray sparks jumping from one spark plug wire to another. Some other possible causes are too rich or lean a fuel mixture during cold running, or a compression ring or valve sticking when cold.

10.3 CAMSHAFT ASSEMBLY

The camshaft is used to open and close the intake and exhaust valves throughout the four strokes of the engine. To do this, the camshaft is driven by the crankshaft. The camshaft assembly includes the camshaft, camshaft timing gear, camshaft bearings, and timing chain, belt, or gears, if used.

Camshaft Design

The camshaft is a long shaft that fits into the block or head on overhead cam engines. Two cams, or *lobes,* are machined on the camshaft for each cylinder. As the camshaft turns, the lobes open and close the valves. See *Figure 10–20.* Several bearing surfaces are also machined on the camshaft. These surfaces are used to support the camshaft at several places throughout its length. The typical camshaft is made of cast or forged steel. The cam and bearing surfaces are hardened to provide protection from excessive wear. In addition, a gear is placed on the camshaft. This gear is used to drive the distributor and the oil pump.

Camshaft Thrust

Camshafts need some means to control the shaft end thrust. One method is to use a *thrust plate* between the camshaft gear and a flange machined into the camshaft. See *Figure 10–21.* The thrust plate is bolted to the block to contain any thrust movement of the camshaft. On certain overhead camshaft designs, the thrust plate is bolted directly to the head.

Camshaft Lobe Design

There are many designs used on camshaft lobes. The contour of the camshaft lobe determines how the valves open and close. Camshaft lobes play an important part in volumetric efficiency. The speed and amount of opening, and speed of closing are controlled by the shape of the cam lobe.

The cam lobe has several parts. See *Figure 10–22.* The amount of lift is measured by the height of the cam lobe. The shape of the ramp determines how rapidly or slowly the valves open or close. For example, on certain camshafts the ramp is designed to open the valve gradually. The valve should close as rapidly as possible, but it should not bounce on the ramp. When operating on the heel, the valve is not opened. The nose is designed to keep the valve open for a certain length of time.

Camshaft Timing to Crankshaft

For the valves to open and close in correct relation to the position of the crankshaft, the camshaft must be timed to the crankshaft. This means that the two shafts must be assembled so that the lobes open the valves at a precise time in relation to the position of the piston and crankshaft. Several methods are used to do this.

There is a set of timing gears on the crankshaft and camshaft. These gears are located on the shaft by using a *keyway.* The keyway locates the gear on the shaft in the correct position. The camshaft and crankshaft are assembled so that two dots line up. See *Figure 10–23.* If they are assembled this way, the camshaft and crankshaft will be in time with each other. Because of the four-stroke design, the camshaft always rotates half as fast as the crankshaft.

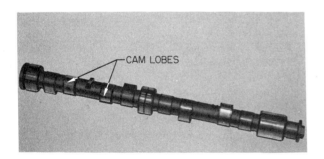

FIGURE 10–20. Cam lobes are machined on the camshaft to lift the valves open at the right time.

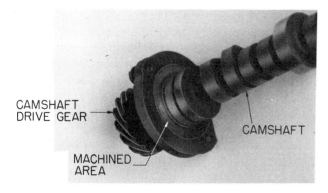

FIGURE 10–21. The thrust plate on a camshaft helps to absorb thrust forces.

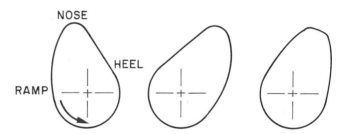

FIGURE 10–22. The shape of the camshaft lobe is designed to raise and lower the valve at a specific time.

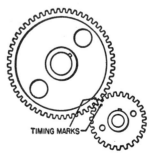

FIGURE 10–23. The camshaft and crankshaft must be timed correctly. Marks must be lined up to be installed correctly. *(Courtesy of Motor Publications, Auto Repair Manual)*

Some engines use a timing chain to connect the camshaft and crankshaft. In this case, two marks are again lined up during assembly. See *Figure 10–24*. When a chain drive is used on some engines, a spring-loaded damper pad is used to keep the chain tight.

Overhead camshafts are also timed by lining up marks shown on the two shafts as shown in *Figure 10–25*. It is important to always review the procedures listed in the maintenance manual when timing the camshaft and crankshaft. A belt tension device is used to keep the belt tight.

Bushings

The camshaft is supported in the cylinder block by several bushings. These bushings are friction-type bearings and are called camshaft bearings by some mechanics. They are designed as one piece and are typically pressed into the camshaft bore in the block, *Figure 10–26*.

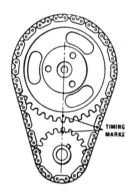

FIGURE 10–24. When a timing chain is used, the two marks on the gears must be aligned. This alignment will time the camshaft to the crankshaft. *(Courtesy of Motor Publications, Auto Repair Manual)*

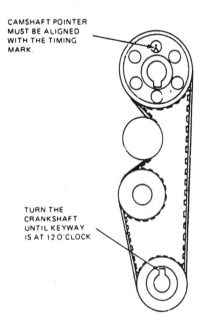

CAMSHAFT POINTER MUST BE ALIGNED WITH THE TIMING MARK.

TURN THE CRANKSHAFT UNTIL KEYWAY IS AT 12 O'CLOCK

FIGURE 10–25. The timing marks are shown for an overhead camshaft with a belt drive. *(Courtesy of Motor Publications, Auto Repair Manual)*

FIGURE 10–26. A camshaft bearing is a full round design, pressed into the block. *(Courtesy of Federal-Mogul Corporation)*

CAR CLINIC

PROBLEM: Camshaft Damage

A car has about 30,000 miles on it. During this time the camshaft has been replaced two times. Why would a camshaft go bad in so few miles?

SOLUTION:

Several conditions cause excessive camshaft wear. The friction and bearing loads on a camshaft are very great. Under these conditions motor oil may be good for only about 5,000 miles. The oil breaks down and cannot lubricate under high stresses. Frequent oil changes will improve this situation. Several manufacturers have also reduced the valve spring tension so as not to wear the camshaft as much. Remember also that high rpm on the engine can also increase the stresses on the camshaft.

10.4 VALVE OPERATING MECHANISM

The valve operating mechanism consists of the lifters which ride on the camshaft, the pushrods, and the rocker arms. These components make up the mechanism used to transfer the camshaft lift to the valve assembly, *Figure 10–27*.

As the engine heats up during operation, the parts of the valve mechanism expand. Because of this expansion, there must be a clearance in the valve mechanism. This clearance is called *valve train clearance*. All engine valve mechanisms must have this clearance.

Lifters

The valve lifters, also called *tappets,* are designed to follow the shape of the camshaft and lobes. The valve lifters ride directly on the camshaft. Lifters are used to change the rotary

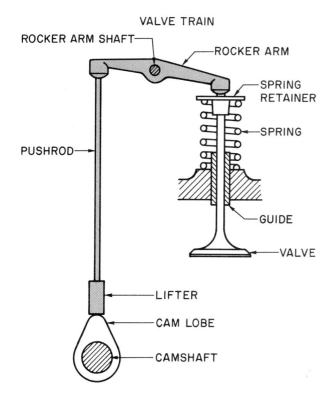

FIGURE 10–27. The lifters, pushrods, and rocker arms make up the valve operation mechanism.

FIGURE 10–28. Adjustments can be made on the rocker arms to control the valve train clearance.

motion of the camshaft to reciprocating motion to open and close the valve.

Several types of lifters are used. They include solid lifters, cam followers, and hydraulic lifters.

Solid Lifters

Solid lifters (used on older engines) transfer motion as a solid piece from the camshaft to the pushrod. Solid lifters are designed as lightweight cylinders. Some are designed as a hollow tube, while others are designed as a solid piece. Solid lifters are used primarily on older engines or on high-performance engines. A disadvantage of solid lifters is that they are noisy and have a distinct tapping sound.

All solid lifters must have some means of adjusting the valve clearance. Adjustments are made on the rocker arm section of the valve mechanism. See *Figure 10–28*.

Cam Followers

Cam followers are sometimes used instead of lifters. Cam followers are also called roller lifters by some technicians. Cam followers resemble solid lifters. The only difference is that followers have rollers that contact the camshaft, rather than metal sliding on the camshaft. Cam followers reduce friction and distribute the load more evenly. They are used primarily on high-compression engines such as diesel and racing engines. The roller is on one end of the cam followers. The other end is machined so the pushrod can be inserted. Cam followers also have a small groove machined into the

side. Generally, there is a small pin in the lifter bore that matches the groove. This design helps eliminate the possibility of having the cam follower spin in its bore. Several designs are used. One of the most common is shown in *Figure 10–29*. In this design, the roller rides directly on the camshaft. The pushrod sits in the cam follower. Engines that use cam followers of this design also have an adjustable valve train clearance.

Hydraulic Lifters

Hydraulic lifters are used to reduce noise and to control the valve clearance. Hydraulic lifters use oil pressure to keep the valve clearance at zero. The main parts of the hydraulic lifter are shown in *Figure 10–30*. The body houses the internal parts of the hydraulic lifter. The plunger moves up

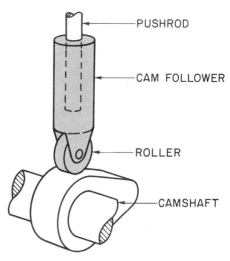

FIGURE 10–29. Cam followers are used in place of solid lifters. They have a roller that rides on the camshaft.

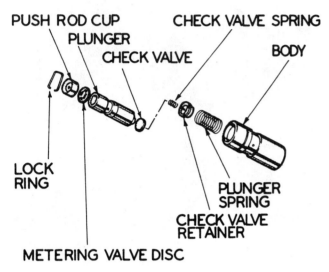

PUSH ROD CUP
PLUNGER
CHECK VALVE
CHECK VALVE SPRING
BODY
LOCK
RING
PLUNGER
SPRING
CHECK VALVE
RETAINER
METERING VALVE DISC

FIGURE 10–30.   The parts of the hydraulic lifter are shown. The body of the lifter holds the other parts inside. *(Courtesy of Motor Publications, Auto Repair Manual)*

and down inside the body. *Figure 10–31* shows the hydraulic lifter operation for an overhead cam engine. The rocker arms push directly on the lifter.

The hydraulic lifter operates as shown in *Figure 10–32*. Referring to Figure 10–32 (A), before the cam lobe starts to lift, the plunger is pushed upward by the internal return spring. Oil is fed into the recessed area called the *oil relief*. The oil pressure comes from the oil system in the engine. During this time, the high pressure chamber is filled with oil. Any clearance within the valve mechanism is now taken up by the oil pressure. Note that the oil passes by the check

ball. The check ball allows oil to pass in one direction only. If oil tries to flow from the high pressure chamber into the plunger, it will be stopped. Some lifters use a check valve rather than a check ball, but the principle is still the same.

When the cam lobe starts to raise the lifter, Figure 10–32 (B), the valve spring pressure, which is felt through the rocker arm, keeps the plunger from moving upward. The body of the lifter, however, is raised by the cam lobe. This causes the pressure in the high pressure chamber inside the lifter to be increased. As the cam lobe continues to lift the body of the lifter, the high pressure locks the system, and the valve is forced to open. A small amount of oil then leaks from the clearance between the plunger and the body, causing the plunger to move down slightly. This is called leak-down. Leak-down is very important. It is controlled precisely by the clearance between the plunger and the body. Its purpose is to allow the valve spring pressure to push the plunger down adequately into the body.

As the cam lobe continues to turn, the pressure on the body is reduced. This is because the cam lobe has passed the lifter. As the pressure decreases, the pressure from the valve spring forces the valve to close. The plunger and the body of the lifter now return to the original position. Again, any clearance in the valve mechanism is taken up by the oil pressure. When the lifter is at the position shown in Figure 10–32 (C), it is ready to repeat the cycle.

Pushrods

Pushrods are designed to be the connecting link between the rocker arm and the valve lifter. They are made as light as possible. Some are designed to have small convex balls on the end. These small balls ride inside the lifter and the rocker

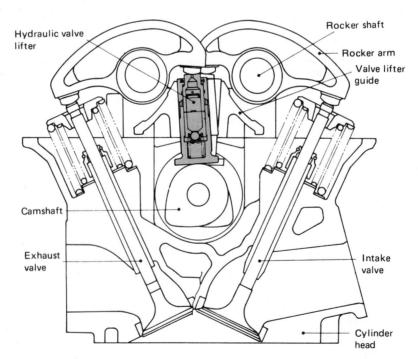

Hydraulic valve lifter
Rocker shaft
Rocker arm
Valve lifter guide
Camshaft
Exhaust valve
Intake valve
Cylinder head

FIGURE 10–31.   On an overhead cam engine, the lifters are set directly above the camshaft. No pushrod is needed. *(Courtesy of Nissan Motor Corporation in USA)*

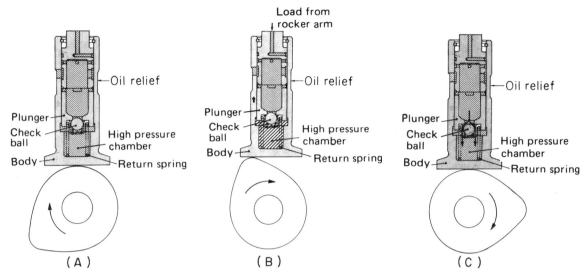

FIGURE 10–32.   The operation of a hydraulic lifter is shown. (A) shows the operation before the cam lobe lifts, (B) shows the operation during cam lobe lifting, and (C) shows the operation after the cam lobe has been lifted. *(Courtesy of Nissan Motor Corporation in USA)*

arm. Pushrods are used only on engines that have the camshaft placed within the block. Overhead camshafts do not need pushrods.

Pushrods are either solid or hollow. On certain engines, the pushrods have a hole in the center to allow oil to pass from the hydraulic lifter to the upper portion of the cylinder head. Rather than having a convex ball, the end of the pushrod on solid lifters is concave. This end then fits into a ball on the rocker arm. *Figure 10–33* shows examples of different types of ends on pushrods.

Rocker Arms

Rocker arms are designed to do two things: (1) change the direction of the cam lifting force and (2) provide a certain *mechanical advantage* during valve lifting. Referring to *Figure 10–34*, as the lifter and pushrod move upward, the rocker arm pivots at the center point. This causes a change in direction on the valve side. This change in direction causes the valve to open downward.

On some engines, it may be important to open the valve more than the actual lift of the cam lobe. This can be done by changing the distances from the *pivot point* to the ends of the rocker arm. The distance from the ends of the rocker arm to the pivot point is not the same. Refer to *Figure 10–35*. Note that the distance from point A to the pivot point is less than the distance from point B to the pivot point. The ratio

between these two measurements is called rocker arm ratio. In this example, the ratio is 1.5 to 1. This means that the valve will open 1.5 times more than the actual lift on the cam lobe.

Rocker arms are designed and mounted in several ways. Some are designed to fit on a rocker arm shaft. Springs, washers, individual rocker arms, and bolts are used in this type of assembly. Other rocker arms are placed on studs that are mounted directly in the cylinder head.

Some overhead camshaft engines use rocker arms in such a way that the camshaft rides directly on top of the rocker arm. See *Figure 10–36*. Other overhead camshaft engines do not use rocker arms. In this type of engine, the camshaft rides directly on top of the valves.

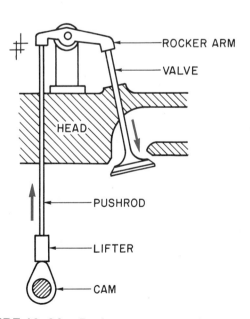

FIGURE 10–34.   Rocker arms are used to change the direction of motion on the valve operating mechanism.

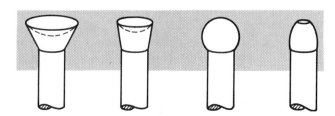

FIGURE 10–33.   Several types of ends are used on pushrods.

ROCKER ARM RATIO

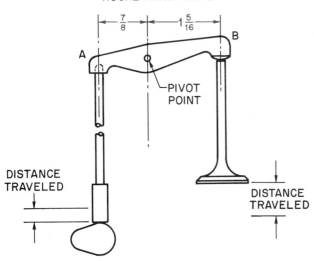

FIGURE 10–35. Rocker arms have different lengths from the center to the ends. This difference produces a rocker arm ratio, which is used to open the valve more than the cam lift.

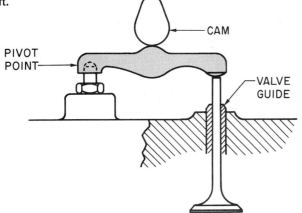

FIGURE 10–36. Certain engines have rocker arms that ride directly under the camshaft. These are used on overhead camshaft engines.

Variable Valve Timing

Recent engine designs have been incorporating a valve mechanism that is called *variable valve timing*. Variable valve timing is incorporated so that the total lift of the valve from its seat can be varied. In addition, the duration of the valve opening can also be changed. By changing the lift and duration of the valve, the engine characteristics also change. Variable valve timing allows for the engine to change combustion characteristics (air-fuel amounts, combustion efficiency, and so on) throughout the rpm range of the engine. The result is a more powerful, more economical, and cleaner-running engine.

In operation, the valves are adjusted according to the load sensed by the engine computer. For example, when the engine computer says that more power is called for, it adjusts the valve mechanism to get the maximum valve lift for the longest duration.

Mechanically, several systems are being used. One system uses the engine computer in conjunction with a control solenoid. The control solenoid controls the amount of oil going into the hydraulic lifter. Depending upon this flow, the lifter will hydraulically lock up to control the lift and duration of valve opening. Another system has several cams located above each valve. A locking mechanism locks up the one that is needed for optimum efficiency. A third system has a hydraulic mechanism placed on the camshaft to allow it to be rotated relative to the drive sprocket. This produces a 20-degree shift in intake timing. As more efficiency and cleaner-burning engines are demanded, more variable valve systems will be designed in the future.

CAR CLINIC

PROBLEM: Car Smokes When Started

A vehicle produces blue smoke when the engine is first started. Once the engine is running and at operating temperature, the smoking stops. What could be the problem?

SOLUTION:

The most common cause of this problem is oil seeping past the exhaust valves when the engine is shut down. The oil then sits in the exhaust manifold until the engine is started. When the engine is started, the oil is burned, producing the blue smoke. Replacing the valve stem seals should solve the problem.

Problems, Diagnosis and Service

PROBLEM: Bad Cylinder Head

Loss of power in one cylinder, white exhaust smoke, loss of coolant and sometimes a blown head gasket.

DIAGNOSIS

This type of problem can often be associated with a crack in the cylinder head or possible warpage of the cylinder head. A crack in the block may also cause coolant to enter the combustion chamber and cause white exhaust smoke. In addition, a warped cylinder head may cause the head gasket to blow. Both of these problems could cause the lack of power in a specific cylinder. Such problems can be diagnosed by performing wet and dry compression tests.

SERVICE

1. With the cylinder head removed, check between each combustion chamber and the valve guides for possible cracks. In most cases, the cracks cannot be observed unless the area has been cleaned with a wire brush. Cracks can be very small and at times may be very difficult to notice.

2. Check the cylinder head for warpage by using a straight-edge and feeler gauge.
   a. Using a steel straight-edge as shown in *Figure 10–37* lay the straight-edge across the length of the head.
   b. Now try to slip a feeler gauge between the head and the straight-edge. These spots show that the head is warped.
   c. Start with a 0.003-inch feeler gauge, then go to a larger feeler gauge, if possible.
   d. Check several spots on the length as well as the width of the head. Also check the warp diagonally.
   e. A typical specification for maximum warp is 0.003 inch for any 6-inch length or 0.007 inch overall. Note that not all manufacturers have the same specification. Generally, maximum warp is between 0.003 and 0.007 inch.
   f. If the cylinder head is warped beyond the manufacturer's specifications, the cylinder head must be machined. This process is called milling the cylinder

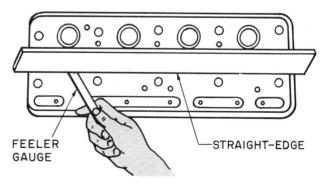

FIGURE 10–37. Check cylinder head flatness using a straight-edge and a feeler gauge.

head. Generally, a specialized machine shop has the correct tools to mill a cylinder head. If the cylinder head is milled (approximately 0.010 inch), the compression ratio will increase slightly. On overhead camshaft engines, milling the head may change the belt or chain tension on the camshaft.

PROBLEM: Loss of Power

Loss of engine power, engine misses on one or more cylinders, and loss of compression on one or more cylinders.

DIAGNOSIS

After an engine has had many miles on it, often the intake and exhaust valve begin to leak compression. In addition, the valve lifter may be worn, causing the valves not to open as far. The valve springs may also be broken or show signs of weakening. There are parts and components on the cylinder head and valve mechanism that can be worn or damaged. Some of the more important components include the intake and exhaust valves, the valve seats, camshaft, valve springs, rocker arms, lifters and pushrods.

SERVICE

Disassembly of Cylinder Head

1. After the cylinder head has been removed from the engine, thoroughly clean the lifters and pushrods.

2. Remove the valve rocker arm mechanism and clean each thoroughly.

3. Check the rocker arms for wear on the valve and the push rod end. If signs of wear are evident on the valve end, some rocker arms can be ground to eliminate the wear. Maximum metal removal is approximately 0.010 inch.

4. Check each push rod for straightness. This can be done by rolling the push rod along a flat surface.

5. Remove the valve using the spring compressors. There are several valve-removing tools available as shown in *Figure 10–38*.
   a. Place the cylinder head in a position so that the compressor tools can be applied to each valve as shown in *Figure 10–39*.
   b. Make sure the spring compressor is matched to the size of the valve.
   c. Slowly compress the valve spring by tightening the valve spring compressor.
   d. When the valve spring is fully compressed, carefully remove the valve keepers and valve retainer.
   e. Slowly release the valve spring compressor.
      CAUTION: Valve springs are under high pressure. Be careful not to release the compressor too fast as the spring may be forced out rapidly and cause injury.
   f. Now carefully remove each valve by pushing it out through the valve guide. If the top of the valve stem is slightly worn, the valves may scrape and damage

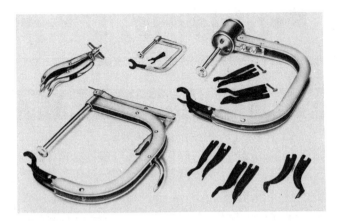

FIGURE 10–38. These valve-removing tools should be used to aid in valve removal and installation. *(Courtesy of Snap-On Tools Company)*

FIGURE 10–39. A valve compressor is used to remove valve springs. *(Courtesy of Chevrolet)*

the valve guides during removal. File the valve stems if needed before removal.

6. Completely remove all carbon deposits from the cylinder head and combustion chamber. On aluminum heads be careful not to damage or scratch the softer aluminum.
   a. Using a small punch, chip away the larger particles of carbon.
   b. Using an electrical drill with a coarse wire wheel, clean the carbon deposits from the combustion chamber. Refer to *Figure 10–40*.
      CAUTION: Be sure to wear a face mask and safety glasses during this process.
   c. Be careful not to damage the seat area of the valves with the wire wheel.

7. Completely remove all carbon deposits from the valves.
   a. Chip off the large particles of carbon with a steel punch. Be careful not to chip the valve surface especially at the fillet.

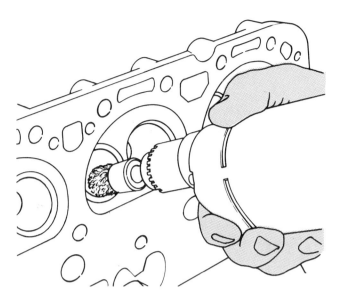

FIGURE 10–40. Clean the combustion chamber by using a drill and wire brush. *(Courtesy of Chevrolet)*

FIGURE 10–41. A valve-grinding machine is used to grind the valves. *(Courtesy of Sioux Tools Inc.)*

b. Using a wire wheel on a power grinder, clean off the remaining valve deposits.

CAUTION: Be sure to wear a face mask and safety glasses during this process.

c. Do not clean the stem of the valve with the wire wheel.

d. Soak the valve in cleaning solvent to soften the remaining carbon and varnish. Use a polishing grade of emery cloth (not coarser than 300 grit) to clean the remaining varnish.

Checking and Grinding Valves and Seats

1. Once the valves have been removed, check the valve face and valve seats for indications of burned surfaces.

2. Using a valve grinder as shown in **Figure 10–41** grind each valve according to the manufacturer's specifications. Most valves are ground at either a 44-, 45-, or 46-degree angle. Other engines may have a 30-degree angle. Refer to the manufacturer's specifications to determine the valve face angle for your vehicle. Generally, the procedure is as follows:

a. Use the valve-grinding machine by first dressing the stone correctly.

b. Place the valve in the holding chuck, and tighten securely.

c. Turn on the machine and move the valve closer to the wheel. Make sure the coolant valve is turned on to allow coolant to flow over the stem.

d. Advance and grind the valve slowly, making sure the valve is not turning blue. If it does, the valve is too hot and too much metal is being ground off at one time.

e. Continue grinding the valve until all pits and signs of wear have been removed.

3. After the valve has been ground, check the valve margin

and compare it with the manufacturer's recommended specifications.

a. Use a vernier caliper to check the margin.

b. The minimum width of valve margins is 1/32 inch. If the width is less than 1/32 inch, the valve should be discarded and replaced with a new valve.

4. Grind the valve seats using a valve seat grinder. Follow the tool manufacturer's procedure to grind the seats correctly. Generally, a 45-degree angle stone is placed on the sleeve of the valve seat grinder. Then a pilot rod is placed down into the valve guide. The valve seat grinder and stone are then placed over the guide and carefully brought down to touch the valve seat.

Note: If the manufacturer calls for an interference fit, different degree angle stones must be used to grind off the upper and lower part of the seat. The valve seat must be a specified width. To adjust the width use a 30-degree or a 60-degree stone as shown in **Figure 10–42**.

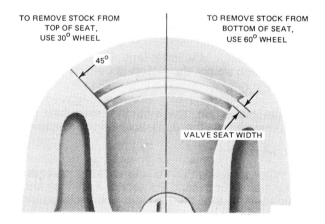

FIGURE 10–42. The valve seat can be repositioned higher or lower in the head using a 30- or 60-degree wheel during grinding. *(Courtesy of Ford Motor Company)*

Checking and Grinding Valve Stems

1. Check the tip of the valve stem for wear from the rocker arms.
   a. If the stem is not square or has nicks and is rounded off, reconditioning is needed.
   b. Use the valve-grinding machine by first dressing the stone correctly.
   c. Place the valve in the holding clamp and tighten the clamp.
   d. Turn on the machine and move the valve closer to the wheel. Make sure the coolant valve is turned on to allow coolant to flow over the stem.
   e. Advance and grind the stem slowly, making sure the valve is not turning blue. If it is, the valve is too hot and too much metal is being ground off at one time.
   f. Grind the stem until all pits and signs of wear have been removed.
   g. If the chamfer has been removed on the valve stem, it may have to be reground. Make sure the chamfer is no wider than 1/32 inch.

2. If the valve face and stem have been ground, the valve will sit at a different height when replaced in the cylinder head. This difference may cause the clearance to change slightly, especially on overhead camshafts. Follow the manufacturer's procedure to check the installed spring height if necessary.

Checking Valve Guides

1. Check the valve guides for wear according to the manufacturer's specifications. These specifications are listed in many of the auto maintenance manuals.
   a. Check the valve guide by determining the maximum dimension at the port end or top end of the guide.
   b. Place a telescoping or small-hole gauge inside the guide.
   c. After removing the gauge, measure it with a micrometer.
   d. Measure the smallest valve stem diameter on the valve. This is usually found where the valve stem touches the top of the valve guide.
   e. Subtract the two readings. This value is called the valve clearance.
   f. Average specifications are: intake, 0.001–0.003 inches; exhaust, 0.0015–0.0035 inches. Note that these readings may vary with different manufacturers and engine makes.
   g. A dial indicator can also be used to check the valve guide clearance. With the dial indicator touching the valve, move the valve back and forth to read the amount of clearance as shown in *Figure 10–43*.

Checking Valve Springs

1. During disassembly of the cylinder head, check each valve spring for possible breakage. Replace as necessary.

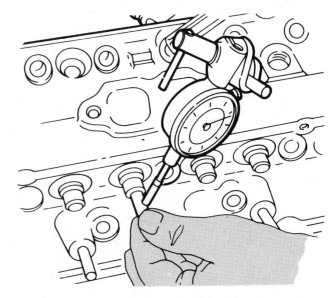

FIGURE 10–43.   To check valve stem clearance use a dial indicator against the valve. *(Courtesy of Chevrolet)*

2. Check the valve springs for alignment and squareness.
   a. Stand the valve spring on a flat surface.
   b. Hold the bottom of the spring against a square as shown in *Figure 10–44*.
   c. Using a feeler gauge or vernier caliper, measure the distance away from the square, the gap, from the spring top to the square.
   d. Compare the distance measured with the manufacturer's specification. The maximum distance allowed varies, but generally it is in the range of 1/16 to 5/64 inch.

3. Check the valve springs for the correct valve spring tension. A valve spring tension tester is normally used as shown in *Figure 10–45*.
   a. After placing the spring in the tester, compress each spring the same amount. There is usually a stop on the handle of the spring tension tester.
   b. Read the tension on the dial and compare the reading with the manufacturer's specifications. The valve

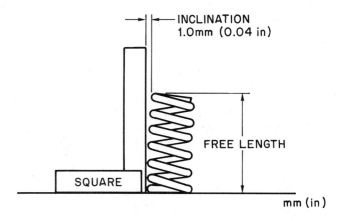

FIGURE 10–44.   Use a square to check spring alignment.

FIGURE 10–45.   Valve spring tension (compression) can be checked on a valve spring tension checker. *(Courtesy of Chevrolet)*

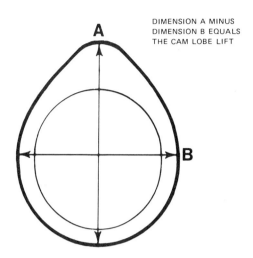

DIMENSION A MINUS
DIMENSION B EQUALS
THE CAM LOBE LIFT

FIGURE 10–46.   The height of the cam (cam lobe lift) can be measured by taking the A dimension, minus the B dimension. *(Courtesy of Ford Motor Company)*

spring tension should usually be within 10% of the specifications listed in the manual. A typical compression pressure reading would be 180 pounds of compression at 1.09 inches of movement.

Camshaft

1. With the camshaft removed from the engine, check each cam lobe for excessive wear by checking the lift of each lobe with a dial indicator or micrometer.
   a. Remove the camshaft from the engine.
   b. Place the camshaft in a set of V blocks so it can be rotated.
   c. Using a dial indicator, rotate the cam to determine the height of the cam lobe.
   d. If a dial indicator is not available, a micrometer can be used. Check the smallest diameter of each cam, and subtract this dimension from the largest diameter at the cam height. See *Figure 10–46*. Compare each cam lobe and the lift. Compare the wear with the manufacturer's specifications. The maximum lobe wear allowed is usually about 0.005 inch.

2. With the camshaft removed from the engine, check for excessive wear or scraping on the thrust plate.

3. The end play of the camshaft should also be checked. To complete this check, the camshaft must be placed in the block.
   a. Place a dial indicator on the end of the camshaft.
   b. Move the camshaft back and forth along its axis, and measure the amount of end play. Typical readings will vary; however, camshaft end play will be from 0.001 inch to as high as 0.010 inch on some engines.

4. When installing the camshaft, make sure the timing marks are aligned according to the service manual specifications.

Automotive maintenance manuals have drawings showing how the timing marks should look. Although each manufacturer's procedure may be different, the camshaft must be timed correctly to the crankshaft.

Lifters

1. If the lifters are to be reused, they should be marked so that they can be installed so they operate on their original cam lobes.

2. Check each lifter for wear at the bottom or the part that rides directly on the camshaft. The lifter bottom should show no signs of wearing, scuffing, scoring, or pitting. Lifters that are concave or flat as shown in *Figure 10–47* must be replaced. Lifters that are slightly convex are not worn. Replace lifters if wear is evident.

3. The outer surface of the lifter should have no signs of wearing. If there is wear, scuffing, or scoring on the outside of the lifter, also check the lifter bores for wear. Replace the lifter if wear is noticeable.

4. If in doubt about lifter quality, leakdown tests can be performed.

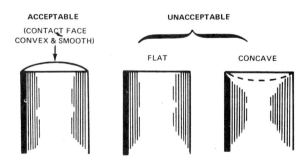

FIGURE 10–47.   Acceptable and unacceptable lifter wear. *(Courtesy of Ford Motor Company)*

a. Two systems can be used to complete a leakdown test. One system uses a special testing fixture, the other can be done on a workbench. If a fixture is available, follow the recommended procedure in the operator's manual.

b. If a testing fixture is not available, disassemble the lifter, removing the plunger spring and oil.

c. Reassemble the filter without the plunger spring and snap ring.

d. Depress the plunger until a light resistance is felt. Note the position of the plunger. Now rapidly depress and release the plunger.

e. Observe the position the plunger returns to. If it stays down or does not return to the previously noted position (in step 4 above), the leakdown rate is excessive. The lifter should then be replaced.

CAUTION: It is acceptable to replace old lifters and still use the old camshaft. However, never use old, worn lifters on a new camshaft.

SUMMARY

The purpose of this chapter was to investigate the design and operation of the cylinder heads and valve assemblies. These parts include the cylinder head, the valve assembly, the camshaft assembly, and the valve operating mechanism. Several service tips and diagnosis checks were also studied.

The cylinder head acts as a cap or seal for the top of the engine. The cylinder head can be made of cast iron or aluminum. Once cast, various surfaces must be machined so that other parts can fit on the cylinder head.

The cylinder head has both intake and exhaust ports to allow fuel and air to enter and leave the engine. In addition, the cylinder head has cooling passages to allow the coolant to flow through the head.

One of the more important parts of the cylinder head is the combustion chamber. Two types of combustion chamber are commonly used. They are the wedge-shaped combustion chamber and the hemispherical combustion chamber. Both are designed to improve the combustion process under certain engine conditions. Some other types of combustion chambers are used for diesel engines only. They include the open, precombustion, and turbulence combustion chambers. These chambers are needed because diesel fuel burns differently than gasoline.

The valve assembly consists of the valves, valve seats, seals, guides, springs, and retainers. There are many parts to the valve. They include the valve face, stem, fillet, margin, and valve head.

Valves can be made of several materials. The selection of material is usually based on the idea that valves must conduct heat rapidly. Nickel, chromium, and manganese are used. Some valves use a liquid sodium inside the valve to help conduct the heat.

Valve guides are used to hold the valve within the cylinder head. They also act as bushings for the valves to slide open and closed. There are two types of valve guides: integral and insert guides. Both have advantages and disadvantages for correct operation.

Valve seals are used to stop oil from seeping past the valve guides. Several types of valve seals are used. These include oil deflectors, positive guide seals, and passive guide seals. Without these seals, oil would flow past the guides into the intake and exhaust stream of gases. This might cause excessive oil consumption.

The valve seat is machined into the cylinder head to allow the valve face to seal against it. The valve seats can be either integral or insert type. These seats should always be checked for cracks and excessive wear. Seats can be ground or resurfaced. An interference angle is machined on the seat

(continued)

SERVICE MANUAL CONNECTION

There are many important specifications to keep in mind when rebuilding the cylinder head and valve mechanism. To identify the specifications for your engine, you will need to know the VIN (vehicle identification number) of the vehicle, the type and year of the vehicle, and the type of engine. Although they may be titled differently, some of the more common cylinder head and valve specifications (not all) found in service manuals are listed below. Note that these specifications are typical examples. Each vehicle and engine will have different specifications.

Common Specification	Typical Example
Camshaft bearing clearance	0.0008–0.0028 inch
Camshaft journal diameter	1.2582–1.2589 inches
Cylinder head warpage limit	0.006 inch
Lifter to bore clearance	0.009–0.0026 inch
Seat angle	45 degrees
Seat width (intake)	0.069–0.091 inch
Valve margin (intake)	1/32 inch
Valve spring out-of-square limit	0.060 inch
Valve stem diameter (intake)	0.3159–0.3167 inch
Valve stem to guide clearance	0.0008–0.0027 inch

In addition, the service manual will give specific directions for many service procedures. Some of the more common procedures include:

- Adjusting valves
- Cylinder head replacement
- Push rod service
- Replacing the camshaft
- Rocker arm service
- Valve guide service
- Valve lifter replacement

Linkage to Future Automotive Technology

ELECTRONIC VALVE TIMING

It is widely accepted that by changing the valve timing, engine performance can be improved. One method being tested is the use of electronic valve timing (EVT). This system uses electropneumatic (electrical and air) actuators to open and close the valves. The actuators are connected to a microcomputer that controls the exact time in which valves open and close. The first figure compares valve lift profiles using the tangential, or mechanical, cam (dotted line) with profiles using electropneumatic actuators (solid lines). The lift profile shows the number of degrees of crankshaft rotation (bottom axis) and the valve lift in millimeters (left axis). The more vertical the lines, the faster the valve opens. Note that the valves can be opened much faster when using EVT. This means that the lift profiles are almost square, especially at lower speeds. The second figure shows a comparison of full-load BMEP (pressure on top of the piston) between conventional valve lift systems and EVT. Engine performance is significantly increased because of improved engine "breathing." In addition, engine performance is improved because of more precise valve timing, or opening and closing the valve at the optimum time. *(Courtesy of Society of Automotive Engineering)*

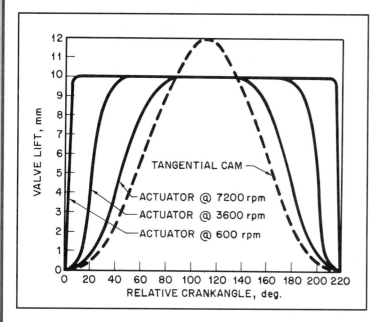

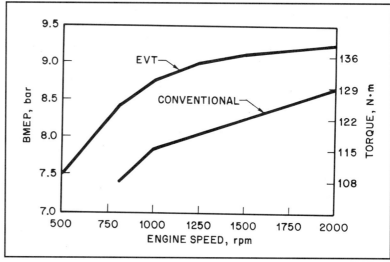

when grinding. The interference angle means that the valve is ground at 45 degrees, while the seat is ground at 46 degrees. This improves the initial seating of the valve.

Valve springs are used to keep the valves closed. They are held in place by retainers and keepers. When the springs are broken or do not have the right tension, valve float and/or valve bounce results. This may damage the engine. In addition, valve springs have vibrations known as harmonics. Special springs are used to reduce this vibration by changing the pitch of the springs or the outside diameter of the spring.

Valve rotators are used to slightly rotate the valve each time it is opened. If this is done, the life of the valve will be increased. This is especially true with leaded fuels. The advantages of valve rotation include minimized deposits, cleaner seats and valve face, reduced valve burning, uniform valve temperatures, and improved valve lubrication.

The camshaft is used to open and close the valves for the four-stroke operation. There are many styles and shapes of cam lobes. The shape determines how quickly the valves open and close. The camshaft is driven by the crankshaft. This is done with timing gears, belts, or chains. Always make sure that the camshaft and crankshaft are timed according to the manufacturer's specifications. The camshaft is held in place with the thrust plate bolted to the cylinder block.

The valve operating mechanism includes lifters, pushrods, and rocker arms. This mechanism is used to change the rotary motion of the camshaft to reciprocating motion to open and close the valves. Because of the heat of expansion, there must be a valve train clearance. This clearance is reduced as the parts heat up.

Several types of lifters are used on the valve mechanism. Solid lifters transfer motion through a solid piece of metal. All solid lifters have some means of adjusting the valve train clearance. This is usually done by moving a small adjusting screw on the rocker arm.

Cam followers are also considered solid lifters. Cam followers use a roller that rides directly on the camshaft. They must also have some means of adjusting the valve train clearance. Cam followers wear less, but they are used in applications requiring stronger valves.

Hydraulic lifters are used on many engines. Hydraulic lifters absorb the valve train clearance by using oil pressure inside the lifter body. As the camshaft lobe starts to raise the lifter, oil inside the lifter locks up and lifts the pushrod, rocker arms, and valves.

Pushrods are defined as the connecting link between the rocker arm and the lifters. Pushrods usually have small convex balls inserted on each of their ends. These convex balls fit into the lifter and rocker arm to allow proper movement. Overhead camshaft engines do not need pushrods.

Rocker arms are designed to change the direction of the cam lifting force and to provide a mechanical advantage for lifting the valve. The purpose of the mechanical advantage is to open the valve more than the actual lift of the camshaft lobe. This is done by making the distance from the center of the rocker arm to each end different lengths.

Service is very important when dealing with the cylinder head and valves. The cylinder head can be checked for flatness, cracks, and warpage. The valve seats can be ground during an overhaul. The valves can also be ground to either a 30 or 45 degree angle, depending upon the manufacturer's specifications. Other important service checks include valve spring tension and alignment, valve guide wear, broken springs, camshaft lobe wear, and lifter wear.

TERMS TO KNOW

Can you explain each of the following terms? Review the chapter until you can use each term correctly.

Siamese ports	Line contact
Wedge-shaped combustion chamber	Keeper
	Valve float
Hemispherical combustion chamber	Valve bounce
	Harmonics
Turbulence	Pitch
Quenching	Inclined surface
Shrouding	Curtain area
Precombustion chamber	Lobe
Poppet-type valve	Thrust plate
Valve face	Keyway
Valve guide	Valve train clearance
Seating	Tappet
Integral guide	Oil relief
Insert guide	Mechanical advantage
Passive seal	Pivot point
Stellite	Variable valve timing
Interference angle	

 REVIEW QUESTIONS

Multiple Choice

1. Which of the following is used to seal the top of the cylinder block and hold the valves?
   a. Tappets
   b. Cylinder head
   c. Lifters
   d. Camshaft
   e. Crankshaft

2. Two cylinders drawing air and fuel from the same port are called:
   a. Double porting
   b. Multiple porting
   c. Siamese ports
   d. Single ports
   e. All of the above

3. Which type of combustion chamber is designed as a half circle?
   a. Hemispherical combustion chamber
   b. Wedge-shaped combustion chamber
   c. Open combustion chamber
   d. Precombustion chamber
   e. Closed combustion chamber

4. When gases are cooled by pressing them in the cylinder area, _____ has occurred.
   a. Turbulence
   b. Quenching
   c. Combustion
   d. Cool down
   e. Convection

5. Which type of combustion chamber is called a turbulence-type combustion chamber?
   a. Hemispherical
   b. Wedge
   c. Precombustion
   d. Open
   e. Closed

6. The _____ combustion chamber is a second small chamber used to ignite a rich mixture of fuel.
   a. Hemispherical
   b. Wedge
   c. Precombustion
   d. Closed
   e. Open

7. The valve assembly consists of:
   a. The valve guides
   b. The valve seats and valves
   c. The springs, retainers, and seals
   d. All of the above
   e. None of the above

8. The _____ on the valve makes direct contact with the valve seat.
   a. Valve stem
   b. Valve face
   c. Valve margin
   d. Valve bottom
   e. Valve side

9. The distance between the valve face and the valve head is called the:
   a. Stem
   b. Fillet
   c. Margin
   d. Seat
   e. Guide

10. Which of the following valve parts are worn when oil leaks into the exhaust stream?
    a. Valve guides
    b. Valve margin
    c. Valve fillet
    d. Valve seat
    e. Valve head

11. Which type of valve seat can be removed and replaced if it is defective?
    a. Insert type
    b. Integral type
    c. Ground seats
    d. Hemi seat
    e. Wedge seat

12. When the valve is ground at a different angle than the seat by one degree, a/an _____ is obtained.
    a. Wrong angle
    b. Interference angle
    c. Poor contact
    d. Side angle
    e. Offset angle

13. Which of the following are used to reduce harmonics in valve springs?
    a. Variable spring pitch
    b. More than one spring
    c. Small spring vibration damper
    d. All of the above
    e. None of the above

14. Camshaft thrust is absorbed by the use of a:
    a. Thrust plate
    b. Thrust gear
    c. Center cam thrust bearing
    d. Special washer
    e. Thrust bearing

15. Camshafts are driven from the crankshaft by:
    a. Timing belts
    b. Timing chains
    c. Timing gears
    d. All of the above
    e. None of the above

16. Which of the following lifters has "leakdown"?
    a. Hydraulic lifters
    b. Cam followers
    c. Solid lifters
    d. Rollers
    e. Solid rollers

17. Which of the following lifters will produce the least wear on the camshaft?
    a. Hydraulic lifters
    b. Cam followers
    c. Solid lifters
    d. Hollow lifters
    e. Slide lifters

18. Rocker arms are designed in an I-head engine to do which of the following?
    a. Change the rotary motion of the camshaft to reciprocating motion for the valves
    b. Reduce wear on the valve face
    c. Hold the valve in place in the cylinder head
    d. Control the speed of the camshaft
    e. All of the above

19. Rocker arm ratio is used on valve mechanisms to:
    a. Open the valve a certain distance
    b. Reduce wear on the valve stem
    c. Increase oil sealing on the valve stem
    d. Increase the valve size
    e. Decrease the valve size

20. When installing the timing gear and camshaft:
    a. Always time the gears according to the manufacturer's specification
    b. Never worry about correct timing of the two gears
    c. Always force the gears together with a rubber hammer
    d. Put the gears 90 degrees apart from each other
    e. Bolt the gears together

21. Valve mechanisms can wear:
    a. On the valve stem
    b. On the valve face and seat
    c. On the valve guide
    d. All of the above
    e. None of the above

The following questions are similar in format to ASE (Automotive Service Excellence) test questions.

---

22. Technician A says a leakdown test can be performed on pushrods. Technician B says a leakdown test can be performed on lifters. Who is right?
    a. A only
    b. B only
    c. Both A and B
    d. Neither A nor B

23. After checking the lift on the lobes of a camshaft, one lobe is found to be 0.002 inch less than the other lobes. Technician A says the camshaft need not be replaced. Technician B says the camshaft should be replaced. Who is right?
    a. A only
    b. B only
    c. Both A and B
    d. Neither A nor B

24. Technician A says valve springs should be checked for weight. Technician B says valve springs should be checked for color. Who is right?
    a. A only
    b. B only
    c. Both A and B
    d. Neither A nor B

25. Technician A says the camshaft cannot wear and thus need not be checked. Technician B says the camshaft lobes will wear and thus should be checked for lift. Who is right?
    a. A only
    b. B only
    c. Both A and B
    d. Neither A nor B

26. Technician A says that to position the valve seat correctly for maximum sealing, grind the bottom of the seat using a 30-degree stone. Technician B says to use a 60-degree stone. Who is correct?
    a. Technician A
    b. Technician B
    c. Both A and B
    d. Neither A nor B

27. Technician A says that engines can have four valves per cylinder. Technician B says that engines can have up to eight valves per cylinder. Who is correct?
    a. Technician A
    b. Technician B
    c. Both A and B
    d. Neither A nor B

28. Technician A says that cam followers should be able to spin in their bore. Technician B says that cam followers do not touch the cam. Who is correct?
    a. Technician A
    b. Technician B
    c. Both A and B
    d. Neither A nor B

29. Technician A says that future engines will have variable valve timing. Technician B says that mechanical mechanisms will be used more and more to open and close valves. Who is correct?
    a. Technician A
    b. Technician B
    c. Both A and B
    d. Neither A nor B

Essay

30. What is quenching in reference to the combustion chamber?

31. What is the purpose of a precombustion chamber?

32. What should be done to the valve if the valve face is damaged?

33. What will be the result if the valve stem-to-guide clearance is too large?

34. What is the purpose of the interference angle on valves?

35. What is the purpose of valve rotators?

36. What is the definition of rocker arm ratio?

Short Answer

37. A crack in the cylinder head can cause the coolant to _____.

38. Two common problems that valves have after extended operational time are _____ and _____.

39. Always check the valves for indications of _____.

40. A common problem with camshafts is that the camshaft lobes will often _____.

41. The _____ of the lifter should always be checked for wear.

MECHANICAL/FLUID ENGINE SYSTEMS

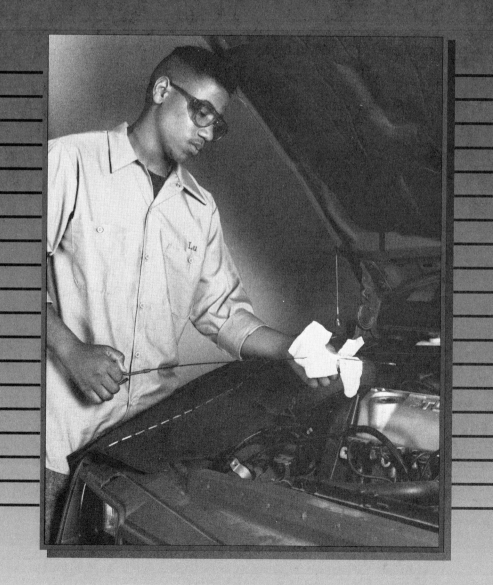

CHAPTER 11

Lubricating Systems

INTRODUCTION   The automobile engine has many moving parts. These parts must be lubricated adequately in order for the engine to operate correctly. During operation many contaminants enter and are produced within the engine. The lubricating system must also clean out these contaminants. To keep the engine well lubricated and able to operate for long periods of time, high-quality lubrication oil is used. The goal of this chapter is to define the purpose, operation, and characteristics of the lubricating system.

OBJECTIVES   After reading this chapter, you should be able to:

- Define the purposes of the lubricating system.
- Identify the contaminants within the engine that must be removed by the lubricating system.
- Analyze the characteristics of lubricating oil.
- Compare the different ways oil can be classified.

- Compare the advantages and disadvantages of using synthetic oils.
- Follow the flow of oil through an engine.
- Examine the parts of the lubricating system in both gasoline and diesel engines.
- Identify problem, diagnosis and service procedures for the lubricating system.

 SAFETY CHECKLIST

When working with lubricating systems, keep these important safety precautions in mind.

✔ Always keep all tools clean and free from oil.

✔ Make sure to wear safety glasses in the service area.

✔ Always use the correct tools when working on the lubrication system.

✔ Always keep the service area floor free of grease and oil.

✔ Never remove an oil pressure sender or gauge from the engine while the engine is running.

Some of the information in this chapter can help you prepare for the National Institute for Automotive Service Excellence (ASE) certification tests. The test most directly related to this chapter is entitled

ENGINE REPAIR (TEST A1).

The content area that closely parallels this chapter is

LUBRICATION AND COOLING SYSTEMS DIAGNOSIS AND REPAIR.

11.1 PURPOSES OF LUBRICATION

Lubricating oil is used in gasoline and diesel engines for many purposes. Lubricating oil is designed to do four major things within the engine. These are to lubricate, cool, clean, and seal various parts within the engine. See *Figure 11–1*.

Oil Lubricates

The most important function of the oil is to lubricate the parts that are moving close together. As engine parts move close together, they produce friction. *Friction* is defined as resistance to motion between two bodies in contact with each other. In an earlier chapter, frictional horsepower (the horsepower used to overcome friction) was defined. Lubricating oil helps to reduce frictional horsepower. If used correctly, lubricating oil can substantially reduce engine wear between two parts.

Oil Cools

Lubricating oil comes directly in contact with vital internal moving engine parts. Lubricating oil is designed to effectively carry away the excess heat being produced. As the lubricating oil passes over a hot engine part, it removes a great amount of heat. The heat is transferred to the crankcase oil reservoir located in the oil pan. Here the heat is dissipated into the oil. If engine lubricating oil is lacking within the engine, the engine may overheat. This is because there is not enough oil to remove the excess heat.

Oil Cleans

It is also very important to keep all engine parts clean and free of carbon and dirt. Clean engine parts will assure proper circulation and cooling of the engine. As particles of dirt get into the engine, the lubricating oil helps to remove these particles and send them to an oil filter. Most of the physical dirt that gets into the engine comes from blow-by. Dust and dirt also come in through the air filter. This dirt must be removed from the engine and sent to the oil filter.

Oil Seals

Lubricating oil inside the engine produces a film on the moving parts. This film acts as a protective sealing agent in the vital ring zone area. Oil located on the cylinder walls and rings helps to produce a seal between the two. The oil actually takes up space between the two moving parts. Without this oil, compression gases would escape into the crankcase area. As was discussed in an earlier chapter, cylinders and rings are deglazed or honed. Honing helps keep the oil on the walls so that sealing can be produced. It is necessary to keep all foreign materials out of this area so that proper sealing can be obtained.

Fluid Friction

Oil, like other matter, is composed of molecules. These oil molecules exhibit two important characteristics for engine lubrication.

1. Oil molecules will stick to metal surfaces more readily than to other oil molecules.

2. Oil molecules will slide against each other freely.

If a film of oil is flowing between two metal surfaces, as in *Figure 11–2*, the top layer of oil molecules will stick to the top piece of metal. The bottom layer of oil molecules will stick to the bottom piece. As the top piece of metal is moved, the internal layers of oil molecules will slide against each other. This action will produce less friction than metal pieces that slide against each other without the oil film.

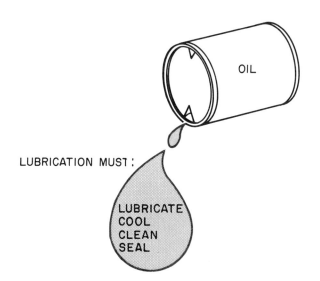

FIGURE 11–1. The purpose of any lubrication system is to lubricate, cool, clean, and seal within the engine.

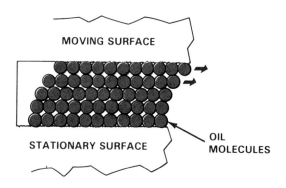

FIGURE 11–2. Oil acts as many small ball bearings. When movement occurs, the internal layers of oil will slide against each other, reducing friction. *(Courtesy of Federal-Mogul Corporation)*

CAR CLINIC

PROBLEM: Removing Engine Sludge

An engine has a heavy amount of sludge inside. What is the best way to remove sludge from an engine?

SOLUTION:

The best way to remove sludge from an engine is to disassemble the engine, clean all the parts, replace worn or damaged parts, and rebuild the engine. Chemicals on the market that remove sludge may cause oil contamination. In addition, there may be other problems in the engine. Removing the sludge will not fix these problems. To avoid sludge buildup, change the oil frequently and be sure that the thermostat is the correct temperature and is operating properly.

11.2   CONTAMINANTS IN THE ENGINE

Many *contaminants* get into the engine oil. These contaminants must be controlled. This means that either the oil must be designed to reduce the amount of contaminants in the engine or the oil must be filtered to reduce the amount of contaminants. To understand the lubricating system better, several contaminants should be defined. These include dust and dirt particles, carbon, water, fuel, oil oxidation, and acid buildup.

Road Dust and Dirt

Road dust and dirt can get into gasoline and diesel engines from the outside. Road dust and dirt enter the engine through the air cleaner and travel into the combustion chamber. They then pass by the rings during blow-by and into the crankcase area. After the dirt gets into the crankcase, it settles in the oil. The typical gasoline engine takes in an excess of 10,000 gallons of dust-carrying air for each gallon of gasoline it consumes. This dust and dirt can be very harmful to the engine. It is the job of the oil system to remove these contaminants.

Carbon and Fuel Soot

Many particles of carbon and soot are not burned completely in the combustion process. Pressures produced by combustion forces some of this unburned fuel and carbon past the rings and into the crankcase area. This process is known as blow-by. Again, if carbon and soot particles were to remain in the oil, the life of the engine could be reduced drastically. The oil must be filtered to remove these particles.

Water Contamination

Water can also contaminate the engine lubrication system. Water can contaminate the lubricating oil because of leaks

in the cooling system or from water vapor. Water vapor is part of the combustion by-products. The blow-by process described earlier forces the water vapor into the crankcase area. As the water vapor enters the crankcase, it cools and condenses into a liquid. Water vapor can also enter the crankcase through several pollution control devices. Air usually has moisture in it. As outside air flows through the crankcase, the moisture from the air is condensed and forms a liquid. Water within the crankcase can produce problems with *sludges* and acids. Sludges are produced when the oil becomes thickened with water and other contaminants.

Fuel Contamination

The performance of motor oil is seriously affected when unburned or partially burned fuel enters the crankcase. Faulty operation of the choke (rich mixture), the fuel pump, poor combustion, bad timing, or worn pistons and rings can all cause fuel to enter the crankcase. Faulty injection and worn engine parts produce the same condition in diesel engines.

Fuel *dilution* of crankcase oil may occur in any engine. The amount may vary from a mere trace to as much as 50%. The presence of fuel in excess of 5% gasoline or 7% diesel fuel may lead to rapid engine wear and deterioration of oil. Fuel contamination of 5% changes the qualities of motor oil. It makes it thinner and less able to stick to the moving parts. This change reduces the ability of the oil to lubricate. See *Figure 11–3*.

Oil Oxidation

Oil *oxidation* occurs within the engine during normal operation. Oil oxidation is defined as the combining of hydrocarbons and other combustion products with oxygen. This is a normal process or by-product of combustion. The result is the actual production of acids within the crankcase. This process produces oil with high *acidity*. Oil oxidation is enhanced or increased in the presence of certain types of metals used in the engine. In fact, certain metals act as a *catalyst*, an agent that speeds up the process, to promote further oxidation and add more corrosive acids to the oil. Increases in oil temperature and in water in the crankcase also enhance

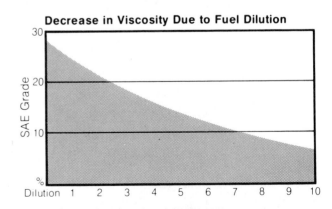

FIGURE 11–3. As fuel contaminates the oil, the oil becomes thinner. This reduction of the viscosity makes the oil less desirable. *(Courtesy of Dana Corporation)*

oil oxidation. Once the process of oil oxidation starts, the situation becomes progressively worse because it is self-accelerating.

Acids in the Engine

Certain *organic* acids are highly corrosive. Other organic acids tend to form gums and lacquers within the engine crankcase. If allowed to become concentrated from not changing oil regularly, the organic acids will attack certain bearing metals. The acids cause pitting and failure. See *Figure 11–4*.

The acids also react with the remainder of the oil to form soft masses. These are referred to as sludges. Sludges cause engine trouble by settling in the oil passageways, in the oil pan, in the filters, and in the oil coolers. The heavier oxidation products form hard *varnish* deposits on pistons, valve stems, and other engine parts. The sludges, acids, and varnish obviously reduce engine life. Therefore, it is very important that oxidation be reduced as much as possible.

11.3   OIL CHARACTERISTICS

As has been discussed, oil has several major jobs to do within the engine. Oil must reduce contaminants within the engine and cool, lubricate, and seal under various conditions.

Viscosity

The *viscosity* of lubrication oil is defined as the oil's *fluidity* or thickness at a specific temperature. Viscosity is also defined

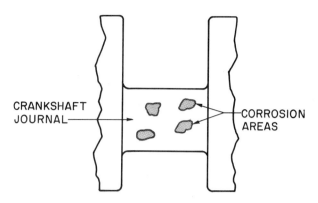

FIGURE 11–4.   As acids get into the engine oil, they tend to cause corrosion and pitting. Note the pitting caused by the acidic oil.

as resistance to flow. Viscosity is measured by a device known as the *Saybolt Universal Viscosimeter*. See *Figure 11–5*. Viscosity is determined at a specific oil temperature. The most common temperatures are 0, 150, and 210 degrees F. A sample of oil is drained from the viscosimeter into a receiving flask. This is done at a specific temperature. The time required for the sample to completely drain is recorded in seconds. The viscosity is given in Saybolt Universal Seconds (SUS) at a particular temperature.

Viscosity Index

As an oil becomes cooler, it also becomes less fluid. As an oil becomes hotter, it becomes thinner. The *viscosity index*

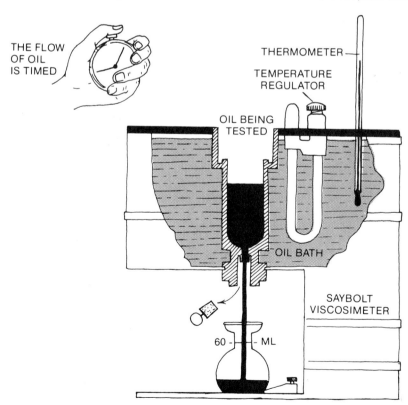

FIGURE 11–5.   A Saybolt Universal Viscosimeter measures the thickness of oil. *(Courtesy of Davis Publications)*

(VI) is used to control oil thickness at different temperatures. The viscosity index is a measure of how much the viscosity of an oil changes with a given temperature. Chemicals are added to oil so that as the temperature of the oil changes the viscosity will not change as much. Usually the higher the viscosity index, the smaller the relative change in viscosity with temperature.

Pour Point

Oil must flow as a liquid in order to be used. Extremely cold conditions may increase oil viscosity until it cannot flow. The temperature at which the oil ceases to flow is defined as the *pour point*. As the oil approaches its pour point, it becomes thicker and more difficult to pump. Additives are put into the oil to control the pour point.

Oxidation Inhibitors

Oxidation inhibitors reduce oxygen. Reduction of oxygen reduces the formation of sludges and varnish produced within the engine. As indicated earlier, any oxygen in the crankcase area may increase oil oxidation in the engine and thus produce acids. Chemicals that help eliminate or absorb oxygen are added to oil during the refining process. If the oxygen is absorbed, less is available to produce oil oxidation. In turn, fewer acids are produced. Note that if oil is not changed regularly, oxidation may increase.

Detergents and Dispersants

Detergents are added to engine oil to help clean particles, dust, dirt, and other foreign materials from the engine. Detergents in the oil loosen and detach deposits of carbon, gum, and dirt. The oil suspends these particles. This characteristic is called *suspendability*. The oil then carries the loosened materials to the filter. Particles that are smaller than the filter size stay in the oil until the oil is changed. Note, however, that detergents also cause a certain amount of increased wear on the engine.

Dispersants are also added to oil. A chemical is added to the oil to keep the small dirt particles dispersed, or separated from each other. Without dispersants, particles tend to collect and form larger particles. These particles, which are heavier and harder to suspend in oil, can block oil passageways and filters. Dispersants greatly increase the amount of contaminants the oil can carry while functioning correctly.

Petroleum manufacturers are now placing more emphasis on dispersants than on detergents. It is felt that if the contaminants can be kept suspended in the oil, they will not deposit on engine parts. This means there is less need for detergent chemicals in the oil.

Other Additives

Antifoaming additives are added to the lubricating oil to reduce foaming of the oil. During normal operation, the oil is pressurized and pumped through the engine. This constant pumping may cause the oil to foam. Any foam produced in the engine reduces lubricating, sealing, cooling, and clean-

ing. Hydraulic lifters also operate poorly with oil that has foam mixed in it. Chemicals are added to the oil to reduce foaming.

Corrosion and *rust inhibitors* are added to oil to reduce, or *inhibit* corrosion of engine parts. Chemicals are added to help neutralize any acids produced. Rust inhibitors are also used to help remove water vapors from engine parts. Oil can then coat the engine parts correctly.

Antiscuff additives are put in the oil to help polish moving parts. This is especially important during new engine break-in periods.

Extreme-pressure resistance additives are added to the lubricating oil to keep oil molecules from splitting apart under heavy pressures. During operation, oil is constantly being pressurized, squeezed, and so on. This may cause the oil molecules to separate and reduce the oil's lubricating properties. The added chemicals react with metal surfaces to form very strong, slippery films, which may be only a molecule or so thick. With these additives, protection is increased during moments of extreme pressure.

CAR CLINIC

PROBLEM: Oil Leak When Car Sits Overnight

Oil leaks from the vehicle when it sits overnight in a driveway. The valve cover gaskets have been replaced several times, but the leak always comes back.

SOLUTION:

A chronic oil leak like this can be caused by too much crankcase pressure. Check the crankcase pressure and compare it with the manufacturer's specifications. If it is above specifications, perform a cylinder leakdown test. This test will check for leaky piston rings. If the piston rings are in good condition, check the condition of the PCV system for correct venting. Fixing one of these two problems should solve leaking valve cover gaskets.

11.4   OIL CLASSIFICATIONS

Lubricating oils are rated by various agencies. These ratings are used so that the correct oil can be selected for the correct application. Three organizations rate oil: *Society of Automotive Engineers* (*SAE* ratings), the *American Petroleum Institute* (*API* ratings), and the federal government (military ratings).

SAE Ratings

SAE ratings are given in terms of the viscosity or thickness of the oil. The SAE has applied the Saybolt Universal Seconds test to their ratings. SAE ratings are determined for different temperatures. Oil is tested for viscosity at 0 degrees, 150 degrees, and 210 degrees F. The most common are 0 and 210 degrees. A rating that has a letter *W* after it means that the viscosity is tested at 0 degrees. If there is no *W* after the rating, the oil has been tested at 210 degrees. For example, in *Figure 11–6*, a 10W oil has a rating of 6,000 to 12,000 seconds at 0 degrees. When the oil temperature is increased to 210 degrees, the oil has a rating of 39 seconds. Multigrade oils that have ratings such as 10W30 meet the viscosity requirements for both the 0 degree and 210 degree ranges. This means that the oil is less affected by temperature changes. Viscosity index improvers are added to make this possible.

It is sometimes difficult to determine exactly which type of oil viscosity to use. Manufacturers include various charts to help determine the best viscosity for the best service. *Figure 11–7* shows such a chart. For example, SAE 10W30 oils should be used in temperatures from about –10 degrees to about 68 degrees F. Other oils are shown for different temperature conditions. The manufacturer's recommendations should always be followed to determine which oil is correct for their engine. Failure to do so will void the new car warranty.

API Ratings

The American Petroleum Institute (API) rates oil on the basis of the type of engine service the oil should be used in. API ratings for gasoline engines include SA, SB, SC, SD, SE, SF, and SG. API diesel ratings are CA, CB, CC, and CD. SA and SB ratings are for light-duty engine operations. There is very little protection against corrosion, scuffing, and deposits. Oils rated SC meet the requirements for vehicles manufactured from 1964 to 1967. SD oils meet the requirements for vehicles manufactured from 1968 to 1979. The SE rating means that the oil can be used in vehicles built in 1972 and in certain 1971 vehicles. Oils rated SF are used in gasoline engines built between 1981 and 1988. Vehicles manufactured in 1989 and later should use oils rated as SG. SG oils have

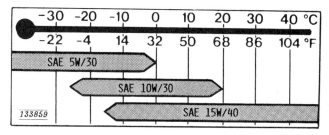

Viscosity: (stable ambient temperatures)

FIGURE 11–7. Car manufacturers recommend certain viscosity ratings for different temperatures. *(Courtesy of Volvo of North America)*

more additives than SF oils. SG oils can withstand higher temperatures, have better control of engine deposits, and provide additional protection against rust and corrosion. Oils meeting the API rating of SG may be used when API ratings of SF, SE, SF/CC, or SE/CC are recommended.

As the automotive manufacturers design engines with higher temperatures and closer clearances, the type of oil used will have to be changed. Other ratings will eventually be used for vehicles that require even more protection against sludge, varnish, wear, and engine deposits.

CA oils are designed for mild- to moderate-duty operation with high-quality fuel used with diesel engines. CB oils are for mild- to moderate-duty operation of diesel engines with lower-quality fuels. More protection is needed against wear deposits and bearing corrosion. CC oils are intended for moderate- to severe-duty supercharged or turbocharged diesel engines. There is more protection against rust, corrosion, and low-temperature deposits. CD oils are designed for protection with supercharged or turbocharged diesel engines in severe-duty service. Protection is given against high-temperature deposits, bearing corrosion, and use of various fuels. Automotive manufacturers usually require the use of CD oils in automotive diesel applications.

Military Ratings

The third rating is associated with military testing and performance. The federal government contracts with an engine manufacturer to build engines for a particular application. When this is done, a military specification is issued for the type of oil recommended in that specific application. Some of the tested ratings are:

1. MIL-L2104 B, MIL-L46152, or MIL-L-6082

2. Supplement 1

3. Series 3

From these tests, an engine manufacturer then recommends a specific type of oil for its engines in the military application. SAE and API ratings are usually included with this recommendation. If there is a military rating stamped on the can, it can be assumed that this oil has been tested for a specific application with military equipment.

VISCOSITY RANGE, SAYBOLT UNIVERSAL SECONDS				
SAE NUMBER	SECONDS AT 0°F MIN.	MAX.	SECONDS AT 210°F MIN.	MAX.
5W		4,000	39	
10W	6,000	12,000	39	
20W	12,000	48,000	39	
20			45	58
30			58	70
40			70	85
50			85	110

FIGURE 11–6. Viscosity is measured in seconds. Oil must have a certain flow rate in seconds for each SAE rating.

These three ratings are normally stated on the oil can. *Figure 11–8* shows a typical can with the ratings stamped in the cover. If the oil can does not have an API rating, the oil probably won't meet the API specifications.

11.5 SYNTHETIC LUBRICANTS

In recent years the use of *synthetic* lubricants has increased. *Synthesize* means to combine parts into a whole or to make complex compounds from a series of individual molecules. Synthetic lubricants are made chemically by mixing alcohol, various acids, other chemicals, and hydrocarbons together. The hydrocarbons can be taken from coal, oil, natural gas, wood, or any agricultural resource. The result is a synthesized product that is capable of meeting and exceeding the lubrication needs of various engines. Synthetic oils are manufactured by combining specific molecules into an end product tailored to do a specific job. They are designed to meet or exceed the SAE and API recommendations.

Advantages of Synthetic Oils

Synthetic oils were initially designed for jet engine use because of the higher temperatures and pressures. They are now used in automobile applications because of their ability to withstand high temperatures with little change in the viscosity of the oil. There are several advantages and disadvantages of using synthetic oil in automotive engines. Some advantages include:

1. *Increased thermal and oxidation stability*. For example, synthetic oils can operate effectively from –60 degrees F to +400 degrees F. Oxidation occurs at about 50 degrees higher than in standard oils.

2. *Less evaporation*. Only about 1% of the oil evaporates over a standard period of time as compared with about 25% for standard lubrication oils.

3. *Less viscosity change with temperature*. This improves cold starting ability and fuel mileage during cold weather.

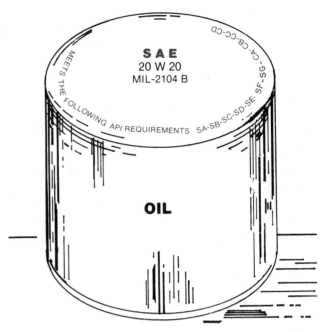

FIGURE 11–8. Each oil can has different ratings. SAE, API, and MIL ratings are printed on the can. *(Courtesy of Davis Publications)*

4. *Improved fuel mileage*. Synthetic oils have increased lubricating properties. The results are less frictional resistance and more horsepower. *Figure 11–9* shows horsepower increases at different RPM.

5. *Reduced oil consumption*. Synthetic oils increase sealing characteristics.

6. *Cleaner engine parts*. Less maintenance is required when engine parts remain cleaner.

7. *Not affected by fuel contamination*.

Disadvantages of Synthetic Oils

Although synthetic oils seem to be better than conven-

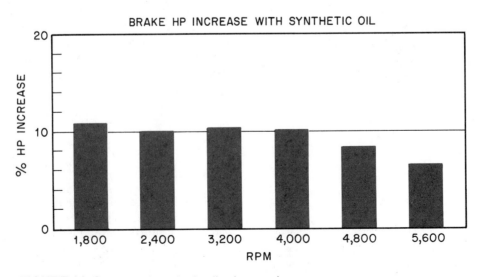

FIGURE 11–9. Use of synthetic oils changes horsepower.

tional oils, there are several disadvantages that should be mentioned. These include:

1. *Poor break-in characteristics.* Because of the increased lubrication property, break-in will not occur correctly. Synthetic oils should not be used until the vehicle has reached about 6,000 miles.

2. *Ineffectiveness in older engines.* Synthetic oils should not be used in engines with bad rings, valve seals, or seals. If used on such engines, the oil may be consumed more rapidly.

3. *Higher cost.* The cost per quart is still higher for synthetic oil than for conventional motor oil. Over the life of the vehicle, however, the total cost for lubrication will be about the same. The savings come from cleaner engines and better fuel mileage. Oil change periods range in the area of 25,000 miles.

4. *Inability to be mixed.* It is not advisable to mix different brands of synthetic oils. This may cause some inconvenience when trying to buy a particular brand.

A great deal of research is being done on synthetic oils. As the temperatures of engines increase in the future, synthetic lubricants will have to be reevaluated to see if they can be used more effectively than conventional oils. Each person will have to decide about the use of synthetic lubricants.

11.6   GREASES

The term grease has long been employed to describe lubricants that are in a semifluid state and are used to reduce friction. Grease is made by adding various thickening agents such as soap to a liquid lubricant such as oil. Greases are commonly used on automotive chassis parts such as the universal joints, wheel bearings, and front end steering parts.

Although greases are suitable for many lubrication jobs, several modifying agents are often added to greases to improve certain properties. Examples of properties that may be improved include: tackiness, oxidation stability, consistency stability, load-carrying capacity, and rust prevention.

Greases can be identified by several methods. One method is by measuring the consistency of grease. See *Figure 11–10*. Consistency is a measure of relative hardness. This property is expressed in terms of the ASTM (American Society for Testing and Materials) penetration or *NLGI (National Lubricating Grease Institute)* grade or consistency number.

The consistency of a grease is an important factor in its ability to lubricate, seal, and remain in place. It is also an important factor in how easily the grease can be applied and removed. Most automotive greases are in the NLGI number 2 grade or range. This means the grease ranges from soft to medium consistency. The NLGI number is sometimes referred to as the *EP (extreme pressure)* number or grade.

The ASTM penetration is a numerical statement of the actual penetration of a grease sample. It is measured in tenths of a millimeter using a standard testing device under standard conditions. The higher the penetration value, the softer the grease.

CLASSIFICATION OF GREASES BY NLGI CONSISTENCY NUMBERS	
NLGI[a] Number	ASTM Worked Penetration @ 25°C (77°F) (tenths of a millimeter)
000	445–475 (Semi-Fluid)
00	400–430 (Semi-Fluid)
0	355–385 (Soft)
1	310–340
2	265–295
3	220–250
4	175–205
5	130–160
6	85–115 (Hard)

[a]National Lubricating Grease Institute (NLGI)

FIGURE 11–10.   Greases are classified by their consistency numbers. *(Courtesy of Phillips 66 Company)*

11.7   LUBRICATING SYSTEM OPERATION

The lubricating system is composed of several parts. These include the oil pan, oil pump, main oil galleries, oil filters, oil pressure regulators, oil coolers, and oil sensors. These parts are needed to make the lubricating system operate correctly.

Oil Pan

The purpose of the oil pan is to hold the excess oil during operation and nonrunning conditions. This reservoir for the oil is located on the bottom of the engine. After the parts of the engine are lubricated, gravity causes the oil to flow back to the oil pan. A plug in the bottom of the oil pan is used to drain the oil. The cooling of the oil takes place within the oil pan.

Oil Flow

Each engine manufactured has a certain flow pattern to get the oil from the oil pan, or *sump*, to the various parts that need lubrication. Flow diagrams are different for each type of engine and for each year manufactured. One type of flow diagram is shown in *Figure 11–11*. The flow of oil starts at the oil pan where the oil is stored and cooled. From there the oil is drawn into the oil pump through the oil screen. In this case, the oil pump is located in the front of the engine on the crankshaft. Other oil pumps are driven from the camshaft or through the distributor shaft. After the oil is pressurized, it is sent to the oil filter to be cleaned. From the oil filter, the oil is sent into passages in the block of the engine. These are referred to as the main oil gallery. From the main oil gallery, oil is sent to all other parts of the engine. There is an oil pressure sensor on the main oil gallery. The oil pressure sensor is used to sense the oil pressure. It is attached to the oil light or gauge on the dashboard.

Oil is sent through drilled passages that come into contact with the main oil gallery to the crankshaft. Here the oil is

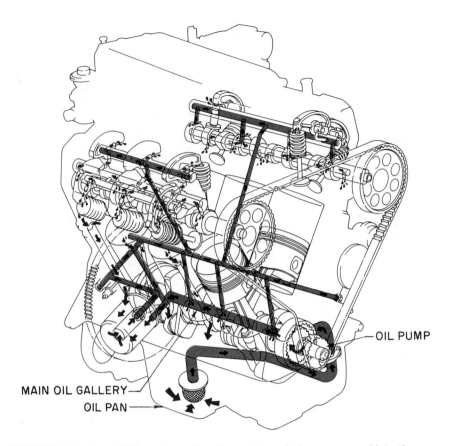

FIGURE 11–11. Oil flows from the oil pan, through the pump, and into the main oil gallery. From there the oil is sent to all the parts of the engine. *(Courtesy of Nissan Motor Corporation in USA)*

used to lubricate the main and connecting rod bearings. *Figure 11–12* shows oil holes drilled in a crankshaft. Oil from the main bearings feeds to the connecting rod bearings and then drops back to the oil pan and sump.

From the main oil gallery, the oil is also sent through drilled passages to the head. On some engines, the oil flows from the main oil gallery, through the lifters, through the pushrods, and up to the rocker arms. Here the oil is used to lubricate the camshafts, rocker arms, and valves. The oil then drains back to the oil pan and sump through holes in the block and cylinder heads.

A second oil flow diagram is shown in *Figure 11–13*. The oil flow is as follows:

1. Oil is drawn from the oil pan, through a wire mesh filter into the oil pump.

2. Oil is then pressurized and sent into the oil filter to be cleaned. Drilled internal passageways are used.

3. Oil is then sent to a main oil gallery to lubricate both the crankshaft and the camshaft. Drilled internal passageways are used.

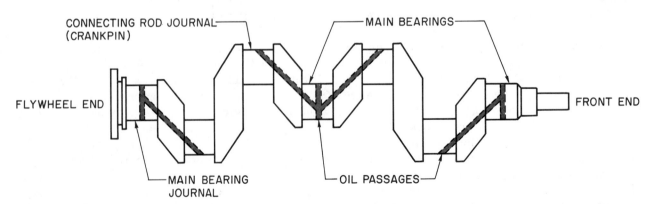

FIGURE 11–12. Oil from the main oil gallery is sent through passages into the crankshaft. The oil at the main bearings is then sent to the connecting rod bearings.

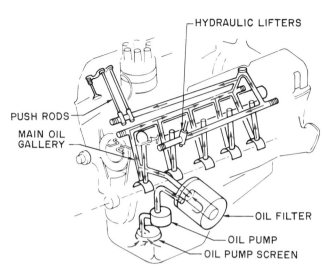

FIGURE 11–13. A typical oil flow diagram for a V-6 or a V-8 engine. *(Courtesy of Motor Publications, Auto Repair Manual)*

4. From the main oil gallery, oil is sent to the hydraulic lifters. Drilled internal passageways are used.

5. From the hydraulic lifters, oil is sent up through the pushrods to lubricate the rocker arms.

6. At this point the oil is no longer under pressure, and it drains back to the oil pan through internal passageways. Some passageways are drilled, while some are cast into the cylinder head and block.

An oil flow diagram for a diesel engine is shown in *Figure 11–14*. Some differences include:

1. Oil is sent to the turbocharger immediately after going through the filter.

2. Oil is sent to the oil cooler immediately after going through the filter.

3. Oil is sent to the rocker arm shaft after going through the oil filter.

Oil Pumps

For the oil to be distributed throughout the engine, it must be pressurized. This is done with an oil pump. The oil pump is located in the crankcase area so that oil can be drawn from the oil pan and sent into the engine. Oil pumps are considered positive displacement pumps. This means that for every revolution on the pump a certain volume of oil is pumped. Therefore, as RPM increases, oil pressure also increases.

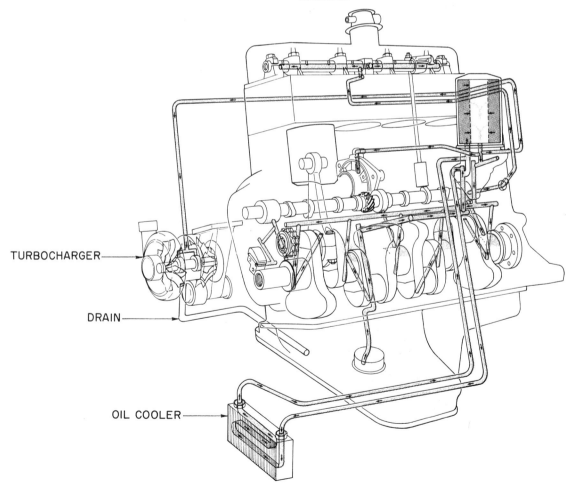

FIGURE 11–14. On certain engines, oil must also flow to the turbocharger and the oil cooler. *(Courtesy of Peugeot Motors of America, Inc.)*

There are several types of pumps. *Figure 11–15* shows how a standard gear-type pump operates. In this case, the oil is drawn in on one side as if into a vacuum. It is then pressurized on the other side. The *eccentric* gear-type pump operates on the same principle. (Eccentric means not having the same center.) *Figure 11–16* shows two gears. The centers of the gears are not at the same position. As the inside gear is turned, a suction is produced on one side, and a pressure is produced on the other side.

Figure 11–17 shows a typical oil pump driven by the crankshaft. The pump is an eccentric type. As the inside gear is turned, the vacuum produced draws oil from the oil pan, through the oil screen, through the tube, and into the oil pump. The oil is then pressurized and sent into the engine.

Oil Pressure Regulating Valve

Because all oil pumps are positive displacement types, a pressure regulator valve must be used. A pressure regulator valve is used to keep the pressure within the oil system at a constant maximum value. As the RPM of the engine changes, the amount of pressure produced by the oil pump also changes. In addition, as the oil gets thicker because of cold weather, oil pressure may increase. The pressure regulator valve maintains a constant maximum pressure. Whenever the pressure exceeds this maximum, the regulator valve opens to reduce the pressure. Normal oil pressures vary according to the engine manufacturer. Check the engine manufacturer's specifications to determine the oil pressure for a particular engine.

Figure 11–18 shows how an oil regulator valve works. As the oil pressure increases in the pump, the pressure pushes against a ball or valve held in place by a spring. When the oil pressure is greater than the spring tension, the ball lifts off its seat. At this point, some of the oil is returned to the suction side of the oil system or to the oil pan. This reduces the

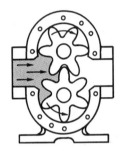
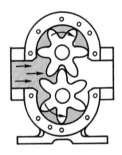
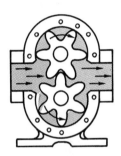

FIGURE 11–15. As the gears turn on the oil pump, a suction is produced on the left side, drawing in oil. The oil is carried around to the other side. As the gears mesh with each other, the oil is squeezed out and pressurized.

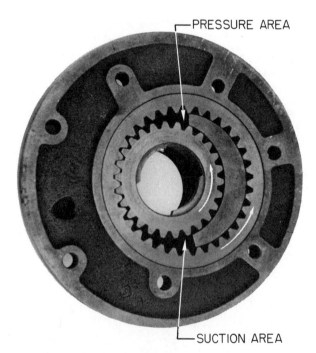

FIGURE 11–16. An eccentric gear pump has two gears. Each has a different center point (eccentric). As they are turned, suction and pressure are produced.

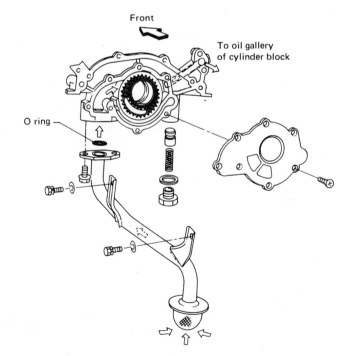

FIGURE 11–17. This eccentric pump is driven directly by the crankshaft. *(Courtesy of Nissan Motor Corporation in USA)*

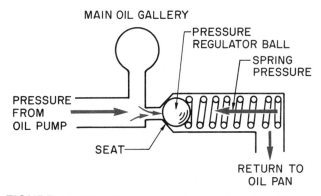

FIGURE 11–18. During normal operation, the oil is sent into the main oil gallery. As oil pressure increases, the ball is lifted off its seat (against spring pressure). Some of the oil is then returned to the oil pan, reducing the oil pressure.

pressure, which seats the ball again. The spring tension is designed to set the oil pressure at the manufacturer's specifications. If a stronger spring is used, the oil pressure will increase. If the spring pressure is less or the spring is broken, the oil pressure will be less. Pressures are normally about 40–60 psi for passenger cars and light trucks. Larger engines may have pressures in the range of 40–70 psi.

Oil Filters

Oil must be filtered and cleaned constantly within the engine. As was mentioned earlier in this chapter, several contaminants get into the oil. Oil filters are used to clean the dirt particles out of the oil. *Figure 11–19* shows a typical oil filter on an engine.

FIGURE 11–19. Oil filters are used to remove dust, dirt, and sludge particles from the oil.

There are two types of oil filtering systems. One is called the full-flow system and one is called the by-pass system. Years ago only the by-pass system was used. However, because of a greater need to filter the oil, full-flow systems are now being used. Full-flow systems filter all of the oil before it enters the engine. By-pass systems filter only a part of the oil during operation.

Bypass Filter

Figure 11–20 shows the bypass system. Approximately 90% of the oil is pumped directly to the engine. Only about 10% is sent into the oil filter to be cleaned. If this filter becomes plugged, no oil can be filtered. Oil will still be pressurized, however, and sent into the engine. Certain diesel applications use this system along with a full-flow filter.

Full-Flow Filter

Figure 11–21 shows the full-flow system. In this system, all of the oil must pass through the oil filter before entering the engine. If dirt plugs the oil filter, the oil pressure will increase before the filter, causing all of the oil to be returned to the crankcase through the regulator valve. To prevent this problem, a relief valve is used. The relief valve is designed to open at about a 5–40 psi difference in pressure across the

CAR CLINIC

PROBLEM: Synthetic Oil

A customer has been using synthetic oil for about 15,000 miles in the vehicle. Now it is noticed that the engine is using a small amount of oil. Is it acceptable to mix regular oil with synthetic oil to keep the oil at the correct level?

SOLUTION:

The manufacturers of synthetic oil recommend that synthetic oil NOT be mixed with regular oil. More important, if the engine is using oil, it may have to be rebuilt. New rings may have to be put on the pistons to eliminate oil consumption. Also, check for valve guide seals leaking into the intake or exhaust. A compression leakdown test will help determine which cause is producing the oil burning.

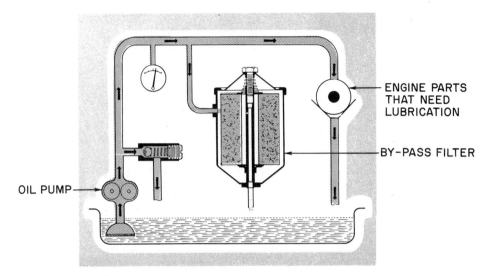

FIGURE 11–20.   A bypass oil filter is used on some engines. In this system, only a small amount of oil is filtered. The filter is a bypass line around the oil system. *(Courtesy of Dana Corporation)*

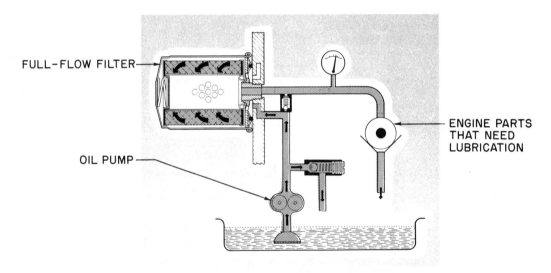

FIGURE 11–21.   When a full-flow oil filter is used, all of the oil must go through the filter before entering the engine passages. *(Courtesy of Dana Corporation)*

filter. This is called *differential pressure*. Differential pressure is the difference in pressure between the inlet and outlet of the filter. The inlet pressure will always be controlled by the regulator valve. As the oil filter plugs up, the pressure on the other side of the filter will drop. When the difference is equal to the relief valve setting, a certain amount of oil will pass through the filter and go into the engine. This means that even if the filter gets plugged, the engine will still receive oil. If the filter is totally plugged, the oil pressure will be slightly less than normal pressure.

Filter Design

Oil filters come in a variety of shapes and sizes. Two common types are the surface and the depth filters. The surface filter is shown in *Figure 11–22*. The oil flows over the surface of the paper material. The contaminants are trapped on

the surface of the paper, but the oil flows through microscopic pores in the paper.

The depth filter material is a blend of cotton thread and various fibers. *Figure 11–23* shows a depth filter. As the oil and dirt flow through the filter material, contaminants are trapped inside the filter material. Depth filters are used less today because they produce more restriction to the oil flow. Today's engines need more oil flow to aid in cooling the engine.

Oil Coolers

Oil coolers are used on certain heavy-duty gasoline engines and many diesel engines. An oil cooler is a device that helps keep the oil cool. Oil temperature should be in the range of 180–250 degrees F. Under normal conditions, oil is cooled by having the right amount of oil in the oil pan. When excess

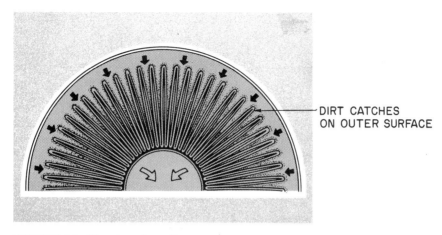

FIGURE 11–22.   A surface filter catches the dirt particles on the surface of the filter material. *(Courtesy of Dana Corporation)*

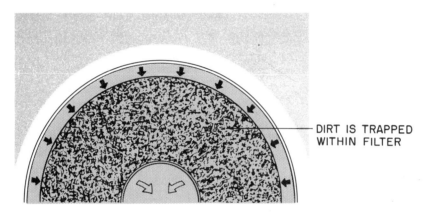

FIGURE 11–23.   A depth filter is made of cotton threads and other fibers. The dirt particles are trapped within the filter. *(Courtesy of Dana Corporation)*

temperatures occur, however, this cooling may not be enough. Oil coolers are used then.

Common oil coolers are designed with many copper tubes that are sealed together. The assembly is then sealed in a shell-type housing. This type of device is called a liquid-to-liquid heat exchanger. This means that the hotter liquid transfers some of its heat to a cooler liquid. Coolant from the engine cooling system passes from one end to the other through the copper tubes. The higher-temperature lubricating oil passes through the shell. Although the two fluids do not mix, the heat in the lubricating oil is transferred to the coolant. The coolant then expels the excess heat through the radiator. *Figure 11–24* shows an example of an oil cooler used on a diesel engine.

Oil Sensors and Gauges

Oil pressure sensors are used to indicate if the oil system has the right amount of pressure. Oil pressure is usually sensed or measured directly from the main oil gallery. This information is sent to the dashboard on the vehicle so the operator can read the pressure. Two types of systems are commonly used. These are the pressure gauge and the oil indicator light. The pressure gauge reads the pressure of the oil within

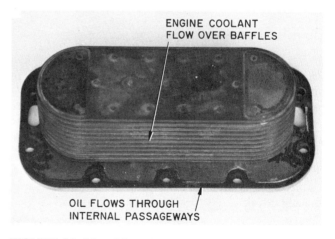

FIGURE 11–24.   Oil coolers are used to keep the oil cool during operation. Oil coolers use a series of metal tubes connected together. Oil flows on one side, while engine coolant flows on the other side.

the system. The oil indicator light system has a light that goes on when oil pressure is low, usually at 7 psi or below.

Electric Oil Gauge

Figure 11–25 shows how an electric oil pressure gauge

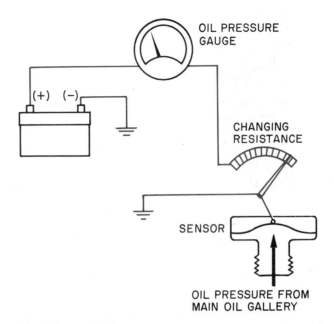

FIGURE 11–25. An electric oil pressure gauge senses oil pressure. As pressure changes, resistance within the circuit also changes, causing the needle to read differently.

works. As oil pressure is sensed from the main oil gallery, the pressure moves an arm in such a way that it changes the resistance of the circuit. This change in resistance causes the oil pressure gauge to read differently for different pressures. The oil sensor is connected to the main oil gallery. Wires are then connected from the sensor to the electric oil gauge on the dashboard.

Bourdon Gauge

The Bourdon pressure gauge is also used to measure and read oil pressure. *Figure 11–26* shows a typical Bourdon gauge. The tube is made of thin brass. The free end is connected to an indicating needle on the gauge dial. As pressure in the oil system increases, the gauge tends to become straighter. This causes the needle to read differently on the dial. This type of gauge reading requires the oil to be sent directly to the gauge. A small copper or plastic tube is usually connected from the engine main oil gallery to the gauge on the dashboard.

Indicator Light

The oil indicator light simply goes on when the oil pressure is low. The light is connected to the ignition switch. There is also a pressure switch on the main oil gallery. When the ignition switch is turned on, the pressure switch is still closed because there is no oil pressure. The light is on then. When the engine starts, oil pressure builds up and opens the switch on the main oil gallery. Opening this switch turns off the oil light. *Figure 11–27* shows two types of oil sensors.

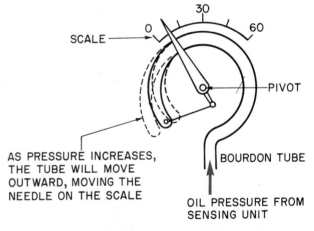

FIGURE 11–26. In a Bourdon pressure gauge, as pressure increases, the tube becomes straighter, giving a different reading.

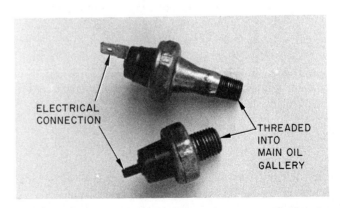

FIGURE 11–27. Oil sensors are used to sense the pressure in the main oil gallery. As pressure increases, a switch in the sensor opens. When pressure is low, the switch closes and turns on the oil indicator light.

Problems, Diagnosis and Service

▷ ☐ SAFETY PRECAUTIONS ☐ ◁

1. The vehicle must be lifted up whenever the oil is changed. When jacking up a vehicle with a hydraulic lift, always use jack stands to support the vehicle if the hydraulic lift should fail.
2. When you change oil or oil filters, oil often spills on the floor. If oil spills, clean up the spill immediately so that you won't slip and fall.
3. Always use proper clothing (shop coats and so on) when working on the lubrication system. Oil spilled on clothing, especially diesel oil, may damage the clothing.
4. When running the engine to check oil pressure, make sure the exhaust fumes are adequately removed by the exhaust system in the building.
5. Used oil from the engine is very toxic and should not be disposed of on driveways or in fields. All used oil from engines should be recycled. Many states have specific recycling information concerning oil. In many states, the retail outlet that sells oil must either recycle the used oil or provide information noting where it can be recycled in your area. Check with your local or state pollution control agency if you are in doubt about how to recycle used oil.

FIGURE 11–28. When changing the oil and filter, always remove the filter and drain it in the appropriate container.

PROBLEM: Changing Oil

The oil has not been changed in the vehicle for a long period of time. If not changed at regular intervals, sludge, varnish deposits, and engine wear could result.

DIAGNOSIS

Refer to the manufacturer's recommended change periods. Depending upon the vehicle year and make, the change periods in miles will vary. Most newer vehicles should have the engine oil changed every 6,000 to 8,000 miles.

SERVICE

When changing the oil, make sure you know the correct quantity of oil. When the oil filter is changed, an additional quart of oil typically must be added.

1. Bring the engine up to operating temperature.
2. Jack up the vehicle and place the jack stands securely under the car.
3. Remove the oil plug.
4. Remove the oil filter and drain as shown in *Figure 11–28*.

5. Let the old oil drain into an appropriate oil pan.
6. Make sure all the oil has been drained before tightening the oil plug.

   CAUTION: Be careful not to strip the threads on the oil plug during installation.

7. Remove the oil filter if necessary.
8. Select the correct oil to use. Make sure the oil viscosity is correct for the application and weather conditions. Again, always refer to the manufacturer's specifications, as use of incorrect oil viscosity may void the manufacturer's warranty. Make sure the API ratings are correct for the application and year of the vehicle.
9. Before replacing a new filter, put oil on the oil filter seal. Then fill the new filter with the correct type of oil. This procedure will eliminate any air in the lubrication system during initial starting. Now replace the oil-filled filter on the engine block. Make sure the oil filter is tight. Be careful not to strip the oil filter threads when replacing a new filter.
10. Remove the vehicle from the jack stands.

11. Add the correct quantity of oil to the engine.

12. Start engine and check for oil pressure. Also check for oil leaks around the filter.

13. Now stop engine and check engine oil level on the dipstick.

PROBLEM: Acid Buildup in the Oil

An engine has been stored for over a year. When the engine was run for a short period of time, it was suspected that a main or connecting rod bearing was bad. During disassembly of the engine, it was noticed that there were small spots of corrosion on the crankshaft journals.

DIAGNOSIS

Used oil that sits in an unused engine may have a buildup of acids over a period of time. The acids come from the combustion process and enter the oil pan because of blow-by past the rings.

SERVICE

To prevent acids from developing in the oil, always change the used oil in an engine before the engine is stored. Do this if the engine is to be stored for more than three months at a time.

PROBLEM: Gasoline in the Oil

Oil pressure seems to have been dropping continuously over a period of several weeks. In addition, the oil seems to be getting thinner.

DIAGNOSIS

These two problems generally suggest that there may be fuel in the oil. Fuel can be detected in the oil by a gaseous smell or reduced viscosity. Fuel can get into the oil in several ways.

1. If the mechanical fuel pump is damaged, oil may seep through the pump and into the crankcase.

2. If the engine is flooded continuously when starting, or if the engine carburetor is set too rich, fuel may get into the oil.

SERVICE

If fuel is found in the oil first determine where it is coming from.

1. Check the fuel pump for correct pressure.

2. If the fuel pump is suspected, remove the fuel pump and check for a gaseous smell where it attaches to the block.

3. Replace the fuel pump if necessary.

4. Check the carburetor for correct settings including the choke and main fuel circuits.

5. Once the problem has been found and repaired, drain the contaminated oil. Remove and replace the filter also.

6. Now replace with the correct type and quantity of oil.

PROBLEM: Water in the Oil

The engine oil appears to be light brown or whitish.

DIAGNOSIS

When the oil becomes light brown or whitish water may have entered the lubrication system. Water can get into the oil from the cooling system. The water usually comes from a cracked cylinder block or head.

SERVICE

If coolant is getting into the lubricating system, the cylinder head may be checked by performing a compression test on the cylinder head. A low compression reading may indicate a cracked head or a broken head gasket. If this is the case, the engine will need to be disassembled and the cylinder head replaced or gasket replaced. If the cylinder head compression test is OK, then the crack most likely is in the cylinder block. In this case the engine will need to be disassembled, and a new block should be installed.

PROBLEM: Low Oil Pressure

The operator of the vehicle has noticed that the oil pressure is low.

DIAGNOSIS

Various components can be damaged that may cause low oil pressure.

1. A broken spring on the regulator valve could be a cause of low oil pressure.

2. If the oil pressure drops suddenly, check the oil level first, then check the oil pressure sensor and the gauge for correct operation.

3. Low oil pressure can also be caused by worn main and connecting rod bearings. Check the age and number of miles on the engine.

SERVICE

1. If a broken spring on the regulator valve is suspected, remove the filter, valve, and spring from the engine. Replace the spring with a new one.

2. If the oil sensor is bad, replace with a new one. This can be done by unscrewing the oil sensor from its location on the main oil gallery. Make sure the electrical or mechanical connections have been removed before removing the oil pressure sensor.

3. If the main and connecting rod bearings are suspected, the engine must be disassembled. To check the clearance

on the main and connecting rod bearings, use Plastigage. Refer to Chapter 9 for the correct procedure.

PROBLEM: Oil Leaks

The engine has developed small oil leaks.

DIAGNOSIS

Oil leaks occur through the engine. When working on the lubrication system, visually check for leaks at these possible trouble spots:

1. The oil plug, which might be stripped or loose. See *Figure 11–29*.

2. The gaskets around the valve covers.

3. All of the bolts that come into contact with the crankcase. Oil can leak around the threads of the bolts. These bolts should have copper, felt, or other sealing washers to stop leaks. These are more common on older engines.

4. The front or rear main seals on the crankshaft.

5. The filter, which might be loose or sealed incorrectly. See *Figure 11–30*.

SERVICE

The type of service will depend upon the exact location of the leak.

FIGURE 11–30. When looking for leaks, check the oil filter gasket for correct sealing. If the filter is leaking, the gasket should be somewhat irregular or should show where it was misaligned to cause the leak.

1. If the oil plug is stripped, a self-tapping oil plug can be installed to help seal this area.

2. If the gaskets on the valve covers are leaking, these covers will need to be removed and replaced with new gaskets.

3. If bolts are contacting the crankcase area and are leaking, thread sealers can be used to help seal the bolts (see Chapter 3).

4. If the rear or front main seals are leaking, they must be replaced. Follow the manufacturer's recommended procedure to replace the crankshaft seals.

5. Check the oil filter for correct installation. Make sure the oil filter was not cross-threaded during installation. If it was, remove the oil filter and replace it with a new one. Oil filters can be removed easily, using the oil filter wrenches shown in *Figure 11–31*.

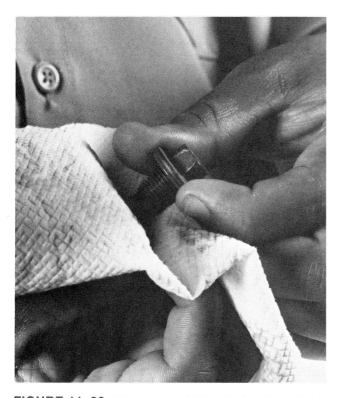

FIGURE 11–29. Always check the oil plug threads for damage before installation. If damaged, replace the plug to eliminate oil leaks.

FIGURE 11–31. Oil filter wrenches such as these are used to remove oil filters from the engine. *(Courtesy of Owatonna Tool Company)*

PROBLEM: Excessive Oil Consumption

The engine uses a lot of oil.

DIAGNOSIS

Oil consumption in the engine can be caused by several internal conditions:

1. Oil can be consumed because the valve guides are worn. Oil then seeps down into the intake valve and is burned in combustion. A bluish exhaust smoke indicates that oil is being burned.

2. Oil can be consumed because the oil control rings are worn. When rings are worn, the oil is not scraped completely from the cylinder walls. This oil is then burned in the combustion chamber and exhausted. Again, a bluish exhaust is evidence of oil burning in the combustion chamber.

3. To determine if the oil consumption is from the exhaust valves or from the rings, perform a compression leak-down test as described in Chapter 9.

Condition	Possible Cause	Correction
EXTERNAL OIL LEAKS	(1) Fuel pump gasket broken or improperly seated.	(1) Replace gasket.
	(2) Cylinder head cover RTV sealant broken or improperly seated.	(2) Replace sealant; inspect cylinder head cover sealant flange and cylinder head sealant surface for distortion and cracks.
	(3) Oil filler cap leaking or missing.	(3) Replace cap.
	(4) Oil filter gasket broken or improperly seated.	(4) Replace oil filter.
	(5) Oil pan side gasket broken, improperly seated or opening in RTV sealant.	(5) Replace gasket or repair opening in sealant; inspect oil pan gasket flange for distortion.
	(6) Oil pan front oil seal broken or improperly seated.	(6) Replace seal; inspect timing case cover and oil pan seal flange for distortion.
	(7) Oil pan rear oil seal broken or improperly seated.	(7) Replace seal; inspect oil pan rear oil seal flange; inspect rear main bearing cap for cracks, plugged oil return channels, or distortion in seal groove.
	(8) Timing case cover oil seal broken or improperly seated.	(8) Replace seal.
	(9) Excess oil pressure because of restricted PCV valve.	(9) Replace PCV valve.
	(10) Oil pan drain plug loose or has stripped threads.	(10) Repair as necessary and tighten.
	(11) Rear oil gallery plug loose.	(11) Use appropriate sealant on gallery plug and tighten.
	(12) Rear camshaft plug loose or improperly seated.	(12) Seat camshaft plug or replace and seal, as necessary.
	(13) Distributor Base Gasket damaged.	(13) Replace Gasket.

FIGURE 11–32. This troubleshooting chart shows many of the common problems, possible causes, and corrections for trouble in the lubricating system. *(Courtesy of Motor Publications, Auto Repair Manual)*

SERVICE

1. If the valve guides are leaking oil, the cylinder head must be rebuilt. Follow the manufacturer's recommended procedure to rebuild the cylinder head.

2. If the oil control rings are bad, the rings must be replaced. Follow the manufacturer's recommended procedure to replace the piston rings.

PROBLEM: Using Synthetic Oil

An engine has been using synthetic oil, and oil consumption has increased.

Refer to *Figure 11–32* for a listing of various lubrication system problems using both synthetic and regular oils.

DIAGNOSIS

Keep the following rules in mind when using synthetic oils.

1. Never use a synthetic oil in an old engine that has an excess amount of wear on the rings.

2. Never mix synthetic oils.

3. Never use synthetic oils for break-in periods.

Condition	Possible Cause	Correction
EXCESSIVE OIL CONSUMPTION	(1) Oil level too high.	(1) Drain oil to specified level.
	(2) Oil with wrong viscosity being used.	(2) Replace with specified oil.
	(3) PCV valve stuck closed.	(3) Replace PCV valve.
	(4) Valve stem oil deflectors (or seals) are damaged, missing, or incorrect type.	(4) Replace valve stem oil deflectors.
	(5) Valve stems or valve guides worn.	(5) Measure stem-to-guide clearance and repair as necessary.
	(6) Poorly fitted or missing valve cover baffles.	(6) Replace valve cover.
	(7) Piston rings broken or missing.	(7) Replace broken or missing rings.
	(8) Scuffed piston.	(8) Replace piston.
	(9) Incorrect piston ring gap.	(9) Measure ring gap, repair as necessary.
	(10) Piston rings sticking or excessively loose in grooves.	(10) Measure ring side clearance, repair as necessary.
	(11) Compression rings installed upside down.	(11) Repair as necessary.
	(12) Cylinder walls worn, scored, or glazed.	(12) Repair as necessary.
	(13) Piston ring gaps not properly staggered.	(13) Repair as necessary.
	(14) Excessive main or connecting rod bearing clearance.	(14) Measure bearing clearance, repair as necessary.

FIGURE 11–32. (CONTINUED)

Condition	Possible Cause	Correction
NO OIL PRESSURE	(1) Low oil level.	(1) Add oil to correct level.
	(2) Oil pressure gauge, warning lamp or sending unit inaccurate.	(2) Inspect and replace as necessary.
	(3) Oil pump malfunction.	(3) Repair or replace oil pump.
	(4) Oil pressure relief valve sticking.	(4) Remove and inspect oil pressure relief valve assembly.
	(5) Oil passages on pressure side of pump obstructed.	(5) Inspect oil passages for obstructions.
	(6) Oil pickup screen or tube obstructed.	(6) Inspect oil pickup for obstructions.
	(7) Loose oil inlet tube.	(7) Tighten or seal inlet tube.
LOW OIL PRESSURE	(1) Low oil level.	(1) Add oil to correct level.
	(2) Inaccurate gauge, warning lamp or sending unit.	(2) Inspect and replace as necessary.
	(3) Oil excessively thin because of dilution, poor quality, or improper grade.	(3) Drain and refill crankcase with recommended oil.
	(4) Excessive oil temperature.	(4) Correct cause of overheating engine.
	(5) Oil pressure relief spring weak or sticking.	(5) Remove and inspect oil pressure relief valve assembly.
	(6) Oil inlet tube and screen assembly has restriction or air leak.	(6) Remove and inspect oil inlet tube and screen assembly. (Fill inlet tube with lacquer thinner to locate leaks.)
	(7) Excessive oil pump clearance.	(7) Inspect and replace as necessary.
	(8) Excessive main, rod, or camshaft bearing clearance.	(8) Measure bearing clearances, repair as necessary.
HIGH OIL PRESSURE	(1) Improper oil viscosity.	(1) Drain and refill crankcase with correct viscosity oil.
	(2) Oil pressure gauge or sending unit inaccurate.	(2) Inspect and replace as necessary.
	(3) Oil pressure relief valve sticking closed.	(3) Remove and inspect oil pressure relief valve assembly.

FIGURE 11–32. (CONTINUED)

SERVICE

If there is excessive consumption when synthetic oils are used, remove the synthetic oil and replace with the correct SAE and API ratings.

Identify the condition on the left side of the chart in Figure 11–32. Then move to the right to see possible causes and the correction.

SERVICE MANUAL CONNECTION

There are many important specifications to keep in mind when working with the lubricating system. To identify the specifications for your engine, you will need to know the VIN (vehicle identification number) of the vehicle, the type and year of the vehicle, and the type of engine. Although they may be titled differently, some of the more common lubricating specifications (not all) found in service manuals are listed below. Note that these specifications are typical examples. Each vehicle and engine will have different specifications.

Common Specification	Typical Example
Engine oil refill	4 quarts (add one quart with filter change)
Normal oil pressure	30–80 lb
Oil pump gear backlash	0.005–0.009 in.
Oil pump gear endplay	0.001–0.004 in.
Oil pump cover screws torque	105 in.-lb
Ring end gap (oil control ring)	.15 in.

In addition, the service manual will give specific directions for various service procedures. Some of the more common procedures include:

- Crankshaft rear oil seal, replace
- Oil pan, replace
- Oil pump, replace

SUMMARY

The lubrication system on both gas and diesel engines is designed to cool, clean, lubricate, and seal the internal parts of the engine. Oil is cooled in the oil pan. As the oil passes through the filter, it is cleaned. Oil must lubricate the many parts of the engine. Oil must also act as a seal around the compression rings.

Gasoline and diesel engines have many contaminants that must be removed. These include road dust and dirt, carbon and fuel soot from combustion, water from water vapor and the cooling system, fuel, and oil oxidation. All contaminants reduce the oil's ability to cool, clean, seal, and lubricate. The oil oxidation process also produces acids in the oil. These acids produce corrosion and damage the engine.

Because of these contaminants, oil must be designed with various characteristics. Viscosity is defined as the thickness of the oil. As temperatures change, the oil viscosity also changes. The viscosity index is a measure of how much the oil viscosity changes with temperature. Pour point is a measure of the temperature at which the oil is too thick to pour. Detergents and dispersants are added to oil to help with the cleaning process. Other chemicals such as antifoaming additives, corrosion and rust inhibitors, antiscuff additives, and extreme-pressure resistance additives are included to improve the quality of the oil during operation.

The SAE (Society of Automotive Engineers) classifies oil according to its thickness or viscosity. API (American Petroleum Institute) rates oil according to the type of service it is used in. The military also rates certain oils for use in specific applications.

The use of synthetic lubricants is increasing. Various chemicals are combined to make synthetic lubricants, which are very stable. Synthetic lubricants have many advantages and disadvantages. These must be studied before deciding to use a synthetic lubricant.

The lubricating system has many parts. Oil is held in an oil pan. This is called the sump. After being pressurized by a gear-type oil pump, the oil passes under pressure to the oil filter. From the oil filter, it is sent into the main oil gallery, which feeds the remaining parts of the engine.

The oil pump is a positive displacement pump that increases pressure with RPM. Several types of pumps are used, including the eccentric gear-type pump. As the pump turns, a suction is created on one side, while a pressure is produced on the other side. The pressure from the oil pump is controlled by the oil pressure regulator. When the oil pressure is greater than the spring pressure of the regulator, oil is returned to the suction side of the pump.

Two types of filters are used on lubricating systems: the full-flow and bypass filter systems. Depending on the engine, either one or both may be used. There are also two types of filters. The surface filter catches the dirt particles as the oil flows through the paper. The depth filter uses cotton and other fibers to catch the dirt particles within the filter.

Oil coolers are used on some engines for cooling the oil. During operation, the oil passes on one side of a series of baffles. Engine coolant passes on the other side. The heat from the lubricating oil is transferred to the cooling system and removed through the radiator.

Oil sensors and gauges are used to monitor the oil pressure being produced within the lubricating system. Electric sensors and gauges sense the pressure in the main oil gallery. On the basis of this pressure, either a gauge or an oil light is used. Other mechanical gauges are used as well. A Bourdon gauge straightens as the pressure increases. This motion is then read on a scale, indicating the correct oil pressure within the engine.

Linkage to Environment

USED MOTOR OIL

Used motor oil contains pollutants, including organic chemicals and metals. When disposed of improperly—in the trash, on the ground, or in a sewer system—the pollutants may reach lakes, rivers, or the ground water. Also, disposing of motor oil in the trash, on the ground, or spreading the oil on roads, is illegal in many states.

Between 5 and 10 million gallons of used motor oil are disposed of improperly each year in any one state. On a national level, the estimate is about 400 million gallons each year. This is the equivalent of 35 Exxon Valdez oil spills!

Recycled oil can be a valuable source of energy. Recycled motor oil can be burned as an industrial fuel or cleaned and reused. All places that sell motor oil in many states must collect used motor oil or post a sign indicating the nearest place that accepts oil. Check the sign where you buy your oil. Many communities and counties provide collection tanks for used oil. Some full-service stations accept used motor oil, often without cost to the consumer.

To recycle your oil, pour the used motor oil into a container. A plastic milk jug with a cap works well. Seal the container, label it, and take it to a used motor oil collection center. Transmission and brake fluids are similar to motor oil and can be mixed with the oil for recycling. However, *never* mix solvents, gasoline, or antifreeze with the used oil. Once the oil has been contaminated with these products, it is difficult or impossible to recycle.

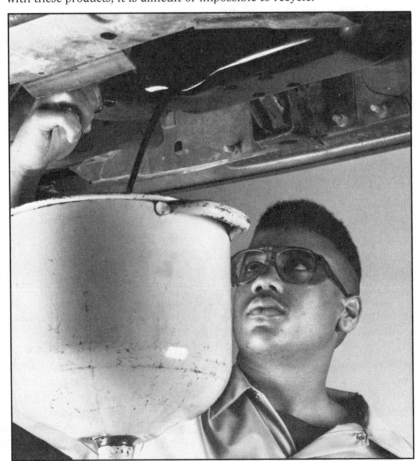

TERMS TO KNOW

Can you explain each of the following terms? Review the chapter until you can use each term correctly.

Friction

Contaminants

Sludge

Dilution

Oxidation

Acidity

Catalyst

Organic

Varnish

Viscosity

Fluidity

Corrosion

Saybolt Universal
    Viscosimeter

Viscosity index

Pour point

Inhibitor

Detergent

Suspendability

Dispersant

Society of Automotive
    Engineers (SAE)

American Petroleum
    Institute (API)

Synthetic

National Lubricating
    Grease Institute (NLGI)

Extreme pressure (EP)

Sump

Eccentric

Differential pressure

REVIEW QUESTIONS

Multiple Choice

1. An engine lubricating system is designed to:
   a. Cool the engine
   b. Clean and seal the engine
   c. Lubricate the engine
   d. All of the above
   e. None of the above

2. Which of the following is not an oil contaminant in an engine?
   a. Road dust
   b. Carbon from combustion
   c. Wheel bearing grease
   d. Oil oxidation
   e. Road dirt

3. The viscosity of oil will _____ as fuel enters the oil.
   a. Increase
   b. Decrease
   c. Remain the same
   d. Heat up
   e. Thicken

4. Acids _____ in an engine's lubricating system.
   a. Cannot be produced
   b. Can be produced
   c. Form from the bearing noise
   d. Form from vibration
   e. None of the above

5. Viscosity is defined as the _____ of oil.
   a. Acidity
   b. Pour point
   c. Oxidation
   d. Thickness
   e. Temperature

6. At what temperatures are oils normally tested for viscosity?
   a. 0 and 100 degrees F
   b. 0, 150, and 210 degrees F
   c. 210 degrees F only
   d. 80 and 100 degrees F
   e. 1,000 to 1,005 degrees F

7. Chemicals added to oil to keep small particles of dirt separated from each other are called:
   a. Detergents
   b. Dispersants
   c. Viscosity index improvers
   d. Filters
   e. Acids

8. Which organization classifies oil by its viscosity?
   a. American Petroleum Institute
   b. Military
   c. Society of Automotive Engineers
   d. All of the above
   e. None of the above

9. An oil with a 10W30 label means the oil has a/an _____ at 0 degrees.
   a. API 30 rating
   b. SAE rating of 10
   c. SAE rating of 30
   d. API CD rating
   e. API SD rating

10. When an oil is manufactured by combining specific molecules into an end product, the oil is said to be:
   a. Synthetic
   b. Oxidized
   c. High in viscosity
   d. Low in viscosity
   e. High in acidity

11. Which type of oil pump has two gears that have different center points?
   a. All oil pumps
   b. Eccentric oil pumps
   c. Differential pressure pumps
   d. Centrifugal
   e. None of the above

12. Which type of filter forces only a small portion of the oil through the filter?
   a. Full-flow filter
   b. By-pass filter
   c. Differential pressure filter
   d. Easy-flow filter
   e. None of the above

13. Which device controls the pressure of the oil directly from the oil pump?
    a. Oil relief valve
    b. Oil regulator valve
    c. Oil screen
    d. Oil pump
    e. Oil pan

14. The difference between the input pressure of the oil filter and the output pressure of the filter is called:
    a. Pressure equalness
    b. Filter difference
    c. Pressure differential
    d. Input vs. output pressure
    e. None of the above

15. Which type of filter catches the dirt and dust particles on the outside of the filter surface?
    a. Depth filter
    b. Round filter
    c. By-pass filter
    d. Surface filter
    e. None of the above

16. The oil cooler takes heat from the oil and transfers it to the _____.
    a. Cooling system
    b. Engine block
    c. Oil sump
    d. All of the above
    e. None of the above

17. Which type of oil gauge straightens a curved tube as the oil pressure increases?
    a. Electric oil gauge
    b. Bourdon gauge
    c. By-pass filter gauge
    d. Curved-tube gauge
    e. Low-pressure differential gauge

18. If the oil pressure drops suddenly, the problem may be the:
    a. Oil crankshaft
    b. Oil regulator valve
    c. Oil pan
    d. Oil passages
    e. Oil seals

19. There iFs no problem when using a full-flow filter for a by-pass filter, or a by-pass filter for a full-flow filter.
    a. False, the two should never be mixed
    b. True, it is OK to interchange the filters
    c. True, but always use a clean filter if they are changed
    d. False, the two can be mixed only after 5,000 miles
    e. False, the two can only be mixed after 10,000 miles

The following questions are similar in format to ASE (Automotive Service Excellence) test questions.

20. A car must be put away for four months for storage. Technician A says the oil should be changed before storage because of acid buildup in the oil. Technician B says keep the old oil in the engine and then change it after the car is taken out of storage. Who is right?
    a. A only
    b. B only
    c. Both A and B
    d. Neither A nor B

21. Fuel has been found in the oil. Technician A says it could be because of too rich a carburetor mixture. Technician B says it could be caused by a bad diaphragm in the mechanical fuel pump. Who is right?
    a. A only
    b. B only
    c. Both A and B
    d. Neither A nor B

22. Technician A says excessive oil consumption can be caused by bad rings. Technician B says excessive oil consumption is caused by bad valve guides. Who is right?
    a. A only
    b. B only
    c. Both A and B
    d. Neither A nor B

23. Oil pressure in a car with enough oil in the engine has dropped. Technician A says the first thing to check is the oil sensor. Technician B says the oil pump is bad and should be replaced immediately. Who is right?
    a. A only
    b. B only
    c. Both A and B
    d. Neither A nor B

24. Technician A says that when the oil gets to be light brown or whitish, fuel is in the oil. Technician B says that whitish oil causes increased oil consumption. Who is right?
    a. A only
    b. B only
    c. Both A and B
    d. Neither A nor B

25. Technician A says that greases that have a higher grade such as 4, 5, or 6, are thinner. Technician B says that 4, 5, and 6 grade greases have poorer lubrication quality. Who is right?
    a. A only
    b. B only
    c. Both A and B
    d. Neither A nor B

26. Technician A says that synthetic oil should never be used as a break-in oil. Technician B says that synthetic oil should never be used in an old engine. Who is right?
    a. A only
    b. B only
    c. Both A and B
    d. Neither A nor B

27. Technician A says that high oil consumption can be caused by a poorly adjusted carburetor. Technician B says that high oil consumption can be caused by having bad main bearings. Who is right?
    a. A only
    b. B only
    c. Both A and B
    d. Neither A nor B

Essay

28. What four things must an oil lubricant do in an engine?

29. List at least three contaminants that can make the oil dirty.

30. How can fuel contaminate oil?

31. What is oil oxidation, and what are the results of oil oxidation?

32. Define two methods used to classify oil.

33. What is an oil dispersant?

34. List three advantages and three disadvantages of using a synthetic oil.

35. What is the difference between a by-pass filter and a full-flow filter?

Short Answer

36. When hydrocarbons combine with oxygen in the oil, the process is called _____.

37. When oil has gasoline mixed with it, the oil pressure has a tendency to _____.

38. Newer vehicles normally should have the oil changed approximately every _____ miles.

39. When oil sits in the engine for a long period of time, the oil has a tendency to build up _____.

40. Two common problems that cause the oil pressure to drop are a damaged _____ and _____.

CHAPTER 12

Cooling Systems

INTRODUCTION   The cooling system is one of the more important systems on the automotive engine. If the cooling system is not operating correctly, the engine may be severely damaged. To understand the cooling system, it is important to study coolant characteristics. The various parts of the cooling system, including the water pump, thermostats, radiators, hoses, pressure caps, fans, and temperature indicators must also be studied.

OBJECTIVES   After reading this chapter, you should be able to:

- Identify the purposes of the cooling system.
- Compare the ways in which heat can be transferred.
- Compare the different types of cooling systems.
- Define the characteristics of coolant and antifreeze.
- Define the proper procedure to dispose of antifreeze.
- Describe the operation of water pumps.

- State the purpose and operation of thermostats and pressure caps.
- Describe the operation of expansion tanks.
- State the purpose and operation of radiators.
- Compare the operation and design of fans, shrouds, and belts.
- Describe the operation of electrical circuits used to control the cooling system.
- Identify various problem, diagnosis and service procedures on the cooling system.

 SAFETY CHECKLIST

When working with cooling systems, keep these important safety precautions in mind.

✔ Never remove the pressure cap when the engine is hot.

✔ Be careful not to touch the hot parts of the engine.

✔ Always dispose of used antifreeze in an approved container. Never pour used antifreeze down the water drain in a building.

✔ When the engine is running, always keep your hands and tools away from the moving belts and spinning fan.

12.1   PRINCIPLES OF THE COOLING SYSTEM

Purpose of the Cooling System

The purpose of the cooling system is to do three things. The first is to maintain the highest and most efficient operating temperature within the engine. The second is to remove excess heat from the engine. The third is to bring the engine up to operating temperature as quickly as possible. If the engine is not at the highest operating temperature, it will not run efficiently. Fuel mileage will decrease, and wear on the engine components will increase.

In heavy-duty driving, an engine could theoretically produce enough heat to melt an average 200-pound engine block in 20 minutes. Even in normal driving conditions, combustion gas temperatures may be as high as 4,500 degrees F. Lubricated parts such as pistons may even run 200 degrees F or more above the boiling point of water (212 degrees F).

Heat Removal

Within the gasoline or diesel engine, energy from the fuel is converted to power for moving the vehicle. Not all of the energy, however, is converted to power. Referring to *Figure 12–1*, of the energy going into the engine, about 25% is used to push the vehicle. About 9% of the heat generated by the fuel is lost through radiation, and 33% is sent out through the exhaust system. The remaining 33% must be removed by the cooling system. If this is done correctly, the temperature of the engine will be at its highest efficiency.

If the engine temperature is too high, various problems will occur. These include:

1. *Overheating of lubricating oil.* This will result in the lubricating oil breaking down.

2. *Overheating of the parts.* This may cause loss of strength of the metal.

3. *Excessive stresses between engine parts.* This may cause increases in friction, which may cause excessive wear.

If the engine temperature is too low, various problems will occur. These include:

1. *Poorer fuel mileage.* The combustion process will be less efficient.

2. *Increases in carbon buildup.* As the fuel enters the engine, it will condense and cause excessive buildup on the intake valves.

3. *Increases in varnish and sludges within the lubrication system.* Cooler engines enhance the buildup of sludges and varnishes.

4. *Loss of power.* If the combustion process is less efficient, the power output will be reduced.

5. *Incomplete burning of fuel.* This will cause fuel to dilute the oil and cause excessive engine wear.

Heat Transfer

The cooling system works on the principles of *heat transfer*. Heat will always travel from a hotter to a cooler object. Heat transfers in three ways: conduction, convection, and radiation. *Conduction* is defined as transfer of heat between

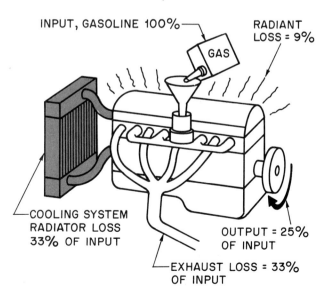

FIGURE 12–1. Approximately 33% of the heat generated by the engine must be removed by the cooling system. *(Courtesy of DCA Educational Products)*

two solid objects. For example, in *Figure 12–2*, heat must be transferred from the valve stem to the valve guide. Since both objects are solid, heat is transferred from the hotter valve stem to the cooler valve guide by conduction. Heat is also transferred from the valve guide to the cylinder head by conduction.

Heat can be transferred by *convection*. Convection is defined as the transfer of heat by the circulation of heated parts of a liquid or gas. The hot cylinder block transfers heat to the coolant by convection. Convection also occurs when the hot radiator parts transfer heat to the cooler air surrounding the radiator.

Radiation is another way that heat is transferred. Radiation is defined as the transfer of heat by converting heat energy to radiant energy. Any hot object will give off radiation. The hotter the object, the greater the amount of radiant energy. When the engine is hot, some of the heat is converted to radiation (about 9% in Figure 12–1). The cooling system relies on these principles to remove the excess heat within an engine.

12.2   TYPES OF COOLING SYSTEMS

Engine manufacturers commonly use two types of cooling systems. These are the air-cooled and liquid-cooled systems.

Air-cooled Engines

Several manufacturers have designed engines that are *air-cooled*. Certain foreign manufacturers still use air-cooled engines. Air-cooled engines have fins or ribs on the outer surfaces of the cylinders and cylinder heads. These fins are cast directly into the cylinders and heads. The fins increase the surface area of the object which, in turn, increases the amount of convection and radiation available for heat transfer. The heat produced by combustion transfers from the internal parts of the engine by conduction to the outer fins. Here the

heat is dissipated to the passing air. In some cases, individual cylinders are used to increase air circulation around the cylinders.

Air-cooled engines require air circulation around the cylinder block and heads. Some sort of fan is usually used to move the air across the engine. A shroud is also used in some cases to direct or control the flow of air across the engine. Air-cooled engines usually do not have exact control over engine temperature; however, they do not use a radiator and water pump. This may reduce maintenance on the engine over a long period of time.

Liquid-cooled Engines

In a *liquid-cooled* engine, the heat from the cylinders is transferred to a liquid flowing through jackets surrounding the cylinders. The liquid then passes through a radiator. Air passing through the radiator removes the heat from the liquid to the air. Liquid-cooling systems usually have better temperature control than air-cooled engines. They are designed to maintain a coolant temperature of 180–205 degrees F.

Liquid Coolant Flow

Figure 12–3 shows the parts of a liquid-cooling system. When the vehicle is started, the coolant pump begins circulating the coolant. The coolant goes through the cylinder block from the front to the rear. The coolant circulates around the cylinders as it passes through the cylinder block.

The coolant then passes up into the cylinder head through the holes in the head gasket. From there, it moves forward to the front of the cylinder head through internal passages. These passages permit cooling of high-heat areas such as the spark plug and exhaust valve areas.

As the coolant leaves the cylinder head, it passes through a thermostat on the way to the radiator. As long as the coolant

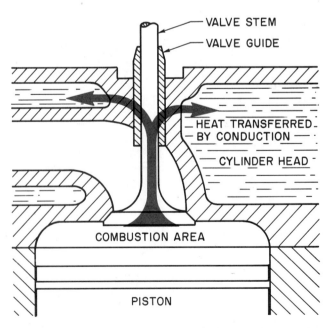

FIGURE 12–2. Heat is transferred by conduction from the valve stem to the valve guide. Both objects are solid.

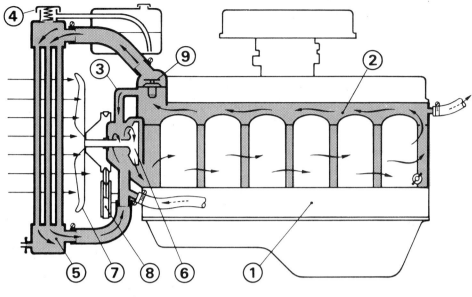

1. CYLINDER BLOCK
2. CYLINDER HEAD
3. BYPASS
4. RADIATOR PRESSURE CAP
5. RADIATOR
6. COOLANT PUMP
7. FAN
8. FAN BELT
9. THERMOSTAT

FIGURE 12–3. Coolant is pumped from the water pump, through the cylinder block and head, through the thermostat into the radiator, and back to the water (coolant) pump. *(Courtesy of First Brands Corporation)*

temperature remains low, the thermostat stays closed. Under these conditions the coolant flows through the *bypass tube* and returns to the pump for recirculation through the engine. As the coolant heats up, the thermostat gradually opens to allow enough hot coolant to pass through the radiator. This will maintain the engine's highest operating temperature.

From the thermostat, the coolant flows to the internal passages in the radiator. These are tubes in the core with small fins on them. The coolant is now being cooled by the air passing through the radiator. From there it returns to the outlet of the radiator and back to the pump. It then continues its circulation through the engine.

12.3 COOLANT CHARACTERISTICS

Antifreeze

Water has been the most commonly used engine coolant, because it has good ability to transfer heat and can be readily obtained. Water alone, however, is not suitable for today's engines for a number of reasons. Water has a freezing point of 32 degrees F. Engines must operate in colder climates. Also, water has a boiling point of 212 degrees F. Engine coolant temperature often exceeds this point. In addition, water can be very *corrosive* and produce rust within a coolant system.

To overcome these problems, *antifreeze* is added to the coolant. An ethylene-glycol-type antifreeze coolant is the most common type used. When purchased on the market, this antifreeze includes suitable corrosion inhibitors. The best percentage of antifreeze to water to use is about 50% antifreeze mixed with 50% water.

CAR CLINIC

PROBLEM: Hot Engine

A car with 45,000 miles on it seems to be overheating. There is a "hot" light on the dashboard. On the highway at 55 mph, the light goes on and then off. Does this mean the engine is very hot? The engine doesn't seem to lose power, and coolant never has to be added.

SOLUTION:

The first and easiest component to replace is the coolant temperature sensor. At times, these coolant sensors will operate incorrectly. Although the sensor is reading "too hot," the engine may be at the correct temperature. Replace the coolant sensor to eliminate the problem.

Antifreeze as a Hazardous Waste Product

Antifreeze is considered a *hazardous waste* product. That is, it is harmful to people and to the environment. Therefore, it must be disposed of according to certain procedures. Antifreeze should not be allowed to enter sewer systems. Antifreeze has various heavy metals and contains contaminants that will harm the environment. The procedures and laws for disposing of antifreeze vary from state to state. In order to determine the exact procedure in your state, call the state pollution control agency. Some states have an office of waste management that might also give specific directions as to antifreeze disposal.

The best method to dispose of antifreeze is to recycle the product. Depending on the city and region, there are various private and public organizations that collect and recycle antifreeze. Some companies are recycling significant quantities of antifreeze each year.

Freezing Points

Figure 12–4 shows what happens to the freezing point of a coolant when different percentages of antifreeze are used. For example, when 100% water is used, the freezing point is 32 degrees F. When 25% antifreeze and 75% water are used, the freezing point of the coolant is about 10 degrees F. At 68% antifreeze, the freezing point of the coolant is about –92 degrees F. As the amount of antifreeze percentage increases from this point, the freezing point goes back toward 0 degrees F.

Boiling Points

The addition of antifreeze in the cooling system increases the boiling point. The *boiling point* of a fluid is the temperature at which a liquid becomes a vapor. Any coolant that becomes a vapor has very poor conduction and convection properties; therefore, it is necessary to protect it from boiling. This protection provides a greater margin of safety against engine cooling system overheating failure.

Figure 12–5 shows how boiling points increase with increases in percentages of antifreeze. For example, when there is no antifreeze, the boiling point is at 212 degrees F. When there is 50% antifreeze in the coolant, the boiling point increases to 226 degrees F. If there is 70% antifreeze, the boiling point increases to about 238 degrees F. It can be seen that antifreeze protects the coolant during both summer and winter operation.

Corrosion

Corrosion in the cooling system can be very damaging to the engine. Corrosion can be produced in several ways. *Direct attack* means the water in the coolant is mixed with oxygen from the air. This process can produce rust particles, which can damage water pump seals and cause increased leakage. *Electromechanical attack* is a result of using different metals in an engine. In the presence of the coolant, different metals may set up an electrical current in the coolant. If this occurs, one metal may deteriorate and deposit itself on the other metal. For example, a core plug may deteriorate to a point of causing leakage. *Cavitation* is defined as high shock pressure developed by collapsing vapor bubbles in the coolant. These bubbles are produced by the rapid spinning of the water pump impeller. The shock waves erode nearby metal surfaces such as the pump impeller.

Mineral deposits such as *calcium* and *silicate deposits* are produced when a hard water is used in the cooling system. Both deposits restrict the conduction of heat out of the cooling system. See *Figure 12–6*. The deposits cover the internal passages of the cooling system, causing uneven heat transfer out of the engine. See *Figure 12–7*. When an ethylene-glycol antifreeze solution is added to the coolant, many of these corrosion problems are eliminated. Chemicals are added to the antifreeze to reduce corrosion. It is usually not necessary to add any corrosion inhibitor to the cooling system. In some cases, mixing different corrosion inhibitors produces unwanted sludges within the cooling system.

Cooling System Leaks

While a full cooling system is essential, leakage ranks very high on the list of cooling system problems. There are numerous sources of leaks. Some leaks can be corrected by tightening hose clamps, but a large percentage of leaks are from small pinholes. These are commonly found in the radiator,

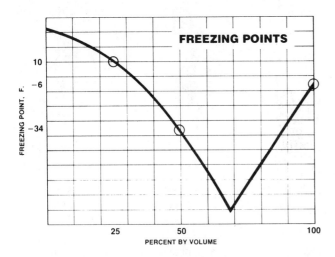

FIGURE 12–4. As the percentage of antifreeze increases, the freezing point of the solution is lowered. This is true up to the point where there is 68% antifreeze and 32% water. Beyond this point, the freezing temperature starts to increase. *(Courtesy of Chevrolet Division, General Motors Corporation)*

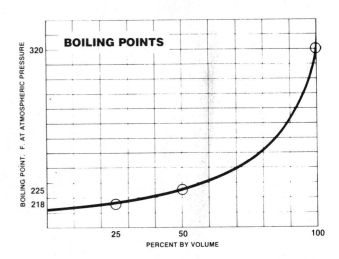

FIGURE 12–5. As antifreeze is added to the coolant, its boiling point increases. *(Courtesy of Chevrolet Division, General Motors Corporation)*

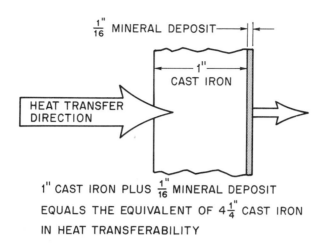

FIGURE 12–6. Mineral deposits inside the cooling system restrict the conduction of heat. Here, a 1/16-inch deposit makes the cast iron equivalent to 4 1/4 inches for heat transfer.

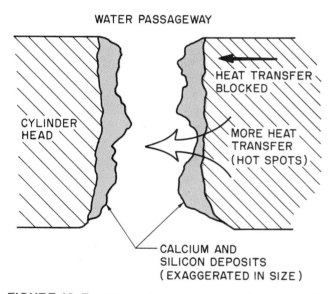

FIGURE 12–7. When minerals such as calcium and silicate build up inside the cooling system, certain areas may not transfer heat, while other areas may transfer heat more rapidly. This uneven heat transfer causes hot spots inside the engine.

CAR CLINIC

PROBLEM: Rust in the Cooling System

An engine has rust in the antifreeze. The antifreeze looks very brown, and water pump bearings keep going out. There is not an overflow tank on this vehicle. What could be the problem?

SOLUTION:

Rust in the cooling system and antifreeze is normally caused by air getting into the radiator when the engine cools. As the coolant cools, it shrinks. An overflow tank normally has sufficient coolant in it to keep the radiator full even at cold temperatures. Without an overflow tank, air will enter the cooling system through the radiator cap. The rust in the coolant also causes wear on the water pump seal and the bearings. The best solution is to purchase an overflow tank and install it on the cooling system. Keep the overflow tank filled to the mark shown on the tank.

freeze plugs, heater core, or around gaskets. To omit leaks, certain antifreezes have stop-leak protection. These products are designed to seal the common pinhole leaks. This will prevent inconvenient breakdown and costly repair bills.

12.4 COOLING SYSTEM PARTS AND OPERATION

Various parts are used to operate the cooling system correctly. These include the water pump, water jackets, thermostats, radiators, transmission coolers, pressure caps, expansion tanks, fans, shrouds, belts, and temperature indicators.

Water Pump

The purpose of the water pump is to circulate the water through the cooling system. The pump is located on the front of the engine. In most vehicles, it is driven by a belt that is attached to the crankshaft. As the crankshaft turns, the fan belt turns the pump, causing coolant to be circulated. See *Figure 12–8*.

The coolant pump is called a *centrifugal pump*. This means that as coolant is drawn into the center of the pump, centrifugal forces pressurize water and send it into the cooling system. See *Figure 12–9*. Centrifugal forces throw the coolant outward from the impeller tips. This type of pump will pump only the coolant that is required by the system. Therefore, it does not require a regulator or relief valve.

The pump consists of a housing, a bearing on a shaft, the impeller, and seal. The housing has a coolant inlet and outlet. The seal is used to keep the water inside the pump. The bearing is used to support the shaft on which the impeller rides. See *Figure 12–10*. This assembly is bolted to the cylinder block. A gasket is used to keep the coolant from leaking. On some engines, there is also a hub where a fan and pulley can be connected to the shaft. Other engines have the fan mounted directly on the radiator. In this case, the fan is operated electrically. Only the drive belt pulley is connected to the water pump shaft.

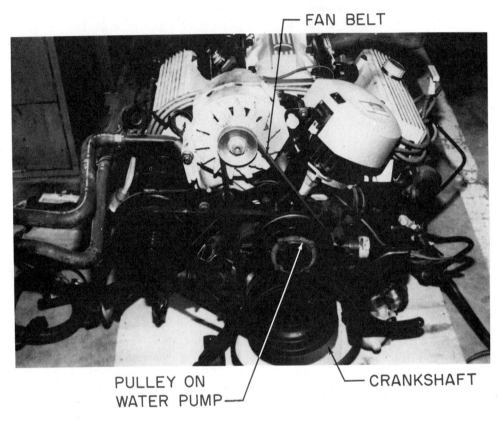

FAN BELT

PULLEY ON
WATER PUMP

CRANKSHAFT

FIGURE 12–8. The water pump is driven from the crankshaft by V belts.

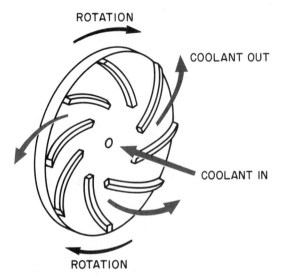

ROTATION

COOLANT OUT

COOLANT IN

ROTATION

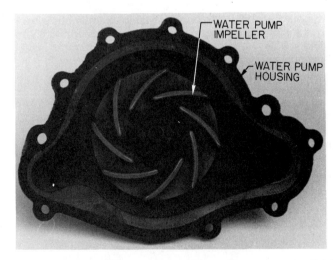

WATER PUMP
IMPELLER

WATER PUMP
HOUSING

FIGURE 12–9. A centrifugal pump takes the fluid into the center of the vanes, and centrifugal forces throw the fluid outward.

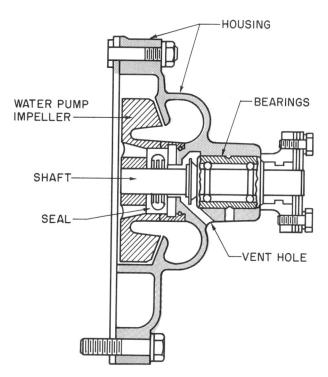

FIGURE 12–10. The water pump consists of a housing, bearings, shaft, and seals.

There is a small hole on the bottom of the water pump housing. This hole allows coolant to escape if the seal leaks. Today it is easier to simply replace the damaged water pump with a rebuilt or new pump. The old pump can then be turned in to get a "core charge" and possibly be rebuilt by a manufacturer.

Water Jackets

Water jackets are defined as the open spaces within the cylinder block and cylinder head where coolant flows. These water jackets are designed to allow coolant to flow to the right spots so that maximum cooling can be obtained. *Figure 12–11* shows internal water jackets used on an engine.

Thermostats

The thermostat is one of the most important parts of the cooling system. The purpose of the *thermostat* is to keep the engine coolant at the most efficient temperature. The thermostat is used to bring the coolant temperature up to operating temperature as quickly as possible. It is designed to sense the temperature of the coolant. If the coolant remains cold, the thermostat will be closed. See *Figure 12–12*. The coolant then goes to the by-pass tube. This allows a small amount of coolant to pass into the radiator to be cooled. The remaining coolant flows through the by-pass tube. This coolant is recirculated without being cooled. If the engine is under a heavier load, more cooling will be necessary. If the

FIGURE 12–11. Water jackets are used to allow the coolant to flow to the right spots within the engine.

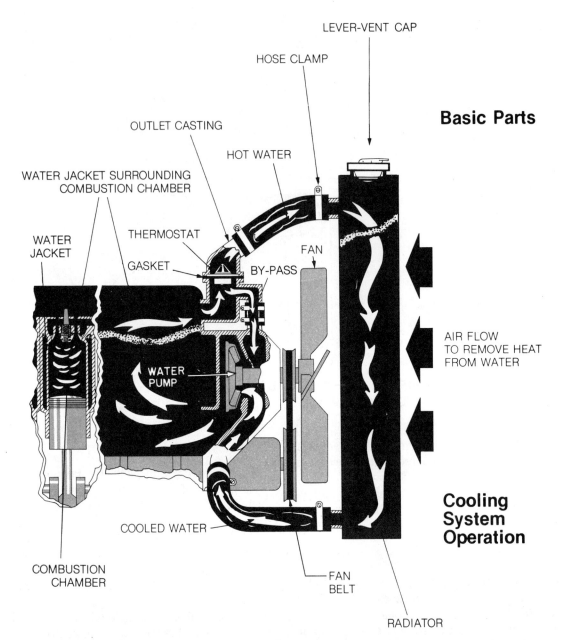

LEVER-VENT CAP

HOSE CLAMP

Basic Parts

OUTLET CASTING

HOT WATER

WATER JACKET SURROUNDING
COMBUSTION CHAMBER

WATER
JACKET

THERMOSTAT

FAN

GASKET

BY-PASS

AIR FLOW
TO REMOVE HEAT
FROM WATER

WATER
PUMP

**Cooling
System
Operation**

COOLED WATER

COMBUSTION
CHAMBER

FAN
BELT

RADIATOR

FIGURE 12–12.   The thermostat is used to open a passageway to the radiator or to force the coolant through a bypass tube. *(Courtesy of Robertshaw Controls Company)*

temperature of the coolant increases to the opening temperature, the thermostat will open slightly. As the temperature of the coolant increases further, the thermostat opens more. This allows more coolant to reduce its temperature through the radiator. When the engine is under full load, the thermostat will be fully open. The maximum amount of coolant will be sent to the radiator for cooling, and a small amount of coolant will continue to flow through the by-pass tube.

Thermostats operate on a very simple principle. A wax pellet material within the thermostat expands and causes the mechanical motion that opens the thermostat. See *Figure 12–13*. This allows coolant to pass through to the radiator. It should be noted that the thermostat is opened only partially when the temperature reaches its opening point. As the cool-

ant temperature increases, the thermostat opens further. Eventually, the coolant is hot enough to cause the thermostat to open fully to get maximum cooling.

Thermostats are designed to open at different temperatures. Common thermostat temperatures are 180 and 195 degrees. Always follow the manufacturer's recommendations for determining the correct thermostat temperature.

The thermostat is usually placed near the front of the engine so its output can go directly to the radiator. *Figure 12–14* shows how the thermostat is placed with the thermostat housing and thermostat cover. Each manufacturer uses a different shape housing and gaskets. When replacing a thermostat remember to keep the temperature-sensitive valve toward the hot side of the engine.

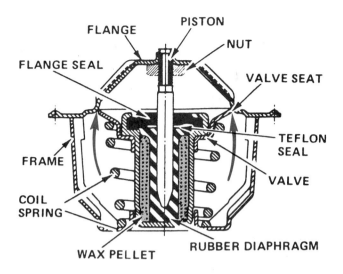

FIGURE 12–13.   As the temperature of the wax pellet increases, the coil spring and the valve lift. The valve lifts off its seat, allowing coolant to pass through the thermostat. *(Courtesy of Chevrolet Division, General Motors Corporation)*

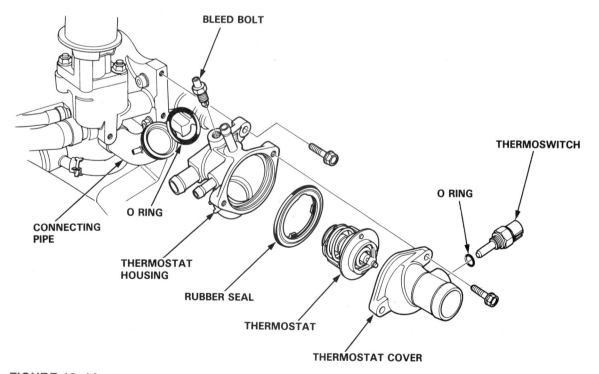

FIGURE 12–14.   The thermostat is held in place between the thermostat housing and thermostat cover. *(Courtesy of Honda Motor Company, Ltd.)*

Radiators

The purpose of the radiator is to allow fresh air to reduce the temperature of the coolant. This is done by flowing the coolant through tubes. As the coolant passes through the tubes, air is forced around the tubes. This causes a transfer of heat from the hot coolant to the cooler air. This process is called heat exchange. In this case, heat is exchanged from a liquid, the coolant, to air. This is called a liquid-to-air *heat exchanger*. *Figure 12–15* shows an internal diagram of a typical radiator. Note that the coolant flows through the tubes, and air flows through the air fins.

Down-Flow and Cross-Flow Radiators

Two types of radiators are commonly used in the automobile: the down-flow radiator and the cross-flow radiator. In the down-flow radiator, coolant flows from the top of the radiator to the bottom. In the cross-flow radiator, the coolant flows from one side of the radiator to the other side. *Figure 12–16* shows a diagram of both the down-flow radiator and the cross-flow radiator. The down-flow radiator is found on most older vehicles. Because newer vehicles are lower in front, the cross-flow radiator has been used on most vehicles manufactured after 1970. Some American and foreign manufacturers, however, still use the down-flow radiator.

Radiator Parts

Radiators are made of several parts. The fins and tubes mentioned earlier are called the *core*. The core and fins on the radiator are made of brass, copper, or aluminum or some combination of those metals. They are used because they transfer heat very rapidly. This characteristic makes the radiator much more efficient. Depending upon the size of the engine and the cooling requirements, one, two, three, or four cores can be used. There are also an inlet and an outlet tank. These tanks hold the coolant before it goes into the radiator or into the block. The inlet tank also has a hose connection to allow coolant to flow from the engine into the radiator. The outlet tank has a hose connection to allow coolant to pass back to the engine. In addition, there is a filler neck attached to one of the tanks. The radiator pressure cap is placed here. *Figure 12–17* shows the common parts of the radiator.

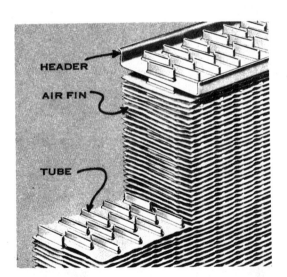

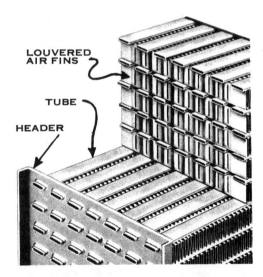

FIGURE 12–15. Inside the radiator there are small tubes through which the coolant flows. The air fins help remove the heat into the air. *(Courtesy of Harrison Radiator Division of General Motors Corporation)*

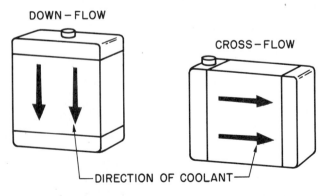

FIGURE 12–16. The down-flow radiator moves the coolant from the top to the bottom. The cross-flow radiator moves coolant from one side to the other.

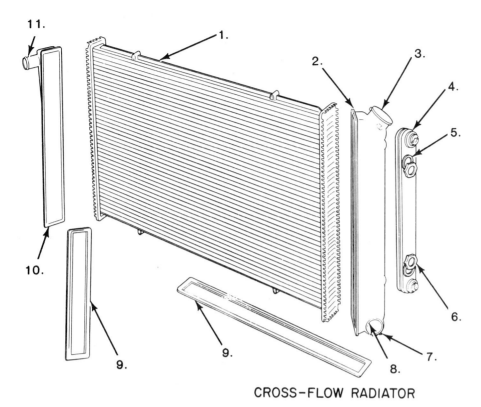

1. RADIATOR CORE ASSEMBLY
2. OUTLET TANK
3. FILLER NECK
4. TRANSMISSION OIL COOLER
5. OIL COOLER GASKETS
6. OIL COOLER ATTACHING NUTS
7. DRAIN COCK
8. OUTLET PIPE
9. GASKETS
10. INLET TANK
11. INLET PIPE

CROSS-FLOW RADIATOR

FIGURE 12–17. The parts of a standard radiator. *(Courtesy of Chevrolet Motor Division, General Motors Corporation)*

Transmission Coolers

Cars that have automatic transmissions must have some means of cooling the transmission fluid. If the transmission fluid gets too hot, the transmission may be severely damaged. Transmission fluid is cooled by passing the fluid out of the transmission, into a tube inside the radiator outlet tank, then back to the transmission. The liquid in the radiator is cool enough to lower the temperature of the transmission fluid. This heat transfer is done by using a liquid- (transmission fluid) to-liquid (engine coolant) heat exchanger. See *Figure 12–18.*

Pressure Caps

Pressure caps are placed on the radiator to do several things. They are designed to:

1. Increase the pressure on the cooling system

2. Reduce cavitation

3. Protect the radiator hoses

4. Prevent or reduce surging

It is very important to maintain a constant *pressure* on

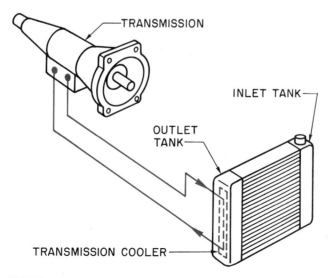

TRANSMISSION

INLET TANK

OUTLET TANK

TRANSMISSION COOLER

FIGURE 12–18. Fluid from the automatic transmission is sent through metal tubes to the radiator to be cooled.

the cooling system. The pressure should be near 15 pounds per square inch. Pressure caps are placed on the radiator to maintain the correct pressure on the cooling system.

Pressure on the cooling system changes the boiling point. As pressure is increased, the boiling point of the coolant also increases. This is shown in *Figure 12–19*. The bottom axis shows pressure. The left vertical axis shows the boiling point. Different solutions of antifreeze are also shown. For example, using water, the boiling point at 0 *psig* (pounds per square inch, on a gauge) is 212 degrees F. If the pressure is increased to 15 psig, the boiling point increases to about 250 degrees F.

Figure 12–20 shows how a pressure cap maintains the constant pressure. As the coolant increases in temperature, it begins to expand. As it expands, the coolant cannot escape. The spring holds a rubber washer against the filler neck. This keeps the fluid in the cooling system and increases the pressure. When the pressure reaches 15 psig, the rubber seal is lifted off the filler neck against spring pressure. The coolant then passes through the pressure cap to a tube that is connected to a recovery bottle. This type of system is called a closed system. An open system allows the coolant to pass through the pressure cap directly to the road surface.

The pressure cap also protects the hoses from expanding and collapsing. When the engine is shut down, the coolant starts to cool. As it cools, the coolant shrinks. Eventually, a *vacuum* is created in the cooling system. This means that

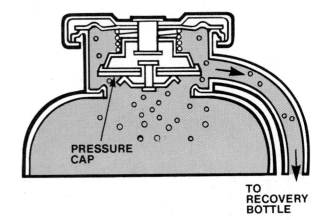

FIGURE 12–20. As the pressure increases on the cooling system, the large spring will eventually be lifted off its seat. This action releases any pressure over 15 pounds per square inch. *(Courtesy of Chevrolet Division, General Motors Corporation)*

the pressure outside the radiator is greater than the pressure inside the radiator. This difference in pressure causes the hoses to collapse. Continued expanding and collapsing of the hoses cause them to crack and eventually leak. The pressure cap has a vacuum valve that allows atmospheric pressure to seep into the cooling system when there is a slight vacuum.

During operation, a small spring holds the vacuum valve closed. When there is a vacuum inside the cooling system, the vacuum valve is pulled down and opened. The vacuum is then reduced within the cooling system. See *Figure 12–21*.

Increasing the pressure also reduces cavitation. *Cavitation* is the production of small vacuum bubbles by the water pump action. Increased pressure reduces this action.

Pressure on the cooling system also reduces *surging*. Surging is defined as a sudden rush of water from the water pump. This could be caused by rapidly increasing the RPM of the engine. Surging can produce air bubbles and agitation of the coolant. Pressure on the cooling system tends to reduce this action.

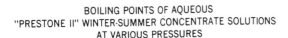
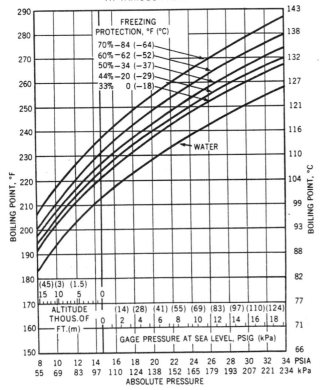

BOILING POINTS OF AQUEOUS
"PRESTONE II" WINTER-SUMMER CONCENTRATE SOLUTIONS
AT VARIOUS PRESSURES

FIGURE 12–19. As the pressure is increased on the cooling system, the boiling point also increases. *(Courtesy of First Brands Corporation)*

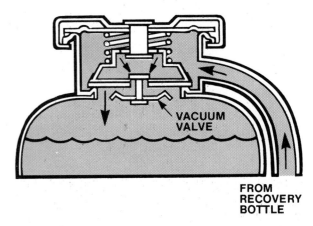

FIGURE 12–21. When the cooling system cools down, a vacuum is produced in the system. The vacuum spring is opened, and the system equalizes the pressure. *(Courtesy of Chevrolet Division, General Motors Corporation)*

Expansion Tank (Closed System)

Many cooling systems use an expansion or recovery tank. Cooling systems with expansion tanks are also called closed-cooling systems. They are designed to hold any coolant that passes through the pressure cap when the engine is hot. *Figure 12–22* shows a typical expansion tank.

As the engine warms up, the coolant expands. This expansion eventually causes the pressure cap to release. The coolant that normally passes to the atmosphere is now sent to an expansion tank. When the engine is shut down, the coolant begins to shrink. Eventually, the vacuum spring inside the pressure cap opens. When this happens, the coolant from the expansion tank is drawn back into the cooling system. (On open systems without an expansion tank, air is drawn into the cooling system.) The major advantage of using this system is that air never gets into the cooling system. Air in the cooling system can cause rust and corrosion, which can damage the cooling system components.

Coolant is added to the expansion tank. There is a small plastic cap on the expansion tank that can be removed. See *Figure 12–23*. Coolant can be added when the engine is hot because the pressure cap does not have to be removed to add the coolant.

Fan Designs

The purpose of the fan is to draw air through the radiator for cooling during low-speed and idle operation. A fan is not needed at faster speeds because air is pushed through the radiator by the vehicle speed. On older vehicles, the fan was driven on the same shaft as the water pump. A belt was used to turn the water pump and fan. Because the fan produces frictional horsepower losses, it has been designed to operate only at certain times on newer cars. It is estimated that the fan on the cooling system can absorb up to 6% of the engine horsepower.

FIGURE 12–23. When a closed system is used, coolant can be added directly to the expansion tank.

Fan Blades

There are usually 4–6 blades on the fan. The fan blades are usually spaced unevenly. See *Figure 12–24*. This is done to reduce vibration and fan noise. If the blades are evenly spaced, they may produce fan noise and vibration that become very annoying to the operator. The fan blades slapping the air actually make the noise. If the blades are spaced irregularly, the noise is broken up and reduced.

Variable-Speed Fan

The fan does not need to be turned when the engine is cold or at high speeds. Variable-speed fans are used to control the time when the fan should turn. *Figure 12–25* shows a typical variable speed fan. As air passes through the radiator,

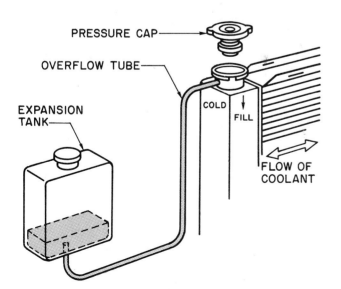

FIGURE 12–22. When the pressure cap releases coolant, it is sent to the expansion tank. When the engine cools, the fluid in the expansion tank is drawn back into the radiator.

FIGURE 12–24. Fan blades are spaced unevenly to reduce vibration and fan noise.

TEMPERATURE
SENSOR

TEMPERATURE SENSOR   COOLING FINS
(BIMETAL STRIP)

FIGURE 12–25. The variable-speed fan senses the temperature of the air coming through the radiator. When the air is hot enough, the inside clutch engages and causes the fan to turn.

its temperature is sensed on the front of the fan clutch. During cold engine operation, the fan is allowed to slip. When the temperature increases to the correct point, a *bimetallic strip* (the thermostatic coil) on the front of the clutch expands. This expansion causes a shaft or valve inside the clutch to turn slightly. As the shaft turns, it opens a hole to allow silicon oil to enter a fluid coupling. This oil causes the fan to lock up against a clutch and start turning. There are several variations of this design; however, the result is the same. *Figure 12–26* shows the internal parts of a typical variable-speed fan.

Electric Fans

Another method used to turn the fan involves using a small motor. See *Figure 12–27*. In this system, the fan is turned on and off according to the engine coolant temperature. When the coolant reaches a certain temperature, usually around 200 degrees F, a sensor tells the electric fan to turn on. If the temperature is less than 200 degrees F, the fan remains off. The advantage of this system is that there are no fan belts. There is no frictional horsepower loss, as with belt-driven fans. There is, however, a small power loss because the alternator must charge the battery more often. This is because the power used to turn the electric motor comes from the electrical system of the vehicle.

Figure 12–28 shows a typical electrical circuit used to turn the electric fan off and on at the correct time. The circuit on the right operates the engine cooling fan motor. In order for the fan motor to start, the engine cooling fan relay (center left) must operate to close the switch. When this switch is closed, the fan motor will turn on. The switch is closed by operating a second circuit. The circuit starts at the fan fuse, then goes through the engine cooling fan relay (coil) and over to the engine coolant temperature switch. This switch is located on the bottom right of the circuit. The engine coolant temperature switch closes because the engine temperature increased to a certain point. When this switch closes the coil in the engine cooling fan relay is energized and starts

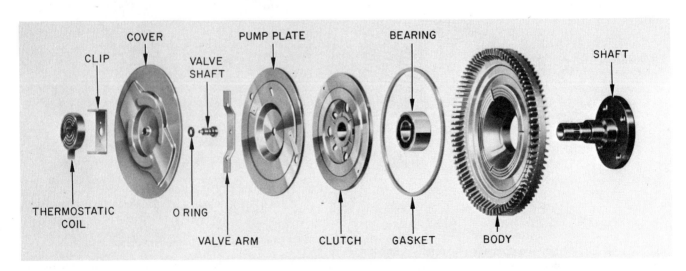

CLIP   COVER   VALVE   PUMP PLATE   BEARING   SHAFT
                   SHAFT

THERMOSTATIC   O RING   CLUTCH   GASKET   BODY
COIL
          VALVE ARM

FIGURE 12–26. The internal parts of a typical variable-speed fan. *(Courtesy of Eaton Corporation)*

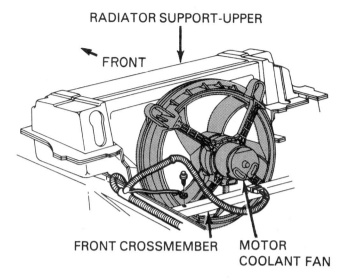

RADIATOR SUPPORT-UPPER

FRONT

FRONT CROSSMEMBER   MOTOR COOLANT FAN

FIGURE 12–27. On certain vehicles, the fan is driven by an electric motor. The motor turns the fan off and on whenever it is needed. This system reduces frictional horsepower losses. *(Courtesy of Chevrolet Division, General Motors Corporation)*

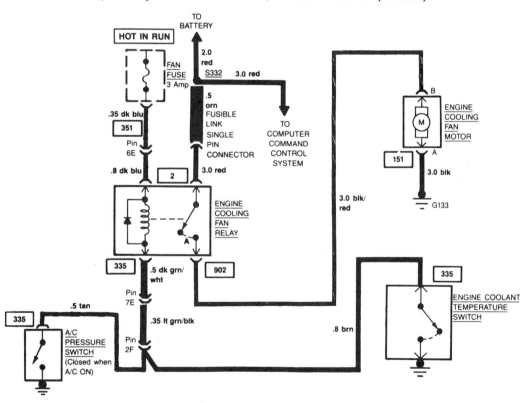

FIGURE 12–28. To start the engine cooling fan motor, the engine coolant temperature switch must close. This energizes the engine cooling fan relay, completing the circuit for the fan motor. *(Courtesy of Motor Publications, Auto Repair Manual)*

the engine cooling fan motor. Each manufacturer has different circuits; however, the basic principle is the same.

Flexible-Blade Fans

Flexible blades are also used to reduce frictional horsepower loss from the fan. See *Figure 12–29*. These flexible blades are made of fiberglass or metal. As the speed of the

engine and vehicle increases, the blades flatten. The blades move less air, causing less frictional horsepower to be lost.

Fan Shrouds

Certain vehicles use a fan *shroud*. A fan shroud is used to make sure the fan pulls air through the entire radiator. If a fan shroud is not used, there may be hot spots in the radiator.

FLEXIBLE
FAN BLADE

FIGURE 12–29. Flexible-blade fans are used to reduce frictional horsepower losses. As the blade speed increases, the blades bend and cut through less air.

See *Figure 12–30*. For example, the fan normally pulls air through the radiator directly in front of the blades. Very little air moves through the corners of the radiator. Using a fan shroud causes air to be pulled evenly through the entire surface area of the radiator.

Fan Belts

The fan belt is used to turn the water pump and the fan. Most fan belts are V-type belts. Friction is produced between the sides of the belt and the pulley. Using the V-type belt produces a larger area of contact. This means that a more positive connection can be made between the belt and the pulley.

Other types of belts are also being used today. One popular type is called the flat serpentine belt. It is about 1 1/2 inches wide and has several grooves on one side. It is flat on the other side. On some engines, this belt is used to reverse the direction of a water pump. This is done because objects can be driven from either side of the belt.

Temperature Indicators

It is important for the vehicle driver to know the engine temperature. Several systems, including a gauge showing the temperature or a warning light, can be used.

The warning light is the simplest system. An indicator is placed in the coolant. As the temperature of the coolant increases to a certain level, the heat from the engine causes an electrical circuit to close inside the sensor. This sensor connects the battery to the warning light on the dashboard. See *Figure 12–31*.

A second type of temperature indicator reads the actual coolant temperature and displays this on the dashboard of the vehicle. See *Figure 12–32*. The electrical indicator and the *Bourdon tube* gauge operate in this manner.

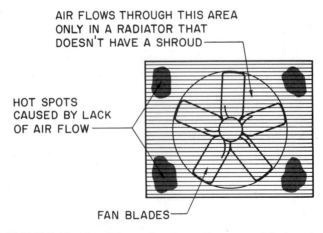

AIR FLOWS THROUGH THIS AREA
ONLY IN A RADIATOR THAT
DOESN'T HAVE A SHROUD

HOT SPOTS
CAUSED BY LACK
OF AIR FLOW

FAN BLADES

FIGURE 12–30. When a fan shroud is not used, hot spots can be created in the corners of the radiator. A fan shroud reduces this possibility.

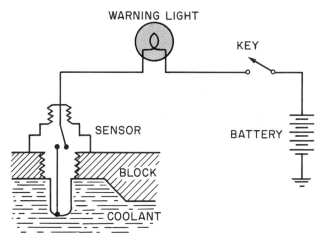

FIGURE 12–31. A warning light operates when the coolant reaches a certain temperature.

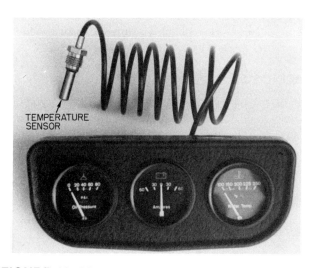

FIGURE 12–32. Electrical temperature gauges use a sensor and a gauge to read the exact temperature inside the engine.

The electrical unit has a sensor placed in the coolant. As the temperature of the engine coolant increases, the electrical resistance of the sensor decreases. As the temperature of the coolant decreases, the electrical resistance of the sensor increases. This increase or decrease in resistance causes the needle in the temperature gauge to read differently with different coolant temperatures.

As pressure changes within the Bourdon tube, the needle reads differently on the dial. Pressure is produced in the tube inside the sensor, which is immersed in the coolant. As the temperature of the coolant increases, a liquid inside the sensor vaporizes. The vapor produces a pressure that is transmitted to the gauge through a tube so a dial can be moved.

CAR CLINIC

PROBLEM: Engine Overheats

A car has recently been overheating on the highway. The problem started suddenly. One person says the problem is the thermostat. But the thermostat was checked and proved to be OK. What might cause an engine to overheat?

SOLUTION:

One of the more common causes of an engine overheating is a bad radiator pressure cap. The radiator pressure cap is designed to keep 15 pounds of pressure on the cooling system. As the pressure of the cooling system increases, the boiling point also increases. If the pressure on the cooling system has been reduced (bad radiator pressure cap), the boiling point is also reduced. Using a pressure cap and cooling system tester, check the cap. It sounds as if the radiator pressure cap cannot hold pressure on the cooling system.

Problems, Diagnosis and Service

1. When working on the cooling system, remember that at operating temperature the coolant is extremely hot, approximately 220 degrees F or hotter. Touching the coolant or spilling the coolant on the body may cause serious injury.

2. When working on the coolant system, for example when replacing the water pump or thermostat, you may spill some coolant on the floor. The antifreeze in the coolant causes it to be very slippery. Immediately wipe up any coolant that spills to reduce or eliminate the chance of injury.

3. Always wear proper clothing and eye protection when using coolant additives to remove silicate and calcium deposits; they may be very corrosive.

4. When working on the fan, water pump, or belts, make sure the engine ignition system is off or the battery is disconnected or both.

5. Whenever the vehicle is running, always keep fingers, tools, and clothing away from the moving fan.

6. When working on the water pump, fan, or belts, be careful not to scrape your knuckles against the radiator, as injury may result.

7. Never remove the pressure cap when the engine is hot. Removing the pressure cap releases the pressure on the cooling system. This reduces the boiling point of the coolant. The coolant will then boil violently and burn or injure a persons' hands or face.

8. When using a chemical cooling system cleaner, be careful not to get the chemical in your eyes or on your skin. Always follow the manufacturer's instructions.

9. Keep antifreeze away from children and animals. Antifreeze has a sweet taste, and, if consumed, it could lead to death in as little as 24 hours. If antifreeze is ingested, see a doctor immediately.

PROBLEM: Correct Amount of Antifreeze

A customer has asked a service technician to check his radiator for the correct amount of antifreeze.

DIAGNOSIS

It is important to have the correct amount of antifreeze in the cooling system for both summer and winter operation. Antifreeze protects the coolant from corrosion in the summer and from freezing in the winter. The correct amount of anti-freeze can be checked by using a cooling system hydrometer. Two typical hydrometers are shown in *Figure 12–33*.

SERVICE

CAUTION: Never remove the radiator cap when the engine is at operating temperature.

1. Remove the radiator cap and draw coolant up into the hydrometer.

2. Read the hydrometer to determine the exact freezing point. Because there are several types of hydrometers, read the directions to find out what the reading means. Usually, the hydrometer indicates the lowest temperature at which the coolant is protected before it will freeze.

PROBLEM: Corrosion in the Cooling System

The coolant in the radiator has turned brownish, and the water pump seal and bearings need to be replaced.

DIAGNOSIS

If the coolant has a rusty color, corrosion may be building up in the cooling system. Corrosion can easily cause the water pump seal and bearings to be damaged. The rust in the system acts as an abrasive on the water pump seal. Corrosion is usually caused by the presence of oxygen in the cooling system. Oxygen can get into the system if the expansion tank is plugged.

SERVICE

1. Drain the coolant from the system.

2. Check the expansion tank for any plugged hoses or leaks.

3. Completely clean the expansion tank.

4. Flush the cooling system completely. Remember that antifreeze must be disposed of according to the state pollution control agency. Never drain the coolant into the sewer system.

5. Remove the water pump, and replace it with a new or rebuilt water pump.

6. Add the correct amount of antifreeze and water, and refill the cooling system.

PROBLEM: Engine Overheats — Hard Water

A customer has complained that the engine overheats easily in hot weather. The problem has been getting worse as time goes on.

DIAGNOSIS

Many problems may cause an engine to overheat. One could be the type of water used in the cooling system. If hard

FIGURE 12–33. A hydrometer is used to check the coolant for protection against freezing.

water is used, there will be a significant amount of silicate and calcium built up on the system. Silicate and calcium buildup have a tendency to restrict heat transfer out of the radiator. This restriction could cause the engine to overheat easily. Also, if there is evidence of corrosion buildup, the temperature sensors may read the wrong temperature.

SERVICE

Check for silicate and calcium buildup by looking down into the radiator and observing the tubes. See *Figure 12–34*. Deposits can be seen building up around each tube. If there appears to be silicate and calcium buildup, the radiator and engine will have to be cleaned. Radiator shops are often fully equipped to clean the internal passageways of the radiator. If there is equipment in the shop, follow the manufacturer's suggested procedure for cleaning radiators and flushing the engine block. If you drain the coolant from the cooling system, make sure to dispose of the coolant correctly. Antifreeze is considered a hazardous waste product.

PROBLEM: Engine Overheats — Faulty Thermostat

A customer has complained that the engine has overheated. The problem came on very rapidly.

DIAGNOSIS

If the engine has overheated and the problem came on rapidly, the thermostat may be faulty. If the thermostat remains closed, no coolant can pass through the thermostat to the radiator.

SERVICE

To remove and check the thermostat use the following procedure:

CAUTION: Make sure the cooling system is at room temperature before starting work.

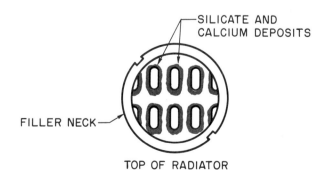

FIGURE 12–34. Deposits of calcium and silicate can be easily seen on down-flow radiators by looking directly into the filler neck. There will be a buildup of deposits around each tube. On other radiators look for deposits in and around the pressure cap.

1. Drain the cooling system and save all coolant.
2. Remove the upper radiator hose from the thermostat.
3. Remove the thermostat housing so the thermostat can be removed.
4. Check the thermostat as shown in *Figure 12–35*.
   a. Suspend the thermostat in a pan of hot water with a thermometer in the water.
   b. Increase the temperature of the water in the pan until the thermostat starts to open. The opening can be observed visually. A thermostat should still be closed at about 10 degrees F below the number stamped on the thermostat.
   c. The thermostat should be fully open about 25 degrees F above the number stamped on it.

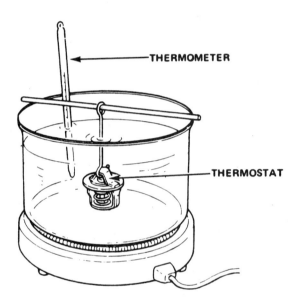

FIGURE 12–35. The thermostat can be checked to determine the temperature at which it will open. Suspend the thermostat in a pot of water and increase the temperature. Observe at what temperature the thermostat opens. *(Courtesy of Honda Motor Company, Ltd.)*

PROBLEM: Leaking Antifreeze

A customer has complained that the cooling system has a leak, and antifreeze is always found under the car after the vehicle sits overnight.

DIAGNOSIS

Cooling systems can be diagnosed for leaks by using a pressure tester. See *Figure 12–36*.

1. Remove the radiator cap.
   CAUTION: Be sure the engine is cool, not hot or at operating temperature.
2. Place the pressure tester on the radiator and seal it like the radiator cap.
3. Pump up the pressure tester to the pressure reading on the cap.
4. With pressure on the system, observe the hoses, water pump, radiator, and so on for small leaks.
5. If no external leaks are evident but the gauge refuses to hold pressure for at least 2 minutes, there may be an internal coolant leak. If this is the case, the engine must be disassembled, and the block and head must be checked for cracks.

SERVICE

If a leak is visually spotted, the component will need to be replaced. If coolant is leaking from the water pump, the water pump seal is damaged. If leakage occurs, replace the water pump using the following general procedure:

1. Make sure the engine is cool or at room temperature.
2. Remove the radiator cap.
3. Drain the coolant from the radiator and cylinder block. Save the coolant if it is to be used again. If not, remember that antifreeze is considered a hazardous waste product and must be disposed of correctly.

FIGURE 12–36. The cooling system can be checked for small leaks by putting the system under pressure.

4. Remove the belts by loosening the appropriate component on the belts. This may include the alternator, air conditioning compressor, and so on.

5. On some engines, the radiator may have to be removed to get at the water pump.

6. Remove the fan if it is driven by the water pump.

7. Remove the bolts holding the water pump to the engine cylinder block.

8. Scrape the old gasket completely off of the block.

9. Replace the old gasket with a new gasket.

10. Replace the water pump with a new or rebuilt pump.

11. Reverse the previous procedure to complete the assembly.

12. Before installing the fan belts, check the inside surface for wear as shown in *Figure 12–37*. Twist the belt slightly to see if there are any cracks on the inside surface.

13. Always check the reinforcement springs inside the lower radiator hose. The spring is there on some vehicles to prevent the rubber hose from collapsing because of water pump suction. If the lower hose is replaced, make sure the spring is not deformed, missing, or out of position. Without the spring, the vehicle is likely to overheat at cruising speed. See *Figure 12–38*.

14. Check the front of the radiator. Keep the front of the radiator clean and free of dirt, bugs, and other debris.

15. After all the parts have been inspected and replaced, add the coolant back into the cooling system. Extra antifreeze may have to be added.

16. Check the fan belts.
    a. Always check the fan belts for wear and correct tension.
    b. Tension on the fan belts can be checked by using the gauge shown in *Figure 12–39*. Position the gauge between the two pulleys as shown. The tighter the belt, the less it will bend from pressure created

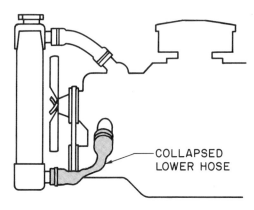

FIGURE 12–38. The lower radiator hose may collapse at cruising speed because of the suction of the water pump. A spring is placed inside the hose to prevent the hose from collapsing.

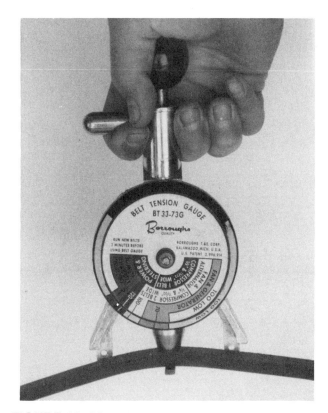

FIGURE 12–39. Fan belts are checked for tension by using this gauge. If the belts are too tight, the bearings may be damaged.

by the gauge. Read the gauge to determine the tightness of the belt.

17. After all parts have been inspected and reassembled, run the engine and pressure test for leaks again.

18. When finished, remove the pressure tester and replace the pressure cap.

PROBLEM: Faulty Radiator Cap

A customer has complained that the engine has overheated. The problem seemed to have happened rapidly.

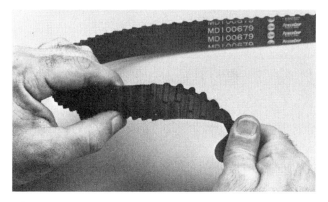

FIGURE 12–37. The belt should be checked for cracks and excessive wear. Bend the belt slightly backward.

DIAGNOSIS

If the engine has overheated and the problem came on rapidly, the radiator cap may be faulty. If the radiator cap doesn't hold the pressure on the cooling system, the boiling point will be reduced, possibly causing the engine to overheat.

SERVICE

To check the radiator cap use the following procedure:

CAUTION: Make sure the cooling system is at room temperature before starting work.

1. Remove the radiator cap.

2. Place the pressure cap on the pressure tester as shown in *Figure 12–40*. Seal the cap on the pressure tester by turning, as if on a radiator.

3. Increase the pressure on the cap, using the pump on the pressure tester.

4. Note the pressure at which the pressure cap releases. As the pressure is increased by the pumping, the pressure will eventually not be able to go higher.

5. Make sure the cap releases pressure at the pressure setting shown on the cap.

6. If the pressure is released at a lower point, the cap is defective. Replace the cap if this occurs.

7. Check the pressure cap vacuum valve also. One method used to check this valve is to observe the upper radiator hose. If the upper radiator hose collapses after the engine

FIGURE 12–40.   The pressure cap tester is used to determine exactly what pressure will open the pressure cap.

has cooled down, the vacuum valve may be defective or clogged. When clogged or damaged, the valve will not allow pressure in the cooling system to equalize when being cooled down. If this is the case, replace or clean the vacuum valve to remedy the problem. See *Figure 12–41*.

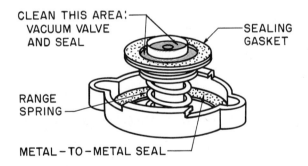

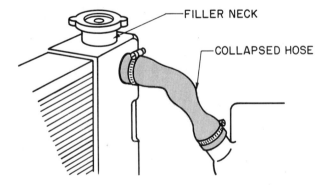

FIGURE 12–41.   If the pressure cap vacuum valve is defective or clogged, the upper radiator hose will collapse when the engine cools down. Clean the valve or replace the pressure cap.

SERVICE MANUAL CONNECTION

There are many important specifications to keep in mind when working with the cooling system. To identify the specifications for your engine, you will need to know the VIN (vehicle identification number) of the vehicle, the type and year of the vehicle, and the type of engine. Although they may be titled differently, some of the more common cooling system specifications (not all) found in service manuals are listed below. Note that these specifications are typical examples. Each vehicle and engine will have different specifications.

Common specification	Typical example
Belt tension	
New	165 lb
Used	100 lb
Cooling system capacity	
Without air conditioner (A/C)	15.3 quarts
With air conditioner (A/C)	15.9 quarts
Radiator cap relief pressure	16 lb
Thermostat opening temperature	196° F

In addition, the service manual will give specific directions for various service procedures. Some of the more common procedures include:

- Checking the variable-speed fan operation
- Setting belt tension
- Thermostat removal and replacement
- Water pump replacement

Linkage to Automotive Manufacturing

Cooling system components require high quality and reliability in manufacturing. These high-efficiency radiators can be made as cross-flow or down-flow radiators. They are composed of a copper and brass soldered core with soldered-on brass tanks. Product engineering and design personnel use up-to-date methods to mathematically analyze and design radiators for a particular application in a vehicle. *(Courtesy of Harrison Radiator Division, General Motors Corporation)*

SUMMARY

The cooling system is designed to maintain the highest operating temperature within the engine. To do this, the cooling system must remove large quantities of heat from the engine. The cooling system uses three means of heat transfer to accomplish this: conduction, convection, and radiation. It is designed to maximize the principles of transferring heat by these three means.

Several types of cooling systems are now being used on the automobile. Air-cooled engines use air passing over fins to cool the engine block and cylinder heads. Heat is dissipated to the air passing around the engine. Liquid-cooled engines circulate a mixture of antifreeze and water through the engine to remove heat. The coolant is pumped with a water pump into the engine block, through internal passages, into the cylinder head, and into a radiator. Air flows through the radiator to remove the excess heat captured by the coolant. A thermostat is used to direct the coolant, which is either recirculated without being cooled or sent to the radiator to be cooled.

To understand the design and operation of the cooling system, it is important to identify coolant characteristics. Antifreeze is added to the coolant to protect it against freezing. Antifreeze also increases the coolant's boiling point, and it reduces corrosion within the cooling system. Corrosion can be caused by oxygen in the system, electromechanical attacks, and the buildup of calcium and silicate deposits. Antifreeze can also reduce leaks. Chemicals are added to the antifreeze to stop pinhole leaks in the cooling system.

The cooling system has many parts that enable it to operate effectively. These include the water pump, water jackets, thermostat, radiator, pressure cap, expansion tanks, fan, shrouds, belts, and temperature indicators.

The water pump is used to circulate the coolant throughout the cooling system. It is called a centrifugal pump. It is usually driven by a belt from the crankshaft. The water jackets are open spaces within the cylinder block. The coolant passes through the water jackets, picking up heat to be removed from the engine. The thermostat is used to control the temperature of the engine. If the coolant is cold, the thermostat remains closed, and directs the coolant back into the water pump to be recirculated. If the coolant is hot, the thermostat opens and sends the coolant to the radiator to be cooled.

The radiator is used to remove heat from the coolant. The coolant passes through small tubes inside the radiator. Air flows across the tubes and removes the heat. Both down-flow and cross-flow radiators are used in vehicles today. Automatic transmission fluid is also passed through a tube in the bottom of the radiator to be cooled. A pressure cap is placed on the radiator to maintain approximately 15 pounds of pressure on the cooling system. The pressure increases the boiling point of the coolant, reduces cavitation, protects radiator hoses, and reduces surging.

An expansion tank is used on some vehicles. When the engine heats up and the coolant increases in temperature, the coolant expands. At times the pressure cap will release excess fluid into the air. An expansion tank collects the excess coolant. Using an expansion tank reduces the amount of oxygen allowed into the system. Corrosion is then greatly reduced.

Several types of fans and fan blades are used on the cooling system. The fan is normally a source of frictional horsepower loss; therefore, it should be operated only when necessary. The variable-speed fan uses silicon oil inside a fan clutch to engage and disengage the clutch. It does this on the basis of coolant temperature. Fans are driven by an electric motor or by using V belts. On electric fans, a sensor tells the fan when to operate. Some fan blades are made of fiberglass. As the speed of the fan increases, the fan blades flatten, reducing frictional horsepower losses. Fan shrouds are used to make sure air flows evenly through the radiator.

Temperature indicators are used to tell the operator the condition of the cooling system. Several types are used. The simplest type turns a light on when the temperature gets too high. A second style reads the engine coolant temperature on a gauge. Two gauges are available: the Bourdon tube gauge and the electrical gauge.

Several diagnosis and service tips about the cooling system should be known. Some of the more important ones include always checking fan belt tension, checking the pressure cap, making sure the thermostat opens at the correct temperature, checking hoses that may be damaged, checking the water pump for leakage and damaged bearings, and checking for calcium and silicate buildup within the radiator.

TERMS TO KNOW

Can you explain each of the following terms? Review the chapter until you can use each term correctly.

Heat transfer	Psig
Conduction	Vacuum
Convection	Surging
Radiation	Bimetallic strip
Air-cooled	Shroud
Liquid-cooled	Bourdon tube
Bypass tube	
Corrosive	
Antifreeze	
Hazardous waste	
Boiling point	
Direct attack	
Electro mechanical attack	
Cavitation	
Calcium deposits	
Silicate deposits	
Centrifugal pump	
Thermostat	
Heat exchanger	
Core	
Pressure	

REVIEW QUESTIONS

Multiple Choice

1. Which of the following is *not* a purpose of the cooling system?
   a. Keeping the engine temperature as low as possible
   b. Removing excess heat from the engine
   c. Bringing the temperature to operating range as quickly as possible
   d. Operating the engine at the best operating temperature for highest efficiency
   e. Protecting the internal parts from overheating

2. Which of the following is transfer of heat when both objects are solid?
   a. Conduction
   b. Convection
   c. Radiation
   d. Surging
   e. Vacuum

3. Heat transfer by _____ means to move heat by circulation of air or liquid.
   a. Conduction
   b. Convection
   c. Radiation
   d. Surging
   e. Vacuum

4. The _____ engine uses air passing over fins to cool the engine.
   a. Liquid-cooled
   b. Air-cooled
   c. Conduction
   d. Radiant
   e. Closed-loop

5. If the coolant is not hot enough to be cooled, it is sent to the _____.
   a. Radiator
   b. Pressure cap
   c. By-pass tube
   d. Differential regulator
   e. Coolant sensor

6. Antifreeze is used to protect the coolant against:
   a. Freezing
   b. Boiling
   c. Corrosion
   d. All of the above
   e. None of the above

7. Which two deposits build up inside the cooling system?
   a. Calcium and water
   b. Silicate and rust
   c. Calcium and silicate
   d. Water and rust
   e. Nitrogen and water

8. What is the most common mixture for antifreeze and water?
   a. 20% water, 80% antifreeze
   b. 50% water, 50% antifreeze
   c. 90% water, 10% antifreeze
   d. 30% water, 70% antifreeze
   e. None of the above

9. The water pump is considered a/an _____ type pump.
   a. Positive displacement
   b. Centrifugal
   c. Eccentric
   d. All of the above
   e. None of the above

10. The water pump is driven by:
    a. Fan belts from the starter
    b. Fan belts from the oil pump
    c. Fan belts from the crankshaft
    d. Fan belts from the transmission
    e. None of the above

11. When the engine gets hot enough, the automotive thermostat:
    a. Closes
    b. Opens
    c. Blocks off the radiator
    d. Tells the radiator to shut down
    e. None of the above

12. The thermostat is _____.
    a. Open all of the time
    b. Closed all of the time
    c. Opened more and more as the temperature increases
    d. Opened to allow coolant to flow to the transmission
    e. None of the above

13. The radiator is considered a _____ type of heat exchanger.
    a. Air-to-liquid
    b. Liquid-to-air
    c. Air-to-air
    d. All of the above
    e. None of the above

14. Which type of radiator is used in vehicles that are lower in front?
    a. Down-flow
    b. Cross-flow
    c. Centrifugal-flow
    d. Up-flow
    e. Side-flow

15. Which of the following is *not* a part of the radiator?
    a. Inlet tank
    b. Outlet tank
    c. Core
    d. Water pump
    e. Cooling baffles, fins, and tubes

16. Pressure on the cooling system will protect the cooling system from:
    a. Cavitation
    b. Increased operating temperatures
    c. Cold weather operation
    d. All of the above
    e. A and B

17. What is the standard pressure on a cooling system?
    a. 60–70 pounds
    b. 10 pounds
    c. 15 pounds
    d. 2–4 pounds
    e. None of the above

18. When an expansion tank is used on the cooling system:
    a. Overflow coolant from the pressure cap enters the expansion tank
    b. Coolant is drawn back into the radiator when the engine cools down
    c. Coolant can be added to the expansion tank
    d. All of the above
    e. None of the above

19. Which system will produce more rust and corrosion in a cooling system?
    a. A cooling system without an expansion tank
    b. A cooling system with an expansion tank
    c. A cooling system without a cross-flow radiator
    d. A cooling system with a radiator cap
    e. A cooling system with a thermostat

20. What is a big disadvantage of using a fan to draw air through the radiator?
    a. Fans make too much noise
    b. Fans vibrate too much
    c. Fans consume frictional horsepower
    d. All of the above
    e. None of the above

21. The electric-driven fan is turned off and on by the:
    a. Temperature of the engine
    b. Pressure of the coolant
    c. Speed of the engine
    d. Pressure of the lubrication
    e. Amount of coolant flow

22. Which method of temperature indicators uses a curved tube that straightens when pressure increases?
    a. The electrical sensor
    b. The Bourdon tube gauge
    c. The silicon oil fan clutch
    d. All of the above
    e. None of the above

23. A fan shroud is used:
    a. To reduce any hot spots in the corners of the radiator
    b. To protect the fan from damage
    c. To protect the radiator from damage
    d. To contain leaks in the cooling system
    e. To protect the hoses

The following questions are similar in format to ASE (Automotive Service Excellence) test questions.

24. Technician A says that brownish coolant is a sign of rust in the cooling system. Technician B says that brownish coolant is caused by the addition of antifreeze in the coolant. Who is right?
    a. A only   c. Both A and B
    b. B only   d. Neither A nor B

25. Technician A says the thermostat can be checked only by keeping it in antifreeze. Technician B says to check the thermostat, remove it, and suspend it in water with a thermometer while heating up the water. Who is right?
    a. A only   c. Both A and B
    b. B only   d. Neither A nor B

26. After checking the engine, it was found that the coolant was boiling at 212 degrees F. Technician A says this is normal. Technician B says the thermostat should be checked with a pressure tester. Who is right?
    a. A only   c   Both A and B
    b. B only   d. Neither A nor B

27. An engine has a large amount of silicon and calcium in the cooling system. Technician A says the silicon is there because of the high quality of the antifreeze. Technician B says the silicon is there because of the aluminum cylinder block. Who is right?
    a. A only   c. Both A and B
    b. B only   d. Neither A nor B

28. Technician A says that antifreeze should be treated as a hazardous waste product. Technician B says that antifreeze should be dumped into the water drain. Who is correct?
    a. A only   c. Both A and B
    b. B only   d. Neither A nor B

29. Technician A says that rust in the cooling system can easily damage the water pump bearings. Technician B says that rust in the cooling system can damage the water pump seal. Who is correct?
    a. A only   c. Both A and B
    b. B only   d. Neither A nor B

30. An engine has a leak in the cooling system. Technician A says to check the cooling system with a pressure tester. Technician B says to check the pressure relief valve in the radiator cap. Who is correct?
    a. A only   c. Both A and B
    b. B only   d. Neither A nor B

31. An engine is overheating. Technician A says that the problem could be a bad thermostat. Technician B says the problem could be silicate and calcium deposits inside the cooling system. Who is correct?
    a. A only   c. Both A and B
    b. B only   d. Neither A nor B

Essay

32. What problems can occur when the engine temperature is too high?

33. What problems can occur when the engine temperature is too low?

34. What is the difference between convection, conduction, and radiation forms of heat transfer?

35. What is the purpose of the by-pass tube on the cooling system?

36. What happens to the freezing point of coolant if the percentage of antifreeze is too high?

37. Describe the purpose and operation of a thermostat.

38. Describe the purpose and operation of a pressure cap.

Short Answer

39. Because antifreeze is considered a hazardous waste product, it should always be _____.

40. The temperature-sensitive valve on a thermostat should always be placed toward the _____ side of the engine.

41. Generally, _____ or _____ type materials are used as the fins on a radiator.

42. On most newer vehicles, the radiator fan is controlled or turned off and on by _____.

43. To check the freezing point of the antifreeze, use a _____.

Fuel Characteristics

INTRODUCTION The correct operation and driving characteristics of automotive engines are directly related to the type of fuel that is used. Today's automotive engines use gasoline as the primary fuel. However, diesel fuel is available for diesel engines. In addition, gasohol and other fuels are constantly being tried to see if they are efficient and clean-burning. This chapter is related to the study of these fuels.

OBJECTIVES After reading this chapter, you should be able to:

- Define the refining process and determine the heating values of different fuels.

- State the characteristics and properties of gasoline.

- Identify the characteristics and properties of diesel fuels.

- Recognize the characteristics of gasohol as a fuel.

- Compare liquid petroleum gas as a fuel with diesel fuel and gasohol fuel.

3.1 REFINING PROCESSES

Hydrocarbons and Crude Oil

Fuels used in vehicles are called *hydrocarbons*. In simple terms, hydrogen and carbon molecules are combined chemically to make different fuels. These combinations of molecules are called hydrocarbons. The oil industry begins the manufacture of automotive fuels by first exploring for crude oil. Crude oil is the thick brown and black, slippery liquid from which all fuels are made. It contains thousands of different chemical combinations of hydrogen and carbon. See *Figure 13–1*.

Crude oil is usually located from 5,000 to 20,000 feet beneath the surface of the earth. It is the oil company's job to find the oil and then get it out of the ground. Large offshore and land oil rigs are used to pump the crude oil to the surface. See *Figure 13–2*.

After the crude oil has been pumped from the ground, it is transported to the refinery to be processed into different fuels. After the fuels have been refined, they are shipped to the proper distributor for sale to the public.

Boiling Points

The *boiling point* of a hydrocarbon is defined as the temperature at which the hydrocarbon will start to become a vapor. If the vapor is cooled below its boiling point, the vapor will *condense*, or become a liquid again. Hydrocarbon boiling points range from –250 degrees F to more than 1,300 degrees F. Most hydrocarbons have a range of boiling points. For example, gasoline molecules start to boil from about 195 degrees F to 390 degrees F. Other fuels have different boiling points.

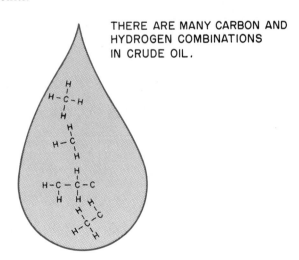

THERE ARE MANY CARBON AND HYDROGEN COMBINATIONS IN CRUDE OIL.

FIGURE 13–1. Crude oil contains many combinations of hydrogen and carbon. Different combinations make different fuels.

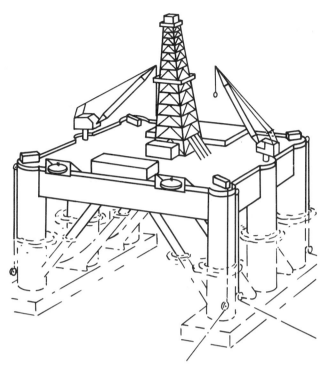

FIGURE 13–2. Large oil rigs such as this one remove crude oil from the ground.

Distillation

Crude oil is converted to usable fuels in a refinery. *Figure 13–3* shows a typical refinery. One of the major processes done in a refinery is that of distillation. *Distillation* is the process in a refinery that separates the different hydrocarbons in the crude oil. Certain hydrocarbons from the crude oil will be used to make gasoline. Other hydrocarbons will be used to make diesel fuels. Others will be used to make many other

products. *Figure 13–4* shows some of the products that can be made from crude oil.

Distillation is done by heating all of the crude oil and the hydrocarbons to the highest boiling point. At the bottom of the column in *Figure 13–5* all hydrocarbons are vaporized. As the vapors rise to the top of the column, they start to cool. The hot vapors are cooled near their boiling points. At this point, they are condensed back to a liquid. For example, on

FIGURE 13–3. A refinery is used to change crude oil into many products used in the automotive industry. One of its primary purposes is distillation, or the breaking down of crude oil into various products. *(Courtesy of API)*

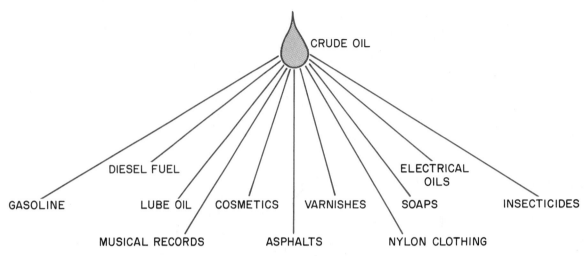

FIGURE 13–4. Many products, including fuels, can be extracted from crude oil. These are just a few of them.

the right side of the column, vapors cool to form gasolines, diesel fuels, heavier oils, and different residues. This column is also called a fractionating column.

From this point, the fuels are cleaned, and chemicals are added to improve the fuels. They are now ready to be transported to the distributors and service stations.

Heating Values

Each of the fuels that are refined has a different heating value. Heating values are measured in Btus. The term *Btu* means British Thermal Unit. It is defined as the amount of heat needed to raise one pound of water one degree F. For example, one Btu is about equal to the heat given off when

one wooden match burns completely. A home on a cold winter day may require 30,000 Btu per hour to be heated.

Gasoline and diesel fuels are compared by the amount of Btus they contain if converted to heat. The higher the heating value of a fuel, the better the combustion and thus the better the fuel mileage. For example, one gallon of gasoline contains about 110,000–120,000 Btu. Diesel fuels typically contain about 130,000 to 140,000 Btu per gallon.

The heating value of a fuel is related to its boiling point during distillation. Normally, the higher the boiling point of a hydrocarbon, the higher the heating value of the fuel. Diesel fuels have a higher boiling point than gasoline. This means that diesel fuels have more Btus per gallon than gasoline.

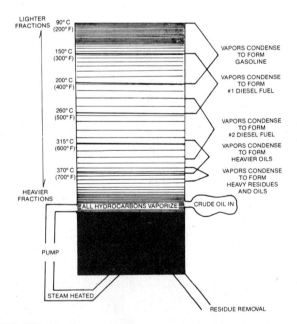

FIGURE 13–5. Distillation vaporizes all hydrocarbons. Then, as they condense at different temperatures, they are separated and removed as specific products. *(Courtesy of Davis Publications, Inc.)*

PROBLEM: Alcohol in the Fuel

Many car owners are concerned about the use of alcohol in fuel such as gasohol. Is there any problem with running high levels of alcohol in the fuel?

SOLUTION:

Alcohol will generally cause engine damage. The amount of damage depends on the percentage of alcohol in the gasoline. Anything above 10% could damage the engine. At 15%, alcohol may damage aluminum parts and cause steel to begin rusting. Alcohol may also dilute the engine oil considerably. Always be aware of how much alcohol is being added to the fuel. If a vehicle has been using gasoline for a long period of time and the owner switches to gasohol (10% alcohol), the alcohol will loosen some gum deposits in the fuel tank and lines and have a tendency to plug up fuel filters.

13.2 PROPERTIES OF GASOLINE

Knocking

The term *knocking* is used when studying fuel and different gasoline qualities. Knocking is a process that happens within the combustion chamber. It sounds like a small ticking or rattling noise within the engine. It can be very damaging to the pistons and rings as well as to the spark plug and valves. Another name for knocking is detonation.

Figure 13–6 shows what happens inside a combustion chamber when detonation occurs. When the spark plug fires to ignite the air-fuel mixture, it produces a flame front. Shortly after ignition, a second explosion (flame front) and ignition of fuel take place on the other side of the combustion chamber. This flame front is produced from low-octane fuel combusting, or burning, too early. When these two energy fronts hit each other, they cause a *pinging* or knocking within the engine. Knocking is usually caused by poor-quality fuel. The temperatures within the combustion chamber are high enough to cause the air and fuel mixture to ignite without the spark plug. Fuels are made to have antiknocking characteristics. Actually, antiknocking fuels need higher temperatures to start burning.

Octane Number

Different types of gasoline are identified by the *octane number*. The octane number is defined as the resistance to burning. For example, the higher the octane number of a gasoline, the higher the temperature needed to ignite the fuel. The lower the octane number, the easier the fuel can start burning. Standard octane ratings range from 85–90 for regular gasoline. Premium gasoline or hi-test gasoline has an octane range from 90–95. Gasolines that have higher octane ratings tend to reduce knocking and detonation.

Types of Octane Ratings

Three types of octane ratings are used in the petroleum industry. They include the research octane, motor octane, and road octane. Research octane is a laboratory measure of gasoline and its antiknock characteristics. The octane is tested under mild engine operating conditions, low speed, and low temperatures. Motor octane is a laboratory measure of the antiknock characteristics of the fuel under severe engine operation. This includes high speed and high temperatures within the engine. Road octane represents actual road driving conditions. Road octane is the one posted on gasoline pumps. It is calculated by taking the average of the research and motor octanes. On gasoline pumps, road octane is stated as research octane plus motor octane divided by two. This is illustrated on the pump as:

$$\text{Octane} = \frac{R + M}{2}$$

where:

R = Research octane
M = Motor octane

Until about the 1970s, the octane numbers of gasoline were increasing. This was because the automotive manufacturers were constantly increasing compression ratios. Higher compression ratios usually meant more efficient combustion. As the compression ratios increased, so did the compression temperatures. If a lower-octane fuel was used in these higher compression ratio engines, knocking always occurred. *Regular gasoline* was used for low-compression engines. *Hi-test* was used for higher compression engines.

Octane Requirements

The octane requirements of automobiles vary a great deal. In fact, as an engine gets older, the octane requirement may increase somewhat. This is because when the engine is new, there is a set compression ratio. As the engine gets older, however, carbon buildup may increase the compression ratio. This means that the engine will need a higher-octane gasoline. See *Figure 13–7*.

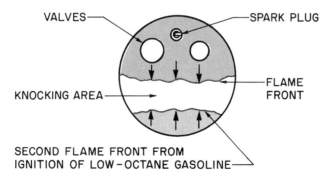

VIEW OF TOP OF CYLINDER

VALVES — SPARK PLUG

KNOCKING AREA — FLAME FRONT

SECOND FLAME FRONT FROM IGNITION OF LOW–OCTANE GASOLINE

TWO FLAME FRONTS COLLIDE

FIGURE 13–6. Detonation results when two flame fronts hit each other. One is from the spark plug combustion, and one is from early fuel ignition caused by poor-quality fuel.

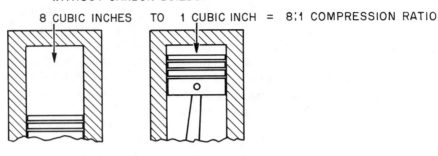

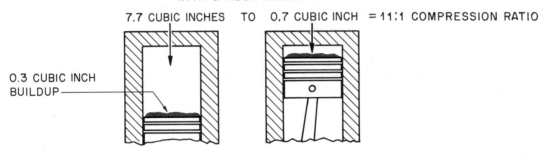

FIGURE 13–7. As an engine gets older, the compression ratio may increase. As carbon builds up on top of the piston, the compression ratio may change.

Many other factors also influence the octane needed in an engine. These include:

1. *Air temperature* — The higher the air or engine temperature, the greater the octane requirements.

2. *Altitude* — The higher the altitude, the lower the octane.

3. *Humidity* — The lower the humidity, the greater the octane needed in the engine.

4. *Spark timing* — The more advanced the spark timing, the greater the octane needed.

5. *Carburetor settings* — The leaner the carburetor, the higher the octane needed.

6. *Method of driving* — If the vehicle is accelerated rapidly, higher octane is needed. Start-and-stop driving also increases combustion deposits and buildup. Higher octane will then be needed.

Adding Lead to Gasoline

One method used to increase the octane of gasoline is by adding a chemical called TEL. This stands for *tetraethyl lead*. Tetramethyl lead, called TML, is also used to increase the octane rating. These chemicals were added during the refining process. They also act as a lubricant on the valves and valve guides. It was found, however, that TEL and TML are dangerous pollutants. The exhaust gases from cars were carrying lead pollution. Today many pollution control devices, particularly catalytic converters, should not be used with leaded fuels.

Removing Lead from Gasoline

In the early 1970s, TEL and TML were removed from gasoline because of pollution. The result was called low-lead or nonleaded gasoline. Other chemicals were added to the gasoline to aid in lubricating the valves.

When the lead was removed from gasoline, the octane ratings fell. Therefore, the automobile manufacturing companies had to reduce their compression ratios. Compression ratios dropped from an average of 12 to 1, down to 8.5 to 1. This made the engine less efficient. Recent engines still have compression ratios from 8 to 1 up to about 9 to 1. One advantage to lowering compression ratios is that the internal combustion temperatures are lower. This means fewer *nitrogen oxides* are produced within the exhaust. Nitrogen oxides are also a source of pollution. Nitrogen oxides are referenced as NO_x and are further discussed in Chapter 23.

The problem with compression ratios and octane ratings exists only in engines that compress an air and fuel mixture. Diesel engines do not have this problem. Diesel engines have increased their compression ratios to as high as 22.5 to 1. This can be done because the compression stroke on a diesel engine compresses only air. Fuel is then injected near top dead center. It is nearly impossible for a diesel engine to detonate, because fuel does not enter the cylinder until the piston is near top dead center. See *Figure 13–8*.

Volatility

Gasoline must vaporize in order to burn effectively. If a fuel does not vaporize completely before going into the combustion chamber, combustion efficiency and fuel efficiency, in turn, will decrease. *Volatility* is defined as the ease with which a gasoline vaporizes. Highly volatile fuels *vaporize* very easily. Fuels that are used in cold weather must be highly volatile. In warm weather, however, gasoline should be less volatile to prevent formation of excess vapor. Excess vapor causes a loss of power or stalling due to vapor lock. Gasolines vary in volatility seasonally.

Vapor Lock

Fuels that have high volatility also have a characteristic known as *vapor lock*. Vapor lock is defined as vapor buildup that restricts the flow of gasoline through the fuel system. Vapor lock occurs from the heating of the fuel, causing it to turn to a vapor. During very warm operating conditions, vapor lock can occur in fuel lines that are near exhaust systems or near other heat sources. When vapor lock occurs the fuel vapors cannot be pumped by the fuel pump. This action blocks the fuel to the carburetor or fuel injection system. To eliminate the potential of vapor lock, additional vapor lines are added to the fuel system to relieve the vapor from the system.

Gasoline Additives

Various additives are put into fuel to change its characteristics. These additives have different properties and uses. Many are added during the refining processes; others can be added by the consumer.

Ethyl alcohol or methanol can be put into gasoline as an *anti-icing* additive. It prevents gasoline from freezing. Winter additives, including *anti-icers*, stop fuel lines and carburetors from icing up in cold weather. For example, the carburetor anti-icers help keep ice from building up on the throttle plates. If ice does build up, missing and stalling will result. The ice is formed when moist air hits a throttle plate that has been cooled by the vaporization of gasoline. The ice then restricts the flow of air into the carburetor.

Oxidation inhibitors are added to gasoline that is being stored for long periods of time. During storage, harmful gum deposits form because of the reaction of certain gasoline chemicals with each other and with oxygen. Oxidation inhibitors help the gasoline to remain more stable. This helps to reduce gum, varnishes, and other deposits in the gasoline.

Gasoline is in constant contact with various metals. These metals are found in the fuel lines, fuel tank, carburetor, and so on. *Rust inhibitors* are added to gasoline to inhibit any reaction between the fuel and the metal. Without rust inhibitors, small abrasive particles will form, plugging the fuel system and filters.

Detergents are added to gasoline to clean certain components inside the fuel system and engine. For example, a fuel that has detergents helps to keep the carburetor, fuel injectors, and the like clean during normal operation.

Ignition control and combustion modifiers are also added to gasoline. These additives help prevent spark plug fouling and *preignition*. Preignition is caused by glowing carbon deposits in the combustion chamber. These deposits ignite the air-fuel mixture before the spark plug fires. See *Figure 13–9*. This causes a pinging or knocking sound as does detonation. Other additives include antirust, antigum, and antiwear chemicals.

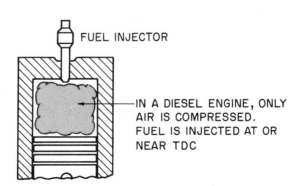

FUEL INJECTOR

IN A DIESEL ENGINE, ONLY AIR IS COMPRESSED. FUEL IS INJECTED AT OR NEAR TDC

FIGURE 13–8. In a diesel engine, only air is compressed. There is no chance that the fuel will ignite too soon.

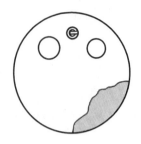

FIRST
IGNITION OCCURS FROM
GLOWING CARBON PARTICLE
BEFORE SPARK IGNITION

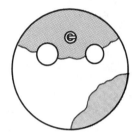

NOW
SPARK IGNITES
REMAINING FUEL

FIGURE 13–9. Preignition occurs when something ignites the fuel before the spark plug does. In this case, ignition is caused by a carbon particle. Preignition also causes pinging.

Engine Run-on

Another characteristic of combustion caused by poor-quality gasoline is called *postignition*. Postignition is defined as having the engine run after the ignition has been shut off. See *Figure 13–10*. For example, a poor-quality gasoline may have many glowing deposits inside the combustion chamber during operation. When the ignition is shut off, these glowing deposits act as the ignition source for the air and fuel still in

CAR CLINIC

PROBLEM: Using Unleaded Fuel in Older Cars

An older vehicle has always used a leaded fuel. Is it OK to run unleaded fuel in such an engine? Could unleaded fuels damage the engine?

SOLUTION:

The biggest problem in using an unleaded fuel in older engines is that it shortens the life of the exhaust valves. The lead in leaded fuels lubricates the valves. In engines designed to use unleaded fuel, the valves are harder, so they don't need as much lubrication. If the engine is going to be used for a long time, try changing the valves to a harder type if they are available. Also, an oiler kit that oils the valves from the top could improve the situation. It is important to get used to the idea that there will eventually be no leaded fuels on the market.

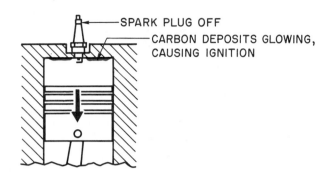

—SPARK PLUG OFF
—CARBON DEPOSITS GLOWING,
CAUSING IGNITION

FIGURE 13–10. Postignition occurs after the ignition has been shut off. A glowing particle of carbon ignites the air-fuel mixture.

the combustion chamber. Postignition is also called dieseling or run-on.

13.3 PROPERTIES OF DIESEL FUEL

Diesel fuels are also a mixture of hydrogen and carbon molecules. However, diesel fuels have more energy per gallon than gasoline. In addition, diesel fuels burn with higher efficiency during combustion.

Diesel fuel is part of a group of fuel oils called distillates. This group of fuel oils make up such products as jet fuels, kerosene, home fuel oil, and diesel fuels.

Three properties are important in the selection of diesel fuel. These include cetane number, distillation endpoint, and sulfur content. Other characteristics, including pour point, flash point, viscosity, and ash content, are also considered.

Cetane Number

There is a delay between the time that fuel is injected into the cylinder and the time that the hot gases ignite. This time period or delay is expressed as a *cetane number*. Cetane numbers range from 30 to 60 on diesel fuels. The cetane number is an indication of the ignition quality of diesel fuel. The higher the cetane number, the better the ignition quality of the fuel. High cetane numbers should be used for starting in cold weather. *Ether*, with a cetane number of 85–96, is often used for starting diesel engines in cold weather. If a low cetane number is used in a diesel engine, some of the fuel might not ignite. The fuel will then accumulate within the cylinder. When combustion finally does occur, this excess fuel will explode suddenly. This may result in a knocking sound as in a gasoline engine.

Distillation Endpoint

Fuels can be burned in an engine only when they are in vaporized form. The temperature at which a fuel is completely vaporized is called the *distillation endpoint*. The distillation endpoint should be low enough to permit complete vaporization at the temperatures encountered in the engine. This means for engines operating at reduced speeds and loads or in cold weather, lower distillation endpoints will give better performance.

Sulfur Content

The *sulfur* content in a diesel fuel should be as low as possible. Sulfur is part of crude oil when it is taken out of the ground. Refining is designed to remove as much sulfur as is practical. There is a direct link between the amount of sulfur present in the fuel and the amount of corrosion and deposit formation within the engine. Sulfur is also contained in the exhaust gases. These gases can pollute the air and cause a significant amount of *acid rain*. Certain tests have shown that increasing sulfur content from 0.25% to 1.25% increases engine wear by 135%. Engine wear is most noticeable on the cylinder walls and piston rings.

Pour Point

Diesel fuels are also rated as to their pour point. Pour point is defined as the temperature at which fuel stops flowing. For cold weather operation, the pour point should be about 10 degrees F below the *ambient* (surrounding air) temperature at which the engine is run.

Cloud Point

The *cloud point* of a diesel fuel is defined as the temperature at which wax crystals start to form in the fuel. Diesel fuels tend to produce wax crystals in very cold weather. The wax crystals plug up fuel filters and injectors.

Viscosity

As we saw in the lubricating system, viscosity is a measure of the resistance to flow. The fuel should have a viscosity that allows it to flow freely in the coldest operation. The viscosity of fuel oil also affects the size of the fuel spray droplets from the fuel injection nozzles. The higher the viscosity, the larger the droplets. The size of the droplets, in turn, affects the *atomization* qualities of the fuel spray.

Fuel oil viscosity is normally checked at 100 degrees F. It is measured in centistokes. This is another unit used to measure viscosity. It is used instead of the Saybolt Universal Second. Additives are incorporated into the fuel during refining to keep the viscosity at the correct level.

Flash Point

The *flash point* of a diesel fuel is defined as the fuel's ignition point when exposed to an open flame. It is determined by heating the fuel in a small enclosed chamber. The temperature at which vapors ignite from a small flame passed over the surface of the liquid is the flash point temperature. The flash point should be high enough for the fuel to be handled safely and stored without danger of explosion.

Ash Content

The ash content of diesel fuels is a measure of the impurities, which include metallic oxides and sand. These impurities cause an *abrasive* action on the moving parts of the engine. The amount of ash content should be kept to a minimum.

ASTM Diesel Fuel Classification

Diesel fuels are classified as either No. 1-D or No. 2-D. The characteristics of each are shown in *Figure 13–11*. This is the American Society for Testing and Materials (ASTM) classifications.

Grade No. 1-D fuels have the lowest boiling ranges (are the most volatile). These fuels also have the lowest cloud and pour points. Fuels within this classification are suitable for use in high-speed diesel engines in services involving frequent and relatively wide variations in loads and speeds. This may include stop-and-go bus and door-to-door operations. They are also used where abnormally low fuel temperatures are encountered.

Grade No. 2-D fuels have higher and wider boiling ranges than 1-D fuels. These fuels normally have higher cloud and pour points than 1-D fuels. They are used in diesel engines in services with high loads and uniform speeds. They are also used in climates where cold starting and cold fuel handling are not severe problems. These fuels satisfy the majority of automotive diesel applications.

ASTM CLASSIFICATION OF DIESEL FUEL OILS		
	NO. 1-D	NO. 2-D
Flash Pt.; °F Min.	100	125
Carbon Residue; %	0.15	0.35
Water and Sediment; (% by volume) Max.	Trace	0.10
Ash; % by Wt.; Max.	0.01	0.02
Distillation, °F 90% Pt.; Max. Min.	550 –	640 540
Viscosity at 100°F; centistrokes Min. Max.	1.4 2.5	2.0 4.3
Sulfur; % Max.	0.5	0.7
Cetane No; Min.	40	40

FIGURE 13–11. The ASTM classifications for the two types of diesel fuels. *(Courtesy of American Society for Testing and Materials)*

13.4 GASOHOL AS A FUEL

Gasohol is a term used to describe a motor fuel that blends 90% gasoline and 10% alcohol. See *Figure 13–12*. The alcohol in gasohol is called *ethanol*. Ethanol is produced by distilling agricultural crops such as corn, wheat, timber, and sugar cane. The purpose of using gasohol is that for every gallon of gasohol sold, 10% of the fuel is renewable, whereas gasoline is considered a nonrenewable source of fuel. The study and use of gasohol grew out of the energy shortage of 1973. There is still a rather large debate going on as to its effectiveness and use in the automobile.

Gasohol Characteristics

Overall, the Btus in a gallon of gasohol are slightly less than in gasoline. Gasoline has about 115,000 Btu per gallon. Ethanol contains only 75,000 Btu per gallon. By adding ethanol to gasoline, the total Btu content is slightly less than that of gasoline. Alcohol, however, has a slightly higher octane than gasoline. The octane of gasohol is normally about 3–4 points higher than that of gasoline. The increase in octane reduces or eliminates engine knock and ping. Gasohol's higher octane also reduces engine postignition and run-on. Testing has shown that when gasohol is used, cleaner burning occurs in the combustion chamber. This tends to reduce harmful carbon deposits and soot buildup, which, in turn, promotes longer engine life. The alcohol in gasohol is also a de-icer (it prevents freezing in cold weather). Gasohol has been used in many parts of the country. Car manufacturers vary in their recommendations concerning the use of gasohol.

Questions about Gasohol

Questions still need to be answered about the use of gasohol. Is the reduced gasoline mileage when using gasohol sufficient to warrant its continued use? Should the United States grow grain to run our automobiles when millions of people are starving in other countries? What effect would gasohol production have on farming and other farm product prices? Can the price of gasohol be competitive with the price of gasoline? Before gasohol becomes widely accepted, these and other questions will have to be addressed in detail.

FIGURE 13–12. Gasohol is made from 90% gasoline and 10% alcohol.

CAR CLINIC

PROBLEM: Eliminate Vapor Lock

A customer has constantly complained about vapor lock. How can vapor lock be reduced?

SOLUTION:

Vapor lock is normally caused when fuel is heated to its vapor point in the lines of the fuel system. Methods used to reduce vapor lock include:

1. Use rubber and fabric lines because they are less of a heat sink than metal lines.
2. Try to direct the hot air away from the area of vapor lock.
3. Devise shields to eliminate hot exhaust heat from radiating to the fuel lines.
4. Check the vapor point on the specific fuel that is being used.

Each vehicle will be somewhat different, so the best solution will depend on the exact car and the exact cause of the problem.

13.5 LIQUID PETROLEUM GAS

LPG Characteristics

Another type of fuel that can be used in the automobile is called liquid petroleum gas, or LPG. LPG is also a hydrocarbon fuel and a by-product of the distillation process. It is made primarily of *propane* and butane. One major difference of LPG is its boiling point. See *Figure 13–13*. LPG has a very low boiling point. In normal ambient pressures, LPG has boiled and is in the vapor form. If the fuel is put under a pressure, the boiling point can be increased. The fuel can then be stored in a pressurized container as a liquid. See *Figure 13–14*. This makes storage much easier but possibly more dangerous in accidents. When the fuel is allowed to come out of the container, it turns back to a vapor.

LPG also has a higher octane rating (about 100 octane) than gasoline. This means that compression ratios could be increased slightly to improve efficiency. However, because the Btu content of LPG per gallon is less, there is slightly less power than with gasoline.

Advantages and Disadvantages of LPG

One of the big advantages of using LPG is that it is extremely clean and pollution-free. This is the reason many lift trucks use LPG fuels inside buildings. The exhaust is not as dangerous as the carbon monoxide that is produced by

Linkage to Service and Education

THE PRICE OF GAS

Gasoline prices seem always to be rising. However, when gasoline prices in the United States are compared with prices in other countries, they seem very low. The figure shows the average gasoline price per gallon in selected countries. Although prices vary with supply and demand, the United States still pays remarkably little for a gallon of gas compared with other countries. Other countries have such high gasoline prices, in part, because they must buy oil from foreign suppliers. Generally, the more oil a country must purchase from foreign suppliers, the greater the cost of the fuel to the consumer. Imagine how many miles people would drive each year in the United States if a gallon of regular gasoline cost $4.25 as in Bulgaria. It would cost $85 to fill a 20-gallon tank. *(Courtesy of Schwaller, Transportation Energy and Power Technology, Delmar Publishers, Inc.)*

PRICE OF REGULAR GASOLINE
IN SELECTED COUNTRIES
IN U.S. DOLLARS EQUIVALENT

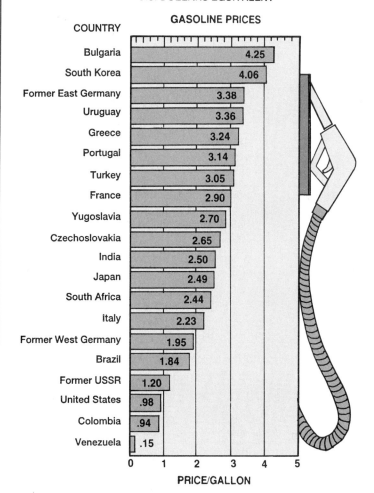

COUNTRY	GASOLINE PRICES
Bulgaria	4.25
South Korea	4.06
Former East Germany	3.38
Uruguay	3.36
Greece	3.24
Portugal	3.14
Turkey	3.05
France	2.90
Yugoslavia	2.70
Czechoslovakia	2.65
India	2.50
Japan	2.49
South Africa	2.44
Italy	2.23
Former West Germany	1.95
Brazil	1.84
Former USSR	1.20
United States	.98
Colombia	.94
Venezuela	.15

PRICE/GALLON

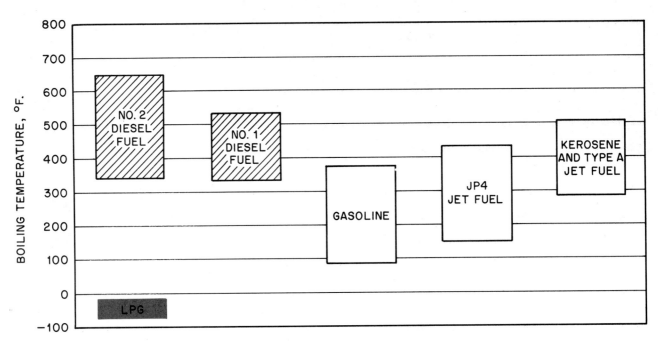

FIGURE 13–13. The boiling point of LPG is considerably lower than that of other fuels. At ambient pressure and temperature, LPG fuel has already boiled and is in a vaporized form.

gasoline. Large fleet operations are probably the biggest users of LPG fuels in the automotive industry. In these operations, the fuel can be containerized and sold in larger quantities. However, the fuel systems must be altered slightly to allow LPG to be used. Regulators, converters, and several other components must be installed to operate the system correctly.

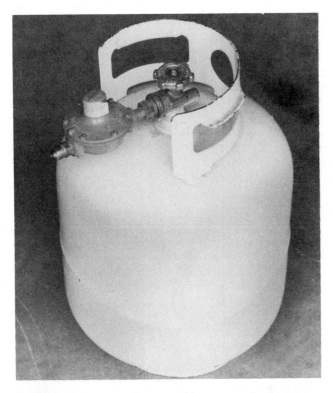

FIGURE 13–14. LPG is stored in a pressurized container to keep it in liquid form.

SUMMARY

Several types of fuel are used today in the automotive engine. The most popular is gasoline, but diesel fuel is also used. Gasohol and LPG are being studied and tested as possible fuels.

These fuels are all considered hydrocarbons. Normally, oil companies explore and locate crude oil under the ground. When it is found, the refinery separates the crude oil into many products. Gasoline, diesel fuel, and LPG all come from the crude oil. Distillation is the process that separates the crude oil into different fuels. The biggest difference between the fuels is that each has a different boiling point. The heating value of each fuel is also different. Heating values are measured in Btus.

Gasoline has many properties. Knocking occurs when a poor-quality fuel ignites on one side of the combustion chamber, and the spark plug ignites the other side. The two flame fronts hitting each other causes knocking. Octane is added to the fuel to reduce knocking. It is important to use the right octane. Temperatures, altitude, humidity, spark timing, carburetor setting, and driving methods all influence the octane rating needed.

Tetraethyl lead was used to increase the octane, but it also produced pollution. In addition, many new emission control devices would not work with lead in the fuel. The lead was removed and no-lead fuels were put in cars. This meant the compression ratios had to be reduced. Reducing compression ratios has had a significant effect on the efficiency of combustion in engines.

Gasoline has many additives. These include anti-icers, carburetor detergents, lubricants for valves, and combustion modifiers.

Poor-quality gasoline can cause postignition. When the

ignition is shut off, the vehicle's engine continues to run. Postignition is produced by glowing carbon deposits inside the combustion chamber.

Diesel fuels are also used in the automotive market. The primary rating of diesel fuel is the cetane number. Cetane is a measure of the delay time between injection and combustion of the fuel. Other characteristics of diesel fuels include distillation endpoint, sulfur content, pour point, cloud point, flash point, and ash content.

Diesel fuels come in two classifications: No. 1-D and No. 2-D. Each has been designed to have a certain cetane number, distillation endpoint, cloud, pour and flash points, and ash content.

Gasohol is being used in some vehicles. It is made from a mixture of 90% gasoline and 10% alcohol. The alcohol comes from distilling corn, wheat, and other farm products. Although many questions still surround the use of gasohol, it is being used in parts of the United States.

Liquid petroleum gas (LPG) is also a hydrocarbon. It is made from hydrocarbons distilled from natural gas or crude oil. If put under a pressure, it becomes a liquid. In ambient pressures, LPG is in a gaseous form. It is made primarily of propane and butane.

TERMS TO KNOW

Can you explain each of the following terms? Review the chapter until you can use each term correctly.

Hydrocarbon
Boiling point
Condense
Distillation
Btu
Knocking
Pinging
Octane number
Regular gasoline
Hi-test
Tetraethyl lead
Nitrogen oxide
Volatility
Vaporize
Vapor lock
Anti-icer
Oxidation inhibitors

Rust inhibitors
Detergents
Preignition
Postignition
Cetane number
Ether
Distillation endpoint
Sulfur
Acid rain
Ambient
Cloud point
Atomization
Flash Point
Abrasive
Ethanol
Propane

REVIEW QUESTIONS

Multiple Choice

1. Crude oil is primarily made of what molecules?
   a. Nitrogen and oxygen
   b. Carbon and hydrogen
   c. Sulfur and nitrogen
   d. Nitrogen and sulfur
   e. Sulfur and carbon

2. What is the major difference between different fuels?
   a. Boiling points
   b. Acid levels
   c. Degree of lubrication
   d. Density
   e. Thickness

3. The process of separating crude oil into different fuels is called _____.
   a. Combustion
   b. Condensing
   c. Distillation
   d. Departing
   e. None of the above

4. When two flame fronts hit each other, a _____ sound is heard.
   a. Knocking
   b. Soft sound
   c. Cracking
   d. Hissing
   e. None of the above

5. The resistance to burning of gasoline is defined as:
   a. Cetane
   b. Octane
   c. Butane
   d. Methane
   e. Ethane

6. Which octane is a result of calculating (R + M)/2?
   a. Road octane
   b. Motor octane
   c. Research octane
   d. All of the above
   e. None of the above

7. Which of the following will influence the octane number needed in an engine?
   a. Carburetor settings
   b. Air temperature
   c. Altitude
   d. All of the above
   e. None of the above

8. Which chemical is added to gasoline to increase the octane number?
   a. Sulfur lead
   b. Distillation chemicals
   c. Tetraethyl lead
   d. Nitrogen
   e. Oxygen

9. When lead was removed from gasoline, what had to be done with the compression ratios?
   a. They were increased
   b. They were kept the same
   c. They were reduced or lowered
   d. They were doubled
   e. None of the above

10. The condition that occurs when the engine ignition is shut off and the engine continues to run is called _____.
    a. Pinging
    b. Knocking
    c. Postfiring
    d. Preignition
    e. Run-on

11. The measure of a diesel fuel's quality is called:
    a. Ash point
    b. Cetane number
    c. Sulfur content
    d. Methane number
    e. Octane number

12. The temperature at which a diesel fuel is completely vaporized is called the:
    a. Distillation endpoint
    b. Flash point
    c. Pour point
    d. Fire point
    e. Boiling point

13. The term *ambient* is defined as:
    a. Surrounding
    b. Closed in
    c. Open
    d. Endpoint
    e. Cetane point

14. A diesel fuel's ignition point when exposed to open flame is defined as:
    a. Pour point
    b. Flash point
    c. Distillation point
    d. Burning point
    e. Firing point

15. What are the two types of diesel fuel classifications?
    a. 1-D and 2-D
    b. 2-D and 4-D
    c. 3-D and 4-D
    d. 4-D and 5-D
    e. 4-D and 1-D

16. Gasohol is a mixture of what percentages of gasoline and alcohol?
    a. 10% gasoline and 90% alcohol
    b. 20% gasoline and 80% alcohol
    c. 30% gasoline and 70% alcohol
    d. 40% gasoline and 60% alcohol
    e. None of the above

17. Gasohol has _____ ratings than gasoline.
    a. Lower octane
    b. Higher octane
    c. 17 higher octane
    d. Higher cetane
    e. Lower cetane

18. If put under a pressure, LPG will change to a _____.
    a. Liquid
    b. Gas
    c. Solid
    d. Semisolid
    e. Semiliquid

The following questions are similar in format to ASE (Automotive Service Excellence) test questions.

19. Technician A says gasoline has an octane rating. Technician B says gasoline has a cetane rating. Who is right?
    a. A only
    b. B only
    c. Both A and B
    d. Neither A nor B

20. Technician A says that resistance to burning is measured with a cetane rating on gasoline. Technician B says that resistance to burning has no type of measurement for gasoline. Who is right?
    a. A only
    b. B only
    c. Both A and B
    d. Neither A nor B

21. Technician A says that preignition is caused by glowing deposits inside the combustion chamber. Technician B says that preignition is caused by bad lubrication. Who is right?
    a. A only
    b. B only
    c. Both A and B
    d. Neither A nor B

22. Technician A says that lead has recently been added to fuel to improve nitrogen oxides. Technician B says that lead has recently been added to fuel to lower the compression ratio. Who is right?
    a. A only
    b. B only
    c. Both A and B
    d. Neither A nor B

23. Technician A says that vapor lock occurs when fuel is too hot. Technician B says that vapor lock is caused by a lack of oxidation. Who is correct?
    a. A only
    b. B only
    c. Both A and B
    d. Neither A nor B

24. Technician A says that anti-icer could be used in the winter. Technician B says that anti-icer is a cleaning agent in the fuel. Who is correct?
    a. A only
    b. B only
    c. Both A and B
    d. Neither A nor B

25. Technician A says that the lack of oxidation inhibitors will cause the fuel filter to plug up. Technician B says that oxidation inhibitors are added to gasoline that is being stored. Who is correct?
    a. A only
    b. B only
    c. Both A and B
    d. Neither A nor B

26. Technician A says that as carbon builds up on top of the piston, the compression ratio decreases. Technician B says that as carbon builds up on top of the piston, detonation decreases. Who is correct?
    a. A only
    b. B only
    c. Both A and B
    d. Neither A nor B

Essay

27. What does the term distillation mean?

28. What is knocking?

29. How does octane of a fuel relate to the burning of fuel?

30. Why are anti-icers added to fuel?

31. State several advantages and disadvantages of using gasohol.

Short Answer

32. When storing gasoline, it is a good idea to add a/an _____ to the fuel.

33. To prevent gasoline from freezing in cold climates, add _____ to the fuel tank.

34. To help keep the carburetor and/or fuel injector system clean, always add _____ to the fuel.

35. Vapor lock can be developed in the fuel system when fuel lines are _____ to the heat source.

36. One of the major processes done in a refinery is that of _____.

CHAPTER 14

Basic Fuel Systems

INTRODUCTION The fuel system is critical to engine operation. This chapter is about the fuel system components and their operation. The fuel system consists of the fuel tank, lines, pumps, filters, carburetors, and injectors. However, because carburetors and injectors have become rather complex, a separate chapter is devoted to each. This chapter deals only with the basic components of the fuel system needed to get the fuel to the carburetor or injectors.

OBJECTIVES After reading this chapter, you should be able to:

■ Identify the total fuel flow on an automobile engine.

■ Analyze the parts and operation of the fuel tank and fuel metering parts.

■ Recognize the parts and operation of mechanical and electrical fuel pumps.

■ State the purpose and operation of fuel filters.

■ Identify common problems, diagnosis, and service procedures in the basic fuel system components.

✔ SAFETY CHECKLIST ✔

When working with basic fuel systems, keep these important safety precautions in mind.

✔ Whenever gasoline is spilled, immediately wipe it up and dispose of the rags in a sealed container.

✔ Never clean any automotive parts with gasoline.

✔ Never smoke in or around an automobile.

✔ Keep all unshielded flames away from the vehicle when the fuel system is being serviced.

✔ Always store the fuel in an approved OSHA container.

14.1 TOTAL FUEL FLOW

The fuel system is made so that fuel can be stored in a fuel tank and be ready for delivery to the engine. *Figure 14–1* shows a total fuel system flow of an engine with a carburetor. The fuel in the fuel tank is ready to be used when the engine needs it. The fuel pump, which is electrically or mechanically driven, draws fuel from the tank and sends it to the carburetor. The purpose of the carburetor is to keep the fuel at the right air-fuel ratio. It is very important to maintain a ratio of 14.7 parts air to 1 part fuel. The air-fuel ratio must be accurate throughout engine operation.

Figure 14–2 shows the total fuel system flow of a fuel-injected engine. The fuel is stored in the fuel tank. The fuel

pump is located in the fuel tank. Fuel is pressurized and sent to the fuel feed pipe, through a fuel filter, and into the fuel injectors. A *pressure regulator valve* keeps the pressure constant on the system.

Figure 14–3 shows a diesel fuel system. Here the fuel goes to the *fuel injector* pump, rather than to the carburetor. On all fuel injector systems on diesel engines, there must be a fuel return line to the fuel tank. This is also shown. Any fuel not used by the engine is returned to the fuel tank or to the suction side of the fuel pump to be used again.

The parts of the fuel gasoline system include the vapor separator, the carbon canister, and the fuel filter. The vapor separator is used to separate any *fuel vapors* and send them back to the fuel tank. The carbon canister is a pollution

Some of the information in this chapter, Basic Fuel Systems, can help you prepare for the National Institute for Automotive Service Excellence (ASE) certification tests. The tests most directly related to this chapter are entitled

ENGINE REPAIR (TEST A1) AND ENGINE PERFORMANCE (TEST A8).

The content areas that closely parallel this chapter are

FUEL AND EXHAUST SYSTEMS DIAGNOSIS AND REPAIR AND FUEL, AIR INDUCTION, AND EXHAUST SYSTEMS DIAGNOSIS AND REPAIR.

control device that holds excess vapors from the tank and carburetor. The carbon canister is studied in detail in the chapter on pollution. The fuel filter, which is located directly before the carburetor or fuel injectors, is used to keep the fuel clean and free of contaminants.

PROBLEM: Oil Level Increases

A customer has noticed when checking the oil that the level has increased. How can the level of oil be increased without adding oil to the crankcase?

SOLUTION:

The level cannot increase without adding some type of fluid. The most likely problem is that fuel (gasoline) is being added to the oil. A quick check is to smell the oil. It should have a gasoline odor. As fuel is added, the oil level appears to increase. Fuel can be added to the oil in two major ways. The fuel pump (if mechanical and located on the side of the engine) can have a leak in the diaphragm. Fuel then passes through the diaphragm into the crankcase area. A second way in which fuel can be added to oil is by having the carburetor or fuel injectors extremely rich during starting. A heavily choked engine will cause raw fuel to slip past the rings and into the crankcase area. To eliminate the problem, either replace the fuel pump or readjust the choke according to the manufacturer's specifications. If the vehicle uses injectors, the computer controls will have to be checked for a rich mixture.

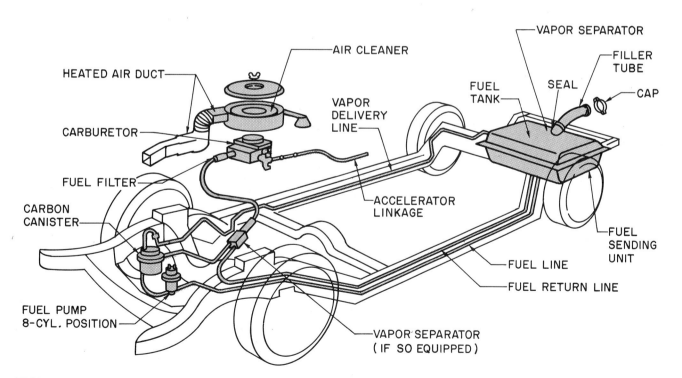

FIGURE 14–1.   The fuel system consists of the fuel tank, fuel lines, fuel pump, carburetor or fuel injectors, fuel filter, and vapor separator. The carbon canister and heated air duct also play a part in the fuel system. *(Courtesy of Ford Motor Company)*

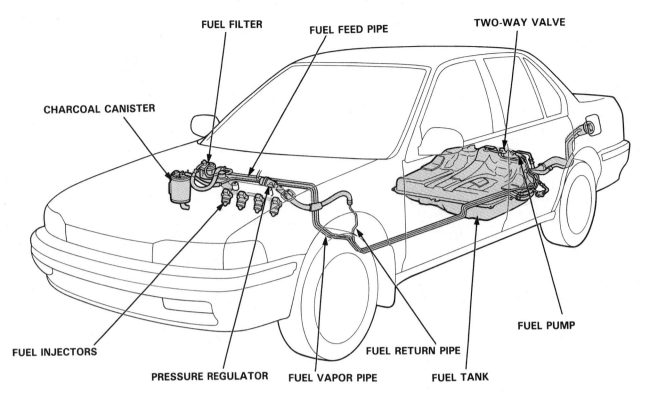

FUEL FILTER   FUEL FEED PIPE   TWO-WAY VALVE

CHARCOAL CANISTER

FUEL PUMP

FUEL INJECTORS

PRESSURE REGULATOR   FUEL VAPOR PIPE   FUEL TANK

FUEL RETURN PIPE

FIGURE 14–2. Total fuel flow for a fuel-injected engine. *(Courtesy of Honda Motor Company, Ltd.)*

14.2   FUEL TANK

The fuel tank is made to hold or store the excess fuel needed by the automobile. It is usually located in the rear of the vehicle, but in cars that have rear-mounted engines, it is located in the front part of the vehicle. *Figure 14–4* shows a fuel tank. The shape of the fuel tank depends on the physical design of the vehicle. The fuel tank must fit around the frame and still be protected from impacts.

The size of the fuel tank depends on the driving range of

the vehicle. Because today's cars get better fuel economy than older cars, fuel tanks are smaller. Generally the tank sizes range from 10 to 25 gallons.

The fuel tank is made of thin sheet metal or plastic. Various parts of the fuel tank are welded or soldered together to make the completed assembly. A lead-tin alloy is placed on the sheet metal to keep gasoline from rusting and corroding the tank.

Inside the fuel tank there are several baffles as shown in *Figure 14–5*. These baffles are used to keep the fuel from

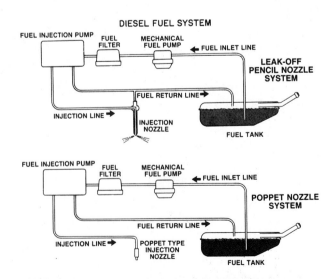

DIESEL FUEL SYSTEM

FUEL INJECTION PUMP   FUEL FILTER   MECHANICAL FUEL PUMP   ← FUEL INLET LINE

LEAK-OFF PENCIL NOZZLE SYSTEM

FUEL RETURN LINE →

INJECTION LINE →   INJECTION NOZZLE

FUEL TANK

FUEL INJECTION PUMP   FUEL FILTER   MECHANICAL FUEL PUMP   ← FUEL INLET LINE

POPPET NOZZLE SYSTEM

FUEL RETURN LINE →

INJECTION LINE →   POPPET TYPE INJECTION NOZZLE

FUEL TANK

FIGURE 14–3. A diesel fuel system has a tank, mechanical pump, fuel filter, and fuel injection pump with injectors. *(Courtesy of General Motors Product Service Training)*

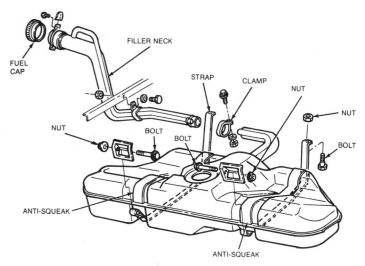

FIGURE 14–4. The fuel tank consists of many parts. They are designed to fit around the frame of the vehicle. *(Courtesy of Chevrolet Division, General Motors Corporation)*

sloshing and splashing around in the fuel tank. The baffles help to restrict fuel movement during rapid starts and stops, cornering, and so on. Without the baffles, small bubbles caused by the constant agitation or movement may form in the fuel. If these bubbles were to get into the fuel system, the engine would perform poorly.

Many fuel tanks also have an expansion tank built into the existing tank. The expansion tank is not filled during a normal fill-up at a gasoline station. When the tank is full and the fuel expands because it becomes warmer (during hot summer days) fuel enters the expansion tank rather than overflowing (see Chapter 24 for more information).

Fuel Cap and Filler Neck

The fuel cap on the fuel tank is used for several reasons. First, the fuel cap keeps the fuel from splashing out of the tank. Second, the cap releases the vacuum created when the fuel is removed by the engine. Third, the cap releases pressure when the fuel tank heats up and expands in hot weather. Fourth, the cap passes vapors to the carbon canister when needed. The filler neck on newer vehicles has a restrictor door so that only unleaded fuel nozzles can be used.

Many designs are used for fuel caps. One common type seals the tank with a cap that has threads, *Figure 14–6*. A ratchet tightening device on the threaded filler cap reduces the chances of incorrect installation. If the wrong cap is used, vapor control will be lost.

The filler neck has internal threads. The cap contains a plastic center extension. This acts as a guide when inserted into the filler neck. As the cap is turned, a large O ring is seated upon the filler neck flange. After the seal and flange make contact, the ratchet produces a clicking noise. This indicates that the seal has been set. Now the vacuum and pressure lines will operate correctly.

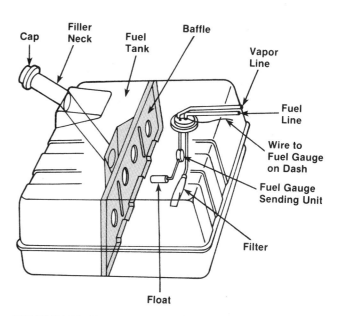

FIGURE 14–5. Baffles are used inside the fuel tank to reduce sloshing and moving of the fuel during cornering and acceleration or deceleration. *(Courtesy of Scharff, Complete Fuel Systems and Emission Control, Delmar Publishers Inc.)*

FIGURE 14–6. The filler cap is used to seal the fuel tank so pressure and vapors can escape.

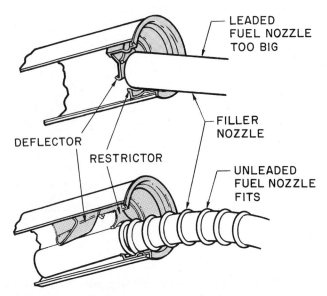

FIGURE 14–7. This restrictor allows only the unleaded fuel nozzle to fit into the filler neck. *(Courtesy of Scharff, Complete Fuel Systems and Emission Control, Delmar Publishers Inc.)*

A *filler neck restrictor* is used on vehicles that require unleaded gasoline. *Figure 14–7* shows the neck restrictor. The smaller hole (produced by the restrictor) prevents the customer from using the larger nozzle at a fuel pump. The larger nozzle is used to deliver only leaded gasoline. Thus, only unleaded fuel can be used in cars that have filler neck restrictors.

Fuel Metering Unit

The operator must know how much fuel is in the tank. This is measured with a fuel metering unit. Many styles are used. One type has a hinged float inside the tank. As the float changes position with different levels of fuel, the sensing unit changes its resistance. The resistance then changes the current in the circuit and the position of the needle on the dashboard gauge. *Figure 14–8* shows a fuel metering unit.

Inside the fuel level sender there is a variable resistor. As the fuel level changes more or less resistance is put into the fuel sensing circuit. *Figure 14–9* shows how the electrical circuit operates. The design uses an electrical bimetallic strip (thermostatic strip) that can be bent or warped by heat. Heat is produced by the electricity flowing in the circuit.

When the tank is empty or low in fuel as shown in Figure 14–9 (A), high resistance is produced at the variable resistor in the fuel tank. Consequently, very little electricity can flow in the circuit. The thermostatic strip remains cool, and there is very little deflection of the pointer.

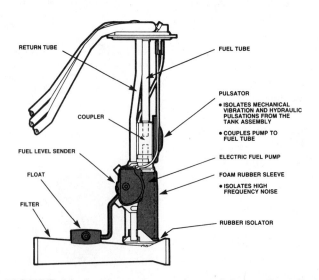

FIGURE 14–8. The fuel metering unit has a float that changes resistance as the fuel level changes. *(Courtesy of General Motors Product Service Training)*

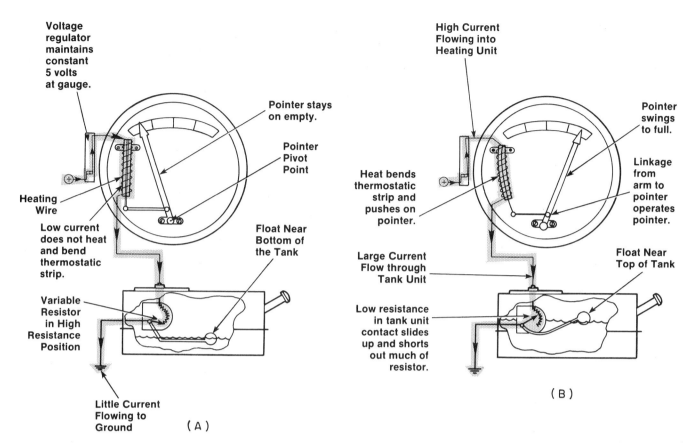

FIGURE 14–9. The electricity in the fuel gauge is controlled by the variable resistor in the fuel tank. *(Courtesy of Scharff, Complete Fuel Systems and Emission Control, Delmar Publishers Inc.)*

When the tank is full as shown in Figure 14–9 (B) a lower resistance is produced at the variable resistor in the fuel tank. This means that more electricity can flow in the bimetallic strip. More electricity produces more heat. The heat bends the thermostatic strip. This causes the pointer to move to a full position.

Diesel Fuel Pickup and Sending Unit

Diesel engines are very sensitive to water contamination. Water can get into the fuel by *condensation*. When a fuel tank is only partially full, water tends to form within the tank. The moisture in the air within the tank condenses on the inside tank wall. This occurs in the fuel tank or in any storage tank between the refinery and the vehicle.

By law in many states, water in diesel fuel should be no more than 1/2 of 1%. That quantity of water will be absorbed by the fuel. Higher levels may have a damaging effect on the injectors.

Hydrocarbon fuels are lighter than water. This means that water will be on the bottom of the tank and not on the top. Pickup systems are made to keep water out of the fuel. Some use a "sock" to absorb the water. Others use a detector to determine if water should be drained from the system.

Figure 14–10 shows a common type of fuel pickup with a water warning system. This unit uses a capacitive probe to detect the presence of water when it reaches the 1–2 gallon level. An electronic module provides a ground through a wire to a light in the instrument panel. The light reads "water in fuel."

PROBLEM: Bad Fuel Filter

An engine is becoming consistently more erratic, and the engine power is reducing. At times the engine shuts down. It seems that the engine isn't getting enough fuel. What would be a quick component to check with these symptoms?

SOLUTION:

The quickest component to check with these symptoms is the fuel filter. Over a period of time, the fuel filter in the main fuel line to the carburetor may become plugged with dirt from the fuel tank. Replace the fuel filter, and the problems will probably be eliminated.

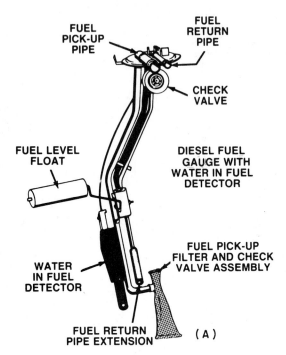

FUEL PICK-UP PIPE

FUEL RETURN PIPE

CHECK VALVE

FUEL LEVEL FLOAT

DIESEL FUEL GAUGE WITH WATER IN FUEL DETECTOR

WATER IN FUEL DETECTOR

FUEL PICK-UP FILTER AND CHECK VALVE ASSEMBLY

FUEL RETURN PIPE EXTENSION

(A)

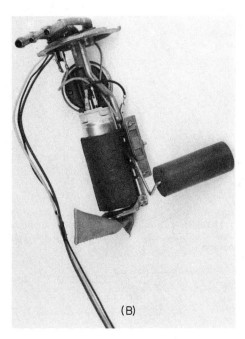

(B)

FIGURE 14–10. This fuel pickup/sending unit has a water-in-fuel warning system. *(Part A Courtesy of General Motors Product Service Training)*

14.3 FUEL PUMPS

The purpose of the fuel pump is to transfer the fuel from the tank to the carburetor or fuel injectors. Gasoline engine fuel pumps are either mechanical or electrical. Both will be studied. Diesel engines have a complex fuel pump. This unit will be studied further in the chapter on fuel injection.

Mechanical Fuel Pumps

A typical mechanical fuel pump is shown in ***Figure 14–11***. This unit is driven by the camshaft. There is a cam or an eccentric lobe on the camshaft. As the camshaft turns, the lobe lifts a lever up and down, causing a pumping action.

FIGURE 14–11. The mechanical fuel pump is used on many vehicles that use carburetors. It is driven by the camshaft.

Fuel is drawn from the tank by a vacuum and is sent to the carburetor.

This pump is called a *diaphragm*-type pump. A diaphragm is used internally to cause the suction and pressure needed to move the fuel. Check valves are used to keep the fuel moving in the right direction.

Check valve operation is shown in ***Figure 14–12***. The check valve is made of a small disc held on a seat by a spring. If a suction is produced on the right side of the valve, the disc will lift off the seat and draw fuel into the pump, Figure 14–12 (A). When a pressure is produced on the back side of the disc, it is forced against the seat. Also, when a pressure is produced on the left side of the valve, the disc will open to allow flow, Figure 14–12 (B).

The same action occurs inside the fuel pump. Referring to ***Figure 14–13***, when the eccentric cam lifts the diaphragm, a suction is produced. This suction causes the inlet check valve to open and draw in fuel. When the diaphragm moves in the opposite direction, a pressure is produced inside the fuel pump. This pressure closes the inlet check valve and forces the fuel through the outlet check valve. This action causes a suction, which draws fuel from the tank. This creates a pressure, which forces the fuel to the carburetor.

Fuel pumps can be checked for two specifications, pressure and capacity. The pressure created by a mechanical fuel pump is low. Each vehicle will be different, but average fuel pump pressures range from 3 to 10 pounds per square inch. The capacity of a fuel pump measures how much volume the fuel pump can deliver in a certain period of time, generally 30 seconds. Average capacity ratings are from 0.5 pint to 1 pint per 30 seconds.

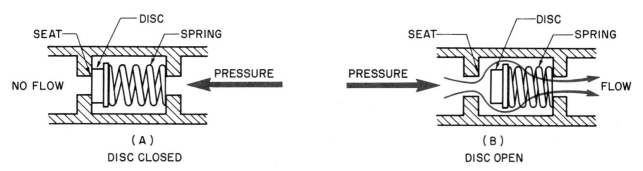

FIGURE 14–12. Check valves are used inside the mechanical fuel pump to control the suction and pressure of the fuel. When a suction is on the left side, the disc lifts off the seat and brings in fuel. Pressure on the right side causes the disc to seat again.

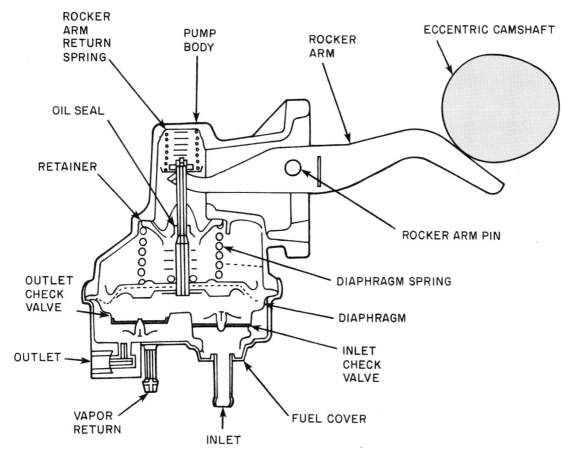

FIGURE 14–13. A diaphragm is used to cause a vacuum. The fuel is drawn in and pressurized. It is then sent through the check valve to the carburetor. *(Courtesy of Scharff, Complete Fuel Systems and Emission Control, Delmar Publishers Inc.)*

Vapor Return Line

Some mechanical fuel pumps have a small connection on the fuel pump called a vapor return. The purpose of this line is to return fuel vapor that has built up in the fuel pump to the fuel tank. As engine and underhood temperatures increase, vapors may develop in the fuel lines. Vapors are removed at this point.

Electrical Fuel Pumps

Electrical fuel pumps can be used instead of mechanical fuel pumps. Electrical fuel pumps have certain advantages over the mechanical type. Electrical fuel pumps work independently on electrical current. They provide fuel when the switch is turned on. Mechanical fuel pumps must have the engine cranking or turning before they deliver fuel. Another advantage is that electrical fuel pumps can be located farther away from the engine. This means that heat from the engine will not produce vapors in the fuel pump. Therefore, there is less risk of vapor lock. Electrical fuel pumps also work well in conjunction with computer-controlled vehicles. In addition, electrical fuel pumps consume less frictional horsepower. Electrical fuel pumps also produce more pressure than the typical mechanical pump. Depending on the engine and

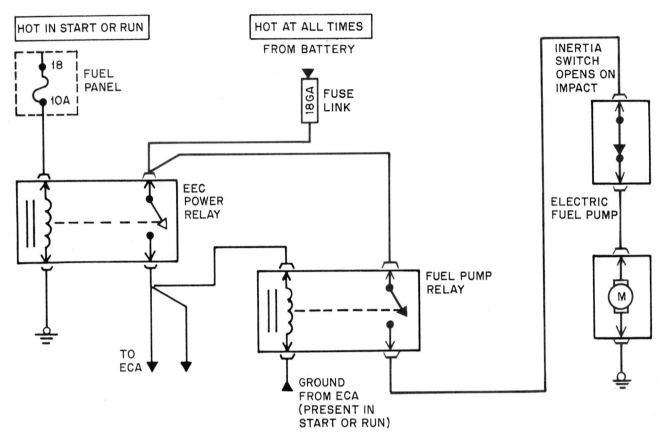

FIGURE 14–14. The circuit to operate the electrical fuel pump has an inertia switch to break the circuit during sudden impacts (accident). *(Courtesy of Scharff, Complete Fuel Systems and Emission Control, Delmar Publishers Inc.)*

manufacturer, average pump pressures range from 15 to 40 psi.

Several styles of the electrical fuel pump are used, including the bellows type and the impeller or roller vane type. The year of manufacture and the type of vehicle will determine which type is used.

The electrical circuit used to operate the electrical fuel pump is shown in **Figure 14–14**. In operation, electricity starts at the battery and flows to the fuse link (center). The fuse link is connected to the fuel pump relay. This relay is immediately energized, and the switch is closed when the vehicle ignition switch is in the start or run position. Electricity then flows through an *inertia switch*, which is normally closed. From there the electricity flows into the electrical fuel pump to turn the fuel pump motor.

The inertia switch is a safety switch that opens the circuit whenever there is sudden impact from a vehicle crash or accident. This keeps the fuel pump from running and spilling gasoline if the car is in an accident.

Bellows-Type Electrical Fuel Pump

In the bellows-type electrical fuel pump, a metal *bellows* is used instead of a diaphragm. A bellows can cause a vacuum or pressure when stretched or compressed. The bellows is moved back and forth by the action of a solenoid. See *Figure 14–15*. When the electrical current is sent to the mag-

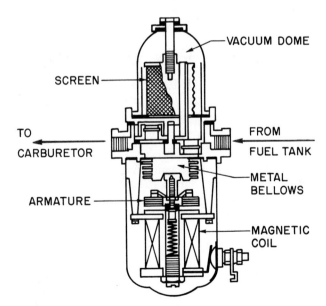

FIGURE 14–15. A bellows-type fuel pump operates from the movement of the armature in the magnetic coil. The bellows is stretched and squeezed to produce the suction and pressure needed to move the fuel.

netic coil, the *armature* is drawn downward. This action causes the metal bellows to expand and stretch. Fuel is drawn in by a vacuum. When the armature reaches its lowest point, the electrical current on the magnetic coil is removed. The return spring then pushes the bellows upward. This causes a pressure that forces the fuel out of the fuel pump and into the carburetor.

Roller Vane Fuel Pump

A second type of fuel pump used on newer vehicles is called the roller vane electrical fuel pump. There are several variations of this type of pump. *Figure 14–16* shows an example of such a pump. The electric motor assembly is operated by electrical current. As the motor turns an impeller, fuel is drawn in by the lower section of the pump. It is pressurized and sent out the top of the pump for delivery to the engine. The impeller at the inlet end serves as a vapor separator. The unit operates at approximately 3,500 RPM. A pressure relief valve keeps fuel pump pressure at a constant pressure such as 60–90 psi. The fuel pump delivers more fuel than the engine can consume even under the most extreme conditions. *Figure 14–17* shows the impeller action.

Fuel Pressure Regulators

Fuel systems that have electrical fuel pumps and fuel injectors may use a fuel pressure regulator. *Figure 14–18* shows such a regulator. It is located as shown in *Figure 14–19*. The

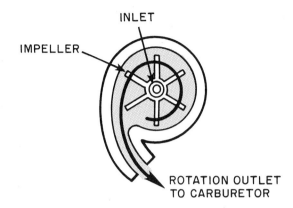

FIGURE 14–17. The impeller in the fuel pump creates suction that draws fuel into the pump. It then pushes it out to the carburetor. *(Courtesy of Scharff, Complete Fuel Systems and Emission Control, Delmar Publishers Inc.*

FIGURE 14–18. A fuel pressure regulator keeps fuel at the right pressure for the system.

fuel pressure regulator regulates the fuel that comes out of the fuel pump, through the fuel filter, and into the injector. It controls the fuel pressure at the fuel injectors. The purpose of the regulator is to keep the pressure of the fuel at the injectors between 60 and 90 psi. Some manufacturers have lower fuel injector pressure.

The fuel pressure regulator operates internally as shown in *Figure 14–20*. The fuel pressure regulator contains a pressure chamber that is separated by a diaphragm. A *calibrated* spring is placed in the vacuum chamber side. Fuel pressure is regulated when the fuel pump pressure overcomes the spring pressure. At this point, a small relief valve in the center opens. This action passes excess fuel back to the fuel tank. Vacuum action on the top side of the diaphragm, along with spring pressure, controls fuel pressure. A decrease in vacuum creates an increase in fuel pressure. A small increase in the intake manifold vacuum creates a decrease in fuel pressure. As an example, when the engine is under heavy load, vacuum is decreased. This condition requires more fuel. A decrease in vacuum allows more pressure to pass the top side of the pressure relief valve. This increases fuel pressure, and thus more fuel is pumped.

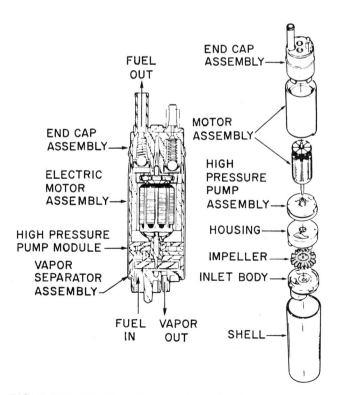

FIGURE 14–16. The roller vane fuel pump has a motor that rotates an impeller to draw fuel in and pressurize it. *(Courtesy of General Motors Corporation)*

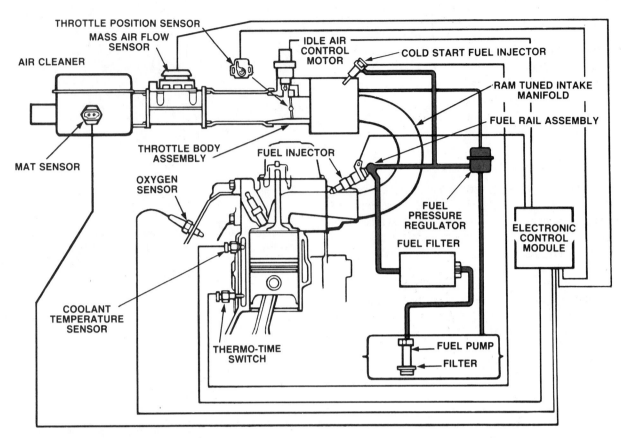

FIGURE 14–19. The fuel pressure regulator is located in a position where it can regulate the fuel going to the injector. *(Courtesy of General Motors Product Service Training)*

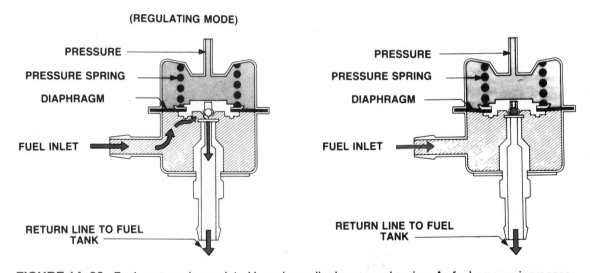

FIGURE 14–20. Fuel pressure is regulated by using a diaphragm and spring. As fuel presure increases, the spring lifts and allows fuel to pass through the check valve, back to the tank. *(Courtesy of General Motors Product Service Training)*

Computers and Fuel Control

Many manufacturers are using computers to control various functions of the engine. Fuel systems are also being controlled by computers. One such system is diagrammed in *Figure 14–21*. This figure shows a diagram of a computer used to control several systems. The left side of the diagram shows the signals being fed into the control unit. The right side of the diagram shows what systems are being controlled by the control unit. In this case, the control unit is operating the fuel pump.

Operation of the fuel pump is controlled by the computer

FUEL PUMP CONTROL

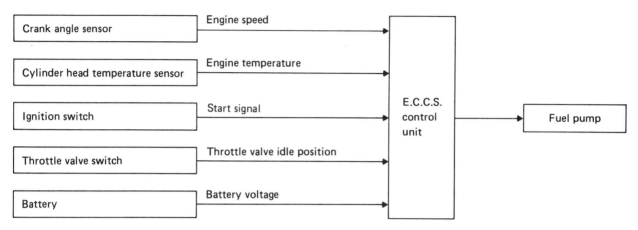

FIGURE 14–21. On computer-controlled engines, the fuel pump is controlled by the computer. Various inputs help determine the operation of the fuel pump. *(Courtesy of Nissan Motor Corporation in USA)*

control unit. This particular manufacturer calls the computer control unit an E.C.C.S. (electronic concentrated engine control system). Several signals are fed into the computer to control the fuel pump. These include the engine speed, temperature, a start signal, the throttle valve idle position, and the battery voltage. The E.C.C.S. unit then takes each of these signals and operates the fuel pump accordingly. More information will be given about computer-controlled systems in later chapters.

CAR CLINIC

PROBLEM: Engine Misses at High Speed

A customer complains that when running at fuel throttle up a slight grade, the vehicle begins to slow down, sputters, and misses. Several items have been repaired and replaced. These include the carburetor, timing, fuel pump, filters, and the Exhaust Gas Recirculation (EGR) valve. (See Chapter 24.) What other areas should be checked?

SOLUTION:

It sounds as if the fuel tank is developing a vacuum, and the fuel is being restricted to the carburetor. Check the fuel tank cap. The caps are designed to vent the tank of fumes and to allow air to come into the tank as the fuel is removed. Also check the carbon canister for damage or lines that are crimped.

14.4 FUEL FILTERS

Purpose of Fuel Filters

Most internal combustion engines consume a mixture of fuel and air to produce power. The key word in the operation of any such engine is cleanliness. Any fuel system using a carburetor or fuel injectors has many small passages and delicate parts that can be damaged by dirt particles. A dirty carburetor or fuel injector can cause erratic performance or complete engine shutdown.

Diesel engines use a fuel injector under very high pressure. Many small openings in the tip of the injectors will be damaged if dirt particles get into the system.

Sources of Gasoline Contaminants

Contaminants may enter the fuel system from various sources. These include:

1. Unfiltered fuel that is pumped into the vehicle tank

2. Loose tank caps or faulty sealing gaskets

3. Rust, a powerful abrasive, that flakes off from the fuel tank and lines

4. Contaminants or dirt particles left in the tanks or lines during manufacturing and assembly

Gasoline Fuel Filters

Depending on the manufacturer, some engines may have one or two filters in the fuel system. The first filter, *Figure 14–22*, located in the gasoline tank, is made of fine woven fabric. This filter prevents large pieces of contaminant from damaging the fuel pump. The tank filter also prevents most water from going to the carburetor or fuel injectors.

The second filter is found in one of several locations. An

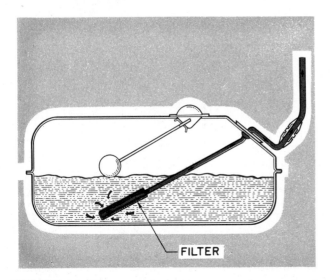

FIGURE 14–22. The first filter in a gasoline engine is located directly in the tank. *(Courtesy of Dana Corporation)*

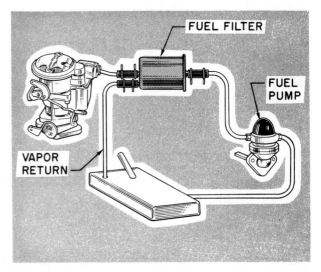

FIGURE 14–23. An in-line filter is used to filter out small particles of dirt and rust. A vapor return line helps to reduce vapor buildup in the system. *(Courtesy of Dana Corporation)*

in-line filter is shown in *Figure 14–23*. Fuel is drawn from the tank into the fuel pump. The fuel pump pressurizes the fuel and sends it to the filter. A return line is used on vehicles that have a vapor lock problem. (Not all filters have this return line.)

Gasoline from the pump flows to the inlet fitting of the filter. Gasoline used by the carburetor passes through the filter and out the center fitting. A small amount of gasoline will exit through the second outlet and return to the tank. The recirculation of gasoline through the vapor line cools the gas and prevents vapor lock.

Figure 14–24 shows the in-carburetor type of fuel filter. This filter has small pleated paper filters with a gasket to provide positive sealing.

Diesel Fuel Contaminants

When diesel fuel is being shipped from the refinery, it can pick up certain fuel contaminants. These include rust, dirt, and water.

Rust usually comes from large storage tanks or vehicle tanks. Rust occurs when there are low fuel levels in the tank over a long period of time. Rust is an abrasive and can cause damage to the injection system.

Water can enter the fuel when it is held in underground storage tanks and when a vehicle tank is being filled on a wet, rainy day. The most common source of water is condensation in the fuel tank. If the fuel tank is not kept filled, warm, moisture-filled air condenses on the cooler inside metal wall of the fuel tank.

Dirt can find its way into the fuel in several ways. Dirt can be found on the tank spouts and dispensing nozzles. The vent system must be in good condition and checked as a source of dirt.

Two other contaminants are sometimes found in fuel. These are bacteria and wax crystals. Bacteria growth takes place in diesel fuel when certain microorganisms begin to

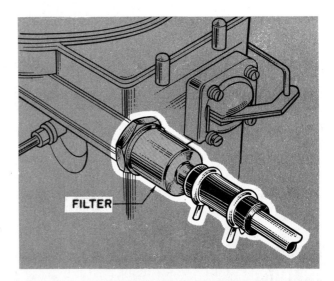

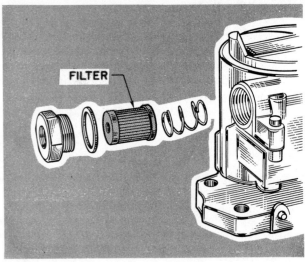

FIGURE 14–24. The filter is attached directly to the carburetor on some engines. *(Courtesy of Dana Corporation)*

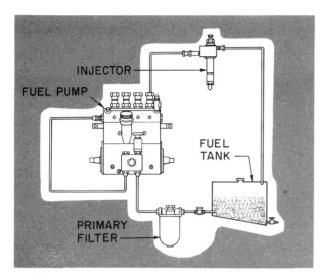

FIGURE 14–25. It is desirable to use a primary filter in the diesel fuel system. *(Courtesy of Dana Corporation)*

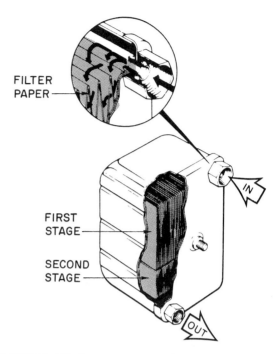

FIGURE 14–26. In some automotive diesel fuel systems, the filters are combined into a single filter. The first- and second-stage filters are built into this filter. *(Courtesy of General Motors Product Service Training)*

grow. They grow at the point where water and diesel fuel meet in the tank. The tank is dark inside, and if the fuel moves very little conditions are ideal for bacteria to grow. As the bacteria grow, they form a "slime" that will eventually be carried to the filter. This slime causes the filter to plug prematurely.

Wax crystals form when the diesel fuel reaches its cloud point temperature. As the wax crystals begin to form, they plug the filters. Less fuel will be sent to the engine, which could cause stalling or complete shutdown.

Diesel Fuel Filters

The most desirable arrangement for diesel engines is the two-filter system. However, many diesel engines used in automotive applications have only one filter, which is called the primary filter, shown in *Figure 14–25*. The primary filter will catch most of the solid contaminants and remove small amounts of water. The secondary filter is much more efficient. It removes all remaining solid particles from the fuel.

On certain engines, the primary and secondary filters are combined, *Figure 14–26*. This is a surface-type filter with pleated paper. The first stage consists of about 400 square inches of filtering area. It removes 94% of the particles 10 *micrometers* and larger. One micrometer is equal to 0.000039 inch. See *Figure 14–27*. The second-stage filter is made of the same paper material. It consists of about 200 square inches of filtering surface. This stage is 98% effective in filtering the fuel already filtered by the first stage.

RELATIVE SIZE OF MICRON PARTICLES MAGNIFICATION 1000 TIMES

1 MICRON = 0.000039
LOWEST VISIBILITY RANGE = 44 MICRONS (.0017)
HUMAN HAIR = 0.003

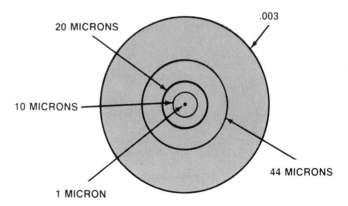

FIGURE 14–27. One micrometer (often referred to as a micron) is equal to 0.000039 inch. It is used to describe filter sizes. *(Courtesy of General Motors Product Service Training)*

Problems, Diagnosis and Service

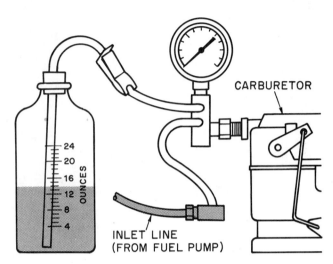

FIGURE 14–28. Fuel pump pressure can be tested by using a gauge and a pint size container. The engine is run, and the amount of fuel measured in the container is compared with the engine specifications.

2. Attach the correct pressure gauge and hose between the carburetor inlet and the disconnected fuel pipe.

3. Start and run the engine.

4. Check the automotive service manual to see if the pressure is within the limits stated in the specifications for that type and year of vehicle.

5. The pressure should remain constant or return very slowly to zero when the engine is shut off.

6. Make sure the hose is placed inside the pint container to check the capacity.

7. Run the engine at idle speed and note how long it takes to fill the container.

8. Depending on the pump being tested, it should take about 20–30 seconds to fill the container.

PROBLEM: Faulty Fuel Pump

The engine has been losing power in a vehicle with a mechanical fuel pump.

DIAGNOSIS

Often, mechanical fuel pumps will fail. In some cases, the fuel pump cannot transfer enough fuel to operate the engine. If the fuel pump is suspected, perform a fuel pump pressure test as shown in *Figure 14–28* as follows:

1. Disconnect the fuel pipe at the carburetor inlet.

SERVICE

If the fuel pump does not meet the specifications stated in the service manual then replace it as necessary, using the following general procedure:

1. Disconnect the negative side of the battery to eliminate the potential for sparks.

2. Disconnect the input and output fuel lines from the fuel pump. Use an open end (flare) wrench to loosen the fuel line connections as shown in *Figure 14–29*. On some flexible lines, the clamp must be removed before the line can be removed.

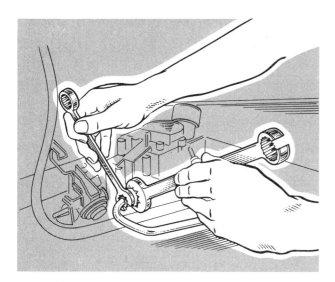

FIGURE 14–29. When removing an in-line filter, always use two wrenches. *(Courtesy of Dana Corporation)*

3. Remove any emission control or vacuum lines that are attached and label for reassembly.

4. Using the correct size socket and ratchet wrench, remove the two bolts holding the fuel pump to the block.

5. After the fuel pump has been removed, make sure the gasket is also removed. In some cases, the gasket must be scraped from the block to eliminate the possibility of leakage later.

6. Replace with a new fuel pump. Make sure new gaskets have been installed.

7. In some cases, it may be difficult to push the fuel pump into place against the block. If this is the case, the eccentric cam is in a position to lift the fuel pump lever. Rotate the engine slightly to eliminate this problem.

8. After the fuel pump has been installed correctly, tighten the bolts to the correct torque specification.

9. Reassemble the fuel lines and vacuum hoses as necessary.

PROBLEM: Faulty Fuel Pump Diaphragm

The level of oil has been increasing recently in a vehicle with a mechanical fuel pump.

DIAGNOSIS

An increased level of oil in the lubrication system may indicate a bad mechanical fuel pump. If the diaphragm is cracked, fuel will leak through the diaphragm and into the crankcase. This condition can be detected by smelling the oil. If it has a gasoline smell, the fuel pump may be damaged and should be replaced. A fuel pressure and capacity test would also show reduced pressures and capacities.

SERVICE

Follow the service procedure above to remove and replace the mechanical fuel pump.

PROBLEM: Plugged Fuel Filter

An engine has stopped completely. Before it stopped, it hesitated and operated sluggishly.

DIAGNOSIS

This type of problem is most likely caused by a plugged fuel filter. The fuel filter increasingly blocks the fuel to the carburetor or fuel injectors. Eventually, the filter totally blocks the fuel to the engine.

SERVICE

Remove and replace the fuel filter, using the following general procedure:

1. Disconnect the negative terminal of the battery to avoid any sparks.

2. Disconnect the fuel lines at the fuel inlet nut. This procedure is shown in *Figure 14–30*.

3. Remove the fuel inlet nut from the carburetor.

4. Remove the filter and spring.

5. Make sure there are no dirt particles around the filter element.

6. Obtain the new filter, and soak it in gasoline for a short period of time.

7. Some filters have a filter check valve. Make sure the check valve is replaced correctly inside the filter.

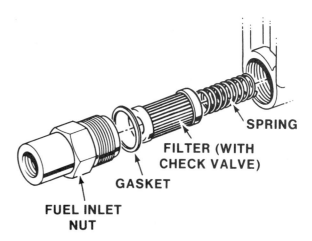

FIGURE 14–30. The fuel filter can be replaced by removing the assembly from the side of the carburetor. *(Courtesy of Oldsmobile Division, General Motors Corporation)*

8. Install the spring, filter, gasket, and fuel inlet nut.

9. Be careful not to strip the threads when inserting the fuel inlet nut. It is very easy to misalign the threads, causing them to be damaged. Always start the fuel inlet nut with your fingers. Use a flare wrench to tighten the nut to the correct torque specifications.

PROBLEM: Low Fuel Pressure

An engine is sluggish and seems to be lacking power. The vehicle has an electrical fuel pump and injectors.

DIAGNOSIS

Problems such as this generally suggest that the fuel pressure feeding into the injectors is not high enough. Fuel pressure can be checked on the fuel manifold as shown in *Figure 14–31*. Each manufacturer has a different method for checking the fuel pressure. In this case, a service bolt is removed and a fuel pressure gauge is installed. The engine is run, and fuel pressure is measured and compared with the manufacturer's specifications. If the pressure is higher than specified check the following:

- A pinched or clogged fuel return hose or piping

- A faulty pressure regulator

If the pressure is lower than specified check the following:

- A clogged fuel filter

- Faulty pressure regulator

- Leakage in the line

- The fuel pump

SERVICE

To check the fuel pressure regulator use the following general procedure:

1. Attach the pressure gauge as shown in Figure 14–31.

2. Start and run the engine at idle.

3. Check that the fuel pressure rises when the vacuum hose from the regulator is disconnected.

4. If the fuel pressure does not rise, check to see if it rises with the fuel return hose slightly pinched.

5. If the fuel pressure still does not rise, replace the pressure regulator.

6. If the fuel pressure regulator is operating correctly, the problem is a poor electrical fuel pump.

Replace the electrical fuel pump using the following general procedure:

1. The entire electrical fuel pump must be replaced.

2. Remove the negative battery cable to eliminate the possibility of sparks.

3. Relieve any fuel pressure in the system.

4. Lift the vehicle on an appropriate hoist.

5. Drain the fuel from the fuel tank and place it in an approved OSHA container.

6. Remove the fuel tank. This procedure may be different and will vary with different vehicles.

7. Loosen, then remove, the assembly that holds the fuel pump in the fuel tank. This procedure is shown in *Figure 14–32*.

    CAUTION: Be careful not to produce any sparks if you use a punch. Several tool manufacturers sell a tool that is designed to remove sending units by using a ratchet. This is a much safer method.

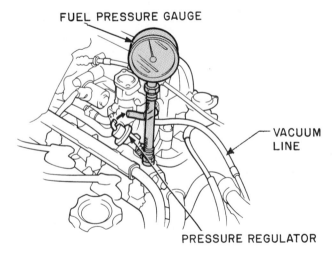

FUEL PRESSURE GAUGE

VACUUM LINE

PRESSURE REGULATOR

FIGURE 14–31. Fuel pressure can be checked on fuel injection engines by attaching a fuel pressure gauge to the fuel manifold. *(Courtesy of Honda Motor Company, Ltd.)*

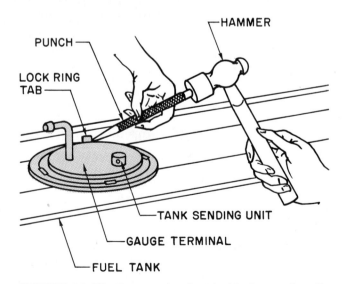

PUNCH

HAMMER

LOCK RING TAB

TANK SENDING UNIT

GAUGE TERMINAL

FUEL TANK

FIGURE 14–32. Remove the electrical fuel pump from the tank by lightly tapping the lock ring tab on top of the fuel tank. Be careful not to produce sparks. *(Courtesy of Scharff, Complete Fuel Systems and Emission Control, Delmar Publishers Inc.)*

8. Lightly tap the lock ring tab in a counterclockwise direction.

9. Remove the fuel pump and tank sending unit.

   CAUTION: Be careful not to produce any electrical sparks, as there are still gasoline vapors in the fuel tank.

10. Inspect hoses, sender, and pump assembly for signs of deterioration. The fuel pump can be checked again by applying 12 volts to the electrical wires. Never operate an electrical fuel pump out of the gasoline container for more than 30 seconds. Listen for bearing noise caused by damaged parts.

11. Reverse the procedure to install a new fuel pump and sending unit assembly. Make sure the O rings and locking assembly are correctly in place.

12. Replace the fuel tank and fuel.

13. Start and run the engine.

PROBLEM: Water in Diesel Fuel

A diesel engine is operating sluggishly and irregularly.

DIAGNOSIS

A common problem on diesel engines is that water gets into the fuel system. Also the filters get dirty and restrict the fuel flow. If water is suspected to be in diesel fuel, drain the water out before operation. Fuel is lighter than water so the water will settle to the bottom. A bottom drain can be used to drain the water out of the system. On some diesel fuel systems there are valves called petcocks at the bottom of the fuel tank and at the bottom of the primary and secondary filter canisters. The petcocks are used to remove the water from the fuel system. They should be drained regularly.

SERVICE

To replace the fuel filters use the following general procedures:

1. Disconnect the negative side of the battery.

2. Locate the primary and/or secondary filters.

3. Using the correct wrench size, carefully remove the filters. Be careful not to spill the fuel that is in the filter canisters.

4. Clean the fuel filter canisters using an approved cleaning solvent as shown in *Figure 14–33*.

5. Replace with new filters. It is best to fill the filter canisters with fuel before reinstalling them on the engine. Filling them could save having to prime the engine later. Be careful not to spill any of the fuel during assembly.

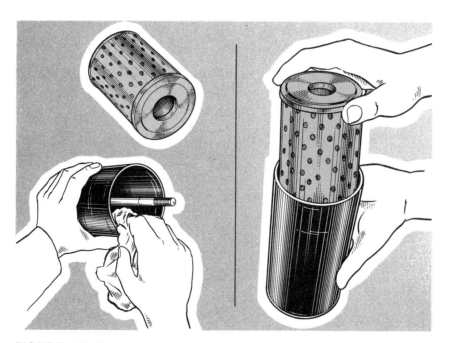

FIGURE 14–33. Always clean the inside of the container before replacing diesel fuel filters. *(Courtesy of Dana Corporation)*

Linkage to Future Automotive Technology

ALTERNATIVE FUEL FOR CARS

Methanol, also known as methyl alcohol, is one of many types of fuel being looked at for future uses in automobiles. Methanol is a liquid hydrocarbon fuel made from natural gas. Actually methanol is lighter than gasoline, but heavier than methane. For use as a fuel it is usually mixed with gasoline in a ratio of approximately 15% gasoline to 85% methanol. Methanol has only about half the energy of gasoline per gallon and burns cleaner. Research suggests that using methanol for fuel would cause less damage to the ozone layer than using gasoline.

METHANOL 85%   GASOLINE 15%

METHANOL:

- Is a liquid.

- Is made from either coal, wood, or natural gas.

- Has less energy per gallon than gasoline. A car will need to fill up twice as much, or tanks will need to be twice as large.

- Has about 60,000 BTU/gallon, while gasoline has about 123,00 BTU/gallon.

- Is cleaner burning than gasoline. It produces less nitrogen oxides.

- Is easy to store. It is a liquid at ambient temperature and pressure.

- Produces more aldehydes.

- Produces less damage to the ozone layer by producing less greenhouse gases.

- Corrodes synthetic gaskets.

- Is more expensive to produce than gasoline.

SERVICE MANUAL CONNECTION

There are many important specifications to keep in mind when working with the basic fuel system. To identify the specifications for your engine, you will need to know the VIN (vehicle identification number) of the vehicle, the type and year of the vehicle, and the type of engine. Although they may be titled differently, some of the more common fuel system specifications (not all) found in service manuals are listed below. Note that these specifications are typical examples. Each vehicle and engine may have different specifications.

Common Specification	Typical Example
Fuel injector resistor	5–7 ohms
Fuel pressure regulator	34–41 psi
Fuel pump pressure	6–8 lb

In addition, the service manual will give specific directions for various service procedures. Some of the more common procedures include:

- Checking fuel pressure regulator
- Fuel filter replacement
- Fuel pump replacement
- Fuel pump testing
- Relieving fuel pressure
- Replacing fuel injectors
- Troubleshooting the fuel system

SUMMARY

The fuel system is critical to the operation of the automobile. The main purpose of the fuel system is to supply fuel to the carburetor or fuel injectors so that a constant 14.7 parts of air can mix with 1 part of fuel. Several components are used to accomplish this task. These include the fuel tank, fuel pump, and fuel filters. Carburetors and fuel injectors are more complex, and a separate chapter is devoted to each major area.

The fuel tank is made to hold excess fuel where it is ready to be used by the carburetor. The fuel tank cap is made to seal the fuel tank. It must operate so that both a vacuum and a pressure are released inside the tank.

A fuel metering unit is located inside the fuel tank. This unit is made to measure the amount of fuel inside the tank. It uses a float device that changes the resistance of an electrical circuit as it moves. Diesel fuel tanks also have a water sensor to determine if there is too much water in the tank. On newer vehicles, the electrical fuel pump is also part of the total unit inside the fuel tank.

Fuel pumps are used to transfer the gasoline or diesel fuel from the tank to the carburetor or fuel injectors. Several

types are used, including the mechanical and the electrical fuel pump. The mechanical fuel pump uses a diaphragm that is moved up and down by a lever connected to a cam device on the camshaft. The up-and-down movement causes a suction and pressure to be created inside the fuel pump. Check valves are used to control the fuel within the fuel pump.

Several types of fuel systems use a vapor return line. As the fuel is heated near the engine, vapor forms. This can cause vapor lock in the fuel system. Vapor return lines eliminate vapor lock.

Electrical fuel pumps are used on many vehicles today. They are located in the rear of the vehicle or inside the fuel tank, so there is less risk of vapor lock. Two types of electrical fuel pumps are used. The bellows-type uses a bellows that is stretched and squeezed. This action creates a suction and pressure. The second type is called a roller vane fuel pump. An electric motor rotates an impeller to pump the fuel from the tank to the engine.

Fuel systems that have electrical fuel pumps with fuel injectors use a pressure regulator. The pressure regulator keeps the fuel pressure at a constant pressure. It is controlled by the intake manifold vacuum.

Computers are also being used to control fuel pumps. Several signals are fed into the computer. The computer then controls the fuel pump accordingly.

Fuel filters are used to stop any contamination from getting into the fuel system. Both gasoline and diesel fuel systems use filters. There are several types used on the gasoline engine. One type of filter is usually placed inside the fuel tank. This filter is made of a fine woven fabric.

The second filter is an in-line filter that can be found in several locations. The filter can be placed directly in the pressure fuel line or on the input to the carburetor. This filter is considered to be a surface filter.

Diesel fuel systems use either one or two filters. One is called the primary, and one is called the secondary. Each filter has a certain micrometer size to allow a certain size particle through the filter.

Always refer to the maintenance manual before working on the fuel system. Several important service suggestions include: (1) be careful when handling gasoline, as it is very explosive; (2) water can be very damaging to a diesel fuel system; (3) always use two wrenches when removing filters connected to the input of the carburetor; (4) fuel pressure can be checked with a pressure gauge and a pint size container; (5) oil that has been mixed with fuel (gasoline) may indicate a bad diaphragm on the fuel pump.

TERMS TO KNOW

Can you explain each of the following terms? Review the chapter until you can use each term correctly.

Fuel injector
Fuel vapor
Pressure regulator valve
Filler neck restrictor *(continued)*

Condensation   Armature
Diaphragm   Calibrated
Bellows   Micrometers
Inertia switch

REVIEW QUESTIONS

Multiple Choice

1. Which of the following is *not* part of the basic fuel system flow?
   a. Fuel tank
   b. Catalytic converter
   c. Fuel pump
   d. Fuel filter
   e. Vapor separator

2. Which system always has a return line back to the fuel pump or tank?
   a. Diesel fuel system
   b. Gasoline fuel system
   c. Contaminated fuel system
   d. All of the above
   e. None of the above

3. The fuel cap is used to:
   a. Help produce a vacuum on the fuel tank
   b. Help produce a pressure on the fuel tank
   c. Relieve the pressure and vacuum on the fuel tank
   d. Clean the fuel
   e. Filter the fuel

4. The fuel metering unit changes the _____ in an electrical circuit when the float changes position.
   a. Resistance
   b. Voltage
   c. Calibration
   d. Filters
   e. Wattage

5. Water in diesel fuel will _____.
   a. Increase the horsepower
   b. Damage the fuel system
   c. Cause vaporization
   d. All of the above
   e. None of the above

6. The mechanical fuel pump is driven from the:
   a. Crankshaft
   b. Distributor shaft
   c. Camshaft
   d. Alternator
   e. Valve system

7. Vapor in the gasoline fuel system is caused by:
   a. Rapidly cooling down the temperature of gasoline
   b. Heating gasoline to its boiling temperature
   c. Pumping gasoline through small holes
   d. Mixing it with nitrogen
   e. None of the above

8. Which of the following is a type of electrical fuel pump?
   a. Bellows-type
   b. Roller vane type
   c. Mechanical diaphragm
   d. All of the above
   e. A and B

9. What is the purpose of using a fuel pressure regulator?
   a. It regulates the oil pressure
   b. It regulates the fuel pressure at the injectors
   c. It controls the thickness of the fuel in cold weather
   d. It controls the temperature of the fuel
   e. None of the above

10. Which of the following is a contaminant that is of concern in diesel fuel?
    a. Wax crystals
    b. Microorganisms
    c. Rust
    d. All of the above
    e. None of the above

11. Fuel filters are _____ inside the fuel tank.
    a. Never placed
    b. Always placed
    c. Sometimes placed
    d. Dissolved
    e. Expanded

12. What is the most desirable arrangement of fuel filters on a diesel engine?
    a. Only one filter should be used
    b. Two filters should be used
    c. Three filters should be used
    d. No filters should be used
    e. Five or more filters should be used

13. One micrometer is equal to _____ inch(es).
    a. 0.0045
    b. 0.000039
    c. 1.3
    d. 1.35
    e. 0.0039

14. Which filter has the smallest micrometer size holes?
    a. The primary filter
    b. The secondary filter
    c. Both filters have the same micrometer size
    d. The combining filter
    e. Filters are not rated by micrometer size

The following questions are similar in format to ASE (Automotive Service Excellence) test questions.

15. Technician A says to check fuel pump pressure, use a compression gauge. Technician B says to check fuel pump pressure, disconnect the fuel line to the carburetor, and use a pint jar and a pressure gauge. Who is right?
    a. A only
    b. B only
    c. Both A and B
    d. Neither A nor B

16. An engine seems to be running irregularly and stalls often. Technician A says the fuel filter needs to be replaced. Technician B says the fuel lines are broken. Who is right?
    a. A only
    b. B only
    c. Both A and B
    d. Neither A nor B

17. A gasoline engine hesitates and runs sluggishly. Technician A says the problem could be the use of high-octane fuel. Technician B says the problem could be a dirty fuel filter. Who is right?
    a. A only
    b. B only
    c. Both A and B
    d. Neither A nor B

18. There is an increase in the oil level in a gasoline engine. Technician A says fuel could be leaking into the oil through the fuel pump. Technician B says fuel cannot get into the oil, and probably too much oil was put into the crankcase. Who is right?
    a. A only
    b. B only
    c. Both A and B
    d. Neither A nor B

19. Technician A says the fuel pressure for a mechanical fuel pump should be about 5–6 pounds. Technician B says the fuel pressure for a mechanical fuel pump should be checked with a vacuum tester. Who is correct?
    a. A only
    b. B only
    c. Both A and B
    d. Neither A nor B

20. Technician A says the fuel pressure for an electrical fuel pump should be about 5–6 pounds. Technician B says the fuel pressure for an electrical fuel pump is measured with a voltmeter. Who is correct?
    a. A only
    b. B only
    c. Both A and B
    d. Neither A nor B

21. Technician A says that the restrictor on the filler neck is to keep unleaded fuel out of the gasoline tank. Technician B says the filler neck has hoses to vent the fuel tank. Who is correct?
    a. A only
    b. B only
    c. Both A and B
    d. Neither A nor B

22. Technician A says the inertia switch is used to shut the fuel off to the injection system during impacts or accidents. Technician B says the inertia switch is used to regulate pressure in the fuel pump during slow deceleration. Who is correct?
    a. A only
    b. B only
    c. Both A and B
    d. Neither A nor B

Essay

23. Why is there a vacuum release on the fuel cap?

24. Describe the operation of the diaphragm-type fuel pump.

25. What are some advantages of using an electrical fuel pump?

26. Why do some cars have a fuel pressure regulator?

27. List the types of contaminants that can enter the fuel system.

28. What is a micrometer?

29. Describe the procedure used to check fuel pump pressure.

Short Answer

30. A _____ valve is used to keep the pressure constant on fuel injection systems.

31. Fuel pumps can be checked for two specifications including _____ and _____.

32. When inserting the fuel inlet nut on the carburetor, always be careful not to _____ the threads on the nut.

33. If the fuel pressure from an electrical fuel pump is lower than specifications, check for _____ and _____.

34. To keep the fuel from splashing around in the fuel tank _____ are placed inside the fuel tank.

CHAPTER 15

Carburetor Systems

INTRODUCTION Carburetors used on gasoline engines are designed to mix the air and fuel at the correct ratio. The most correct air-fuel ratio is 14.7 parts of air to 1 part of fuel. A carburetor's job is to maintain this ratio during all engine operations. There are many types of carburetors and accessories. Over the years many changes have been incorporated into the carburetor. In fact, carburetors are now being controlled by computers. Also, there are many variations to the basic carburetor, circuits, and electronic controls.

OBJECTIVES After reading this chapter, you should be able to:

- Define the basic principles of carburetion.
- Define the different types of vacuum produced from a carburetor.
- Compare the different types of carburetors used on automotive engines.
- Analyze carburetor circuits, including the float, idle, low-speed, main metering, power, acceleration, and choke circuits.

- State the design and purpose of common carburetor accessories.
- Identify how carburetors are controlled by electronic controls and computers.
- Define the difference between open and closed loop operation.
- State various problems, diagnosis, and service procedures regarding carburetors.

  SAFETY CHECKLIST

When working with the carburetor system, keep these important safety precautions in mind.

✔ Immediately wipe up any spilled gasoline and dispose of the rags in a sealed container.

✔ Never clean any external carburetor parts with gasoline.

✔ Never smoke in or around an automobile or when working on the carburetor system.

✔ Always store the fuel in an approved OSHA container. Never store gasoline in an open container.

✔ Always keep an approved fire extinguisher nearby when working on the carburetor.

✔ Always wear OSHA-approved safety glasses when working on carburetor systems.

 CERTIFICATION CONNECTION

Some of the information in this chapter can help you prepare for the National Institute for Automotive Service Excellence (ASE) certification tests. The tests most directly related to this chapter are entitled

> **ENGINE REPAIR (TEST A1) AND ENGINE PERFORMANCE (TEST A8).**

The content areas that closely parallel this chapter are

> **FUEL AND EXHAUST SYSTEMS DIAGNOSIS AND REPAIR AND FUEL, AIR INDUCTION, AND EXHAUST SYSTEMS DIAGNOSIS AND REPAIR.**

15.1 CARBURETOR PRINCIPLES

Air-Fuel Ratio

Research has shown that if the gasoline engine operates on an accurate and precise air-fuel ratio, engine efficiency will be improved. However, many things cause the air-fuel ratio to be upset or changed from the optimum 14.7:1. The following factors may change the air-fuel ratio:

1. Air density and altitude

2. Acceleration of the vehicle

3. Deceleration of the vehicle

4. Temperature of the air

5. Moisture content of the air

6. Speed of the engine or vehicle

7. Load on the engine

8. Overall condition and efficiency of the engine

The carburetor must be designed to operate under different conditions. *Figure 15–1* shows how the air-fuel ratio changes with different speeds. Air-fuel ratios range from 9 to 1 during idle to 18 or 19 to 1 during deceleration. When the vehicle is started and at idle, the air-fuel ratio is about 12 to 1. This is a very rich mixture and produces poor fuel economy. As the engine speed is increased to move the vehicle to 40 mph, the air-fuel ratio settles at about 15 to 1. As the speed of the vehicle increases to 60 mph or above, the air-fuel ratio drops off again to about 12 to 1. Also, when the vehicle is accelerated or decelerated, the air-fuel ratio changes accordingly. Deceleration produces a leaner mixture, while acceleration produces a richer mixture.

Atomization

Carburetors operate on the principle that as more air flows through the carburetor, more fuel is added. However, the fuel must be in an *atomized* state. Fuel that is atomized is in very small mistlike droplets. The fuel is then *vaporized*. When a liquid is changed to a vapor, it is vaporized. Vaporization occurs after the fuel is atomized. This can be done by increasing the temperature of the fuel. Fuel in a vaporized state mixes very well with the air that is passing through the carburetor. *Figure 15–2* shows how atomized particles of fuel are surrounded by 14.7 parts of air for the most efficient combustion. Fuel that is in a liquid state, not vaporized or atomized, mixes poorly with the air passing through the carburetor.

Venturi

Air is drawn into the engine by the action of the piston moving downward on the intake stroke. When the piston moves down and the intake valve is opened, a *vacuum* is produced. This vacuum causes air to be drawn or pushed into the engine. The air, however, passes through the carburetor and *venturi* as it goes into the engine. (The vacuum can also be called a pressure differential. At the venturi, there is actually a lower pressure than above the venturi. For simplicity, the word *vacuum*, rather than pressure differential, will be used throughout this chapter.)

A venturi is a streamlined restriction that partly closes the carburetor bore. See *Figure 15–3*. Air is drawn into the engine by the intake manifold vacuum. As the air enters the venturi, it is forced to speed up, or increase in velocity, in order to pass through the restriction. This restriction causes an increase in vacuum by the venturi. The vacuum is also

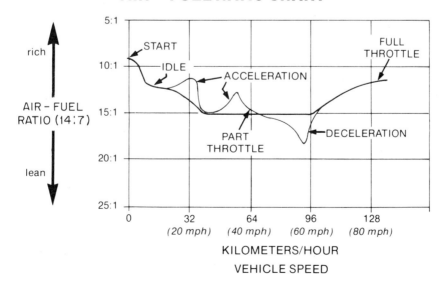

AIR — FUEL RATIO CHART

FIGURE 15–1. Air-fuel ratios will change with different driving speeds. Acceleration and deceleration points are also shown. *(Courtesy of Davis Publications, Inc.)*

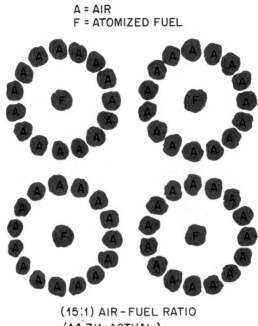

A = AIR
F = ATOMIZED FUEL

(15:1) AIR-FUEL RATIO
(14.7:1 ACTUAL)

FIGURE 15–2. When air and fuel are mixed correctly, 14.7 particles of air will surround 1 part of fuel. The fuel mixes best in the atomized state.

felt slightly below the major restricted area, and it continues to be reduced farther down the bore.

As the engine speed increases during acceleration, more air goes into the carburetor. This causes the venturi vacuum to increase because the greater the velocity of air passed through the venturi, the greater the vacuum. The vacuum produced at the venturi is used to draw in the correct amount of fuel. As the vacuum increases, more fuel is drawn in. As it decreases, less fuel is drawn in.

The venturi also aids fuel atomization and vaporization by exposing the fuel to air. The fuel is added in the center of the strongest vacuum point of the venturi. *Figure 15–4* shows fuel being added to the air flow through the carburetor. A discharge tube is located near the venturi. As the air flows through the venturi, the vacuum draws the fuel from a bowl into the stream of air going into the engine.

Throttle Plate

The flow of air and fuel through the carburetor is controlled by the throttle plate, *Figure 15–5*. The throttle plate, which is made of a circular disc, is placed directly in the flow of air and fuel, below the venturi. Its purpose is to control the amount of air and fuel that enters the engine. The throttle

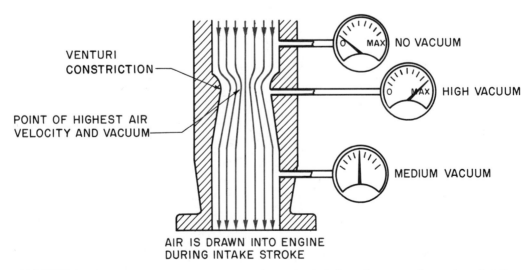

VENTURI
CONSTRICTION

POINT OF HIGHEST AIR
VELOCITY AND VACUUM

NO VACUUM

HIGH VACUUM

MEDIUM VACUUM

AIR IS DRAWN INTO ENGINE
DURING INTAKE STROKE

FIGURE 15–3. A venturi is a restriction in the path of air flow. A vacuum is produced at the point of greatest restriction.

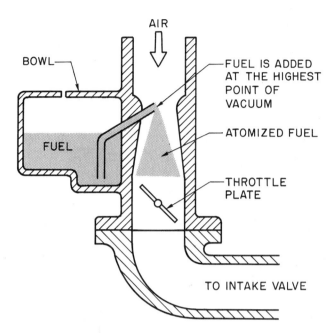

FIGURE 15–4. The vacuum that is produced at the venturi is used to draw in the fuel from the carburetor.

plate is connected to the driver's throttle. As the driver's foot is depressed, the throttle plate opens to a vertical position. During this condition, there is very little restriction of air and fuel. This is a maximum load and speed condition. As the driver's foot is removed, a spring closes the throttle plate and restricts the amount of air and fuel going into the engine. This is a low speed and load condition. *Figure 15–6* shows a throttle plate from a carburetor.

Types of Vacuum Available

The vacuum that is produced around the venturi and throttle plates is used to operate various components on the vehicle. Many components must operate according to the position of the throttle. Ports within the carburetor bore are connected to vacuum motors, exhaust gas recirculating (EGR) valves, ignition components, emission controls, and so on. (See Chapter 24 for information on the EGR value.)

One type of vacuum is called *ported vacuum*, as shown in *Figure 15–7*. This vacuum is tapped off the carburetor above the position of the throttle plate. During idle conditions, the vacuum is very low. As the throttle opens, more of the port is exposed to the air flow through the carburetor. This opening causes a higher vacuum.

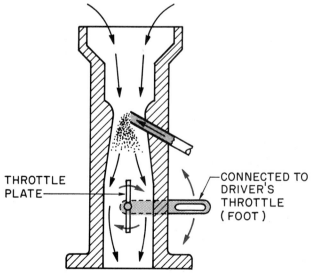

FIGURE 15–5. A throttle plate is put in the base of the carburetor to control the amount of air and fuel flowing into the engine.

FIGURE 15–6. The throttle plate is a circular disc attached to a center rod. As the rod is turned, the throttle plate opens and closes.

PORTED, VENTURI, AND INTAKE MANIFOLD VACUUM

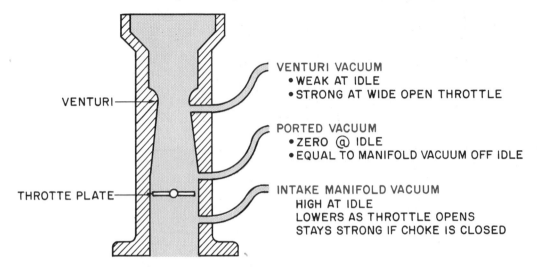

VENTURI

THROTTLE PLATE

VENTURI VACUUM
• WEAK AT IDLE
• STRONG AT WIDE OPEN THROTTLE

PORTED VACUUM
• ZERO @ IDLE
• EQUAL TO MANIFOLD VACUUM OFF IDLE

INTAKE MANIFOLD VACUUM
HIGH AT IDLE
LOWERS AS THROTTLE OPENS
STAYS STRONG IF CHOKE IS CLOSED

FIGURE 15–7.   Various types of vacuum can be tapped off the carburetor to operate ignition, emission, and other components.

Intake manifold vacuum is also used to operate similar components on the engine and vehicle. Intake manifold vacuum is tapped off the carburetor below the position of the throttle plate. During idle conditions, the vacuum is very high. As the throttle opens, intake manifold vacuum decreases. *Figure 15–8* shows how both types of vacuum are used to operate one variation of the EGR valve.

Note that the vacuum can also be directly tapped off the venturi. This arrangement is often called a *venturi vacuum*. It is used to operate certain emission control components.

It operates in a manner similar to that of the ported vacuum except the vacuum increases at higher RPM.

15.2   TYPES OF CARBURETORS

Many types of carburetors have been built in the past. Different load conditions, engine shapes, and air-fuel requirements require different types of carburetors. Carburetors are designed with different drafts, different numbers of barrels, different types of venturi, and different flow rates.

Carburetor Draft

Draft is defined as the act of drawing or pulling air. Carburetors are classified as having different directions of draft. For example, a downdraft carburetor has air flowing down

CAR CLINIC

PROBLEM: Car Stalls on Turns

After about 15,000 miles, the customer notices that the car seems to stall on right turns. The carburetor has recently been rebuilt.

SOLUTION:

A vehicle that stalls on turns usually has fuel-level problems in the carburetor. Start by checking the float levels. When the float level is too low, the fuel may slosh to one side when the car turns. Too high a float level may interfere with the carburetor venting system. Also, on certain carburetors the lower section of the carburetor may become loose. If this is the case, centrifugal forces during turning will cause the carburetor to tilt to one side. This would create a severe vacuum leak that could cause the engine to stall. To check, simply move the top part of the carburetor back and forth to see if it is loose.

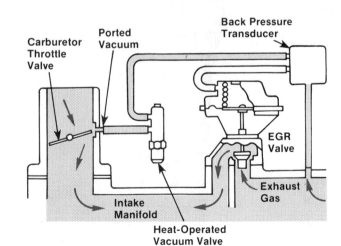

FIGURE 15–8.   This circuit shows how both ported and intake manifold vacuums are used to operate the EGR (exhaust gas recirculating) valve. *(Courtesy of Scharff, Complete Fuel Systems and Emission Control, Delmar Publishers Inc.)*

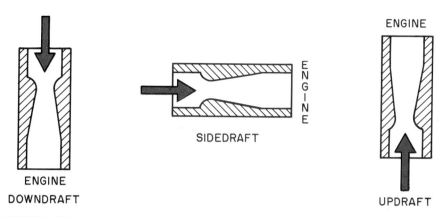

FIGURE 15–9. Carburetors are classified by the type of draft used. Downdraft, sidedraft, and updraft carburetors are used.

vertically into the engine. Most engines today have a downdraft carburetor. *Figure 15–9* shows a schematic of the different drafts used on carburetors.

The sidedraft carburetor is designed so that air flows through the carburetor horizontally. Many foreign sports cars use a sidedraft carburetor because it is placed on the side of the engine rather than on the top. The engine compartment can then be more streamlined.

An updraft carburetor brings the air and fuel into the engine in an upward direction. Not many automobiles use this type. Updraft carburetors are used in forklifts and other industrial engine applications.

Carburetor Barrels

A *carburetor barrel* is defined as the passageway or bore used to mix the air and fuel. One barrel consists of the throttle plate, venturi, and air horn. This design is used on small engines that do not require large quantities of fuel.

A two-barrel carburetor has two throttle plates and two venturis. The area where the air comes into the carburetor is common on both barrels. *Figure 15–10* shows the throttle plates from a two-barrel carburetor. A two-barrel carburetor is used on many intermediate load applications. Many newer small vehicles also use two-barrel carburetors. These carburetors, however, have one barrel that is very small in diameter and one that is larger.

A four-barrel carburetor has four barrels to mix the air and fuel. In most driving conditions, the engine operates on two of the barrels. When additional power is needed, the other two barrels add fuel to increase the amount of horsepower and torque produced by the engine. *Figure 15–11* shows a four-barrel carburetor.

Modern engines are designed to be fuel-efficient. In the past, when fuel efficiency was not a concern, many four-barrel carburetors were used. As the need to increase fuel mileage increased, however, the use of four-barrel carburetors decreased. Today, four-barrel carburetors are used on engines that require high horsepower and torque loads.

One of the most common four-barrel carburetors is called

FIGURE 15–10. Carburetors are also classified by stating the number of barrels. This is a two-barrel carburetor. There is a throttle plate for each barrel.

FOUR BARRELS

FIGURE 15–11.   A four-barrel carburetor has four barrels and four throttle plates.

the quadrajet as shown in *Figure 15–12*. In this carburetor the mixture control is tied into the on-board computer, called the ECM (electronic control module).

Types of Venturis

Carburetors are also classified by the type of venturi used. *Figure 15–13* shows the different types used. The single venturi is used on many small single-cylinder engines such as those used in gardening equipment.

The double (dual) venturi is called the secondary or boost venturi. This design increases the venturi effect which, in turn, increases the efficiency of the carburetor. The bottom of the center venturi is located at the greatest restriction area of the next larger venturi. In this arrangement, the vacuum developed in the venturi is multiplied. This causes better vaporization and atomization and more control of fuel entering the carburetor.

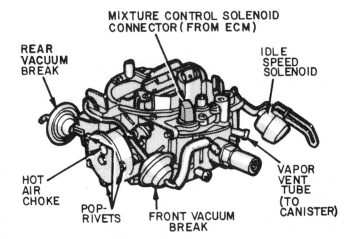

MIXTURE CONTROL SOLENOID
CONNECTOR (FROM ECM)

REAR VACUUM BREAK

IDLE SPEED SOLENOID

HOT AIR CHOKE

POP-RIVETS

FRONT VACUUM BREAK

VAPOR VENT TUBE (TO CANISTER)

FIGURE 15–12.   This is a typical four-barrel carburetor, called the quadrajet. *(Courtesy of Motor Publications, Auto Engine Tune-up & Electronics Manual)*

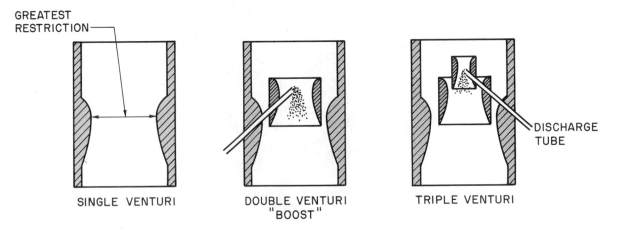

GREATEST RESTRICTION

SINGLE VENTURI

DOUBLE VENTURI "BOOST"

TRIPLE VENTURI

DISCHARGE TUBE

FIGURE 15–13.   Carburetors have several types of venturis. One, two, and three venturis can be used. These can also be called boost venturis.

The third type of venturi is called the triple venturi. Even more control and atomization occurs with this design. The fuel discharge tube is located inside the smallest venturi for maximum control and atomization.

Some carburetors are built with a variable or changing venturi. As the throttle is depressed, the venturi increases in size. As the throttle is released, the venturi decreases in size. Some American cars and several foreign cars use variable venturi carburetors.

CAR CLINIC

PROBLEM: Engine Runs On

A customer has a vehicle with a carburetor. When the engine is hot and shut off, it continues to run. The points have been replaced. The carburetor has been cleaned. What could be another cause of dieseling, or run on?

SOLUTION:

Quite often the throttle solenoid on the carburetor either is not working or is not adjusted correctly. The throttle solenoid is an electrical device that helps set the position of the throttle during engine operation. When the engine ignition is shut off, the throttle solenoid is released and the throttle valve is completely closed. Vehicles without a throttle solenoid are shut off with the throttle position at idle. If the pistons continue to draw in fuel, and if there is a hot spot in the cylinder, the engine may run on. Shutting off the throttle valve completely with the throttle solenoid valve reduces this possibility. Check to see that the throttle solenoid valve operates and is adjusted correctly.

15.3 CARBURETOR CIRCUITS

Carburetors are studied by analyzing different circuits of operation. There are several carburetor circuits. These include the float, idle, low-speed, main metering, power, acceleration, and choke circuits. Most carburetors use these circuits for operation.

There has been an increase in the number of changes made on the carburetor. Emission controls and standards have had an impact on carburetor designs. Carburetors have been changed and altered drastically to meet these standards. This section looks at the basics of each of these circuits.

Float Circuit

The float circuit is made to provide a source of fuel in a bowl for the carburetor. The carburetor float circuit maintains the correct fuel level for all conditions of operation. The circuit includes a fuel bowl that contains a supply of fuel, a float, and a float-operated valve to control the level of fuel in the bowl. There are also bowl vents to maintain correct fuel bowl pressure.

The bowl is a cast part of the carburetor. It holds the fuel to be used in the carburetor. It is like a reservoir of fuel. There is a float inside the float bowl, *Figure 15–14*. The float, which is made of a brass or plastic bulb, floats on top of the fuel. The float is connected to a needle valve. The needle valve fits into the fuel inlet.

As the fuel in the bowl is used, the float drops slightly, see *Figure 15–15*. As the float drops, it opens the needle valve to allow more fuel to enter the float bowl chamber. As the fuel enters, the float lifts and causes the needle valve to close off the fuel inlet port. During operation, the fuel is kept at almost a constant level. The float tries to hold the needle valve partly closed. The incoming fuel makes up for the fuel being used at the venturi.

It is important to maintain the exact amount of fuel inside the bowl. The level of fuel in the bowl controls the amount of fuel entering the venturi area. If the fuel level is too high,

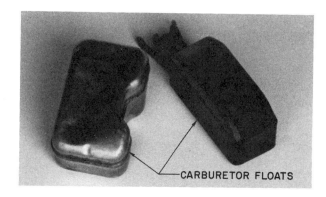

FIGURE 15–14. Brass or plastic floats are used to keep the right amount of fuel inside the bowl area.

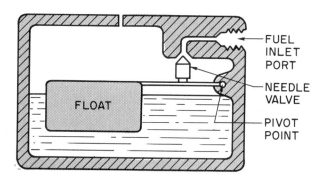

FIGURE 15–15. The float system keeps the correct amount of fuel in the float bowl. When fuel is used, the float drops slightly. This opens the needle valve and more fuel enters. As the fuel enters, the float rises and shuts off the fuel inlet.

the extra fuel adds pressure. This pressure increases the amount of fuel entering the venturi, causing a rich condition, see *Figure 15–16*. If the fuel level is too low, less fuel will enter the venturi. This will cause a lean condition. Both conditions are damaging to the engine.

Float Bowl Venting

As fuel is removed from the float chamber or bowl, air must replace the fuel. If there is no air for replacement, a vacuum will develop inside the float chamber. This will upset the air-fuel ratio. Two vents are used. One vent is connected to the carbon canister, which is a pollution control device. Fumes from the carburetor float bowl area are sent to the carbon canister.

A second tube is connected from the float bowl to the top of the air horn, *Figure 15–17*. This is called the internal vent. Almost all carburetors have this vent. Its purpose is to keep the pressure on top of the fuel the same as that going into the carburetor air horn. For example, if the air cleaner is dirty and produces a drop in pressure (an increase in vacuum), less air will be going into the air horn and through the venturi. This means that less fuel should be going into the carburetor for normal operation. This lower pressure is also felt inside the bowl area through the internal vent. However, if atmospheric pressure were felt inside the bowl, it would be higher than that before the venturi. This would cause a higher pressure (as compared with the top of the air horn) on the float area. The air-fuel mixture would now be richer. The internal vent equalizes these pressures.

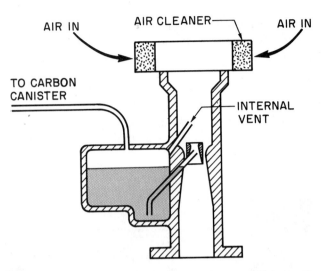

FIGURE 15–17. An internal vent is used to keep the pressure in the float bowl the same as that going into the engine.

Idle Circuit

During idle conditions, there is not enough air entering the venturi to cause a vacuum to move the fuel. The throttle plate is almost all the way closed as shown in *Figure 15–18*. During this condition, there is a large vacuum below the throttle valve. This vacuum causes fuel to be drawn from the carburetor float bowl through internal passages to the idle port. The idle port is below the throttle plate. As fuel is drawn from the float bowl to the idle port, air is drawn in through

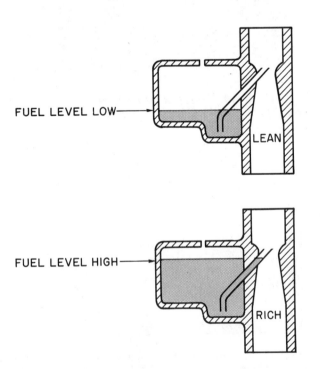

FIGURE 15–16. If the float level is too low, the mixture will be too lean. If the float level is too high, the mixture will be too rich.

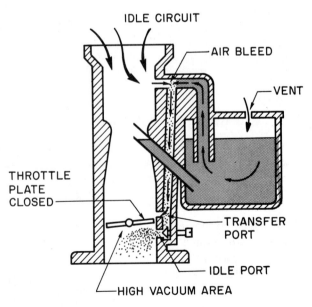

FIGURE 15–18. During idle conditions, the throttle plate is closed. Fuel is drawn in from the intake manifold vacuum through the idle port. *(Courtesy of Ignition Manufacturers Institute)*

an air-bleed passageway near the top of the carburetor. Only a small amount of air passes by the throttle plate. During this condition, the air-fuel mixture needs to be rich to keep the engine idling.

On older engines there is an idle mixture needle valve. This valve is used to control or adjust the amount of air and fuel at idle, see *Figure 15–19*. There is a certain amount of adjustment available on these carburetors. More current carburetors, however, have limiting caps on the idle screws. This limits the amount of adjustment available on the idle mixture screws. On newer carburetors, the idle mixture screws are sealed with steel plugs to eliminate all adjustment.

Single-barrel carburetors have only one idle circuit. Most two-barrel carburetors have two idle circuits. On four-barrel engines, only the two primary barrels use an idle system. The secondary barrels do not have an idle circuit.

Some carburetors have a transfer slot between the transfer port and idle port. This slot helps to maintain the correct air-fuel ratio during low-speed conditions. There are times during idle when more air is needed. Additional air is transferred from above the throttle plate to below it through the transfer slot.

Propane Mixture Test

Today there is an effort to reduce emissions on all vehicles. Newer carburetors are being adjusted to run much leaner than in the past. A slightly leaner mixture has a tendency to reduce emissions. One method used to help adjust carburetors so that they run leaner is called the Propane Enrichment Idle Fuel Mixture Check. To perform the test, a bottle of propane is connected to the engine intake manifold or carburetor, see *Figure 15–20*. The propane enriches the fuel mixture, and the idle speed then increases. At this point the idle speed is adjusted to an "enriched RPM." The propane is then shut off, and the idle mixture adjustments are made.

Low-Speed Circuit

The low-speed circuit is used to provide the correct air-fuel mixture during very low speeds from idle to 15–25 mph. (Speeds will vary with each carburetor.) During this condition, the throttle port is open slightly. *Figure 15–21* shows the position of the throttle plate during low-speed operation. Now a small amount of air flows past the throttle plate. This is still not enough air, however, to cause a vacuum at the venturi. Therefore, fuel must enter through the idle port and the transfer port. When the throttle plate is opened, it gradually exposes the transfer port to the intake manifold vacuum. This causes the fuel to be discharged through the transfer and idle ports. Some manufacturers call the transfer port operation the off idle operation. Carburetors have one, two, or three off idle ports, depending upon the manufacturer.

Main Metering Circuit

As the operator demands more speed, the carburetor transfers from the idle or low-speed circuit to the main

FIGURE 15–19. On older carburetors the air-fuel mixture can be adjusted during the idle by using the idle mixture adjustment screws located at the base of the carburetor.

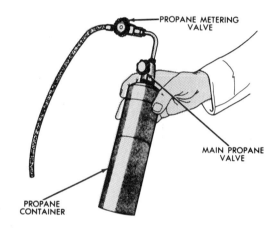

FIGURE 15–20. This propane tank is used to help adjust the carburetor idle mixture adjustments to produce leaner mixtures. It is called the propane enrichment test. *(Courtesy of Motor Publications, Auto Engine Tune-up and Electronics Manual)*

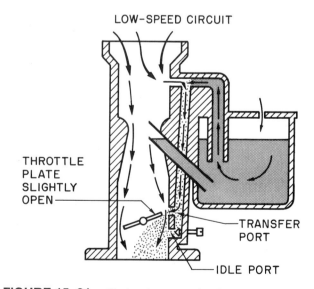

FIGURE 15–21. During low speeds, the throttle plate is slightly open. Fuel enters the carburetor through the idle and transfer ports.

metering circuit. This circuit operates the vehicle from about 25 to 60 mph. This range varies, depending upon the type of vehicle and the manufacturer.

During main metering, the throttle plate is opened enough so that air moves rapidly past the venturi, see *Figure 15–22*. As the air passes, a vacuum is created. The vacuum draws fuel from the float bowl area, through a tube, and into the flow of air. The tube is called the main nozzle, high-speed nozzle, or discharge tube. Very little vacuum is felt inside the idle and transfer ports. During this time, the operator opens the throttle plate to increase speed, and more air enters the venturi. More air means more vacuum, and thus, more fuel.

Power Circuit

The size of the discharge tube controls the maximum amount of fuel allowed into the engine during main metering operation. When more fuel is required, for example, when pulling heavy loads, the power circuit supplies it. *Figure 15–23* shows the addition of a metering rod in the circuit. The metering rod is located in the hole that leads to the discharge tube. This hole is called a main jet.

The metering rod has different diameters on the end. When the thickest diameter of the metering rod is inserted in the jet, only a certain amount of fuel can pass through the jet. When the metering rod is lifted, the thinner diameter is in the main jet. Now more fuel can pass through the jet and into the engine. The carburetor is operating on the main metering circuit when the thickest diameter is inserted. When more fuel is needed under heavier loads, the metering rod is lifted, allowing more fuel to enter the venturi.

Figure 15–24 shows a tapered metering rod and jet compared with the step-type metering rod. Note that the metering rod is tapered. In addition, the metering rod jet has a tapered hole. As the rod lifts out of the jet, more and more

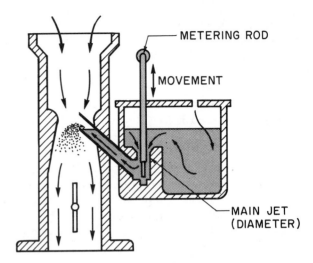

FIGURE 15–23. The metering rod is used to increase the size of the main jet during high-power conditions. The metering rod is lifted so that the end with the smaller diameter fills the main jet. Now more fuel can enter into the carburetor for increased loads. *(Courtesy of Ignition Manufacturers Institute)*

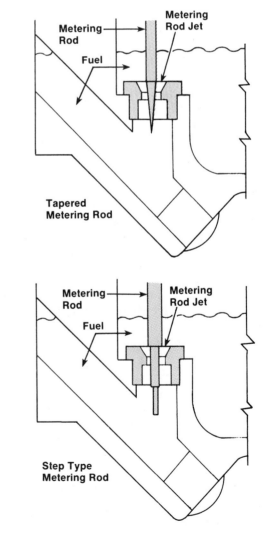

FIGURE 15–24. The main metering jet can be either tapered or stepped. *(Courtesy of Scharff, Complete Fuel Systems and Emission Control, Delmar Publishers Inc.)*

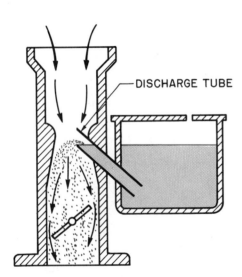

FIGURE 15–22. During normal medium-speed driving, the throttle plate is open enough for the venturi to create a vacuum. Fuel is drawn in by this vacuum through the discharge tube.

fuel is allowed to pass into the venturi. Now the metering rod has an infinite number of positions to deliver fuel.

In certain engines and in certain conditions, the main jets and metering rod can be changed. This is usually necessary if the engine is operated continuously at higher altitudes or under excessive loads.

Mechanically Controlled Metering Rod

The metering rod can be controlled in several ways. One method is to control the metering rod mechanically. The metering rod movement is connected to the movement of the throttle. As the throttle is depressed during medium loads, the metering rod is not moved. Then as the operator pushes the throttle plate fully open, the metering rod is lifted. As it lifts upward, the smaller-diameter end of the metering rod is moved into the main jet. This causes more fuel to pass through the main jet and into the discharge tube. When the operator decelerates, the metering rod returns to its original position.

Vacuum-controlled Metering Rod

A second method used to control the movement of the metering rod is to use vacuum. Compared with the mechanical metering rod, the vacuum-controlled metering rod provides more metering rod movement with less throttle action. When the throttle is nearly closed, engine manifold vacuum is high. This vacuum pulls a spring-loaded piston downward. The metering rod now provides maximum restriction in the main jet.

When the throttle is opened, there is a corresponding decrease in manifold vacuum. The spring pressure then raises the piston and metering rod. See **Figure 15–25**. This permits an increased flow of fuel through the main jet. As the throttle opens farther, the spring pressure pushes the piston and metering rod up even farther. This produces less restriction in the main jet. The maximum amount of fuel will now flow through the carburetor. The vacuum-operated metering rod also operates when the throttle is opened quickly during acceleration.

Certain carburetors use both the mechanically and vacuum-operated systems. New carburetion systems use computers to control the movement of the metering rod. Computer-controlled carburetors will be discussed later in this chapter.

Acceleration Circuit

When the throttle is opened quickly during acceleration, a large volume of air enters the engine. This causes the air-fuel ratio to be very lean, and the engine may stall. An acceleration pump is used to supply extra fuel during acceleration. The acceleration pump is connected to the linkage of the throttle. As the throttle is depressed, the acceleration pump forces fuel under pressure into the stream of air entering the carburetor.

There are many pump designs. One system is shown in **Figure 15–26**. This system has the pump lever connected to the throttle movement. When the throttle is depressed, the pump plunger is forced down. The cup seal forces fuel through a discharge passage, through a pump discharge spring and ball, and into the flow of air just before the venturi. When the operator decelerates, the pump return spring forces

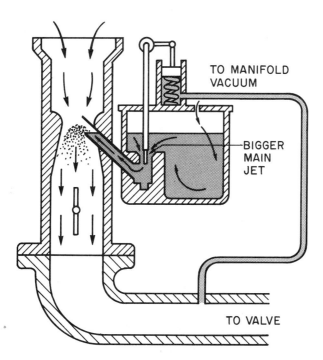

FIGURE 15–25. The metering rod can be controlled by the engine vacuum. As the vacuum decreases under heavy load, the vacuum is reduced and the metering rod is lifted.

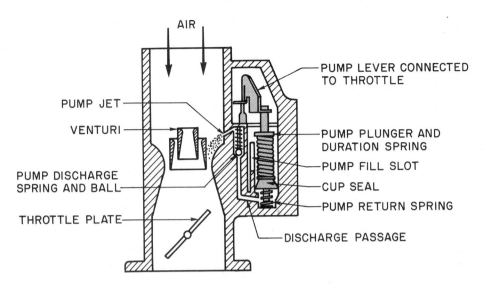

FIGURE 15–26. An acceleration pump is used to force the fuel into the air stream during acceleration. The pump is connected to the mechanical motion of the throttle.

the pump plunger upward. During this upward motion, more fuel is brought into the area below the cup seal.

The discharge spring and ball allow the fuel to flow in only one direction. If the engine backfired, pressure would build up inside the venturi. The spring and ball would now seat. This action would stop any backfire pollutants from getting into the acceleration system.

This particular system also has a pump fill slot. The plunger is located within the fuel bowl. A slot is cut into the plunger well to allow fuel to enter the area below the plunger. Certain systems use an intake *check ball* (valve) to allow fuel to flow into the plunger well. When the plunger moves down during acceleration, the ball is seated and fuel cannot pass back into the bowl area.

Duration Spring

On many acceleration pumps, there is a duration spring. This spring is used to lengthen the time of the pump down-stroke. It *meters* the fuel with the opening time of the throttle valve. The duration spring also prevents damage to the diaphragms on the accelerator pump caused by trying to compress liquid fuel. During operation, the duration spring delays the plunger motion slightly. The movement of the plunger by the throttle motion pushes down on the duration spring. The duration spring then pushes down on the plunger to force fuel into the carburetor. *Figure 15–27* shows the plunger and duration spring.

Choke Circuit

When the engine is cold, a richer air-fuel mixture is needed to keep the engine running. A rich mixture is required for starting because fuel atomization is very poor in a cold engine. Much of the gasoline condenses on the cold engine parts before entering the cylinder area. A choke valve is used to

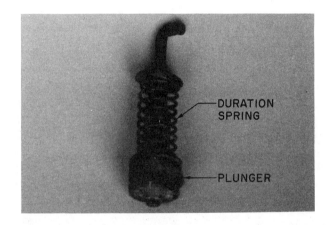

FIGURE 15–27. The duration spring is used to lengthen the time of the acceleration pump downstroke.

provide the richer mixture. The choke valve is located directly on top of the air horn, see *Figure 15–28*. It is used to block the air going into the carburetor. As the valve closes, intake manifold vacuum is felt up through the venturi area. This higher vacuum draws increased amounts of fuel through the discharge tube and into the engine.

Manual Choke Control

Several methods are used to control the opening and closing of the choke plate. The simplest method is to manually control the choke. When the engine is cold, the operator pulls a choke control knob on the dashboard. A wire cable is connected from this knob to the choke plate. This action closes the choke plate. As the engine warms up, the operator must slowly push the knob back in or the air-fuel ratio will be too rich. This system was used on many older vehicles and many foreign sports cars.

FIGURE 15–28. The choke valve is used to restrict the air flow into the carburetor during cold starting conditions.

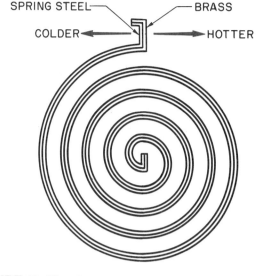

FIGURE 15–30. Some chokes are adjusted by positioning a bimetallic strip with a slight tension. As the spring heats up, it decreases its tension and opens the choke plate.

Automatic Choke Control

The choke can also be controlled automatically. As the temperature of the engine increases after starting, the choke should be opened accordingly. When the engine is at operating temperature, the choke should be fully open. Automatic chokes operate on vacuum diaphragms, small pistons, and electric controls.

A vacuum diaphragm system is shown in *Figure 15–29*. The choke valve is connected to a thermostatic coil rod. This rod is connected to a thermostatic coil that is made of a *bimetallic strip*. The coil is located close to the intake manifold. As the coil cools, it increases in tension. When the coil warms up, the tension is reduced. When the engine is cold, the thermostatic coil has greater tension. The increased tension closes the choke plate, putting the choke circuit into operation. As the engine warms up, the thermostatic coil decreases its tension and the choke valve slowly opens, see *Figure 15–30*.

Thermostatic coils are adjusted in many ways. On some systems, the coil can be tightened or loosened for adjustment. A plastic plate on the outside of the thermostatic coil shows the direction for a leaner or richer mixture, see *Figure 15–31*. On other carburetors, the thermostatic coil rod may have to be bent to get the correct adjustment.

The system shown in Figure 15-29 also has a *vacuum diaphragm* unit. Vacuum is used to open the choke slightly when the engine is cold. A vacuum-operated piston is used on some carburetors. If the choke plate is closed completely, the engine will not get any air. This may cause an overchoked, or rich, condition. The choke plate needs to be slightly open when at full choke. This is done by using a diaphragm that

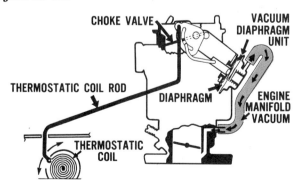

FIGURE 15–29. The choke plate is controlled by a vacuum diaphragm unit. *(Courtesy of Ignition Manufacturers Institute)*

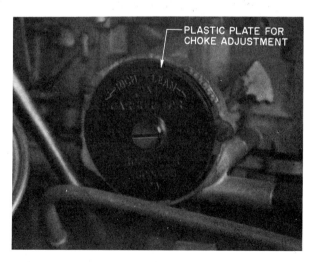

FIGURE 15–31. Some carburetors have a plastic adjustment cover on the outside housing of the thermostatic coil. Turning the plastic cover either increases or decreases the tension of the thermostatic coil.

is controlled by engine manifold vacuum. Before the engine is started, the choke plate is completely closed. When the engine starts, engine manifold vacuum pulls against the vacuum diaphragm. This action pulls the choke valve slightly open so a small amount of air can get into the carburetor. As the engine heats up and the thermostatic coil decreases its tension, the choke plate starts to open. The vacuum diaphragm unit is no longer in effect. This system is also referred to as the choke unloader system.

CAR CLINIC

PROBLEM: Black Smoke During Starting

An engine has become hard to start and produces large amounts of black smoke when it is cold. Also, the fuel mileage has been decreasing each month. What could be the problem?

SOLUTION:

Black smoke is always a sign of an extremely rich mixture in the carburetor. Make sure the choke is adjusted properly. The choke should be set so that the choke plate is just closed. Make sure the bimetallic strip is not holding the choke closed under high spring pressure. Also, the choke should be fully open when the engine is at operating temperature. Often, the choke must be readjusted by bending the choke rod. In some cases, if this doesn't solve the problem, the bimetallic spring controlling the choke valve must be replaced.

15.4 CARBURETOR ACCESSORIES

There have been many changes in carburetor designs. Many accessories have been used during different years on carburetors. Certain accessories are used on cars with air conditioning and with manual or automatic transmissions. The increased emphasis on emission and pollution control has produced more accessories. This section introduces some of the more common accessories used on carburetors.

Hot Idle Compensator

During times when the engine is very hot and underhood temperatures are very high, fuel vapors have a tendency to collect in the intake manifold. The addition of these fuel vapors can cause the air-fuel mixture to be too rich. This may cause the engine to have a rough idle and a tendency to stall at low or idle speeds. The hot idle compensator is used to open a bleed circuit. This circuit permits more air to enter the manifold below the throttle plate. The hot idle compensator helps to dilute the rich air-fuel mixture.

Figure 15–32 shows the hot idle compensator valve. It is made from a bimetallic strip attached to the valve on top of the bleed circuit. It is usually located directly on top of the carburetor. As the temperature of the engine increases to about 120 degrees F, the bimetallic strip starts to bend and open the valve. This permits additional air to enter the intake manifold. When operating temperatures go below 120 degrees F, the valve is closed and the extra air flow is stopped below the throttle plate.

Idle Speed Adjusting Screw

On most carburetors there is an idle speed adjusting screw. Its purpose is to adjust the speed of the idle when the engine is warm. A metal bracket is attached to the throttle plate. The operator's foot pedal is attached to this plate. There is

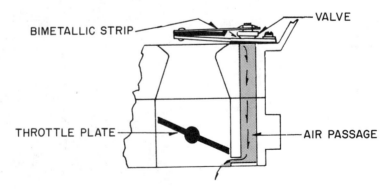

HOT IDLE COMPENSATOR

VALVE

BIMETALLIC STRIP

THROTTLE PLATE

AIR PASSAGE

FIGURE 15–32. The hot idle compensator valve uses a bimetallic strip to open an air bleed circuit. The extra air dilutes the rich air-fuel mixture. *(Courtesy of Ignition Manufacturers Institute)*

also a small adjusting screw located either on the frame of the carburetor or the bracket. As the screw is adjusted, the position of the throttle plate is opened or closed. This action will either increase or decrease the idle speed. Once the operator accelerates, the idle speed adjusting screw does not affect the operation of the throttle plate.

Fast Idle Cam

When the engine is operating on the choke circuit, the engine idle must be increased or the engine will stall. The idle is increased mechanically with a fast idle cam. *Figure 15–33* shows a fast idle cam. There is a connecting rod linkage attached from the choke plate rod to the fast idle cam. The fast idle cam is a small, stepped cam. When the choke plate closes, the fast idle cam is lifted. The idle speed adjusting screw now rides on a higher spot on the cam. This action causes the idle speed to be increased during choked conditions. When the engine heats up and the choke is opened, the fast idle cam drops down from gravity. Now the idle speed is reduced to normal conditions.

When an engine is started during cold conditions, the throttle must be depressed in order for the choke to close. If it is not depressed, the choke will not engage and the high-speed cam will not increase the idle. Also, once the engine is running at fast idle (on the cam), the throttle must be depressed or opened in order for the fast idle cam and the choke plate to be released.

Idle Stop Solenoid

Most current engines with emission controls idle at higher speeds, use leaner air-fuel mixtures, have slightly retarded timing, and have higher cooling temperatures. These conditions increase the tendency of the engine to run on or diesel after the ignition switch has been turned off. One way to stop this condition is to remove the air and fuel completely when the engine is shut down.

In the past, the position of the idle screw always kept the throttle plate slightly open. Air and fuel could enter the engine as it slowed to a stop. With this system, the throttle plate is completely closed when the engine is shut down. Now there is less chance for run-on. This is done by using an idle stop *solenoid*, also called a TSCV (throttle solenoid control valve).

When the engine is running, the solenoid is energized and the plunger is extended, see *Figure 15–34*. The plunger sets the position of the throttle plate. When the ignition switch is shut off, the plunger retracts. The throttle plate now closes completely, shutting off all air and fuel going into the engine. Idle adjustment is made by turning the center of the solenoid plunger in or out.

Electric-assisted Choke

Certain carburetors have an electric-assisted choke. Its purpose is to decrease the time the choke is closed. While the choke is closed, the engine's production of hydrocarbons and carbon monoxide emissions increases. This can be reduced by decreasing the amount of time the choke is closed. A heating element is placed in the thermostatic coil assembly. The addition of the heat from the electric heating element plus the heat from the intake manifold causes the choke to open earlier.

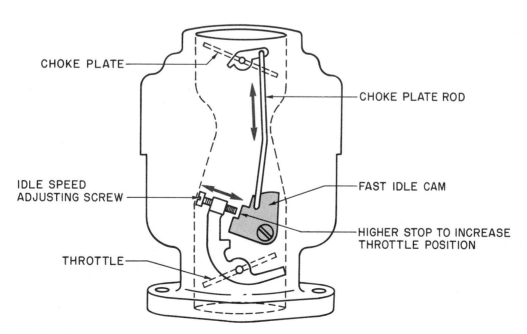

CHOKE PLATE

CHOKE PLATE ROD

IDLE SPEED ADJUSTING SCREW

FAST IDLE CAM

HIGHER STOP TO INCREASE THROTTLE POSITION

THROTTLE

FIGURE 15–33.   The fast idle cam is used to increase the idle speed during choked conditions.

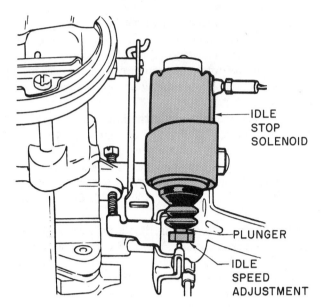

FIGURE 15–34. An idle stop solenoid is used to control the position of the idle setting when the ignition is turned off and on. *(Courtesy of Echlin Manufacturing Company)*

Offset Choke Plate

An offset choke plate is used when the choke is opened and closed by a thermostatic spring. In *Figure 15–35*, the plate is offset on the center shaft of the choke. Air trying to enter the engine can easily push the long side down and flow into the carburetor. During starting, the offset choke plate allows a small amount of air to enter the carburetor during each vacuum pulse. As the engine warms up, changing speeds cause the opening of the choke plate to vary. This action helps to regulate the position of the choke.

Other Accessories

A variety of small carburetor accessories is used to improve the operation of the engine. Each has a special purpose and operation. They include:

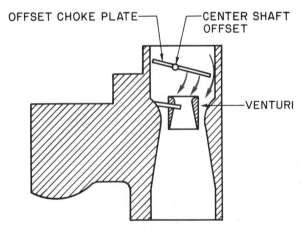

FIGURE 15–35. The choke plate is offset on certain carburetors. Air trying to enter the engine can easily push the long side down and flow into the carburetor.

1. *Anti-icing vents* — used to send warm air to a spot in the carburetor that may ice up because of evaporation.

2. *Idle enrichment valves* — used to enrich the idle mixture to reduce emissions. A small vacuum diaphragm mounted near the carburetor top is used.

3. *Secondary throttle linkage* — used to engage the secondary barrels of a carburetor. Mechanical linkage is used to engage the secondary throttles when the primary throttles are about one half or more open.

4. *Deceleration* dashpots — used to slow down the motion of the throttle during deceleration. If the throttle closes too fast, a very rich condition could cause the engine to stall.

5. *Hot water chokes* — used to apply heat to the thermostatic housing. The choke is released earlier so that less pollution is produced.

6. *Altitude compensators* — used to keep the air-fuel mixture correct at different altitudes. A bellows is usually used to sense altitude differences, causing the air-fuel ratio to be adjusted.

7. *Poppet valve choke plates* — used on some manual chokes. A small poppet valve and spring are placed on the choke plate. When the choke is fully closed, a small amount of air can still get through the poppet valve.

Other connections are also made to the carburetor. These connections are used to sense or control other systems. *Figure 15–36* shows two complete carburetors. Note the many connections, adjustments, and accessories shown.

 **CAR CLINIC**

PROBLEM: **Sticky Carburetor Needle Valve**

A vehicle has been stored over winter. When taken out of storage in the spring, the engine doesn't start. There seems to be a lack of fuel available at the carburetor. A check of the fuel pump shows that the pump is working. What could be the problem?

SOLUTION:

Quite often, the cause of this problem is a sticky needle valve in the carburetor bowl area. Because the engine and carburetor have not been used regularly, the needle valve may stick in the closed position. Then there is a lack of fuel in the carburetor float area. If there is no fuel in the bowl area, the engine will not be able to start. Check by removing the float bowl to check for gasoline. If the bowl is dry, then the problem is the carburetor float valve.

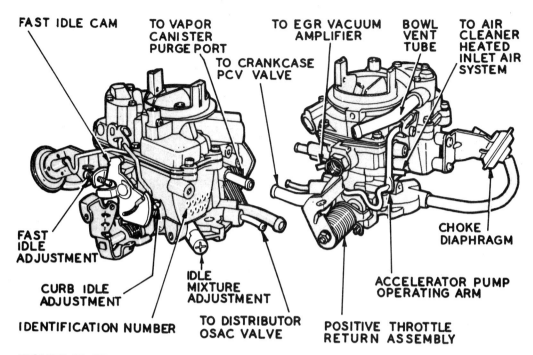

FAST IDLE CAM

TO VAPOR CANISTER PURGE PORT

TO CRANKCASE PCV VALVE

TO EGR VACUUM AMPLIFIER

BOWL VENT TUBE

TO AIR CLEANER HEATED INLET AIR SYSTEM

FAST IDLE ADJUSTMENT

CURB IDLE ADJUSTMENT

IDLE MIXTURE ADJUSTMENT

IDENTIFICATION NUMBER

TO DISTRIBUTOR OSAC VALVE

POSITIVE THROTTLE RETURN ASSEMBLY

ACCELERATOR PUMP OPERATING ARM

CHOKE DIAPHRAGM

FIGURE 15–36. Two complete carburetors are shown including many of the connections, accessories, and adjustments. *(Courtesy of Motor Publications, Auto Engine Tune-up & Electronics Manual)*

15.5 ELECTRONIC CARBURETOR CONTROLS

In recent years, computers have been used to control various components on the engine. This is also true in the fuel system. Control of fuel by computers is referred to as fuel management. A small computer is placed on board the vehicle. During normal operation, many sensors electronically feed signals into the computer, which acts as a brain. On the basis of these input signals, the computer sends out a signal to operate a certain component.

Each car manufacturer now uses computerized systems.

The systems are referred to by many different names for several reasons. Manufacturers often have their own names for their own systems. Also, as the computerized systems have been improved, the names have been changed. Computers that are used to manage spark, timing, fuel injection, and so on are referred to by various other terms. The following is a partial list of computer systems used to manage fuel.

General Motors has a computerized system called CCC (computer command control). The CCC is able to control many systems, including the carburetor system. The computer used in the CCC system is called the electronic control module (ECM) shown in *Figure 15–37*.

FIGURE 15–37. A computer is used to control fuel. The computer is part of a system called Computer Command Control, manufactured by General Motors.

Ford Motor Company calls their current system the EEC IV (electronic engine control IV). This is the fifth generation of computer systems designed by Ford. The computer used in this system is called the electronic control assembly (ECA).

Chrysler Corporation also has well-developed computer systems. Their computerized system is called the oxygen feedback system. The computer used in this system is called the combustion control computer.

American Motors calls their system the ECU, or electronic control unit.

Figure 15–38 shows a schematic of the General Motors fuel management system. The computer ECM is part of the total CCC system. The computer is designed to manage fuel so that higher gasoline mileage can be obtained while producing less emissions. However, before studying this system, two terms must be defined. These are closed and open loop operation.

Closed and Open Loop

The computer systems used on automobiles today can operate in either a closed or open loop mode. All computerized systems managing fuel or ignition can operate in the *closed loop mode*. In this mode an oxygen sensor is placed in the exhaust system (see Figure 15–38) to get an indication of the air-fuel ratio of the engine. The term *closed loop* describes the relationship between three components: the oxygen sensor, the computer, and the fuel-metering control device (carburetor). The oxygen sensor sends electrical signals telling the computer what the air-fuel mixture is. The computer sends a command to the fuel-metering control device to adjust the air-fuel ratio as close to 14.7:1 as possible. This adjustment usually causes the air-fuel ratio to go too far in the opposite direction. The oxygen sensor senses this over-adjustment and sends a signal to the computer to adjust back toward the 14.7:1 ratio. This cycle occurs so quickly that the air-fuel ratio never gets very far from the optimum of 14.7:1 in either direction. This cycle repeats continuously.

The closed loop mode is the most efficient operating mode. The computer is designed and programmed to keep the system in the closed loop as much as possible. The computer reads three criteria to keep the system in closed loop:

1. The oxygen sensor must reach a temperature of at least 600 degrees F.

2. The engine coolant temperature must reach a predetermined temperature of 150 degrees F.

3. The engine must have been running for a certain period of time. The time varies from system to system. The range of time is from several seconds to several minutes.

Open loop operation is used whenever the optimum air-fuel ratio will not work. For example, during starting and warm-up conditions a richer mixture is needed. Also, a richer mixture is needed at wide-open throttle. During these conditions the computer uses coolant temperature, engine load, barometric pressure, and engine speed to determine exactly what the air-fuel ratio should be. On the basis of these inputs, the computer sends a command to the fuel mixture control

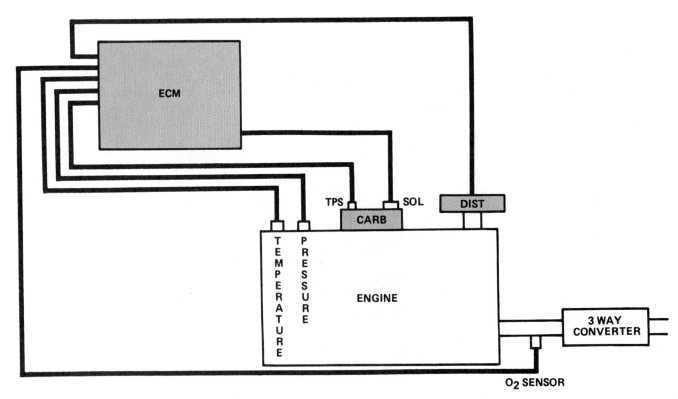

FIGURE 15–38. This schematic shows the inputs and output on a fuel management system. *(Courtesy of General Motors Product Service Training)*

to set a predetermined air-fuel ratio (not 14.7:1). The air-fuel ratio will not change until one of the inputs changes. In the open loop mode, the computer does not use the oxygen sensor for input. Thus, open loop operation is generally not as efficient as closed loop operation. In addition, more emissions are produced. Thus, the computer is designed to put the system into the closed loop mode as soon and as much as possible. Certain failures in the system cause the computer to go out of closed loop operation.

Carburetor Solenoid

An electrical solenoid in the carburetor controls the air-fuel mixture. The solenoid is connected to the ECM. The ECM sends a signal to the solenoid. The solenoid, in turn, controls a metering rod and an idle air bleed valve. With the use of the computer, the air-fuel ratio can be accurately controlled throughout the entire operating range of the engine.

Figure 15–39 shows a mixture control (M/C) solenoid. The mixture control solenoid is an electrical unit that controls fuel flow from the bowl to the main discharge tube or nozzle.

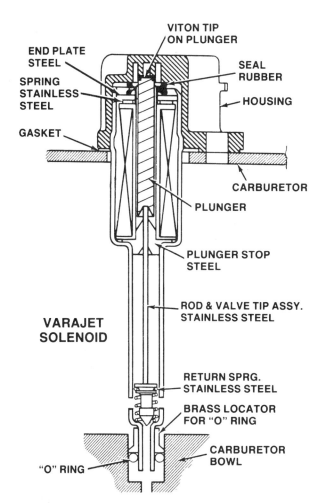

FIGURE 15–39. The M/C (mixture control) solenoid is controlled by the computer. It keeps adjusting the size of the main jet for different air-fuel conditions. *(Courtesy of General Motors Product Service Training)*

The idle circuit air bleed is also controlled by the solenoid. The solenoid coil and plunger are mounted vertically in the carburetor. The stem and valve end reach to the bowl floor where the solenoid controls a passage between the bowl and the discharge tube. It acts as a metering valve that opens and closes. This happens at a rapid rate of 10 times per second.

The upper end of the solenoid rod plunger opens and closes the idle air bleed. When the solenoid is energized, the plunger moves down. This opens the idle air bleed and closes the discharge tube passage. Both the idle and main metering systems become lean or rich together.

O₂ Sensor (Oxygen Sensor)

A sensor is located in the exhaust stream close to the engine. It is known as an oxygen sensor. It measures the amount of oxygen in the exhaust gas. *Figure 15–40* shows an oxygen sensor. There is a direct relationship between the air-fuel mixture and the amount of oxygen in the exhaust gas. The oxygen sensor determines whether the exhaust is too rich or too lean. It sends a low-voltage (below 450 millivolts) signal to the ECM when the mixture is lean. A high-voltage (above 450 millivolts) signal is sent to the ECM when the mixture is rich.

The ECM then signals the mixture control (M/C) solenoid to deliver a richer or leaner mixture. As the carburetor makes an air-fuel change, the oxygen sensor immediately senses that change and again signals the ECM. This goes on continually during the engine operation.

This process is a closed loop operation. Closed loop operations deliver an accurate 14.7 to 1 air-fuel ratio to the engine.

Temperature Sensor

A temperature sensor is also used with the ECM, *Figure 15–41*. The sensor is located in the cooling system and is connected to the ECM. Whenever the engine is cold, there

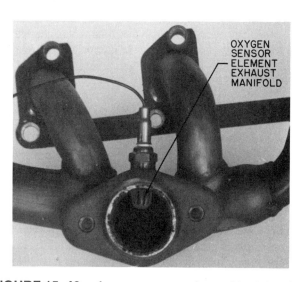

FIGURE 15–40. An oxygen sensor is used to determine the amount of oxygen in the exhaust. This information is sent to the computer to help control the air-fuel ratio.

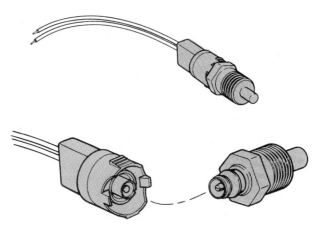

FIGURE 15–41. A temperature sensor is used to sense the temperature of the engine coolant. This information is sent to the computer to help control the air-fuel ratio. *(Courtesy of General Motors Product Service Training)*

is no need for the oxygen sensor to control the air-fuel ratio. Under these conditions, the ECM tells the carburetor to deliver a richer mixture. The mixture is based on what has been programmed into the ECM and what other sensors are telling the computer. This is an open loop operation. The sensor's resistance is lowered as coolant temperature increases. The resistance is raised as the temperature decreases.

After the engine reaches operating temperature, the temperature sensor signals the ECM to read what the oxygen sensor is providing. If other requirements are met, closed loop operation begins.

Pressure Sensor

The load on the engine also affects the air-fuel mixture needed in the engine. As a load is placed on the engine, a richer air-fuel mixture is needed. This can be measured by sensing the intake manifold vacuum, shown in *Figure 15–42*. A pressure sensor located in the intake manifold detects changes in the manifold pressure. As the pressure changes, a flexible resistor attached to a diaphragm also changes its resistance. This pressure change causes a voltage change that the ECM can read. This voltage change signals the ECM that

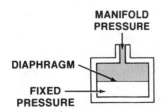

FIGURE 15–42. A pressure sensor located in the intake manifold detects changes in manifold pressure or vacuum. *(Courtesy of General Motors Product Service Training)*

there is an increase in load. The ECM takes this signal into account to determine the exact air-fuel ratio required.

Throttle Position Sensor

The position of the throttle opening is another factor in determining what air-fuel ratio is needed. The more the throttle is open, the richer the mixture required by the engine. *Figure 15–43* shows the TPS (throttle position sensor). It is a variable resistor that sends a signal to the ECM. Depending on the position of the throttle, the ECM will signal the carburetor solenoid to increase or decrease the air-fuel mixture.

The throttle position sensor is a variable resistor mounted in the float bowl. As the position of the throttle changes, the voltage also changes. At closed throttle, the voltage is about 1 volt or less. As the throttle opening increases, the voltage increases to about 5 volts at wide-open throttle.

Engine Speed Sensor

Engine speed also has a direct bearing on the air-fuel mixture. When the engine is operating at a low speed, less fuel is needed. When the engine operates at a higher RPM, more fuel is needed. This adjustment is made by using an engine speed sensor. A tachometer signal from the distributor is sent to the ECM. Refer to the schematic in Figure 15–38. This signal tells the ECM the RPM of the engine. The computer considers this signal when setting the exact air-fuel ratio needed.

Idle Speed Control

Since the increase in emission standards, idle speed must be controlled more precisely. The CCC system controls the idle speed for drivability as well as for fuel economy and emission control. This is done by using the ECM and a reversible

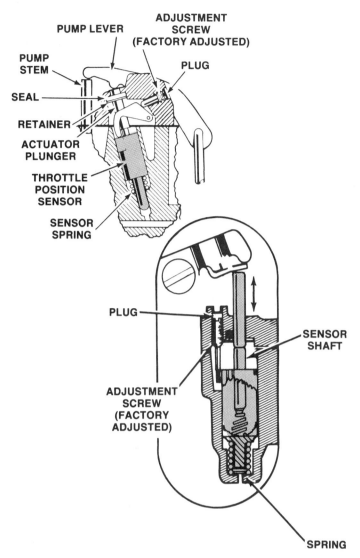

FIGURE 15–43. A throttle position sensor is used to determine the exact position of the throttle. This information then helps the computer determine the exact air-fuel ratio needed. *(Courtesy of General Motors Product Service Training)*

electric motor. The ECM maintains a selected idle speed regardless of the load imposed on the engine. A plunger that acts as a movable idle stop changes the idle speed. The plunger is positioned by a small electric motor. A throttle contact switch tells the ECM to operate only when the throttle lever is closed. When the throttle lever moves away from the throttle contact switch, the ECM is instructed not to operate. The driver now has control of the engine speed. See *Figure 15–44*.

Figure 15–45 shows a schematic of the ECM and identifies the inputs and the outputs to the electric motor. Note that the throttle switch is considered an input to the ECM. Also, many of the inputs are the same as those used with the carburetor solenoid. The following controls are considered input signals to the ECM:

1. *Distributor* — sensing RPM.

2. *Oxygen sensor* — sensing oxygen in exhaust.

3. *Temperature sensor* — sensing coolant.

4. *Pressure sensor* — sensing manifold pressure and load.

5. *Throttle position sensor* — sensing throttle position.

The *battery signal* is used to sense the system's operating voltage. If the voltage signal falls below a predetermined level, the ECM will instruct the idle speed control plunger to extend. This will increase the engine speed, which will, in turn, increase the generator speed so that generator output will increase.

The *park-neutral switch* tells the ECM when the transmission has shifted. When the transmission shifts, the load on the engine changes. The idle speed must then be changed. This prevents different idle speeds at neutral, drive, and reverse conditions.

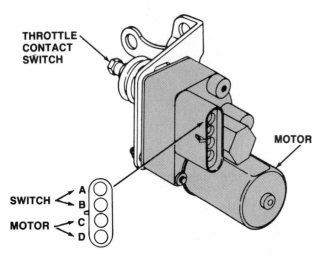

THROTTLE
CONTACT
SWITCH

MOTOR

SWITCH
A
B

MOTOR
C
D

Idle Speed Control Motor

FIGURE 15–44.   The idle speed control motor is operated by signals from the ECM. An internal motor positions an inside plunger. When the throttle lever is moved away from the throttle contact switch, the computer is instructed not to control the idle speed control motor. *(Courtesy of General Motors Product Service Training)*

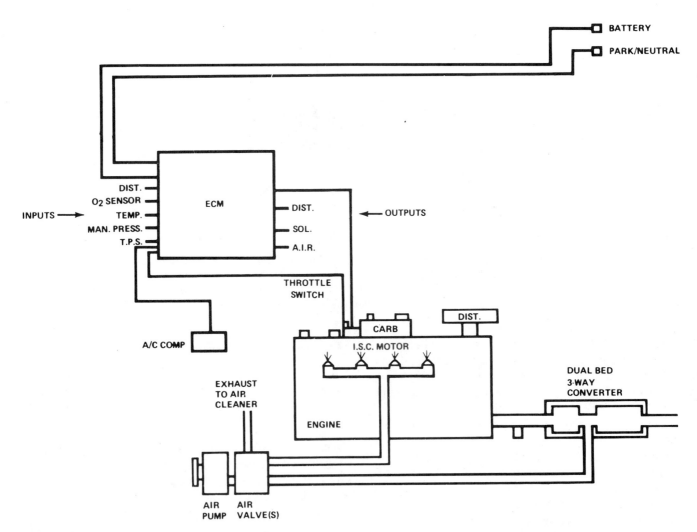

FIGURE 15–45.   This schematic shows the inputs and outputs used to control the idle speed control motor. *(Courtesy of General Motors Product Service Training)*

Problems, Diagnosis and Service

1. The cleaner used to clean carburetors is extremely toxic. When cleaning carburetors, always wear protective gloves, safety glasses, and protective gowns to eliminate any possibility of injury.
2. When adjusting the carburetor with a screwdriver or other tool, always approach the carburetor from the side. Approaching from the front may cause injury if the tool is accidently dropped into the spinning fan.
3. When setting any adjustment on the carburetor, always put the car in park, with the emergency brake on and the wheels blocked.
4. Often vehicles must have the color of the exhaust checked. When checking the color of exhaust with the engine running, make sure there is adequate ventilation for the exhaust fumes.
5. When checking the electrical components on or near the carburetor always use a battery-operated tester to eliminate any sparks. Sparks could cause a fire if near gasoline fumes.
6. Make sure there are no unshielded flames, such as a cutting torch, around or near a vehicle when the carburetor is being serviced.
7. If even a small quantity of gasoline must be stored for a short period of time, always store the fuel in an approved OSHA container. Never store gasoline in an open container. It may spill and possibly cause a fire.

PROBLEM: Too Rich Mixture

A vehicle with a standard carburetor has difficulty starting and emits black smoke.

DIAGNOSIS

Black smoke is usually a result of a rich air-fuel mixture. The exhaust can be observed when the engine is accelerated or running normally. Also, black carbon will build up inside the exhaust pipe. These are all indications of too rich an air-fuel mixture. The rich mixture can be a result of several faults. The two usually associated with a rich mixture are poorly adjusted floats and choke.

SERVICE

Float Adjustment

Floats must be adjusted according to the manufacturer's specifications. Many automotive repair manuals and tune-up manuals have such carburetor specifications. Too high a float level will cause a rich mixture, black smoke, and poor gasoline mileage. Too low a float level will cause a lean mixture and may possibly damage the internal parts of the engine. If the floats are off as little as 1/32 of an inch the air-fuel ratio will be off.

Floats are commonly checked and adjusted by removing the top of the carburetor and holding the floats and air horn in a set position. Generally two adjustments are made. These include the float drop and the float level or height. Often the exact type of float adjustment is shown in the carburetor rebuild kit. *Figure 15–46* shows an example of adjusting the float level and the float drop. These measurements are made and compared with manufacturer's specifications. To adjust, a float arm (also called a tang) is bent to get the exact specification.

While the float is off for adjustments also check the float for small pinhole leaks. This can be done by shaking the float to see if there is fuel inside it. Some floats can be weighed with a scale to check for fuel absorption.

Checking and Adjusting the Choke

Another possible cause of a rich air-fuel mixture is the choke. If the choke is set too rich, the engine will start hard and produce black smoke.

1. When adjusting the choke, check that it is fully open when the engine is at operating temperature and fully closed when the engine is cold, before starting. Because there are so many variations and accessories on carburetors, always refer to the manufacturer's specifications and procedures. These can be found in the automotive service and repair manuals. Generally, the part that is adjusted is the tension on the bimetallic coil attached to the choke plate.
2. Over a period of time, the characteristics of the bimetallic strip on the choke may change. This change may cause the choke to open and close at different temperatures. If the choke cannot be adjusted to compensate for the change, the bimetallic strip may have to be replaced.

PROBLEM: Float Valve Stuck

An engine that has a carburetor has fuel spilling out of the top of the bowl area.

DIAGNOSIS

This type of problem often means that the float valve is stuck in the open position. It often gets stuck because a piece of dirt is lodged in the float valve.

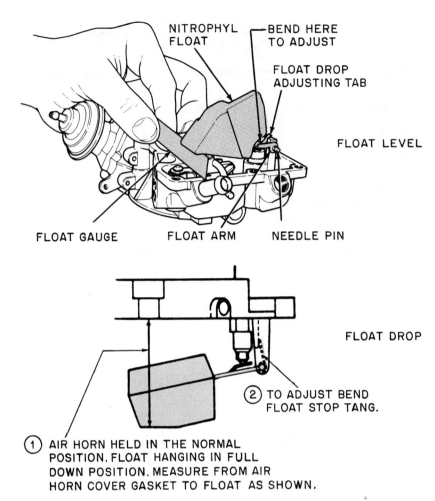

NITROPHYL FLOAT

BEND HERE TO ADJUST

FLOAT DROP ADJUSTING TAB

FLOAT LEVEL

FLOAT GAUGE   FLOAT ARM   NEEDLE PIN

FLOAT DROP

② TO ADJUST BEND FLOAT STOP TANG.

① AIR HORN HELD IN THE NORMAL POSITION. FLOAT HANGING IN FULL DOWN POSITION. MEASURE FROM AIR HORN COVER GASKET TO FLOAT AS SHOWN.

FIGURE 15–46. These are typical examples of how to measure float drop and float level. *(Courtesy of Motor Publications, Auto Engine Tune-up and Electronics Manual)*

SERVICE

1. Remove the main fuel line to the carburetor.

2. Remove the accelerator linkage to the carburetor.

3. Remove any choke or other linkage that will restrict the removal of the air horn from the carburetor.

4. Remove the top of the carburetor by loosening and removing all screws.

5. Remove the float and float pins.

6. At this point, the needle valve can be seen.

7. Use a small needle nose pliers to remove the valve.

8. Check for dirt particles, and clean the needle valve and passageways.

9. Make sure the needle valve moves in the hole without sticking.

10. After cleaning, assemble the carburetor in the reverse order.

PROBLEM: Idle Mixture Adjustment

An engine is running rough at idle. The vehicle has an older engine with a carburetor.

DIAGNOSIS

On older vehicles, the carburetor idle mixtures may need to be adjusted. The idle mixture adjustment screws are adjusted as far in as possible with the highest idle. The standard is usually 1 to 1 1/2 turns out. Always check the manufacturer's specifications.

SERVICE

1. Begin by turning the needle valves in to a seated position. Be careful not to turn in too hard as the seat may be damaged.

2. Turn the idle mixture adjustment screws 1 1/2 turns out. The engine should be off during this adjustment.
   CAUTION: Set the parking brake for safety.

3. Start the engine and run it to operating temperature, making sure the choke is open.

4. Turn the idle screws in until a slight drop in engine RPM is observed. This can be done by using a tachometer attached to the engine's electrical system.

5. Now turn the screws out until a slight drop is observed in RPM.

6. Adjust the idle mixture screws between these two points to get the smoothest idle.

7. This procedure may vary with each vehicle and manufacturer. More accurate idle adjustments can be made using a propane mixture test.

PROBLEM: Dirty Carburetor

A vehicle has poor fuel economy, loss of power, flat spots during accelerations, and irregular idle.

DIAGNOSIS

Often it is necessary to rebuild the carburetor. For example, flat spots occur during acceleration because of a faulty acceleration pump. Irregular operation may be caused by the idle transfer port being plugged with dirt or varnish deposits from the fuel. This condition is sometimes called off idle stumble. These and other problems are caused because of constant use, dirty fuel, and wear to the carburetor. The carburetor needs to be rebuilt.

When rebuilding a carburetor it will first be necessary to buy a carburetor rebuild kit. This kit contains the gaskets, valves, instructions, and so on necessary to rebuild the carburetor. To obtain the correct carburetor kit you will need to know the type of vehicle, year, and other pertinent information, including the number of the carburetor. This number is usually found on a small metal tag attached to the carburetor.

SERVICE

A carburetor rebuild kit usually has parts to replace the seals, needle valves, gaskets, acceleration plunger, and other components. Always clean the internal parts of the carburetor with carburetor cleaner. Carburetor cleaner will also clean off varnish on the internal parts of the carburetor circuits.

CAUTION: Carburetor cleaner is toxic and harmful to human skin. Always wear safety glasses, gloves, and use an approved container to hold the carburetor cleaner solution. Use the following general procedure to rebuild the carburetor.

1. After the carburetor has been removed from the engine, carefully disassemble the carburetor. Make sure to remove the concealment plugs or limiter caps.

CAUTION: Do not remove the throttle plates from the shaft. The screws that hold the throttle plates to their shafts are "staked" (positioned exactly). Attempts to remove the throttle plates may damage the carburetor.

2. Carefully inspect all parts for damage and wear.

3. Using an approved container and special carburetor cleaner, soak each part. Follow the directions on the carburetor cleaner container.

4. Wash all cleaner from the parts and dry. Using compressed air, blow out all air passageways and air bleed circuits.

5. Reassemble the carburetor according to the procedures listed in the rebuild kit.

6. On all rebuilt carburetors it is necessary to readjust the idle mixture adjustments. This adjustment can be made by using artificial propane enrichment. The following general procedure shows how to complete a propane enrichment test. Always check the service manual for the exact procedure.

   a. Remove the concealment plugs or limiter caps from the carburetor.

   b. Start the engine and allow to reach normal operating temperature.

   c. Disconnect and plug vacuum hose at EGR valve.

   d. Disconnect vacuum hose from heated air door or choke diaphragm, then connect hose from metering valve on enrichment tool fitting.

   e. Remove PCV valve from cylinder head.

   f. Disconnect and plug 3/16 inch diameter control hose at canister.

   g. Check with manufacturer's procedure as to other components that need to be removed or plugged.

   h. After setup according to manufacturer's procedure, open main propane valve fully. Now, open propane metering valve slowly until maximum idle RPM is obtained. NOTE: Too much propane will cause engine speed to drop. Adjust metering valve to obtain maximum idle RPM.

   i. With propane flowing, adjust idle speed to specified enriched RPM by turning idle speed screw.

   j. Adjust metering valve to obtain maximum RPM. If there has been a change in maximum RPM, readjust idle speed screw to specified enriched RPM.

   k. Turn off main propane valve and allow engine speed to stabilize.

   l. Adjust mixture screw to obtain smoothest idle at specified curb idle RPM. Allow time between adjustment for engine speed to stabilize.

   m. Turn on main propane valve and adjust valve to obtain maximum engine RPM. If maximum engine speed differs by more than 25 RPM from specified enriched RPM, repeat steps i thru m.

   n. When the adjustment is correct, turn off both propane valves, stop engine, and remove tool.

   o. Install concealment plug, and perform the idle speed adjustment according to specifications.

PROBLEM: Incorrect Idle Speed

The idle on the engine is too high. The transmission makes noise when shifting from forward to reverse.

DIAGNOSIS

On most vehicles the curb idle adjustment must be made occasionally. If the curb idle is too high, the transmission has a difficult time shifting from forward to reverse. If the curb idle speed is too low, the engine will shut down during idle.

SERVICE

The curb idle speed on the idle stop solenoid is adjusted by turning the inside hex nut on the plunger on the solenoid or by positioning the solenoid. Use the following general procedures to check the solenoid:

1. Check the solenoid by holding the throttle about one-quarter open with the engine off.

2. Apply battery voltage to the solenoid with a jumper wire. The plunger should extend.

3. Remove the jumper wire, and the solenoid should retract.

To check the idle and shutdown adjustments:

1. Connect a tachometer to the engine. Set the brake and block the drive wheels.

2. Start the engine and warm it up to normal operating temperature.

3. Check the manufacturer's specifications for transmission position (drive or park). Also check whether the air conditioning should be on or off.

4. Make sure the plunger on the solenoid is fully extended.

5. Adjust the solenoid body or plunger screw to obtain the specified slow curb idle speed.

6. Disconnect the solenoid lead wire to de-energize the solenoid and retract the plunger.

7. Adjust the carburetor idle speed screw of the solenoid to obtain the specific shutdown idle. Reconnect the solenoid and return to the curb idle speed position.

PROBLEM: Carburetor-Computer Controls

On a vehicle equipped with a computer to manage fuel, a CHECK ENGINE light comes on on the dashboard.

DIAGNOSIS

Today, there are many electrical components used on computerized systems. Often these components fail. The type of failure is usually an open, a short, or a voltage value that stays too high or too low for too long. The computer is able to monitor these faults.

There are two methods used to diagnose these faults in computerized control systems.

1. *Demand diagnostics* — This method performs various diagnostic procedures only on demand from an outside control. In this case, a service technician initiates the computer to go through certain diagnostic procedures. These procedures are stored in the computer memory. When variations from standards are found, service codes are signaled to the service technician. Various scanners and electronic testers are also used to perform similar diagnostics.

2. *Ongoing diagnostics* — Most manufacturers have ongoing diagnostic systems. Problems are signaled to the driver by a flashing CHECK ENGINE light on the dash. A trouble code associated with that problem is also stored in the computer's RAM (random access memory). As long as power is supplied to the computer, the codes remain stored in the memory.

   If the problem is intermittent, the CHECK ENGINE light will go out. However, the trouble code will remain in the memory as long as power is applied.

SERVICE

Assessing stored trouble codes and other diagnostic information can be done easily. The technician grounds a test lead under the dash while the engine is running. The connector is often called the assembly line communication link (ALCL). It is also called the assembly line diagnostic link (ALDL). The location of the ALCL will vary with each manufacturer. Some are under the dash, while others are under the hood. *Figure 15–47* shows one example. The test lead is on the passenger side of the vehicle. The CHECK ENGINE light shown in *Figure 15–48* then flashes on and off. The

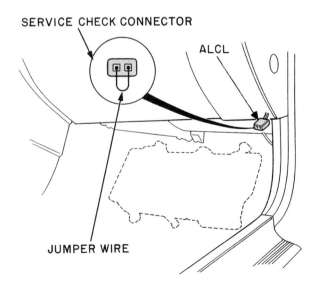

FIGURE 15–47.   To determine the trouble code on certain vehicles, use a jumper wire on the service check connector. *(Courtesy of Honda Motor Company, Ltd.)*

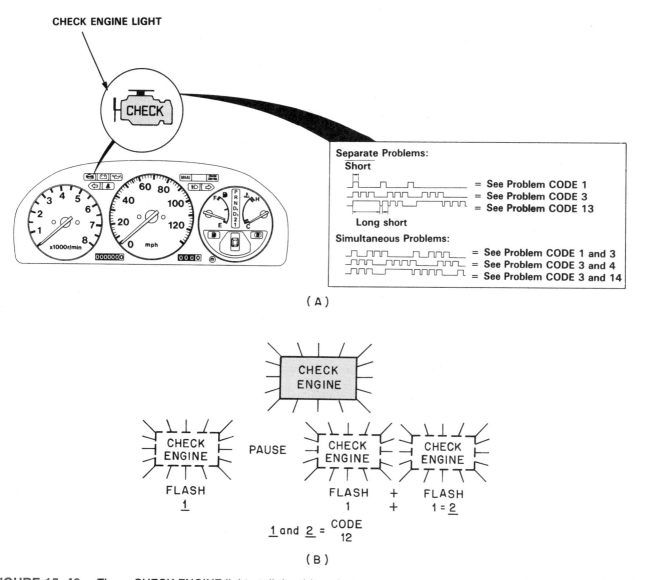

FIGURE 15–48. These CHECK ENGINE lights tell the driver that a trouble code has been placed in the computer. The trouble code is identified by observing the on-and-off sequence of the CHECK ENGINE light. *(Courtesy of (A) Honda Motor Company, Ltd. and (B) General Motors Corporation)*

exact sequence depends on the engine. Two systems are shown for comparison. The system shown in 15–48 (A) is able to show both separate problems and simultaneous problems. For example, this manufacturer uses long blinks for the first digit in the trouble code and short blinks for the second digit. Figure 15–48 (A) also shows a graphical representation of the blinking light. In Figure 15–48 (B) only one code is shown using a series of blinks and pauses.

There are certain codes to help diagnose the fuel system. For example, if the light in Figure 15–48 (A) flashes four times, pauses for a moment, then flashes three more times, it means the trouble code 43 has been stored. *Figure 15–49* identifies the problem for code 43 as the fuel supply system. Each manufacturer also has different codes. *Figure 15–50* shows another manufacturer's trouble code numbers.

SERVICE MANUAL CONNECTION

There are many important specifications to keep in mind when working with carburetor systems. To identify the specifications for your engine, you will need to know the VIN (vehicle identification number) of the vehicle, the type and year of the vehicle, and the type of engine. Although they may be titled differently, some of the more common carburetor system specifications (not all) found in service manuals are listed below. Note that these specifications are typical examples.

Continued

SERVICE MANUAL CONNECTION Continued

Each vehicle and engine may have different specifications.

Common Specification	Typical Example
Automatic choke setting	1 notch rich
Choke unloader setting	0.280 inch
Curb idle speed	
Manual transmission	550 RPM
Automatic transmission	
(in drive)	600 RPM
Fast idle cam setting	0.175 inch
Fast idle speed	
Manual transmission	2100 RPM
Automatic transmission	
(in drive)	2200 RPM
Float level	0.600 inch
Mixture adjustment	1 1/4 turns
Propane enrichment	
(gain in RPM)	10–100 RPM

In addition, the service manual will give specific directions for various service procedures. Some of the more common procedures include:

- Adjusting idle speed
- Carburetor overhaul
- Fast idle speed adjustment
- Idle speed and mixture adjustments
- Propane enrichment idle fuel mixture check

SELF-DIAGNOSIS INDICATOR BLINKS	SYSTEM INDICATED
0	ECU
1	OXYGEN CONTENT
3	MANIFOLD ABSOLUTE PRESSURE
5	
4	CRANK ANGLE
6	COOLANT TEMPERATURE
7	THROTTLE ANGLE
8	TDC POSITION
9	No.1 CYLINDER POSITION
10	INTAKE AIR TEMPERATURE
12	EXHAUST GAS RECIRCULATION SYSTEM
13	ATMOSPHERIC PRESSURE
14	ELECTRONIC AIR CONTROL
15	IGNITION OUTPUT SIGNAL
16	FUEL INJECTOR
17	VEHICLE SPEED SENSOR
20	ELECTRIC LOAD DETECTOR
30	A/T FI SIGNAL A
31	A/T FI SIGNAL B
41	OXYGEN SENSOR HEATER
43	FUEL SUPPLY SYSTEM

FIGURE 15–49. After determining the code from the CHECK ENGINE light, refer to this chart to determine the system fault. *(Courtesy of Honda Motor Company, Ltd.)*

TROUBLE CODE IDENTIFICATION

The "SERVICE ENGINE SOON" light will only be "ON" if the malfunction exists under the conditions listed below. It takes up to five seconds minimum for the light to come on when a problem occurs. If the malfunction clears, the light will go out and a trouble code will be set in the ECM. Code 12 does not store in memory. If the light comes "on" intermittently, but no code is stored, go to section B - Symptoms. Any codes stored will be erased if no problem is detected within 50 engine starts. A specific engine may not use all available codes.

The trouble codes indicate problems as follows:

TROUBLE CODE 12	No distributor reference signal to the ECM. This code is not stored in memory and will only flash while the fault is present. This is a normal code with ignition "on," engine not running.	TROUBLE CODE 34	Vacuum sensor or Manifold Absolute Pressure (MAP) circuit - The engine must run up to two minutes, at specified curb idle, before this code will set.
TROUBLE CODE 13	Oxygen Sensor Circuit - The engine must run up to four minutes at part throttle, under road load, before this code will set.	TROUBLE CODE 35	Idle speed control (ISC) switch circuit shorted. (Up to 70% TPS for over 5 seconds.)
TROUBLE CODE 14	Shorted coolant sensor circuit - The engine must run two minutes before this code will set.	TROUBLE CODE 41	No distributor reference signal to the ECM at specified engine vacuum. This code will store in memory.
TROUBLE CODE 15	Open coolant sensor circuit - The engine must run five minutes before this code will set.	TROUBLE CODE 42	Electronic spark timing (EST) bypass circuit or EST circuit grounded or open.
TROUBLE CODE 21	Throttle Position Sensor (TPS) circuit voltage high (open circuit or misadjusted TPS). The engine must run 10 seconds, at specified curb idle speed, before this code will set.	TROUBLE CODE 43	Electronic Spark Control (ESC) retard signal for too long a time; causes retard in EST signal.
		TROUBLE CODE 44	Lean exhaust indication - The engine must run two minutes, in closed loop and at part throttle, before this code will set.
TROUBLE CODE 22	Throttle Position Sensor (TPS) circuit voltage low (grounded circuit or misadjusted TPS). Engine must run 20 seconds at specified curb idle speed, to set code.	TROUBLE CODE 45	Rich exhaust indication - The engine must run two minutes, in closed loop and at part throttle, before this code will set.
TROUBLE CODE 23	M/C solenoid circuit open or grounded.	TROUBLE CODE 51	Faulty or improperly installed calibration unit (PROM). It takes up to 30 seconds before this code will set.
TROUBLE CODE 24	Vehicle speed sensor (VSS) circuit - The vehicle must operate up to two minutes, at road speed, before this code will set.	TROUBLE CODE 53	Exhaust Gas Recirculation (EGR) valve vacuum sensor has seen improper EGR control vacuum.
TROUBLE CODE 32	Barometric pressure sensor (BARO) circuit low.	TROUBLE CODE 54	M/C solenoid voltage high at ECM as a result of a shorted M/C solenoid circuit and/or faulty ECM.

FIGURE 15–50. General Motors uses this chart to identify the trouble code flashed on the dashboard. *(Courtesy of Motor Publications, Auto Engine Tune-up and Electronics Manual)*

SUMMARY

The purpose of this chapter was to introduce basic carburetor principles, study carburetor circuits, analyze carburetor accessories, and study computer-controlled carburetors.

The carburetor works on several main principles. It is designed to keep the air-fuel ratio close to 14.7 parts of air to 1 part of fuel. The carburetor must also change the fuel into tiny droplets or a spray for best atomization. The venturi is the main component that is used to draw fuel into the air flow. The throttle plate is used to control the amount of air and fuel flowing into the engine.

Three methods are used to identify types of carburetors. The carburetor draft refers to the direction in which air flows through the carburetor. The number of barrels refers to the number of throttle plates, idle circuits, and choke plates used. The number of venturis also helps determine the type of

carburetor used. One, two, and three venturis may be used in any one carburetor.

Several circuits are built into the carburetor to obtain the best performance. The float circuit keeps the level of fuel in the float bowl at the correct level. It uses brass or plastic floats and a needle valve for operation. The idle circuit controls the fuel during idle and very low speed operation. When the throttle plate is closed, fuel is brought in through an idle port below the throttle by the intake manifold vacuum. The low-speed circuit uses an additional transfer port to increase fuel flow during low speeds. The main metering circuit uses a stepped metering rod to control the amount of fuel during intermediate driving conditions. The power circuit is used for increased power. The metering rod is lifted so that more fuel can enter the main jet. The acceleration circuit uses a mechanical pump to squirt extra fuel for acceleration. The

Linkage to Science and Mathematics

BERNOULLI'S THEOREM

A venturi in a carburetor works on a simple scientific principle called Bernoulli's theorem. Bernoulli's theorem states that when a fluid (air or a liquid) flows through a pipe, pressure will remain constant unless the diameter of the pipe changes. At the venturi in a carburetor the throat diameter narrows. The figure illustrates this principle. Note how the diameter of the pipe changes in the center.

In order to keep the flow rate constant, the fluid must flow faster through the restriction. When the velocity of the fluid increases at the restriction, the static pressure is reduced in the center (low pressure area). The reduction of static pressure (called a vacuum) is the energy used to draw fuel from the carburetor bowl into the throat of the carburetor. *(Courtesy of Schwaller, Transportation Energy and Power Technology, Delmar Publishers Inc.)*

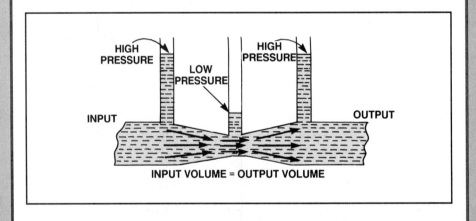

choke circuit increases the amount of fuel during cold starting conditions.

Various carburetor accessories are used to reduce emissions and to make the carburetor more efficient. The hot idle compensator bleeds air into the intake manifold to dilute the air-fuel ratio during hot idle conditions. The idle speed adjusting screw adjusts the speed of the idle by mechanically adjusting the position of the throttle plate. The fast idle cam increases the idle when the choke is engaged. The idle stop solenoid completely shuts off the fuel and air when the engine ignition is shut off. The electric-assisted choke uses an electric heater in the choke to heat up the thermostatic spring quickly. The offset choke plate allows a small amount of air to pulse into the carburetor during fully choked conditions. Other accessories used on carburetors include anti-icing vents, idle enrichment valves, secondary throttle linkage, dashpots, hot water chokes, altitude compensators, and poppet valve choke plates. Each accessory has a special purpose and improves carburetor performance.

Carburetors are now being controlled by computers. Fuel management is needed as a result of stricter emission standards. A common type of fuel management system is called the CCC (computer command control). This system uses an ECM (electronic control module). Various data are sent into the computer. These include oxygen in the exhaust, coolant temperature, intake manifold pressure/vacuum, engine speed, battery voltage, and park-neutral conditions. On the basis of these inputs, the air-fuel ratio is controlled at idle and during normal driving. This is done by operating a metering control solenoid and an idle speed control motor.

Many service checks can be performed on the carburetor. A carburetor that is operating correctly will deliver a 14.7 to 1 air-fuel ratio throughout its operation. If this ratio changes drastically, poor fuel mileage, increased emissions, and irregular operation will result.

TERMS TO KNOW

Can you explain each of the following terms? Review the chapter until you can use each term correctly.

Atomized	Vacuum diaphragm
Vaporized	Solenoid
Vacuum	Dashpot
Venturi	Closed loop
Ported vacuum	Open loop
Intake manifold vacuum	Battery signal
Venturi vacuum	Park–neutral switch
Draft	
Carburetor barrel	
Check ball	
Meter	
Bimetallic strip	

REVIEW QUESTIONS

Multiple Choice

1. The main purpose of the carburetor is to mix the air-fuel ratio to:
   a. 12.3 to 1
   b. 14.7 to 1
   c. 20 to 1
   d. 25.3 to 1
   e. 30.2 to 1

2. Atomization is used to help _____ the fuel.
   a. Cool
   b. Vaporize
   c. Weigh
   d. Pressurize
   e. Reduce the weight of

3. A restriction in the flow of air in a carburetor is called a _____.
   a. Barrel
   b. Pressure
   c. Venturi
   d. Dashpot
   e. None of the above

4. Fuel is drawn into the carburetor by a _____ produced by a venturi.
   a. Pressure
   b. Vacuum
   c. Temperature difference
   d. Vacuum pump
   e. Hydraulic pressure

5. What controls the amount of air and fuel going into the carburetor during normal operation when the engine is warm?
   a. Throttle plate
   b. Air horn
   c. Bowl
   d. Position of the choke
   e. Position of the dashpot

6. Which of the following is a method used to identify a type of carburetor?
   a. Number of barrels
   b. Number of venturis
   c. Type of draft
   d. All of the above
   e. None of the above

7. A carburetor that has two throttle plates is called a:
   a. Two-barrel carburetor
   b. Two-venturi carburetor
   c. Two-draft carburetor
   d. All of the above
   e. None of the above

8. During idle, what causes the fuel to enter into the air flow?
   a. Fuel pressure
   b. Intake manifold vacuum
   c. Air horn pressure
   d. Injector valve
   e. Accelerator pump

9. The idle port is positioned _____ the throttle plate.
   a. Below
   b. Above
   c. Even with
   d. To the right of
   e. To the left of

10. Too high a float level will produce a _____ .
    a. Lean mixture
    b. 14.7 to 1 mixture
    c. Rich mixture
    d. High pressure in the venturi
    e. Low pressure in the venturi

11. Which vent on the float bowl is used to equalize pressure between the bowl and the air horn?
    a. External vent
    b. Internal vent
    c. Bypass vent
    d. All of the above
    e. None of the above

12. Idle mixture adjustment screws are used on _____ .
    a. Older carburetors
    b. Newer carburetors
    c. All carburetors
    d. Electronic carburetors
    e. Fuel injectors

13. When the carburetor is operating on the low-speed circuit, fuel enters the air flow:
    a. Two inches above the throttle
    b. Below the throttle
    c. By accelerator pump pressure
    d. All of the above
    e. None of the above

14. When the carburetor is operating on the low-speed circuit, fuel is drawn into the air stream by the:
    a. Venturi
    b. Intake manifold vacuum
    c. Fuel pump pressure
    d. Air cleaner
    e. Fuel pump

15. Which of the following carburetor circuits uses a metering rod?
    a. Idle
    b. Low-speed
    c. Main metering
    d. Choke
    e. Acceleration

16. Which of the following carburetor circuits uses the small diameter end of a metering rod?
    a. Main metering
    b. Low-speed
    c. Idle
    d. Power
    e. Choke

17. The metering rod can be controlled by:
    a. Vacuum
    b. Mechanical linkage
    c. The computer
    d. All of the above
    e. None of the above

18. Which circuit is used for high speed and heavy loads?
    a. Power circuit
    b. Acceleration circuit
    c. Main metering circuit
    d. Idle circuit
    e. Choke

19. The acceleration circuit operates:
    a. Only when the choke is on
    b. Only during idle
    c. Only when the throttle linkage moves to increase fuel
    d. When the throttle closes
    e. Only when the engine is cold

20. What is used to lengthen the time of the downstroke on the acceleration pump?
    a. Vacuum diaphragm
    b. Duration spring
    c. Bimetallic strip
    d. Fuel pump
    e. Choke plate

21. Chokes can be controlled by:
    a. Manual means
    b. Thermostatic coils
    c. Vacuum diaphragms
    d. All of the above
    e. None of the above

22. When brass and spring metal are made into a strip, it is called a _____ .
    a. Two-metal strip
    b. Diaphragm strip
    c. Bimetallic strip
    d. Cold spring
    e. Bent spring

23. What circuit is used to increase the air during idle and when the engine is hot?
    a. Idle speed adjustment
    b. Fast idle cam
    c. Hot idle compensator
    d. Choke
    e. Main

24. The fast idle cam is used only during:
    a. Choked conditions
    b. Main metering conditions
    c. Power conditions
    d. High-speed conditions
    e. Low-speed conditions

25. Which accessory helps to eliminate run-on and dieseling?
    a. Fast idle cam
    b. Idle stop solenoid
    c. Hot idle compensator
    d. Antichoke valve
    e. None of the above

26. The electric-assisted choke is used to:
    a. Heat up the thermostatic coil more quickly
    b. Shut off the choke immediately with a solenoid
    c. Sense the temperature of the choke for the computer
    d. Increase the engine speed
    e. Decrease the engine speed

27. When the computer sends a set of programmed instructions to the carburetor to tell it what to do, it is said to be in:
    a. Open loop operation
    b. Closed loop operation
    c. Intermediate loop operation
    d. High-speed loop
    e. Low-speed loop

28. The computer on the CCC system controls:
    a. The metering control solenoid
    b. The idle speed control motor
    c. The choke plate
    d. All of the above
    e. A and B

29. Which of the following is *not* used as an input on the ECM when it is used for fuel management?
    a. Coolant temperature
    b. RPM
    c. Throttle position
    d. Coolant fan speed
    e. Exhaust oxygen

30. Idle mixture adjustment screws should be turned:
    a. Out about 1 1/2 turns
    b. All the way in
    c. Out at least 4 1/2 turns
    d. Out 3 1/2 turns
    e. Out 5 turns

31. The choke should be adjusted so it is _____ when the engine is at operating temperature.
    a. Fully open
    b. Fully closed
    c. Partly open
    d. Two-thirds closed
    e. None of the above

The following questions are similar in format to ASE (Automotive Service Excellence) test questions.

32. Technician A says that black smoke coming from the exhaust is an indication of a lean mixture. Technician B says that black smoke coming from the exhaust is an indication of a bad fuel pump. Who is right?
    a. A only
    b. B only
    c. Both A and B
    d. Neither A nor B

33. Technician A says that when the floats are set too high the engine will run rich. Technician B says that when the floats are set too high the engine will run lean. Who is right?
    a. A only
    b. B only
    c. Both A and B
    d. Neither A nor B

34. Technician A says the choke should be checked only when the engine is cold. Technician B says the choke should be checked only when the engine is warm. Who is right?
    a. A only
    b. B only
    c. Both A and B
    d. Neither A nor B

35. Technician A says the choke should be fully open when the engine is cold. Technician B says the choke should be fully closed when the engine is at operating temperature. Who is right?
    a. A only
    b. B only
    c. Both A and B
    d. Neither A nor B

36. Technician A says that a propane enrichment test is used to adjust the curb idle RPM. Technician B says it is used to adjust the idle mixture adjustment after rebuilding the carburetor. Who is correct?
    a. A only
    b. B only
    c. Both A and B
    d. Neither A nor B

37. Technician A says that trouble codes on computerized systems are determined by a flashing light on the dashboard. Technician B says that trouble codes can be identified by grounding a service check connector under the dashboard. Who is correct?
    a. A only
    b. B only
    c. Both A and B
    d. Neither A nor B

38. Technician A says that closed loop means that the computer uses the oxygen sensor for an input. Technician B says that open loop means that the engine temperature is below 150 degrees F. Who is correct?
    a. A only
    b. B only
    c. Both A and B
    d. Neither A nor B

39. Technician A says that the ported vacuum is taken below the throttle plate. Technician B says that the intake manifold vacuum is taken above the throttle plate. Who is correct?
    a. A only
    b. B only
    c. Both A and B
    d. Neither A nor B

Essay

40. Describe at least three things that may change the air-fuel ratio.

41. What is the difference between atomizing and vaporizing?

42. What is the purpose of a venturi?

43. What is the difference between the main metering circuit and the power circuit on a carburetor?

44. What is the purpose of the fast idle cam?

45. What is the purpose of the oxygen sensor?

46. Describe the purpose and operation of the throttle position sensor.

47. What are some of the input signals to the ECM on computer-controlled carburetors?

Short Answer

48. If the float on a carburetor is adjusted too high, it causes the air-fuel mixture to be _____.

49. Fuel spilling out of the top of the carburetor may be a sign that the _____ is stuck in the open position.

50. Two adjustments that can be done on a carburetor are adjusting the _____ and the _____.

51. There are two methods used to diagnose faults in computerized control systems. These are _____ diagnostics and _____ diagnostics.

52. The three most common types of vacuum produced from a carburetor are the _____, the _____, and the _____ vacuum.

CHAPTER 16

Injection Systems

INTRODUCTION   In the past few years, many changes have occurred in the design of fuel systems. One change is to use fuel injection rather than carburetion to mix the fuel. Fuel injection has always been used in diesel engines. It has been used on gasoline engines for several years now. The reason for using fuel injection is to control the air-fuel ratio of the engine more precisely. The purpose of this chapter is to study different fuel injection systems used on automobile engines.

OBJECTIVES   After reading this chapter, you should be able to:

- Define the purposes of using fuel injection systems on engines.
- State the different types of fuel injection systems used.
- Analyze the throttle body fuel injection system.
- Analyze the types of sensors used on computerized fuel injection systems.
- Analyze the port injection system.
- State the different mode of operation on fuel injection systems.
- Analyze high-pressure fuel injection systems used in diesel engines.

- Describe the operation of the injector nozzles used on high-pressure injection systems.
- Identify the operation of governor systems used on high-pressure diesel injection systems.
- Explain how electronic controls are used on diesel fuel injection systems.
- State various problems, diagnosis, and service procedures used on injection systems.

✔ SAFETY CHECKLIST ✔

When working with injection systems, keep these important safety precautions in mind.

✔ Immediately wipe up any spilled gasoline and dispose of the rags in a sealed container.

✔ Never smoke in or around an automobile.

✔ Always store the fuel in an approved OSHA container. Never store gasoline in an open container.

✔ Always keep an approved fire extinguisher nearby when working on the fuel injection system.

✔ Always wear OSHA-approved safety glasses when working on the fuel injection system.

16.1 CLASSIFICATIONS OF FUEL INJECTION SYSTEMS

Direct and Indirect Fuel Injection

Fuel injection systems can be divided into two major types: the high-pressure (direct) injection system used on diesel engines and the low-pressure (indirect) systems used on gasoline engines. See *Figure 16–1*. Direct fuel injection means the fuel is injected directly into the combustion chamber. Indirect fuel injection means the fuel is injected either into the port before the intake valve or into the intake manifold by a *throttle body* (throttle body injection, TBI) injector. When fuel is injected into the combustion cham-

ber, the pressure of the injection must be increased to high values. High-pressure injection must be used because the injection occurs during the compression stroke. The injection pressure must be much higher than the compression pressure for correct atomization. Indirect pressure injection systems inject fuel either into the port before the intake valve or into the throttle body. The area of injection is low in pressure, and thus low-pressure injection can be used.

Port and Throttle Body Fuel Injection

Two types of indirect fuel injection are used. When the fuel is injected into the port, it is called port fuel injection (PFI). In this case, there is one fuel injector for each cylinder and set of valves. When the fuel is injected into the center of the throttle body where the carburetor used to be, it is called throttle body injection (TBI). In this case, only one fuel injector is used on the system. The fuel injector feeds all of the cylinders of the engine. These two systems are also called multiple-point (port) and single-point (throttle body) fuel injection.

Timed and Continuous Fuel Injection

Fuel injection systems are also classified by the type of injection action. Some injection systems are defined as timed fuel injection. This means that fuel injection occurs at a precise time. Both gasoline and diesel engines use the timed injection system. Diesel engines have high-pressure timed injection systems. Gasoline engines have low-pressure timed injection systems.

Continuous injection is another method of defining the type of injection. Certain gasoline engines have used continuous fuel injection in the past. They are designed to spray a continuous flow of fuel into the engine. Diesel engines do not have a continuous injection system.

In addition to these classifications, fuel injection can be either mechanical or electronic. Diesel engines utilize mech-

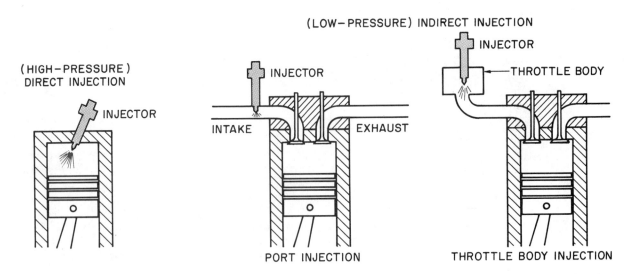

FIGURE 16–1. There are several types of fuel injection. Fuel can be injected either into the combustion chamber, into the intake port, or into a throttle body.

anical fuel injection. Initially, gasoline engines used mechanical fuel injection. Because of stricter *emission standards* and the increased use of computers on gasoline engines, however, today's fuel injection systems are almost totally electronic.

16.2 GASOLINE ELECTRONIC FUEL INJECTION SYSTEMS

Fuel Injection Defined

Fuel injection is defined as the process of injecting fuel before the valves so that the 14.7 to 1 air-fuel ratio can be maintained in the combustion chamber. Carburetors have been used in the past to mix the correct amount of fuel with the air. With the increased emphasis on pollution and emissions, however, more precise methods are needed. Fuel injection can precisely measure the amount of fuel to maintain the exact air-fuel ratio.

Fuel injection systems operate in conjunction with electronic computers. As discussed in the previous chapter, the electronic control module (ECM) takes in data from many sensors. On the basis of this information the ECM tells the fuel injector to inject the exact amount of fuel at the correct time.

Fuel Injection and Air-Fuel Ratio

When the air-fuel ratio is at 14.7 to 1, conditions are ideal for complete combustion. Complete combustion helps to ignite the mixture, assuring release of all the heat energy in the fuel. If combustion is complete, very little unburned fuel is left. The 14.7 to 1 air-fuel ratio is known as the *stoichio-*

metric ratio. This is called the best ratio for achieving both optimum fuel efficiency and optimum emission control under ideal conditions.

There are three primary pollutants caused by poor combustion. These are carbon monoxide (CO), hydrocarbons (HC), and nitrogen oxides (NO_x). These pollutants will be discussed in detail later in this textbook. As air-fuel ratios are changed, these pollutants increase or decrease. *Figure 16–2* shows the relationship between air-fuel ratios and pollution characteristics. Referring to this chart, it is easy to understand why it is very important to maintain a precise 14.7 to 1 air-fuel ratio. The stoichiometric ratio is the optimum ratio to minimize undesirable emissions.

Nonstoichiometric Air-Fuel Ratio Conditions

There are certain operating conditions when special air-fuel ratio requirements have priority over those of emission control. These conditions include times when the engine is cold and times when there is low manifold vacuum. Low manifold vacuum is a result of an increased load put on the engine.

Cold engine operation occurs whenever the engine is below normal operating temperature and is started or operated. During this condition, the cold inner surfaces of the intake manifold cause some of the fuel in the air-fuel mixture to condense. If the intake air is also below the desirable temperature of 70 degrees F, its ability to vaporize the fuel and mix with it is reduced. During cold engine operation, a richer mixture is needed. The rich mixture replaces the fuel that is lost through condensation or poor vaporization. The rich mixture also aids prompt starting and smooth responsive

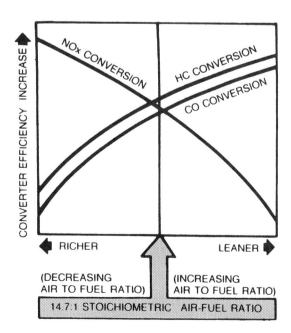

FIGURE 16–2. When the air-fuel mixture is lean, there is an increase in NO_x. When it is rich, HC and CO increase. Fuel injection can be designed to increase control over these pollutants. *(Courtesy of Chrysler Corporation)*

performance during warm-up periods.

Low manifold vacuum is produced when the load on the engine is increased. When the operator needs more power from the engine, the throttle is pushed down. This opens the throttle plate. When the throttle plate is open, the *intake manifold vacuum* is reduced. Any reduction in manifold vacuum is a positive indication that the engine is being asked to take on an added load. During this time, a richer mixture is needed. A richer-than-stoichiometric ratio helps provide excess fuel for the increased load. This condition is similar to acceleration. Once the engine and load stabilize, the air-fuel mixture is returned to the optimum ratio. Although carburetion systems provide for this increased air-fuel ratio, electronic fuel injection can more precisely limit the enrichment to the degree needed and for the exact duration required.

Throttle Body Injection

The throttle body injection (TBI) system uses a computer to control the amount of fuel injected into the manifold. It is considered an indirect type of injection. Air is drawn into the engine and passes by the injector nozzle. The exact amount of fuel is added for the conditions of operation, *Figure 16–3*.

Fuel Injector

A typical TBI system uses a solenoid-operated fuel injector controlled by the computer. The throttle body injector is centrally located on the intake manifold, usually near the top center of the fuel charging assembly. Here air and fuel are mixed correctly. Fuel is supplied to the injector from the electric fuel pump located in the fuel tank. The incoming fuel is directed to the low end of the injector assembly. An electrically operated solenoid valve in the injector is used to control fuel delivery from the injector nozzle. As shown in *Figure 16–4*, when there is no electrical current from the electronic control module (ECM) to the solenoid, a spring closes a ball-type metering valve inside the injector nozzle. This prevents fuel from flowing through the nozzle.

When the solenoid valve is energized by the computer, the spring-loaded metering valve moves to its full open position. Fuel under pressure from the fuel pump is injected in a *conical* spray pattern into the throttle body bore. The throttle body bore is located directly above the throttle plate. The volume of fuel flow is changed by varying the length of time the injector is held open by the ECM. Manufacturers may refer to the computer systems differently. Examples include electronic computer control system (ECCS), electronic engine control (EEC), and logic module.

Injector Pulse Width or Duration

The length of time the injector is open (turned on) and emitting fuel is called the *pulse width*. The pulse width is measured in milliseconds (ms). The injector is pulsed electronically by the distributor for each piston stroke. The correct

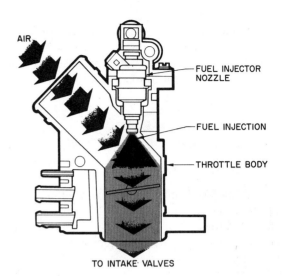

FIGURE 16–3. The throttle body injector injects fuel into an air stream going into the engine. *(Courtesy of Chrysler Corporation)*

amount of fuel is *metered* into the engine by controlling how long and when to pulse or turn on the injector. This is controlled by the computer.

Fuel Pressure Regulator

The fuel pressure must be regulated in order for the TBI to work correctly. This is done by a fuel pressure regulator. *Figure 16–5* shows how the fuel pressure regulator is built into the fuel circuit. The throttle body injector is located directly above the throttle body bore. Fuel from the fuel tank is pressurized and sent into the fuel inlet. From the fuel inlet the fuel is sent to the TBI. There is usually an excessive amount of fuel available at the injector. Excess fuel passes through the injector and into the fuel pressure regulator

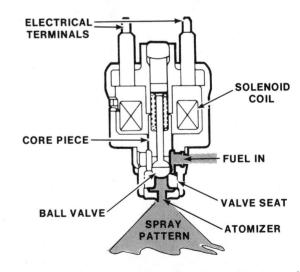

FIGURE 16–4. The throttle body injector is operated by a solenoid. When energized, the ball valve is lifted off its seat, and fuel flows into the engine. A spring keeps the ball on the seat when the injector is not energized. *(Courtesy of Rochester Products Division, General Motors Corporation)*

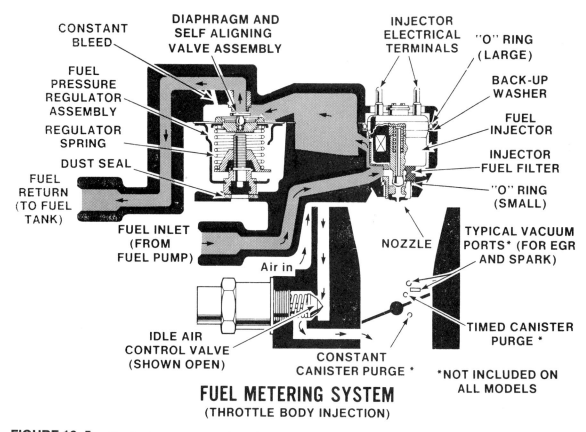

FUEL METERING SYSTEM
(THROTTLE BODY INJECTION)

FIGURE 16–5.   The fuel pressure regulator is used to control the pressure of the fuel at the throttle body injector. If fuel pressure increases too much, the fuel will pass by the regulator and back to the fuel tank. *(Courtesy of Chevrolet Division, General Motors Corporation)*

assembly. The fuel pressure regulator is an integral part of the throttle body injection unit. *Figure 16–6* shows such a unit.

The fuel pressure regulator is a mechanical device that maintains approximately 11 psi across the tip of the injector. The exact pressure depends upon the manufacturer. Some are as high as 36 psi. When the fuel pressure exceeds the regulator setting, it pushes the spring-loaded diaphragm down. This uncovers the fuel return port. As the fuel pressure drops below the regulator setting, the spring tension pushes the diaphragm up. This closes off the fuel return port to maintain the pressure of the fuel.

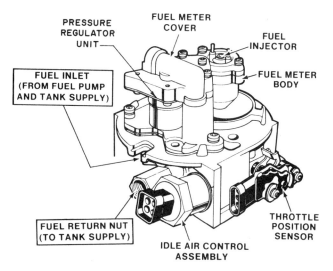

FIGURE 16–6.   The fuel pressure regulator can be designed as an integral part of the throttle body injection unit. *(Courtesy of Chevrolet Division, General Motors Corporation)*

Vacuum Assist

A vacuum assist is used on some, but not all, fuel pressure regulators. The vacuum assist is used to change the fuel pressure during different operating conditions. For example, when the throttle plate is open, a greater vacuum is felt on the injector tip. Therefore, less fuel pressure is needed to make the fuel flow at the same rate. A vacuum line is connected from above the throttle plate to the bottom of the fuel pressure regulator. This vacuum line reduces the spring pressure, which causes the fuel pressure regulator to open sooner, or at a lower pressure.

Types of Sensors

Various sensors are used to feed information into the computer on the computerized injection system. The following is a list of various types of sensors used.

1. *Potentiometer* — A potentiometer is a sensor that can change the voltage in relationship to mechanical motion. For example, as the throttle is moved to change the fuel setting, a throttle position sensor changes voltage. The computer is able to read the change in voltage, thus affecting the fuel setting.

2. *Thermistor* — A *thermistor* is a sensor that can change its electrical resistance on the basis of a change in temperature. For example, the computer needs to know the air temperature outside. The air charge temperature (ACT) sensor is able to tell the computer the outside temperature on the basis of the electrical resistance in the circuit.

3. *Magnetic pickup* — A *magnetic pickup* sensor is used to sense the position of the crankshaft within its 360 degrees of rotation. In operation, a small magnet is placed in the crankshaft. As the crankshaft spins, the small magnet induces a charge of electricity. This charge or pulse of electricity is fed to the computer to operate the crankshaft position sensor (CP) and the vehicle speed sensor (VSS).

4. *Voltage generator* — A voltage generator sensor is able to produce a voltage based on various inputs such as oxygen. For example, the EGO or exhaust gas oxygen sensor is a small voltage generator. It is mounted in the exhaust flow. It is able to pick up exhaust gases that are lean or rich. It is very sensitive to the presence of oxygen. Lean mixtures produce smaller output voltages (0–0.4 volts), while richer mixtures produce larger output voltages (0.6–1.0 volts).

5. *Frequency generator* — A frequency generator is a sensor that can read various pressures and convert these pressures to an electrical voltage, read by the computer. The conversion from pressure to voltage is done through an electrical generating device using capacitors, oscillators, and amplifiers. The computer needs to know the manifold absolute pressure (MAP) and the barometric pressure (BP). Frequency generators are used to read these pressures for the computer.

Throttle Position Sensor (TPS)

The throttle position sensor (TPS) contains a variable resistor that is used to regulate an input voltage on the basis of the angle of the throttle valve. The ECM uses this signal as a reference to determine idle speeds and air-fuel ratios.

Idle Air Control (IAC)

On certain throttle body injection systems, an idle air control (IAC) is used. Some manufacturers call this system the automatic idle speed motor (AIS). The purpose of the idle air control system is to control engine RPM at idle, while preventing stalls due to changes in engine load. Changes in engine load may be caused from accessory loads, such as air conditioning, during idle.

An IAC assembly motor is mounted on the throttle body unit. It provides control of bypass air around the throttle valve. By extending or retracting a *pintle*, a controlled amount of air is routed around the throttle valve. See **Figure 16–7**.

If the RPM of the engine is lower than desired during operation, more air is diverted around the throttle valve. This increases the RPM. If the RPM is higher than desired, less air is diverted around the throttle valve. This decreases RPM. The ECM monitors the manifold vacuum and adjusts the fuel delivery as idle requirements change.

During idle, the ECM uses the information from several input signals to calculate the desired pintle position. If the RPM drops below a value stored in the ECM's memory, and the throttle position sensor indicates that the throttle is closed, the ECM calculates the desired pintle position. The ECM will increase or decrease RPM to prevent stalling.

Throttle Body Injector (TBI) Controls

Throttle body injection systems utilize several sensors that send information to the ECM. These sensors include

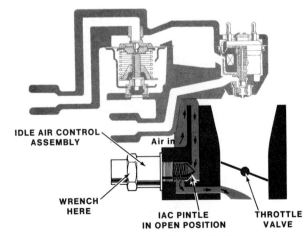

IDLE AIR CONTROL SYSTEM

FIGURE 16–7. Idle air control (IAC) is achieved by controlling the air passing around the throttle valve. The IAC is attached directly to the throttle body. *(Courtesy of Rochester Products Division, General Motors Corporation)*

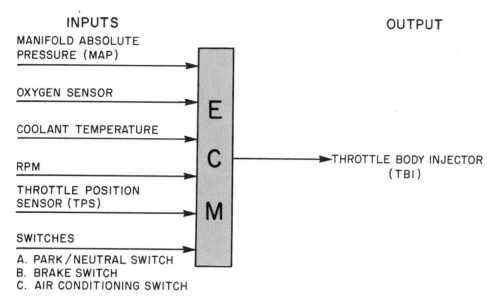

FIGURE 16–8. The throttle body injector is controlled by the ECM. Several inputs are needed to obtain the correct control of the TBI.

manifold absolute pressure (MAP), oxygen in the exhaust (oxygen sensor), coolant temperature (coolant sensor), engine speed (RPM), and throttle position sensor (TPS). See *Figure 16–8*. Information sent to the ECM from these sensors tells the TBI unit exactly how much fuel should be metered at a specific time. Other inputs are also used to provide information to the ECM. These include a park-neutral safety switch, brake switch, and air conditioning switch.

Manifold Absolute Pressure (MAP)

Manifold absolute pressure (MAP) is a sensor used to measure the absolute pressure (vacuum) inside the intake

manifold. In order to understand MAP, absolute pressure and gauge pressure must be studied.

Gauge pressure is defined as pressure on a scale (psig) starting with zero at atmospheric pressure or 14.7 atmospheres. *Absolute pressure* is defined as pressure on a scale (psia) starting with zero at zero atmospheric pressure. *Figure 16–9* shows the differences between absolute pressure and gauge pressure. Zero psig is the same as 14.7 psia. One advantage of using the absolute scale is that there are no vacuum readings. A vacuum on the psig scale is a pressure on the psia scale.

Intake manifold vacuum can now be stated as a pressure. Manifold absolute pressure (MAP) is a pressure reading on

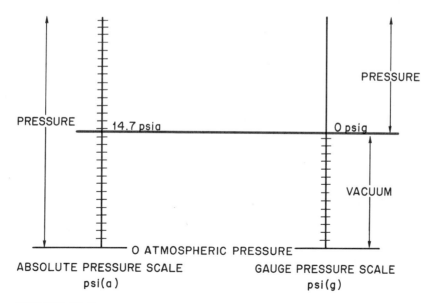

FIGURE 16–9. Manifold absolute pressure can be understood by comparing different types of pressure scales. Psig and psia scales are used. A vacuum on the psig scale is a pressure on the psia scale.

the psia scale. It would be considered a vacuum on the psig scale. Note that as manifold pressure increases, vacuum decreases. Manifold absolute pressures are used in the study of computer-controlled combustion (CCC) systems.

The MAP sensor uses a flexible-type resistor. When the resistor is flexed because of an increase in manifold pressure, its resistance changes. This change causes a voltage change that the ECM uses to control the TBI.

Crossfire Injection

Certain engines utilize a pair of throttle body injection units. These are mounted on the front and rear of a single manifold cover. This arrangement allows each TBI unit to supply the correct air-fuel mixture through a crossover port. The port is located inside the intake manifold and feeds the cylinders on the opposite side of the engine, thus the term *crossfire injection*.

Modes of Operation

All electronic fuel injection systems operate on either a closed or open loop mode. During closed loop operation, the computer uses various inputs including the oxygen sensor to produce an air-fuel ratio close to 14.7 to 1. During the open loop mode, the computer is programmed to provide an air-fuel ratio best suited for conditions such as starting and wide-open throttle. In addition, many other modes of operation are designed into the system for starting, initial running, flooding, and other conditions. The exact titles vary with each manufacturer and the year of the vehicle. Some common terms for modes of operation are listed below.

1. *Synchronized mode* — When in the synchronized mode, the throttle body injector is being pulsed once for each reference pulse from the distributor. The pulses of fuel injection are synchronized with the distributor pulses. The injector sprays once for each firing of the cylinder. All closed loop operation is in the synchronized mode.

2. *Nonsynchronized mode* — In this mode, the throttle body injector is pulsed every 12.5 milliseconds. The pulses are independent of the distributor reference pulses. This mode is usually used when the engine is under special conditions such as wide open throttle (open loop). During this condition, the injector must open and close extremely rapidly. The injector is not mechanically able to open and close this fast, so the computer takes over and pulses the injector every 12.5 seconds.

3. *Cranking mode* — During the cranking mode an enriched air-fuel ratio is required. In order to provide the enriched mixture the computer senses the outside air temperature and sets the pulse width of the injector accordingly. For example, when the outside air temperature is very cold, the pulse width is longer, making an enriched air-fuel ratio. If the outside air temperature is warmer, the pulse width is calibrated to a short period of time, reducing the enriched mixture.

4. *Clear flood* — At times the engine may be flooded and not able to start. At this point, if the throttle is pushed down, say to 80% of wide open throttle, the computer goes into the clear flood mode. In the clear flood mode, the computer calibrates the injector pulse to produce a lean air-fuel ratio, say 20:1. The computer keeps the system in this mode until the engine starts or the throttle is moved to less than 80% of wide open throttle.

5. *Run* — Once the engine is started and running at curb idle, say 600 RPM, the computer immediately puts the system into open loop operation. (Chapter 15 discusses open and closed loop operation). During this condition the computer is monitoring three conditions to get the system into closed loop operation as soon as possible. These include:

   a. The oxygen sensor must reach 570 degrees F.
   b. The engine coolant temperature must reach 150 degrees F.
   c. A specified amount of time must have passed since the engine was started.

When these three conditions are met, the computer puts the fuel injection system into its closed loop mode of operation. At this point, the computer is using the oxygen sensor to help make decisions about the air-fuel ratio.

CAR CLINIC

PROBLEM: Too High Idle

A car that has a 2.5-liter engine with fuel injection has just been purchased. The vehicle should normally get about 35 mpg, it is only getting about 25 mpg. The idle is very high, and the car is very hard to slow down. What can be done?

SOLUTION:

GM cars that use a computer and fuel injection typically have few controls for idle. On some vehicles, the programmable read only memory (PROM) may be programmed for different altitudes. The engine is getting too much fuel and is running very rich. In this case, the PROM should be replaced. Go to the manufacturer to get the PROM. The manufacturer is the only source for the correct PROM.

16.3   PORT FUEL INJECTION SYSTEMS

Port fuel injection is another way of electronically injecting fuel into a gasoline engine. Port fuel injection is designed to have a small fuel injector placed near the intake port of each cylinder. See *Figure 16–10*. Each injector is controlled by the ECM, and the metering is based on several inputs, as with throttle body injection.

One of the biggest advantages of using port injection over TBI is the ability to get the same amount of fuel to each cylinder. When a throttle body injector or carburetor is used, the intake manifold acts as a sorting device to send fuel to each cylinder. As air flows through the curved ports in the intake manifold, air, being lighter than fuel, is sorted evenly. However, fuel, which is heavier than air, tends to collect at certain spots inside the intake manifold. This causes some cylinders to be richer than others during operation, *Figure 16–11*.

Types of Port Fuel Injection

Several types of port fuel injection (PFI) are used. The standard type of PFI has a double-fire fuel injection. This means that all injectors are pulsed one time each engine revolution. Two injections of fuel are mixed with incoming air to produce the charge for each combustion cycle. On some engines, groups of injectors are fired at the same time.

A second type of PFI is referred to as sequential fuel injection (SFI). On certain applications, the injectors are pulsed sequentially (one-by-one) in spark plug firing order.

A third type of PFI is called the tuned port injection (TPI). *Tuned ports* are a way of identifying the type of ports used to get the air through the intake manifold to the intake port. Tuned ports mean that each port is designed with equal and minimum restriction. This design assures that the same amount of air will be delivered to each cylinder.

Port Fuel Injection Flow Diagram

Figure 16–12 shows a complete schematic of a port fuel injection system. Various components of this system that differ from carburetion and the TBI system will be discussed. Although port fuel injection systems may be designed differently by other manufacturers, the basic principles remain the same.

The port fuel injector is located just in front of the intake valve. It is controlled by the ECM. Fuel from the fuel pump

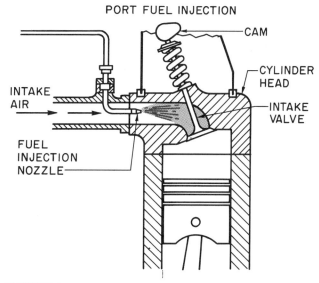

FIGURE 16–10. Port fuel injection has an injector located near the intake port. The fuel is injected directly into the port before the intake valve.

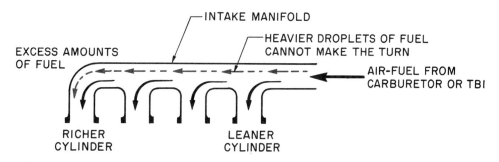

FIGURE 16–11. When throttle body injection or carburetion is used, fuel delivered to the cylinder may vary because of the design of the manifold. This problem can be overcome by using port fuel injection.

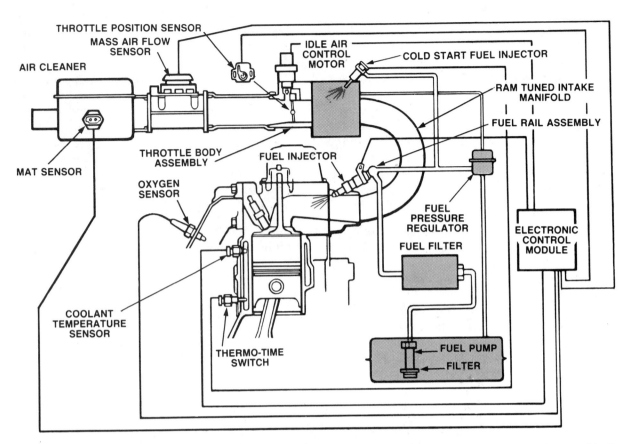

FIGURE 16–12. This schematic shows a port fuel injection system. Many of the sensors were also used in the TBI and carburetion systems. *(Courtesy of General Motors Product Service Training)*

and filter in the tank is sent through a fuel filter into the injector. As with the TBI system, a fuel pressure regulator controls the pressure of the fuel being sent to the injector. Other components that have already been studied as part of the carburetion or TBI section include the oxygen sensor, coolant temperature sensor, throttle position sensor, and the idle air control motor.

Manifold Air Temperature (MAT)

In order for the ECM to meter the correct amount of fuel during all driving conditions, the temperature of the air coming into the intake manifold is sensed. As the temperature of the air changes, the amount of oxygen per cubic foot also changes. In Figure 16–12, the MAT sensor is located on the air cleaner. The temperature of the incoming air is used as a signal and sent to the ECM.

Port Fuel Injectors

The fuel injectors used with PFI inject fuel directly before the intake valve, *Figure 16–13*. Nozzle spray angle is 25 degrees. Two O rings are used for installation. One O ring is used to seal the injector nozzle to the intake manifold. The second O ring is used to seal the injector with the fuel inlet connection. Both O rings also prevent excessive injector vibration.

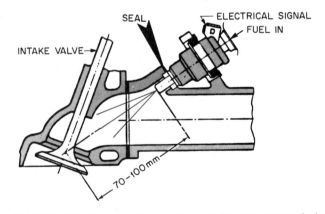

FIGURE 16–13. Fuel is injected at the correct angle in the intake port. *(Courtesy of General Motors Product Service Training)*

The injector is designed as shown in *Figure 16–14*. It is a solenoid-operated injector, consisting of a valve body and a *needle valve* that has a specially ground pintle. A solenoid winding is operated electrically by the ECM. When an electric pulse is sent to the injector, the magnetic field inside the solenoid lifts the needle valve from its seat. The ECM controls the length of the pulse, which establishes the pulse width or the amount of injection. A small helical spring closes the

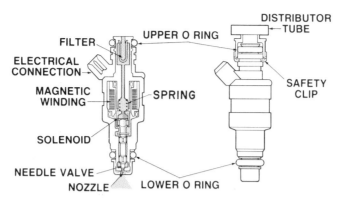

FIGURE 16–14. The solenoid for port fuel injection is a solenoid-operated needle valve. When the solenoid is energized, the needle valve lifts to inject fuel. *(Courtesy of General Motors Product Service Training)*

FIGURE 16–15. Port fuel injectors.

needle valve when the electrical signal is removed. *Figure 16–15* shows a port fuel injector.

Fuel Rails

Fuel must be sent to each injector from the fuel pump. The fuel is sent into a fuel rail, *Figure 16–16*. Here the fuel is distributed to each injector. The pressure regulator shown in *Figure 16–17* keeps the pressure inside the fuel rail at approximately 35 psi on this particular system. The injectors are locked in place using retainer clips.

Throttle Blade

The throttle blade controls the volume of air that enters the engine, *Figure 16–18*. The throttle blade is controlled by the position of the operator's foot. As the foot is depressed, the blade opens and allows more air into the engine. As the foot is released, the blade closes and reduces the amount of air allowed into the engine. Some engines also have a coolant passage that allows engine coolant to flow through the throttle body unit. The purpose of this coolant flow is to

FIGURE 16–16. The fuel rail is used to send the fuel to each port fuel injector.

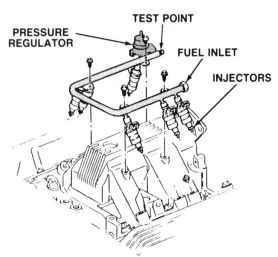

FIGURE 16–17. The fuel pressure regulator is located directly on the fuel rail. *(Courtesy of General Motors Product Service Training)*

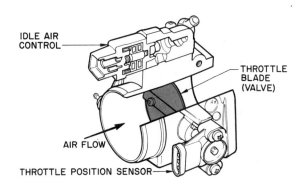

FIGURE 16–18. The throttle body consists of the throttle blade (valve), which controls the air flow, and the throttle position sensor. *(Courtesy of General Motors Product Service Training)*

increase the temperature of the incoming air to assist in preventing throttle blade icing in cold weather operation.

The throttle body also supports and controls the movement of the throttle position sensor (TPS). As was stated earlier,

the TPS is used to send a signal to the ECM. This signal gives the position of the throttle under all operating conditions.

Idle Air Control (IAC)

Attached to the throttle body is an idle air control (IAC). The IAC is used to control the amount of air during idle conditions. The ECM controls idle speed by moving the IAC valve in and out as shown in *Figure 16–19*. The ECM does this by sending the IAC voltage pulses called "counts" to the proper motor winding. The motor shaft and valve move a given distance for each count received.

For example, to increase the idle speed the ECM sends enough counts to retract the IAC valve and allow more air to flow around the throttle blade. The increase in air flow into the engine causes the idle to increase. (A corresponding increase in fuel metered by the ECM must also occur.) To decrease the idle speed, the ECM sends the correct number of counts to the IAC to extend the valve and reduce air flow. *Figure 16–20* shows the throttle body unit with the idle air control valve and the throttle position sensor.

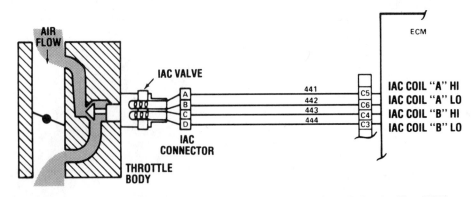

FIGURE 16–19. The idle air control is attached to the throttle body. The ECM controls the motor windings to open or close the IAC valve. *(Courtesy of General Motors Product Service Training)*

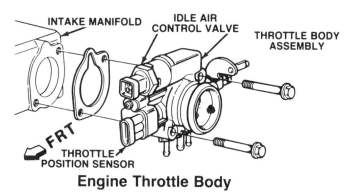

Engine Throttle Body

FIGURE 16–20. On this throttle body the throttle position sensor and the idle air control valve are attached. *(Courtesy of General Motors Product Service Training)*

Cold Start Injector

Additional fuel is required to start a cold engine. If there is sufficient fuel, correct fuel vaporization and atomization for combustion will occur. The cold start injector is used to provide additional fuel during cranking. This circuit is important when engine coolant temperatures are low. During this time, the main injectors are not pulsed "ON" long enough to provide the amount of fuel needed to start the engine.

Figure 16–21 shows how the cold start system operates. During cranking, fuel is injected into the cylinder ports through the individual fuel injectors. Additional fuel is injected into a separate passage within the inlet manifold by the cold start injector. This passage has small individual orifices by each cylinder. These small passages send extra

fuel to each cylinder. Air is also sent through the passage from the throttle body.

Thermal-Time Switch

The cold start injector is controlled by the thermal-time switch. This switch is connected to the starter solenoid. The cold start injector operates only during cranking or starting of the engine. The cold start injector also operates only at coolant temperatures below 95 degrees F (35 degrees C) and can operate only a certain length of time.

The switch is made of a bimetallic material and opens at a specified coolant temperature. The bimetallic material is heated by a winding inside the thermal switch. This arrangement allows the cold start injector to stay on for a specific

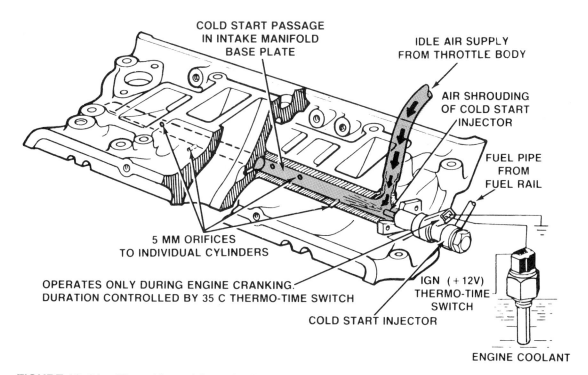

FIGURE 16–21. The cold start injector is placed on the intake manifold to help in cold starting conditions. *(Courtesy of General Motors Product Service Training)*

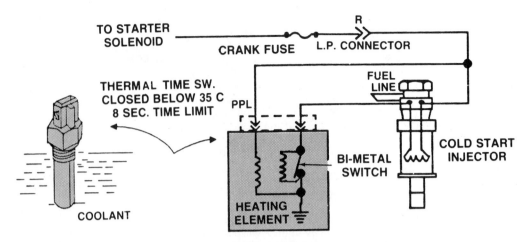

FIGURE 16–22. The thermal-time switch controls the time the cold start injector is on. The switch operates only during cranking or starting the engine. A small heating element also heats the bimetal switch to limit the "ON" to 8 seconds. *(Courtesy of General Motors Product Service Training)*

amount of time (8 seconds). The time the thermal switch stays closed varies inversely with the coolant temperature. As the coolant temperature goes up, the cold start valve on-time goes down. *Figure 16–22* shows an example of the cold start injector circuit and the thermal-time switch.

Mass Air Flow (MAF)

Mass air flow is defined as the total amount (mass) of air going into the engine. This amount depends on the altitude of the vehicle, temperature of the air, density of the air, and moisture of the air. All of these variables cause the air-fuel

ratio to change. In order to maintain a stoichiometric air-fuel ratio of 14.7 to 1, these variables must be known. They are measured by a mass air flow sensor.

Figure 16–23 shows an MAF sensor. It consists of the following:

1. A flow tube that houses the parts

2. A sample tube that directs air to a sensor

3. A screen that breaks up the air flow

4. A ceramic resistor that measures the temperature of the incoming air (air temperature sending resistor)

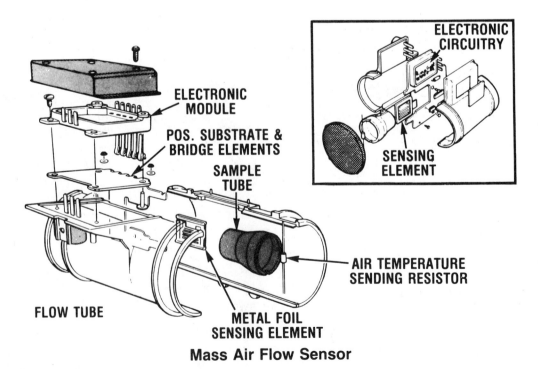

Mass Air Flow Sensor

FIGURE 16–23. The mass air flow (MAF) sensor determines the exact amount (mass) of air flowing into the engine. *(Courtesy of General Motors Product Service Training)*

5. A metal foil sensing element that senses air mass

6. An electronic module that determines the mass air flow from the sensing element

This type of sensor can compensate for altitude and humidity. In operation, air mass is determined by measuring the amount of electrical power needed to keep the temperature of the sensing element 75 degrees C (167 degrees F) above the incoming air. As air enters the unit, it passes over and cools the sensing element. When the element is cooler, it requires more electrical power to keep the element at 75 degrees C (167 degrees F) above the incoming air temperature. The electrical power requirement is a measure or indication of the mass air flow. The power is converted to a digital signal as a frequency. This signal is sent to the ECM and used to calculate engine load. Using mass air flow, engine temperature, and RPM, the ECM can calculate the exact amount of fuel to be metered to provide a stoichiometric ratio of 14.7 to 1.

Modes of Operation

Like throttle body injection systems, port fuel injection systems operate in various modes. Depending on the manufacturer and the year of the vehicle, these modes are much the same as those of throttle body injection. Additional modes include:

1. *Starting mode* — When the engine is turned on, the computer turns on the fuel pump relay. If it does not read a cranking signal in 2 seconds, it turns off the fuel pump relay, thus shutting off the fuel pump.

2. *Acceleration mode* — Rapid increases in the throttle opening or a drop in manifold pressure will signal the computer to enrich the air-fuel mixture.

3. *Deceleration mode* — Rapid decreases in the throttle opening or manifold pressure will signal the computer to lean out the air-fuel mixture.

4. *Battery voltage correction mode* — On some port fuel injection systems, if the battery voltage drops below a specific value, the computer will compensate for a weak ignition spark. The computer will
   a. enrich the air-fuel mixture,
   b. increase the throttle opening to increase the idle slightly, and
   c. increase the ignition dwell.

5. *Fuel cutoff mode* — When the engine is shut off, the injectors could continue to be pulsed as the engine RPM slows to a stop. This continued pulsing may cause dieseling. To avoid the problem, the computer is designed to immediately stop pulsing the injectors the second the ignition is shut off.

6. *MPG lean cruise* — When the engine is at cruising conditions the computer is able to improve the fuel economy. This is done by taking the system out of closed loop operation and leaning out the air-fuel mixture to improve the fuel economy.

7. *Modular strategy or mode* — At times it may be necessary to operate the engine during special conditions. These conditions may include:
   - Cold engine
   - Overheated engine
   - High altitude

During these conditions it may be necessary to compensate air-fuel ratios just to keep the vehicle drivable. The computer compensates the air-fuel ratio enough to keep the engine operating.

8. *Limited operational strategy or mode (LOS)* — At times a component within the system may fail. The failure may prevent the engine from operating in a normal closed loop mode. When this happens, the computer enters an alternate mode designed to protect other system components, still keeping the vehicle drivable until service can be completed. Often this mode is referred to as "Limp Home Mode," "Backup Mode," or "Fail Safe Mode."

CAR CLINIC

PROBLEM: Smelly Exhaust on Fuel Injection Engines

The exhaust from a fuel injected vehicle smells much like rotten eggs. This smell usually occurs during acceleration. What could be the cause of the smell?

SOLUTION:

The most common cause of the rotten egg smell is a rich mixture of fuel. The three-way catalytic converter is probably not up to temperature yet. Whenever the air-fuel mixture is rich, the rotten egg smell is produced. If the smell is also there after the engine is at operating temperature, check the air-fuel mixture. On fuel injection vehicles, the PROM may have to be checked and perhaps replaced.

16.4   HIGH-PRESSURE DIESEL FUEL INJECTION SYSTEMS

All diesel engines being manufactured today use injection systems. The injection of diesel fuel is considered mechanical, direct (into the cylinder), and timed. In other words, diesel fuel is injected at a precise time into the top of the cylinder, during the compression stroke of the diesel engine. In order to do this, the pressure to produce atomized fuel must be very high. Injection systems inject fuel in the range of 4,000–10,000 psi.

This type of injection system requires study in several major areas. These include: (1) pressurizing the fuel, (2) timing the fuel, (3) atomizing the fuel, and (4) metering the fuel. *TAMP* is a term used to remember *T*iming, *A*tomizing, *M*etering, and *P*ressurizing. In addition, diesel fuel injection systems also use *governors* for speed control.

There have been many changes through the years to diesel fuel injection design. Each of the TAMP principles can be accomplished in many ways. In addition, electronic controls have been added to get precise fuel control. However, the basic principles of fuel injection remain much the same. One of the more common types of fuel injection pump is called the rotor-distributor-type injection pump.

Fuel Pump Components

Figure 16–24 shows a cutaway of a standard high-pressure fuel injection pump. The pump has several components including the:

1. Drive shaft

2. Housing

3. Metering valve

4. Hydraulic head assembly

5. Transfer pump

6. Pressure regulator assembly

7. Distributor rotor

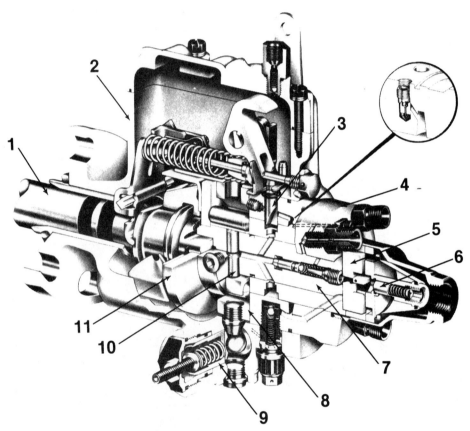

MAIN COMPONENTS

1. DRIVE SHAFT
2. HOUSING
3. METERING VALVE
4. HYDRAULIC HEAD ASSEMBLY
5. TRANSFER PUMP BLADES
6. PRESSURE REGULATOR ASSEMBLY
7. DISTRIBUTOR ROTOR
8. INTERNAL CAM RING
9. AUTOMATIC ADVANCE (OPTIONAL)
10. PUMPING PLUNGERS
11. GOVERNOR

FIGURE 16–24. This high-pressure fuel injection pump is used on automotive diesel engines. It is designed to inject high-pressure fuel into the combustion chamber during the compression stroke. (*Courtesy of Society of Automotive Engineers*)

8. Internal cam ring

9. Automatic advance (optional)

10. Pumping plungers

11. Governor

Fuel Flow Diagram

To understand high-pressure fuel systems, the schematic in *Figure 16–25* will be analyzed. Fuel is drawn from the supply tank, through a master water separator, through a master filter, and into the transfer pump. The transfer pump is located inside the fuel pump unit. The transfer pump pressurizes the fuel and sends it to the head passage area. The pressure of the diesel fuel at this point acts on the cam ring to aid in advancing the fuel timing.

Fuel is sent through the head passage to the metering valve. The metering valve is positioned by the governor to meter the correct amount of fuel to the distributor rotor. Inside the distributor rotor, pumping plungers produce the high pressure needed for injection. When the high pressure is produced, fuel is sent through a delivery valve to each injector nozzle. There is an injector nozzle for each cylinder. Any excess fuel from the nozzle or governor area is returned to the fuel tank. Timing occurs in the distributor rotor, atom-izing occurs at the nozzle, metering occurs at the metering valve, and pressurizing occurs at the distributor rotor.

Transfer Pump

The purpose of the transfer pump is to transfer the diesel fuel from the fuel tank to the fuel pump. The transfer pump is located on the main shaft of the fuel injection pump. As the fuel injection pump is rotated by the engine, the transfer pump also rotates.

The transfer pump is a positive displacement vane-type pump. *Figure 16–26* shows a transfer pump. The inside diameter of the liner is eccentric to the rotor axis. This causes the blades to move in the rotor slots. This blade movement changes the volume between the blade segments. As the blade is rotated, a suction and pressure are created in the inlet slot and outlet groove.

Pressure Regulator Assembly

The pressure of the transfer pump increases with the RPM of the main shaft. When too much pressure is created, some of the fuel is bypassed back to the inlet side of the transfer pump. This is done by the regulator assembly. As flow increases, the regulating spring is compressed. Eventually the regulating spring is compressed until the edge of the

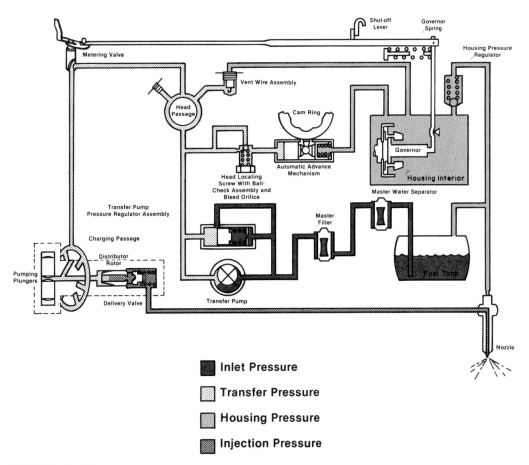

FIGURE 16–25.   This flow diagram shows the flow of fuel from the fuel tank to the injector. *(Courtesy of Stanadyne Diesel Systems Division)*

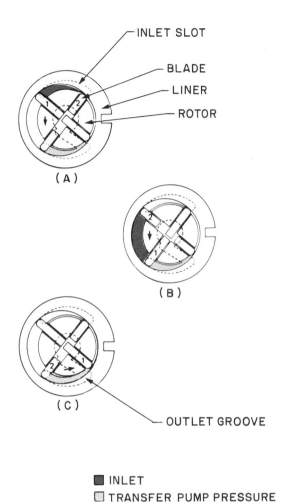

INLET SLOT
BLADE
LINER
ROTOR

(A)

(B)

(C)

OUTLET GROOVE

■ INLET
□ TRANSFER PUMP PRESSURE

FIGURE 16–26. This vane-type pump is used to transfer fuel from the fuel tank to the injection pump. As the vanes rotate in an eccentric housing, a suction and pressure are created. *(Courtesy of Stanadyne Diesel Systems Division)*

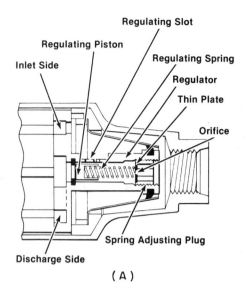

Regulating Slot
Regulating Piston
Regulating Spring
Inlet Side
Regulator
Thin Plate
Orifice

Spring Adjusting Plug

Discharge Side

(A)

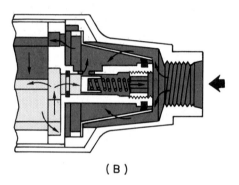

(B)

■ INLET
□ TRANSFER PUMP PRESSURE

FIGURE 16–27. The pressure regulator is used to maintain the correct transfer pump pressure. As the pressure increases with RPM, the regulating spring will compress. Eventually the regulating piston moves to open a regulating slot. Fuel is bypassed back to the suction side of the pump. *(Courtesy of Stanadyne Diesel Systems Division)*

regulating piston uncovers the pressure regulating slot. Diesel fuel is now transferred back to the inlet side of the pump. See *Figure 16–27*.

Charging Cycle

After the fuel is pressurized by the transfer pump, it must be charged. The charging cycle is defined as that part that brings in the correct amount of fuel to be pressurized. In *Figure 16–28*, pressurized fuel from the transfer pump is sent through internal passages into a circular fuel passage. From the circular fuel passage the fuel is sent past the metering valve. The position of the metering valve determines exactly how much fuel will be sent to the injectors. From the metering valve the fuel is sent into a charging passage. This is a circular passage with holes that line up with holes in the rotor. When the holes line up during rotation, the metered fuel is sent to the center of the rotor. *Figure 16–29* shows a breakdown of the rotor. Remember that the rotor is being turned by the engine.

When the fuel is sent to the center of the rotor, it forces the small plungers outward. The metered fuel is now in a pumping chamber. If only a small amount of fuel is admitted to the pumping chamber, as in idle, the plungers move out only a short distance. If more fuel is admitted to the pumping chamber, the plungers move out farther. The fuel injection pump is now ready for the discharge cycle.

Discharging Cycle

Figure 16–30 shows a circular cam with the plungers and rollers placed in the center. As the rotor turns, the ports from the circular passages are closed off. The fuel inside the rotor is captured. As the center rotor continues to turn, the rollers are forced inward by the shape of the cam. This produces a high pressure (injection pressure) because the fuel is being squeezed inside the rotor.

Figure 16–31 shows the flow of fuel during the discharge cycle. When the fuel is fully pressurized, it flows past a delivery

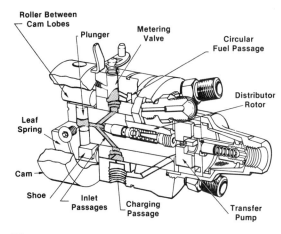

□ Transfer Pump Pressure

FIGURE 16–28. During the charging cycle, fuel passes the metering valve and enters the area below the plunger. Fuel is now ready to be pressurized in the discharge cycle. *(Courtesy of Stanadyne Diesel Systems Division)*

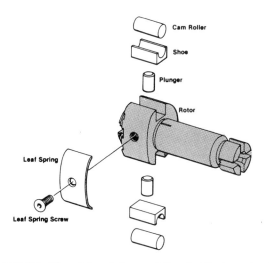

FIGURE 16–29. A breakdown of the distributor rotor. The plunger, rotors, and cam rollers are used to produce the high pressure. *(Courtesy of Stanadyne Diesel Systems Division)*

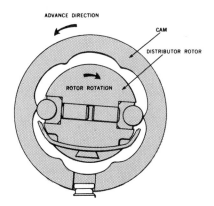

FIGURE 16–30. This circular cam and rotor is used to produce the high-pressure fuel injection. As the rotor and rollers turn inside the cam, the shape of the cam pushes the rollers in to produce the high pressure. *(Courtesy of Stanadyne Diesel Systems Division)*

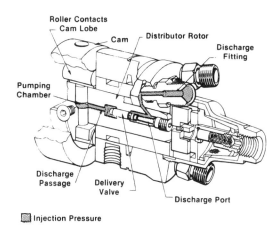

▨ Injection Pressure

FIGURE 16–31. Fuel flow during the discharge cycle. Fuel pressure created from the cam and rollers is sent through a delivery valve to each discharge fitting. From there the fuel is sent to each injector. *(Courtesy of Stanadyne Diesel Systems Division)*

valve to a discharge port. As the rotor continues to turn, the discharge port lines up with a port that goes to each discharge fitting and finally to the injector. The high-pressure fuel is now being distributed to each cylinder. Delivery of the fuel continues until the cam rollers pass the innermost point on the cam lobe and begin to move outward.

Delivery Valve

The purpose of the delivery valve is to shut off the flow of fuel during injection. It is important to end injection rapidly. If the injection does not end rapidly, the injector will dribble fuel into the combustion chamber. The result will be poorly timed and atomized fuel.

The delivery valve operates in a bore in the center of the distributor rotor. When injection starts, fuel pressure created by the rollers and cam moves the delivery valve slightly out of its bore. *Figure 16–32* shows this action. Pressure from the cam and rollers pushes the delivery valve to the right. Fuel now passes to the discharge port and to the injectors. Delivery ends when the pressure on the plunger side is reduced quickly. The pressure is reduced because the cam rollers pass the highest point on the cam lobe.

At this point, there is a drop in pressure on the left side of the delivery valve, while a high pressure still exists on the right side of the delivery valve. This difference in pressure causes the delivery valve to close rapidly. This action reduces the high pressure to the injector very rapidly. Once the pressure has been reduced, the discharge port closes completely, and the fuel that remains is maintained until the next injection.

Return Fuel Oil Circuit

Excess fuel from the transfer pump is discharged into a vent passage. It is returned to the interior housing of the governor. See *Figure 16–33*. The amount of fuel sent back

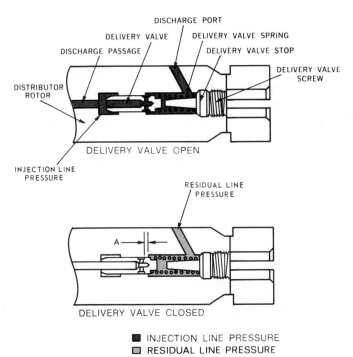

FIGURE 16–32. The delivery valve is used to rapidly shut off the fuel to the injectors. *(Courtesy of Stanadyne, Diesel Systems Division)*

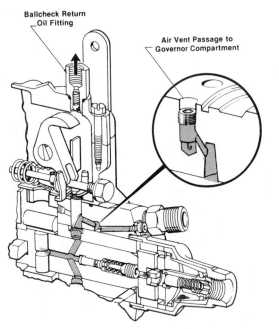

FIGURE 16–33. Fuel flow back to the housing is controlled by the size of the vent wire in the passage. *(Courtesy of Stanadyne, Diesel Systems Division)*

to the housing depends on the specifications. The amount of return fuel oil is controlled by the size of a wire used in the vent assembly. The smaller the wire, the more return flow, and vice versa. The vent wire is available in several sizes.

Metering Valve

The metering valve is used to control the exact amount of fuel being sent into the circular charging passage. *Figure 16–34* shows examples of two metering valves. As the valves are turned, the position of the metering edge changes with respect to the holes in the housing. This means either a larger quantity or lesser quantity of fuel will be delivered to the circular charging head.

Governor Principles

A governor is a speed-sensing device that tells the metering valve how much fuel to put into the engine. *Figure 16–35* shows the principles of any governor operation. Two forces are working against each other. A spring force pushes in one direction. A centrifugal force from several weights produces the second force. The weights are turned by the engine. The center point is connected to the engine throttle or metering valve.

The governor tries to keep the RPM of the engine the same. The speed of the engine is controlled by the tension adjusted on the spring. If the engine is running at 3,000 RPM under no load, a balance has been established between the centrifugal force and the weight force. When the engine encounters a load, the RPM drops. This causes the centrifugal forces to be reduced. There is now an unbalanced condition between the two forces. The spring will now push the metering rod to add more fuel. As more fuel is added to the engine,

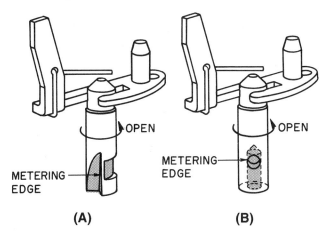

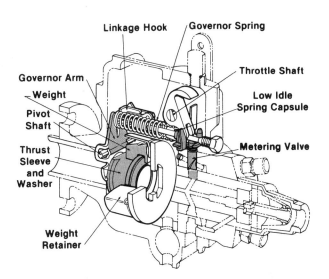

FIGURE 16–34. The metering valve is used to control or meter the exact amount of fuel for each injection. (A) One uses a helix (angled cut) to meter fuel. (B) The other uses a hole to meter fuel. *(Courtesy of Society of Automotive Engineers)*

FIGURE 16–36. On a fuel injection pump, weights move a thrust sleeve. The sleeve is connected through a linkage to the governor spring. This spring sets the metering rod in the correct position. *(Courtesy of Stanadyne, Diesel Systems Division)*

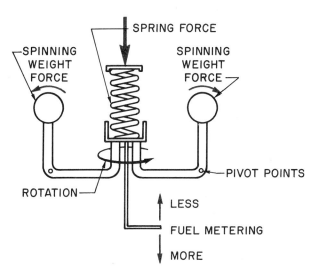

FIGURE 16–35. Any governor is a speed-sensing device. Centrifugal forces from spinning weights oppose spring forces. The resultant force controls the metering of the fuel.

valve. As the weights move outward from a decrease in load, they move the thrust sleeve and washer to the left. This action pushes the lower section of the governor arm to the left. The governor arm is supported on a pivot shaft. Movement to the left on the bottom of the governor arm causes movement to the right on the top of the governor arm. This movement pushes against the governor spring. The throttle shaft also moves to the right. This action reduces the amount of fuel sent through the metering valve.

If the load is increased, the reverse occurs: (1) the governor weights drop in, (2) the governor spring pushes the governor arm to the left, (3) the throttle shaft moves to the left, (4) the metering valve increases its flow, (5) RPM increases to handle the extra load.

Automatic Fuel Injection Advance

The advance mechanism will advance or retard the delivery of fuel to each injector. As the RPM of the engine increases, the fuel should be advanced. Advancing the fuel assures that combustion will take place when the piston is at the most effective position during all RPM and loads.

Figure 16–37 shows the operation of an advance mechanism. Advance is accomplished by moving the cam ring clockwise. When the cam is moved counterclockwise, the injection is retarded. The cam ring is controlled by the position of two pistons. One is called the spring piston and the other is called the power piston. The pressure from these two pistons positions the advance cam screw to either advance or retard the injection.

Governor housing pressure is applied to the spring piston. Governor housing pressure is controlled by the pressure

the RPM will increase back to 3,000 to handle or carry the load.

If the load is removed, the reverse happens. As the load is removed, the engine RPM increases. This causes the centrifugal forces to be greater than the spring forces. This action moves the metering valve to reduce the fuel setting. The RPM is subsequently reduced to the 3,000 originally set.

Governor Operation

Figure 16–36 shows the mechanical system and how it operates. The governor weights are located inside the weight retainer. The governor spring is connected to the throttle shaft. The throttle shaft controls the position of the metering

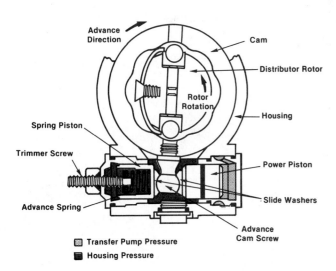

FIGURE 16–37. Advance on a fuel injection system is accomplished by moving the cam ring. The ring is moved by using two pressures working against each other. *(Courtesy of Stanadyne, Diesel Systems Division)*

regulator on the housing. This uses a ball check valve to control the pressure inside the housing.

Transfer pump pressure is applied to the power piston. As the engine speed increases, the transfer pump pressure increases. This increase causes an unbalanced pressure, which moves the cam ring clockwise. The fuel injection is now being advanced. When the engine speed decreases and transfer pump pressure is reduced, the advance spring pushes the advance cam screw to the right. The fuel injection is now being retarded. A trimmer screw is provided to adjust the advance spring. This controls the start of cam movement.

Fuel Injector Nozzles

The fuel injector nozzle is used to inject the fuel directly into the combustion chamber. See *Figure 16–38*. During the injection process, the fuel must be finely atomized. The injector nozzle is designed to atomize the fuel correctly.

There are several types of injector nozzles. The most common are the pintle nozzle and the hole nozzle. *Figure*

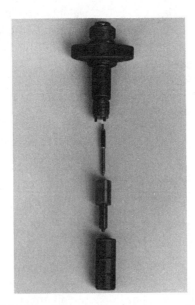

FIGURE 16–38. There are many types of fuel injector nozzles. The nozzles are used to inject and atomize the fuel inside the combustion chamber.

16–39 shows both types of nozzles. The pintle nozzle has a small needle valve located in the center of the tip protruding into the combustion chamber. The needle valve or stem is used to open and close a small hole for injecting fuel. The hole nozzle has a valve stem that opens and closes several holes leading to the combustion chamber. The most common type of nozzle in the automotive market is the hole nozzle. Although there are many designs used to accomplish atomization, the principles are much the same.

Nozzle Operation

In operation, high-pressure fuel delivered from the fuel injection pump is fed through steel lines to the injector. Once at the injector, the fuel is fed through internal passages to the nozzle assembly. See *Figure 16–40*. The nozzle assembly has a stem that keeps the holes closed off when there is no pressure from the injection pump. A spindle assembly and large spring are used to hold the nozzle closed.

As fuel pressure is increased by the injection pump, this pressure is felt on the stem or needle valve of the nozzle. See *Figure 16–41*. As the pressure continues to increase, the stem or needle valve will lift against spring tension. When this happens, fuel is injected rapidly into the cylinder. As the fuel is injected, the pressure drops. When the pressure drops below the spring pressure, the stem or needle valve is rapidly forced closed by the injector spring. This action "pops" the injector. This means that the injection stroke is started and stopped very rapidly. This improves the atomization and timing of fuel into the combustion chamber.

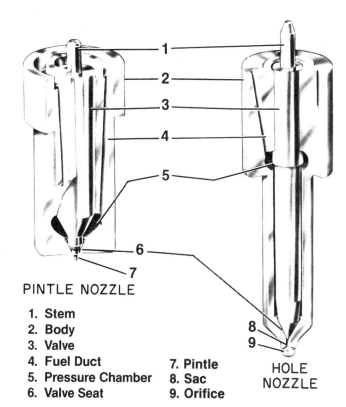

PINTLE NOZZLE

1. Stem
2. Body
3. Valve
4. Fuel Duct   7. Pintle
5. Pressure Chamber   8. Sac
6. Valve Seat   9. Orifice

HOLE NOZZLE

FIGURE 16–39. Several nozzle tips are used to inject the fuel into the cylinder. Both the hole and pintle nozzles are used. *(Courtesy of United Technologies, formerly American Bosch)*

1. Protection Cap Gasket
2. Nozzle Holder Body
3. Nozzle Gasket
4. ADB Nozzle Assembly
5. Dowel Pin
6. Nozzle Cap Nut
7. Spindle Assembly
8. Spring Adjusting Retaining Cap Nut
9. Protection Cap
10. Retaining Screw Gasket
11. Retaining Screw

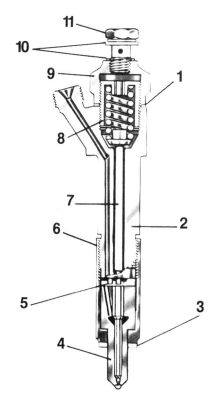

FIGURE 16–40. Fuel from the fuel injection pump is sent into the injector. As the pressure increases, the needle valve is lifted against the spring pressure. Fuel under high pressure now enters the combustion chamber. *(Courtesy of United Technologies, formerly American Bosch)*

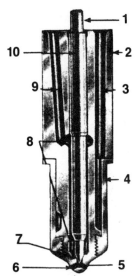

1. Stem (Needle Valve)
2. Body
3. Coolant Duct
4. Coolant Sleeve
5. Spray Hole Chamber
6. Spray Hole
7. Valve Seat
8. Pressure Chamber
9. Fuel Duct
10. Valve

FIGURE 16–41.   As the pressure from the fuel pump increases, the needle valve will eventually open and allow fuel to pass into the combustion chamber. *(Courtesy of United Technologies, formerly American Bosch)*

16.5   DIESEL ELECTRONIC CONTROL SYSTEMS (DECS)

In order to meet emission standards, diesel engines also use computers to control the fuel and emission systems. One type of computer system is called the diesel electronic control system (DECS). This system uses an electronic control module to control various inputs and outputs. *Figure 16–42* shows a schematic of the inputs and outputs on the fuel system.

Fast Idle Solenoid

The fast idle solenoid is a plunger-type solenoid. When extended, it pushes on the throttle linkage of the fuel injection pump. This action increases the spring pressure on the governor and slightly increases the engine speed. It is energized with temperatures below 100 degrees F, and above 248 degrees F for overheating. The fast idle solenoid is operated whenever the air conditioning is on.

Housing Pressure Cold and Altitude Advance (HPCA and HPAA)

It is desirable to advance the fuel injection pump on a cold engine and at higher altitudes. Advancing helps to reduce emissions, white smoke, and noise. Cold starting is also improved. The HPCA and HPAA solenoid operates with the fuel injection pump return line pressure regulator. The solenoid operates at cooling temperatures below 98.6 degrees F and above 4,000 feet above sea level.

When energized, the solenoid pushes the injector housing check ball off its seat. This causes the housing pressure to drop, which results in advanced fuel injection pump timing.

Altitude Fuel Limiter (AFL)

At altitudes above 4,000 feet, the fuel must be limited. The AFL is a solenoid that, when activated, limits the travel of the metering valve at wide open throttle.

Metering Valve Sensor (MVS)

The metering valve sensor is a variable resistor that sends a metering valve position signal to the ECM. The resistance is lowest at wide open throttle. Voltage output will be about 5 volts. As the metering valve closes, the resistance will increase, changing the voltage signal back to the ECM.

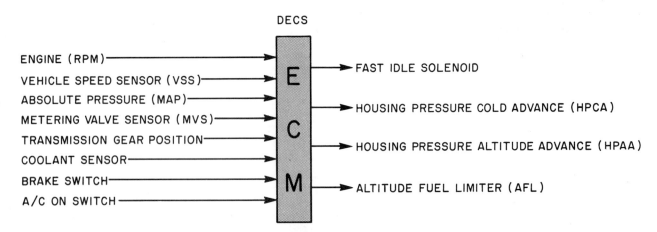

FIGURE 16–42.   The diesel electronic control system (DECS) is used to control the fuel injection system. Both input and output systems are shown.

Problems, Diagnosis and Service

▶ ◼ SAFETY PRECAUTIONS ◼ ◀

1. Always disconnect the battery and place the vehicle in park when working on fuel system parts.
2. When running an engine during a check of a specific part of the fuel injection system, always make sure the exhaust fumes are being exhausted, the brake is on, and the vehicle is in park.
3. Never work with the electrical components when gasoline has been spilled or there are gasoline fumes nearby.
4. When checking the electrical components on or near the fuel injection system, always use a battery-operated tester to eliminate any sparks. Sparks could cause a fire if near gasoline fumes.
5. Make sure there are no unshielded flames, such as a cutting torch, around or near a vehicle when the fuel injection system is being serviced.
6. When working on the fuel system, never use a drop light to inspect fuel system components; use a flashlight to reduce the possibility of sparks.

CAUTION: When working on vehicles that have computers in them, always follow the manufacturer's suggested service procedure. Standard test lights and unfused jumper wires may damage the computer. Never use these tools unless recommended by the manufacturer.

NOTE: Many computer controls are used on fuel injection systems. Each year the manufacturers improve these systems. In addition, each car manufacturer uses a different set of procedures for troubleshooting and for diagnosing problems in the computer fuel injection system. The following diagnosis and service hints are only general in nature, but they give an idea of how to diagnose and troubleshoot fuel injection systems.

PROBLEM: Faulty PROM

A vehicle has a CHECK ENGINE light on the dashboard. After grounding the test terminal under the dashboard and determining the code, it was found that the PROM needs to be checked.

DIAGNOSIS

The computer used on each vehicle has a PROM. The word PROM stands for programmable read only memory. The

PROM is a programmed set of data put into the computer by the manufacturer. It includes programmed data related to the vehicle's weight, engine size, transmission, axle ratio, and so on. If any diagnostic procedure calls for the computer to be replaced, the calibration unit (PROM) should be checked to see if it is the proper one and if it is installed correctly. If it is the correct one, the PROM should be removed and placed in the new computer.

SERVICE

1. Locate the computer in the vehicle and remove.
2. Make sure the ignition switch is in the off position and the battery is disconnected.
3. Remove the cover over the PROM.
4. Using a special PROM removal tool, remove the PROM carefully.
   CAUTION: Avoid touching the PROM with your hands, as the oils on your hand can affect the PROM operation.
5. Make sure all of the electrical pins and terminals are straight.
6. Install the PROM in the new computer making sure the reference marks match between the computer and the PROM.
7. Make sure the PROM is securely fastened and fully inserted into the socket.
8. Reinstall the computer into the mounts, and connect the electrical connectors to the computer.

PROBLEM: Open Coolant Sensor Circuit

A vehicle's CHECK ENGINE light on the dashboard has come on.

DIAGNOSIS

1. Using a test wire, ground out the test terminal under the dashboard of the vehicle.
2. Read the code flashing on the test light.
3. The code flashes once, then pauses, then flashes five times.
4. Using the list of codes in *Figure 16–43*, determine the problem to be an open coolant sensor circuit (code 15).

SERVICE

Use the diagnostic chart in *Figure 16–44* to complete the service procedure on the coolant sensor circuit. Additional

CODE	CIRCUIT AFFECTED
■■ 12	NO DISTRIBUTOR (TACH) SIGNAL
☐ 13	O₂ SENSOR NOT READY
☐ 14	SHORTED COOLANT SENSOR CIRCUIT
☐ 15	OPEN COOLANT SENSOR CIRCUIT
■■ 16	GENERATOR VOLTAGE OUT OF RANGE
☐ 18	OPEN CRANK SIGNAL CIRCUIT
☐ 19	SHORTED FUEL PUMP CIRCUIT
■■ 20	OPEN FUEL PUMP CIRCUIT
☐ 21	SHORTED THROTTLE POSITION SENSOR CIRCUIT
☐ 22	OPEN THROTTLE POSITION SENSOR CIRCUIT
☐ 23	EST/BYPASS CIRCUIT PROBLEM
☐ 24	SPEED SENSOR CIRCUIT PROBLEM
☐ 26	SHORTED THROTTLE SWITCH CIRCUIT
☐ 27	OPEN THROTTLE SWITCH CIRCUIT
☐ 28	OPEN FOURTH GEAR CIRCUIT
☐ 29	SHORTED FOURTH GEAR CIRCUIT
☐ 30	ISC CIRCUIT PROBLEM
■■ 31	SHORTED MAP SENSOR CIRCUIT
■■ 32	OPEN MAP SENSOR CIRCUIT
■■ 33	MAP/BARO SENSOR CORRELATION
■■ 34	MAP SIGNAL TOO HIGH
☐ 35	SHORTED BARO SENSOR CIRCUIT
☐ 36	OPEN BARO SENSOR CIRCUIT
☐ 37	SHORTED MAT SENSOR CIRCUIT
☐ 38	OPEN MAT SENSOR CIRCUIT
☐ 39	TCC ENGAGEMENT PROBLEM
■■ 44	LEAN EXHAUST SIGNAL
■■ 45	RICH EXHAUST SIGNAL
■■ 51	PROM ERROR INDICATOR
▼ 52	ECM MEMORY RESET INDICATOR
▼ 53	DISTRIBUTOR SIGNAL INTERRUPT
▼ 60	TRANSMISSION NOT IN DRIVE
▼ 63	CAR AND SET SPEED TOLERANCE EXCEEDED
▼ 64	CAR ACCELERATION EXCEEDS MAX. LIMIT
▼ 65	COOLANT TEMPERATURE EXCEEDS MAX. LIMIT
▼ 66	ENGINE RPM EXCEEDS MAXIMUM LIMIT
▼ 67	SHORTED SET OR RESUME CIRCUIT
.7.0	SYSTEM READY FOR FURTHER TESTS
.7.1	CRUISE CONTROL BRAKE CIRCUIT TEST
.7.2	THROTTLE SWITCH CIRCUIT TEST
.7.3	DRIVE (ADL) CIRCUIT TEST
.7.4	REVERSE CIRCUIT TEST
.7.5	CRUISE ON/OFF CIRCUIT TEST
.7.6	"SET/COAST" CIRCUIT TEST
.7.7	"RESUME/ACCELERATION" CIRCUIT TEST
.7.8	"INSTANT/AVERAGE" CIRCUIT TEST
.7.9	"RESET" CIRCUIT TEST
.8.0	A/C CLUTCH CIRCUIT TEST
-1.8.8	DISPLAY CHECK
.9.0	SYSTEM READY TO DISPLAY ENGINE DATA
.9.5	SYSTEM READY FOR OUTPUT CYCLING OR IN FIXED SPARK MODE
.9.6	OUTPUT CYCLING
.0.0	ALL DIANOSTICS COMPLETE
■■	TURNS ON "SERVICE NOW" LIGHT
☐	TURNS ON "SERVICE SOON" LIGHT
▼	DOES NOT TURN ON ANY TELLTALE LIGHT

NOTE: CRUISE IS DISENGAGED WITH ANY "SERVICE NOW" LIGHT OR WITH CODES 60-67.

FIGURE 16–43. Diagnostic codes are used on computer-controlled systems to aid in diagnosing problems. Each manufacturer has a different set of codes. For example, if code 13 is displayed, there may be trouble in the oxygen sensor. Code 32 shows that there is an open in the MAP sensor circuit. *(Courtesy of Motor Publications, Auto Engine Tune-up and Electronics Manual)*

diagnostic charts for each component on a computerized fuel management system can be found in the service manual.

PROBLEM: Idle Speed Control

A vehicle's CHECK ENGINE light on the dashboard has come on. After the lead in the test terminal under the dashboard was grounded, the problem was identified as being the idle speed control.

DIAGNOSIS

Certain manufacturers use a pinpoint test along with a set of codes. Pinpoint tests are used to get more specific readings of individual components in the system. Voltmeter readings are taken at different points and compared with the manufacturer's specifications. The procedures and readings can be found in many of the service manuals used today. Since there are so many variations, it is important to follow the exact procedure in the manual for the particular year and make of the vehicle.

SERVICE

1. Locate the year and model of the vehicle.
2. After determining the problem component (idle speed control) find the pinpoint procedure for this component.
3. As shown in *Figure 16–45*, there may be several pinpoint procedure tests (1 of 3, 2 of 3, 3 of 3).
4. Follow the procedure as stated on the pinpoint procedure.

PROBLEM: Faulty ISC or TPS

A vehicle with port fuel injection is continually stalling.

DIAGNOSIS

For diagnosing various problems in port fuel injection systems such as "continually stalling," troubleshooting guides are available in many of the service manuals for reference. *Figure 16–46* shows an example of a typical "Troubleshooting Guide for Port Fuel Injection Systems." In this particular case, the problem may be either in the idle speed control (ISC) or the throttle position sensor (TPS).

SERVICE

The exact service will depend on the components that need to be tested, serviced, or replaced. Follow the manufacturer's recommended procedure for service and replacement of the faulty component. If the remedy suggests that various vacuum and pressure hoses be inspected for leaks, various vacuum hose diagrams are also available. The service and repair manuals have drawings for each vehicle, the model, year, and

CODE 15
OPEN COOLANT SENSOR CIRCUIT

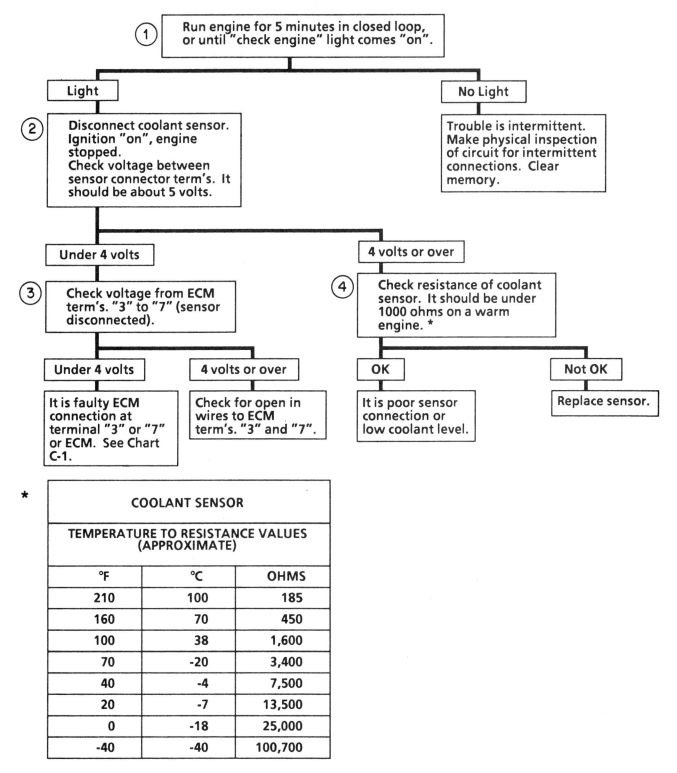

① Run engine for 5 minutes in closed loop, or until "check engine" light comes "on".

Light

② Disconnect coolant sensor. Ignition "on", engine stopped. Check voltage between sensor connector term's. It should be about 5 volts.

No Light

Trouble is intermittent. Make physical inspection of circuit for intermittent connections. Clear memory.

Under 4 volts

③ Check voltage from ECM term's. "3" to "7" (sensor disconnected).

4 volts or over

④ Check resistance of coolant sensor. It should be under 1000 ohms on a warm engine. *

Under 4 volts

It is faulty ECM connection at terminal "3" or "7" or ECM. See Chart C-1.

4 volts or over

Check for open in wires to ECM term's. "3" and "7".

OK

It is poor sensor connection or low coolant level.

Not OK

Replace sensor.

*

COOLANT SENSOR		
TEMPERATURE TO RESISTANCE VALUES (APPROXIMATE)		
°F	°C	OHMS
210	100	185
160	70	450
100	38	1,600
70	-20	3,400
40	-4	7,500
20	-7	13,500
0	-18	25,000
-40	-40	100,700

FIGURE 16–44.   Codes are used to diagnose different ECM systems. Here code 15 indicates trouble in the coolant sensor system. Diagnostic charts are then used to locate the exact problem.   *(Courtesy of General Motors Product Service Training)*

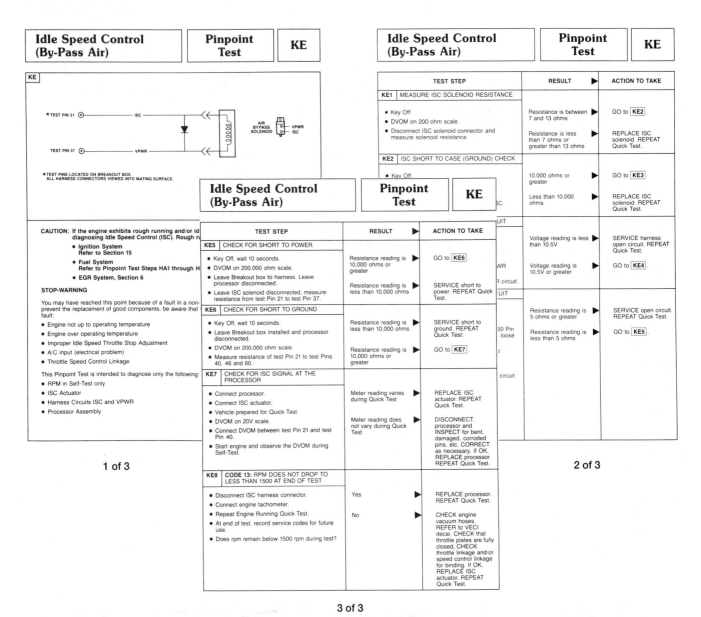

FIGURE 16–45. These pinpoint tests are used to help the service technician troubleshoot various components in computerized systems. *(Courtesy of Motor Publications, Auto Engine Tune-up and Electronics Manual)*

the hose connections. *Figure 16–47* shows an example of the vacuum hose routing for a specific type of vehicle.

Certain companies also manufacture special diagnostic instruments for checking the computerized systems. *Figure 16–48* shows such an instrument. These test instruments can be connected directly into the computer system (ALCL) test terminal (under the dashboard or in the engine compartment) to make rapid and accurate diagnostic checks. These hand-held testers are also known as scanners. They are manufactured by several companies.

At times all of the components may check out OK, but the problem still exists in the vehicle. When this happens the fault may be in the wiring harness used to hold all of the wires together. *Figure 16–49* shows a typical wiring harness used on a computerized fuel management system. Often, this wiring harness will vibrate against the vehicle frame and cause one of its circuits to stop operating. The exact point of contact is very difficult to locate. Visually inspect the wiring harness and make sure all the electrical connections are complete. You may have to refer to recent manufacturer's service bulletins to determine exactly where the wiring harness is rubbing against the frame.

TROUBLESHOOTING GUIDE FOR PORT FUEL INJECTION SYSTEMS

Condition	Possible Cause	Remedy
Preliminary checks		Check fuel system for fuel leaks.
		Check battery state of charge.
		Check all wiring and connections.
		Check cooling system level.
		Check ignition system.
		Check air cleaner and preheat system.
		Check fuel system pressure.
		Check fuel lines for restrictions.
		Check vacuum hoses for leaks and restrictions.
Hard start, cold or rough idle, cold	CTS	Check coolant level or replace sensor.
	Fuel pressure bleed down	Check for fuel leak or defective fuel pump.
	Cold start injector	Check cold start injector; service or replace as required.
	Leaking manifold gasket or base gasket	Replace defective gasket.
	ACT/MAT Sensor	Replace defective ACT/MAT sensor.
	Wrong PCV valve	Replace PCV valve.
	Warm-up regulator	Replace warm-up regulator.
	Injector	Check injectors for variation in spray pattern; clean or replace injectors as required.
	Mass air flow sensor	Check air flow meter, fuel pump contacts.
	Pressure regulator	Check pressure regulator for setting and bleed down.
Hesitation or surging, hot or cold	CTS	Check coolant level or replace sensor.
	Low fuel system pressure	Check fuel filter and fuel pump; service or replace as required.
	Restricted air intake system	Check air cleaner and preheat system; service or replace as required.
	TPS defective or not adjusted correctly	Check TPS; adjust or replace as required.
	Mass airflow sensor	Check airflow meter, fuel pump contacts
	ACT/MAT sensor	Replace defective ACT/MAT sensor.

FIGURE 16–46. This troubleshooting guide will help the service technician locate and solve problems in computerized port fuel injection systems. *(Courtesy of Scharff, Complete Fuel Systems and Emission Control, Delmar Publishers Inc.)*

TROUBLESHOOTING GUIDE FOR PORT FUEL INJECTION SYSTEMS (CONTINUED)

Condition	Possible Cause	Remedy
	Air leak in air intake system	Check gaskets, hoses and ducting; service or replace as required.
	Defective oxygen sensor	Replace oxygen sensor.
	Defective computer	Replace computer.
Hard start, hot	Bleeding injector	Inspect injector for dripping; service, or replace as required.
	Leaking intake manifold gasket or base gasket	Replace defective gasket.
	MAP sensor	Check MAP sensor and vacuum hose; service or replace as required.
	Pressure regulator	Check pressure regulator for setting and bleed down; service or replace as required.
Rough idle, hot	MAP sensor	Check MAP sensor and vacuum hose; service or replace as required.
	CTS	Check coolant level or replace sensor.
	TPS	Check TPS; adjust or replace as required.
	Injector	Check injector for variation in spray pattern; clean or replace injector as required.
	Oxygen sensor	Replace oxygen sensor.
	Defective computer	Replace computer.
	ISC/IAC	Check idle speed control device; service or replace as required.
Stalling	ISC/IAC	Check idle speed control device; service or replace as required.
	TPS	Check TPS; adjust or replace as required.
	MAP Sensor	Check MAP sensor and vacuum hose; service or replace as required.
Poor power	Dirty injector	Check injector spray pattern; clean or replace injector as required.
	Fuel pump	Check fuel pump pressure; replace fuel pump.
	Fuel pump pickup strainer	Check strainer; replace as required.
	Fuel filter	Check fuel filter; replace as required.
	Pressure regulator	Check pressure regulator for setting and bleed down; service or replace as required.

FIGURE 16–46. (CONTINUED)

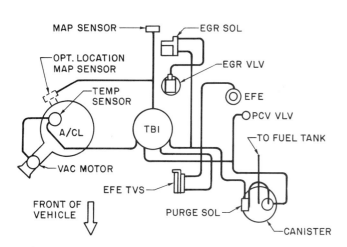

FIGURE 16–47. Always refer to the specification manuals for routing of vacuum hoses. Check vacuum circuits for leaks and for damage or broken parts. *(Courtesy of Motor Publications, Auto Engine Tune-up and Electronics Manual)*

FIGURE 16–48. Various manufacturers sell test instruments used to diagnose computer-controlled systems. These instruments can save the technician valuable time and money. *(Courtesy of Owatonna Tool Company)*

FIGURE 16–49. Often the wiring harness may short out against the frame, causing irregular vehicle operation.

SERVICE MANUAL CONNECTION

There are many important specifications to keep in mind when working with injection systems. To identify the specifications for your engine, you will need to know the VIN (vehicle identification number) of the vehicle, the type and year of the vehicle, and the type of engine. Although they may be titled differently, some of the more common injection system specifications (not all) found in service manuals are listed below. Note that these specifications are typical examples. Each vehicle and engine may have different specifications.

Common Specification	Typical Example
Curb idle speed	
Manual transmission	900 RPM
Automatic transmission	850 RPM in neutral
Electrical power to choke unit	7.5 volts ac
Fuel control solenoid	28–66 ohms
Fuel pressure regulator	36 psi
Idle speed control motor	
adjustment	1.06 volts
Injector resistance	1.5–2.5 ohms
Oxygen sensor voltage	0–0.99 volts
Throttle body injector torque	200 in.-lb
Throttle position sensor	
pinpoint test	More than 1900 ohms

In addition, the service manual will give specific directions for various service and testing procedures. Some of the more common procedures include:

- Coolant sensor replace

- Pinpoint test, barometric pressure

- Pinpoint test, idle speed control

- Throttle position sensor (TPS) adjust

- Trouble code diagnosis (all codes stated)

SUMMARY

Fuel injection is the process of injecting fuel into the flow of air going into the engine. There are several types of fuel injection, including throttle body, port, and high-pressure diesel fuel injection. In addition, fuel injection systems are classified as either direct or indirect, timed or continuous, and port or throttle body injection.

As the demand for cleaner engines and better fuel economy has increased, automotive manufacturers have converted many fuel systems to fuel injection. The main goal of using fuel injection is to maintain a stoichiometric ratio of 14.7 to 1. However, there are also nonstoichiometric conditions such as when the engine is cold and during low manifold vacuum. Fuel injection is extremely precise compared with the standard carburetion systems.

Throttle body injection is designed so that an injector injects fuel directly into the air as it comes through the throttle body. It uses a throttle body injector that is controlled by a computer. The injector is able to produce a conical spray pattern when a solenoid lifts a metering valve. Fuel pressure is regulated by a fuel pressure regulator.

The throttle body injection system uses several other components for correct operation. A vacuum assist is used to monitor the vacuum. A signal is sent from the vacuum assist to the electronic control module to meter the right amount of fuel. A throttle position sensor is used to determine the exact position of the throttle. The idle air control is used to control engine RPM at idle. The manifold absolute pressure sensor signals the amount of manifold vacuum (absolute pressure) to the ECM. All of these components work in conjunction with the ECM to control the throttle body injector for all operations.

A second type of fuel injection is called port fuel injection. Here a small fuel injector is placed just before each intake valve. More accurate fuel control is obtained with this system than with the throttle body injection system. There are several types of port injection, including double-fire injection, sequential fuel injection, and tuned port injection.

The port fuel injector is a solenoid-operated valve with a pintle. Fuel is sent to the fuel injector through a fuel rail. The amount of air going into the intake manifold is controlled by the throttle body.

Several additional sensors are used in port fuel injection. The manifold air temperature sensor tells the ECM the temperature of the incoming air. Idle air control is used to control the amount of air bypassing the throttle blade during idle. The cold start injector is used to increase the amount of fuel during cold starting conditions. A thermal-time switch is used to tell the cold start injector when to operate. The mass air flow sensor tells the ECM the amount of air entering the engine. All of these components are integrated into the ECM to control the exact amount of fuel being delivered to the injectors.

High-pressure, direct, timed fuel injection is used on diesel engines. High pressure (4,000–10,000 psi) is needed to inject fuel into the cylinder during the compression stroke. High-pressure injection systems are designed to time, atomize, meter, and pressurize the fuel. The system consists of a drive shaft, housing, metering valve, transfer pump, distributor rotor, internal cam ring, automatic advance, pumping plungers, and a governor.

The transfer pump is used to draw the fuel from the fuel tank to the injection pump. Regulator valves are used to control the amount of pressure. The fuel is charged inside a rotor. As the rotor turns, a set of rollers and an internal cam ring are used to create the high pressure. The high pressure is sent to each piston through fuel lines. A delivery valve is used to assure that the fuel shuts off rapidly.

The governor is used to maintain correct speed by using

(continued)

Linkage to Science and Mathematics

USING A MANOMETER TO MEASURE PRESSURES

One instrument used to accurately measure pressure and vacuum in engine systems is a manometer. Manometers are most often used to measure pneumatic pressures and vacuum readings when testing engines at the manufacturing plant. A manometer is shown. It consists of a U-shaped tube with a fluid inside. Water is used for lower readings, while mercury is used for higher readings. A scale is used between the tubes. When a pressure or vacuum is connected to one end of the tube, the fluid has a tendency to move. The movement on the scale is an indication of the amount of vacuum or pressure. To read a manometer, add the inches of fluid movement dropped on one side to the inches of fluid movement lifted on the other side. A conversion table for psig, water, and mercury readings is shown. *(Courtesy of Schwaller, Transportation, Energy and Power Technology, Delmar Publishers Inc.)*

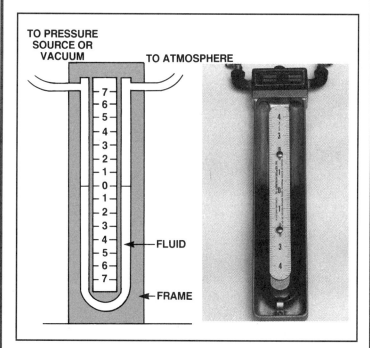

Conversion between psig, water, and mercury readings		
1" of water	=	0.0735" of mercury
1" of water	=	0.0361 psig
1" of mercury	=	0.491 psig
1" of mercury	=	13.6" of water
1 psig	=	27.7" of water
1 psig	=	2.036" of mercury

a centrifugal weight force against a spring pressure. The balance of these two forces controls the position of the metering valve. An automatic advance is used on some injectors to advance the fuel injection time as rpm increases.

Fuel injector nozzles are used to inject the high-pressure fuel into the cylinder. A nozzle consists of high-pressure spring designed to hold a needle valve in the closed position. The high pressure from the fuel pump lifts the needle valve off its seat to inject the fuel.

Diesel engines are also incorporating computers for fuel control. The system is called the diesel electronic control system (DECS). Several sensors are used to control the fuel. A fast idle solenoid controls the amount of fuel at idle by controlling the governor spring tension with a solenoid. Advance timing is accomplished by rotating the cam ring. This is done by using two hydraulic pressures working against each other. Both altitude and cold starting conditions are improved by advance timing the fuel injection. This is done by reducing the housing pressure.

A series of codes is used to diagnose computer-controlled systems. The computer has built-in diagnostic checks that can also be made. When identifying a code, refer to a diagnostic chart. It is important to follow the chart to check voltages and other readings. These readings are then compared with the manufacturer's specifications.

TERMS TO KNOW

Can you explain each of the following terms? Review the chapter until you can use each term correctly.

Throttle body	Magnetic pickup
Emission standards	Pintle
Stoichiometric ratio	Gauge pressure
Cold engine operation	Absolute pressure
Low manifold vacuum	Crossfire injection
Intake manifold vacuum	Tuned ports
Conical	Needle valve
Throttle plate	Governor
Pulse width	
Metered	
Thermistor	

 REVIEW QUESTIONS

Multiple Choice

1. Gasoline fuel injection is considered:
   a. Indirect
   b. High pressure
   c. Direct
   d. Nonmetered
   e. Governed

2. Which type of fuel injection has one fuel injector feeding all pistons?
   a. Port fuel injection
   b. Direct fuel injection
   c. Throttle body injection
   d. All of the above
   e. None of the above

3. The correct stoichiometric ratio is:
   a. 12.2 to 1
   b. 14.7 to 1
   c. 16.7 to 1
   d. 18.1 to 1
   e. 19.2 to 1

4. Metering of throttle body fuel injection is controlled by the:
   a. Operator only
   b. Fuel pump
   c. Computer
   d. Cooling system
   e. Lubrication system

5. The fuel injector in the throttle body fuel injection system is opened and closed by using:
   a. Battery voltage
   b. A solenoid
   c. The operator's foot
   d. Mechanical linkage from the carburetor
   e. Lubricating oil pressure

6. The amount of fuel injection from a throttle body injector is measured by the:
   a. Pulse width
   b. Pulse frequency
   c. Size of the battery
   d. Temperature of the fuel
   e. Speed of the tires

7. The fuel pressure regulator in throttle body fuel injection is located on:
   a. The cooling thermostat
   b. The fuel pump
   c. The fuel rails
   d. The exhaust manifold
   e. The carburetor

8. The throttle position sensor is used as a/an _____ the ECM.
   a. Input to
   b. Output from
   c. Frequency sensor from
   d. Voltage from
   e. Speed sensor from

9. Which of the following units bypasses air around the throttle plate on the TBI system?
   a. Throttle position sensor
   b. Gauge pressure unit
   c. Manifold absolute pressure
   d. Idle air control
   e. Absolute pressure unit

10. Which of the following measures absolute pressure inside the manifold?
    a. MAF
    b. IAC
    c. MAP
    d. TPS
    e. None of the above

11. Which pressure scale starts at zero, when the atmospheric pressure is at 14.7psi?
    a. Psig
    b. Psia
    c. CCC
    d. Port pressure
    e. None of the above

12. Which fuel system would eliminate fuel droplets forming inside the intake manifold because the fuel is heavier than air?
    a. Throttle body
    b. Port
    c. Carburetors
    d. Central fuel system
    e. Controlled-combustion fuel system

13. Manifold air temperature is used as an _____.
    a. Input to the ECM
    b. Output from the ECM
    c. Input to the MAP
    d. Output from the MAP
    e. None of the above

14. The port fuel injector opens and closes because of the operation of a _____.
    a. Plunger
    b. Set of rollers
    c. Regulator
    d. Solenoid
    e. High-pressure diaphragm

15. The cold start injector on a port fuel injection system operates:
    a. Only during cold starting
    b. To add extra fuel during starting
    c. On the basis of the temperature of the coolant
    d. All of the above
    e. None of the above

16. The thermal-time switch operates along with the:
    a. Manifold air temperature
    b. Cold start fuel injector
    c. Mass air flow
    d. Carburetor
    e. High-pressure fuel injector

17. Which system has a sensing element that must be kept 75 degrees C (167 degrees F) above the temperature of the incoming air?
    a. Mass air temperature
    b. Manifold absolute pressure
    c. Idle air control
    d. Mass air flow
    e. None of the above

18. Diesel engines use injection systems that are classified as:
    a. Direct
    b. High-pressure
    c. Timed
    d. All of the above
    e. None of the above

19. Which of the following is not done on a diesel fuel injection system?
    a. Timed injection
    b. Atomized injection
    c. Pressurized injection
    d. Metered injection
    e. Produce continuous injection

20. High pressure is produced on a diesel fuel injection system by using a set of:
    a. Rollers inside a cam ring
    b. Bearings on a cam
    c. Plungers pushing outward
    d. Eccentric pumps
    e. None of the above

21. The purpose of the transfer pump on a diesel fuel injection system is to:
    a. Produce the high pressure
    b. Produce the governor action
    c. Produce the regulation action
    d. All of the above
    e. None of the above

22. Which item is used to measure and control the right amount of fuel in a diesel fuel injection system?
    a. Transfer pump
    b. Cam ring
    c. Plunger and rollers
    d. Metering valve
    e. Delivery valve

23. The delivery valve is used to control:
    a. The start of injection
    b. The middle of injection
    c. The end of injection
    d. The total pulse width
    e. Governor pressure

24. A governor is a device that can sense a change in:
    a. Load
    b. Speed
    c. Metering valve setting
    d. Spring forces
    e. Vehicle speed

25. When spring force is greater than centrifugal weight force on a governor, the fuel setting will:
    a. Increase
    b. Decrease
    c. Remain about the same
    d. Decrease and then immediately increase
    e. Increase and then immediately decrease

26. When the diesel fuel injection system is advanced, what object is moved or rotated?
    a. The transfer pump
    b. The delivery valve
    c. The cam ring
    d. The nozzle
    e. None of the above

27. The fuel nozzle is used to:
    a. Inject fuel into the combustion chamber
    b. Atomize the fuel in the combustion chamber
    c. Start and stop injection rapidly
    d. All of the above
    e. None of the above

28. Which of the following is used on the DECS?
    a. Altitude fuel limiter
    b. Housing pressure cold advance
    c. Housing pressure altitude advance
    d. All of the above
    e. None of the above

29. When diagnostic work is done on a computer-controlled system, a series of _____ are used.
    a. Codes
    b. Subsystems
    c. Voltage readings that are displayed on the dashboard
    d. Special instructions that are displayed on the dashboard
    e. None of the above

The following questions are similar in format to ASE (Automotive Service Excellence) test questions.

30. Technician A says when the air-fuel ratio is constant during starting, the computer system is in a closed loop mode. Technician B says when the air-fuel ratio is constant during starting, the computer system is in an open loop mode. Who is right?
    a. A only
    b. B only
    c. Both A and B
    d. Neither A nor B

31. Technician A says the PROM is a set of data that tells the fuel injector when to shut off. Technician B says the PROM is a speed sensor. Who is right?
    a. A only
    b. B only
    c. Both A and B
    d. Neither A nor B

32. The air-fuel ratio is being held constant. Technician A says the system is in a closed loop mode. Technician B says the system is in an open loop mode. Who is right?
    a. A only
    b. B only
    c. Both A and B
    d. Neither A nor B

33. Technician A says that the PROM is a set of programmable data for each specific car. Technician B says that the PROM is the same for all cars being manufactured. Who is right?
    a. A only
    b. B only
    c. Both A and B
    d. Neither A nor B

34. Technician A says that hand-held scanners can be connected to the ALCL. Technician B says that hand-held scanners are used to check fuel pressures. Who is right?
    a. A only
    b. B only
    c. Both A and B
    d. Neither A nor B

35. Technician A says that during closed loop operation, the oxygen sensor is not being used as an input. Technician B says that open loop operation doesn't start until the engine reaches 150 degrees F. Who is right?
    a. A only
    b. B only
    c. Both A and B
    d. Neither A nor B

36. Technician A says that the computer enriches the fuel during cold starting. Technician B says that the computer has no effect on the air-fuel ratio during closed loop operation. Who is right?
    a. A only
    b. B only
    c. Both A and B
    d. Neither A nor B

37. Technician A says that a coolant sensor is considered a thermistor type of sensor. Technician B says that the magnetic pickup type sensor is used to sense barometric pressure. Who is right?
    a. A only
    b. B only
    c. Both A and B
    d. Neither A nor B

Essay

38. What is the difference between direct and indirect fuel injection?

39. What is the difference between port and throttle body injection?

40. Describe the difference between continuous and timed injection.

41. Describe the purpose and operation of the idle air control.

42. What is the purpose of the fuel rails?

43. Describe the purpose and operation of the mass air flow sensor.

44. What is the difference between diesel and gasoline fuel injection?

Short Answer

45. The crankshaft position sensor and the vehicle speed sensor use a _____ pickup to produce the electronic signal.

46. When the fuel injectors are being pulsed independently from the distributor reference pulses, the system is in the _____ mode.

47. When the throttle is pushed to 80% of wide open throttle, during starting, the computer system is in the _____ mode.

48. The abbreviation PROM stands for _____ _____ _____ _____ .

49. Often, when a problem occurs in a computerized fuel injection system, the computer goes into _____ _____ _____ .

CHAPTER 17

Air Intake and Exhaust Systems

INTRODUCTION   For an engine to operate correctly, air must flow into and out of the engine without restriction. Air intake and exhaust systems are designed to clean the air coming in and reduce the noise coming out. This chapter deals with the components and operation of the air intake and exhaust systems.

OBJECTIVES   After reading this chapter, you should be able to:

- Analyze the use and operation of air filter systems.
- Define the use and operation of intake manifolds.
- State the purpose and operation of using turbochargers on gasoline and diesel engines.
- Define the operation of exhaust systems.
- Describe various problems, diagnosis, and service procedures on the intake and exhaust systems.

✔ SAFETY CHECKLIST ✔

When working with the air intake and exhaust system, keep these important safety precautions in mind.
✔ Never smoke in or around an automobile.
✔ Always keep an approved fire extinguisher nearby when working on the air cleaner, turbocharger, or fuel system.
✔ Keep your fingers away from the turbocharger immediately after the engine is shut down, as the compressor may still be spinning.
✔ Be careful not to cut your hands on the sharp edges of the air intake housings and ductwork.
✔ Always wear OSHA-approved safety glasses.

17.1   AIR INTAKE SYSTEMS

Purpose of Air Filters

The average gasoline engine brings in and exhausts approximately 10,000 gallons of air for every gallon of fuel consumed. The intake air must be clean. *Airborne* contaminants can shorten engine life or even cause premature failure. For example, the dirt that gets into the engine causes excessive wear on the rings, pistons, bearings, and valves. Depending on the amount of dirt getting into the engine, its life can be shortened from 1/3 to 1/2.

As was indicated when studying fuel, the correct amount of air is very important for correct engine operation. Engines must breathe freely to provide maximum power. Air filters are used on every engine to trap contaminants, yet provide a free flow of air into the engine. Air filters that are dirty and not replaced can cause large restrictions to the air. This condition will cause the engine to run excessively rich. Fuel mileage can be substantially reduced by a dirty air cleaner. Exhaust emissions will also be increased.

The type of dirt and contaminants that enter the engine is determined by how and where the engine is used. The most common contaminants are leaves, insects, exhaust soot, dust, and road dirt. The geographic location of the vehicle also affects the amount of airborne contaminants. In dusty conditions, there may be more dirt than at high-altitude conditions.

Some of the information in this chapter can help you prepare for the National Institute for Automotive Service Excellence (ASE) certification tests. The tests most directly related to this chapter are entitled

ENGINE REPAIR (TEST A1) AND ENGINE PERFORMANCE (TEST A8).

The content areas that closely parallel this chapter are

FUEL AND EXHAUST SYSTEMS DIAGNOSIS AND REPAIR AND FUEL, AIR INDUCTION, AND EXHAUST SYSTEMS DIAGNOSIS AND REPAIR.

All of these variables determine the exact type of filter needed and the degree of filtration.

Dry-Type Air Filters

The dry-type air filter is made of a paper element. *Figure 17–1* shows an example of a dry-type air filter. This filter permits air to flow into the engine with little resistance. However, it traps and holds contaminants inside the paper. When the dry-type air filter becomes plugged with dirt, it is replaced with another filter.

There are several types of dry-type air filters. The light-duty paper-type air cleaner is shown in *Figure 17–2*. These

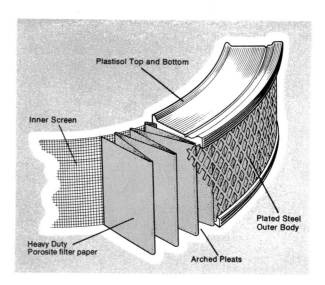

FIGURE 17–2. A paper-type filter is made of pleated paper, steel mesh, and seals on the top and bottom. *(Courtesy of Dana Corporation)*

filters are generally used on passenger vehicles and small pickup trucks. The filter element is made of paper. These filters are usually small because of space restrictions under the hood. The efficiency of this type of filter is near 98% for most driving conditions. Because of the high efficiency, the dry air filter has replaced the oil bath air cleaner. The filter can be designed in many shapes to fit different types of air cleaners. The design depends on the type of ducting and housing used on the engine.

A second type of light-duty air cleaner is called the polyurethane filter. This filter is sometimes called the foam filter, *Figure 17–3*. It is normally placed on the outer cover over a dry-type paper element. It consists of a polyurethane wrapper stretched over a metal support. The material has thousands of pores and interconnecting strands that create a mazelike contaminant trap. It may be used dry or with a thin coat of oil. In both cases, this filter has about the same efficiency as a paper-type element. The advantage to this filter is that it can be removed, cleaned, and reused. Many polyurethane filters are used as *aftermarket* equipment. After-

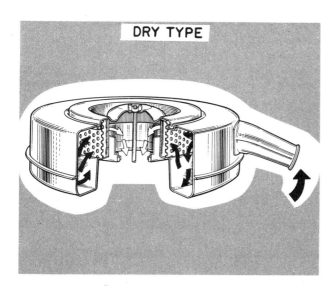

FIGURE 17–1. The dry-type air filter permits air flow into the engine with little restriction. *(Courtesy of Dana Corporation)*

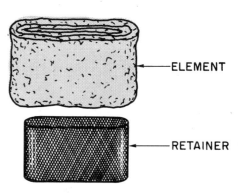

FIGURE 17–3. The polyurethane-wrapped filter stretches over a metal support.

market equipment parts are sold to consumers by local parts dealers.

There is also a series of heavy-duty filters used on certain equipment. Heavy-duty air cleaners are used in very dirty and contaminated areas. However, because the automobile is normally driven on paved roads, there is less call for heavy-duty air cleaners in cars.

Intake Ducting

On vehicles using carburetors, air cleaners are typically placed directly on top of the carburetor. *Figure 17–4* shows such an example. The air is drawn into the fresh-air intake, through a temperature-controlled valve, and into the air cleaner. From the air cleaner, the air is drawn directly into the venturi of the carburetor.

When manufacturers started using fuel injection and other configurations on the automobile, the intake ducting was also changed. Intake ducting is also different on engines that are *turbocharged*. *Figure 17–5* shows two examples of different ducting. The air cleaners are light-duty paper elements. They are located for easy maintenance and service. The intake ducting has several clamps and rubber ducting to get the air into the engine.

Resonator

Certain engine applications use a *resonator* on the intake ducting. *Figure 17–6* shows a resonator used in a diesel engine application. The purpose of the resonator is to reduce induction noise produced on the intake system.

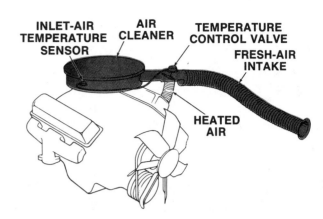

FIGURE 17–4. Intake ducting can take many forms. A simple type is shown with the air cleaner mounted directly on top of the carburetor. *(Courtesy of Chrysler Corporation)*

Intake Manifolds

The intake manifold is used to transfer or carry the air or fuel or both from the air cleaner to the intake valve. *Figure 17–7* shows a typical intake manifold for a V-8 diesel engine. On four- and six-cylinder engines, the intake and exhaust manifolds form an assembly.

The intake manifold is designed to deliver the right amount of air and fuel to each cylinder under all driving conditions. It would be best if all intake ports were the same length (tuned ports). However, on many engines with carburetors this design is compromised to reduce the cost. The most common manifolds are made of a one-piece casting of either cast iron or aluminum.

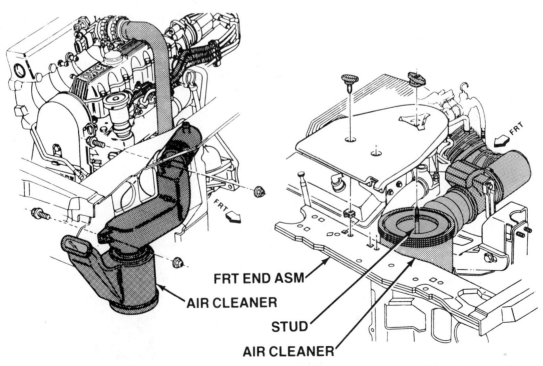

FIGURE 17–5. Intake ducting will change as different types of engines are designed. Two different ducting arrangements are shown. *(Courtesy of General Motors Product Service Training)*

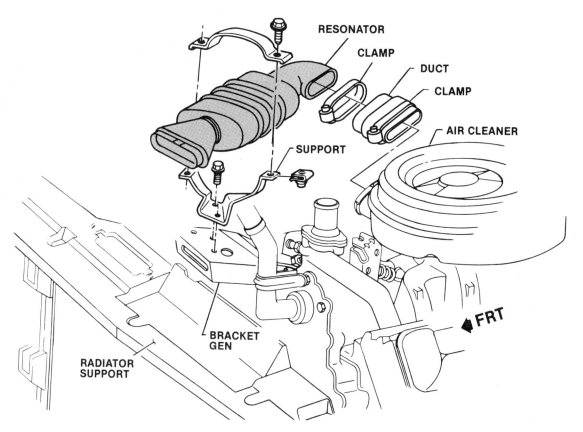

FIGURE 17–6.   A resonator is used to reduce the intake noise. *(Courtesy of General Motors Product Service Training)*

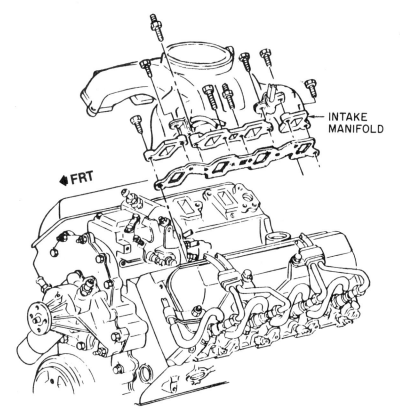

FIGURE 17–7.   A typical V-8 manifold for a diesel engine. *(Courtesy of General Motors Corporation)*

On four-cylinder engines, the intake manifold has either four *runners* or two runners that break into four near the intake manifold, *Figure 17–8*. On in-line six-cylinder engines, there are either six runners or three that branch off into six near the intake manifold. On V-configuration engines (V-6 and V-8), both open and closed intake manifolds are made. Open intake manifolds have an open space between the bottom of the manifold and the valve lifter valley. Closed intake manifolds act as the cover to the intake lifter valley.

Wet and Dry Manifolds

Manifolds can also be either wet or dry. Wet manifolds have coolant passages cast directly into the manifold. Dry manifolds do not have coolant passages.

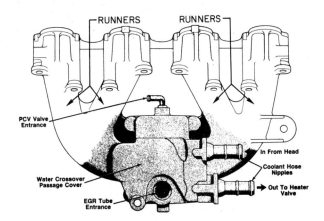

FIGURE 17–8. The intake manifold for an in-line four-cylinder engine can have two or four runners. Two runners are shown here. *(Courtesy of Chevrolet Division, General Motors Corporation)*

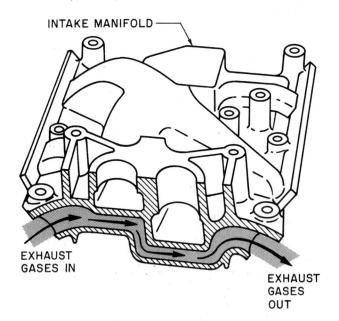

FIGURE 17–9. A crossover manifold is used to transfer the exhaust from one side of the engine to the other to be exhausted. The exhaust heat causes better vaporization of the fuel in the carburetor.

Exhaust Crossover Intake Manifold

On some manifolds, there is an exhaust crossover passage. This passage allows the exhaust from one side of the engine to cross over through the intake manifold to the other side to be exhausted. The exhaust crossover provides heat to the base of the carburetor to improve the vaporization of the fuel while the engine is warming up. See *Figure 17–9*. The crossover also reduces carburetor icing.

PROBLEM: Air Intake Restriction

Customers often complain that the engine isn't running correctly. Technicians usually say that the problem may be in the air intake. What are the symptoms of an air intake restriction?

SOLUTION:

One of the most common problems today in all automobiles is air intake restrictions. If the owner does not change the air filter at regular intervals, the dirty air filter restricts the air as it tries to enter the engine. Common symptoms of an air intake restriction are:

1. The engine is hard to start.

2. The engine has a loss of power.

3. The coolant temperature decreases.

4. The exhaust smoke increases in density and is black.

5. The oil consumption and fuel usage increase significantly.

17.2   TURBOCHARGING

With the increased use of fuel injection and computer-controlled combustion systems, turbochargers have become common components on gasoline and diesel engines. In the past, only large engines had turbochargers. Today, with the precise control afforded by computers, turbochargers are making smaller engines more efficient and capable of producing more power. In order to study turbochargers, supercharging must first be defined.

Supercharging Defined

When the piston moves downward on the intake stroke, a vacuum is created. This vacuum causes air and fuel to be drawn into the engine. This process is called a *naturally aspirated* or normally aspirated engine. The amount of air entering the engine is based on atmospheric pressure. Most engines are considered to be naturally aspirated. However, with the increased use of smaller engines, there may be a lack of power for certain driving conditions.

To overcome this lack of power, an engine can be supercharged. *Supercharging* an engine means to deliver a greater volume of air to the cylinders than that delivered from the suction of the pistons alone. The engine is not naturally aspirated; it is supercharged. When more air is forced into the cylinders, there must be a corresponding increase in fuel. Fuel is needed to maintain a 14.7 to 1 air-fuel ratio. If these conditions occur, then a great increase in power will result. In some cases, up to 50% more power can be obtained by supercharging an engine.

Blower

Either a blower or turbocharger can be used to supercharge an engine. A blower is a mechanical air pump that forces air into the engine. It is driven by a set of gears or belts from the crankshaft. It produces a substantial frictional loss on the engine because it requires horsepower from the engine to operate. Blowers are used on certain heavy-duty diesel engines, and on high-performance racing engines.

Turbocharging Principles

A turbocharger is a device that uses the exhaust gases, rather than engine power to turn an air pump or compressor. The air pump then forces an increased amount of air into the cylinders. Both diesel and gasoline engines in the automotive market use turbochargers. *Figure 17–10* shows a typical schematic of air and exhaust in a turbocharged engine. High-velocity exhaust gases pass out of the exhaust ports. From there they pass through a *turbine*-driven pump. Here the exhaust gases cause the exhaust turbine to turn very rapidly. The exhaust turbine causes the intake *compressor* to turn very rapidly also. As the compressor turbine turns, it draws in a large amount of fresh air. The intake air is pressurized and forced into the intake port. The increase in pressure in the intake manifold is called *boost*. Boost may produce pressure in the intake manifold of about 6–10 psi or more, depending on the manufacturer.

If a corresponding amount of fuel is added, a large increase in power will result. *Figure 17–11* shows a chart that compares a turbocharged and a normally aspirated engine. Note that both the torque and horsepower have been increased at all RPM. For example, at 5,000 RPM the normally aspirated engine produces about 80 hp. At this RPM, the turbocharged

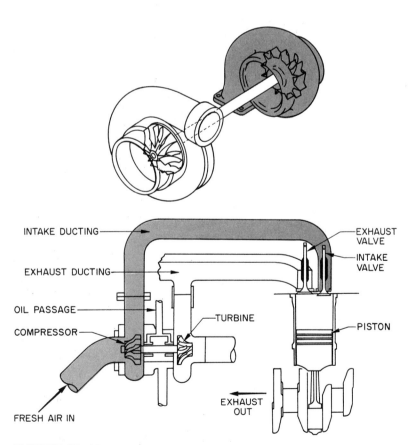

FIGURE 17–10.   A turbocharger uses the exhaust gases to turn an air pump or compressor. The compressor turbine forces extra air into the engine. *(Courtesy of Peugeot Motors of America, Inc.)*

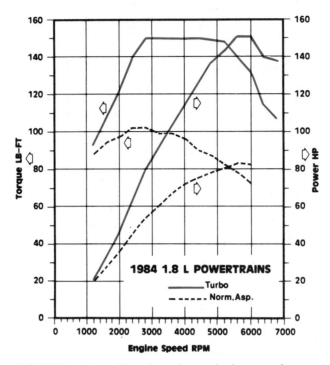

FIGURE 17–11. This chart shows the increase in power and torque when an engine is turbocharged. *(Courtesy of General Motors Product Service Training)*

engine can produce about 140 hp. *Figure 17–12* shows a turbocharger used on an automobile.

Turbocharged Engine Changes

A few internal changes are necessary on turbocharged engines. These include strengthening the pistons, using different piston rings, and making sure the bearings can withstand the extra load. However, turbocharged and nonturbocharged engines share basically the same compression ratios and emission control devices.

Turbocharger Ducting

The inlet ducting is changed when a turbocharger is used. See *Figure 17–13*. The exhaust gases pass through the exhaust manifold and into the exhaust turbine on the turbocharger. From the exhaust turbine, the exhaust gases are

FIGURE 17–12. A complete turbocharger unit for an automobile.

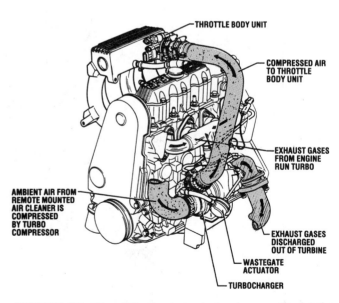

FIGURE 17–13. When using a turbocharger, the intake ducting will be different. Here the ducting is designed so the turbocharger can be located on the lower side of the engine. *(Courtesy of General Motors Product Service Training)*

sent through the exhaust system into the environment. As the compressor turbine turns, air is drawn through the air cleaner into the intake manifold. The pressurized air is sent through ducting to the throttle body unit. Here the air and fuel are mixed in the correct proportion.

Turbocharger Lag

One problem associated with a turbocharged engine is called *lag*. Lag is defined as the time it takes for the turbocharger to increase the power. It is the delay between a rapid throttle opening and the delivery of increased boost. There is a lag between the time the operator calls for the extra power and the actual power produced. This is because it takes time for the turbine speed to increase and produce the necessary power. Turbochargers on automobiles operate at about 10,000 RPM at idle. They run most efficiently at about 100,000 to 150,000 RPM under maximum boost. It takes time for the turbocharger to increase to this speed for best efficiency.

Turbocharger Wastegate

A wastegate is connected to the turbocharger. The wastegate is used to bypass the exhaust gases when the turbocharger boost is too high. Too much pressure or too high a boost may cause excessive detonation or engine damage, or may even destroy the engine. The wastegate causes the exhaust gases to bypass the exhaust turbine. When this happens, there is less power turning the compressor turbine; thus, the turbocharger action is reduced. *Figure 17–14* shows a typical wastegate flow diagram. When the wastegate is

closed, exhaust gases pass through the exhaust turbine. The engine is now being turbocharged. When the wastegate is opened, the exhaust gases bypass the turbine.

Wastegate Control

The wastegate is normally closed. It opens to bypass exhaust gases to prevent an overboost condition. The wastegate opens when pressure is applied to the *actuator*. The actuator is controlled by a wastegate control valve that is pulsed on and off by the ECM. See *Figure 17–15*. Under normal driving conditions, the control solenoid is energized 100% of the time. This means the exhaust gases pass through the exhaust turbine. During rapid acceleration, there may be an increase in boost pressure. As the boost increases, it is sensed by the MAP (manifold absolute pressure) sensor. The ECM now pulses the wastegate control valve above a boost of 15 psi. With the wastegate pulsing on and off, the manifold pressure decreases. If an overboost condition does occur, the ECM will also reduce the fuel delivery. *Figure 17–16* shows the wastegate actuator attached to the turbocharger.

Turbocharger Construction

Figure 17–17 shows a complete turbocharger. The shafts on the intake and exhaust turbines are connected together. The intake turbine is designed to act as a centrifugal compressor. The exhaust turbine acts as a fan, causing the shaft to turn. A housing surrounds both turbines. Flanges are attached to the housing for mounting.

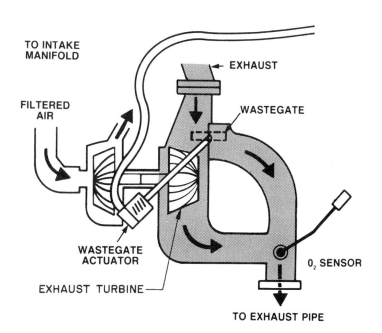

FIGURE 17–14. A wastegate is used to bypass the exhaust gases during times of high boost. *(Courtesy of General Motors Product Service Training)*

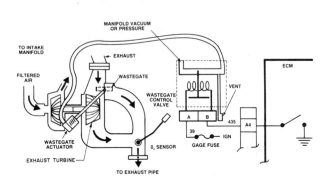

FIGURE 17–15. The wastegate is controlled by a wastegate actuator and manifold vacuum along with the electronic control module (ECM). *(Courtesy of General Motors Product Service Training)*

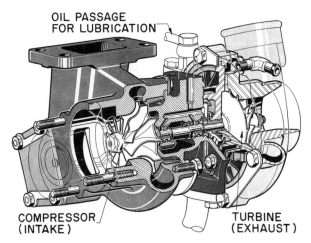

FIGURE 17–17. A cutaway view of a turbocharger. Note the location of the oil passages for lubrication. *(Courtesy of Peugeot Motors of America, Inc.)*

FIGURE 17–16. The wastegate is controlled by the wastegate actuator, which is located on the turbocharger.

Intercoolers

An *intercooler* is considered a heat exchanger. It exchanges heat from air to air and is often used on turbocharged engines. The intercooler is designed to remove the heat from the intake air charge. In effect, the intercooler is placed between the turbocharger and the combustion chamber. As it cools down the intake air, the air increases in density. This allows for more air and fuel molecules to be forced into the combustion chamber at a given boost pressure. The result is more power from the engine.

In operation, as the turbocharged air is pressurized, it increases in temperature. However, when this air is fed through the intercooler, fresh air from outside can cool the intake air charge down somewhat. *Figure 17–18* shows a typical example of an intercooler on an engine.

FIGURE 17–18. An intercooler can be used on turbocharged engines to reduce the temperature of the intake charge going into the combustion chamber. *(Courtesy of Motor Magazine)*

PROBLEM: Stopping the Turbocharger

What is the best way to shut off an engine with a turbocharger? Some say to just shut the engine down after any RPM, while others say to let the engine idle for a short period of time. Who is right?

SOLUTION:

Turbocharged engines should be shut down by first idling the engine for a short period of time. This procedure lets the turbocharger in the turbine slow down after being at high speed. During this slow-down time, the engine is still running and is thus sending oil to the turbocharger bearings. If the engine is shut down immediately after high-speed operation, the oil pressure will not be available at the turbocharger bearings, which may cause damage. This problem has become common enough for the marketing of "add-on" oilers that continue to circulate oil after the engine has been turned off.

17.3   EXHAUST SYSTEMS

The exhaust system collects the high-temperature gases from each combustion chamber and sends them to the rear of the vehicle to be *dispersed*. An exhaust manifold, heat riser, mufflers, and pipes are used to accomplish this. A catalytic converter is also used.

Exhaust Manifold

The exhaust manifold is connected to the cylinder head of the engine. The exhaust gases from the exhaust valves pass directly into the exhaust manifold. The exhaust manifold is made of cast iron that can withstand rapid increases in temperature and expansion. See *Figure 17–19*. Under full-

load conditions the exhaust manifold may be red hot, yet cold water can be splashed on the manifold while driving.

Volumetric efficiency was defined in an earlier chapter as the efficiency of air moving in and out of the engine. Exhaust manifolds can be designed to improve volumetric efficiency. This can be done by designing the manifolds with more or less restriction.

Several types of exhaust manifolds are used. Four-cylinder engines use either three- or four-runner manifolds. On three-runner manifolds, the two center cylinders feed one runner. Four-runner manifolds have a runner for each cylinder, and provide better volumetric efficiency. On six-cylinder engines, the exhaust manifold is either a four or six runner. Again, the four-runner manifold has two of the center cylinders feeding one runner. On V-6 and V-8 engines, there is an exhaust manifold on each side.

Headers may be used on certain racing engines. Headers are welded steel tubing used for exhaust. They are designed to allow a smooth, even flow of exhaust gases out of the engine. This smooth flow assures that each cylinder has equal exhaust back pressure. It also assures that each cylinder is completely cleaned of exhaust (scavenged). It has been found that headers improve only high-speed and load performance. They have a small effect on normal driving performance.

Heat Riser

Most engines manufactured have a type of heat riser attached to the exhaust manifold. The heat riser is a valve. Its purpose is to restrict the exhaust gases during starting and warm-up periods. This restriction tends to increase the engine to operating temperature more quickly by aiding in vaporization of fuel. On in-line engines, the heat riser also helps to vaporize the fuel during cold starting.

The heat riser is controlled by a flat spring. When the engine is cold, the spring and a counterweight cause a valve in the exhaust manifold to close. As the spring heats up, it relaxes. This causes the counterweight to open the valve and allow normal exhaust. *Figure 17–20* shows how the exhaust gases are routed to improve vaporization.

Vacuum-controlled Heat Valve

On V-8 engines, the manifold heat control valve is located on one bank of the exhaust manifold. When the engine is

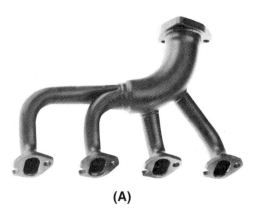

(A)

(B)

FIGURE 17–19.   The exhaust manifold is used to collect the exhaust gases and send them to the exhaust pipe. *(Part A courtesy of Masco Industries)*

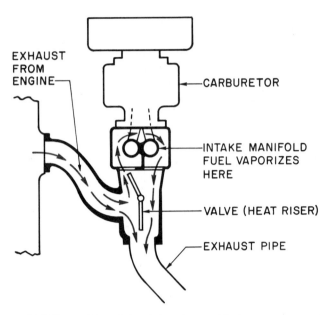

FIGURE 17–20. A heat riser is used to increase vaporization of fuel during starting. During cold starting, exhaust gases are routed internally to increase the temperature at the base of the carburetor.

cold, the heat control valve closes and directs some of the hot gases up through the intake manifold to the other side of the engine (crossover intake manifold). When the engine is warm, the valve opens and exhaust gases pass out each side normally. The valve is actuated by a vacuum-controlled motor. As the temperature of the engine increases, vacuum is removed from the motor and the heat valve opens. See *Figure 17–21*.

Exhaust Piping

The exhaust pipe is the connecting pipe between the exhaust manifold and the muffler or catalytic converter. Many types of exhaust piping are used on vehicles. The shape depends on the configuration of the engine, size of the engine, and undercarriage of the car. Exhaust piping can also be single or dual design.

Exhaust Muffler

The muffler is used to dampen the exhaust sound of the engine. Two types are primarily used. One uses a series of baffled chambers to reduce the sound. The other uses a per-

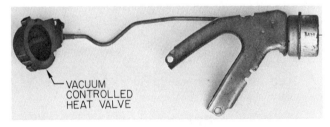

FIGURE 17–21. A vacuum-controlled heat valve keeps the riser closed until the engine coolant is hot. The vacuum is then removed, and the valve opens.

forated straight pipe enclosed in fiberglass and a shell. The straight pipe, which is also called a "glass pack," reduces exhaust back pressure, but it does not reduce the sound as much as the baffle type. Glass packs are illegal in most states because they alter emissions considerably.

Resonator

A resonator is another type of muffler. Most of the noise from an exhaust system is sound vibration. These vibrations cause louder noise. Resonators provide additional sound protection at critical points in the exhaust flow. They are used to absorb excessive sound vibration.

Tail Pipe

The tail pipe is a tube that is used to carry the exhaust gases from the muffler or resonator to the rear of the automobile. Many shapes and sizes are used, depending on the vehicle. The tail pipe is supported by a series of hangers that allow the exhaust system to flex and move during driving. Rubber connectors help isolate the vibration from the rest of the vehicle.

CAR CLINIC

PROBLEM: High Exhaust Back Pressure

A customer owns a car with a diesel engine. Recently an automotive technician suggested that the rough idle noticed by the driver could be caused by high exhaust back pressure. What are the effects of high exhaust back pressure on diesel engines?

SOLUTION:

High exhaust back pressure is developed by some type of restriction in the exhaust system. A rusted muffler, plugged tail pipe, or bent exhaust system may have caused the high back pressure. The symptoms on the engine of having high back pressure include:

1. Higher engine temperature

2. A decrease in power

3. Exhaust smoke becoming denser

4. Rough idle

5. Excessive carbon buildup on the valves, injectors, and pistons

6. Contaminated oil

If these symptoms appear, the exhaust system should be inspected and repaired or replaced.

Problems, Diagnosis and Service

PROBLEM: Dirty Air Cleaner

An engine is losing power slightly, and excessive black smoke is coming from the exhaust.

DIAGNOSIS

Excessive black smoke may indicate a dirty air cleaner. A dirty air cleaner restricts the amount of air that can enter the engine. Less air creates a very rich air-fuel ratio. The rich mixture produces excessive black smoke.

SERVICE

Use the following service procedures and suggestions when working with the air cleaner and intake ducting.

1. Replace dirty air cleaners at least every 10,000 miles or at tune-up time. More frequent replacement may be necessary in dusty conditions.
2. Remove the air cleaner cover by removing the wing nut or other housing.
3. Remove the air cleaner element.
4. Clean the air cleaner housing when replacing the filter. All dirt and grease should be removed from the housing using a solvent that is not flammable.
5. If you have a polyurethane filter around the outside of the air cleaner, use soap and water to clean the filter. Be sure to dry the polyurethane filter before installation.
6. Use a light coat of oil on the polyurethane filter. The light coat of oil will help to capture more of the dirt and dust particles that flow through the air cleaner element.
7. While the air cleaner is removed, inspect all intake ducting for cracks or leaks, and replace where necessary.

Any leak that occurs in the air inlet may also bring in dirty, unfiltered air. The dirty air can damage the engine.

8. Always use the correct filter suggested by the manufacturer.
9. Replace the filter in the same position as the old filter.
10. Tighten all wing nuts and other fasteners securely when replacing the air cleaner. Be careful not to tighten the wing nut too much as the carburetor or ductwork may be damaged.

PROBLEM: Damaged Fresh Air Duct

An engine is hard to start. In addition, there is hesitation and poor drivability.

DIAGNOSIS

The fresh air duct shown in *Figure 17–22* is designed to deliver cool air to the engine when the air under the hood is hot. Bringing too-hot air into the engine may cause starting or drivability problems such as vapor lock or hesitation.

SERVICE

1. Check the fresh air duct by unclamping and removing it. Bend the duct slightly to inspect between the bellows for tears or rips.
2. Make sure clamps are not damaged and that they seal the fresh-air duct securely.
3. If the duct appears to be torn or ripped, replace as necessary.

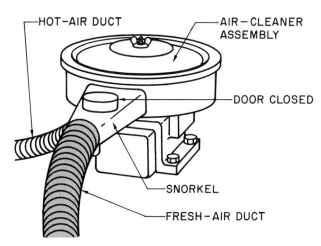

FIGURE 17–22. The fresh air duct should be checked for cracks. This is done by removing the duct and slightly bending it to observe cracks and damaged sections.

PROBLEM: Plugged Crossover Passage

An engine hesitates and has poor fuel economy.

DIAGNOSIS

These two problems suggest that the intake manifold crossover passage may be plugged. During normal operation, this crossover passage has air and fuel passing through it. The exhaust heat nearby aids in fuel vaporization. However, the passage can become plugged because of being too cool. This causes carbon to build up significantly in the passageway. To check for blockage:

1. Let the engine idle for several minutes.

2. Carefully touch the manifold crossover area with your finger.

3. If the manifold is relatively cool, the passage is probably plugged. If it is not plugged, the crossover area should be hot.

   CAUTION: Be careful not to touch the manifold too long as it may burn your fingers.

   Figure 17–23 shows an example of a service technician touching the crossover passage area.

SERVICE

If the passage is plugged, use the following general procedure to remove the intake manifold and clean the passageway. The exact procedure will depend on the engine and manufacturer.

1. Remove all linkages and electrical connections to the

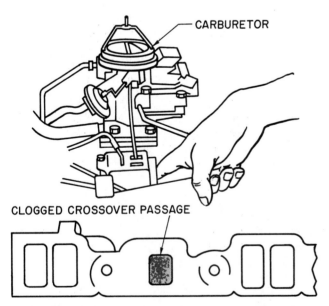

CLOGGED CROSSOVER PASSAGE

FIGURE 17–23. The exhaust crossover passage may become plugged. To check it, touch your finger to the intake manifold where the crossover passage is located. If it is cold (when the engine is hot), the passage is plugged.

carburetor or throttle body injection system. Mark and label accordingly.

2. Remove the bolts holding the intake manifold to the block.

3. Once removed, check for carbon buildup in the crossover passageway. Clean the carbon out of the passageway, using a wire brush or other suitable tool.

4. Remove and clean all gasket material on both the block and the intake manifold.

5. Replace all intake manifold gaskets with new ones.

6. Carefully place the intake manifold gaskets on the block.

7. Secure all bolts and torque to specifications.

8. Replace all linkage and wires.

PROBLEM: Exhaust Restriction

An engine has a loss of power, and an exhaust sound is heard near the engine.

DIAGNOSIS

Often a loss of power will occur when the exhaust is restricted. The restriction can be caused by having the vehicle hit a curb (or other object) causing the exhaust pipe to bend inward. The effect is that the exhaust is restricted and cannot be removed from the engine adequately. In addition, various cracks may form around and near the exhaust manifold. Depending on the type of exhaust manifold, either a weld may have broken or the exhaust manifold may have cracked. Check the following when checking for cracks and for restrictions in the exhaust system:

CAUTION: Never run an engine in an unventilated area. When in a building, always connect the exhaust pipe to the building exhaust system to remove all gases.

1. Check the exhaust manifold for cracks. Cracks generally occur around each runner on the exhaust manifold.

2. Check the heat riser for movement. The heat valve should be able to move freely. On some engines, the heat riser has rusted closed and may cause a restriction, longer warm-ups, and hesitation when cold.

3. Check the exhaust manifolds and exhaust pipes for any leaks or dents in the system that may restrict the flow of gases.

4. Exhaust restrictions can be found by checking the exhaust back pressure. Each manufacturer has a different procedure for checking exhaust back pressure. Generally, a gauge is placed on the exhaust system, near the exhaust manifold. Exhaust back pressure is then read. Typically, if the exhaust back pressure is above 2 psi, an exhaust restriction is indicated. Of course, the back pressure specifications will be different for each type of vehicle and manufacturer.

SERVICE

When servicing the exhaust system use the following general procedures. These procedures may vary depending on the vehicle and the manufacturer.

CAUTION: Never work on an exhaust system that is hot. Always wait until the engine has cooled to surrounding temperature.

1. To remove the exhaust manifold, remove the wire attached to the oxygen sensor, if used.

2. Remove the bolts holding the exhaust manifold to the cylinder head.

3. Remove the exhaust manifold.

4. Check the entire exhaust manifold for cracks.

5. Check the exhaust manifold gaskets for breaks.

6. If there is a crack in the manifold repair and replace as necessary.

7. Check the exhaust pipe for cracks, leaks, and dents.

8. If the exhaust pipe is damaged, replace as necessary.

9. Check and replace any exhaust or tail pipes that are broken or that leak.

10. Many exhaust systems are supported by free-hanging rubber mountings. This arrangement permits some movement of the exhaust system, but it does not permit transfer of noise into the passenger compartment. Annoying rattles and noise vibrations in the exhaust system are usually caused by misalignment of parts. Loosen all bolts and nuts. Then realign the exhaust system parts. Working from the front to the rear of the engine, tighten each part.

PROBLEM: Damaged Turbocharger

Various problems can occur with turbochargers. Some of the more common problems include:

1. Engine lacks power

2. Black exhaust smoke

3. Excessive oil consumption

4. Blue exhaust smoke

5. Noisy turbocharger

6. Oil leaks at compressor or turbine seals or at both.

DIAGNOSIS

Be aware of different sounds made by the turbocharger. Different noise levels during operation may signal air restrictions or dirt built up in the compressor housing. Some of the common diagnostic checks to determine turbocharger problems include:

1. Restricted air intake duct to turbocharger.

2. Air leak in duct from compressor to intake manifold.

3. Restricted exhaust system.

4. Air leak at intake manifold to engine mating surface.

5. Restricted turbocharger center housing.

6. Dirt on compressor wheel and/or diffuser vanes.

7. Damaged turbocharger.

8. Exhaust gas leak in turbine inlet exhaust manifold or exhaust manifold.

9. Restricted turbocharger oil drain line.

10. Restricted turbocharger center housing.

11. Restricted PCV system.

12. Incorrect wastegate boost pressure. Overboost can be caused by:
    a. A sticking wastegate or wastegate actuator
    b. A control valve stuck in the closed position
    c. A cut or pinched vacuum hose
    e. A fault within the computer

    Underboost can be caused by:
    a. The wastegate sticking open
    b. The control valve sticking open
    c. A faulty computer (ECM) unit

SERVICE

CAUTION: A turbocharged engine has exhaust pipes located high in the engine compartment. Care must be taken to avoid accidental contact with hot exhaust pipes to avoid injury.

Various service procedures are used to correct problems dealing with turbochargers. Because of the detail and complexity of these procedures, only general service procedures are listed here.

1. The wastegate-boost pressure test is used to determine the amount of boost pressure created under acceleration conditions. Follow the manufacturer's recommended procedure for testing wastegate-boost pressure. Generally, the wastegate control valve can be checked by using a vacuum tester. For example, the actuator should begin to move at 4 psi and obtain full travel at 15 psi. Readings will be determined by manufacturer recommendations.

2. Inspecting the turbocharger internal condition.
    a. Check for mechanical movement of the wastegate.
    b. Spin the compressor wheel, checking for binding, drags, and other poor conditions.
    c. Inspect internal housing for sludge and dirt and clean accordingly.
    d. Inspect compressor oil seal for damage or leakage. Replace as necessary.

e. Check turbocharger main shaft for radial and axial clearances as described in the service manuals.
f. Check the journal bearing and thrust bearing clearances as described in the service manuals. See *Figure 17–24*.
g. Check the external condition of the compressor and turbine blades as shown in *Figure 17–25*. Checks should be made for cracked, broken, or bent blades. Replace turbine or compressor blades as necessary.

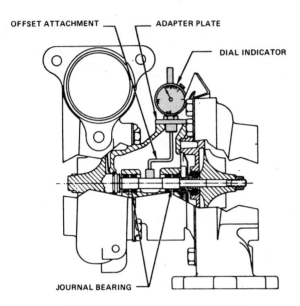

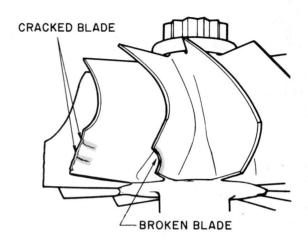

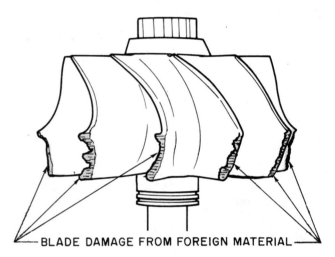

CHECKING JOURNAL BEARING

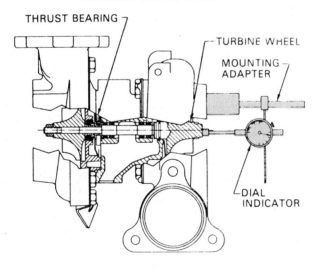

CHECKING THRUST BEARING

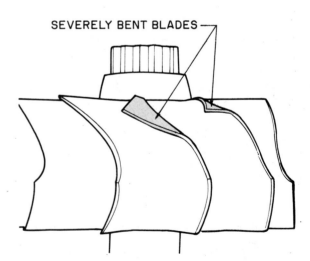

FIGURE 17–24. Both the journal bearing and thrust bearing clearances on the turbocharger should be checked. *(Courtesy of Motor Publications, Auto Tune-up and Electronics Manual)*

FIGURE 17–25. When inspecting turbochargers, always check for cracked, broken, or bent turbine and/or compressor blades. *(Courtesy of Motor Publications, Auto Tune-up and Electronics Manual)*

Linkage to Automotive History

OIL BATH AIR CLEANERS

A great deal of research has been done to perfect the type and method of air filtration on automotive engines. Years ago, oil bath air cleaners were used. A typical oil bath air cleaner used on vehicles built in the 1940s and early 1950s is shown. In operation, as the air was drawn through the air cleaner, it was forced to flow through a pool of oil. The dirt particles were removed in two ways. First, the dirty air was forced to make a 180 degree turn at the oil pool. The heavier dirt particles were thrown into the oil by centrifugal force at this point. Secondly, the dirt particles had a tendency to stick to the oil vapors inside the wire mesh, located above the oil pool. With these two stages of filtration, old oil bath air cleaners were able to filter about 94–96% of the dirt from the air. Today's dry-type air filters are even more efficient. They filter close to 99% of the dirt from the air.

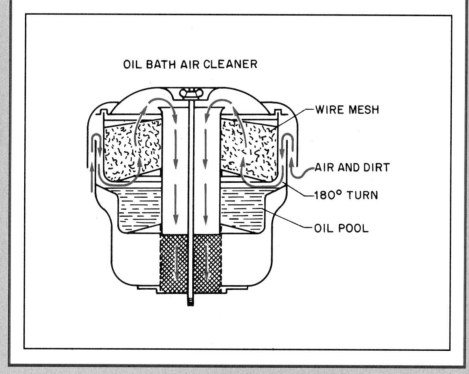

OIL BATH AIR CLEANER

WIRE MESH
AIR AND DIRT
180° TURN
OIL POOL

SERVICE MANUAL CONNECTION

There are many important specifications to keep in mind when working with injection systems. To identify the specifications for your engine, you will need to know the vehicle identification number (VIN) of the vehicle, the type and year of the vehicle, and the type of engine. Although they may be titled differently, some of the more common air intake and exhaust system specifications (not all) found in service manuals are listed below. Note that these specifications are typical examples. Each vehicle and engine may have different specifications.

Common Specification	Typical Example
Exhaust back pressure	2 psi
Turbocharger bearing axial clearance	0.001–0.003 in.
Turbocharger bearing radial clearance	0.003–0.006 in.
Turbocharger to exhaust manifold torque	16–19 lb-ft
Turbocharger RPM	120,000
Wastegate boost pressure	9 psi

In addition, the service manual will give specific directions for various service and testing procedures. Some of the more common procedures include:

- Turbocharger assembly/replace

- Turbocharger internal inspection

- Turbocharger wastegate-boost pressure test

- Wastegate actuator replace

SUMMARY

This chapter dealt with the design and components of the air intake and exhaust systems. It included study in air filters, intake ducting, turbochargers, wastegates, exhaust manifolds, and heat risers.

Air filters are designed to keep dirt and other contaminants out of the engine. To do this, dry-type air filters can be used. Dry-type filters are highly efficient, but they cannot be cleaned. They must be replaced. There are several types of dry filters, including the paper-type and the polyurethane type.

The intake ducting is used to transfer the air from outside the engine to the filter and finally to the engine. Many designs are used, depending on the configuration of the engine and air cleaner. Some intake ducting also includes a resonator to reduce the intake noise.

The intake manifold is used to transfer the air and/or fuel from the air cleaner to the intake valve. Several designs are used. The runner on the intake manifold is the port that carries the flow of air and/or fuel. Manifolds can also be wet or dry. Wet manifolds have coolant passing through them.

Turbochargers are being used more on smaller engines. In order to understand turbocharging, supercharging must first be defined. Supercharging forces air into the cylinder. The engine is not naturally aspirated. A turbocharger supercharges an engine by using hot exhaust gases to turn a compressor turbine. The compressor turbine compresses the air to get a boost in intake pressure.

Turbocharged engines must use stronger pistons, different rings, and bearings that can withstand the extra load. Ducting on turbocharged engines is also different from that on naturally aspirated engines.

The turbocharger wastegate is used to open a bypass tube. This tube is used so that if the boost pressure gets too high, the exhaust gases will bypass the turbocharger turbine. This gives the turbocharger protection under rapid acceleration. The wastegate is controlled in conjunction with the ECM.

The exhaust system is used to collect and carry the exhaust gases to the rear of the vehicle to be dispersed. The exhaust manifold collects the exhaust from each cylinder. The exhaust pipe transfers the gases to the catalytic converter and muffler. The tail pipe transfers the exhaust gases from the muffler to the atmosphere near the rear of the vehicle.

TERMS TO KNOW

Can you explain each of the following terms? Review the chapter until you can use each term correctly.

Airborne	Compressor
Aftermarket	Boost
Turbocharged	Lag
Resonator	Actuator
Runner	Intercooler
Naturally aspirated	Disperse
Supercharging	Header
Turbine	

REVIEW QUESTIONS

Multiple Choice

1. If dirt gets into the engine, the engine life may be:
   a. Increased by 1/2
   b. Decreased by 1/3
   c. Affected very little — nothing to worry about
   d. Increased by 1/3
   e. None of the above

2. A dirty air cleaner will produce:
   a. White exhaust smoke
   b. More power in the engine
   c. Black smoke
   d. A rich mixture
   e. Both c and d

3. One of the disadvantages of a paper-type air cleaner is that:
   a. It must be cleaned with oil
   b. It must be replaced and cannot be cleaned
   c. It usually doesn't fit correctly
   d. It must be replaced every 5,000 miles
   e. It cannot be removed

4. Which of the following is a type of dry air cleaner?
   a. Paper
   b. Polyurethane
   c. Runner
   d. Timed
   e. Both a and b

5. Which type of air cleaner can be cleaned?
   a. Paper
   b. Polyurethane
   c. Runner
   d. Timed
   e. Both a and b

6. Which of the following is used primarily to reduce noise on the intake system?
   a. Intake manifold
   b. Intake ducting
   c. Intake resonator
   d. Intake filter
   e. Catalytic converter

7. How many runners may an intake manifold for a four-cylinder engine have?
   a. One
   b. Two
   c. Three
   d. Four
   e. Both b and d

8. An engine that uses atmospheric pressure to force the air into the engine is called a _____ engine.
   a. Supercharged
   b. Turbocharged
   c. Naturally aspirated
   d. Blown
   e. None of the above

9. Which type of component uses exhaust gases to turn a turbine that forces air into the cylinder?
   a. Blower
   b. Wastegate
   c. Turbocharger
   d. Intake manifold
   e. Runner

10. The wastegate bypasses exhaust gases when:
    a. Turbine speed is low
    b. Turbine speed is high
    c. Too much fuel is added
    d. Too much boost pressure is sensed by the MAP
    e. The load is removed

11. On a turbocharged engine:
    a. The pistons must be strengthened
    b. The rings must be strengthened
    c. The bearings must be strengthened
    d. All of the above
    e. None of the above

12. On a turbocharged engine, the delay between a rapid throttle opening and the delivery of boost is called:
    a. Turbocharger efficiency
    b. Volumetric efficiency
    c. Turbocharger lag
    d. Wastegate control
    e. Speed control

13. Steel tubes of the same length that are welded into an exhaust manifold are called:
    a. Turbocharging
    b. Headers
    c. Exhaust resonators
    d. All of the above
    e. None of the above

14. Which device is used to block off the flow of exhaust gases to improve vaporization during cold starting?
    a. Wastegate
    b. Blower
    c. Turbocharger
    d. Intake actuator
    e. Heat riser

15. After approximately how many miles should the air cleaner be replaced (under normal driving conditions)?
    a. 4,000
    b. 10,000
    c. 50,000
    d. 80,000
    e. 100,000

The following questions are similar in format to ASE (Automotive Service Excellence) test questions.

16. Technician A says that an exhaust restriction can be checked by testing for exhaust back pressure. Technician B says that an exhaust restriction can be checked by observing the timing. Who is right?
    a. A only
    b. B only
    c. Both A and B
    d. Neither A nor B

17. Technician A says that all air cleaners can be cleaned with gas and replaced. Technician B says that there are no air cleaners on older or newer vehicles that can be cleaned. Who is right?
    a. A only
    b. B only
    c. Both A and B
    d. Neither A nor B

18. A turbocharged engine is exhausting black smoke. Technician A says it could be caused by an air restriction. Technician B says it could be caused by a bad ECM (electronic control module). Who is right?
    a. A only
    b. B only
    c. Both A and B
    d. Neither A nor B

19. An engine is lacking power. Technician A says it could be caused by a dirty air cleaner. Technician B says it could be caused by a restriction in the air intake system. Who is right?
    a. A only
    b. B only
    c. Both A and B
    d. Neither A nor B

20. An engine with a turbocharger is lacking power. Technician A says the problem may be a broken compressor blade. Technician B says the problem may be dirt in the compressor. Who is correct?
    a. A only
    b. B only
    c. Both A and B
    d. Neither A nor B

21. An engine with a turbocharger needs to be inspected. Technician A says that the radial clearances should be checked on the main shaft. Technician B says that axial clearances should be checked on the main shaft. Who is correct?
    a. A only
    b. B only
    c. Both A and B
    d. Neither A nor B

22. Technician A says the wastegate operation can be checked with a dial indicator. Technician B says it can be checked with a micrometer. Who is correct?
    a. A only
    b. B only
    c. Both A and B
    d. Neither A nor B

23. Technician A says that a turbocharger with a broken compressor blade will not affect engine performance. Technician B says that a turbocharger with a bent blade need not be replaced. Who is correct?
    a. A only
    b. B only
    c. Both A and B
    d. Neither A nor B

Essay

24. Describe the purpose and operation of a turbocharger.

25. What is the difference between a wet- and dry-type manifold?

26. What is the definition of supercharging?

27. What is the purpose and operation of a wastegate on a turbocharger?

28. What is the purpose of the vacuum-controlled heat valve?

Short Answer

29. An engine with a turbocharger can produce increased _____ and _____.

30. An intercooler is considered an _____ to _____ heat exchanger.

31. When the exhaust is producing black smoke, this may be an indication of a dirty _____.

32. If the intake manifold crossover passage is plugged, it will cause the engine to _____.

33. An exhaust restriction can be found by checking and measuring the exhaust _____.

ELECTRICAL
ENGINE SYSTEMS

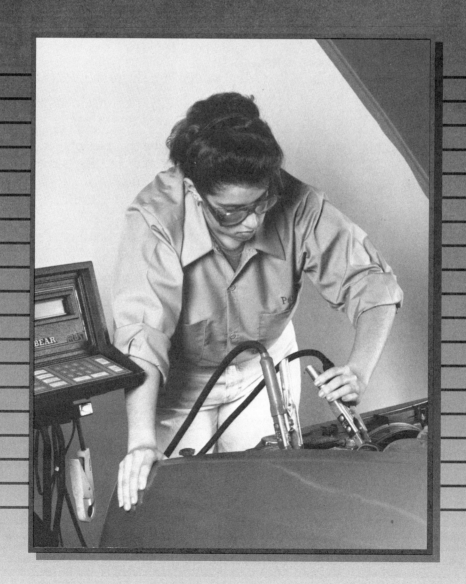

CHAPTER 18

Electrical and Computer Principles

INTRODUCTION   Electricity, electronics, and computers are being used more and more to control the automobile. The electronic control module (ECM), the electronic engine control (EEC IV) and the oxygen feedback system, discussed in Chapter 15 are examples of electronics and computers used in the automobile. In addition, storage batteries, ignition systems, charging systems, and starting systems use electricity to operate. Therefore, the study of automotive technology must include a discussion of electrical and computer principles. This chapter will help you understand electricity, electronics, the use of computers, and how they are applied to automotive systems.

OBJECTIVES   After reading this chapter, you should be able to:

- Define electricity in terms of voltage, amperage, and resistance.

- Calculate both Ohm's and Watt's laws.

- Define voltage drop, simple circuits, and symbols.

- Analyze series, parallel, and series-parallel circuits.

- Analyze electrical schematics.

- Apply magnetism principles to electro-magnetic induction.

- Explain the principles of a simple generator.

- Identify the fundamentals of basic electronics.

- Describe the uses of diodes, transistors, integrated circuits, and microprocessors in the automobile.

- Identify basic computer communications terminology.

18.1   INTRODUCTION TO ELECTRICITY

Atomic Structure

The heart of all information concerning electricity is in the study of *atoms* and atomic structure. Everything — water, trees, buildings — is made up of atoms. They are very small, about a millionth of an inch across. There are millions of atoms in a single breath of air.

The structure of atoms can be illustrated as shown in *Figure 18–1*. Each atom has at its center a nucleus that contains both *protons* and neutrons. The nucleus is the major part of the atom. Protons are said to carry a positive charge (+). Neutrons carry no charge and are not considered in the study of electricity. Also present in the atom are *electrons*, which orbit around the nucleus. Electrons are very light in comparison to the nucleus. They carry a negative charge (–).

There is an attraction between the negative electrons and the positive protons. The attractive force and the centrifugal forces cause the electron to orbit the nucleus or protons in the center, *Figure 18–2*.

The number of electrons in all orbits and the number of protons in the nucleus will try to remain equal. If they are equal, the atom is said to be balanced or neutral. *Figure 18–3* shows several atoms for comparison.

Valence Ring

In the study of electricity, we are concerned only with the electrons in the outer orbit. The outer orbit of the atom is called the *valence ring*. It holds the outermost electrons. Actually, electrons in the valence ring can easily be added or removed. Generally, an atom with several electrons missing will try to gain or capture other electrons. This will make the

Some of the information in this chapter can help you prepare for the National Institute for Automotive Service Excellence (ASE) certification tests. The tests most directly related to this chapter are entitled

ENGINE REPAIR (TEST A1) AND ELECTRICAL SYSTEMS (TEST A6).

The content areas that closely parallel this chapter are

IGNITION SYSTEM DIAGNOSIS AND REPAIR,BATTERY AND STARTING SYSTEM DIAGNOSIS AND REPAIR, GENERAL ELECTRICAL SYSTEM DIAGNOSIS, BATTERY DIAGNOSIS AND SERVICE,STARTING SYSTEM DIAGNOSIS AND REPAIR, AND CHARGING SYSTEM DIAGNOSIS AND REPAIR.

atom balanced. Also, if an atom has an excess amount of electrons in the valence ring, it may try to get rid of these electrons. This will also help balance the atom.

Certain materials can lose or gain electrons rather easily. This depends upon the number of electrons needed in the valence ring to balance the atom. If an atom loses electrons easily, the material is called a good *conductor*. If the atom cannot lose electrons easily, the material is called a good *insulator*. Insulators and conductors can be defined as:

1. Three or fewer electrons — conductor

2. Five or more electrons — insulator

3. Four electrons — semiconductor

Materials that have four electrons in the outer orbit can be considered either a conductor or an insulator. These materials are called *semiconductors*. They are used in solid-state components, which will be discussed later in this chapter.

Electricity Defined

Electricity can be defined as the movement of electrons from atom to atom. This can happen only in a conductor. An example is shown in *Figure 18–4*. Copper atoms are shown with only the valence ring. Copper is a good conductor. If an excess amount of positive charges, or protons, is placed

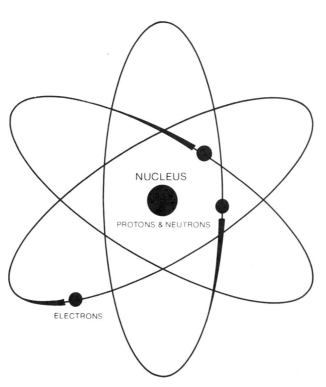

FIGURE 18–1.   An atom with protons, neutrons, and electrons.

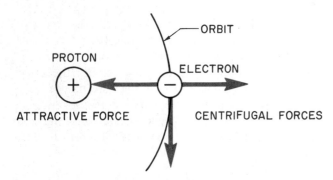

FIGURE 18–2. When an attractive force equals the centrifugal force, the electron will orbit around the proton.

COMPARISON OF DIFFERENT ATOMS

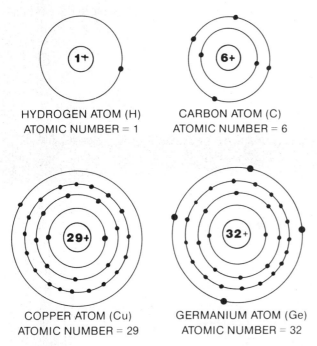

HYDROGEN ATOM (H)
ATOMIC NUMBER = 1

CARBON ATOM (C)
ATOMIC NUMBER = 6

COPPER ATOM (Cu)
ATOMIC NUMBER = 29

GERMANIUM ATOM (Ge)
ATOMIC NUMBER = 32

FIGURE 18–3. Different atoms have different numbers of protons and electrons. Hydrogen is the simplest atom, while germanium is much more complex.

on the left, one of the positive atoms will try to pull the outer electron away from the copper atom on the far left.

This action will make the far left copper atom slightly positively charged. There is one more proton than electron in the total atom. This positively charged atom will then pull an electron from the one on its right side. This atom also becomes positively charged. In total, when this action continues to happen, electrons will be flowing from the right to the left. Remember, there must be an abundant amount of protons on the left and electrons on the right.

Electron Theory

In Figure 18–4 the electrons were flowing from a negative point to a positive point. When electricity is defined this way, it is called the *electron theory*. This means that electricity will flow from a negative point to a more positive point. This is one method of defining the direction of electrical flow.

Conventional Theory

Electricity can be defined another way. Electricity can be defined as flow from a positive point to a more negative point. This is called the *conventional theory*. For example, referring to Figure 18–4, while negative charges are flowing from right to left, positive charges are flowing from left to right. This means that electrical charges could also flow from positive to negative. In the automotive field, this method has been used to define the direction of electrical flow. It is only important to be consistent with the method you choose. If electron theory is used, stay with electron theory. If conventional theory is used, stay with conventional theory.

Amperage Defined

The measurement of the amount of electrons flowing from a negative point to a positive point in a given time period is called *amperage*. This term is also called *current*. Amperage, or current, is analogous to water flowing through a pipe (electrons flowing through a wire). Amperage is defined as the amount of electrons passing any given point in the cir-

ELECTRON MOVEMENT IN A COPPER WIRE

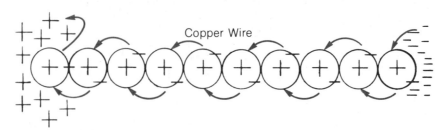

FIGURE 18–4. When (+) charges are placed on one end of a copper wire and (–) charges are placed on the other end, electrons will move through the wire. This is called the flow of electrons, or electricity.

cuit in one second. The letter used to identify amperage, or current, is *I*. This stands for *I*ntensity of current flow. It is measured in units called amperes.

Voltage Defined

Voltage is defined as the push or force used to move the electrons. Referring to Figure 18–4, the difference between the positive and negative charges is called voltage. This difference in charges has the ability to move electrons through the wire. *Figure 18–5* illustrates the definition of voltage.

Other terms are used to describe voltage. They include potential difference, electromotive force (emf), and pressure. When the term *voltage* is compared to a water system, water pressure is used to push water through a pipe. (Voltage is used to push electrons through a wire.) Voltage is represented by the letter *E*, which stands for *E*lectromotive force, and is measured in units called volts.

Resistance Defined

The third component in electricity is called *resistance*. Resistance is defined as opposition to current flow. Because of their atomic structure, certain materials offer poor conductivity. This will slow down the electrons. Actually, as the electrons move through a wire, they bump into other atoms in the conductor. As this occurs, the material heats up and causes even more resistance.

Various types and values of resistors are designed to control the flow of electrons. This depends upon how much current is needed to flow through a circuit. Resistance is identified by the letter *R*, which stands for *R*esistance to electron flow. It is measured in units called ohms. When comparing resistance to a water circuit, flow valves and faucets control or restrict water flow. (Resistance in an electrical circuit controls or restricts electron flow.)

Ohm's Law

The three electrical components just described interact with each other. For example, if the resistance decreases and the voltage remains the same, the amperage will increase. If the resistance stays the same and the voltage increases, the amperage will also increase. These relationships can be identified by a formula called *Ohm's Law*. Ohm's Law is a mathematical formula that shows how voltage, amperage, and resistance work together. The triangle shown in *Figure 18–6* is a graphical way of showing this formula. It shows that if two electrical components are known, the third can easily be found.

For example, if resistance (R) and voltage (E) are known, cover the unknown (I) to see the formula. The amperage can be found by dividing the resistance into the voltage. If the amperage and resistance are known, voltage can be found by multiplying the amperage by the resistance. In actual practice, many electrical circuits are designed so that control of the current, or amperage, can be obtained by changing the voltage or resistance. In addition, when using the ECM (electronic control module), a certain resistance will set up a voltage signal to be sent to the ECM.

Watt's Law

Wattage is another term used to help analyze electrical circuits. It is measured using *Watt's Law*. Wattage is a measure of the power (P) used in the circuit. Wattage is a measure of the total electrical work being done per unit of time. When voltage (E) is multiplied by amperage (I), the result is wattage (P). Wattage, which is a measure of electrical power, may also be referred to as kilowatts (kW). One thousand watts equals 1 kilowatt. *Figure 18–7* illustrates the relationship between voltage, amperage, and wattage. If the amperage and wattage are known, cover the voltage to see the formula. If the voltage and wattage are known, amperage can be calculated.

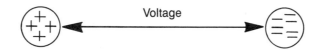

FIGURE 18–5. When there is a difference in charges from one side of a conductor to another, the difference is called voltage.

OHM'S LAW
Voltage (E) = Amperage (I) × Resistance (R)

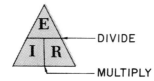

FIGURE 18–6. Ohm's Law states that Voltage (E) = Amperage (I) × Resistance (R).

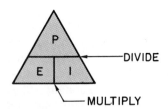

FIGURE 18–7. Watt's Law states that Wattage (P) = Voltage (E) × Amperage (I).

CAR CLINIC

PROBLEM: Fan Runs After Engine Turns Off

A customer complains that every time the engine is shut off, a small fan continues to run under the hood. Is there a problem with the wiring, or is the fan designed to shut off after the engine cools?

SOLUTION:

Many manufacturers have added electrical fans to smaller and intermediate-sized cars to keep the fuel from boiling, possibly causing vapor lock. Normally, these fans are designed to run up to 10 minutes after a hot vehicle has been shut off.

18.2 BASIC CIRCUITS

Circuits are used to show the operation of electrical components in the electrical systems in the automobile. A circuit normally consists of several components. First, a power source is needed to provide the necessary voltage. Second, wire is needed to provide a path for the flow of electrons. Third, a load, which can be any resistance, is needed. Lights, radios, starter motors, spark plugs, CCC sensors, batteries, and wiper motors are all examples of loads. The load provides the resistance in the circuit.

Simple Circuit

The simplest circuit consists of a power source (a battery), a single unit or load to be operated (a light), and the connecting wires. *Figure 18–8* shows a simple circuit. Note that the wires must be connected to complete the circuit. In this case, electricity flows from the positive terminal on the battery, through the wire to the light, and back to the negative terminal of the battery.

Voltage Drop

When testing and troubleshooting an electrical circuit, the technician usually measures *voltage drop*. Voltage must

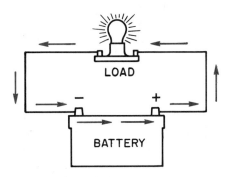

FIGURE 18–8. A simple circuit shows amperage flowing through the light to make it operate.

be present for amperage to flow through a resistor. Voltage is dropped across each resistor that it pushes amperage through. To determine the voltage drop across any resistor, simply use Ohm's Law. In this case, however, use only the voltage, amperage, and resistance at that particular resistor. Voltage drop at any resistor is shown as:

$$\text{Voltage Drop} = \text{Resistance} \times \text{Amperage} \ (I \times R)$$
$$\text{(at any one resistor)}$$

Voltage drop can be measured by using a voltmeter. Usually, the voltmeter leads are placed across the component to be checked or across the component to ground.

Opens, Shorts, and Grounds

Electrical systems may develop an *open, shorted,* or *grounded circuit*. Each of these conditions will render the circuit ineffective.

An open circuit is one that has a break in the connection. Refer to *Figure 18–9*. This is called a break in continuity. If the circuit is open, there is not a complete path for the current to flow through. An open circuit acts the same as if the circuit had a switch in the open position. Voltage drop across an open circuit is always the same as the source, or maximum voltage.

A shorted circuit is one that allows electricity to flow past part of the normal load. An example of this is a shorted coil. See *Figure 18–10*. The internal windings are usually insulated from each other. However, if the insulation breaks and allows the windings to touch each other, part of the coil will

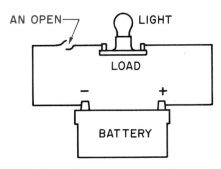

FIGURE 18–9. An open in the circuit will stop all current from flowing through the circuit.

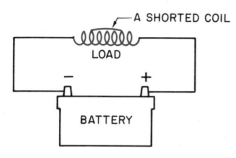

FIGURE 18–10.   A shorted circuit bypasses part of the load.

be bypassed. Any load can be partially or fully bypassed by having a shorted circuit. If a load is fully bypassed, the voltage dropped across the load will be zero.

A grounded circuit is a condition that allows current to return to the battery before it has reached its intended destination. An example is a grounded tail light. See *Figure 18–11*. If a wire leading to the light were broken and touching the frame, the electricity would be grounded back to the battery. Grounded circuits can cause excessive current to be drained from the battery.

Series Circuit

A *series circuit* consists of two or more resistors connected to a voltage source with only one path for the electrons to follow. An example is shown in *Figure 18–12*. The series circuit has two resistors placed in the path of the electrons. The resistors are shown as R_1 and R_2. (The jagged line is a

symbol used to represent a resistor.) All of the amperage that comes out of the positive side of the battery must go through each resistor, then back to the negative side of the battery. In a series circuit, the resistors are added together to get the total resistance (R total).

Series circuits are characterized by the following facts:

1. The resistance is always additive. R total is equal to $R_1 + R_2 + R_3$, and so on.

2. The amperage through each resistor is the same. Amperage is the same throughout the circuit.

3. The voltage drop across each resistor will be different if the resistance values are different.

4. The sum of the voltage drops of all the resistors equals the source voltage.

Parallel Circuit

Parallel circuits provide two or more paths for the current to flow through. Each path has separate resistors and operates independently from the other parallel paths. In a parallel circuit, amperage can flow through more than one resistor at a time. An example of a parallel circuit is shown in *Figure 18–13*. Note that if one branch of the circuit breaks or has an open circuit, the remaining resistors can still operate. The resistance in a parallel circuit is calculated by the formula

$$R \text{ total } = \frac{1}{1/R_1 + 1/R_2 + 1/R_3 + 1/R_4, \text{ etc.}}$$

Total resistance in a parallel circuit will always be less than the resistance of the smallest resistor. Most circuits on the automobile are parallel circuits. If more resistors are added to the circuit, the total resistance will decrease. A parallel circuit can be characterized by the following:

1. The total resistance is less than the resistance of the lowest resistor.

2. The amperage flowing through the resistors is different for each if the resistance values are different.

3. The voltage drop across each resistor is the same. This is also the source voltage.

4. The sum of the separate amperages in each branch equals the total amperage in the circuit.

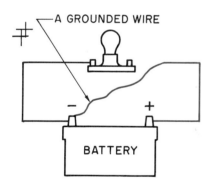

FIGURE 18–11.   A grounded wire can cause excessive drain on the battery.

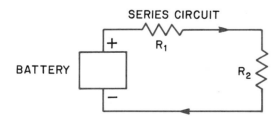

FIGURE 18–12.   A series circuit with two resistors for current to flow through.

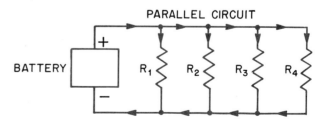

FIGURE 18–13.   A parallel circuit showing there is more than one path for the current to follow.

Series-Parallel Circuit

A series-parallel circuit is designed so that both series and parallel combinations exist within the same circuit. **Figure 18–14** shows four resistors connected in a series-parallel circuit. To calculate total resistance in this circuit, first calculate the parallel portions, then add the result to the series portions of the circuit. Total current flow will be determined by the total resistance and the total source voltage.

Ground Symbol

A ground symbol is sometimes used when analyzing a circuit. This means that the circuit is connected to the steel structure of the vehicle. The ground symbol is shown in **Figure 18–15**. The symbol indicates that the electricity is returning to the battery through the frame of the vehicle. Any steel structure of the vehicle can actually act as the wire that returns electricity to the battery. This could include the body sheet metal, frame, engine block, or transmission case.

Electrical Symbols

A more complete listing of symbols used in automotive circuits can be found in **Figure 18–16**. Many symbols are used in the wiring diagrams in this textbook and in the automotive repair manuals. It is important to become familiar with these symbols in order to analyze more involved circuits.

Testing Electrical Circuits

Once an electrical circuit is understood, it can be easily tested for faulty components, opens, grounds, shorts, and other problems. Electrical circuits are commonly tested using a voltmeter, an ohmmeter, or an ammeter.

When using a *voltmeter* keep these rules in mind:

■ Always ground the negative lead and probe the circuit with the positive lead.

■ When connecting the test lead the power should be off. After connecting the leads, turn the power on.

■ Voltmeters are always connected in parallel with the circuit.

■ Use a voltmeter when testing for an open circuit or failed component.

■ Use a digital volt-ohmmeter with a 10-megohm or higher impedance rating when testing a circuit that has solid-state components.

When using an *ohmmeter* keep these rules in mind:

■ Always select the highest range before making your ohmmeter check.

■ When checking solid-state components always use a digital ohmmeter with a 10-megohm impedance rating to prevent damage to the components.

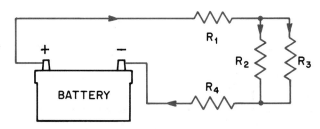

FIGURE 18–14. A series-parallel circuit. Resistors R_2 and R_3 are in parallel. The total resistance of R_2 and R_3 in parallel is added to R_1 and R_4, which are in series with R_2 and R_3.

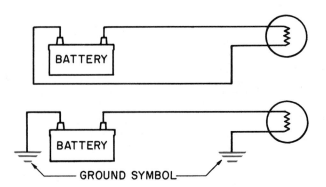

FIGURE 18–15. Ground symbols are used to make a circuit drawing easier to read.

■ Either the component being checked should be removed from the circuit, or that part of the circuit should be disconnected.

When using an *ammeter* keep these rules in mind:

■ Always start with the highest scale on the ammeter and work down until you are on the correct scale.

■ Always connect the ammeter in series with the circuit.

AUTOMOTIVE ELECTRICAL SYMBOLS			
SYMBOL	**REPRESENTS**	**SYMBOL**	**REPRESENTS**
(ALT)	ALTERNATOR	HORN	HORN
(A)	AMMETER		LAMP OR BULB (PREFERRED)
	BATTERY – ONE CELL		LAMP OR BULB (ACCEPTABLE)
	BATTERY – MULTICELL	(MOT)	MOTOR – ELECTRIC
12 V	THE LONG LINE IS ALWAYS POSITIVE POLARITY	—	NEGATIVE
BAT	BATTERY – VOLTAGE BOX	+	POSITIVE
	BIMETAL STRIP		RELAY
	CABLE – CONNECTED		RESISTOR
	CABLE – NOT CONNECTED		RESISTOR – VARIABLE
	CAPACITOR	IDLE STOP	SOLENOID – IDLE STOP
	CIRCUIT BREAKER	B SOL STARTING MOTOR	STARTING MOTOR
	CONNECTOR – FEMALE CONTACT		
	CONNECTOR – MALE CONTACT		
	CONNECTORS – SEPARABLE – ENGAGED		SWITCH – SINGLE THROW
	DIODE		SWITCH – DOUBLE THROW
H E I	DISTRIBUTOR	(TACH)	TACHOMETER
	FUSE		TERMINATION
(FUEL)	GAUGE – FUEL	(V)	VOLTMETER
(TEMP)	GAUGE – TEMPERATURE	or	WINDING – INDUCTOR
	GROUND – CHASSIS FRAME (PREFERRED)		
	GROUND – CHASSIS FRAME (ACCEPTABLE)		

FIGURE 18–16. Various symbols used in electrical circuits.

The Electrical Schematic

The electrical schematic is the service technician's key to solving many of the electrical problems in circuits. A schematic can be considered a road map used to follow the current through the circuit. The schematic shows the symbols used to indicate a junction, splice, a male or female connector, components, fusible links, fuses, and any other elements in the circuit. It tells the service technician how current gets from one point to another, through switches, fuses, and so on.

Remember that a schematic is not drawn to scale. For example, a 4-foot length of wire in the vehicle may be represented by a 2-inch line on the schematic. Also, the actual location and physical appearance of the components are not the same as in the vehicle. In most cases, schematics are read from the top down or from left to right. *Figure 18–17* shows one of two schematics used to analyze an antilock brake system. This schematic uses some of the following symbols.

- Wires are color-coded (for example, BK/GN means black with green strip).

- A number in front of the color shows the metric size of the wire.

- Relays such as the ABS relay and the ABS control module are boxed in.

- Test connector points are shown for reference.

- Fuses are enclosed in a dotted box.

- Certain wires have arrows to show direction of electricity.

- Ground points are shown by G300, G100, etc.

- Connector points are shown by C100, C329, etc.

- In-line splices are shown by S316, S318, etc.

A more complete listing of symbols used on schematics is shown in *Figure 18–18*.

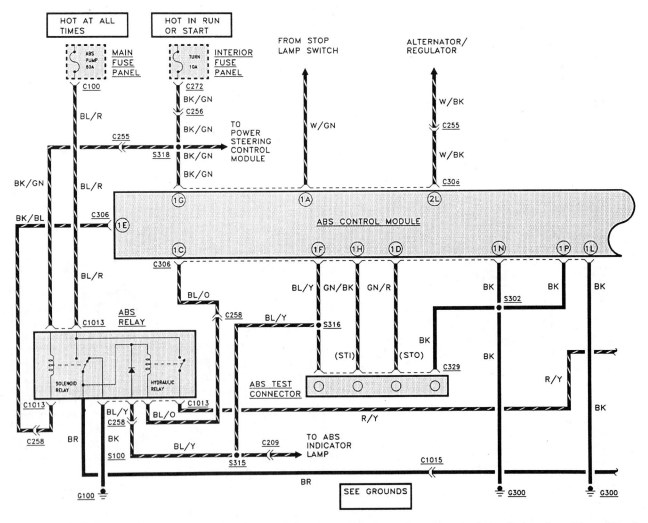

FIGURE 18–17. A schematic such as this is a tool used to understand various electrical circuits in automobiles. *(Courtesy of Motor Publications, Wiring and Diagram Manual, Chrysler Motors, Eagle/Jeep, Ford Motor Company)*

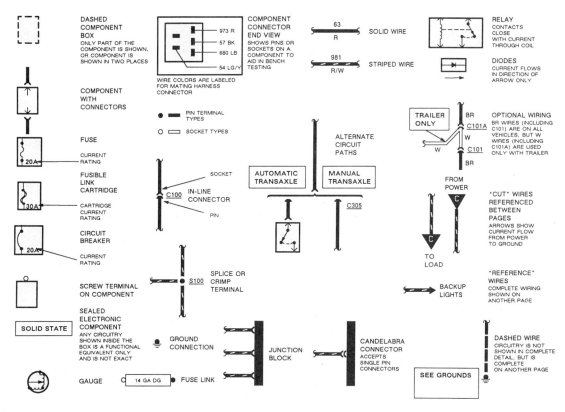

FIGURE 18–18. Some common symbols used on schematics in service manuals. *(Courtesy of Motor Publications, Wiring and Diagram Manual, Chrysler Motors, Eagle/Jeep, Ford Motor Company)*

CAR CLINIC

PROBLEM: Key Off, Battery Drain

On a computer-controlled vehicle there is a small amount of battery drain when the key is in the OFF position. What is causing this drain, and is it normal?

SOLUTION:

With the increasing use of electronics and computer memories, there will normally be a small amount of battery drain when the key is in the OFF position. Use a 1-ohm, 10-watt resistor hooked in series with the negative battery terminal and cable, and a digital volt-ohmmeter (DVOM) to check the battery drain. Measure the voltage drop across the resistor. If there is a voltage drop, then there is a small amount of current drain with the key in the OFF position. The current can be calculated using Ohm's Law. Divide the voltage drop by 1 ohm (the resistance of your test resistor) to get the current drain. An acceptable battery drain when the key is OFF should be around 100 milliamps.

18.3   MAGNETISM

One area of study in automotive systems is that of magnetism. The principles of magnetism are integrated into motors, generators, solenoids, and other electrical systems in the automobile. Magnetism can be best understood by observing some of its effects.

The effects of magnetism were first observed when fragments of iron ore, referred to as lodestones, were attracted to pieces of iron. It was further discovered that a long piece of iron would align itself so that one end always pointed toward the earth's north pole. This end of the bar was called the north (N) pole, and the other end was called the south (S) pole. The bar was called a bar magnet.

Domains

Inside the bar magnet are many small *domains*. Domains are minute sections in the bar where the atoms line up to produce a magnetic field. Most of the domains must be lined up in the same direction in the bar magnet to form a magnetic field. *Figure 18–19* shows a bar of metal with the domains located randomly and a bar with the domains lined up.

Lines of Force

Magnets can be further defined by the *lines of force* being produced. The magnetic field is defined as invisible forces that come out of the north pole and enter the south pole. See

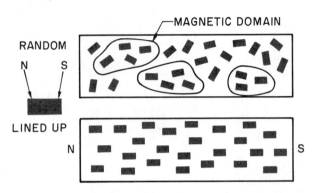

FIGURE 18–19. There is no magnetism in a metal bar when the domains are not lined up. When they are lined up, magnetism is produced.

Figure 18–20. The shape of the magnetic lines of force can be illustrated by sprinkling iron filings on a piece of paper on top of the bar magnet. When the paper is tapped, the iron filings align to form a clear pattern around the bar magnet. Note that the lines of force never touch each other. Also note that the lines of force are more concentrated at the ends of the magnet.

Repulsion and Attraction

If two bar magnets are placed together at unlike poles, they will snap together. If the ends have the same poles, they will repel each other. This is shown in *Figure 18–21.*

Electromagnetism

The bar magnet that was mentioned previously is called a permanent magnet. There are also temporary magnets that can be made from electricity. This can be done by wrapping an electrical wire around an unmagnetized bar to make an electromagnet. This is called *electromagnetism.*

When any wire has electricity flowing through it, a magnetic field develops around the wire. See *Figure 18–22.* If the wire is then placed in the shape of a coil, as shown in *Figure 18–23*, the magnetic field in the center of the coil will be additive. If a nonmagnetized bar is placed in the center of the coil, the bar will also be magnetized, *Figure 18–24.*

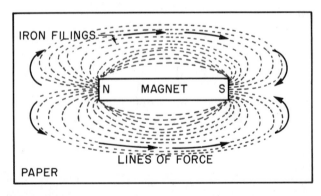

FIGURE 18–20. A bar magnet and iron filings show the invisible lines of force around a magnet. Magnetic lines of force always flow from the north pole to the south pole.

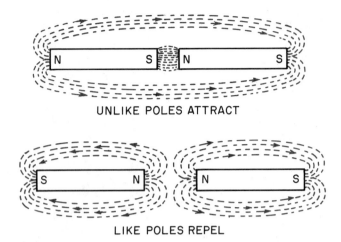

FIGURE 18–21. Unlike poles will attract each other. Like poles will repel each other.

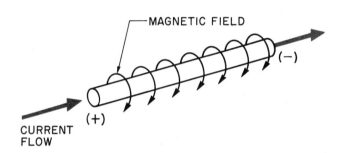

FIGURE 18–22. Electricity flowing through a wire will produce a small magnetic field around the wire.

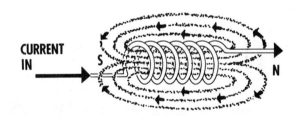

FIGURE 18–23. When electrical current passes through a conductor, a magnetic field is developed around the conductor. If the conductor is formed in the shape of a coil, the magnetic field is additive in the center. *(Courtesy of Delco-Remy Division of General Motors Corporation)*

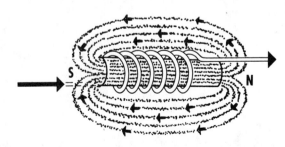

FIGURE 18–24. When a coil of wire has current passing through it, north and south poles are created. The strength of the magnetic field can be increased by inserting an iron bar. *(Courtesy of Delco-Remy Division of General Motors Corporation)*

Electromagnetic Induction

Through experimentation it was discovered that a conductor moving across or cutting a magnetic field would produce a voltage. This is called *electromagnetic induction*. Actually, an electromotive force (emf) will be induced or generated within the wire. Internally, a generator is converting mechanical energy to electrical energy. In the simplest form, *Figure 18–25* shows how voltage is produced with a magnet.

The direction of current flow produced by the voltage can be reversed if the movement is also reversed. In fact, if the wire were moved back and forth rapidly, the result would be alternating current.

Figure 18–26 shows a complete simple generator used to produce voltage in a wire. Note that rather than using permanent magnets, electromagnets are used. Also, 12 volts have been applied to produce the electromagnets. This voltage is called the field voltage. If the center wire moves up, a voltage will be produced on the voltmeter. If the wire moves down, a reverse voltage will be produced. This means the positive and negative points will have been reversed.

Note that three things are necessary to induce a voltage in a generator. These include:

1. a magnetic field producing lines of force,

2. conductors that can be moved, and

3. movement between the conductors and the magnetic field so that the lines of force are cut.

If any one of the preceding factors increases or decreases, the induced voltage will also increase or decrease. Note also that a conductor can be stationary while the lines of force

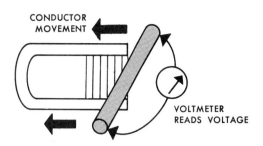

FIGURE 18–25.   As a conductor moves or cuts through a magnetic field, a voltage is produced. If the voltage is applied to a circuit with a load or resistance, a complete circuit can be produced. *(Courtesy of Delco-Remy Division of General Motors Corporation)*

are moved. This will still induce a voltage because the lines of force will be cut.

18.4   SOLID-STATE COMPONENTS AND COMPUTERS

Semiconductors

One area of electrical study that has grown recently is that of electronics. Electronics is the study of solid-state devices such as diodes, transistors, and integrated circuits. Solid-state devices are those that have no moving parts except internal electrons.

To begin, let's review the study of conductors and insulators presented earlier in this chapter. It was mentioned that any material that has four electrons in its outer orbit is called a semiconductor. See *Figure 18–27*. This means that it could be either a good conductor or a good insulator.

SIMPLE GENERATOR

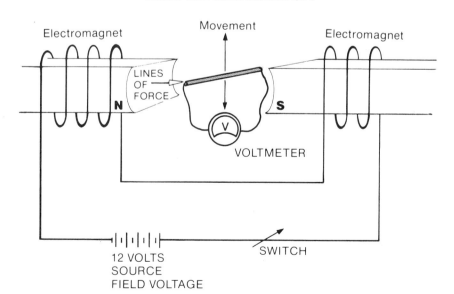

FIGURE 18–26.   If a conductor is moved perpendicular to the lines of force from the magnet, a voltage will be induced in the conductor. *(Courtesy of Davis Publications, Inc.)*

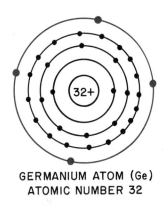

GERMANIUM ATOM (Ge)
ATOMIC NUMBER 32

FIGURE 18–27.   Semiconductors have only four electrons in their outer orbit. *(Courtesy of Davis Publications, Inc.)*

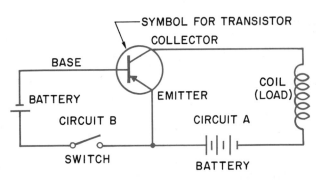

FIGURE 18–29.   A transistor can control the on-off sequence of the coil. Circuit B controls circuit A.

Semiconductors are also called solid-state devices. Because of their characteristics, semiconductors are often used as switches. Circuits can be turned off and on by semiconductors with no moving parts.

Diodes

The *diode* is a semiconductor that permits current to flow through a circuit in one direction but not in the other. *Figure 18–28* shows a circuit with a diode. The alternator produces a current that flows back and forth 60 times per minute. This is called ac voltage. In the battery, however, direct current (dc) voltage is used to charge the battery. The battery is considered the load. The diode can be used to convert the ac to dc. In Figure 18–28, electricity is able to flow in the direction of the arrow. If electricity tries to flow in the opposite direction, it will be stopped. There will be no current flow in the reverse direction.

Transistors

The *transistor* is also a type of semiconductor. In this case, the transistor has some semiconductor material added to it. A circuit using a transistor is shown in *Figure 18–29*. In operation, the circuit to be turned off and on is identified as circuit A. Circuit B is the controlling circuit. The transistor has three wires. These are called the base, emitter, and collector.

If a small amount of current flows (when the switch is closed) in the emitter-to-base circuit, the resistance between the emitter and collector circuits will be zero. Circuit A is then turned on to operate the coil. (This could be a primary coil in an ignition system.) When the current stops flowing in circuit B (switch open), the resistance between the emitter and collector is very high. This resistance shuts off circuit B.

Transistors can also be used to amplify an on-off sequence of a signal. A small amount of current flowing on and off in circuit B can control a large amount of current flowing in circuit A. The on-off sequence will be amplified from circuit B to circuit A.

Integrated Circuits

Over the past several years, engineers have found ways of making diodes and transistors extremely small. Because they are smaller, many diodes, transistors, and other semiconductors can be placed on a board called an integrated circuit. See *Figure 18–30*. These circuits may contain many semiconductors. More recently, the chip has been designed to incorporate even smaller components on the integrated board. Some applications that use *integrated circuits* and chips in the automobile include solid-state ignition, electronic fuel injection, electronic engine systems, computer-controlled combustion, and speed and cruise controls. Other circuits are constantly being developed to make the automobile even more controlled by electronic components. Many of these will be discussed in other chapters in this book.

Microprocessors

With the addition of integrated circuits and chips, the automobile is using more and more *microprocessors*. Microprocessors are small computers that can be used for a variety of tasks. They contain logic and control circuits. Various sensors relay input information to the microprocessor. Engine speed, temperature, outside weather conditions (barometric pressure), load and weight distribution of the vehicle, vehicle speed, throttle position, and so on can be fed into the microprocessor. The microprocessor uses this input information to control the vehicle to its optimum performance.

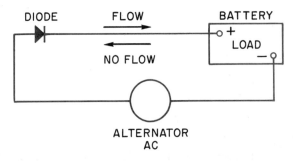

FIGURE 18–28.   A diode in a circuit allows electricity to flow in only one direction.

FIGURE 18–30. Integrated circuits and chips are used in many applications in the automobile today.

On-Board Automotive Computers

Because of the development of integrated circuits and microprocessors, automotive computers have become commonplace. The automotive computer is able to receive information from vehicle sensors and other components. It then makes decisions on the basis of that information and takes actions as a result of those decisions. The microprocessor inside the computer does the calculations and makes decisions of exactly what to control.

Computers in automobiles are generally treated as a "black box." When they don't work, they are replaced. The automotive service technician must first confirm whether the computer is working correctly or not. The troubleshooting processes discussed in earlier chapters help to do this. However, there are various terms and systems that will help the service technician understand and work with these computers.

Communicating with a Computer

Computers communicate by voltage, or electrical, signals. Voltage signals transmit information in three ways:

- by changing voltage levels or amounts

- by changing the shape of the voltage pulses

- by changing the speed at which the signals switch levels

In addition, voltage causes current to flow to working devices such as solenoids, relays, and lamps.

Analog and Digital Computer Signals

Computer communications involve two kinds of signals: analog and digital signals. An *analog* signal is a continuously variable signal and can be represented by any voltage within a given range. For example, temperature- and pressure-sensing signals (coolant temperature, oil pressure) give off an analog signal. Analog signals are generally used when a certain condition is gradually or continuously changing.

The second type of signal, called the *digital* signal, has specific values, usually two. There is no ability for the signal to represent any in-between values. Digital signals are useful when there is a choice between only two alternatives such as one or zero, yes or no, on or off, high or low, and so on. Digital signals are often shown graphically as a square wave signal. *Figure 18–31* shows a graphical comparison of analog and digital signals.

Binary Codes

A computer is able to string a series of digital signals into useful combinations of binary numbers. *Binary codes* are made up of combinations of 1 and 0. Each digital signal (1 or 0) is called a *bit*. For example, voltage above a certain given value converts to a 1. Voltage below a certain value converts to a 0. A combination of eight bits is called a word or a *byte*.

Figure 18–32 shows how a typical byte can be determined. For each bit, 1 or 0 is represented. Eight bits are shown making up the total binary number of 11001011. Under each bit a power is also shown. The power, a numerical value, is used to represent each bit that has a 1. The power starts from the right side and increases to the left. Starting with 1 on the right side, each number is doubled. This is called the power. To determine the numerical value of the byte, multiply each bit (1 or 0) by the power, then add the powers together. In this case the numerical value of the binary number 11001011 is 203.

Most automotive computers are using 8-bit microprocessors. However, computers that have 16 bits are becoming more and more common. The 16-bit computer is able to com-

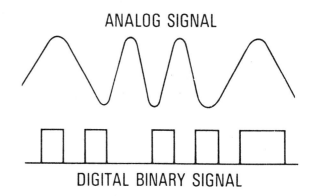

FIGURE 18–31. Analog signals are continuously changing, whereas digital signals are either off or on. *(Courtesy of General Motors Product Service Training)*

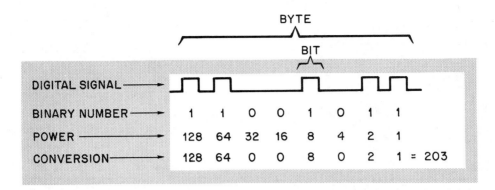

FIGURE 18–32. Digital signals, or bytes, can be converted to numeral values.

municate much more information than an 8-bit computer.

Binary codes also enable the computer to perform mathematical functions very rapidly. The ability of these computers to manipulate large series of digital signals almost instantaneously makes them ideal for automotive use. In order for a computer to be able to perform mathematical functions, there must be a relationship between decimal numbers and binary numbers. *Figure 18–33* shows the binary number made of zeros and ones for each number from 1 to 10.

Computer Memory

The microprocessor in a computer is not able to store any information. However, memory chips are placed in the computer to allow it to store binary code information until it is needed. Basically, three types of memory are used in computers. The exact titles will vary; however, the following are very common.

- ROM (read-only memory)

- RAM (random access memory)

- PROM (programmable read-only memory)

ROM (read-only memory) contains permanent information that cannot be changed. When the computer is manufactured,

DECIMAL	BINARY
0	0
1	1
2	10
3	11
4	100
5	101
6	110
7	111
8	1000
9	1001
10	1010

FIGURE 18–33. Each decimal number on the left has a corresponding binary number on the right.

the programs that control the microprocessor are stored in the ROM. The ROM is soldered into the computer and generally cannot be removed by a service technician.

RAM (random access memory) can be both read from and written into. It is often used for temporary storage of information that changes. For example, if the computer receives information from the coolant temperature sensor, it may be stored in RAM and then read out each time it is needed. The RAM can also be called the "learning" portion of the computer or microprocessor.

There are two types of RAM — a nonvolatile RAM and a volatile RAM. The nonvolatile RAM holds its information even after the power has been removed. A good example of the type of information stored in a nonvolatile RAM is the information necessary for digital displays on the dashboard. The volatile RAM will be erased when the power is shut off. In an automotive computer system, a volatile RAM can be connected to the battery through a fuse or fusible link after the ignition has been shut off. This arrangement is called keep-alive RAM. However, if the battery goes dead the keep-alive RAM will lose its information.

PROM (programmable read-only memory) is much like ROM only it can be removed from the computer and is easily accessed. The PROM chip can be removed from the computer, and a new chip with a different programming can be installed. Other types of memory may also be referenced in the automotive literature, including:

- KAM (keep-alive memory), similar to RAM

- E-PROM, a PROM that reverts to an unprogrammed state when any light strikes it.

Clock Generator/Pulses

A great deal of information must be transmitted by the computer. To aid in this process a precise time interval is needed to allow a computer to transmit each bit of information. A clock generator is installed in the computer that provides periodic pulses, like a clock that ticks thousands of times each second. The microprocessor, its memories, and its interfaces all use these pulses as a reference to time the digital signals. The generated clock pulses are sometimes referred to as the baud rate. A computer that has a baud rate of 5000 can transmit 5000 bits per second.

Interfaces

Computers in automobiles also need several support functions. One is called the interface. An interface circuit is used to allow the computer to read input signals to the computer. A second interface is also used to produce the necessary output from the computer to other components such as the carburetor and fuel injector. The major function of the interface is to translate any analog signals coming into the computer to digital signals. In addition, the interface also changes any digital outputs from the computer to analog signals to operate and control components on the engine.

Data Links

Computers send and receive digital signals through what are called *data links*. Data links allow the computer to communicate with both input and output sensors. In addition, computers can communicate with one another using data links. Some data links transmit data in only one direction. Other data links can transmit in both directions.

To get an idea how the flow of information in a computer occurs, refer to *Figure 18–34*. Data are brought in on the left side of the diagram. These data come from the input sensors such as the oxygen, engine speed, engine temperature, and coolant temperature sensors. The data are then sent into the input interface, converted to digital signals, then translated and sent to the microprocessor. On the basis of ROM, RAM, and PROM memory data, a certain result is sent out of the microprocessor. The output signal goes through the output interface and finally is sent to the component that is being controlled. For example, the port fuel injector's pulse width is changed. All of the systems — ROM, RAM, PROM,

microprocessor, and so on — are controlled by the clock pulses.

SUMMARY

This chapter investigated the basic principles of electricity and how they are related to the automobile. Electricity is defined as the movement of electrons. Voltage, amperage, and resistance are components used to control electricity. Both Ohm's and Watt's laws were defined to help determine the relationships between voltage, amperage, resistance, and power.

Several circuits, including the series, parallel, and series-parallel circuits, were studied. Each type of circuit has specific characteristics. Types of circuits, voltage drop, opens, shorts, and grounds were also defined.

As part of the study of electricity, magnetism was defined. Domains, lines of force, electromagnetism, and simple generators were discussed. The principles concerning magnetism are directly related to automobile systems such as starting and charging, ignition, and electronic controls.

Semiconductors are becoming a significant part of the automobile. Diodes, transistors, integrated circuits, and microprocessors are being used in all systems studied on the automobile.

To make the automotive engine more efficient on-board computers are used. Computers communicate with electrical signals. Both analog and digital signals can be used. Signals can be strung together using binary codes. Codes are then stored in various types of memory such as ROM (Read Only Memory), RAM (Random Access Memory), and PROM (Programmable Read Only Memory). Both permanent (ROM and PROM) and temporary storage (RAM) systems are used. In addition, computers also must be able to connect into other systems. Interfaces and data links, are also used.

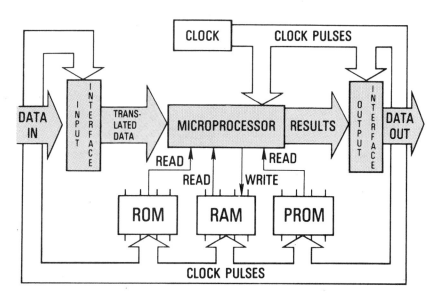

FIGURE 18–34. This diagram shows how all of the computer components operate together. Each part is controlled by the clock pulses to keep the flow of information orderly. *(Courtesy of General Motors Product Service Training)*

Linkage to
Future Automotive Technology

ELECTRIC VECHICLES AND SOLAR POWER

One area that is receiving much attention recently is to propel a car by solar power. Solar cells are used to convert the sun's energy directly into electricity. As the sun's radiant energy strikes the solar cells, the radiant energy is converted to electrical energy. The electrical energy is then stored in batteries. The electricity in the batteries is used to turn a drive motor for propulsion.

More-efficient solar cells are being developed. In addition, battery technology is constantly improving. With these two technologies, solar-powered vehicles may soon become a reality. A solar-powered vehicle is shown. The small crystalline solar cells are placed on the upper surface of the vehicle body. The solar cells are shown being installed on the back panel of the vehicle. To maximize the energy use, a great deal of research is also being done to reduce frictional horsepower losses. Improved bearings, a lower coefficient of drag, and reduced tire rolling resistances are all being researched to make solar-powered vehicles an alternative vehicle for the future. *(Courtesy of General Motors)*

TERMS TO KNOW

Can you explain each of the following terms? Review the chapter until you can use each term correctly.

Atom
Proton
Electron
Valence ring
Conductor
Insulator
Semiconductor
Electricity
Electron theory
Conventional theory
Amperage
Current
Voltage
Resistance
Ohm's Law
Wattage
Watt's Law
Voltage drop
Open circuit
Shorted circuit
Grounded circuit

Series circuit
Parallel circuit
Voltmeter
Ohmmeter
Ammeter
Domain
Lines of force
Electromagnetism
Electromagnetic induction
Diode
Transistor
Integrated circuit
Microprocessor
Analog
Digital
Binary code
ROM
RAM
PROM
Data link

 REVIEW QUESTIONS

Multiple Choice

1. Which of the following components has a negative charge in the atom?
   a. Protons
   b. Electrons
   c. Neutrons
   d. Watts
   e. Volts

2. Which of the following materials has been identified as being a good conductor?
   a. A material with four electrons in the valence ring
   b. A material with three electrons in the valence ring
   c. A material with five or more electrons in the valence ring
   d. Glass
   e. Wood

3. Which theory says that electricity flows from a positive point to a negative point?
   a. Conventional theory
   b. Magnetism theory
   c. Diode theory
   d. Electron theory
   e. Valence ring theory

4. Which theory says that electricity flows from a negative point to a positive point?
   a. Conventional theory
   b. Magnetism theory
   c. Diode theory
   d. Electron theory
   e. Valence ring theory

5. Pressure, or push, on the electrons is defined as:
   a. Amperage
   b. Voltage
   c. Wattage
   d. Resistance
   e. Magnetism

6. Wattage is found by multiplying the voltage by the:
   a. Resistance
   b. Power
   c. Amperage
   d. Protons
   e. Neutrons

7. Current is also called:
   a. Amperage
   b. Voltage
   c. Wattage
   d. Resistance
   e. Magnetism

8. Which circuit has only one path for the electricity to flow in?
   a. Series-parallel circuit
   b. Parallel circuit
   c. Series circuit
   d. Open circuit
   e. None of the above

9. A break in a wire is referred to as:
   a. A short
   b. An open
   c. A ground
   d. A series circuit
   e. A parallel circuit

10. What is necessary to produce an induced voltage?
    a. A magnetic field
    b. A conductor
    c. Movement between a conductor and magnetic field
    d. All of the above
    e. None of the above

11. A wire with electricity flowing through it:
    a. Has no magnetic field around it
    b. Has a magnetic field around it
    c. Is usually considered an open circuit
    d. Is usually considered grounded
    e. Has maximum wattage

12. Which of the following devices can amplify an off-on signal?
    a. Diode
    b. Resistor
    c. Transistor
    d. Voltmeter
    e. Resistance meter

13. Which of the following devices causes electricity to flow in only one direction?
    a. Diode
    b. Resistor
    c. Transistor
    d. Voltmeter
    e. Resistance meter

14. In a parallel circuit, the voltage drop is _____ at each resistor.
    a. The same
    b. Different
    c. 0
    d. The same as the amperage
    e. None of the above

15. Which circuit on a transistor is considered to be the control part?
    a. Base
    b. Emitter
    c. Collector
    d. Negative terminal
    e. Positive terminal

The following questions are similar in format to ASE (Automotive Service Excellence) test questions.

16. Technician A says that inputs such as vehicle speed and engine temperature are fed to the microprocessor. Technician B says that inputs such as engine speed and barometric pressure are fed to the microprocessor. Who is right?
    a. A only
    b. B only
    c. Both A and B
    d. Neither A nor B

17. Technician A says that a transistor is the same as a diode. Technician B says that a transistor is the same as a resistor. Who is right?
    a. A only
    b. B only
    c. Both A and B
    d. Neither A nor B

18. Technician A says that voltage drop is the same as resistance. Technician B says that voltage drop is the amount of voltage dropped across each resistor. Who is right?
    a. A only
    b. B only
    c. Both A and B
    d. Neither A nor B

19. There is a break in an electrical wire. Technician A says this is called a short. Technician B says this is called a ground. Who is right?
    a. A only
    b. B only
    c. Both A and B
    d. Neither A nor B

20. Technician A says that a voltmeter must be hooked up in series in a circuit. Technician B says that an ammeter must be hooked up in series. Who is correct?
    a. A only
    b. B only
    c. Both A and B
    d. Neither A nor B

21. Technician A says that RAM memory in the computer is temporary storage. Technician B says that ROM memory is temporary storage. Who is correct?
    a. A only
    b. B only
    c. Both A and B
    d. Neither A nor B

22. Technician A says that the microprocessor in a computer can read digital signals with an input interface. Technician B says that the output interface is needed to convert analog signals to digital signals. Who is correct?
    a. A only
    b. B only
    c. Both A and B
    d. Neither A nor B

23. Technician A says that on an electrical schematic ground wires are shown. Technician B says that an electrical schematic does not show the color code on wires. Who is correct?
    a. A only
    b. B only
    c. Both A and B
    d. Neither A nor B

Essay

24. Define Ohm's Law.

25. Define and state the difference between an open, short, and ground.

26. Define voltage drop.

27. What are three characteristics of a series circuit?

28. What are three characteristics of a parallel circuit?

29. Define the purpose and operation of a diode.

30. What is the difference between a diode and a transistor?

Short Answer

31. If an electrical circuit has 12 volts and 18 amps, the circuit resistance is _____ .

32. If the resistance of a component in an electrical circuit is 320 ohms, and 0.014 amp is flowing through that component, the voltage drop across the component is

_____ .

33. What is the total resistance of a parallel circuit that has five resistors, with each resistor having a resistance of 7 ohms? _____

34. What is the total resistance of a series circuit with the resistors of $R_1 = 4$ ohms, $R_2 = 4$ ohms, $R_3 = 6$ ohms, $R_4 = 8$ ohms, $R_5 = 2$ ohms, $R_6 = 12$ ohms? _____

35. Computers communicate with two types of signals, which are called _____ and _____ signals.

CHAPTER 19

Automotive Batteries

INTRODUCTION   The battery is a very important part of the automobile. It is used to supply electricity for many systems and components within the vehicle. The purpose of this chapter is to study the operation and maintenance of the automotive storage battery.

OBJECTIVES   After reading this chapter, you should be able to:

- Identify the purpose of the automotive battery.

- Analyze the internal parts, construction, and operation of the battery, including chemical action and specific gravity.

- Determine the methods used to rate batteries.

- Identify the methods used to test and maintain the battery.

- Analyze the various problems, diagnosis, and service procedures used on batteries.

✔ SAFETY CHECKLIST ✔

When working with automotive batteries, keep these important safety precautions in mind.
✔ Never smoke in or around an automobile or when working on the battery.
✔ Always keep an approved fire extinguisher nearby when working on the battery.
✔ When working on batteries, always remove rings, watches, and other jewelry to avoid electrical shock.

✔ Always wear safety glasses when working on the battery system.
CAUTION: Battery acid is considered a hazardous waste product. Batteries should not be thrown away, as damage to the environment may result. All stores that sell batteries normally take old batteries and dispose of them correctly. When buying a new battery, bring your old battery to the seller for correct disposal.

19.1 BATTERY DESIGN AND OPERATION

Purpose of the Battery

The purpose of the battery is to act as a reservoir for storing electricity. The battery receives, stores, and makes electrical energy available to the automobile. It is called a storage battery because it stores or holds electricity. The battery is

considered an *electrochemical* device. This means that it uses chemicals to produce and store electricity (electrochemical). Energy in the battery is stored in a chemical form. The chemical energy is released as electrical energy for use in the automobile. The purpose of the battery is to provide sufficient electrical energy to crank the starter and operate the ignition system, computers, solenoids, lights, and other electrical components.

Some of the information in this chapter can help you prepare for the National Institute for Automotive Service Excellence (ASE) certification tests. The tests most directly related to this chapter are entitled

> **ENGINE REPAIR (TEST 1) AND ELECTRICAL SYSTEMS (TEST 6).**

The contents areas that closely parallel this chapter are

> **BATTERY AND STARTING SYSTEM DIAGNOSIS AND REPAIR, GENERAL ELECTRICAL SYSTEM DIAGNOSIS, BATTERY DIAGNOSIS AND SERVICE, STARTING SYSTEM DIAGNOSIS AND REPAIR, AND CHARGING SYSTEM DIAGNOSIS AND REPAIR.**

Types of Batteries

Batteries can be subdivided into two major groups: primary and secondary batteries. *Primary batteries* are those that are nonrechargeable. Examples of primary batteries include those used in flashlights, calculators, smoke alarms, and radios. Various metals and chemicals are used to manufacture primary batteries.

Secondary batteries are those that can be discharged and recharged repeatedly. This can be done by reversing the normal current flow through the battery. The automobile battery is called a secondary battery because it can be charged and discharged many times.

Battery Cells

Batteries are made by putting together a number of cells. A *battery cell* is defined as that part of a battery that stores chemical energy for later use. In its simplest form, a battery cell consists of three components. These include a positive plate (one type of metal), a negative plate (another type of metal), and an *electrolyte* solution. When these three components, two dissimilar metals and an electrolyte solution, are placed together, electricity can be produced.

All batteries, both primary and secondary, have cells. The difference between battery cells is the type of metals and electrolyte chemicals used in the cells. For example, a 2-volt primary battery cell uses different metals and chemicals than a 9-volt primary battery cell.

Lead-Acid Battery

Figure 19–1 shows a simple cell. The positive plate is made of a metal called lead peroxide (PbO_2). The negative plate is made of a metal called sponge lead (Pb). The electrolyte solution is made of a mixture of sulfuric acid and water (H_2SO_4). This is called a lead-acid battery cell. The metals are made of different types of lead, and the electrolyte is made of acid. When these three components are arranged as shown, approximately 2.1 to 2.5 volts are produced across the positive and negative plates. If an electrical circuit were placed across this voltage source, electrons would flow from the negative plate, through the circuit, back to the positive plate.

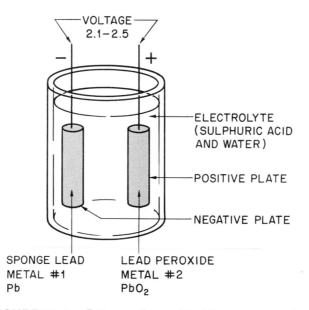

FIGURE 19–1. Battery cells consist of three components. These include two different metals and an electrolyte solution. When these two metals are placed together in the electrolyte solution, a voltage can be produced across the metals.

SYMBOL FOR BATTERY CELL

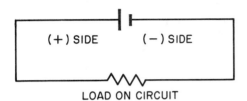

FIGURE 19–2. The symbol for a battery cell. The long line represents the positive (+) side of the battery. The short line represents the negative (–) side.

Battery Cell Symbol

The electrical symbol of a battery is shown in ***Figure 19–2***. The longer line represents the positive plate. The shorter line represents the negative plate.

Combining Battery Cells

The automobile requires 12 volts to operate. Battery cells can be connected to produce different voltages. When battery cells are connected in series, the voltage is additive. For example, in order to produce a 6-volt lead-acid battery, three 2-volt cells are connected in series. A 12-volt battery has six 2-volt cells connected in series. See ***Figure 19–3***.

Whenever battery cells are placed in parallel, the voltage remains the same. However, the amperage that the battery can produce is increased. This is called *amperage capacity*. This means that the battery can produce a certain amperage faster than a single cell could produce that amperage. See ***Figure 19–4***.

Chemical Action in a Battery

Figure 19–5 shows how the chemical reactions occur inside the battery cell. During *discharging*, or when a load is applied, the lead peroxide (PbO_2) is separated. The sulfuric acid (H_2SO_4) and water are separated. Some of the sulfate (SO_4) combines with the negative-plate sponge lead (Pb). Some of the sulfate (SO_4) combines with the lead (Pb) part of the positive plate. The remaining oxygen (O_2) combines with the hydrogen (H_2) left from the electrolyte. If the battery continues to be discharged, the two metals will eventually change to leadsulfate ($PbSO_4$) and the electrolyte will become water (H_2O).

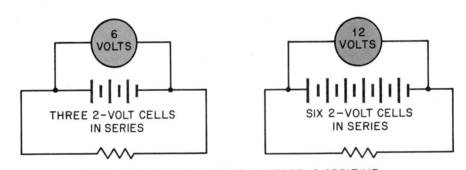

WHEN CELLS ARE IN SERIES, VOLTAGE IS ADDITIVE

FIGURE 19–3. When three 2-volt cells are placed in series, the total voltage is 6 volts. When six 2-volt cells are placed in series, the voltage is 12 volts.

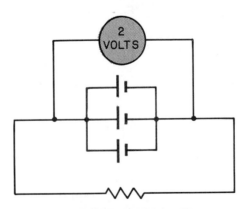

WHEN CELLS ARE IN PARALLEL,
VOLTAGE REMAINS THE SAME,
BUT AMPERAGE CAPACITY INCREASES.

FIGURE 19–4. When 2-volt cells are connected in parallel, the voltage remains the same, but the amperage capacity increases.

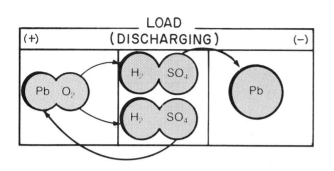 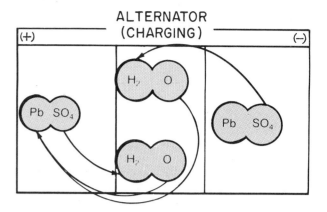

FIGURE 19–5. The chemical action that takes place in a battery during discharging and charging. *(Courtesy of Davis Publications, Inc.)*

During *charging*, the chemical and electrical actions are just the reverse. This is done by using the generator or alternator on the vehicle. At the end of a charge, the battery cell is the same chemical as it was before discharge.

When a battery is discharged and recharged, it has gone through a *cycle*. For example, if the vehicle's lights had been left on overnight, the battery would be in a discharged state and would have to be recharged. The discharging and recharging constitute a cycle. Generally, a battery can go through only so many cycles before it becomes damaged. A damaged battery loses its ability to hold electricity. In a normal automotive application, most batteries are able to last between 3 and 5 years. Of course, it depends on how many and how severe the cycles were. A battery can be designed using different chemicals to allow more cycles in its lifetime. This type of battery is called a *deep cycle battery*.

Explosive Gases

Hydrogen and oxygen gases are released during the process of charging and discharging a battery. The gases escape the battery through the vent caps. The more rapidly a battery is charged or discharged, the greater the possibility of producing these gases. These gases can be very explosive. It is always important to keep any sparks or open flame away from a battery that is being charged or discharged. Always charge batteries in a well-vented room.

Electrolyte

The electrolyte in a battery is a combination of water and sulfuric acid. Normally, the ratio of acid to water is 40% acid to 60% distilled water. This combination of water and acid is the best electrolyte solution for the battery. During normal operation, the water will evaporate. The acid does not usually evaporate. Distilled water is the only ingredient that should be added to a battery. The right amount of acid will always be in the battery unless it is tipped over and spilled.

Specific Gravity

The condition of the battery electrolyte can be checked by measuring its *specific gravity*. Specific gravity is defined as the weight of a solution compared with the weight of water. The specific gravity of water is rated as 1.000. Any solution heavier than water is expressed in terms of the ratio of its density to the density of water. Sulfuric acid is heavier than water. Adding sulfuric acid to water causes the density to exceed that of water, or 1.000.

Figure 19–6 shows how the specific gravity of water and acid change when they are mixed. The specific gravity of water (1.000) mixed with acid (1.835) is equal to an electrolyte solution of 1.270.

The condition or state of charge can be determined by measuring the specific gravity. *Figure 19–7* shows different

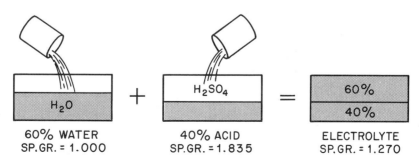

FIGURE 19–6. The ratio of water to acid is about 60% to 40%. The specific gravity of the two causes the electrolyte solution to have a specific gravity of about 1.270.

SPECIFIC GRAVITY READINGS AT 80° F	
1.260–1.280	Fully charged
1.235–1.260	¾ charged
1.205–1.235	½ charged
1.170–1.205	¼ charged
1.140–1.170	Poorly charged
1.110–1.140	Dead

FIGURE 19–7. The specific gravity reading can determine the condition of a charge on a battery.

specific gravity readings for different battery conditions. Specific gravity is measured with a hydrometer, which will be discussed later in this chapter.

Maintenance-free Batteries

In a standard battery, antimony (a metallic substance) is added to the lead plates to strengthen them. This also aids the battery in producing certain gases during charging and discharging. Calcium, rather than antimony, is used in maintenance-free batteries. A trace of tin is also included. Lead-calcium batteries normally discharge less gas than lead-acid batteries unless they are grossly overcharged. They do not have filler caps and never need water.

The purity of the lead-calcium plates reduces self-discharging and makes the battery harder to overcharge. Overcharging is a major cause of water loss in the battery. Because of these characteristics, the battery has no filler holes and smaller vent holes than a standard battery. The vent holes are located below a small cover on the top or side of the battery. Most of the battery breathing takes place through a series of *baffles* inside the battery. These baffles collect acid vapor and condense it back into the solution. Corrosion outside the battery is also reduced. Acid vapors that help cause outside corrosion are kept inside the battery.

Future Battery Developments

Newer chemicals are being tested for use in batteries. Some manufacturers use an electrolyte in the form of a gel to reduce further gassing. In fact, manufacturers are experimenting with different materials inside the battery to increase the *cell density*. Cell density is a measure of how many watts can be discharged per hour, per pound of battery. For example, the lead-antimony battery has a cell density of 3–4 watt-hours/pound. The lead-calcium battery has a cell density of 6–8. A zinc-chloride (experimental) battery has a cell density of 10–15. Future batteries may have cell densities of 45–50 watt-hours/pound.

Battery Construction

Figure 19–8 shows the internal parts and construction of a typical battery. Following the diagram, first a grid is manufactured as the base of the positive and negative plates. Lead peroxide and sponge lead, called the active materials, are manufactured and spread on the grid. The result is a completed plate.

Connectors are used to assemble the plates into a group of cells. Note that the plates are placed in parallel to increase the amperage capacity. Both positive and negative groups are manufactured. Separators are then placed between the groups to keep the plates from touching each other. One cell, or element, is now complete. This cell is capable of producing about 2.1 to 2.5 volts. Amperage capacity can be increased by adding more plates to each cell.

Once the elements, or cells, are completed, they are connected in series and placed in a plastic container. A one-piece cover is placed on top of the container and sealed. Here the battery posts are on top. Many batteries have the battery posts on the side as shown in *Figure 19–9*. The electrolyte is added, and the vent caps are installed. The battery is now complete.

CAR CLINIC

PROBLEM: Frozen Battery

A car has been stored over the winter in an outside garage. During the winter an inspection was made, and it was found that the battery had cracked and the fluid inside had frozen. What could cause a frozen battery?

SOLUTION:

Batteries are able to freeze only if the battery is discharged severely. Electrolyte has a lower freezing point than water. The electrolyte changes to water when the battery is discharged. Then the water is able to freeze. When water freezes, it expands, cracking the case. Always store the battery inside a building to prevent this problem, and keep the battery charged.

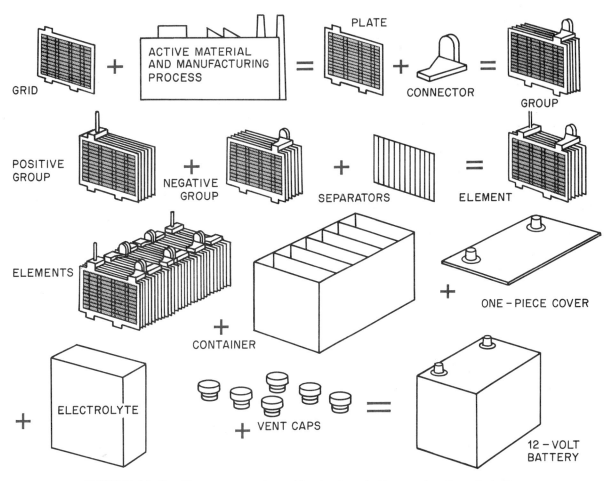

FIGURE 19–8. The components and basic steps in the construction of a battery.

FIGURE 19–9. Battery posts can be either on top of the battery or on the side. Here, side-mounted battery connectors are used in place of posts.

19.2 BATTERY RATINGS

Several ratings are used to identify the size and amperage capacity of the battery. Certain battery applications require cranking ability, while others may require long periods of high-amperage output. Because of these application differences, batteries are rated by (1) cold-cranking performance, (2) reserve capacity, (3) ampere-hour ratings, and (4) watt-hour ratings.

Cold-cranking Performance Rating

The cold-cranking performance rating is a measure of the battery's ability to crank an engine under cold weather conditions. During cold weather operation, the engine is more difficult to crank. It takes much more amperage to crank a cold engine than to crank a warm engine. This rating indicates the number of cranking amperes the battery can deliver at 0 degrees F for a period of 30 seconds. During this time, the cell voltage cannot drop below 1.2 volts, or the total battery voltage below 7.2 volts. This rating is listed, for example, as 500 CCA (cold-cranking amperes). When buying a battery, you should compare this rating with other batteries in the same range.

Reserve Capacity Rating

The reserve capacity rating is expressed in minutes. It measures a battery's ability to provide emergency power for ignition, lights, and so on if the charging system is not working. This rating involves a constant discharge at normal temperatures. The reserve capacity rating is defined as the number of minutes a fully charged battery at 80 degrees F can be discharged at 25 amperes and still maintain a minimum voltage of 1.75 volts per cell or 10.5 volts for the total battery. The higher the reserve capacity rating, the longer the battery can provide the emergency power for lights and accessories. A typical reserve capacity rating might be 125 minutes.

Ampere-Hour Rating

The ampere-hour rating is another measure of the battery's capacity. It is obtained by multiplying a certain flow of amperes by the time in hours during which current will flow. This is usually expressed as a "20-hour rating." Again, the test is run at 80 degrees F, and until the cell voltage drops below 1.75 volts or the total battery voltage drops below 10.5 volts.

The amount of amperage used in this test is 1/20 of the published 20-hour capacity in ampere-hours. For example, if a battery is rated at 105 ampere-hours, its discharge amperage is 5.25 (1/20, or 0.05, of 105 equals 5.25). To pass the test, this battery would be discharged at 5.25 amps for 20 hours and still have a total voltage above 10.5.

CAR CLINIC

PROBLEM: Electronics Damaged by Use of Jumper Cables

A vehicle had a dead battery and needed to be jump started by another vehicle. The jump start damaged several electronic components. What caused the electrical components to be damaged?

SOLUTION:

While they were being connected to the battery cables, the jumper cables were momentarily reversed, and a spark was produced at the battery terminal. Reversing the polarity caused excessive reverse voltage to be applied to many electronic components and circuits. This reverse voltage may have caused some of the electronic components to be damaged. It is very important when using jumper cables never to reverse the polarity, even for a brief moment. Vehicles today have numerous electronic circuits that can be damaged easily. Always follow the exact recommended procedure when using jumper cables to jump start another vehicle.

Watt-Hour Rating

The watt-hour rating is measured by multiplying the ampere-hour rating by the voltage of the battery. It is much the same as the ampere-hour rating, except watts are measured instead of amperes.

19.3 BATTERY MAINTENANCE AND TESTING

Hydrometer Testing

A *hydrometer* is used to measure the specific gravity of batteries that have filter caps. *Figure 19–10* shows a typical hydrometer. The hydrometer is made of a weighted float inside a glass tube. A bulb syringe is used to draw the electrolyte into the glass tube. Some hydrometers also have a temperature indicator or thermometer inside the float.

The object of the hydrometer is to determine the density of the electrolyte. The heavier, or denser, the electrolyte, the greater the percentage of acid. The lighter or less dense the electrolyte, the less the percentage of acid. If the electrolyte is denser, the float inside the hydrometer will not sink as deep into the solution. If the electrolyte is less dense, the float will sink deeper into the solution. The amount the float sinks into the solution is a measure of the specific gravity.

Figure 19–11 shows an example of how the hydrometer is used. The electrolyte solution is drawn into the glass tube. The depth the float sinks into the solution is read by reading the specific gravity stated at the top of the fluid. The inside of the float has a specific gravity scale to show the exact reading. Never take specific gravity readings immediately after the battery has been filled with water. The water and acid will not be completely mixed, and the reading will be incorrect.

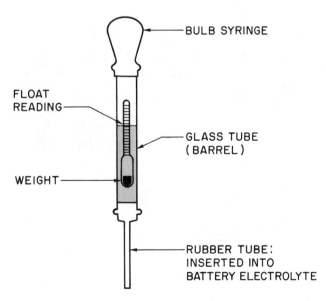

FIGURE 19–10. A hydrometer is used to measure the specific gravity of the battery electrolyte. Fluid is drawn into the glass tube, and the float reading tells the specific gravity of the electrolyte.

FIGURE 19–11. The specific gravity reading is measured on a hydrometer by lining up the level of the fluid with the floating bulb. The specific gravity reading is read on the floating bulb.

Temperature and Specific Gravity

The temperature of the electrolyte will have an effect on the exact specific gravity. Specific gravity readings must be changed to compensate for temperature. For each 10 degrees above 80 degrees F, 0.004 points must be added to the specific gravity reading. For every 10 degrees below 80 degrees F,

0.004 points must be subtracted from the measured specific gravity reading. For example, *Figure 19–12* shows a hydrometer correction scale. If the electrolyte solution is at 100 degrees F and the specific gravity is measured at 1.218, the corrected specific gravity will be 1.226. (For each 10 degrees above 80 degrees F, 0.004 points are added. 1.218 + 0.008 points = 1.226 corrected specific gravity reading.)

Battery Freezing

The freezing point of the electrolyte depends on its specific gravity. A fully charged battery will never freeze. As the battery discharges and the specific gravity gets close to 1.000 or pure water, the chance of the electrolyte freezing increases. If the electrolyte freezes, the battery case may crack and damage the battery. The table shown in *Figure 19–13* indicates the freezing temperatures of electrolytes at various specific gravities.

Specific Gravity on Maintenance-Free Batteries

Since there are no filler vents on a maintenance-free battery, another method is used to measure specific gravity. Refer to *Figure 19–14*. On certain batteries, specific gravity is determined by a float device built into the battery. A small colored ball floats when the specific gravity is correct or in the right range. If the specific gravity is below the required level, the ball sinks. If the green dot is seen, the specific gravity is correct. If the indicator is black, the specific gravity is low. The battery should be charged. If the indicator shows light yellow, the battery electrolyte is too low. The battery may be damaged and should be replaced.

Other maintenance-free batteries have a test indicator that is also located on the top of the battery. When the test indicator shows "OK," the battery is satisfactory. This is shown by a blue or other color on the test indicator. If the test indicator is colorless, charging is necessary.

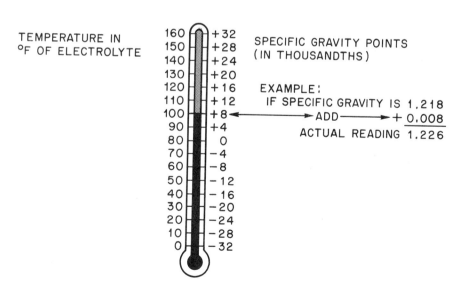

FIGURE 19–12. Specific gravity readings must be corrected for temperature according to this table.

VALUE OF SPECIFIC GRAVITY	FREEZING TEMP. DEG. F.	VALUE OF SPECIFIC GRAVITY	FREEZING TEMP. DEG. F.
1.100	18	1.220	−31
1.120	13	1.240	−50
1.140	8	1.260	−75
1.160	1	1.280	−92
1.180	−6	1.300	−95
1.200	−17		

FIGURE 19–13.   The freezing temperature of the electrolyte will change with different specific gravity readings.

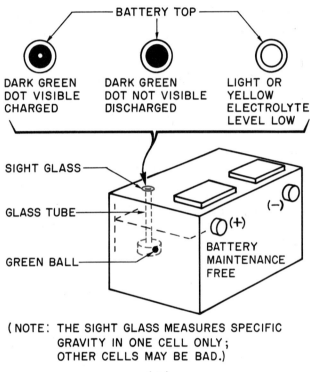

(NOTE: THE SIGHT GLASS MEASURES SPECIFIC GRAVITY IN ONE CELL ONLY; OTHER CELLS MAY BE BAD.)

(A)

(B)

FIGURE 19–14.   Specific gravity of some maintenance-free batteries is determined by an indicator. If the green dot can be seen, the specific gravity is correct. If there is a black spot, the specific gravity is too low, and the battery needs a charge. If the indicator is yellow, the battery might need to be replaced. *(Courtesy of Chrysler Corporation, Sales and Marketing)*

Battery Open Circuit Test

An open circuit battery voltage test can be done easily by measuring total battery voltage across the positive and negative terminals. This is done after the battery has been stabilized or charged fully. This test will quickly determine the general state of charge and battery condition. This test uses a voltmeter placed across a battery that is disconnected. The voltmeter should read more than 12 volts. If there is a bad cell, the overall voltage will be less. *Figure 19–15* shows the relationship between open circuit voltage and percent of charge.

Load Tests

Several types of load tests can be performed on a battery. A light load test places a small 10–15 ampere load on the battery for a specific amount of time. The voltage of the cells

is then checked against the manufacturer's specification. The specifications are listed in the service and repair manuals. The high-discharge and cold-cranking tests place a larger load, 300–500 amperes, on the battery for a short period of time, usually 15 seconds. The amount of amperes placed on the battery depends on its size. Voltage readings are again

OPEN CIRCUIT VOLTAGE					
Voltage	11.7	12.0	12.2	12.4	12.6 or more
% charge	0%	25%	50%	75%	100%

FIGURE 19–15.   When testing for open circuit voltage, use these voltage readings to determine the percent of charge.

taken to determine the voltage of each cell or the total battery. These readings are compared with specifications to determine the condition of the battery. The reserve-capacity test places the same load on the battery as the ampere-hour rating test. This rating is a time or minutes measurement.

Slow Charging Batteries

Batteries can be brought back to a fully charged state by two methods: the slow and fast charges. The slow charge is defined as charging the battery at a low ampere rating over a long period of time. Slow charging a battery is much more effective than fast charging. Slow charging causes the lead sulfate of the discharged battery plates to convert to lead peroxide and sponge lead throughout the thickness of the plate. See *Figure 19–16*.

The slow charge ampere rate is 1 ampere per positive plate in one cell. For example, if the cell has eleven plates, there are six negative and five positive plates. The slow charge ampere rate would then be 5 amps until the battery is fully charged. This may be in excess of 24 hours.

Fast Charging Batteries

Batteries can also be charged using a higher rate of amperes. Fast charging a battery changes the lead sulfate only on the outside of the battery plates. The internal parts of the plate are still lead sulfate. See *Figure 19–17*. Fast charges are used to "boost" the battery for immediate cranking power. *Figure 19–18* shows a table of time and charge rates for different specific gravity readings. Use this table only as a guideline.

SLOW CHARGE

ENLARGED VIEW OF (+) PLATE

$PbSO_4$ (LEAD SULFATE) CHANGED TO PbO_2 THROUGH ENTIRE PLATE THICKNESS

PbO_2 PbO_2
PbO_2 PbO_2
PbO_2

FIGURE 19–16. A slow charge will change the lead sulfate back to lead peroxide throughout the entire thickness of the plate.

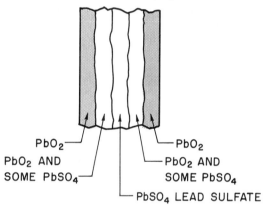

FAST CHARGE

ENLARGED VIEW OF (+) PLATE

PbO_2 PbO_2
PbO_2 AND SOME $PbSO_4$ PbO_2 AND SOME $PbSO_4$
$PbSO_4$ LEAD SULFATE

FIGURE 19–17. When a battery is fast charged, only the outer surface of the plate changes to lead peroxide. The inner part of the plate is still lead sulfate.

SPECIFIC GRAVITY READING	CHARGE RATE AMPERES	BATTERY CAPACITY – AMPERE-HOURS			
		45	55	70	85
Above 1.225	5	★	★	★	★
1.200–1.225	35	30 min.	35 min.	45 min.	55 min.
1.175–1.200	35	40 min.	50 min.	60 min.	75 min.
1.150–1.175	35	50 min.	65 min.	80 min.	105 min.
1.125–1.150	35	65 min.	80 min.	100 min.	125 min.

BATTERY HIGH RATE CHARGE TIME SCHEDULE

★ Charge at 5-ampere rate until specific gravity reaches 1.250 @ 80°F.

FIGURE 19–18. This table shows the charging rates for different specific gravity ratings and battery capacity ratings. Use this chart as a guideline when fast charging a battery. Charge at 5-ampere rate only until the specific gravity reaches 1.250 at 80 degrees F. At no time during charging should the electrolyte temperature be higher than 125 degrees F.

Problems, Diagnosis and Service

PROBLEM: Corroded Battery Terminals

The engine in a vehicle is not able to start. The battery seems to be in good condition and is still operating the accessories.

DIAGNOSIS

Often, dirty battery terminals restrict the heavy flow of electricity, during starting, from the terminal to the battery post. Refer to *Figure 19–19*. Corrosion can build up on the top and side-type battery terminals. To check the condition of the battery post and connector, a voltmeter can be used. Check the voltage drop across or between the battery post and the connector. Any voltage drop indicates a resistance is present between the two, and corrosion exists.

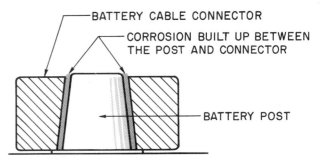

FIGURE 19–19. Corrosion can develop between the battery post and the cable connector. Use a wire brush to clean off the corrosion on the post and the cable connector.

SERVICE

1. Always use the correct battery tools when working on automotive batteries. See *Figure 19–20*. To clean the battery post use the following general procedure:
   a. Remove the negative terminal, then the positive terminal of the battery.
   b. Using a wire brush, clean both the post and the connectors, removing all corrosion.
   c. Clean the remaining corrosion using a small amount of baking soda and water solution.

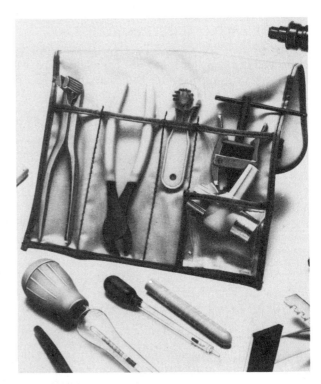

FIGURE 19–20. Always use the proper tools when servicing a battery. *(Courtesy of Snap-On Tools Corporation)*

2. Battery terminal clamps that are corroded beyond repair can be replaced. Remove the clamps from the battery post. Cut off the old clamp and strip about 3/4 inch of insulation from the cable. Clean the exposed copper wire strands and install a top or side-mounted replacement clamp or terminal. See *Figure 19–21*.

PROBLEM: Overcharging the Battery

A battery continually needs water to keep the electrolyte to the correct level.

DIAGNOSIS

A battery that continually needs water is being overcharged by the alternator or is overcharging because it will not accept a charge.

SERVICE

Various checks need to be completed:

1. The regulator on the charging system needs to be checked for correct voltage and current output (see Chapter 21).

2. Perform a load test on the battery. *Figure 19–22* shows one manufacturer's procedure for testing a battery. In this case, when the battery is load tested, the voltage cannot drop below 9.6 volts.

3. If the battery has fill holes, check the specific gravity.

   CAUTION: Be careful not to spill any electrolyte when using the hydrometer tester.

4. When adding water, keep these rules in mind:
   a. Never add sulfuric acid to a battery to increase its specific gravity readings. Add only water.
   b. Check the level of water in the battery by removing the vent caps (if not a maintenance-free battery).

   c. Using distilled water, add water to each cell until the water is level with the lower inside ring of the vent hole.
   d. Make sure the level of water is the same in each cell.
   e. Replace the vent caps, and dry off any water spilled on the top of the battery.

PROBLEM: Storing a Battery

A battery needs to be stored over a long period of time. What procedure should be followed?

DIAGNOSIS

Batteries will self-discharge as shown in *Figure 19–23*. It is best to store a battery that is not in use in a cool location. The cool temperature retards the chemical reaction and reduces self-discharging.

SERVICE

When storing a battery over a long period of time, use these general rules:

1. Store in a cool, dry location.

2. Store the battery on wood or other nonconductive material.

3. Before storage, prepare the battery as follows: Keep the outer case of the battery clean from dirt and grime. A certain amount of battery leakage can occur through dirt and grime. Clean the battery case with a solution of water and baking soda.

PROBLEM: Dirty Battery Casing and Top

A battery seems to be losing its charge when sitting for a long time.

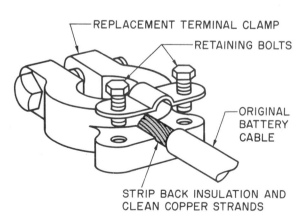

—REPLACEMENT TERMINAL CLAMP
—RETAINING BOLTS
—ORIGINAL BATTERY CABLE
STRIP BACK INSULATION AND CLEAN COPPER STRANDS

FIGURE 19–21.   The cable connectors on the ends of battery cables can be replaced. Remove the old connector, cut back the insulation, and replace the connector with a new one.

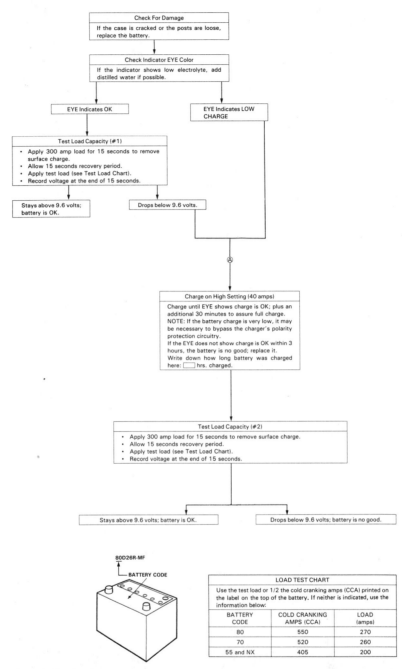

FIGURE 19–22. Use this procedure when checking a battery. Note that after each load test, the battery voltage must be at least 9.6 volts. (*Courtesy of Honda Motor Company, Ltd.*)

DIAGNOSIS

Acid, dirt, corrosion, or cracks on the top of the battery can cause a slow discharge or leakage of the energy stored in the battery. If enough of this leakage occurs, there is a good chance the battery will be too weak to start the engine.

SERVICE

1. Use the following general procedures to check for leakage:
   a. Make sure the engine is off.
   b. Using a voltmeter, connect the black clip to the negative side of the battery.
   c. Lightly touch the red clip to various parts of the battery top and sides (not the battery posts).
   d. Carefully watch the meter for any voltage readings. There should be no voltage readings.
   e. A voltage reading, regardless of how small, indicates leakage. To correct the leakage, thoroughly clean the battery with a water and baking soda solution. Dry thoroughly, and retest the battery for leakage.

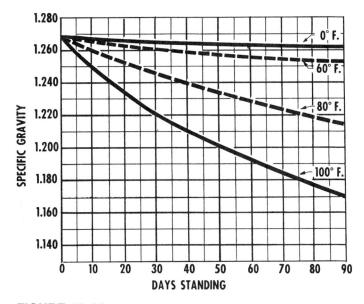

FIGURE 19–23. Batteries will self-discharge depending on the temperature around the battery. Colder conditions slow down any chemical action that would take place during self-discharging. *(Courtesy of Delco-Remy Division of General Motors Corporation)*

2. Use the following general procedure to charge a battery.

   CAUTION: Be extremely careful not to cross the jumper or charging cables. Always connect positive to positive and negative to negative. If the cables are crossed, you may damage various electrical components, including the computer in the vehicle.

   a. At no time during charging a battery should the electrolyte temperature exceed 125 degrees F. (The battery will feel very hot to the touch.)
   b. Make sure the top of the battery is clean.
   c. Remove the vent caps if applicable to allow gases to escape easily.
   d. Determine if the battery will be slow or fast charged. This will determine the amperage rating needed.
   e. Each battery charger manufacturer may have a slightly different procedure. *Figure 19–24* shows a typical battery charger.
   f. With the battery charger disconnected from the power (110 volts), attach the positive lead of the charger to the positive terminal of the battery. If the battery terminal posts on the top cannot be identified as positive or negative, the larger-diameter top terminal post is usually the positive side. It may also have a plus sign (+) near it or be painted red.
   g. Attach the negative lead of the battery charger to the negative terminal on the battery.
   h. At this point, plug in the charger to 110 volts and set the amperage readings (according to the specific charger instructions).
   i. Some battery chargers may also have a timer that should now be set.

   j. The time required to charge a battery will vary depending on several factors:
      - *Size of battery* — The larger the battery, the more time for charging.
      - *Temperature* — It takes longer to charge a colder battery than a warmer battery.

FIGURE 19–24. Each battery charger may have a slightly different procedure to charge the battery. Always follow the battery charger manufacturer's recommended procedure for charging batteries. *(Courtesy of Snap-On Tools Corporation)*

- *Charger capacity* — Battery chargers vary as to how much current they can put into the battery. Small chargers can only put around 10-12 amps into the battery. Other chargers can put up to 30 amps in.
- *State-of-charge* — The more discharged the battery, the greater the time needed for charging.

k. After the battery is charged, shut the charger off.

l. Remove the power cord (110 volts).

m. Now remove the positive and negative terminal leads between the battery and the battery charger.

CAUTION: The purpose of having the charger unplugged from the terminal leads is to prevent an explosion. Any small spark could ignite explosive gases around the battery.

PROBLEM: Jump Starting a Battery

A vehicle has been left with the lights on while parked. The battery is now dead and will not start the vehicle.

DIAGNOSIS

Batteries that have been temporarily discharged may be jump started by another vehicle's battery. The battery voltage of the second car should be enough to jump start the discharged battery.

CAUTION: When jump starting a battery that has a computer in the vehicle, make sure the battery cables do not get crossed. If they do, they could produce a spark and damage the computer beyond repair.

SERVICE

Use the following general procedure in an emergency for jump starting a battery:

1. *Figure 19–25* shows an example of the connections for jump starting a battery.

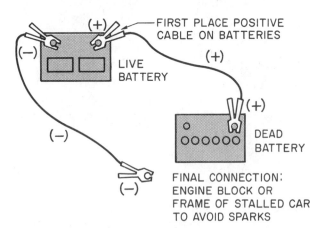

FIGURE 19–25. When boosting or jump starting a car, always connect the jumper cables as shown. Make the final connection between the engine block or frame to avoid sparks around or near the battery.

2. Make sure the engine is off.

3. Connect the positive terminal of the discharged battery to the positive terminal of the good battery. It is very important that the positive terminals are connected together.

4. The negative cable should be connected between the engine block, ground, or frame to avoid sparks around or near the battery.

CAUTION: Do not connect directly to the negative terminal of the dead or discharged battery.

5. Now start the engine of the live battery. The live battery's vehicle should be kept running during starting to avoid draining its battery.

6. In some cases, if the battery is extremely discharged, it may have to accept a charge for several minutes before starting.

7. Now reverse the directions exactly when removing the jumper cables.

SERVICE MANUAL CONNECTION

There are many important specifications to keep in mind when working with automotive batteries. To identify the specifications for your engine, you will need to know the VIN (vehicle identification number) of the vehicle, the type and year of the vehicle, and the type of engine. Although they may be titled differently, some of the more common battery specifications (not all) found in service manuals are listed below. Note that these specifications are typical examples. Each vehicle and engine may have different specifications.

Common Specification	Typical Example
Ampere-hour rating	105 ampere-hours
Cold-cranking amps (CCA)	550 amperes
Hydrometer reading	1.280
Test load	270 amperes
Voltage after test load applied	9.6 volts minimum

In addition, the service manual will give specific directions for various service and testing procedures. Some of the more common procedures include:

- Battery charging (procedure/time/amperage)
- Battery diagnosis
- Battery replacement
- Cold-cranking tests
- Light load tests
- Measuring specific gravity

Linkage to Future Automotive Technology

BATTERIES OF THE FUTURE

Researchers are continually looking for ways to make new and more efficient batteries. The need for better batteries has increased since interest in battery-powered and solar-powered vehicles has increased. It is estimated that battery-operated vehicles might account for 20% of all new car sales in the early part of the twenty-first century.

Three major battery characteristics are being researched: cell density (watt-hours per pound), operating temperature, and cell life cycles. The table below compares six types of batteries. Watt-hours per pound is probably the most important factor. The higher this value the more energy can be stored for each pound of battery weight. The high temperatures needed for some batteries show that more research must be completed on sealing, corrosion, and battery placement in the vehicle.

	Lead-antimony	Calcium-lead	Zinc-chloride	Sodium-sulfur	Lithium-sulfur	Molten sodium
Cell density (watt-hours/lb)	3–4	6–8	10–15	15–18	15–18	45
Operating temperature	Near ambient	Near ambient	Near ambient	572°–662°F	716°–842°F	482°–626°F
Cell life cycles (no. of cycles)	500	600	600	400	500	2000–3000

SUMMARY

This chapter analyzed the storage battery and its design. The purpose of the storage battery is to store energy chemically so it can be used later as electrical energy. Two types of batteries are manufactured: the primary battery and secondary battery. The secondary battery can be recharged and is the type used in the automobile.

Batteries are made by combining a series of cells. A cell is made by using two metals and an acid. The positive plate metal is lead peroxide. The negative plate metal is sponge lead. The acid is a mixture of water and sulfuric acid. When these three components are placed together, approximately 2 volts are produced. This is called a lead-acid battery. Cells are added in series and parallel to get 12 volts and a larger amount of amperage capacity.

The combination water and acid is called an electrolyte. During discharging and charging, the electrolyte gives off explosive gases. Also, as the battery discharges, the two metals turn into lead sulfate, and the electrolyte turns chemically into water.

The amount of acid in the electrolyte is measured by the specific gravity. Specific gravity is a measure of the weight of the electrolyte compared with the weight of water. Water has a specific gravity of 1.000. A fully charged battery has a specific gravity of 1.270. As the battery is discharged, the specific gravity decreases.

The maintenance-free battery is used to reduce the gassing and maintenance. There are no caps on the battery for adding water. The chemicals inside are designed to reduce gassing and evaporation of water.

There are several types of battery ratings. The ratings usually tell the technician the amperage capacity or the ability of the battery to produce amperage. The cold-cranking performance rating is used to measure the cranking ability of the battery when the engine is cold. The reserve capacity rating measures how long the battery can supply electricity for emergency power when the engine is shut down. The ampere-hour rating measures the discharge of the battery at a specific amperage for a 20-hour period. The watt-hour rating is measured by multiplying the ampere-hour rating by the voltage of the battery.

Several tests and maintenance procedures can be performed on the battery. The hydrometer test is used to measure the specific gravity of the battery. When taking this test, the readings must be corrected for temperature. Also, note that if the battery's specific gravity gets too low, it may freeze and crack the battery.

Load tests are used to measure the battery's ability to handle an electrical load. The light load test places a small amperage on the battery to discharge it. The battery voltage is measured to determine its state or condition. The high-discharge or cold-cranking test places a larger amperage load on the battery, about 300–500 amps. Voltage is then measured to determine the battery's condition. The reserve-capacity test places a continuous load on the battery. The battery is discharged until the battery voltage drops below a certain point. The measurement is made in minutes.

Batteries can either be slow or fast charged. Slow charged batteries get a better and deeper charge. Fast charge batteries use more amperage initially to charge the battery, but the time of charge is relatively short.

There are many service tips that should be observed when working on batteries. Important tips include never work around a battery without safety glasses, use baking soda and water to flush battery acid from the eyes, use the proper tools when working on a battery, never smoke around a charging battery, and never spill acid on other parts or clothes.

TERMS TO KNOW

Can you explain each of the following terms? Review the chapter until you can use each term correctly.

Electrochemical
Primary battery
Secondary battery
Battery cell
Electrolyte
Amperage capacity
Discharging
Charging

Cycle
Deep cycle battery
Specific gravity
Baffles
Cell density
Hydrometer
Slow charge

 REVIEW QUESTIONS

Multiple Choice

1. The positive plate of the lead-acid battery is made of:
   a. Lead oxide
   b. Lead peroxide
   c. Sponge lead
   d. Sulfuric acid
   e. None of the above

2. The negative plate of the lead-acid battery is made of:
   a. Lead oxide
   b. Lead peroxide
   c. Sponge lead
   d. Sulfuric acid
   e. None of the above

3. The purpose of the battery is to store _____ energy for use later as electrical energy.
   a. Radiant
   b. Chemical
   c. Thermal
   d. Nuclear
   e. Mechanical

4. Which type of battery can be recharged?
   a. Primary battery
   b. Antimony battery
   c. Secondary battery
   d. Sulfur battery
   e. None of the above

5. As a lead-acid battery is discharged, the negative plate is converted to:
   a. Lead sulfate
   b. Sponge lead
   c. Water
   d. Sulfuric acid
   e. None of the above

6. As a lead-acid battery is discharged, the positive plate is converted to:
   a. Lead sulfate
   b. Sponge lead
   c. Water
   d. Sulfuric acid
   e. None of the above

7. When battery cells are placed in series, the voltage of the battery will:
   a. Be reduced to zero
   b. Be additive
   c. Remain the same
   d. Increase by one half of each cell voltage
   e. None of the above

8. When battery cells are placed in parallel, the amperage capacity of the battery will:
   a. Be reduced to zero
   b. Be increased
   c. Remain the same
   d. Decrease
   e. None of the above

9. What is the ratio of water and sulfuric acid in a lead-acid battery?
   a. 10% water, 90% acid
   b. 20% water, 80% acid
   c. 30% water, 70% acid
   d. 50% water, 50% acid
   e. None of the above

10. What is the specific gravity of a fully charged battery?
    a. 1.000–1.002
    b. 1.128–1.130
    c. 1.270–1.295
    d. 1.940–2.300
    e. 1.750–2.100

11. Cell density of a battery is a measure of the:
    a. Electrolyte amount
    b. Watt-hours/pound produced from the battery
    c. Amperage capacity
    d. Active materials in the battery
    e. Specific gravity

12. Which battery rating is used to measure the battery's ability to provide electricity when the engine is shut off?
    a. Cold-cranking performance
    b. Reserve capacity rating
    c. Ampere-hour rating
    d. Watt-hour rating
    e. None of the above

13. The object of a hydrometer test is to determine the _____ of the battery.
    a. Voltage
    b. Amperage
    c. Wattage
    d. Specific gravity
    e. Amount of lead sulfate

14. What correction is needed to compensate for the temperature of the electrolyte when taking specific gravity readings?
    a. Increase 0.004 for each 10 degrees above 80 degrees F.
    b. Increase 0.008 for each 10 degrees above 80 degrees F.
    c. Decrease 0.004 for each 10 degrees above 80 degrees F.
    d. Decrease 0.004 for each 1 degree above 80 degrees F.
    e. None of the above.

15. Which type of charge will give the battery the deepest and most effective charge?
    a. Fast charge
    b. Boost charge
    c. Intermediate charge
    d. Slow charge
    e. No charge

16. What should be used when battery acid gets into the eyes?
    a. Water only
    b. Lead sulfate
    c. Sulfuric acid
    d. Baking soda and water
    e. Sponge lead

17. When a battery is stored or not used, it is better to store the battery in a _____ location.
    a. Warm
    b. 80 degrees or above
    c. Cool
    d. Damp, moist
    e. None of the above

The following questions are similar in format to ASE (Automotive Service Excellence) test questions.

18. Technician A says that maintenance-free batteries cannot be charged. Technician B says that maintenance-free batteries can be checked for specific gravity using a hand-held hydrometer. Who is right?
    a. A only
    c. Both A and B
    b. B only
    d. Neither A nor B

19. Battery acid has just been spilled on a person's clothing. Technician A says to wash the acid off with baking soda and water. Technician B says to wash the acid off with vinegar. Who is right?
    a. A only
    b. B only
    c. Both A and B
    d. Neither A nor B

20. While being charged, a battery becomes very hot. Technician A says the heat is normal, and there is no need for concern. Technician B says that the battery could be overcharging, and the amount of charge should be reduced. Who is right?
    a. A only
    b. B only
    c. Both A and B
    d. Neither A nor B

21. Technician A says the larger battery terminal is positive and the smaller terminal is negative. Technician B says the smaller battery terminal is positive and the larger terminal is negative. Who is right?
    a. A only
    b. B only
    c. Both A and B
    d. Neither A nor B

22. Technician A says that a battery can be checked for leakage around a dirty battery case. Technician B says that a battery case can be cleaned with baking soda. Who is right?
    a. A only
    b. B only
    c. Both A and B
    d. Neither A nor B

23. Technician A says the amount of a charge is determined by the size of the jumper cables. Technician B says the time of charge is determined by the size of the battery. Who is right?
    a. A only
    b. B only
    c. Both A and B
    d. Neither A nor B

24. A battery continually needs additional water. Technician A says it's OK to add acid to the battery. Technician B says the battery may not be able to accept a charge any longer. Who is right?
    a. A only
    b. B only
    c. Both A and B
    d. Neither A nor B

25. A battery will not start the engine, but the lights and horn still work. Technician A says the problem is a corroded battery cable connector. Technician B says the problem is that the electrolyte has a specific gravity of 1.280. Who is right?
    a. A only
    b. B only
    c. Both A and B
    d. Neither A nor B

Essay

26. What is the difference between primary batteries and secondary batteries?

27. What is a definition of the specific gravity of a battery?

28. Define cell density of a battery.

29. What is the definition of the cold-cranking performance rating of a battery?

30. What is the purpose of a hydrometer when used with a battery?

31. What happens to the specific gravity as temperature increases?

Short Answer

32. At what amperage could a 120 ampere-hour rated battery be discharged for a period of 20 hours? _____

33. A battery has a specific gravity of 1.165 and has an electrolyte temperature of 100 degrees F. The actual specific gravity of the battery is _____.

34. On maintenance-free batteries, the vent holes are located _____.

35. What is the watt-hour rating of a 12-volt battery that has a 100 ampere-hour rating? _____.

36. At the completion of a battery open circuit test, the voltmeter should read _____ volts across the battery terminals.

CHAPTER 20

Ignition Systems

INTRODUCTION   In order for proper combustion to take place, the air and fuel mixture must be ignited. The ignition system is designed to produce a spark in the combustion chamber at a precise moment. This chapter discusses the components that make up the ignition system. These include the coil, points, spark plugs, advance mechanisms, and electronic and computer systems for ignition.

OBJECTIVES   After reading this chapter, you should be able to:

- Identify the parts and operation of the conventional ignition system that uses contact points.

- Define the operation of the primary and secondary circuits.

- Examine the operation and purpose of advance mechanisms.

- Identify spark plug design and operation.

- Analyze the electronic spark control systems used on vehicles today.

- Define the parts and operation of distributor-less ignition systems.

- State common problems, diagnosis, and service procedures used on the ignition system.

✔ SAFETY CHECKLIST ✔

When working with the ignition system, keep these important safety precautions in mind.

✔ To eliminate the possibility of electrical shock, never crank an engine with one of the spark plug wires off.

✔ Always use the correct tools when working with the ignition system.
✔ Always wear approved OSHA safety glasses when working on the ignition system.
✔ Always use the correct tools when working on the ignition system.

20.1 CONTACT POINT (CONVENTIONAL) IGNITION SYSTEMS

Purpose of the Ignition System

The air and fuel in the combustion chamber must be ignited at a precise point in time during the four-stroke cycle. This is done by causing an electrical spark to jump across a gap on a spark plug. About 5,000 to 50,000 volts are needed to force the electrical current to jump across the spark plug gap. However, there is only a 12-volt battery within the automobile. The ignition system is used to increase the voltage to the necessary amount at the right time for the spark to occur. In addition, the time of spark must also be altered as speed and load increase or decrease. Advance and retard mechanisms are used to accomplish this.

The ignition system has been developed and changed as the automobile has changed. The conventional ignition system using a mechanical set of points and condensers has

Some of the information in this chapter can help you prepare for the National Institute for Automotive Service Excellence (ASE) certification tests. The tests most directly related to this chapter are entitled

ENGINE REPAIR (TEST A1) AND ENGINE PERFORMANCE (TEST A8).

The content area that closely parallels this chapter is

IGNITION SYSTEM DIAGNOSIS AND REPAIR.

Conventional Ignition System Components and Operation

There are two separate circuits in the ignition system: the *primary circuit* and the *secondary circuit*. The primary circuit is considered the low-voltage circuit. Low voltage is battery voltage, or about 12 volts. The secondary circuit is called the high-voltage circuit. Components in this circuit operate at voltages between 5,000 and 50,000 volts, depending on the type of system being used.

The primary circuit operates as shown in *Figure 20–1*.

1. *The battery* is used to provide a source of electrical energy needed to operate the system. The negative side is grounded to the frame, and the positive side is fed directly to the ignition switch.

2. *The ignition switch* connects or disconnects the flow of electricity to the ignition system. The ignition switch will direct the current through a bypass route during cranking and through the ballast resistor during normal operation. The ballast resistor can also be a resistive-type wire.

3. *The ballast resistor* controls the current flow to the coil during normal operation. The resistor reduces the voltage available to the coil at low engine speeds. It increases the voltage at higher RPM when the voltage requirement increases.

been updated to an electronic ignition system using semiconductors and transistors. From this development, electronic ignition systems now work directly with computer-controlled systems. In order to analyze these ignition systems, the conventional ignition system will be briefly analyzed and compared with the newer computer-controlled systems.

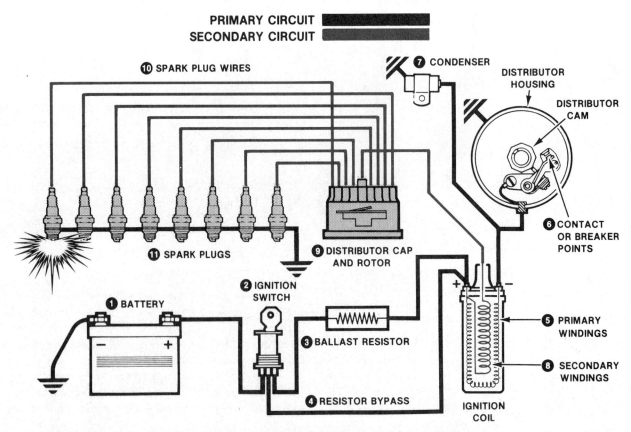

FIGURE 20–1. Both primary and secondary circuits are used in the ignition system. The primary circuit operates on 12 volts, and the secondary circuit operates on 5,000 to 50,000 volts. *(Courtesy of Sun® Electric Corporation)*

4. *The resistor bypass circuit* is used only when the engine is being cranked. During this time, more voltage is needed at the coil to produce spark. When the operator stops cranking the engine, the electrical current flows through the ballast resistor.

5. *The primary coil windings* are used to convert the electrical energy into a magnetic field. When electricity passes through the primary windings, a strong magnetic field is produced. This magnetic field also surrounds the secondary windings.

6. *Breaker points* are used to close and open the primary circuit. As the distributor shaft rotates, it also causes a distributor cam to rotate. The *distributor cam* causes a small set of points to open and close at each cam lobe position. When the points are closed, current flow in the primary circuit causes the magnetic field to build up in the coil. When the points are opened, the current flow stops. This causes the magnetic field in the coil to collapse. The sudden collapse of the primary magnetic field produces a strong induced voltage in the secondary windings.

7. *The condenser* is used to reduce the amount of arcing when the points open the primary circuit. Whenever an electrical circuit is broken, it produces arcing. This arcing can cause the points to be pitted or corroded. The condenser helps to reduce corrosion on the points.

The secondary circuit is called the high-voltage circuit. Depending on the system, the voltage in the secondary circuit may be as high as 50,000 volts. The components in the secondary circuit operate as shown in Figure 20–1.

8. *The secondary coil windings* are used to capture the voltage produced by the collapsing primary magnetic field. There is approximately a 12:20,000 volt (1:1,666) ratio of windings between the primary and the secondary circuits. This means that for each volt in the primary windings, there are about 1,666 volts in the secondary windings. This will produce 20,000 volts on the secondary

circuit. This high voltage available at the secondary windings is fed to the coil tower when the primary magnetic field collapses.

9. *The distributor cap and rotor* are used to distribute the surges of high voltage available at the coil tower. The high-voltage surge is sent from the coil to the center of the distributor by the coil wire. The surges are then directed, one at a time, to each outer terminal of the distributor cap by the rotor. The rotor is turned by the distributor shaft.

10. *The spark plug wires* are used to connect the high-voltage surge to each spark plug. They are arranged in the firing order of the engine.

11. *The spark plugs* provide a predetermined gap within the combustion chamber so that each time a high-voltage surge is delivered, a quality spark will occur in the combustion chamber.

Dwell

Dwell is defined as the length of time the points remain closed. ***Figure 20–2*** shows the dwell on a typical engine. As the distributor cam rotates, the points are opened and closed. Dwell is important because during dwell the magnetic field is increasing. As the dwell time increases, the magnetic field buildup increases, producing a greater secondary voltage. ***Figure 20–3*** shows the different dwells for different cylinder engines. Four-cylinder engines have a greater amount of time that the points remain closed (greater dwell). This causes a greater magnetic field buildup around the primary coil, which produces a greater secondary voltage.

Distributor

The distributor is used to hold many of the ignition components. It has a center shaft that is driven by the main camshaft of the engine. This is done by using a small helical gear that meshes with a similar gear on the camshaft. On many engines, there is also a slot on the bottom of the distributor shaft. This slot is used to turn the oil pump. It must be aligned during installation. In addition to a helical

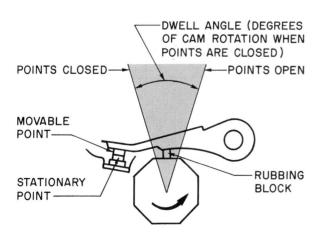

FIGURE 20–2.   Dwell is defined as the length of time the points are closed in degrees of rotation

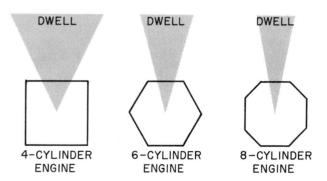

FIGURE 20–3.   Four-cylinder engines have a greater dwell time than eight-cylinder engines.

gear, certain manufacturers use a simple slot or offset slot to turn the distributor shaft.

The distributor is used to turn the distributor cam. In addition, the distributor holds the contact points, condenser, and advance mechanisms, and supports the rotor and distributor cap. *Figure 20–4* shows a typical distributor for a conventional ignition system.

Distributor Rotor and Cap

The distributor rotor and cap are used to distribute the secondary voltage to each spark plug. *Figure 20–5* shows a rotor and cap used on an eight-cylinder engine. They are made from insulating materials such as Bakelite, plastic, or epoxy that are easily shaped. Conductors are placed inside the material to allow high-voltage electricity to pass through.

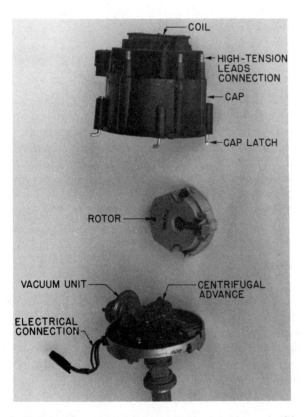

FIGURE 20–4. The distributor holds the primary ignition parts, the rotor, and the distributor cap.

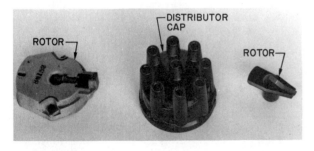

FIGURE 20–5. Examples of rotors and a distributor cap used on an eight-cylinder engine.

The high voltage produced each time the points open is sent from the high-voltage terminal on the coil to the center of the distributor cap, which is called the coil tower. The high voltage is then sent inside the cap to the rotor, which is being turned by the distributor shaft. As the rotor revolves inside the cap, it distributes the high voltage to each cylinder according to the firing order of the engine. There are many shapes and sizes of rotors used on older engines.

CAR CLINIC

PROBLEM: Engine Misses In Damp Weather

An engine operates fine in dry weather. When it rains or the weather is very damp, the engine starts to run very rough. A loss of power is also noticed.

SOLUTION:

The most common problem that causes the engine to misfire in damp weather is poor plug wires. If the wires are bad (have poor insulation) they will short between each other and to ground when the surrounding air has high moisture content. The best way to check this is to run the engine at night (so you can see the shorted sparks) in damp weather. If it is not damp outside, spray a light mist around the engine with a garden hose.

20.2 ADVANCE MECHANISMS

Purpose of Advancing the Spark

Ignition timing is defined as the time in degrees of crankshaft rotation that the spark occurs during idle. This is called the initial timing. The initial timing is adjusted when the engine is at idle. It is usually adjusted several degrees before top dead center (BTDC). As the engine speed and load increase, the timing must also increase.

As the engine speed increases, the piston moves faster and the time of spark must also be advanced. This is because the crankshaft will move farther during the time the combustion occurs. There must be enough time for the combustion to be complete. In *Figure 20–6*, when the engine is at 1,200 RPM, the spark occurs about 6 degrees BTDC. At 23 degrees after top dead center (ATDC), the combustion ends. This will produce an even power pulse to the piston on the power stroke. As the engine is run faster, say at 3,600 RPM, the timing must be increased to as far as 30 degrees BTDC so the combustion can end at 23 degrees ATDC. Of course, these figures will vary with different engines. The principle, however, is the same.

Load also affects when the timing should occur. If the load is increased, different amounts of air and fuel are needed in

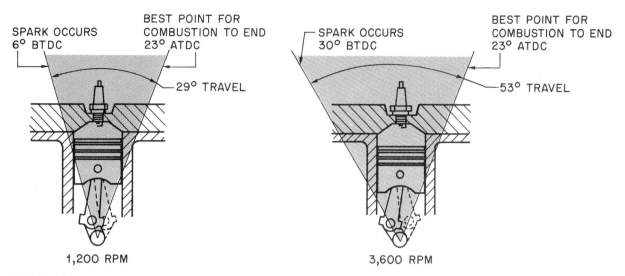

FIGURE 20–6. The speed of the engine determines how much spark advance is needed. As the engine speeds up, more advance is required to complete the combusion on time.

the combustion chamber. It takes longer for the combustion to occur, and the timing must be adjusted.

Initial Timing

The initial timing is set by adjusting the distributor. When the distributor is placed in the engine, the distributor shaft gear meshes with the engine camshaft. The distributor housing can, however, be rotated. When the housing is rotated, the timing of the engine will be either advanced or retarded. Timing is set by using a timing light attached to the number one cylinder. When the number one cylinder fires, the timing light flashes. If this light is pointed toward the timing marks on the crankshaft of the engine, the exact timing of the engine can be determined. See *Figure 20–7*.

Centrifugal Advance

The centrifugal advance increases or decreases the timing on the basis of the speed of the engine. There are two weights on the distributor shaft, *Figure 20–8*. Springs are used to hold them inward. As these weights turn, their centrifugal force causes them to spin outward. The outward movement of the weights causes the time in which the points open and close to be different. On some engines, weight movement causes the breaker plate (the plate the points are attached to) to move so the points open earlier. On other engines, the movement of the weights causes the position of the distributor cam to change. This causes the cam to open the points at a different time. *Figure 20–9* shows the effect of engine RPM and the increase in timing advance.

Vacuum Advance

The vacuum advance is used to increase the timing of the engine as the load increases. As load is applied to the engine, the intake manifold vacuum is reduced. The change in the intake manifold vacuum is used to advance the timing.

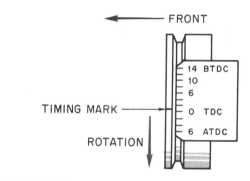

FIGURE 20–7. Timing marks are used to help determine the spark advance of the engine.

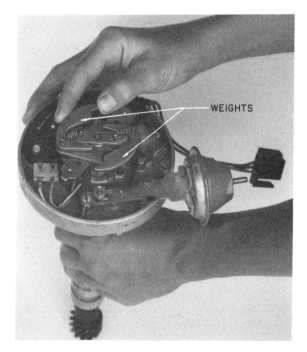

FIGURE 20–8. Centrifugal weights are used to advance the timing of the spark on the basis of RPM.

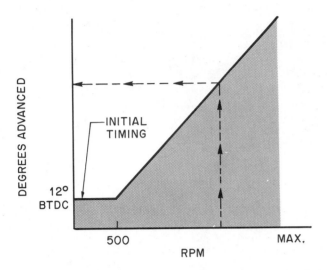

FIGURE 20–9.   This chart shows the effect of engine RPM and the increased timing of the spark. The initial timing is set at idle.

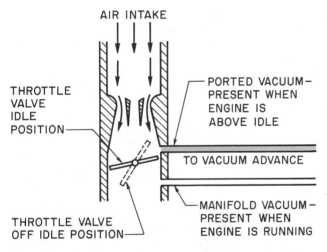

FIGURE 20–10.   Ported vacuum is taken from slightly above the throttle plate.

A diaphragm is attached to the side of the distributor. One side of the diaphragm is mechanically attached to the breaker plate by a small rod. The other end of the diaphragm is attached to the intake manifold vacuum. The intake manifold vacuum used is considered *ported vacuum*. Ported vacuum is present only when the engine is above idle. It is taken from slightly above the throttle plate when the throttle plate is in the closed position. See *Figure 20–10*. A spring is used to force the diaphragm and breaker plate to a retarded position. As the engine throttle is opened for increased load, the vacuum pulls back on the diaphragm against spring pressure. This rotates the breaker plate and advances the engine spark. See *Figure 20–11*. *Figure 20–12* shows how the vacuum advance is added to the centrifugal advance to obtain the total advance of the engine.

Advance and Emissions

Since the introduction of emission control devices, many systems have been added to control the spark more effectively. The goal has been to retard the spark during idle, or to delay the advance. By controlling the advance more accurately, combustion chamber temperatures have been raised. This reduces the amount of hydrocarbon emissions.

Many systems have been used. The following systems are the most common:

1. *Spark delay* — a valve placed in the vacuum line from the distributor vacuum advance to the carburetor. The spark delay is used to delay the spark during acceleration.

2. *Temperature-sensing vacuum control valve* — used to increase the advance when the engine coolant temperatures are too high. Advancing the engine causes the RPM to increase, which helps to cool the engine.

3. *Dual diaphragm vacuum advance* — used to apply both the ported and manifold vacuum to the advance. Its purpose is to improve starting and to retard initial timing to reduce exhaust emissions.

4. *Solenoid retard-advance* — used to control the timing by using a solenoid to operate the advance for starting.

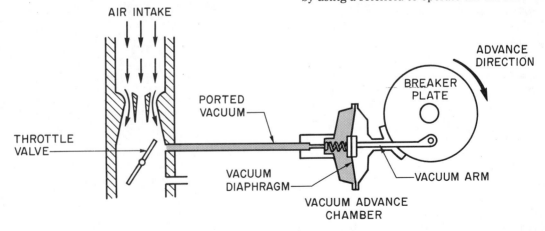

FIGURE 20–11.   Vacuum is used to rotate the breaker plate so the timing can be retarded or advanced on the basis of load.

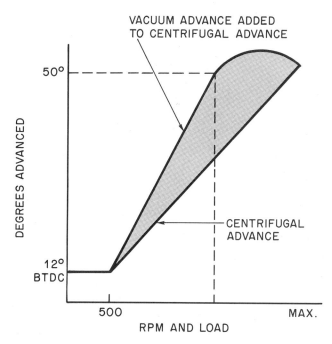

FIGURE 20–12.   Vacuum advance is added to centrifugal advance during engine operation.

CAR CLINIC

PROBLEM: Spark Knock

A GM engine is constantly knocking when the vehicle goes up hill. This started after about 50,000 miles. Using a higher-octane fuel helps a little, but the engine manufacturer says a lower-octane fuel is OK. Many ignition parts have already been replaced with no improvement.

SOLUTION:

On GM engines, the ignition is controlled by the PROM in the vehicle computer. The original PROM may have allowed too much advance on the ignition under engine load and octane conditions. The new PROM advances timing less at low intake manifold pressures, when knock is hard to control. Check with the manufacturer and replace the PROM.

20.3   SPARK PLUGS

Spark Plug Design

The purpose of the spark plug is to provide a place for a spark that is strong enough to ignite the air-fuel mixture to occur inside the combustion chamber. This is done by causing

a high voltage to arc across a gap on the spark plug. Spark plugs are designed as shown in *Figure 20–13*. The center electrode, often made of copper or platinum or a copper-platinum alloy, is a thick metal wire that runs through the plug. Its purpose is to conduct electricity from the high-voltage wire to the combustion chamber area. The insulator is a porcelain-like casing that surrounds the center electrode. The upper and lower portions of the center electrode are exposed. The metal casing is a threaded casing used for installing the spark plug into the cylinder head. It has threads and is hex-shaped to fit into a spark plug socket. The side electrode is a short, thick wire made of nickel alloy. It extends about 0.020–0.080 inch away from the center electrode. Its position creates the gap for the spark to jump across.

Spark Plug Heat Range

The heat range of a spark plug refers to its thermal characteristics. The thermal characteristics of a plug are a measure of how fast the plug can transfer combustion heat away from its firing end to the cylinder head of the engine, *Figure 20–14*. Plugs are considered to be cold or hot. There is a certain amount of thermal temperature at the time of the spark. If the plug tip temperature is too cold, the plug may foul out with carbon, oil, and other combustion deposits. If the plug tip temperature is too hot, preignition occurs and the plug and piston may be damaged. *Figure 20–15* shows the effect on the engine when plugs are too hot or cold. The tip temperature is shown as the vertical axis. The load on the engine is shown as the horizontal axis. When too cold a plug is used, carbon and oil fouling occur at idle conditions. When the plug is too hot, electrode burning and preignition occur at full load.

The spark plug heat range is changed by changing the length of the insulator nose. Hot plugs have relatively long insulator noses with a long heat flow path to the cylinder head. Cold plugs have a short insulator nose with a short heat flow path to the cylinder head. *Figure 20–16* shows the difference in design of hot and cold plugs.

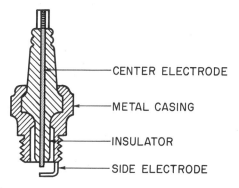

FIGURE 20–13.   A spark plug is made of a center electrode, an insulator, a metal casing, and the side electrode. *(Courtesy of Champion Spark Plug Company)*

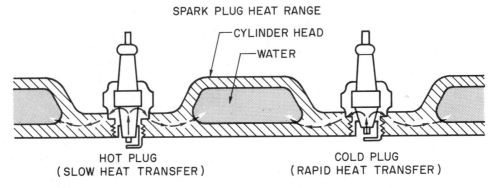

FIGURE 20–14. Plug heat ranges are based on the length of time it takes to remove the heat from the tip of the spark plug.

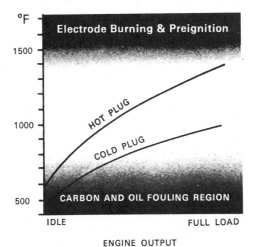

FIGURE 20–15. When plugs are too cold, they may foul out. If plugs are too hot, they may cause preignition. *(Courtesy of Champion Spark Plug Company)*

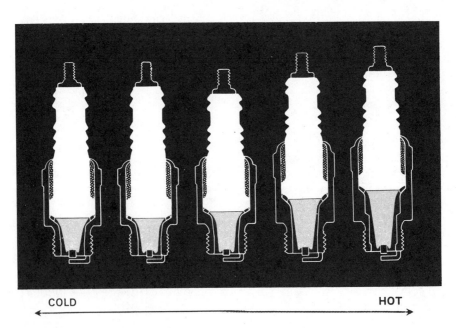

FIGURE 20–16. Spark plug heat ranges are changed by changing the length of the insulator nose inside the spark plug. *(Courtesy of Champion Spark Plug Company)*

Factors Affecting Spark Plug Temperatures

Many operational factors also affect the temperature of spark plugs. *Figure 20–17* shows some of the factors. Insulator tip temperature is shown on the left axis of each graph. Different factors are listed on the bottom axis of each graph. Each graph shows the type of relationship. Ignition timing causes spark plug temperature to change. Figure 20–17 (A) shows that as the engine is over-advanced, tip temperature

increases. Figure 20–17 (B) shows that as coolant temperature increases, the tip temperature also increases. Figure 20–17 (C) shows that as more detonation occurs from lower-octane fuel, tip temperature also increases. Figure 20–17 (D) shows that clean spark plugs have higher tip temperatures than spark plugs with deposits. Figure 20–17 (E) shows that as the air-fuel ratio changes from rich to lean, insulator tip temperatures also change.

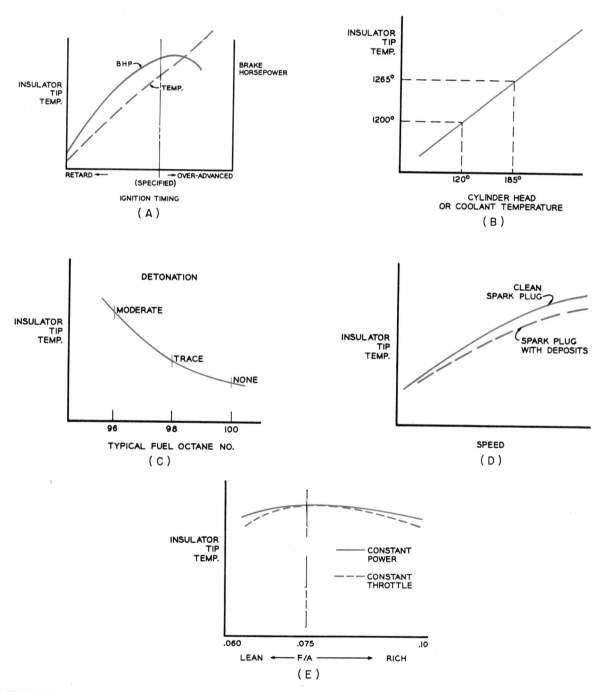

FIGURE 20–17. Many factors affect the temperature of the spark plug. These include advance (A), coolant temperature (B), detonation (C), condition of spark plugs (D), and air-fuel ratio (E). *(Courtesy of Champion Spark Plug Company)*

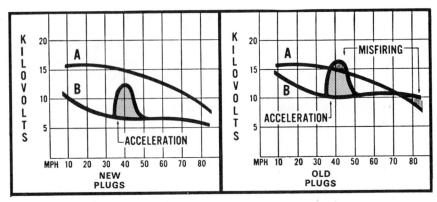

A Voltage available from ignition system
B Voltage required to fire new spark plugs

A Voltage available from ignition system
B Voltage required to fire old spark plugs

FIGURE 20–18. When old plugs are used, voltage requirements are higher. There may be times in which older plugs misfire. *(Courtesy of Champion Spark Plug Company)*

Factors Affecting Spark Plug Voltages

The voltage required by spark plugs also changes with various factors. *Figure 20–18* shows how new and old plugs require a different voltage from the ignition system. On the chart, line A is the voltage available from the ignition system. Line B is the kilovolts required to fire the spark plug. When old plugs are used, the voltage required to spark is greater. Older plugs may misfire at certain times.

Other factors also affect the voltage requirements. *Figure 20–19* shows some of these factors. Figure 20–19 (A) shows that as compression pressures increase, voltage requirements also increase. Figure 20–19 (B) shows that as plug gap is

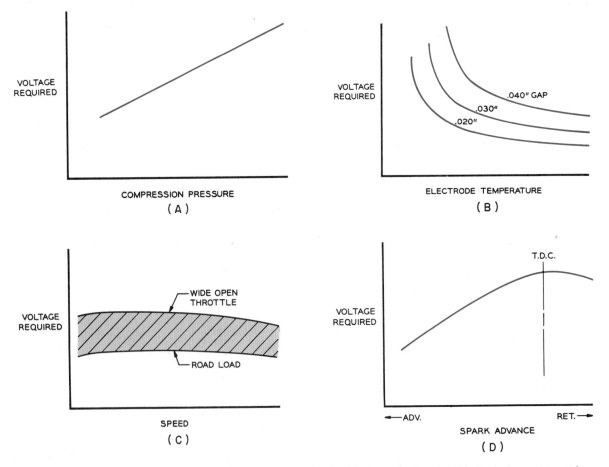

FIGURE 20–19. Many factors affect the voltage required of the spark plug. These include compression pressures (A), plug gap (B), speed/load (C), and timing advance (D). *(Courtesy of Champion Spark Plug Company)*

widened, voltage requirements increase. Figure 20–19 (C) shows that as the throttle or load is increased, the voltage requirements also increase. Figure 20–19 (D) shows that as the engine timing is advanced, voltage requirements decrease.

Variations in Spark Plug Design

Automotive manufacturers require many variations in the spark plug. These may include:

1. The number of threads on the spark plug

2. The design of the gasket for sealing the spark plug to the cylinder, or the use of a tapered seat rather than a gasket

3. The type of resistor element inside the plug to eliminate interference in radios and TVs

4. The type of electrode used to establish the spark plug gap

Manufacturers base their spark plug numbering system on these and other design features. Each spark plug manufacturer uses a different system. Take for example the spark plug manufacturer's number R V 18 Y C 4. These numbers indicate the following:

R = a resistor type plug
V = the type of shell design
18 = the heat range
Y = firing end design
C = firing end design
4 = wide gap designation

PROBLEM: Pinging Problem

A four-cylinder engine has a problem with pinging at high speeds and hot temperatures. The timing has been checked and is right on specifications. All of the advance mechanisms, including the weights and the vacuum systems, have been checked. What other problem might cause pinging?

SOLUTION:

The only items not checked were the spark plugs. Check the spark plugs and make sure they are the correct ones for the engine. If a spark plug range is too hot, the tip of the plug might not be cooling enough. This could cause pinging at high speeds and temperatures. The only other solution might be a large amount of carbon buildup on the top of the piston. This could cause the compression ratio to increase, which would cause compression temperatures to increase and cause preignition.

20.4 ELECTRONIC AND COMPUTER IGNITION SYSTEMS

Purpose of Electronic Ignition Systems

Two of the biggest problems with the conventional ignition system are the wear on the points and the speed at which the primary current is stopped. Conventional ignition systems use a set of contact points. With the introduction of solid-state components and transistors in the 1970s, however, many manufacturers converted the conventional ignition system to solid state. These ignition systems were developed and improved over a period of time. Systems were called capacitive discharge ignition systems, breakerless ignition systems, solid-state ignition systems, electronic ignition systems, and high-energy ignition systems. But they all had one thing in common. They used semiconductors (transistors) in circuits to open the primary circuit faster. The secondary circuit remained much the same, except that higher voltages were produced.

Transistors Used in Ignition Systems

Transistors are used to open and close the primary side of the ignition system. It was found that a transistor can open and close a circuit much faster than a set of breaker points. The magnetic field will then collapse much faster, producing a higher voltage in the secondary circuit. The secondary voltage may be as high as 60,000 volts with a transistor ignition system. This will improve the combustion and emission characteristics of the engine.

Triggering the Primary

Figure 20–20 shows how a simple transistor is used to trigger the primary side of the ignition coil. A small signal voltage is used to trigger the emitter-base circuit. This voltage signal is produced by a pickup coil and *reluctor* that act much like a small generator. The pickup voltage is a precisely timed signal. It triggers the electronic circuitry and transistors in the control unit. This interrupts the current flowing in the primary circuit, causing the ignition coil's magnetic field to collapse. The difference is that the emitter-collector circuit can be stopped very rapidly. This causes the magnetic field to collapse rapidly, producing a higher secondary voltage. The electronic circuit is much more complex than just one transistor. Dwell and timing advance can also be designed electronically into the system. *Figure 20–21* shows some of the more common types of reluctors used to trigger the transistor.

Figure 20–22 shows an example of the control unit. A complex electronic circuit inside turns the primary ignition coil on and off. The input includes the pickup coil signal, and the output is the primary side of the ignition coil. A vacuum advance and a centrifugal advance are still used on this system.

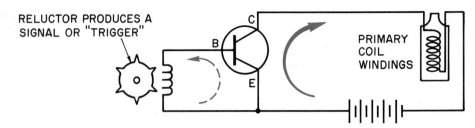

FIGURE 20–20. The transistor in a solid-state ignition system is used to turn off and on the primary side of the ignition coil. A small signal voltage triggers the transistor.

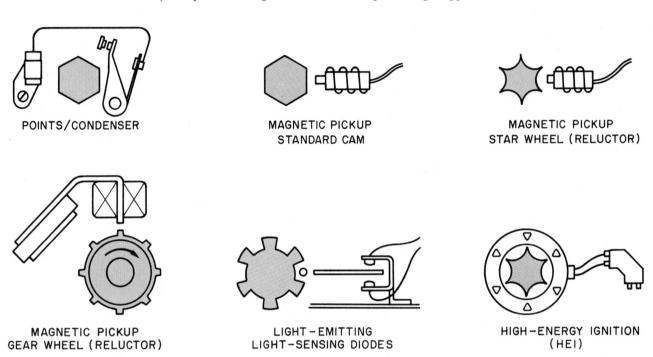

POINTS/CONDENSER

MAGNETIC PICKUP
STANDARD CAM

MAGNETIC PICKUP
STAR WHEEL (RELUCTOR)

MAGNETIC PICKUP
GEAR WHEEL (RELUCTOR)

LIGHT–EMITTING
LIGHT–SENSING DIODES

HIGH–ENERGY IGNITION
(HEI)

FIGURE 20–21. There are many types of reluctors used to trigger the transistor.

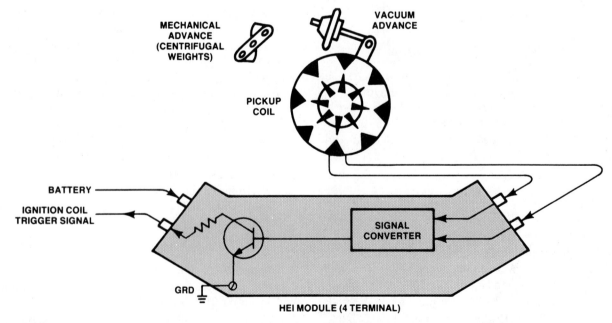

FIGURE 20–22. The control unit in a high-energy ignition (HEI) system uses the signal produced from the reluctor to turn the transistor on and off. The transistor controls the primary coil current. *(Courtesy of General Motors Product Service Training)*

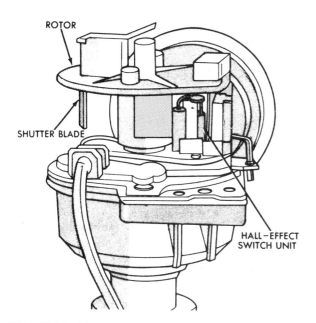

FIGURE 20–23. This Hall-effect sensor is used to sense and determine the position of the crankshaft for the computer. *(Courtesy of Motor Publications, Auto Engine Tune-up and Electronics Manual)*

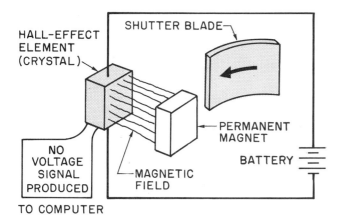

FIGURE 20–24. As the shutter blade passes in front of the magnet, it reduces the magnetic field, thus increasing the voltage and signal of the Hall-effect element.

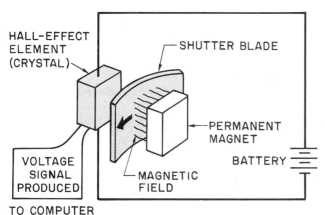

Hall-Effect Pickup

On electronic and computer-controlled ignition systems other types of electrical pickup devices are used. One such device is called the *Hall-effect* switch or sensor. Its purpose is to provide a signal each time a piston reaches top dead center. Hall-effect sensors are also able to read various positions within the 360 degrees rotation of the crankshaft. The signal produced by the switch is then used for ignition timing. One advantage of the Hall-effect sensor is that it provides a digital signal for the computer. *Figure 20–23* shows an example of a typical Hall-effect pickup inside a distributor. It consists of three parts. There is a permanent magnet, a shutter wheel, and a Hall-effect element. The permanent magnet is stationary. The Hall-effect element, or pickup, also called a crystal, is also stationary. The shutter wheel is rotated by the distributor shaft. As shown in *Figure 20–24*, a voltage is applied to the Hall-effect element producing an output voltage. When the shutter blade is not between the magnet and the crystal, the magnetic field has the effect of reducing the signal. This produces a weak voltage in the crystal (about 0.4 volts). However, when the shutter blade (vane) is between the magnet and the Hall-effect crystal, the magnetism is reduced, producing a higher voltage (12 volts) in the Hall-effect element. Through internal circuitry, the signal is then amplified and sent to the computer. *Figure 20–25* shows the Hall-effect pickup and the shutter blade.

Crankshaft Position Sensor

On some electronic and computer ignition systems, a crankshaft position (CP) sensor is used to trigger the ignition system or the computer. It is also used on many computer systems to provide a signal for ignition timing and engine speed. For example, Ford Motor Company uses a PIP (profile ignition pickup) for this purpose. *Figure 20–26* shows an example of a typical crankshaft position sensor. It is made of three parts: the pulse ring, the crankshaft position sensor, and the clamp assembly. The pulse ring is mounted and rotates on the crankshaft. Its purpose is to act as a trigger wheel to provide engine speed information. The crankshaft

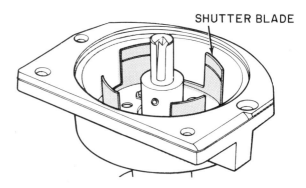

FIGURE 20–25. The position of the Hall-effect pickup is shown. *(Courtesy of Motor Publications, Auto Engine Tune-up and Electronics Manual)*

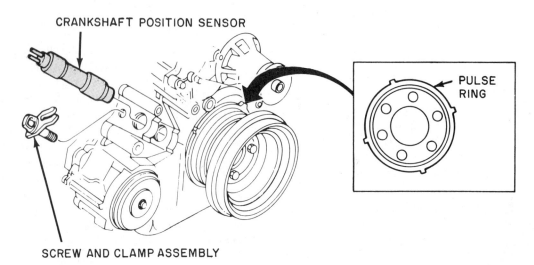

FIGURE 20–26. The crankshaft position sensor is located near the front of the crankshaft and is able to determine the crankshaft position for the computer. *(Courtesy of Ford Motor Company)*

position sensor is mounted near the pulse ring. Its purpose is to pick up an electrical signal from the pulse ring and send the signal to the electronic or computer ignition system. It does much the same as the magnetic pickup on older electronic ignition systems. The clamp assembly holds the sensor securely in the front of the cylinder block.

Other types of crankshaft position sensors are also used. They can be designed to read various positions on the 360 degrees rotation of the crankshaft. One is shown in *Figure 20–27*. It is called a permanent magnet pulse generator. Depending on the manufacturer and the year of the computer, the ECM (electronic control module) is able to read and separate each of the pulses.

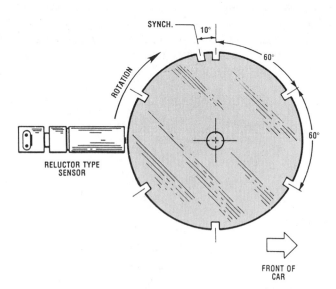

FIGURE 20–27. The permanent magnet pulse generator is able to read various positions of the crankshaft for the computer.

Detonation Sensors

The use of computers to control spark timing can be improved if the computer can sense detonation during the combustion process. If detonation or "knock" can be sensed, the optimum ignition timing can be controlled by the computer. A knock (*detonation*) *sensor* is a device that is able to pick up small, high-frequency vibration in the engine. When knock does occur (from poor fuel, cylinder temperature, and so on), a high-frequency vibration is caused by the spark knock. This high frequency (5,000–6,000 hertz, or cycles per second) can be converted to a voltage signal for the computer. The knock sensor uses a piezoelectric crystal to sense knock. This crystal is able to produce an electrical signal (about 0.3 volts) when a vibration occurs. The knock sensor is generally threaded into a hole near the combustion chamber.

Computer-controlled Spark

The next logical step in the development of electronic ignition systems is to incorporate the computer to control the spark. An example of this system is the computer command control (CCC) and the (EEC) electronic engine control systems. The CCC and EEC systems use several inputs from different sensors. These inputs are combined, and decisions are made on the amount of fuel to be added to the engine and, in this case, the amount of spark advance to be allowed. The centrifugal weights and the vacuum advance are controlled by the computer. *Figure 20–28* shows another system in block diagram. The ECCS stands for electronic constant engine control system. There are several inputs to the computer. These include engine speed, amount of air, temperature of the engine, throttle position, vehicle speed, start signal, engine knocking, and battery voltage. On the basis of these inputs, the power transistor in the electronic ignition system is operated to give the correct spark timing.

IGNITION TIMING CONTROL

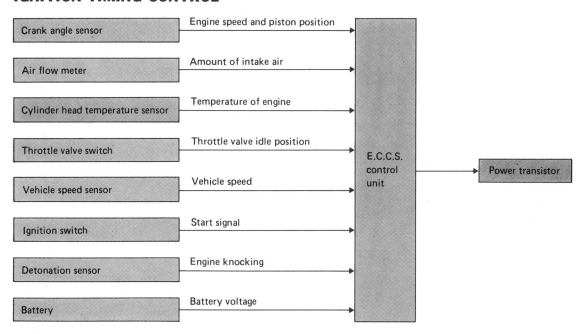

FIGURE 20–28. A computer-controlled spark system uses many inputs to electronically control the exact timing of the spark. *(Courtesy of Nissan Motor Corporation in USA)*

PROBLEM: Fouled Plug

A customer has an engine that consistently fouls out on number 5 cylinder. The vehicle has 76,000 miles on it. The number 5 plug is very wet, oily, and carbon-filled. Even a new plug will foul out in a short time. Why would only one plug foul out and not the others?

SOLUTION:

The most common cause of having just one plug foul out is a bad spark plug or spark plug wire. Since the plug has been changed, it would be wise to check the spark plug wires. This can be done on an electronic engine diagnosis scope or analyzer. When was the last time the spark plug wires were changed? They do eventually go bad. Replace the spark plug wires with a new set to eliminate the problem.

Electronic Spark Timing (EST)

Electronic spark timing uses many signals sent into the computer to electronically control the spark. This electronic advance is much more exact and reliable than conventional advance mechanisms. *Figure 20–29* shows how the timing

of the spark occurs in an HEI (high-energy ignition) system. To help understand the operation, a relay with a double set of contact points is shown in the HEI module. Solid-state circuitry is used in the module, but adding the relay makes it easier to visualize how EST functions.

During cranking, the relay is in the de-energized position. The pickup coil is connected to the base of the transistor. When the pickup coil applies a positive voltage to the transistor, it turns on. When the voltage is removed, the transistor turns off. It then accomplishes what the contact points did in the old ignition systems. When the transistor turns on, current flows through the primary winding of the ignition coil. When the transistor turns off, the primary current stops and the spark will be developed. The EST circuit is located inside the ECM (electronic control module). Several inputs are also shown for reference. The condition shown is for starting the engine. Timing is not being electronically controlled at this point.

Figure 20–30 shows how the timing is controlled when the engine is running. At about 200 RPM, the ECM applies about 5 volts to the bypass line. This voltage enters the HEI module at pin B and energizes the relay, causing it to shift. This is actually done electronically. The EST line from the ECM is now connected directly to the transistor base. The HEI system is now controlled by the signal from the ECM. The time at which the spark occurs is now determined by a circuit in the ECM based on the many inputs to the ECM. Timing is now controlled electronically.

Figure 20–31 shows a typical HEI (high-energy ignition) system used with EST (electronic spark timing). Note that the distributor and coil are combined into one unit. The unit

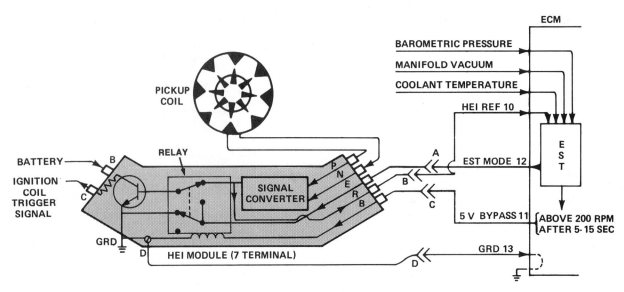

FIGURE 20–29.   This circuit shows how timing of the spark is produced during cranking of the engine. *(Courtesy of General Motors Product Service Training)*

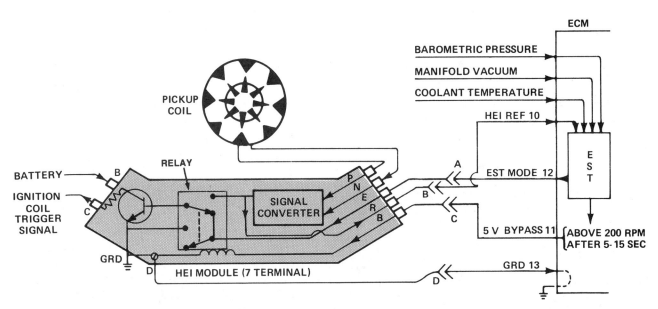

FIGURE 20–30.   This circuit shows how timing of the spark is produced while the engine is running. *(Courtesy of General Motors Product Service Training)*

is referred to as an HEI-EST distributor with an internal coil. The coil is placed on top of the distributor. The electronic control unit is placed inside the distributor. Electrical wires from the control module are attached to the connectors.

Computer-controlled Coil Ignition System (C³I)

Another advance in ignition systems is called the computer-controlled coil ignition system. It is considered to be a *distributorless ignition* system. This system consists of an electronic

control module (ECM), ignition (coil) module, and electro-magnetic camshaft and crankshaft position sensors. This system has eliminated the distributor and conventional ignition coil. It uses a microprocessor that receives and alters information from the crankshaft and camshaft position sensors. This information is processed to determine the proper firing sequence. The system then triggers each of three inter-connected coils on six-cylinder engines (two on four-cylinder engines) to fire the spark plugs. Ignition timing is again determined by the ECM, which monitors crankshaft position, engine RPM, engine temperature, and the amount of air the

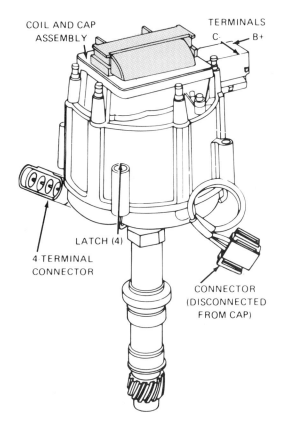

FIGURE 20–31. In this HEI (high-energy ignition) system, the coil and the distributor are combined into one unit. *(Courtesy of Motor Publications, Auto Engine Tune-up and Electronics Manual)*

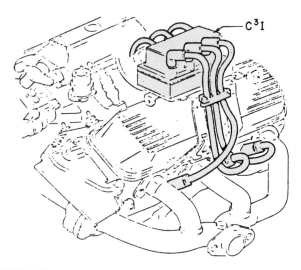

FIGURE 20–32. This computer-controlled coil ignition system (C³I) has eliminated the distributor and conventional ignition coil. It uses several sensors that feed information to the ignition module, which, in turn, triggers the coils to produce the high voltage. *(Courtesy of Motor Publications, Auto Engine Tune-up and Electronics Manual)*

Distributorless Ignition System (DIS), (Ford)

It is out of the scope of this book to discuss all the variations on distributorless ignition systems in detail. However, to aid in understanding the basic concepts, the distributorless ignition system (DIS) by Ford Motor Company is further discussed.

Ignition System Purpose

As discussed in the earlier part of this chapter, the purpose of an ignition system is to ignite the air-fuel mixture. The

engine is consuming. It then signals the ignition module to produce the necessary spark at the right time. *Figure 20–32* shows a typical C³I ignition module installation.

Direct Ignition System (DIS), General Motors

Another computer-controlled ignition system used by one manufacturer is called the DIS (direct ignition system). It is considered a distributorless type ignition system. It consists of two separate ignition coils on four-cylinder models and three separate ignition coils on six-cylinder engines. In addition to the coils, the following are also used: (1) a DIS module, (2) a crankshaft sensor, (3) electronic spark timing as part of the ECM (electronic control module).

A "waste spark" method of distribution is used on this system. Each cylinder is paired with its opposing cylinder in firing order. Thus, one cylinder on the compression stroke fires, while its opposing cylinder on the exhaust stroke fires. It requires less voltage to fire the plug on the exhaust stroke. Thus most of the available voltage is sent to the compression-stroke cylinder. The process is reversed as the cylinder roles are reversed. This system is represented in *Figure 20–33*, which shows a four-cylinder DIS exploded view of the module. Note that there are two coils, one for cylinders 2 and 3, one for cylinders 1 and 4.

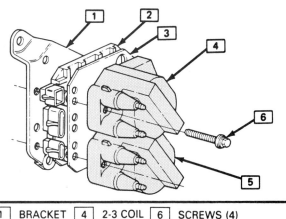

1	BRACKET	4	2-3 COIL	6	SCREWS (4)
2	MODULE	5	1-4 COIL		4.5 N·m (40 LBS. IN.)
3	SHIELD				

FIGURE 20–33. This direct ignition system (DIS) uses two coils, one for firing cylinders 2 and 3, and one for firing cylinders 1 and 4. *(Courtesy of Motor Publications, Auto Engine Tune-up and Electronics Manual)*

ignition spark must be there at the correct time and in the correct sequence. The computer in Ford's system, called the EEC IV, is used to provide this information. In this system, the ignition timing is adjusted constantly. Many factors affect ignition timing including engine RPM, coolant temperature, EGR flow rate, intake air temperature and volume, throttle position, manifold absolute pressure, barometric pressure, and engine knock. The EEC IV module monitors these conditions through various sensors.

Spark Plug Firing

Spark plugs are generally fired in pairs. This means that one spark plug fires during the compression stroke, and its companion plug fires during the exhaust stroke. The next time that coil is fired, the plug that was on the exhaust will be on compression. The one that was on compression will be on exhaust. The spark plug in the exhaust cylinder is wasted, but little of the coil energy is lost.

Ignition System Components

Several components are used on Ford's DIS system. These include the:

- battery
- ignition switch
- DIS module
- EEC IV module
- spark plugs
- spark plug wires
- PIP sensor (profile ignition pickup, or crankshaft sensor)
- CID sensor (cylinder identification sensor)
- ignition coils (contains both primary and secondary coils)

Many of these components have been discussed previously, thus only certain components will be further defined. *Figure 20–34* shows several of these components and their location on the engine.

PIP Sensor

The function of the PIP, or crankshaft sensor, is to detect the position and speed of the crankshaft. The PIP sensor uses a Hall-effect type of pickup, shown in *Figure 20–35*. It is mounted to the engine block near the crankshaft pulley and hub assembly. It consists of three vanes that interrupt the magnetism. The digital signal produced (also shown) is on for 60 degrees, then off for 60 degrees, on 60 degrees, off 60

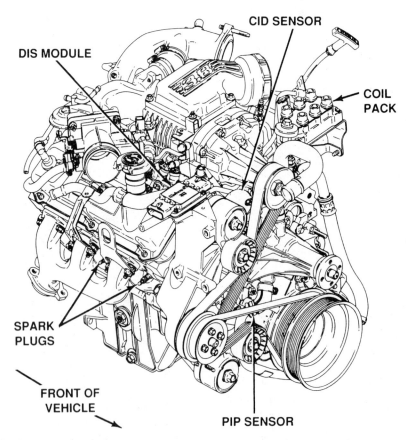

FIGURE 20–34. Ford's distributorless ignition system components are shown for reference. *(Courtesy of Ford Motor Company)*

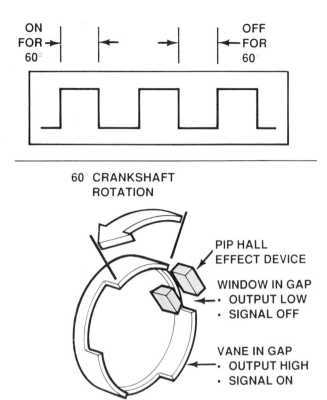

FIGURE 20–35. The PIP uses a Hall-effect pickup to generate a digital signal. *(Courtesy of Ford Motor Company)*

degrees, on 60 degrees, and finally off for 60 degrees. This makes up one complete crankshaft revolution of 360 degrees. Note also that the leading edge of the digital signal (the first ON signal) always occurs at 10 degrees BTDC. This is the base timing of the engine.

CID Sensor

The function of the CID sensor is to detect the position of the engine camshaft. Camshaft position is used to identify when piston 1 is 26 degrees ATDC of its compression stroke. The DIS module uses the CID signal to select the proper coil to fire. The CID sensor is much like the PIP sensor. It uses a Hall-effect pickup as shown in *Figure 20–36*. The differences are that the CID is driven by the camshaft, and there is only one vane on the sensor. Thus the digital signal is on 180 degrees and off 180 degrees of camshaft rotation.

Ignition Coils

The function of the coil is to take a low voltage (12 volts) and produce a high voltage (32,000 volts). There is both a primary and a secondary circuit in each coil. If a four-cylinder engine is used, there are two coils. If a six-cylinder engine is used, there are three coils. Each coil has two high-voltage towers. (Remember that two plugs are being fired each time.) Each tower supplies one plug. All coils are mounted together in a single coil pack. *Figure 20–37* shows a coil pack for a six cylinder and the internal circuits of that coil pack.

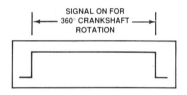

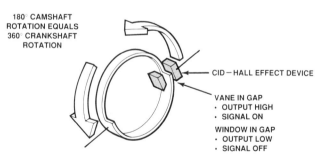

FIGURE 20–36. The CID (cylinder identification) sensor uses a Hall-effect pickup driven from the camshaft to determine the location of number 1 piston. *(Courtesy of Ford Motor Company)*

DIS Module

The functions of the DIS module are to:

■ select which coil to fire,

■ control current in the primary coils,

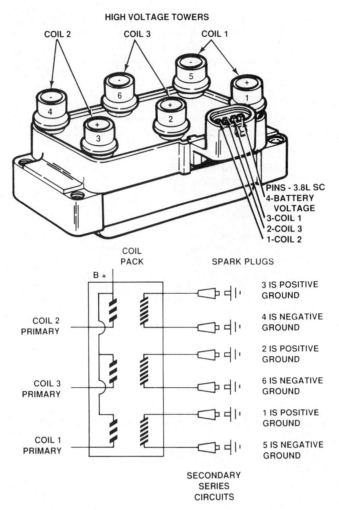

FIGURE 20–37.   An ignition coil pack is shown along with the internal circuitry. *(Courtesy of Ford Motor Company)*

■ generate a diagnostic signal for the EEC IV, and

■ provide an ignition ground circuit.

The DIS module has several inputs and outputs. The inputs include:

■ battery voltage

■ CID sensor input

■ PIP sensor input

■ spark timing signal from the EEC IV

The outputs include:

■ an ignition ground

■ ground path for the primary circuit for coil 1

■ ground path for the primary circuit for coil 2

■ path for the diagnostic circuit and tachometer

In its basic operation, a spark timing signal is sent from the EEC IV to the DIS. On the basis of the information from the various sensors, the DIS opens the ground path to the primary of one of the coils. Note that in each coil, there is a primary and secondary circuit. When the spark timing signal is shut off in the DIS, the primary circuit is broken rapidly. This causes the primary circuit to collapse rapidly, causing the secondary voltage to be produced. The secondary voltage is then sent out to two spark plugs for ignition. The system is actually much more complex electronically. However, more detail is out of the scope of this book.

Problems, Diagnosis and Service

1. When replacing parts or doing other work on the ignition system, always make sure the ignition system is off. If it is left on, a spark may be produced, causing gasoline fumes to ignite, causing a safety hazard.
2. If it is necessary to crank the engine when working on the distributor, disconnect and ground the coil wire to make sure you will not get a shock from the high-voltage wire.
3. Never use only your hands to pull high-tension wires off the spark plug when the engine is running. Use the correct pliers to remove the plug wires.
4. When removing spark plug wires and spark plugs, always remove them after the engine has cooled down. The spark plugs and wires are often located near the exhaust manifold, which may burn your hands if hot.
5. When working on the ignition system when the engine is running, always keep your hands away from the spark plug wires. In addition, be careful not to drop any tools into the fan or pulleys on the front of the vehicle.

PROBLEM: Open Circuit in Primary Coil

An engine was running fine then suddenly stopped running. Although the engine can crank, it will not fire the spark plugs.

DIAGNOSIS

A common problem is to have the ignition coil primary develop an open circuit because of high current or getting too hot. This will cause the total ignition system to shut down. This can be checked by using an ohmmeter. An open circuit will show infinite resistance on the primary. Check the resistance between the positive side of the primary circuit and the negative side of the primary circuit.

SERVICE

If it is determined that the ignition coil is bad, it must be replaced. Use the following general procedure to replace the ignition coil.

1. Disconnect the battery.
2. Disconnect both the negative and positive connections to the primary coil.
3. Carefully remove the secondary wire on the top of the coil.

4. Remove the coil and replace with a new one.
5. Reverse the procedure and test accordingly.
6. When reconnecting the wires, make sure the positive side of the coil primary is connected to the ignition switch. The coil will then operate with the correct polarity. If it is connected backward, the coil output will be reduced by approximately one-half. Whatever the vehicle ground polarity, that side of the coil goes toward the ignition points.

PROBLEM: Engine Misfires

A vehicle has a conventional ignition system. The engine is missing badly.

DIAGNOSIS

Various parts may be damaged on a conventional ignition system. Use the following diagnostic checks to determine the condition of the ignition system:

1. As contact points become pitted, the engine may misfire erratically. This is because the points are not breaking the primary circuit fast enough.
2. If a ballast resistor or resistive wire is shorted out, the points may burn prematurely because of the increased amount of current in the primary circuit.
3. If the condenser is bad, the points may corrode faster.
4. Check the distributor cam lobes for excessive wear. If these cam lobes are worn, the points will open and close at the incorrect time.
5. Check the distributor bearings for wear. Bad bearings will affect the mechanical opening and closing of the points.
6. Check for moisture or moisture spots on the inside top of the distributor cap. Moisture condensing inside the distributor cap may also cause the engine to misfire or not start at all.
7. A cracked distributor cap can cause the engine to misfire or not start at all. A cracked distributor cap can be found by removing the distributor cap and carefully observing the inside of the cap for small cracks. See *Figure 20–38*.
8. Check the springs on the centrifugal advance. If these springs break, the engine will be advanced at the wrong time. Always check the spring weights for the correct tension and lubricate all moving parts.
9. Check the vacuum diaphragm for leakage. A leaking vacuum diaphragm on the distributor will prevent the vacuum advance from operating. This will cause a lack

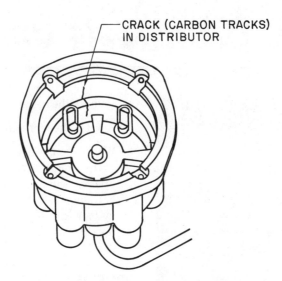

FIGURE 20–38.   Always check the inside top of the distributor cap for small cracks or carbon tracks, which may cause the engine to misfire.

of power, poor fuel economy, and increased exhaust emission. Use a vacuum tester to check the diaphragm as shown in *Figure 20–39*.

SERVICE

The procedure will depend on the exact nature of the fault. Refer to the service manual for the manufacturer's suggested procedure for the defective part.

PROBLEM: Damaged Spark Plug Wires

An engine has a very irregular misfire. Often the misfire seems to increase in wet or moist conditions. Often when the hood of the vehicle is lifted at night, one can see sparks coming from the spark plug wires.

DIAGNOSIS

If sparks are continually jumping from one spark plug wire to another, the insulation could be bad. The wires will have to be replaced.

SERVICE

The spark plug wires often must be cut to the correct length after purchasing the new set. Replace only one spark plug wire at a time so that the wires don't get mixed up. Use

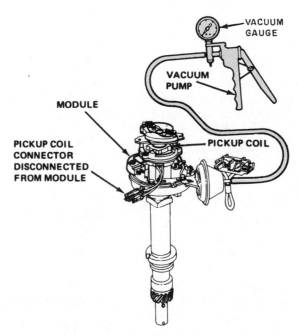

FIGURE 20–39.   Use a vacuum guage to test the condition of the vacuum advance. *(Courtesy of Motor Publications)*

the following procedure if the plug wires have been mixed up and cannot be replaced in the correct order.

CAUTION: Carelessly pulling spark plug wires off the spark plugs, bending them sharply, or stretching them will damage the new wires and cause the engine to misfire.

1. With all plug wires removed, remove the number 1 spark plug. The number 1 spark plug can be determined by looking in the maintenance manual.

2. Slowly crank the engine until the number 1 spark plug is at top dead center (TDC) on the compression stroke. Top dead center can be determined by observing the timing marks and lining them up correctly. When turning the engine to get to TDC on the compression stroke, a slight pressure should be felt if a finger is placed over the spark plug hole.

3. Remove the distributor cap and notice the location of the rotor. At this point (TDC for the number 1 spark plug), the rotor should be pointing at the number 1 spark plug wire on the distributor cap.

4. Place a spark plug wire on the correct hole on the distributor and on the number 1 spark plug.

5. With the distributor cap removed, observe the direction of rotation of the rotor as the engine is cranked.

6. Place the distributor cap back on the distributor.

7. Using the firing order listed on the intake manifold or in the maintenance manual, continue placing the spark plug wires on the distributor and the corresponding spark plug. For example, if the firing order is 1, 5, 3, 6, 2, 4, then after number 1 fires, the next cylinder to fire is number 5. Place a spark plug wire from the next hole in the distributor cap (remember the distributor rotation) to spark plug number 5. Continue this procedure until all spark plug wires have been replaced.

PROBLEM: Damaged Spark Plugs

An engine has a steady miss in one or more cylinders.

DIAGNOSIS

Use the following diagnostic checks to determine the condition of the spark plugs:

1. Often the spark plugs may be damaged, or they may need to be replaced. *Figure 20–40* shows different spark plug conditions. When diagnosing the exact problem with spark plugs, match the spark plugs with the correct characteristics. Replace the spark plugs if necessary.

2. Check the spark plug heat range against the manufacturer's specifications. When purchasing new spark plugs, make sure the number on the spark plug is the same as the number recommended by the manufacturer.

3. Always make certain the plug gaps are adjusted to the manufacturer's specifications. These can be found in the service and repair manuals.

4. Note that electronic ignition systems use wide spark plug gaps.

5. Always follow the recommended diagnosis and service procedures listed in the service and repair manuals to troubleshoot and diagnose electronic and computer-controlled spark systems.

SERVICE

After determining the exact cause of the spark plug failure, replace the plugs as necessary. Depending on the exact engine and manufacturer, the replacement of spark plugs can be very easy or extremely difficult. Make sure to use the correct tools to remove and replace necessary components in order to get at the spark plugs. Remember that when removing spark plugs, always use a spark plug socket that has a small rubber cushion inside the socket. This will prevent the spark plug from cracking when you apply torque to the wrench. Always torque to manufacturer's specifications, normally around 12–25 pound-feet.

PROBLEM: INCORRECT IGNITION TIMING

An engine is running but produces a pinging or knock especially during acceleration.

DIAGNOSIS

Often an engine that has a ping or knock may have the timing slightly advanced. Timing can be changed easily by readjusting the position of the distributor in the block.

SERVICE

Use the following general procedure to set the timing of an engine:

1. Use a timing light, *Figure 20–41*, to check the timing of an engine.

2. Attach the clip-on leads to the battery, making sure to attach positive to positive and negative to negative.

3. Place an inductive lead over the number 1 cylinder spark plug wire.

4. Slightly loosen the bolt that holds down the distributor. Do not remove the bolt, as the distributor will be too loose.

5. Start the engine and allow it to idle. On some engines you may have to remove and plug the vacuum advance lines to disable the vacuum advance system.

6. As the engine idles, every time the number 1 spark plug fires, the timing light will flash. When the engine is running the flashes look like a strobe light.

Match Plug End Condition Description At Right with Correct Illustration on Left

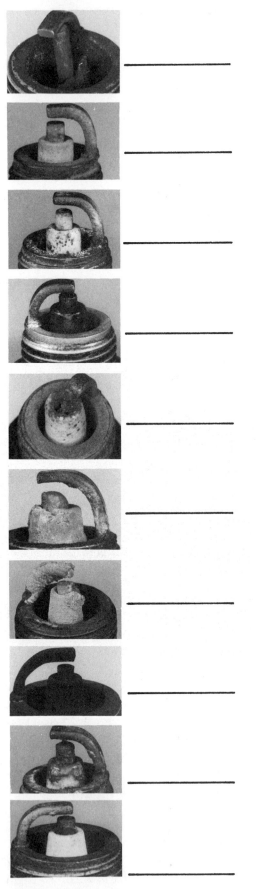

1 CRACKED INSULATOR

Small portion broken off or vertical crack in the insulator.

Check ignition timing, replace plug.

2 NORMAL

Brown to greyish tan color and slight electrode wear.

Service plug or replace with same range.

3 SPLASHED DEPOSITS

Leopard-like deposits. Occurs shortly after long delayed tune-up.

Service and reinstall plugs.

4 OIL DEPOSITS

White or yellowish deposits on one side of plug.

Check engine condition. Use non turbo action plug.

5 PREIGNITION

Melted electrodes. Center electrode generally melts first and ground electrode follows.

Check engine conditions and timing, use colder plug.

6 WORN OUT

Electrodes eroded, heavy deposits, pitted insulater.

7 MODIFIER DEPOSITS

Powdery white or yellow deposits that build up on shell, insulator and electrodes.

Service plug or replace with same range.

8 CARBON DEPOSITS

Dry soot, or oily deposits.

Check engine condition or use hotter plug.

9 HIGH SPEED GLAZING

Insulator usually has yellowish varnish-like color.

Service plug or replace with colder type.

10 TOO HOT

Blistered, lily white insulator, eroded electrodes and absence of deposits.

Reset ignition timing or use colder plug.

FIGURE 20–40. The condition of the spark plug can tell many things about the engine. The condition of the spark plug should always be checked to see if problems are developing in the engine. *(Courtesy of Champion Spark Plug Company)*

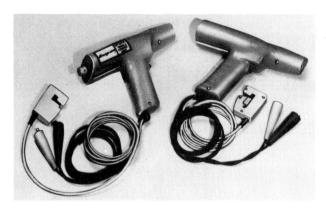

FIGURE 20–41.   A timing light is used to adjust the time of the spark. The light is attached to the battery and to the number 1 spark plug wire. When the plug fires, the light flashes to show the timing marks. *(Courtesy of Snap-On Tools Company)*

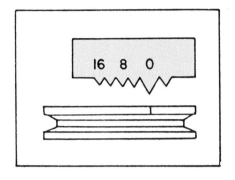

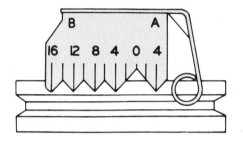

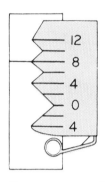

FIGURE 20–42.   These are examples of how the timing marks might look on different vehicles. *(Courtesy of Motor Publications, Auto Engine Tune-up and Electronics Manual)*

7. Now carefully shine the timing light on the timing marks on the front of the engine during idle.

   CAUTION: Be careful not to get the wires near the spinning fan or near the electric fan.

   Figure 20–42 shows several examples of the timing marks on engines.

8. When the light shines on the timing marks on the front of the engine during idle, the amount of advance or retarded condition can be observed.

9. With the distributor base loosened, as the distributor is turned, advancing or retarding the ignition can be easily observed by the timing light flashes.

10. Set the timing marks (by turning the distributor) to the exact amount of advance BTDC, as suggested by the manufacturer.

11. Shut the engine off and tighten down the distributor base.

12. Remove the timing light. The ignition advance should now be set correctly.

PROBLEM: Electronic Ignition Fault Parts

An engine with an electronic ignition system is misfiring badly.

DIAGNOSIS

Many engines today use electronic ignition systems. Diagnosis procedures are different for each of these systems. In addition, there is a constant flow of service bulletins that help the service technician troubleshoot and diagnose the ignition system. *Figure 20–43* shows an example of one of many troubleshooting charts available to help the service technician diagnose problems. As each step is performed, the problem will eventually be found by taking voltage and resistance readings and testing for spark.

Many of the ignition system components are checked on the electronic oscilloscope. Several procedures can, however, be followed when diagnosing the electronic ignition system.

1. Using an ohmmeter, check the spark plug wire resistance. The resistance should be 5,000 ohms per inch or less. If the resistance of the wire is greater, replace the wire.

2. Spark plug wires should be checked for road salt, deposits, dirt, damaged boots, and cuts and punctures.

3. Various tests can be made to check voltage to the spark plug. Because several methods can be used, follow the specific manufacturer's recommendation to determine if spark exists.

4. In many maintenance and service manuals, specific connections are shown for ohmmeter tests. *Figure 20–44 (A)* shows how to test an HEI system for the primary and

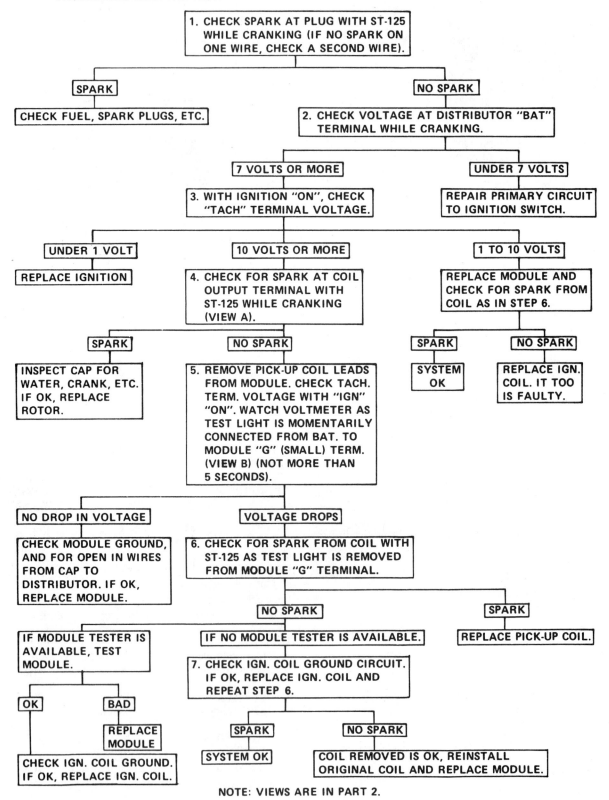

ENGINE CRANKS, BUT WILL NOT START
NOTE: IF A TACHOMETER IS CONNECTED TO THE TACHOMETER TERMINAL, DISCONNECT IT BEFORE PROCEEDING WITH THE TEST.

1. CHECK SPARK AT PLUG WITH ST-125 WHILE CRANKING (IF NO SPARK ON ONE WIRE, CHECK A SECOND WIRE).

SPARK

CHECK FUEL, SPARK PLUGS, ETC.

NO SPARK

2. CHECK VOLTAGE AT DISTRIBUTOR "BAT" TERMINAL WHILE CRANKING.

7 VOLTS OR MORE

3. WITH IGNITION "ON", CHECK "TACH" TERMINAL VOLTAGE.

UNDER 7 VOLTS

REPAIR PRIMARY CIRCUIT TO IGNITION SWITCH.

UNDER 1 VOLT

REPLACE IGNITION

10 VOLTS OR MORE

4. CHECK FOR SPARK AT COIL OUTPUT TERMINAL WITH ST-125 WHILE CRANKING (VIEW A).

1 TO 10 VOLTS

REPLACE MODULE AND CHECK FOR SPARK FROM COIL AS IN STEP 6.

SPARK

INSPECT CAP FOR WATER, CRANK, ETC. IF OK, REPLACE ROTOR.

NO SPARK

5. REMOVE PICK-UP COIL LEADS FROM MODULE. CHECK TACH. TERM. VOLTAGE WITH "IGN" "ON". WATCH VOLTMETER AS TEST LIGHT IS MOMENTARILY CONNECTED FROM BAT. TO MODULE "G" (SMALL) TERM. (VIEW B) (NOT MORE THAN 5 SECONDS).

SPARK

SYSTEM OK

NO SPARK

REPLACE IGN. COIL. IT TOO IS FAULTY.

NO DROP IN VOLTAGE

CHECK MODULE GROUND, AND FOR OPEN IN WIRES FROM CAP TO DISTRIBUTOR. IF OK, REPLACE MODULE.

VOLTAGE DROPS

6. CHECK FOR SPARK FROM COIL WITH ST-125 AS TEST LIGHT IS REMOVED FROM MODULE "G" TERMINAL.

NO SPARK

SPARK

REPLACE PICK-UP COIL.

IF MODULE TESTER IS AVAILABLE, TEST MODULE.

IF NO MODULE TESTER IS AVAILABLE.

7. CHECK IGN. COIL GROUND CIRCUIT. IF OK, REPLACE IGN. COIL AND REPEAT STEP 6.

OK

BAD

REPLACE MODULE

CHECK IGN. COIL GROUND. IF OK, REPLACE IGN. COIL.

SPARK

SYSTEM OK

NO SPARK

COIL REMOVED IS OK, REINSTALL ORIGINAL COIL AND REPLACE MODULE.

NOTE: VIEWS ARE IN PART 2.

FIGURE 20–43.   Because of the complexity of many of the ignition systems, various diagnosis charts are available in the service and repair manuals. Follow the correct diagnosis chart to help troubleshoot the electronic ignition system. *(Courtesy of Motor Publications, Auto Engine Tune-up and Electronics Manual)*

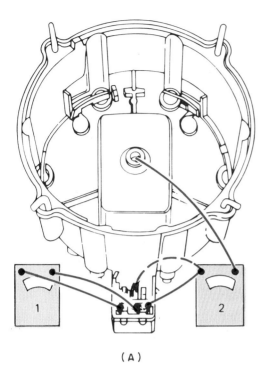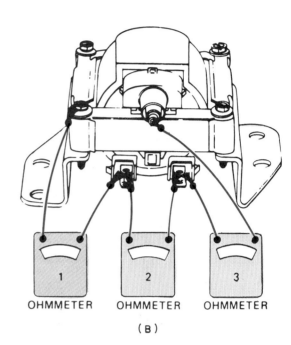

(A)   (B)

FIGURE 20–44.   (A) This ohmmeter check will help to determine the condition of the primary and second ary coil. (B) This check will help determine the condition of the electronic distributor pick-up. *(Courtesy of Motor Publications, Auto Engine Tune-up and Electronics Manual)*

secondary coils using the ohmmeter. ***Figure 20-44 (B)*** shows how to check the electronic pickup using an ohmmeter. Compare the results with those suggested in the service manuals.

SERVICE

The service for each problem will vary. Follow the service procedures in the service manual for the exact type of ignition system.

PROBLEM: No Distributor Reference Pulse

A vehicle that has a C³I distributorless ignition system has a CHECK ENGINE light on.

DIAGNOSIS

After grounding the "test" terminal under the dashboard or after using a scanner, it is determined that Code 12 is the problem. Code 12, according to this manufactuer is "No distributor reference pulses to the ECM."

SERVICE

At this point it will be necessary to refer to the manufacturer's diagnosis chart shown in ***Figure 20–45***. Follow the exact diagnosis chart as illustrated until the problem is found and corrected. (NOTE: for each code listed by the manufacturer there is a diagnosis chart to follow to aid the service technician in repairing the problem.)

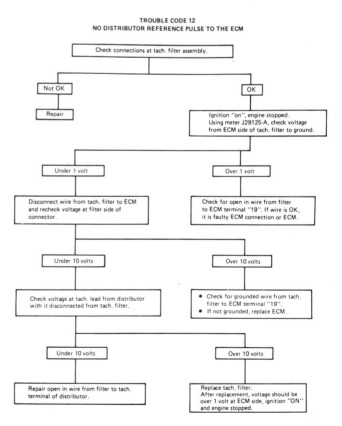

FIGURE 20–45.   This diagnosis chart can be used to help the service technician diagnose and repair Code 12, "No distributor reference pulses to the ECM" on a C³I ignition system. *(Courtesy of Motor Publications, Auto Engine Tune-up and Repair Manual)*

SERVICE MANUAL CONNECTION

There are many important specifications to keep in mind when working with ignition systems. To identify the specifications for your engine, you will need to know the VIN (vehicle identification number) of the vehicle, the type and year of the vehicle, and the type of engine. Although they may be titled differently, some of the more common ignition system specifications (not all) found in service manuals are listed below. Note that these specifications are typical examples. Each vehicle and engine may have different specifications.

Common Specification	Typical Example
Full advance	10 degrees at 3,000 RPM
Firing order	1-3-4-2
HEI distributor cap/coil resistance (depending on the exact connection)	500–1500 ohms
Ignition timing BTDC (before top dead center)	
Manual transmission	10 degrees
Automatic transmission	12 degrees
Spark plug gap	0.060 inch
Spark plug torque	10–15 lb-ft
Starting of centrifugal advance	0 degrees at 600 RPM

In addition, the service manual will give specific directions for various service and testing procedures. Some of the more common procedures include:

- Ignition lock replace
- Ignition switch replace
- Ignition timing
- Module replacement
- Pinpoint test-spark knock
- Pinpoint test-spark timing test
- Spark plug removal and replacement

SUMMARY

The many types of ignition systems used on vehicles today were studied in this chapter. The purpose of the ignition system is to convert the 12 volts produced by the battery to 20,000 to 50,000 volts for use at the spark plug. To do this, primary and secondary systems are used in the ignition system. The primary circuit operates on low voltage and includes the ignition switch, primary coil windings, resistive wire, condenser, and contact points. The secondary circuit operates on high voltages of 20,000 to 30,000 volts and includes the high-voltage windings in the coil, the rotor, distributor cap, spark plug wires, and spark plugs.

The ignition switch is used to turn the ignition system on and off. The ignition coil is used to change the 12 volts to 5,000–50,000 volts. The breaker points act as a primary circuit switch to turn the circuit on and off. The length of time in distributor degrees of rotation that the points remain closed is defined as dwell.

The points mechanism is held in place on the distributor and is opened and closed by the distributor cam.

The secondary components in the ignition system operate on higher voltages. The rotor and distributor cap are used to distribute the high-voltage spark. The high voltage then passes through the spark plug wires to the spark plugs.

Spark timing must be changed when the speed or load is increased. This is done by using advance mechanisms. Two types are used. The centrifugal advance increases the advance of the spark as the engine speed increases. The vacuum advance increases the spark advance as the load is increased. It is connected to the engine intake manifold, which is sensitive to engine load. Several systems are incorporated to help retard the spark during certain conditions. These include spark delay systems, temperature-sensing vacuum control valves, dual diaphragm vacuum advance, and solenoid retard-advance systems.

One critical component in the ignition system is the spark plug. Spark plugs have heat ranges. These are determined by how long it takes to transfer the heat at the tip of the plug to the cylinder head. The longer it takes, the hotter the heat range.

Spark plugs are affected by many conditions. Spark plug temperature is affected by the amount of advance, coolant temperature, detonation, plug condition, and air-fuel ratio. Spark plug voltage is affected by plug condition, compression pressures, plug gap, load, and engine timing.

Because of the wear and maintenance on conventional ignition systems, manufacturers have developed electronic and computer-controlled ignition systems. Electronic ignition systems use transistors to open and close the primary circuit much faster. More voltage, about 30,000 to 60,000 volts, is produced. The only additional component is a reluctor, which is used to signal or trigger the transistor on and off at the right time. These systems require minimal maintenance, mostly checking parts for abnormal wear.

Once electronic systems had been improved, the next logical step was to control the spark with computers. Spark advance is controlled by the CCC, computer control combustion system. The computer is used to signal the exact triggering of the transistor so that correct spark advance is produced. The signal is based on several inputs to the computer, including engine speed, amount of air, throttle position, engine knocking, start signal, battery voltage, engine coolant temperature, vehicle road speed, and air intake temperature. Two of the more common distributorless ignition systems are the DIS (direct ignition system) manufactured by General Motors and the DIS (distributorless ignition system) by Ford.

(continued)

Linkage to Automotive Performance and Testing

ELECTRONIC ANALYZERS

Computerized technology on engines often requires electronic engine analyzers to help the service technician diagnose and repair problems. These analyzers are able to check emissions, timing, ignition components, and computer systems.

In addition to electronic analyzers, complete diagnostic centers are now being used. Advanced diagnostic service centers are able to check more than 200 elements of engine systems and electrical performance. The diagnostic center is then able to print out the type of problem and suggested service needed. *(Courtesy of Sun® Electric Corporation and The Firestone Tire and Rubber Company)*

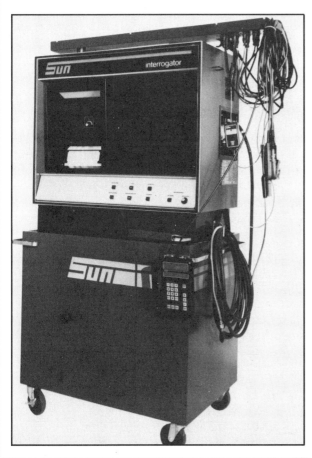

These systems use crankshaft sensors, cylinder identification sensors, DIS modules, and Hall-effect systems to operate the distributorless ignition systems.

There are many service tips and suggestions for working on the ignition system. Conventional ignition systems typically require more service than electronic or computer-controlled systems. Dwell must be adjusted, and the breaker points must be changed periodically. The condenser may also fail. Electronic ignition systems require little maintenance. Dwell is built directly into the circuits. Because of the complexity of computer-controlled systems, it is important to refer to the specific type of ignition system and the appropriate service and repair manual for diagnosis.

TERMS TO KNOW

Can you explain each of the following terms? Review the chapter until you can use each term correctly.

Primary circuit	Reluctor
Secondary circuit	HEI
Breaker point	Hall-effect
Distributor cam	Detonation sensor
Dwell	Distributorless ignition
Ported vacuum	

 REVIEW QUESTIONS

Multiple Choice

1. The primary circuit on the ignition system operates on _____ volts.
   a. 5
   b. 7
   c. 12
   d. 20,000
   e. 50,000

2. The secondary circuit on the ignition system operates on _____ volts.
   a. 5
   b. 7
   c. 12
   d. 20,000
   e. 70,000

3. Which of the following components is not part of the primary circuit?
   a. Condenser
   b. Rotor
   c. Points
   d. Ballast resistor
   e. Large size windings in the coil

4. Which of the following components is not part of the secondary circuit?
   a. Points
   b. Condenser
   c. Ballast resistor
   d. All of the above
   e. None of the above

5. Dwell is defined as:
   a. The length of time in degrees the points are closed
   b. The length of time in degrees the points are open
   c. Point gap in thousandths of an inch
   d. The voltage at the secondary circuit
   e. The voltage at the primary circuit

6. Which type of advance is used to increase the timing as speed increases?
   a. Contact point advance
   b. Centrifugal advance
   c. Vacuum advance
   d. Ported advance
   e. Computer advance

7. Which type of advance is used to increase the timing as load increases?
   a. Contact point advance
   b. Centrifugal advance
   c. Vacuum advance
   d. Ported advance
   e. Computer advance

8. A plug that is fouling out with carbon and soot may be:
   a. Too hot a plug
   b. Too high a voltage on the plug
   c. Too cool a plug
   d. Too long a plug
   e. Too short a plug

9. The tip temperature of the plug will increase with:
   a. An over-advanced engine
   b. An increase in coolant temperature
   c. Clean spark plugs
   d. All of the above
   e. None of the above

10. The spark plug voltage required will increase with:
    a. Decreases in compression
    b. Decreases in spark plug gap
    c. Decreases in load on the engine
    d. All of the above
    e. None of the above

11. What component is used to open and close the ignition primary circuit on an electronic ignition system?
    a. A condenser
    b. A diode
    c. A computer
    d. A transistor
    e. A set of contact points

12. What is an average voltage on the secondary for an electronic ignition system?
    a. 10,000 volts
    b. 20,000 volts
    c. 12 volts
    d. 50,000 volts
    e. 6 volts

13. Which of the following is used to trigger the electronic circuit to open and close the primary windings in the coil?
    a. Conductor
    b. Reluctor
    c. Condenser
    d. Transistor
    e. Secondary coil windings

14. The spark on a computer-controlled ignition system is timed by:
    a. The centrifugal weights
    b. The vacuum advance
    c. The computer or electronic control module
    d. The springs on the weights
    e. None of the above

15. As the breaker points become corroded, the speed at which the magnetic field collapses:
    a. Increases
    b. Remains about the same
    c. Decreases
    d. Is proportional to the voltage
    e. None of the above

16. When diagnosing the secondary circuit, which of the following should be checked?
    a. Moisture in the distributor cap
    b. Cracks in the distributor cap
    c. Condition of the spark plug wires
    d. All of the above
    e. None of the above

The following questions are similar in format to ASE (Automotive Service Excellence) test questions.

---

17. Technician A says that as the contact points become pitted, the gasoline engine mileage goes down. Technician B says that as the contact points become pitted, the voltage to the spark plug is decreased. Who is right?
    a. A only
    b. B only
    c. Both A and B
    d. Neither A nor B

18. Technician A says that moisture inside a distributor cap will have no effect on the ignition system operation. Technician B says that moisture inside a distributor cap will cause the spark plug voltage to increase and improve ignition system operation. Who is right?
    a. A only
    b. B only
    c. Both A and B
    d. Neither A nor B

19. Technician A says that the resistance of the spark plug wire can be checked with an ohmmeter. Technician B says that the resistance of the spark plug wire cannot be checked at all. Who is right?
    a. A only
    b. B only
    c. Both A and B
    d. Neither A nor B

20. An engine seems to start but seems to miss on #3 cylinder. Technician A says the problem is #3 spark plug. Technician B says the problem is a bad distributor bearing. Who is right?
    a. A only
    b. B only
    c. Both A and B
    d. Neither A nor B

21. Sparks are noticed jumping from spark plug wire to wire. Technician A says the problem is too high a voltage to the spark plugs. Technician B says the problem is the ignition switch. Who is right?
    a. A only
    b. B only
    c. Both A and B
    d. Neither A nor B

22. Technician A says that when the coil fires on a DIS system, it actually fires two cylinders at the same time. Technician B says that when the coil fires on a DIS system, both cylinders are on the compression stroke at the same time. Who is right?
    a. A only
    b. B only
    c. Both A and B
    d. Neither A nor B

23. Technician A says that the Hall-effect pickup is not used on electronic or computerized ignition systems. Technician B says the Hall-effect pickup is used as a sensing device on the PIP, or crankshaft position, sensor. Who is right?
    a. A only
    b. B only
    c. Both A and B
    d. Neither A nor B

24. Technician A says that cracks that occur in a distributor cap may cause a misfire. Technician B says that only voltage tests can be made on the distributor and coil. Who is right?
    a. A only
    b. B only
    c. Both A and B
    d. Neither A nor B

25. Technician A says that the Hall-effect pickup is a device that uses voltage to produce a digital signal for the EEC IV. Technician B says that the Hall-effect pickup uses a magnet. Who is right?
    a. A only
    b. B only
    c. Both A and B
    d. Neither A nor B

Essay

26. What is the difference between the primary and secondary ignition circuits?

27. Define the term *dwell*.

28. State two types of advance, and identify how they operate.

29. Describe spark plug heat ranges.

30. Identify two things that affect spark plug temperature.

31. What is a reluctor and why is it used?

32. State the purpose of electronic spark timing.

Short Answer

23. The _____ sensor is able to provide a digital signal within the 360 degrees of crankshaft rotation.

34. The sensor used to provide a digital signal for timing and engine speed is called the _____ position sensor.

35. The "knock" sensor can also be called a _____ sensor.

36. An open circuit on the ignition coil primary will show _____ ohms when tested with an ohmmeter.

37. If there is a slight knock or pinging heard in the engine, the ignition timing may be too far _____.

CHAPTER 21

Charging Systems

INTRODUCTION The purpose of this chapter is to study the charging system. This includes the study of generators, alternators, regulation, and troubleshooting of the charging system.

OBJECTIVES After reading this chapter, you should be able to:

- Identify the purpose of the charging system.

- Analyze the principles of converting the mechanical energy of the engine to electrical energy for charging.

- Define the parts and operation of dc generators.

- State the operation of dc regulation on a generator.

- Identify how three-phase voltages from the alternator are rectified.

- State the operation of solid-state electronic and computerized regulation systems.

- Identify the purpose of high output alternators.

- Identify basic problems, diagnosis, and service procedures on the charging system.

✔ **SAFETY CHECKLIST** ✔

When working with the charging system, keep these important safety precautions in mind.
✔ Never work on the alternator when the engine is running.
✔ When working on the alternator, always make sure the battery is disconnected.
✔ Make sure all electrical wires from the testing instrument are away from the cooling fan and pulleys.
✔ Always wear OSHA-approved safety glasses when working on the alternator.

21.1 GENERATOR PRINCIPLES

Purpose of the Charging System

A charging system is used on all automobiles to convert the mechanical energy of the engine to electrical energy. The electrical energy is used to operate the vehicle during normal driving conditions and to charge the battery. Each time electrical energy is removed from the battery, the battery must be recharged. If it is not recharged, the battery will eventually become discharged. The charging system is used to accomplish this. In addition to charging, it is important to be able to regulate the amount of charge. If too little charge is produced, the battery will have a low charge. If the charging system puts too much back into the battery, the battery may

Some of the information in this chapter can help you prepare for the National Institute for Automotive Service Excellence (ASE) certification tests. The tests most directly related to this chapter are entitled

ELECTRICAL SYSTEMS (TEST 6) AND ENGINE PERFORMANCE (TEST 8).

The content areas that closely parallel this chapter are

CHARGING SYSTEMS DIAGNOSIS AND REPAIR, AND ENGINE ELECTRICAL SYSTEMS DIAGNOSIS AND REPAIR.

be overcharged and damaged. The regulation of the charge ensures that the exact amount of electricity needed is being generated.

Producing Electricity

A generator uses three things to change mechanical energy to electrical energy. These are a magnetic field, a conductor or wire, and movement between the two. This principle is called electromagnetic induction. *Figure 21–1* shows a simple generator used to produce electricity. When wire is wound around a metal core, a magnetic field is produced. The magnetic lines of force are moving from the north pole to

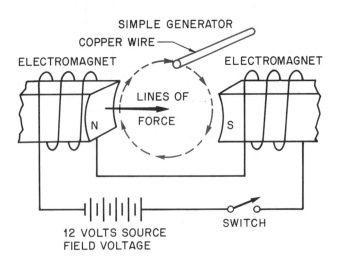

FIGURE 21–1. A simple generator is made of a set of poles, copper wire, and movement between the poles and the wire in which the wire cuts magnetic lines of force. All three are needed to produce a voltage.

the south pole. When a wire or conductor is moved to cut the magnetic field, a voltage is produced within the wire. This voltage is used to push electrons back to the battery for charging. It is also used to supply current to the rest of the vehicle during normal operation.

Generated voltage (and, therefore, current available) can be increased by increasing any one of the three components in the generator. If the magnetic field is increased, the voltage will increase. If the amount of copper wire is increased, the voltage will increase. If the speed of motion is increased, the voltage will increase.

Difference between Generators and Alternators

For years the automotive charging system used a generator to charge the battery. Today an alternator is used. The difference between a generator and an alternator is the method of physical construction. A generator has stationary poles, and the wire moves across the field. An alternator has moving poles (magnetic field) and a stationary wire. Although both produce electricity, the alternator is much more efficient.

There are also several minor differences that will be discussed in this chapter. Generators use brushes and a *commutator* to remove the produced voltage from the rotating windings. The alternator uses diodes to *rectify* the voltage to dc.

CAR CLINIC

PROBLEM: **Electrical System Totally Fails**

The entire electrical system on a new vehicle with 500 miles on it began to lose voltage. While driving on the highway, the owner noticed at night that the lights seemed to become dimmer. The radio and other electrical components also seemed to lose power. What could be the problem?

SOLUTION:

Since the vehicle is new, one of the electrical connections on the alternator may have come loose. The first and most obvious connection to check is the main wire between the alternator and the battery (red). If this connection is broken or faulty, any electrical current produced by the alternator will not get to the battery or the other electrical systems. When the battery is drained of all its electrical energy, the electrical circuits also lose power. Check the BAT wire to make sure that it has a solid electrical connection. Also check the alternator drive belt tension. A loose belt will slip and reduce alternator output.

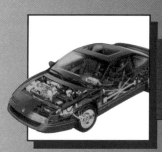

Total Vehicle

The automobile is a very sophisticated group of technologies that are assembled together. Because of the great number of mechanical and electrical systems, proper service is a must. The automotive technician of today must understand not only the parts, nomenclature and operation, but must also understand the diagnosis and service procedures for each system in the vehicle. For more information about this topic refer to chapters 1, 7, 8, 9 and 10 in the textbook.

(Courtesy of Ford Motor Company)

Engine

Diagnosis and service on the automobile engine requires a great deal of knowledge. Correct disassembly, diagnosis and service procedures should always be followed. For more information about this topic refer to chapters 1, 7, 8, 9 and 10 in the textbook. (Courtesy of Volkswagen of America)

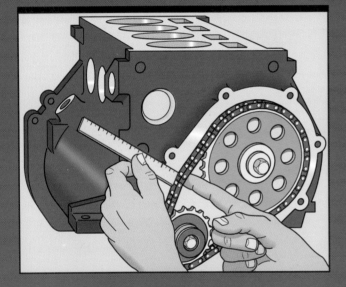

If the timing chain is worn, it may jump and cause the engine to be out of time. The timing chain will wear if the engine lubrication is not changed regularly or if the engine is used in excessive horsepower and torque applications. For more information about this topic refer to chapters 8, 9, 10 and 11 in the textbook. (Courtesy of Ford Motor Company)

This engine has four valves per cylinder, an aluminum block and twin dual camshafts. For more information about this topic refer to chapters 6, 8 and 10 in the textbook. (Courtesy of Motor Magazine)

Service

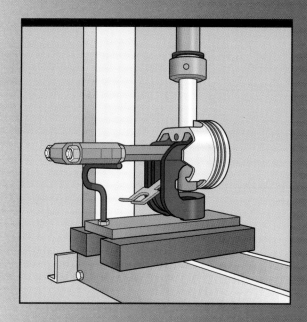

Various service procedures can be completed on engines today. Here a piston pin is being removed for inspection and possible replacement. For more information about engine service refer to chapter 9 in the textbook.

Today's internal combustion engine uses many new designs. For example, four valves are used on this engine to aid engine breathing. For more information about engine types and valve arrangements refer to chapters 7 and 10 in the textbook. (Courtesy of Motor Magazine)

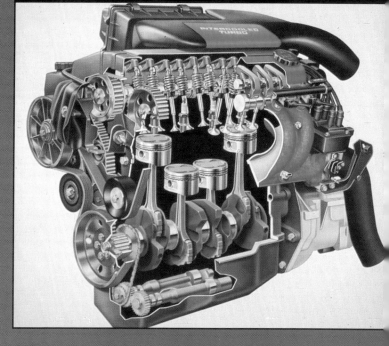

Some engine manufacturers use deep skirts on the cylinder block to increase its strength. This design also reduces mechanical noise. For more information about cylinder blocks refer to chapters 6, 8 and 9 in the textbook. (Courtesy of Motor Magazine)

Transmission

Today's standard, automatic and electronic transmissions requires in-depth knowledge of problem identification, diagnosis and service. For more information about this topic refer to chapters 25 and 26 in the textbook. (Courtesy of General Motors Corporation)

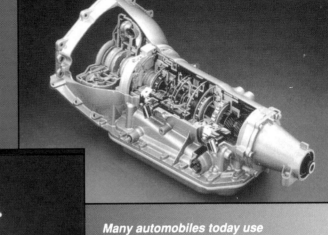

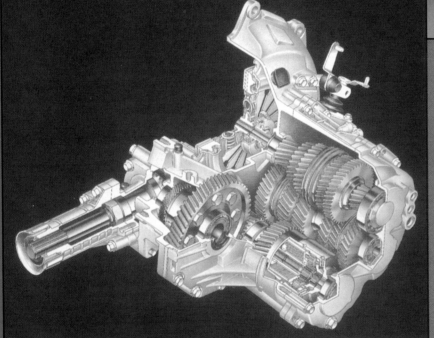

Many automobiles today use front wheel drive automatic transmissions. This front wheel drive automatic transmission also has the differential mounted within the same housing. For more information about automatic transmissions refer to chapters 25 and 26 in the textbook. (Courtesy of General Motors Corporation)

Many front wheel drive automatic transmissions use a heavy duty chain to transfer the torque from the torque converter to the transmission. This chain must be inspected for wear as shown. For more information about automatic transmissions refer to chapter 26 in the textbook. (Courtesy of Oldsmobile Division, General Motors Corporation)

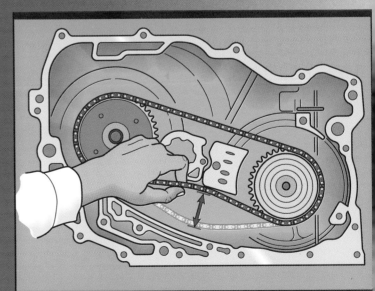

Service

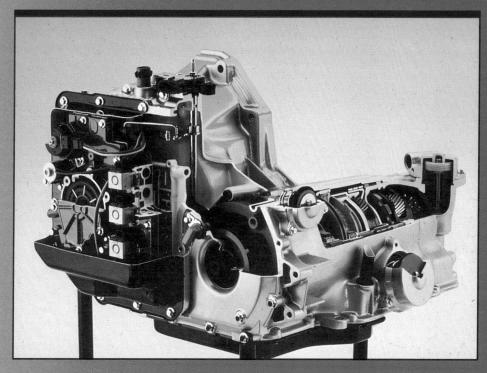

Now that computers have been placed on automotive vehicles, electronic controls can be placed on the transmission as well. Most of the shifting and movement of shift valves are controlled by an on-board computer for the electronic transmission. For more information about this topic refer to chapters 25 and 26 in the textbook.
(Courtesy of Motor Magazine)

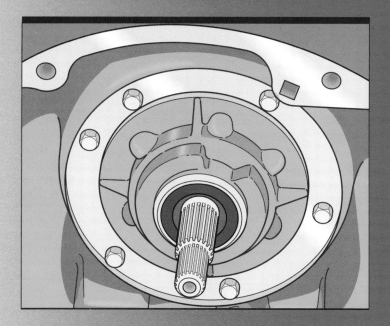

The oil pump is often located on the front of the transmission, behind the torque converter. It is easily removed by removing the bolts that keep it in place. A rubber "O" ring on the outer diameter of the oil pump seals the oil within the transmission. For more information about automatic transmission refer to chapter 26 in the textbook.

Suspension,

All antilock braking systems must have a sensor on each wheel to determine its speed. This wheel sensor is used to tell the computer the exact speed of each wheel. With this information the computer can control the hydraulic pressure accordingly in the braking system. For more information about antilock braking systems refer to chapter 28 in the textbook.
(Courtesy of Chrysler Corporation)

Braking systems often require diagnosis and service. Often the wheel cylinder may leak hydraulic brake fluid. A hone is used to clean up the internal surface of a wheel cylinder to improve sealing of the wheel cylinder parts. For more information about wheel cylinder service refer to chapter 28 in the textbook.

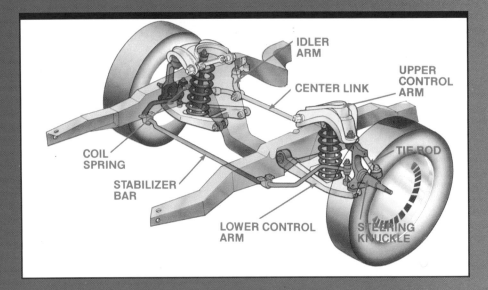

The front suspension and steering system have many parts that must be inspected and serviced throughout the life of the vehicle. Improperly serviced suspension and steering systems cause the vehicle to ride poorly and driver control is reduced. For more information about suspension and steering systems refer to chapters 29 and 30 in the textbook.
(Courtesy of Erjavac/Automotive Technology: A Systems Approach)

Steering and Brakes

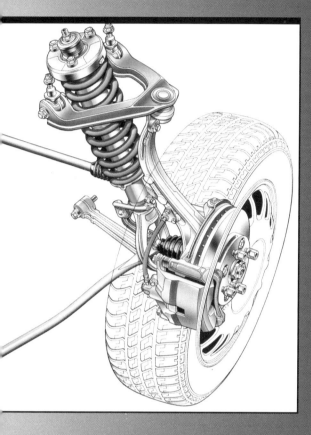

In order to obtain maximum ride comfort and safety, proper service and diagnostic procedures should always be followed when working on the suspension and steering system. For more information about this topic refer to chapters 28, 29, 30 and 31 in the textbook. *(Courtesy of Motor Magazine)*

On front wheel drive vehicles, a strut suspension system is used. When removing or replacing the strut, alignment will be affected. The alignment (camber) can be set by using the cam washers to position the strut to the front wheel. For more information about wheel alignment refer to chapter 30 in the textbook.

Sophisticated alignment equipment should always be used to align the vehicle for proper ride, comfort, and safety. For more information about wheel alignment refer to chapters 28, 29, 30 and 31 in the textbook. *(Courtesy of Hunter Engineering Company)*

Electrical Service

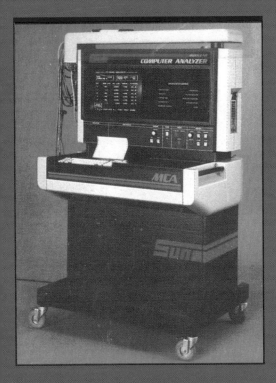

Electrical ignition systems can be precisely checked and diagnosed by using computer analyzers. For more information about electrical diagnosis refer to chapters 18, 19, 20, 21 and 22 in the textbook. (Courtesy of Hunter Engineering Company)

The automobile today is controlled by various electronic sensors, circuits and computers. The automotive service technician must have a sound knowledge of electrical principles and troubleshooting procedures to diagnosis and service many of the electrical problems found in the automobile. For more information about automotive computers refer to chapters 18, 19, 20, 21, 22 and 34 in the textbook. (Courtesy of Cleveland Institute of Electronics)

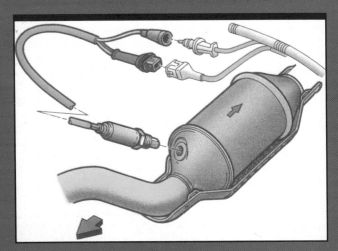

An oxygen sensor is used to measure the oxygen in the exhaust flow. Based upon the oxygen in the exhaust, electrical signals are sent to the on-board engine computer to control the air fuel ration and ignition timing. For more information about oxygen sensors refer to chapters 15 and 16 in the textbook. (Courtesy of Volkswagen United States, Inc.)

Many of the electrical circuits are connected together using a wiring harness. At times, wires in the harness may short out against the frame of the vehicle, causing irregular vehicle operation. Follow the exact service manual procedure to diagnosis and service electrical problems in the automobile. For more information about electrical diagnosis refer to chapters 18, 19, 20, 21, 22 and 34 in the textbook.

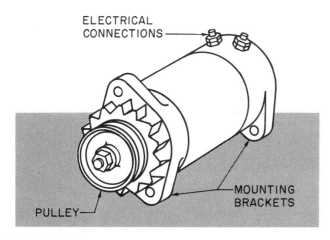

FIGURE 21–2. A generator is used on older vehicles to produce a voltage for charging the battery.

21.2 DC GENERATORS

Although all vehicles being manufactured today use an alternator, many vehicles still have generators. It is important to study these systems so the newer electronic systems can be understood. *Figure 21–2* shows a typical dc generator. It is driven by a belt from the crankshaft.

Dc Generator Parts

The dc generator is made of several parts. These are shown in *Figure 21–3*. The poles are stationary and produce the magnetic field needed to generate electricity. This circuit is called the *field circuit*. Rotating inside the field poles is an *armature*. Voltage is produced in the armature as it rotates within the magnetic field.

Ac and Dc Voltages

The voltage produced within the armature is ac, or alternating current. Ac voltage is continually changing back and forth as shown in *Figure 21–4*. The current flows first in a positive direction, then in a negative direction. Dc voltage is continuous, or flows in one direction. Dc voltage is always flowing in a positive or negative direction.

Rectifying Ac Voltages

The ac voltage within the armature must be converted to dc voltage for automotive circuits. A commutator and a set of brushes are used to accomplish this. The commutator is also called a split-ring commutator. Ac voltage is changed to dc voltage when it goes from the commutator to the brushes. The brushes are made of carbon and rub against the commutator. The voltage at the brushes is dc voltage that can be used to charge the battery or operate the vehicle circuits. *Figure 21–5* shows the armature, the commutator, and the brushes.

A graph of the voltage rectified by the split-ring commutator is shown in *Figure 21–6*. Note that although the voltage is pulsating from zero to a maximum point, it continually

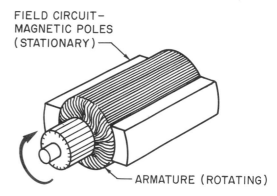

FIGURE 21–3. A dc generator has several parts, including the poles (which are stationary) and the armature (copper wire), which rotates inside the poles.

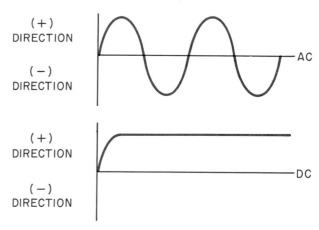

FIGURE 21–4. Ac voltages alternate from a positive direction to a negative direction and back. Dc voltages always have current flow in only one direction. These graphs illustrate the differences between ac and dc voltages.

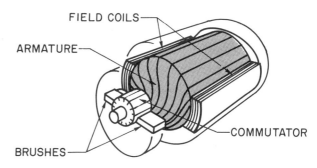

FIGURE 21–5. The generator is made of an armature, field coils, the commutator, and the brushes. *(Courtesy of Delco-Remy Division of General Motors Corporation)*

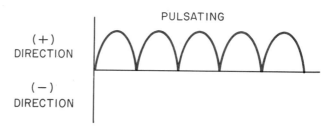

FIGURE 21–6. The dc voltage that is changed by the split-ring commutator is pulsating dc and is illustrated in the graph.

goes in the same direction. It does not reverse direction as ac voltages do.

Purpose of Regulating Voltage

The output of the dc generator must be regulated and controlled. Regulation is needed to protect the generator or alternator, the battery, and the electrical circuits in the automobile from too much voltage or current. It is very important to keep the voltage output of the generator or alternator slightly above 12 (about 13.5) volts. If the voltage is too high, the light bulbs may burn out and the battery may overheat. Too low a voltage will cause poor charging of the battery and incorrect operation of the electrical circuits. The voltage regulator is used for this control.

Voltage Regulator

The following discussion on voltage regulators pertains only to dc generators. This type of voltage and current regulation is no longer used with the newer alternators, which use electronic and computerized regulation. However, its discussion will help the service technician better understand the reason for many of the new electronic components used in regulators today.

Figure 21–7 shows a three-unit, or coil, regulator. A coil with a set of points or contacts is also called a *relay*. It has three coils inside. They are called the cutout relay, the current regulator, and the voltage regulator. When these coils are energized, the contact points close. As semiconductors were used more, automotive manufacturers improved these circuits. Depending on the vehicle make and year, three, two, or one coil could be used. Today, all regulators are solid-state. Some are built into the alternators, and no relay coils are used.

Cutout Relay

The cutout relay is used to protect the generator when it is not charging as much voltage as the battery is producing. If the battery voltage is greater than the generator voltage, the cutout relay will open. This action stops any current from going backwards into the generator. This could cause the

battery to discharge unnecessarily. When the generator increases its voltage above the battery voltage, the coil is energized and closes the set of contacts on top of the cutout relay. Now the generated voltage forces electrons from the generator to the battery or into the vehicle circuits or both. See *Figure 21–8A*. If the battery is fully charged, the generated voltage supplies current only to the circuits in the vehicle. If the generator stops producing voltage, the cutout relay will de-energize, and the contact points will open. This

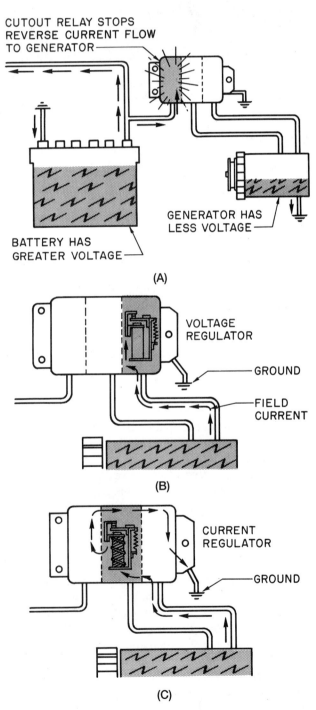

CUTOUT RELAY STOPS REVERSE CURRENT FLOW TO GENERATOR

BATTERY HAS GREATER VOLTAGE

GENERATOR HAS LESS VOLTAGE

(A)

VOLTAGE REGULATOR

GROUND

FIELD CURRENT

(B)

CURRENT REGULATOR

GROUND

(C)

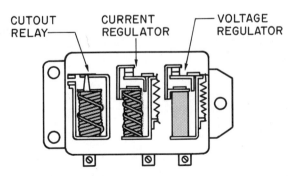

CUTOUT RELAY — CURRENT REGULATOR — VOLTAGE REGULATOR

FIGURE 21–7. A three-unit voltage regulator has a cutout relay, a current regulator, and a voltage regulator. These units were used on older vehicles before electronic regulators were developed. *(Courtesy of Delco-Remy Division of General Motors Corporation)*

FIGURE 21–8. Older voltage regulators for dc generators used a (A) cutout relay, (B) voltage relay, and (C) current relay to control the output. *(Courtesy of Delco-Remy Division of General Motors Corporation)*

will protect the generator from receiving any unnecessary battery voltage.

Voltage Relay

The voltage relay controls the generator's field current so the voltage doesn't get too high. The field current controls the strength of the magnetic field. If the field current increases, its magnetic field will also increase. Voltage output will now increase. If the field current decreases, the magnetic field will also decrease. Voltage output will now decrease.

A voltage-sensitive coil is used to control field current. When voltage is too high, say 15 volts, the relay coil is energized. This opens the voltage relay contact points. This action limits the amount of current that can flow into the field windings. The voltage output will now decrease. See *Figure 21–8B*. When the generator output decreases to 12 volts or lower, the voltage relay closes again so full current can flow to the field windings.

Current Relay

At times the electrical system may demand more current than the generator can produce. This can happen if too much load is placed on the vehicle's electrical circuits. The current relay controls the amount of generator current output. Here a current-sensitive coil is used, *Figure 21–8C*. During normal operation, current output from the generator passes into the current regulator, through the contact points, and back to the field windings. When too much current is demanded by external circuits, the coil is energized. This opens the points and again limits the field current. Many regulator designs have been used on different vehicles. All circuits, however, must control three things: the reverse current protection (cutout), voltage control, and current control.

PROBLEM: Overcharged Battery

The battery on a customer's car (1982 Ford) seems to always overcharge. The battery seems very hot after operation, and the customer has replaced the battery once. What could be the problem?

SOLUTION:

The problem is most likely tied to the voltage regulator. The voltage regulator is used to monitor and control the amount of current and voltage going back into the battery during charging. On older cars, the voltage regulator can be adjusted. If the voltage regulator is overcharging or cannot be adjusted on a newer car, it should be replaced. This should solve the problem.

21.3 ALTERNATORS

An alternator, rather than a generator, is used on today's vehicles to charge the battery and operate the electrical circuits. This is because the alternator is much more efficient than a generator. Alternators are much smaller, lighter in weight, and produce more current than generators. The alternator has a set of rotating poles and a stationary set of windings. In addition, there is no split-ring commutator. Solid-state diodes are used to convert ac to dc voltages. The alternator is made of a stator, rotor, and slip-ring and brush assembly. Many modern (late-model) alternators have the regulator built into the housings as a complete unit.

Stator

The *stator*, *Figure 21–9,* is made of a circular, *laminated* iron core. There are three separate windings wound on the core. The windings are arranged so that a separate ac voltage *waveform* is induced in each winding as the rotating magnetic field cuts across the wires.

Rotor

The *rotor*, *Figure 21–10,* is made of a coil of wire wound around an iron core on a shaft. When current is passed through the windings, the assembly becomes an electromagnet. One side is a north pole, and the other side is a south pole. Iron claws are placed on both ends. Each projection has the same polarity as the ends of the coil. When the claws are meshed together from each side, pairs of north and south poles are formed around the circumference of the rotor, *Figure 21–11*. The number of north and south poles is determined by the manufacturer. Four, six, and seven sets of poles are common in alternators today. The poles are designed to rotate inside the stator, producing the voltage needed to charge the battery.

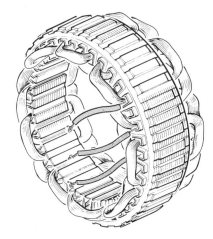

FIGURE 21–9. Alternators use a stator, or stationary set of windings, to generate voltage. *(Courtesy of Lucas Industries, Inc.)*

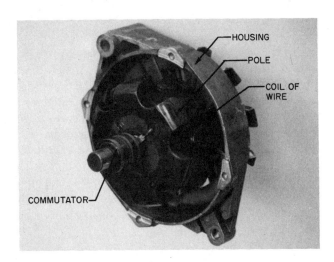

FIGURE 21–10. The rotor is made of a coil of wire wound around an iron core.

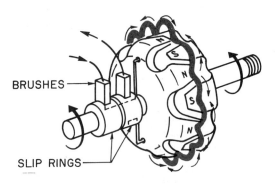

FIGURE 21–11. The coil of wire on the rotor has two end plates meshed together. Seven sets of north and south poles produce the magnetic fields.

Slip-ring and Brush Assembly

The ends of the rotor coil are connected to *slip-rings* that are mounted on the shaft. Current is supplied from the battery through the brushes and slip-rings to energize the rotor field windings. This produces the magnetic field needed for making the north and south poles in the alternator.

Three-Phase Voltage

As the rotor revolves inside the stator windings, voltage is produced in the stator. Three separate windings are spaced evenly inside the stator. The voltage produced is called *three-phase* voltage. Each winding produces a separate voltage. This is shown in *Figure 21–12*. The voltages, just like the windings, are 120 degrees apart from each other.

The three-phase stator windings can be connected in one of two ways. The star connection is also called the wye connection. This is the most common hookup in an alternator. The delta connection is used for higher-output alternators. Each winding produces a separate voltage. The dark solid voltage line (Figure 21–12) is produced from coil (A). The lighter solid voltage line is produced from coil (B). The dashed voltage line is produced from coil (C). Each voltage is separate and independent. However, it is still ac voltage and must be converted, or rectified, to dc for use in the automobile.

Rectifying Three-Phase Ac Voltage

The three-phase voltage in the alternator stator windings must be converted, or rectified, to dc. Six diodes are used to do this. Three are considered positive diodes, and three are considered negative diodes. Diodes allow current to flow in only one direction. (See Chapter 18.) *Figure 21–13* shows

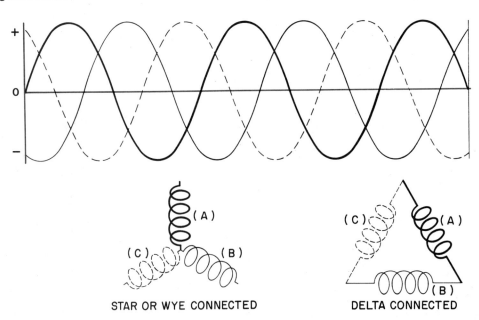

STAR OR WYE CONNECTED   DELTA CONNECTED

FIGURE 21–12. The voltage produced by the alternator is considered three-phase. Each phase is produced by a separate set of stator windings. This graph shows the three-phase voltage produced. Also, the stator can be connected as a star, or wye, connection or as a delta connection. *(Courtesy of Lucas Industries, Inc.)*

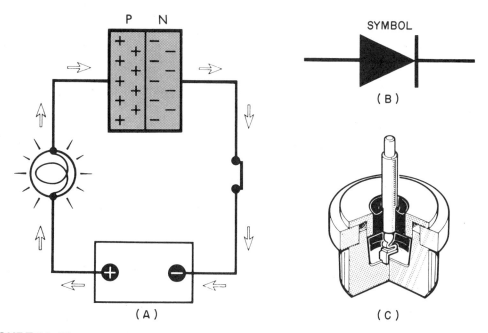

FIGURE 21–13.   Diodes are used to convert ac voltages to dc for use in the automobile. Diodes allow current to flow in only one direction. (A) shows a diode circuit, (B) a diode symbol, and (C) a cross-sectional view of a diode. *(Courtesy of Lucas Industries, Inc.)*

a diode circuit (A), the electrical symbol for a diode (B), and a cross-sectional view of a diode (C).

Figure 21–14 shows a circuit that uses six diodes to rectify three-phase ac voltage to dc. Coils (A), (B), and (C) produce an ac voltage. Each voltage is sent to the rectifier. No matter where the current enters the rectifier, it is sent out on top to the positive side of the battery. The current at the battery has been rectified to dc.

Current Flow in a Three-Phase Rectifier

In Figure 21–14, the first half-cycle produced from coil (A) passes current from point 1 to diode (C) to the positive side of the battery. The current returns to coil (A) through diode (D) and coil (B). On the negative half-cycle, coil (A) passes current from point 2, through coil (B), through diode (A), to the positive side of the battery. The current returns from the battery through diode (F) to point 1 on coil (A). The voltage produced by coil (A) is now rectified to dc. It goes through the battery in the same direction.

Coil (B) works the same way. The first half-cycle produced by coil (B) passes current from point 4 to diode (A) to the positive side of the battery. The current returns to coil (B) through diode (E) and coil (C). On the negative half-cycle, coil (B) passes current from point 3, through coil (C), to diode (B), to the positive side of the battery. The current returns from the battery through diode (D) to point 4 on coil (B). The voltage produced by coil (B) is now rectified to dc.

The flow through the rectifier can be followed the same way for coil (C). It is also rectified to dc. *Figure 21–15* shows the resultant dc voltage wave that is produced by rectifying three-phase ac voltage. It is called pulsating dc and is considered *full-wave rectification*.

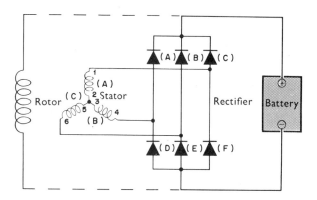

FIGURE 21–14.   Six diodes are used to convert three-phase ac to pulsating dc. *(Courtesy of Lucas Industries, Inc.)*

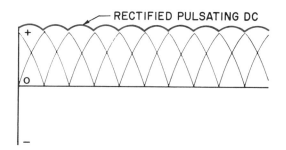

FIGURE 21–15.   The voltage that is rectified on an alternator is called pulsating dc. It is made by rectifying all three phases of ac to dc in the rectifier. *(Courtesy of Lucas Industries, Inc.)*

Higher-Output Alternators

Alternators are generally rated by the amount of amperage that they can produce. Voltage generally remains at 12–14 volts. As more and more electrical components are being placed on vehicles, amperage demand continues to increase. Thus, higher-output alternators are being used on many vehicles today. For example, average alternator output ratings ranged between 40 and 60 amps several years ago. Today vehicles require alternators that can produce 80–110 amps. In order to produce the higher amperage, the alternator rotor is made slightly larger. This allows the magnetic field to be stronger. In addition, more stator windings are put into the alternator, thus increasing its amperage output.

There are certain charging systems that allow the voltage to increase as well. For example, on some vehicles that use heated windshields, 50–70 volts are needed to heat the windshield. In order to produce this voltage, all other circuits are operated directly from the battery. Then, the voltage of the alternator can be increased by the voltage regulator or computer to the necessary voltage. Each system is different, so it is necessary to refer to the manufacturer's service manual for service and diagnosis.

21.4 ALTERNATOR REGULATION

Many types of regulators have been used on automotive charging systems. As more solid-state circuitry was developed, the regulation systems slowly changed from relays and coils to electronics. Today regulators are all electronic and require very little maintenance.

All regulators are designed to control the amount of current sent into the field windings. *Figure 21–16* shows the relationship between rotor speed, field current, and the regulated voltage. The solid line represents the regulated voltage from the alternator. The dotted line represents the field current. As the rotor speed increases, the field current is reduced to keep the regulated voltage controlled.

In dc generators, a relay was used to control the amount of current to the field windings. In electronic regulators, the switching of the field current is controlled by transistors turning off and on. No cutout relay is needed because diodes in the rectifying circuit prevent current from flowing in the reverse direction.

Two-Unit Regulators

When alternators were first introduced in the automobile, the regulator was designed using relays and diodes. *Figure 21–17* shows an example of a typical alternator wiring diagram. The cutout relay has been removed. When diodes are used, the battery voltage cannot force current back into the alternator. The diodes prevent current flow in this direction.

There are still two relays. One relay is called the field relay. The second relay is called the voltage relay. In Figure 21–17, when the ignition key is turned on, the battery is connected to terminal 4 of the regulator. Current now flows through the indicator lamp on the dashboard. This lights the lamp to show no charging. Current also flows from terminal 4 to the voltage regulator through its contacts, and to terminal F over to the field windings. The field windings are now energized to produce a strong north and south pole.

When the engine starts, the alternator starts to produce voltage. This voltage is used to charge the battery or operate other electrical circuits. One phase of the voltage is also sent to terminal R on the alternator. This voltage sends a current to terminal 2 on the regulator and to the field relay, closing its set of points. When the points close in the field relay, this action causes the battery voltage to be connected directly to the field windings. This is done by connecting terminal 3, through the field relay points, to the points in the voltage relay, and finally to terminal F to the field windings.

When the points close, battery voltage is impressed directly on terminal 4. This action stops the current flowing in the

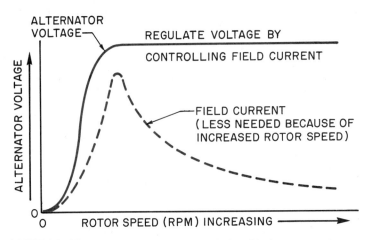

FIGURE 21–16. This chart shows the relationship between rotor speed, current in the field windings, and output voltage. As the rotor speed increases, field current is reduced to keep the regulated voltage controlled.

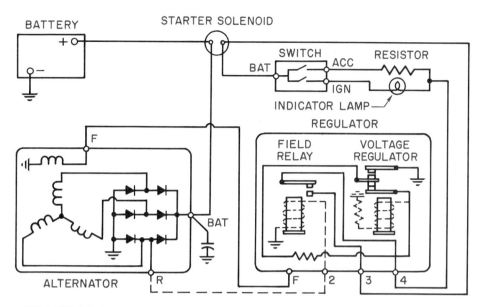

FIGURE 21-17. When alternators were first introduced, a two-unit regulator was used. Diodes replaced the cutout relay, but a field relay and a voltage relay were still used. *(Courtesy of Delco-Remy Division of General Motors Corporation)*

switch circuit, turning off the indicator lamp. This indicates that a voltage is being produced by the alternator.

As the voltage from the alternator increases because of high speed or too much current sent to the field windings, the bottom set of contacts on the voltage regulator opens. This action causes the field current to be sent through the resistor. The resistor reduces the field current, causing the generated voltage to be reduced. In operation, the voltage regulator action is very rapid when maintaining an accurate voltage.

When the alternator speed increases rapidly and there is a chance of excessive voltage, the upper contact on the voltage regulator is forced down. Now all current to the field windings is grounded through the set of contact points. This action stops current flow to the field windings, reducing the alternator output.

Electronic Regulators

As solid-state circuitry was developed, voltage regulators eventually became totally electronic. *Figure 21-18* shows an alternator with the voltage regulator built directly into the alternator. *Figure 21-19* shows a complete charging circuit for the alternator. The action of the regulator is similar to relay types, except transistors are used to turn the field windings off and on.

A *zener diode* is used to tell the circuit exactly when too much voltage is being produced by the alternator. The zener diode is identified as D2. When the alternator voltage is too high, the zener diode turns on. When the zener diode turns on, transistor TR1 turns off, shutting off the current to the field windings. The reverse happens when the voltage drops to an acceptable level. Although the action is more complicated, the concept of controlling the field current is the same.

Alternator Construction

Alternators are designed today as complete integral units. *Figure 21-20* is an exploded diagram of an alternator. Note the position of each part previously discussed in this chapter. Housings are used on both ends for support. They also include the necessary bearings for supporting the rotor. The rotor has six fingers on the north pole and six fingers on the south

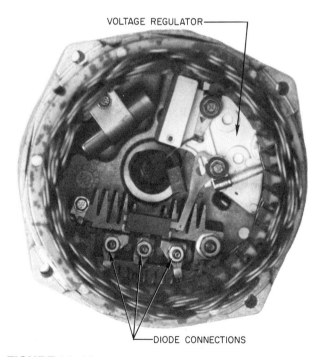

FIGURE 21-18. Voltage regulators are totally electronic today. Transistors turn the field windings off and on for control.

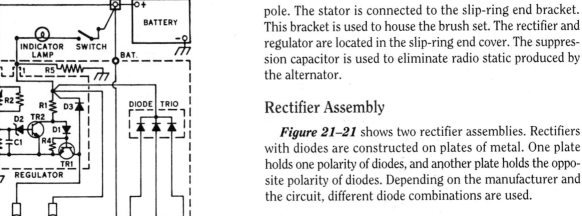

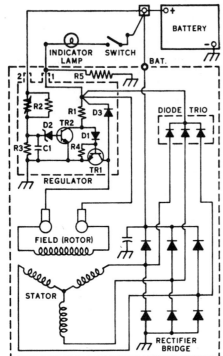

FIGURE 21–19. This is a complete circuit of an alternator, field windings, electronic voltage regulator, and diodes for rectification. *(Courtesy of Motor Publications, Auto Repair Manual)*

pole. The stator is connected to the slip-ring end bracket. This bracket is used to house the brush set. The rectifier and regulator are located in the slip-ring end cover. The suppression capacitor is used to eliminate radio static produced by the alternator.

Rectifier Assembly

Figure 21–21 shows two rectifier assemblies. Rectifiers with diodes are constructed on plates of metal. One plate holds one polarity of diodes, and another plate holds the opposite polarity of diodes. Depending on the manufacturer and the circuit, different diode combinations are used.

Computerized Regulation

Beginning in 1985, some manufacturers used the computer to regulate the charging circuit. The computer is now able to control the alternator's output. The computer essentially replaced the voltage regulator. In order to regulate the alternator output, the internal circuitry for regulation is much the same. *Figure 21–22* shows one vehicle manufacturer's system used to control the alternator. In this system, the ECU (electronic control unit) monitors various sensors. Various components on the engine will require or demand more output from the alternator. Many of these components have sensors that tell the computer that more output is needed by the alternator. In addition, there is also an ELD (*electric load detector*). This sensor is used to detect the exact amount of electrical load required by the various components on the engine. The result is improved fuel economy and more efficient operation of the charging system.

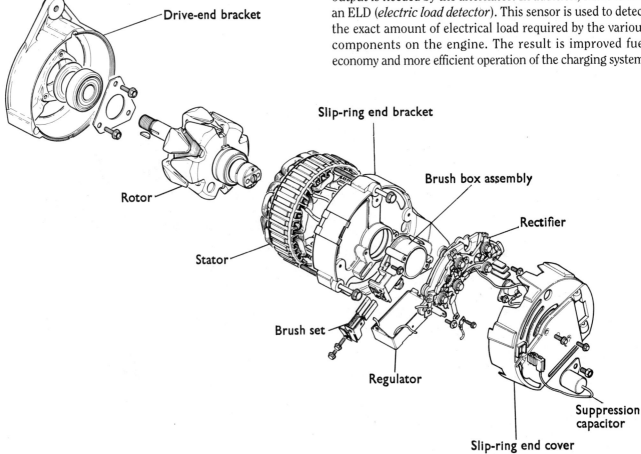

FIGURE 21–20. An exploded diagram of an alternator. *(Courtesy of Lucas Industries, Inc.)*

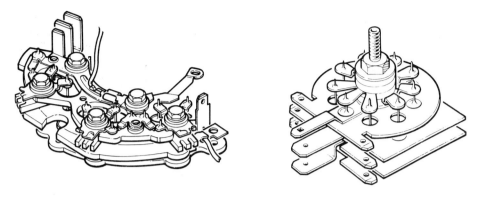

FIGURE 21-21. Rectifier packs are designed in many styles. Usually the diodes are grouped together on a plate for correct operation and polarity. *(Courtesy of Lucas Industries, Inc.)*

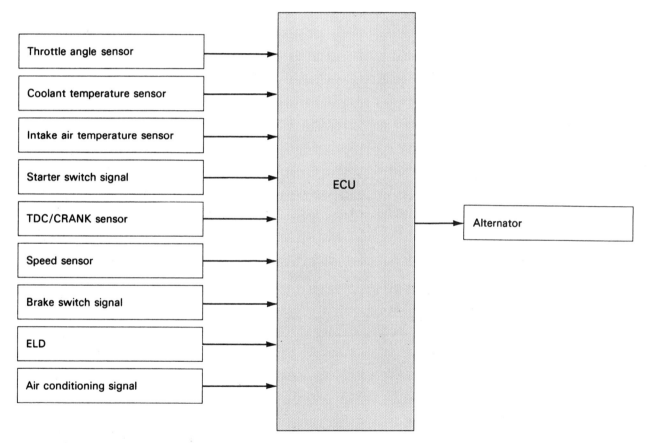

FIGURE 21-22. Many vehicles today use the on-board computer to regulate the output of the alternator. Various sensors are fed into the ECU to control the output of the alternator. *(Courtesy of Honda Motor Company, Ltd.)*

Problems, Diagnosis and Service

PROBLEM: Incorrect Alternator Belt Tension

A squealing sound comes from the front of the engine during acceleration.

DIAGNOSIS

Often the squealing sound is made because the alternator belts are not tightened to the correct tension, or the belts have been tightened too much. If they are too tight there will be excess pressure on the alternator bearings. The bearings may then have to be replaced.

SERVICE

Figure 21–23 shows one manufacturer's procedure for checking belt tension.

1. Loosen the alternator adjustment bolt and the pivot bolt so the alternator can move.
2. Lightly pry back the alternator, tightening the belt tension.
3. Make sure the belt is loose enough to produce the specific deflection between the alternator and the crankshaft. (NOTE: On certain late-model vehicles, there is a half-inch square opening in the belt tension bracket. This square opening, shown in *Figure 21–24*, allows the use of either a torque wrench or drive socket. This approach eliminates stress on the components.)
4. Holding the alternator at this position, tighten the adjustment bolt and the pivot bolt to the manufacturer's torque specifications.

PROBLEM: Defective Diodes

An alternator on an engine seems to rattle during operation.

DIAGNOSIS

A rattling noise from the alternator can be caused by several things. Generally the problem is caused by worn or dirty bearings, loose mounting bolts, a loose drive pulley, a defective stator, or defective diodes. If any of these is the cause, it will be necessary to remove the alternator and perform various procedures.

SERVICE

1. Remove the alternator wires and external connections.
2. Remove the pivot and adjusting bolts from the alternator.
3. Carefully remove the alternator from the engine.

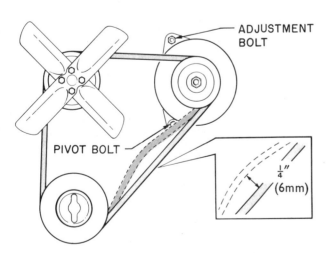

FIGURE 21–23. When checking the charging circuit, always make sure the belt tension on the alternator is correct. *(Courtesy of Lucas Industries, Inc.)*

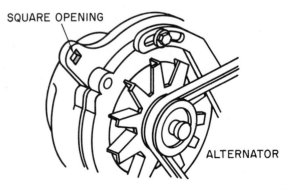

FIGURE 21–24. The alternator can be moved for tightening the belt tension by placing a ratchet in the square opening on the alternator housing.

4. Check the alternator for bad bearings. Bad bearings can be determined by rotating the armature and feeling for rough turning. Bearings should be replaced if there is any evidence of wear.

5. Refer to the manufacturer's procedure to disassemble the alternator. *Figure 21–25* shows a completely disassembled alternator from one manufacturer. Use the following general procedure to disassemble the alternator:
   a. Carefully remove the bolts that hold the alternator to the brackets on the engine.
   b. Scribe marks on the alternator front and rear housings to retain the proper position during reassembly. On some alternators, the regulator can be removed from the rear of the assembly by removing several small screws.

c. Remove the through-screws that hold the front and rear housing together.

d. Pry the assembly apart, making sure to keep the stator assembly with the rear half.

e. Remove the center rotor assembly from the end housing.

f. Remove the regulator and other parts of the assembly as necessary.

g. Reverse this procedure for reassembly.

6. The rotor can be checked for shorts or opens with an ohmmeter as shown in *Figure 21–26*. The ohmmeter is used to check for shorts between the rotor shaft, frame poles, and windings.

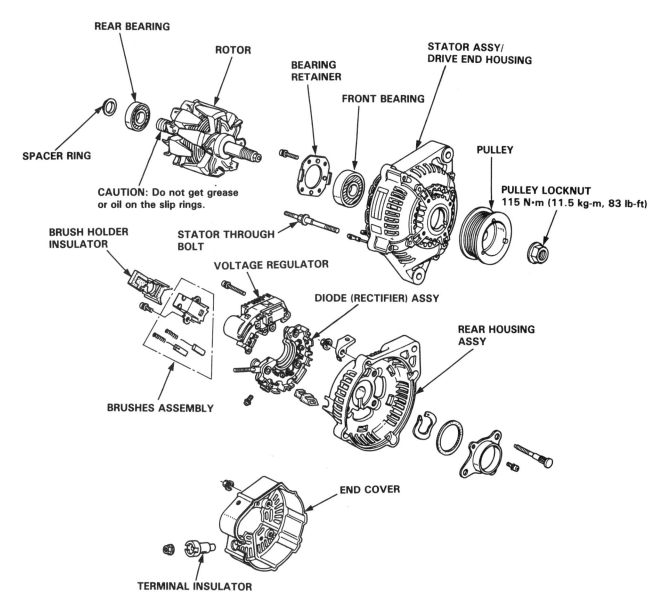

FIGURE 21–25. When disassembling the alternator, follow the manufacturer's recommended procedure. *(Courtesy of Honda Motor Company, Ltd.)*

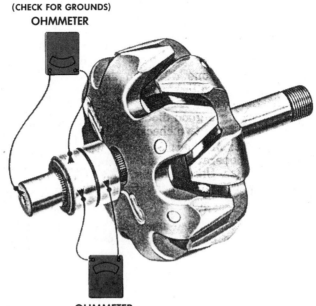

(CHECK FOR GROUNDS)
OHMMETER

OHMMETER
(CHECK FOR SHORTS AND OPENS)

FIGURE 21–26. The rotor can be checked by using an ohmmeter. Grounds, shorts, and opens can be checked. *(Courtesy of Delco-Remy Division of General Motors Corporation)*

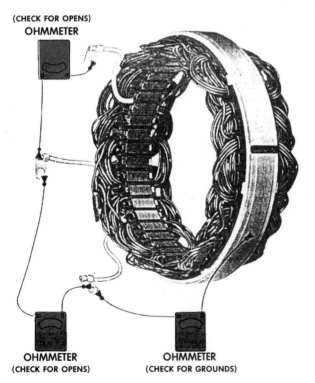

(CHECK FOR OPENS)
OHMMETER

OHMMETER
(CHECK FOR OPENS)

OHMMETER
(CHECK FOR GROUNDS)

FIGURE 21–27. The stator can be checked using an ohmmeter. All three windings should be checked for grounds and opens. *(Courtesy of Delco-Remy Division of General Motors Corporation)*

7. A stator can be checked for shorts or opens as shown in *Figure 21–27*. The ohmmeter is used to check each winding.

8. Inspect the brushes for excessive wear, damage, or corrosion. If there is any doubt about their condition, replace the brushes. Also measure the brushes for wear and compare with manufacturer's specifications. If the brushes have worn down below the service limit, replace the brushes.

9. Bad diodes can also cause a rattling noise during operation. This is because if one diode has shorted out, one-third of the alternator stator will not be charging or under load. Thus, in one revolution of the alternator, two-thirds of the revolution is under load while one-third is not. This causes a vibration to occur in the rotor shaft, which sounds like bad bearings or a rattling noise.

   a. An ohmmeter is used to check for defective diodes. When placed across the diode, high resistances should be noted in one direction and low resistances should be noted in the reverse direction. If both readings are very low or very high, the diode is defective.

   b. On some vehicles six diodes are used. On others, eight may be used. *Figure 21–28* shows how one manufacturer recommends checking these diodes. Check for continuity in each direction, between the B and P terminals (of each diode pair), and between the E (ground) and P terminals (of each diode pair). All diodes should have continuity in only one direction.

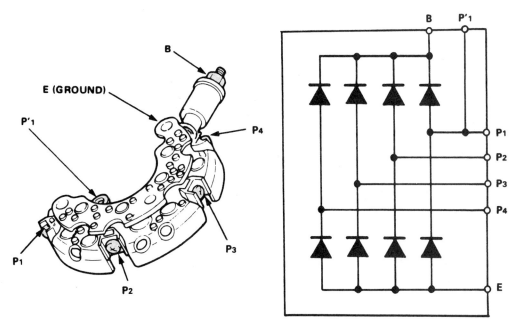

FIGURE 21–28. When checking diodes, always check each diode for continuity. If any one diode is either shorted or opened, replace the entire rectifier assembly. *(Courtesy of Honda Motor Company, Ltd.)*

If any of the diodes fails, replace the rectifier assembly. Diodes are not available separately.

c. On some regulators, a diode trio is also used. Its purpose is to rectify current entering the voltage regulator and field or rotor windings. The schematic diagram shown in Figure 21–19 shows a diode trio. These diodes should also be checked for continuity. Remember that a diode can either be shorted or opened. An open diode will have a high (infinite) resistance in both directions. A shorted diode will have a low (zero) resistance in both directions.

PROBLEM: Faulty Alternator or Regulator

The battery on a vehicle does not seem to be getting a full charge from the alternator. At times during operation the headlights seem to dim easily.

DIAGNOSIS

Various tests can be run on the alternator when it is on the vehicle. Four of them are:

■ Voltmeter test of charging system

■ Alternator amperage output under maximum load using the *VAT* (voltage-amperage tester)

■ Regulator voltage test, used to check the regulator, using the VAT

■ Regulator bypass test, used to short out the regulator to find the fault, using the VAT

The first test can be done using a voltmeter. Use the following general procedure to test the voltage output using a voltmeter only.

1. Run the engine at idle for about 15 minutes to get the engine warm.

2. Stop the engine, and place a voltmeter on the alternator. Clip the black lead to the negative side of the battery. Attach the positive side of the meter to the positive post on the battery.

   CAUTION: Keep wires and body parts away from any part of the engine while it is running.

3. Start the engine and gradually increase the engine speed to about 1,800 RPM. Note the voltage reading on the meter scale.

4. If the meter pointer climbs steadily and comes to an abrupt halt within a range of 13.5 to 15.5 volts for a 12-volt system, the entire charging system is most likely operating correctly.

5. If the meter climbs but stops below the correct range of 13.5–15.5 volts or above it, or if the meter fluctuates and will not stop, the regulator is most likely defective.

6. If the meter does not climb to the correct range, the alternator is most likely defective.

The other tests are done with a VAT, shown in *Figure 21–29*. Each manufacturer of these testing instruments has specific procedures for testing the charging system.

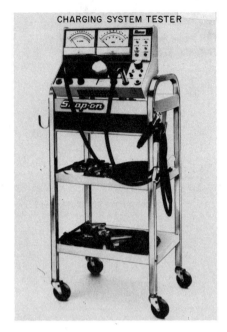

FIGURE 21–29. Charging systems can be checked using this tester. Both voltage and amperage can be checked to determine the charging system condition. *(Courtesy of Snap-On Tools Corporation)*

SERVICE

Use the following general procedure to test the charging system with a VAT.

1. First make sure the battery is in good shape.

2. *Figure 21–30* shows a typical hook-up between the VAT, the battery, and the alternator. Connect as shown. Put selector switch on the "starting" position.

3. Start the engine, and turn off all the accessories.

4. Move the selector switch to the "charging" position. Remove the inductive pickup, and zero the ammeter. Now reconnect the inductive pickup to the alternator output wire.

5. Increase the engine speed to 2,000 RPM, and hold at this RPM. Make sure the cooling fan is not on.

6. Now apply a "load" with the carbon pile, so the voltage drops back to not less than 12 volts.

7. At this point, check the maximum amperage reading and compare it with the chart in *Figure 21–31*. You should subtract from 5 to 10 amperes from the maximum reading because of engine operation. For example, if the engine is running at 2,000 RPM, the alternator speed is about 5,000 RPM. At this alternator speed the alternator should produce about 63 amperes minimum (after subtracting 5–10 amps). If the reading is below this number, the alternator needs to be replaced or rebuilt.

8. Check the regulator voltage test by turning the selector knob to the correct setting.

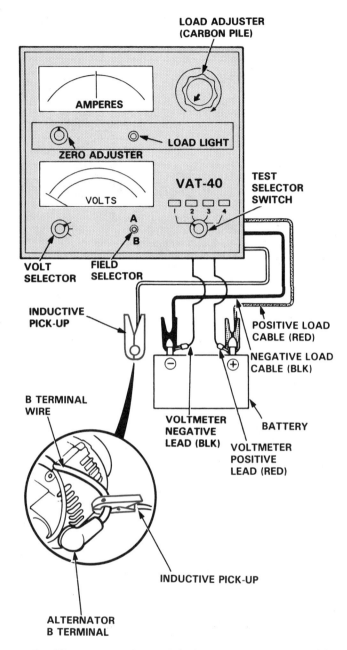

FIGURE 21–30. The VAT (voltage-amperage tester) is used to check the output of the charging system. *(Courtesy of Honda Motor Company, Ltd.)*

9. Run the engine again at 2,000 RPM, and check the voltage on the VAT. Generally the voltage should be between 13.5 and 14.5 volts. This is the normal voltage output for a fully charged battery. If the voltage is steady and within this range, the regulator is OK. If the voltage is higher or lower than this, the voltage regulator should be replaced.

10. A regulator bypass test can also be performed. This test is done by shorting out the regulator and operating the alternator. Direct battery voltage is used to excite the rotor field. Each manufacturer suggests different ways of shorting out the regulator. Some involve shorting a

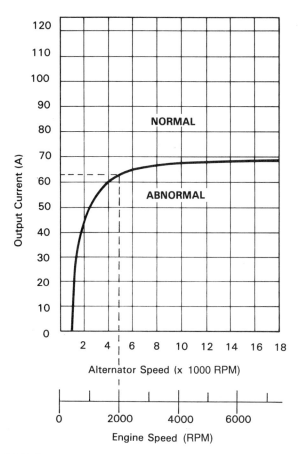

FIGURE 21–31. After checking the amperage output of the alternator, compare the readings with this chart to determine if the alternator is faulty. *(Courtesy of Honda Motor Company, Ltd.)*

test tab to ground on the rear of the alternator. Others require the use of a jumper wire to connect the battery voltage to the field. Check the service manual for the correct procedure. Now perform the voltage and current test previously mentioned. If the charging voltage and current increase to normal levels with the regulator bypassed, the problem is most likely the regulator. If the voltage and current remain the same when the regulator is bypassed, then the problem is most likely the alternator.

SUMMARY

The charging system was covered in this chapter. Generator principles, the dc generator, alternators, and voltage regulators were covered.

Three things are needed to produce electricity. These include a magnetic field, electrical wire, and having the wire cut across the magnetic lines of force. Both dc generators and alternators are designed to accomplish this. As any one of the three factors increases, the output voltage will also increase. If any one of the three decreases, the voltage output will also decrease.

One method used to convert mechanical energy into

SERVICE MANUAL CONNECTION

There are many important specifications to keep in mind when working with charging systems. To identify the specifications for your engine, you will need to know the VIN (vehicle identification number) of the vehicle, the type and year of the vehicle, and the type of engine. Although they may be titled differently, some of the more common charging system specifications (not all) found in service manuals are listed below. Note that these specifications are typical examples. Each vehicle and engine may have different specifications.

Common Specification	Typical Example
Alternator adjusting bolt torque	18 lb-ft
Alternator belt tension (deflection)	0.33–0.47 inch
Alternator brush length	0.22 inch, lower limit
Alternator output amperage at 12 volts	65 amps hot
Alternator voltage	12.5–14.5 volts

In addition, the service manual will give specific directions for various service and testing procedures. Some of the more common procedures include:

- Alternator belt adjustment
- Alternator overhaul
- Alternator regulator testing
- Alternator replacement
- Brush inspection
- Charge warning light test
- Checking output voltage of alternator
- Rectifier test
- Rotor slip ring test
- Stator test

electrical energy involves using a dc generator. Here the magnetic field is stationary. The wire rotates within the magnetic field. A split-ring commutator is used to remove the voltage produced in the rotating part. The split-ring commutator is also used to convert the ac in the rotor to dc for use in the automotive electrical system.

The charging system must have a regulator. A regulator is used to control the voltage and amperage. The regulator uses a cutout relay to stop the battery voltage from forcing current back into the generator when it is at a low charge. In operation, the regulator controls the amount of current

(continued)

Linkage to Automotive History

CONTROL FOR DIRECT CURRENT GENERATORS

Years ago, all automobiles used direct current generators and mechanical contact regulators. With these components it was difficult to get efficient voltage and current regulation at all speeds. The illustration shows that as the speed of the generator increased, eventually the voltage would increase beyond the voltage regulator limit. This voltage could damage many electrical components in the vehicle. Thus, some means had to be developed to regulate voltage at higher speeds. To do this a "bucking field" generator was used. A bucking field generator used a special field coil wound in the direction opposite that of the other field coils. The bucking field coil had a tendency to slow down the generation of electricity at high speeds. With today's sophisticated electronic technology and the use of alternators, voltage and current regulation are easily maintained at all operating speeds.

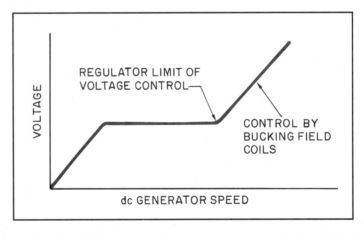

being sent to the field windings. If more current goes to the field windings, generator output increases. If less current goes to the field windings, generator output decreases.

The regulator used for dc charging systems has three relays. The cutout relay is used to stop the flow of reverse current from the battery back to the generator. The voltage relay controls the exact amount of voltage output from the generator. The amperage relay controls the maximum amperage being produced by the generator.

Alternators are much like generators, but they are more efficient. In an alternator, the field windings rotate, and the wire where the voltage is produced is stationary. Several sets of magnetic poles are usually used. Seven sets of north and south poles are very common. The commutator used on an alternator is called a slip-ring type. Its purpose is to connect electricity to the rotating fields.

Alternators also produce three-phase voltages, rather than single-phase voltages as in the generator. These three phases are rectified to pulsating dc by using six diodes. This is called three-phase full-wave rectification.

Alternator output must also be regulated. Voltage and current regulation are built into the circuits. There is no need for a cutout relay because the diodes prevent any reverse current flow from the battery back to the alternator. Depending on the year and manufacturer, voltage regulators may have electrical relays or, as in the present system, be fully solid-state. Zener diodes and transistors are used to regulate the alternator output.

During servicing of alternators and generators, four major symptoms can be observed: (1) the battery may be getting a low charge; (2) the battery may be getting too high a charge; (3) the indicator lamp may be faulty; (4) the alternator may be noisy. These faults can be caused by bad diodes; grounded, open, or shorted circuits; bad bearings; or a faulty regulator. Always follow the manufacturer's recommended procedures and specifications when troubleshooting the charging circuit.

TERMS TO KNOW

Can you explain each of the following terms? Review the chapter until you can use each term correctly.

Commutator
Rectify
Field circuit
Armature
Relay
Stator
Laminated
Waveform
Rotor
Slip-ring
Three-phase
Full-wave rectification
Zener diode
Electric load detector
VAT

REVIEW QUESTIONS

Multiple Choice

1. The charging system is used to convert _____ energy to electrical energy.
   a. Radiant
   b. Mechanical
   c. Chemical
   d. Nuclear
   e. Thermal

2. What is necessary to produce a voltage in an alternator or generator?
   a. Conductors
   b. Magnetic field
   c. The conductors cutting the magnetic field
   d. All of the above
   e. None of the above

3. In order to increase the output of a generator or alternator:
   a. Increase the magnetic field strength
   b. Increase the amount of wire or conductors
   c. Increase the speed of movement between the magnetic field and the wire
   d. All of the above
   e. None of the above

4. The field circuit in a generator is also called:
   a. The magnetic core
   b. Field poles
   c. Slip-ring commutator
   d. Diode
   e. Voltage circuit

5. Which component is used to extract the voltage produced in the armature on a dc generator?
   a. Slip-ring commutator
   b. Diode
   c. Split-ring commutator
   d. Laminations
   e. Stator

6. Voltage produced inside the dc generator or alternator is always:
   a. Dc, and must be converted to ac
   b. Ac, and must not be converted to dc
   c. Dc, and must not be converted to ac
   d. Ac, and must be converted to dc
   e. Greater than the battery voltage

7. A voltage regulator on a charging system is always controlling the:
   a. Diodes
   b. Ac voltage
   c. Strength of the magnetic field
   d. Speed of operation
   e. Zener diode

8. Which of the following relays is used on a dc generator system to stop the reverse flow of electricity when the generator is at a low charge?
   a. Voltage relay
   b. Current relay
   c. Field relay
   d. Cutout relay
   e. All of the above

9. Which of the following components are rotating on an alternator?
   a. Magnetic north and south poles
   b. Slip-rings
   c. Magnetic pole fingers
   d. All of the above
   e. None of the above

10. The alternator produces:
   a. Single-phase voltages
   b. Double-phase voltages
   c. Three-phase voltages
   d. Dc without diodes
   e. Ac without rectification being needed

11. How many diodes are used on an alternator?
   a. 1
   b. 3
   c. 4
   d. 5
   e. 6

12. Regulators used in current charging systems today:
   a. Use two relays
   b. Are all solid state
   c. Use one relay
   d. Have no voltage regulator
   e. Use three relays

13. A zener diode is used to:
   a. Close off the field current
   b. Tell the transistors when there is too much voltage
   c. Generate voltage
   d. Rectify three-phase voltages
   e. Rectify single-phase voltages

14. Which of the following is not a problem in a charging system?
   a. Diodes shorting out
   b. Field windings grounding
   c. Bad bearings
   d. Too high RPM
   e. Brushes wearing down

The following questions are similar in format to ASE (Automotive Service Excellence) test questions.

15. Technician A says that if a constant 11 volts is being produced by the alternator, the system is alright. Technician B says that if a constant 14 volts is being produced by the alternator, the system is alright. Who is right?
   a. A only
   b. B only
   c. Both A and B
   d. Neither A nor B

16. A noise seems to be coming from an alternator, as if a bearing is damaged. Technician A says that the bearings should be replaced. Technician B says that the diodes should be checked. Who is right?
   a. A only
   b. B only
   c. Both A and B
   d. Neither A nor B

17. An alternator does not have enough current output. Technician A says the problem is bad brushes. Technician B says the stator is reversed. Who is right?
   a. A only
   b. B only
   c. Both A and B
   d. Neither A nor B

18. An alternator is not charging correctly. Technician A says the problem is in the brushes and they may be worn. Technician B says the problem is that the alternator frame has too much magnetism. Who is right?
   a. A only
   b. B only
   c. Both A and B
   d. Neither A nor B

19. Technician A says that six diodes can be checked with an ohmmeter. Technician B says that the diodes can be checked with a voltmeter. Who is right?
   a. A only
   b. B only
   c. Both A and B
   d. Neither A nor B

20. Technician A says the charging system voltage can be checked with a voltmeter. Technician B says the charging system output can be checked with a VAT. Who is right?
   a. A only
   b. B only
   c. Both A and B
   d. Neither A nor B

21. An alternator is producing a rattling noise as it is in operation. Technician A says the problem is faulty bearings. Technician B says the problem is a faulty diode. Who is right?
    a. A only
    b. B only
    c. Both A and B
    d. Neither A nor B

22. Technician A says that charging voltage can be checked using the VAT. Technician B says that the VAT checks for continuity. Who is right?
    a. A only
    b. B only
    c. Both A and B
    d. Neither A nor B

Essay

23. What three things are necessary to produce a voltage?

24. What is the difference between a dc generator and an alternator?

25. Describe the definition of rectifying.

26. What is the purpose of a stator?

27. What is a zener diode, and how is it used in an electronic regulator?

28. Describe how to check the output of an alternator.

Short Answer

29. Higher-output alternators generally have higher _____ ratings.

30. On computerized regulation systems, an _____ is used to sense the exact amount of electrical load.

31. A squealing sound from the alternator system means that the _____ needs to be adjusted.

32. A bad diode in the regulator may cause the alternator _____ to be damaged.

33. Two tests that can be performed on the alternator when it is in the vehicle are the _____ and the _____.

CHAPTER 22

Starting Systems

INTRODUCTION The starter system is a type of electrical circuit that converts electrical energy into mechanical energy. The electrical energy contained in the battery is used to turn a starter motor. As this motor turns, the engine is cranked for starting. This chapter is concerned with the starting system, its components, operation, and service.

OBJECTIVES After reading this chapter, you should be able to:

- Identify the principles of starter motors.

- List the parts of the starter motor and state their purpose.

- Compare the operation and parts of different starter drive and clutch mechanisms.

- Describe the purpose and operation of the solenoid and related circuits.

- Describe the purpose of a crank signal on computerized vehicles.

- Describe various problems, diagnosis, and service and repair procedures for the starting system.

 SAFETY CHECKLIST

When working with starting systems, keep these important safety precautions in mind.
✔ Always wear OSHA-approved safety glasses around the automotive shop.
✔ Always use the correct tools when working on the starter.

✔ Always remove rings, bracelets, and other jewelry to eliminate the possibility of getting an electrical shock.
✔ Be careful not to cut your hands on the edges of the starter.

22.1 STARTER SYSTEM OPERATING PRINCIPLES

Purpose of the Starter System

Although energy cannot be created, it can be changed from one form to another. In the starter system, the starter motor is used to convert electrical energy from the battery to mechanical energy to crank the engine. Several parts are needed to do this. These include the starter motor, a drive and clutch mechanism, and a solenoid that is used to switch on the heavy current in the circuit.

A considerable amount of mechanical power is necessary to crank and start a car engine. About 2 horsepower, or approximately 250 to 500 amps of electricity, is normally needed. The amperage is higher on a diesel engine, but the basic principles are the same. Because of the high amounts of current, heavy cables must be used to carry this current. A switch on the dashboard is used to energize the heavy-current circuits. *Figure 22–1* shows a complete electrical circuit of the starting system. It includes the starter to cranking motor, solenoid, drive and clutch mechanisms, electrical wire, and ignition switch. Each component will be studied in more detail in this chapter.

Some of the information in this chapter can help you prepare for the National Institute for Automotive Service Excellence (ASE) certification tests. The tests most directly related to this chapter are entitled

ENGINE REPAIR (TEST A1), ELECTRICAL SYSTEMS (TEST A6), AND ENGINE PERFORMANCE (TEST A8).

The content areas that closely parallel this chapter are

BATTERY AND STARTING SYSTEM DIAGNOSIS AND REPAIR, STARTING SYSTEM DIAGNOSIS AND REPAIR, AND ENGINE ELECTRICAL SYSTEMS DIAGNOSIS AND REPAIR.

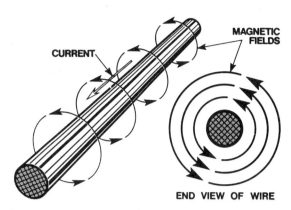

FIGURE 22–2. When current passes through a conductor, a magnetic field is built up around the conductor. The magnetic field surrounds the conductor. *(Courtesy of Lucas Industries, Inc.)*

produce a magnetic field. The lines of force between the two poles flow from the north pole to the south pole. A wire carrying electricity is placed within the magnetic field. When this is done, the two magnetic fields below the wire travel in the same direction. Above the wire, the lines of force travel in opposite directions. The result is a stronger magnetic field on the bottom of the wire and a weaker magnetic field on the top. This difference in magnetic fields causes the wire to move upward.

There is another way to define this movement. Magnetic lines of force traveling in the same direction tend to repel each other. Magnetic lines of force are often compared to a stretched elastic band. If there is any distortion, the bands (magnetic lines of force) will try to realign themselves. This causes the wire to move away from the area where the lines of force are concentrated.

In a starter, the wire is wound into loops. *Figure 22–4* shows how a loop of wire would be turned if it were placed within a magnetic field. The electricity flows into point B and loops around to come out at point A. The wire is placed on the center axis. The direction of the magnetic field around

Magnetic Field around a Conductor

When current is passed through a conductor, a magnetic field is built up around the conductor. This is shown in *Figure 22–2*. When current passes from the back of the wire to the front, a magnetic field is created. It circles around the conductor in a counterclockwise direction. The lines of magnetic force are formed in a definite pattern. If the current is reversed, the magnetic lines of force will flow in a reverse or clockwise direction.

Producing Motion from Electricity

A starter motor has a north pole and a south pole. This is shown in the top of *Figure 22–3*. The north and south poles

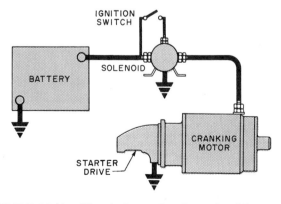

FIGURE 22–1. The starter system is made of the starter, or cranking motor, the solenoid, the ignition switch, and the starter drive mechanism. *(Courtesy of Delco-Remy Division of General Motors Corporation)*

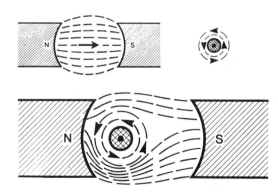

FIGURE 22–3. A north pole and a south pole are needed to create the action in a motor. If the current-carrying conductor is placed within the magnetic field, the wire tends to move. This movement is caused by differences in the magnetism on top of and below the wire. *(Courtesy of Lucas Industries, Inc.)*

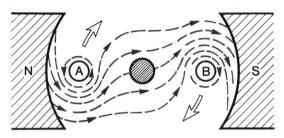

FIGURE 22–4. When a loop of wire with current flowing in the wire is placed within a magnetic field, the loop will turn because of the direction of the magnetic fields. *(Courtesy of Lucas Industries, Inc.)*

the left and right conductors is opposite. When this condition occurs, the magnetic lines of force strengthen below the left side and above the right side. The concentration of magnetic lines of force causes the wire loop to turn in a clockwise direction on the center axis. When electricity is passed through wire, electrical energy is converted to mechanical energy.

The Principle of Commutation

In Figure 22–4, when the loop has rotated one-half revolution, point A is positioned at the south pole and point B is positioned at the north pole. Because the magnetic field around point B is clockwise, magnetic distortion occurs above B and below A. This means that the wire loop will reverse direction to return to the original position.

To keep the loop turning in the same direction, the electrical current in the loop must be reversed precisely at the right time. This is done by using a *commutator.* Commutation, or current reversal, is achieved by joining the ends of the loop to two metal segments. The contact surface between the battery and the segments is formed by the brushes.

Figure 22–5 shows a simple starter with a commutator and brushes. The loop of wire is shown as having a black side and a white side. Both ends of the loop of wire are connected to a segment of metal. On the top diagram the white half of the loop (on the right) is connected to the positive side of

the battery. The current will flow from the positive terminal on the battery, through the loop, and return to the negative side of the battery. This will produce a magnetic field around the wire in the loop. In this position, the direction of the magnetic field on the black half is counterclockwise and of the white half is clockwise. This causes the loop to turn.

In the lower drawing, the loop has moved through a half turn. The white section is now on the left, and the black section is on the right. Because of the position of the metal segments under the brushes, the current is now reversed in the loop. This causes the magnetic field around both sides to reverse in relation to the top drawing. The magnetic field around the conductor will now keep the loop turning in the same direction.

Producing the North and South Poles

The north and south poles are created by using soft iron that can be easily magnetized. This is done by wrapping a coil of wire around the soft iron core and passing current through the wire. These coils are called field coils or poles. The soft iron core is specially shaped to concentrate the magnetic lines of force in the space provided. *Figure 22–6* shows the main magnetic fields. In this case, the north pole is formed on the left, and the south pole is formed on the right. The lines of magnetic force always flow from the north pole to the south pole.

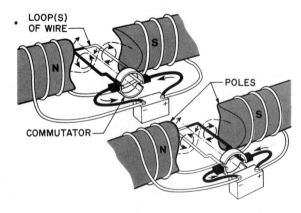

FIGURE 22–5. A simple starter motor consists of a set of poles, a loop of wire, and a commutator. *(Courtesy of Lucas Industries, Inc.)*

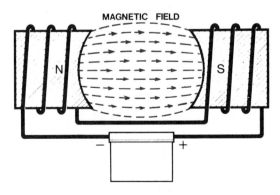

FIGURE 22–6. All starter motors have a set of north and south poles that are produced by winding wire around a soft iron core. *(Courtesy of Lucas Industries, Inc.)*

PROBLEM: Bad Starter Bearings

A vehicle has 60,000 miles on it. No work has been done on the starter system. There have been times recently when the engine would not even crank over. It sounds as if the solenoid is trying to engage the starter pinion, but the starter just won't turn over.

SOLUTION:

Quite often the starter bushings will wear. When the bushings wear, the armature sits lower in the starter field windings, often scraping on them. Remove the starter and check the no-load speed test. This should show that the starter bushings are bad and should be replaced.

22.2 STARTER MOTORS

Parts of the Starter

The parts of the starter motor will now be considered in more detail. All starters have a set of field coils. Coils are made of copper or aluminum strips wound in the correct direction to produce the poles. Typically, four field coils are used on a starter. *Figure 22–7* shows an example of the field

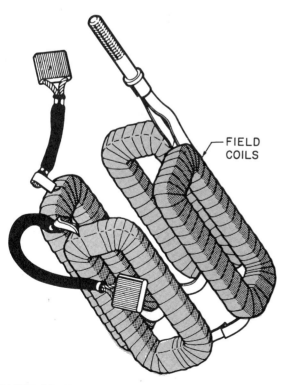

FIGURE 22–7. Four field coils are used on a starter motor. *(Courtesy of Lucas Industries, Inc.)*

coils. These coils are assembled over the soft iron core. The iron core, or shoe, is attached to the inside of a heavy iron frame on the motor. See *Figure 22–8*. The iron frame and *pole shoes* provide a place for the field coils. They also provide a low-resistance path for the magnetic lines of force.

Series Wound Field Circuits

The four field coils in the starter can be connected in several ways. Two common connections are the series and the series-parallel wound field. The one selected is determined by the application, engine speed, torque requirements on the starter, cable size, battery capacity, and current-carrying capacity of the brushes.

Figure 22–9 shows the series wound circuit. Here the field coils are connected in series. The four field coils are wound in different directions to produce alternate north and south poles. The electrical current flows from the battery into each coil, then to the *armature* windings. All four field coils are in series with the armature windings.

Series-Parallel Wound Field Circuits

Another type of electrical circuit used in starters is called the series-parallel field connection. This arrangement is shown in *Figure 22–10*. The electrical current comes into the starter and splits. The field circuit consists of two paths

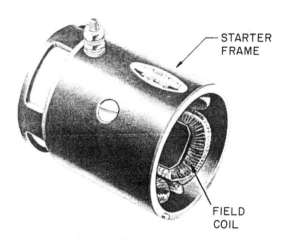

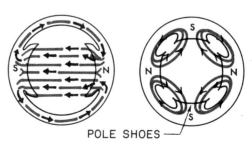

FIGURE 22–8. The four field coils are attached to the starter frame. The shoes provide a place for the field coils. *(Courtesy of Delco-Remy Division of General Motors Corporation)*

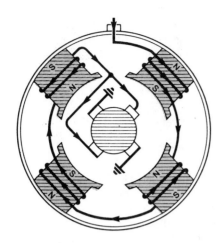

FIGURE 22–9. A series wound circuit in the starter has all four coils in series with the armature. *(Courtesy of Lucas Industries, Inc.)*

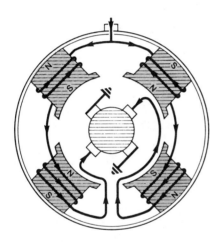

FIGURE 22–10. A series-parallel wound circuit in the starter has two paths for the current to flow through the poles. *(Courtesy of Lucas Industries, Inc.)*

for the current. The field windings, however, are still in series with the armature, while one field coil is in parallel with the armature windings. This is sometimes called a *shunt* coil connection. It is used to control the maximum speed of the starter during operation.

Armatures

The armature is the rotational part of the starter. Earlier in this chapter, the armature was called the loop of wire. There are many loops of wire in the armature. Each wire loop is connected to the copper segments arranged in a barrel shape. See *Figure 22–11*. The segments are insulated from each other and from the armature shaft. These segments of copper form the commutator and provide the running surface for the brushes.

The armature assembly consists of a stack of iron *laminations*, or layers, located on a steel shaft. The steel shaft is supported by bearings located on the end plates of the starter. The iron laminations are used to concentrate the

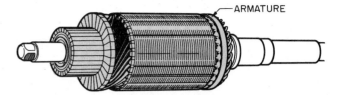

FIGURE 22–11. The armature in a starter is the rotational part that has many loops of wire with a commutator. *(Courtesy of Lucas Industries, Inc.)*

magnetic field. Laminations are also used to reduce the heating effect of *eddy currents*. Eddy currents are small electrical currents that are produced inside the iron core. The windings are made of heavy copper ribbons that are inserted into the slots in the iron laminations. *Figure 22–12* shows an actual armature used in a starter motor.

Brushes

Brushes are used to make electrical contact between the armature, which rotates, and the battery, which is stationary. Brushes are made from a high percentage of copper and carbon. This material minimizes electrical losses due to overheating. *Figure 22–13* shows an example of the brushes held in place on the starter end plate. Each brush uses a small metal spring to force the brush against the commutator during operation. There are typically four brushes. Two brushes are used to feed electricity into the armature. Two brushes are grounded and used to return the electricity to ground, which is the negative side of the battery.

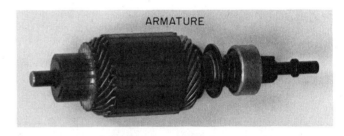

FIGURE 22–12. An armature used in a starter motor.

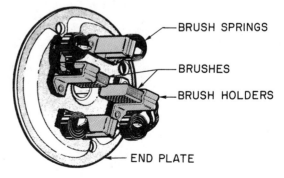

FIGURE 22–13. Brushes are held in place on the end plate of the starter. *(Courtesy of Lucas Industries, Inc.)*

CAR CLINIC

PROBLEM: Starter Drag

A vehicle with about 30,000 miles on it starts OK the first time. After the engine is hot, however, it usually takes several times to crank the engine. The starter seems to be very sluggish and seems to have a drag.

SOLUTION:

Check the condition of the starter bearings. If they are in good condition, check the current on the starter when it is hot. Suspect high current draw. If the starter and solenoid have no electrical faults, exhaust gases may be heating up the starter, causing it to drag and be sluggish. A heat baffle may be needed between the starter and the exhaust pipe. Also, make sure that as the car is moving forward, there is sufficient air flowing over the starter to help cool it.

22.3   DRIVE AND CLUTCH MECHANISMS

Purpose of Drives and Clutches

The starting system uses several types of drives and clutches. The purpose of the drive is to engage and disengage the *pinion gear* from the flywheel. The pinion gear is the small gear located on the armature shaft. When the engine is running, the pinion gear cannot be in contact with the flywheel. When the starter is cranked, however, the pinion gear must slide on the shaft and engage the flywheel, only at that time.

When the engine starts to turn on its own power, the fly-

wheel turns faster. Now the pinion gear must be removed rapidly. Several types of drives and clutches are used for this purpose. Two popular types include the *inertia drive* and the *overrunning clutch drive*. Most manufacturers use a design similar to one of these two drives.

Inertia Drives

There are several types of *inertia* drives. Inertia drives are also called Bendix drives. Although they may differ considerably in appearance, each drive operates on the principle of inertia. Inertia is a physical property of an object. An object at rest tends to stay at rest. An object in motion tends to remain in motion. Inertia is used to move the pinion gear to engage the engine ring gear when the starter motor is energized.

Figure 22–14 shows an inertia drive system. There is a pinion gear, a screw sleeve, the armature shaft, and springs. All the parts of the drive mechanism are assembled onto the armature drive shaft. The drive shaft has a spline that meshes with the internal spline on the screw sleeve. Thus, the screw sleeve can move along the axis of the armature shaft.

When the armature turns during starting, the armature shaft and the screw sleeve rotate. The inertia of the pinion (remaining at rest) causes the screw sleeve to turn inside the pinion. This causes the pinion to move out and engage with the flywheel ring gear. As soon as the engine fires and runs under its own power, the flywheel is driven faster by the engine. As the pinion gear is forced faster, it is moved back along the screw sleeve and out of engagement with the flywheel. At this point, the starter switch is released. The spring is used to absorb excessive twisting of the shaft. On certain drives, a compression spring is used to reduce the shock at the moment of engagement.

Overrunning Clutch Drives

A second type of drive is called the overrunning clutch drive. This type of drive is also referred to as a roll-type drive,

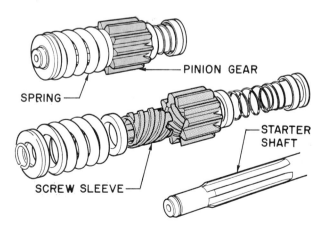

FIGURE 22–14.   An inertia drive system is used on some starter systems to engage the pinion gear with the ring gear. *(Courtesy of Lucas Industries, Inc.)*

or *sprag* (small angular wedges) drive. The sprag drive uses a series of 30 sprags, rather than rollers. It is commonly used on diesel engines and on some gasoline engines. The roller clutch drive is shown in *Figure 22–15*. It consists of a drive and driven member and a series of cylindrical rollers. These rollers are placed in wedge-shaped tracks in the clutch housing. As shown in *Figure 22–16*, when the armature shaft rotates during cranking, the small rollers become wedged against the collar attached to the pinion gear. This wedging action locks the pinion gear with the armature shaft. The pinion gear now rotates with the shaft, cranking the engine.

When the engine starts, *Figure 22–17*, the flywheel spins the pinion faster than the armature. This action releases the rollers, unlocking the pinion gear from the armature shaft. The pinion then "overruns" safely and freely until it is pulled out of mesh. The overrunning clutch is moved in and out of mesh by linkage operated by the solenoid.

Gear Reduction Starter Drives

On certain vehicles a gear reduction system is used between the starter and the pinion gear. Its purpose is to increase the amount of torque during starting of the engine. The gears are designed to reduce the speed of the pinion gear (keeping the starter at the same speed), thus producing more torque at the flywheel ring gear.

Several types of gearing are used on starter systems today. One system uses a planetary gear arrangement. The planetary gear system includes a set of planet pinion gears, a planet pinion carrier, a sun gear, and a ring gear. In operation, one of the three gears needs to be blocked up. In this case the ring gear is locked up. As the sun gear rotates, the planet pinion gears also rotate within the ring gear. This causes the planet pinion carrier to rotate also. The planet pinion carrier is attached to the output of the system and turns the overrunning clutch.

Another system uses a single *reduction gear* as shown in *Figure 22–18*. In this case, the armature drive gear turns a reduction gear. The reduction gear then turns the pinion shaft, overrunning clutch, and drive pinion.

22.4   SOLENOIDS

Definition of a Solenoid

A *solenoid* is an electromechanical device that switches electrical circuits on and off. *Figure 22–19* shows the operation of a solenoid. When current flows through the electrical coil, a magnetic field is created inside the coil. If a soft iron core of metal is placed near the center of the coil, the metal core tends to center itself inside the coil. If a spring is used to hold the metal core outside the center, it again tries to center itself. Thus, when current passes through the coil, the metal core will move. This process, then, converts electrical energy into mechanical energy. The movement of the metal core is used to open and close electrical circuits. Therefore, a solenoid is considered an electromechanical switch.

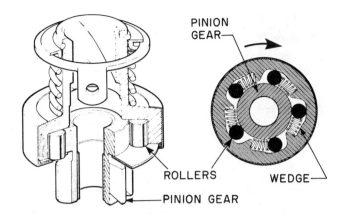

FIGURE 22–15.   A roller clutch, also called the overrunning clutch, is used on some starter systems to engage the pinion gear with the ring gear. *(Courtesy of Lucas Industries, Inc.)*

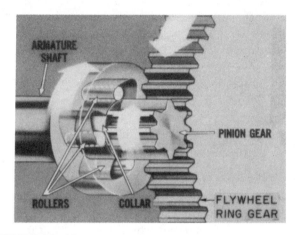

FIGURE 22–16.   When the armature shaft rotates during cranking, small rollers become wedged, causing the pinion gear to lock up and rotate the ring gear. *(Courtesy of Delco-Remy Division of General Motors Corporation)*

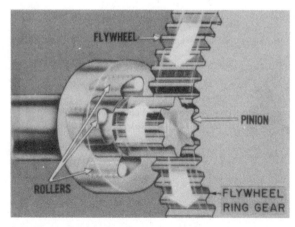

FIGURE 22–17.   When the engine starts, the flywheel spins the pinion gear faster, which releases the roller in the wedge. *(Courtesy of Delco-Remy Division of General Motors Corporation)*

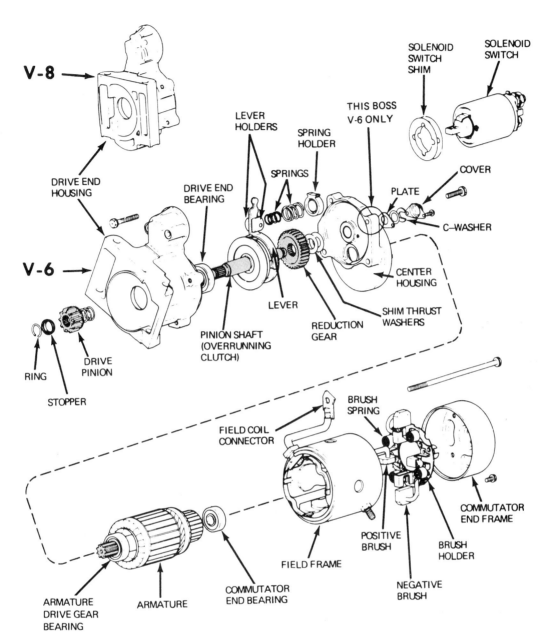

V-8

DRIVE END HOUSING

V-6

LEVER HOLDERS

SPRINGS

SPRING HOLDER

THIS BOSS V-6 ONLY

SOLENOID SWITCH SHIM

SOLENOID SWITCH

DRIVE END BEARING

COVER

PLATE

C-WASHER

CENTER HOUSING

LEVER

REDUCTION GEAR

SHIM THRUST WASHERS

RING

STOPPER

DRIVE PINION

PINION SHAFT (OVERRUNNING CLUTCH)

FIELD COIL CONNECTOR

BRUSH SPRING

POSITIVE BRUSH

BRUSH HOLDER

NEGATIVE BRUSH

COMMUTATOR END FRAME

FIELD FRAME

ARMATURE DRIVE GEAR BEARING

ARMATURE

COMMUTATOR END BEARING

FIGURE 22–18. A reduction gear is used to reduce the speed of the pinion, thus increasing the torque to the flywheel ring gear. *(Courtesy of Motor Publications, Auto Repair Manual)*

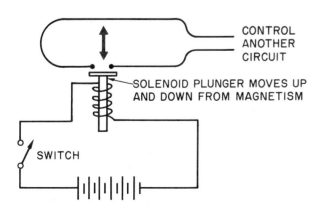

CONTROL ANOTHER CIRCUIT

SOLENOID PLUNGER MOVES UP AND DOWN FROM MAGNETISM

SWITCH

FIGURE 22–19. A solenoid is a device that converts electrical energy to mechanical energy by the use of magnetism.

Solenoid Operation

Figure 22–20 shows the internal operation of a solenoid used on certain vehicles. The solenoid is used to start and stop the heavy current that flows to the starter motor during cranking. The electrical winding is placed around the iron core. This core is called the armature or plunger. On the bottom of the armature is a set of moving contacts. On the bottom of the solenoid is a set of fixed contacts connected to the heavy-current terminals. When the solenoid windings are energized, the center armature is forced downward magnetically. This causes an electrical connection between the two fixed contact points. When the current is stopped in the windings, the armature returns to its original position.

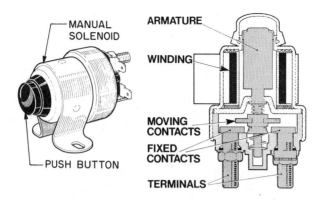

FIGURE 22–20. When the solenoid is operated, a plunger or armature moves in and makes contact with two terminals used to switch the motor on. *(Courtesy of Lucas Industries, Inc.)*

Some older armatures can also be pushed manually to accomplish the same result.

Closing and Hold-on Coils

Many solenoids contain two coils. One is called the closing, or pull-in, coil. One is called the hold-on coil. This is shown in the electrical circuit in *Figure 22–21*. The heavy-gauge winding is called the closing coil, or pull-in winding. It has low resistance. The finer or thinner coil is the hold-on winding. It has higher resistance.

The closing coil has less resistance. This means that there will be more current and more force in the coil. This force is needed along with the hold-on coil to move the center plunger. Once the plunger movement has been completed, much less magnetism is needed to hold the plunger in. When the contact disc touches the terminals, the pull-in winding is shorted out, thus no current flows through the winding. This reduces current draw on the battery during cranking.

Solenoid Drive Linkage

On many vehicles, there is a linkage attached to the opposite end of the plunger on the solenoid. This linkage is used to engage the pinion with the flywheel gear. *Figure 22–22*

shows an example of this linkage. Any movement of the plunger results in a similar but opposite movement of the pinion gear. The movement of the linkage is designed so the pinion gear meshes completely before the solenoid makes contact with the terminals. This assures that the gears are meshed before the starter turns.

On occasion, the pinion gear and flywheel gear may not instantly mesh, because the teeth butt up against each other. A spring on the overrunning clutch assembly will overcome this problem. When the teeth butt up against each other, the plunger and operating lever move their full distance. However, the pinion gear may still not be meshed. When the starter begins to turn, the teeth immediately mesh and cause the engine to crank.

The gear teeth on the pinion gear also have a slight edge (*chamfer*) cut on the end of each tooth. This also helps the pinion and ring gear to mesh more smoothly.

22.5 STARTER CIRCUIT OPERATION

Starter Circuit

Now that all of the components have been studied on the starting system, the complete circuit can be analyzed. *Figure 22–23* shows the complete operation of the starting circuit.

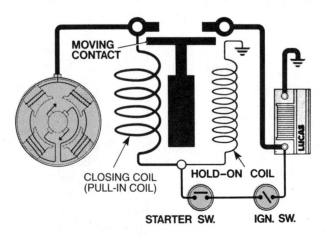

FIGURE 22–21. The two windings used in a solenoid close the plunger and hold the plunger in. *(Courtesy of Lucas Industries, Inc.)*

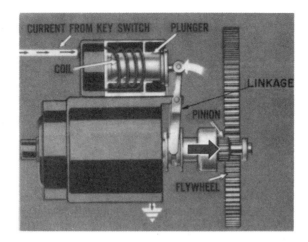

FIGURE 22–22. Linkage is used to engage the pinion gear with the flywheel gear. *(Courtesy of Delco-Remy Division of General Motors Corporation)*

Electrical energy is made available by the battery. A large, heavy cable of wire is connected from the battery to the starter solenoid. The ignition switch is also connected to the positive side of the battery.

A neutral safety switch is also included in the circuit. This switch remains open except when the transmission is in park or neutral. When the transmission is in any gear, the switch is open and the engine cannot be cranked. When the transmission is in park, the switch is closed and the engine can be cranked.

If the transmission is in park and the start switch is closed, electrical current passes to the solenoid. The solenoid is now energized, and the plunger moves. This causes the linkage to engage the pinion gear and crank the engine.

When the ignition switch is closed, current causes the solenoid to engage the starter. At the same time, the mechanical linkage engages the pinion gear with the ring gear. When the engine starts, the pinion gear is pushed away from the ring gear. When the ignition switch is released, the solenoid also releases. The starter circuit is now ready to operate again when the switch is turned to the crank position.

Starting System Computer Signal

On some engines that use computerized controls, a start or *crank signal* is sent to the computer. Its purpose is to tell the computer that the engine is starting to crank. The computer will then enrich the air-fuel mixture accordingly, to either the carburetor or the injectors. On some engines, a cold start injector is used during starting. In order to get the crank signal to the computer, a wire is fed from the starter solenoid circuit to the computer.

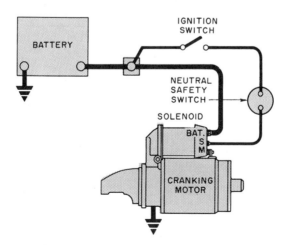

FIGURE 22–23. The complete electrical circuit of the starter system. *(Courtesy of Delco-Remy Division of General Motors Corporation)*

Problems, Diagnosis and Service

PROBLEM: Faulty Solenoid

The engine in a vehicle will not start. When the ignition switch is engaged, the solenoid seems to click but the starter will not turn.

DIAGNOSIS

If the solenoid engages but the starter does not turn, the solenoid moving contact may be corroded. On certain starters, this moving contact can be cleaned and replaced in the solenoid. To check, use a battery jumper cable to bypass the solenoid. Connect the jumper cable across the heavy-current lines, between the input and output of the solenoid. If the starter turns, then the solenoid is defective. Often the problem occurs because each time the solenoid is turned on, a copper washer makes contact with two electrical connections. When the solenoid is turned off, there is always a small amount of electrical arcing on the washer and contacts. This causes corrosion and eventually increases the resistance enough so that electrical contact cannot be made.

SERVICE

Use the following general procedure to remove the solenoid and replace or repair the moving contact.

1. Disconnect the battery.
2. Generally the solenoid is located either directly on top of the starter or on the side of the engine compartment on the wheel well. Remove all wires from the solenoid and mark them for reassembly later.
3. Remove the solenoid from the vehicle.
4. Some solenoids can be disassembled. If this is the case, disassemble the solenoid, being careful not to break any electrical connections.
5. Using sandpaper or a file or both, clean both internal heavy-current contacts in the solenoid. Also clean the small washer that makes contact between the two heavy-current contacts.
6. While the solenoid is apart, both the hold-in and pull-in windings can be checked for resistance and voltage drops. Refer to the manufacturer's specifications for the correct readings.
7. After cleaning the contact points and checking the hold-in and pull-in windings, reassemble the solenoid.
8. Attach the solenoid back on the starter or to the wheel well.
9. Attach all electrical wires to their correct location.
10. Engine should now start.

PROBLEM: Faulty Starter Motor

An engine will not start when the ignition switch is closed. At first, the problem happened only occasionally. Now, each time the vehicle is stopped, it is not able to start again.

DIAGNOSIS

Often the starter has a bad set of brushes, bad bearings, a bad electrical contact, or windings in the starter have either shorted out or grounded. This means the starter must either be replaced or rebuilt. Several checks can be made on the starter to determine if it needs to be rebuilt.

1. A voltmeter can be used to check various points in the starter circuit. Refer to *Figure 22–24*.
2. The voltage drop in the starter can be checked with a voltmeter during cranking. Excessive voltage drop could mean the resistance in the starter circuit is too high. Several checks can be made. *Figure 22–25* shows three checks. The voltage drop can be checked between the vehicle frame and the grounded battery terminal post (A), between the vehicle frame and the starter field frame (B),

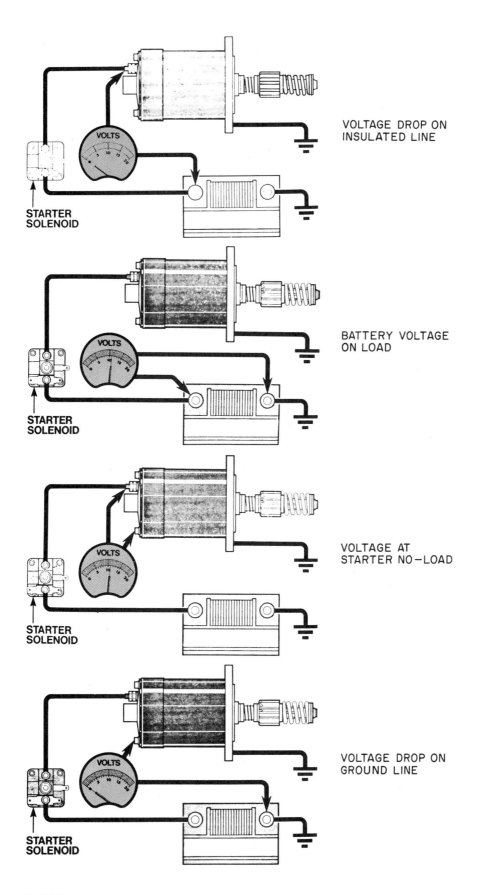

VOLTAGE DROP ON
INSULATED LINE

STARTER
SOLENOID

BATTERY VOLTAGE
ON LOAD

STARTER
SOLENOID

VOLTAGE AT
STARTER NO-LOAD

STARTER
SOLENOID

VOLTAGE DROP ON
GROUND LINE

STARTER
SOLENOID

FIGURE 22–24. Several voltage checks can be made to test the voltage drop on the starter circuits. *(Courtesy of Lucas Industries, Inc.)*

VOLTAGE DROP CHECKS

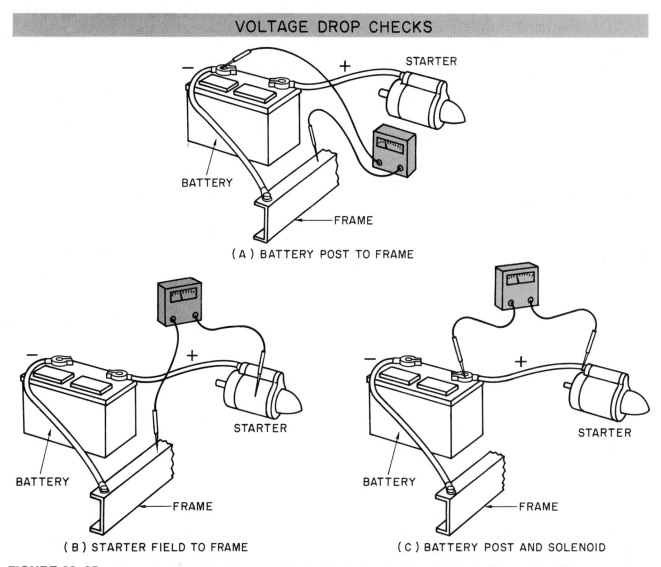

FIGURE 22–25.   Several voltage drops can be checked to determine the condition of the engine. Voltage can be checked (A) between the frame and the negative battery terminal, (B) between the frame and the starter field frame, and (C) between the positive side of the battery and the solenoid terminal.

or between the ungrounded battery terminal post and the battery terminal on the solenoid (C). If any of these readings shows more than 1/10 (0.1) volt drop when the starting motor is cranking, the electrical connections will need to be cleaned. A light coating of grease on the battery cables and terminal clamps will retard further corrosion. If the starter still does not crank the engine, the starter will need to be rebuilt.

3. The free speed test can also be performed on the starter. Using the circuit shown in *Figure 22–26*, a tachometer can be used to measure the speed of the starter per minute. Failure of the motor to perform to specifications may be due to bad bearings or high-resistance connections. During this test, check the amperage, volts, and RPM and compare the results with the manufacturer's specifications.

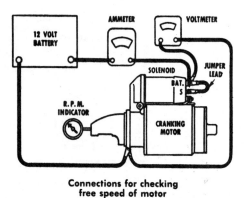

**Connections for checking
free speed of motor**

FIGURE 22–26.   The free speed test can be performed on a starter when it is out of the vehicle. Voltage amperage and RPM are compared with specifications given by the manufacturer. *(Courtesy of Motor Publications, Auto Repair Manual)*

SERVICE

Use the following general procedure and checks when rebuilding a starter motor.

1. Disconnect the battery.

2. Using the correct tools, remove the starter from the engine. Often this procedure is listed in the service manuals.

3. If the solenoid is attached to the starter make sure all wires have been disconnected and marked for reassembly.

4. Disassemble the starter by removing the through bolts.

5. Remove both ends of the starter to expose the internal parts.

6. If the starter appears inoperative, the field coils can be checked for shorts, opens, or grounds. Use an appropriate ohmmeter to measure the resistance of the field coils. Compare the results with manufacturer's specifications.

7. Check the armature end play and compare the readings with the manufacturer's specifications. Shims may be needed to correct excessive end play. Depending on the manufacturer, the clearance should be between 0.010 and 0.140 inches. See *Figure 22–27*. Also, make sure that during assembly of the starter, the small friction disc on the end of the pinion gear is replaced in the same position.

8. Check the starter brushes for excessive wear. Check the manufacturer's specifications for the amount of wear allowed on the brushes. Use a vernier caliper as shown in *Figure 22–28* to check the brush length. Replace the brushes if necessary.

9. Check the brushes to be sure the brush springs are providing the correct tension. Depending on the manufacturer, the tension may be from 30 to 100 or more ounces (2–6 lb). Check the manufacturer's specifications

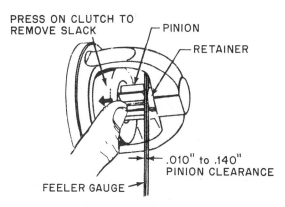

FIGURE 22–27. The starter can be checked for end play between the pinion gear and the retainer. *(Courtesy of Motor Publications)*

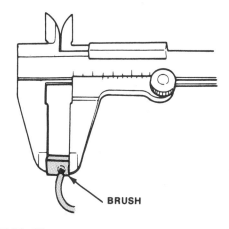

FIGURE 22–28. Use a vernier caliper to check the starter brushes for excessive wear. *(Courtesy of Honda Motor Company, Ltd.)*

for the exact amount required for each starter. If the tension is not within the specifications, replace the springs. *Figure 22–29* shows an example of how to check spring tension.

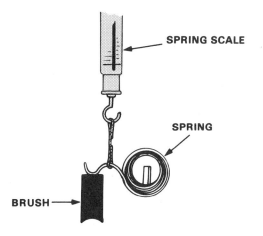

FIGURE 22–29. Use a small spring scale to check the spring tension for the starter motor brushes. *(Courtesy of Honda Motor Company, Ltd.)*

10. With the starter disassembled, check the roller clutch drive for smoothness, instantaneous lock-up and free movement along the shaft. Check for broken or distorted springs on the starter linkage mechanism. Also check the condition of the pinion gear and the ring gear on the flexplate as shown in *Figure 22–30*. If any of these conditions exist, replace the roller clutch or spring mechanism, or both.

11. Bushings in the end plates wear and need to be replaced in the starter. If the bushings wear excessively, the starter armature may rub on the pole shoes, causing damage to the starter. If the bushings are bad, the starter will require very high current draw during cranking. A growling or scraping sound may also be heard during cranking. Replace the bushings if wear is suspected.

12. The starter armature can be checked for short circuits by using a growler, *Figure 22–31*. A growler is a tool that creates a magnetic field around the armature. A hacksaw blade is placed on top of the armature. When it vibrates, it indicates a short in the armature.

13. Check the armature commutator segments for evidence of burning. This can be identified by observing the commutator and looking for burned copper on the commutator. If there is evidence of burning, the commutator can be cut down on a lathe or sanded lightly with number 500 or 600 sandpaper. The normal procedure is to cut down or turn the commutator with light cuts until the worn or bad spots are removed. See *Figure 22–32*. After cutting the armature, remove the burrs with sandpaper.

14. There may be other checks that can be done on the starter circuits and components. These depend on the car manufacturer and the style of the starter. After you have made all the checks on the starter, make sure to clean all parts before reassembly.

15. Lubricate all bushings in the starter with high-temperature grease before assembly.

FIGURE 22–30.   When rebuilding the starter, always check the condition of the pinion gear and the ring gear on the flexplate. *(Courtesy of Motor Publications, Auto Repair Manual)*

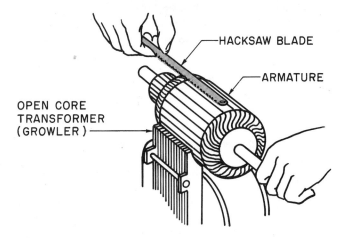

FIGURE 22–31.   A growler is used to check for shorts in the armature.

16. Reassemble the starter as recommended by the manufacturer.

17. Start and run the engine.

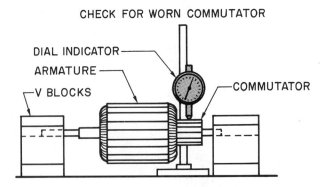

FIGURE 22–32.   If the commutator is burned or worn, it can be turned on a lathe and cleaned up.

Linkage to
Science and Mathematics

Cranking motors have cemf (counter electromotive force). As the motor operates, the armature windings are forced to rotate around a magnetic field. At this time, all conditions necessary to *induce* a voltage in the armature are present: a conductor, a magnetic field, and motion between the two. Thus, as the motor turns it also produces a voltage and current (cemf) in the armature windings that are opposite in direction to the battery current. Thus, as cemf increases, it opposes the current necessary to produce torque in the cranking motor. So the higher the cemf the less torque produced inside the starter motor.

Motor speed and torque also relate to cemf. As the speed of the armature increases, cemf also increases. As the speed of the cranking motor increases, the current and torque of the cranking motor decrease. Thus maximum torque on a cranking motor is produced at zero RPM.

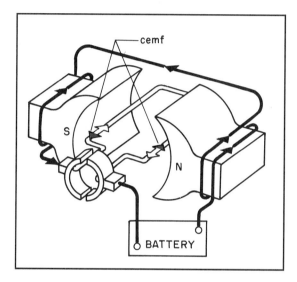

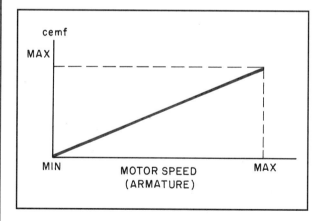

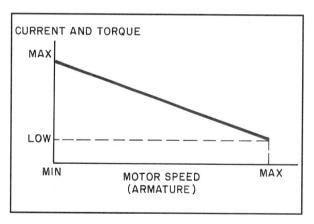

SERVICE MANUAL CONNECTION

There are many important specifications to keep in mind when working with starting systems. To identify the specifications for your engine, you will need to know the VIN (vehicle identification number) of the vehicle, the type and year of the vehicle, and the type of engine. Although they may be titled differently, some of the more common starting system specifications (not all) found in service manuals are listed below. Note that these specifications are typical examples. Each vehicle and engine may have different specifications.

Common Specification	Typical Example
Cranking current	350 amps
Cranking voltage	8.5 volts
Free speed test	77 amps
Starter brush length	
New	0.59–0.61 inch
Service limit	0.39 inch
Starter brush spring tension	40–80 ounces
Starter commutator runout	
New	0–0.001 inch
Service limit	0.002 inch

In addition, the service manual will give specific directions for various service and testing procedures. Some of the more common procedures include:

- Overrunning clutch inspection
- Solenoid replacement
- Starter brush replacement
- Starter overhaul
- Starter replacement
- Testing starter current

SUMMARY

The purpose of the starting system is to convert electrical energy in the battery to mechanical energy to crank the engine. This is done by using a starter motor, ignition switch, solenoid, and starter drive mechanism.

In order to understand the starting system, several principles are important. Whenever a wire carries electrical current, a magnetic field is built up around the conductor. If this conductor is placed within a strong magnetic field made from a north and south pole, the wire will move. If the wire is placed in the shape of a loop on an axis, the loop will revolve. A commutator is used to provide the correct path for electricity into the loop of wire. The north and south poles are made by using electromagnets.

A starter typically has four windings that make up the field coils. These coils are wound on pole shoes and attached to the starter housing. The rotating part of the starter is called the armature. It is made of many turns of wire. The connections between the armature and the poles can either be series wound or series-parallel wound. The type of circuit will depend on the starter speed, load, size of the engine, cable size, and so on. The armature core is made of iron laminations to reduce eddy currents. Brushes are used to rub on the commutator for continuous connections to the armature.

The starter uses several types of drive mechanisms. Their purpose is to engage the pinion gear to the flywheel gear for cranking the engine. The inertia drive system uses a pinion gear on a screw sleeve to engage the two gears. When the starter begins to turn, the pinion gear slides outward and meshes with the ring gear.

The overrunning clutch drive uses a set of rollers that become wedged in the drive housing when the starter begins to turn. When the engine fires and turns faster than the starter, the pinion gear unlocks from the wedges and spins freely. This protects the starter from being turned at high RPM by the engine, if the operator continues to crank the engine. If the engine does turn the starter, it will be damaged.

The solenoid is used for several purposes. The solenoid makes the electrical contact for the high current used to crank the starter. The solenoid also moves the pinion gear in mesh with the ring gear. There are typically two windings in the solenoid. One is called the pull-in or closing winding. The other is called the hold-in winding. When the solenoid closes the electrical contacts for the starter, the pull-in winding pulls the solenoid plunger in. Then it is shorted out when contact is made. Only the hold-in winding is used during cranking.

When the operator cranks the engine by using the ignition switch, the solenoid is energized. This action closes the moving contacts in the solenoid and makes the electrical connection to the starter. As the starter cranks, the pinion gear is in mesh with the ring gear, thus cranking the engine. When the ignition switch is released, the starter motor stops turning and drive linkage is released, removing the pinion gear from the ring gear.

Several checks can be used to determine the condition of the starter circuit. A voltmeter is used to check voltage drops. The free speed test tells the current, voltage, and RPM when the starter is removed from the vehicle. Other checks include observing the spring tension, brush wear, bushing wear, and solenoid operation.

TERMS TO KNOW

Can you explain each of the following terms? Review the chapter until you can use each term correctly.

Commutator	Laminations
Pole shoes	Eddy currents
Armature	Pinion gear
Shunt	Inertia

(continued)

Inertia drive   Solenoid
Overrunning clutch drive   Chamfer
Sprag   Crank signal
Reduction gear

 REVIEW QUESTIONS

Multiple Choice

1. The starter system converts:
   a. Mechanical energy to chemical energy
   b. Thermal energy to electrical energy
   c. Mechanical energy to electrical energy
   d. Electrical energy to mechanical energy
   e. Thermal energy to mechanical energy

2. Any wire that has electrical current passing through it:
   a. Moves toward a north pole
   b. Moves toward a south pole
   c. Has a magnetic field around it
   d. Has no magnetic field around it
   e. Reduces its internal resistance

3. What causes the movement to occur on the armature of a motor?
   a. Two magnetic fields opposing and aiding each other
   b. Thermal energy forces
   c. A north pole pushing against a south pole
   d. Gravity
   e. Eddy currents

4. The _____ keep(s) the current flowing in the correct direction in the armature.
   a. Eddy currents
   b. Stator
   c. Commutator
   d. Brushes
   e. Solenoids

5. The north and south poles in a starter are:
   a. Made of permanent magnets
   b. Made from electromagnets
   c. Repelling each other
   d. Turned off during starting
   e. Operated in pulses

6. The _____ holds the field windings.
   a. Solenoid
   b. Brushes
   c. Hold-on coil
   d. Pole shoes
   e. Sprags

7. Eddy currents can be reduced in the armature by using a core made of:
   a. Plastic   d. Carbon
   b. Silicon   e. Laminations
   c. Copper

8. Which type of starter drive mechanism uses the principle that an object tends to remain at rest or stay in motion?
   a. Overrunning clutch
   b. Roller clutch
   c. Inertia drive
   d. Sprag drive
   e. All of the above

9. Which type of starter drive mechanism uses a series of sprags?
   a. Overrunning clutch
   b. Inertia drive
   c. Bendix drive
   d. Roller clutch
   e. None of the above

10. On the overrunning clutch, when the engine starts and turns faster than the starter:
    a. The rollers are not being wedged in
    b. The pinion gear moves out of mesh with the ring gear
    c. The starter will not be forced to turn faster
    d. All of the above
    e. None of the above

11. A solenoid is used to convert:
    a. Mechanical energy to thermal energy
    b. Electrical energy to chemical energy
    c. Electrical energy to mechanical energy
    d. All of the above
    e. None of the above

12. When the plunger is energized and the contact disc makes electrical contact inside the solenoid:
    a. The hold-in winding releases
    b. The starter motor begins to turn
    c. The pinion gear is disengaged
    d. The ring gear stops turning
    e. Brushes release contact on the armature

13. Which coil in the solenoid is shorted out when the starter motor begins to turn?
    a. The field coils
    b. The hold-in coil
    c. The pull-in coil
    d. All of the above
    e. None of the above

14. Which of the following is *not* considered a service check on the starter system?
    a. Checking the voltage drop of the starter
    b. Checking for opens on the field poles
    c. Checking the amount of wear on the brushes
    d. Checking the operation of the diodes in the circuit
    e. Checking the condition of the commutator

15. Which of the following is *not* considered a service check on the starter system? Checking the
    a. Bushings for wear
    b. Circuit for grounds and opens
    c. Drive mechanism for voltage drop
    d. Commutator for signs of wear
    e. Drive mechanism for damaged springs

The following questions are similar in format to ASE (Automotive Service Excellence) test questions.

---

16. Technician A says that if the commutator is slightly burned, it must be replaced. Technician B says that if the commutator is slightly burned, it may be machined on a lathe to remove the burn spots. Who is right?
    a. A only
    b. B only
    c. Both A and B
    d. Neither A nor B

17. When tested on a growler, the hacksaw blade vibrates at a specific spot. Technician A says that the armature has a short in it. Technician B says that the field poles have a short in them. Who is right?
    a. A only
    b. B only
    c. Both A and B
    d. Neither A nor B

18. The spring tension on the brushes on the starter is weak and below specifications. Technician A says that the springs should be bent to obtain more tension. Technician B says that the weaker spring tension will not cause any damage and that they need not be replaced. Who is right?
    a. A only
    b. B only
    c. Both A and B
    d. Neither A nor B

19. The armature of the starter has been rubbing on the field coils. Technician A says the problem is the spring tension of the brushes. Technician B says the problem is misalignment of the solenoid. Who is right?
    a. A only
    b. B only
    c. Both A and B
    d. Neither A nor B

20. A set of starter brushes has worn down to the service limit. Technician A says to replace the starter brushes with new ones. Technician B says the starter brush springs should be checked for tension. Who is right?
    a. A only
    b. B only
    c. Both A and B
    d. Neither A nor B

21. In a cranking test on the starter, the voltage read is about 9 volts. Technician A says to replace the starter. Technician B says the amperage should be about 15 amps. Who is right?
    a. A only
    b. B only
    c. Both A and B
    d. Neither A nor B

22. Various electrical checks can be made on a starter. Technician A says that one test is a voltage drop on the ground line. Technician B says that one test is battery voltage on the load. Who is right?
    a. A only
    b. B only
    c. Both A and B
    d. Neither A nor B

23. Technician A says that armature end play always needs to be checked during starter overhaul. Technician B says that resistance of the field coils should be checked. Who is right?
    a. A only
    b. B only
    c. Both A and B
    d. Neither A nor B

Essay

24. Describe how magnetism is produced in a coil of wire.

25. What is the definition of commutation?

26. What is the purpose of pole shoes on a starter?

27. What is the purpose of using laminations of steel on the armature?

28. Describe the operation of the inertia drive clutch.

29. What is the purpose of the solenoid?

30. What is the purpose of the hold-in and pull-in coil on the solenoid?

Short Answer

31. A _____ is cut on the end of the pinion gear to allow the teeth to mesh more easily.

32. On certain vehicles a _____ system is used between the starter and the pinion gear to increase torque.

33. On computerized engines, the crank signal causes the air-fuel ratio to become _____ during cranking.

34. Voltage drop in the starter can be checked using a _____.

35. To measure the speed of the starter in RPM, a _____ test can be performed.

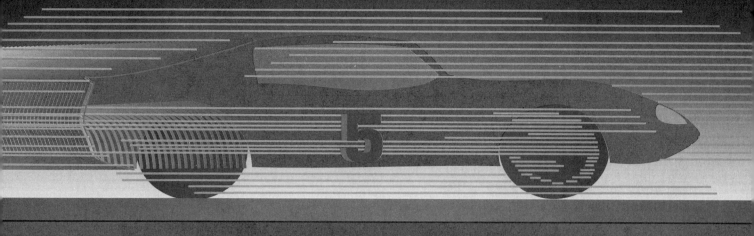

EMISSION
CONTROL SYSTEMS

CHAPTER 23

Characteristics of Air Pollution

INTRODUCTION   Before the late 1960s very little emphasis was placed on pollution in our society. All industries, including the automotive manufacturers, were producing goods without concern for how the waste products affected the environment. Any product that is manufactured produces waste. By the mid-1960s, there was serious concern about how these pollutants could be reduced. In the early 1960s, government emission standards were set. Because of these standards, automobile emission controls were developed to reduce pollution. This chapter is about the problem of air pollution, the types of pollutants being produced, and how our society is improving the air quality in the environment.

OBJECTIVES   After reading this chapter, you should be able to:

- State why there is a problem with pollution in our society.

- Compare the definitions and effects of the major types of air pollution produced by the automobile.

- Identify how pollution is being controlled through certification of new cars, regulation agencies, emissions requirements, exhaust gas analyzers, and fuel economy standards.

23.1   POLLUTION IN OUR SOCIETY

Defining the Air Pollution Problem

Pollution is defined as the contamination of the environment by harmful products. If these *contaminants* are in large enough numbers, they can harm plants, animals, and humans. There are many sources of pollution. Industries, power plants, home heating, gasoline and diesel vehicles, and refuse disposal plants all produce pollution. There are many forms of pollution such as chemical, thermal, radiation, air, water, and noise. Pollution is also produced by natural causes such as volcanos and brush fires.

One of the greatest sources of pollution in our society in the past has been the automobile, with both gasoline and diesel engines. Today, however, automobile pollution has been reduced drastically. This chapter is primarily concerned with air pollution produced by the automobile.

Air pollution is a by-product of any combustion process. Air pollution is produced when coal, oil, or natural gas is burned. Since the automobile uses both diesel fuel and gasoline, it is a source of air pollution.

Smog

Smog is the result of having too much pollution suspended in the air. Smog is defined as a fog made heavier and darker by the addition of smoke and chemicals to the air. Both the smoke and chemicals are floating in the air.

Photochemical Smog

There are known types of smog. One type is called *photochemical smog*. The word photochemical means the mixing of sunlight with the chemicals in the air. See *Figure 23–1*. This combination causes photochemical smog. Photochemical smog is more dangerous to plants, animals, and humans than plain smog. For example, when photochemical smog is breathed into the body, these chemicals and acids cause coughing and irritate the nose, throat, and lungs. This pollution has been linked to such health problems as asthma, skin damage, cancer of internal organs, emphysema, and heart and circulatory problems.

504

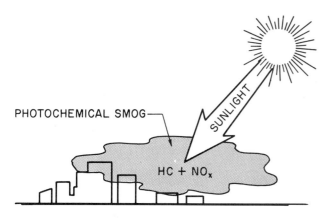

FIGURE 23–1. When sunlight mixes with HC and NO$_x$, photochemical smog is produced.

Temperature Inversion

Under normal weather patterns, the warm air near the ground tends to rise and cool. When this happens, the smog and pollution in the air *dissipate* and are reduced. During a temperature inversion, the warm air becomes trapped and cannot rise. A temperature inversion happens when a layer of warm air acts as a cap or lid to the air near the ground or surface of a city. In this case, the warm air prevents the smog and air pollutants from rising and dissipating into the atmosphere. The inversion layer is usually within 1,000 feet of the surface of the ground. Temperature inversions are common in cities that are located in large valleys. See *Figure 23–2*. Los Angeles and Denver are examples of places where temperature inversions occur.

Units Used to Measure Pollution

In order to control pollution on automobiles, measurements are taken to determine how much pollution actually exists. Several units have been used to measure pollution. One common unit is a measurement in grams of pollution per mile of operation. This unit is abbreviated as g/mi. For example, a vehicle driving down the road may produce 1.5 grams of a certain type of pollution per mile of operation.

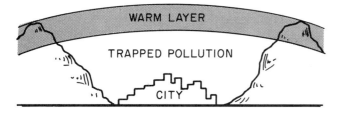

FIGURE 23–2. When a warm layer of air traps the air around a city, a temperature inversion results. The temperature inversion causes the pollutants to stay trapped in the air around the city.

Another unit used to measure the amount of pollution is parts per million. It is abbreviated as ppm. This unit represents the number of parts of pollution per million parts of air being put into the atmosphere. This unit is also referred to as micrograms per cubic meter (μg/m^3). Both of these units are used as guidelines to control the exact amount of pollution that a vehicle is allowed to emit into the air.

A third method of referring to the amount of pollution is to use percentages. For example, the exhaust of a gasoline engine has about 2–3% carbon monoxide. This means that about 2–3% of the exhaust volume is carbon monoxide.

Other units also appear in many readings. These may include grams per hour, grams per ton mile, and grams per horsepower. The reason there are so many units is that many manufacturers like to make comparisons between different engines and different applications. These units make it easier to make comparisons.

CAR CLINIC

PROBLEM: **Pollution and Computers**

A customer asks why computers are needed to manage engines. What relationship does the computer have with reducing pollution and vehicle emissions?

SOLUTION:

Computers are able to react and make decisions much faster and more precisely than components used on older engines. All manufacturers have now added computers for combustion and pollution control. By using computers to control combustion, the manufacturers can reduce exhaust emissions to such a low level that common exhaust gas analyzers cannot measure them. In addition, many of the mechanical pollution control components used several years ago are no longer needed and are being replaced by computer controls. The result is that computers help to reduce vehicle emissions, thus contributing to a cleaner environment.

23.2 TYPES OF POLLUTANTS

Carbon Monoxide

Carbon monoxide is considered a deadly poison gas that is colorless and odorless. When people inhale carbon monoxide in small quantities, it causes headaches and vision difficulties. In larger quantities, it causes sleepiness and, in many cases, death.

Carbon monoxide (CO) is a by-product of combustion. Carbon monoxide emissions are increased as the combustion process becomes less efficient. During perfect combustion, the by-products are water (H_2O) and carbon dioxide (CO_2). Carbon monoxide forms in the engine exhaust when there is insufficient oxygen to form the carbon dioxide. Thus, whenever the engine operates in a rich air-fuel mixture, increased CO is the result. The best way to reduce CO is to increase the amount of oxygen in the combustion chamber. Carbon monoxide is not one of the chemicals that produces photochemical smog.

In general, carbon monoxide concentration is much lower in diesel exhaust than in gasoline exhaust. *Figure 23–3* shows the carbon monoxide percentages in gasoline and diesel exhaust for different air-fuel ratios. Note that CO is considerably lower in diesel engines than in gasoline engines. This is because diesel engines are typically operated with a leaner air-fuel ratio than gasoline engines.

Hydrocarbons

Hydrocarbons (HC) are another type of pollution produced by the automobile combustion process. Hydrocarbons are also called *organic materials*. Fossil fuels are made of various hydrogen and carbon molecules. Unburned hydrocarbons emitted by the automobile are largely unburned portions of fuel. Any fuel that is partially burned contains hydrocarbons. For example, gasoline in the combustion chamber burns extremely rapidly. Some of the hydrogen and carbon molecules near the sides of the combustion chamber may get partially burned. This action produces HC in the exhaust. All petroleum products produce small traces of HC during the combustion process. For example, gasoline in the fuel tank and carburetors also gives off traces of HC.

Most hydrocarbons are poisonous at concentrations above several hundred parts per million. Although they are not as dangerous by themselves as CO, hydrocarbons are the main ingredient in the production of photochemical smog.

Nitrogen Oxides

Nitrogen oxides (NO_x) are formed by a chemical union of nitrogen molecules with one or more oxygen molecules.

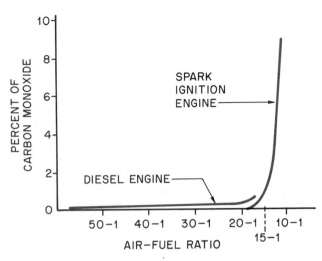

FIGURE 23–3. As the air-fuel ratio changes, the percentage of carbon monoxide also changes. *(Courtesy of General Motors Corporation)*

Nitrogen oxides form freely under extreme heat conditions. As the combustion process becomes leaner, combustion temperatures typically increase. Higher temperatures cause nitrogen oxides to be produced. When the combustion temperatures reach 2,200–2,500 degrees F, the nitrogen and oxygen in the air-fuel mixture combine to form large quantities of nitrogen oxide, *Figure 23–4*.

Nitrogen oxide by itself does not appear to have any important harmful effects on air pollution. However, nitrogen oxide reacts with hydrocarbons to form harmful irritating *oxides* and gives photochemical smog its characteristic light brown color. Nitrogen oxide is also considered a major greenhouse gas. (See the Linkage to Environment at the end of this chapter.)

Gasoline engines that are running very lean with higher temperatures produce nitrogen oxides. Diesel engines generally produce higher concentrations of nitrogen oxides because their internal temperatures are usually higher than gasoline engines. The best method of reducing the emission

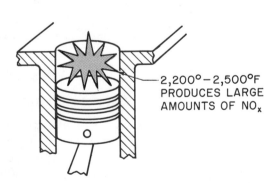

FIGURE 23–4. Whenever combustion temperatures increase into the 2,200–2,500 degree F range, large quantities of NO_x are produced.

of nitrogen oxides is to reduce the temperature of the combustion process. Doing this, however, will result in less efficient burning and increases in HC and CO emissions.

To illustrate this, **Figure 23–5** shows how the three emissions discussed are affected by the air-fuel ratio and conversion efficiency. For example, as the air-fuel ratio becomes leaner, nitrogen oxide conversion efficiency decreases, thus producing more of this particular pollution form. The CO and HC emissions increase (conversion efficiency decreases on the chart) as the air-fuel mixture becomes richer. By observing this chart, it can be seen that the best air-fuel ratio for any engine is in the "window" area, or close to 14.7:1. Manufacturers now use computer controls to obtain an accurate air-fuel ratio.

Sulfur Dioxide

Sulfur dioxide (SO_2) is another form of air pollution. Sulfur is present in many of the hydrocarbon fuels that are used in engines and power plants. Diesel fuel has slightly more sulfur than gasoline; therefore, sulfur emissions are greater with diesel engines than with gasoline engines. When sulfur gets into the atmosphere, it breaks down and combines with water in the air to produce sulfuric acid. This acid is very corrosive and produces the commonly known acid rain form of pollution. NO_x also contributes significantly to the acid rain problem.

Particulate Matter

Particulates are defined as a form of solid air pollution such as microscopic solid particles of dust, soot, and ash. They can be solid or liquid matter that floats in the atmosphere. Examples of particulate substances are lead and carbon produced by burning leaded gasoline. These particulates are absorbed directly into the body and can cause severe health hazards.

Engines that use unleaded fuel produce very little particulate matter. Engines that have the carburetor set very rich, however, may also produce carbon particulates that could be a health hazard.

Particulate matter is damaging because it reduces air visibility and allows less sunlight to reach the ground. Particulates carry damaging materials such as sulfuric acids to the surfaces they strike. There is also some evidence that particulate matter is having an effect on weather patterns.

Additional Diesel Pollutants

The diesel engine uses different fuels, has different compression ratios, and uses a different ignition system than the gasoline engine. Because of these characteristics, diesel engines present two other emission concerns. Diesel engines in general have an exhaust odor that can be considered a nuisance. These exhaust odors have recently been measured so that proper technological steps can be taken to reduce them. In addition, smoke is evident on many diesel engines. The blue-white smoke is caused by liquid droplets of lubricating or fuel oil. This indicates that maintenance is required. The black-gray smoke often seen on diesel vehicles is caused by unburned carbon particles. This is caused largely by inaccurate air-fuel ratios. Black smoke will increase as the load is increased. In some cases, smoke charts have been developed to measure the amount of smoke being emitted by diesel engines.

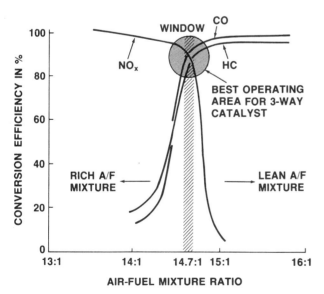

FIGURE 23–5. Whenever steps are taken to reduce HC and CO emissions, NO_x emissions increase. It is very important to keep the air-fuel ratio close to 14.7 to 1 for more effective emission control. *(Courtesy of General Motors Product Service Training)*

CAR CLINIC

PROBLEM: Sunlight and Photochemical Smog

In discussions about pollution and the environment, often the term *photochemical smog* is used. Exactly what is photochemical smog?

SOLUTION:

Photochemical smog is a by-product of combining three ingredients. When nitrogen oxides (NO_x) and hydrocarbons (HC) are mixed in the presence of sunlight, the result is photochemical smog. Thus, the sunlight helps to produce the photochemical smog. Nitrogen oxides and hydrocarbons are both by-products of gasoline and diesel engine combustion. Photochemical smog is dangerous because it irritates the eyes and corrodes metals and other materials. It is also dangerous to one's health.

23.3 CONTROLLING POLLUTION

New Car Certification

One method of reducing pollution from automobiles is to set certain emission standards for new vehicles. Standards are established by the *Environmental Protection Agency* (*EPA*). Families of cars are given emissions tests. They are tested for HC, CO, and NO_x emissions. Tests are performed under cold start, normal, and hot-start conditions. If the vehicle passes the emission standards set by the EPA, it can be offered for sale to the public.

Progress in Reducing Emissions

Much has been done recently to the automobile to reduce emissions. From 1970 to 1980 a number of *emission control* devices were placed on all vehicles. These devices drastically reduced the amount of CO, particulate matter, HC, and NO_x in the atmosphere. In fact, there was approximately a 37% drop in carbon monoxide, a 50% drop in particulate matter, and an 11% drop in HC emissions for this 10-year period.

Although these emissions were reduced, NO_x increased during this 10-year period. When pollution standards were started in 1968, the automotive manufacturers tried to reduce HC and CO. As these were reduced, however, the engine combustion process became leaner, increasing the production of NO_x. Only in the past 8–12 years have efforts been made to reduce NO_x in vehicles.

As more and more computer controls were put on engines, emissions were further reduced. Today's engines are very efficient, controlling all emissions (including nitrogen oxides well within the standards set by the federal government).

Another factor that helps to reduce exhaust emissions is a tune-up. During a recent EPA test, cars were tested for carbon monoxide and hydrocarbon emissions before and after a tune-up. *Figure 23–6* shows the results. After a tune-up, carbon monoxide emissions dropped an average of 66%.

Regulating Agencies

Several regulating agencies were established in the 1960s to help identify standards and regulations for automobiles. California became the first state to use air pollution standards. California also established the Air Resources Board (ARB), which helps to enforce the emission standards. California standards are typically much stricter than those of other states.

In 1968 the Clean Air Act was passed by the U.S. Congress. This act set allowable levels of HC, CO, and NO_x. The EPA is the agency responsible for enforcing the Clean Air Act. Many other states also passed their own laws. These laws must be approved by the EPA. These laws were based on different altitude operation, such as in mountainous regions. As a result, there were several emission standards. These included (1) California vehicles, (2) federal 49 state vehicles, (3) high-altitude vehicles.

The manufacturers must be able to meet the standards set by the EPA or other agency. It is up to the manufacturer, however, to determine the type of technology used to reduce emissions.

Emission Requirements

Emission requirements were established by the EPA for each year vehicle. *Figure 23–7* shows an example of the emission standards set by the EPA (Federal Mandated Standards) for various years. Newer vehicles (last 5 years) have stricter standards than earlier years to help reduce emissions even further. In addition to the federally mandated standards, many states also have their own emission standards. Often these emission standards are based on the year of the vehicle and the GVW (gross vehicle weight). Usually hydrocarbons and carbon monoxide emissions are listed. *Figure 23–8* shows the standards for one of approximately 33 states that have their own emission standards. Most of the service manuals used today have these standards available

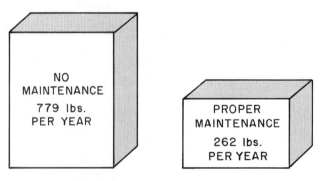

CARBON MONOXIDE REDUCTIONS
WITH MAINTENANCE

FIGURE 23–6. In an EPA test, cars checked at random were producing 779 pounds of carbon monoxide per year. Given a tune-up, their CO emissions dropped an average of 66%. (*Courtesy of Motor Magazine*)

FEDERAL MANDATED STANDARDS

USE THIS CHART ONLY IF THE STATE IN WHICH THE VEHICLE IS OPERATED HAS NOT SET ITS OWN EMISSIONS STANDARDS

Year	Hydrocarbon (HC)[1]	Carbon Monoxide (CO)[1]	Nitrogen Oxides (NOx)[1]
1970–71	4.1	34.0	—
1972	3.0	28.0	—
1973–74	3.0	28.0	3.1
1975–76	1.5	15.0	3.1
1977–79	1.5	15.0	2.0
1980	.41	7.0	2.0
1981–82	.41	3.4[2]	1.0[3]
1983–84	.41	3.4	1.0[4]
1985–91	.41	3.4	1.0

[1]—Grams per mile.
[2]—On select engine families, a waiver to 7.0 was allowed.
[3]—For diesel engines or innovative technology, a waiver to 1.5 was allowed. For smaller manufacturers', a waiver to 2.0 was allowed.
[4]—For diesel engines or innovative technology, a waiver to 1.5 was allowed.

FIGURE 23–7.   Emission standards have been established by the EPA and must be met by all manufacturers. *(Courtesy of Motor Publications, Motor Emission Control Manual)*

Connecticut

MAXIMUM ALLOWABLE MOTOR VEHICLE GASOLINE ENGINE HC & CO LIMITS

Vehicle Classification (GVW)[1]	Year	Hydrocarbon (HC) ppm[2] At Idle	Carbon Monoxide (CO) % At Idle
6000 Lbs. Or Less	1968–69	750	7.5
	1970	650	7.0
	1971	650	6.0
	1972	575	6.0
	1973–74	425	6.0
	1975–79	300	3.0
	1980	275	2.5
	1981–91	220	1.2
6001 To 8500 Lbs.	1968–69	850	7.0
	1970–73	700	5.5
	1974–78	500	4.0
	1979	300	3.0
	1980	275	2.5
	1981–91	220	1.2
8501 to 10,000 Lbs.	1968–69	850	7.0
	1970–73	700	5.5
	1974–78	500	4.0
	1979–91	300	3.0

[1]—GVW: Gross Vehicle Weight.
[2]—ppm: parts per million.

FIGURE 23–8.   In addition to the federal mandated emission standards, many states also have their own emission standards for HC and CO. *(Courtesy of Motor Publications, Motor Emission Control Manual)*

for the service technician. Emission control standards are often placed on the vehicle's hood, *Figure 23–9*. These are used to identify the type of vehicle and to help service technicians identify the amount of emissions allowed for each vehicle. These labels are often referred to as *vehicle emission control information (VECI).*

Infrared Exhaust Analyzer

It is very important to keep the engine emission levels within federal and state standards. These emission levels can be tested by using an *infrared exhaust analyzer.* There are two types of infrared exhaust gas analyzers. There is the two-gas analyzer and the *four-gas analyzer.* The two-gas analyzer is able to read the amount of hydrocarbon and carbon monoxide emissions. The four-gas analyzer gives much more information. This analyzer is able to read the levels of four chemicals:

1. HC (hydrocarbons)

2. CO (carbon monoxide)

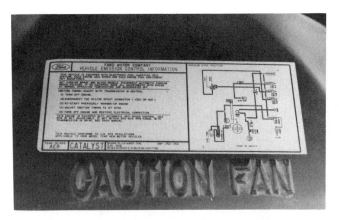

FIGURE 23–9. Certain pollution control information can be found under the hood of the vehicle.

3. CO_2 (carbon dioxide)

4. O (oxygen)

Although O is not considered a dangerous emission, it provides useful data about combustion efficiency. Also, CO_2 is considered a major greenhouse gas. (See the Linkage to Environment at the end of this chapter.) The four-gas analyzer is used on all newer vehicles. It provides accurate information for the service technician to evaluate the condition and adjustments needed on the engine. The following list gives examples of the type of problems and conditions that can be diagnosed using an exhaust gas analyzer:

1. Ignition system condition and problems

2. Vacuum hose condition and leaks

3. Air filter condition

4. Catalytic converter condition

5. Computer control system problems

6. Fuel injection or carburetor condition

7. Valve and piston conditions

8. Condition of pollution devices (e.g., PCV, EGR)

The exhaust gas analyzer operates as shown in *Figure 23–10*. A sample of gas is taken from the exhaust pipe while the engine is running at curb idle. As the exhaust gases pass into the tube, they eventually go through an infrared beam of light. At this point, a signal is generated and sent to the internal circuitry in the analyzer. The signal represents the percentage of carbon monoxide, hydrocarbons, etc. , in the exhaust. The analyzer electronically processes this signal to be read out on meters or on a cathode ray tube (CRT).

Various companies manufacture infrared exhaust analyzers. Always refer to the specific manufacturer's recommended procedure.

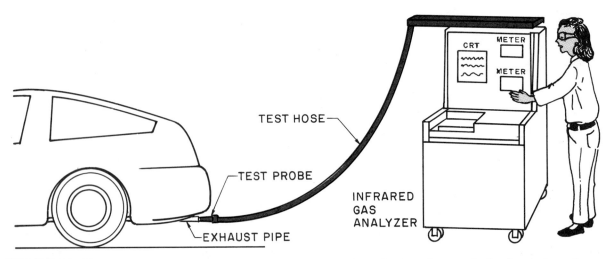

FIGURE 23–10. An infrared exhaust gas analyzer can be used to check various emission levels from the exhaust gases.

Fuel Economy Standards

As the emission requirements became stricter, the fuel economy of vehicles was reduced. In 1973 the United States faced an "energy crisis." There were severe supply and demand problems, especially in obtaining petroleum for gasoline. The supply of gasoline was much less than the demand. This resulted in federally mandated economy standards.

Congress enacted the Energy Policy Conservation Act. This act set standards for the manufacturers to follow. These standards are referred to as *CAFE (Corporate Average Fuel Economy)*. *Figure 23–11* shows the corporate average fuel economy for cars through several years. While certain vehicle lines may obtain less than the standard, others in the fleet will obtain higher than the standard.

In order for the manufacturers to meet both the fuel economy and emission level standards, it is necessary to control HC, CO, and NO_x emissions. This must be done while maintaining or increasing fuel economy standards and performance. This is accomplished with the use of electronic fuel-air control, the catalytic converter, and the addition of port fuel injection on engines.

SUMMARY

Pollution is a harmful contamination of the environment. It is produced by many sources, with combustion of hydro-carbon fuels being a major source. Air pollution is of greatest concern when discussing the automobile.

Pollution produces photochemical smog. Photochemical smog results when NO_x, HC, and sunlight are combined, producing irritation to the nose, throat, and lungs. One reason for increases in the smog is temperature inversions. A temperature inversion occurs when a warm layer of air traps pollutants near the ground. Several units can be used to measure the amount of pollution. These include grams of pollution per mile, parts per million, and percentages.

Several major types of pollution are produced by automobiles. Carbon monoxide is a colorless, odorless gas that is produced by a lack of oxygen. It is deadly in large quantities. Hydrocarbons are also produced when incomplete combustion occurs. Nitrogen oxides are produced when there are high temperatures within the combustion process. Usually temperatures of 2,200–2,500 degrees F produce large quantities of NO_x. Sulfur dioxides are produced because the crude oil carries sulfur before refining. Sulfur and nitrogen oxides also contribute to the acid rain problem. Particulates are solid forms of air pollution, either water or air that floats in the atmosphere. Diesel engines also produce odors and smoke that are considered forms of pollution.

Many methods have been used to reduce pollution from the automobile. New cars must now be certified by the EPA

(continued)

FUEL ECONOMY STANDARDS

MODEL YEAR	MPG	TOTAL IMPROVEMENT OVER THE 1974 MODEL YEAR
1978	18.0	50%
1979	19.0	58%
1980	20.0	67%
1981	22.0	83%
1982	24.0	100%
1983	26.0	116%
1984	27.0	125%
1985	27.5	129%
1986	26.0*	116%
1987	26.0	116%
1988	26.0	116%
1989	26.5	120%
1990	27.5	129%

*Reduced from 27.5% by the federal government in 1986

FIGURE 23–11.   Automotive manufacturers must meet CAFE (corporate average fuel economy) standards.

Linkage to Environment

THE GREENHOUSE EFFECT

One major environmental issue facing our society today is called the greenhouse effect. The greenhouse effect is defined as a process in which the temperature of the earth's atmosphere continually increases. It is also called global warming. Research has shown that global warming can cause major weather patterns to change, growing seasons to be altered, and basic changes in the way in which we live. Global warming is caused by increasing cer-tain gases in the atmosphere. These gases are shown in the table below. Burning of any fossil fuel (gasoline, die-sel fuels, natural gas, and so on) produces various greenhouse gases. Unfortunately, automobiles are a significant contributing factor. Because the automobile uses refrigerants and burns oil (gasoline) it has become a major contributor to global warming. Automobiles produce greenhouse gases such as carbon dioxide, methane, and nitrous oxide. In addition, the refrigerants used in air conditioning systems produce chlorofluorocarbons, known as CFCs. *(Courtesy of Worldwatch Institute)*

Gas	Atmospheric concentration (ppm)	Annual increase (percent)	Life span (years)	Relative efficiency (CO_2=1)	Current greenhouse (percent)	Principal sources of gas
Carbon dioxide	351.3	0.4	x^1	1	57	
Fossil fuels					44	Coal, oil, natural gas
Biological					13	Deforestation
Chlorofluoro-carbons	0.000225	5	75–111	15,000	25	Foams, aerosols, refrigerants, solvents
Methane	1.675	1	11	25	12	Wetlands, rice, fossil fuels, livestock
Nitrous oxide	0.31	0.2	150	230	6	Fossil fuels, fertilizers, deforestation

[1] Carbon dioxide is a stable molecule with a 2–4 year average residence time in the atmosphere.

for control of HC, CO, and NO_x. Considerable progress has been made in reducing these pollutants by using many pollution devices on the automobile engine. Many regulating agencies and acts have been established by Congress to help enforce the regulations in different states. Emission requirements were established by the EPA. Each manufacturer must design and manufacture vehicles that pass these standards. In addition, fuel economy standards were implemented to improve the fuel mileage of vehicles. The CAFE (Corporate Average Fuel Economy) standards must be met by each manufacturer.

TERMS TO KNOW

Can you explain each of the following terms? Review the chapter until you can use each term correctly.

Pollution
Contaminants
Smog
Photochemical smog
Dissipate
Carbon monoxide
Hydrocarbon
Organic material
Nitrogen oxide
Oxide
Particulates
Environmental Protection Agency (EPA)
Emission control
Infrared exhaust analyzer
Four-gas analyzer
Vehicle emission control information (VECI)
Corporate Average Fuel Economy (CAFE)

REVIEW QUESTIONS

Multiple Choice

1. Photochemical smog is created when _____ mixes with NO_x and HC emissions.
   a. CO
   b. Particulates
   c. Sunlight
   d. Smog
   e. None of the above

2. Which of the following are considered acceptable units for measuring emissions from the automobile?
   a. Parts per million
   b. Grams per mile
   c. Percentages
   d. All of the above
   e. None of the above

3. Which of the following emissions from the automobile is a deadly, odorless, tasteless gas that can cause death?
   a. CO
   b. NO_x
   c. HC
   d. SO_x
   e. None of the above

4. Which of the following emissions from the automobile is a contributor to acid rain?
   a. CO
   b. NO_x
   c. HC
   d. All of the above
   e. None of the above

5. Which of the following emissions from the automobile increases with combustion temperatures above 2,200 degrees F?
   a. CO
   b. NO_x
   c. HC
   d. SO_x
   e. Particulates

6. As combustion efficiency increases to reduce HC and CO emissions, what happens to NO_x?
   a. NO_x increases
   b. NO_x decreases
   c. There is no effect on NO_x
   d. NO_x is completely eliminated
   e. None of the above

7. Another term for HC is _____.
   a. CO
   b. Organic materials
   c. NO_x
   d. Particulates
   e. SO_x

8. Lead in gasoline is considered what type of pollution?
   a. NO_x
   b. CO
   c. HC
   d. Particulate
   e. Photochemical smog

9. What is the CAFE for the newest vehicles being manufactured?
   a. 22.5 mpg
   b. 27.5 mpg
   c. 31.5 mpg
   d. 38.5 mpg
   e. CAFE has nothing to do with miles per gallon.

10. What agency will help enforce emission standards on automobiles?
    a. U.S. Congress
    b. U.S. CAFE
    c. EPA
    d. ARB
    e. None of the above

The following questions are similar in format to ASE (Automotive Service Excellence) test questions.

---

11. Technician A says that as the engine air-fuel ratio becomes leaner, nitrogen oxides increase. Technician B says that as the engine air-fuel ratio becomes richer, hydrocarbons increase. Who is right?
    a. A only
    b. B only
    c. Both A and B
    d. Neither A nor B

12. Technician A says that photochemical smog is caused by sulfur mixing with sunlight. Technician B says that photochemical smog is caused by lead compounds mixing with sunlight. Who is right?
    a. A only
    b. B only
    c. Both A and B
    d. Neither A nor B

13. Technician A says that nitrogen oxide, carbon monoxide, and sulfur emissions are all checked before the manufacturer sells the vehicle. Technician B says that nitrogen oxide, carbon monoxide, and hydrocarbon emissions are all checked before the manufacturer sells the vehicle. Who is right?
    a. A only
    b. B only
    c. Both A and B
    d. Neither A nor B

14. Technician A says that amounts of air pollution can be measured in parts per million. Technician B says that amounts of air pollution can be measured in grams per mile. Who is right?
    a. A only
    b. B only
    c. Both A and B
    d. Neither A nor B

15. A four-gas exhaust analyzer is being used on an engine. Technician A says that carbon monoxide and hydrocarbons can be tested. Technician B says that carbon dioxide and oxygen can be tested. Who is right?
    a. A only
    b. B only
    c. Both A and B
    d. Neither A nor B

16. Technician A says that there are federal mandated standards for emission amounts. Technician B says that there are state standards for emission amounts. Who is right?
    a. A only
    b. B only
    c. Both A and B
    d. Neither A nor B

17. Technician A says that the exhaust emission levels can be tested with a voltmeter. Technician B says that exhaust emission levels can be tested with an infrared exhaust analyzer. Who is right?
    a. A only
    b. B only
    c. Both A and B
    d. Neither A nor B

18. Technician A says that to check exhaust emissions on older vehicles, the four-gas analyzer should be used. Technician B says that to check the exhaust emissions on newer vehicles, the two-gas analyzer should be used. Who is right?
    a. A only
    b. B only
    c. Both A and B
    d. Neither A nor B

Essay

19. Define carbon monoxide.

20. How is photochemical smog produced?

21. What three forms of air pollution are commonly checked on a car?

22. What does CAFE stand for?

Short Answer

23. The gas from an engine that is considered odorless, colorless, and deadly is called _____.

24. One of the most effective methods used by automotive manufacturers to reduce pollution on new vehicles is the _____.

25. Emission standards are often based on the _____ of the vehicle.

26. The two most common types of exhaust analyzers are the _____ gas and the _____ gas analyzer.

27. A/an _____ is used to check the exhaust emissions of a vehicle.

CHAPTER 24

Emission Control Systems

INTRODUCTION During the middle 1960s, our society was very concerned about the amount of pollution produced by both industries and automobiles. Because of this interest, it became mandatory that emission controls be installed on all automobiles. The automobile has been analyzed very carefully to determine the types of pollution that it produces. Usually the fuel tank, exhaust gases, crankcase area, and carburetor produce the majority of pollution in the automobile. Automobile emissions can be controlled with various devices. This chapter examines emission control systems in detail.

OBJECTIVES After reading this chapter, you should be able to:

- Explain how the PCV system works.

- Describe how evaporative emission controls operate.

- Identify the purpose of the carbon canister.

- Examine how the intake and exhaust emissions are controlled.

- Define several devices that are used to control combustion efficiency.

- Examine electronic and computer control of emissions.

- Identify common problems, diagnosis, and service procedures used on pollution control devices.

SAFETY CHECKLIST

When working with the emission control system, keep these important safety precautions in mind.

✔ Always wear OSHA-approved safety glasses when working on emission control systems.

✔ Always be careful not to burn your hands on hot emission control components.

✔ Always use the correct tools when working on emission control systems.

✔ When running the engine, make sure there is adequate ventilation for the exhaust fumes.

CERTIFICATION CONNECTION

Some of the information in this chapter can help you prepare for the National Institute for Automotive Service Excellence (ASE) certification tests. The test most directly related to this chapter is entitled

ENGINE PERFORMANCE (TEST A8).

The content area that closely parallels this chapter is

EMISSION CONTROL SYSTEMS DIAGNOSIS AND REPAIR.

24.1 POSITIVE CRANKCASE VENTILATION (PCV) SYSTEM

Purpose of Crankcase Ventilation

Figure 24–1 shows where most of the pollution comes from in an automobile. During normal engine operation, a considerable amount of dirty air passes through the engine crankcase. This air is a result of a process called *blow-by*. Blow-by is a product of the combustion process. See *Figure 24–2*.

Every time combustion occurs, a certain amount of blow-by (from combustion) escapes past the piston rings. This blow-by produces a small *crankcase pressure*. The gases from blow-by are very acidic. If they are allowed to stay in the crankcase area, the acids will attack the oil and metal within the engine. To help prevent this on older engines, air was drawn into the engine through the oil filler cap. The air flowed through the crankcase area, picking up the acidic gases. It was then directed out through a tube into the atmosphere. This tube was referred to as the draft or breather tube. Obviously, these gases are a great source of air pollution from the automobile.

Positive Crankcase Ventilation System Operation

Crankcase emissions are easily controlled by the *positive crankcase ventilation (PCV)* system. Refer to *Figure 24–3*. In this system, any crankcase vapors produced are directed back into the base of the carburetor to be reburned.

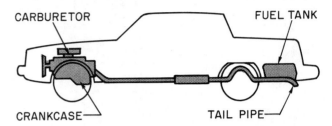

FIGURE 24–1. Sources of pollution on the automobile include the carburetor, crankcase, tail pipe, and fuel tank.

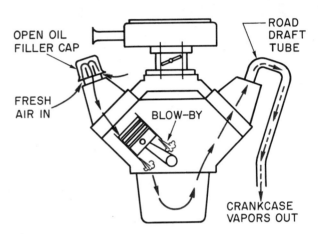

FIGURE 24–2. Crankcase ventilation was accomplished in older vehicles by passing the vapors in the crankcase out of the engine through a draft tube.

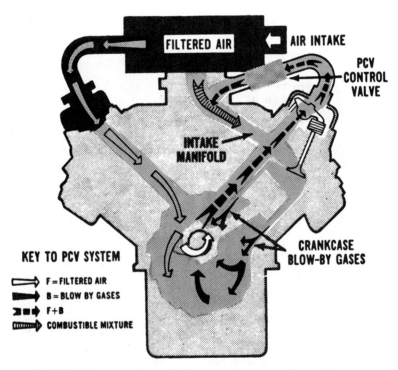

KEY TO PCV SYSTEM

F = FILTERED AIR
B = BLOW BY GASES
F + B
COMBUSTIBLE MIXTURE

FIGURE 24–3. A closed PCV system brings air through the air cleaner, through the closed oil filler cap, and into the crankcase. The vapors are then sent through a PCV valve and back into the base of the carburetor to be reburned. *(Courtesy of Motor Publications, Emission Control Manual)*

With this system, which is called a closed system, air is drawn through the carburetor air cleaner assembly, into the engine valve compartment and crankcase. These vapors are then drawn up through a vacuum-and-spring-controlled ventilating valve (PCV valve) and into the intake manifold. The vapors are then mixed with the air-fuel mixture and burned in the combustion process.

Not all PCV systems were designed like this. Earlier systems, which were called open systems, did not bring the fresh air through the carburetor air cleaner assembly. The air came through the open oil filler cap. Any air that entered the open system contained dirt and other materials. The open system was replaced by the closed system shown in Figure 24-3.

PCV Valve Operation

If crankcase vapors are allowed to flow into the carburetor during all loads and engine RPM, the crankcase gases will upset the basic carburetor air-fuel ratios. During idle and low speeds, less vapor must be burned. Therefore, a PCV valve is placed in the flow just before the carburetor. A PCV valve is shown in *Figure 24-4*. *Figure 24-5* shows the internal operation of the PCV valve. Two forces are working against each other. Vacuum from the intake manifold is working against spring pressure inside the valve. When the engine is stopped, no intake manifold vacuum exists. During this time, the PCV valve is held closed by the force of the internal spring. The tapered valve is moved fully to the right, closing off the entrance to the valve.

When the engine is at idle or is decelerating, vacuum in the intake manifold is very high. The tapered valve plunger is drawn to the left. This action closes off the metered opening. Little crankcase vapor is allowed to enter the carburetor.

When the engine operates at normal loads and speeds, the vacuum in the intake manifold drops. This drop allows the spring to push the plunger to the right. This action causes the metered opening to increase in size. The amount of crankcase vapor sent back to the intake manifold is now increased.

During acceleration or heavy loading, the intake manifold vacuum is very low. The spring moves the tapered valve fully to the right. Now the maximum amount of crankcase vapor can enter the carburetor. Therefore, when the engine is at low speeds, little crankcase vapor is sent to the carburetor. As the engine speed and load increase, more and more of these vapors are allowed to enter the carburetor.

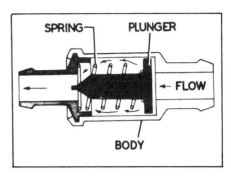

FIGURE 24-5. A typical PCV valve. Spring pressure pushes the valve to the right, while intake manifold vacuum pulls the plunger to the left. *(Courtesy of Motor Publications, Emission Control Manual)*

PROBLEM: Oily Air Cleaner

A customer says that the air cleaner is getting oil in it. The filter must be replaced about every 1,500 miles. What could be the problem?

SOLUTION:

The oil gets into the air cleaner through the PCV system. Crankcase vapors are normally sent through the PCV valve to the carburetor to be burned. However, if the PCV valve is plugged or blocked, the engine cannot breathe correctly. Crankcase vapors now come through the closed oil filter cap tube into the air cleaner. This causes the filter to be soaked with oil. Check the PCV valve by shaking it. It should rattle if it is not plugged. Replace if necessary.

24.2 EVAPORATIVE EMISSION CONTROLS

Any gasoline released from the fuel tank or carburetor in a liquid or vapor form is also pollution. These liquids and vapors are made of hydrocarbons. A variety of devices are being used to help reduce these emissions. These systems are called evaporative emission controls. *Figure 24-6* shows the typical parts to the evaporative emission controls.

Carbon Canister

The *carbon canister* is used to store any vapors from the fuel tank or carburetor. Refer to *Figure 24-7*. The carbon canister is made of a bed of activated charcoal (carbon). Warm weather can cause the fuel to expand in the fuel tank. This

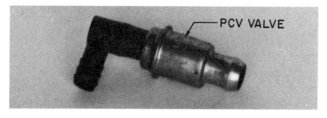

FIGURE 24-4. A PCV valve is located in the positive crankcase ventilation system to control the flow of vapors back to the carburetor.

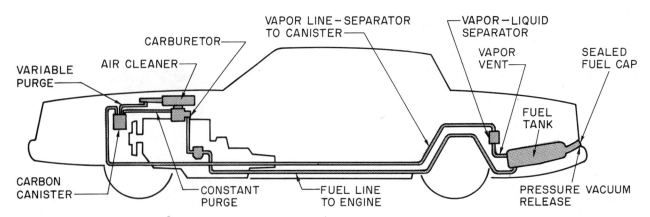

FIGURE 24–6. Typical evaporative emission control systems. Vapors and liquids from the fuel tank and carburetor are being controlled.

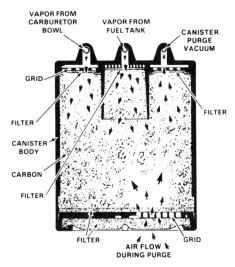

FIGURE 24–7. A schematic of a charcoal (carbon) canister used to store fuel vapors. *(Courtesy of Motor Publications, Emission Control Manual)*

expansion causes the vapors to be forced out of the tank and into the carbon canister. The carbon absorbs or stores gasoline vapors from the fuel tank and carburetor when the engine is not running.

When the engine is running, the clean vapors in the carbon canister are sent back to the carburetor to be burned. As shown in *Figure 24–8*, when the engine is operating, vacuum inside of the *purge* line draws air through the air cleaner. Air then passes through the filter at the bottom of the canister and into the activated charcoal. This action evaporates the gasoline vapors trapped within the charcoal. The remaining fumes are carried to the intake manifold and burned during combustion.

Computer-controlled Carbon Canister

More and more emission control systems are being controlled by computers. The process of purging the carbon

canister can also be controlled by the computer. *Figure 24–9* illustrates one such system. The fuel vapors from the fuel tank are first sent to the carbon canister for storage. When pressure in the fuel tank is higher than the set value, the two-way valve will open and allow the vapors to enter the canister. Canister purging is done by drawing fresh air from the bottom of the canister, through the canister, through the purge control diaphragm valve, then into a port near the throttle (butterfly valve). From this point the vapors are sent into the combustion chamber for burning.

The amount of flow is controlled by the purge control diaphragm valve and the purge cut-off solenoid valve. Depending on various input signals to the electronic control unit (ECU), the computer controls a signal sent to the purge cut-off solenoid valve. This signal in turn controls the vacuum sent to the purge control diaphragm valve. The position of this valve (controlled by the vacuum) then controls the amount of vapors being sent back to the throttle body.

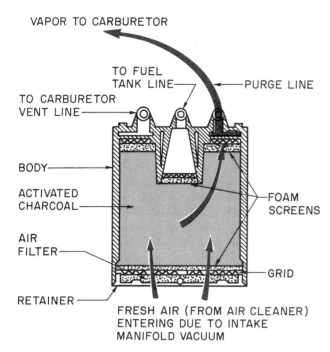

FIGURE 24–8. Arrows show the flow of air and vapors during canister purging or when the engine is running. *(Courtesy of Motor Publications, Emission Control Manual)*

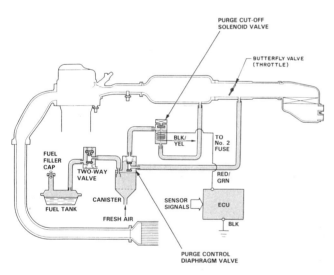

FIGURE 24–9. This system uses a computer to control the purging of the fuel vapors from the carbon canister to the intake of the engine. *(Courtesy of Honda Motor Company, Ltd.)*

Vapor-Liquid Separator

It is important that only vapors, not liquid fuel, enter the carbon canister. Liquid fuel may leak out when the engine is stopped, or excess fuel may enter the carburetor during running conditions. Certain conditions may cause liquid gasoline to enter the carbon canister. For example, a full fuel tank that expands from heat or a vehicle that accidentally rolls over may cause fuel to enter the carbon canister. To prevent this, a vapor-liquid separator is used.

One type of vapor-liquid separator passes the vapors through open-cell foam. Liquid gasoline cannot pass through the foam. As shown in **Figure 24–10**, the vapors will pass through the open-cell filter material and be sent to the carbon canister. The separator is usually located directly on or near the fuel tank. Figure 24–6 shows the location of the vapor-liquid separator near the fuel tank.

A second type of vapor-liquid separator is called the float type. **Figure 24–11** shows an example of this type of separator. Vapors come into the separator from the fuel tank and cause the float to rise. The float forces the needle into its seat, closing off the vent line until the liquid fuel drains back into the tank.

Rollover Check Valve

Another method of controlling the liquid gasoline is by using a rollover check valve. This valve is located in series with the main vapor line from the fuel tank to the canister. If the vehicle rolls over in an accident, a small stainless steel

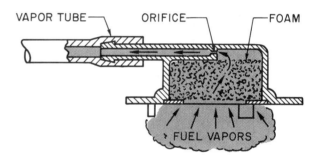

FIGURE 24–10. A vapor-liquid separator. This system uses a foam to separate the liquid and vapors. *(Courtesy of Motor Publications, Emission Control Manual)*

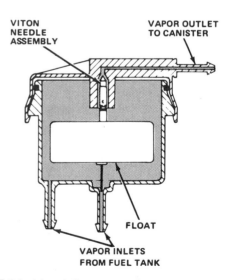

FIGURE 24–11. A float-type of vapor-liquid separator. Fuel entering the valve raises the float. The raised valve forces the needle valve to seal off the vent line to the carbon canister. *(Courtesy of Motor Publications, Emission Control Manual)*

ball will force the plunger to close off the vent line. See *Figure 24–12*.

Fuel Tank

Most fuel tanks are sealed with a special pressure-vacuum relief filler cap. This is shown in *Figure 24–13*. The relief valves in the cap are used to regulate pressure or vacuum in the fuel tank. Excess pressure or vacuum could be caused by some malfunction in the evaporative emission control system or by excess heating or cooling. The fuel tank is allowed to "breathe" through the filler cap when gasoline expands or contracts from heating or cooling.

When pressure in the fuel tank rises above 0.8 psi, the pressure cap opens to let the pressure in the fuel tank escape. If the vacuum in the fuel tank is greater than 0.1 Hg (inches of mercury), the valve is also activated.

Some fuel tanks are designed to allow for expansion when the tank has been filled. The tank shown in *Figure 24–14* has a built-in expansion tank. The orifices leading to the expansion tank are so small that it takes 10–15 minutes for gasoline from the main tank to enter the expansion tank. The expansion tank area will accept some fuel from the main fuel tank after it is filled at the fuel pump. This also provides room for fuel expansion and vapors in the main tank.

Vapor Control from Carburetor

The carburetor float bowl is also vented into the carbon canister. Fuel vapors are produced in the float bowl, especially when the engine is shut off. During this time, heat is transferred from the engine to the carburetor. This heat causes excess vapor to be produced inside the carburetor bowl. *Figure 24–15* shows the carburetor bowl area connected with a line to the carbon canister.

When the engine is shut off, vapors from the float bowl are sent to the bowl vent valve. This valve is open when the engine is off. The carburetor vapors now go directly to the carbon canister to be stored. When the engine starts, a vacuum line from the carburetor closes off the bowl vent valve. The valve stops the vapors coming from the carburetor to the carbon canister.

When the engine is running, the idle purge line draws stored vapors out of the carbon canister to the carburetor. These vapors are burned during combustion.

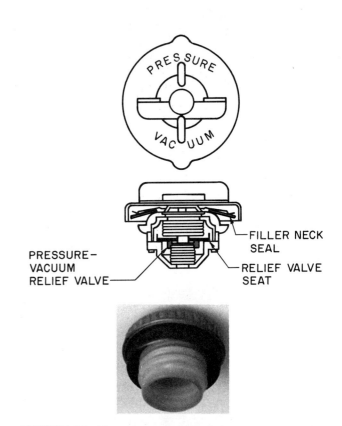

FIGURE 24–13. The pressure-vacuum relief cap opens with either high pressure or vacuum in the fuel tank. This action will prevent the tank or other components in the fuel system from being damaged.

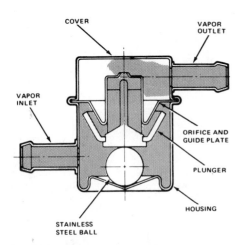

FIGURE 24–12. A rollover check valve (stainless steel base) will stop any liquid fuel from entering the carbon canister if the vehicle rolls over in an accident. *(Courtesy of Motor Publications, Emission Control Manual)*

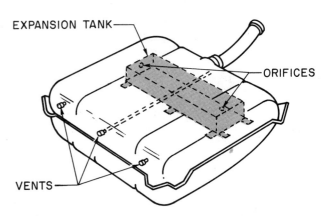

FIGURE 24–14. An expansion tank is used on certain vehicles to allow for fuel expansion when the tank is filled with gasoline.

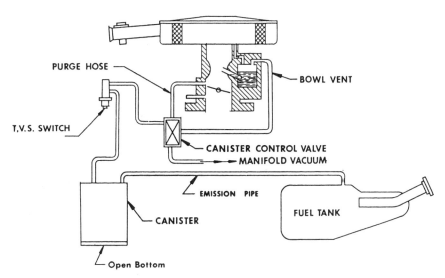

FIGURE 24–15.   A complete evaporative control system. This type of evaporative control system uses a bowl vent valve. *(Courtesy of Motor Publications, Emission Control Manual)*

Some carburetors use an insulator, *Figure 24–16*, to reduce heat transfer from the engine intake manifold to the carburetor and float bowl. The insulator is normally placed directly below the base of the carburetor on the intake manifold.

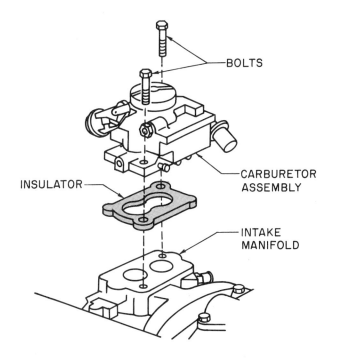

PROBLEM: Erratic Engine Operation

An engine has developed several problems. The engine has 22,000 miles on it. The system uses computer-controlled EFI (electronic fuel injection). The complaints are that the engine stops after cold starting, stops at idle after deceleration, surges during cruise, and has a rough idle. What would be a good starting point for troubleshooting?

SOLUTION:

Erratic engine operation such as this indicates a bad or inoperative EGR valve. The symptoms suggest the EGR valve is providing too much flow of exhaust back into the intake. Too little EGR flow would produce problems with spark knock, engine overheating, and emission test failure. Make sure the vacuum system on the EGR valve operates. Use a vacuum pump to check the diaphragm. Also make sure the EGR valve passages are clean from carbon buildup. Repair or replace the EGR valve to eliminate the erratic engine operation.

FIGURE 24–16.   Some carburetors use an insulator to reduce heat transfer from the intake manifold to the carburetor. This reduces the formation of vapors in the carburetor float bowl.

24.3   INTAKE AND EXHAUST EMISSION CONTROLS

In addition to the pollution controls already mentioned, certain changes can be made to the intake and exhaust systems. These particular systems alter or change the intake temperatures, the exhaust hydrocarbons, the nitrogen oxides, and the carbon monoxide.

Heated Air Intake

Automotive manufacturers have made the air-fuel mixture leaner over the past few years. Leaner air-fuel mixtures have lower hydrocarbon and carbon monoxide emissions. This is true especially during idle conditions. Faster warm-up and quicker choke action have also helped reduce emissions. During starting, the carburetor usually produces a richer mixture than what is actually needed. If the amount of time the choke is used could be reduced, less emissions would result. It is also known that a lean air-fuel mixture will ignite easier when the air is warm.

To accomplish this, air going into the carburetor can be preheated. *Figure 24–17* shows how a heated air intake system operates. This system is also referred to as a thermostatically controlled air cleaner. When heated air is required, the air control motor attached to the air cleaner assembly closes off cold air coming into the engine. All air coming into the engine now passes over the exhaust manifold and through the hot air pipe. The area where the air is heated is called the *heat stove*.

The motor is operated by the vacuum of the engine and a bimetallic strip. When the engine is off, no vacuum is produced in the vacuum chamber. This is shown in *Figure 24–18*. In this position, the control damper assembly is closing off the hot air pipe. When the engine starts, vacuum is produced. The vacuum lifts the diaphragm and closes off the

air inlet. Now only warm air drawn over the exhaust manifold can enter the carburetor.

Temperature can also be used to control the direction of air flow. This is done by a temperature sensor located on the base of the air cleaner. When the engine is operating, and the underhood temperature is below 85 degrees F, the temperature-sensing spring closes the air bleed valve. This admits full engine vacuum to the vacuum chamber. Now all outside air below 85 degrees F (cold air) is shut off. Only warm air can enter the carburetor.

When the underhood temperature reaches about 135 degrees F, the bimetallic strip spring in the temperature sensor opens the air bleed valve. This reduces any vacuum in the vacuum chamber. The diaphragm spring now pushes the control damper assembly in a position to close off the hot air pipe.

When the air temperature under the hood is between 85 and 135 degrees F, the control damper assembly is between a fully open and fully closed position. The actual opening and closing temperatures can vary somewhat, depending on the manufacturer. Also, when the engine is accelerated heavily, vacuum to the chamber will drop off instantly. This causes the spring to snap the damper downward, closing off the hot air tube. This action will allow maximum air flow through the *snorkel tube*. Under heavy acceleration, engines need all the intake air they can get for good performance.

Exhaust Gas Recirculation (EGR)

When combustion temperatures are in the range of 2,200 to 2,500 degrees F, nitrogen mixes with oxygen and produces oxides of nitrogen (NO_x). This type of emission has a detrimental effect on the environment. The method used to reduce oxides of nitrogen is to cool down the combustion process. This is done by using an *exhaust gas recirculation (EGR) valve*.

In operation, part of the exhaust gas (usually less than

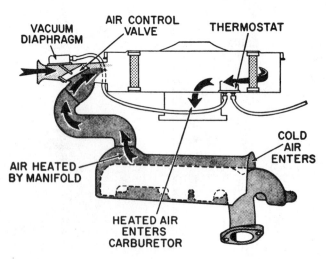

FIGURE 24–17.   Heated air is obtained on a thermostatically controlled air cleaner by drawing the air going into the air cleaner across the exhaust manifold. *(Courtesy of Motor Publications, Emission Control Manual)*

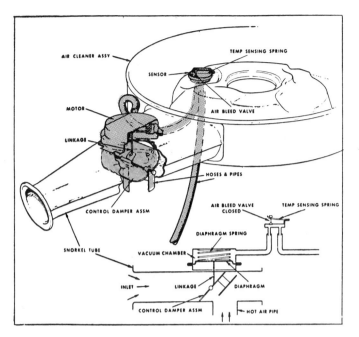
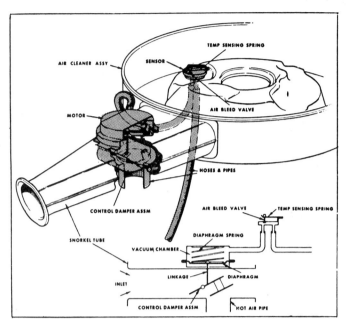
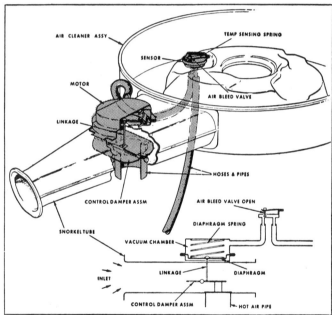

FIGURE 24–18. The control damper, the temperature sensor, and the spring control when and how much warm air will enter the air cleaner. *(Courtesy of Motor Publications, Emission Control Manual)*

10%) is sent back through the intake manifold. The exhaust gases, which are considerably cooler than the combustion temperature, cool down the process of combustion. *Figure 24–19* shows the EGR valve. This valve is located near the back of the carburetor on the intake manifold. The exhaust is picked up on the crossover passageways in the intake manifold. On in-line engines, an external line must be connected from the exhaust side to the intake side.

The EGR valve is controlled by engine vacuum. As shown in *Figure 24–20*, exhaust gases are present at the base of the EGR valve. The *pintle* valve opens or closes to regulate the exhaust gases flowing to the intake manifold.

The EGR valve also has a diaphragm, which is controlled by spring pressure against a vacuum from the carburetor. When the throttle valve is at a specific position, it uncovers the carburetor vacuum port. This action pulls the diaphragm upward against spring pressure. The EGR valve is now opened, allowing exhaust gases to enter the intake manifold.

When the engine is at idle, the throttle valve has not yet uncovered the port. During this condition, no vacuum is available to operate the EGR valve. The EGR valve remains closed during idle or heavy deceleration.

A temperature-sensitive control is sometimes placed between the EGR valve and the carburetor. Exhaust gas

FIGURE 24–19. The EGR valve located on the intake manifold recirculates exhaust gases back into the intake for cooler combustion and fewer NO$_x$ emissions.

recirculation is not needed below certain temperatures. If it is allowed to occur, it will cause poor engine performance. *Figure 24–21* shows the location of the temperature control. The EGR temperature control senses the temperature of the engine coolant. When the engine temperature reaches a certain point, the EGR temperature control opens and allows the vacuum to operate the EGR valve.

Some EGR valves also have a back-pressure *transducer* that senses pressure in the exhaust manifold to change the amount of opening.

Computer-controlled EGR System

With the use of computers controlling engine functions, the EGR valve can also be controlled. Normally the EGR valve is either open or closed. With computer control, the EGR valve can be either open, closed, or anywhere in between. The result is more precise control of the EGR valve. This results in improved engine efficiency.

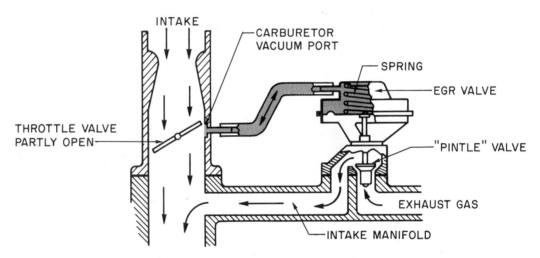

FIGURE 24–20. The EGR valve controls the amount of exhaust flowing back into the intake.

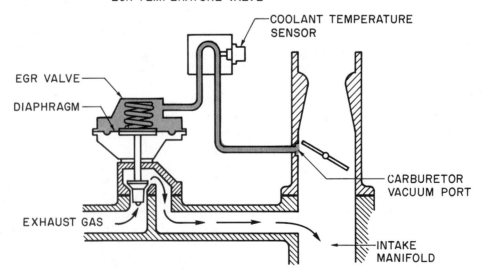

FIGURE 24–21. The EGR valve can also be controlled by a temperature valve. The EGR valve is designed to be closed below a certain temperature in the engine.

Several designs are used to control the EGR valve position. However, an ECU (electronic control unit) or ECM (electronic control module) is needed to control the EGR valve. The computer can control the EGR valve by several methods. Three popular methods are

1. by bleeding off the vacuum from the carburetor using a solenoid,

2. by using an EGR control solenoid to control the vacuum, and

3. by using solenoids directly attached to the EGR valve. One manufacturer calls this an IEEGR (integrated electronic exhaust gas recirculating) valve, shown in *Figure 24–22*.

No matter which system is used, the solenoids are operated by signals from the computer. The output signal to the solenoids is controlled by several input signals to the computer. Some of the devices used to produce input signals include the throttle position sensor, the engine temperature sensor, and the manifold pressure sensor.

Figure 24–23 illustrates a computerized control system for the EGR valve. In operation, the ECU (electronic control unit) contains memories for ideal EGR valve lifts for various operating conditions. The EGR valve lift sensor detects the amount of EGR valve lift and sends this information to the ECU. The ECU then compares it with the ideal EGR valve lift (determined by the input signals). If there is any difference between the two, the ECU reduces current to the EGR control solenoid valve. This reduced current in turn reduces the vacuum applied to the EGR valve. The result is that the EGR

FIGURE 24–22. Some vehicles with computer control use an integrated electronic exhaust gas recirculating (IEEGR) valve. *(Courtesy of CTS Corporation, Electromechanical Group)*

changes the amount of exhaust gases passing back into the intake air flow.

Air Injection System

One method used to reduce the amount of hydrocarbons (HC) and carbon monoxide (CO) in the exhaust is by forcing fresh air into the exhaust system after combustion. This additional fresh air causes further oxidation and burning of the unburned hydrocarbons and carbon monoxide. The process is much like blowing on a dwindling fire. Oxygen in the air combines with the HC and CO to continue the burn-

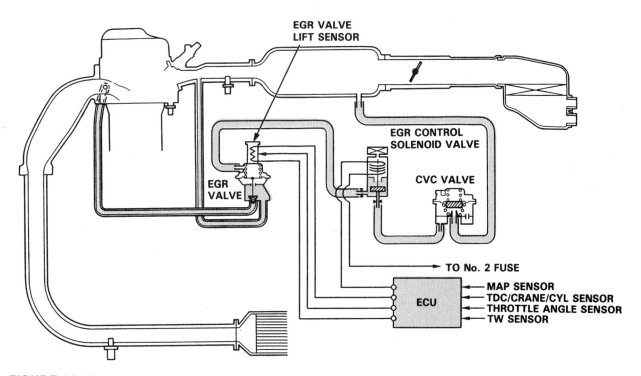

FIGURE 24–23. This system uses a computer to control the movement of the EGR valve. *(Courtesy of Honda Motor Company, Ltd.)*

ing, which reduces the HC and CO concentrations. This allows them to oxidize and produce harmless water vapor and carbon dioxide.

This method of cleaning the exhaust does not affect the efficiency of combustion. However, a small amount of frictional horsepower (up to 3 hp) is needed to operate the air injection pump. This acts as a form of horsepower loss to the engine.

These systems, which are referred to as *air injection reactors (AIR)*, thermactors, air guards, and so on, use an air pump, air manifolds, and valves to operate. A typical system is shown in *Figure 24–24*.

The air pump is driven by a belt from the crankshaft. The air pump produces pressurized air that is sent through the exhaust manifold to the injection tubes located at each cylinder. The air is then injected directly into the exhaust

flow. *Figure 24–25* shows where the air is injected into the exhaust flow. This is only one setup. The air can be injected at the base of the exhaust manifold as shown, or it can be injected directly through the head at the exhaust port. One other way to use this air is to inject it into the exhaust catalytic converter in the exhaust system.

Air Pump

The air pump is a rotating vane (also called an eccentric-type) *positive displacement pump*. See *Figure 24–26*. A relief valve is placed on the pump to control the amount of pressure the pump can develop. When pressure inside the pump exceeds a predetermined level, the relief valve opens and allows the excess pressure to escape.

As each rotating vane passes the intake chamber, a vacuum

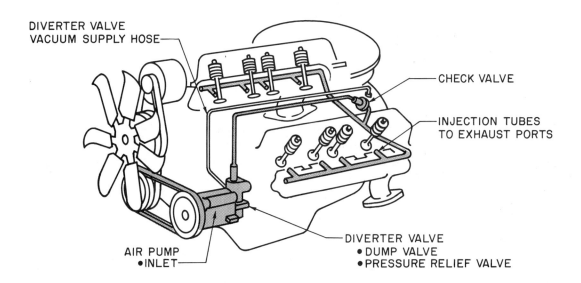

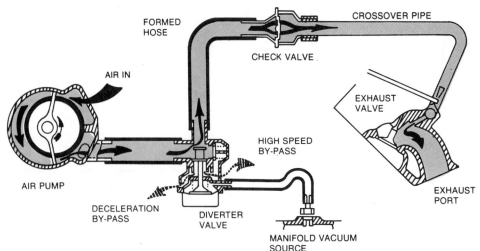

FIGURE 24–24.   A typical air injection system injects air (oxygen) directly into the exhaust flow. This air will assist the burning of any unburned hydrocarbons and carbon monoxide in the exhaust system. *(Courtesy of Motor Publications, Emission Control Manual)*

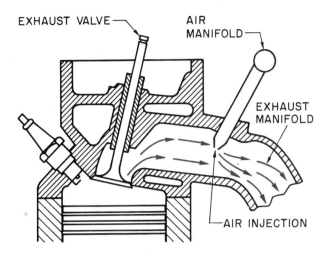

FIGURE 24–25. Air is injected directly into the exhaust gases in the air injection system. This extra fresh air will cause the unburned hydrocarbons and carbon monoxide to burn more completely, reducing emissions.

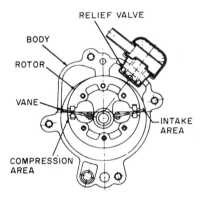

FIGURE 24–26. A cutaway view of an air injection system pump. This is a positive displacement pump using vanes to produce the air pressure. *(Courtesy of Motor Publications, Emission Control Manual)*

there is a high intake manifold vacuum. The high vacuum produces a rich air-fuel mixture from the carburetor. The mixture is too rich to be ignited in the combustion chamber. It will, therefore, go out the exhaust valve and into the exhaust manifold. If excess air were pumped into this rich mixture, violent burning action might be produced. This could cause a backfire and possibly damage the exhaust system.

The diverter valve operates as shown in *Figure 24–28*. During normal operation, pressurized air enters the inlet

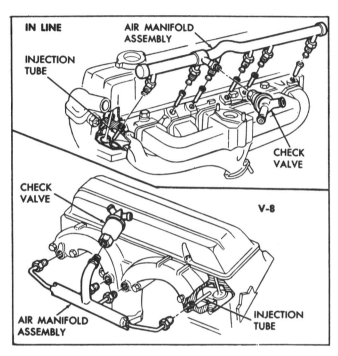

FIGURE 24–27. Check valves are used in the air injection system to control any reverse flow of exhaust gases. The check valve allows air flow in one direction but not in the other. *(Courtesy of Motor Publications, Emission Control Manual)*

is produced. This vacuum draws in a fresh charge of air. The vane carries the air charge around to the compression area. Because of the shape of the internal housing, the air charge is compressed and sent to the exhaust chamber. The pressurized air is then sent to the manifold and finally to the exhaust manifolds.

Check Valve

A check valve is also placed in the air injection system. This check valve is used to prevent back flow of exhaust gases. Backfire may occur whenever the exhaust pressure is greater than the air pump pressure. A check valve is shown in *Figure 24–27*.

Diverter Valve

The diverter valve is used to bypass the air from the air injection pump when the throttle is closed quickly. It is also called the deceleration or gulp valve. During this condition,

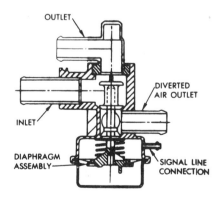

FIGURE 24–28. A diverter valve, or deceleration valve, is used to stop the flow of pumped air to the exhaust during deceleration periods. This action eliminates the possibility of backfire damage. *(Courtesy of Motor Publications, Emission Control Manual)*

and goes directly to the exhaust manifold through the outlet. When deceleration occurs, the high vacuum is felt at the vacuum signal line. This vacuum causes the metering valve to rise, closing off the line to the outlet and the exhaust manifold. Pressurized air is then directed internally to the diverted air outlet.

Aspirator Valve

The *aspirator valve* is a system that permits air to be injected into the exhaust without the use of an air pump. This unit consists of a steel tube containing a one-way aspirator valve that is attached to the exhaust manifold. **Figure 24–29** shows the external connections on the aspirator valve.

This unit uses exhaust pressure pulsations to draw fresh air into the exhaust system. The additional air reduces carbon monoxide and, to a lesser degree, hydrocarbon emissions.

The aspirator valve is shown in **Figure 24–30**. During the exhaust pulses, when the pressure in the exhaust system is positive (view A), the aspirator valve is closed. Air is not sent into the exhaust to reduce emissions. When the exhaust has a negative pressure during the pulses (view B), the aspirator valve opens and allows a small amount of air to enter the exhaust. This small amount of fresh air is first brought through the carburetor. It has an effect similar to that of injecting air into the exhaust. This action reduces emissions.

Catalytic Converters

Catalytic converters provide another method of treating exhaust gases. Catalytic converters are located in the exhaust system between the engine and the muffler. They are used to convert harmful pollutants such as HC, CO, and NO_x into

harmless gases. In operation, the exhaust gases pass over a large surface area that is coated with some form of *catalyst*. A catalyst is a material that causes a chemical reaction without becoming part of the reaction process. The catalyst is not chemically changed in the process.

The catalyst used on a catalytic converter depends on the exact type of pollutant being removed. When exhaust gases are passed through a bed of platinum- or palladium-coated pellets or through a coated honeycomb core, the HC and CO react with the oxygen in the air. The result is the formation of water and carbon dioxide. When the metal rhodium is used as the catalyst, the NO_x in the exhaust gases is reduced to harmless nitrogen and oxygen. In this case, rhodium is known as a reducing catalyst.

The reaction within the catalyst produces additional heat in the exhaust system. Temperatures up to 1,600 degrees F are normal. This additional heat is necessary for the catalyst to operate correctly. Because of these high temperatures, catalytic converters are made of stainless steel. Special heat shields are used to protect the underbody from excessive heat. Each car manufacturer has its own unique heat shielding.

It is important that only unleaded fuel be used with a catalytic converter. Leaded gasoline will destroy the effectiveness of the catalyst as an emission control device. Under normal conditions, the catalytic converter will not require maintenance. It is important, however, to keep the engine properly tuned. If it is not properly tuned, engine misfiring may cause overheating of the catalyst. This heat may cause damage to the converter. This situation can also occur during engine testing. If any spark plug wires have been removed and the engine is allowed to idle for a prolonged period of time, damage may occur.

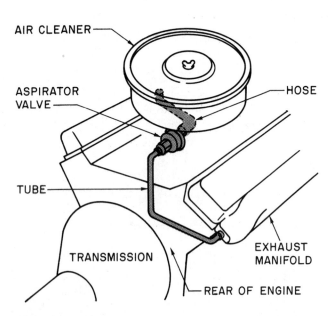

FIGURE 24–29.   External connections for the aspirator air injection system.

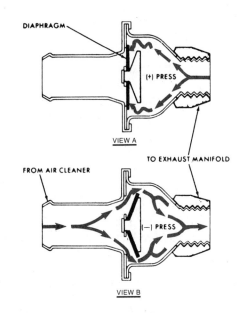

FIGURE 24–30.   The aspirator valve works in response to the positive and negative pulses in the exhaust. *(Courtesy of Motor Publications, Emission Control Manual)*

Types of Catalytic Converters

There are two types of catalytic converters: the two-way converter and the three-way converter. Both types can employ either a *monolith* or a pellet design. The monolith and pellet designs are shown in *Figures 24–31* and *24–32*, respectively.

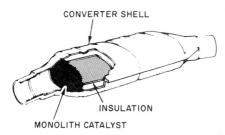

FIGURE 24–31. The two-way monolith catalytic converter uses a catalyst made like a honeycomb to allow gases to pass through. *(Courtesy of Motor Publications, Emission Control Manual)*

Two-Way Catalytic Converter

The two-way catalytic converter reduces carbon monoxide and hydrocarbon particles. It does not reduce any nitrogen oxide emissions. Figures 24–31 and 24–32 are examples of the two-way catalytic converter. Here, only platinum and palladium are used as catalysts to reduce hydrocarbons and carbon monoxide.

Three-Way Catalytic Converter

The three-way catalytic converter is designed to reduce nitrogen oxide emissions. An additional catalyst bed coated with platinum and rhodium is used. The bed not only helps reduce hydrocarbons and carbon monoxide but also lowers the levels of nitrogen oxide emissions.

Figure 24–33 shows a three-way monolith catalytic converter. The front bed, or inlet, is treated with platinum and rhodium and is termed a reducing catalyst. The rear bed is coated with palladium and platinum and is referred to as the oxidizing catalyst.

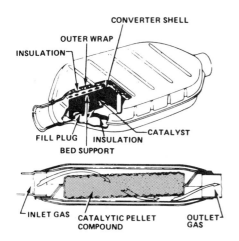

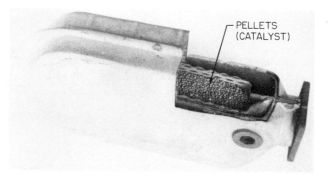

FIGURE 24–32. The two-way pellet-type catalytic converter uses pellets as the catalyst. Exhaust gases are forced through the catalyst pellets. *(Courtesy of Motor Publications, Emission Control Manual)*

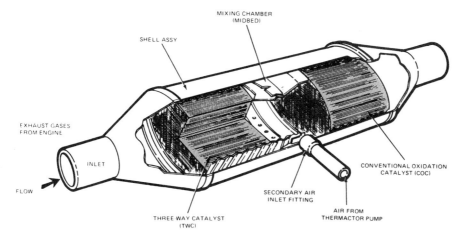

FIGURE 24–33. A three-way, dual-bed, monolith catalytic converter. Secondary air from the air injection system is used to cause greater oxidation of the emissions. *(Courtesy of Motor Publications, Emission Control Manual)*

In Figure 24–33, exhaust gases first pass through the reducing catalyst. This causes the levels of NO_x to be reduced. Pressurized air from the air injection system is forced into the space between the catalyst beds. Extra air supplies additional oxygen. The extra air causes more oxidation of the gases.

As the treated exhaust gases from the first bed continue, they eventually pass through the conventional oxidation catalyst made of palladium and platinum. Here, hydrocarbons and carbon monoxide emissions are reduced.

CAR CLINIC

PROBLEM: **Deceleration Problem**

A vehicle makes a jerking motion while decelerating. The problem happens only when the engine is warmed up.

SOLUTION:

Normally, any jerking during deceleration is caused by incorrect air and fuel mixtures. The jerking could also be caused by too much ignition timing advance. A third possible cause might be the EGR valve. A quick way to check the EGR valve is to disconnect the valve and run the engine. If it still has a jerking motion on deceleration, reconnect the EGR valve (if it's OK) and check the advance. Try retarding the ignition timing slightly and see if the jerking stops. If the jerking is still there, the air-fuel ratio will have to be checked with an exhaust gas analyzer.

24.4 CONTROLLING COMBUSTION AND AIR-FUEL MIXTURES

Many other types of emission control systems are used on the automobile today. These systems are designed to change or control the air-fuel ratio or the combustion process, or both. Knowledge of the fuel and ignition system is necessary to understand this information.

Idle Limiters

Certain types of carburetors have an idle limiter screw. Its purpose is to assure that the carburetor will deliver a leaner air-fuel mixture, especially during idle. The idle mixture adjustment screw is adjusted leaner by the manufacturer. Then, the idle limiter cap is installed. The cap permits only a small idle mixture adjustment. The cap should be removed only during carburetor repair. *Figure 24–34* shows the idle limiter screw in one model of carburetor. On late-model carburetors, the idle mixture screw is completely sealed. No adjustment is possible on newer carburetors except by authorized technicians.

Combustion Chamber

Combustion chambers have also been changed to produce fewer emissions. During combustion, the layer of air and fuel mixture next to the cooler cylinder head and piston head typically does not burn. The metal surfaces chill this area below the combustion temperature. A certain amount of unburned fuel is swept out of the cylinder on the exhaust stroke.

These emissions can be controlled by reducing the S-V ratio of the combustion chamber. The S-V ratio is the ratio between the surface (S) area and the volume (V) of the combustion chamber. A wedge-design combustion chamber has

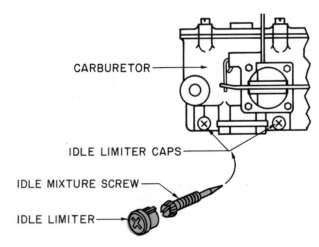

FIGURE 24–34. The idle limiter is located at the base of the carburetor. It assures a leaner air-fuel mixture during idle conditions. This leaner mixture reduces emissions. On newer carburetors, the idle mixture screw is sealed so adjustments cannot be made.

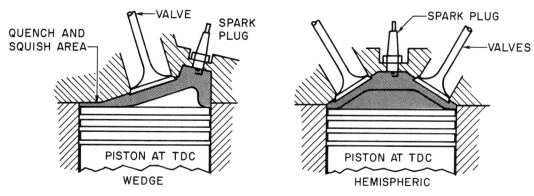

FIGURE 24–35. The wedge and the hemispheric combustion chambers. The hemispheric combustion chamber has a lower S-V (surface-to-volume) ratio, which produces less pollution in the cylinder.

the highest S-V ratio. The hemispheric combustion chamber has a lower S-V ratio. *Figure 24–35* shows the wedge and the hemspheric combustion chambers.

Combustion chambers have also been changed to reduce close clearances that tend to quench the flame before all of the air-fuel mixture is burned. Quench heights have been increased. This permits more complete burning of the air-fuel mixture in these areas. On late-model engines, manufacturers have gone to a more "open" style combustion chamber to reduce exhaust emissions.

Lower Compression Ratios

During the 1960s, the compression ratio of engines being built was about 9.5 to 1. In fact, compression ratios were being increased each year to produce more power. Higher compression ratios also produced higher combustion temperatures. These higher temperatures then increased the amount of nitrogen oxide being produced. Because of this problem, automobile manufacturers have lowered the compression ratios to about 8 to 1. Reducing the compression ratio reduces peak combustion temperatures, which, in turn, reduces the amount of nitrogen oxide produced. However, reducing compression ratios also reduces engine performance and efficiency to some extent.

Intake Manifolds

Intake manifolds have been modified to assure more rapid vaporization of fuel during warm-up periods. The exhaust crossover flow area of the intake manifold between the inlet and exhaust gases has been made thinner. The time required to get the heat from the exhaust gases into the inlet gases has been reduced.

Ignition Timing

Ignition timing of the automobile engine is very important to the reduction of emissions. For example, during part throttle operation, the distributor vacuum advance normally advances the ignition timing. This provides more time for the leaner air-fuel mixture to burn. The added time, however, also allows more NO_x to develop. Several systems have been incorporated to control vacuum advance under certain driving conditions such as reverse, neutral, or low forward speeds. These include the TRS (transmission-regulated spark) and CCC (computer command control). For example, the CCC system does not use mechanical or vacuum advance for distributor spark control or timing. It is all done by the computer.

Control of Vacuum Advance: TRS System

A *transmission-regulated spark* (TRS) system is one method used to regulate the vacuum at low speeds. As shown in *Figure 24–36*, the system works so that the solenoid valve is normally open. This allows the distributor to have full vacuum advance when the transmission is in high gear only. In the lower gears, the transmission switch is closed. This closes the solenoid valve. When the transmission switch is closed, vacuum to the distributor vacuum advance is shut off. Now there is no vacuum advance applied to the distributor during lower speeds.

Electronic Spark Control

Automotive manufacturers have recently designed and incorporated electronic control of spark and timing. These systems do not use the conventional mechanical and vacuum advance. A number of sensors are used in their place. Basic timing is provided by a magnetic pickup coil sensor in the distributor. As shown in *Figure 24–37*, signals such as barometric pressure, manifold vacuum, and coolant temperature are fed into a solid-state computer. On the basis of these input signals, the computer determines and provides the optimum spark advance within milliseconds.

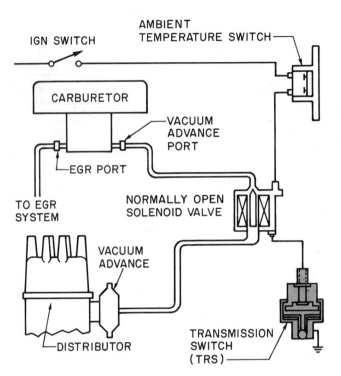

FIGURE 24–36. A transmission-regulated spark (TRS) system. A signal from the transmission operates the normally open solenoid valve to stop vacuum advance during low speeds.

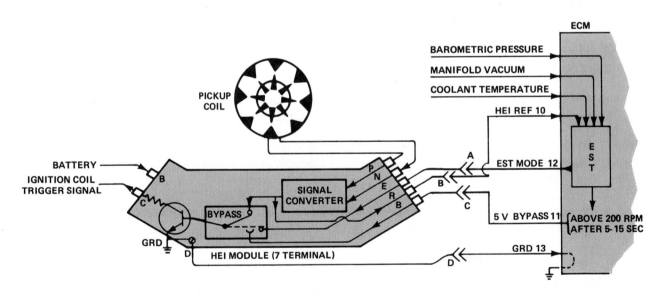

FIGURE 24–37. On the electronic spark timing (EST) system, various sensors feed information into the computer to control the spark advance for optimum emission control. *(Courtesy of General Motors Product Service Training)*

Computer Command Control

The use of computers to control spark advance has led to the development of computer command control systems, EFI, and ECCS (electronic concentrated engine control systems) used on automobiles today. These systems provide very sensitive and precise control of air-fuel ratios and ignition system timing advance.

A computer system is shown in *Figure 24–38*. This system is capable of sensing up to 11 variables and controlling 6 functions with the information. Other systems, including injection timing, injection of air into the exhaust manifold, injection of air into the converter, and idle speed, can also be controlled. Precise control of these systems makes possible a sizable reduction in emissions.

E.C.C.S. CHART

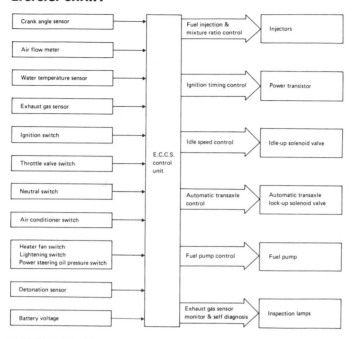

FIGURE 24–38. This schematic shows a closed loop electronic control system that monitors and controls a wide range of units and functions to help reduce emissions. This system is called the electronic concentrated engine control system. *(Courtesy of Nissan Motor Corporation in USA)*

The computer used on automobiles is also tied into some of the existing emissions control equipment. These include carbon canister purge control, EGR control, and EFE control.

1. The carbon canister purge is controlled by a computer. A solenoid is placed in the manifold vacuum purge line. The computer controls when the purging takes place. For a more detailed description, refer to Section 24.2, Evaporative Emission Controls.

2. The EGR valve can also be controlled by the computer. On the basis of the coolant temperature, mass air flow, engine RPM, and throttle position, the computer will cycle the EGR valve open and closed. For a more detailed description, refer to Section 24.3, Intake and Exhaust Emission Controls.

3. The *EFE (early fuel evaporation)* is used to cause exhaust gases on one side of a V engine to be directed over to the other side. The excess heat causes the fuel to evaporate faster, reducing emissions. The EFE system is also controlled by the computer.

CAR CLINIC

PROBLEM: Converter Temperatures

A customer has complained that the catalytic converter is running very hot. The temperature on the converter is about 800–900 degrees F. Is this normal, or is something wrong with the engine?

SOLUTION:

Catalytic converters are designed to operate at this temperature and at times even hotter. The heat is needed to help reduce the NO_x emissions. However, if the temperature gets hotter and the catalytic converter glows red, there may be a problem. The first thing to check is a blockage in the catalytic converter. This will cause the temperature to increase significantly.

Problems, Diagnosis and Service

1. After the engine has been running, the EGR valve may be very hot. Let the engine cool down so that your hands will not be seriously burned.
2. Never weld anything on or near the gasoline tank, even if the fuel has been removed. There may still be gasoline fumes inside the tank that could cause an explosion.
3. When checking the heated intake air system, be careful not to burn your hands. The tube is connected to the exhaust manifold and can be very hot.
4. The catalytic converter normally operates at a higher temperature than the exhaust. Always be extra careful when working around the catalytic converter so as to eliminate the possibility of severe burns.
5. Always use compressed air and an air hose to blow out valves, tubes, or other clogged passageways on emission control devices. Never blow these out with your mouth as you may be exposed to toxic liquids.
6. At times when diagnosing the emission control system, the engine must be running. Be careful not to drop anything into the spinning parts or in the fan blades. Remember also to stay clear of the electric fan. It may go on unexpectedly, causing injury.

PROBLEM: Faulty EGR or PCV Valve

An engine is running rough, has a very irregular and rough idle, and stalls.

DIAGNOSIS

Often the EGR or the PCV valve may be defective. If either is defective, the air-fuel ratio may be off and will produce an irregular or rough idle. *Figure 24–39* shows an emission system troubleshooting guide.

On most vehicles with computer-controlled systems, trouble codes are shown on the instrument panel when a fault is detected. If you use a scanner or if you ground a trouble code test lead terminal under the dashboard, the CHECK ENGINE light will flash a trouble code that indicates the problem area. Refer to the manufacturer's service manual for the correct identification of codes for each vehicle.

SERVICE

1. When servicing the emission control systems, always check the condition of emission control vacuum hoses and tubes for leaks, small cracks, or bad sealing. Any leak could cause a pressure or vacuum leak. This in turn may cause incorrect operation of the emission control devices.

2. Hoses, vacuum diaphragms, and tubes can be checked with a vacuum tester as shown in *Figure 24–40*. To check a component, remove the hose attached to the device to be checked. Using the vacuum tester, apply vacuum to the component by pumping the vacuum tester. The device should be able to hold a vacuum without leaking. Leakage can be observed easily on the vacuum scale.

3. Always check the specification manual for the correct hookup of vacuum hoses. Most service manuals have sections that show the vacuum hose routing. *Figure 24–41*

SYMPTOM	SUB SYSTEM	CATALYTIC CONVERTER	EGR SYSTEM	POSITIVE CRANKCASE VENTILATION SYSTEM	EVAPORATIVE EMISSION CONTROLS
ROUGH IDLE			①	②	
FREQUENT STALLING	AFTER WARM-ING UP		①		
POOR PERFORMANCE	FAILS EMISSION TEST	①			②
	LOSS OF POWER	①			

FIGURE 24–39. To help troubleshoot the emission control system, look for the symptom on the left. Then read across to the most likely problem. Number 1 is the first or most likely source of the problem. Number 2 is the second most likely source of the problem. *(Courtesy of Honda Motor Corporation, Ltd.)*

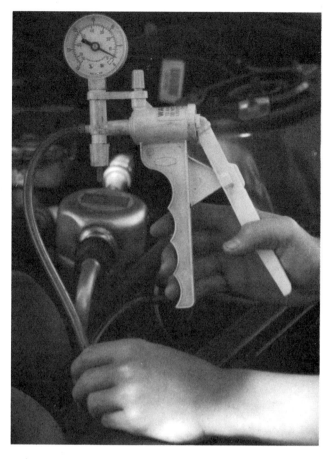

FIGURE 24–40.   A vacuum tester can be used to check for vacuum leaks and the condition of diaphragms and other pollution control equipment.

shows two typical examples of vacuum hose routing diagrams.

4. Since there are several types of EGR valve systems, refer to the manufacturer's specifications and procedure for correct testing and service of each. On some engines, the CHECK ENGINE light will come on to indicate a certain trouble code. For example, on vehicles made by one manufacturer, Code 12 indicates "Exhaust Gas Recirculating System." Check the EGR valve using the following general procedure:

a. Place a finger under the EGR valve and lift up on the diaphragm plate.

   CAUTION: Be careful not to burn your fingers or hands.

   The plate should move up and down freely without binding or sticking. If it doesn't move freely, replace the valve.

b. Check the vacuum by connecting a vacuum gauge to the EGR valve signal line using a T fitting. Start the engine and run it at part throttle. The vacuum gauge should read at least 5 inches Hg (the reading will be different for each vehicle) at part throttle and at normal engine operating temperature. If the gauge reads less, check the hoses and vacuum source, and repair as needed.

c. With the engine running as in step b, disconnect the vacuum hose to the EGR valve. The diaphragm plate should move, and the engine speed should increase. If the plate does not move, replace the EGR valve.

d. Reconnect the vacuum hose. The EGR valve diaphragm plate should move, and the engine speed should decrease.

e. If the diaphragm moves but there is no change in the engine speed, check the manifold passages for blockage. If the passages are clean, the EGR valve is defective.

f. The intake manifold can be cleaned with the EGR valve removed. Use a suitable screwdriver, scraper, and wire brush to remove deposits.

g. On certain vehicles, there is a replaceable filter on the EGR valve. Replace this filter at the manufacturer's recommended intervals.

h. Replace either the EGR valve assembly or the filter before starting engine.

5. The PCV valve may also be defective, thus producing a rough idle. Use the following general procedures when servicing the PCV valve:

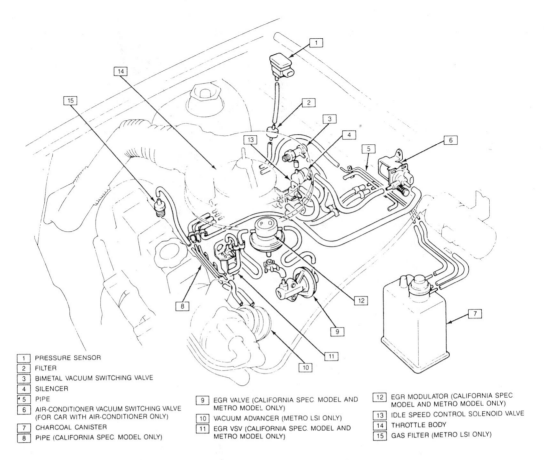

1 PRESSURE SENSOR		
2 FILTER		
3 BIMETAL VACUUM SWITCHING VALVE		
4 SILENCER		
5 PIPE	9 EGR VALVE (CALIFORNIA SPEC. MODEL AND METRO MODEL ONLY)	12 EGR MODULATOR (CALIFORNIA SPEC MODEL AND METRO MODEL ONLY)
6 AIR-CONDITIONER VACUUM SWITCHING VALVE (FOR CAR WITH AIR-CONDITIONER ONLY)	10 VACUUM ADVANCER (METRO LSI ONLY)	13 IDLE SPEED CONTROL SOLENOID VALVE
7 CHARCOAL CANISTER	11 EGR VSV (CALIFORNIA SPEC. MODEL AND METRO MODEL ONLY)	14 THROTTLE BODY
8 PIPE (CALIFORNIA SPEC. MODEL ONLY)		15 GAS FILTER (METRO LSI ONLY)

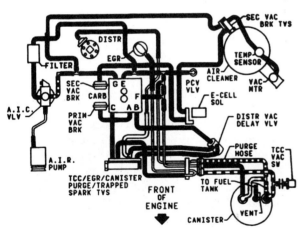

FIGURE 24–41. Vacuum hose routing diagrams are available in many of the maintenance and service manuals. Refer to these diagrams when checking for correct vacuum connections. *(Courtesy of Motor Publications, Emission Control Manual)*

a. Check the PCV valve for correct operation by removing the valve, running the engine, and observing a small vacuum. See *Figure 24–42*. A hissing sound should also be heard. If there is no hissing sound, no vacuum, or if there is a slight pressure, the PCV valve may be damaged or plugged. If this is the case, remove the valve and replace it with a new one.

b. A plugged PCV valve can cause rough idle, stalling at low speeds, oil leaks, oil in the air cleaner, or sludge in the engine. The PCV valve can easily be checked by shaking it lightly. When it is shaken, a PCV valve should make a slight clicking noise, indicating that the valve is free to move. If there is no clicking, the valve may be plugged or inoperative. Replace the valve if necessary.

c. The PCV system can also be checked using the PCV system tester, shown in *Figure 24–43*. Other testers can also be used. This tester is connected into the PCV vacuum system while it is operating. On the basis of the amount of vacuum, various colors will read out on the tester body. Green indicates the system is operating correctly. Yellow indicates the system is partially plugged. Red indicates the system is fully plugged. The system is then serviced accordingly.

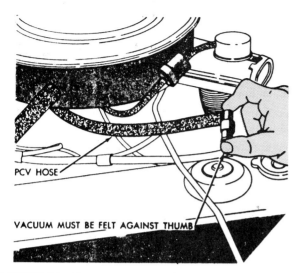

FIGURE 24–42. When checking the PCV valve, remove the valve and run the engine at idle. A strong vacuum should be felt at the end of the PCV valve. *(Courtesy of Motor Publications, Emission Control Manual)*

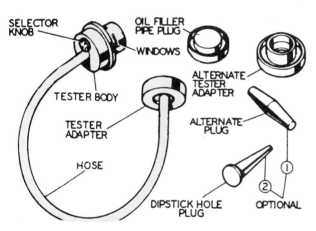

FIGURE 24–43. This PCV system tester measures vacuum in the system. It reads out the condition using several colors to indicate whether the system is operating correctly or not. *(Courtesy of Motor Publications, Emission Control Manual)*

PROBLEM: Faulty Fuel Tank Cap

The fuel tank on a vehicle is beginning to collapse.

DIAGNOSIS

A collapsing fuel tank usually indicates that the fuel tank cap is defective. A defective cap will cause the tank to collapse because as the fuel is removed during normal driving, no air can get into the tank to replace the volume of fuel.

SERVICE

To remedy the problem, remove the filler cap and replace it with a new one.

PROBLEM: Faulty Diverter Valve

The engine produces a backfire.

DIAGNOSIS

Often an engine with a diverter valve may backfire if the valve is operating incorrectly. The diverter valve may be putting excess air into the combustion chamber. The result would be backfiring.

SERVICE

Use the following general procedure to test the diverter valve:

1. Start the engine and run it until it reaches normal operating temperature.

2. Disconnect the vacuum hose from the diverter valve to ensure the presence of a vacuum at the hose.

3. Reconnect the hose to the valve. Air should be vented through the diverter valve for at least 1 second.

4. Momentarily accelerate the engine to full throttle while observing the diverter valve. Each time the engine is accelerated, air should be discharged from the diverter valve muffler for about 1 second. If the diverter valve fails to perform as outlined, the valve is defective and should be replaced with a new one.

PROBLEM: Defective Air Injection Reactor (AIR) Pump

The air injection reactor pump is making loud noises.

DIAGNOSIS

The air injection reactor (AIR) pump often will become defective. The result is that there may be excessive belt, bearing, or knocking noises from the pump.

SERVICE

Use the following general procedures to service the AIR pump:

1. Check for the correct tension on the air injection reactor pump belt. This can be done using the belt tension checker discussed in Chapter 12.

2. There should be no air leaks in the AIR system components. Look for air leaks at the hoses and the air injection tubes on the exhaust manifold. If there are any leaks, replace the components as necessary.

3. Check the mounting bolts for looseness and to see if the pump is aligned correctly.

4. After removing the belt, check for a seized air pump. Replace if necessary.

5. Check for loose air pump hoses.

6. Check for a defective pressure relief valve.

7. Inspect the check valves for air flow in only one direction. Replace as necessary.

PROBLEM: Damaged Heated Air Intake

An engine usually runs rough, hesitates, or stalls during cold starting conditions.

DIAGNOSIS

The heated intake air system may be damaged and operating incorrectly. If it is damaged, the carburetor will not get warm air (drawn across the exhaust manifold) during cold starting. The result is that the air-fuel ratios may be slightly off during cold starting.

SERVICE

When this system is defective, several checks can be made:

1. Check the hoses that feed the vacuum to the vacuum motor for cracks and leaks.

2. Check the hose that feeds the warm air from the exhaust manifold to the air cleaner housing. This tube often rips, breaks, or cracks, depending on its type.

3. The vacuum motor can be checked with the vacuum tester.

4. First disconnect the vacuum hoses that lead to the vacuum motor. When a vacuum from the vacuum tester is applied to the motor, the linkage and control damper should move freely, and the damper should remain in position.

5. If the damper assembly returns slowly, there is a leak in the motor and it should be replaced.

PROBLEM: Faulty Carbon Canister

Fuel is leaking from the carbon canister. What is the necessary service on the carbon canister?

DIAGNOSIS

Often, the carbon canister is overlooked when a vehicle is serviced. If it is not operating correctly or if fuel is leaking, there may be cracks in the hoses, the purge valve may be defective, or the filters may need to be replaced.

SERVICE

Use the following suggestions when inspecting the carbon canister:

1. Replace the filter on the carbon canister according to the manufacturer's recommended time intervals.

2. Check the carbon canister for cracks or fuel leaking from the fittings. Repair and replace where necessary.

3. Check the purge valve using a vacuum pump as shown in *Figure 24–44*. Refer to the exact manufacturer's procedure to perform this test. Replace as necessary.

PROBLEM: Carbon Canister Purge Valve

The vehicle is using an excessive amount of gasoline and is emitting black smoke from the exhaust pipe.

DIAGNOSIS

One problem that can occur with the carbon canister purge systems is a purge valve that fails. Commonly, when this valve fails, it allows excessive engine vacuum to enter the vapor-liquid separator in the fuel tank. This excessive vacuum results in liquid gasoline being drawn up to the intake manifold of the engine. The gasoline enters the intake and is thus burned. Although the carburetor or fuel injection system may be working correctly, the engine gets a very rich air-fuel mixture.

SERVICE

Use the following suggestions when testing and servicing the carbon canister purge valve.

1. To check the purge valve, remove all fuel and vacuum lines attached to the valve.

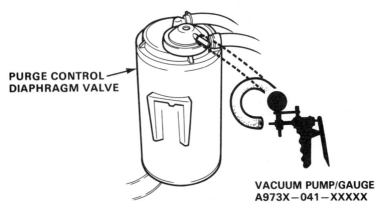

PURGE CONTROL DIAPHRAGM VALVE

VACUUM PUMP/GAUGE
A973X—041—XXXXX

FIGURE 24–44.   Use a vacuum tester to check the condition of the purge control diaphragm valve. *(Courtesy of Honda Motor Company, Ltd.)*

2. Turn the valve on one end and shake it. If liquid gasoline is present, then the valve is faulty and should be replaced.

3. The purge valve can also be tested by using a vacuum pump. Refer to the manufacturer's suggested procedure to perform this test.

4. If the purge valve is replaced, also replace the carbon canister. It may be contaminated with liquid gasoline.

5. It may now be necessary to clear a trouble code of "rich exhaust" from the computer. Refer to the appropriate service manual for the correct procedures.

PROBLEM: Faulty Catalytic Converter

An engine has a significant power loss at lower speeds.

DIAGNOSIS

At times the catalytic converter can become plugged because of the use of leaded fuel in the engine. The honeycomb core may also disintegrate as shown in *Figure 24–45*.

SERVICE

Use the following procedures to service the catalytic converter.

1. Check to see if the customer has been using leaded fuel in the engine. Also check to see if the restrictor ring has been removed from the fuel tank inlet. If leaded fuel has been used or if the restrictor has been removed, the catalytic converter will need to be replaced.

2. A rotten egg smell is often produced by vehicles that have a catalytic converter. This odor is generally caused from too rich a mixture in the carburetor. If this smell persists, check the carburetor adjustments or try using another type of fuel to eliminate the odor.

3. Pellets coming out of the exhaust indicate that the catalytic converter is damaged internally. Replace as necessary.

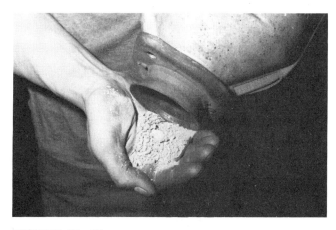

FIGURE 24–45. This catalytic converter's honeycomb core has disintegrated, blocking the exhaust flow from the engine. *(Courtesy of Motor Magazine)*

SERVICE MANUAL CONNECTION

There are many important specifications to keep in mind when working with emission control systems. To identify the specifications for your engine, you will need to know the VIN (vehicle identification number) of the vehicle, the type and year of the vehicle, and the type of engine. Although they may be titled differently, some of the more common emission control system specifications (not all) found in service manuals are listed below. Note that these specifications are typical examples. Each vehicle and engine may have different specifications.

Common Specification	Typical Example
Air pump drive belt (on belt tension gauge)	3/8 inch
Carbon monoxide (CO)	3.4 grams per mile
Filler cap relief valve opening	0.8 psi
Hydrocarbons (HC)	0.41 grams per mile
Nitrogen oxides (NO_x)	1.0 grams per mile
Thermostatic air cleaner check valve closing temperature	80 degrees F

In addition, the service manual will give specific directions for various service and testing procedures. Some of the more common procedures include:

- Carbon canister servicing
- Catalytic converter replace
- Exhaust gas recirculating valve testing
- Oxygen sensor replace
- Ported vacuum switches testing
- Positive crankcase ventilation system servicing
- Vacuum control valves testing
- Vacuum hose routings

SUMMARY

This chapter covered the operation of the crankcase ventilation system, evaporative systems, and intake and exhaust controls. In addition, several devices designed to control combustion more effectively to reduce emissions were also studied.

The positive crankcase ventilation system is used to prevent crankcase vapors from entering the atmosphere. This is done by using a PCV valve. Blow-by gases are produced by the combustion process. These blow-by gases are then sent through a PCV valve and back to the intake manifold of the engine for reburning. This prevents any crankcase emissions from entering the atmosphere.

(continued)

Linkage to Environment

EFFECTS OF CARBON MONOXIDE

Many types of automotive pollutant gases can be dangerous to one's health. One such pollutant is carbon monoxide. Carbon monoxide is produced from automobile exhaust. It displaces oxygen in the bloodstream, which results in carbon monoxide poisoning.

The concentration of carbon monoxide in air is measured in parts per million (ppm). This term means that in one million parts of air a certain number of the parts are composed of carbon monoxide. Generally, with 100 ppm carbon monoxide in the air for less than one hour of exposure no symptoms are noticeable. Mild carbon monoxide poisoning is noticeable as a headache or drowsy feeling. Increasingly severe stages of carbon monoxide poisoning include throbbing headaches, vomiting, collapse, and coma. At a concentration of 600 ppm death may occur. The figure shows how different levels of exposure to carbon monoxide will affect a person over certain time periods. The bottom axis is the duration of exposure. The vertical axis is the amount of carbon monoxide in ppm. Each line shows the effect of various carbon monoxide levels over different time periods. For example, if the concentration of carbon monoxide were 300 ppm (300 ppm line), it would take about 8–9 hours of exposure to reach the coma stage.

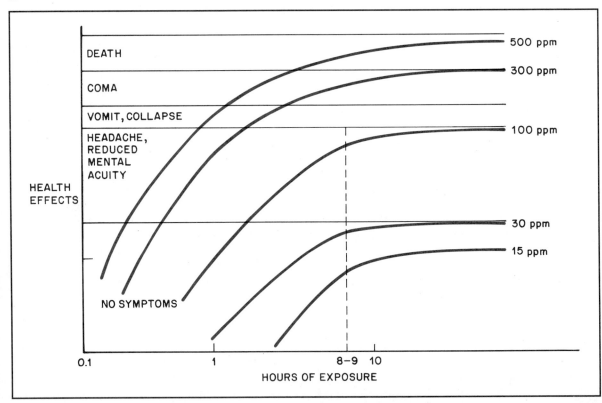

Another area of emissions from the automobile is that produced from fuel. This emission is made of hydrocarbons. Several devices are used to prevent any hydrocarbon vapors from being released into the atmosphere. The carbon canister (also called the charcoal canister) is a small canister used to hold carbon. The fuel vapors from the fuel tank and carburetor are sent to the carbon canister to be absorbed. During engine operation, some of these vapors are sent directly into the intake to be burned in the combustion process.

Other components are also used to control evaporative emissions. A vapor-liquid separator is used to stop any raw fuel from entering the canister. The rollover check valve is used to stop liquid fuel from going into the canister if the vehicle rolls over in an accident. Many fuel tanks also have an expansion tank to allow for fuel expansion.

Another set of emission controls is designed to control the intake and exhaust of the engine. The heated air intake system is used to heat the intake air for the most efficient operation during cold starting. Air is drawn over the exhaust manifold to heat the air. The EGR (exhaust gas recirculator) is used to reduce NO_x. It allows cooler exhaust gases to flow back into the intake to reduce combustion temperatures. The AIR (air injection reactor) system forces excess air into the exhaust to continue burning emissions that have been partially burned within the combustion chamber. This system uses an air pump driven by the crankshaft and a set of tubes to each exhaust port. Several other devices are used as part of an AIR system. These include check valves, diverter valves, and aspirator valves.

A catalytic converter is also used on vehicles today. The catalytic converter uses a catalyst to change the chemistry of the exhaust. All three emissions, including HC, CO, and NO_x, can be controlled by the converter. Two types of catalytic converters are used: the two-way and three-way converters. Pellet and monolith designs are used for the converters.

Emissions can also be controlled by changing the combustion at various operational speeds and loads. Idle limiters are used on certain carburetors to prevent tampering with precise carburetor air-fuel mixture adjustments, which affect emissions at idle. Combustion chambers are being reshaped to reduce emissions. Lower compression ratios allow for non-leaded fuels. Intake manifolds are being designed to enhance vaporization of fuel quicker. Timing is also being electronically adjusted and controlled to help reduce emissions.

In addition to the changes mentioned, computer controls are now being used to control emissions even more accurately. Computers that monitor various inputs such as engine and vehicle speed, coolant temperature, position of the crankshaft, load, air flow into the engine, intake air temperature, and throttle position, are being added to vehicles. These inputs help the computer to precisely control the fuel and timing advance for optimum performance and reduced emissions.

There are many service procedures used on emission control systems. Each manufacturer has its own procedures and set guidelines to follow. On computer-controlled systems, codes are used to identify problems in the system.

TERMS TO KNOW

Can you explain each of the following terms? Review the chapter until you can use each term correctly.

Blow-by
Crankcase pressure
Positive crankcase ventilation (PCV)
Carbon canister
Purge
Heat stove
Snorkel tube
Exhaust gas recirculation (EGR)
Pintle
Transducer
Air injection reactor (AIR)
Positive displacement pump
Aspirator valve
Catalytic converter
Catalyst
Monolith
Transmission-regulated spark (TRS)
Early fuel evaporation (EFE)

REVIEW QUESTIONS

Multiple Choice

1. Crankcase pressures are produced by:
   a. The cooling system
   b. The ignition system
   c. Power output
   d. Blow-by
   e. The starter

2. The PCV valve _____ the amount of vapor being burned in the combustion chamber during low speeds.
   a. Increases
   b. Decreases
   c. Doubles
   d. Has no effect on
   e. None of the above

3. The carbon canister stores:
   a. Fuel vapor from the fuel tank
   b. Fuel vapor from the carburetor
   c. Blow-by vapors
   d. All of the above
   e. A and B

4. The carbon canister:
   a. Stores fuel vapors
   b. Has a filter
   c. Has a purge line back to the carburetor
   d. All of the above
   e. None of the above

5. Which of the following stops raw fuel from entering the carbon canister?
   a. Check valve
   b. Vapor-liquid separator
   c. Air pump
   d. PCV valve
   e. Idle limiter screws

6. Which device is used to allow a place for expanding fuel in a full tank of gasoline in warm weather?
   a. Check valve
   b. Rollover valve
   c. Expansion tank
   d. PCV valve
   e. AIR system

7. Warming up the intake air during cold starting will:
   a. Reduce emissions
   b. Increase emissions
   c. Reduce fuel consumption
   d. Cause rough idling
   e. Increase power

8. The "heat stove" is used on what pollution control device?
   a. AIR
   b. PCV
   c. Thermostatically controlled air cleaner
   d. Transmission-controlled spark
   e. CCC

9. Which of the following pollution control devices is designed to reduce the NO_x emissions?
   a. AIR
   b. PCV
   c. EGR
   d. TCS
   e. None of the above

10. On the EGR system _____ is/are sent back to the intake.
    a. Exhaust gases
    b. Blow-by
    c. Extra spark
    d. Liquid coolant
    e. Catalyst

11. Which pollution control system forces air into the exhaust stream to help burn emissions?
    a. AIR   d. TCS
    b. PVC   e. CCC
    c. EGR

12. Which of the following will have little or no effect on the combustion process?
    a. PCV
    b. Carbon canister
    c. AIR
    d. Evaporative emission systems
    e. Heated air intake systems

13. What type of system allows air to be injected into the exhaust without the use of a positive displacement pump?
    a. CCC
    b. Aspirator system
    c. Carbon canister
    d. All of the above
    e. None of the above

14. Which of the following systems change(s) the exhaust system to reduce emissions?
    a. Two-way catalytic converter
    b. Three-way catalytic converter
    c. Diverter valve
    d. AIR system
    e. A, B, and D

15. Which of the following can be found in a catalytic converter?
    a. A monolith catalyst
    b. A pellet catalyst
    c. An air connection from the AIR system
    d. A platinum catalyst
    e. All of the above

16. Which catalytic converter system uses air from the AIR system?
    a. Two-way converter
    b. Three-way converter
    c. Four-way converter
    d. All of the above
    e. None of the above

17. Carburetors today:
    a. All have idle limiters
    b. Have no pollution controls on them
    c. All are designed to use lead
    d. All of the above
    e. None of the above

18. Which compression ratio is for engines that are designed to reduce emissions?
    a. 12:1   d. 8:1
    b. 11:1   e. 4:1
    c. 10:1

19. Which of the following has/have been changed to enhance vaporization of the fuel?
    a. Combustion chambers
    b. Intake manifolds
    c. Exhaust flow
    d. Catalytic converters
    e. PCV systems

20. Which of the following is/are part of the computer-controlled systems to reduce pollution?
    a. EGR valves
    b. Carbon canister
    c. EFE (early fuel evaporation)
    d. All of the above
    e. None of the above

The following questions are similar in format to ASE (Automotive Service Excellence) test questions.

21. Technician A says that the PCV valve should not rattle when it is shaken. Technician B says that if the PCV valve rattles when shaken, the PCV valve is not plugged. Who is right?
    a. A only
    b. B only
    c. Both A and B
    d. Neither A nor B

22. Technician A says that the EGR valve can be tested by pushing up inside of the valve and seeing if the diaphragm moves freely. Technician B says that the EGR valve can be checked using the vacuum tester. Who is right?
    a. A only
    b. B only
    c. Both A and B
    d. Neither A nor B

23. Technician A says that the charcoal canister has no filter to be changed. Technician B says that the charcoal canister has a filter that should be changed at regular recommended intervals. Who is right?
    a. A only
    b. B only
    c. Both A and B
    d. Neither A nor B

24. Technician A says that a collapsed fuel tank is caused by too much vacuum in the tank. Technician B says a collapsed fuel tank is caused by a bad fuel tank cap. Who is right?
    a. A only
    b. B only
    c. Both A and B
    d. Neither A nor B

25. Technician A says computer controls can be used on the EGR system. Technician B says computer controls can be used on the PCV system. Who is right?
    a. A only
    b. B only
    c. Both A and B
    d. Neither A nor B

26. Fuel is leaking near the front of the engine. Technician A says the problem could be the carbon canister. Technician B says the problem could be the EGR valve system. Who is right?
    a. A only
    b. B only
    c. Both A and B
    d. Neither A nor B

27. A vehicle has a plugged catalytic converter. Technician A says the problem is caused from using leaded fuel. Technician B says the problem could be a plugged PCV system. Who is right?
    a. A only
    b. B only
    c. Both A and B
    d. Neither A nor B

28. Technician A says a common problem with the AIR system is oil leakage from the bearings. Technician B says a common problem with the AIR system is loose drive belts. Who is right?
    a. A only
    b. B only
    c. Both A and B
    d. Neither A nor B

Essay

29. Describe the purpose and operation of the PCV system.

30. Describe the purpose and operation of the EGR system.

31. What is the carbon canister used for?

32. What is a heat stove used for on a pollution control system?

33. Describe the operation of a catalytic converter.

34. Define the S-V ratio when dealing with combustion chambers.

35. List several ways in which pollution has been reduced by changing the combustion chamber or air-fuel mixtures, or both.

Short Answer

36. The on-board computer on a vehicle is used to _____ the carbon canister.

37. With the use of the on-board computer, the EGR valve can be either open, closed, or _____.

38. If the PCV valve is bad, it most likely will produce a _____ idle.

39. If the heated intake air system is damaged, the engine will run rough during _____ conditions.

40. If the catalytic converter is plugged, the engine will have a _____.

POWER TRANSMISSION SYSTEMS

CHAPTER 25

Manual Transmissions

INTRODUCTION   Torque that is produced at the end of the crankshaft by the engine must be transmitted to the driving wheels. To accomplish this, torque must first pass through the clutch and transmission. This chapter is about these two components.

OBJECTIVES   After reading this chapter, you should be able to:

- Identify the purpose and operation of the clutch.
- Define the purpose of the standard, or manual, transmission.
- Analyze the purpose of different gear ratios.
- Describe the operation and gear selection of the manual transmission.
- State the purpose and operation of synchronizers.

- Identify transmission lubricants.
- Compare different types of transmissions.
- Identify the operation of linkages and accessories used on manual transmissions.
- State common problems, diagnosis, and service suggestions pertaining to manual transmissions.

✔ SAFETY CHECKLIST ✔

When working with manual transmissions, keep these important safety precautions in mind.

✔ Always wear OSHA-approved safety glasses when working on the manual transmission.

✔ Always use the proper tools when working on manual transmissions.

✔ Be careful not to crush your fingers or hands when lifting a transmission, as it is very heavy.

✔ When working on the transmission, always support the vehicle safely on the hoist or on the jack stands.

✔ Always use a transmission jack stand when removing a transmission from a vehicle.

Some of the information in this chapter can help you prepare for the National Institute for Automotive Service Excellence (ASE) certification tests. The test most directly related to this chapter is entitled

MANUAL DRIVE TRAIN AND AXLES (TEST A3).

The content areas that closely parallel this chapter are

CLUTCH DIAGNOSIS AND REPAIR, TRANSMISSION DIAGNOSIS AND REPAIR, AND TRANSAXLE DIAGNOSIS AND REPAIR.

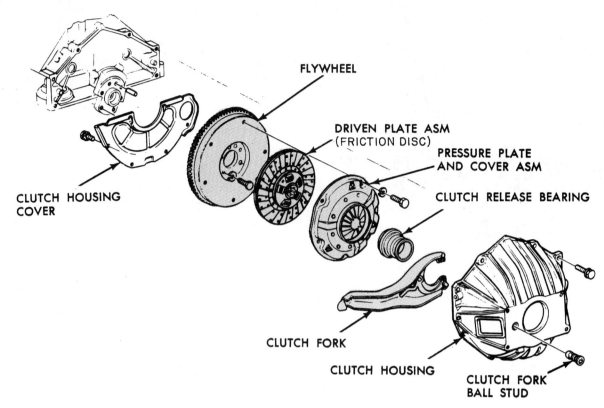

FIGURE 25–1.   The main parts of the clutch. *(Courtesy of Chevrolet Motor Division, General Motors Corporation)*

25.1   CLUTCH SYSTEMS

Purpose of Clutches

All standard or manual transmissions have a *clutch* to engage or disengage the transmission. While the engine is running, there are times when the driving wheels must not turn. The clutch is used as a mechanism to engage or disengage the transmission and driving wheels. If clutches were not used, every time the vehicle came to a stop, the engine would stop. Since this is not practical, the operator can engage or disengage the clutch when needed.

The clutch is designed to engage the transmission gradually. This will eliminate jumping abruptly from no connection at all to a direct solid connection to the engine. This is done by allowing a certain amount of slippage between the input and the output shafts on the clutch. Several components are needed to do this. These include the pressure plate, driven plate or friction disc, flywheel, clutch release bearing, clutch fork, and clutch housing. These are shown in *Figure 25–1*.

Figure 25–2 shows the basic principle of engaging a clutch. The left side is considered the drive member, or input, to the clutch. It is composed of the flywheel and *pressure plate*. The output is the center driven member, or *friction disc*. The output of this shaft drives the transmission. When the pressure plate is withdrawn, the engine can revolve freely and is disconnected from the driven member and the transmission. When the pressure plate moves in the direction of

the arrows, however, the friction disc is forced to turn at the same speed of the input, or driving, member. *Figure 25–3* shows the actual components including the flywheel, pressure plate, and friction disc.

Pressure Plate Assembly

The pressure plate is designed to squeeze or clamp the friction disc between itself and the flywheel. The pressure plate has several components, *Figure 25–4*. They include the cover, a series of springs, release fingers, and the pressure plate. The pressure plate and the flywheel have smooth machined surfaces to clamp the clutch disc. The pressure plate cover is bolted to the flywheel and turns at exactly the

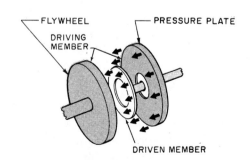

FIGURE 25–2.   When the clutch is engaged, the driven member is squeezed between the two driving members. The transmission is attached to the driven member. *(Courtesy of General Motors Corporation)*

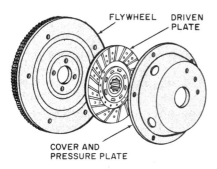

FIGURE 25–3. The actual components of a typical clutch system. *(Courtesy of General Motors Corporation)*

same speed as the flywheel. The springs are used to squeeze or clamp the friction disc between the two plates. Several types of springs are used. The *diaphragm spring* shown in *Figure 25–5* is the type currently used. It consists of a series of spring plates used to force or clamp the friction disc.

Pressure plates also have some form of linkage used to engage or disengage the friction disc, *Figure 25–6*. When the release levers are pushed in at the center, the pressure plate surface is moved to the right. This action disengages the friction disc. When there is no force on the release levers, the pressure plate springs force the pressure plate to tighten down and squeeze the friction disc to start it rotating.

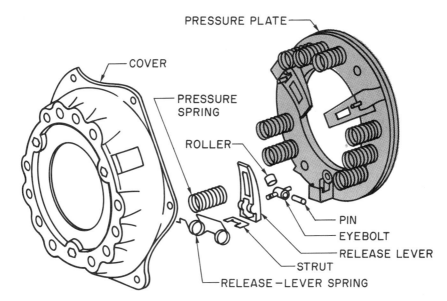

FIGURE 25–4. The pressure plate is constructed of several parts. *(Courtesy of Chevrolet Division, General Motors Corporation)*

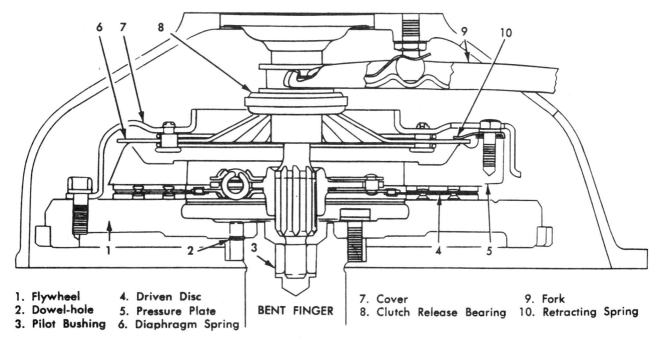

1. Flywheel
2. Dowel-hole
3. Pilot Bushing
4. Driven Disc
5. Pressure Plate
6. Diaphragm Spring

BENT FINGER

7. Cover
8. Clutch Release Bearing
9. Fork
10. Retracting Spring

FIGURE 25–5. The diaphragm spring is also used to help force the pressure plate against the clutch driven disc. *(Courtesy of Chevrolet Division, General Motors Corporation)*

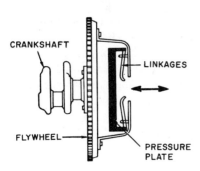

FIGURE 25–6. All clutches must have some type of linkage to engage and disengage the clutch. *(Courtesy of General Motors Corporation)*

Friction Disc

The friction disc is the output of the clutch system. When the clutch assembly spins, it drives the manual transmission. The clutch is made of several parts. These are shown in *Figure 25–7*. The center of the clutch has a spline hole for the transmission input shaft connection. The grooves on both sides of the clutch disc lining prevent sticking of the plate to the flywheel and pressure plate. Frictional facings are attached to each side of the clutch disc. These are made of various materials. Several years ago they were made of cotton and asbestos fibers, woven or molded together. However, because of increased concern for the dangerous effects of *asbestos* (see Chapter 2), other materials are also being used. Fiberglass is now gaining in popularity as one material used on friction discs. On some clutches copper wires are also woven into the material for additional strength.

The clutch has a flexible center to absorb the *torsional vibration* of the crankshaft. Steel compression springs permit the disc to rotate slightly in relation to the pressure plate.

The cushion springs are raised to eliminate chatter when the clutch is engaged. These springs cause the contact pressure on the facings to rise gradually as the springs flatten out when the clutch is engaged.

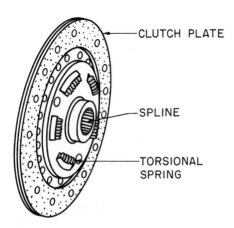

FIGURE 25–7. The clutch disc has torsional springs to eliminate jerky starting.

Clutch Release Bearing (Throwout Bearing)

The clutch release bearing, also called a throwout bearing, is a ball-thrust bearing held within the clutch housing. The bearing is moved by the clutch pedal and linkage to engage or disengage the pressure plate. When the clutch pedal is pressed down, the clutch release bearing pushes against the revolving pressure plate release levers. This action disengages the clutch. When the clutch pedal is released, the clutch release bearing moves back. The springs in the pressure plate now engage the clutch disc, *Figure 25–8*.

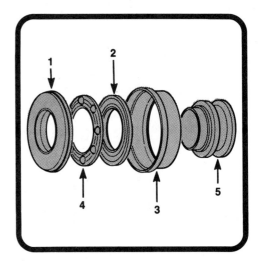

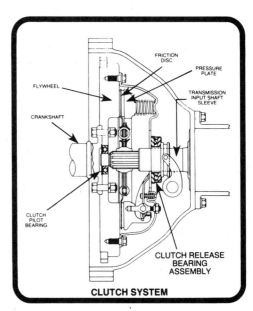

FIGURE 25–8. The main elements in the clutch release bearing are the two washer-shaped rings (1,2) in which the raceways for the balls are machined. A steel housing (3) holds the rings and balls (4) together. The bearing is pressed onto the carrier (5) to complete the assembly. The clutch bearing is located on the transmission input shaft sleeve. *(Courtesy of Federal-Mogul Corporation)*

Clutch Linkage

The purpose of the clutch linkage is to engage and disengage the clutch. As the operator moves the clutch pedal down, the clutch release bearing pushes against the release levers to disengage the clutch. Depending on the design of the vehicle, several clutch linkages are used. These may include the rod and lever, the cable type, and the hydraulic linkage. The rod and lever system is shown in *Figure 25–9*. As the clutch is pushed in, the clutch fork moves to the left. Note the pivot points. When the clutch fork moves to the left, the clutch release bearing moves to the right. This action disengages the clutch from the pressure plate.

The cable type of linkage uses a flexible cable connected from the clutch pedal to the clutch fork. As the clutch pedal is pressed down, the flexible cable forces the clutch fork to move. *Figure 25–10* shows how the cable is attached to the clutch fork.

The hydraulic system consists of a master cylinder and a *slave cylinder*. When pressure is applied to the clutch pedal, hydraulic pressure is built up in the master cylinder. The pressure is sent through hydraulic tubing to the slave cylinder. Here the pressure is used to move the clutch fork to engage or disengage the clutch disc, *Figure 25–11*.

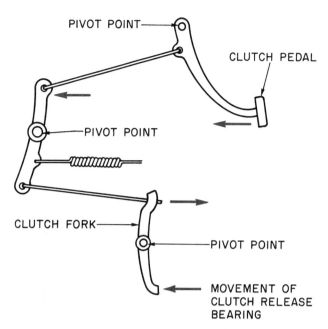

FIGURE 25–9.   This rod and level system is used to engage and disengage the clutch.

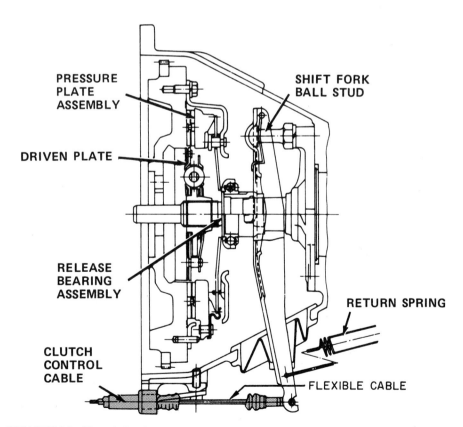

FIGURE 25–10.   A flexible cable can be used to disengage the clutch. *(Courtesy of American Isuzu Motors, Inc.)*

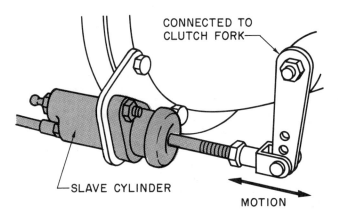

FIGURE 25–11. A slave cylinder can be used to engage and disengage the clutch fork.

CAR CLINIC

PROBLEM: Poor Shifting

A customer indicates that the five-speed manual transmission has been difficult to downshift into first gear and is getting worse. The vehicle is used mostly in the city. Downshifting into first gear makes driving much easier in traffic. It is becoming more difficult to make the downshift and gears are clashing.

SOLUTION:

Manual transmissions have synchronizers to enable ease of downshifting. The synchronizers are used to get both gears at the same speed before engaging them. Replace the first gear synchronizer, and the problem should be eliminated.

25.2 DESIGN OF TRANSMISSIONS

Purpose of the Transmission

The purpose of a transmission is to apply different torque forces to the driving wheels. Vehicles are required to perform under many types of loads. Stopping and starting, heavy loads, high speeds and small loads are examples of the different demands placed on the vehicle. The transmission is designed to change the torque applied to the driving wheels for different applications. In addition, the transmission is used to reverse the vehicle direction for parking and to provide neutral (no power) to the wheels. Normally, less torque is needed with higher speeds and smaller loads. When slower speeds and higher loads are used, more torque is needed.

Levers and Forces

In order to understand how gears in a transmission work, levers and forces must first be defined. A *lever* is a device that changes forces and distances. For example, in *Figure 25–12 (A)*, a lever has an input, a *fulcrum*, and an output. When a force is applied to one side over a certain distance, a resulting force is produced with a certain distance. Force times distance on the input will always equal force times distance on the output. Therefore, work input always equals work output.

If the fulcrum is positioned farther to the right as shown in *Figure 25–12 (B)* several things occur. First, the work input will again equal the work output. However, the output force will be much greater, while the input distance will be much greater. By changing the position of the fulcrum, different forces can be obtained while giving up distance.

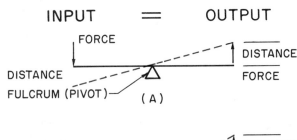

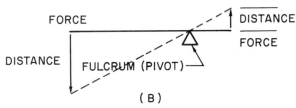

FIGURE 25–12. When the pivot point is moved to the right as in (B), increased forces can be obtained. However, the distance traveled is less. Force times distance input will always equal force times distance output.

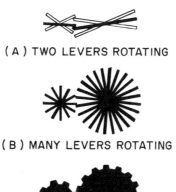

(A) TWO LEVERS ROTATING

(B) MANY LEVERS ROTATING

(C) GEARS ROTATING

FIGURE 25–13. Gears can be used to increase torque just as levers are used to increase force. *(Courtesy of General Motors Corporation)*

Torque and Torque Multiplication

The principle of levers can also be applied to gears. A gear can be considered a set of spinning levers. A set of gears can increase or decrease torque the same way that levers increase or decrease force. This is shown in *Figure 25–13 (A)*. One lever is pushing a second lever. The length of each lever determines how much force will be created on them. For example, if the short lever pushes against the longer lever, the longer lever will move less distance but will have more force. If a series of levers is attached as shown in Figure 25–13 (B), then a continuous torque is developed. When applied to gears as shown in Figure 25–13 (C), a small gear can increase torque in a larger gear. However, as with levers, the larger gear moves less distance than the input gear.

Gear Ratios

The amount of torque increased from the input to the output depends on the relative size of the gears. The difference in size between the input and output gears is called the gear ratio. The best way to show a gear ratio is by counting the number of teeth on each gear. *Figure 25–14* shows a set of gears. The input gear has 12 teeth and the output gear has 24 teeth. It will take two revolutions of the input gear to get the output gear to turn once. The speed of the output gear will be half the speed of the input gear. However, the torque will be doubled on the output. The gear ratio is stated as 24 to 12, or 2 to 1. This means that the input gear will turn two times while the output gear will turn one time.

Manual Transmission Parts

The transmission is a case of gears located behind the clutch. The output of the clutch drives the set of gears. The case is attached to the clutch housing. There are several shafts

GEAR RATIO = 2:1
(2 REVOLUTIONS INPUT TO
1 REVOLUTION OUTPUT)

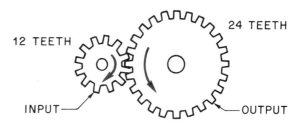

24 TEETH

12 TEETH

INPUT

OUTPUT

FIGURE 25–14. Gear ratios are determined by comparing the number of teeth on the output with the number of teeth on the input. This gear ratio is 24 to 12, or 2 to 1.

with different-sized gears inside the case. As the gears are shifted to different ratios, different torques can be selected for different operational conditions. *Figure 25–15* shows a diagram of the internal parts of a manual transmission. Although there are many parts in the transmission, the main ones include the drive, or input gear, the countershaft gear (also called the cluster gear) with four gears on it, the main shaft with two gears on it, and the reverse idler gear. The countershaft gears all turn at the same speed. The low and reverse gear and the second and high-speed gear are able to slide on the main shaft spline.

Gear Selection

First gear is selected by connecting the gears so as to produce the greatest torque and the lowest output speed. This condition is used to start the vehicle moving or to go up a very steep hill. This is done as shown in *Figure 25–16*.

NEUTRAL

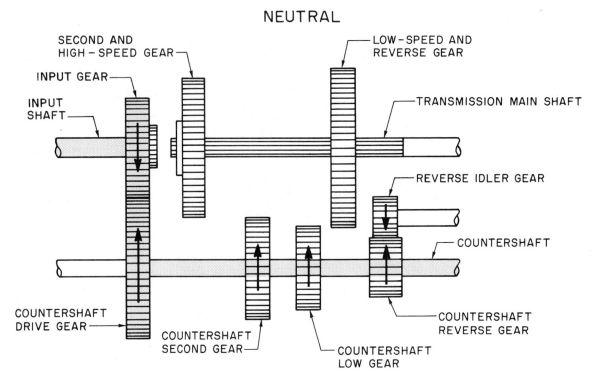

FIGURE 25–15. The main parts of a transmission are shown for reference.

FIRST

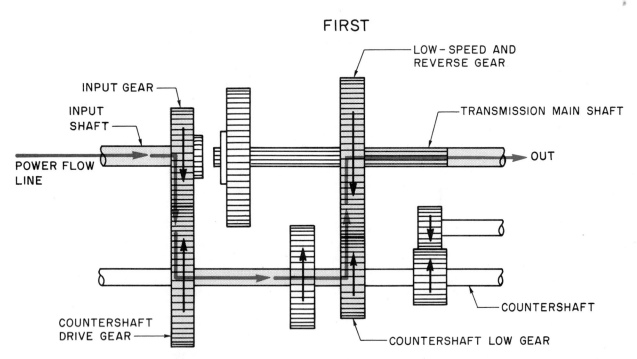

FIGURE 25–16. Low or first gear is selected by moving the low and reverse gear in mesh with the countershaft low gear.

When the shift lever is moved to low or first gear, the low and reverse gear on the main shaft meshes with the low gear on the countershaft. Power is now transmitted from the input shaft to the countershaft. From the countershaft, the power is transmitted to the main shaft. Because of the gear ratios, the input shaft speed is about three times as fast as the speed of the output main shaft. However, the output shaft has about three times as much torque as the input shaft.

Second gear is selected by connecting the second and high-speed gear on the main shaft in mesh with the second gear on the countershaft. See *Figure 25–17*. Note that the gears used for low or first gear have been disengaged and are

SECOND

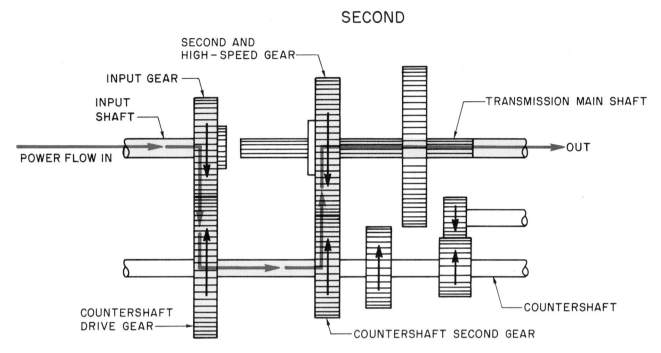

FIGURE 25–17.   Second gear is selected by meshing the second and high-speed gear with the clutch gear.

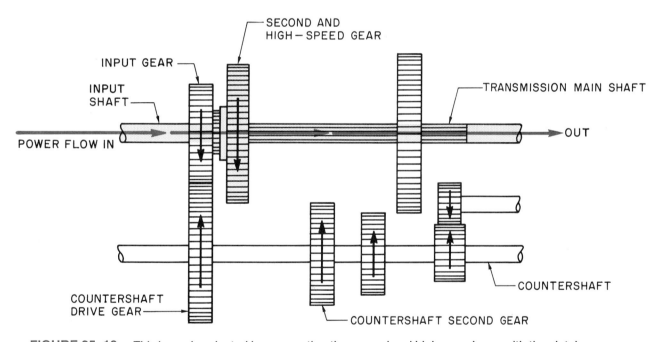

FIGURE 25–18.   Third gear is selected by connecting the second and high-speed gear with the clutch gear.

not in mesh. In this case, the ratio of input shaft to output shaft is about 2 to 1. The speed has been increased slightly, while torque has been decreased.

Third gear is selected by connecting the second and high-speed gear directly to the input shaft. This causes the input and output to rotate at the same speed, *Figure 25–18*. The ratio is now 1 to 1. In this condition, maximum speed with minimum torque is produced.

Reverse gear is selected by connecting the low-speed and reverse gear with the reverse *idler gear*. When the extra idler gear is added to the gear train, the direction of the output speed reverses. Reverse is considered a very low-speed, high-torque gear arrangement.

Types of Gears

Several types of gears are used in manual transmissions. Spur gears are found in older transmissions. These gears are typically very noisy. In order to reduce noise, helical gears are now used. Helical gears have the teeth at an angle. This produces a smoother meshing of teeth between the two gears. It also causes more surface contact between the teeth, which makes them much stronger. Most manual transmissions use helical gears. A third type of gear is called the internal gear. The gear teeth are machined inside a ring. A fourth type of gear is called the compound gear. A compound gear is of several gears of different sizes placed on a shaft. All the gears spin at the same speed. The countershaft gear in a manual transmission is called a compound gear. *Figure 25–19* shows examples of different types of gears.

Purpose of Synchronizers

During normal shifting patterns, gears must be engaged and disengaged. Most gears, however, are not turning at the same speed before being engaged. To eliminate gears clashing with each other during normal downshifting or upshifting, *synchronizers* are used. Synchronizers are used in all forward speeds in most of today's manual transmissions. There are several types of synchronizers, but they all work on a similar principle. If the gear speeds can be synchronized or put at the same speed, they will mesh easily and there will be little clash or clatter.

Synchronizer Operation

Figure 25–20 shows how a synchronizer operates. The assembly is made of an input gear, several cone surfaces, a ring gear sliding sleeve, the hub, several spring-loaded steel balls, and the internal gear. The goal is to mesh the input gear with the internal gear. If the internal gear turns, then the output shaft will also turn.

For ease of understanding, view the input gear as spinning and the output shaft, hub, and internal gear as not spinning. As the shift fork is moved to the left, it moves the ring gear sliding sleeve and the hub to the left. The hub and the ring gear are splined together. As the movement to the left continues, the two cone surfaces eventually begin to rub together. This action brings both objects to the same speed. The internal gear is still not in mesh with the input gear at this point. As the shift fork is moved farther to the left, the ring gear sliding sleeve continues to move while the hub remains in the same position. As the ring gear continues to move left, it eventually meshes easily with the input gear because both are spinning at the same speed.

In most transmissions, the synchronizers are moved rather than the gears. This type of transmission is called a constant mesh type. *Figure 25–21* shows this principle. The gears are meshed at the start, but they are spinning on bearings on the output shaft. When the first gear synchronizer is moved to the left, it brings the output shaft to the same speed as the first gear. When the second gear synchronizer is moved to the right, it brings the second output shaft to the same speed as second gear. When the third gear synchronizer is moved to the left, the output shaft is brought to the same speed as the input gear. For simplicity, the reverse gear is not shown here.

Although many synchronizers may differ in appearance, the basic design is the same. Most synchronizers use a synchronizer ring (called a blocker ring) to replace the internal cone. Keys, rather than the small spring-loaded balls are used on some synchronizers. *Figure 25–22* shows a disassembled synchronizer.

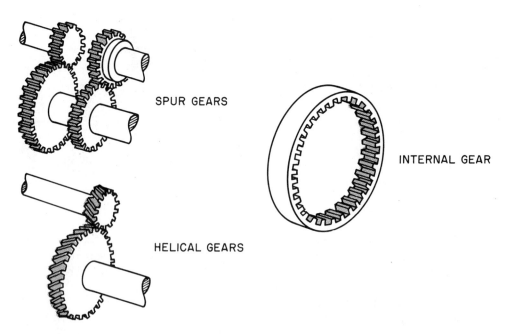

SPUR GEARS

HELICAL GEARS

INTERNAL GEAR

FIGURE 25–19. Several types of gears are used in manual transmissions. These may include the spur, helical, and internal gears.

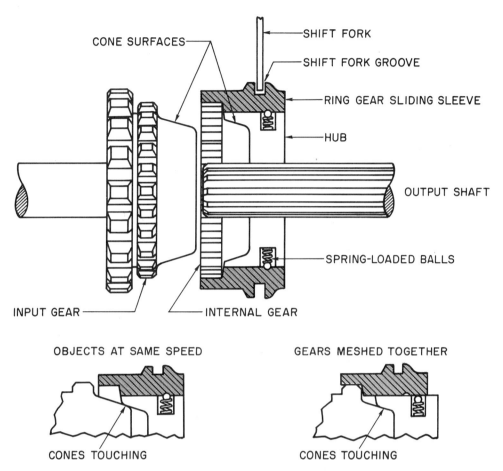

FIGURE 25-20. On a synchronizer, as the hub and internal gear assembly are moved to the left, the cone surfaces begin to touch. This brings both shafts to the same speed. As the shift fork continues to move, it eventually slides the ring gear sliding sleeve in mesh with the input gear.

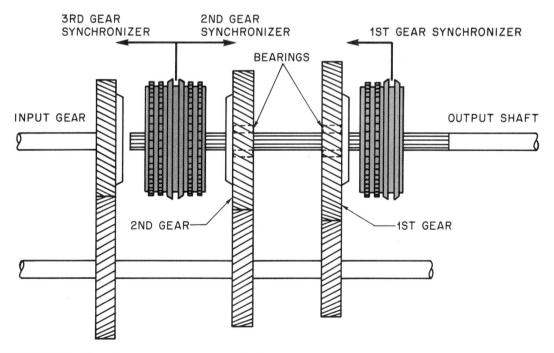

FIGURE 25-21. In most manual transmissions, the gears are always meshed. However, the synchronizers actually engage and disengage the gears on the main output shaft for correct operation.

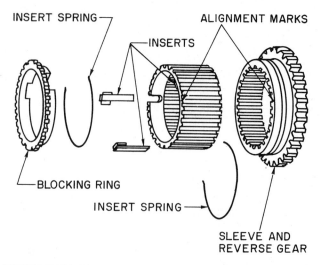

FIGURE 25–22. A disassembled synchronizer.

Overdrive Systems

The purpose of an *overdrive* system in a transmission is to decrease the speed of the engine during high vehicle speed operation. If this is done, the engine fuel mileage will improve. However, the torque at high speeds will be reduced. On transmissions without overdrive, the highest gear ratio is usually 1 to 1. On overdrive transmissions, the ratio may be 0.8 to 1 as shown in *Figure 25–23*. This means the engine crankshaft has slowed down slightly. This is typically done by adding another gear in the gear train. The size of the gear and the direction of power through the transmission cause the engine to slow slightly at the higher vehicle speeds. On older transmissions, the overdrive gear was engaged by mechanical means. On modern transmissions, a synchronizer clutch or electrical solenoid is used to engage the overdrive gear. If the transmission has an overdrive gear, the gear shift knob often has the letters *OD* or similar representation stamped on it.

Transmission Case

The transmission case is used to hold the gears for proper shifting. The case is bolted to the clutch housing with several bolts. It is made of aluminum or cast iron for strength and support. The transmission case also includes an extension housing that contains the transmission output shaft. The housing is bolted to the rear of the transmission case. *Figure 25–24* shows the complete transmission with the case and the extension housing. The housing is used as an engine mount base and holds a rear seal to the transmission. The extension housing also includes a hole for the speedometer cable. The speedometer cable is driven from the output shaft by the speedometer gear.

Transmission Lubrication

Many transmissions use gear oil for lubrication. Gear oil is a type of lubrication used to keep gears well lubricated. Each manufacturer typically recommends its own type of gear oil. In addition, gear oils have different SAE viscosities. Typical viscosity ranges recommended by manufacturers are from 75 to 90 or more, depending on the outside temperature. The viscosity recommendation increases as the outside temperature increases.

Today, manufacturers are also recommending motor oils for use in manual transmissions. For example it is not uncommon for a manufacturer to recommend engine oil 5W-30 SG for the transmission fluid. The exact viscosity is determined by the outside temperature, as with engine oil. See Chapter 11 for more detail on viscosities and API oil ratings. In addition, some manufacturers also recommend automatic fluid such as Dextron II ATF. Refer to the service manual for the recommended type.

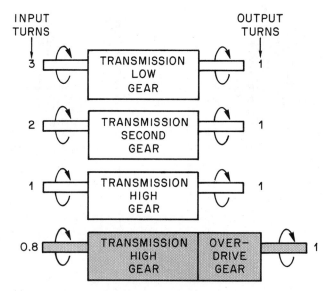

FIGURE 25–23. An overdrive gear has a ratio of approximately 0.8 to 1. This means that the input shaft is going slower than the output shaft. This ratio reduces engine speed and improves fuel mileage. However, torque at high speeds is reduced.

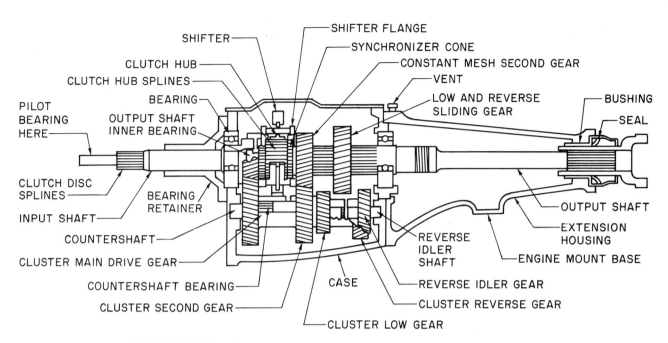

FIGURE 25–24.   A complete transmission, case, and extension housing.

25.3 TYPES OF TRANSMISSIONS

Purposes of Different Transmissions

Now that basic transmission components have been studied, other styles and types can be discussed. Vehicle designs have been changing over the past several years. Front wheel drive vehicles are now very popular. In addition, many manufacturers are using smaller engines. Because of these changes, several types of transmissions have been developed. These include four-speed, five-speed, and transaxle transmissions.

Four-Speed Transmissions

The four-speed manual transmission has an additional gear set to produce four forward gears rather than three. With four gears, a wider range of torque characteristics is available. Increased torque range is usually needed for smaller engines. *Figure 25–25* shows an example of a four-speed transmission. The major difference is that the countershaft has four forward gears rather than three. Synchronizers are also used to perform the shifting.

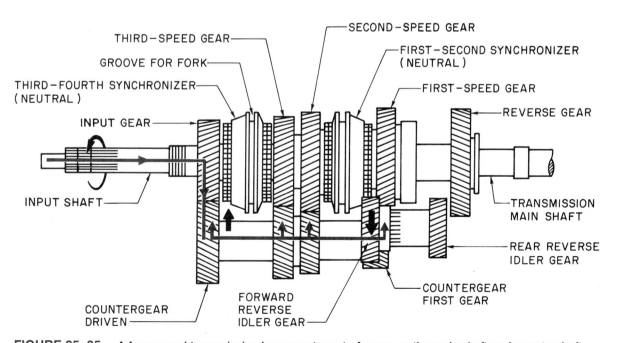

FIGURE 25–25.   A four-speed transmission has an extra set of gears on the main shaft and countershaft.

Five-Speed Transmissions

Five-speed transmissions are used for small engine displacements. With five gears, the range of torque is increased so that a smaller engine can be used. *Figure 25–26* shows an example of a five-speed transmission. In order to get five speeds, an additional set of gears is added to the transmission. Synchronizers are again used to engage and disengage the gears. In each gear shown, the transmission of mechanical energy is from the input shaft, to the countershaft, to the

specific gear on the main or upper shaft, through the synchronizer, and to the output shaft. In this particular case, the fifth gear is considered an overdrive gear. Fourth gear is direct drive.

Transaxle System

The *transaxle* system is used on front wheel drive vehicles that have the transmission and final drive gearing placed together. It is mounted on the rear of the engine in such a

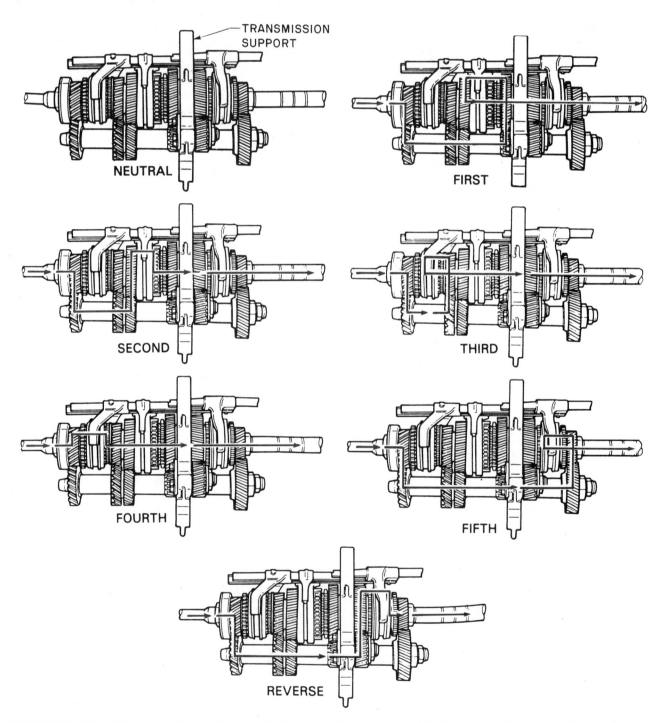

FIGURE 25–26.   A five-speed transmission, with the power flow for each of the five gears. *(Courtesy of American Isuzu Motors, Inc.)*

way that the output of the transaxle feeds directly to the front wheels. There are many designs used for transaxles. The principles are much the same. *Figure 25–27* shows an example of a typical four-speed transaxle. The countershaft, called the input cluster gear, is attached directly to the clutch system. The gears are in constant mesh with synchronizers that are used to engage and disengage each gear. The output of the main shaft is used to drive the differential. *Figure 25–28* shows a complete breakdown of a five-speed transaxle. Note

that in addition to the individual parts, there are several major assemblies. These include the countershaft assembly (item 21), the mainshaft assembly (item 17), and the differential assembly (item 22). Note that the synchronizers are placed on the mainshaft and countershaft assemblies. When servicing similar transaxles, the service technician will need to become familiar with all the major parts and assemblies. The differential is discussed in a later chapter.

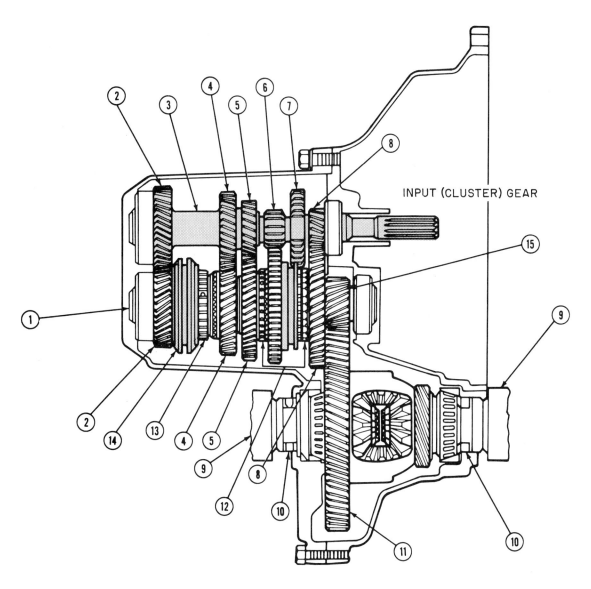

LEGEND:

1. MAINSHAFT
2. 4TH SPEED GEARS
3. INPUT CLUSTER
4. 3RD SPEED GEARS
5. 2ND SPEED GEARS
6. REVERSE GEAR
7. REVERSE IDLER GEAR
8. 1ST SPEED GEARS

9. HALF SHAFTS
10. DIFFERENTIAL OIL SEALS
11. FINAL DRIVE RING GEAR
12. 1ST/2ND SPEED SYNCHRONIZER
   BLOCKER RINGS
13. 3RD/4TH SPEED SYNCHRONIZER HUB
14. 3RD/4TH SPEED SYNCHRONIZER SLEEVE
15. PINION GEAR – PART OF MAINSHAFT

FIGURE 25–27. A four-speed transaxle has the differential attached to the manual transmission. Most front wheel drive vehicles have similar designs. *(Courtesy of Ford Motor Company, Parts and Service Division)*

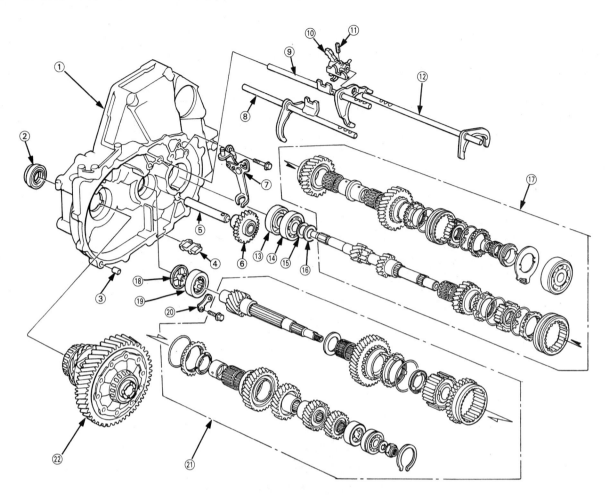

①	CLUTCH HOUSING	⑨	3rd/4th SHIFT FORK	⑰	MAINSHAFT ASSEMBLY
②	OIL SEAL	⑩	5th/REVERSE SHIFT PIECE	⑱	OIL GUIDE PLATE
③	DOWEL PIN	⑪	SPRING PIN	⑲	NEEDLE BEARING
④	MAGNET	⑫	5th SHIFT FORK	⑳	RETAINING PLATE
⑤	REVERSE IDLER GEAR SHAFT	⑬	OIL SEAL	㉑	COUNTERSHAFT ASSEMBLY
⑥	REVERSE IDLER GEAR	⑭	BALL BEARING	㉒	DIFFERENTIAL ASSEMBLY
⑦	REVERSE SHIFT FORK	⑮	SPRING WASHER		
⑧	1st/2nd SHIFT FORK	⑯	WASHER		

FIGURE 25–28.   This five-speed transaxle system has the synchronizers placed on the mainshaft and countershaft. *(Courtesy of Honda Motor Company, Ltd.)*

25.4   LEVERS, LINKAGES, AND ACCESSORIES

Shifting Forks

On the manual transmission the gears must be moved or shifted to engage different gears. Shifting forks are used to move the synchronizers back and forth to engage the gears. There are several types of shifting forks. *Figure 25–29* shows an example of a disassembled shifting fork mechanism. It is positioned in such a manner that it fits over the synchronizer assembly.

Figure 25–30 shows the third and fourth gear shifting fork assembly as a whole. As the operator moves the shift linkage, the fork moves the synchronizer for a specific gear.

Detent springs, balls, and rollers are used to hold the shifting fork in the correct gear position to ensure full engage-

ment. *Figure 25–31* shows examples of detent springs and balls and rollers used on a manual transmission. A small groove is cut in the shift fork shaft. As the shift fork moves to its fully engaged position, the detent spring forces the detent roller down into the groove. The pressure from the spring holds the shift fork in place so it doesn't become disengaged from the gear.

Shift Mechanisms

There are many designs of shifting mechanisms. The style and design depend on the position of the shift lever, the vehicle style, the year of the vehicle, the manufacturer, the number of gears, and the type of transmission. Certain vehicles have the shift lever on the steering wheel column, while others have a floor shift system. Both mechanical

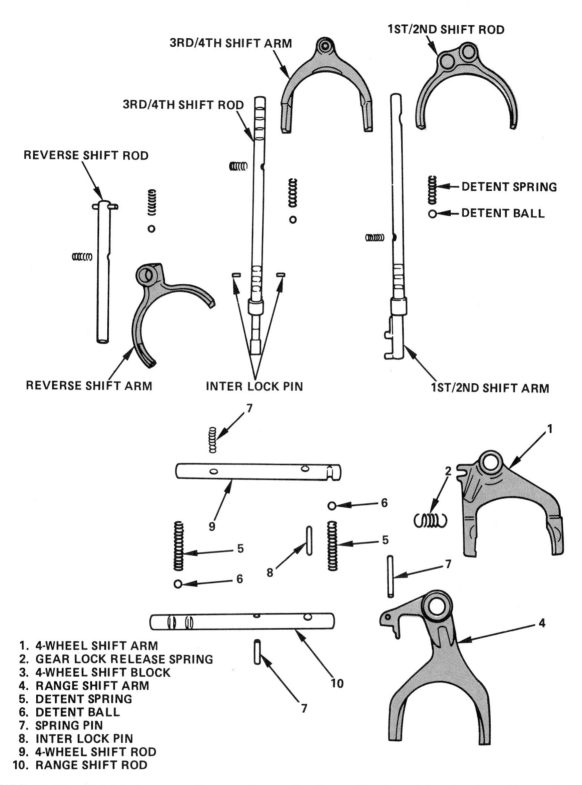

3RD/4TH SHIFT ARM

1ST/2ND SHIFT ROD

3RD/4TH SHIFT ROD

REVERSE SHIFT ROD

DETENT SPRING

DETENT BALL

REVERSE SHIFT ARM

INTER LOCK PIN

1ST/2ND SHIFT ARM

1. 4-WHEEL SHIFT ARM
2. GEAR LOCK RELEASE SPRING
3. 4-WHEEL SHIFT BLOCK
4. RANGE SHIFT ARM
5. DETENT SPRING
6. DETENT BALL
7. SPRING PIN
8. INTER LOCK PIN
9. 4-WHEEL SHIFT ROD
10. RANGE SHIFT ROD

FIGURE 25–29.   Clutch forks are used to move the synchronizers. *(Courtesy of American Isuzu Motors, Inc.)*

linkage and cables can be used to transfer the shift lever movement to the shifting forks. ***Figure 25–32*** shows a typical floor shift mechanism. As the shift (change) lever is moved to select the correct gear, one of the two shafts (cables) is moved. To select between a group of forward gears or reverse

gear the "select cable" is moved. To shift from one forward gear to another, the "shift cable" is moved. Each cable is fed through a tube attached to the frame. This allows it to slide in and out of the tube. The moving cable is then attached to the transmission shift forks to shift the gears. Refer to the

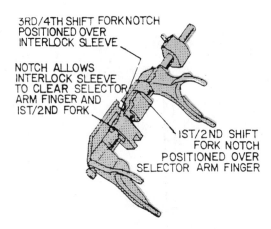

FIGURE 25–30. The third and fourth gear shift fork assembly. *(Courtesy of Motor Publications, Domestic Transmission Manual)*

specific maintenance manual specifications for the type and correct adjustment of the shift mechanisms.

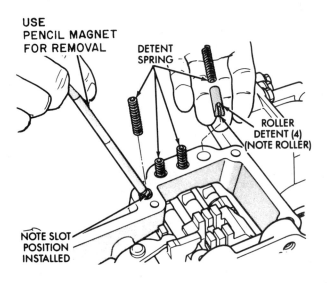

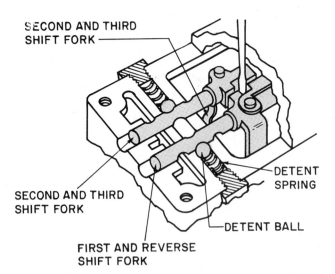

FIGURE 25–31. These detent springs, balls, and rollers are used to hold the shift fork in gear. *(Courtesy of Motor Publications, Domestic Transmission Manual)*

CAR CLINIC

PROBLEM: Clutch Chatter

An older vehicle with about 70,000 miles on it has a standard or manual transmission. When the clutch pedal is released, a noticeable chatter is felt in the vehicle. What could be the problem?

SOLUTION:

Clutch chatter is most often caused by oil getting on to the clutch and pressure plate surface. The friction of the clutch against the flywheel and pressure plate causes the oil to become very sticky. This causes the chatter when the clutch pedal is released and the clutch tries to engage. Most often the oil comes from a leaky rear main seal on the engine. Replace the rear main seal on the engine to eliminate this problem.

Other Accessories

The speedometer in most vehicles is driven from the output shaft on the manual transmission. A small drive gear is attached to the output shaft. The speedometer gear is then inserted into a hole in the transmission extension housing. The speedometer gear meshes with the gear attached to the transmission output shaft. On most vehicles, there is also an electrical hookup for the backup light switch and overdrive solenoid.

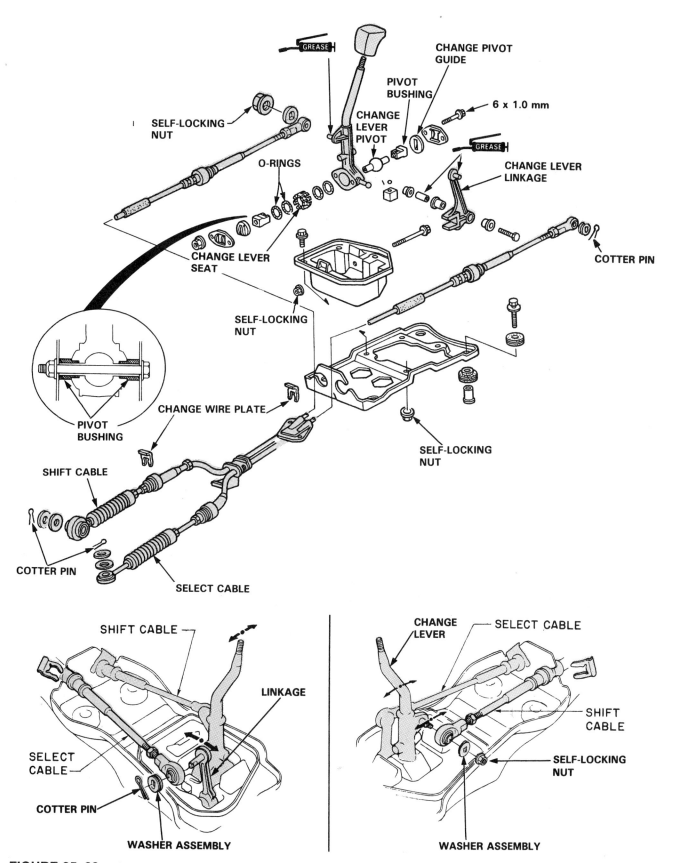

FIGURE 25–32.   A complete shift mechanism for a five-speed transaxle with a floor shift. *(Courtesy of Honda Motor Company, Ltd.)*

Problems, Diagnosis and Service

▷ ▶ ⬜ SAFETY PRECAUTIONS ⬜ ◀ ◁

1. When working under the vehicle on the transmission, make sure that no oil or antifreeze has been spilled. You may slip and seriously injure yourself.
2. Always disconnect the battery cables from the battery before working on any part of the manual transmission. This will eliminate any possibility of the engine accidentally being cranked during maintenance.
3. The manual transmission external housing is often used to support the rear of the engine. Always support the bottom of the engine adequately before removing the transmission. Special engine supports on the top of the engine can also be used.
4. On many vehicles, asbestos has been used as a material in the clutch friction disc. Be careful not to breathe any of the asbestos dust particles into your lungs. The dust particles are generally found in and around the clutch housing and inside the clutch and friction disc cover.
5. When installing gears, bearings, and gear shafts, be careful not to pinch your fingers between the part and the housing.
6. When removing or installing snap rings, always use a snap ring pliers. Snap rings have a high degree of spring tension. If not installed with a correct tool, a snap ring may fly off and injure your eye, face, or body.

PROBLEM: Faulty Clutch Mechanism

As the vehicle is accelerated and the clutch pedal released, the clutch seems to be slipping. In addition, as the clutch is engaged, a scraping sound is heard.

DIAGNOSIS

This problem is usually caused by several defective components. The clutch disc may slip because:

1. It is worn down and cannot be adjusted any further.
2. The clutch linkage is not adjusted correctly.

The scraping sound may come from two sources:

1. The clutch release (throwout) bearing may be damaged. This is normally damaged by constantly applying a slight pressure to the clutch pedal. This causes the clutch release bearing to spin constantly.
2. The clutch disc may be worn so badly that the rivets are scraping on the clutch pressure plate or on the flywheel. *Figure 25–33* shows a clutch trouble diagnosis chart.

If there are other problems with the clutch system refer to this chart for the condition, probable cause, and correction.

SERVICE

If the clutch linkage is correctly adjusted, the clutch and related components will need to be removed, serviced, and replaced if necessary. Each clutch system to be disassembled uses a different procedure. Refer to the service manual for the correct procedure. Use the following general procedure to remove and disassemble the clutch and related components.

1. Using the proper safety precautions position the car so that the transmission can be removed.
2. Remove the drive shaft(s).
3. Check to see if the rear of the engine is supported by the transmission. If it is, the engine must be supported while the transmission is being worked on. *Figure 25–34* shows an engine support used in the upper portion of the engine compartment.
4. Drain the gear oil from the transmission.
5. Disconnect the linkage used to shift the transmission.
6. Remove the speedometer cable from the transmission.
7. Remove any electrical wires attached to the transmission and mark for reassembly.
8. Support the transmission with a transmission jack stand.
9. Remove the bolts holding the transmission to the clutch housing. The transmission should now be easily removed and set on the workbench.
10. Disconnect the clutch linkage from the clutch fork.
11. At this point the clutch release bearing should be in a position to be removed easily.
12. Remove the bolts holding the clutch housing to the engine block.
13. At this point, the clutch pressure plate assembly should be observable.
14. Insert the clutch plate alignment tool into the clutch plate and crankshaft to support its weight when the bolts are removed. Using the correct wrench size, remove the clutch pressure plate.

CAUTION: The pressure plate is very heavy. Be careful not to drop the pressure plate on your feet.

The clutch disc should now be loose and easily removed.

CAUTION: Be careful not to breathe any of the asbestos particles from the clutch disc.

CLUTCH TROUBLE DIAGNOSIS

CONDITION	PROBABLE CAUSE	CORRECTION
Fails to Release (Pedal pressed to floor — shift lever does not move freely in and out of reverse gear or grinding noise shifting into Reverse)	a. Improper linkage adjustment. b. Improper pedal travel. c. Loose linkage or worn cable. d. Faulty pilot bearing. e. Faulty driven disc. f. Fork off ball stud. g. Clutch disc hub binding on clutch gear spline. h. Clutch disc warped or bent. i. Pivot rings loose, broken or worn.	a. Adjust linkage. b. Trim bumper stop and adjust linkage. c. Replace as necessary. d. Replace bearing. e. Replace disc. f. Install properly and* lubricate fingers at release bearing with wheel bearing grease. g. Repair or replace clutch gear and/or disc. h. Replace disc (run-out should not exceed .020"). i. Replace cover and pressure plate assembly. *Very lightly lubricate fingers
Slipping	a. Improper adjustment (no lash). b. Oil soaked driven disc. c. Worn facing or facing torn from disc. d. Warped pressure plate or flywheel. e. Weak diaphragm spring. f. Driven plate not seated in. g. Driven plate overheated.	a. Adjust linkage to spec. b. Install new disc and correct leak at its source. c. Replace disc. d. Replace pressure plate or flywheel. e. Replace pressure plate. (Be sure lash is checked before replacing plate.) f. Make 30 to 40 normal starts. CAUTION: Do Not Overheat. g. Allow to cool — check lash.
Grabbing (Chattering)	a. Oil on facing. Burned or glazed facings. b. Worn splines on clutch gear. c. Loose engine mountings. d. Warped pressure plate or flywheel. e. Burned or smeared resin on flywheel or pressure plate.	a. Install new disc and correct leak. b. Replace transmission clutch gear. c. Tighten or replace mountings. d. Replace pressure plate or flywheel. e. Sand off if superficial, replace burned or heat checked parts.
Rattling — Transmission Click	a. Weak retracting springs. b. Release fork loose on ball stud or in bearing groove. c. Oil in driven plate damper. d. Driven plate damper spring failure.	a. Replace pressure plate. b. Check ball stud and retaining. c. Replace driven disc. d. Replace driven disc.
Release Bearing Noise with Clutch Fully Engaged	a. Improper adjustment. No lash. b. Release bearing binding on transmission bearing retainer. c. Insufficient tension between clutch fork spring and ball stud. d. Fork improperly installed. e. Weak linkage return spring.	a. Adjust linkage. b. Clean, relubricate, check for burrs, nicks, etc. c. Replace fork. d. Install properly. e. Replace spring.
Noisy	a. Worn release bearing. b. Fork off ball stud (heavy clicking). c. Pilot bearing loose in crankshaft.	a. Replace bearing. b. Install properly and lubricate fork fingers at bearing. c. See Section 6 for bearing fits.
Pedal Stays on Floor When Disengaged	a. Bind in cable or release bearing. b. Springs weak in pressure plate. c. Springs being over traveled.	a. Replace cable. b. Replace pressure plate. c. Adjust linkage to get proper lash, be sure proper pedal stop (bumper) is installed.
Hard Pedal Effort	a. Bind in linkage. b. Driven plate worn. c. Friction in cable.	a. Lubricate and free up linkage. b. Replace driven plate. c. Replace cable.

FIGURE 25–33. Use this chart to determine the cause of various clutch problems. *(Courtesy of Chevrolet Motor Division, General Motors Corporation)*

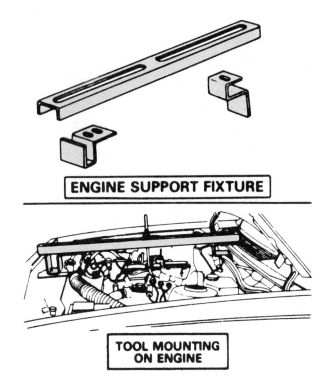

ENGINE SUPPORT FIXTURE

TOOL MOUNTING ON ENGINE

FIGURE 25–34. When a manual transmission is removed the engine may need to be supported by special engine support fixtures. *(Courtesy of Motor Publications, Domestic Transmission Manual)*

15. Check the condition of the clutch release (throwout) bearing. If there is any restriction while turning the bearing, replacement will be necessary. The bearing should turn smoothly.

16. Check the condition of the clutch disc. If it is worn beyond the manufacturer's specifications, replace it.

17. Check the condition of the pressure plate and flywheel surface. If the friction disc is worn too thin, it may score and scratch the pressure plate and flywheel surfaces. This will cause grooves to be cut into the pressure plate. If they are scored and scratched, the pressure plate and flywheel will have to be machined or replaced. Refer to the manufacturer's service manual for further service in this area.

18. Check for excessive wear or bent diaphragm spring fingers when the clutch is disassembled. If the spring fingers are worn, the pressure plate must be replaced.

19. Clean all parts and begin reassembly.

20. Attach the friction disc and pressure plate to the flywheel. The friction disc and pressure plate must be correctly aligned before installing the transmission. Use the following procedure to align the disc correctly.
   a. Place the friction disc in the correct position on the flywheel.
   b. Using the correct bolts, attach the pressure plate. However, do not tighten the bolts at this point. The

clutch disc must still be loose enough to be moved slightly for alignment.
   c. Using the correct alignment tool (it should look the same as the transmission mainshaft) align the pressure plate assembly and clutch disc to the flywheel. The alignment tool positions the disc with the flywheel so that the transmission mainshaft can be inserted easily into the clutch disc and flywheel. *Figure 25–35* shows how the alignment tool will position the friction disc with the pressure plate. Make sure the end of the alignment tool is completely inserted into the end of the crankshaft before tightening the pressure plate bolts.
   d. Using the correct torque specifications, tighten the pressure plate bolts.
   e. Remove the alignment tool.

21. Replace the flywheel housing and torque to specifications.

22. Insert the clutch release (throwout) bearing.

23. Reattach the clutch linkage.

24. Insert the transmission into the clutch assembly. If the alignment procedure was done correctly, the transmission will slip into place easily.

25. Tighten the bolts between the transmission and the flywheel housing to stated torque specifications.

26. Replace all linkages, wires, driveshafts, and so on.

27. At this point the clutch mechanism needs to be adjusted. If the clutch linkage is adjusted incorrectly, the clutch may not engage completely and it will slip or be hard to shift. Each vehicle has a different procedure for adjusting the clutch mechanism. *Figure 25–36* illustrates several common measurements taken. Refer to the manufacturer's specifications and the suggested procedures to adjust clutch linkage.

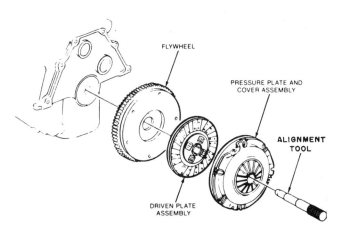

FLYWHEEL

PRESSURE PLATE AND COVER ASSEMBLY

ALIGNMENT TOOL

DRIVEN PLATE ASSEMBLY

FIGURE 25–35. Before tightening the pressure plate, insert the correct alignment tool. This will help align the pressure plate, friction disc, and flywheel correctly so that the transmission can be inserted easily. *(Courtesy of Motor Publications, Auto Repair Manual)*

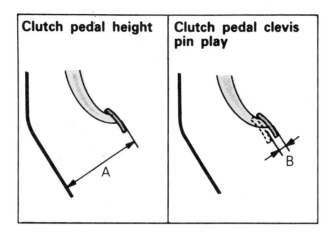

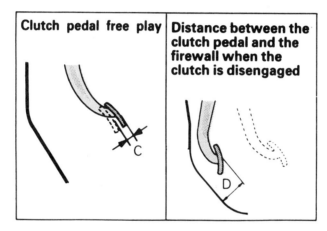

FIGURE 25–36.   These checks are normally made when adjusting the clutch. *(Courtesy of Motor Publications, Domestic Transmission Manual)*

28. Adjust the shifting linkage according to manufacturers specifications. Also make sure the linkage is not damaged or bent. If the linkage is not adjusted properly, the transmission may slip out of gear, or hard shifting may result. Again, each vehicle has a different procedure. A typical procedure, however includes:
    a. Place the transmission in neutral.
    b. Place a gauge pin in the shift levers for alignment.
    c. Tighten the linkage to manufacturer's specifications.

PROBLEM: Oil on Clutch Surface

As the clutch pedal is released and the clutch engaged, during acceleration, a jerking motion occurs. The clutch does not engage the transmission smoothly.

DIAGNOSIS

If the rear main oil seal in the engine leaks oil, the oil may get on the friction disc. When this happens, the oil becomes very sticky and causes a jerking motion during release of the clutch and engagement of the transmission.

SERVICE

To repair, the rear main seal on the engine must be replaced. Refer to Chapter 9 for service details.

PROBLEM: Defective Synchronizer

A manual transmission is difficult to shift. During shifting, a grinding noise or clashing of gears is usually heard.

DIAGNOSIS

Gears that clash during shifting usually indicate a bad or defective synchronizer. The transmission will need to be removed, disassembled, and overhauled accordingly. *Figure 25–37* shows a manual transmission trouble diagnosis chart. If there are other problems with the manual transmission refer to this chart for the condition, probable cause, and correction.

SERVICE

There are many service procedures used on manual transmissions. When working on the transmission always

TROUBLE DIAGNOSIS	DIAGNOSIS	
CONDITION	**POSSIBLE CAUSE**	**CORRECTION**
Hard Shifting	1. Clutch. 2. Synchronizers worn or broken. 3. Shift shafts or forks worn.	1. Adjust. 2. Replace. 3. Replace.
Slips Out of Gear	1. Shift shafts worn. 2. Bearings worn. 3. Drive gear retainer broken or loose. 4. Excessive play in synchronizers.	1. Replace. 2. Replace as necessary. 3. Tighten or replace retainer. 4. Replace.
Noisy in All Gears	1. Insufficient lubricant. 2. Worn countergear bearings. 3. Worn or damaged drive gear and countergear. 4. Damaged drive gear or main shaft. 5. Worn or damaged countergear.	1. Fill to correct level. 2. Replace countergear bearings and shaft. 3. Replace worn or damaged gears. 4. Replace damaged bearings or drive gear. 5. Replace countergear.
Noisy in Neutral	1. Damaged drive gear bearing. 2. Damaged or loose pilot bearing. 3. Worn or damaged countergear. 4. Worn countergear bearings.	1. Replace damaged bearing. 2. Replace pilot bearing. 3. Replace countergear. 4. Replace countergear bearings and shaft.
Noisy in Reverse	1. Worn or damaged reverse idler gear or idler bushing. 2. Worn or damaged reverse gear. 3. Damaged or worn countergear.	1. Replace reverse idle gear assembly. 2. Replace reverse gear. 3. Replace countergear assembly.
Leaks Lubricant	1. Excessive amount of lubricant in transmission. 2. Loose or broken drive gear bearing retainer. 3. Drive gear bearing retainer gasket damaged. 4. Center support gaskets either side. 5. Rear extension seal. 6. Speedo driven gear.	1. Drain to correct level. 2. Tighten or replace retainer. 3. Replace gasket. 4. Replace gaskets. 5. Replace. 6. Replace O ring seal.

FIGURE 25–37. When troubleshooting a manual transmission, always refer to the manufacturer's diagnosis information as shown here. *(Courtesy of American Isuzu Motors, Inc.)*

use the correct tools. Common tools other than the standard wrenches include a snap ring pliers, gear pullers, drift punches, and a hammer. Use the following general service procedures when replacing synchronizers or rebuilding manual transmissions.

1. Use the same procedure for removing the transmission as previously discussed.

2. With the transmission on a workbench, remove the bolts holding the side and top covers on the transmission.

3. Remove the main drive gear. See *Figure 25–38*. Snap rings may have to be removed first. *Figure 25–39* shows the mainshaft removed from the transmission case.

4. Remove the countershaft. This may require removing the woodruff key from the rear of the transmission case.

5. Remove all other gears inside the case.

6. Follow the manufacturer's recommended procedure to remove and replace the synchronizer assembly.

7. With the transmission disassembled, various checks can be performed. Although there are many procedures, the following are common checks on most transmissions:
   a. Check for wear and missing or damaged teeth on all gears and synchronizers. Check all internal bearings. Check the synchronizer sleeves to see that they slide freely on their hubs. A small presence of metal in the

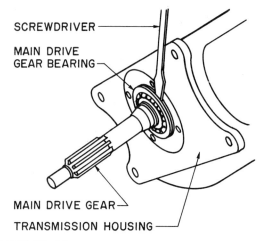

FIGURE 25–38.   To disassemble the transmission, the main drive gear must be removed first.

transmission fluid may indicate gear or synchronizer wear. Replace where necessary.
   b. Inspect the reverse gear bushing for wear, and replace if necessary.
   c. Remove all gears on the main- and countershaft according to manufacturer's recommended procedures.
   d. Check the runout of the output shaft, as shown in *Figure 25–40*.

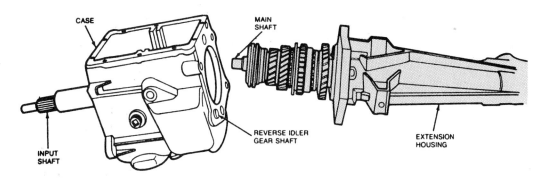

FIGURE 25–39.   After the snap ring has been removed, the mainshaft can be removed from the transmission case. *(Courtesy of Motor Publications, Domestic Transmission Manual)*

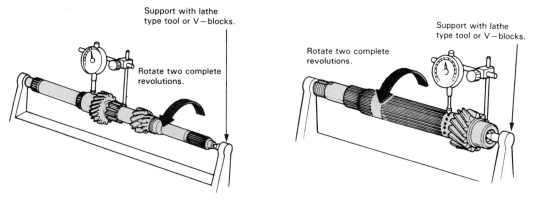

FIGURE 25–40.   The mainshaft and countershaft runout can be checked with a dial indicator when the transmission is disassembled. *(Courtesy of Honda Motor Company, Ltd.)*

e. On many manual transmissions, the thrust clearance needs to be checked with a dial indicator before reassembly. *Figure 25–41* shows how to check thrust clearance. If the thrust clearance is not correct, it must be adjusted during reassembly.

f. Often gear end play, synchronizer clearance, and bearing position need to be adjusted during reassembly. The adjustments are normally controlled by the thickness of various shims, snap rings, and thrust washers. For example, as shown in *Figure 25–42*, various snap rings are available with different markings. Depending on the clearance needed, a certain snap ring is used to maintain the clearance.

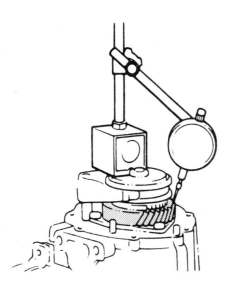

FIGURE 25–41. Gear thrust clearance can be checked with a dial indicator. *(Courtesy of Motor Publications, Domestic Transmission Manual)*

IDENTIFICATION MARK

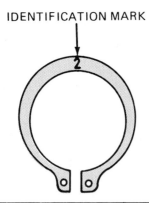

Thickness		Identification Mark
Millimeters	Inches	
1.5	0.059	1
1.55	0.061	2
1.6	0.063	3
1.65	0.065	4

FIGURE 25–42. End play on gears and synchronizers can be adjusted by using different sizes of snap rings. *(Courtesy of Motor Publications, Domestic Transmission Manual)*

SUMMARY

The purpose of this chapter was to learn about the manual or standard transmission. This chapter studied the principles and operation of the clutch system, the basic transmission, including synchronizers and overdrives, and the levers and linkages used on the transmission.

(continued)

GEAR TEETH DESIGN

The design of gear teeth used on a transmission is very scientific and precise. A great deal of engineering goes into the exact shape of the tooth on a gear. The figure shows some of the more common measurements and terminology of standard gear teeth. The gear teeth are designed so that minimum contact and wear will occur as the gears mesh with one another. In this figure a mating tooth is also shown. Note where the gear teeth touch each other during meshing. By studying gear design it becomes apparent that proper lubrication is important to reduce gear wear. Also, if a bearing on the gear shaft is worn, the two gears may not mesh correctly, causing wear and possible damage to both gears.

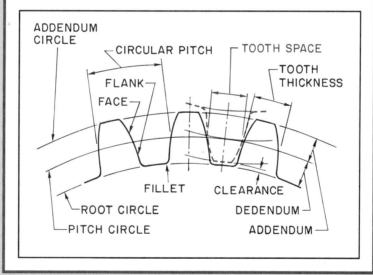

The clutch is used to engage and disengage the transmission. It is composed of the friction disc, the pressure plate, the clutch linkage, and the clutch release bearing. In operation, when the operator pushes the clutch pedal down, the linkage and clutch release bearing push against springs so the pressure plate is brought away from the friction disc. Under these conditions, the engine is not connected to the transmission. When the operator releases the clutch, the mechanism causes the pressure plate to squeeze the friction disc between the flywheel and the pressure plate. Because the friction disc is squeezed between the two, it causes the disc to rotate. The output of the friction disc then drives the transmission.

On some vehicles, rather than using mechanical linkages to move the pressure plate, a slave cylinder is used. A hydraulic cylinder operated by the clutch pedal moves the clutch fork in and out to engage or disengage the friction disc.

Transmissions are used to produce different torque capabilities at the driving wheels. When the vehicle is starting, or going up a steep hill, high torque and low speed are needed. When the vehicle is moving fast along a straight highway, low torque and high speed are required. A transmission is designed to give these different torque requirements.

Torque can be changed by using different gears and gear ratios. Spur, helical, and internal gears are used in a transmission. Typically, when a smaller gear drives a bigger gear, torque is multiplied. First, second, third, fourth, or fifth gear is determined by moving different-sized gears in mesh with the input gear on the transmission. A three-speed transmission will typically have several gear ratios. First gear is normally 3 to 1. Second gear is 2 to 1, and third gear is 1 to 1. Reverse is also a very low gear ratio. When four- and five-speed transmissions are used, more gear ratios are available.

To eliminate the clashing and grinding of gears, transmissions today have synchronizers. Synchronizers are used to get both gears spinning at the same speed before meshing. In late model transmissions, all gears are in mesh. The synchronizers engage and disengage to produce the power flow through the transmission.

On some transmissions, an overdrive gear set is used. Overdrive reduces the speed of the engine somewhat to produce better fuel mileage. A 0.8 to 1 gear ratio is typically used when in the highest gear.

Transaxles are used on front wheel drive vehicles. When the engine is mounted in the front, a transaxle is used to transmit the output of the transmission to the front wheels for driving. The differential is usually included inside the case. The output of the differential is used to drive the front wheels.

All transmissions have some form of linkage from the foot pedal to the clutch release bearing. Most vehicles have mechanical linkages. Cable linkage is also used to move the shift forks that are placed around the synchronizers. Several other components are also placed on the transmission. These include the speedometer cable, backup light switch, and solenoids to control overdrive.

There are many diagnosis and service suggestions that are important for manual transmissions. Possible areas of service include the synchronizers, bearings, clutch linkage adjustment, ar d gears. Service may also be necessary on the clutch disc, pressure plate, and throwout bearing.

TERMS TO KNOW

Can you explain each of the following terms? Review the chapter until you can use each term correctly.

Clutch	Lever
Pressure plate	Fulcrum
Friction disc	Idler gear
Diaphragm spring	Synchronizer
Asbestos	Overdrive
Torsional vibration	Transaxle
Slave cylinder	Detent springs

 REVIEW QUESTIONS

Multiple Choice

1. The purpose of the clutch system is to:
   a. Start the engine
   b. Engage the crankshaft to the oil pump
   c. Engage the engine to the transmission
   d. Reduce the speed of the overdrive
   e. Increase the speed of the synchronizers

2. What device squeezes the friction disc against the flywheel?
   a. Torsional springs
   b. Clutch linkage
   c. Clutch release bearing
   d. Pressure plate
   e. Synchronizers

3. The clutch release bearing pushes against the _____ to disengage the friction disc.
   a. Pressure plate release levers
   b. Pressure plate springs and linkage
   c. Flywheel
   d. Transmission case
   e. Torsional springs

4. _____ are placed on the friction disc to eliminate a jerky or chatter motion when the clutch is engaged.
   a. Asbestos springs
   b. Torsional springs
   c. Splines
   d. Gears
   e. Pressure plates

5. Which device is/are used to push the clutch release bearing in and out of engagement?
   a. Clutch disc
   b. Torsional springs
   c. Clutch fork
   d. Synchronizers
   e. Pressure plate

6. The purpose of the standard or manual transmission is to:
   a. Increase torque output at the right time
   b. Change the speed of the output shaft
   c. Decrease the input shaft at high speeds in overdrive
   d. All of the above
   e. None of the above

7. On a set of gears, if the input gear has 12 teeth and the output gear has 24 teeth, what is the gear ratio?
   a. 3 to 1
   b. 2 to 1
   c. 1 to 1
   d. 1 to 3
   e. 1 to 0.2

8. If a smaller gear is used to drive a larger gear, the:
   a. Torque output will be decreased
   b. Torque output will be increased
   c. Speed output will be increased
   d. Input speed will be decreased
   e. None of the above

9. When reverse gear is selected in a transmission:
   a. Two extra gears are added to the gear train
   b. Three extra gears are added to the gear train
   c. One extra gear is added to the gear train
   d. The overdrive gear is always used
   e. The clutch is always disengaged

10. What is the gear ratio for a three-speed transmission in first gear?
    a. About 1 to 4
    b. About 1 to 5
    c. About 1 to 3
    d. About 3 to 1
    e. About 2 to 1

11. In high or third gear on a three-speed transmission, the countershaft:
    a. Is driving all gears
    b. Is freewheeling and not driving any gears
    c. Is driving the second and first gears
    d. All of the above
    e. None of the above

12. Which type of gear has the teeth at an angle to the gear axis, rather than parallel to the gear axis?
    a. Spur gear
    b. Helical gear
    c. Spur gear that is internal
    d. Synchronizer gear
    e. Overdrive gear

13. In current transmissions that use synchronizers, the countershaft gears in the transmission:
    a. Are not in mesh during shifting
    b. Are always in mesh during shifting
    c. Are not spinning
    d. Must first engage the reverse gear
    e. Mesh only after the synchronizer engages

14. The center of a synchronizer assembly that slides on the main shaft is called the:
    a. Cone
    b. Synchronizer ring
    c. Synchronizer sleeve
    d. Hub
    e. Key

15. What type of gear actually engages inside the synchronizer assembly?
    a. External clutch gear
    b. External spur gear
    c. Internal gear
    d. All of the above
    e. None of the above

16. The shift forks on a synchronized transmission control or move the:
    a. Hub
    b. Synchronizer sleeve
    c. Synchronizer keys
    d. Synchronizer cones
    e. Splines

17. What would be a common gear ratio in highest gear with a transmission using an overdrive system?
    a. 1 to 1
    b. 1 to 1.8
    c. 1 to 2
    d. 2 to 1
    e. 0.8 to 1

18. Which type of transmission would be used on a front wheel drive vehicle?
    a. two-speed
    b. six-speed
    c. Transaxle
    d. All of the above
    e. None of the above

19. The shift lever for the operator of the vehicle:
    a. Moves the shifting forks
    b. Has several types of linkages used to shift the transmission
    c. Can be on the column of the steering or on the floor
    d. All of the above
    e. None of the above

20. Which component is not attached to the transmission?
    a. Speedometer cable drive
    b. Backup lights
    c. Oil seals
    d. Oil pan
    e. Extension housing

21. Gear clashing during shifting may be caused by:
    a. A bad speedometer cable
    b. A misaligned clutch
    c. Damaged or worn synchronizers
    d. A worn clutch release bearing
    e. A leaky rear seal

22. If the clutch chatters or causes a jerky motion when engaged, the problem could be caused by:
    a. A leaky rear transmission seal
    b. Bad synchronizers
    c. Oil leaking from the engine to the friction disc
    d. A broken extension housing
    e. A bad clutch release bearing

> *The following questions are similar in format to ASE (Automotive Service Excellence) test questions.*

23. Technician A says that if oil leaks on the clutch disc, the clutch will slip during engagement. Technician B says that if oil leaks on the clutch disc, the clutch will chatter during engagement. Who is right?
    a. A only
    b. B only
    c. Both A and B
    d. Neither A nor B

24. Technician A says that gear clashing is caused by misalignment of the shift linkage. Technician B says that gear clashing is caused by a bad synchronizer. Who is right?
    a. A only
    b. B only
    c. Both A and B
    d. Neither A nor B

25. During assembly of the transmission to the clutch assembly, the transmission cannot be inserted into the clutch assembly. Technician A says that the transmission mainshaft is damaged. Technician B says that the clutch disc is not properly aligned. Who is right?
    a. A only
    b. B only
    c. Both A and B
    d. Neither A nor B

26. A small amount of ground metal filings are found in a transmission. Technician A says that they are clutch particles, not filings. Technician B says that these filings are metal and indicate possible gear wear. Who is right?
    a. A only
    b. B only
    c. Both A and B
    d. Neither A nor B

27. Technician A says that gear end play on a manual transmission is set by different thickness snap rings. Technician B says the bearings must be adjusted when reassembling a manual transmission. Who is right?
    a. A only
    b. B only
    c. Both A and B
    d. Neither A nor B

28. Technician A says that runout can be checked on the mainshaft. Technician B says that runout can be checked on bearings. Who is right?
    a. A only
    b. B only
    c. Both A and B
    d. Neither A nor B

29. When adjusting the clutch mechanism, Technician A says to adjust the throwout bearing. Technician B says to adjust the flywheel. Who is right?
    a. A only
    b. B only
    c. Both A and B
    d. Neither A nor B

30. A vehicle has a grinding noise during clutch engagement. Technician A says the problem is most likely the synchronizer. Technician B says the problem is a badly worn clutch, scraping against the pressure plate. Who is right?
    a. A only
    b. B only
    c. Both A and B
    d. Neither A nor B

Essay

31. What is the purpose of a pressure plate?

32. Define torsional vibration.

33. What is the purpose of the clutch release bearing?

34. Describe the gear ratios for first, second, third, and fourth gears.

35. Describe the purpose and basic operation of a synchronizer.

36. Why are overdrive systems used on transmissions?

37. What is a transaxle?

Short Answer

38. Asbestos is being replaced with _____ on clutch discs.

39. A popular type of transmission lubricant is identified as _____.

40. The _____ springs are used to hold shifting forks in the correct position.

41. A scraping sound during clutch engagement may be caused by _____.

42. Oil on the clutch disc and pressure plate will cause the vehicle to _____ when the clutch is engaged.

CHAPTER 26

Automatic Transmissions

INTRODUCTION The automatic transmission is designed to shift gears automatically from low to high without the driver's control. Several major components are used in the automatic transmission. These include the torque converter, planetary gear system, hydraulic components, different types of clutches and bands, and various controlling parts. This chapter explains how these components are used in the automatic transmission.

OBJECTIVES After reading this chapter, you should be able to:

■ Identify the purpose and operation of the torque converter and lockup system.

■ Explain the purpose and operation of the planetary gear system used on automatic transmissions.

■ Analyze the different types of clutches and bands used on automatic transmissions.

■ State the purpose and basic operation of the hydraulic systems used on automatic transmissions.

■ Define the purpose and operation of various standard and computerized control devices used on automatic transmissions.

■ Identify common problems, diagnosis, and service suggestions for automatic transmissions.

 SAFETY CHECKLIST

When working with automatic transmissions, keep these important safety precautions in mind.
✔ Always wear OSHA-approved safety glasses when working on the automatic transmission.
✔ Always use the proper tools when working on automatic transmissions.
✔ Always use the special tools that are recommended for automatic transmissions.
✔ Be careful not to crush your fingers or hands, as the transmission is very heavy.

26.1 BASIC DESIGN AND REQUIREMENTS

Purpose of the Automatic Transmission

The purpose of the automatic transmission is to connect the rotational forces of the engine to the drive wheels and to provide correct torque multiplication. This must be done at varying loads, speeds, and driving conditions. For example, to get the car started, low speed and high torque are required. As the speed increases, the torque requirements decrease. The automatic transmission is designed to produce the correct torque needed for these varying driving conditions.

Major Parts of the Automatic Transmission

The torque converter is used for the same reason that a clutch is used in a standard transmission. The torque converter connects the engine to the transmission gearing. At times, the engine and gears must be directly connected. At other

Some of the information in this chapter can help you prepare for the National Institute for Automotive Service Excellence (ASE) certification tests. The test most directly related to this chapter is entitled

AUTOMATIC TRANSMISSION/ TRANSAXLE (TEST A2).

The content areas that closely parallel this chapter are

GENERAL TRANSMISSION/TRANSAXLE DIAGNOSIS, TRANSMISSION/ TRANSAXLE MAINTENANCE, IN-VEHICLE TRANSMISSION/TRANSAXLE REPAIR, AND OFF-VEHICLE TRANSMISSION/TRANSAXLE REPAIR.

times (at a stop light), the two must be disconnected. In addition, the torque converter multiplies the torque sent to the transmission for varying loads.

The planetary gear system is used to produce the correct gear ratio for different torque and speed conditions. Low speeds, drive, and reverse gear ratios can be achieved by using the planetary gear system.

Various hydraulic controls are used to lock up parts of the gear system in an automatic transmission. Clutches, bands, and other components help to control which gears are used in the planetary gear system.

The automatic transmission uses several hydraulic control valves to operate the clutches and bands for correct operation. Complex hydraulic circuits have been incorporated into the automatic transmission to accomplish this goal.

26.2 TORQUE CONVERTER

In a standard transmission, a clutch is used to engage and disengage the engine from the transmission. This mechanism is called a friction drive. In the automatic transmission, a *fluid coupling* is used to engage and disengage the engine from the transmission. This coupling is called the *torque converter*. It uses a hydraulic, or fluid, coupling.

Fluid Coupling

A common way of describing a fluid coupling is by using two electric fans. In *Figure 26–1*, one fan produces a pressure and blows the air against the other fan. The air pressure produces enough energy to rotate the second fan. This action couples the input and output. The first fan is called the pump, and the second fan is called the *turbine*. The faster the pump turns, the better the fluid lockup between the input and output. In the actual torque converter, a pump and turbine are used, and transmission oil, rather than air, is used.

Parts of the Torque Converter

Several parts make up a torque converter to produce the fluid or, in this case, hydraulic coupling. *Figure 26–2* shows the major parts of the torque converter. These include the pump (also called impeller), the turbine, and the guide wheel or *stator*. Note that each part is made of a series of vanes to direct oil through the torque converter. These parts are contained in a sealed housing that is completely filled with oil. Motion and power are transferred by the pressure of the mass of the flowing oil. There is no direct mechanical contact between the input and the output drives, only a fluid connection. Because of this type of connection, torque converters operate essentially wear-free.

Operation of the Torque Converter

Figure 26–3 shows the operation of the torque converter. The entire torque converter is bolted to the engine crankshaft through a flexplate. See *Figure 26–4*. As the engine turns, the entire outside housing of the torque converter turns. The

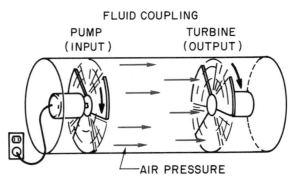

FIGURE 26–1. A torque converter produces a fluid coupling in a manner similar to the operation of two fans. The pressure from the pump fan causes the blades on the second fan, or turbine, to turn. The input and output are now connected.

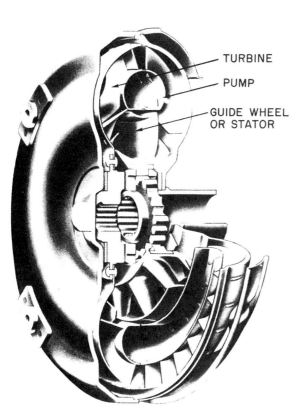

FIGURE 26–2. The major parts of the torque converter are the pump, turbine, and guide wheel or stator. *(Courtesy of Sachs Automotive Products Company)*

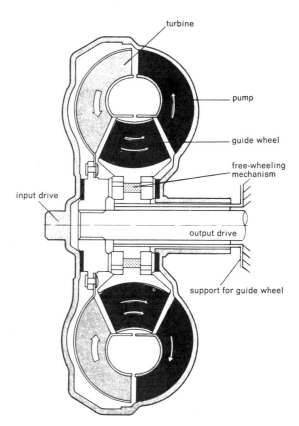

FIGURE 26–3. As the pump rotates, oil is sent to the turbine, through the stator or guide wheel, and back to the pump. This action produces a hydraulic coupling. *(Courtesy of Sachs Automotive Products Company)*

pump vanes are attached directly to the inside of the housing of the torque converter. This connection causes the pump vanes to turn. As the pump rotates, the oil in the pump vanes is forced to the *periphery*, the outer edges of the pump, by

centrifugal force. The oil now reaches the turbine vanes with high velocity (just like the air hitting the fan as shown in Figure 26–1). The high-velocity oil causes the turbine vanes to rotate and to lock up hydraulically with the pump.

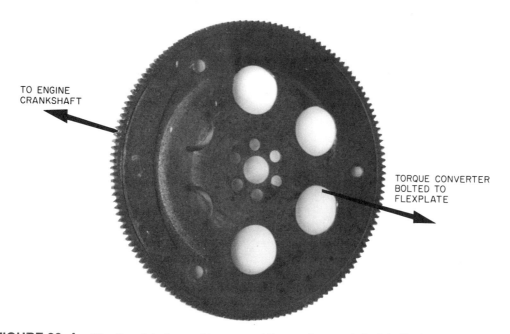

FIGURE 26–4. The flexplate is used to connect the engine crankshaft to the torque converter.

Within the turbine vanes, the oil flow is changed to mechanical rotation by the sharply curved vanes of the turbine. The turbine is connected to the output drive of the torque converter. The stator or guide wheel is used to direct the oil flow back to the pump in the most efficient manner. In effect, the oil flows in a circular fashion throughout the torque converter as shown in *Figure 26–5* (much like a spring bent into a circle).

Torque Multiplication

The torque converter is capable of producing different torque ratios. When starting, the torque converter multiplies torque. The torque may be increased 2–3.5 times the engine torque. As the speed of the turbine blades increases, the torque is continuously reduced until the torque ratio is 1 to 1. At this point, the pump and turbine are spinning at the same speed.

Torque on the turbine wheel is a direct result of how the oil is deflected from the blades. In *Figure 26–6*, when oil hits the turbine vane, the vane is forced to deflect. It has a greater *deflection angle* when the turbine vane is stationary. The greater the deflection angle, the greater the torque on

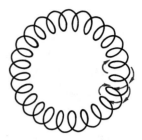

OIL FLOWS INSIDE THE TORQUE CONVERTER FROM THE PUMP, TO THE TURBINE, TO THE STATOR AND BACK TO THE PUMP.

FIGURE 26–5. Oil flows in a circular fashion throughout the torque converter.

the turbine wheel. When the turbine wheel is stopped, there is a maximum deflection angle. As the turbine blade increases in speed, the oil is not deflected as much. This is because the turbine blade is now moving to the right. Since the turbine blade is also moving, there is less deflection. Less deflection means less torque multiplication.

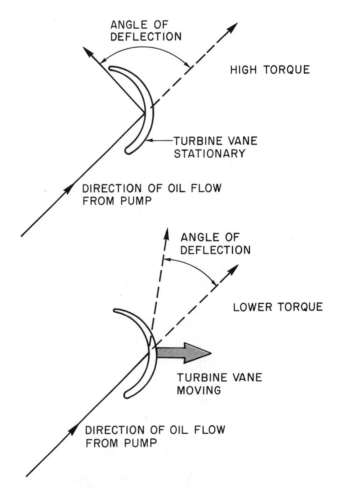

FIGURE 26–6. Torque is multiplied inside the torque converter. The greater the angle of deflection of oil, the greater the torque. As the speed of the turbine increases, the torque decreases.

Figure 26–7 shows the oil flow through all three components inside the torque converter. Figure 26–7 (A) shows the pump rotating with the turbine and guide wheel (stator) stopped. Notice that there is maximum angle of deflection of oil, causing greater torque multiplication.

The oil flows from the torque converter to the stator. Here the oil flow direction wants the stator to turn to the left, but the stator cannot turn that way. The stator is designed so that it can rotate only to the right. It is supported by a one-way, freewheeling sprag or roller clutch drive system. See *Figure 26–8*. The sprag clutch drive system allows rotation in one direction but locks up in the opposite direction. The oil then is redirected to the correct angle to reenter the pump.

As the speed of the turbine increases, the angle of deflection decreases, producing less torque multiplication. This is shown in Figure 26–7 (B). The stator is still not moving because there is still pressure to move it to the left. Notice that the pattern of oil flow is becoming straighter.

Figure 26–7(C) shows the pump and turbine at approximately the same speed. During this condition, the oil flow has no deflection. The speed of the oil and the turbine blade, moving to the right, are the same. There is no torque multiplication at this point. However, the oil flow is now hitting the back of the stator or guide wheel blades. If left this way, the oil will not flow back to the pump correctly. To eliminate this problem, the stator starts to turn to the right. The freewheeling action of the stator is in effect.

Torque Converter Lockup

Torque converters never operate without any loss. There is usually a certain slip between the turbine speed and the pump speed. The pump speed may be 2–8% faster than the turbine speed. In most transmissions, this loss is not accounted for, but it does reduce gasoline mileage.

Most newer automatic transmissions have a lockup system

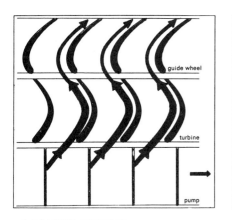 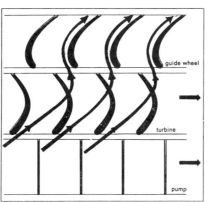 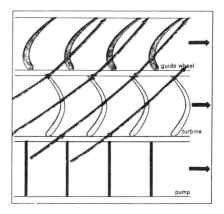

(A) HIGH TORQUE;
GREAT DEFLECTION ANGLE;
LOW OUTPUT SPEED.

(B) MEDIUM TORQUE;
MEDIUM DEFLECTION ANGLE;
MEDIUM OUTPUT SPEED.

(C) LOW TORQUE
LOW DEFLECTION ANGLE;
HIGH OUTPUT SPEED.

FIGURE 26–7. (A) High torque multiplication. (B) Medium torque multiplication. (C) Low torque multiplication. *(Courtesy of Sachs Automotive Products Company)*

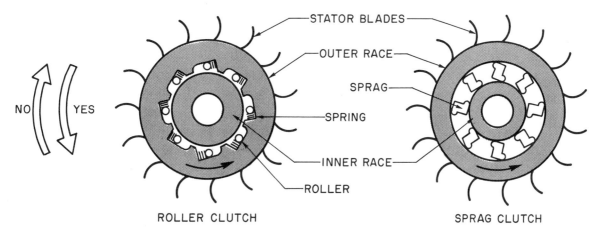

FIGURE 26–8. The stator must turn in one direction only. It is prevented from turning in the other direction by either a roller or sprag clutch drive system. When the inner hub is held stationary, the outer stator vanes can rotate only in a counterclockwise direction. When forced in the opposite direction, the stator vanes cannot turn.

between the torque converter turbine and the engine. The effect of locking up these two components is similar to direct drive. Actually, the torque converter is no longer a part of the power flow. It is being bypassed. The overall effect is that during high gear operation, there is no transmission slippage, and fuel efficiency improves.

Figure 26–9 shows a schematic of the parts and oil flow through the torque converter during clutch on (lockup) and clutch off. Note that several parts are added to the torque converter. A lockup piston is placed between the torque converter turbine and the torque converter cover. This piston

is made of a lockup plate assembly, a friction disc, and a damper spring. On the left or outside of the lockup plate assembly is the friction disc. This friction disc matches up with a machined surface on the inside of the torque converter cover. A damper spring is used to attach the lockup piston to the turbine. It is used to help dampen engine power pulses coming from the drive train.

There are two modes of operation. The first mode operates during the first several gears (not high gear). During this time, the *lockup clutch* is disengaged or in the clutch off position. Refer to Figure 26–9 (A). Oil pressure from the

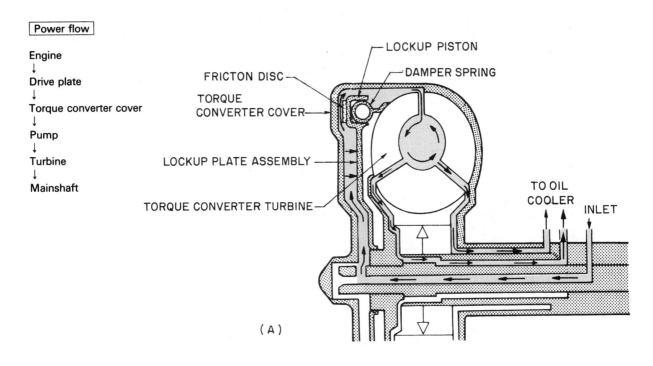

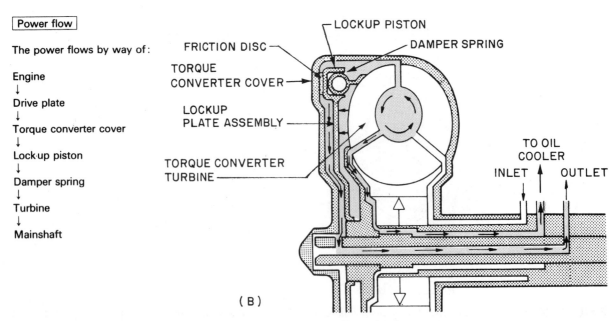

FIGURE 26–9. Most torque converters have a lockup mechanism. Its purpose is to lock up the torque converter in high gear to improve fuel economy. *(Courtesy of Honda Motor Company, Ltd.)*

transmission is sent between the lockup plate and the torque converter cover. The effect is that the oil allows for a certain amount of slippage between the two. During this condition, the friction disc is not in contact with the torque converter cover.

Figure 26–9 (B) shows the second mode, when the system is in the clutch on (lockup) mode. During this condition, the oil pressure between the converter cover and the lockup plate assembly is discharged. The converter oil then exerts pressure through the piston, against the converter cover. As a result, the friction disc now works against the converter cover. This action firmly locks the converter cover directly to the turbine.

The oil pressure from the transmission to the lockup clutch is controlled by a converter clutch shuttle valve. This valve is also called an apply valve. The shuttle valve is controlled by the computer and is discussed later in this chapter.

Torque Converter Location

On rear wheel drive vehicles, the torque converter is located directly behind the engine. The transmission is located directly behind the torque converter. The torque converter and transmission are one combined unit.

On certain front wheel drive cars, a different arrangement

is used. The torque converter is located alongside the transmission. A large heavy chain is used to connect the torque converter to the transmission. See *Figure 26–10*.

26.3 PLANETARY GEAR SYSTEM

Purpose of the Planetary Gear System

The *planetary gear system* is used to produce different gear ratios within the automatic transmission. The output of the torque converter (turbine) is considered the input to the planetary set of gears. Power flow comes from the torque converter, through a hydraulic clutch, to the planetary gear system. The planetary gear system produces either low speeds, drive, or reverse. In addition, certain automatic transmissions may have D1, D2, D3, and overdrive. More than one planetary gear system can also be used on transmissions to produce more gear ratios.

Parts of the Basic Planetary Gear System

All planetary gear systems have several major parts. They include the:

1. Sun gear
2. Ring gear

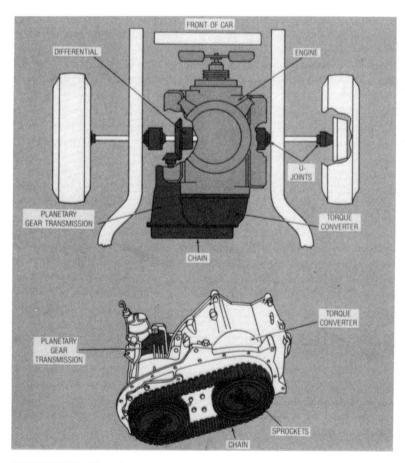

FIGURE 26–10. On front wheel drive vehicles, a heavy chain is used on some transmissions to connect the torque converter to the transmission case. *(Courtesy of General Motors Corporation)*

3. Planet gears (also called pinion gears)

4. Planet gear carrier

Figure 26–11 shows a simple planetary gear system. The sun gear is the center gear. The planet (pinion) gears are held in position by the *planet carrier*. The ring gear is an internal gear that surrounds all of the planet gears. All gears are helical in design and are in constant mesh.

Operation of the Planetary Gear System

To select different gear ratios, one of three gears, the sun, ring, or planets, is held stationary. The input and output then occur on the remaining gears. For example, if the ring gear is held stationary and the input is the sun gear, the carrier is the output with a lower speed. The most common arrangement for low gear is to have the sun gear held stationary, the input on the ring gear, and the output on the carrier.

Eight combinations can be produced in a planetary gear system. These are shown in *Figure 26–12*. In addition, direct drive occurs when any two gears of the planetary gear system are turned at the same speed. The third gear must then rotate at the same speed. In this condition, the planet gears do not rotate on their shafts. The entire unit is locked together to form one rotating part. Neutral occurs when all members of the planetary gear system are free. When the transmission is placed in park, a small pawl is engaged with the teeth on the planet carrier.

Overdrive conditions can also be obtained by using planetary gears. Overdrive can be used when the sun gear or

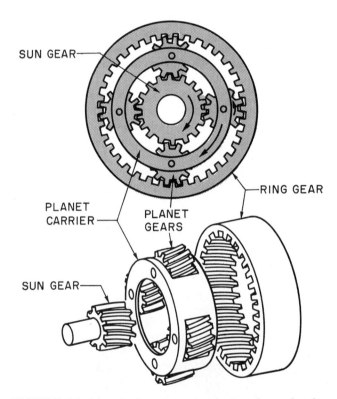

FIGURE 26–11. A planetary gear system is made of a sun gear, a ring gear, several planet gears, and a planet carrier.

GEAR COMBINATIONS								
GEAR	1	2	3	4	5	6	7	8
RING	Output	Hold	Input	Hold	Input	Output	HOLD ANY TWO GEARS	FREE ALL GEARS
CARRIER	Input	Input	Output	Output	Hold	Hold		
SUN	Hold	Output	Hold	Input	Output	Input		
SPEED CHANGE (Input to Output)	Increase	Increase	Lower	Lower	Increase Reverse	Lower Reverse	Direct Drive	Neutral

FIGURE 26–12. Eight combinations of gear ratios can be produced in a planetary gear system. By holding one gear stationary and changing the input and output, various gear ratios can be achieved.

the ring gear is held stationary. Input would be as shown in Figure 26–12, condition 1 or 2.

Variations in the Planetary Gear System

There are several variations to the basic planetary gear system. One type of planetary gear system is called the simple type. It has two sets of planet gears. Another type of planetary gear system uses two sets of planet gears, two sun gears, and a planet carrier. *Figure 26–13* shows this system, called the compound planetary gear system. On certain transmissions, two complete sets of planetary gears are used.

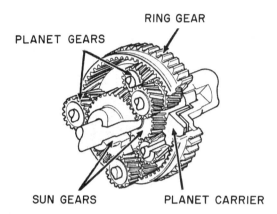

FIGURE 26–13. A compound planetary gear system has two sets of planet gears and two sun gears. *(Courtesy of Chrysler Corporation)*

PROBLEM: Towing Problem

A person would like to use a vehicle with a six-cylinder engine to tow a trailer and boat. What problems might occur using the standard radiator and transmission?

SOLUTION:

The most common problem when towing a boat or trailer is engine overheating. The engine must do more work, so the engine will run hotter and the transmission will be under more stress. The transmission is cooled by the engine coolant. If the engine is running hotter, the transmission fluid is also hotter. Damage to the transmission could result.

The best protection is to have the manufacturer install a towing package. The most common package includes an extra transmission cooler placed on the front of the radiator. Some manufacturers also recommend changing the rear end differential to a different ratio. The cost is much higher, but the engine will not be loaded as much.

26.4 CLUTCHES, BANDS, AND SERVO PISTONS

Purpose of Clutches and Bands

The planetary gear system provides the gear ratios, but the clutches and bands control which gears are held or released. The clutches and bands are used to lock up the correct gear to get the right gear ratio. Depending on which clutch or band is activated, one member of the planetary gear system is held, while the other is driven.

Multiple-Disc Clutch

One common clutch used in automatic transmissions is called the *multiple-disc clutch*. It is made of a series of friction discs placed between steel discs or plates. The exact number of discs depends on the vehicle manufacturer. See *Figure 26–14*. The friction discs or composition-faced plates have rough gripping surfaces. The steel discs have smooth metal surfaces. These two components make up the input and output of the clutch. The clutch pack also has a piston and return springs.

When fluid pressure is applied to the clutch, the piston moves and compresses the clutch pack together. The action locks up the input and output of the clutch. When the pressure is released, the springs help to remove the pressure on the discs. This action unlocks the clutch. *Figure 26–15* shows an exploded view of the multiple-disc clutch. This type of clutch could be used to connect two shafts together. For example, the torque converter output must be connected and disconnected to the planetary gear system. The mechanism that makes this connection is called the forward clutch, and it uses a multiple-disc clutch.

Transmission Band

Another type of clutch is called the *transmission band*. It is made of a flexible piece of steel wrapped around a clutch housing or drum. The inside of the band has a friction surface to help grip the clutch housing. The band is tightened or loosened to hold or free the clutch housing or drum. If the

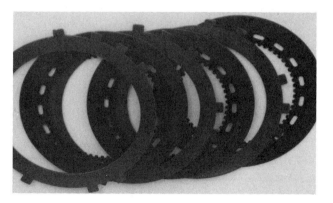

FIGURE 26–14. Multiple-disc clutches use both a friction disc and a steel disc. When pressure is applied, the two lock up and transmit the necessary torque.

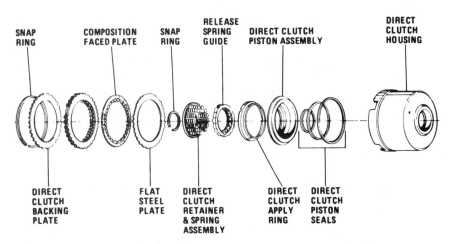

FIGURE 26–15. An exploded view of the multiple-disc clutch with the piston and other operational parts. *(Courtesy of Motor Publications, Automatic Transmission Manual)*

clutch housing is attached to the sun gear, control of the sun gear is made by this transmission band. *Figure 26–16* shows a band type of clutch used on a transmission.

Servo Piston

The *servo* piston is used to control the transmission band operation. In *Figure 26–17*, the band is controlled by a servo piston. The servo piston is made of the case, piston, stem, spring, and cover. When oil pressure from the hydraulic system is applied, it pushes the servo piston to the right. This action causes the stem to move and tighten the band. When oil pressure is removed, the spring pushes the servo piston back and releases the band. The band clearance can be changed by turning the adjusting screw.

Accumulator

An *accumulator* is a device that cushions the motion of the clutch and servo actions. This is typically done by using a smaller piston inside a servo piston. The smaller piston makes contact with the linkage quicker, thus acting as a cushion.

Overrunning Clutch

The overrunning clutch is used to prevent backward rotation of certain parts of the planetary gear system during shifting. The overrunning clutch shown in *Figure 26–18* is made of the inner hub, outer cam, and a series of rollers and springs. It operates the same as a sprag drive, allowing rotation in only one direction.

It is difficult to get a smooth upshift from low to drive on most transmissions. If one band releases slightly before the second band engages, the engine may have a rapid increase in RPM. The overrunning clutch provides smooth engagement and disengagement without any delay. This improves the shift quality and timing from low to drive gear.

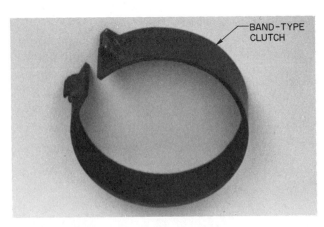

FIGURE 26–16. A transmission band is used to lock up a clutch housing.

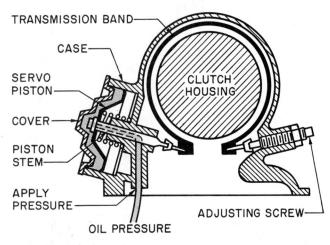

FIGURE 26–17. A servo piston is used to operate the transmission band.

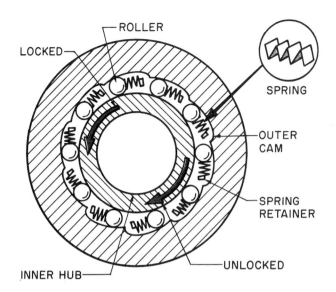

FIGURE 26–18. The overrunning clutch assembly is used to provide a smooth shift from low to drive.

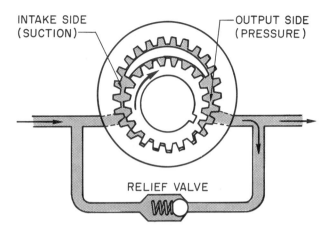

FIGURE 26–19. A gear-type, eccentric pump is used to produce the needed oil pressure in the automatic transmission.

26.5 HYDRAULIC SYSTEM

Purpose of the Hydraulic System

The automatic transmission is controlled by the hydraulic system. When the operator shifts into drive, low, reverse, or any other gear, hydraulic pressure is used to lock up different clutches and bands on the planetary gear system. The torque converter also uses transmission fluid.

Oil Pump

All pressurized oil in the automatic transmission is produced by the transmission oil pump. It creates the pressure used to lock up the clutches or operate the servo to lock up the transmission bands. It also sends oil to the torque converter.

Several types of oil pumps are used on automatic transmissions. These may include the gear, vane type, or rotor type. These are all positive displacement pumps. *Figure 26–19* shows how a common oil pump operates. It uses a gear-type, eccentric pump. As the inside gear is turned, a suction is created on the left side. Automatic transmission fluid is drawn in between the gear teeth. The oil is then carried to the other side of the pump. Pressure is produced here by forcing the oil out from between the gear teeth. The relief valve is used to bypass high-pressure oil back to the suction side. This happens only when higher RPM is producing oil pressure above the recommended pressure.

The oil pump usually is built into the front of the transmission case, directly behind the torque converter. The pump is driven by the torque converter. The torque converter is inserted into the transmission body. Two *tangs*, or feet, on the torque converter come into contact with the center gear of the oil pump. *Figure 26–20* shows an oil pump and body near the front of the transmission.

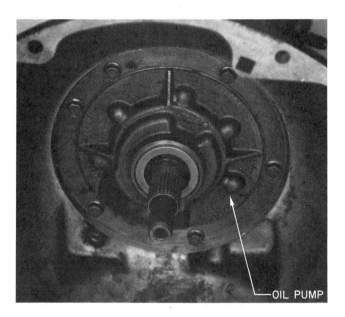

FIGURE 26–20. The oil pump on most transmissions is located directly in front of the transmission and is driven by the torque converter.

Automatic Transmission Fluid

In the transmission there are high shearing and pressure conditions. The automatic transmission fluid must withstand extreme pressure, friction, and shearing stresses. In addition, both cold and hot conditions, which might change viscosity, may exist. Because of all these conditions, the automatic transmission fluid must have the following:

1. Corrosion inhibitors
2. Detergents
3. Pour-point depressants
4. Friction modifiers
5. Antifoam agents
6. Viscosity-index improvers

Because of these special characteristics and requirements, only the recommended fluid should be used. The fluid is generally reddish or brownish. It is often identified as *automatic transmission fluid (ATF)*. Two types of automatic transmission fluid are recommended by most vehicle manufacturers. One type is referred to as Dexron II ATF. Another type is called Mercon ATF. Always follow the manufacturer's recommendation when selecting ATF.

Valve Body

The oil from the oil pump is sent to the *valve body*. The valve body is usually located on the underside of the transmission case and is covered by the transmission oil pan. The oil is sent through many passageways inside the valve body to the various parts of the transmission. The oil is then used to lock up or release the clutches. A series of valves, controls, and springs inside the valve body control the shifting of the automatic transmission. *Figure 26–21* shows a typical valve body.

Oil Cooler

A great deal of friction is produced on most transmissions. Friction tends to increase the temperature of the transmission fluid. If the temperature of the transmission fluid is allowed to get too high, the lubricating properties of the ATF may deteriorate and the transmission may fail. To overcome this potential problem, the transmission oil is cooled by an oil cooler. Oil is typically sent out of the transmission to a heat exchanger placed inside the radiator. Transmission fluid operates about 40–50 degrees F hotter than engine coolant. Most heat is produced by the friction in the clutch and the torque converter. Engine coolant absorbs thermal energy from the transmission to cool the fluid. Vehicles that have excess loads placed on them may also have an additional external cooler on the front of the radiator.

CAR CLINIC

PROBLEM: Hard Shifting and Loss of Transmission Fluid

A customer complains of continually adding transmission fluid to the automatic transmission without signs of leaking. Also the customer complains of very hard downshifting during closed throttle.

SOLUTION:

The vacuum modulator on the automatic transmission cushions shifting and is connected to a vacuum source on the engine intake manifold. When the modulator diaphragm ruptures, the shifting will become hard and engine vacuum will draw transmission fluid into the engine where it is burned in combustion. Here the transmission fluid will be burned with the fuel. The solution is to replace the vacuum modulator.

26.6   TRANSMISSION CONTROLS

Purpose of Transmission Controls

Several controls are used to lock up or release the clutches and transmission bands to control the shifting. In addition, the torque converter clutch must be controlled. The type of valves used are determined by the year and manufacturer of the transmission. Pressure regulator valves, kickdown valves, shift valves, governors, throttle valves, vacuum modulators, and manual valves are used. A working knowledge of these valves will help you to visualize the internal operation of

FIGURE 26–21.   The valve body is used to house the transmission controls. It is also used to direct the oil to the proper part for correct operation.

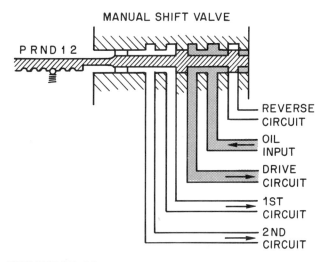

MANUAL SHIFT VALVE

P R N D 1 2

REVERSE
CIRCUIT
OIL
INPUT
DRIVE
CIRCUIT
1ST
CIRCUIT
2ND
CIRCUIT

FIGURE 26–22. When the gear shift lever is moved, a manual shift valve is operated inside the transmission valve body. The movement of this valve causes different hydraulic circuits to be put into operation.

different transmissions. Certain valves are also used to increase the smoothness and quality of shifting.

Pressure Regulator Valve

The *pressure regulator valve* is used to regulate the amount of oil pressure. Various oil pressures are required within the transmission. Certain pressures are needed to control locking of clutches and other valves. The pressure regulator valve uses a *spool valve* to control these pressures. The pressure from the transmission oil pump is sent to the regulator valve so that correct pressures can be maintained throughout the transmission.

Manual Shift Valve

Manual shifting is done by placing the vehicle shift lever in the proper position inside the car. Depending on the vehicle, park, reverse, neutral, drive, and low are common positions to place the shift lever. Many cars also have a D1 and D2. When the operator shifts the lever, a set of shift linkages causes a *manual shift valve* to move inside the valve body. *Figure 26–22* shows the valve that is moved. It is very similar to a spool valve.

Throttle Valve

Under heavy acceleration, it is necessary to increase the force on the transmission bands and clutches to reduce slippage. This can be done by increasing the oil pressure to the servo that controls the transmission band. The *throttle valve (TV)* is used to increase pressure. As the throttle is increased, the throttle linkage is used to change the position of the valve.

Different positions produce different pressures. This valve is used in conjunction with the shift valve.

Governor

The governor is used to help shift the transmission on the basis of vehicle speed. For example, when the vehicle is in low or first gear, it must automatically shift to second or drive at a certain speed. Also, as the vehicle slows to a stop, the transmission must downshift. This is done by using a governor assembly as shown in *Figure 26–23*. The speed of the vehicle is sensed by the governor from the output shaft on the transmission. A set of small weights moves out and in from centrifugal force. Centrifugal force is working against a spring force. These two forces acting against each other cause the valve to open and close a set of hydraulic ports. The output oil pressure controlled by the governor is sent to the *shift valve* to make the necessary shift.

Shift Valve

The throttle valve and the governor do not actually send oil to the clutches. The oil is first sent to the shift valve. Here, governor oil pressure works against throttle valve oil pressure to position the shift valve. *Figure 26–24* shows a simplified example of this. Governor oil pressure enters at the bottom.

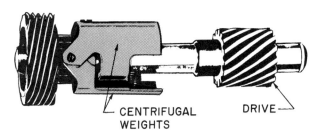

CENTRIFUGAL WEIGHTS   DRIVE

FIGURE 26–23. The governor is used to sense road and engine speed and to shift the transmission accordingly. *(Courtesy of Oldsmobile Division, General Motors Corporation)*

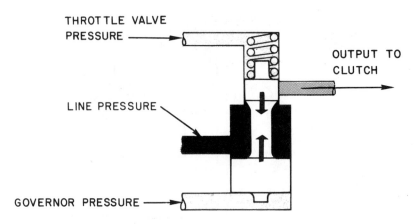

FIGURE 26–24. A shift valve is controlled by the throttle valve oil pressure working against the governor oil pressure. Its position tells exactly when and to which clutch to send the oil pressure. *(Courtesy of Chrysler Corporation)*

Throttle valve pressure enters at the top. These two pressures balance the valve. Any time this balance is disturbed, the shift valve moves upward or downward. Line pressure (pressure used to control the clutches) is also directed to the center of the shift valve. This pressure does not enter into shift valve movement. This pressure is simply ready to be directed to the correct clutch in the planetary gear system to lock up or release the correct clutch. The shift valve is actually more complicated than this and has several outputs to different clutches.

Vacuum Modulator

Another way in which engine load can be determined to help shifting is by using a *vacuum modulator* valve instead of the throttle valve. Both valves are used in vehicles today.

As the throttle opening is increased, the intake manifold vacuum decreases. The intake manifold vacuum is sent to the transmission and is hooked to a vacuum diaphragm. Spring pressure acting against the vacuum causes a rod to be moved. The rod controls the position of the throttle valve. *Figure 26–25* shows a vacuum modulator.

Kickdown Valve

A kickdown valve is used on some transmissions. This valve, which is also called a detent valve, is part of the throttle valve assembly. It operates by using a variable-shaped cam that controls the position of the throttle valve. Under full load, or when the throttle is pushed all the way to the floor, the kickdown valve positions the throttle valve in such a position as to shift to a lower gear.

Ball Check Valves

Ball check valves are used to control the flow of oil in the transmission. Check valves prevent flow until a certain

pressure is reached. They also close passages to prevent back flow of transmission fluid. *Figure 26–26* shows the action of a ball check valve.

Oil Flow Circuits

Many oil flow circuits are outlined in the service manuals. *Figure 26–27* shows a typical oil flow circuit. It is not necessary to understand the complete flow and operation of this diagram. It is more important to observe how all the com-

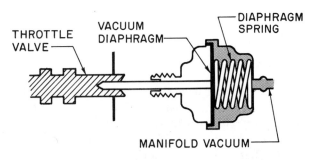

FIGURE 26–25. The vacuum modulator is used to sense engine load on the basis of intake manifold vacuum.

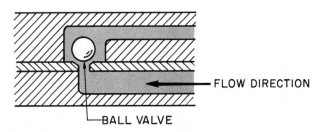

FIGURE 26–26. Ball check valves are used to control the direction of oil flow through the passageways.

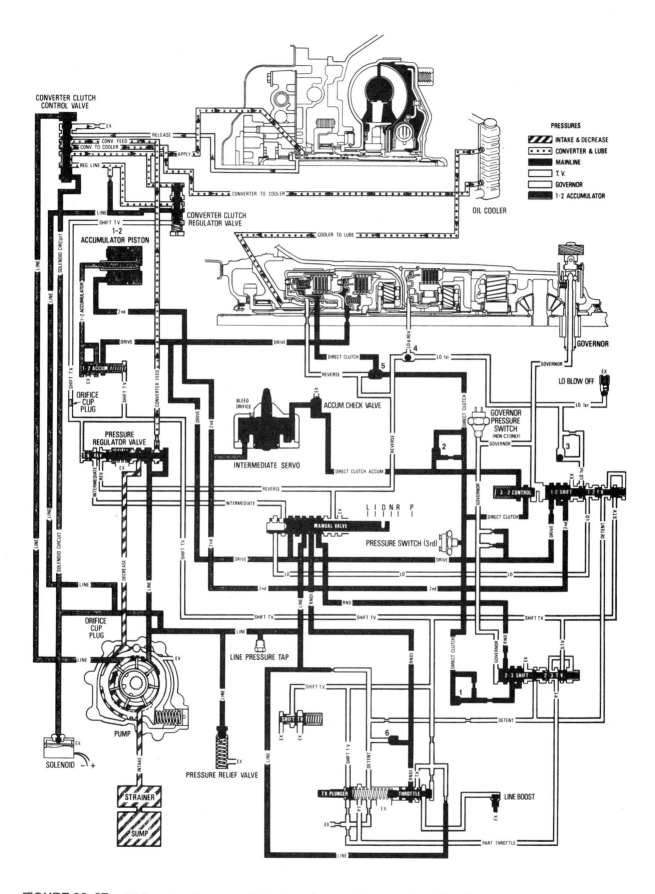

FIGURE 26–27. Oil flow circuits are used to help understand the complete oil flow in an automatic transmission. *(Courtesy of Oldsmobile Division, General Motors Corporation)*

ponents work together to control the oil in the automatic transmission. Note that most of the major components have already been discussed. These components include the oil pump, manual and shift valves, accumulator, regulator valve, servo, governor, oil cooler, clutches, torque converter, pressure relief valve, ball check valves, and converter clutch control valve.

Torque Converter Clutch Valve

As mentioned earlier, the torque converter is locked up at certain times. The oil pressure used to lock up the torque converter is controlled by:

1. a *torque converter clutch (TCC) valve* located in the center of the circuit, and

2. the converter signal, located in the lower right side of the circuit and controlled by the converter clutch shift valve.

Figure 26–28 illustrates the operation of these valves. To begin, when the TCC is not energized, its upper spring pressure positions the valve so that oil pressure is sent to the release circuit, into the lockup clutch, through the torque converter, and back to the TCC valve. The arrows show the direction of flow of oil through the circuit. At this point the converter clutch shift valve is not sending a hydraulic signal to the TCC.

In *Figure 26–29* the position of the converter clutch shift valve is changed (moved to the right). This is a function of the position of the shift lever. The result is that oil pressure is now sent to the bottom of the TCC. The pressure pushes the TCC upward into a new position. In this position, oil

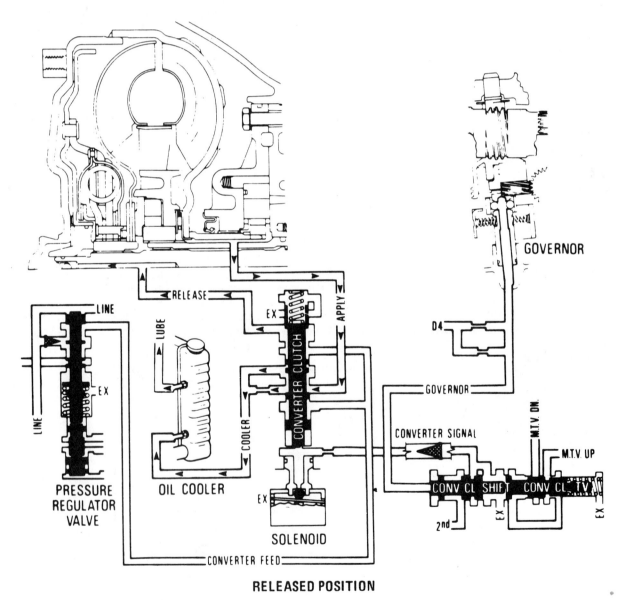

RELEASED POSITION

FIGURE 26–28.   The converter clutch (or torque converter clutch, TCC) is used to control the oil flowing to the lockup torque converter during the released condition. *(Courtesy of Motor Publications, Domestic Transmission Manual)*

pressure now exits the apply circuit. The resulting oil pressure is used to move the clutch lockup plate assembly to the left. This action locks up the torque converter.

The TCC is also controlled by the on-board computer. The ECM (electronic control module), for example, controls the operation of the solenoid on the bottom of the TCC. Normally, the solenoid is positioned so the oil is bled off. When all conditions are met, the ECM energizes the solenoid. The result is that the converter signal pressure is no longer bled off. Now the oil pressure is able to build up and move the TCC. The result is that the TCC is positioned to apply oil so the clutch is locked up. Although the circuitry is more complicated, *Figure 26–30* shows the common inputs to the ECM used to control the TCC solenoid.

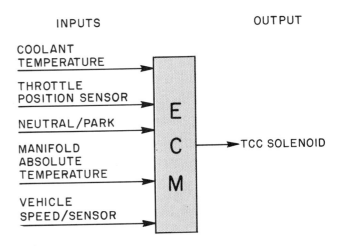

FIGURE 26–30. The torque converter clutch (TCC) is controlled by several inputs.

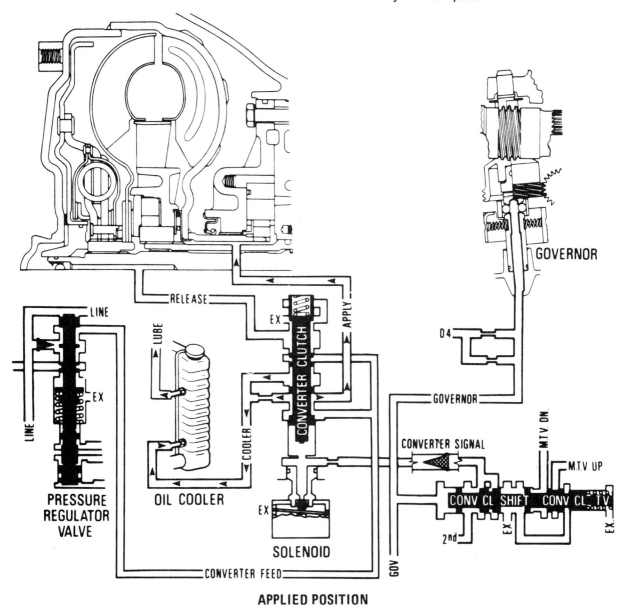

APPLIED POSITION

FIGURE 26–29. With the shift lever in the correct position and the ECM energizing the solenoid, the TCC (torque converter clutch) is positioned to apply the torque converter lockup clutch. *(Courtesy of Motor Publications, Domestic Transmission Manual)*

Neutral Start Switch

On most vehicles, there is an electrical neutral start switch. This switch protects the vehicle from starting when the shift linkage is in any position except neutral or park. If the vehicle were able to start in a forward gear, a possible safety hazard could exist.

Electronic and Computer-controlled Transmissions

Computers and electronics are becoming more integrated into automatic transmissions. In the past several years, various manufacturers have developed transmissions that use a computer to control the shifting and torque converter clutch. The computer works in conjunction with the ECM (electronic control module). In this case, the computer control is called the *power control module (PCM)*. *Figure 26–31* is a diagram of one such system. Various inputs to the PCM (or ECM) help determine the control of the automatic transmission. These include:

1. *VSS* (vehicle speed sensor) — Senses vehicle speed, which is necessary to determine shift points.
2. *TPS* (throttle position sensor) — Senses throttle position, which is necessary to determine shifting times.
3. *Coolant sensor* — Senses engine coolant temperature, used to determine TCC operation times.
4. *Low gear pressure switch* — Switch that senses transmission oil pressure in low gear, used for shifting points.
5. *Fourth gear pressure switch* — Switch that senses transmission oil pressure in fourth gear, used for shifting points.
6. *Brake switch* — Senses whether the brakes are applied or not. Used to disengage the TCC when the brakes are applied.

7. *Cruise control switch* — Senses whether the vehicle is in cruise control or not, for control of TCC system.
8. MAT (manifold absolute pressure) — Senses the amount of throttle opening for shifting points.
9. EST (electronic spark timing) — Senses the timing of the spark, used for shifting times.

On the basis of these inputs, the PCM controls three major solenoids:

1. Shift solenoid A
2. Shift solenoid B
3. TCC (torque converter clutch) solenoid

The TCC valve works the same as previously described. The shift solenoids are attached to hydraulic valves inside the valve body. These valves, as in older transmissions, control the hydraulic fluid to various clutches and bands working with the planetary gear system.

When solenoids A and B are turned off or on by the computer, the shift solenoids work together (in tandem) to produce the four forward speeds. In operation, a gear is selected by the computer on the basis of specific input information. Then solenoids A and B are operated to control different hydraulic circuits inside the hydraulic valve body. *Figure 26–32* shows which solenoids are turned on and off for each of four gears forward. For example, when the computer wants the transmission to shift from first to second gear, solenoid A is turned off while solenoid B is turned on. *Figure 26–33* shows the location of various pressure switches and solenoids on the valve body inside the automatic transmission. *Figure 26–34* shows an example of hydraulic circuitry, working together with the PCM and the two shift solenoids.

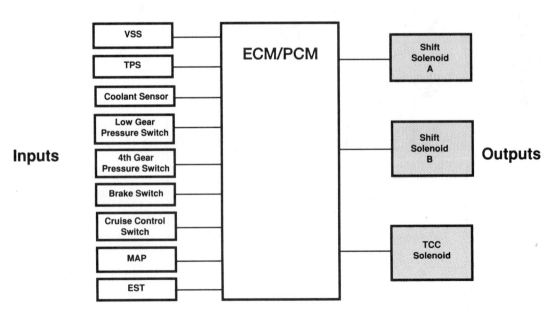

FIGURE 26–31. Computers are able to control the shifting and operation of the TCC, using various inputs to the ECM (electronic control module) or the PCM (power control module). *(Courtesy of General Motors Corporation)*

Gear	Solenoid	
	A	B
1st	On	On
2nd	Off	On
3rd	Off	Off
4th	On	Off

FIGURE 26–32. When shift solenoids are turned off or on, various hydraulic circuits are operated to shift from one gear to another. *(Courtesy of General Motors Corporation)*

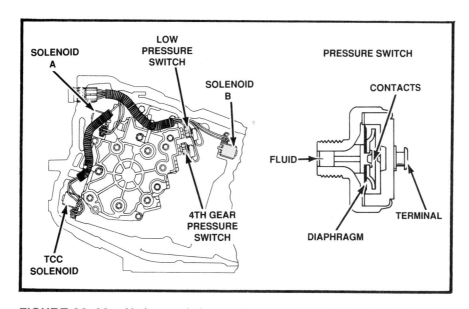

FIGURE 26–33. Various switches and solenoids are placed on the hydraulic valve body to control shifting and TCC operation on automatic transmissions. *(Courtesy of General Motors Corporation)*

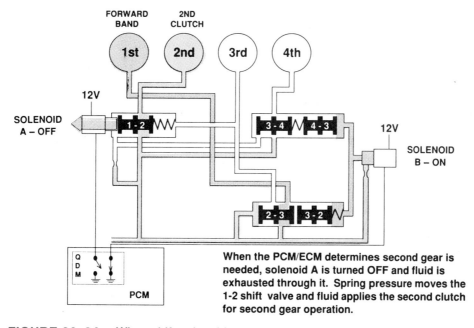

When the PCM/ECM determines second gear is needed, solenoid A is turned OFF and fluid is exhausted through it. Spring pressure moves the 1-2 shift valve and fluid applies the second clutch for second gear operation.

FIGURE 26–34. When shift solenoids are energized, various hydraulic circuits operate to engage different gears. *(Courtesy of General Motors Corporation)*

Problems, Diagnosis and Service

SAFETY PRECAUTIONS

1. When you are working on the automatic transmission, the vehicle must be supported on a hoist or hydraulic stand. Always follow the correct procedure when lifting the vehicle, and always use extra jack stands for safety.

2. The automatic transmission is often used as the rear support for the engine. Never remove the automatic transmission without first adequately supporting the engine in the vehicle.

3. When you remove the automatic transmission, you may spill ATF fluid onto the floor. To eliminate any possibility of slipping, which could cause serious injury, wipe up any spilled fluid immediately.

4. Transmission fluid operates above the temperature of the radiator. Be very careful when checking the fluid when the vehicle has just been stopped. A serious burn could result.

5. When disconnecting the torque converter from the flywheel, the flywheel must be turned. The ring gear on the flywheel is very sharp and could accidently scrape your knuckles and hands. Be very careful, and use the correct tools when removing the torque converter.

6. When installing gears, bearings, and gear shafts, be careful not to pinch your fingers between the part and the housing.

7. When removing or installing snap rings, always use a snap ring pliers. Snap rings have a high degree of spring tension. If not installed with a correct tool, they may fly off and cause eye, face, or bodily injury.

8. At times it is necessary to keep the vehicle running and in gear to test an automatic transmission. Always make sure the emergency brake is applied when testing the transmission.

9. At times it may be necessary to run the engine and automatic transmission on a lift, in gear. Be careful of the rotating front or rear wheels while servicing the vehicle in this mode of testing.

PROBLEM: **Low Transmission Fluid Level from Leaks**

A vehicle has a slight transmission leak. Lately, when the engine is cold, the transmission seems to slip when accelerating.

DIAGNOSIS

When the transmission fluid is low and the transmission is cold, there is the possibility of slippage in the transmission

bands. If the fluid level gets too low, complete loss of drive may occur, especially when the transmission is cold. This condition will further damage the transmission internally. The leak is most likely in the front or rear seal on the transmission.

Always check the transmission fluid for the correct level. The fluid level should be checked when the transmission is at operating temperature (about 200 degrees F) and in park or neutral while the engine is running. Refer to **Figure 26–35**.

CAUTION: When adding fluid do not overfill, as foaming and loss of fluid may occur through the vent.

SERVICE

If the transmission fluid is leaking from the front, the front seal is damaged or not sealing. The front seal is located behind the torque converter on the oil pump housing. Replace the seal according to the manufacturer's recommended procedure. Use the following general procedure to remove the transmission.

CAUTION: Remove the ground cable on the battery before starting removal.

1. Remove the transmission dipstick.

2. Lift the car up on a suitable car hoist or jack. Remember to follow the safety guidelines when operating the car hoist.

3. Remove the drive shaft from between the transmission and the differential. On front wheel drive vehicles, remove the front axles.

4. Remove the shift linkage connected to the transmission.

5. Remove and mark all electrical connections to the transmission.

6. Remove the transmission cooler lines.

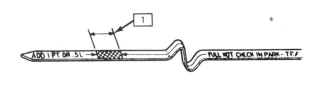

1 LEVEL TO BE IN CROSS-HATCHED AREA ON FLUID LEVEL INDICATOR BLADE. CHECK AT OPERATING TEMPERATURE.

FIGURE 26–35. Follow the manufacturer's recommendation when checking the fluid level. *(Courtesy of Oldsmobile Division, General Motors Corporation)*

7. Remove the speedometer cable.

8. Remove any vacuum connections to the transmission and mark for reassembly.

9. Drain the fluid from the transmission into a suitable container by removing the drain plug (if equipped) or by removing the transmission oil pan.

10. Remove the flywheel undercover.

11. Remove the bolts holding the torque converter to the flywheel. There are usually three bolts. Mark the flywheel and converter for reference during installation.

12. Using a suitable jack, lift the rear of the engine so as to take the weight off the rear transmission mount.

13. Remove the transmission mount from the transmission.

14. Place a transmission jack stand under the transmission to support it once it has been disconnected from the engine block.

15. Attach an engine support fixture as shown in *Figure 26–36*. This fixture is used to support the engine while the transmission is removed from the vehicle.

16. Slowly and carefully lower the engine until the bolts between the transmission torque converter housing and the block of the engine can be removed.

    CAUTION: Lowering the engine too far could press the distributor cap or other parts against the firewall and cause them to break or be damaged.

17. After the bolts between the transmission housing and the block have been removed, slowly lower the transmission jack stand and transmission away from the engine.

    CAUTION: Be careful not to drop the torque converter, as it is very heavy and filled with transmission fluid.

18. Use a suitable converter-holding tool to secure the converter.

19. With the transmission on the bench remove the torque converter and place aside.

20. The front seal is used to seal the transmission fluid where the torque converter inserts into the transmission. Remove the front seal using a suitable tool or seal puller.

21. Install a new front seal. Make sure a suitable liquid sealant has been placed around the outside of the seal.

22. To install the transmission, reverse the removal procedure.

PROBLEM: Dirty Transmission Fluid

A vehicle's transmission fluid has been checked and seems to be dirty. There are no apparent driving problems. However, there is varnish or gum on the dipstick.

DIAGNOSIS

It is recommended that the automatic transmission fluid and filter be changed at regular intervals. Refer to the owner's manual in the vehicle to determine when to change the fluid and filter.

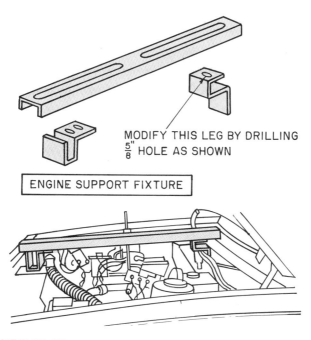

MODIFY THIS LEG BY DRILLING $\frac{5}{8}$" HOLE AS SHOWN

ENGINE SUPPORT FIXTURE

FIGURE 26–36.   Always install an engine support fixture before removing the automatic transmission. *(Courtesy of Motor Publications, Domestic Transmission Manual)*

SERVICE

Use the following general procedure to change the fluid and filter on the transmission.

1. Using a suitable jack, support the vehicle so that work can be done easily on the bottom of the transmission. The vehicle is usually placed on a car hoist.

   CAUTION: Follow all safety procedures when lifting a vehicle up on a hoist.

2. Drain the transmission fluid into a suitable container by loosening the oil pan and letting the transmission fluid drain out. There may also be a drain plug or filler tube connection that can be removed. Make sure to dispose of the automatic transmission fluid according to state or local regulations (see Chapter 2).

3. Using the correct size socket wrench, remove the transmission oil pan. At this point, the transmission filter can be observed.

4. Remove the oil filter and replace it with a new one. Replace the oil filter and gaskets in their proper positions. Failure to do so may damage the transmission. See *Figure 26–37*.

5. To reassemble, reverse the preceding procedure.

PROBLEM: Damaged Clutches or Bands

A vehicle has hard shifting from first to second gear.

DIAGNOSIS

Generally, this type of problem (and other shift problems) may indicate damaged clutches or bands. Several diagnostic checks can be done. When diagnosing transmission shift problems always check the following:

1. Periodically inspect the automatic transmission cooler lines for signs of damage. Worn or crimped lines may cause ATF loss or restriction. Prevent future damage by

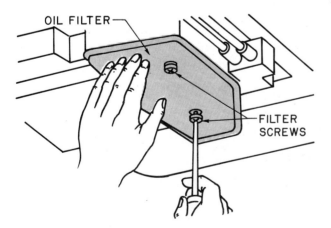

FIGURE 26–37. Replace the filter and oil at the recommended intervals. Always replace the filter and gasket in the correct and proper positions.

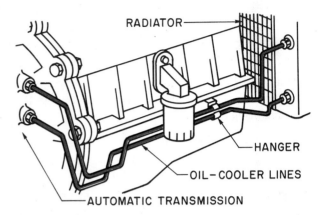

FIGURE 26–38. Inspect the transmission cooler lines for damage or leakage. Support the lines with the correct type of hanger.

supporting the lines with the proper clamp or hanger as shown in *Figure 26–38*.

2. Check the ATF for a burned odor, darkened color, or metal particles. A burned odor may indicate overheating and, possibly, damaged clutches. Metal particles may indicate damaged gears or extremely worn clutches.

3. If the engine cooling system is not working properly (overheating), the transmission may operate at higher temperatures as well. Higher oil temperature may damage the clutches and transmission bands. Check the cooling system if overheating is suspected.

4. Bubbles in the transmission fluid indicate the presence of a high-pressure leak in the transmission. A leak such as this may be in the valve body, valve, or hydraulic passageways. If such a leak is suspected, the transmission hydraulic system will need to be checked and repaired. Normally, the valve body can be replaced as a unit.

5. A poorly tuned engine that has low or insufficient vacuum may cause shifting problems. This is because several components on the transmission operate off a vacuum. Before testing any part of the automatic transmission, make sure that the engine vacuum is correct.

6. Inspect all linkages to the transmission for binding and damage. Incorrect linkage adjustments may cause bad shifting.

7. Numerous diagnosis flowcharts are available for further transmission diagnosis. *Figure 26–39* is an example of one such chart. Charts are usually available for each make and year of transmission.

SERVICE

There are two general categories of service for an automatic transmission.

1. In-vehicle adjustments and service

2. Overhaul

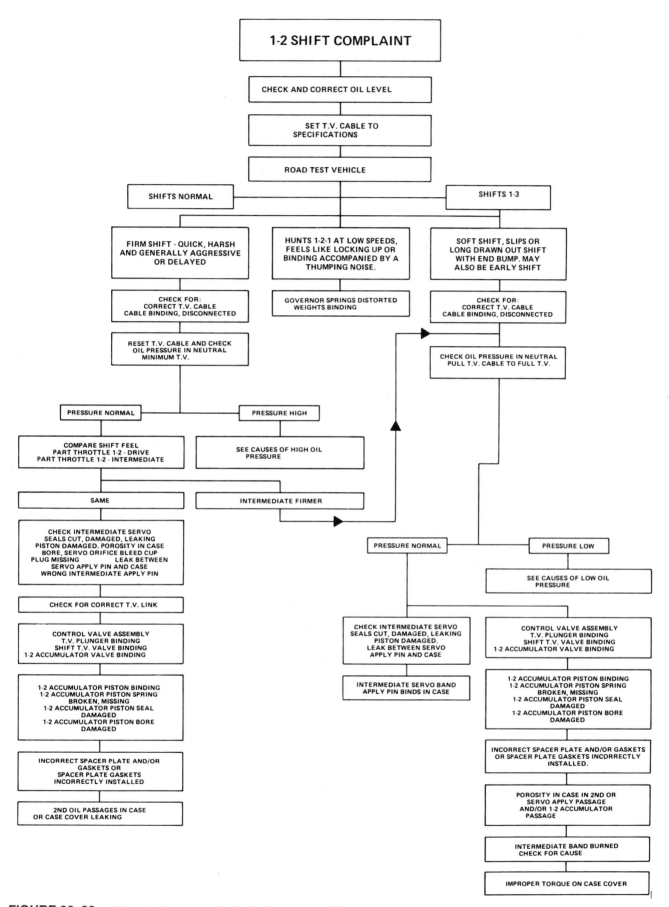

FIGURE 26–39. Flowcharts are used to help diagnose problems in automatic transmissions. *(Courtesy of Oldsmobile Division, General Motors Corporation)*

In-vehicle Adjustments and Service

Depending on the vehicle and manufacturer, the following types of adjustments and service can be made with the transmission in the vehicle:

1. Manual linkage adjustments

2. Downshift linkage adjustments

3. Neutral start switch adjustments

4. Bands adjust

5. Valve body replace

6. Governor replace

7. Extension housing replace

8. Vacuum regulator valve adjust

Each procedure will be different with each manufacturer. Refer to the appropriate service manual to determine the exact procedure for the vehicle.

Overhaul

Depending on the vehicle and manufacturer, the following types of service can be made with the transmission out of the vehicle:

1. Transmission disassemble

2. Governor assembly

3. Front end play check

4. Oil pump disassembly and assembly

5. Forward clutch disassembly and assembly

6. Sun gear and sun drive shell service

7. Valve body service

8. Low and reverse roller clutch service

9. Transmission assembly

Each procedure will be different with each manufacturer. Refer to the appropriate service manual to determine the exact procedure for the vehicle.

The following are selected examples of both in-vehicle and out-of-vehicle service checks and adjustments that are done on automatic transmissions:

1. On front wheel drive vehicles that use a chain drive, check the chain for excessive wear. See *Figure 26–40*.

2. Various air pressure checks are recommended during disassembly of automatic transmission. These checks determine the condition of various passageways and components. See *Figure 26–41*.

3. Often the manual shift linkage must be adjusted. Each procedure will be different. *Figure 26–42* shows a typical linkage being adjusted.

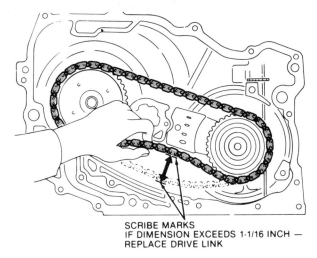

SCRIBE MARKS
IF DIMENSION EXCEEDS 1-1/16 INCH —
REPLACE DRIVE LINK

FIGURE 26–40. Check front wheel drive transmissions for chain wear and replace the chain if necessary. *(Courtesy of Oldsmobile Division, General Motors Corporation)*

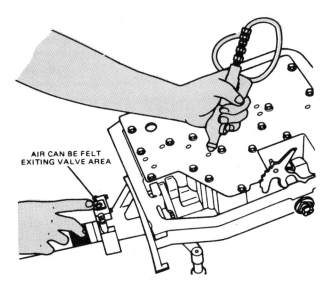

AIR CAN BE FELT
EXITING VALVE AREA

FIGURE 26–41. Air passageways can be checked in the transmission by using an air hose with 40 psi. *(Courtesy of Motor Publications, Domestic Transmission Manual)*

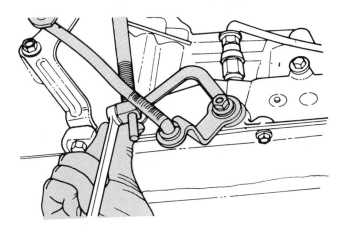

FIGURE 26–42. Various adjustments can be made on the linkage of each automatic transmission. *(Courtesy of Motor Publications, Domestic Transmission Manual)*

4. Various checks can be made in the clutch mechanism. *Figure 26–43* shows an example of measuring the intermediate clutch clearance. *Figure 26–44* shows an example of measuring the forward clutch snap ring clearance with a feeler gauge.

5. Torque converter end play can be checked using a dial indicator. *Figure 26–45* shows this check. Note that a special tool is used to perform this test.

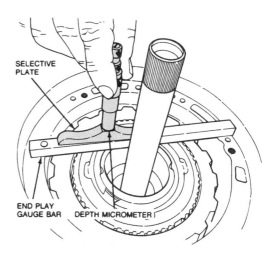

FIGURE 26–43. The clutch clearances can be checked using an inside micrometer. *(Courtesy of Motor Publications, Domestic Transmission Manual)*

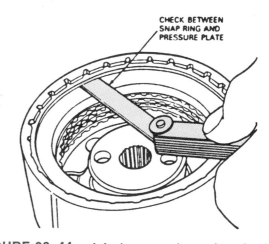

FIGURE 26–44. A feeler gauge is used to check the forward clutch snap ring clearance. *(Courtesy of Motor Publications, Domestic Transmission Manual)*

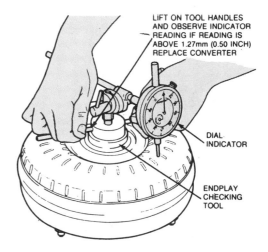

FIGURE 26–45. Use a dial indicator to check the torque converter end play. *(Courtesy of Motor Publications, Domestic Transmission Manual)*

SERVICE MANUAL CONNECTION

There are many important specifications to keep in mind when working with automatic transmissions. To identify the specifications for your engine, you will need to know the VIN (vehicle identification number) of the vehicle, the type and year of the vehicle, and the type of transmission. Although they may be titled differently, some of the more common automatic transmission specifications (not all) found in service manuals are listed below. Note that these specifications are typical examples. Each vehicle and engine may have different specifications.

Common specification	Typical example
Bands adjustment (front) after 10 lb-ft of torque applied (backoff)	4 1/4 turns
Downshift linkage adjustment	0.050–0.070 inch
Fluid change period	30,000 miles
Oil pan bolts, torque	12 lb-ft
Oil pressure (minimum throttle valve)	66–74 psi
Oil pump clearance, gears to cover	0.0005–0.0035 inch
Transmission fluid capacity	
Pan only	4.0 quarts
Total	12.0 quarts

In addition, the service manual will give specific directions for various service and testing procedures. Some of the more common procedures include:

- Adding fluid to dry transmission
- Bands adjustment
- Governor replacement
- Oil pump replacement
- Speedometer gear replace
- Throttle downshift linkage adjustment
- Transmission replacement

Linkage to
Future Automotive Technology

CONTINUOUSLY VARIABLE TRANSMISSION

One innovation that is promising for the future is the continuously variable transmission (CVT). The CVT is a type of transmission that has no gears for changing torque and speed requirements. Instead, two variable-speed pulleys or cones change speed ratios as the RPM changes. Normally, as the drive pulley or cone increases in speed, its running diameter gets larger. As the driven pulley increases in speed, its running diameter gets smaller. The combination of these pulleys or cones produces infinite speed ratios between the input and output of the transmission. The CVT enables the engine to operate at the most efficient RPM for the best fuel mileage. In one test comparing a CVT with a five-speed transmission, the CVT used 11.5% less fuel, produced 33% fewer hydrocarbon emissions, and 20% fewer CO emissions. The figure illustrates the drive and driven pulley in a CVT.

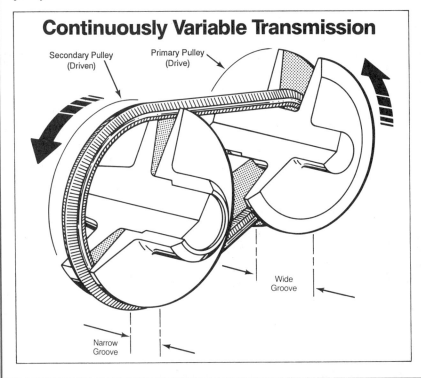

Continuously Variable Transmission

Secondary Pulley (Driven)

Primary Pulley (Drive)

Wide Groove

Narrow Groove

SUMMARY

This chapter discussed the purpose, parts, and operation of the automatic transmission. The purpose of the automatic transmission is to connect the engine to the drive wheels. It is made of several major parts and systems. These include the torque converter, planetary gear system, hydraulic system, and controls.

The torque converter connects the engine to the transmission and multiplies the torque at lower speeds. It is considered a fluid coupling. The torque converter is made of several parts, including the pump, turbine, and stator. As the engine turns, the pump forces oil centrifugally into the turbine blades. The turbine blades then turn the transmission gears. The stator is used to correctly redirect the flow of oil back to the pump.

When the turbine blade is stopped under load, the oil deflection is greatest. The angle of deflection produces the amount of torque produced on the turbine blades. As the speed of the turbine increases, the angle of deflection decreases. Torque is also decreased as speed increases.

The torque converter is placed in front of the transmission case on rear wheel drive vehicles. On front wheel drive vehicles, the torque converter is located to the side of the transmission case. A large chain from the torque converter to the transmission is used to transfer the torque.

Different gear ratios are produced in the transmission by using a planetary gear system. The planetary gear system is made of several parts. These include the sun gear, ring gear, planet gears, and planet gear carrier. If any one of these is held stationary, different gear ratios can be produced.

Several types of clutches and bands are used to lock up or hold the correct gear in the planetary gear system. The multiple-disc clutch uses a set of friction discs working against a set of metal discs. Oil pushes a piston against the discs to lock up the system. One of the planetary gears is connected to the discs, which then lock up.

A transmission band is used to lock up a clutch housing or ring gear. The band is wrapped around the housing. A servo is operated hydraulically to engage and disengage the transmission band. Some transmissions also use an accumulator to cushion the action of the servo.

To aid in smoothness of shifting, an overrunning clutch is used on transmissions. This clutch is used to provide smooth engagement and release of the other clutches.

The heart of the automatic transmission is the hydraulic system. Oil is used to operate and control the transmission. Oil pressure is produced by the oil pump, which is located in the front of the transmission case. There are several styles of oil pumps, including the gear, rotor, and vane-type pumps. All use an eccentric design to produce suction and pressure for pumping oil. The oil pump is driven by the torque converter with two tangs.

The fluid used in the hydraulic system must undergo high pressures, stresses, temperatures, and shearing forces. Special automatic transmission fluid (ATF) is used. Refer to the manufacturer's recommendations to determine the exact type to use.

Most of the hydraulic controls are housed in the valve body. The valve body has many small passageways and holes that transfer the oil to the correct part. The oil is also sent to the radiator to be cooled. At the radiator, a heat exchanger extracts heat from the transmission fluid to the radiator coolant.

Many control valves are used on the transmission oil circuits. The pressure regulator valve is used to control the exact pressure for the different components. The manual shift valve is used to tell the transmission what gear is to be used. Its operation is controlled by the operator moving the gear shift lever. The throttle valve is used to help shift gears, based on engine load and amount of throttle. The governor is used to help shift gears, based on vehicle speed. On the basis of the speed and load of the vehicle, the shift valve operates the clutches to lock and unlock the exact gear in the planetary gear system.

Several other valves are also used. The vacuum modulator tells the transmission the amount of load, determined by intake manifold vacuum. The kickdown valve is used to downshift when the operator pushes the throttle fully to the floor. Various ball check valves are used to control the direction of oil flow and prevent back flow.

Today's automatic transmissions use a lockup system between the torque converter turbine and the engine. In the past, there has always been a certain amount of slippage between the engine and the torque converter turbine. The lockup system eliminates slippage. Lockup occurs based upon a hydraulic circuit in the automatic transmission. A torque converter clutch valve located in the transmission is used to aid lockup.

Computers are also used to control automatic transmissions. Generally, computers are used to control the shifting and the torque converter clutch. The computer works in conjunction with an ECM to determine the exact time for shifting and for torque converter clutch lockup.

There are several major considerations when servicing the automatic transmission. Filters and ATF should be checked and changed at the correct intervals. When the transmission oil smells burned or contains fine metal particles, the clutches might be damaged. The engine temperature also affects the operation and temperature of the transmission fluid. Before checking any part of the transmission, always be sure the engine is running correctly. Various other diagnosis and service tips can be found in the appropriate service manuals.

TERMS TO KNOW

Can you explain each of the following terms? Review the chapter until you can use each term correctly.

Fluid coupling	Stator
Torque converter	Periphery
Turbine	Deflection angle

(continued)

Valve body

Planetary gear system

Planet carrier

Overdrive

Multiple-disc clutch

Transmission band

Servo

Accumulator

Tang

Automatic transmission
   fluid (ATF)

Lockup clutch

Pressure regulator valve

Spool valve

Manual shift valve

Throttle valve (TV)

Shift valve

Vacuum modulator

Torque converter clutch
   (TCC) valve

Power control module (PCM)

 REVIEW QUESTIONS

Multiple Choice

1. Which of the following is not considered a major part in an automatic transmission?
   a. Torque converter
   b. Planetary gear system
   c. Oil pump
   d. Power steering gear
   e. Hydraulic valves

2. Which of the following parts is/are used as the input inside the torque converter?
   a. Turbine
   b. Pump
   c. Stator
   d. Seal
   e. All of the above

3. The output of the torque converter is taken off the:
   a. Turbine
   b. Stator
   c. Pump
   d. Seal
   e. All of the above

4. The coupling between the engine and transmission on the automatic transmission is considered:
   a. An air coupling
   b. A fluid coupling
   c. An electrical coupling
   d. A mechanical coupling
   e. All of the above

5. As the turbine speed decreases, the angle of deflection:
   a. Increases
   b. Decreases
   c. Remains the same
   d. Causes the stator speed to change
   e. Causes the pump speed to increase

6. Which of the following is a part of a planetary gear system?
   a. Sun gear
   b. Planet carrier
   c. Planet gears
   d. Ring gear
   e. All of the above

7. The planetary gear system is able to produce a/an _____ in output speed.
   a. Increase
   b. Decrease
   c. Reverse direction
   d. All of the above
   e. None of the above

8. Which of the following uses a set of friction discs and steel discs pressed together to engage a clutch?
   a. Transmission band
   b. Overrunning clutch
   c. Multiple disc
   d. Servo
   e. Accumulator

9. What component aids in the operation of the transmission band?
   a. Servo piston
   b. Accumulator
   c. Vacuum modulator
   d. Multiple-disc
   e. Torque converter

10. What component is used to help smooth the shifting from one gear to another?
    a. Overrunning clutch
    b. Servo
    c. Sun gear
    d. Ring gear
    e. Torque converter

11. The oil pump on the automatic transmission uses the _____ type of design.
    a. Eccentric
    b. Vane
    c. Gear
    d. All of the above
    e. None of the above

12. The oil pump on the transmission housing is located:
    a. Inside the planetary gear system
    b. On the hydraulic circuit body
    c. On the front of the transmission case
    d. On the drive shaft
    e. None of the above

13. Which component is used to turn the oil pump on an automatic transmission?
    a. Planetary gear system
    b. Accumulator
    c. Servo
    d. Crankshaft
    e. Torque converter

14. Which component in the automatic transmission houses the valves and contains the many oil passageways?
    a. The accumulator
    b. The modulator valve
    c. The valve body
    d. The planetary gear system
    e. None of the above

15. Which of the following components helps to cool the transmission fluid?
    a. Radiator
    b. Torque converter
    c. Accumulator
    d. Planetary gear system
    e. Valve body

16. Which of the following transmission control valves is used to measure vehicle speed and, in turn, direct oil flow to shift gears?
    a. Manual shift valve
    b. Shift valve
    c. Throttle valve
    d. Governor
    e. Modulator valve

17. Which of the following transmission control valves uses intake manifold vacuum to measure vehicle load?
    a. Shift valve
    b. Modulator valve
    c. Manual shift valve
    d. Throttle valve
    e. Governor

18. Which type of valve is used to control or direct oil flow and prevent back flow of oil?
    a. Ball check valve
    b. Governor
    c. Throttle valve
    d. Shift valve
    e. Modulator valve

19. If the transmission fluid has a burned odor, the trouble may be in the _____ on the automatic transmission.
    a. Torque converter
    b. Clutches
    c. Seals
    d. Governor
    e. Shift valve

20. What parts may need service on the automatic transmission?
    a. Filter may be dirty
    b. Clutches may be worn
    c. Seals may leak
    d. All of the above
    e. None of the above

The following questions are similar in format to ASE (Automotive Service Excellence) test questions.

21. Technician A says that if the engine coolant is too hot, the transmission may be overheated and damaged. Technician B says that the cooling system has no effect on the operation or temperature of the transmission. Who is right?
    a. A only
    b. B only
    c. Both A and B
    d. Neither A nor B

22. Bubbles are noticed in the transmission fluid. Technician A says that there is too much transmission fluid, and foam is being produced. Technician B says that there is an internal leak in the hydraulic system. Who is right?
    a. A only
    b. B only
    c. Both A and B
    d. Neither A nor B

23. Transmission fluid is leaking from the front of the transmission housing. Technician A says to remove and replace the transmission filter. Technician B says to replace the oil pump. Who is right?
    a. A only
    b. B only
    c. Both A and B
    d. Neither A nor B

24. Technician A says the transmission fluid level should be checked when the transmission is at operating temperature. Technician B says it should be checked when the transmission is cold. Who is right?
    a. A only
    b. B only
    c. Both A and B
    d. Neither A nor B

25. Technician A says that adjusting the shift linkage is considered an in-vehicle adjustment. Technician B says that checking the snap ring end play is an in-vehicle adjustment. Who is right?
    a. A only
    b. B only
    c. Both A and B
    d. Neither A nor B

26. A vehicle has a computerized automatic transmission. Technician A says that solenoid A is not used to control shifting. Technician B says that solenoid B is the only one used to control shifting. Who is right?
    a. A only
    b. B only
    c. Both A and B
    d. Neither A nor B

27. Technician A says that when the apply circuit is energized on the TCC system, the torque converter is locked up. Technician B says that when the release circuit is energized on the TCC system, the torque converter is not locked up. Who is right?
    a. A only
    b. B only
    c. Both A and B
    d. Neither A nor B

28. A vehicle's ATF has a burned smell. Technician A says the clutches are bad. Technician B says the bands are bad. Who is right?
    a. A only
    b. B only
    c. Both A and B
    d. Neither A nor B

Essay

29. What is the purpose of the torque converter?

30. What is the deflection angle on automatic transmissions?

31. Describe the purpose and operation of a planetary gear system.

32. What are the purposes of clutches and bands in an automatic transmission?

33. What is the purpose of the valve body in an automatic transmission?

34. What is the purpose of using a governor in an automatic transmission?

35. Describe the purpose and operation of a neutral start switch.

Short Answer

36. On automatic transmission lockup systems, the torque converter is locked to the _____.

37. Lockup on the torque converter is accomplished by _____ pressure.

38. The two most common types of ATF include _____ and _____.

39. One type of computer used to control shifting in electronic transmissions is called the _____ module.

40. How many computer-controlled solenoids are normally used in an electronic transmission? _____

CHAPTER 27

Drive Lines, Differentials, and Axles

INTRODUCTION   To get the vehicle moving, power or torque must be transferred from the transmission to the drive wheels. This is done by using drive lines, differentials, and axles. The purpose of this chapter is to define the parts, operation, and diagnosis and service of these components.

OBJECTIVES   After reading this chapter, you should be able to:

- State the parts and operation of rear wheel drive shafts and universal joints.

- State the parts and operation of front wheel drive shafts and constant velocity universal joints.

- Identify the parts and operation of differentials, including the nonslip (limited slip) differentials.

- State the correct lubrication used in differentials.

- Describe common problems, diagnosis, and service tips used with drive lines, differentials, and axles.

✔ SAFETY CHECKLIST ✔

When working with drive lines, differentials, and axles, keep these important safety precautions in mind.

✔ Always wear OSHA-approved safety glasses when working on drive lines, differentials, and axle components.

✔ Always use the proper tools when working on drive lines, differentials, and axles.

✔ Immediately wipe up any oil that is spilled on the floor.

✔ Always disconnect the battery before working on any part of the drive lines and differential.

✔ Never try to lift heavy drive lines or differentials without proper lifting equipment.

Some of the information in this chapter can help you prepare for the National Institute for Automotive Service Excellence (ASE) certification tests. The test most directly related to this chapter is entitled

MANUAL DRIVE TRAIN AND AXLES (TEST A3).

The content areas that closely parallel this chapter are

TRANSAXLE DIAGNOSIS AND REPAIR, DRIVE (HALF) SHAFT AND UNIVERSAL JOINT DIAGNOSIS AND REPAIR, AND REAR AXLE DIAGNOSIS AND REPAIR.

27.1   REAR DRIVE SHAFTS AND OPERATION

Purpose of the Drive Shaft

The torque that is produced from the engine and transmission must be transferred to the rear wheels to push the vehicle forward and reverse. The *drive shaft* must provide a smooth, uninterrupted flow of power to the axles. The drive shaft and differential are used to transfer this torque. *Figure 27–1* shows the location of the drive shaft and differential.

There are several functions of the drive shaft. First, it must transmit torque from the transmission to the axle. During operation, it is necessary to transmit maximum low-gear torque developed by the engine. The drive shaft must also be capable of rotating at the very fast speeds required by the vehicle.

The drive shaft must also operate through constantly changing angles between the transmission and the differential and axles. The rear axle is not attached directly to the frame of the vehicle. It rides suspended by the springs and travels in an irregular floating motion. As the rear wheels roll over bumps in the road, the differential and axles move up and

down. This movement changes the angle between the transmission and the differential.

The length of the drive shaft must also be capable of changing while transmitting torque. Length changes are caused by axle movement due to torque reaction, road deflections, braking loads, and so on. *Figure 27–2* shows the movements that the drive shaft may undergo during normal driving operation.

Purpose of Universal Joints

Universal joints (U-joints) are used to permit the drive shaft to operate at different angles. *Figure 27–3* shows a drawing and a photograph of a simple universal joint. Note that the rotation can be transmitted when two shafts are at different angles. This type of universal joint is called the cross and bearing type *Cardan universal joint,* or four-point joint. It consists of two *yokes* and a journal assembly with four *trunnions.* A yoke is a Y-shaped assembly that is used to connect the U-joint together. The trunnion is a protrusion on the journal assembly. The journal assembly is also called a *cross* and bearing assembly or spider.

Universal Joint Parts

The universal joint is made of several parts. The center of the universal joint is called the cross and bearing assembly. Its purpose is to connect the two yokes. The yokes are attached directly to the drive shafts. Four *bearing caps* are placed on the universal joint. Each cap is placed on a trunnion part of the universal joint. Each bearing cap is a needle-type bearing that allows free movement between the trunnion and yoke. The needle bearing caps are attached to the yokes by several methods. They can be pressed into the yokes, bolted to the yokes, or held in place with bolts, nuts, U-bolts, or metal

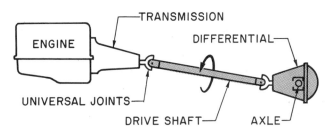

FIGURE 27–1.   The drive shaft is used to transmit the power from the engine and transmission to the differential and axles on rear wheel drive vehicles.

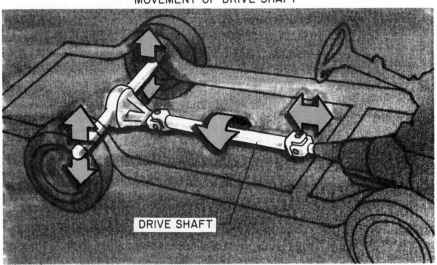

FIGURE 27–2.   The drive shaft must be designed to allow for both up and down motion on the differential and shortening and lengthening between the differential and transmission. *(Courtesy of Dana Corporation)*

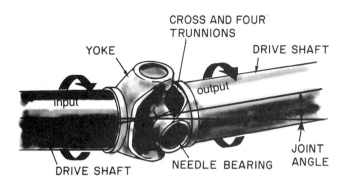

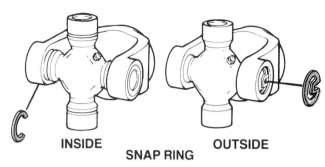

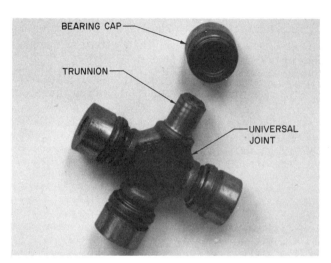

FIGURE 27–3. Universal joints allow the drive shaft to turn through different angles. *(Courtesy of Drivetrain Service Division, Dana Corporation)*

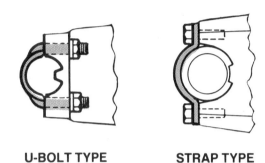

FIGURE 27–4. Universal joints are held in the yoke in several ways. Snap rings, U-bolts, and straps are used. *(Courtesy of Dana Corporation)*

straps. Snap rings are also used to hold bearing caps in place. See *Figure 27–4*. On most replacement universal joints, there is a lubrication fitting to put grease into the needle bearings.

Slip Joints

The drive shaft must also be able to lengthen and shorten during operation with irregular road conditions. A *slip joint* is used to compensate for this motion. The slip joint is usually made of an internal and external spline. It is located on the front end of the drive shaft and is connected to the transmission. See *Figure 27–5*. The slip joint can also be placed in the center of the drive shaft.

Drive Shaft Vibration

Vibration is the most common drive shaft problem. It can be either transverse or torsional. As shown in *Figure 27–6*, transverse vibration is the result of an unbalanced condition acting on the shaft. This condition is usually caused by dirt or foreign material on the shaft, and it can cause a rather noticeable vibration in the vehicle.

Torsional vibration occurs from the power impulses of the engine or from improper universal joint angles. It causes a noticeable sound disturbance and can cause a mechanical

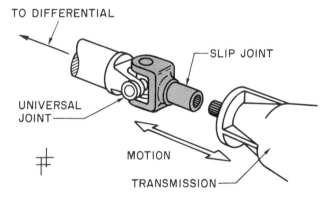

FIGURE 27–5. The slip joint is designed to allow the drive shaft to shorten and lengthen when the differential goes over an irregular road surface.

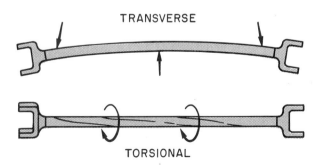

FIGURE 27–6. Vibration in the drive shaft can be either transverse or torsional. Both types of vibration can cause damage to the universal joints.

shaking. In excess, both types of vibration can cause damage to the universal joints and bearings.

Drive Shaft Velocity and Angles

The popular cross and bearing assembly universal joint has one disadvantage. When the U-joint transmits torque through an angle, the output shaft increases speed and slows down twice in each revolution of the shaft. The rate at which the speed changes depends on the steepness of the universal joint angle. The speed changes are not normally visible during rotation. However, they may be felt as torsional vibration due to improper installation, steep and/or unequal operating angles, and high speeds.

Figure 27–7 shows how the output shaft changes speed. The input path and bearings rotate in a circular motion when viewed from the end of the drive shaft. The output path and bearings rotate in an elliptical motion or path. The output path is viewed at an angle instead of straight on because it is at an angle from the input shaft. Therefore it looks like an ellipse.

In operation, the input shaft speed has a constant velocity. The output shaft speed accelerates and decelerates (catching up and falling behind in rotation) during one complete revolution. In *Figure 27–8*, from 0 to 90 degrees rotation, the output shaft accelerates. From 90 to 180 degrees rotation, the output shaft decelerates. From 180 to 270 degrees rotation, the output shaft accelerates again. From 270 to 360 degrees rotation, the output shaft decelerates. The input and output shafts complete one rotation at exactly the same time. The greater the output angle, the greater the change in velocity of the output shaft for each revolution.

The torsional vibrations mentioned before travel down the drive shaft to the next universal joint. At the second

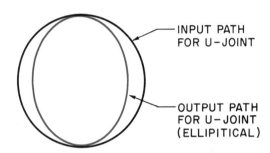

FIGURE 27–7. The input path of the universal joint is circular. The output path of the universal joint is elliptical. The elliptical path causes the output shaft to accelerate and decelerate within each drive shaft revolution.

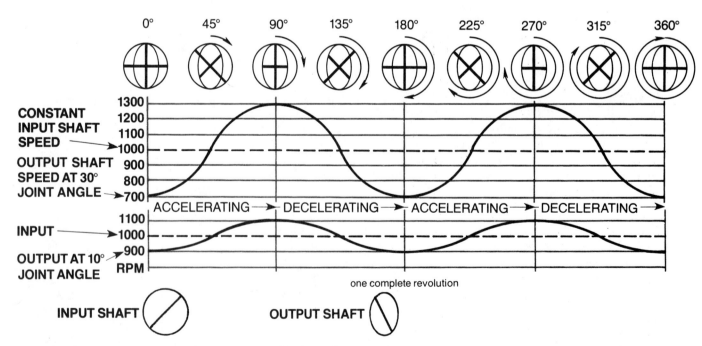

FIGURE 27–8. Within one revolution of a drive shaft with the universal joint at an angle, the output speed accelerates and decelerates two times. The greater the angle of the universal joint, the greater the change in speed. *(Courtesy of Drivetrain Service Division, Dana Corporation)*

universal joint angle, similar acceleration and deceleration occur. However, these take place at equal and reverse angles to the first joint. See *Figure 27–9*. Now the speed changes cancel each other when the two operating angles are equal. Drive shafts must have at least two universal joints, and operating angles must be small and equal. Any variations from this may cause excessive needle bearing and trunnion wear.

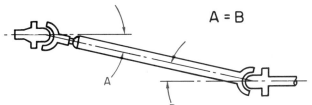

FIGURE 27–9.   To offset the velocity changes in a drive shaft, a second universal joint is used at an equal and opposite angle.

Drive Shaft Construction

There are several designs for drive shafts. The type depends on several factors. These include the length of the vehicle, the amount of power the engine must transmit, the RPM of the drive shaft, and the year of the vehicle. *Figure 27–10* shows a typical drive shaft. In most cases, a universal joint is placed on both sides. The most common location for the slip joint is on the output of the transmissions. On certain vehicles, the slip joint is located in the center of the drive shaft.

Center Bearing

On many large vehicles, it may be necessary to use a center bearing for support on the drive shaft. *Figure 27–11* shows a typical center bearing assembly. When a center bearing is used, there will be two drive shafts and usually more than two universal joints. The bearing assembly supports the end of the first drive shaft by being bolted directly to the frame of the vehicle.

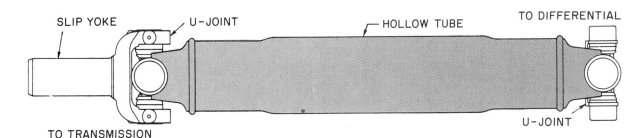

FIGURE 27–10.   The parts of a standard drive shaft. *(Courtesy of Chevrolet Division, General Motors Corporation)*

CENTER BEARING ASSEMBLY

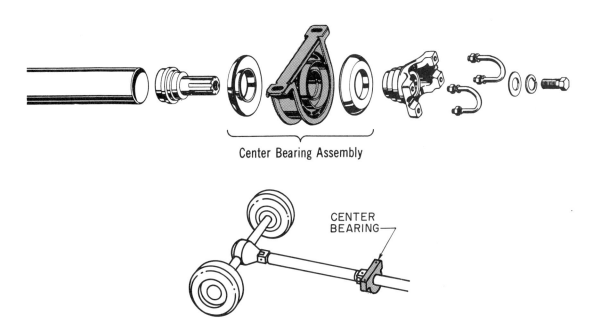

FIGURE 27–11.   The center bearing is used to support longer drive shaft systems. The center bearing assembly is attached directly to the frame. *(Courtesy of Universal Joint Division, Dana Corporation)*

PROBLEM: Noise in Driveshaft

A car has developed a squeaky noise in the drive shaft. The noise is not heard all the time. However, when the car is shifted into reverse and then into forward again, a slight clunk is heard and the sound returns.

SOLUTION:

The most common cause of noise in the drive shaft is a bad universal joint. When it is worn, the U-joint squeaks. The squeak comes from the lack of lubrication in the U-joint needle bearings. Remove the drive shaft and check the U-joints. When moving the U-joints to check them, check for any irregular bumps or motion. Replace the U-joints, if necessary.

27.2   FRONT WHEEL DRIVE SYSTEMS

Requirements of Front Wheel Drive Systems

A front wheel drive vehicle presents several unique problems for the drive shafts and joints. The drive shaft must be able to do three things. First, it must allow the front wheels to turn for steering. Second, it must be able to telescope, an action similar to that of a slip joint on rear drive vehicles. Third, it must transmit torque continuously without vibration. Because of these characteristics, a cross and bearing universal joint would not work well, especially during sharp turning. A *constant velocity (CV) joint* is used instead. See *Figure 27–12*.

Constant Velocity Joints

The constant velocity drive is designed much the same as a set of bevel gears. Balls and grooves are used, rather than gears. See *Figure 27–13*. Balls and grooves connect the input and output shafts. If the balls are placed in elongated grooves, the result is called a constant velocity (CV) joint. With this type of joint, there will be no speed or velocity changes on

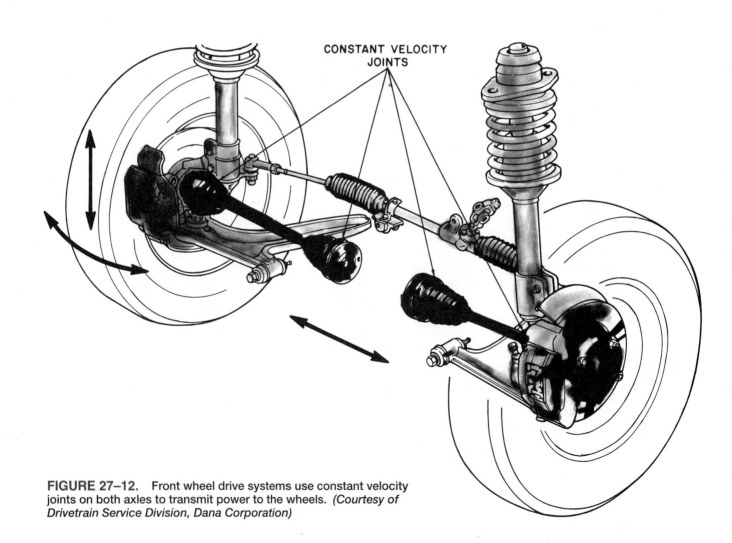

CONSTANT VELOCITY JOINTS

FIGURE 27–12.   Front wheel drive systems use constant velocity joints on both axles to transmit power to the wheels. *(Courtesy of Drivetrain Service Division, Dana Corporation)*

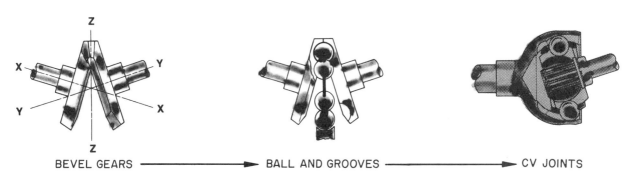

FIGURE 27–13. Constant velocity joints act much the same as bevel gears or ball and groove connections. *(Courtesy of Drivetrain Division, Dana Corporation)*

the output shaft as with cross and bearing type universal joints.

Types of CV Joints

There are two types of CV joints. *Figure 27–14* shows the ball-style and the *tripod*-type CV joints. The ball style uses a series of balls, a cage, and inner and outer races. The tripod uses a tulip assembly and three rollers. Both perform well in front wheel drive cars.

The typical front wheel drive car uses two drive shaft assemblies. One assembly drives each wheel. Each assembly has a CV joint at the wheel end. This CV joint is called the fixed joint or outboard joint. A second joint on each shaft is located at the transaxle end. This CV joint is called the inboard or plunging joint. This may be either a ball or a tripod CV joint. It allows the slip motion that is required when the drive shaft shortens or lengthens because of irregular surfaces. See *Figure 27–15*.

Other Applications for Constant Velocity

On certain makes of cars, the engine is located in the rear. On these cars, constant velocity joints may also be used. *Figure 27–16* shows such a system. Two drive shafts are used on this system. In addition, two constant velocity joints are used on each drive shaft.

FIGURE 27–14. Two types of constant velocity joints are commonly used. These are the ball style and the tripod type. *(Courtesy of Drivetrain Service Division, Dana Corporation)*

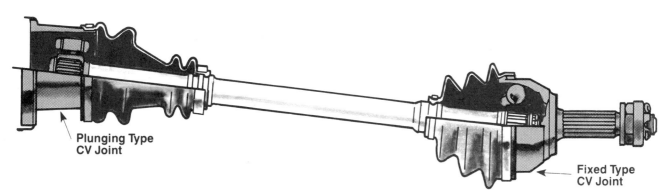

FIGURE 27–15. The plunging CV joint is used on the transaxle end. The fixed-type CV joint is used on the wheel end. *(Courtesy of Drivetrain Service Division, Dana Corporation)*

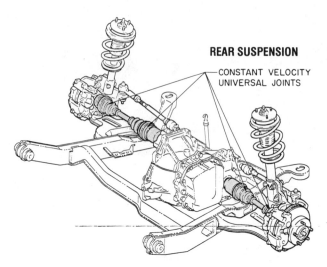

FIGURE 27–16. Constant velocity joints are also used on certain types of rear engine vehicles. *(Courtesy of Pontiac Division, General Motors Corporation)*

FIGURE 27–17. A differential transmits torque from the drive shaft to the axles and drive wheels. *(Courtesy of Masco Industries)*

CAR CLINIC

PROBLEM: Rear End Whine

A car has a noticeable whine in the rear end or differential at 30–45 mph. When the engine decelerates, the whine stops. What could be the problem?

SOLUTION:

The whine is probably coming from the ring and pinion gear in the differential. However, the rear wheel bearings may also be bad. Check the rear wheel bearings first. If they are OK, check the differential ring and pinion gear. Check for wear and backlash specifications. The ring and pinion gear will probably have to be replaced.

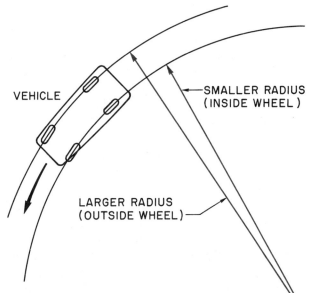

FIGURE 27–18. The differential is needed because the rear wheels turn at different speeds around a corner.

27.3 DIFFERENTIALS AND AXLES

Purpose of the Differential

The purpose of the *differential*, shown in *Figure 27–17*, is to transmit the torque from the drive shaft to the axles and drive wheels of the vehicle. On front wheel drive vehicles, the differential is located inside the transaxle and is a part of the total assembly. Torque is transmitted from the engine, through the transmission, and through the drive shaft. The differential then splits the torque and sends it to the drive wheels.

In addition, the differential allows the rear wheels to turn at different speeds during cornering. *Figure 27–18* shows why the wheels turn at different speeds on corners. The inside

rear wheel turns at a smaller radius than the outside rear wheel. The differential is designed to keep the power transmitting equally to both wheels while they are traveling at different speeds.

Differential Main Parts

Figure 27–19 shows the main parts of the differential:

1. *Drive pinion* — The drive pinion is the main input shaft to the differential. It is driven from the drive shaft.

2. *Ring gear* — The ring gear is driven from the drive pinion. Its purpose is to drive the remaining parts of the differential.

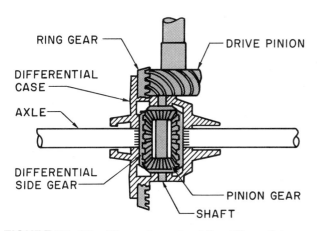

FIGURE 27–19. The main parts of the differential.

3. *Differential case* — The differential case holds several bevel gears. The entire differential case is driven from the ring gear, which is bolted to it.

4. *Two differential side gears and two pinion gears* — These four gears are placed inside the differential case. All four gears are meshed together. The pinion gears have a shaft running through their center. The shaft is secured to the differential case. Thus, as the differential case turns, the shaft rotates (end to end) at the same speed as the differential case. Since all four gears are meshed, the differential side gears also rotate at the same speed.

5. *Axle* — The axles are attached to the differential side gear by a spline on the axle and inside the differential side gear. As the differential side gear rotates, the axles also rotate, causing the vehicle to move.

Differential Operation

When the vehicle is moving straight down the road, the transmission of power comes from the drive pinion to the ring gear and differential case. As the differential case turns, the pinion (also called bevel) gears inside the case also move with the case. However, although the pinion gears are meshed during this condition, they are not rotating among themselves. In fact, the pinion gears are not spinning on their shafts at this point.

As the car goes around a left corner, the left axle slows down and the right axle speeds up. During this slowing down and speeding up, the bevel or pinion gears inside the differential case begin to rotate among themselves. The pinion gears are now rotating or turning on the shaft. The pinion gear is said to walk around the differential side gears. When the vehicle returns to a straight line, both axles are spinning at the same speed, but the gears are no longer turning among themselves. As the car goes around a right corner, the right axle slows down and the left axle speeds up. Again the pinion gears inside the differential case begin turning among themselves. (The pinion gear walks around the differential side gears.) This is necessary so that the axles will spin at different speeds while still transmitting power.

Complete Differential

Figure 27–20 shows a complete differential. In addition to the parts already mentioned, several other parts are included. These are:

1. *Pinion gears* — This differential shows four pinion gears for more torque-carrying capabilities.

2. *Adjusters* — As they are turned in and out, adjusters move the entire differential case (gear case) from side to side. This adjustment is used to change the gear backlash between the drive pinion and the ring gear, and to preload bearings.

3. *Bearings* — Various bearings are used to support each shaft.

4. *Thrust washers* — Thrust washers are used to absorb any side thrust produced by the gears in the differential.

5. *Spacer* — A spacer is used on the drive pinion shaft to adjust the position of the drive pinion in relation to the ring gear.

6. *Carrier* — The carrier housing is used to hold all the differential parts together.

Limited Slip Differential

On a standard differential, equal torque is transmitted to the rear wheels if the loads on the two wheels are the same. However, if one wheel hits a patch of ice or other slippery surface, the torque on the two wheels will be different. In this case, one wheel may spin freely while the other wheel produces torque.

To eliminate this condition, *limited slip differentials* are used. Limited slip differentials use a set of clutches or cones to lock up both wheels. The clutches or cones apply a pressure to the side gears. This additional pressure prevents one wheel from spinning more rapidly than the other. The clutch assembly or cone assembly is located inside the differential case, usually between the side gears and the carrier housing or differential case.

Figure 27–21 shows a limited slip differential system. Three additional parts are shown. These include the:

1. *Clutch plate* — used to produce the necessary friction to lock up both wheels.

2. *Preload spring* — used to produce the pressure against the clutches.

3. *Pressure ring* — a surface against which the clutches rub for the side gear.

Although there are many designs, the principles of operation remain the same. Springs or some other force must push clutches or cones against a surface to lock the side gears to the differential case.

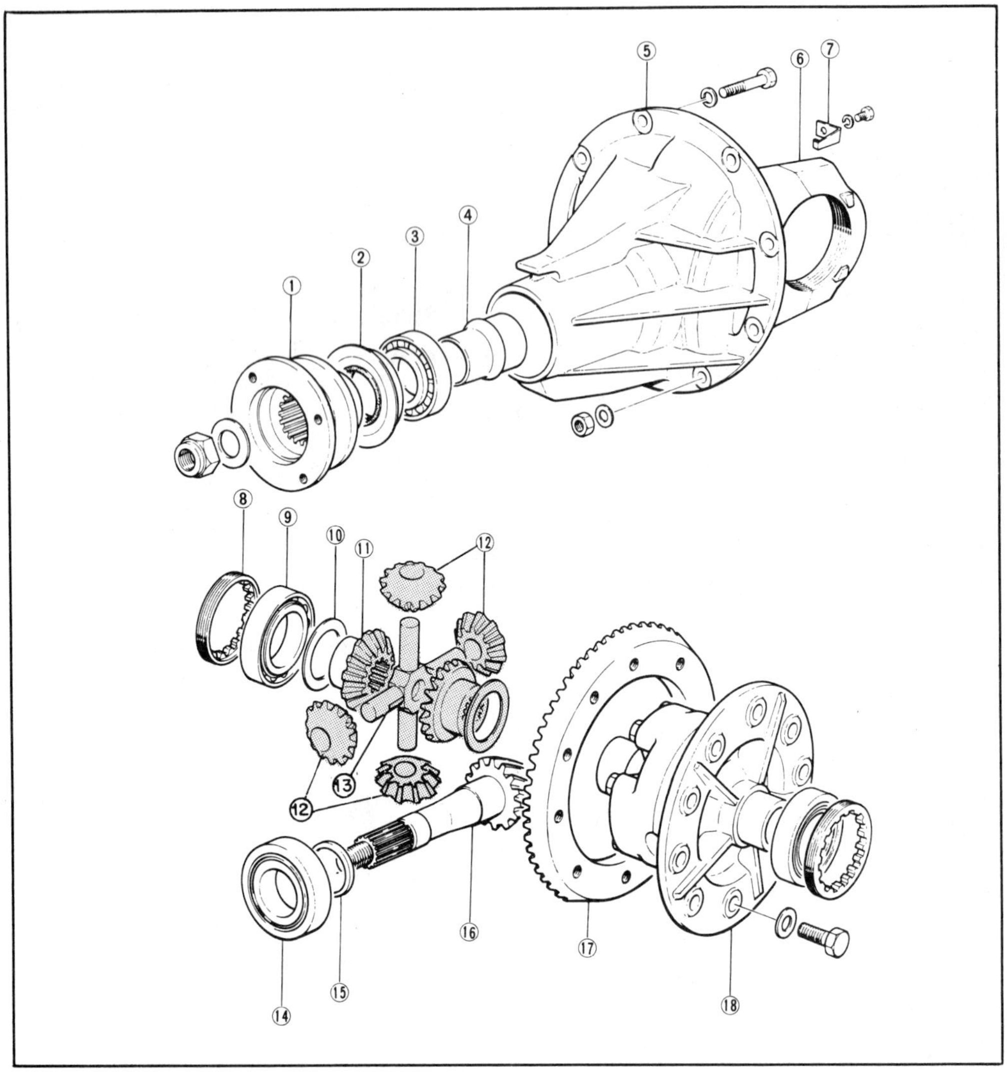

Rear axle components
1. Companion flange
2. Oil seal
3. Front bearing
4. Collapsible spacer
5. Gear case
6. Bearing cap
7. Adjuster lock plate
8. Adjuster
9. Differential bearing
10. Thrust washer
11. Side gear
12. Pinion gears
13. Spider
14. Rear bearing
15. Spacer
16. Drive pinion
17. Ring gear
18. Carrier

FIGURE 27–20.   The differential assembly can also use four pinion gears. *(Courtesy of Mazda Motor Corporation)*

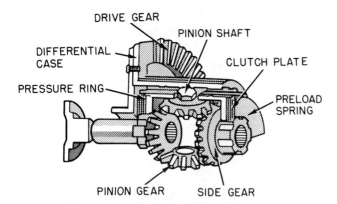

DRIVE GEAR
PINION SHAFT
DIFFERENTIAL CASE
CLUTCH PLATE
PRESSURE RING
PRELOAD SPRING
PINION GEAR
SIDE GEAR

FIGURE 27–21.   A limited slip differential uses a clutch plate, springs, and a pressure ring to lock up the two side gears. *(Courtesy of Chrysler Corporation)*

Differential Lubrication

The differential uses several types of lubricants. The exact type depends on the year of the vehicle and whether the differential is separate or combined into the transaxle. Also, the viscosity will also change with the weather condition. On rear wheel drive vehicles, where the differential is separate, a *hypoid gear oil* such as 80W-90 can be used. In addition, Dexron II ATF is used in many vehicles. On vehicles in which a transaxle is used, several types of lubricants are recommended including Dexron II ATF and 5W-30 grade SF engine oil.

Limited Slip Lubricant

On certain axles equipped with locking clutches or limited slip differentials (Dana Trac-Lok, Sure-Grip, Traction-Lok, and others) a *friction modifier* is added to the gear oil. Generally 4 ounces of special friction lubricant are needed on these differentials. For example, one manufacturer recommends replacing 4 ounces of standard differential lubricant with 4 ounces of Mopar hypoid gear oil additive modifier with every refill. Without the correct amount of modifier, the slip between the axles will be incorrect. Too much modifier allows the clutch packs (shown in *Figure 27–22*) to slip too much.

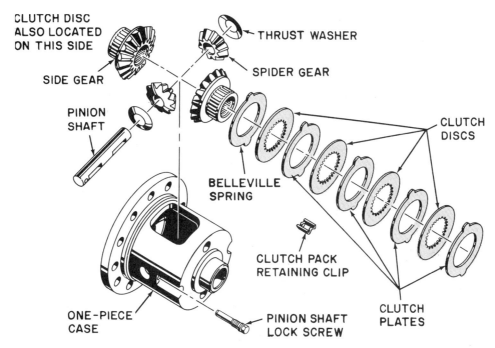

FIGURE 27–22. Limited slip differentials need a special friction modifier added to the lubricant to aid the set of clutch discs on both sides of the differential. *(Courtesy of Motor Magazine)*

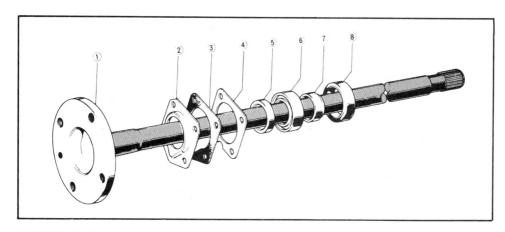

Rear axle shaft

1. Rear axle shaft
2. Bearing retainer
3. Gasket
4. Shim
5. Spacer
6. Bearing
7. Bearing collar
8. Oil seal

FIGURE 27–23. The axle is used to transmit the power from the differential side gears to the wheels. *(Courtesy of Mazda Motor Corporation)*

Too little modifier makes the differential chatter because it becomes too sticky. To determine the exact type of differential lubricant refer to the service manual or owner's manual.

Rear Axle

The rear axle is used to connect the differential to the rear wheels. The rear axle shown in ***Figure 27–23*** is attached to the side gears inside the differential case. The two are connected by an internal and external spline. As the side gears are turned inside the differential case, the axles are also turned.

The axle is supported in the axle tube shown in ***Figure 27–24***. Bearings, gaskets, shims, oil seals, bearing retainers, bearing collars, and spacers are used to support the shaft and keep differential lubricant from leaking out of the assembly.

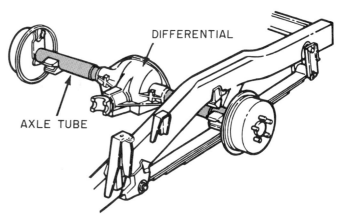

FIGURE 27–24. The axle fits inside the axle tube. *(Courtesy of Chevrolet Division, General Motors Corporation)*

Problems, Diagnosis and Service

PROBLEM: Worn Universal Joints

A vehicle with a rear drive has a noticeable clunk when shifting from forward to reverse. In addition, there seems to be a small ticking sound when the vehicle is in forward gear and low speeds.

DIAGNOSIS

The most likely cause of this problem is bad or worn universal joints. There are several diagnostic checks that tell if the universal joints are bad or worn.

1. Check the universal joint trunnion for brinelling. Brinelling is the process of producing grooves in the trunnion from the needle bearings. Refer to *Figure 27–25*. If brinelling has occurred, replace the universal joints.

2. If there is no obvious brinelling, move the bearing caps around on the trunnion. Also move the universal joint in the drive shaft yoke. If there is any restriction of movement, small bumps during movement, or scraping during movement, replace the universal joints.

3. Check the universal joints for end *galling* (wear on the end of the trunnion and inside the bearing caps).

FIGURE 27–25.   Brinelling, grooves from needles marking and burning into the trunnion, is caused by improper angles, lack of lubrication, or too much load. *(Courtesy of Dana Corporation)*

SERVICE

Use the following general procedure to disassemble and reassemble with new universal joints.

CAUTION: The vehicle must be positioned so that the drive shaft can be removed. Follow all safety procedures when putting the vehicle on a hoist.

1. Remove the drive shaft by removing the two U-bolts that attach the rear universal joint to the differential yoke.

2. Pull the drive shaft away from the yoke and pull backward to remove the assembly. Certain vehicles have two drive shafts that must be removed. In this case the center bearing will need to be removed along with the drive shafts.

3. Remove the snap rings and retainer plates that hold the bearings in the yoke and drive shaft.

4. Select a wrench or socket with an outside diameter slightly larger than the U-joint bearing cap diameter. Select another socket with an inside diameter slightly larger than the U-joint trunnion diameter.

5. To remove the U-joint from the drive shaft, place the sockets on opposite ends of the bearing caps on the U-joint. The smaller socket will become the bearing pusher, and the larger socket will become the bearing receiver.

6. Close the vise with the assembly between the jaws.

7. As the vise is closed, one bearing will be pushed out of the drive shaft yoke and into the larger socket. The other bearing cap will be pushed to the center.

8. To remove the opposite bearing, place it in the vise with the pusher socket on the exposed trunnion of the U-joint.

Then tighten the vise jaws, pressing the bearing cap back through the drive shaft into the larger, receiving socket.

9. The spider or cross of the U-joint should now be easily removed.

10. Obtain the correct replacement kit from the parts center. Since there are many types and sizes of U-joints, it is possible to accidently obtain the wrong replacement kit. Always double check the numbers on the universal kit to make sure they are correct.

11. Begin reassembly by packing the bearing caps with the correct type of grease. Note that certain universal joints do not require grease. Refer to the manufacturer's recommendation. Note also that too much grease may damage the seals on the U-joint.

12. Using the pusher socket, press one bearing cap part way into the drive shaft yoke. Position the spider into the partially installed bearing cap.

   CAUTION: Make sure that no needle bearings have fallen to the center of the bearing cap. The grease should be used to hold them in place. Refer to *Figure 27–26*.

13. Now position the second bearing cap into the drive shaft yoke. Place the assembly in the vise so that the bearing caps can be pressed in by the jaws of the vise.

14. As the vise is tightened, press the bearing caps into the drive shaft. Make sure the spider and trunnion are in such a position as to avoid binding or damage to the needle bearings.

15. Use the pusher socket to push the bearing caps far enough into the yoke so the snap rings can be installed.

16. When installing the snap rings, make sure they are completely touching the trunnion. Note that some late model cars use an injected nylon retainer on the universal joint bearing cap. When service is necessary, pressing the bearing cap out as described previously will shear the nylon retainer. Replacement U-joints must be the steel snap-ring type. See *Figure 27–27*, which shows the retaining rings being installed. (NOTE: If the bearing caps cannot be pushed in far enough to allow the retainers to be inserted, a needle bearing has been caught in the base of the cap. The U-joint must be removed and replaced again.)

17. Lubricate the spider or cross and bearing caps if required. See *Figure 27–28*.

18. Replace any other U-joints that are worn.

19. Install the drive shaft and test the vehicle.

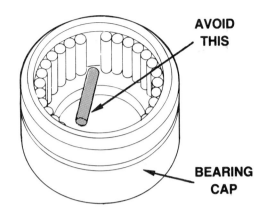

FIGURE 27–26.   Make sure that all needle bearings are lined up inside the cap. *(Courtesy of Dana Corporation)*

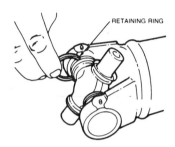

FIGURE 27–27.   Retaining rings should be installed on the universal joints to hold the spider in place. *(Courtesy of Motor Publications, Auto Repair Manual)*

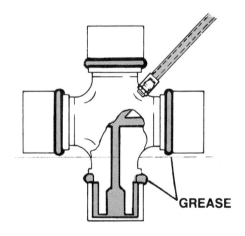

FIGURE 27–28.   The universal joints should be lubricated before installation. Grease must flow from all four bearing seals. *(Courtesy of Dana Corporation)*

PROBLEM: Faulty Differential

A vehicle has developed a humming noise in the differential.

DIAGNOSIS

A humming noise in the differential is usually an indication that the differential needs to be checked and inspected for gear backlash, gear wear, or bad bearings. When the differential is noisy or is suspected of being damaged, first make sure the noise is not any of the following:

1. Road noise

2. Tire noise

3. Front bearing noise

4. Transmission and engine noise

5. Drive shaft and U-joint noise

If tests show that the differential or rear axle is noisy, the noise is most likely coming from one of several bad parts. These include the rear wheel bearings, differential side gear and pinion, side bearing, or ring and pinion gear.

Also check if the vehicle has different-sized tires on the rear wheels. Excessive wear may develop in the differential, because the differential will act as if the vehicle is cornering. Also, limited slip differentials will have excessive wear on the clutches or cones when different-sized tires are used.

SERVICE

Use the following general procedure to disassemble and inspect the differential components:

1. Lift the vehicle with appropriate hoist.

2. Loosen the differential cover bolts and allow lubricant to drain into a suitable container.

3. Remove the housing cover.

4. Remove rear axles and propeller shaft.

5. Scribe reference marks on differential bearing and bearing caps. These are to be used during reassembly. Remove bearing cap bolts.

6. Using a suitable tool, pry differential case, bearing races, and shims out of the housing.

7. Additional disassembly procedures can be found in the service manuals.

Perform the following checks, inspection, and adjustments on the differential. Note that on transaxle systems, the service is similar.

Figure 27–29 shows the wear characteristics on the ring gear. Also check the condition of the pinion gear. In extreme cases, the ring and pinion gear may be damaged severely. *Figure 27–30* shows a pinion gear damaged by lack of lubrication. On the basis of these and other gear wear pat-

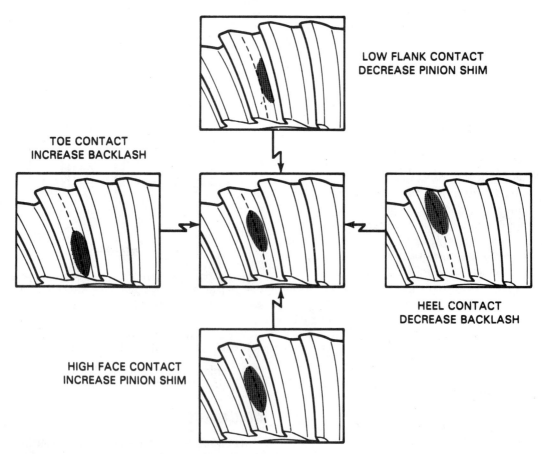

LOW FLANK CONTACT
DECREASE PINION SHIM

TOE CONTACT
INCREASE BACKLASH

HEEL CONTACT
DECREASE BACKLASH

HIGH FACE CONTACT
INCREASE PINION SHIM

FIGURE 27–29.   Excessive wear will result on the ring gear if the differential backlash is incorrect. Adjust the backlash by using shims and adjusters. *(Courtesy of Motor Publications, Auto Repair Manual)*

FIGURE 27–30. This pinion gear was damaged by a lack of lubrication in the differential. *(Courtesy of Motor Magazine)*

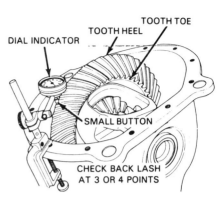

FIGURE 27–31. A dial indicator should be used to check the backlash between the ring gear and the pinion. *(Courtesy of Motor Publications, Auto Repair Manual)*

terns, several checks and adjustments can be made on the differential.

1. Backlash adjustment is made by mounting a dial indicator on the ring gear as shown in *Figure 27–31*. The pointer is set to zero. The backlash is checked by moving the ring gear back and forth. Note the amount of space (backlash) indicated on the dial indicator. If the backlash is greater than that allowed by the manufacturer, loosen the right-hand nut one notch and tighten the left-hand nut one notch. If the backlash is less than the allowable minimum, loosen the left-hand nut one notch and tighten the right-hand nut one notch. The adjustment nuts are located on the sides of the bearing caps.

2. The position of the drive pinion can also be checked and adjusted. A shim pack is placed between the pinion head and the inner race of the rear bearing. Increasing the shim pack will move the pinion close to the ring gear. Decreasing the shim pack will move the pinion away from the ring gear. See *Figure 27–32*.

3. Check the clearance between the side gear and pinion gear in the differential case using a dial indicator. See *Figure 27–33*. Clearance should generally be in the range of 0.001–0.006 inch. If clearance is more than the maxi-

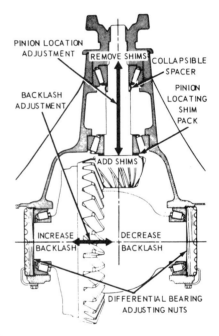

FIGURE 27–32. This drawing shows the direction of movement when adjusting the ring gear and pinion gear. Shims are used to position the pinion gear, and bearing adjusting nuts are used to position the ring gear. *(Courtesy of Motor Publications, Auto Repair Manual)*

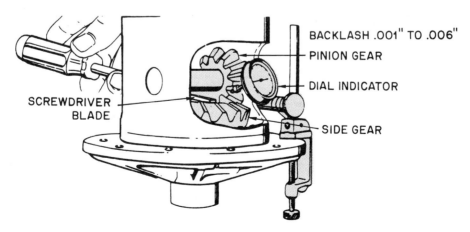

FIGURE 27–33. Gear backlash can be measured between the side and pinion gears in the differential case using a dial indicator. *(Courtesy of Motor Publications, Auto Repair Manual)*

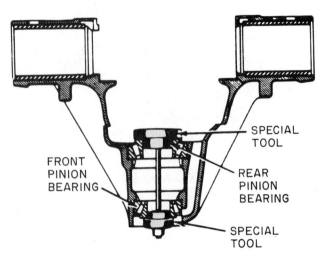

FIGURE 27–34. Pinion gear depth is checked using a special tool and dial indicator. It is adjusted by using shims. *(Courtesy of Motor Publications, Auto Repair Manual)*

mum, shims must be added. If the clearance is less than the minimum, shims need to be removed. Generally, a 0.002-inch shim will change the clearance about 0.001 inch.

4. During assembly of the differential it is necessary to check the pinion depth. Various special tools are available, or a dial indicator can be used. Shims are used to control the position of the pinion gear. *Figure 27–34* shows one method used to check this measurement. Follow the manufacturer's specific procedures to perform this task.

5. Check the side gear-to-case clearance by using a set of feeler gauges. Common measurements are between 0.000 and 0.006 inch. If the clearance exceeds specifications, the differential case will need to be replaced. Refer to *Figure 27–35*.

6. Follow the manufacturer's recommended procedure for reassembly.

FIGURE 27–35. Side gear-to-case clearance is checked by using two feeler gauges. *(Courtesy of Motor Publications, Auto Repair Manual)*

7. Make sure the correct lubricant is used in the differential. Also, limited slip differentials require about 4 ounces of friction modifier. Refer to the manufacturer's recommendations.

PROBLEM: Worn CV Joints

A front drive vehicle is producing a humming noise during driving. Also, a popping or clicking sound is heard on sharp turns.

DIAGNOSIS

Generally, a humming noise indicates the early states of insufficient or incorrect lubrication at the CV joints. If the noise is more of a vibration, then one or both of the drive shafts may be bent. *Figure 27–36* shows a drive shaft that has excessive axial runout.

The popping or clicking noise indicates possible CV joint wear in the outer, or wheel-end, joint. The clicking noise is produced when the CV joint is being extended during turning.

SERVICE

Various service checks, inspection, and measurements can be taken to service CV joints. Use the following general procedure when servicing CV joints.

1. Remove the wheel, damper fork, and steering knuckle from the front of the brake and strut assembly. Refer to *Figure 27–37*. Also drain lubricant from transaxle.

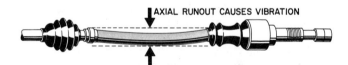

FIGURE 27–36. A bent front wheel drive shaft may cause vibration during operation. *(Courtesy of Motor Magazine)*

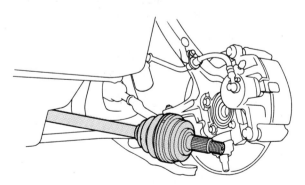

FIGURE 27–37. In order to remove the CV joints, the front wheel, brake assembly, and strut must be moved. *(Courtesy of Honda Motor Company, Ltd.)*

2. Using a suitable screwdriver, pry the shaft from the transmission differential case as shown in ***Figure 27–38***. (NOTE: Do not pull on the drive shaft, as the CV joint may come apart.)

3. Inspect the condition and straightness of the drive shafts. A straightedge can be used to check for straightness. There should be no bend or axial runout. If there is, the axle must be replaced.

4. Once the drive shaft is removed, carefully work the CV joint back and forth about 40 degrees while rotating the shaft. If there are any bumps, scrapes, or resistance while moving the CV joint throughout its range of motion, it must be replaced.

5. Remove the rubber boot by disconnecting the boot band or clamp. If welded, it may have to be cut. Take care not to cut or rip the boot, as it will leak grease.

6. Mark the spider and drive shaft so they can be reinstalled in their original position.

7. If the CV joint is OK, clean all parts thoroughly.

8. Thoroughly pack the CV joints and boots with high-quality grease. See ***Figure 27–39***. Use the manufacturer's recommended grease type.

9. Assemble the CV joint back onto the drive shaft according to the manufacturer's recommended procedure. ***Figure 27–40*** shows how the parts are assembled. Make sure there is adequate lubrication for the CV joint.

10. Install the boot and clamp accordingly.

11. Reinstall the drive shaft and CV joints into the transaxle, making sure the set ring is pushed into the set ring groove, ***Figure 27–41***.

12. Refill the transaxle with the recommended lubricant and test it.

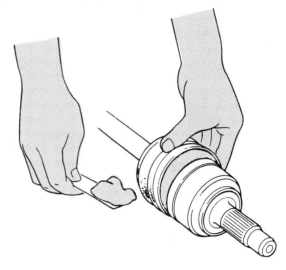

FIGURE 27–39. When servicing CV joints the boots and universal joints must be packed with the recommended grease. *(Courtesy of Honda Motor Company, Ltd.)*

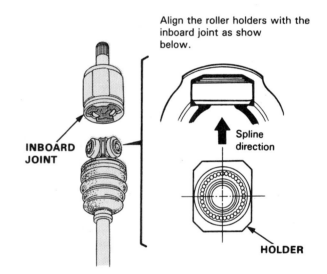

FIGURE 27–40. During assembly of the CV joint, the axle, boot, and joint are pushed up into the inboard joint. *(Courtesy of Honda Motor Company, Ltd.)*

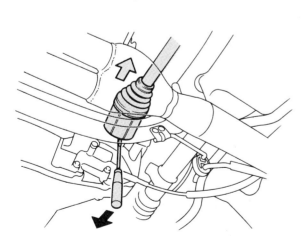

FIGURE 27–38. To service CV joints, the drive shaft must be pried from the transaxle. *(Courtesy of Honda Motor Company, Ltd.)*

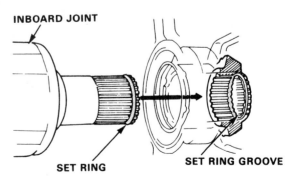

FIGURE 27–41. When inserting the drive shaft into the transaxle make sure the set ring engages with the set ring groove. *(Courtesy of Honda Motor Company, Ltd.)*

Linkage to Science and Mathematics

HYPOID GEAR RATIOS

The differential on a car uses a hypoid gear. A hypoid gear, shown in the figure, has the center line of the pinion and ring gear at different levels. The pinion gear is dropped down slightly so that the drive shaft of the vehicle can be lower. If the drive shaft is lower, then there is a lower hump or tunnel inside the passenger compartment. Hypoid gears also run very quietly and allow several teeth to absorb the drive force at one time.

The teeth on both the pinion and ring gear are curved, causing a wiping action during meshing. The number of teeth on both the pinion and ring gear determines the ratio between the two. For example, if the pinion gear has 11 teeth and the ring gear has 32 teeth, the gear ratio is 2.91:1. This means that the pinion gear must turn 2.91 times to get the ring gear to turn 1 time. Common ratios for differential hypoid gears are 2.91:1, 3.00:1, 3.50:1, and 4.50:1. By changing hypoid gear ratios, torque and fuel economy are affected. Generally, as the ratios increase, more torque output is produced. As the ratios are decreased, fuel economy is improved.

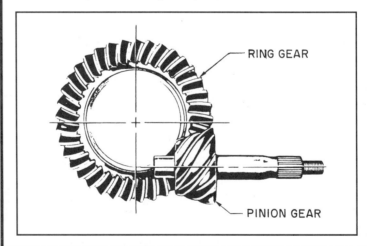

RING GEAR

PINION GEAR

SERVICE MANUAL CONNECTION

There are many important specifications to keep in mind when working with drive lines, differentials, and axles. To identify the specifications for your engine, you will need to know the VIN (vehicle identification number) of the vehicle, the type and year of the vehicle, the type of engine and the type of transmission. Although they may be titled differently, some of the more common drive line, differential, and axle specifications (not all) found in service manuals are listed below. Note that these specifications are typical examples. Each vehicle may have different specifications.

Common Specification	Typical Example
Differential carrier backlash	0.003–0.006 inch
Nominal pinion locating shim	0.030 inch
Pinion bearing preload	
(new with seal)	16–29 in.-lb
Pinion nut torque	140 lb-in.
Rear axle capacity	4.4 pints
Ring gear and pinion backlash	0.008–0.015 inch
Ring gear runout	0.004 inch maximum
Side bearing clearance	
shim thickness	0.002 inch

In addition, the service manual will give specific directions for various service and testing procedures. Some of the more common procedures include:

- Backlash inspection
- Bearing replacement
- Differential disassembly and reassembly
- Drive shaft assembly and greasing
- Drive shaft removal
- Oil seal removal
- Pinion gear removal

placed inside bearing caps and placed on the trunnions. The universal joint is held in place by bolts or straps or by being pressed into the yoke.

The drive shaft must also have a slip joint. Irregular road conditions cause the distance from the transmission to the differential to change. A slip joint compensates for this lengthening and shortening.

Vibration is the most common drive shaft problem. Both torsional and transverse vibration are common. Transverse vibration is a result of an unbalanced condition. Torsional vibration is a result of the power pulses from the engine. Vibration can cause excessive wear on the universal joints. Torsional vibration can also be caused by too great an angle or unequal angles on the universal joints.

Because of their length, some drive shafts use a center bearing. Usually, two drive shafts are used, with the center bearing supporting the end of the first drive shaft. The center bearing is bolted to the frame for support.

Front wheel drive systems require constant velocity joints to be used. Here the speed of the drive shaft will be constant throughout its complete revolution. Two types of constant velocity joints are used: the ball-style and the tripod. Slip motion is also necessary and is designed into the CV joints.

The differential is used to transmit the torque from the drive shaft to the drive wheels. The torque must be distributed to both wheels. The differential includes a ring gear, pinion gear, differential case, bevel gears, and side gears. The torque is transmitted to each part before going to the axle. When the vehicle is going around a corner, the differential side gears and bevel gears work together to keep torque equal on both the inner and outer wheel.

The limited slip differential is designed to provide equal torque to the rear wheels when one wheel is slipping on ice or other slippery surface. Clutches or cones are used to lock up the two side gears connected to the axles. With these gears locked up, equal torque will be applied to both wheels during these abnormal conditions.

The rear axle is connected to the side gears inside the differential. As the differential side gears are turned, the axles also turn. The axle and side gear are splined together. The axle is then held in place in the axle tube by bearings. In addition, seals and gaskets are used to keep the differential lubricant inside the axle tube and differential.

SUMMARY

The purpose of this chapter was to explain how torque is transmitted through the drive train to the wheels. In order to do this, power must be sent through the drive shaft, differential, and axles.

Rear wheel drive vehicles use a drive shaft with universal joints to transmit the power to the differential. During normal operation, the drive shaft must transmit torque through a variety of angles. Universal joints are used to allow this to happen. Universal joints are made with two yokes and a cross assembly with trunnions on the end. Needle bearings are

TERMS TO KNOW

Can you explain each of the following terms? Review the chapter until you can use each term correctly.

Drive shaft	Constant velocity (CV) joint
Cardan universal joint	Tripod
Yoke	Differential
Trunnion	Limited slip differential
Cross	Hypoid gear oil
Bearing cap	Friction modifier
Slip joint	Galling

REVIEW QUESTIONS

Multiple Choice

1. Which of the following is used to transmit the torque to the differential?
   a. Axles
   b. Universal joints
   c. Drive shaft
   d. Axle bearings
   e. B and C

2. Which of the following is/are used to allow the drive shaft to rotate through changing angles?
   a. Differential side gears
   b. Differential ring gear
   c. Universal joints
   d. Slip joint
   e. None of the above

3. Which of the following are used to allow the length of the drive shaft to change (lengthen and shorten) during operation?
   a. Differential side gears
   b. Bearings
   c. Universal joints
   d. Differential ring gears
   e. Slip joints

4. Which of the following is/are part of the universal joint?
   a. Yoke
   b. Trunnion
   c. Needle bearings
   d. All of the above
   e. None of the above

5. _____ vibration is caused by the power pulses of the engine.
   a. Transverse
   b. Elongated
   c. Trunnion
   d. Torsional
   e. Velocity

6. Cardan universal joints have one major disadvantage. That is that:
   a. The input shaft continually slows down during operation.
   b. The output shaft continually slows down during operation.
   c. There is always excessive wear on the tripods.
   d. The output shaft changes velocity in each revolution because of the angle of operation.
   e. The input shaft changes velocity in each revolution because of the angle of operation.

7. A _____ is used on vehicles that require a long drive shaft distance.
   a. Center bearing
   b. Single universal joint
   c. Double slip joint
   d. Constant velocity joint
   e. All of the above

8. Front wheel drive systems:
   a. Use constant velocity joints
   b. Use two drive shafts
   c. Must have a slip joint on each wheel
   d. All of the above
   e. None of the above

9. Which type of joint on a drive system does not have a velocity change within one revolution?
   a. Cross/bearing type
   b. Constant velocity
   c. Cardan type
   d. All of the above
   e. None of the above

10. The fixed-type constant velocity joint is used:
    a. On the inboard side of the drive shaft
    b. On the outboard side of the drive shaft
    c. On rear wheel drive systems
    d. On the inside of the differential
    e. On rear axles

11. Which of the following is/are *not* a part of the differential?
    a. Pinion gear
    b. Ring gear
    c. Side and bevel gears
    d. Universal joints
    e. Differential case

12. The differential is used on the drive train of a vehicle:
    a. To transmit equal power during cornering
    b. To allow for changing angles of the drive train
    c. To reduce the velocity changes during rotation
    d. To support the axles only
    e. None of the above

13. When the vehicle is moving in a straight line and there is equal resistance at each wheel:
    a. The differential case is turning
    b. The side gears and bevel gears are in mesh but are not rotating with each other
    c. The ring gear is turning
    d. All of the above
    e. None of the above

14. The adjusters on the differential are used to change the backlash between the pinion gear and the _____.
    a. Side gears
    b. Axles
    c. Differential case
    d. Bevel gears
    e. Ring gear

15. To eliminate one wheel spinning on ice or other slippery surface, the _____ is/are used.
    a. Double ring gear
    b. Universal joints
    c. Limited slip differential
    d. Spacer
    e. Bearing

16. The axle and differential side gears are attached by:
    a. Bolts
    b. A strong welded section
    c. An internal and external spline
    d. Grease seals
    e. Gaskets

17. The process of needle bearings producing grooves in the trunnion is called:
    a. Metal wear
    b. Brinelling
    c. End galling
    d. Yoke
    e. Torsional vibration

18. Which of the following is not a service concern on drive shafts and differentials?
    a. Correct lubricant in U-joints
    b. Adjustment between ring gear and pinion gear
    c. Backlash adjustment
    d. End galling
    e. Piston scraping

The following questions are similar in format to ASE (Automotive Service Excellence) test questions.

19. Technician A says that backlash can be checked on the differential by using a vernier caliper to measure the correct clearance. Technician B says that backlash can be checked by using a dial indicator. Who is right?
    a. A only   c. Both A and B
    b. B only   d. Neither A nor B

20. Technician A says that too much lubrication can damage the seals in the U-joint. Technician B says that too much lubrication can damage the spider in the U-joint. Who is right?
    a. A only   c. Both A and B
    b. B only   d. Neither A nor B

21. A humming noise is heard in the rear end of the vehicle. Technician A says the differential backlash may be out of adjustment. Technician B says the differential ring gear may be damaged or worn. Who is right?
    a. A only   c. Both A and B
    b. B only   d. Neither A nor B

22. Technician A says that the U-joints can be replaced by using common tools in the automotive shop. Technician B says that the universal joints are replaced by using special presses and hydraulic jacks. Who is right?
    a. A only   c. Both A and B
    b. B only   d. Neither A nor B

23. A vehicle with front wheel drive has a vibration coming from the front end. Technician A says the problem is a shock absorber. Technician B says the problem is a bent drive shaft. Who is correct?
    a. A only   c. Both A and B
    b. B only   d. Neither A nor B

24. A vehicle has a clunk when shifting from reverse to forward. Technician A says the problem is the end play in the CV joint. Technician B says the problem is a bad universal joint. Who is correct?
    a. A only   c. Both A and B
    b. B only   d. Neither A nor B

25. A differential needs to be inspected and possibly rebuilt. Technician A says it is important to check the ring gear-to-pinion gear backlash. Technician B says it is important to check the side gear-to-pinion gear clearance. Who is correct?
    a. A only   c. Both A and B
    b. B only   d. Neither A nor B

26. A vehicle has a limited slip differential. Technician A says there is a set of clutches in the differential. Technician B says that a friction modifier is needed in the lubricant. Who is correct?
    a. A only   c. Both A and B
    b. B only   d. Neither A nor B

Essay

27. Define the purpose of universal joints.

28. What is the purpose of a slip joint?

29. What is the difference between constant velocity joints and Cardan universal joints?

30. State the purpose of a differential.

31. What is a limited slip differential?

32. What is galling on universal joints?

Short Answer

33. Each bearing cap is placed on the _____ of the universal joint.

34. On rear wheel drive vehicles the differential lubrication used is _____.

35. Lubricants that are used for limited slip differentials typically have a _____ modifier added to the lubricant.

36. The process of producing grooves in the trunnion from the needle bearings on universal joints is called _____.

37. A humming noise in the rear axle area can mean that the _____ are worn.

VEHICLE SUSPENSION AND CONTROL SYSTEMS

CHAPTER 28

Braking Systems

INTRODUCTION The automobile braking system is used to control the speed of the vehicle. The system must be designed to enable the vehicle to stop or slow down at the driver's command. The brake system is composed of many parts, including friction pads on each wheel, a master cylinder, wheel cylinders, and a hydraulic control system. This chapter discusses the total braking system used on the automobile.

OBJECTIVES After reading this chapter, you should be able to:

- Identify the principles of friction, hydraulic circuits, and basic braking system operation.

- State the name and operation of all braking system components.

- Analyze the purpose and operation of power brake systems.

- State the principles of operation of antilock braking systems.

- Analyze various problems, diagnosis, and service tips and procedures used on braking systems.

 SAFETY CHECKLIST

When working with the braking system components, keep these important safety precautions in mind.

✔ Always wear OSHA-approved safety glasses when working on braking systems.

✔ Always use the proper tools when working on braking systems.

✔ Be careful not to breathe the dust particles left in a drum brake assembly when removing the brakes. The dust may contain asbestos and cause serious injury to your lungs.

✔ Always wipe up any brake fluid that has been spilled to eliminate the possibility of slipping and causing injury.

Some of the information in this chapter can help you prepare for the National Institute for Automotive Service Excellence (ASE) certification tests. The test most directly related to this chapter is entitled

BRAKES (TEST A5).

The content areas that closely parallel this chapter are

HYDRAULIC SYSTEM DIAGNOSIS AND REPAIR, DRUM BRAKE DIAGNOSIS AND REPAIR, DISC BRAKE DIAGNOSIS AND REPAIR, POWER ASSIST UNITS DIAGNOSIS AND REPAIR, AND MISCELLANEOUS DIAGNOSIS AND REPAIR.

28.1 BRAKING SYSTEM PRINCIPLES

Friction

Friction is defined as a resistance to motion between two objects. When two surfaces rub against each other, there is friction. See *Figure 28–1*. The amount of friction depends on two things: the roughness of the surfaces and the amount of pressure between the two surfaces.

Heat Energy

When there is friction, *kinetic energy* (energy in motion) is converted to thermal (heat) energy. The larger the amount of kinetic energy that must be brought to rest, the greater the amount of heat produced. The energy of motion, or kinetic energy, depends on the weight of the vehicle and the speed of the vehicle. Brakes must also then be able to remove the heat that is produced.

Friction and Braking Systems

In any braking system, the amount of friction is controlled by the operator. By varying friction, the vehicle can be stopped, and its speed can be modified on curves, grades, and in different driving conditions. The control of friction is obtained by forcing a stationary brake shoe or pad against a rotating drum or disc. As the driver presses harder on the brake pedal, friction increases.

When the wheel is being slowed down by the brake friction, the tire is also slowed down. However, friction is also produced between the tire and the road. The friction on the brakes must be matched by the friction of the tires and the road. If the wheels cannot produce the friction, the tire will lock up and skid. A car stops better when the wheels are not locked. Locked wheels can produce dangerous results, especially since there is no driver control of the friction between the tires and the road. *Computer-controlled brakes* are now being used to control the slowing down of each wheel without skidding.

Basic Operation of Drum Brakes

A drum brake assembly consists of a cast drum that is bolted to and rotates with the wheel. Inside the drum, there is a *backing plate* that has a set of *brake shoes* attached to it. Other components are also attached to the backing plate, including a hydraulic cylinder and several springs and linkages. The brake shoes are lined with a frictional material. The frictional material contacts the inside of the drum when the brakes are applied. See *Figure 28–2*. When the brakes are applied, the brake shoes are forced out and produce friction against the inside of the drum.

Shoe Energization

When the brakes are applied, it is important for the shoe to be *self-energizing*. When the brake shoe is engaged, the frictional drag acting around the shoe tends to rotate the shoe about its hinged point as shown in *Figure 28–3*. When the drum rotates in the same direction, the frictional drag

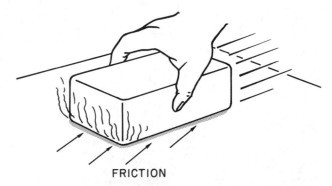

FIGURE 28–1. When two surfaces rub together, friction is produced. Brakes produce friction to stop or slow down the vehicle.

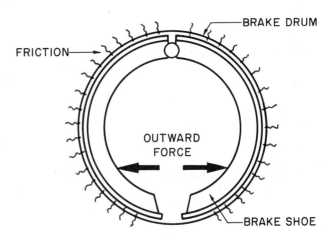

FIGURE 28–2. On a drum brake system, the shoes are forced outward against a brake drum to produce the necessary friction.

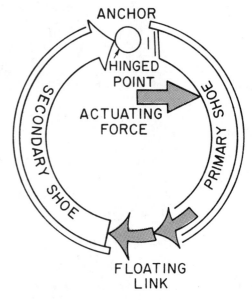

FIGURE 28–3. When the brakes are applied, the primary shoe reacts first. Then the primary shoe pushes against the secondary shoe to produce additional friction. *(Courtesy of EIS Brake Parts, Division Standard Motor Products, Inc.)*

between the two will cause the shoe to become tighter against the inside of the drum. This action is called self-energizing.

Servo Type Brakes

A *servo* is a device that converts a relatively small force into a larger force. In most vehicles today, *servo brakes* are used to cause the brake shoes to move outward from a hydraulic pressure inside a cylinder. The pressure is produced by the operator's foot. The motion is the outward push of the brake shoes against the drum.

Primary and Secondary Shoe Operation

In a drum brake system, there is a primary and secondary shoe as shown in Figure 28–3. When the brakes are applied, the *primary shoe* reacts first. It has a weaker return spring. The shoe lifts off the anchor and contacts the drum surface. The anchor normally acts as a stop. As the shoe begins to contact the drum, the shoe is energized, forcing it to rotate deeper into the drum.

During this time, there is also action on the *secondary shoe*. As the primary shoe moves, it tends to push or move the secondary shoe at the bottom. This motion forces the secondary shoe in the same direction as the drum. Note that the secondary shoe cannot move upward because it is forced against the anchor. This causes the secondary shoe to also be energized. The servo brake system then acts or behaves as if it were one continuous shoe.

The actuating force from the hydraulic cylinder pushes on only one shoe. A small amount of pressure is usually produced against the secondary shoe by the hydraulic cylinder. This force is not, however, used to energize the brakes, except in a reverse direction.

Basic Operation of Disc Brakes

Many vehicles use *disc brakes* along with drum brakes. On many vehicles, disc brakes are used on the front of the vehicle, while drum brakes are used on the rear wheels. Disc brakes resemble the brakes used on a ten-speed bicycle. The friction is produced by pads. This is shown in *Figure 28–4*. These pads are squeezed or clamped against a rotating wheel. The wheel, also called the rotor, is attached to the rim and tire. The rotor is made of cast iron that is machined on both sides. The pads are attached to metal plates that are actuated by pistons from the hydraulic system.

Caliper Operation

The pistons in a disc brake system are contained or held in place by the *caliper*. The caliper does not rotate because it is attached to the vehicle's steering mechanism. The caliper is a housing that contains hydraulic pistons and cylinders. It also contains seals, springs, and fluid passages that are used to produce the movement of the piston and pads.

The pads act perpendicular to the rotation of the rotor. See *Figure 28–5*. This is different from the drum brake

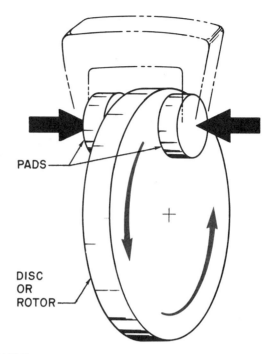

FIGURE 28–4. A disc brake sytem uses two pads reacting against a rotor to produce the friction and stop the vehicle. *(Courtesy of EIS Brake Parts, Division Standard Motor Products, Inc.)*

system. Disc brakes are said to be non-self-energized. This means that they require more force to achieve the same braking effort. For this reason, disc brakes are usually used with power brakes.

Fixed Caliper Design

There are two types of caliper designs: the fixed caliper and the floating caliper. The *fixed caliper* design has the

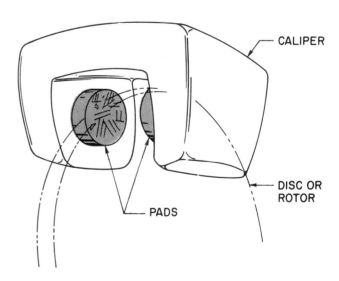

FIGURE 28–5. On a disc brake system, the pads work perpendicular to the rotor. *(Courtesy of EIS Brake Parts, Division Standard Motor Products, Inc.)*

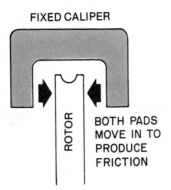

FIGURE 28–6. The fixed caliper remains stationary, and pads move in and out to produce friction. There are two pistons on this system. *(Courtesy of EIS Brake Parts, Division Standard Motor Products, Inc.)*

caliper assembly attached directly to the frame or steering components. Each pad is actuated by a piston. *Figure 28–6* shows the fixed caliper design.

Floating Caliper Design

The *floating caliper* design has the main housing of the caliper able to slide in and out a small amount on the mountings. There is a piston on only one side. The other has only a friction pad. When the brakes are applied, the hydraulic pressure within the cylinder pushes the piston in one direction. The entire caliper housing is free to slide in the opposite direction. As the pads contact the rotor, the force of the piston pad is matched by an equal force from the pad on the other side of the caliper. *Figure 28–7* shows a floating caliper design.

Fluids

Fluids play an important part in braking systems. Brake fluid is used to transfer the motion of the operator's foot to the cylinders and pistons at each brake. Fluids cannot be compressed, while gases are compressible, as shown in *Figure 28–8*. Any air in the brake hydraulic system will compress

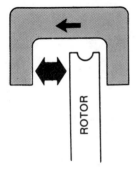

FIGURE 28–7. The floating caliper is permitted to slide in and out a small amount on its mountings. There is only one piston on this system. *(Courtesy of EIS Brake Parts, Division Standard Motor Products, Inc.)*

FIGURE 28–8. Hydraulic fluid is used in brake systems because it is noncompressible. Air, however, is compressible and must be removed from the hydraulic system. *(Courtesy of Delco Moraine Division, General Motors Corporation)*

as the pressure increases. This action will reduce the amount of force that can be transmitted. This is why it is very important to keep all air out of the hydraulic system. To do this, air must be bled from brakes. This is called *bleeding* the brake system.

Hydraulic Principles

The automotive braking system uses hydraulic pressure to transfer the force of the operator's foot to press the friction surfaces together. In *Figure 28–9*, when the foot pedal is pressed down, a pressure is built up in the master cylinder. This pressure is then transferred throughout the hydraulic lines to each wheel cylinder. Note that the pressure at each point in the system is the same.

Force and Pressure

There is a specific relationship between the force of the pedal and the piston area in a closed *hydraulic system*. If a force of 100 pounds were applied to a piston with an area of 1 square inch, a pressure of 100 pounds per square inch would be produced. Also, as shown in *Figure 28–10*, if there are other pistons in the hydraulic system, they may produce different pressures because of their size. A 1/2-square-inch piston produces 50 pounds of force. The 1-square-inch piston produces 100 pounds of force. The 2-square-inch piston produces 200 pounds of force. This example shows that a certain force applied to a hydraulic system can produce different forces, depending on the piston size.

Very little movement of fluid occurs in the hydraulic system. It is the pressure and the forces that do the job needed in the braking system. In actual practice, the fluid is used only to transfer the force and pressure of the operator's foot to the piston and friction pads.

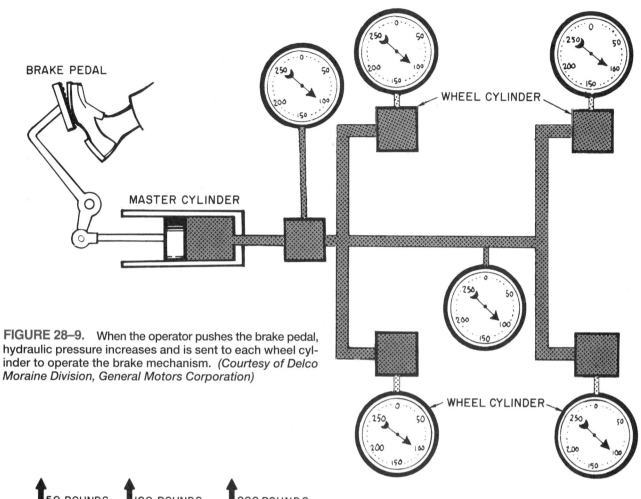

BRAKE PEDAL

WHEEL CYLINDER

MASTER CYLINDER

WHEEL CYLINDER

FIGURE 28–9. When the operator pushes the brake pedal, hydraulic pressure increases and is sent to each wheel cylinder to operate the brake mechanism. *(Courtesy of Delco Moraine Division, General Motors Corporation)*

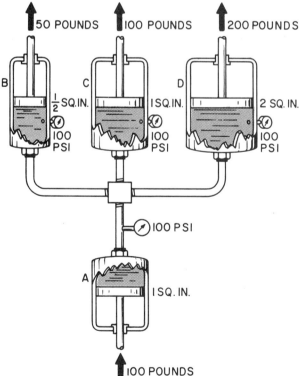

50 POUNDS   100 POUNDS   200 POUNDS

B   C   D

½ SQ. IN.   I SQ. IN.   2 SQ. IN.

100 PSI   100 PSI   100 PSI

 100 PSI

A   I SQ. IN.

100 POUNDS

FIGURE 28–10. Pressures in the hydraulic system can be changed by changing the size of the piston. *(Courtesy of EIS Brake Parts, Division Standard Motor Products, Inc.)*

CAR CLINIC

PROBLEM: Rear Brake Noise

A vehicle with 80,000 miles on it is producing a scraping noise on the rear right brake when it is raining or very damp outside. What could be the problem?

SOLUTION:

Brake linings can become glazed and covered with road dirt and grease under wet and damp conditions. Glazed linings are very hard, which can produce noises. In addition, some of the brake retainer parts and mechanisms may be worn or locked up. Remove the rear brake and check all parts, including the drums, for wear and correct operation. Also, consider replacing the brake linings.

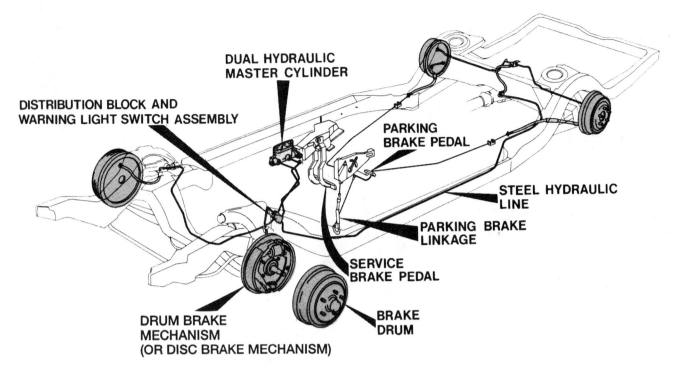

FIGURE 28–11. A common brake system and the major parts are shown on the vehicle. *(Courtesy of Delco Moraine Division, General Motors Corporation)*

28.2 BRAKING SYSTEM COMPONENTS AND OPERATION

Total System Operation

A common brake system is shown in *Figure 28–11*. In this system, drum brakes are used on all wheels. The system starts at the brake pedal, which is attached to the *master cylinder*. The master cylinder is used to produce the necessary pressure in the hydraulic system. Hydraulic lines are connected from the master cylinder, through the distribution block and warning light switch, to the individual wheels. Here the hydraulic pressure is sent to each *wheel cylinder*, which finally moves the drum brake mechanism. In addition to the hydraulic system, there is also a parking brake system that uses mechanical linkage to the rear wheels. Either the pedal mechanism or the hand parking brake can be used.

Master Cylinder Operation

The purpose of the master cylinder is to convert the mechanical force of the operator's foot to hydraulic pressure. The main components of the master cylinder are shown in *Figure 28–12*. Although many designs are used for master cylinders, the principles remain the same. The important parts include:

1. the push rod, which is moved by the movement of the operator's foot;

2. the piston, which produces the pressure;

3. the primary and secondary sections, which help produce the pressure;

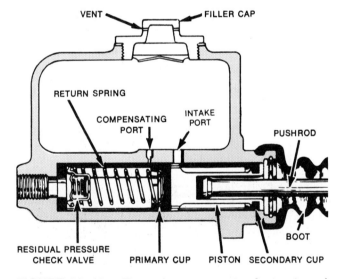

FIGURE 28–12. The main components of a master cylinder. *(Courtesy of EIS Brake Parts, Division Standard Motor Products, Inc.)*

4. the return spring, which returns the pedal after braking; and

5. the compensating and intake ports, which enhance the speed of the fluid flow.

Forward Stroke

When the operator pushes the brake pedal, the piston (pushrod) moves to the left as shown in *Figure 28–13*. This action causes the pressure on one side of the piston to be

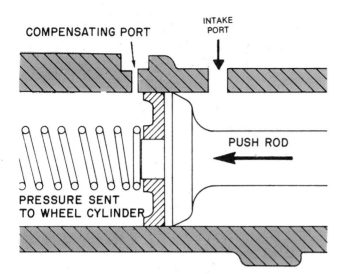

FIGURE 28–13. Once the pushrod moves past the compensating port, pressure starts to build up. This pressure is then sent to the wheel cylinders. *(Courtesy of EIS Brake Parts, Division Standard Motor Products, Inc.)*

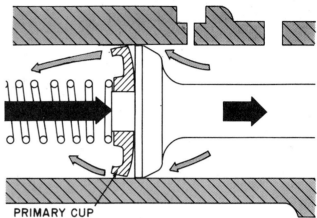

FIGURE 28–15. As the piston moves back during the return stroke, a small amount of brake fluid will pass around the primary cup to equalize the pressure. *(Courtesy of EIS Brake Parts, Division Standard Motor Products, Inc.)*

increased. Pressure is first produced when the primary cup passes the compensating port. The vacuum produced on the backside is relieved because brake fluid is drawn in from the reservoir above the piston through the intake port. The reservoir is also needed because as the brake pads and linings wear, there will be more fluid displacement during braking. The reservoir holds this extra amount of fluid when needed.

Return Stroke

During the return stroke, the brake pedal is pushed back to its original position. The spring is used to move the piston back. During this action, a low pressure is created on the left side of the piston. Refer to *Figure 28–14*. The piston moves back faster than the fluid coming from the brake lines. If the operator immediately reapplied the brakes, there would not

be enough fluid for them to operate correctly. In order to remedy this, fluid must be able to flow from the secondary to the primary port of the master cylinder.

The shape of the primary cup allows this to happen. *Figure 28–15* shows that as the piston is moved to the right during the return stroke, a certain amount of fluid passes around the primary cup. This can happen only when there is a lower pressure on the left side of the cup. The piston cup serves as a one-way valve. Under these conditions, the piston, pushrod, and brake pedal will return very quickly, allowing for successive rapid brake strokes.

To make up for the extra brake fluid passed to the left of the piston, a certain amount of fluid is drawn from the reservoir into the secondary area of the piston. See *Figure 28–16*.

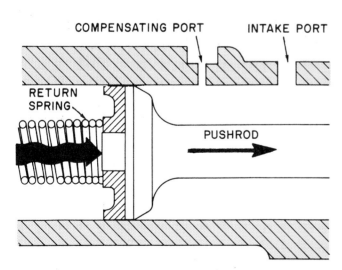

FIGURE 28–14. The return spring is used to push the master cylinder piston back to its original position. *(Courtesy of EIS Brake Parts, Division Standard Motor Products, Inc.)*

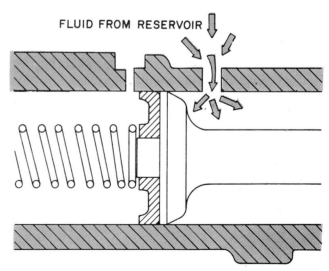

FIGURE 28–16. Any extra brake fluid needed on the right side of the primary cup will be admitted through the intake port. *(Courtesy of EIS Brake Parts, Division Standard Motor Products, Inc.)*

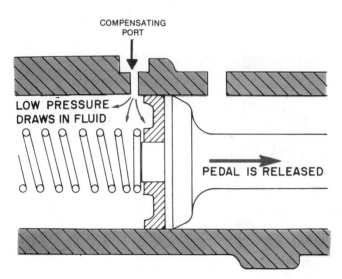

FIGURE 28–17. The compensating port allows excess fluid to return to the reservoir when the pedal is released. *(Courtesy of EIS Brake Parts, Division Standard Motor Products, Inc.)*

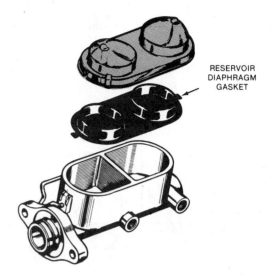

FIGURE 28–18. The reservoir diaphragm gasket keeps dirt out of the reservoir and allows the brake fluid to rise and fall during normal braking operation. It is also vented to the atmosphere. *(Courtesy of EIS Brake Parts, Division Standard Motor Products, Inc.)*

Compensating Port

Now that the piston has been fully returned, the fluid from the brake lines will continue to enter the area left of the piston. This area is now, however, full of brake fluid from the return stroke. If there were no place for the fluid from the lines to go, the brakes would not release as necessary. Another passage, called the *compensating port*, is used. The compensating port allows the excess fluid to return to the reservoir when the pedal is released. The compensating port is uncovered only when the piston is fully returned. See *Figure 28–17*.

Residual Pressure Check Valve

In the past, a *residual pressure* check valve was used on drum brake systems. In theory, it was felt that a small amount of pressure on the brake lines would be beneficial. This could reduce the possibility of air getting into the system. Also, a slight pressure on the system would take up any slack in the linkages in the brake mechanism at each wheel. A small pressure check valve was placed inside the primary area of the master cylinder. Since disc brakes don't employ shoe return springs, these valves are omitted. Also, in some drum brake systems, the check valve has been eliminated by improved design of the wheel cylinders.

Reservoir Diaphragm Gasket

A flexible rubber gasket is used between the reservoir and the master cylinder cap. It is used to stop moisture and dirt from getting into the brake fluid reservoir. The reservoir must be vented to the atmosphere because of the rising and falling of the brake fluid level during brake operation. The diaphragm gasket separates the brake fluid from the air above it, while remaining free to move up and down with fluid level changes. *Figure 28–18* shows a typical reservoir diaphragm gasket.

Dual Master Cylinder

The dual master cylinder provides two separate and distinct pressure chambers in one bore. This design was required by federal law in the late 1960s. Should a failure occur in one master cylinder piston, the second piston will still work. *Figure 28–19* shows a typical dual master cylinder in the applied position. One chamber is used for the front brakes, and the other chamber is used for the rear brakes. Note that on this system the bypass holes act as the compensating port.

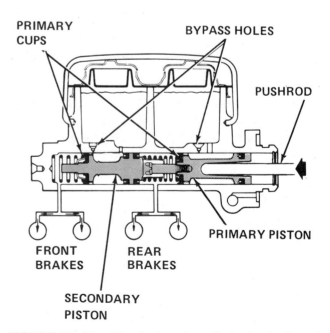

FIGURE 28–19. The dual master cylinder has both a primary and secondary piston to produce pressure. If one master cylinder fails, the other will stop the vehicle. *(Courtesy of Delco Moraine Division, General Motors Corporation)*

The operation of the dual master cylinder is the same as that of the single cylinder just described, except that two cylinder pressures are being developed. One cylinder is actuated by the pushrod. The second cylinder is operated by a spring and the "plug" of fluid between the two. This system is sometimes called a *tandem* master cylinder.

Diagonal Brake System

Another variation in brake systems is the diagonal brake system. In the diagonal system, the right-front and left-rear brakes are connected to one chamber of the master cylinder. The left-front and right-rear brakes are connected to the other master cylinder chamber. The purpose of this system is again to make sure that there is still braking on two wheels if the master cylinder fails to work.

Additional Brake Fluid Components

Several other designs are used on brake fluid systems. These all depend on the type of vehicle and the year the vehicle was manufactured. They include the quick-take-up master cylinder, warning light switches, and proportioning and metering valves.

1. *Quick-take-up master cylinder* — This system has a master cylinder with two different bore sizes. Its purpose is to displace a larger amount of brake fluid during the initial stages of brake pedal movement. This helps to take up shoe return spring linkage more quickly.

2. *Warning light switches* — A warning light switch is cast directly into the master cylinder. This switch senses the pressure in the master cylinder. If one half of the system has failed, the pressure in the other half will be greatly increased. This pressure trips an electrical switch and lights up a warning light.

3. *Proportioning valve* — The *proportioning valve* is used to proportion the pressure to the rear brakes and the front brakes. It is located in the brake line after the master cylinder. The harder the brakes are applied, the more weight that shifts to the front of the vehicle. If the pressure is equal to all wheels, the back wheels may lock up, causing loss of vehicle control. As the force on the brake pedal increases, the proportioning valve causes the pressure to the rear brakes to be less than to the front brakes. This action reduces the possibility of rear wheel skidding.

4. *Metering valve* — The metering valve is used on systems that have both disc and drum brakes. The metering valve keeps the front discs from operating until the rear drums have started to work. This is needed because the disc system operates faster than the drum brakes. In operation, the fluid to the front disc brakes must go through the metering valve. The metering valve acts like a regulator valve. It holds back the fluid to the front brakes until a certain amount of pressure has been developed. When this pressure is reached, the metering valve opens, and the system operates normally.

Brake Lines

Brake lines are used to carry the brake fluid and pressure from the master cylinder to the individual cylinders. The brake lines are made of double-walled, rust-resisting steel except where they have to flex. Flexing usually occurs between the chassis and the front wheels. Here flexible high-pressure hoses are used. All brake lines are designed for high pressure by using double-flared ends and connectors.

Brake Linings

Brake linings provide the friction against the drum to stop the car. There are many kinds of linings. The lining is attached to the shoe either by riveting or by bonding. The primary shoe has the shorter length lining. The secondary shoe has a full-length lining because it carries a bigger load. In addition, most brake linings used today are ground so that they are slightly thicker at the center. This design improves the ease with which the lining comes in contact with the drum. When the shoe pressure is increased, the lining and shoe flex slightly to produce full contact. *Figure 28–20* shows a typical brake lining as well as the thickest part of the lining.

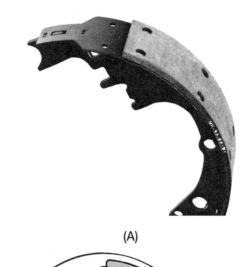

(A)

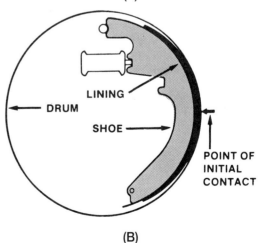

(B)

FIGURE 28–20. When a brake shoe is applied on a drum brake system, the initial point of contact is near the center. *(Courtesy of (A) Ferodo America and (B) Allied Aftermarket Division, Allied Automotive)*

Drum Brake Wheel Cylinder

The purpose of the wheel cylinder is to convert hydraulic pressure to mechanical force. *Figure 28–21* shows a typical wheel cylinder for a drum brake system. The assembly includes two pistons, two cups, two boots, a bleeder screw, and an internal spring. When two pistons are used, it is called a duo servo system. When the brakes are applied, hydraulic pressure inside the wheel cylinder forces both pistons outward, causing the brakes to be applied.

Duo Servo Drum Brake Assembly

There are many variations on the drum brake assembly. One common type, the duo servo drum brake, is shown in *Figure 28–22*. The parts include:

1. Primary shoe — produces friction for stopping (the forward shoe)

2. Secondary shoe — produces friction for stopping (the rear shoe)

3. Return springs — pull the shoes back away from the drum after the brakes have been released

4. Wheel cylinder — produces the mechanical motion to move the brake shoes

5. Hold-down spring and cup — hold the brake shoes against the backing plate

6. Anchor — used for self-energization and as a stop for the brake shoes

7. Connecting spring — holds the brake shoes together on the bottom

8. Star wheel adjuster — adjusts the distance between the brake shoe linings and the drum

9. Brake drum — absorbs the friction produced by the brake shoes and reduces the speed of the wheels

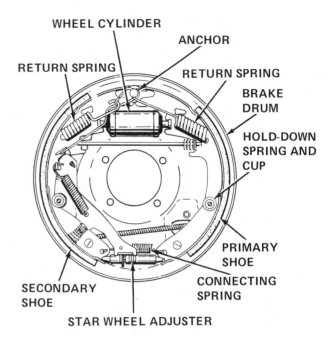

FIGURE 28–22. A duo servo drum brake and associated parts. *(Courtesy of Delco Moraine Division, General Motors Corporation)*

Brake Shoe Adjustment

Drum brakes may be adjusted either manually or by automatic adjusters to compensate for lining wear. Manually adjusted brakes have an adjusting screw, which is normally called a *star wheel adjuster,* for this purpose. As the star wheel is turned by an external adjusting tool, excess clearance is removed.

Automatically adjusted brakes are designed so that as the shoes move in and out during normal operation, excess lining clearance is removed. One method is to use a set of eccentric cams. Refer to *Figure 28–23*. As the brake shoes travel outward, the adjuster pin follows the shoe. This rotates the adjuster cam on the backing plate. When the brake is released, the adjuster will remain in the new position.

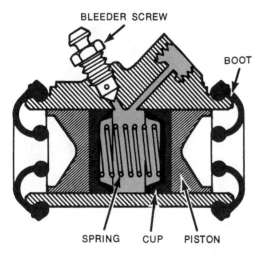

FIGURE 28–21. The standard wheel cylinder, with each part identified. *(Courtesy of EIS Brake Parts, Division Standard Motor Products, Inc.)*

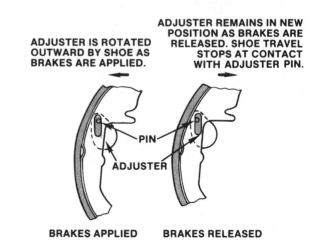

FIGURE 28–23. A set of eccentric cams is used on some brake systems to adjust the brakes automatically. *(Courtesy of Allied Aftermarket Division, Allied Automotive)*

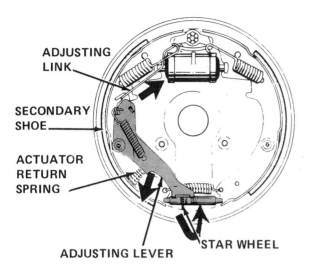

FIGURE 28–24. Certain types of brake systems use an adjusting lever that works against the star wheel to adjust the brakes. *(Courtesy of EIS Brake Parts, Division Standard Motor Products, Inc.)*

A second method of automatically adjusting brakes is to use the ratchet adjuster. *Figure 28–24* shows this system. The adjusting lever acts like a ratchet on the star wheel. Each time the brake shoe moves outward, the ratchet mechanism tries to advance the star wheel to make the adjustment. This happens whenever the brake is applied when the vehicle is moving in reverse.

Parking Brakes

The parking brake is a hand- or foot-operated mechanical brake designed to hold the vehicle while it is parked. A simple parking brake system is shown in *Figure 28–25*. The system uses a series of mechanical cables that are operated by the parking brake pedal. When the parking brake is applied, the parking brake cables and equalizer apply a balanced pull on the parking brake levers in the rear wheels. The levers and the parking brake strut move the brake shoes outward against the brake drum. This position is held until the parking brake pedal is released.

Disc Brake Assembly

As with the drum brake assembly, there are many arrangements for disc brake assemblies. *Figure 28–26* shows a floating-caliper type of disc brake assembly. The parts include:

1. Inboard and outboard shoe and lining — produce the friction against the rotor

2. Rotor — attached to the wheel and used to absorb the friction to slow down the wheel

3. Piston — produces the pressure from the hydraulic system to force the shoes against the rotor

4. Piston seal — seals the brake fluid inside the piston bore

5. Boot — keeps dust and dirt out of the piston bore

6. Mounting bracket — holds the assembly on the vehicle

7. Bleeder screw — used to remove air from the hydraulic fluid

Although the parts on other vehicles may look different, the principles of operation are still much the same. *Figure 28–27* shows a complete assembly of a disc brake system along with two discs.

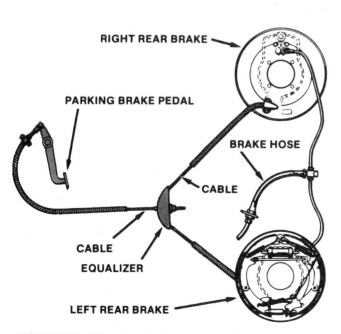

FIGURE 28–25. A typical integral parking brake system. *(Courtesy of Allied Aftermarket Division, Allied Automotive)*

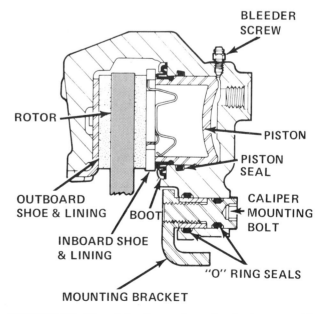

FIGURE 28–26. A floating-caliper disc brake assembly, with all parts identified. *(Courtesy of Delco Moraine Division, General Motors Corporation)*

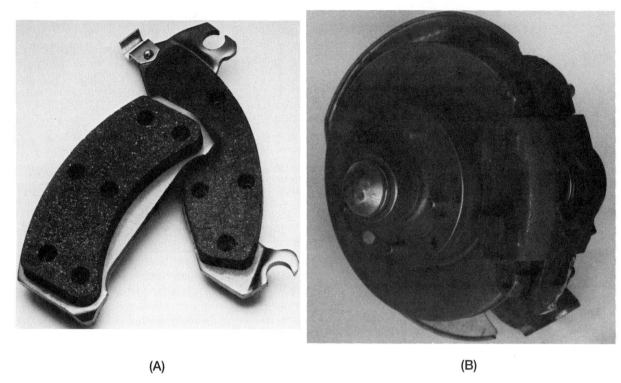

(A)   (B)

FIGURE 28–27.   A complete assembly of a disc brake system and two discs. *(Courtesy of Ferodo America)*

Brake Fluid

A wide variety of materials is used within a standard braking system. Several types of metal, rubber, and plastics that come in contact with the brake fluid are used. Brake fluid must be compatible with all materials in the brake system and maintain stability under varying conditions, both in temperature and pressures. Because of these conditions, brake fluid must possess the following characteristics:

1. *Viscosity* — must be free-flowing at all temperatures.

2. *High boiling point* — must remain liquid at high operating temperatures without vaporization.

3. *Noncorrosive* — must not attack metal, plastic, or rubber parts.

4. *Water tolerance* — must be able to absorb and retain moisture that collects in the system. This characteristic is called hygroscopic. Water causes pitting in the brake system.

5. *Lubricating ability* — must lubricate pistons and cups to reduce wear and internal friction.

6. *Low freezing point* — must meet a certain freezing point as established by Federal Motor Vehicle Safety standards.

It is best to refer to the vehicle manufacturer's recommendations to determine the exact type of brake fluid to use. The Department of Transportation (DOT) specifies brake fluid for vehicles. Manufacturers recommend a specific DOT specification. For example, when a vehicle has a combination of disc and drum brakes, generally a DOT-3 is recommended. DOT-4 is recommended for vehicles with four wheel disc brakes. Heavy-duty applications may require DOT-5 brake fluid.

Brakelight Switches

The brakelight switch is a spring-loaded electrical switch that comes on when the brake pedal is depressed. There are generally two types of switches.

1. *Mechanically operated switches* — used on most recent model vehicles.

2. *Hydraulically operated switches* — used on older vehicles.

The mechanically operated brakelight switch is operated by contact with the brake pedal. It is usually attached to a bracket on the brake pedal. The hydraulic switch is operated by hydraulic pressure developed in the master cylinder. In both types, there is no electrical current through the switch when the brakes are not being applied. When the brakes are applied, the circuit through the switch closes and causes the brakelight to come on. *Figure 28–28* shows examples of various mechanically and hydraulically operated switches.

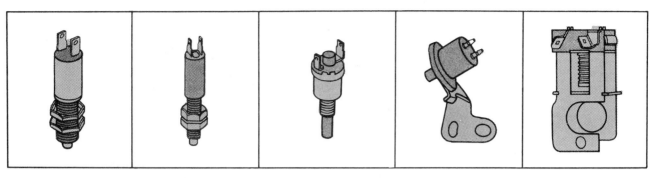

Mechanically Operated Switches

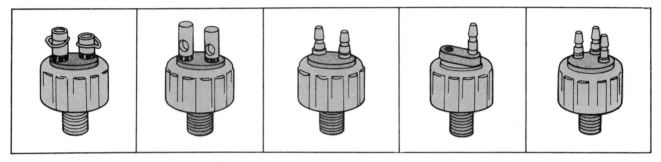

Hydraulically Operated Switches

FIGURE 28–28. There are many brakelight switches used. Both the mechanically operated and hydraulically operated switches are common. *(Courtesy of Allied Aftermarket Division, Allied Automotive)*

CAR CLINIC

PROBLEM: Warped Front Disc Brake Rotors

What is the most common reason the rotors on front disc brakes warp? A customer has noticed that there is a pulsing as the brakes are applied or a shimmy of the steering on light brake application.

SOLUTION:

Several factors can cause the discs on front disc brakes to warp. These include:

1. Overtightening the front wheel lugs.

2. Having the rotors machined too far so that the heat of friction cannot be removed.

3. Hitting cold water in the road immediately after the brakes have been used excessively.

In most cases, the front rotor will have to be machined to make the rotor an even thickness and true, without runout.

28.3 POWER BRAKES

Power brakes are used today on many passenger cars. Power brakes are designed to have an extra pressure called a booster. The boost is produced either by a vacuum or by hydraulic fluid acting as an extra force for the brake pedal. When the brake pedal is applied, the booster unit multiplies the pedal force for the master cylinder. This means the operator puts less force on the brake pedal, making it easier to stop the car. The booster unit is placed between the brake pedal and the master cylinder. The master cylinder and the rest of the brake system parts are all identical to those in a regular brake system.

Vacuum-assisted Brakes

Intake manifold vacuum can be used as the booster in a power brake system. In *Figure 28–29*, power brakes use a diaphragm with a vacuum placed on each side. The center shaft of the diaphragm is connected to the master cylinder. If a vacuum is placed on both sides of the center diaphragm, the diaphragm will not move. However, if the vacuum is removed and atmospheric pressure is admitted to the right side of the diaphragm, the center shaft will be forced to the left. This motion can then be used to operate the master cylinder. When vacuum is returned to the right side of the diaphragm, the brakes are released. The brake pedal is used

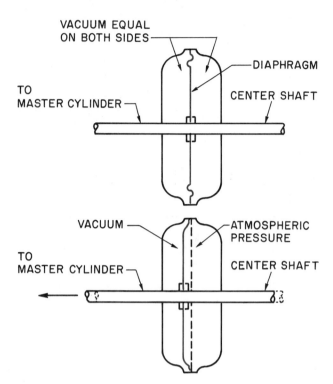

FIGURE 28–29. Power brakes use a vacuum to produce the push against the pushrod on the master cylinder.

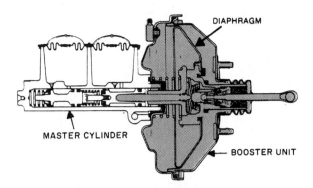

FIGURE 28–30. The booster unit for power brakes is attached directly to the master cylinder. *(Courtesy of EIS Brake Parts, Division Standard Motor Products, Inc.)*

to open, hold, or close two internal valves to allow atmospheric pressure or vacuum to enter the right side of the diaphragm. An example of a booster unit attached to the master cylinder is shown in *Figure 28–30*.

As shown in *Figure 28–31*, the power brake system operates in one of three modes. These include apply, hold, and release. Normally, the entire inside of the canister is under a vacuum. When the driver steps on the brake pedal, the mechanism closes the vacuum valve and opens the air valve. Air is allowed to come into the right side of the diaphragm through air filters. Now the diaphragm is forced to move to the left. As braking increases, the back pressure on the hydraulic system in the master cylinder is felt on the brake pedal. This gives the driver the feel of braking. When the driver stops the pedal movement and holds a position, both valves are closed. Any further pedal movement, either applying or releasing, causes the mechanism to unseat the appropriate valve. For example, if the driver releases the brake pedal, the vacuum valve will open, causing the diaphragm to return to its original position.

Vacuum Check Valve

The vacuum is obtained from the intake manifold on the engine. Since fluctuations occur in the intake manifold vacuum, there is a reservoir in the system to act as a storage for vacuum. The reservoir is the large canister surrounding the diaphragm. See *Figure 28–32*. Also, there is a check valve between the manifold and the reservoir. This check valve prevents the vacuum from escaping the reservoir during conditions of wide-open throttle. The check valve is also a

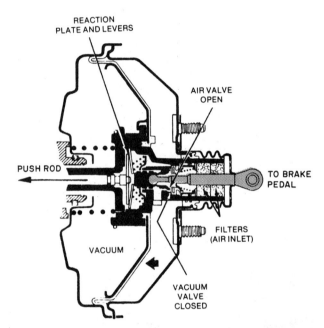

FIGURE 28–31. When the operator pushes the brake pedal, vacuum on the right is released, which pushes the pushrod to the left. *(Courtesy of EIS Brake Parts, Division Standard Motor Products, Inc.)*

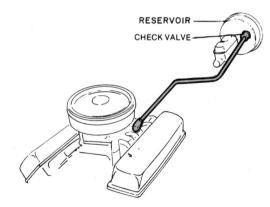

FIGURE 28–32. Vacuum for power brakes is taken directly from the intake manifold. *(Courtesy of EIS Brake Parts, Division Standard Motor Products, Inc.)*

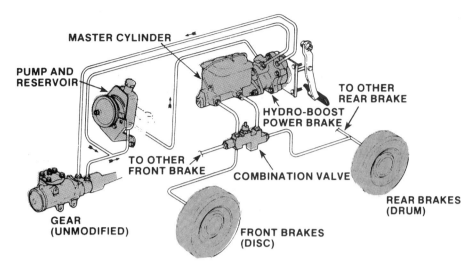

FIGURE 28–33. A hydro-boost system uses hydraulic pressure from the steering pump to produce the increased pressure working on the master cylinder. *(Courtesy of Allied Aftermarket Division, Allied Automotive)*

safety device in the event of a leaking supply line or other vacuum failure.

Hydro-boost Brakes

Hydro-boost brakes are designed to use hydraulic pressure from the power steering pump to boost the pressure for the master cylinder. This system does the same job as a vacuum booster and is connected in the brake system much the same way. One reason the hydro-boost unit is used is because of federal regulations. These regulations require that the vehicle stop in fewer number of feet with less pressure on the brake pedal. This could be done with vacuum boost systems, but the size of the vacuum diaphragm would have to be increased. The trend today is to make parts smaller, not larger.

In certain applications, the hydro-boost has many advantages over vacuum boosters. Hydro-boost systems work well with diesel and turbocharged engines, which have, at times, inadequate vacuum available. In addition, its compact size allows it to be installed where underhood space is at a premium, such as in vans or compact cars. Also, because its boost is much higher than that of vacuum units, it can be used where greater master cylinder pressures are required. Light-to-medium-duty trucks and cars equipped with four-wheel disc brakes are good examples.

Hydro-boost Operation

Figure 28–33 shows a hydro-boost system. Pressure from the steering pump and reservoir is sent to the hydro-boost. Note its small size as compared with the vacuum-boost system. Hydraulic fluid is used to multiply the pressure for the master cylinder.

The hydro-boost system works with the use of a spool valve that is built into the unit. The spool valve shown in *Figure 28–34* is operated or moved by the movement of the brake pedal. The position of the spool valve directs the high-pressure

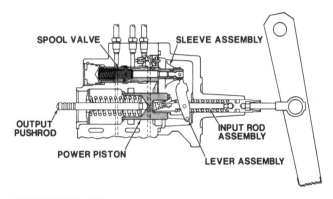

FIGURE 28–34. The hydro-boost unit uses a spool valve inside the master cylinder. *(Courtesy of General Motors Product Service Training)*

fluid either back to the steering system or to the power piston. This directs the high-pressure fluid to a cavity behind the power piston. The pressure forces the power piston forward, applying the pressure to the output pushrod. The output pushrod is used to operate the master cylinder.

Variations in Power Brake Systems

Although the principles remain the same, there are two variations for power-assisted brakes. These variations are determined by the type of manufacturer, the application, and the year of production. These variations are:

1. Tandem power head — a power brake booster with two diaphragms in tandem or series. This provides additional boost to the master cylinder.

2. Dual power brake system — a power brake system that uses both a vacuum-assisted and hydraulically assisted (hydro-boost) design. This system is used on heavy-duty applications such as buses and trucks.

CAR CLINIC

PROBLEM: Car Pulls to Left

A vehicle has been pulling to the left recently when the brakes are being applied. The brake fluid seems to be down a little. The vehicle has drum brakes on both the front and rear and has 56,000 miles on it. What could be the problem?

SOLUTION:

The most likely cause of this problem is that the front wheel cylinder on the left side is leaking. The brake fluid leaking out of the wheel cylinder is getting on the brake shoes and drum. The heat from the friction of the brakes causes the brake fluid to be very sticky. This causes the left front wheel to brake more than the right, causing the vehicle to pull to the left. Remove, service, and replace the front wheel cylinder with a new wheel cylinder kit to eliminate the problem.

28.4   ANTILOCK BRAKING SYSTEMS

Purpose of Antilock Braking Systems (ABS)

In a conventional brake system if the brake pedal is depressed excessively, the wheels can lock up before the vehicle comes to a stop. During this condition driver control is reduced. Research has shown that the quickest stops occur when the wheels are prevented from lockup. The amount of lockup on a tire is referred to as *slip*. When a tire locks up completely during a stop, there is 100% slip. When a tire is rolling freely, there is 0% slip. Through research it has been found that maximum braking force is generated when the tire slips about 10–30%. This means that some tire rotation is necessary to achieve maximum braking. Various factors affect slip on a tire. These include:

1. Vehicle weight (loaded versus unloaded)
2. Type of road surface (dirt, blacktop, concrete)
3. Road condition (dry, wet, smooth, bumpy)
4. Axle load distribution
5. Sudden changes in the tire-road friction (e.g., puddles, loose dirt, ice on one side)
6. Braking in a turn

Antilock braking systems (*ABS*) are designed to prevent wheel lockup under heavy braking conditions on any type of road condition. The result is that, during heavy braking, the driver:

- retains directional stability (control of steering)
- stops faster
- retains maximum control of vehicle

ABS General Description

Under normal conditions, the ABS on a vehicle operates much the same as standard brake systems with a split or dual master cylinder. If, during braking, a wheel lockup condition begins to occur, the system will enter the antilock mode. When the braking system is in this mode, hydraulic pressure is released (in a pulsing fashion) on the wheel that is locking up. The amount of pressure released controls the wheel slip to about 10–30%, thus preventing lockup.

Figure 28–35 illustrates the basic components of the ABS.

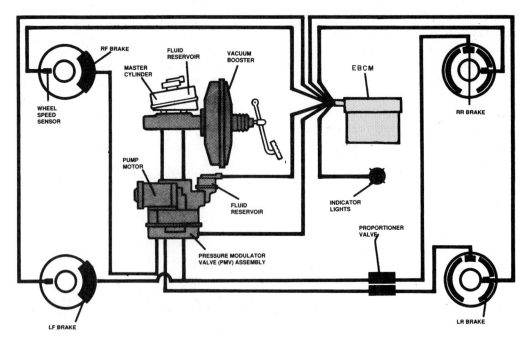

FIGURE 28–35.   Antilock braking systems have various components. *(Courtesy of General Motors Corporation)*

These include hydraulic circuits, an electrical system, and various other components.

Wheel Speed Sensors

A *wheel speed sensor* is located at each wheel. Its purpose is to sense the speed of each wheel. The speed is converted to an electrical signal and sent to the computer, called the *ABCM* (antilock brake control module).

Figure 28–36 shows several examples of front and rear wheel sensor assemblies. The exact type will depend on the manufacturer and whether the vehicle is front or rear wheel drive.

The wheel speed sensor assemblies are made of a wheel speed sensor and a toothed wheel (also called a tonewheel). As the toothed wheel passes by the sensor, a small ac voltage is produced. *Figure 28–37* shows that a permanent magnet is used as part of the wheel speed sensor to produce the volt-

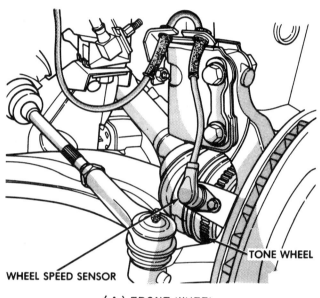

WHEEL SPEED SENSOR   TONE WHEEL

(A) FRONT WHEEL

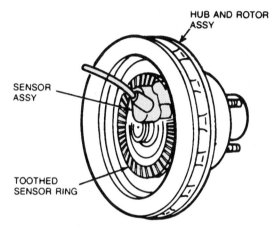

HUB AND ROTOR ASSY

SENSOR ASSY

TOOTHED SENSOR RING

(B) REAR WHEEL

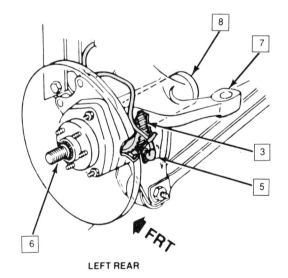

LEFT REAR

1	SENSOR, RIGHT FRONT WHEEL SPEED
2	KNUCKLE, FRONT STEERING
3	RING, TOOTHED (PART OF 4 AND 6)
4	HUB AND BEARING ASSEMBLY, FRONT

(C)

RIGHT FRONT

5	SENSOR, LEFT REAR WHEEL SPEED
6	SPINDLE, REAR DRIVESHAFT
7	KNUCKLE, SUSPENSION
8	SHAFT, REAR WHEEL

(D)

FIGURE 28–36. Wheel sensors have several configurations. *(Courtesy of (A) Chrysler Motors, (B, C, and D) Motor Publications, Auto Repair Manual)*

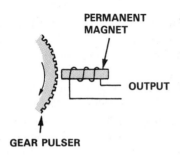

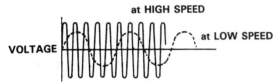

FIGURE 28–37. A permanent magnet is used to produce a voltage, which in turn senses the wheel speed. *(Courtesy of Honda Motor Company, Ltd.)*

age. Higher speeds will produce a higher frequency. Lower speeds will produce a lower frequency.

Pressure Modulator Assembly

The *pressure modulator* assembly shown in ***Figure 28–38*** contains the wheel circuit modulator (solenoid) valves used to control or modulate the hydraulic pressure to the brake calipers.

Pump Motor

The pressure modulator assembly also contains a hydraulic pump motor. The pump motor takes low-pressure brake fluid from the fluid reservoir and pressurizes it for storage in an accumulator or for direct use in the antilock braking system. When the pressure on a caliper has been released because of an impending wheel lockup, pressure must be restored after the pressure has been released. The result is the production of a pulsing effect on the brakes. The pump motor helps to provide this extra buildup or increase in pressure.

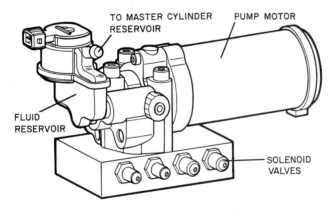

FIGURE 28–38. The pressure modulator valve is used to control the pressure to the calipers. *(Courtesy of General Motors Corporation)*

Master Cylinder

The master cylinder works the same as that on a standard braking system (during normal braking). During antilock condition, it works with the pressure modulator assembly to control or modulate the hydraulic pressure to the calipers on each wheel.

Antilock Brake Control Module (ABCM)

The ABCM is also called EBCM (electronic brake control module) by certain manufacturers. The ABCM is a small control computer that receives wheel speed information. On the basis of the wheel speed information (if one wheel is decelerating too fast), the ABCM sends an electronic signal to the pressure solenoids. The solenoids then control the hydraulic pressure to the calipers.

ABS Operation

There are several modes of operation on antilock braking systems. Each manufacturer may refer to these modes differently. The basic operation is still similar. The following typical modes are described:

1. Normal conditions
2. Pressure hold
3. Pressure drop
4. Pressure increase

The normal condition mode operates when all four wheels are breaking or slowing down equally. The other three conditions (pressure hold, drop, and increase) work when an impending lockup is sensed by the computer. The cycle of pressure hold, drop, and increase occurs very rapidly, from 3–20 times per second.

Normal Conditions

Refer to ***Figure 28–39***. Under normal conditions, when the brake pedal is depressed fluid pressure is sent out of the master cylinder to the modulator assembly. Inside the modulator assembly there are two modulator valves for each wheel caliper. One is an input, one an output modulator valve. Pressure from the master cylinder then goes through the normally open input modulator valves and into each caliper. The output modulator valve on the return line of the caliper is closed. Thus, no fluid is being sent back to the master cylinder.

The modulator valves, when energized by the computer, are able to switch from a normally open to a closed position. ***Figure 28–40*** shows the two conditions of each of eight modulator valves. Each of the eight valves operates separately.

Pressure Hold

When the ABCM determines that the wheel sensor shows an impending lockup, the first stage of the cycle is *pressure hold*. This means that no additional pressure can be produced

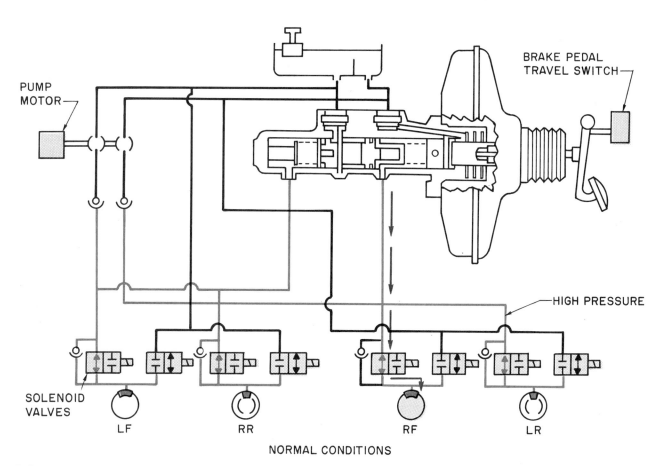

FIGURE 28–39. During normal conditions the pressure to each caliper is produced from the master cylinder. *(Courtesy of General Motors Corporation)*

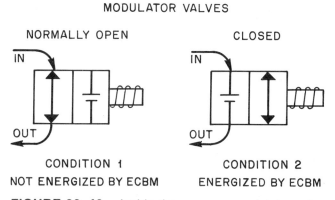

FIGURE 28–40. Inside the pressure modulator valve there are small valves controlled by the computer. They are in either the normally open or the closed position.

from the master cylinder as the brake is applied further. The computer simply shuts off the pressure to the affected wheel. Refer to *Figure 28–41*. The condition shows that the RF (right front) wheel is going to lock up. The ABCM energizes the input modulator valve so as to shut off further pressure from the driver. Note also, the output modulator valve is still closed, thus maintaining constant pressure in the caliper.

Pressure Drop

Refer to *Figure 28–42*. The next stage is called *pressure drop*. If the ABCM senses that the right front wheel will still lock up, it energizes the output modulator valve. This valve moves from a closed position to an open position. The result is that the internal pressure in the caliper is being relieved. The hydraulic brake fluid is now being sent back to the master cylinder.

Pressure Increase

If, at this point, the ABCM senses that the lock up has been activated, the pressure needs to be increased again. See *Figure 28–43*. Thus, the outlet modulator valve is de-energized, and the inlet modulator valve is energized. The modulator valve mode at this point is the same as normal conditions.

However, there is a brake pedal travel switch that tells the computer the brake pedal is still being applied by the driver. When the pedal travel reaches 40% travel, the computer senses this signal. The result is that the computer turns on the pump motor. The source of the hydraulic pressure to the right front wheel now comes from the pump pressure and pedal pressure. This mode continues until either the pressure hold or pressure drop mode returns.

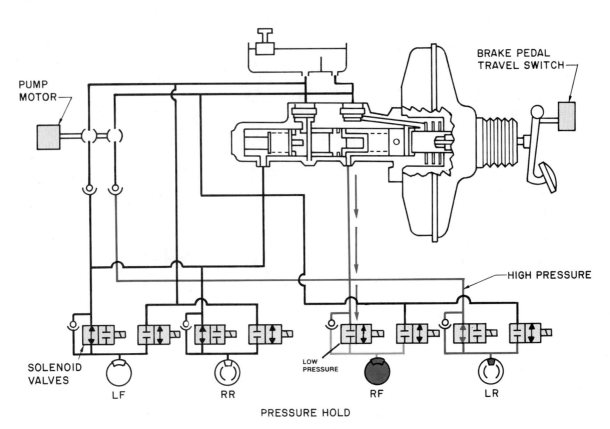

FIGURE 28–41.   When an impending lockup is sensed by the computer, the first mode of operation is called pressure hold. In this mode, pressure is held constant at the caliper. *(Courtesy of General Motors Corporation)*

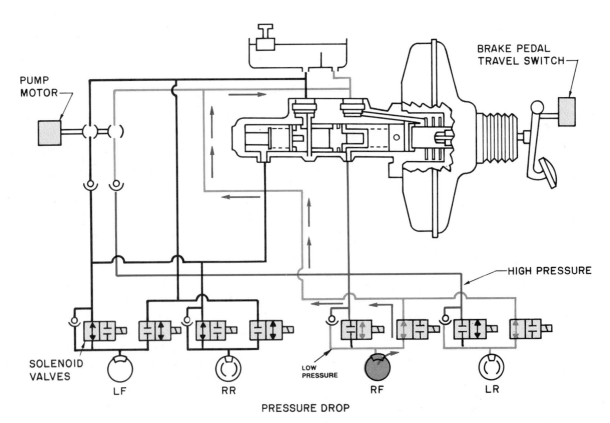

FIGURE 28–42.   During the pressure drop mode, hydraulic pressure at the caliper is released. *(Courtesy of General Motors Corporation)*

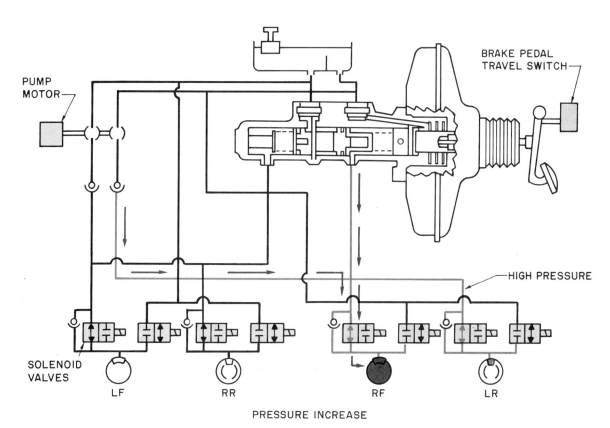

FIGURE 28–43. During the pressure increase mode, fluid pump pressure is used to increase the hydraulic pressure again in the caliper. *(Courtesy of General Motors Corporation)*

ABS Driving Characteristics

Several driving characteristics may be different in an ABS from those in a conventional braking system.

1. *Pedal feel* — Antilock braking systems have the ability to reduce total pedal travel during normal braking. The result is a feeling of short pedal travel during normal braking. When the vehicle is not in motion, the pedal will feel springy.

2. *Component noise* — During antilock braking, brake pressures are modulated by cycling electrical (solenoid) valves. These cycling valves can be heard as a series of popping or ticking noises. In addition, the cycling may be felt as a pulsation in the brake pedal. The cycle of pressure build, hold, and drop can occur very rapidly, up to 20 times per second. Generally the pulsing does not cause pedal movement, although during hard braking, the vehicle may seem to be pulsing slightly. ABS operation occurs during all speeds except below 3–5 mph. Thus, wheel lockup may occur at the very end of an antilock stop. This is normal.

3. *Tire noise and marks* — During antilock braking, some wheel slip is desired (10–30%). Slip may result in some "chirping" of the wheel. This will depend on the road surface. Complete wheel lock normally leaves black tire

marks on dry pavement. When in operation, antilock braking will leave noticeable light patch marks on the pavement.

Additional Components on Antilock Braking Systems

Depending on the vehicle, manufacturer, and year, there are additional components used on antilock braking systems. Some include:

1. *Antilock warning lamp* — placed on the dashboard instrument cluster; used for monitoring ABS

2. *Fluid level sensor* — located on the reservoir cap; senses the level of hydraulic brake fluid

3. *Pressure accumulator* — located on the pressure modulator valve assembly; stores high pressure from the fluid pump

4. *Pressure switch* — located on the accumulator; senses pressure in the accumulator

5. *Self-diagnostic function* — located in the ABCM; provides various diagnostic checks on the antilock braking system

6. *Piston travel switches* — located in the master cylinder; signal ABCM about piston travel for fault detection

Problems, Diagnosis and Service

1. The springs that are used on drum brakes are under high pressure during installation. Always use the correct tools and wear safety glasses when removing or installing these springs.
2. When bleeding the brakes, brake fluid must be forced out of the hydraulic system, along with the air. To eliminate the possibility of spilling the fluid, use a hose connected from the bleeding valve to a canister to catch the excess brake fluid.
3. Be careful not to crush your fingers or hand when the disc brake assembly is being moved during disassembly.
4. At times the brake drums or pads may drag on the drum or rotor. This causes the brake assembly to become very hot. Be careful not to burn your hands when servicing brake systems. Wait for the parts to cool down.
5. When working on the brake system, the vehicle must be jacked up and correctly supported with a hoist or hydraulic or air jack. Use the correct safety procedure when lifting the vehicle.

PROBLEM: Air in the Hydraulic System

When the operator of the vehicle applies the brakes, the brakes seem to be very spongy and soft.

DIAGNOSIS

Spongy or soft brakes are an indication of air in the hydraulic system. When the brakes are applied the air compresses, which gives a spongy feeling. Air can get into the brakes during service or if one of the wheel cylinders is leaking. Often older vehicles that are stored during the winter may leak fluid from a wheel cylinder. Then, when the brakes are pumped, air enters into the hydraulic system. To overcome air in the brakes, the hydraulic system must be bled.

SERVICE

Use the following general procedure when bleeding the brakes:

1. With the vehicle placed properly on the jack stand, have another person pump the brakes inside the vehicle, then press down on the brake pedal. The operator should feel a spongy brake pressure from the air being compressed.
2. Start bleeding each wheel cylinder, starting with the farthest from the master cylinder. Some vehicle manufacturers recommend a special procedure, so refer to the service manual.
3. With the pressure applied to the brake system and using the correct size flare wrench, release the hydraulic pressure by opening the bleed valve on the back of the wheel cylinder. A rubber hose should be attached to the end of the bleed valve so the hydraulic brake fluid can be directed into a can.

   CAUTION: Be careful not to get any brake fluid in your eyes.

   The brake fluid should have small bubbles of air mixed with it at this time.

4. When the valve is opened, the operator's foot should go to the floor. When the pedal is completely to the floor, tighten the bleed valve before the operator lets the pedal spring back. If the valve is not closed first, air will be drawn back into the hydraulic system at the wheel cylinder.
5. Have the operator pump the brakes again. There should be less of a spongy feeling.
6. Continue bleeding air on the wheel cylinder farthest from the master cylinder until there are no more air bubbles in the brake fluid. Also, there should be a firmer and more solid brake pressure when the brake is applied.

   CAUTION: It is important to continually check the brake fluid level in the master cylinder to be sure there is always enough brake fluid in the system.

7. Depending on the exact nature of the problem, one or more wheel cylinders may have to be bled. Bleed each wheel cylinder as previously described.

PROBLEM: Faulty Wheel Cylinder

As the operator applies the brakes on a drum brake system the vehicle pulls to the left.

DIAGNOSIS

One of the most common problems that causes the vehicle to pull to the left or right is a leaky wheel cylinder. A leaky wheel cylinder will usually have brake fluid on the inside surface of the tire. This can be visually checked. The leaky wheel cylinder will also cause the wheel to grab first when the brakes are applied. As hydraulic fluid gets on the brake lining, it becomes sticky. This causes the vehicle to pull to the left. Any of the four wheel cylinders can leak.

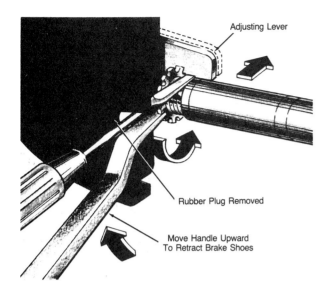

FIGURE 28–44. To back off the self-adjusters on most rear drum brakes, push in the adjusting lever and loosen the star wheel. *(Courtesy of Motor Publications, Motor Magazine)*

SERVICE

Use the following general procedure to replace the wheel cylinder on drum brakes.

1. With the car's emergency brake on, jack up the vehicle following the safety guidelines.

2. Remove the hubcap and remove the wheel.

3. At this point, check the brake hoses for leaks, cuts, cracks, twists, and loose supports. Replace where necessary.

4. Remove the brake drum. If it is the front brake drum, the front wheel bearings and hub must also be removed. When removing drums, it may be necessary to back off the adjusting screw or release the shoe adjusting cams to provide ample lining-to-drum clearance. If this is not

done, the brake drum may be very difficult to get off. *Figure 28–44* shows how the adjusting level can be lifted to allow the star wheel to be turned. If the wheel cylinder is being replaced on the rear wheel, remember to release the emergency brake.

5. With the brakes exposed, remove the springs that hold the brake shoes in place.

CAUTION: Always use the correct tools to remove the return springs and hold-down springs.

Remove all other parts on the brake drum assembly. The exact parts will be determined by the manufacturer and the type of vehicle. To aid in disassembly, always use wheel cylinder clamps as shown in *Figure 28–45*. This clamp is used to hold the wheel cylinder piston in place during disassembly and reassembly.

6. At this point check all springs and other parts for loss of tension and damage. Replace weak springs and other badly damaged parts.

7. Remove the link between the brake drums and the wheel cylinder.

8. When replacing or rebuilding a wheel cylinder always purchase a wheel cylinder repair kit. Never use old parts on the wheel cylinder.

9. Remove the two rubber boots on either side of the wheel cylinder.

10. Pull out the pistons, cups, springs, and expanders from inside the wheel cylinder.

11. Flush and keep all wheel cylinder parts in clean brake fluid. Any dirt that gets into the hydraulic system may cause wear on the pistons and cups.

12. When rebuilding wheel cylinders, make sure there is no grease or oil on the parts. Grease may damage the rubber parts.

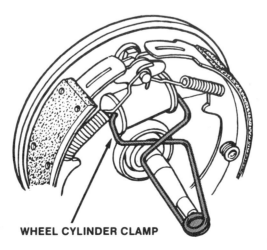

WHEEL CYLINDER CLAMP

FIGURE 28–45. Use a wheel cylinder clamp to hold the wheel cylinder in place during repair. *(Courtesy of Allied Aftermarket Division, Allied Automotive)*

FIGURE 28–46. A hone can be used to clean up the internal surface of the wheel cylinder. Lubricate the surfaces with brake fluid while honing. *(Courtesy of EIS Brake Parts, Division Standard Motor Products, Inc.)*

13. Inspect the wheel cylinder bore for scoring, pitting, and corrosion. An approved cylinder hone, *Figure 28–46*, may be used to remove light roughness or deposits in the bore. Aluminum wheel cylinders and certain other wheel cylinders should not be honed. Check the manufacturer's service manual. Honing will help the cups seal better within the cylinder. Follow the manufacturer's recommended procedure for this operation.

14. Replace with the new cylinder kit and reassemble the drum brake assembly using the correct tools.

15. Adjust the brake linings by tightening the star wheel until there is a very slight drag between the drum and the brake lining.

16. Another method used to measure the inside of the brake drum is a suitable brake drum-to-shoe gauge. With the brake drum off the wheel, adjust the shoes to this dimension. See *Figure 28–47*.

17. Once the brakes have been reassembled it will be necessary to bleed the brakes. Use the general procedure described above.

PROBLEM: Worn Brake Pads or Linings

As the brakes are applied, there is a scraping sound of metal to metal. Also, for a considerable amount of time before this, there was a high-pitched squeaking sound when the brakes were applied.

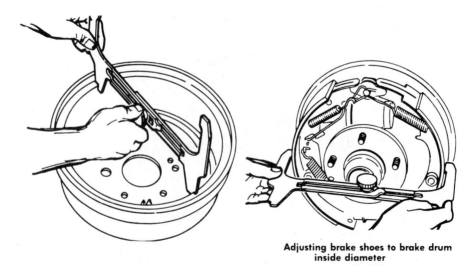

Adjusting brake shoes to brake drum
inside diameter

FIGURE 28–47. To adjust the brake shoes, measure the drum first, then set the brake shoes to this dimension. *(Courtesy of Motor Publications, Auto Repair Manual)*

DIAGNOSIS

Scraping sounds coming from the brakes are usually an indication of excessive wear on the brake pads or brake linings. If there is a metal scraping sound, it usually indicates that the brake pads or linings have been worn down to the metal, thus scraping the brake drum or disc. Also, on many vehicles using disc brakes there is a sensor spring to determine when the brake pads are worn and need replacement. See *Figure 28–48*.

SERVICE

When the brake linings or pads need to be replaced, there are various checks to make. Use the following as a guideline when servicing brake components.

Drum Brakes

1. After safely placing the vehicle on a hoist or hydraulic jack, remove the wheels and expose the brake linings or pads.

2. Check brake drums for wear and distortion as shown in *Figure 28–49*. If the drums are out of specifications, have

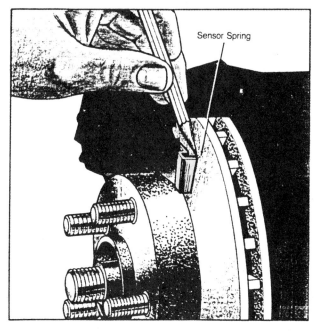

FIGURE 28–48. The sensor spring will squeak if the disc brake pads wear too far. *(Courtesy of Motor Publications, Motor Magazine)*

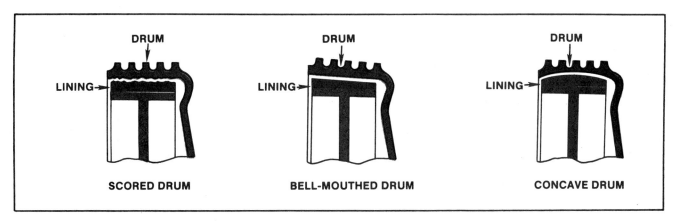

Drum Conditions

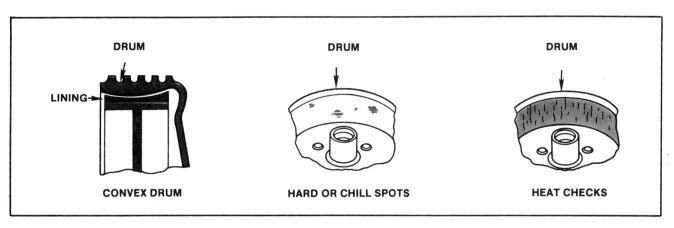

Drum Conditions

FIGURE 28–49. Check the drum for excessive wear as shown. *(Courtesy of Allied Aftermarket Division, Allied Automotive)*

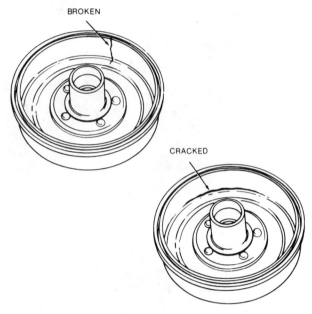

FIGURE 28–50. Inspect the drums for cracks. *(Courtesy of EIS Brake Parts, Division Standard Motor Products, Inc.)*

them machined to correct specifications. Typically, the maximum amount to be taken off is about 0.060 inch.

3. Check the brake linings for excessive wear. New brake linings have approximately 0.250 inch of thickness to the width of the lining. When worn excessively, the lining has been worn down to the metal or rivets. Replace as necessary.

4. *Figure 28–50* shows areas where the drum on drum brakes could crack. Always check drums carefully for such cracks before reinstalling them in the vehicle.

5. Use only precision equipment to refinish or machine drums. Always follow the manufacturer's instructions for use of this equipment. See *Figure 28–51*.

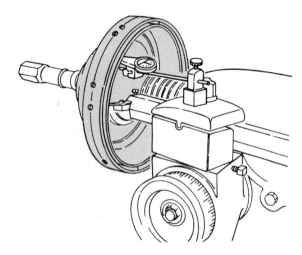

FIGURE 28–51. Use the correct procedure and equipment to recondition the internal surface of the drum brake. *(Courtesy of EIS Brake Parts, Division Standard Motor Products, Inc.)*

FIGURE 28–52. To remove the caliper assembly, loosen and remove the locator pins holding the caliper assembly to the frame.

Disc Brakes

1. After the brake pads and disc have been exposed, check and inspect disc brakes for cracks or chips on the pistons, amount of wear on the pads, even wear on the brake pads, damage to the rotor, damaged seals, and cracks in the caliper housing.

2. Remove the caliper assembly and pads as shown in *Figure 28–52*. Generally the caliper is held in place by bolts or by steel locator pins. Follow the manufacturer's suggested procedure to remove.

3. Check the disc brake rotor for scoring, runout, parallelism, and thickness. Runout, for example, can be checked using a dial indicator as shown in *Figure 28–53*.

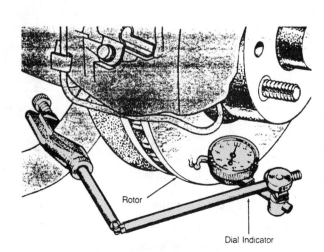

FIGURE 28–53. Runout on the disc of a disc brake system can be checked using a dial indicator. *(Courtesy of Motor Publications, Motor Magazine)*

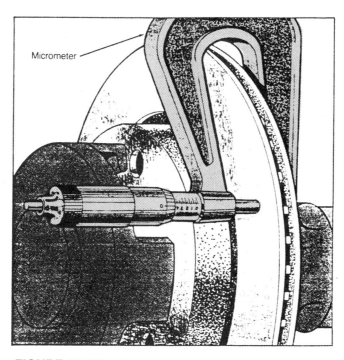

FIGURE 28–54. Use a suitable micrometer to check the thickness variation of the disc on a disc brake system. At least six or more measurements should be taken and compared with the manufacturer's specifications. *(Courtesy of Motor Publications, Motor Magazine)*

4. Certain discs may be out-of-round or may vary in thickness. Measure the thickness at six or more locations around the circumference of the lining contact surface. Use a suitable micrometer. If there is a difference greater than the manufacturer's specification, have the disc machined. See *Figure 28–54*.

5. Scoring and grooving will sometimes occur on the disc as shown in *Figure 28–55*. The rotors will require reconditioning for maximum performance to be developed.

6. If the caliper on a disc brake is leaking or sticking, it will need to be reconditioned. Follow the same general procedure described earlier for drum brake wheel cylinders.

7. Check to see if the piston inside the caliper moves freely with the caliper bore. Road dirt and rust can cause the piston to stick in the bore. When removing the seal use a soft object such as a pencil so as not to scratch the cylinder walls. See *Figure 28–56*.

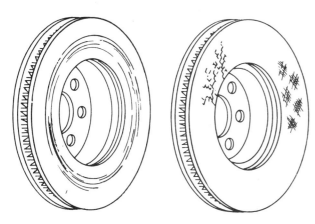

FIGURE 28–55. Check the rotors for signs of scoring or grooving and for signs of overheating. Overheating also causes a slight bluing on the rotor. *(Courtesy of EIS Brake Parts, Division Standard Motor Products, Inc.)*

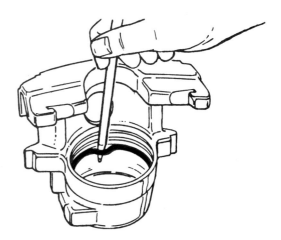

FIGURE 28–56. When removing the seal inside the cylinder on disc brakes, use a soft pointed tool so as not to scratch the cylinder surfaces. *(Courtesy of EIS Brake Parts, Division Standard Motor Products, Inc.)*

PROBLEM: Faulty Antilock Brakes

A vehicle with an antilock brake system has the antilock brake light on continuously. It should go off several seconds after the engine has started or the ignition switch is in the run position. But it stays on all the time.

DIAGNOSIS

Antilock braking systems have a built-in diagnostic system that helps the service technician identify and locate problems. Various diagnostic checks must be performed to determine the problem in antilock braking systems.

1. The first check is to visually inspect the brake system for leaks, low fluid, and disconnected wires. *Figure 28–57* shows a typical visual inspection chart to follow.

2. Generally each manufacturer has a functional check that must also be made to help diagnose the antilock braking system. A typical function check flow chart is shown for reference in *Figure 28–58*.

3. As part of functional check the service technician determines if there are any trouble codes stored in the computer memory. *Figure 28–59* shows one manufacturer's trouble code table. The trouble codes are read in a manner similar to that used for engine trouble codes. Often the light used to check the trouble code is located directly on the computer in the trunk area.

4. On the basis of the results of this check the service technician then goes to a flow chart dealing with the specific trouble code. *Figure 28–60* shows a typical flow chart relating to a faulty wheel speed sensor signal.

SERVICE

The service necessary on antilock braking systems is much the same as that for conventional brakes. However, often wheel sensors, wiring, the pressure modulating valves, and associated parts may need replacement. Refer to the manufacturer's service manual for correct service procedures on these parts.

VISUAL INSPECTION

ITEM	INSPECT FOR	CORRECTIVE ACTION
Brake Fluid Reservoir	Low fluid Level	Add fluid as required. Determine cause of fluid loss and repair.
ABCM	Proper connector engagement. External Damage	Repair as required Verify defect and repair as required.
Hydraulic Assembly	Proper Connector Engagement External Leaks Damaged wiring/connectors Control Pressure Switch Fluid Level Sensor Defect	Repair as required Repair Leaks as required Repair as required Repair as required Repair as required
Pump/Motor Assembly and Hoses	Proper assembly Damaged/Leaking Hoses Damaged wiring/connector	Install components properly Repair hoses as required Repair as required
Parking Brake	Full release Park Brake Switch	Operate manual release lever to verify operation. Adjust cable or repair release mechanism as required Verify correct operation. Repair as required
Front & Rear Wheel Speed Sensors	Proper connector engagement Broken or damaged wires	Repair as required Go to appropriate ABS Code chart and verify fault. Correct as required
OVPR & Pump/Motor Relays	Proper connector engagement Loose wires or terminals	Repair as required Repair as required
Pump/Motor Ground	Corroded, broken or loose eyelets	Repair as required

VERIFY PROPER OPERATION AFTER REPAIRING ANY DEFECT. IF PROBLEM IS STILL PRESENT, PROCEED TO FUNCTIONAL CHECK

FIGURE 28–57.   Visually inspect the antilock braking system before completing other diagnostic checks. *(Courtesy of Chrysler Motors)*

FUNCTIONAL CHECK

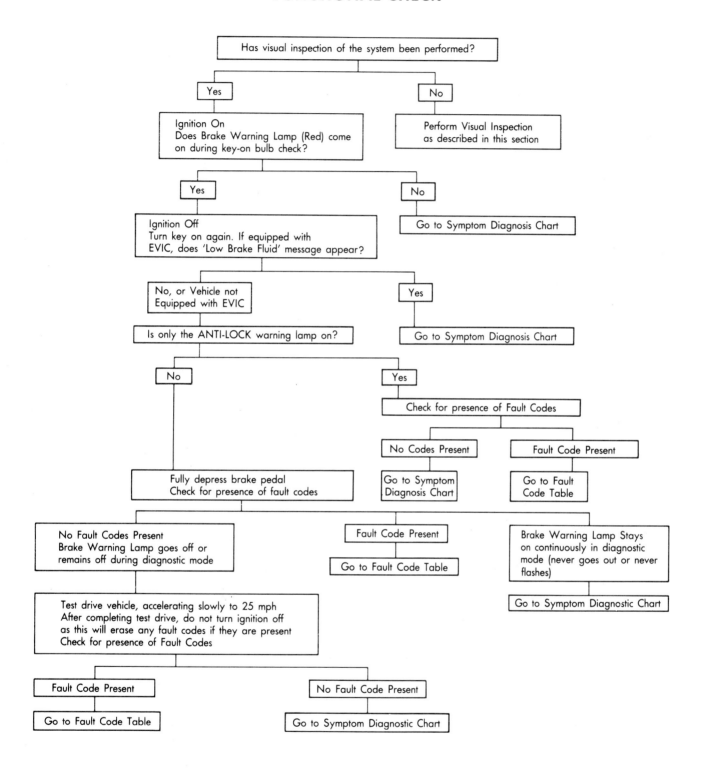

FIGURE 28–58. This flow chart shows how to perform a functional check to help diagnose the antilock braking system. *(Courtesy of Chrysler Motors)*

FAULT CODE TABLE

Fault Code:	Description:
1	Left Front ABS Wheel Circuit Valve
2	Right Front ABS Wheel Circuit Valve
3	Right Rear ABS Wheel Circuit Valve
4	Left Rear ABS Wheel Circuit Valve
5	Left Front Wheel Speed Sensor
6	Right Front Wheel Speed Sensor
7	Right Rear Wheel Speed Sensor
8	Left Rear Wheel Speed Sensor
9	Left Front/Right Rear Wheel Speed Sensor
10	Right Front/Left Rear Wheel Speed Sensor
11	Replenishing Valve
12	Valve Relay
13	Excessive Displacement or Circuit Failure
14	Piston Travel Switches
15	Brake Light Switch
16	ABCM Error

FIGURE 28–59.   During a functional check the service technician checks for one or more of the trouble codes stored in the computer memory. *(Courtesy of Chrysler Motors)*

FAULT CODES 9 AND 10
DIAGONAL WHEEL SPEED SENSOR SIGNAL
Code 9: LF/RR   Code 10: RF/LR

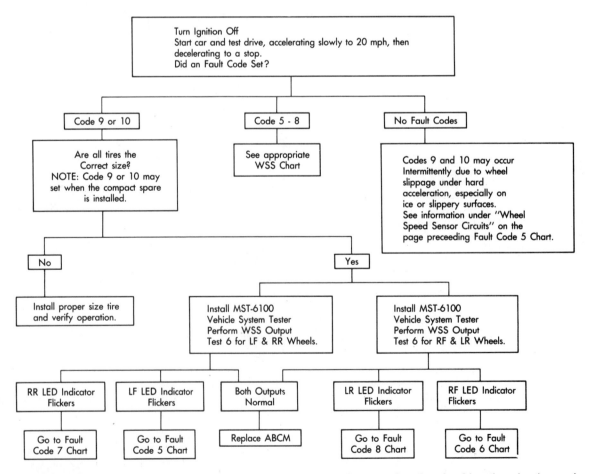

FIGURE 28–60.   This flow chart shows the correct diagnostic procedure for checking the wheel speed sensors. *(Courtesy of Chrysler Motors)*

Linkage to Science and Mathematics

PASCAL'S LAW

All fluid power circuits (including braking systems) follow certain predictable patterns. Pascal's Law helps to explain hydraulic principles of braking systems. This law states that

> *A pressure applied to a confined fluid is transmitted undiminished to every portion of the surface of the containing vessel.*

On the left diagram below, when a force is applied to the handle, the piston is forced downward. The pressure created in the fluid is equal and undiminished in all directions. Pascal's Law also states that pressure on a fluid is equal to the force applied, divided by the area.

This can be shown as

$$P = \frac{F}{A}$$

Where P = pressure in psi
  F = force applied in pounds
  A = area to which the force is applied

Thus 100 pounds of force on a 1-square-inch piston produces 100 pounds per square inch.

When a force (driver's foot) presses down on the brake pedal, a pressure is built up in the master cylinder. This pressure is then transferred throughout the hydraulic lines to each wheel cylinder.

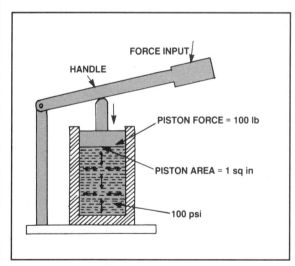

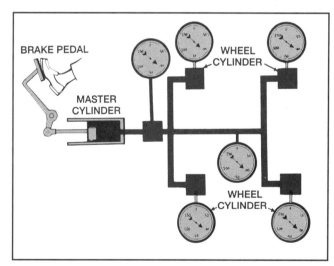

SERVICE MANUAL CONNECTION

There are many important specifications to keep in mind when working with braking systems. To identify the specifications for your engine, you will need to know the VIN (vehicle identification number) of the vehicle, the type and year of the vehicle, and the type of engine. Although they may be titled differently, some of the more common braking system specifications (not all) found in service manuals are listed below. Note that these specifications are typical examples. Each vehicle may have different specifications.

Common Specification	Typical Example
Brake drum inside diameter	10.00 inches
Caliper bore diameter	2.59 inches
Caliper bore maximum cut	0.002 inch
Clearance between sensor face and flange	1.8 inches
Rotor finish	10–80
Rotor lateral runout	0.003 inch
Rotor nominal thickness	0.870 inch
Rotor thickness variation and parallelism	0.0005 inch

In addition, the service manual will give specific directions for various service and testing procedures. Some of the more common procedures include:

- Brake pads replace
- Brake system bleeding
- Caliper overhaul
- Caliper replace
- Electronic controller replace
- Hydraulic pump motor replace
- Sensor replace
- Shoe and lining replacement

SUMMARY

This chapter covered the principles and operation of braking systems. Braking systems operate on the principle of friction. Friction is the resistance to motion between two objects. The brakes produce friction to slow or stop a vehicle. In any braking system, the amount of friction is controlled by the operator. As the operator pushes harder on the brake pedal, friction is increased, and the vehicle slows.

Several types of brake systems are used on vehicles. The drum brake assembly has a cast drum bolted to the wheel. A set of brake shoes is inside the drum. As the brakes are applied, the shoes move out against the inside of the drum, producing the friction needed to control the vehicle. Current drum brake systems are designed for self-energization. This means that as the brake is applied and the drum rotated, the shoe gets tighter against the inside of the drum. Both a primary and a secondary shoe action are designed into the brake system.

A second type of brake system is called the disc brake. In this system, pads are forced against a rotor to stop the vehicle. This is much like a bicycle brake system, only more complex. The caliper is used to hold the two disc pads in place. A fixed or a floating caliper may be used, depending on the vehicle design and manufacturer.

Brake systems also use a hydraulic system to transfer the operator's foot pressure to the brakes. The hydraulic system uses servos and different sizes of pistons to produce the forces and pressures needed.

The braking system uses a master cylinder to convert the mechanical force of the operator's foot to hydraulic pressure. There are several principles of operation during the forward stroke and the return stroke of the piston in the master cylinder. The compensating port allows excess fluid to return to the reservoir. A residual pressure check valve is used to keep a small amount of pressure on the hydraulic system. The reservoir diaphragm gasket is used to keep moisture and dirt from getting into the system.

Other types of master cylinders are also used. The dual master cylinder provides two separate pressure chambers. It is required on certain vehicles by law. One chamber is used for the front brakes and one chamber is used for the rear brakes. In the diagonal system, the left-front and right-rear brakes are connected to one chamber. The other chamber is connected to the remaining wheels.

Other designs are also used on master cylinders. These include the quick-take-up master cylinder, warning light switches, proportioning valve, and metering valves. Depending on the manufacturer and year, the vehicle may have any one of these designs.

Once the pressure has been developed in the master cylinder, brake lines are used to transfer it to the wheel cylinders. The brake linings then move outward to produce the necessary friction.

Drum brakes use a wheel cylinder to operate and move the brake linings. The wheel cylinder converts hydraulic pressure to mechanical force. The most common type of brake assembly is called the duo servo drum brake. It includes both the primary and secondary shoe, return springs, the wheel cylinder, hold-down springs and cup, anchor, connecting springs, star wheel adjuster, and brake drum.

Brake shoes must be adjusted either manually or by automatic adjusters. When adjusted correctly, the brakes move only a certain distance before touching the brake drum.

Disc brakes are used more extensively on the front wheels of most American vehicles. The common parts of a disc brake are the inboard and outboard shoe or lining, the rotor, pistons, piston seals, boots, mounting brackets, and bleeder screws.

Brake fluid is a very important part of braking systems.

Brake fluid must have a certain viscosity, a certain boiling point, be noncorrosive, have water tolerance, be a good lubricant, and have a low freezing point. Always refer to the manufacturer's specifications when buying brake fluid.

Many vehicles with disc brakes use power brakes as well. Power brakes are designed to have an additional pressure exerted on the hydraulic system. This is done either by using vacuum or by using hydraulic pressure from the power steering system. Vacuum-assisted power brakes use vacuum from the intake manifold. Vacuum is fed to the diaphragm and used to increase the pressure in the master cylinder. Hydro-boost brakes use pressure from the power steering. The extra pressure also works against the master cylinder.

Most vehicles today also use antilock braking systems. In operation, small sensors are placed on each wheel to determine their speed. This information is sent to a computer called the antilock brake control module (ABCM). If one wheel were to lockup during braking (possibly causing a serious accident), the computer would be able to sense one wheel slowing down too fast. The computer would then send a signal to the hydraulic system to release the hydraulic pressure on that particular brake or wheel. To operate correctly, four wheel sensors, a pressure modulator assembly, a pump motor, master cylinder, and an antilock brake control module (ABCM) must be used.

There are many service tips that are used on brake systems. Service procedures are available in the manufacturer's service manuals. Several important service tips include using correct tools and checking all parts, including the disc, rotors, drum and shoes, springs, brake lines, and so on for damage and excessive wear. In addition, brakes should be bled and adjusted according to the manufacturer's specifications. At times, both the master cylinder and wheel cylinder may also be rebuilt.

TERMS TO KNOW

Can you explain each of the following terms? Review the chapter until you can use each term correctly.

Friction	Master cylinder
Kinetic energy	Wheel cylinder
Computer-controlled	Compensating port
brakes	Residual pressure
Backing plate	Tandem
Brake shoes	Proportioning valve
Self-energizing	Star wheel adjuster
Servo brake	Slip
Primary shoe	Antilock braking system
Secondary shoe	(ABS)
Disc brake	Wheel speed sensor
Caliper	ABCM
Fixed caliper	Pressure modulator
Floating caliper	Pressure hold
Bleeding	Pressure drop
Hydraulic system	

REVIEW QUESTIONS

Multiple Choice

1. Friction on the automobile brakes depends on which of the following?
   a. Power steering pressure
   b. Tire size
   c. Speed of vehicle
   d. Pressure between the drum and linings
   e. Amount of spring pressure on the parking brake

2. Brake shoes are used on _____.
   a. Front disc brakes
   b. Drum-type brakes
   c. Brakes with a caliper
   d. The back of the master cylinder
   e. Piston-type brakes

3. When a brake shoe becomes tighter against the drum from rotation, this is called:
   a. A master cylinder
   b. Wheel cylinder
   c. Hydraulic pressure
   d. Self-energization
   e. Compensating system

4. The _____ is located to the front of the wheel on vehicles with drum brakes.
   a. Secondary shoe
   b. Caliper
   c. Master cylinder
   d. Primary shoe
   e. Relief valve

5. Which of the following uses a caliper?
   a. Disc brakes
   b. Drum brakes
   c. Master cylinder
   d. Star adjuster
   e. Compensating port

6. The pads on a disc brake system are _____ the rotor.
   a. Perpendicular to
   b. Parallel to
   c. Never touching
   d. Attached to
   e. None of the above

7. The _____ is/are directly attached to the steering assembly and frame on a disc brake system.
   a. Floating caliper   d. Pads
   b. Linings   e. Master cylinder
   c. Fixed caliper

8. Hydraulic fluid used on a braking system:
   a. Transfers the pressure from the master cylinder to the wheel cylinder
   b. Cannot be compressed
   c. Must withstand very high pressures
   d. Is pressurized in the master cylinder
   e. All of the above

9. The purpose of the master cylinder is to:
   a. Reduce pressure on the brakes during braking
   b. Produce the pressure on the brakes during braking
   c. Produce the necessary friction during braking
   d. Be used as a parking brake
   e. Adjust the brakes

10. The _____ allows fluid to flow from the reservoir to the master cylinder.
    a. Forward stroke
    b. Compensating port
    c. Primary cup
    d. Wheel cylinder
    e. Brake linings

11. Brake fluid passes around the primary cup in the master cylinder:
    a. During the return stroke
    b. During the forward stroke
    c. During acceleration
    d. During parking brake action
    e. During rapid stopping

12. A small amount of pressure is kept on the hydraulic fluid on certain brake systems:
    a. To stop the car completely
    b. By the compensating port
    c. By the residual pressure check valve
    d. By the parking brake
    e. By the springs in the wheel cylinder

13. Two wheels braking from one chamber and two wheels braking from a second chamber:
    a. Use a dual master cylinder
    b. Use a diagonal brake system
    c. Protect the system if one master cylinder fails
    d. All of the above
    e. None of the above

14. A _____ is used to reduce the pressure to the rear wheels during braking.
    a. Proportioning valve
    b. Compensating valve
    c. Relief valve
    d. Metering valve
    e. None of the above

15. The primary shoe is_____.
    a. Shorter than the secondary shoe
    b. Longer than the secondary shoe
    c. The same length as the secondary shoe
    d. Placed to the rear on the wheel cylinder
    e. Placed with the disc against the drum

16. Brake shoes can be adjusted_____.
    a. Manually
    b. Automatically
    c. Using the star wheel
    d. All of the above
    e. None of the above

17. On a disc brake system, the pads are forced against the _____.
    a. Rotor
    b. Parking shoe
    c. Bleeder screw
    d. Piston seal
    e. Piston

18. Which of the following is *not* a good characteristic of brake fluid?
    a. Must have extremely low viscosity (thick)
    b. Must have a high boiling point
    c. Must be able to absorb or retain moisture
    d. Must be able to lubricate
    e. Must have a low freezing point

19. Power brakes use _____ for increasing the pressure.
    a. Vacuum
    b. Lubricating oil
    c. Cooling system fluid
    d. The RPM of the engine
    e. The operator's foot

20. Which of the following is a mode of operation on power braking systems?
    a. Apply mode
    b. Hold mode
    c. Release mode
    d. All of the above
    e. None of the above

21. Hydro-boost brake systems use _____ to increase the pressure for the master cylinder.
    a. Vacuum
    b. Power steering fluid
    c. Cooling system fluid
    d. The RPM of the engine
    e. The operator's foot

22. Which of the following is a good service tip when working on brakes?
    a. Bleed the system of air.
    b. Replace linings that show excessive wear.
    c. Keep all wheel cylinder parts clean and coated with brake fluid.
    d. All of the above
    e. None of the above

> *The following questions are similar in format to ASE (Automotive Service Excellence) test questions.*

23. Technician A says that a spongy brake pedal is caused by air in the hydraulic system. Technician B says that a spongy brake pedal is caused by a weak return spring. Who is right?
    a. A only
    b. B only
    c. Both A and B
    d. Neither A nor B

24. When a car is being stopped, it pulls to the right. Technician A says that the left wheel cylinder is leaking. Technician B says that the right wheel cylinder is leaking. Who is right?
    a. A only
    b. B only
    c. Both A and B
    d. Neither A nor B

25. The left front wheel cylinder has just been replaced. Technician A says that the brake system should not be bled of air. Technician B says that the brakes must be bled to remove the air. Who is right?
    a. A only
    b. B only
    c. Both A and B
    d. Neither A nor B

26. A wheel cylinder is leaking slightly. Technician A says that the wheel cylinder should be honed and the old parts replaced. Technician B says a new wheel cylinder kit should be put in after the cylinder is honed slightly. Who is right?
    a. A only
    b. B only
    c. Both A and B
    d. Neither A nor B

27. During braking a scraping sound is heard. Technician A says the problem is the bearings. Technician B says the brake pads are worn and touching the disc. Who is correct?
    a. A only
    b. B only
    c. Both A and B
    d. Neither A nor B

28. Technician A says to always perform a visual inspection before servicing any component on an antilock braking system. Technician B says to always perform a functional check when servicing the ABS. Who is correct?
    a. A only
    b. B only
    c. Both A and B
    d. Neither A nor B

29. Technician A says that on an ABS, the hydraulic system is being pulsed by the pressure modulator valves. Technician B says four speed sensors feed data into the ABCM to determine wheel speeds. Who is correct?
    a. A only
    b. B only
    c. Both A and B
    d. Neither A nor B

30. A vehicle is producing a squeaking sound during braking. Technician A says that the sound is produced by a sensor spring that squeaks if the brakes are worn too much. Technician B says the sound is being made from a bad wheel bearing. Who is correct?
    a. A only
    b. B only
    c. Both A and B
    d. Neither A nor B

Essay

31. Describe the process of bleeding the brakes.

32. What are the primary and the secondary shoes?

33. Describe the operation of a floating caliper.

34. What is a compensating port in the master cylinder?

35. Describe the purpose and operation of the proportioning valve.

36. Describe the operation of power brakes as compared with manual brakes.

Short Answer

37. In a hydraulic system, a force of 400 pounds was placed on the input piston, with an area of 1 square inch. Therefore there would be a force of _____ lbs on a 1/2-square-inch output piston in the same hydraulic system.

38. On an ABS the _____ is measured at each wheel, and this information is sent to the computer.

39. Two driving characteristics that may be noticed with antilock braking systems are that _____ and _____.

40. When the right front wheel cylinder is leaking, it causes the car to pull to the _____.

41. In order to remove the air from the hydraulic circuit in a braking system the system must be _____.

CHAPTER 29

Suspension Systems

INTRODUCTION The suspension system of a car is used to support its weight during varying road conditions. The suspension system is made of several parts and components. These include both the front and rear suspensions, the shock absorbers, and the MacPherson strut system. The objective of this chapter is to analyze the parts and operation of different suspension systems.

OBJECTIVES After reading this chapter, you should be able to:

- Define the parts and operation of the front suspension system.
- Define the parts and operation of the rear suspension system.
- Analyze the purpose, parts, and operation of different types of shock absorbers.
- Compare the MacPherson strut suspension with other suspension systems, including parts and operation.

- Define the operation of computer-controlled suspension systems.
- Identify the purpose and operation of automatic level control and air suspension systems.
- State common problems, diagnosis, and service suggestions concerning different types of suspension systems.

✔ **SAFETY CHECKLIST** ✔

When working with the suspension system components, keep these important safety precautions in mind.
✔ Always wear OSHA-approved safety glasses when working on suspension systems.
✔ Always use the proper tools when working on suspension systems.

✔ Always use the correct procedure for lifting the vehicle when working on the suspension system components.
✔ Be careful not to injure yourself when lifting heavy parts of the suspension system.

29.1 FRONT SUSPENSION

Purpose of the Front Suspension

The purpose of the front suspension is to support the weight of the vehicle. The suspension must also be designed to provide a smooth passenger ride over varying road conditions and speeds.

There are several types of front-end suspension systems. Automobiles commonly use the independent front suspension system. This means that each wheel is independent from the other. For example, if the left wheel goes over a bump in the road, only the left wheel will move up and down. See *Figure 29–1*. Certain types of trucks and other heavy-duty vehicles may use an I-beam suspension. This system has one main

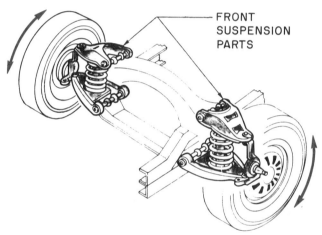

INDEPENDENT FRONT SUSPENSION

FIGURE 29–1. The front suspension is called independent front suspension. This means that each wheel acts independently when going over a bump. *(Courtesy of Dana Corporation)*

beam connecting each front wheel. This system is not independent front suspension.

Parts of the Front Suspension System

Although there are different types of front suspension systems, many of the parts are the same. *Figure 29–2* shows a common type of front suspension system and the related parts. These parts include the:

1. Ball joints (both upper and lower)
2. Control arms, shaft bushings, and shims
3. Sway bar, bushings
4. Strut rod, bushings
5. Coil springs
6. Stabilizers
7. Shock absorbers
8. Steering knuckle and spindle

These parts are assembled to provide the entire front suspension. Each of these parts becomes a vital link in the front suspension operation. They must work properly to ensure driving safety and comfort.

Ball Joints

The *ball joints* are used to connect the spindle and steering knuckle to the upper and lower control arms. They are designed to do several things. The ball joints must carry the weight of the vehicle. They provide a pivot for the wheel to turn. They also allow for vertical movement of the control arms when the vehicle goes over irregularities in the road. *Figure 29–3* shows a typical set of ball joints for upper and lower control arms.

The frame of the upper ball joint is either riveted or bolted to the upper control arm. The steering knuckle is attached to the tapered stud and is held in place with a nut. The lower ball joint is usually bolted, riveted, or pressed into the lower

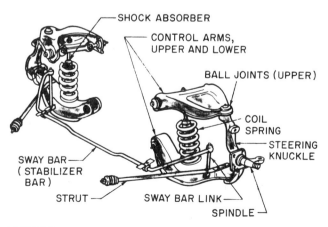

FIGURE 29–2. The parts of the front suspension. *(Courtesy of Dana Corporation)*

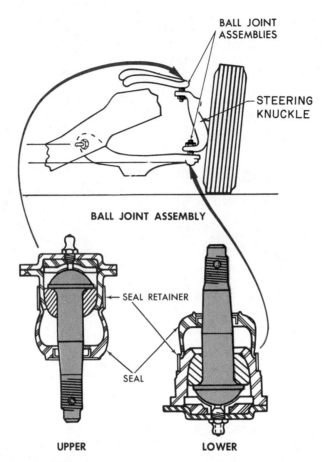

FIGURE 29–3. Ball joints are used to connect the control arms to the steering knuckle. *(Courtesy of Chevrolet Division, General Motors Corporation)*

control arm. The steering knuckle is placed on the tapered stud and held in place with a nut. A rubber boot is placed around the assembly to keep grease in and dirt out.

Control Arms

There are two *control arms*: an upper and a lower control arm. Several arrangements are used for the control arms.

There are single pivot control arms, double pivot control arms, and long and short control arms. *Figure 29–4* shows a comparison of control arms. The type of control arm depends on the year and manufacturer of the vehicle.

The other end of the control arm is attached to the frame of the vehicle. *Figure 29–5* shows how upper control arms are attached to the frame. The upper control arm has a shaft

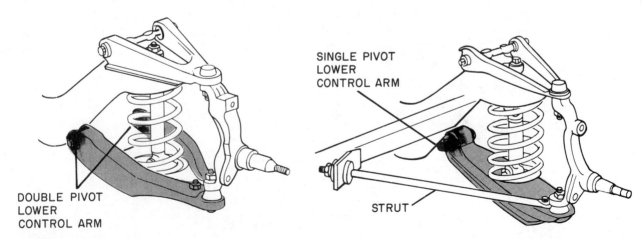

FIGURE 29–4. Either a single or a double lower control arm can be used. The single lower control arm also uses a strut for support. *(Courtesy of Dana Corporation)*

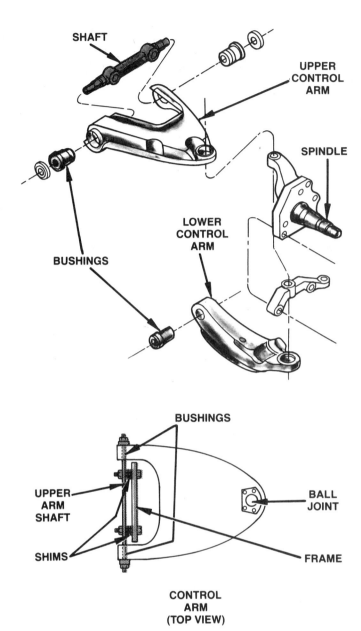

FIGURE 29–5. The parts of the upper control arm. The upper control arm is attached to the frame by bushings, shims, and the upper control arm shaft. *(Courtesy of Dana Corporation)*

that is bolted to the frame. The ends of the shaft carry bushings that are attached to the control arm. Shims are used to adjust the position of the shaft on the frame for alignment of the front suspension. The lower control arm is attached to the frame by bushings and bolts.

Sway Bar and Link (Stabilizer Bar and Link)

The *sway bar* and sway bar link are also called the *stabilizer bar* and link. The sway bar link connects the lower control arm to the sway bar. The sway bar twists like a *torsion bar* during turns. It transmits cornering forces from one side of the vehicle to the other. This helps to equalize the wheel loads and prevent excessive leaning of the car on turns. The

sway bar link and sway bar are attached to the frame with rubber bushings and bolts.

Strut Rods

The *strut rod* is used on vehicles that have single-pivot lower control arms. They can be located either in front of or behind the control rod. They are designed to retain the lower control arms in their intended positions. They also provide a method of keeping the wheel in the right position for alignment. *Figure 29–6* shows the position of the strut rod. The sway bar and the sway bar link are also shown.

Coil Springs

The coil springs are used to support the car's weight, maintain the car's *stance,* or height, and position all the other suspension parts correctly. Thus, if a spring sags a slight amount, the tires, shocks, ball joints, and control arms all work outside their normal positions. This condition may cause excessive or abnormal wear throughout the suspension systems.

Springs may be very flexible or very stiff. The purpose of the springs is to absorb road shock and then return to their original position. A stiff spring gives a rough ride. A flexible spring may cause the vehicle to bounce too much. The best combination is to use a softer spring with a shock absorber.

Torsion Bars

Another method used to provide the desired ride and handling characteristics is to use torsion bars rather than springs. Torsion bars are made so that as the car goes over bumps, the torsion bar will twist. The resistance to twisting produces an effect similar to that produced by springs. A torsion bar is attached to each side of the vehicle. One end of the torsion bar is attached to the frame. The other end of

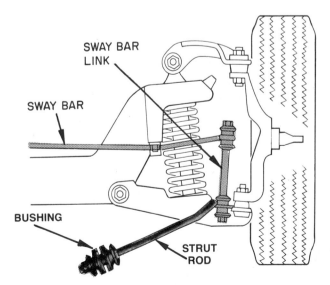

FIGURE 29–6. The strut rod is used to support the single-pivot lower control arm. *(Courtesy of Dana Corporation)*

the torsion bar is attached to the lower control arm. As the lower control arm moves because of bumps in the road, the torsion bar twists and reduces the car's motion. *Figure 29–7* shows a typical torsion bar installation. Other arrangements have also been used. *Figure 29–8* shows a torsion bar connected between the back wheels. As the rear drive shaft moves up and down, it causes the torsion bar to twist. Certain torsion bars are also adjustable for setting the vehicle height.

Steering Knuckle and Spindle

Two other parts of the front suspension include the *steering knuckle* and the *wheel spindle*. The wheel spindle is the unit that carries the hub and bearing assembly with the help of the knuckle. In some vehicles, the steering knuckle and wheel spindle are one unit. *Figure 29–9* shows an example of the steering knuckle and spindle. The steering knuckle is attached to the two control arms with ball joints. The wheel spindle carries the entire wheel load. Bearings are used to reduce friction between the wheel and the spindle. The inner bearing on the spindle is usually larger than the outer bearing. It absorbs the greatest load because the wheel is placed as close to the knuckle as possible.

Front Wheel Bearings

The front wheel bearings are also considered part of the front suspension. There are two bearings on each front wheel spindle to support the wheel. Both bearings are called tapered roller bearings. On certain types of front end suspension systems, ball bearings are used as well. The inner race of the bearing rides on the spindle. The outer race is lightly pressed into the wheel hub.

CAR CLINIC

PROBLEM: Noise Heard in Front Suspension

The customer complains that there is a noise coming from the front end. The noise occurs only when entering or exiting the driveway at the customer's home. What is the problem?

SOLUTION:

Noise such as this is often associated with the front ball joints. Test drive the vehicle, making slow turns, especially up and down a driveway ramp. The most likely cause of the problem is a worn lower ball joint on the left or the right side of the vehicle. Inspect the ball joints and replace where necessary.

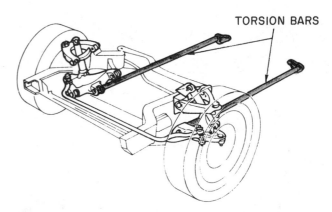

FIGURE 29–7. Torsion bars are used in place of springs on some vehicles. *(Courtesy of Dana Corporation)*

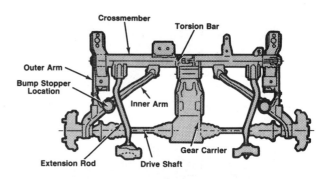

FIGURE 29–8. The torsion bar can also be located between the two rear wheels. In this case, the torsion bar is located between the outer arms on the rear suspension. *(Courtesy of Dana Corporation)*

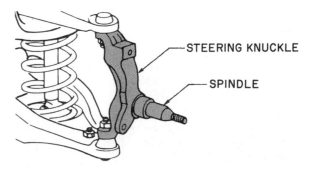

FIGURE 29–9. The spindle holds the wheel bearings and is attached to the steering knuckle. *(Courtesy of Dana Corporation)*

29.2 REAR SUSPENSION

The rear suspension system is an integral part of the total suspension system. There are typically two types of rear suspension systems. These are the solid axle type and the *independent rear suspension* type.

Purpose of Rear Suspension

All rear suspension systems serve the same purpose. They are designed to keep the rear axle and wheels in their proper

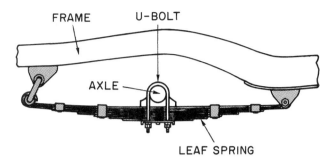

FIGURE 29–10. Both ends of the rear leaf spring are attached to the frame. The axle is attached to the rear spring by a U-bolt. *(Courtesy of Dana Corporation)*

position under the car body. The rear wheels must always track exactly straight ahead. The rear suspension axle allows each of the rear wheels to move up and down somewhat independently from the frame. This helps to maintain alignment and good vehicle control and provides passenger comfort. The spring assembly must also absorb a large amount of rear end torque from acceleration (on rear drive vehicles), side thrust from turning, and road shock from bumps.

Leaf Spring

The most common type of spring used on rear suspensions is called the leaf spring. It consists of one or more leaves and usually has its ends formed into eyes for connection to the vehicle frame. A U-bolt is used to hold the rear axle to the spring. This type of spring is called the semi-elliptical spring. The ends are higher than the center arch as shown in *Figure 29–10*. One end of the spring is fixed to the frame. The other end of the spring is mounted to the frame by a spring *shackle* and bushing. The bushings are used to dampen noise and vibration from the road to the frame of the car. The spring shackle allows the spring to change length slightly during driving. During normal operation, the spring also bends

because of acceleration, braking, or road conditions. The leaf spring supports the car frame, but it allows independent movement of the rear wheels. *Figure 29–11* shows the individual parts of a leaf spring.

Coil Spring Rear Suspension

In a coil spring rear suspension, the spring is placed between a bracket mounted on the axle and the vehicle frame. The coil design is much the same as the front wheel coil spring. In addition to the coil springs, control arms and bushings are used. Control arms provide stability to the rear wheels during driving. The control arms are attached with bushings to the rear axle housing and the car frame. *Figure 29–12* shows a coil spring rear suspension system.

Independent Rear Suspension

Independent rear suspension is used on many front wheel drive cars. Independent rear suspension means that each rear wheel is independent in its movement. This is much the same as the front suspension system. Although there are many designs for independent rear suspension, most systems include coil springs, control arms, struts, and stabilizer bars.

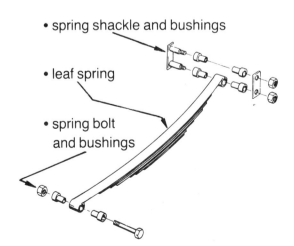

FIGURE 29–11. The parts of a leaf spring. *(Courtesy of Dana Corporation)*

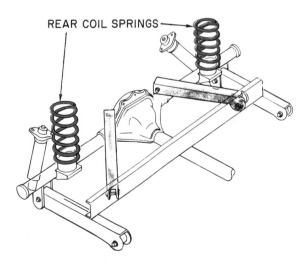

FIGURE 29–12. The rear suspension can also use coils rather than leaf springs. *(Courtesy of Dana Corporation)*

CAR CLINIC

PROBLEM: Alignment and MacPherson Strut

A service technician has removed and replaced the MacPherson struts. After this procedure, the wheel alignment was off. What is the problem?

SOLUTION:

When MacPherson struts are removed, the lower mounting bolts must be removed. This procedure will disturb the camber setting of the wheel assembly. Before removing the two lower mounting bolts, be sure to mark the position of the lower mounting bolt eccentric cam. If this is done, the front end can be reassembled, and the alignment can be put back to its original position by realigning the marks. However, it is still wise to check the camber after replacing the struts.

29.3 SHOCK ABSORBERS

Purpose of Shock Absorbers

Shock absorbers are hydraulic devices that help to control the up, down, and rolling motion of a car body. One shock absorber is used on each wheel. Each shock must control one wheel and axle motion. The car's springs support the body, but the shock absorbers work with the springs to control movements of the car body. A shock absorber can be considered a damper that controls energy stored in the springs under load. For this reason, shock absorbers are also called *oscillation* dampers.

The shock absorber is placed parallel to the upward and downward motion of the car. It has two tasks:

1. to prevent excessive rolling and bouncing of the car body and

2. to rapidly terminate the oscillation of the wheels and axle when they start moving up and down.

These two factors are of major importance for driving comfort and safety.

Figure 29–13 shows how a shock absorber works. When there is a rise or bump in the road surface, the car axle immediately rises. Now the spring is compressed and starts to push the car body up. The impact acting on the vehicle is absorbed by the spring. The spring prevents the axle from touching the car body. After the springs have been compressed, they try to expand. This helps separate the car body from the axle. This entire action causes an oscillation motion to develop.

The oscillation motions are also shown. The shock absorber is placed between the axle and the car body. It is designed to reduce the number of oscillations produced after hitting a bump. For comparison, the oscillations are also shown when a shock absorber is placed between the car body and the axle.

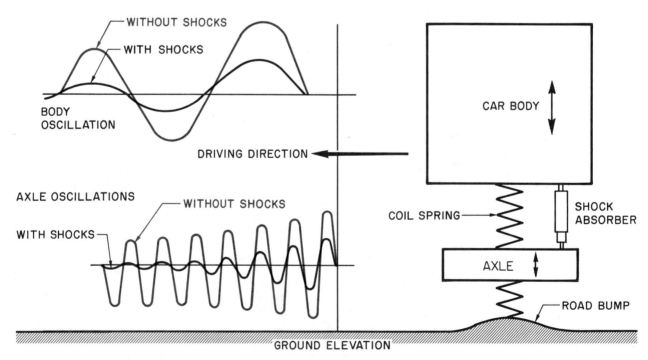

FIGURE 29–13. As the axle goes over a bump, the spring is compressed. The oscillations that are produced are shown with and without a shock absorber. *(Courtesy of Sachs Automotive Products Company)*

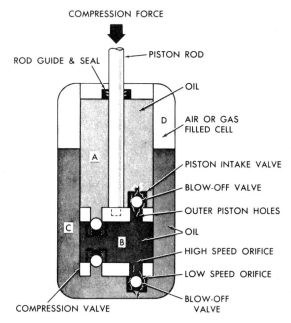

FIGURE 29–14.   Under a compression force, the oil is forced through small valves into reservoirs C and A. *(Courtesy of Chevrolet Division, General Motors Corporation)*

Shock Absorber Operation

The shock absorbers are made to force a noncompressible liquid through small openings. *Figure 29–14* shows how they work. When a compression force is produced from a road bump, the piston rod is forced down. A pressure is produced in the oil below the piston in chamber B. The oil pressure forces oil outward and through both the blow-off valve and the piston intake valve. Oil can only pass through these passageways at a certain speed. The pressure forces oil out into chamber C. During this time, air is being compressed in area D. The damping force originates from the resistance of oil flow at the narrow passages of the valve parts. In addition, oil passes into chamber A. Oil must flow into this chamber because it is getting larger as the piston is moved downward.

When the shock absorber rebounds, oil flows in the reverse direction. *Figure 29–15* shows the flow of oil when the shock absorber rebounds or returns to its original position. During rebounding, the piston rod is forced to extend out and upward. This action causes a vacuum to be produced inside chamber B. This vacuum draws oil from chamber A into chamber B through the rebound valve. Oil also flows from chamber C into chamber B. Air in chamber D then expands to compensate for the loss of oil in chamber C. Since a part of the oscillating energy is converted to heat energy, shock absorbers that are working correctly get warm during operation.

Parts of a Shock Absorber

There are many types of shock absorbers, but the main principles of operation are the same. Although they may be

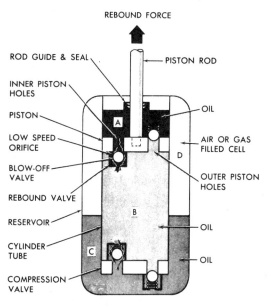

FIGURE 29–15.   During rebound force, oil is forced from reservoirs C and A into B. *(Courtesy of Chevrolet Division, General Motors Corporation)*

different sizes, the parts are much the same. *Figure 29–16* shows a typical shock absorber. It is called the double-tube shock absorber. The more important parts include:

1. *Ring joint* — used to attach the shock to the axle and frame.

2. *Piston rod seal* — used to keep oil from leaking past the rod and into the atmosphere during pressure conditions.

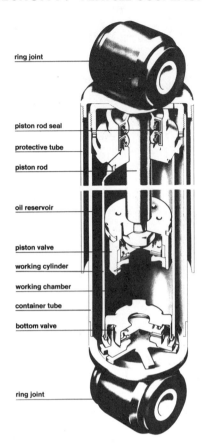

ring joint

piston rod seal

protective tube

piston rod

oil reservoir

piston valve

working cylinder

working chamber

container tube

bottom valve

ring joint

FIGURE 29–16. The parts of a shock absorber. *(Courtesy of Sachs Automotive Products Company)*

3. *Piston valve* — used to control the flow of oil and produce the pressure and vacuum in the chamber above the piston during compression and rebound.

4. *Bottom valve* — used to control the flow of oil into the oil reservoir during compression and rebound.

5. *Protective tube* — used to keep dirt and road dust away from the seals and piston rod.

6. *Container tube* — used to house the internal parts of the shock absorber.

7. *Working chamber* — area where the pressure and vacuum are produced.

Compression and Expansion Valve Operation

The compression and expansion valves are shown in more detail in *Figure 29–17*. The shock absorber is compressed by the oscillation of the vehicle. The oil displaced by the downward-moving piston rod flows into the reserve chamber above the piston. The oil also flows through the bottoming valve at a certain flow rate, damping the motion.

The shock absorber is expanded by the oscillation of the vehicle. During this condition, the piston valve controls the damping. The piston valve resists the oil that is trying to flow from above the piston to the working chamber. The upward motion of the piston is retarded. The bottom valve allows the necessary oil to be sucked easily from the oil reservoir.

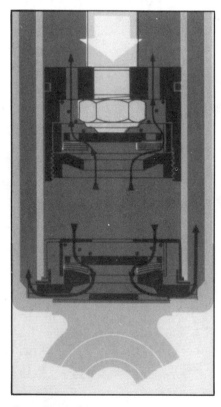

Compression

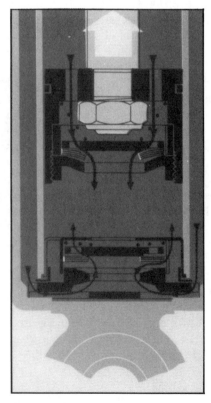

Expansion

FIGURE 29–17. The compression and expansion forces cause oil to flow through the piston valve. The resistance to this flow through the valve causes the motion to be dampened. *(Courtesy of Sachs Automotive Products Company)*

Spiral-grooved Shock Absorbers

When the oil is passed through the valves rapidly, some *aeration,* or foaming, is produced in the oil. Aeration is the mixing of air with the oils. When aeration occurs, the shock develops lag (piston moving through an air pocket that offers no resistance). This causes the shock absorber to work incorrectly and produces a poor ride.

One method used to reduce aeration is to use a spiral-grooved reservoir tube. The spiral grooves on the shock reservoir tend to break up the air bubbles. This action reduces lag.

Gas-filled Shock Absorbers

Gas-filled shocks are also used to reduce aeration. If a pressure gas replaces the air in the shock absorber, air cannot mix with the oil to produce aeration. ***Figure 29–18*** shows two types of gas-filled shock absorbers. Note that both compression and expansion valves are built into the piston. The deflection disc is used to help separate the oil and the gas. When oil is forced through the small holes in the valve, high-pressure jets of oil are produced. These jets of oil are deflected by the deflection disc before they get to the gas. This action reduces foaming and aeration. The separating disc, which is also shown, is arranged so that it completely separates the oil from the gas. It is movable to allow for differences in volume during compression and expansion.

Purpose of Air Shock Absorbers

When an increased amount of load is placed in the car, the springs may not be able to support the vehicle correctly. This is shown in ***Figure 29–19***. This condition can cause several problems. These include:

1. Increased intensity of light beams to oncoming drivers even when the lights are on dim

2. A change in steering geometry

3. Reduction of comfort for the passengers

4. Less steering control for the driver

5. The possibility of bottoming out on bumps

One way to overcome these problems caused by heavy weight is to use air shock absorbers.

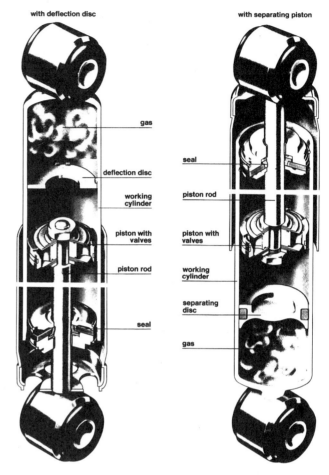

FIGURE 29–18. Gas-filled shock absorbers are used to reduce aeration. *(Courtesy of Sachs Automotive Products Company)*

Operation of Air Shock Absorbers

Figure 29–20 shows an air shock absorber. The unit is made by including an air chamber in the shock. A *bellows* is used to keep the air chamber sealed from the outside while the shock absorber is in different positions. The pressure inside the air chamber determines the amount of load that the vehicle can carry. The entire unit also uses the typical shock absorber system discussed previously.

The air is admitted to the air chamber by use of a standard tire valve. Pressure is produced by a small air pump called

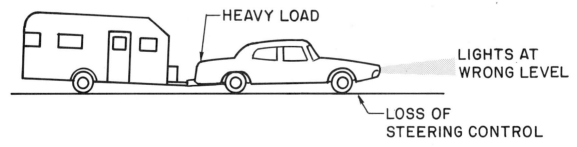

FIGURE 29–19. Heavy load in the rear of the vehicle can cause steering geometry to change, reduce steering control, and increase intensity of light beams to oncoming drivers. *(Courtesy of Sachs Automotive Products Company)*

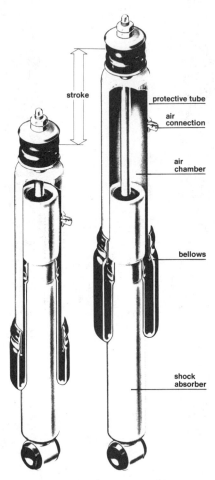

FIGURE 29–20. Air shocks are used to level the stance of the car. Air is forced into a chamber to lift the shock and level the car. *(Courtesy of Sachs Automotive Products Company)*

an air compressor. A height-sensing control valve is also used. *Figure 29–21* shows a typical installation. Other common components include an air reserve tank, different types of air compressors, and the control valve.

Automatic Level Control

The automatic level control system is used to adjust the carrying load of the car when weight is added or removed from the vehicle. The system consists of several components. These include the air compressor, air dryer, manual switch, exhaust solenoid compressor relays, electronic height sensor, and the shock absorbers and air line fittings.

1. The air compressor is a positive-displacement, single-piston pump. It is powered by a 12-volt dc permanent-magnet motor. The casting contains intake and exhaust valves for correct operation.

2. The air dryer is used to dry the air by using a chemical. When air passes through this chemical, moisture is absorbed.

3. A manual switch is used to control the compressor on certain systems. When it is in the off position, the shock absorbers act like standard shocks. When it is in the auto position, the load-leveling system is in operation.

4. The exhaust solenoid is used to exhaust air from the system and to control maximum output pressure from the air compressor.

5. The compressor relays are used to control the different functions of the system.

6. The electronic height sensors are used to measure the amount of drop and rise when weight is changed in the

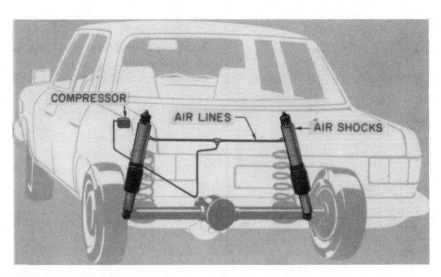

FIGURE 29–21. Air shocks use a small compressor to produce air for extra support. *(Courtesy of Sachs Automotive Products Company)*

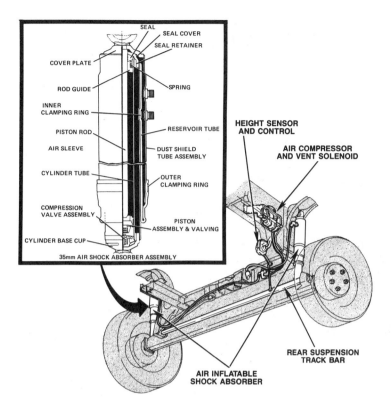

ELECTRONIC AUTOMATIC LOAD LEVELING

FIGURE 29–22. Height sensor and control units are used to measure the amount of load placed in the vehicle. The sensor tells the air compressor how much air should be used in the air shocks. *(Courtesy of Chrysler Corporation)*

vehicle. This signal is then sent to the compressor relays to change the amount of air sent to the system.

7. The shocks are the same as previously mentioned. The air lines connect the air compressor to the shocks.

A similar system is shown in *Figure 29–22*. A height sensor linked to the rear suspension track bar monitors load changes. Solid-state circuitry then either turns on the compressor to inflate the shock absorbers or exhausts the air to maintain the desired pressure. The parts of the air shock absorber assembly are also shown for reference.

Air Suspension

Another type of suspension used on vehicles is called the air suspension system, *Figure 29–23*. Although there are shock absorbers, the system also uses four air springs, one on each wheel. As the front and rear height sensors feed information to the control module, the correct amount of air is sent to each air spring.

System operation is maintained by the addition or removal of air in the air springs. There is a predetermined height for both the front and rear sections of the car. The height sensors will lengthen or shorten, depending on the amount of suspension travel. As weight is added, the body settles. As weight is removed, the body rises. The height sensors signal the control module. The control module then activates the air compressor through relays to change the amount of air in the air springs.

Active Suspension Systems

Now that most vehicles have them, computers are taking on more and more control of vehicle systems. One emerging design is called *active suspension systems*. Active suspension systems use a computer to control body roll, pitch, brake dive, acceleration squat, and ride height. The system can also lower the entire car body for improved aerodynamics during highway driving. The vehicle can also be raised to increase ground clearance. This feature might be practical during heavy snow conditions.

AIR SUSPENSION

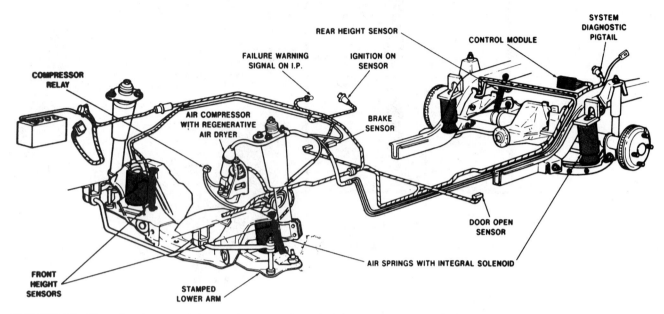

FIGURE 29–23. An air suspension system uses front height sensors, a rear height sensor, a control module, and air springs to keep the vehicle level under varying loads. *(Courtesy of Motor Publications, Auto Repair Manual)*

In order to accomplish these adjustments, the shock absorbers have been replaced with hydraulic actuator and pressure sensors. The hydraulic actuators are placed on each wheel as part of the suspension system. See *Figure 29–24.* The hydraulic actuator, along with a spring, support the weight of the vehicle. The system is designed to react to various road conditions and to make instant adjustments to keep the operator's ride as smooth as possible.

Figure 29–25 shows a simplified schematic of the active suspension system and the hydraulic system. In operation, as the vehicle starts to go over a bump in the road, the wheel is forced upward. The upward movement causes the pressure in the hydraulic system to increase. The increase in pressure is sensed by the pressure control valves. This pressure is then converted to an electronic signal and sent to the suspension computer. The computer then immediately sends an electronic signal back to the pressure control valves to release the pressure in the hydraulic actuator. As the pressure is

ACTIVE SUSPENSION SYSTEM

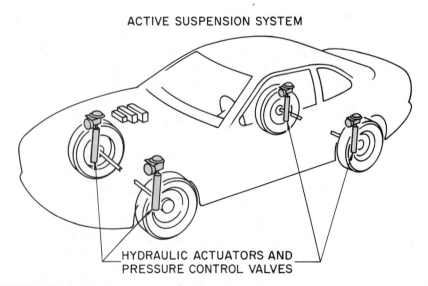

FIGURE 29–24. In an active suspension system, a hydraulic actuator is placed on each wheel to control the movement of the vehicle body over variations in road surface.

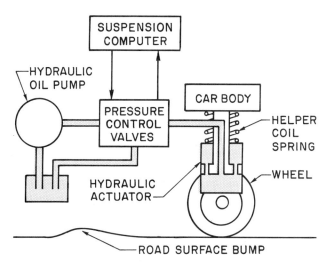

FIGURE 29–25. When the wheel goes over a bump, an increase in pressure is felt. The computer immediately alters the hydraulic pressure so the vehicle body remains at a constant position.

released, the hydraulic actuator retracts. This results in keeping the vehicle level as the tire rides up on a bump.

As the vehicle then goes over the downside of the bump, the pressure inside the hydraulic actuator decreases. This decrease in pressure is sent to the computer as an electronic signal. The computer then increases the pressure inside the hydraulic actuator, keeping the body of the vehicle from moving. The hydraulic pump, driven by the engine, is used to produce the hydraulic pressure in the system. In actual operation, the pressure decreases and increases fast enough to keep the vehicle body in one position over a bump.

PROBLEM: Clunking Noise during Braking

The customer complains that when the vehicle's brakes are applied, there is a clunk from the front end. What could be the problem?

SOLUTION:

Often a clunking noise is heard during braking if there is an excessively worn control arm bushing. If the bushing is worn, the control arm is able to move back and forth during braking or rapid acceleration. The clunking sound comes from the control arm shifting back and forth because of the braking momentum. Check the bushing in the control arms for wear. Look for shiny wear spots on the control arm as well. The solution is to replace the bushing in the control arms.

29.4 MACPHERSON STRUT SUSPENSION

General Description of the MacPherson Strut Suspension

One other popular type of independent suspension system is called the *MacPherson strut suspension.* Many imported and domestic vehicles utilize this system on front wheel drive vehicles. Certain vehicles also use this system on the rear wheels. There is also a modified version of the MacPherson strut system. The MacPherson strut system is favored where space and weight savings are important. It is used by American, European, and Japanese auto manufacturers.

Parts of the MacPherson Strut Suspension

Figure 29–26 shows a complete MacPherson strut suspension system. It is very much like a regular shock absorber and spring combined. The only difference is that the strut assembly is used as a structural part of the vehicle's suspension system. A more detailed drawing is shown in *Figure 29–27*. The system consists of the strut tube, suspension spring, dust shield, *jounce* bumper, upper spring seat, and upper mount and bearing assembly.

The MacPherson strut suspension has eliminated the need for several common suspension parts. There is no upper control arm, and the upper ball joint is not needed. There is a

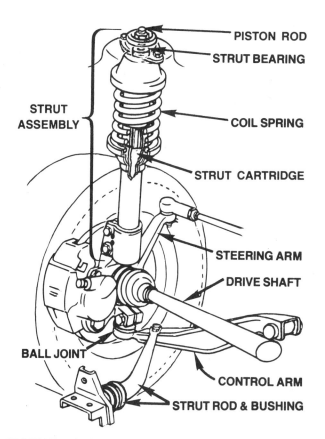

FIGURE 29–26. The basic parts of the complete MacPherson strut suspension system. *(Courtesy of Dana Corporation)*

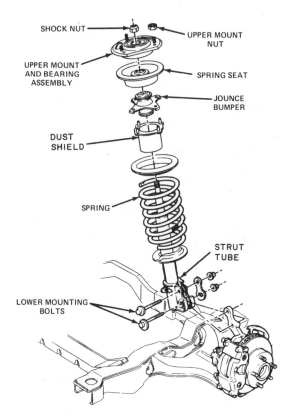

FIGURE 29–27. The detailed parts of the MacPherson strut suspension. *(Courtesy of General Motors Product Service Training)*

lower ball joint, but the ball joint does not carry as much load as in other suspension systems. It is isolated from the vehicle weight. Vehicle weight is supported at the top of the strut assembly. The strut bearing is bolted directly to the shock tower. The shock tower is the part of the car body to which the MacPherson strut is attached. *Figure 29–28* shows the shock tower built into the car body. The lower part of the strut assembly is attached by bolts to the steering knuckle. The steering knuckle is attached to the lower control arm through a ball joint.

The lower control arm is bolted to the frame with conventional rubber bushings. The lower control arm ball joint is riveted to the lower control arm.

Operation of the MacPherson Strut Suspension

During turning, the entire strut assembly is turned. The strut assembly can turn because there is a bearing assembly on top of the strut assembly and a ball joint on the bottom of the assembly. The upper bearing and mount assembly takes the place of the upper control arm. The steering arm and linkage, disc brake caliper, and lower control arm ball joint are all attached to the steering knuckle. The drive shaft is connected directly to the wheel spindle through the steering knuckle. The spring is used for the same purpose as on other suspension systems. It is used to support the vehicle weight and maintain the car stance and height. The shock absorber,

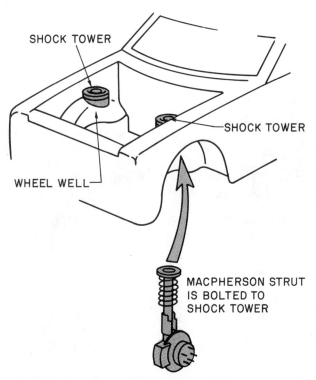

FIGURE 29–28. The MacPherson strut suspension is bolted to the shock tower. The shock tower is part of the wheel well.

which is built into the system, helps to smooth out the oscillations from the spring.

Advantages of Using MacPherson Strut Suspension

There are several advantages of using the MacPherson strut suspension systems. These include:

1. They weigh less than the conventional two control arm system.

2. The system spreads the suspension load over a wider span of the car's chassis.

3. They take up less room in the engine compartment, which allows room for other components.

4. There are fewer moving parts than in the conventional two control arm system.

Modified MacPherson Strut Suspension

Another type of MacPherson strut suspension is called the modified system. *Figure 29–29* shows such a system. The system is basically the same, except the spring is placed between the frame and the lower control arm. With the spring located here, minor road vibrations are absorbed by the chassis rather than fed back to the driver through the steering system. A lower ball joint supports the vehicle weight. This system also eliminates the upper control arm, bushings, and upper ball joints used on the conventional suspension system.

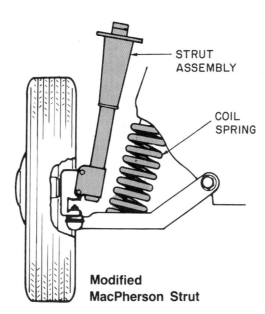

STRUT ASSEMBLY

COIL SPRING

Modified MacPherson Strut

FIGURE 29–29. The modified MacPherson strut suspension has the strut assembly separated from the coil assembly. *(Courtesy of Dana Corporation)*

Problems, Diagnosis and Service

SAFETY PRECAUTIONS

1. The suspension system has many parts that are under high pressure and tension. These include the shocks, springs, and torsion bars. When these parts are removed incorrectly, they may spring out violently, causing serious injury. Make sure all tension has been removed from these components before removing them from the vehicle.
2. Never use high-pressure air to dry off bearings after they have been cleaned. Never spin the bearing with a high-pressure air hose, as the balls could dislodge and cause serious injury.
3. When removing MacPherson strut components, remember that some parts may have high tension on them. Remove the tension or pressure before removing these components from the vehicle. To do this, extra support will be needed.
4. Parts of the suspension system are very heavy. Be careful not to crush your fingers or hands when moving the parts and assemblies.
5. Many parts and assemblies must be removed in the correct sequence. Incorrect disassembly may cause parts to drop or to spring out unexpectedly. Always follow the manufacturer's suggested procedure when removing suspension parts from the vehicle.

PROBLEM: Worn Suspension Components

As the vehicle goes down the road at higher speeds, there is a shimmy in the front end suspension.

DIAGNOSIS

Various components on the suspension system may cause the vehicle to shimmy. Probable causes include the ball joints, shock absorbers, and worn tie rod ends. *Figure 29–30* shows two charts that will help diagnose problems in the suspension system. If any of these components are worn excessively, the front suspension loosens up, and the vehicle may shimmy at different speeds. In addition, various noises may be heard from the front suspension if there is excessive wear on these parts.

Figure 29–31 shows a simple diagnostic flow chart to determine the condition of ball joints. *Figure 29–32* shows a similar troubleshooting chart for shock absorbers. Use these charts to help diagnose shimmy and noise problems in the front suspension system.

SERVICE

Use the following general procedure to service front suspension parts.

Ball Joints

Ball joints can be checked for wear by inspecting the lower section of the ball joint. New ball joints will have a 0.050-inch clearance between the end of the grease *zerk* and the body of a ball joint. The grease zerk is a small fitting used to allow grease to enter the bottom of the ball joint. Refer to *Figure 29–33*. Replace the ball joint if the clearance is less than 0.050 inch. Use the following general procedure to replace a ball joint.

1. Raise the vehicle and support it at the frame. Then remove the wheel and tire.

FRONT WHEEL SHIMMY	
a. Tire and wheel out of balance	a. Balance tires
b. Worn or loose wheel bearings	b. Adjust wheel bearings
c. Worn tie rod ends	c. Replace tie rod end
d. Worn ball joints	d. Replace ball joints
e. Incorrect front wheel alignment	e. Check and align front suspension
f. Shock absorber inoperative	f. Replace shock absorber

FIGURE 29–30. Most front suspension problems produce either a shimmy or various noises. These problems can be diagnosed as shown on these charts. *(Courtesy of Chevrolet Division, General Motors Corporation)*

2. Position a suitable jack under the lower control arm spring seat, and raise the jack to compress the coil spring.

   CAUTION: The jack must remain in place when the ball joint is being replaced to hold the spring and control arm in position.

3. Remove the cotter pins and nuts holding the ball joint stud to the steering knuckle. Now disconnect the joint from the knuckle using a pickle fork.

4. The ball joint must now be removed from the control arm. Remove the heads of the rivets that hold the ball joint to the control arms. Certain ball joints may have to be pressed out of the control arm. The ball joint should now be removable.

5. Place a new ball joint in the control arm. The new ball joint may have to be pressed or bolted in.

6. Install the ball joint stud into the steering knuckle and torque the nut to the manufacturer's specifications.

7. Install the cotter pin.

8. Grease the new ball joint.

9. Replace the wheel and tire.

10. Remove the vehicle from the jack and test it.

Shock Absorbers

Bad shock absorbers have the following characteristics:

1. Continuous bouncing of the body with every road bump

2. Oscillation of the body with rough surface roads

3. Lifting of the body when the car is accelerated

Bad shock absorbers cannot be repaired. In all cases, the shocks are replaced with new ones. Use the following general procedure to replace shock absorbers.

1. Raise and support the vehicle as needed.

2. Hold the shock absorber shaft with a suitable wrench.

3. Remove the upper retaining nut.

4. Remove the lower bolts that hold the shock absorber pivot arm to the control arm. Pull the shock absorber from the coil spring. Replace the shock absorber with a new one by reversing the removal procedures.

5. The rear shock absorbers are removed in much the same manner except the vehicle is supported in the rear. On some vehicles, the upper retaining nut may be located in the trunk area.

   CAUTION: On some vehicles, the rear springs may have to be supported by a jack to remove the shock absorber. Refer to the manufacturer's suggested procedure before removing rear shock absorbers.

PROBLEM: Faulty Wheel Bearings

While driving down the road, the driver notices a slight growling noise coming from the front end of the vehicle. There is also a slight vibration.

DIAGNOSIS

This type of problem is often diagnosed as a bad wheel bearing. When testing for bad wheel bearings follow these general procedures:

1. Drive the car at low speed on a smooth road.

2. Turn the car to develop left and right motions, traffic permitting.

3. The noise should change because of the cornering loads being produced.

NOISE IN FRONT END

a. Ball joints need lubrication	a. Lubricate ball joint
b. Shock absorber loose or bushings worn	b. Tighten bolts and/or replace bushings
c. Worn control arm bushings	c. Replace bushings
d. Worn tie rod ends	d. Replace tie rod ends
e. Worn or loose wheel bearings	e. Adjust or replace wheel bearings
f. Loose stabilizer bar	f. Tighten all stabilizer bar attachments
g. Loose wheel nuts	g. Tighten the wheel nuts to proper torque

FIGURE 29–30. (CONTINUED)

4. Jack up the wheels to verify the roughness at the wheels. Check for loose or worn wheel bearings with the weight of the car off the wheel. This procedure is shown in *Figure 29-34*.

5. Rotate the wheel and verify roughness as the wheel turns.

SERVICE

If the wheel bearings seem rough or produce vibration in the front suspension, use the following general procedure to remove and replace the wheel bearings.

1. Remove wheel from hub.

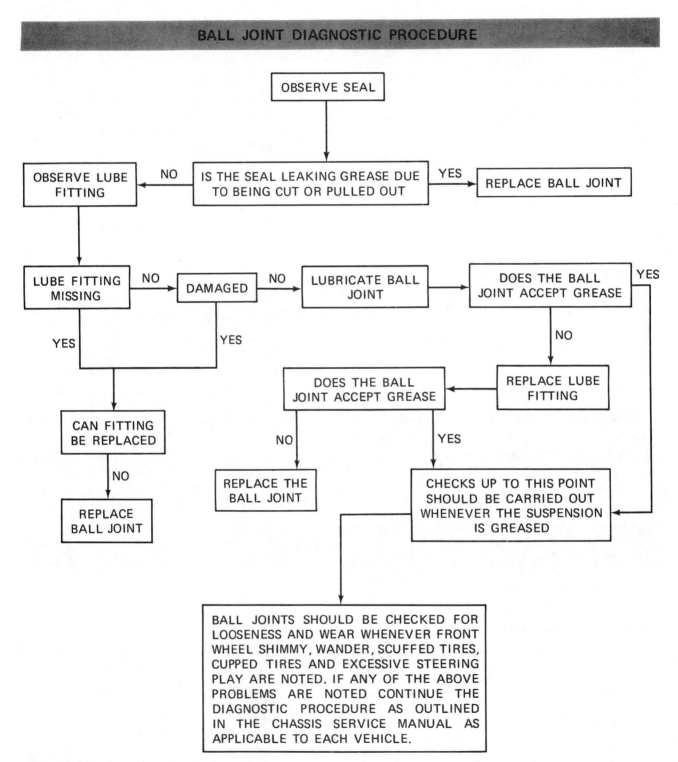

FIGURE 29-31. Follow this ball joint diagnostic procedure to determine problems in the ball joints. *(Courtesy of Chevrolet Division, General Motors Corporation)*

2. Remove the small cover over the hub nut.

3. Remove the cotter pin.

4. Remove the spindle nut.

5. On disc brakes, pull off the caliper assembly.

6. Now pull off the drum or disc from the spindle assembly. The outside bearing will be pulled off as well.

7. Remove the inner seal that is pressed into the hub.

8. Using suitable tools remove the inside bearing from the hub. Typically a hammer and punch can be used.

TROUBLESHOOTING CHART		
TROUBLE	**POSSIBLE CAUSE**	**WHAT TO DO**
1. Shock absorber breaks down	Vehicle spring suspension travel limit stop defective. Shock absorber performs improperly.	Check rubber stop on the spring suspension travel; if necessary, replace it. Replace shock absorber.
2. Shock absorber noises (rattling, rumbling)	Shock absorber mounting loose. Protective tube loose. Protective tube grazes on cylinder tube. Shock absorber worn.	Fasten shock absorber properly. Replace shock absorber. Check offset between top and bottom shock absorber mountings. Exchange shock absorber.
3. Shock absorber inefficient	Oil loss due to defective seals or worn valves.	Exchange shock absorber.
4. Shock absorber leaky	Defective piston rod seal. **Attention! There is a difference between an oil mist, which is harmless, and fresh oil - shock absorber offset.**	Exchange shock absorber. see § 2 also.
5. Shock absorber works too hard	Wrong shock type absorber installed. Valves not in order.	Install correct type according to vehicle specification. Exchange shock absorber.
6. Shock absorber works too smooth	Wrong shock absorber installed. Shock absorber worn out.	Install correct type according to vehicle specification. Install new shock absorber.
7. Bad driving quality	Damping efficiency fades.	Install new shock absorber.
8. Washing out (flattening) of tire profile	Damping efficiency has vanished or ceased to exist.	Install new shock absorber.

FIGURE 29–32. This troubleshooting chart can be used to solve problems with the shock absorbers. *(Courtesy of Sachs Automotive Products Company)*

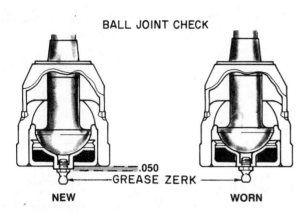

FIGURE 29–33. Ball joints can be checked for wear. There should be a 0.050-inch clearance between the grease zerk and the body of the ball joint. *(Courtesy of Dana Corporation)*

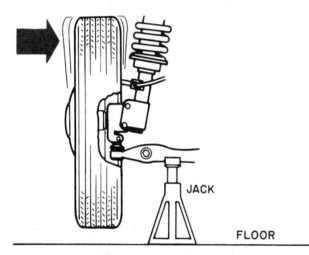

FIGURE 29–34. Check for loose or worn wheel bearings with the weight of the car off the wheel. *(Courtesy of Dana Corporation)*

Remember to push on the part of the bearing that is pressed into the hub.

9. Clean the grease from the bearings and from the inside of the hub.

10. Check the condition of both the inner and outer bearings. The following conditions indicate a damaged bearing. Always check bearings carefully for each condition.

   ■ *Galling* — metal smears on roller ends caused by overheating, lubricant failure, or overload

   ■ *Step wear* — wear pattern on roller ends caused by fine abrasives

   ■ *Indentations* — surface depressions on race and rollers caused by hard particles of foreign materials

   ■ *Etching* — bearing surfaces appear gray or grayish-black

   ■ *Heat discoloration* — bearing surfaces appear faint yellow to dark blue, resulting from overload and lubricant breakdown

   ■ *Brinelling* — surface indentations in raceway caused by rollers either under impact loading or vibration while bearing is not rotating

11. Replace bearings that are damaged or show signs of wear.

12. Repack new bearings with grease. Make sure that grease has been repacked completely into the bearings before installation. When handling bearings always use the guidelines listed in *Figure 29–35*.

13. Install new bearings. The inner bearing will need to be pressed into the drum or disc hub. Make sure to put pressure only on the outer race of the bearing during installation.

14. Install the disc or drum hub onto the spindle.

15. Front wheel bearings must be adjusted correctly so that the right amount of load is placed on the bearings. Use the following procedure to adjust the wheel bearings.
   a. Rotate the wheel. While the wheel is rotating, torque the spindle nut to approximately 12 lb. (Check the manufacturer's specifications for the correct torque.)
   b. Back off the nut until it is just loose, then retighten it by hand.
   c. Loosen the spindle nut until the cotter pin can be inserted. Do not, however, loosen the nut more than 1/2 flat on the nut. With the bearing properly adjusted, there should be about 0.001–0.005 inch end play.
   d. Check the front wheel rotation to see if the wheel rotates smoothly and easily, without excessive friction or noise.
   e. Insert the spindle nut cover and wheel.
   f. Remove the vehicle from the jack or hoist and test it.

PROBLEM: Damaged Strut Assembly

A front wheel drive vehicle produces a noise as the vehicle goes over a bump.

DIAGNOSIS

Often the front wheel drive suspension system may be damaged or worn. Generally, the problem is in the strut assembly.

1. A weak strut assembly on the MacPherson strut suspension can be checked by pushing downward, then quickly releasing near the fender over each strut. Any tendency to bounce more than once means the shock may be in poor condition and should be replaced.

2. Worn strut rod bushings may be checked by firmly grasping the strut rod and shaking it. Any noticeable play indicates excess wear, and replacement is needed.

HANDLING BEARINGS:	
Things To Remember	**Things To Avoid**
1. Remove all outside dirt from housing before exposing bearing.	1. Working in dirty surroundings.
2. Treat a used bearing as carefully as you would a new one.	2. Using dirty, brittle or chipped tools.
3. Work with clean tools in clean surroundings.	3. Using wooden mallets or working on wooden bench tops.
4. Handle with clean, dry hands or, better, clean canvas gloves.	4. Handling with dirty, moist hands.
5. Use clean solvents and flushing oils.	5. Using gasolines containing tetraethyl lead, as they may be injurious to health.
6. Lay bearings out on clean paper.	6. Spinning uncleaned bearings.
7. Protect disassembled bearings from rust and dirt.	7. Spinning bearings with compressed air.
8. Use clean rags to wipe bearings.	8. Using cotton waste or dirty cloths to wipe bearings.
9. Keep bearings wrapped in oilproof paper when not in use.	9. Exposing bearings to rust or dirt at all times.
10. Clean inside of housing before replacing bearing.	10. Scratching or nicking of bearing surfaces.

FIGURE 29–35. Bearings should be handled with care. Always follow these guidelines. *(Courtesy of Chevrolet Division, General Motors Corporation)*

SERVICE

Use the following general procedure to remove and replace the strut.

1. Raise and support the front of the vehicle, using all safety precautions mentioned earlier.
2. Remove the wheel and tire.
3. Support the lower control arm with a suitable jack stand.
4. Remove the brake hose bracket.
5. Mark the eccentric bolt position to the strut bracket to retain correct camber wheel alignment during reassembly.
6. Remove the strut-to-knuckle bolts.
7. Remove the cover from the upper end of the strut at the shock tower area.
8. Remove the nuts from the upper strut assembly.
9. Remove the strut assembly from the vehicle.
10. Reverse the procedure to install the strut.

11. Torque all bolts and nuts to the correct manufacturer's specifications.
12. It will probably be necessary to check the camber adjustment after the strut has been removed and replaced. Refer to Chapter 30.

PROBLEM: Damaged Rear Suspension Components

While driving down the road, the customer hears noise from the rear suspension system.

DIAGNOSIS

Various problems can occur in the rear suspension system.

1. Visual inspection of the rear suspension system can reveal loose, worn, or broken parts. Leaf springs should bow upward at the ends. If the leaf springs are flat, they either have broken or have lost tension. Replace as necessary.
2. Check the coil springs for spots and cracks. Inspect the mounting plates for broken or missing pads. Make sure each coil is an equal distance from the coils above and

SERVICE MANUAL CONNECTION

There are many important specifications to keep in mind when working with suspension systems. To identify the specifications for your vehicle, you will need to know the VIN (vehicle identification number) of the vehicle, the type and year of the vehicle, and the type of engine. Although they may be titled differently, some of the more common suspension system specifications (not all) found in service manuals are listed below. Note that these specifications are typical examples. Each vehicle may have different specifications.

Common Specification	Typical Example
Ball joint nut torque	88 lb-ft
Caliper-to-knuckle torque	58–72 lb-ft
Maximum allowable movement at wheel outer rim diameter (14-inch wheel)	0.020 inch
Rear wheel bearing adjustment (end play)	0.004 inch
Starting torque on lower ball joint	26–87 lb-in.
Tie rod end torque	11–25 lb-ft
Wheel hub end play	0.008 inch

In addition, the service manual will give specific directions for various service and testing procedures. Some of the more common procedures include:

- Ball joint inspection
- Coil spring replace
- Hub and bearing replace
- Rear wheel bearing adjust
- Shock absorber replace
- Spindle replace
- Stabilizer bar replace
- Steering knuckle replace
- Sway bar replace

below it. (Some springs are manufactured so that the spring coils are closer at the top.)

3. Check the vehicle for "dog tracking." This means that the rear wheels track to the right or left of the front wheels. This condition can be checked by visually observing the alignment of the vehicle as it moves down the road. Possible causes for this condition and suggested service are shown in *Figure 29–36*.

SERVICE

Depending on the damaged or worn part, replace as necessary. Refer to the manufacturer's service manual for correct procedures.

"DOG" TRACKING

LEAF TYPE REAR SPRING

a. Rear leaf spring broken
b. Bent rear axle housing
c. Frame or underbody out of alignment

a. Replace spring
b. Replace housing
c. Align frame

COIL TYPE REAR SPRING

a. Damaged rear suspension arm and/or worn bushings
b. Frame out of alignment
c. Bent rear axle housing

a. Replace suspension arm and/or bushings
b. Align frame
c. Replace housing

FIGURE 29–36. Dog tracking (rear wheels not tracking the same as the front wheels) can be caused by several problems in the rear suspension. *(Courtesy of Chevrolet Division, General Motors Corporation)*

TWIN I-BEAM SUSPENSION

Twin I-beam independent suspension utilizes two I-beams on the front of the vehicle. In addition, there are two coil springs and two radius arms. One end of each I-beam pivots on a bushing, which is mounted on a pin attached to the frame. Each coil spring is mounted between the I-beam and the frame. A radius arm is attached to the free end of the I-beam. It is used to steady the I-beam just as a strut rod steadies a control arm in other systems. The free end of the I-beam also has the steering knuckle or wheel spindle attached to it.

Twin I-beam suspension is used often in light-duty trucks. It is an excellent suspension for controlling the ride, damping out bumps, and reducing sway on heavier vehicles. This type of suspension also increases directional control of the vehicle.

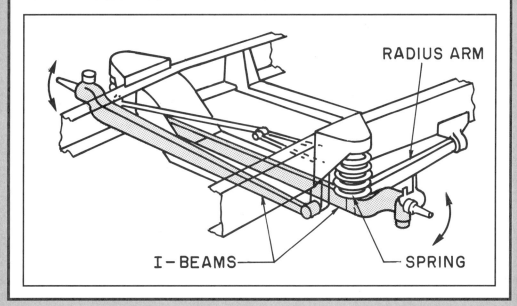

SUMMARY

This chapter dealt with suspension systems. The major areas that were studied included the front suspension, rear suspension, shock absorbers, MacPherson strut suspension, and service and troubleshooting information.

The front suspension system is used to support the front of the vehicle and provide a smooth ride for the passengers. The system is called an independent front suspension system (each wheel acts independently of the other). This is done by using several major components. Ball joints are used to connect the spindle and steering knuckle to the control arms. There are upper and lower control arms. Bushings are used to attach the control arms to the frame. With the use of control arms and ball joints, the wheel can turn, as well as move up and down during operation.

Several other components play an important part in the front suspension system. Sway bars and links are used to help transmit cornering forces from one side of the vehicle to the other. Strut rods are used help retain the lower control arm in its position. Coil springs are used to support the weight of the car and to help position the car correctly. Torsion bars are used on some vehicles in place of springs. A torsion bar is made of a long spring steel rod that is connected to the frame on one end and the lower control arm on the other. As the vehicle moves up and down, the torsion bar twists. The twisting produces much the same effect as that produced by springs. The spindle is used to carry the wheel bearings for the wheel. The spindle is connected to the control arms by the steering knuckle. These parts play a combined role as part of the front suspension system.

The rear suspension system is used to support the rear of the vehicle. It must also keep the rear wheels in line with the front wheels. The rear suspension also uses springs. Both coil and leaf springs are used. The leaf springs are made of spring steel. Each end is mounted to the frame of the vehicle. The axle is attached to the upper center of the leaf spring by a U-bolt. One end of the leaf spring uses a shackle. The shackle is a small link between the end of the leaf spring and the frame. It allows the spring to lengthen and shorten slightly when going over bumps.

All suspension systems, both front and rear, use shock absorbers. A shock absorber is a device that is placed on each wheel to dampen or slow down the bouncing of the car caused by bumps in the road. It is made by using a series of hydraulic cylinders, a piston, and valves. As the vehicle goes over bumps, the piston moves up and down. This action causes hydraulic oil to be forced through small valves. The valves only allow a certain amount of oil to pass through. The net result is that the number of oscillations after hitting a bump in the road is reduced. The shock absorber action happens both on upward and downward motions.

Several designs have been used on shock absorbers. Spiral grooves are placed on the cylinders to reduce aeration of the oil inside. Gas-filled shocks are also used to reduce aeration. Certain types of shock absorbers are called air shocks. Air shocks have small air lines attached to the cylinders. A compressor produces air pressure that is used to raise or lower the shock absorber. When there is extra load on the car, the air shocks can be pressurized to keep the vehicle level.

The automatic level control system can also be used to keep the vehicle level with changing loads. The system uses an air compressor, air dryer, electrical switches and relays, and electronic height sensor to operate. When an extra load is placed on the system, the right amount of air is admitted to each shock to keep the vehicle level.

The air suspension system is also used to maintain level conditions on the car with varying loads. This system uses air springs rather than air shocks. The remaining parts of the system, however, work in a manner similar to the automatic level control system.

MacPherson strut suspension systems are now being used on many smaller cars, both imported and domestic. The Mac-Pherson strut suspension is favored where space and weight savings are important. This system is much like a shock absorber and spring built into one unit. The system has eliminated the need for upper control arms and upper ball joints. The entire unit is attached to the lower control arm on the bottom and to the shock tower (part of the body or fender well) on the top. The entire unit turns when the vehicle is turned. An upper bearing is needed to allow for the turning action. There are also certain modifications to the MacPherson strut suspension that are being used on vehicles today.

Diagnosis and service are important parts of the suspension system. Ball joints should always be checked for wear. Front wheel bearings should be checked for damage and handled according to the manufacturer's guidelines. Shocks should be checked for leakage, excessive bouncing, and broken parts. The struts and sway bars and links should be checked for damaged bushings or broken parts. Many of these parts can be checked by visual inspection. Damage to any of these parts may cause uneven tire wear, poor handling, or uncomfortable rides.

TERMS TO KNOW

Can you explain each of the following terms? Review the chapter until you can use each term correctly.

Ball joint
Control arms
Sway bar
Stabilizer bar
Torsion bar
Strut rod
Stance
Steering knuckle
Wheel spindle
Independent rear
  suspension

Shackle
Shock absorber
Oscillation
Aeration
Bellows
Active suspension
  systems
MacPherson strut
  suspension
Jounce
Zerk

REVIEW QUESTIONS

Multiple Choice

1. The front suspension system on cars is called:
   a. Independent front suspension
   b. Rigid suspension
   c. I-beam suspension
   d. Leaf spring suspension
   e. Strut suspension

2. How many ball joints are used on each side of the standard front suspension system?
   a. 1   d. 4
   b. 2   e. 5
   c. 3

3. The ball joints are attached to the:
   a. Steering knuckle   d. All of the above
   b. Upper control arms   e. None of the above
   c. Lower control arms

4. Which of the following help to transmit cornering loads to the opposite wheel?
   a. Strut rods   d. Ball joints
   b. Control arms   e. Coil springs
   c. Sway bars and links

5. To keep the single-pivot lower control arm held in place, _____ are used.
   a. Coil springs   d. Strut rods
   b. Leaf springs   e. Stabilizer bars
   c. Ball joints

6. Which of the following are used instead of coil springs on the front suspension?
   a. Shock absorbers
   b. Ball joints
   c. Torsion bars
   d. Stabilizer bars
   e. Sway bar and link

7. Front wheel bearings are of the _____ type.
   a. Tapered-roller or ball-bearing
   b. Needle-bearing
   c. Bushing
   d. Triple-ball
   e. None of the above

8. The inner race of the wheel bearings rides on the:
   a. Steering knuckle   d. Control arm
   b. Ball joint   e. Spindle
   c. Stabilizer bar

9. The rear suspension systems used on cars:
   a. Never need service
   b. Use a solid axle
   c. Can be independent rear suspension
   d. All of the above
   e. B and C

10. One end of the leaf spring is attached to the frame. The end of the leaf spring is attached to:
    a. The shackle   d. The wheel
    b. The frame   e. The bearing
    c. The axle

11. Shock absorbers will help to:
    a. Reduce the number of oscillations of motion
    b. Provide a smoother ride
    c. Increase the stability of the car
    d. All of the above
    e. None of the above

12. Which of the following is/are *not* considered part of the shock absorber?
    a. Piston rod and piston   d. Bottom valve
    b. Piston valves   e. Container tube
    c. Strut

13. Which of the following helps to reduce or dampen the motion of a shock absorber?
    a. The position of the valves
    b. The amount of oil that can pass through the valve
    c. The size of the piston
    d. The type of material on the valves
    e. The addition of air or aeration of oil

14. Which of the following is considered a problem with shock absorbers?
    a. They can heat up too much
    b. They produce aeration inside, causing poor performance
    c. They don't support the car properly
    d. They leak transmission fluid
    e. They lock up, causing a rough ride

15. Gas-filled shock absorbers are designed:
    a. To reduce aeration
    b. To improve safety
    c. For automatic leveling
    d. All of the above
    e. None of the above

16. Which of the following systems uses an air pump and compressed air to level the car?
    a. Air shock absorbers
    b. Automatic leveling systems
    c. Leaf spring systems
    d. MacPherson strut systems
    e. Air suspension systems

17. The air suspension system uses which of the following?
    a. Shock absorbers
    b. Automatic height sensors
    c. Control module
    d. All of the above
    e. None of the above

18. A bellows is used on the _____.
    a. Springs
    b. Air shock absorbers
    c. MacPherson strut suspension
    d. Standard shock absorbers
    e. Torsion bars

19. The air suspension system forces air into the:
    a. Shock absorbers
    b. Air springs
    c. Bellows
    d. Stance
    e. Coil springs

20. The upper portion of the MacPherson strut suspension:
    a. Is attached to the shock tower
    b. Uses a bearing
    c. Turns as the car turns
    d. All of the above
    e. None of the above

21. Which is an advantage of a MacPherson strut suspension system?
    a. It is lighter
    b. It takes up more room
    c. It is heavier
    d. It requires increased maintenance
    e. It has more moving parts

22. The MacPherson strut suspension system
    a. Uses a standard shock absorber
    b. Requires no maintenance
    c. Uses extra control arms
    d. Uses extra ball joints
    e. Uses no bearings

23. To check the condition of the ball joint, there should be a difference of _____ inch between the grease zerk and the body of the ball joint.
    a. 0.010
    b. 0.020
    c. 0.030
    d. 0.040
    e. 0.050

24. To check for loose wheel bearings, the car must be:
    a. Driven on a straight line at high speed
    b. Placed on a jack with the weight removed
    c. Placed on the road surface and shaken
    d. Turned in one direction only
    e. Loaded down with extra weight

25. A bad set of shocks causes which of the following?
    a. Car lifts when accelerated
    b. Car has more oscillations after a bump
    c. Car has less stability on the road
    d. All of the above
    e. None of the above

26. Front wheel shimmy can be caused by:
    a. Tires being in balance
    b. Worn tie rods
    c. Worn ball joints
    d. All of the above
    e. B and C

The following questions are similar in format to ASE (Automotive Service Excellence) test questions.

27. Technician A says that the front wheel bearings should be adjusted as tightly as possible by tightening the spindle nut to 100 lb-ft. Technician B says that there should be approximately 0.500-inch play in the front wheel bearings. Who is right?
    a. A only
    b. B only
    c. Both A and B
    d. Neither A nor B

28. Technician A says that there is no check for testing the conditions of ball joints. Technician B says that ball joints can be checked for a clearance between the end of the grease zerk and the body of the ball joint. Who is right?
    a. A only
    b. B only
    c. Both A and B
    d. Neither A nor B

29. There is a continuous bouncing of the vehicle body when the car goes over a bump. Technician A says the problem is bad shock absorbers. Technician B says the problem is a bad steering knuckle. Who is right?
    a. A only
    b. B only
    c. Both A and B
    d. Neither A nor B

30. Technician A says there is no way to check the condition of a ball joint. Technician B says that a dial indicator can be used to check the movement of a ball joint. Who is right?
    a. A only
    b. B only
    c. Both A and B
    d. Neither A nor B

31. A shimmy is felt in the front suspension of a vehicle as it drives down the road. Technician A says the problem is the shock absorbers. Technician B says the problem is the ball joints. Who is correct?
    a. A only
    b. B only
    c. Both A and B
    d. Neither A nor B

32. A car is dog tracking as it moves down the road. Technician A says the problem is the front shock absorbers. Technician B says the problem is the frame out of alignment with the wheels. Who is correct?
    a. A only
    b. B only
    c. Both A and B
    d. Neither A nor B

33. When handling bearings, Technician A says to keep bearings wrapped in oil-proof paper when not in use. Technician B says that when cleaning bearings use clean solvent and flushing oils. Who is correct?
    a. A only
    b. B only
    c. Both A and B
    d. Neither A nor B

34. A noise is heard in the front suspension of the vehicle as it goes over a bump. Technician A says the problem is a worn shock absorber. Technician B says the problem is a worn tire. Who is correct?
    a. A only
    b. B only
    c. Both A and B
    d. Neither A nor B

Essay

35. What is the purpose of the sway bar?

36. Define the purpose and operation of a torsion bar.

37. Describe how to check the condition of shocks.

38. What is the purpose of gas-filled shocks?

39. What are several advantages of MacPherson strut suspension systems?

40. Describe the purpose of a wheel spindle.

41. What is the purpose of ball joints?

Short Answer

42. Active suspension systems are able to control body _____ and _____.

43. On an active suspension system the computer is controlling _____.

44. New ball joints should have a clearance of about _____ inch between the end of the grease zerk and the body of the ball joint.

45. A car that has continuous bouncing of the body with every road bump has worn _____.

46. A damaged wheel bearing should be checked for several conditions. Two things to check for are _____ and _____.

CHAPTER 30

Steering Systems

INTRODUCTION The steering system is used to control the direction of the vehicle. The steering system is designed to control the front wheels over all types of road conditions, through turns, and at different speeds. It is made of a linkage system that is attached to the front wheels, the steering wheel, and the steering gear. Manual and power steering units are used. The purpose of this chapter is to analyze the parts and operation of the steering system components.

OBJECTIVES After reading this chapter, you should be able to:

- Define the parts and operation of the standard steering system.

- Examine the operation of the steering gear.

- Define front end geometry including caster, camber, toe, steering axis inclination, turning radius, and four wheel alignment.

- Identify the operation of power steering units and pumps.

- State common problems, diagnosis, and service procedures on the steering system.

✔ **SAFETY CHECKLIST** ✔

When working with the steering system components, keep these important safety precautions in mind.

✔ Always wear OSHA-approved safety glasses when working on steering systems.

✔ Always use the proper tools when working on steering systems.

✔ Follow all safety rules when jacking up a vehicle to work on the steering system. Also make sure to support the vehicle with extra jack stands.

✔ Any power steering fluid that is spilled should be immediately wiped up to avoid slipping and falling.

30.1 STEERING SYSTEM PARTS AND OPERATION

Parts on a Steering System

The steering system is composed of three major subsystems, *Figure 30–1*. They are the steering column and wheel, the steering gear, and the steering linkage. As the steering wheel is turned by the operator, the steering gear transfers this motion to the steering linkage. The steering linkage turns the wheels to control the vehicle direction.

Although there are many variations to this system, these three major assemblies make up the steering system. Other variations may include power steering and rack and pinion steering.

Steering Wheel and Column

The purpose of the steering wheel and column is to produce the force necessary to turn the steering gear. The steering column is made of many parts. The exact type of steering

Some of the information in this chapter can help you prepare for the National Institute for Automotive Service Excellence (ASE) certification tests. The test most directly related to this chapter is entitled

SUSPENSION AND STEERING (TEST A4).

The content areas that closely parallel this chapter are

STEERING SYSTEMS DIAGNOSIS AND REPAIR AND WHEEL ALIGNMENT DIAGNOSIS, ADJUSTMENT, AND REPAIR.

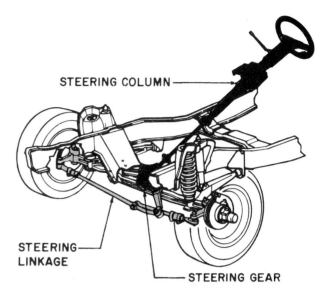

FIGURE 30–1. The three main parts of the steering system are the steering column, steering gear, and steering linkage. *(Courtesy of Dana Corporation)*

wheel and column depends on the year of the car and the manufacturer. Major parts shown in *Figure 30–2* include:

1. The steering wheel — produces the turning effort

2. The lower and upper covers — conceal parts

3. The universal joints — rotate at angles

4. Support brackets — hold the steering column in place

5. Assorted screws, nuts, bolts, pins, and seals — make the steering wheel and column perform correctly

Differences in the steering wheel and column include energy-absorbing or collapsible steering columns, tilt steering wheels, steering lock systems, and location of turn signals and flasher controls.

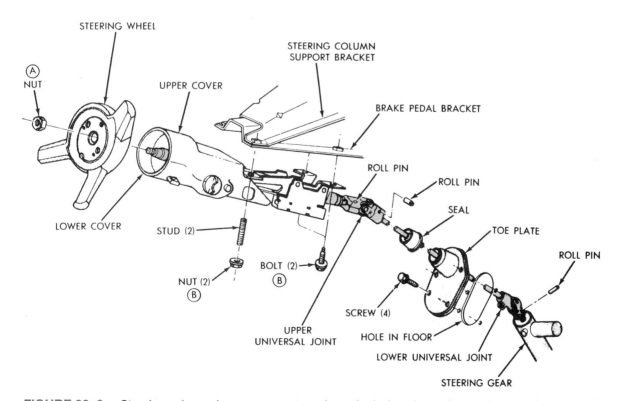

FIGURE 30–2. Steering columns have many parts and vary in design, depending on the manufacturer and the year of the vehicle. *(Courtesy of Motor Publications, Auto Repair Manual)*

Manual Steering Gear

The purpose of the steering gear is to change the rotational motion of the steering wheel to reciprocating motion to move the steering linkage. Two styles are currently in use. These are the pitman arm or recirculating ball steering gear, and the rack and pinion steering gear.

Pitman Arm Steering Gear

One of the most common types of manual steering gears is called the *pitman arm* steering gear. Many manufacturers call this the recirculating ball and worm system. *Figure 30–3* shows such a system. In operation, as the steering shaft is turned, the wormshaft also turns. The wormshaft has spiral grooves on the outside diameter. The ball nut, which has mating spiral grooves inside, is placed over the wormshaft. Small steel balls circulate in the mating grooves and ball guides. As the balls move through the grooves and out, they return to the other side through the guides. This system provides a low-friction drive between the wormshaft and the ball nut.

Teeth on the ball nut mesh with the teeth on the sector shaft. The sector shaft is also known as the pitman shaft. As the wormshaft is rotated, the ball nut moves back and forth, to the left and right. As the ball nut moves back and forth, it causes the sector shaft, or pitman shaft, to rotate through a partial circle. The sector shaft is connected directly to the pitman arm, which controls the steering linkage.

Rack and Pinion Steering Gear

The *rack and pinion system* is fast becoming a standard system on most front wheel drive cars sold in the United States. The rack and pinion system is used in conjunction with MacPherson struts and gives more engine compartment room for transverse-mounted engines.

Rack and pinion steering consists of a flat gear (the rack) and a mating gear called the pinion, *Figure 30–4*. When the steering wheel and shaft turn, the pinion meshes with the teeth on the rack. This causes the rack to move left or right in the housing. This motion moves the remaining steering linkage to turn the front wheels. This system is very practical for small cars that require lighter steering capacity. It is a direct steering unit that is more positive in motion (less lost motion) than the standard steering linkages. *Figure 30–5* shows the complete rack and pinion system with the housing and tie rods.

Steering Ratio

When the steering wheel is turned, a certain effort is needed. The amount of effort is determined by the mechan-

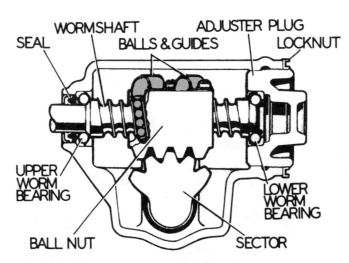

FIGURE 30–3. The manual steering gear uses a recirculating ball and worm system. *(Courtesy of Motor Publications, Auto Repair Manual)*

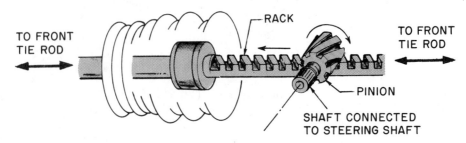

FIGURE 30–4. The rack and pinion uses a flat gear called the rack and a pinion gear attached to the steering column. *(Courtesy of Dana Corporation)*

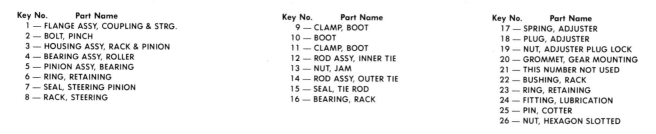

Key No. Part Name
1 — FLANGE ASSY, COUPLING & STRG.
2 — BOLT, PINCH
3 — HOUSING ASSY, RACK & PINION
4 — BEARING ASSY, ROLLER
5 — PINION ASSY, BEARING
6 — RING, RETAINING
7 — SEAL, STEERING PINION
8 — RACK, STEERING

Key No. Part Name
9 — CLAMP, BOOT
10 — BOOT
11 — CLAMP, BOOT
12 — ROD ASSY, INNER TIE
13 — NUT, JAM
14 — ROD ASSY, OUTER TIE
15 — SEAL, TIE ROD
16 — BEARING, RACK

Key No. Part Name
17 — SPRING, ADJUSTER
18 — PLUG, ADJUSTER
19 — NUT, ADJUSTER PLUG LOCK
20 — GROMMET, GEAR MOUNTING
21 — THIS NUMBER NOT USED
22 — BUSHING, RACK
23 — RING, RETAINING
24 — FITTING, LUBRICATION
25 — PIN, COTTER
26 — NUT, HEXAGON SLOTTED

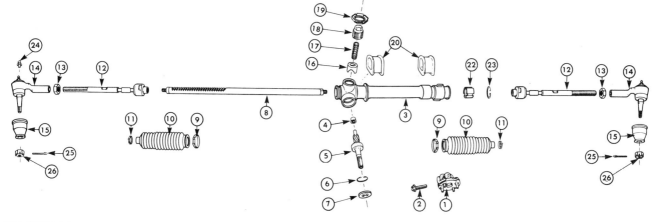

FIGURE 30–5. All parts of the rack and pinion system, referenced with numbers and part names. *(Courtesy of General Motors Product Service Training)*

ical advantage of the steering gear. *Steering ratio* is defined as the ratio between the degrees turned on the steering wheel and the degrees turned on the front wheels. The ratio is stated for exactly one degree of movement on the front wheels. For example, a 30 to 1 steering ratio means the steering wheel will turn 30 degrees for each degree of front wheel turn. The lower the ratio, the harder the steering. Lower steering ratios are called quick steering. The higher the ratio the easier the steering. When the steering ratio increases, however, the steering wheel must be turned farther to make a turn.

The steering ratio used on a car depends on several factors and differences in the steering system. These include:

1. Manual or power steering
2. Weight and size of the vehicle
3. Type of steering gear
4. Size of the steering wheel

Standard Steering Linkage

The steering linkage is defined as the pivoting parts necessary to turn the front wheels. The linkage connects the motion produced by the pitman shaft to the front wheels on the vehicle.

The parts of a standard steering linkage are shown in *Figure 30–6*. The motion from the steering gear and sector shaft (pitman shaft) causes the pitman arm to rotate through a partial circle (reciprocating motion or back and forth). This motion causes the *center link* to move back and forth also. The idler arm is attached to the frame of the vehicle for support. Tie rods are connected to each side of the center link.

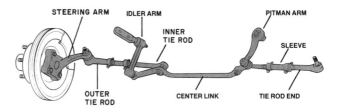

FIGURE 30–6. The steering linkage is made of tie rods, an idler arm, a center link sleeve, and the pitman arm. *(Courtesy of Dana Corporation)*

As the center link moves, both tie rods also move. The tie rods are then attached directly to the wheel for turning. Sleeves are placed on each tie rod for adjustment.

Pitman Arm

Pitman arms can be of the wear or nonwear type. The wear-type pitman arm has a tapered ball stud that is connected to the center link. The other end is mounted on the steering gear sector shaft. The nonwear-style pitman arm has a tapered hole and seldom needs replacement. *Figure 30–7* shows the different types of pitman arms.

Center Link

The center (drag) link can be designed in several ways. *Figure 30–8* shows several styles. The major difference is the method in which the other linkage is connected to the center link. The point of connection can be the pivot point, stud end, bushing end, or open taper end (nonwear).

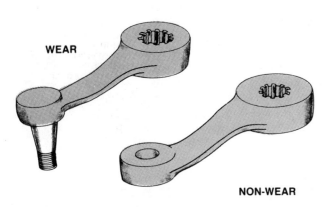

FIGURE 30–7. A vehicle can use one of two types of pit-man arms: the wear or the nonwear type. *(Courtesy of Dana Corporation)*

Idler Arm

Idler arms come in different designs as well. They differ mainly on the wear end of the arm. The different types include the bushing, taper, threaded, and constant torque types of idler arm. *Figure 30–9* shows the different styles of idler arms.

The constant torque type of idler arm shown in *Figure 30–10* is manufactured to precision tolerances and uses synthetic bearings. The bearings reduce friction and absorb road shock. The bearings are preloaded and preset at the factory. This type of idler arm has very low friction characteristics and is used on many new vehicles.

The taper type of idler arm is shown in *Figure 30–11*. It contains synthetic bearings, heat-treated tapered support

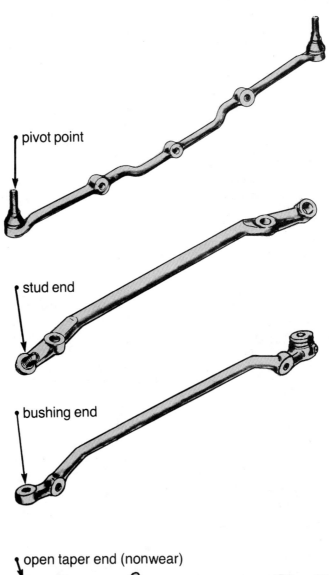

FIGURE 30–8. Different types of center links are used by different manufacturers. *(Courtesy of Dana Corporation)*

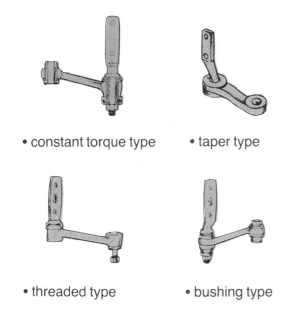

• constant torque type   • taper type

• threaded type   • bushing type

FIGURE 30–9. Different types of idler arms are used on the steering linkage. *(Courtesy of Dana Corporation)*

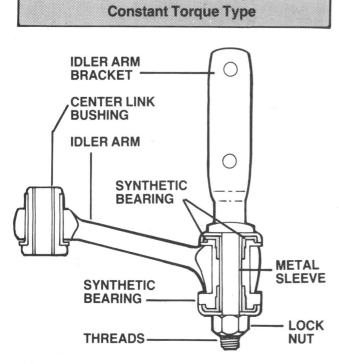

FIGURE 30–10. The constant torque type idler arms use precision tolerances and synthetic bearings. *(Courtesy of Dana Corporation)*

brackets, and a compensating spring. The compensating spring takes up clearances produced by wear. The spring also maintains the steering resistance desired for good vehicle handling.

The bushing type of idler arm is shown in *Figure 30–12*. It uses a resilient, lubricated bushing. These bushings are designed to accept high shock loads and maintain good vehi-

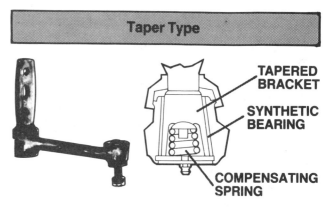

FIGURE 30–11. The taper type idler arm contains a tapering bracket, synthetic bearings, and a compensating spring. *(Courtesy of Dana Corporation)*

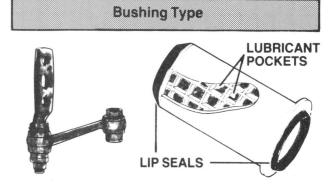

FIGURE 30–12. The bushing type idler gear has lubricant pockets for lubrication. *(Courtesy of Dana Corporation)*

cle handling. The special waffle design bushing traps the lubricant. Seals are used on the end to make the unit self-contained.

Tie Rods and Adjusting Sleeve

Tie rod assemblies consist of an inner tie rod end, an outer tie rod end, and an *adjusting sleeve*. The adjusting sleeve looks like a piece of internally threaded pipe. See *Figure 30–13*. The unit has a slot that runs through the center. Adjusting sleeves also have two crimping, or squeezing, clamps. These are located at each end to lock the tie rod together after adjustment.

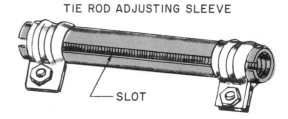

FIGURE 30–13. This sleeve is attached to the tie rods to make adjustments for length. *(Courtesy of Dana Corporation)*

The adjusting sleeve has threads inside. One end of the thread has a left-hand thread and the other end has a right-hand thread. This arrangement allows adjustment without disassembling the tie rods.

The tie rod ends have a rounded ball stud to allow both lateral and vertical movement. *Figure 30–14* shows an example of the rounded ball stud. The tension spring inside the tie rod end is used to reduce road shock throughout the steering system. On some tie rod ends, there is also a grease *zerk*. The zerk is the fitting through which grease is applied.

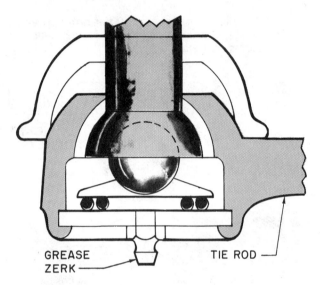

FIGURE 30–14. A rounded ball stud is used on the end of the tie rods. *(Courtesy of Dana Corporation)*

CAR CLINIC

PROBLEM: Rack and Pinion Steering Difficulty

A customer has complained that the steering system on the vehicle is becoming harder and harder to turn. The customer notices gear clunking when turning sharp turns. What is the problem?

SOLUTION:

This type of problem is most often produced by worn rack and pinion gears on the steering column. Over a period of time the rack and pinion gears may wear, causing the pinion to slip or jump teeth on the rack. Normally, this can be easily identified by increasing amounts of slack in the steering wheel. The solution is to replace the rack and pinion steering gears.

30.2   FRONT END GEOMETRY AND ALIGNMENT

Purpose of Wheel Alignment

Alignment is defined as the balancing of all forces created by friction, gravity, centrifugal force, and momentum while the vehicle is in motion. It is very important for the wheels of the vehicle to contact the road correctly. Wheel alignment is a check of how the wheels contact the pavement. The main purpose of wheel alignment is to allow the wheels to roll without scuffing, dragging, or slipping on the road. Good alignment results in:

1. Better fuel economy

2. Less strain on the front-end parts

3. Directional stability

4. Easier steering

5. Longer tire life

6. Increased safety

There are typically five angles that affect the steering alignment. These are caster, camber, toe, steering axis inclination, and turning radius.

Caster

Caster is defined as the backward or forward tilt at the top of the spindle support arm. Backward tilt is called positive caster. Forward tilt is called negative caster. Caster angle is the distance between the center line of the spindle support arm and the true vertical line. An example of caster is an ordinary furniture caster or a bicycle. See *Figure 30–15*. The furniture caster is an example of negative caster. The bicycle is an example of positive caster. Both examples tend to keep the rolling object going in a straight line. For example, a person can take his or her hands off the handle bars and still go in a straight line. The *lead* is defined as the distance at ground level between the two center lines. *Figure 30–16* shows the lead.

Caster is designed into the front-end suspension of a car to do several things. Caster:

1. aids in the directional stability of the car by making the front wheels maintain a straight-ahead position,

2. aids in returning the front wheels to a straight-ahead position when coming out of a turn, and

3. offsets the effect of road crown or curvature of the road.

Too much caster causes hard steering, excessive road shock, and wheel shimmy. Too little caster causes wander, weave, and instability at high speeds. Unequal caster causes pulling to the side of least caster.

While positive caster does aid in directional stability, it also increases steering effort by the driver. This can be compen-

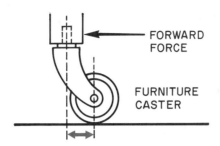

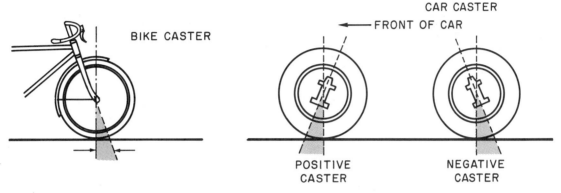

FIGURE 30–15.   Caster is defined as the backward or forward tilt of the spindle support arm. It is much like a furniture caster.

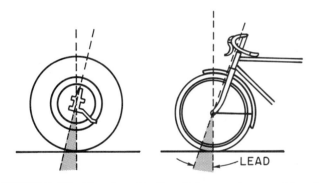

FIGURE 30–16.   Lead is the distance at ground level between the two center lines. A bicycle is shown as an example. *(Courtesy of Dana Corporation)*

sated for by power steering. Cars with manual steering usually require a caster setting of near zero or even a negative angle. Negative caster settings are required on some newer cars.

Camber

Camber is defined as the inward and outward tilt of the front wheels at the top. *Figure 30–17* shows an example of both negative and positive camber. Camber is measured as an angle in degrees from the center line of the wheel to a true vertical line. The purpose of checking camber is to make sure the tire is vertical to the road. This position will make the tire tread uniform on both sides of the tire. This results in equal distribution of load and wear over the whole tire tread. When the camber setting is correct:

1. there will be maximum amount of tire thread in contact with the road surface,

2. the road contact area of the tire will be directly under the point of load, and

3. the steering will be easier because the vehicle weight is placed on the inner wheel bearing and spindle.

When the camber is incorrect:

1. there will be wear on the ball joint and wheel bearings,

2. the steering will pull to one side, and

3. there will be excessive tire wear. This wear is shown in *Figure 30–18*. Too much negative camber will cause wear

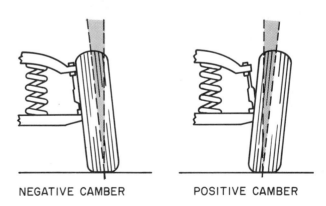

FIGURE 30–17.   Negative and positive camber. *(Courtesy of Dana Corporation)*

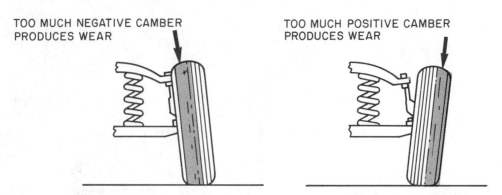

FIGURE 30–18. When the camber is incorrect, wear will increase on the sides of the tire. *(Courtesy of Dana Corporation)*

on the inside of the tire. Too much positive camber will cause wear on the outside of the tire.

Wear on tires with incorrect camber is further explained in *Figure 30–19*. Referring to this figure, notice the rolling radii at different parts of the wheel. At each point, the tire is rolling at different diameters. This causes the wheel to act as a cone. The cone has several rolling diameters and tends to want to roll in a circle. But since it is forced to roll in a straight line, the outer or smaller diameter tries to roll faster. This results in the outer parts of the tread being ground off by slipping and scuffing.

Toe

Toe is defined as the difference in the distance between the front and back of the front wheels. *Figure 30–20* shows toe. When dimension B is smaller than A, it is called a toe-in condition. When dimension B is greater than A, it is called a toe-out condition. Toe is measured in inches or parts of an inch.

When a vehicle is moving forward, certain forces are developed. Braking and the rolling resistance of the tires force the front wheel outward in front. Vehicles are generally set with just a small amount of toe-in to help overcome these forces. Once in motion, clearances in the steering linkage allow the front of the tires to swing out. At this point, there

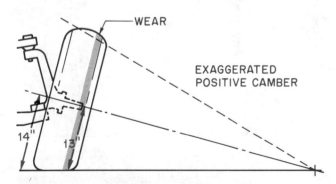

FIGURE 30–19. When camber is excessive, wear occurs because the tire is rolling at different radii. *(Courtesy of Hunter Engineering Company)*

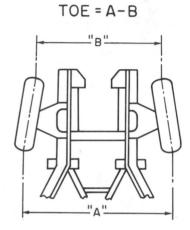

TOE = A – B

FIGURE 30–20. Toe is the difference in the distances between the front and back of the front tires. *(Courtesy of Dana Corporation)*

should be zero amount of toe-in. In front wheel drive vehicles, the tires may be purposely toed out to allow for other forces. Front wheel drive vehicles tend to return the wheels to their proper straight-ahead position. Incorrect toe adjustment will cause the tires to wear excessively and will cause harder steering.

Steering Axis Inclination

Steering axis inclination is defined as the inward tilt of the spindle support arm ball joints at the top. Steering axis inclination angle is the distance between the ball joint center line and true vertical. This angle is not adjustable. It is shown in *Figure 30–21*. The purposes of having a steering axis inclination angle are to:

1. reduce the need for excessive camber,

2. provide a pivot point about which the wheel will turn, producing easy steering,

3. aid steering stability,

4. lessen tire wear,

5. provide directional stability, and

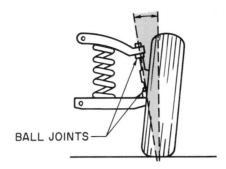

FIGURE 30–21. Steering axis inclination is the angle between the true vertical and the center line of the ball joints. *(Courtesy of Dana Corporation)*

6. distribute the weight of the vehicle more nearly under the road contact area of the tire.

Included Angle

Certain manufacturers use the term included angle to illustrate information about steering axis inclination. The included angle is defined as the sum of the steering axis inclination angle and the camber. For example, *Figure 30–22* shows the included angle. Certain alignment charts specify the included angle instead of the steering axis inclination angle.

Scrub Radius

Scrub radius is the distance between the center line of the ball joints and the center line of the tire at the point where the tire contacts the road surface. The greater the scrub radius, the greater the effort required to steer, and the less the stability on the steering. During turning, when the ball joint center line is inside the tire contact point, the tire doesn't pivot where it touches the road. Instead, it has to move forward and backward to compensate as the driver turns the

steering wheel. Steering effort is greatly increased because the tires scrub against the road during turns. *Figure 30–23* shows scrub radius. Note that both positive camber and steering axis inclination combine to reduce scrub radius to a minimum.

Turning Radius

Turning radius, also called toe-out on turns, is defined as the amount one front wheel turns more sharply than the other. It is measured in degrees. The major purpose for having the correct turning radius is to make the front wheels pivot around a common center. This is shown in *Figure 30–24*. As the car turns around a corner, the outside wheel turns a radius of 18 degrees. The inside wheel turns a radius of 20 degrees. If the turning radius is incorrect, the front wheels will scrub against the road surface on turns.

Turning radius is usually not adjustable. On certain vehicles, however, it can be checked. Turning radius is checked after all other alignment checks have been made. A turning radius that is out of specifications usually indicates that some part of the steering linkage is bent or alignment is incorrect.

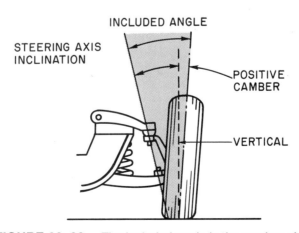

FIGURE 30–22. The included angle is the camber plus the steering axis inclination angle. *(Courtesy of Hunter Engineering Company)*

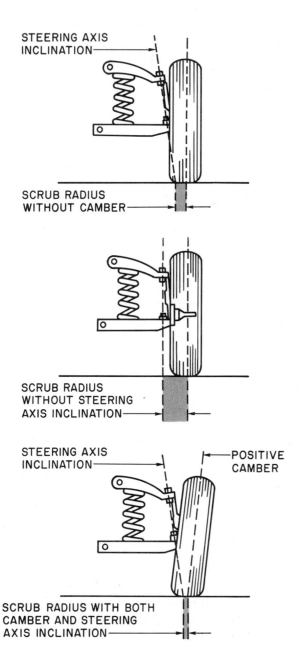

FIGURE 30–23. Scrub radius is the distance at the road surface between the center line of the tire and the center line of the ball joints. *(Courtesy of Dana Corporation)*

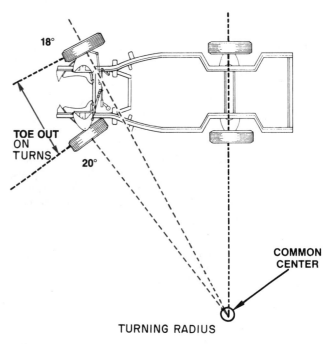

FIGURE 30–24. Turning radius is the amount one wheel turns more sharply than the other. *(Courtesy of Dana Corporation)*

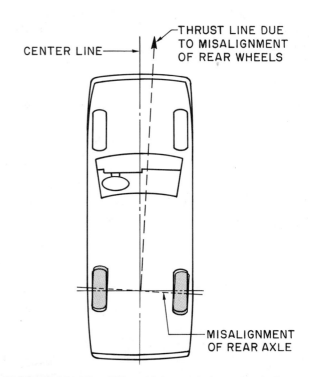

FIGURE 30–25. This vehicle needs four wheel alignment because the rear wheels are not in line with the front wheels.

Four Wheel Alignment

In the past, the only type of alignment done on vehicles was front wheel alignment. However, recently there has been an increased need to align both the front and rear wheels. In the service industry this is called all wheel alignment or *four wheel alignment.* An example of the need for four wheel alignment is shown in *Figure 30–25.* The rear axle on this car is not perpendicular to the center line. When the thrust line is different from the center line, the car will veer off to one side. This type of problem can be diagnosed by alignment of all four wheels.

Several major vehicle design changes have caused the need for four wheel alignment. They include the following:

1. Many vehicles today have front wheel drive. Front wheel drive vehicles are more sensitive to tracking problems than rear wheel drive vehicles. Front wheel drive vehicles demand that the rear wheels track directly behind the front wheels.

2. Modern tires are designed to allow for greater steering forces than older tires. The result is that there is less tolerance for misalignment between the front and rear wheels.

3. Modern tires are also more wear-resistant. Thus, tires are more sensitive to misalignment.

4. Independent rear suspension makes it easier for the rear wheels to become misaligned because of bad road conditions.

The alignment machine shown in *Figure 30–26* is able to perform four wheel alignment. These machines are extremely sophisticated and use computers to help the service technician align the wheels of the vehicle. Specific alignment procedures are stored in the computer for most vehicles. The computer also stores the alignment specifications for vehicles built over the past 25 years. *Figure 30–27* shows a close-up view of the specifications for a four wheel alignment vehicle. Alignment specifications and adjustments are shown for both the front and rear wheels.

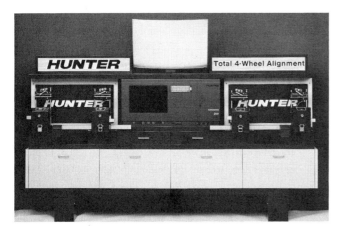

FIGURE 30–26. This computerized alignment machine gives directions and alignment procedures for most vehicles on the road today. *(Courtesy of Hunter Engineering Company)*

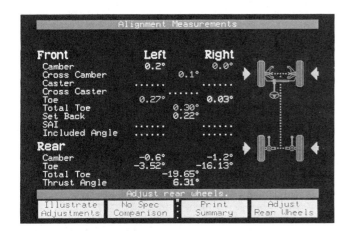

FIGURE 30–27. The computerized alignment machine stores alignment specifications for most vehicles on the road today. *(Courtesy of Hunter Engineering Company)*

CAR CLINIC

PROBLEM: Front End Shimmy

What are the causes of front end shimmy? A car with 77,000 miles on it seems to have a bad shimmy. What should be checked first?

SOLUTION:

Shimmy can be caused by several problems, including:

1. Not enough caster.

2. Toe-in out of specifications.

3. Loose steering linkage parts.

4. Too much play in the steering gear.

5. Bad shocks.

6. Bad suspension parts.

7. A combination of any of the above.

These items should be checked carefully to determine the cause of shimmy on the front wheels.

30.3 POWER STEERING

Purpose of Power Steering

With manual steering, the driver is creating the forces needed to turn the steering gear. The only advantage that can be produced is by changing the steering ratio. Power steering is used on many vehicles to make steering easier for the driver, especially on heavier vehicles. The power steering system is designed to reduce the effort needed to turn the steering wheel. It reduces driver fatigue and increases safety during driving. Power steering systems are used both on the pitman arm steering gear system and the rack and pinion steering system.

Major Parts on Power Steering Systems

Although there are many designs of power steering systems, there are two major parts in all power steering system designs. These are a hydraulic pump and the steering unit. These two units are connected by high-pressure hoses. See *Figure 30–28*. The hydraulic pump is used to produce fluid pressure. The pump is driven by a belt running from the crankshaft. It supplies the hydraulic pressure needed to operate the steering gear.

The power steering unit is an integral part of either the steering gear or the rack and pinion arrangement. The hydraulic pressure is used to assist the motion of the steering

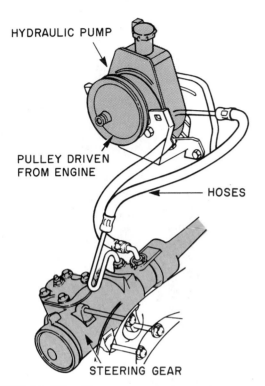

FIGURE 30–28. The power steering system uses a hydraulic pump and the steering unit to provide added pressure to turn the wheels. *(Courtesy of Chevrolet Division, General Motors Corporation)*

gear or the rack and pinion gear. *Figure 30–29* shows a typical rack and pinion steering gear arrangement.

Power Steering Pump

All power steering pumps are called constant displacement or positive displacement pumps. They deliver different pressures, depending on the type and make of the vehicle.

They use special power steering fluid that is recommended by the manufacturer. Automatic transmission fluid should not be used in power steering systems except in small quantities and then only to bring the fluid level up to the fill mark. If more transmission fluid is used in an emergency situation, the system should be drained, flushed, and refilled with power steering fluid as soon as possible.

The fluid is stored in a reservoir that is attached to the pump. There is usually a filter in the reservoir to prevent foreign matter from entering the system. A pressure relief valve is used to control excess pressure when the speed of the pump is increased. *Figure 30–30* shows a power steering pump.

The pump can be of several designs. Three types of pumps are commonly used: the vane type, slipper type, and roller type. These are shown in *Figure 30–31*. All three types work on the same principle. The center of the pump turns within an *eccentric* area. A suction is produced on one side of the

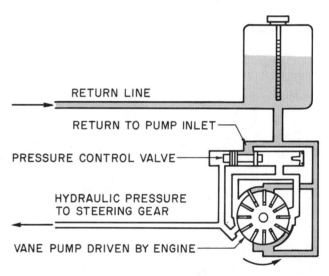

FIGURE 30–30. The parts of a power steering pump.

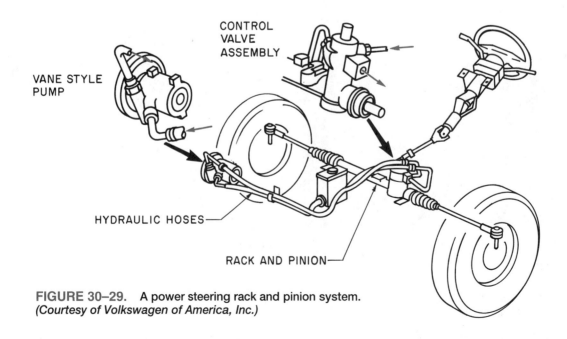

FIGURE 30–29. A power steering rack and pinion system. *(Courtesy of Volkswagen of America, Inc.)*

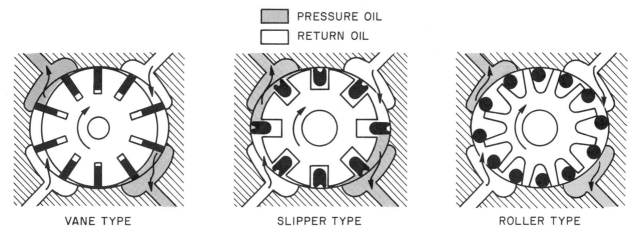

PRESSURE OIL
RETURN OIL

VANE TYPE   SLIPPER TYPE   ROLLER TYPE

FIGURE 30–31. There are three types of power steering pumps: the vane type, slipper type, and roller type.

pump housing. A pressure is produced on the other side of the housing.

Integral Power Steering Gear

In *Figure 30–32*, the sector shaft is turned by the piston and ball nut assembly. Normally, as the worm gear is turned by the steering wheel, the oil pressure is sent to the unit from the power steering pump. Oil is sent to both sides of the piston. This keeps the piston in a stable position. When the car is moving in a straight line, the pressures are equal on both sides of the piston. When the steering wheel is turned, higher oil pressure is directed to one side or the other to assist movement of the piston and ball nut assembly. Assisting the movement of this assembly makes it easier for the driver to turn the steering wheel.

Control Valves

Power steering control valves are built directly into the power steering gear assembly. The purpose of the control valve is to direct the oil pressure to one side or the other on

the piston and ball nut assembly. When the steering wheel is turned, the control valve is positioned in such a way as to direct oil to the correct location. Two types of valves are commonly used: the rotary spool and sliding spool valves.

Sliding Spool Valve

The sliding spool valve is shown in *Figure 30–33*. As the steering wheel and the worm gear are turned, the sliding spool valve is moved slightly by linkage attached to the worm gear shaft. As this movement occurs, the internal spool opens a set of ports to allow high-pressure fluid to enter the correct side of the piston and ball nut assembly. Oil flows through internal passageways to get to the piston assembly. When the steering wheel is turned the other way, the oil is sent to the other side of the piston.

Rotary Spool Valve

The rotary spool valve is also used on many vehicles to control the direction of oil through the steering gear. The rotary spool valve is shown in *Figure 30–34*. When the steer-

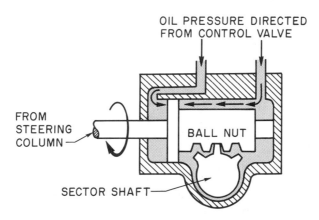

OIL PRESSURE DIRECTED FROM CONTROL VALVE

FROM STEERING COLUMN

BALL NUT

SECTOR SHAFT

FIGURE 30–32. The parts of an integral power steering gear. Oil pressure pushes the ball nut to assist steering.

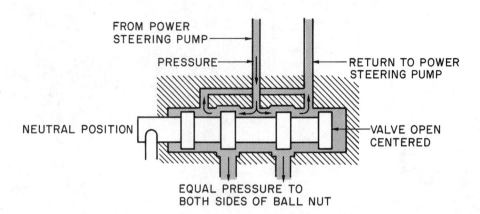

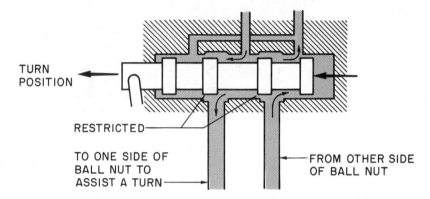

FIGURE 30–33. The sliding spool valve is used to direct the hydraulic pressure to the correct side of the ball nut for a left or right turn.

ing wheel is turned, a twisting effort is produced through a torsion bar to rotate the internal spool slightly. This is done on an internal spline. As the spool rotates slightly, a different set of ports is opened and closed to allow oil pressure to flow to the correct side of the piston assembly. If the steering wheel is turned in the opposite direction, the oil will flow to the opposite side of the piston assembly. *Figure 30–35* shows a cutaway view of a typical power steering gear assembly.

Rack and Pinion Power Steering

The rack and pinion power steering principles are much the same as the integral power steering principles. The major difference is that the pressure from the control valve operates the rack assembly. A power cylinder and piston assembly are placed on the rack. See *Figure 30–36*. Oil pressure from the control valve then pushes or assists the movement

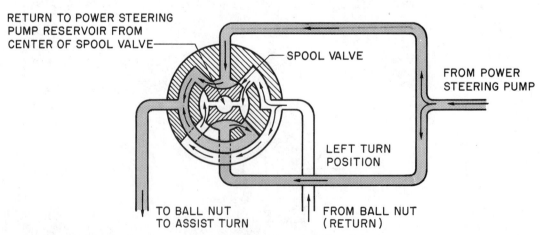

FIGURE 30–34. The rotary spool valve controls the direction of hydraulic pressure by twisting slightly to open or close different ports.

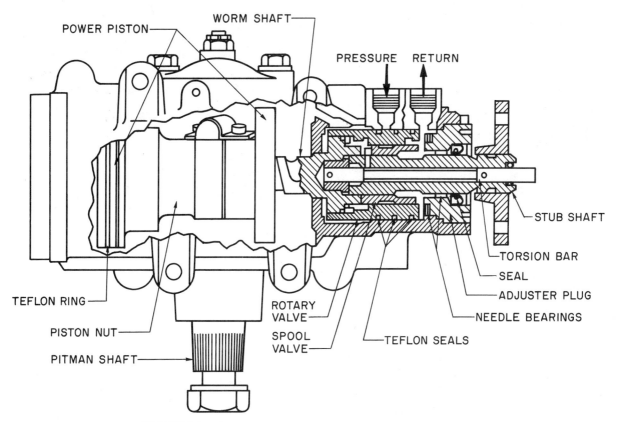

FIGURE 30–35. A complete power steering gear assembly.

of the rack. The control valve is attached to and is operated from the pinion gear as in other power steering systems.

Electronic Steering

Several manufacturers are now using *electronic steering* systems to control the steering on a vehicle. In operation, an electrical motor is placed inside the rack and pinion steering system. As the motor is turned, it assists the movement of the rack and pinion components. The result is that the steering effort is greatly reduced and is taken over by the electric motor.

The electric motor is able to rotate in both directions. The motor is controlled by a sensor placed on the rack and pinion housing, near the steering column. As the driver begins to turn the steering wheel, hydraulic pressure is built up. The increase in pressure is sensed by the steering effort sensor. The sensor then is able to select the direction of the motor movement and turn the motor off and on accordingly.

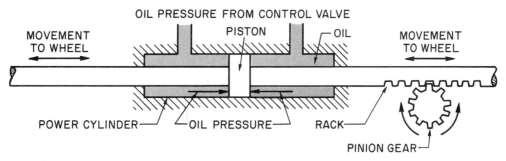

RACK AND PINION POWER STEERING

FIGURE 30–36. Power steering is accomplished on rack and pinion steering by a piston and power cylinder attached to the rack.

Problems, Diagnosis and Service

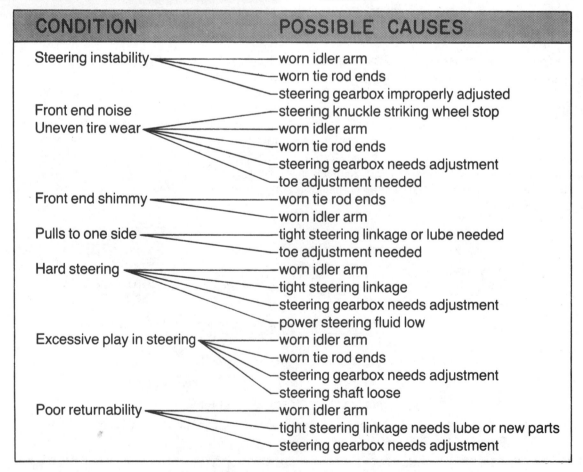

1. When removing the steering wheel, use the correct puller for safe removal.
2. The tie rods may be stuck in place. Always use the correct tools to remove tie rods (e.g., pickle fork for removal).
3. Make sure the battery is disconnected to eliminate the possibility of the engine accidently cranking over when you are checking the belt tension on the power steering unit.
4. When checking the tire rod ends and steering mechanisms, be careful not to pinch your fingers between parts, as serious injury may result.
5. Many parts and assemblies must be removed in the correct sequence. Incorrect disassembly may cause parts to drop or spring out unexpectedly. Always follow the manufacturer's suggested procedure when removing steering system parts from the vehicle.

PROBLEM: Worn Steering Linkages

On a rear wheel drive vehicle, the steering wheel has excessive play.

DIAGNOSIS

Problems such as this are generally in the steering linkages and gear or in the steering column. Other problems, such as poor alignment, may also cause excessive play. *Figure 30–37* shows a list of problems and their possible causes that can be used to diagnose similar steering system problems. Use this chart as a guideline for initial diagnosis of steering problems. When diagnosing the steering system, do the following preliminary checks:

1. Check all tires for proper inflation pressures and approximately the same tread wear.
2. Check the front wheel bearings for proper adjustment.
3. Check for loose or damaged ball joints, tie rod ends, and control arms. Make sure all grease zerks have been lubricated.

CONDITION	POSSIBLE CAUSES
Steering instability	worn idler arm
	worn tie rod ends
	steering gearbox improperly adjusted
Front end noise	steering knuckle striking wheel stop
Uneven tire wear	worn idler arm
	worn tie rod ends
	steering gearbox needs adjustment
	toe adjustment needed
Front end shimmy	worn tie rod ends
	worn idler arm
Pulls to one side	tight steering linkage or lube needed
	toe adjustment needed
Hard steering	worn idler arm
	tight steering linkage
	steering gearbox needs adjustment
	power steering fluid low
Excessive play in steering	worn idler arm
	worn tie rod ends
	steering gearbox needs adjustment
	steering shaft loose
Poor returnability	worn idler arm
	tight steering linkage needs lube or new parts
	steering gearbox needs adjustment

FIGURE 30–37.   Each condition has several causes that need to be checked when troubleshooting the steering system. *(Courtesy of Dana Corporation)*

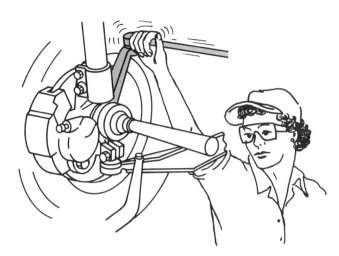

FIGURE 30–38. The tie rod ends can be checked for wear by grasping the rod firmly and forcing it up and down. There should be no lost motion.

4. Check for runout of wheels and tires.

5. Check to see if excess loads have been placed on the vehicle.

6. Consider the condition and type of equipment being used to check the alignment.

7. Check the tie rod end for wear. This can be found by grasping the tie rod end firmly and forcing it up and down or sideways to check for any lost motion. *Figure 30–38* shows a service technician performing this diagnostic check. If there is lost motion or sloppiness in movement, the tie rods will need to be replaced.

SERVICE

Steering Gear and Linkages

The following are common service items on steering gears and linkages.

1. When replacing tie rods, first remove the retaining nut and cotter pin. Before removing the tie rods, measure the distance from the adjusting sleeve to the tie rod end center point. This allows a preliminary toe setting by placing the new tie rod end in approximately the same position. Refer to *Figure 30–39*.

2. Loosen the tie rod adjusting sleeve clamp nuts.

3. Remove the tie rod end nut and cotter pin.

4. Use a pickle fork to remove the tie rod from the steering knuckle. A pickle fork is shown in *Figure 30–40*.

5. The steering gear can be checked and adjusted for correct clearance or lash. Lash is the clearance between the sector shaft and the ball nut. Refer to the correct maintenance manual for the procedure. *Figure 30–41* shows the position of the lash adjuster screw located on top of

the steering gear. The general procedure for adjusting the clearance is as follows:

a. If power steering is used, rotate the wormshaft through the complete range of travel. This is done to bleed air from the system. Then refill the reservoir to the top.

b. Place the steering gear in the center of its movement.

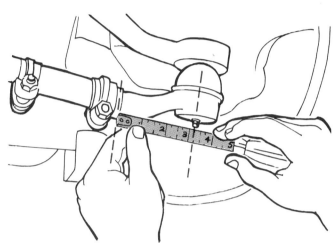

FIGURE 30–39. Before removing a tie rod, check the distance from the adjusting sleeve to the ball nut grease zerk. This measurement gives a preliminary toe setting when you put the tie rod back in the same position. *(Courtesy of Dana Corporation)*

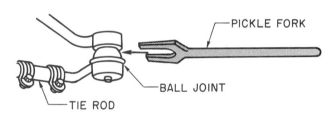

FIGURE 30–40. A pickle fork can be used to separate the tie rod ball joints correctly.

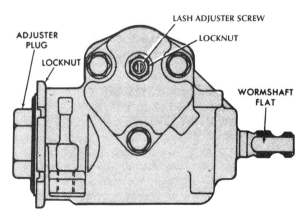

FIGURE 30–41. The lash adjuster screw is located on top of the steering gear assembly. Its purpose is to adjust the clearance between the sector shaft and the ball nut. *(Courtesy of Motor Publications, Auto Repair Manual)*

c. Loosen the lock nut on the adjusting screw.
d. Tighten the adjusting screw until all backlash is removed; then tighten the lock nut.
e. Operate the unit through its range of motion.
f. Loosen the lock nut and the adjusting screw again.
g. Tighten the adjusting screw again until all backlash is again removed.
h. Now tighten the adjusting screw an additional 3/8 of a turn. Now tighten the lock nut.

Steering Columns

Many types of steering systems are used on vehicles. Each type has a different disassembly and assembly procedure. Refer to the manufacturer's service manual for the correct procedure. The following general service items can be done on steering columns:

1. Use a wheel puller to remove the steering wheel to get at the horn and turn signal mechanisms.

2. The universal joints can be replaced. However, the procedure and the parts required will depend on the manufacturer.

3. Electrical and mechanical problems can be serviced in the turn signal and flasher systems and the tilt mechanisms.

PROBLEM: Faulty Power Steering Pump

A buzzing sound comes from the power steering unit when the steering wheel is turned.

DIAGNOSIS

A buzzing sound from the power steering unit is caused either by a lack of fluid or by air in the power steering hydraulic system. Check the power steering system for the following common problems:

1. Steering column U-joint binding that needs lubrication.

2. Loose power steering belt, which causes momentary steering difficulty. When it is loose, the belt will squeal when the engine is accelerated. This shows that the belt is slipping on the pulleys.

3. Loose mounting bolts in the steering gear, which cause abnormal steering wheel kickback and poor control.

4. Leaky power steering lines. Check for loose fittings and damaged hoses.

5. A lack of hydraulic pressure, which can be caused by internal leaks past piston rings or valve body, worn seals, or misaligned housing bore.

SERVICE

To bleed the system of air, start the engine and turn the steering wheel throughout its range. Keep checking the level of the power steering fluid as needed. Turn the steering wheel throughout its range again and add fluid. Continue this procedure until all the air has been removed from the hydraulic system.

PROBLEM: Faulty Rack and Pinion Steering

A vehicle with rack and pinion steering system has excessive play and looseness in the steering wheel.

DIAGNOSIS

Many components can cause similar problems on vehicles that have a rack and pinion steering system. Always check the rack and pinion steering systems for leaks at the end seals, rack seals, and pinion shaft seals. *Figure 30–42* shows a diagnosis chart that can help the service technician determine the possible cause and correction. Two easy checks to diagnose rack and pinion steering are:

1. Check the rack housing bolts attached to the crossmember. *Figure 30–43* shows the bolts in question. Look for movement between the rack housing and the crossmember. This usually indicates worn mount bushings and can cause loose steering.

2. Check the inner tie rod sockets. This can be done by having someone move the steering wheel back and forth slightly. Then place your hand on the flex-type bellows. Feel for looseness and wear in the inside connection. See *Figure 30–44*. Repair as necessary.

SERVICE

Many service procedures are needed to repair the rack and pinion steering gear. The service procedures are different for each type and year of vehicle. For complete procedures for removal, disassembly, assembly, and overhaul refer to the service manual.

PROBLEM: Incorrect Steering Alignment

The tires on a vehicle are wearing abnormally fast, and there is a definite pattern of wear on the tire tread.

DIAGNOSIS

One of the more common problems that produces rapid tire wear is incorrect wheel alignment. The alignment of both the front and the rear tires needs to be checked. *Figure 30–45* shows a diagnose chart for alignment. Match the type of tire wear on the tire to the symptoms. Then identify a probable cause.

RACK & PINION DIAGNOSIS		
CONDITION	**POSSIBLE CAUSE**	**CORRECTION**

Hard steering - excessive effort required at steering wheel.	1. Low or uneven tire pressure.
	2. Tight outer tie rod end or ball joints.
	3. Incorrect front wheel alignment.
	4. Bind or catch in gear.
		1. Inflate to specified pressures.
		2. Lube or replace as required.
		3. Align to specifications.
		4. Remove gear, disassemble, and inspect.
		  a) Replace damaged or badly worn components (OPH)*.
		  b) If housing and tube assembly, rack, or pinion are damaged, replace with service assembly (THP)**.

Poor returnability.	1. Tight ball joints or end housing pivots.
	2. Bent tie rod(s).
	3. Incorrect front wheel alignment.
	4. Bind or catch in gear.
		1. Lube or replace as required.
		2. Replace bent tie rod(s). Align front end.
		3. Align front end.
		4. Remove gear, disassemble, and inspect.
		  a) Replace damaged or badly worn components (OPH)*.
		  b) If housing and tube assembly, rack, or pinion are damaged, replace with service assembly (THP)**.

Excessive play or Looseness in steering system.	1. Front wheel bearings loosely adjusted. 2. Worn couplings or steering shaft U-joints. 3. Worn upper ball joints. 4. Loose steering wheel on shaft, tie rods, steering arms, or steering linkage ball studs. 5. Worn outer tie rod ends. 6. Loose frame to gear mounting bolts. 7. Deteriorated mounting grommets. 8. Excessive internal looseness in gear. 9. Worn rack bushing(s).	1. Adjust or replace as required. 2. Replace worn part(s). 3. Replace. 4. Tighten to specified torque. 5. Replace outer tie rod ends. 6. Tighten to specified torque. 7. Replace mounting grommets. 8. Readjust gear. If still loose, disassemble and inspect. 9. Replace rack bushing(s).

* (OPH) One-piece housing only   ** (TPH) Two-piece housing only

FIGURE 30–42. Use this diagnosis chart to help troubleshoot the power steering rack and pinion system.

FIGURE 30–43. Check the rack and pinion housing bolt to the crossmember for looseness or worn bushings. *(Courtesy of Motor Magazine)*

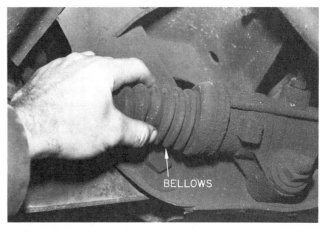

FIGURE 30–44. Check the rack and pinion tie rods by pinching the bellows and feeling for looseness or wear. *(Courtesy of Motor Magazine)*

ALIGNMENT DIAGNOSIS CHART			
SYMPTOM	**PROBABLE CAUSE**	**SYMPTOM**	**PROBABLE CAUSE**
• Excessive tire wear on outside shoulder.	• Excessive positive camber.	• Car tends to wander either to the right or left.	• Improper toe setting. Looseness in steering system or ball-joints. Uneven caster. Tire pull.
• Excessive tire wear on inside shoulder.	• Excessive negative camber.		
• Excessive tire wear on both shoulders.	• Rounding curves at high speeds. Underinflated tires.	• Vehicle swerves or pulls to side when applying brakes.	• Uneven caster. Brakes need adjustment. Out-of-round brake drum. Defective brakes. Underinflated tire.
• Saw-tooth tire wear.	• Too much toe-in or toe-out.		
• One tire wears more than the other.	• Improper camber. Defective brakes. Defective shock absorber.	• Car tends to pull either to the right or left when taking hands off steering wheel.	• Improper camber. Unequal caster. Tires worn unevenly. Tire pressure unequal.
• Tire treads cupped or dished.	• Out-of-round tires. Out-of-balance condition. Defective shock absorber.		
• Front wheels shimmy.	• Defective idler arm bushing. Out-of-round tires. Out-of-balance condition. Excessive positive caster. Uneven caster.	• Car is hard to steer.	• Tires underinflated. Power steering defective. Too much positive caster. Steering system too tight or binding.
• Vehicle vibrates.	• Defective tires. One or more of all 4 tires out-of-round. One or more of all 4 tires out-of-balance. Drive shaft bent. Drive shaft sprayed with undercoating.	• Steering has excessive play or looseness.	• Loose wheel bearings. Loose ball joints or kingpins. Loose bushings. Loose idler arm. Loose steering gear assembly. Worn steering gear or steering gear bearings.

FIGURE 30–45.   Diagnosis charts can help the service technician troubleshoot alignment problems. *(Courtesy of Hunter Engineering Company)*

SERVICE

It is out of the scope of this textbook to describe complete alignment procedure. Specialized alignment equipment and computerized instruments should always be used to check and adjust for correct alignment. Computers are being used today to help determine exact procedures, measurements needed, and specifications for alignment. *Figure 30–46* shows a four wheel alignment machine.

Several additional service notes on alignment include:

1. All wheel alignment angles are interrelated. The adjustment order should be caster, camber, and toe.

2. The alignment angles can be adjusted by several methods, depending on the car. *Figure 30–47* shows that *shims,* eccentric bolts, cams, and *slotted frame* adjustments can be used to change the alignment of the front wheels.

3. Alignment is somewhat different on the MacPherson strut and other front wheel drive suspension systems. Depending on the manufacturer, certain adjustments cannot be made on the front suspension. Camber, for example, is sometimes built into the suspension and cannot be changed. On other vehicles, there is no caster adjustment. Refer to the vehicle manufacturer to determine exactly what adjustments can be done. *Figure 30–48* shows one method used to adjust camber on a knuckle-strut assembly. This method has an elongated bolt hole. A cam washer is placed on the end of the bolt to adjust for camber.

FIGURE 30–46.   Today, alignment is done with sophisticated computerized equipment on all four wheels. *(Courtesy of Hunter Engineering Company)*

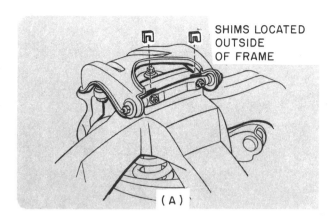

SHIMS LOCATED
OUTSIDE
OF FRAME

(A)

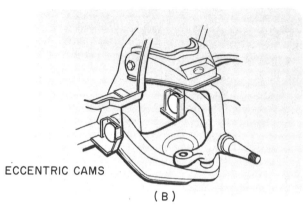

ECCENTRIC CAMS

(B)

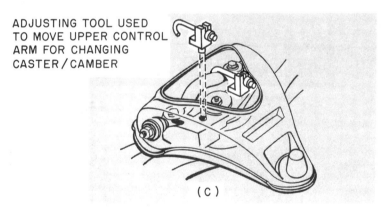

ADJUSTING TOOL USED
TO MOVE UPPER CONTROL
ARM FOR CHANGING
CASTER / CAMBER

(C)

FIGURE 30–47. Shims, eccentric cams, and slotted frame bolts are used to adjust the steering angles. Other methods can also be used. *(Courtesy of Hunter Engineering Company)*

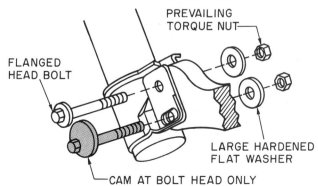

KNUCKLE-STRUT ATTACHMENT

PREVAILING
TORQUE NUT

FLANGED
HEAD BOLT

LARGE HARDENED
FLAT WASHER

CAM AT BOLT HEAD ONLY

FIGURE 30–48. The cam washer (also called eccentric washer) is used to adjust the camber on the MacPherson strut suspension.

Linkage to Automotive Technology

FOUR WHEEL STEERING SYSTEMS

Several car manufacturers are designing four wheel steering systems in which both the front and the rear wheels are able to turn. Four wheel steering works well with front wheel drive vehicles. Without drive mechanisms on the rear wheels, rear wheel steering systems can easily be attached.

In operation, the rear wheels can be turned approximately 5 degrees in either direction. Above a certain speed, say 22 mph, the rear wheels steer in the same direction as the front wheels. The result is that the vehicle has very quick response for lane changes, sharp curves in the highway, and so on. Vehicle body motion during these types of curves is also reduced, giving the passenger a more comfortable ride. Then, at lower speeds, say below 22 mph, the rear wheels steer in the opposite direction of the front wheels. This results in improved maneuverability for U-turns, parallel parking, and the like.

There are several components shown in the figure that make the system operate. These include: (1) speed sensors, (2) a motorized power cylinder on the rear wheels for turning, (3) a steering angle transfer shaft, and (4) a computerized control unit.

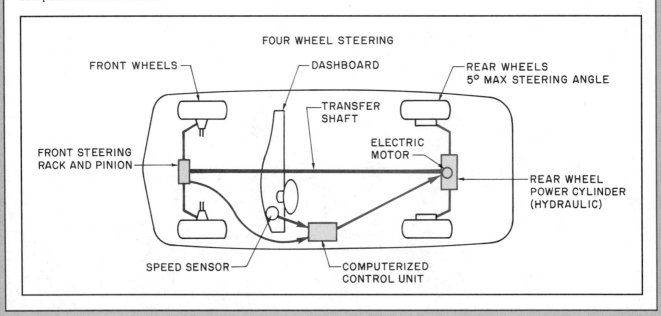

SUMMARY

The steering system is made of three major components. These include the steering column, the steering gear, and the steering linkage. The steering column and wheel are used to produce the necessary force to turn the front wheel. The steering gear is used to change the motion of the steering wheel to reciprocating motion on the steering linkage. The steering linkage is used to connect the steering gear to the front wheels.

There are two types of steering gears currently in use. These include the pitman arm style and the rack and pinion style. The pitman arm style uses a wormshaft with a spiral groove in it. A ball nut is placed over the wormshaft. The ball nut also has an internal spiral groove. Small steel balls are placed inside the groove. This assembly provides a low-friction drive between the wormshaft and the ball nut.

As the ball nut is moved, it meshes with the sector shaft. The sector shaft causes the pitman arm to move. Thus, as the wormshaft is turned by the driver, the end result is the moving of the pitman arm.

The rack and pinion steering system uses a flat gear called a rack. It is meshed with a mating gear called a pinion. The pinion is attached to the steering column. As the steering column is turned, the rack moves back and forth to force the wheel to turn.

Steering ratio is the ratio of the degrees turned on the steering wheel to the degrees turned on the front wheels. The ratio is for exactly one degree of motion on the front wheels. The steering ratio can be changed by changing the gear ratio between the wormshaft and the ball nut or between the pinion and the rack.

The steering linkage is used to connect the pitman arm to the front wheels. The components include the idler arm, center link, tie rods, and pitman arm. There are many styles and differences between each part. The style depends on the manufacturer and the year of the vehicle.

Wheel alignment is defined as the balancing of all forces created by friction, gravity, centrifugal force, and momentum while the wheel is in motion. There are five angles that are related to wheel alignment. These include caster, camber, toe, steering axis inclination, and turning radius. Caster is the forward or backward tilt of the spindle support. Camber is the inward or outward tilt of the wheel. Toe is the inward or outward pointing of the front wheels. Steering axis inclination is the inward tilt of the spindle support arm ball joints at the top. Turning radius is the amount in degrees that one front wheel turns more sharply than the other front wheel while the vehicle is turning.

Power steering is used to assist the driver when turning the vehicle. Power steering is accomplished by using hydraulic pressure produced by a positive displacement pump. The pressure produced is used to help turn the steering gear or push the rack on a rack and pinion system. The power steering pump is run by a belt from the crankshaft. Power steering fluid is used as the hydraulic fluid. Automatic transmission fluid should be used only in emergency situations. There are several designs of pumps including the vane, slipper, and roller types.

The hydraulic pressure in a power steering system is sent to the integral gear. Here the hydraulic pressure is used to help move the ball nut. A sliding spool or a rotary spool valve is used to direct the hydraulic pressure to the correct area for both a left and right turn. Rack and pinion power steering is accomplished by using hydraulic pressure as well. A piston is placed on the rack, inside a cylinder. Hydraulic pressure pushes the piston one way or the other to turn left or right.

TERMS TO KNOW

Can you explain each of the following terms? Review the chapter until you can use each term correctly.

Pitman arm

Rack and pinion system

Steering ratio

Center link

Idler arm

Adjusting sleeve

Zerk

Alignment

Caster

Camber

Toe (in, out)

Steering axis inclination

Scrub radius

Turning radius

Four wheel alignment

Eccentric

Electronic steering

Shim

Slotted frame

 REVIEW QUESTIONS

Multiple Choice

1. The three major components of the steering system are the steering column, steering gear, and
   a. Pitman arm
   b. Steering toe
   c. Steering linkage
   d. Rack and pinion
   e. Steering wheel

2. Universal joints are used in the _____ on a typical steering system.
   a. Steering wheel
   b. Steering column
   c. Pitman arm
   d. Tie rods
   e. Steering linkage

3. The pitman arm steering gear uses:
   a. Recirculating balls
   b. A sector shaft
   c. A ball nut
   d. All of the above
   e. None of the above

4. Which of the following is/are *not* adjustable on a steering system?
   a. Tie rods
   b. Camber
   c. Steering gear
   d. Toe in
   e. Pitman arm

5. The purpose of the steering gear is to:
   a. Change rotary motion to rotary motion
   b. Change reciprocating motion to rotary motion
   c. Change rotary motion to reciprocating motion
   d. Adjust camber
   e. Adjust caster

6. Which type of steering system uses a flat gear?
   a. Tie rod system
   b. Rack and pinion system
   c. Integral gear system
   d. Universal system
   e. Scrub system

7. When the steering wheel turns 60 degrees and the front wheel turns 3 degrees, the steering ratio is:
   a. 15 to 1
   b. 20 to 1
   c. 25 to 1
   d. 30 to 1
   e. 60 to 1

8. Which of the following is part of the steering linkage?
   a. Idler arm
   b. Center link
   c. Tie rod
   d. All of the above
   e. None of the above

9. The adjusting sleeve is attached to the:
   a. Pitman arm
   b. Tie rods
   c. Center link
   d. Idler arm
   e. U-joint

10. Which of the following is defined as the backward and forward tilt of the spindle support arm?
    a. Caster
    b. Camber
    c. Toe
    d. Steering axis inclination
    e. Turning radius

11. Which of the following is defined as the inward and outward tilt of the front wheels at the top?
    a. Caster
    b. Camber
    c. Toe
    d. Steering axis inclination
    e. Turning radius

12. Which of the following is defined as the distance between the front and back of the front wheels?
    a. Caster
    b. Camber
    c. Toe
    d. Steering axis inclination
    e. Turning radius

13. Which of the following is defined as the toe-out on turns or the amount one wheel turns more sharply on turns?
    a. Caster
    b. Camber
    c. Toe
    d. Steering axis inclination
    e. Turning radius

14. The included angle is a combination of the steering axis inclination and the _____.
    a. Toe in
    b. Caster
    c. Camber
    d. Turning radius
    e. Toe out

15. Power steering can be used:
    a. Only on pitman arm steering systems
    b. Only on rack and pinion steering systems
    c. Both A and B
    d. Neither A nor B
    e. Only when the vehicle is extremely light

16. The power steering pump is driven from the:
    a. Steering linkage
    b. Crankshaft by a belt
    c. Differential
    d. Drive shaft
    e. Steering gear

17. The control valves used in power steering are placed:
    a. On the external steering linkage
    b. In the integral gear and pitman arm assembly
    c. In the steering wheel
    d. On the rack and pinion
    e. All of the above

18. Which of the following spool valves changes passageways by rotating?
    a. The sliding spool valve
    b. The rotary spool valve
    c. The positive displacement spool valve
    d. The linkage spool valve
    e. The vane spool valve

19. Power steering on a rack and pinion steering system pushes which component?
    a. The pitman arm
    b. The rack
    c. The pinion
    d. The U-joint
    e. The spool valve

20. Which of the following are methods used to adjust the alignment on a car?
    a. Shims
    b. Eccentric bolts
    c. Cams
    d. All of the above
    e. None of the above

21. Which of the following cannot be adjusted?
    a. Camber
    b. Steering axis inclination
    c. Steering gear lash
    d. Caster
    e. Toe

The following questions are similar in format to ASE (Automotive Service Excellence) test questions.

22. A buzzing sound is heard from the power steering unit. Technician A says that the fluid is low. Technician B says that there may be air in the power steering fluid. Who is right?
    a. A only
    b. B only
    c. Both A and B
    d. Neither A nor B

23. Technician A says that one alignment adjustment will not affect the other alignment adjustments. Technician B says that one alignment adjustment is interrelated with all the other alignment adjustments and will affect the others. Who is right?
    a. A only
    b. B only
    c. Both A and B
    d. Neither A nor B

24. When working on the steering system, several preliminary checks should be made. Technician A says that the tires should be properly inflated as they may affect the steering system. Technician B says that loose ball joints may affect the steering system. Who is right?
    a. A only
    b. B only
    c. Both A and B
    d. Neither A nor B

25. A squealing sound is heard when the engine is accelerated. Technician A says the problem is a loose power steering belt. Technician B says the problem is loose tie rods. Who is right?
    a. A only
    b. B only
    c. Both A and B
    d. Neither A nor B

26. A vehicle has excessive play in the steering wheel. Technician A says the problem is power steering belts. Technician B says the problem is worn tie rods. Who is correct?
    a. A only
    b. B only
    c. Both A and B
    d. Neither A nor B

27. Technician A says a cam washer is used to adjust the camber on MacPherson strut systems. Technician B says a cam washer is used to adjust the alignment angles on rear wheel drive vehicles. Who is correct?
    a. A only
    b. B only
    c. Both A and B
    d. Neither A nor B

28. To remove a tie rod, technician A says to use a pickle fork. Technician B says tie rods are attached to the bearings. Who is correct?
    a. A only
    b. B only
    c. Both A and B
    d. Neither A nor B

29. A car has hard steering. Technician A says the problem is a worn idler arm. Technician B says the problem is too much power steering fluid. Who is correct?
    a. A only
    b. B only
    c. Both A and B
    d. Neither A nor B

Essay

30. Describe how a rack and pinion steering system operates.

31. What is a pitman arm?

32. Define the term *steering ratio*.

33. List the parts and operation of the standard steering linkage.

34. What is the purpose of the idler arm?

35. What is the purpose of the adjusting sleeve on the tie rods?

36. Define the term *caster*.

37. Define the term *camber*.

38. How does a sliding spool valve operate in a power steering system?

Short Answer

39. Front wheel drive vehicles, better tires, and independent rear suspension vehicles are all reasons why vehicles use _____ alignment.

40. A/an _____ is placed inside the rack and pinion on an electronic steering system.

41. Excessive steering play can be caused by _____.

42. A buzzing sound in the power steering unit typically means that _____.

43. Abnormally fast tire wear is a sign of _____.

CHAPTER 31

Tires and Wheels

INTRODUCTION Tires serve several important purposes. They are designed to carry the weight of the vehicle sufficiently, transfer braking and driving torque to the road, and withstand side thrust over varying speeds and conditions. This chapter explains how tires are designed, constructed, sized, and serviced.

OBJECTIVES After reading this chapter, you should be able to:

- Use tire terminology to define how tires are constructed.
- Identify different characteristics of tires.
- Compare different types of tires, including ply, radial, and spare tires.
- Identify how tires are sized.
- Analyze the purpose and operation of wheels and rims.
- Analyze several problems, diagnosis, and service procedures.

 SAFETY CHECKLIST

When working with tires and wheels, keep these important safety precautions in mind.

✔ Never try to lift a tire without proper posture and lifting technique. Keep the tire close to your body, and lift with your legs.

✔ Always wear OSHA-approved safety glasses when working on tires and rims.

✔ Always use the correct tools when working on tires and rims.

Some of the information in this chapter can help you prepare for the National Institute for Automotive Service Excellence (ASE) certification tests. The test most directly related to this chapter is entitled

SUSPENSION AND STEERING (TEST A4).

The content area that closely parallels this chapter is

WHEEL AND TIRE DIAGNOSIS AND REPAIR.

31.1 TIRE CONSTRUCTION AND CHARACTERISTICS

Differences in Tires

Different tire designs have been used on automobiles over the years to meet many demands. Originally, most vehicles used a tube-type tire. However, tube tires were eventually replaced by tubeless-type tires. From that point on, different tread designs, internal construction, and belts and ply designs have been used on tires.

Parts of a Tire

Although they seem simple, tires have several parts. *Figure 31–1* shows a cutaway view of a tubeless tire. The top or outside of the tire is called the *tread*. Its purpose is to produce the friction for braking and torque for driving. The outside

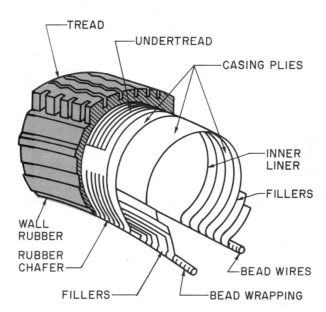

FIGURE 31–1. The tire has many components. Each component plays an important part in tire operation. *(Courtesy of Chevrolet Division, General Motors Corporation)*

sides of the tire are called the wall. On many tires, the wall is made of a white material and is called the white wall. This is for the external looks of the tire. The undertread is located directly below the tread. The layers of material, called *plies*, are formed over a spacing device and then rubberized. The number of plies varies according to the use. For example, most automobile tires have two or four plies. Heavier vehicles such as vans and station wagons may use tires with up to eight plies for strength. The *carcass* is the strong, inner part of the tire that holds the air. The carcass is made of the layers or plies of fabric. It gives the tire its strength.

The sidewall and tread material is *vulcanized* into place. Vulcanizing is defined as the process of heating rubber under pressure to mold the rubber into a desired shape. The *bead* wires, casing, and remaining parts are used for strength and durability. The tire is then attached to the wheel rim, and an air valve is used to admit the necessary air for pressure.

Tube and Tubeless Tires

The tube-type tire is mounted on the wheel rim with a rubber inner tube placed inside the casing. The inner tube is inflated with air. This causes the tire casing to resist change in shape. The tubeless tire is mounted directly on the rim. The air is retained between the rim and tire casing when inflated.

A tube tire cannot be used without a tube. Some service technicians will, however, use a tube in a tubeless tire in emergency situations. Tubes are sometimes installed by the technician to eliminate the hard-to-find slow leak. Tubes are also used when imbedded dirt or rust prevents a tubeless tire from seating properly on the rim. However, using tubes for these reasons should be avoided if at all possible. Tubes are

also useful with wire spoke wheels. The spokes tend to loosen in their sockets with long use, producing small leaks.

Tire Characteristics

Tires have several characteristics that are important in understanding their design. These include:

1. *Tire traction — Traction* is defined as a tire's ability to grip the road and to move or stop the vehicle.

2. *Ride and handling* — Tires are measured by their ride and handling ability. This is an indication of the degree of comfort a tire delivers to the passenger. It is also a measure of the responsiveness provided to the driver's steering actions.

3. *Rolling resistance — Rolling resistance* is a term used to describe the pounds of force required to overcome the resistance of a tire to rotate. As rolling resistance of a tire decreases, fuel mileage typically increases.

4. *Noise* — All tires make a certain amount of noise. Tires can be made "quiet" by scrambling or changing the size, length, and shape of the tread elements. Scrambling prevents the sound frequency buildup that would develop if all of the patterns of the tread were spaced evenly.

Cords

Within the tire, there are layers of plies or belts. These layers have *cords* running through them for strength. *Figure 31–2* shows examples of several cords used inside the plies. *Figure 31–3* lists the advantages of different types of cords. Because newer synthetic fibers are constantly being developed,

FIGURE 31–2. Cords are used inside the plies for strength. *(Courtesy of Cooper Tire and Rubber Company)*

Types of Tire Cords		
CORD TYPE	TENSILE STRENGTH, PSI	ADVANTAGES
Rayon	94,000	Soft ride, resilient, inexpensive
Polyester	104,000	Soft ride, more heat-resistant, inexpensive
Nylon	122,000	High heat resistance, excellent impact resistance, minimum flex, won't absorb water
Fiberglass	407,000	Greatest strength, soft ride

FIGURE 31–3. Different types of cords have different advantages. *(Courtesy of Chevrolet Division, General Motors Corporation)*

more advantages and better driving characteristics will continually occur in tire design.

Radial and Bias Tires

There are typically three ways that the plies of the tire can be laid down. They can be positioned as a *bias*, belted bias, or belted *radial* tire. *Figure 31–4* shows the differences. The bias ply tire has layers of cord material running at an angle from bead to bead. Each cord used runs opposite to the cord below it. This tire provides strength. The plies tend, however, to work against each other during operation. This action produces heat. In addition, bias ply tires tend to produce a certain amount of rolling resistance. These characteristics increase the wear on the tread and shorten the tire life.

The belted bias tire uses additional belts wrapped around the circumference of the body of the plies. The actual cords within the belts are manufactured at an angle. The design and addition of these belts add strength and stiffness to the

Bias Ply Tire

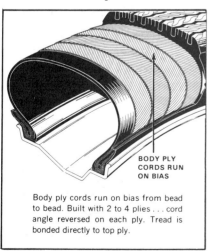

Body ply cords run on bias from bead to bead. Built with 2 to 4 plies . . . cord angle reversed on each ply. Tread is bonded directly to top ply.

Belted Bias

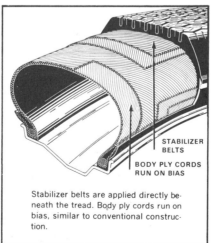

Stabilizer belts are applied directly beneath the tread. Body ply cords run on bias, similar to conventional construction.

Radial

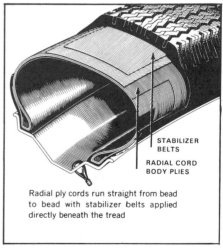

Radial ply cords run straight from bead to bead with stabilizer belts applied directly beneath the tread

FIGURE 31–4. Tires can be bias ply, belted bias, or radial design. The difference is in how the plies are laid down on the tire. *(Courtesy of Firestone Tire and Rubber Company)*

tread. Because this tire typically has less rolling resistance than the bias ply tire, it lasts longer.

The cord material in the body of a belted radial or radial ply tire runs from bead to bead. It is not at an angle as in the other tires. Additional belts are added for strength and durability. The belted radial tire allows the belts to hold more of the tread on the pavement during cornering and straight driving. In addition, the tire does not *squirm*. Squirm means that as the tire hits the road, it is moving or being pushed together. Less squirm results in better traction, less rolling resistance, less heat buildup, longer life, and better fuel mileage. In addition, in newer radials special materials are used in the cords to increase comfort and driveability.

Tread Design

The tread of the tire must be made to work on all types of conditions. For example, cars operate on smooth pavement, gravel, wet pavement, and icy pavement. In addition, steering traction is different from rear wheel drive traction. Today, tire designs are a compromise between these conditions and cost considerations.

Tire treads have been developed to give better traction in wet conditions. The water must be squeezed from the contact area on the road surface. Treads have been developed to move the water away from the tread as efficiently as possible as the tire rolls. Of course, as the tire tread wears, the efficiency is reduced. *Figure 31–5* shows an example of different tread designs.

Technology is gradually changing snow tires as well. Some manufacturers have developed *hydrophilic* tread compounds. Hydrophilic means attraction to water. A tread composed of part of this compound will literally stick to a wet or icy surface.

Tire Performance

Choosing the right tire is becoming an important task for the consumer. Tires can be designed for various characteristics. For example, one tire manufacturer designs tires for the following characteristics.

1. Treadwear — gives more life on the tread of the tire

2. Ride comfort — gives the passengers a more comfortable ride

3. Snow traction — gives more traction on snow

4. Wet traction — gives more traction on wet surfaces

5. Handling — gives improved handling during cornering

6. High speed — gives more control at higher speeds

Many tires are sold as *all-season* tires. This type of tire gives equal importance to each characteristic above. However, an operator may need to have certain characteristics improved.

When one tire characteristic is improved, other characteristics have a tendency to be reduced. This relationship is shown in *Figure 31–6*. This diagram is called a tire performance polygon. Four tires (four polygons) are shown for reference. The farther the points on the polygon get from the center, the better the characteristic. The all-season tire is designed for all-around use. Note that each characteristic point on this tire has been given a value of 100. The other numbers indicate the degree of improvement or reduction of the specific characteristic.

The other three tires are compared with the all-season tire. The other three tires, V-rated, H-rated, and S-rated are all designed for higher speeds, better handling, and improved wet traction. The result is that these tires lose comfort, treadwear, and snow traction characteristics. Knowing this, consumers can choose which performance characteristics are most important to their driving needs and which they are willing to sacrifice.

Tire Valves

The tire valve is used to admit and exhaust the air into and out of the tire. *Figure 31–7* shows a typical tire valve. It has a central core that is spring loaded. This allows air to flow in only one direction, inward. When the small pin is depressed, air flows in the reverse or outward direction. When the valve core becomes defective, it can be unscrewed for removal and replaced. An airtight cap on the end of the valve produces an extra seal against valve leakage.

Puncture-sealing Tires

Puncture-sealing tires are made to permanently seal tread punctures up to 3/16 inch in diameter. This is shown in *Figure 31–8*. A resultant sealer is applied to the inside of the tire at the manufacturer. It is a special rubber compound. If a puncturing object penetrates the tire tread into the sealant layer, it picks up a coating of the sealant. When the punc-

DIFFERENT TREAD TYPES

FIGURE 31–5.   Tire treads vary and are purchased according to the conditions of the road.

TIRE PERFORMANCE POLYGON

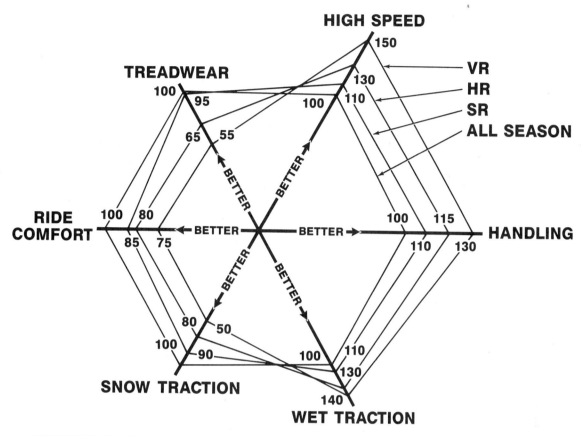

FIGURE 31–6. This polygon shows that tires can be designed for improved high speed, handling, and wet traction. However, snow traction, treadwear, and ride comfort characteristics are reduced. *(Courtesy of Cooper Tire and Rubber Company)*

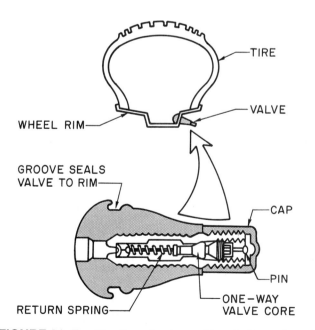

FIGURE 31–7. The tire valve is used to admit or exhaust air from the tire. A small one-way valve is used to cause air to flow in only one direction.

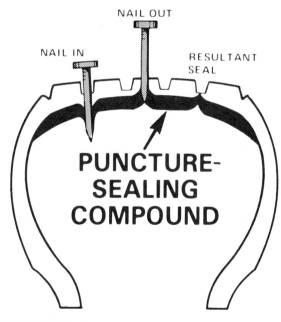

FIGURE 31–8. Puncture-sealing tires are used to permanently seal tread punctures up to 3/16 of an inch. *(Courtesy of Oldsmobile Division, General Motors Corporation)*

COMPACT SPARE

- Temporary Use Only
- Inflate to 60 PSI

FIGURE 31–9. The compact spare tire is used to save weight and space in smaller vehicles. *(Courtesy of Oldsmobile Division, General Motors Corporation)*

turing object is removed or thrown from the tire by centrifugal force, the sealant adheres to it. The sealant is then pulled into the opening in the tread, causing it to seal.

Compact Spare Tire

Many vehicles today are built smaller than in the past. Smaller cars have less trunk space. Many smaller cars use the compact spare tire to save space and weight. A compact spare tire is shown in *Figure 31–9*. It is called a temporary use only spare tire. This tire has a narrow 4-inch-wide rim. The wheel diameter is usually one inch larger than the road wheels. It should be used only when one of the road tires has failed. Inflation pressure is much higher on the compact spare tire, about 60 psi, and the top-rated speed is lower than on regular tires.

CAR CLINIC

PROBLEM: Car Pulls to One Side During Acceleration

The rear end of a vehicle with a limited slip differential seems to pull to one side during acceleration. Limited slip differentials are designed to provide equal push on both rear wheels. What could be the problem?

SOLUTION:

The first thing to check is the rear tires. Make sure that the tires are both the same diameter. The tires have most likely been mismatched. Using a limited slip differential with two tire sizes will cause the car to pull to one side.

31.2   IDENTIFYING TIRES

Metric Tire Sizes

Tires are sized according to the application in which they are to be used and their physical size. The size of the tire must be molded into the side of the tire. Most tires today are sized according to metric standards. In the past, however, there were other ways of identifying tire sizes. *Figure 31–10* shows how metric sizing works. The tire has several designations:

1. The first letter of the size tells if the tire is used for passenger (P), temporary (T), or commercial (C) use.

2. The second designation tells the section width of the tire. The section width is the distance in millimeters from one side of the tire to the other side of the tire when it is inflated normally. For example, the tire shown in Figure 31–10 has a width of 185 mm.

3. The third designation tells the *aspect ratio*. The aspect ratio is found by dividing the section height by the section width. The aspect ratio in Figure 31–10 means the tire's height is 80% of the width. This is called the profile of the tire. Lower profile tires make the car closer to the road and reduce wind drag beneath the car body.

4. The next designation tells the construction type. R means radial tire, B means belted, and D means diagonal (bias).

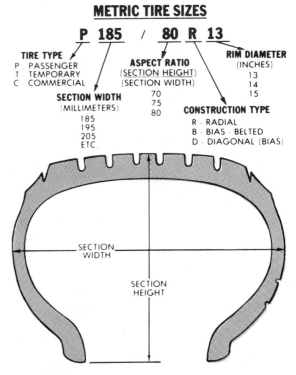

FIGURE 31–10. Tires are sized according to metric sizes. Each designation helps to identify the type and size of tire. *(Courtesy of Oldsmobile Division, General Motors Corporation)*

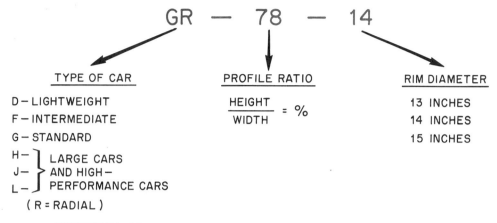

FIGURE 31–11.   Several designations may be used to identify tire size.

5. The last designation gives the wheel rim in inches. The most common car rim sizes are 13, 14, and 15 inches in diameter.

Other Tire Sizing

Some manufacturers may also use other designations. One common type of designation is called the numeric identification. For example, a tire sized as 7.75-14 means the approximate cross section of the tire in inches is 7.75. The rim diameter is 14 inches. The alphanumeric system is shown in *Figure 31–11*. The first letter or letters indicate the type of car the tire is to be used on. The number 78 is the *profile ratio* (height-to-width ratio). The third designation is the rim diameter in inches.

Tire Placard

A *tire placard* is permanently located on many vehicles. The placard is normally located on the rear face of the driver's door. Refer to the placard for tire information. It lists the maximum vehicle load, tire size (including spare), and cold inflation pressure (including spare). *Figure 31–12* shows a tire placard.

UTQG Designation

UTQG (uniform tire quality grading) symbols are required by law to be molded on the sidewall of each new tire sold in the United States. A typical grading may be 90 CB, 170 BC, or 140 AA. The number indicates the comparative tread life. A tire marked 140 should wear 40% longer than a tire marked 100. The first letter indicates comparative wet traction. A is best and C is worst. The second letter is a measure of the resistance to heat. Again, A is the best and C is the worst.

Some tire manufacturers use the *Department of Transportation (DOT)* designation. The DOT specification number indicates that the tire has met various tests of quality established by the Department of Transportation. *Figure 31–13* shows an example of the many numbers and ratings molded into the tire sidewall.

TPC Specification Number

On most vehicles originally equipped with radial tires, a TPC (tire performance criteria) specification number is molded into the sidewall. This shows that the tire meets rigid size and performance standards developed for that particular automobile. It assures a proper combination of endurance,

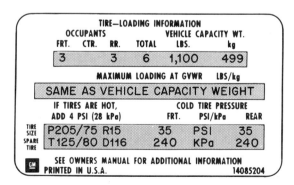

FIGURE 31–12.   The tire placard is used to list maximum vehicle load, tire size, and inflation data. *(Courtesy of Oldsmobile Division, General Motors Corporation)*

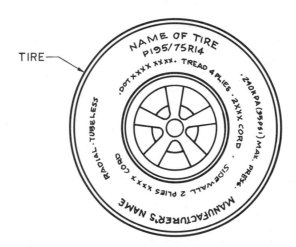

FIGURE 31–13. Several numbers are used to identify the type and style of tire used on the vehicle. These include the tire size, load capacity, name of the tire, manufacturer, number of plies, type of tire (radial or tubeless), and cord information.

handling, load capacity, ride, and traction on wet, dry, or snow-covered surfaces.

Load Range

Tires are measured for the amount of load they can withstand. They are typically identified by letter codes. The codes used are A, B, C, D, E, F, G, H, I, J, L, M, and N. As the size of the tire increases, the *load range* also increases. On some tires, the load range is stated in pounds for a specific tire pressure. For example, the load range molded into the tire may be, "Max Load, 585 kg (1,290 lb) at 240 kPa (35 psi)."

CAR CLINIC

PROBLEM: Tire Wear on Outside

Tires on a vehicle are wearing on the outside edges. The alignment has been checked, and all adjustments are within specifications. The alignment shop says this is normal. Is it normal?

SOLUTION:

Tires should not wear on the outside edges. This type of wear indicates that either the toe-in or the camber is too high. Some vehicles may have to be bent or parts may have to be replaced to adjust the camber. Try a second alignment shop because alignment machines can be inaccurate if they are not serviced properly.

31.3 WHEELS AND RIMS

Drop Center Wheels

Tires are mounted on rims made of steel, aluminum, or other strong material. The parts of the wheel are shown in *Figure 31–14*. The mounting holes are used to attach the wheel to the lugs on the axles. The wheel is called a *drop center wheel*. This means that the center of the wheel is made so that it has a smaller diameter than the rim. The wheel has

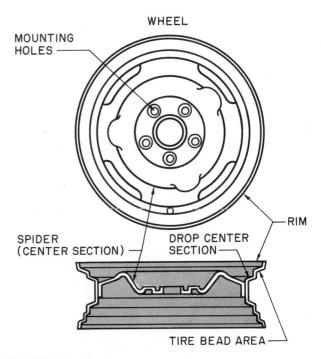

FIGURE 31–14. The wheel is used to support the tire. It has several parts and areas for identification.

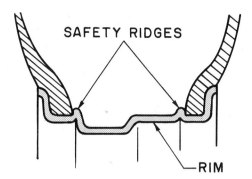

FIGURE 31–15. Safety rims have small ridges in the rim to stop the tire from getting into the dropped area during a blowout.

CAR CLINIC

PROBLEM: Shimmy Problems

A GM travel van with about 15,000 miles on it seems to have a severe shimmy when the vehicle hits a bump. This is especially noticeable on high-speed highway turns. The bias ply tires from the manufacturer are on the vehicle. The alignment has been checked and adjusted. The shimmy disappeared for about 500 miles, then returned.

SOLUTION:

The problem could be caused by two things. First, is the vehicle used on bumpy roads? Severe bumps may cause the alignment to go out of specifications even after 500 miles. The second cause could be the tires. The weight distribution of large vehicles may cause the problem. It is extremely important for the tires to grip the road under all conditions. The better the grip, the less chance of shimmy. With a lot of weight in the rear of a van, the road grip on ply tires may not be enough. Try replacing the tires with a good set of radial tires. This will most likely solve the problem.

a dropped center so that the tire can be easily removed. During removal and installation, the bead of the tire must be pushed into the dropped area. Only then can the other side of the tire be removed over the rim flange.

Safety rims are also being used on vehicles today. The safety rim has small ridges built into rim. See *Figure 31–15*. These ridges are to keep the tire from getting into the dropped center when a blowout occurs while driving and the tire becomes deflated. If the tire stays up on the rim, there is more driving stability than if the tire gets into the dropped center. Thus, safety is improved.

Wheel Sizes

The most common sizes for wheels are 13-, 14-, and 15-inch diameters. The exact wheel size used on a vehicle is determined by the automotive manufacturer. Certain cars use different size wheels, which may include 12- or 16-inch wheel rims. The width of the wheel rims is usually 4.5, 5, or 6 inches. The large wheel rim sizes are usually used on heavy-duty and larger vehicles.

Special Wheels

A variety of wheels are being manufactured today. They are normally made of steel or aluminum. Generally, wheels are one of three types: the disc wheel, the cast aluminum wheel, and the wire wheel. See *Figure 31–16*. All three are currently being used by manufacturers. The consumer can also purchase a *mag wheel*. This type of wheel uses a light magnesium metal for the rim. The term mag is used today, however, to represent almost any type of wheel that uses special material and designs.

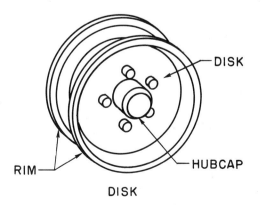

DISK

CAST ALUMINUM

WIRE WHEEL

FIGURE 31–16. Generally, wheels are of three types: the disc, cast aluminum, and wire wheel.

Problems, Diagnosis and Service

1. To service tires and wheels, you must raise the vehicle off the floor. Always follow the correct procedure when using the hoist to lift the car. If a hydraulic jack is used, remember to use extra jack stands for support. Always block the other wheels to eliminate the possibility of the vehicle moving forward or backward.
2. When removing a tire from its rim, remember to use the correct tools and procedure. There is a great deal of pressure on the tire sides, and this pressure could cause serious injury during removal.
3. Always tighten the wheel nuts on the vehicle to the correct torque specifications and sequence. This will prevent the wheel nuts from coming loose and possibly causing serious injury during driving.
4. When a tire is being inflated after it has been replaced on the rim, the bead will often pop into place. Keep your fingers away from the bead during inflation. Also, never inflate the tire over 40 psi, because older rims may come apart and cause serious injury.
5. Tires that are underinflated often will get very hot when driven at high speeds. Always be careful not to touch the hot tire immediately after running at high speeds. It may burn your hands.
6. Be careful when handling a tire that has shredded at high speeds along a highway. There may be sharp metal wires protruding from inside the bead.

PROBLEM: **Uneven Wear on Tires**

The front tires of a vehicle are wearing unevenly and now need to be replaced.

DIAGNOSIS

Uneven tire wear can be produced from several causes. Generally, it is caused by improper inflation, not rotating the tires, or misalignment. To determine the cause of uneven wear, perform the following diagnostic checks:

1. Before checking any problem with tires, make sure the front suspension, steering, and brake systems are working and adjusted correctly.

2. Incorrect front end and rear tire geometry and operation can also cause excessive and uneven wear on the tires. Observe the tire wear patterns to determine the problem as shown in *Figure 31–17*. If the problem appears to be in alignment, have the vehicle aligned according to the manufacturer's recommended procedure before proceeding.

3. Tires can be checked for excessive wear by observing the treadwear indicators or *tread bars*. See *Figure 31–18*. They look like narrow strips of smooth rubber across

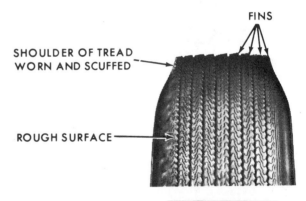

FINS

SHOULDER OF TREAD WORN AND SCUFFED

ROUGH SURFACE

CORNERING WEAR

IRREGULAR DEPRESSIONS

FEATHERED EDGE

ONE SIDE OF TREAD WORN

MULTI-PROBLEM

TOE-IN WEAR

CAMBER WEAR

FIGURE 31–17. Tire wear can be caused by incorrect alignment and front end geometry. *(Courtesy of Chevrolet Division, General Motors Corporation)*

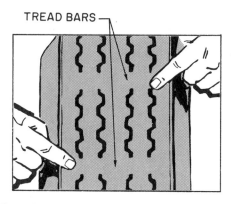

FIGURE 31–18. Check the tread bars on tires. If the tread bars show, the tire is ready to be replaced. *(Courtesy of Tire Industry Safety Council)*

the tread. They will appear on the tire when it is worn down, either evenly or unevenly. When these tread bars are visible, the tire is worn and should be replaced.

4. Tires must be inflated correctly. The recommended tire pressure is calculated according to the type of tire, weight of the vehicle, and ride. In addition, tire inflation may change with temperatures. For example, cold weather reduces tire inflation pressure approximately 1 pound for every 10 degrees drop in temperature. Always check tire inflation in both summer and winter conditions.

5. Check the tires for overinflation. Overinflation of tires increases tire tension and prevents proper deflection of the sidewalls. These conditions result in wear in the center of the tread. The tire also loses its ability to absorb road shocks. Refer to *Figure 31–19*.

6. Underinflation of tires distorts the normal contour of the tire body, causing the tire to bulge outward. It also increases internal heat. Heat may weaken the cords and cause the ply to separate. See Figure 31–19.

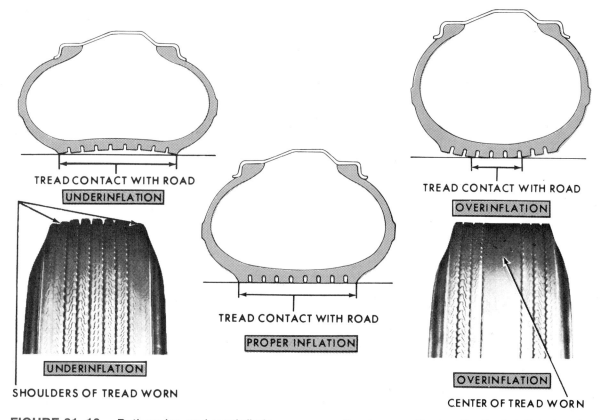

FIGURE 31–19. Both under- and overinflation can cause tire damage. Be sure the tire is inflated to the correct pressure recommended by the manufacturer. *(Courtesy of Oldsmobile Division, General Motors Corporation)*

```
INFLATION PRESSURE CONVERSION CHART
        (KILOPASCALS TO PSI)
```

kPa	psi	kPa	psi
140	20	215	31
145	21	220	32
155	22	230	33
160	23	235	34
165	24	240	35
170	25	250	36
180	26	275	40
185	27	310	45
190	28	345	50
200	29	380	55
205	30	415	60

Conversion: 6.9 kPa = 1 psi

FIGURE 31–20. Both psi (pounds per square inch) and kPa (kilopascals) can be used to measure the inflation of tires. *(Courtesy of Oldsmobile Division, General Motors Corporation)*

7. Tire inflation can be measured in pounds per square inch (psi) or kilopascals (kPa). *Figure 31–20* shows the relationship between the two units.

8. Check whether the tires have been rotated according to the manufacturer's recommended time interval and procedure. There are two acceptable patterns for rotating tires. See *Figure 31–21*. Rotation is shown for a car with and without a spare tire. These procedures do not include the temporary use only spare tire.

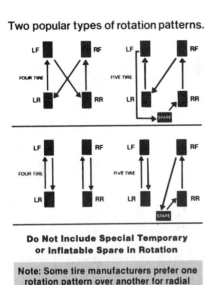

Two popular types of rotation patterns.

Do Not Include Special Temporary or Inflatable Spare In Rotation

Note: Some tire manufacturers prefer one rotation pattern over another for radial tires. Check with your tire dealer for the rotation pattern best suited for your particular tires.

FIGURE 31–21. Tires can be rotated to distribute the wear. Two common rotational patterns are shown. Follow the manufacturer's recommendations when rotating tires. *(Courtesy of Tire Industry Safety Council)*

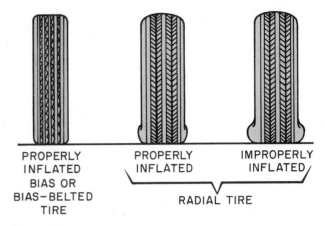

FIGURE 31–22. Different tire types will appear different when properly and improperly inflated.

9. Check whether the weight of the vehicle has been increased with extra loads or objects. Always check the owner's manual for the maximum safe load limit the tires can handle as well as the tire inflation necessary.

10. A visual inspection of the tires can also tell if the inflation is correct or not. *Figure 31–22* shows how tires should look when they are properly inflated.

SERVICE

If it has been determined that the tires are producing uneven wear because of inflation, inflate tires to the correct specification. Refer to the owner's manual. If the tires must be replaced, the following service items should be remembered.

1. Tires should be checked for inflation at least once a month and before long trips. Use an acceptable and accurate pressure gauge. Check the tires when they are cold, and check the spare tire as well.

2. When replacing tires with those not having a TPC (tire performance criteria) specification number, use the same size, load range, and construction type (bias, belted bias, or radial) as the original tires on the car. A different type of tire may affect the ride, handling, speedometer and odometer readings, and vehicle ground clearance.

3. Tires and wheels are match-mounted at the assembly plant on some vehicles. This means that the stiffest part of the tire radially, or the "high spot," is matched to the smallest radius, or "low spot," on the wheel. This is done to provide the smoothest possible ride. The high spot is marked with a yellow paint mark on the outer sidewall. The low spot of the wheel is at the location of the valve stem. Always mount the wheel so the tire and wheel markings are matched. See *Figure 31–23*.

4. When removing and replacing tires, use a quality tire changer. Follow the procedures recommended by the manufacturer of the machine. Use the following general procedure to change a tire.
   a. Remove the air from the tire.

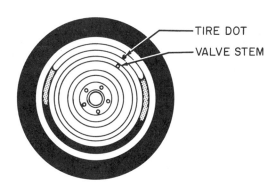

FIGURE 31–23. Align the dot on the tire with the valve stem to get the smoothest ride possible after dismounting a tire. *(Courtesy of Oldsmobile Division, General Motors Corporation)*

b. Remove the valve stem from the tire.
c. Unseat the tire from the rim. See *Figure 31–24*.
d. Using the proper tools and pneumatic rams remove the tire from the rim. See *Figure 31–25*.
e. Check the rim for cracks or bends caused by hitting curbs and so on. It is dangerous to weld a cracked rim or to heat it for straightening. See *Figure 31–26*. Replace the rim rather than trying to repair it.
f. If the rim has no cracks or is not bent, clean the rim using a wire brush as shown in *Figure 31–27*.

FIGURE 31–25. Use a tire changer to remove the tire from the rim.

FIGURE 31–24. Use a tire changer to break the bead of the tire before removal.

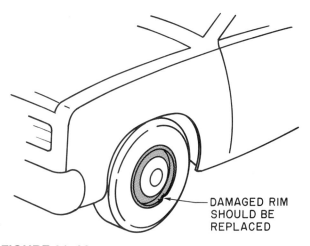

FIGURE 31–26. Never try to repair a rim that has been bent or broken. Always replace the rim.

FIGURE 31–27. Clean the rim with a wire brush before installing a new tire.

g. Rubber compound should be liberally applied to the bead of the new tire. See *Figure 31–28*.

h. Using the tire changer assembly, install the new tire onto the rim.

i. Reinstall the air valve.

j. Inflate to specifications, and check for leaks.

   CAUTION: Do not inflate the tire over 40 psi to set the bead. If the bead will not set, deflate the tire, push down the bead, and reinflate. Make sure rubber compound has been applied to the rim of the tire. If over-inflated, the bead may jump over the rim and injure your hands.

k. Install the tire and rim back on the tire. The tire lug nuts must be tightened in a specific sequence. Using an incorrect tightening sequence may cause the wheel, brake drum, or rotor to bind or bend. See *Figure 31–29* for the correct sequence.

PROBLEM: Defective Radial Tire Belt

A vehicle is pulling to one side. The pulling begins at less than 10 miles per hour.

DIAGNOSIS

This may indicate a defective radial tire. Typically, a belt has shifted inside the tire body. To check this condition:

1. Make sure the suspension, steering, and brake systems are adjusted correctly.

2. Jack up the car, and spin the tire. See *Figure 31–30*.

3. If the tread seems to wobble from side to side, replace the tire.

FIGURE 31–28. Apply rubber compound on tire rim to aid in sealing.

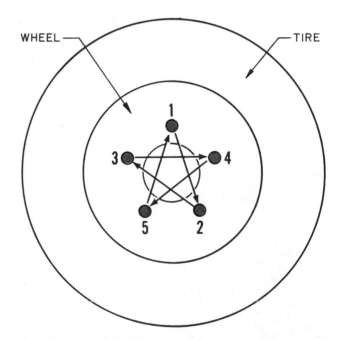

FIGURE 31–29. Wheel nuts should be tightened in the correct sequence and to proper torque specifications. *(Courtesy of Oldsmobile Division, General Motors Corporation)*

SERVICE

Use the same general procedure to remove and replace a tire as previously listed.

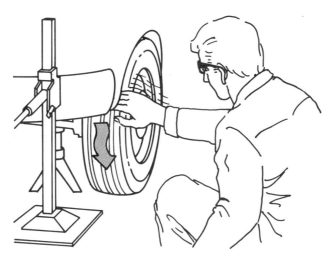

FIGURE 31–30. The tire can be checked for a defective belt by lifting the car and spinning the wheel. The tread will wobble from side to side if the belt is defective.

PROBLEM: Tires Not Balanced Correctly

As the car goes down the road, there is a shimmy or vibration in the front of the vehicle. It is felt in the steering wheel.

DIAGNOSIS

Often the tires get out of balance and must be balanced to get rid of shimmy or vibration. Tires must be balanced correctly in order to run smoothly and evenly at all speeds. A rim that is out-of-round may also produce a shimmy or vibration. When the shimmy is noticed in the steering wheel the front tires are out of balance. When the rear wheels are out of balance, the shimmy is noticeable in the seat and floor of the vehicle.

Wheels get out of balance for two common reasons:

1. Tires wear unevenly, producing an unbalanced tire.

2. The car hits a bump, and the balance weights fall off.

There are two types of balancing, static and dynamic. *Static balance* is the equal distribution of weight around the axis of rotation. The tire is not spinning during the balancing process. The tire will have no tendency to rotate itself, regardless of position. Wheels that are statically unbalanced cause a hopping or bouncing action. This is called wheel tramp. Severe wheel tramp can cause excessive wear and damage to the tire.

Dynamic balancing is the equal distribution of weight about the place of rotation. The tire is spinning during balancing. Tires are tested and checked in balancing machines as shown in *Figure 31–31*. When a tire is spinning, it tends to move from side to side if it is out of balance. Wheels that are not dynamically balanced cause the car to shimmy or vibrate when it is moving. Typically the vibration or shimmy will occur at a specific speed.

FIGURE 31–31. Tires are dynamically balanced by spinning them on this tire balancing machine. *(Courtesy of Hunter Engineering Company)*

A violent jolt, caused by hitting a curb or the like, may also cause a shimmy or vibration. In order to check for this condition, wheel (rim) runout must be measured. *Wheel runout* is a measure of the out-of-roundness of the rim. This can be measured by a dial indicator. See *Figure 31–32*. Both inboard and outboard measurements should be taken on the rim. *Figure 31–33* shows where the measurements should be taken. Radial and lateral (axial) runout on the rim can be taken with the tire on or off the rim. Compare the runout (radial and lateral) with the manufacturer's recommendations. Replace if necessary.

SERVICE

If the tires need to be balanced, follow the procedures listed by the manufacturer of the balancing machine. If the rim must be replaced because of runout, use the general procedure mentioned earlier.

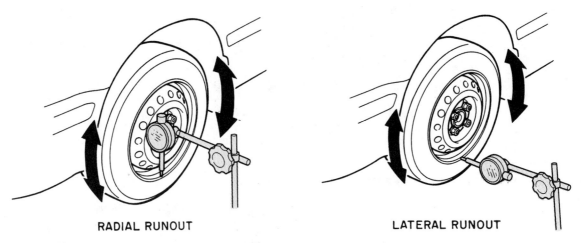

RADIAL RUNOUT   LATERAL RUNOUT

FIGURE 31–32. Wheel runout can be checked using a dial indicator. Both radial and lateral (axial) runout should be measured. *(Courtesy of Honda Motor Company, Ltd.)*

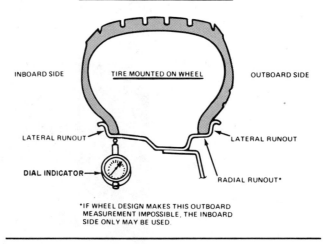

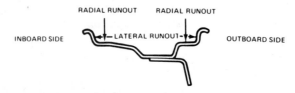

FIGURE 31–33. Wheel runout can be checked with a dial indicator at the positions shown. *(Courtesy of Oldsmobile Division, General Motors Corporation)*

Linkage to Automotive Performance and Testing

TIRE AND WHEEL PERFORMANCE

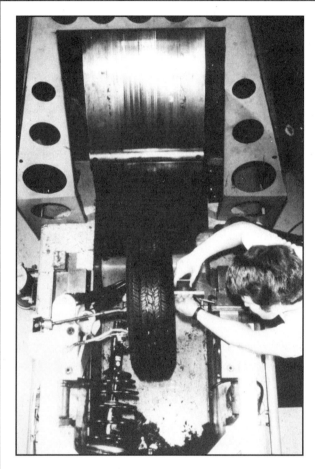

Tires must be tested for many characteristics. At the GM Proving Grounds in Milford, Michigan, tires are tested for traction, cornering, structural durability, uniformity, and road hazard resistance. Other tests include dynamometer testing of wheels under overload conditions and corrosion-resistance testing of wheel attachments. *(Courtesy of General Motors Proving Grounds)*

SERVICE MANUAL CONNECTION

There are many important specifications to keep in mind when working with tires and wheels. To identify the specifications for your vehicle, you will need to know the VIN (vehicle identification number) of the vehicle, the type and year of the vehicle, and the exact type of tire used. Although they may be titled differently, some of the more common tire and wheel specifications (not all) found in service manuals are listed below. Note that these specifications are typical examples. Each vehicle may have different specifications.

Common Specification	Typical Example
Front and rear wheel axial runout	
Steel wheels	0.039 inch
Aluminum wheels	0.045 inch
Inflation pressures	32 psi
Rim diameter	14 inches
Tire cord tensile strength	122,000 psi
Tire loading	1,100 lb
Tire sizing	P 185/80 R 13
Tire width	205 mm
Wheel nut torque	80 lb-ft

In addition, the service manual will give specific directions for various service and testing procedures. Some of the more common procedures include:

- Balancing tires and wheels
- Inflation of tires
- Measuring wheel runout
- Selecting replacement tires
- Tire chair use
- Tire mounting and dismounting
- Tire rotation
- Wheel removal

SUMMARY

This chapter discussed the components and design of tires and wheels. There are many types of tires. The differences are made by changing the tread, belts, cords, plies, beads, and materials within the tire. Both tube and tubeless tires are still manufactured. Tires are designed to have several characteristics. These include tire traction, ride and handling, rolling resistance, and noise.

There are three main types of tires. These are the bias ply tire, the belted bias tire, and the belted radial tire. The bias ply tire is designed with layers of cord material running at angles from bead to bead. The belted bias tire has additional belts wrapped around the circumference of the body of the

tire. The radial tire has the cords running radially from bead to bead. The radial tire also uses belts made of different materials around the circumference of the tire.

There are many tread designs for tires. Treads are designed mostly to improve the traction on different types of surfaces. This may include wet, dry, gravel, or icy conditions. The air is held inside the tire with the use of a tire valve. It is a one-direction valve that allows air into the tire but not out unless the valve is released.

Tire manufacturers also make tires that are puncture-proof and tires that are for temporary use only.

Tires can be identified in a variety of ways. Metric sizes of tires are molded into the sidewall and tell the application, the width in millimeters, the aspect ratio, the type (radial, belted, and so on), and the wheel rim size in inches. Numeric and alpha designations are also used to size tires. In addition, many manufacturers use a tire placard, which is placed on the door of the vehicle, to show maximum vehicle load, tire size, inflation pressure, and so on. Other designations of tires include the UTQG designation, TPC specification number, and load ranges.

The tire is placed on the wheel for support. The design of the wheel is called a drop center wheel. This means the center of the wheel has a smaller radius than the rim. This makes it easier to remove the tire from the wheel. The most common wheel sizes are 13, 14, and 15 inches.

There is a great deal of information concerning tire diagnosis and service. One of the most important service tips is to keep the tires properly inflated. Under- or overinflation will damage the tire very quickly and reduce its mileage. Before diagnosing tires, make sure the steering, suspension, and brakes are in proper working order. Other service tips include: replace tires when the tread bars are showing, check wheel runout, check for misaligned belts, and balance tires according to the manufacturer's specifications.

TERMS TO KNOW

Can you explain each of the following terms? Review the chapter until you can use each term correctly.

Tread	Aspect ratio
Plies	Profile ratio
Carcass	Tire placard
Vulcanized	Department of Transportation (DOT)
Bead	
Traction	Load range
Rolling resistance	Drop center wheel
Cords	Safety rims
Bias	Mag wheel
Radial	Tread bars
Squirm	Static balance
Hydrophilic	Dynamic balancing
All-season tires	Wheel runout

REVIEW QUESTIONS

Multiple Choice

1. Which part of the tire is used to produce the traction between the tire and road?
   a. Cord
   b. Carcass
   c. Tread
   d. Belts
   e. Bead

2. Which part of the tire is used to hold the air inside the tire housing?
   a. Cord
   b. Carcass
   c. Tread
   d. Belts
   e. Bead

3. As the rolling resistance of a tire increases, the fuel mileage of the vehicle:
   a. Will increase
   b. Will decrease
   c. Will remain the same
   d. Will increase then decrease as speed increases
   e. None of the above

4. _____ are used within the tire plies or belts of a tire to increase the strength of the tire.
   a. Rims
   b. Cords
   c. Tubes
   d. Beads
   e. Valves

5. Which type of tire uses plies that are crisscrossed over each other?
   a. Radial
   b. Radial belted
   c. Bias
   d. Bias radial
   e. All of the above

6. Which type of tire has the lowest rolling resistance?
   a. Bias
   b. Bias ply
   c. Bias belted
   d. Tube bias
   e. Radial belted

7. The _____ tread tire has compounds used to attract water to the tread.
   a. Tubeless
   b. Hydrophilic
   c. Belted
   d. Corded
   e. Tube

8. The compact spare tire should be used:
   a. Whenever possible because it has low rolling resistance
   b. Only on rough surfaces
   c. Only in the city
   d. Only when another tire is damaged and cannot be used
   e. Only on wet surfaces

9. Which of the following is *not* molded into the side of a tire for sizing and identification on metric tire sizes?
   a. Wheel size
   b. Aspect ratio
   c. Application
   d. Tire speed
   e. Construction type (radial, bias, etc.)

10. Most information about a car's tires can be found on the:
    a. Steering wheel
    b. Engine block
    c. Tire placard
    d. Undercarriage of the vehicle
    e. Steering system

11. The maximum load a tire can safely withstand is called the:
    a. Load range
    b. Aspect ratio
    c. Profile
    d. Carcass
    e. Construction type

12. Wheels are made with _____ to aid in removing and installing the tires on the wheels.
    a. Cords
    b. Vulcanized rubber
    c. A dropped center
    d. 16-inch rims
    e. Flexible material

13. Which systems are important to check before diagnosing tire problems?
    a. Steering systems
    b. Brake systems
    c. Suspension systems
    d. All of the above
    e. None of the above

14. Which of the following is critical for correct tire operation and wear?
    a. Correct tire material
    b. Correct tire inflation
    c. Correct molding on the side of the tire
    d. Correct casing material
    e. None of the above

15. Which of the following can indicate excessive tread wear on a tire?
    a. Tire inflation
    b. Tread bars
    c. Valve condition
    d. Rim condition
    e. Dropped wheel condition

16. Which of the following will affect tire inflation?
    a. Hotter temperatures
    b. Colder temperatures
    c. Amount of pressure inside the tire
    d. All of the above
    e. None of the above

The following questions are similar in format to ASE (Automotive Service Excellence) test questions.

17. The vehicle is pulling to the right. Technician A says that the problem could be a defective radial. Technician B says that the problem could be in the dynamic balancing. Who is right?
    a. A only
    b. B only
    c. Both A and B
    d. Neither A nor B

18. Technician A says that it is not important for the steering system to be correctly aligned before diagnosing tire problems. Technician B says that it is very important for the steering system to be correctly aligned before diagnosing tire problems. Who is right?
    a. A only
    b. B only
    c. Both A and B
    d. Neither A nor B

19. Technician A says that the tread bars are used to show that the tire is in balance. Technician B says that the tread bars are used to show out-of-round on the tire. Who is right?
    a. A only
    b. B only
    c. Both A and B
    d. Neither A nor B

20. Technician A says that the tire pressure need not be changed for colder or warmer climates. Technician B says that the tire pressure should be changed for colder or warmer climates. Who is right?
    a. A only
    b. B only
    c. Both A and B
    d. Neither A nor B

21. A vehicle has a shimmy in the front wheels. Technician A says the car needs to have the front wheel balanced. Technician B says that the rims should be checked for runout. Who is correct?
    a. A only
    b. B only
    c. Both A and B
    d. Neither A nor B

22. Technician A says that the tires need rotation after balancing. Technician B says that the tires need rotation after 100,000 miles. Who is correct?
    a. A only
    b. B only
    c. Both A and B
    d. Neither A nor B

23. Technician A says that the rims should be cleaned with a wire brush when the wheels are off. Technician B says that rubber compound should be applied to new tires before they are put on the rim. Who is correct?
    a. A only
    b. B only
    c. Both A and B
    d. Neither A nor B

24. A car has uneven wear on the tires. Technician A says to check the inflation pressure of the tires. Technician B says to check the power steering system. Who is correct?
    a. A only
    b. B only
    c. Both A and B
    d. Neither A nor B

Essay

25. List the parts of a tire and describe their purpose.

26. Describe at least three characteristics that tires are designed for.

27. Describe the difference between radial and bias tires.

28. Describe how tires are identified.

29. What is the purpose of a tire placard?

Short Answer

30. Tires are manufactured and designed for various characteristics including _____, _____, _____, _____, _____, and _____.

31. Which type of tire is designed for all of the above characteristics? _____

32. Three types of wheels made today are the _____, the _____, and the _____.

33. Uneven tire wear can be attributed to _____.

34. A shimmy in a moving vehicle is a sign of _____.

VEHICLE ACCESSORY SYSTEMS

CHAPTER 32

Air Conditioning Systems

INTRODUCTION   Many automobiles today have air conditioning. Air conditioning removes the warm air inside the passenger compartment to the outside. This chapter is about air conditioning principles and the parts necessary for air conditioning on cars.

OBJECTIVES   After reading this chapter, you should be able to:

- Identify the principles of air conditioning.
- Examine the heat and refrigerant flow of an air conditioning unit.
- Describe the purpose and operation of the common parts of an air conditioning system.
- Examine the environmental effects of using R-12 refrigerants.

- State the basic operation of computerized A/C systems.
- Identify various problems, diagnosis, and service procedures used with A/C systems.

✔ **SAFETY CHECKLIST** ✔

When working with air conditioning systems, keep these important safety precautions in mind.

✔ Never discharge any refrigerant into an enclosed area having an open flame.

✔ When removing the air compressor, be careful not to injure your hands and fingers.

✔ Always wear OSHA-approved safety glasses to prevent refrigerant R-12 from contacting the eyes.

✔ Refrigerant containers purchased on the market are under high pressure. Always handle these containers with care, and be careful not to drop the containers.

✔ Always use the correct tools when working on air conditioning systems.

32.1   AIR CONDITIONING PRINCIPLES

There are several principles that help to understand air conditioning. These principles deal with heat flow, refrigerant, pressure, vaporization, and condensation.

Purpose of Air Conditioning

During normal summer driving conditions, a great amount of heat enters the passenger compartment. This heat comes from the engine and from the sun or outside air temperature. Air conditioning (A/C) systems are designed to remove this excess heat so that passengers are comfortable. *Figure 32–1* shows an example of heat flow. Heat is admitted into the passenger compartment from outside. The heat is removed by forcing it to flow through a heat exchanger in the passenger compartment. A fluid then absorbs the heat and transfers it to a second heat exchanger outside the passenger compartment.

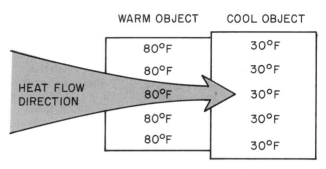

FIGURE 32–2. Heat always flows from a warmer to a colder object. Air conditioning systems are designed to cause air to flow internally from warmer to colder areas.

Heat Flow

An air conditioning system is designed to pump heat or Btus from one point to another. Heat can also be defined as Btu. Btu were discussed in Chapter 12. All materials or substances have heat in them down to –459 degrees F. At this temperature (absolute zero), there is no more heat. Also, heat always flows from a warmer to a colder object. For example, if one object were at 30 degrees F and another object were at 80 degrees F, heat would flow from the warmer object (80°F) to the colder object (30°F). The greater the temperature difference between the objects, the greater the amount of heat flowing. This is shown in *Figure 32–2*.

Heat Absorption

Objects can be in one of several forms. They can be in either a solid, a liquid, or a gas form. When objects change from one form to another, large amounts of heat can be transferred. For example, an ice cube is a solid form. When an ice cube melts, it absorbs a great amount of heat. In fact, all solids soak up huge amounts of heat without getting warmer when they change from a solid to a liquid.

The same thing happens when a liquid changes to a *vapor*. Large amounts of heat can be absorbed. For example, in *Figure 32–3* a tea kettle with a thermometer set inside is warmed. As the burner heats up the water, the temperature of the water starts to rise. It continues to rise until it has reached 212 degrees F. At this point, the temperature will stay at 212 degrees F even when additional heat is applied. The water is changing to a vapor and is soaking or absorbing large quantities of heat. Although this heat does not appear on the thermometer, it is there. It is called *latent heat*, or hidden heat.

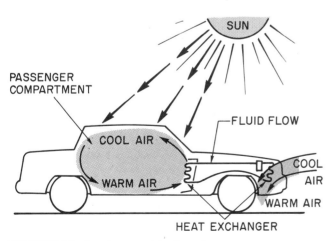

FIGURE 32–1. Heat inside the passenger compartment is sent through heat exchangers to the outside by use of a fluid.

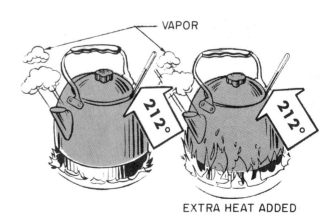

FIGURE 32–3. Heat is absorbed in large quantities when a liquid is changed to a vapor as in the boiling kettle of water. The water in the tea kettle will stay at 212 degrees F even if more heat is applied below the kettle. *(Courtesy of United Delco, Division of General Motors Corporation)*

Condensation

Condensation is the process of changing a vapor back to a liquid. Condensation is usually done by cooling the substance down, below its boiling point. All substances will condense at the same point at which they are boiled. When a vapor is condensed, the heat removed from it is exactly equal to the amount of heat necessary to make it a vapor in the first place.

Pressure and Boiling Points

Pressure also plays an important part in air conditioning. Pressure on a substance such as a liquid changes its boiling point. The greater the pressure on a liquid, the higher the boiling point. If a pressure is placed on a vapor, it will condense at a higher temperature. In addition, as the pressure on a substance is reduced, the boiling point can also be reduced. For example, the boiling point of water is 212 degrees F. The boiling point can be increased by increasing the pressure on the fluid. It can also be decreased by reducing the pressure or placing the fluid in a vacuum.

Pressure on a fluid will also concentrate any heat in the substance. As the pressure on a fluid is increased, the temperature of the fluid tends to increase. For example, refer to *Figure 32–4*. If 37 psi is exerted on a certain volume of vapor, the temperature of the vapor will be 40 degrees F. If the volume is reduced by increasing the pressure, say to 70 psi, the temperature of the vapor will be increased to 70 degrees F, without adding extra heat. This principle is also used in air conditioning systems.

Refrigerant-12 (R-12)

A *refrigerant* is used to transfer heat from the inside of the car to the outside. It is called R-12. This refrigerant has a boiling point of –21.7 degrees F. This means that it changes from a liquid to a vapor at –21.7 degrees F. If one were to place a flask of R-12 inside a refrigerator, it would boil and draw heat away from everything surrounding it. See *Figure 32–5*. If the refrigerant were then pumped outside (along with the heat it absorbed), the inside of the refrigerator would be cooler. Note that the boiling temperature of R-12 is too low to operate inside an air conditioning system. The boiling point in an air conditioning system is changed by altering the pressure of R-12. If the pressure is increased R-12 has a boiling point of from 30 to 60 degrees F. This is the most appropriate temperature range for freon to operate at.

Another important quality of R-12 is that it dissolves in oil. This quality is needed because R-12 circulates through the system with oil. Special oil is added to the air conditioning refrigerant to lubricate the compressor.

Refrigerant and the Environment

Over the past few years research has shown that freon is one of the major contributors to reducing the *ozone layer* above the earth. The ozone layer is a transparent shield of gases surrounding the earth. It protects the earth from harmful radiation from the sun. In addition, it helps keep the earth at an average temperature of 15 degrees C. When the ozone layer is reduced, increases of skin cancer result. Also, reducing the ozone layer causes global warming, known as the greenhouse effect.

The major greenhouse gases are carbon monoxide (CO_2), methane (CH_4), nitrous oxide (NO_2), and chlorofluorocarbons (*CFCs*). CFCs come from foams, aerosols, refrigerants, and solvents. Freon, a refrigerant, is classified as a chlorofluorocarbon, or CFC. In fact, R-12 is often referred to in the literature as CFC-12. R-12 is a major contributor to the greenhouse effect.

In 1987 many governments agreed to phase out, over a 10-year period, the use of products that produce CFCs. Thus, new types of refrigerants are being tested and considered to replace R-12.

One new type of refrigerant that will replace R-12 is called *HFC-134a* (hydrofluorocarbon-134a). This refrigerant will

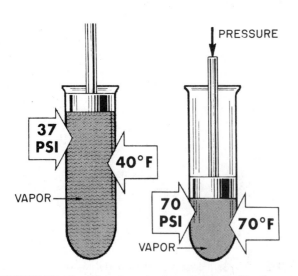

FIGURE 32–4. If a vapor is compressed with pressure from 37 to 70 psi, its temperature will increase from 40 degrees F to 70 degrees F. *(Courtesy of United Delco, Division of General Motors Corporation)*

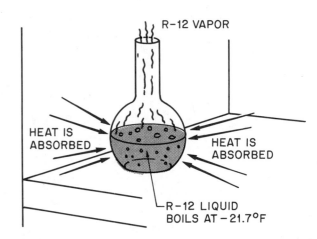

FIGURE 32–5. If R-12 were placed in a flask inside a refrigerator, it would boil at –21.7 degrees F, absorbing all heat surrounding it.

not harm the ozone layer as does R-12. This new refrigerant is also better for transferring heat. New types of oils are also being tested and are now available that can be mixed with the refrigerant. There are several drawbacks to using HFC-134a. Some include:

1. Certain design changes in air conditioning systems will have to be made to work with the new type of refrigerant.

2. The HFC-134a system is generally less efficient than R-12, and larger components will be required.

3. The refrigerant requires a different refrigerant oil and desiccant.

4. HFC-134a is not interchangeable with R-12. Different gauges, charging and recycling equipment, and tools for servicing air conditioning systems will have to be used.

Researchers are continuing to determine what health effects are produced by 134a. As more research and testing are completed all automotive air conditioning systems will eventually be designed to use HFC-134a or a similar refrigerant.

Recycling the Refrigerant

R-12 can be prevented from escaping into the atmosphere; it can be recovered using various recycling tools. One such system is called the air conditioning refrigerant recovery and recycling system *(ACR3)*. During the recovery phase, the ACR3 system pulls refrigerant from the automotive air conditioning system. During the recycling phase, the ACR3 system cleans and dries the refrigerant. After it has been recycled, the cleaned R-12 can be stored for use at a later date. *Figure 32–6* shows a typical ACR3 system. Note the refillable storage tank located on the back. Follow the manufacturer's procedure when using similar machines to recover and recycle R-12.

CAR CLINIC

PROBLEM: Musty Smell in Driver Compartment

A customer says that the interior of the car smells musty. Also, at times, when the air conditioning is turned on, the windows fog up. What is the problem?

SOLUTION:

In humid weather a great deal of moisture forms in the air conditioner evaporator. This moisture normally drains from the evaporator housing through tubes to the outside. If the water cannot drain, mold and mildew will form, causing an unpleasant odor. Make sure the evaporator housing drain is clear and water drips freely from the housing when the air conditioning is operating. Also make sure all hoses and tubes leading to the outside are clear of debris. The odor can be controlled by spraying a disinfectant or deodorant (available from most automotive parts stores) into the air intake in front of the windshield on most cars while the air conditioning is on.

32.2   REFRIGERATION CYCLE OPERATION

Basic Heat Transfer

Heat exchangers are used to transfer heat in an air conditioning unit. *Figure 32–7* shows how heat exchangers are used to pump heat from inside the car to the outside. When cool refrigerant is sent through the evaporator, which is located inside the passenger compartment, it cools the air

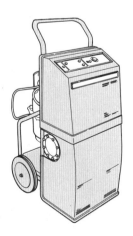
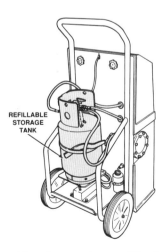

REFILLABLE STORAGE TANK

FIGURE 32–6. This machine is an air conditioning refrigerant recovery and recycling (ACR3) system. It is used to recover and recycle used R-12. *(Courtesy of General Motors Corporation)*

BASIC HEAT EXCHANGER

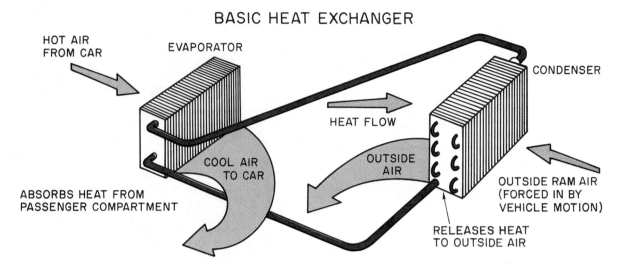

FIGURE 32-7.   Heat transfer in an air conditioning system is done by heat exchangers. The evaporator absorbs heat into a liquid refrigerant. The condenser gives off heat from the refrigerant.

passed over the evaporator fins. The refrigerant is boiling and vaporizes, absorbing the hot air from the car. The refrigerant vapor is then pumped outside the passenger compartment to a second heat exchanger. This one is called the condenser. Here, cooler outside air is forced through the fins on the condenser. The air is cooler than the refrigerant. Heat is now transferred from the refrigerant to the passing air, causing it to heat up. The heat in the car has essentially been pumped, via the refrigerant, from the inside to the outside of the car.

Purpose of Compressor

All automotive air conditioning systems have several major parts. These include the compressor, condenser, expan-

sion tube or expansion valve, and evaporator. *Figure 32–8* shows the flow inside an air conditioning system using all components.

The compressor is the heart of the air conditioning system. It has several purposes. First, the compressor is used to move the refrigerant. Second, the compressor is used to compress the refrigerant to change its boiling point. As the R-12 flows through other components, it undergoes various changes in pressure and temperature. These changes are required for proper heat transfer to take place.

The compressor is powered by the car engine, through a clutch turned by a belt. It has an intake side (suction) and a discharge side (exhaust). When the R-12 enters the compressor, it is a gas at low temperature and low pressure. When the R-12 leaves the compressor, it is still a gas but it is at a

BASIC SYSTEM SCHEMATIC

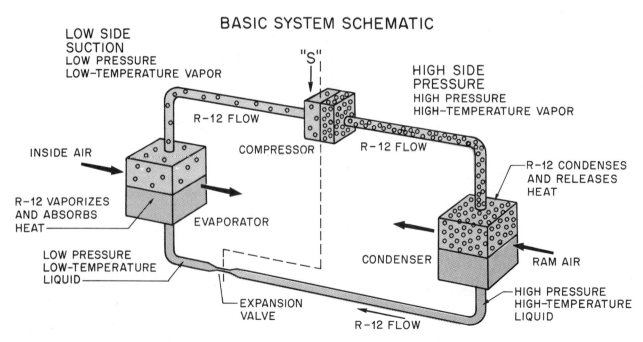

FIGURE 32-8.   This schematic shows how the temperature and pressure of the R-12 change throughout the air conditioning cycle.

very high pressure. Compressing the gas has also increased its temperature well above that of the outside air. The temperature of the gas must be higher than that of the outside air so that heat will flow in the correct direction, from inside the refrigerant to the outside air.

Purpose of Condenser

The *condenser* is basically a heat exchanger. It consists of a series of tubes and fins. As the hot R-12 gas flows through the tubes, it warms the fins. The fins provide enough surface area to transfer heat effectively. Heat transfer now takes place rapidly between the condenser and the outside air. During this rapid heat loss, R-12 is reduced in temperature below its boiling point. (Remember, the boiling point is well above –21.7 degrees F because the vapor has been pressurized.) R-12 now condenses back into a liquid. As R-12 exits the condenser, it is a liquid at high pressure and high temperature.

Purpose of Expansion Valve

Next the liquid R-12 flows through an *expansion valve*. This valve is a restriction in the R-12 flow. As a hot liquid R-12 enters the valve, the restriction causes the pressure to build up behind it. As the liquid passes through the valve, there is a large pressure drop. This pressure drop changes the boiling point of the R-12. Now the R-12 is at a condition where it is ready to boil or evaporate just before it enters the evaporator.

Purpose of Evaporator

The *evaporator* is another version of a heat exchanger. In the evaporator the heat is transferred from the passenger compartment air to the liquid refrigerant. Since the R-12 entering the evaporator is at a lower temperature, it makes the evaporator fins "cold." Thus, warm car air circulating around the cold fins releases heat into the evaporator. As the

heat is applied to the refrigerant, the R-12 boils and changes to a vapor again. As it boils (just like the tea kettle earlier), it is able to absorb huge quantities of heat. The result is a rapid heat loss in the inside passenger air. When the R-12 exits the evaporator, it is once again a gas, at low temperature and low pressure. The system then continues to recycle back to the compressor, repeating the cycle.

High Side and Low Side

Every air conditioner has two sides. There is a high side and a low side. The high side is that portion of the system where the R-12 is at high pressure. The low side is that portion of the system where the R-12 is at low pressure. A dotted line is used in Figure 32–8 to show the dividing line between the high and low pressures. The high side includes the system between the discharge end of the compressor and the restriction of the expansion valve. It includes the condenser. The low side includes the portion from the restriction or expansion valve, through the evaporator, to the intake end of the compressor.

32.3   SYSTEM VARIATIONS

All air conditioning systems use the basic components that were just explained. In addition, several other components are integrated into every system to keep it working properly. These components and their location make up the basic differences between one air conditioning system and another.

Accumulator Orifice Tube System

The accumulator orifice tube system uses an additional *accumulator* and a tube for the expansion valve. The accumulator is located between the output of the evaporator and the input of the compressor. See *Figure 32–9*. The accumu-

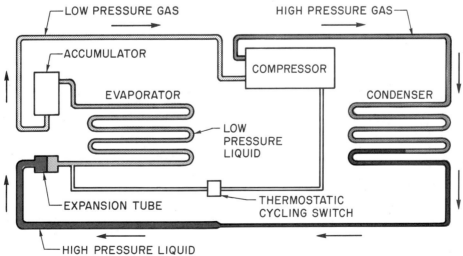

FIGURE 32–9.   An accumulator is used on some air conditioning systems to collect excess refrigerant and filter the refrigerant.

lator performs several vital functions in the air conditioning system.

1. It collects excess R-12 liquid, permitting only R-12 gas to enter the compressor.

2. It contains a filtering element with a built-in *desiccant* (moisture-absorbing material) that helps to reduce moisture from the R-12.

3. It contains a filter screen that traps any foreign matter before it can reach the compressor.

In addition, this system uses an orifice tube as the expansion valve. It is used to create the pressure drop needed just before the R-12 enters the evaporator.

Cycling Clutch System

Another type of air conditioning system uses a receiver-filter-dryer along with a thermostatically controlled clutch. The receiver-filter-dryer is much the same as the accumulator in the preceding system. It is located on the high side of systems. See *Figure 32–10*. In addition to performing filtration and moisture removal, it acts as a reservoir, storing any excess R-12 in the system.

This system also uses an expansion valve rather than an expansion tube to create the required pressure drop. In this system, the expansion valve controls the flow of R-12 entering the evaporator. This metering function is achieved by a sensing bulb. The sensing bulb measures the temperature of the R-12 leaving the evaporator. In turn, on the basis of this temperature, it changes the expansion valve opening to increase or decrease the flow rate.

This system also uses a compressor clutch. The compressor clutch transmits power from the car engine to the compressor. It is turned off and on by a magnetic coil. The magnetic coil is operated by another electrical circuit. The cycling clutch system engages or disengages the compressor according to the demands of the system. The cycle is controlled by a thermostatic switch that senses the temperature at the evaporator. A pressure-sensing switch is used on some models, rather than a temperature-sensing switch.

Control Valve System

Certain air conditioning systems use valves to control the operation of the air conditioning unit. *Figure 32–11* shows a typical control valve system. This system uses a noncycling clutch. The compressor operates continuously. Control devices are used to adjust the temperature, pressure, and flow rate of the R-12 to maintain the required cooling rate. Several control valves are used. At times, as the pressure changes inside the evaporator, it has a tendency to reduce the temperature and freeze up. (The evaporator pressure directly controls the evaporator temperature.) The control valve operates to keep the pressure at a predetermined pressure.

In this system, a POA (pilot-operated absolute) valve or an STV (suction throttling valve) can be used. In addition, an EPR (evaporator pressure regulator) could be used. The valve used depends on the vehicle manufacturer. The control valve opens and closes to regulate the flow of R-12. Controlling the pressure also controls the temperature of the R-12, to slightly above 32 degrees F, as it exits the evaporator.

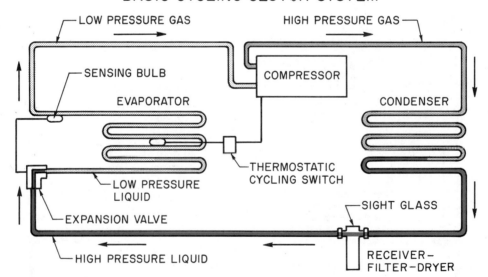

FIGURE 32–10. Certain air conditioning systems use a receiver-filter-dryer. This device is placed on the high side of the system and is used to filter, remove moisture from, and act as a reservoir for R-12. A cycling clutch is also used on this system to turn the compressor off and on.

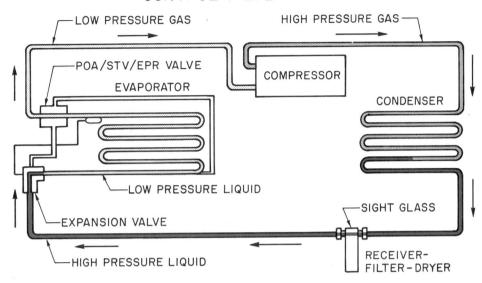

FIGURE 32–11.   Some air conditioning systems use several control valves to operate the system. Either a POA (pilot-operated absolute) valve or an STV (suction throttling valve) is used in this system.

CAR CLINIC

PROBLEM: A/C Blows Out Warm Air

The customer complains that the air conditioner works fine when the vehicle is first started in the morning. However, after about 5–10 minutes of driving, warm air begins to blow out of the vents.

SOLUTION:

This type of problem could be produced by many defective parts. One easy component to check is the temperature control door. This door adjusts to control either warm air from the cooling system or cold air from the air conditioning system. If this door is out of adjustment, it may be allowing warm air from the heater to be distributed in the passenger compartment. The warm air would come into the car after the engine was heated to operating temperature, after about 5–10 minutes. Check the service manual for the correct procedure to adjust the cable. Adjusting the cable may solve the problem easily.

On some vehicles the door may be controlled by either vacuum or electric motors. These motors can also become defective and cause the same problem. Check the condition of the vacuum and electric motors, if they are used. If the problem is still not solved, further diagnostic procedures will have to be completed.

32.4   AIR CONDITIONING PARTS

Once the cycle of operation is understood, each component can be analyzed as to its design and function. This section analyzes the internal operation of several air conditioning components.

Suction Throttling Valve (STV)

Figure 32–12 shows the suction throttling valve (STV). This valve is used to determine the temperature of the evaporator core by controlling the evaporator pressure. In this manner, the valve protects the core against freeze-up. Freeze-up could result in partial or complete loss of cooling capacity.

The valve, which is located in the evaporator outlet line, operates on a spring pressure versus evaporator pressure principle. R-12 vapor flows through the valve inlet. The vapor pressure works against the piston. The piston then pushes against the diaphragm. The spring pressure pushes against the other side of the piston and diaphragm. Evaporator pressure is now working against spring pressure. Any increase in temperature, and thus pressure of R-12, will push the piston to the left, against the spring pressure. This action opens the valve and allows an increase in the amount of vapor flowing to the compressor. In turn, the evaporator pressure will lower and allow the piston to close. The evaporator pressure, and thus the temperature, is controlled to a predetermined setting, with a "throttling" effect.

The temperature lever on the dash may be moved to mix heated air with the maximum cooled air. This will temper

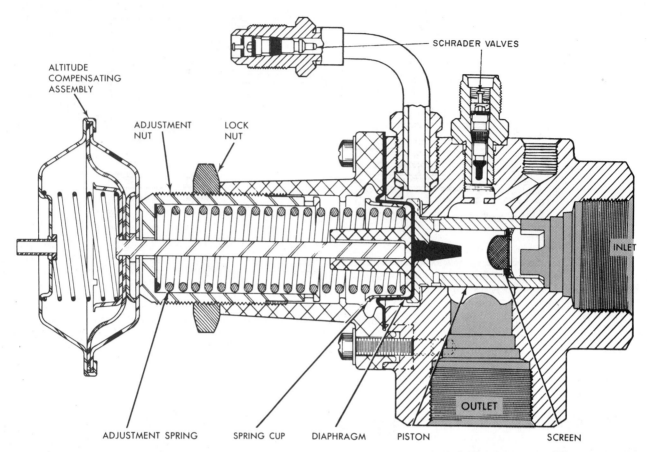

FIGURE 32–12. A suction throttling valve is used to control the temperature and pressure of the R-12. *(Courtesy of United Delco, Division of General Motors Corporation)*

the outlet air to a desired temperature. Any movement on the lever also controls a vacuum valve that sends a vacuum to the altitude compensating assembly shown on the STV. Loss of vacuum at this point causes the internal spring pressure to be increased. Now the minimum evaporator pressure will increase. This increase results in less evaporator cooling capacity. This feature guards against evaporator freeze-up when operating at higher elevations. Two other ports that have *Schrader valves* are also used. The Schrader valve is a spring loaded valve similar to a tire valve. One is used to obtain a system pressure, while the other is used to connect to the oil bypass line from the bottom of the evaporator.

Pilot-operated Absolute (POA) Valve

The function of the POA valve is to control the evaporator pressure. See *Figure 32–13*. This is done much the same way as the STV, by restricting the evaporator outlet. Although the end result is the same, this system uses a pilot valve and a bellows to control the pressure. In operation, evaporator pressure is forced into (A) against the piston. The piston is held in place by the piston spring pressure. When evaporator pressure gets too high, the piston slowly lifts and allows evaporator pressure to pass through (B) to the outlet. During this time, evaporator pressure also flows through the piston bleed hole into area (C) and finally to the bellows area (D).

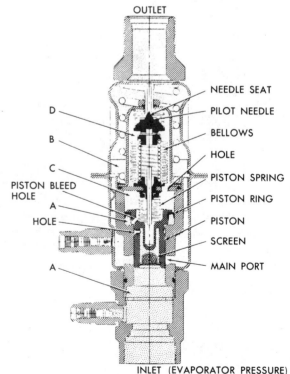

FIGURE 32–13. A pilot-operated absolute valve is used to accurately control the evaporator pressure. This is done by using a series of bleed holes, bellows, and a needle valve. *(Courtesy of United Delco, Division of General Motors Corporation)*

The bellows position controls a needle valve. In operation, the assembly balances out the internal pressures to maintain a predetermined, accurate evaporator pressure. In turn, evaporator temperature will be controlled.

Evaporator Pressure Regulator (EPR) Valve

The main function of the evaporator pressure regulator (EPR) valve is to keep the evaporator pressure low enough to prevent moisture on the evaporator core from freezing. At the same time, it also provides maximum cooling efficiency.

The EPR valve is installed on the suction passage of the compressor. The valve is operated by a gas-filled bellows. As long as the evaporator pressure is above a certain psi, it works against a diaphragm to compress a spring and hold the valve open. When the pressure drops below a certain point, the valve tends to close. When the valve closes evaporator pressure, and thus evaporator temperature, increases (preventing evaporator core freeze-up).

Compressors

Many compressors are used in automotive air conditioning systems. The compressor is located in the engine compartment. Its purpose is to draw low-pressure vapor from the evaporator and compress this vapor into a high-temperature, high-pressure vapor. It is also used to circulate the R-12 throughout the system. The compressor is belt-driven by the engine crankshaft.

There are many types of compressors. One type of compressor works on a *swash plate* pump arrangement. As shown in *Figure 32–14*, the swash plate is attached to the center shaft at an angle. As the center shaft turns, the swash plate also turns. This action causes six small pistons attached to the swash plate to move back and forth. The pistons are attached to the swash plate by large ball bearings. A suction and a pressure are created on the ends of the pistons. A reed valve is used to control the direction of the suction and pressure. An oil pump provides oil pressure to the moving parts.

Compressor Clutch

In all air conditioning systems, the compressor is equipped with an electromagnetic clutch as part of the pulley. It is designed to engage and disengage the pulley to the compressor. Figure 32–14 shows an electromagnetic clutch attached to the compressor. The clutch is engaged by a magnetic field. It is disengaged by springs when the magnetic field is broken. When the controls call for compressor operation, the electrical circuit to the clutch is energized. The pulleys are connected to the compressor shaft. *Figure 32–15* shows the main parts in an electromagnetic compressor clutch.

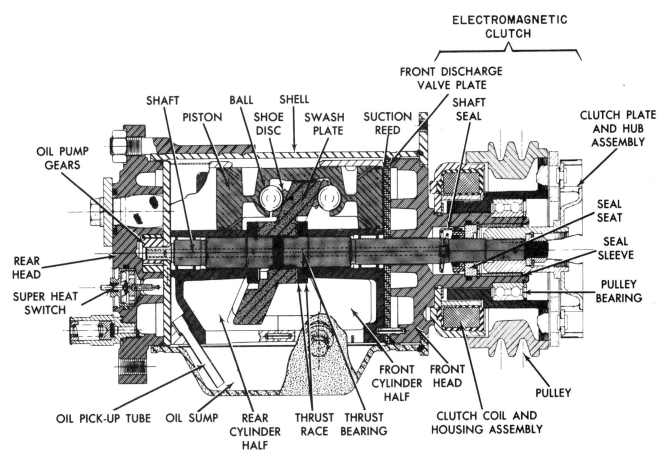

FIGURE 32–14. The compressor in an air conditioning system uses a swash plate pump arrangement to move six pistons back and forth. The piston movement produces a suction and a pressure to control the flow of R-12. *(Courtesy of United Delco, Division of General Motors Corporation)*

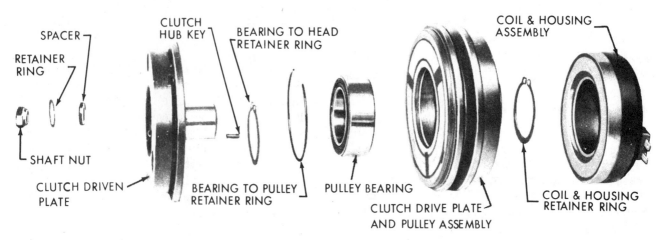

FIGURE 32–15. The main parts of the electromagnetic compressor clutch. When engaged, the drive plate and pulley assembly are forced by magnetism to work against the clutch driven plate. The driven plate drives the compressor main shaft. *(Courtesy of United Delco, Division of General Motors Corporation)*

Receiver-Dehydrator

The receiver-dehydrator (dryer) shown in **Figure 32–16** is a storage tank for liquid refrigerant. R-12 flows from the condenser into the tank. Here a bag of desiccant (moisture-absorbing material) removes moisture from the R-12. The R-12 then flows through a filter screen into the outlet. A sight glass is generally located on the top of the unit. The sight glass shows if there is enough refrigerant in the system. Some sight glasses are located directly in the line from the condenser.

Thermostatic Expansion Valve

The thermostatic expansion valve controls the supply of liquid R-12 to the evaporator. The valve could be considered a variable expansion valve. As shown in **Figure 32–17**, it is controlled by two opposing forces. A spring pressure works against the power element pressure on a diaphragm. The balance between these two forces positions the seat and orifice

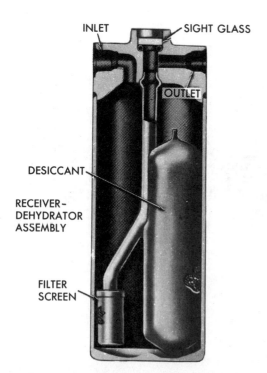

FIGURE 32–16. The receiver-dehydrator assembly is used to filter and remove moisture from the R-12. The desiccant is the moisture-absorbing material. *(Courtesy of United Delco, Division of General Motors Corporation)*

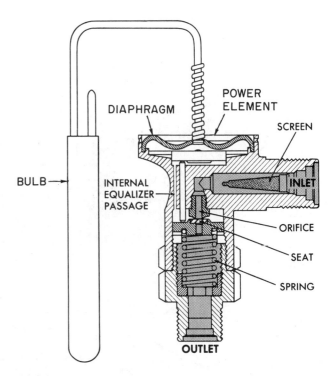

FIGURE 32–17. A thermostatic expansion valve is used to control the size of the expansion valve. The temperature of the evaporator outlet is sensed by the bulb. This causes the power element to move. The pressure from the power element against the spring pressure sets the correct size. *(Courtesy of United Delco, Division of General Motors Corporation)*

to a certain size expansion valve. The power element is sensing the temperature of the evaporator outlet.

In operation, a decrease in the temperature of the evaporator outlet lowers the bulb temperature. When the bulb temperature decreases, the pressure in the power element is reduced. This lower pressure causes the seat to move closer to the orifice, restricting the flow of R-12 to the evaporator. The operation is reversed when the evaporator temperature increases.

Thermostatic Switch

The *thermostatic switch* is used to cycle the electromagnetic clutch off and on. This switch senses evaporator temperature. See *Figure 32–18*. The opening and closing of the internal contacts cycle the compressor. When the temperature of the evaporator approaches the freezing point, the thermostatic switch opens. This action disengages the compressor clutch. The compressor remains off until the evaporator temperature rises to a preset temperature. At this temperature, the switch closes, and the compressor resumes operation.

Ambient Switch

The *ambient* switch is used to sense outside air temperature. It is designed to prevent compressor clutch engagement when the air conditioning is not required. The switch is in series with the electromagnetic compressor clutch.

Thermal Limiter and Superheat Switch

The thermal limiter and superheat switch are designed to protect the air conditioning compressor against damage when the refrigerant is partially or totally lost. During this condition, the superheat switch heats up a resistor to melt a fuse in the thermal switch. The compressor ceases to operate and is protected from damage.

Low-Pressure Cut-off Switch

The low-pressure cut-off switch is located on the pressure side of the compressor. If low pressure is sensed, the switch opens a set of contact points. The electromagnetic clutch is now inoperative.

Water Control Valve

A water control valve is used in many air conditioning systems. See *Figure 32–19*. Its function is to regulate the flow of engine coolant to the heater core. On most vehicles, the water valve is closed when the air conditioning controls are set at maximum cooling.

Muffler

A muffler, *Figure 32–20*, is used to reduce the compressor noise. It is located on the discharge side of the compressor. A complete air conditioning system, with the location of several common parts highlighted, is shown in *Figure 32–21*.

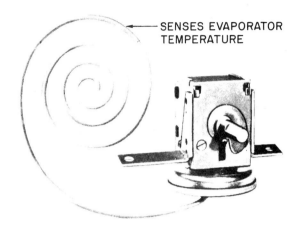

FIGURE 32–18. A thermostatic switch is used to cycle the clutch system on and off. *(Courtesy of United Delco, Division of General Motors Corporation)*

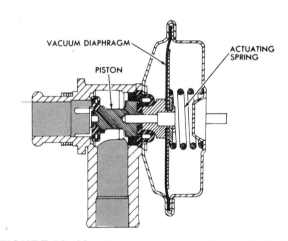

FIGURE 32–19. On some cars a water control valve is used to regulate the flow of engine coolant to the heater core during air conditioning. *(Courtesy of United Delco, Division of General Motors Corporation)*

FIGURE 32–20. A muffler is used on air conditioning systems to reduce the noise of the compressor. *(Courtesy of United Delco, Division of General Motors Corporation)*

Electronic Temperature Control Air Conditioning Systems

Computers can be used to control the air conditioning and heating system. It would be impossible to describe each of the many systems used on automobiles today. However, most electronic temperature control air conditioning systems

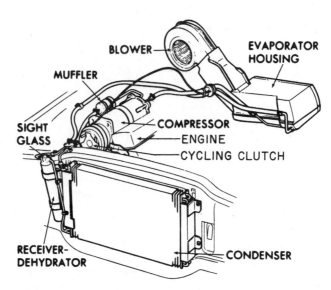

FIGURE 32–21. The parts of the air conditioning system and their locations. *(Courtesy of United Delco, Division of General Motors Corporation)*

have certain common components and operations. *Figure 32–22* shows a diagram of how the air control module (*ACM*) works. The ACM is an electronic module in the vehicle that uses several inputs to control various outputs. It is generally located immediately behind the heating and air conditioning

controls on the dashboard. Note that the ACM controls the compressor clutch (AC clutch). When the clutch is turned off and on by the ACM, the air conditioning system is controlled. The result is that the air in the vehicle can be monitored and controlled by the ACM. Many other electronic

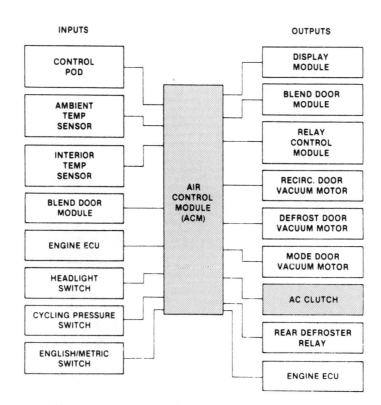

FIGURE 32–22. Automotive air conditioning systems use computers for control. Note that one output is the compressor clutch being turned off and on. *(Courtesy of Motor Publications, Air Conditioning and Heating Manual)*

circuits are used with air conditioning systems. For example, they are used to

- control blower speeds,

- operate blend doors to mix the cool and warm air,

- turn defrost systems off and on,

- operate floor and panel doors, and

- operate cooling and engine coolant fans at different times and speeds.

Figure 32–23, for example, shows an electronic circuit for controlling a two-speed coolant fan on an air conditioning system. For low-speed operation, the low-speed coolant fan relay is operated by the ECM. The fan is turned on when the:

1. coolant temperature exceeds 213 degrees F,

2. vehicle speed exceeds 47 mph, or

3. A/C compressor is in operation.

With the low-speed coolant fan relay energized, power comes through the low-speed switch, through a coolant fan resistor, and into the coolant fan. The resistor reduces voltage, causing the coolant fan to run at low speed.

For high-speed operation, the high-speed coolant fan relay is operated by the ECM. The fan is turned on when the:

1. coolant temperature exceeds 226 degrees F, and

2. A/C coolant fan pressure switch reads 275 psi or higher.

During high-speed operation, the resistor is bypassed. The result is that higher voltage is available at the fan for high speed.

Numerous other electronic circuits are used in air conditioning systems. For complete descriptions of other electronic temperature control circuits, refer to the manufacturer's service manual.

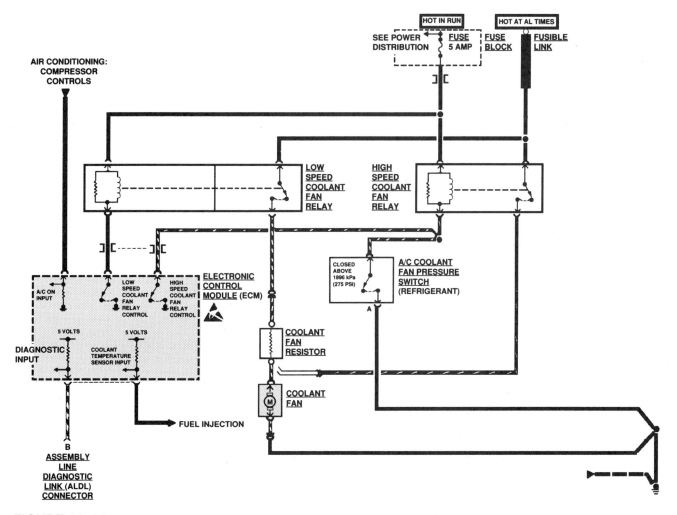

FIGURE 32–23. The ECM is used to control the low- and high-speed coolant fan on air conditioning systems. *(Courtesy of General Motors Corporation)*

Problems, Diagnosis and Service

PROBLEM: Lack of Cold Air

A vehicle with an air conditioning system is not producing cold air at the dashboard outlets.

DIAGNOSIS

Various general diagnostic checks can be performed on air conditioning systems to solve for similar problems.

1. Check the outer surfaces of the radiator and condenser to make sure that airflow is not blocked by dirt, leaves, or other foreign material. Check between the condenser and radiator for foreign material and check the outer surfaces.

2. Check for restrictions or kinks in the evaporator core, condenser core, refrigerant hoses and tubes.

3. Check for refrigerant leaks. It is customary to leak-check the refrigerant system whenever similar problems are encountered. *Figure 32–24* shows a propane leak detector. The tube is placed where there is a suspected leak. Refrigerant gas drawn into the sampling tube attached to the torch causes the torch flame to change color in proportion to the size of the leak.

4. *Figure 32–25* shows an electronic leak detector. This tester is used in areas that are hard to see or inaccessible.

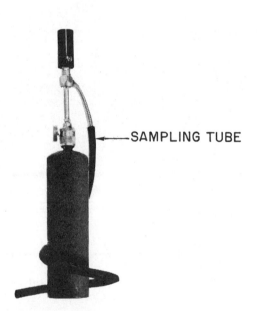

— SAMPLING TUBE

FIGURE 32–24. A propane leak detector can be used to check for refrigerant leaks. Any refrigerant gas drawn into the sampling tube will cause the torch flame to change colors. *(Courtesy of United Delco, Division of General Motors Corporation)*

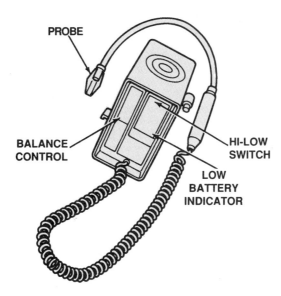

FIGURE 32–25. This electronic leak detector can be used in areas that are inaccessible or are hard to see. *(Courtesy of General Motors Corporation)*

CAUTION: Be careful not to inhale the gas (phosgene gas) produced by this process. It is very dangerous.

Always follow the manufacturer's instructions regarding calibration, operation, and maintenance of this detector.

5. Check all air ducts for leaks or restrictions. Low air flow may indicate a restricted evaporator.

6. Check for proper drive belt tension.

7. Check the air discharge temperature and compare it with the manufacturer's specifications.

8. One common cause for lack of cold air is insufficient refrigerant. At temperatures higher than 70 degrees F, insufficient refrigerant can be observed by viewing a sight glass. The sight glass is usually located in the top of the receiver-dehydrator. *Figure 32–26* shows the location of the sight glass. A shortage of liquid refrigerant is indicated after about 5 minutes of compressor operation by the appearance of slow-moving bubbles (vapor) in the line. A broken column of refrigerant may appear in the glass, indicating insufficient charge. *Figure 32–27* shows a diagnosis chart for the sight glass check.

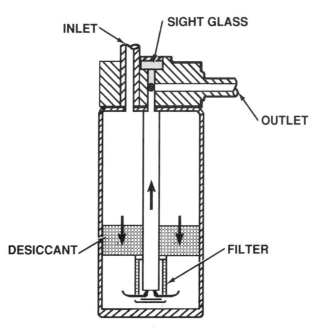

FIGURE 32–26. The sight glass on top of the dehydrator can help to diagnose insufficient refrigerant in the system. *(Courtesy of General Motors Corporation)*

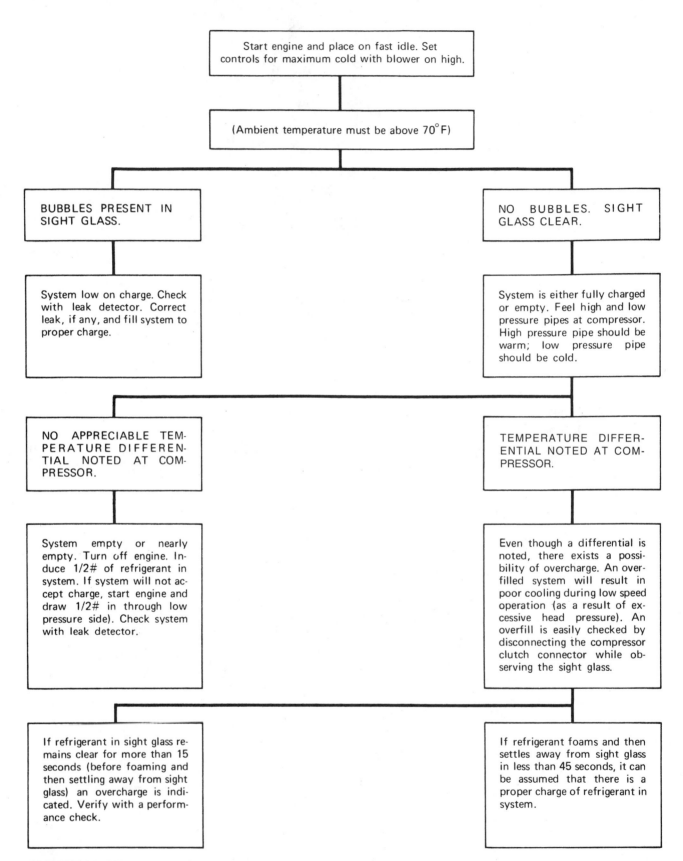

FIGURE 32–27. This diagnosis chart can be used to troubleshoot the air conditioning system by starting with the sight glass. *(Courtesy of United Delco, Division of General Motors Corporation)*

SERVICE

If it has been determined that there is insufficient refrigerant, the system will need to be recharged, Typically a manifold gauge set, shown in *Figure 32–28*, is used for charging, discharging, evacuating, and diagnosing trouble in the air conditioning system. The left gauge measures the low side, the right gauge the high side. The center manifold is common to both sides and is used for evacuating or adding refrigerant to the system. *Figure 32–29* shows one of several hookups for charging the air conditioning system refrigerant. The following general procedure is used to charge the refrigerant:

1. With the A/C mode control lever OFF, start the engine and bring to operating temperature.

2. Invert the R-12 drum, open the valve and allow 1 pound of refrigerant to flow into the system through the low-side service fitting.

3. After the refrigerant has entered the system, immediately engage the compressor by setting the A/C control heat to NORM and the blower speed to high. The remainder of the refrigerant charge is now being brought into the system.

4. Turn off the R-12 valve, and run the engine for 30 seconds to clear the lines and gauges.

5. With the engine running, remove the low-side charging hose adapter from the accumulator service fitting. Unscrew the adapter rapidly to avoid excessive R-12 loss.

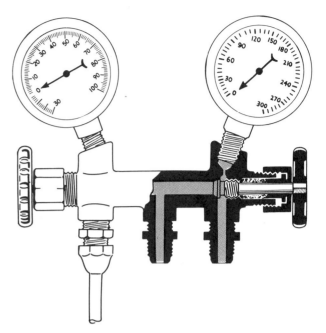

FIGURE 32–28. A manifold gauge set is used to check air conditioning system pressures, to help charge and discharge the system, and to evacuate the system. *(Courtesy of United Delco, Division of General Motors Corporation)*

6. Replace the protective cap on the accumulator service fitting.

7. Turn the engine off.

8. Leak-check the system, and test the air temperature at the dash panel.

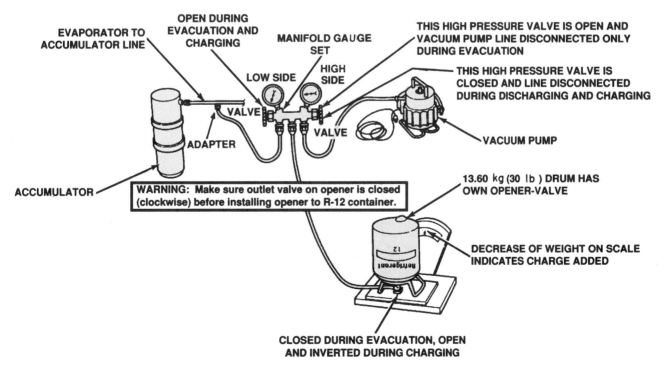

FIGURE 32–29. This schematic shows the hook-up between the manifold gauge set and the A/C components for charging the system. *(Courtesy of General Motors Corporation)*

PROBLEM: **Faulty Air Conditioning Components**

The air conditioner does not work.

DIAGNOSIS

Many components in an air conditioning system can fail. Air conditioning systems vary widely from vehicle to vehicle. Because of this variation, no universal or standard diagnostic procedure exists. However, the following diagnostic checks are common to most systems.

Compressor/Clutch Diagnosis

1. The most common reasons for a compressor failure are inadequate lubrication and contamination. Proper lubrication is critical to correct compressor operation. Contamination usually comes from having moisture in the R-12. Whenever an air conditioning system is open to the atmosphere, it will absorb moisture from the air. All moisture must then be evacuated from the system, and the system must be recharged. Evacuation and recharging are done using the manifold gauge set discussed previously. Follow the procedure listed in the service manual for evacuating and charging the air conditioning system.

CAUTION: Be careful not to touch the R-12 or get refrigerant in your eyes.

Compressor malfunctions appear in one of four ways: noise, seizure, leakage, or low inlet and discharge pressure.

2. *Figure 32–30* shows an example of a diagnosis chart for troubleshooting a compressor that is not engaging or not operating. Many other diagnosis charts are available. Refer to the manufacturer's service manuals for more diagnosis charts.

3. On certain types of air conditioning compressors, the oil of the compressor must be checked periodically. *Figure 32–31* shows how a dipstick is placed in the compressor to correctly check the oil.

4. Problems with the compressor clutch can usually be traced to the compressor. A worn or poorly lubricated compressor will put a strain on the clutch. Low voltage can also cause damage to the compressor clutch.

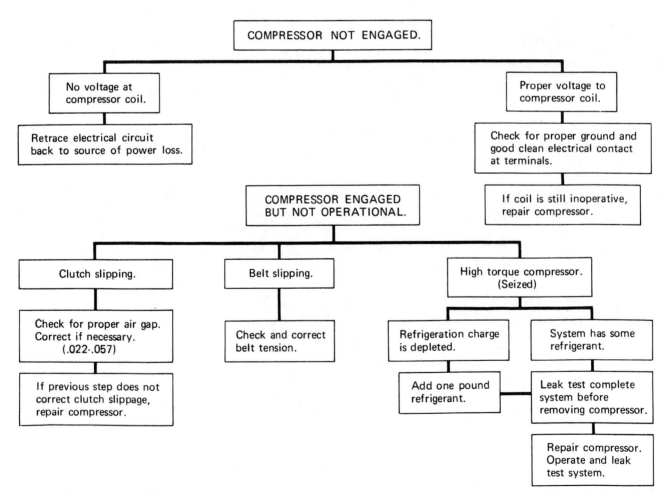

FIGURE 32–30.   If the compressor is not operating or engaging, follow this diagnosis chart to determine the problem. *(Courtesy of United Delco, Division of General Motors Corporation)*

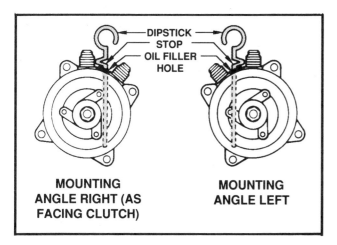

FIGURE 32–31. Some A/C compressors use a dipstick to check the oil inside the compressor. *(Courtesy of General Motors Corporation)*

Diagnosis of Other A/C Components

1. When the *evaporator* is defective, the trouble shows up as an inadequate supply of cool air. A core partially plugged by dirt, a cracked case, a leaking seal, or leaks on the bottom, are generally the cause. Evaporator leaks are mostly the result of pinhole leaks that develop in the bottom section from corrosion. Corrosion will result if moisture enters the system and mixes with the R-12. External corrosion can be caused by atmospheric moisture, especially in areas that have high salt conditions.

2. The *condenser* may malfunction in two ways: it may leak refrigerant, or it may be restricted. Check as previously described.

3. The *receiver-dehydrator* (dryer) may fail because of a restriction inside the body. High pressures on the pressure side indicate a restriction at that point. Also, receiver-dehydrators frequently need to be replaced. These units become used up in normal service. The desiccant becomes saturated with absorbed moisture.

4. The *thermostatic switch* may fail and cause the compressor to run continuously or to shut off completely. Either may cause the evaporator to freeze up. Check the switch for correct adjustment according to the manufacturer's service manual.

5. There may be a *suction throttling valve* (STV) on some older vehicles. The suction throttling valve may need adjustment. It must keep the evaporator pressure above 29–30 psi. If the pressure falls below the specifications, the evaporator core may freeze up.

6. *Expansion valve* failures are usually indicated by low suction and discharge pressure and insufficient cooling.

7. *Figure 32–32* shows a typical A/C system diagnosis chart to help solve many of the problems found in air conditioning systems.

SERVICE

Most of the service for each of the above components is involved with cleaning or removal and replacement. The simplest and most effective cure for surface contamination is flushing the system with water. Flushing will remove debris and corrosive materials. Additional service includes discharging, evacuating, and recharging the system. Follow the manufacturer's service manual for each service needed.

SERVICE MANUAL CONNECTION

There are many important specifications to keep in mind when working with air conditioning systems. To identify the specifications for your vehicle, you will need to know the VIN (vehicle identification number) of the vehicle, the type and year of the vehicle, and the type of engine used. Although they may be titled differently, some of the more common air conditioning system specifications (not all) found in service manuals are listed below. Note that these are typical examples. Each vehicle may have different specifications.

Common Specification	Typical Example
A/C compressor belt tension (pounds on suitable belt tension gauge)	115 newtons
Compressor air gap	0.015–0.025 inch
Compressor discharge pressure	140–210 psig
Discharge air temperature on panel	35–46 degrees F
Evaporator suction (low-pressure side) pressure	18–21 psig
Refrigerant capacity	2.5 lb
Refrigerant oil viscosity	500
Total system capacity	8 ounces

In addition, the service manual will give specific directions for various service and testing procedures. Some of the more common procedures include:

- Accumulator replace
- Charging the air conditioning system
- Checking compressor oil level
- Condenser replace
- Discharging and evacuating system
- Leak tests
- Oil charging
- Performance test

A/C DIAGNOSIS		
CONDITION	**PROBABLE CAUSE**	**CORRECTION**
No cooling blower does not operate	Gas fuse blown Fuse link blown Heater fuse blown Blower motor faulty Blower resistor faulty Blower switch faulty Wiring or ground faulty	Replace fuse and check for short Replace fuse link and check for short Replace fuse and check for short Check blower motor Check blower resistor Check blower switch Repair as necessary
Magnetic clutch does not engage	Fuse link blown Magnet clutch relay faulty Magnet clutch faulty A/C fuse faulty ECM fuse faulty Thermistor faulty A/C amplifier faulty Pressure switch faulty Wiring or ground faulty Refrigerant empty	Replace fuse link and check for short Check relay Check magnetic clutch Replace fuse and check for short Replace fuse and check for short Check thermistor Check amplifier Check switch Repair as necessary Check refrigerant pressure
Compressor does not rotate properly	Drive belt loose or broken Compressor faulty	Adjust or replace drive belt Replace compressor
Insufficient cooling	Condenser clogged Drive belt slipping Magnetic clutch faulty Compressor faulty Expansion valve faulty Thermistor faulty A/C amplifier faulty Insufficient or too much refrigerant Air or excessive compressor oil in refrigeration system Receiver/clogged	Check condenser Check or replace drive belt Check magnetic clutch Check compressor Check expansion valve Check thermistor Check amplifier Check refrigerant charge Evacuate and charge refrigeration system Check receiver
Bubbles present in sight gas	Insufficient refrigerant	Check for leak with gas leak detector
No bubbles present in sight gas	Empty or too much refrigerant	Evacuate and charge system. Then check for leaks with gas leak detectors
No temperature difference between compressor inlet and outlet	Empty or nearly empty refrigerant gone or nearly gone	Evacuate and charge system. Then check for leaks with gas leak detector
Temperature between compressor inlet and outlet is noticeably different	Too much refrigerant	Discharge excess refrigerant to specified amount
Immediately after air conditioner is turned off, refrigerant in sight glass stays clear	Too much refrigerant	Discharge excess refrigerant to specified amount
When air conditioner is turned off, refrigerant foams and then stays clear	Empty or too much refrigerant	Evacuate and charge system. Then check for leaks with gas leak detector
Insufficient velocity of cool air	Evaporator clogged or frosted Air leakage from cooling unit or air duct Air inlet blocked Blower motor faulty A/C amplifier faulty	Clean evaporator fins or filters Repair as necessary Repair as necessary Replace blower motor Check amplifier
A/C switch indicator flashing	Drive belt slipping A/C amplifier faulty	Check or replace drive belt Check amplifier
Cool air comes intermittently	Magnetic clutch slipping Expansion valve faulty Excessive moisture in the system A/C amplifier faulty Wiring connection faulty	Check magnetic clutch Check expansion valve Evacuate and charge system Check amplifier Repair as necessary
Cool air comes out only at high speeds	Condenser clogged Drive belt slipping Insufficient or too much refrigerant Air in refrigeration system Expansion valve faulty Leak in system	Check condenser Check or replace drive belt Check refrigerant charge Evacuate and charge refrigeration system Check expansion valve Leak test system

FIGURE 32–32. Use this diagnosis chart to help determine the condition, possible cause, and correction for most A/C problems. *(Courtesy of General Motors Corporation)*

Linkage to Science and Mathematics

SCIENTIFIC PRINCIPLES OF AIR CONDITIONING

Air conditioning systems are designed around several scientific and physical principles about heat, gases, and pressures.

Heat

- Heat always flows from an area of higher temperature to an area of lower temperature.

- The greater the temperature differential, the faster heat flows.

- Heat continues to flow until the two temperatures are equal.

Liquids and Gases

- A specific amount of heat must be absorbed into the liquid to change liquid to a gas, or vapor.

Pressure and Temperature Relationship of Heat and Gases

- If a pressure acting on a liquid is increased, the boiling point of the liquid increases.

- If a pressure acting on a liquid is decreased, the boiling point of the liquid decreases.

Pressure Temperature Relationship of Refrigerants

- For every pressure increase in a refrigerant, a corresponding temperature increase will occur. See the table.

Because of these laws, performance pressures in air conditioning systems will change at different temperatures. In service manuals for air conditioning systems, pressures are always given for at least five different ambient (outdoor) temperatures. *(Courtesy of General Motors Corporation)*

°F	Pounds of Pressure
− 40	11.0*
− 35	8.3*
− 30	5.5*
− 25	2.3*
− 20	0.6*
− 15	2.4
− 10	4.5
− 5	6.8
− 0	9.2
5	11.8
10	14.7
15	17.7
20	21.1
25	24.6
30	28.5
32	30.1
35	32.6
40	37.0
45	41.7
50	46.7
55	52.0
60	57.7
65	63.7
70	70.1
75	76.9
80	84.1
85	91.7
90	99.6
95	108.1
100	116.9
105	126.2
110	136.0
115	146.5
120	157.1
125	167.5
130	179.0
140	204.5
150	232.0

* Inches of Vacuum

SUMMARY

The purpose of this chapter was to discuss and explain the operation of air conditioning systems used in automobiles. When heat gets into the passenger compartment, it is removed by an air conditioner.

It is necessary to understand several principles of heat flow, pressure, and temperature in order to understand air conditioning. Heat always flows from a hotter to a colder object. Heat can also be absorbed in large quantities when a liquid turns into a gas. This is done by boiling the liquid and evaporating it into a vapor. When the vapor is cooled, it condenses back to a liquid form. Pressure also has a direct effect on the boiling point. As a vapor is compressed under a pressure, its temperature increases.

A refrigerant called R-12 is used. This refrigerant has a boiling point of −21.7 degrees F. Air conditioning systems are designed to change the pressure of the R-12, causing the boiling point to change. When the refrigerant boils, it absorbs large quantities of heat.

Heat transfer in an air conditioning system is done by heat exchangers. An evaporator and a condenser are normally used. Several other components are also used in an air conditioner. These include a compressor and an expansion valve. Heat is removed from the passenger compartment in the following sequence. As R-12 passes through the evaporator in the passenger compartment, it boils and converts to a vapor. A large amount of heat is absorbed into the R-12. The refrigerant is then sent to the compressor to be compressed. The pressure heats up the R-12. The hot R-12 is sent to the condenser, where air flows through the heat exchanger. The air picks up the heat and transfers it outside of the vehicle. The vapor has now been changed to a liquid. The liquid is sent to an expansion valve where the pressure is reduced through the valve. The reduction in pressure causes the boiling point to drop. The liquid is now sent to the evaporator to be boiled again by the heat of the passenger compartment. The refrigerant continues to cycle through the system.

Several air conditioning systems are used. One system uses an accumulator and an orifice tube. A second system uses a cycling clutch to turn the compressor off and on. A third system uses several controls to operate the system at the maximum efficiency.

Other parts may also be used on an air conditioning system. A suction throttling valve (STV) is used to determine the temperature of the evaporator. This control protects the system from freezing up. The valve uses a spring pressure that works against evaporator pressure. When the valve is operating, the evaporator controls the temperature of the R-12 to maximum efficiency.

A second system uses a POA (pilot-operated absolute) valve. It also controls the evaporator outlet. Evaporator pressure works against a piston to open or close the valve. A third system uses an evaporator pressure regulator (EPR) valve. The valve is operated by a gas-filled bellows to control R-12 temperature. Again, this unit is used to prevent core freeze-up.

Many types of compressors are used on air conditioning systems. One popular type uses a swash plate pump to create a suction and pressure on the R-12.

Some air conditioning units also use other controls. The receiver-dehydrator is used to store liquid refrigerant. The thermostatic expansion valve is used to control the size of the expansion valve, on the basis of the temperature of the evaporator. The thermostatic switch is used to turn the electromagnetic clutch off and on. The ambient switch is used to sense outside air temperature. It controls the time when the compressor cannot be electromagnetically engaged. The thermal limiter and superheat switches are designed to protect the air conditioner compressor when the refrigerant is low. The low-pressure cut-off switch is used to shut off the compressor when there is low refrigerant pressure. The water control valve is used to regulate the engine coolant to the heat core.

Electronic temperature control air conditioning systems are also being used today. These systems use an air control module (computer) to control the air conditioning system. Various inputs are needed such as engine coolant temperature, vehicle speed, air compressor operation, and dashboard settings. Based upon these inputs, the computer is able to control blower speeds, blend doors, defrost systems, floor and panel doors, cooling and engine cooling fans, and compressor clutches.

Diagnosis and service procedures are very important on the air conditioning system. The two biggest dangers to an air conditioning system are dirt and moisture. Other problems in the air conditioning system include a damaged compressor, controls that are not adjusted correctly, and accumulators and filters being used up. Follow the manufacturer's recommendations and procedures when working with air conditioning equipment.

TERMS TO KNOW

Can you explain each of the following terms? Review the chapter until you can use each term correctly.

Vapor	Expansion valve
Latent heat	Evaporator
Condensation	Accumulator
Refrigerant	Desiccant
Ozone layer	Schrader valve
CFC	Swash plate
HFC-134a	Thermostatic switch
ACR3	Ambient
Condenser	ACM

REVIEW QUESTIONS

Multiple Choice

1. At what temperature is there a total lack of heat in any substance?
   a. Boiling point
   b. Absolute zero
   c. Freezing point
   d. 88 degrees F
   e. −21.7 degrees F

2. Heat will always flow from a _____ substance.
   a. Colder to a colder
   b. Hotter to a hotter
   c. Hotter to a colder
   d. Colder to a hotter
   e. None of the above

3. At what point can large quantities of heat be absorbed into a liquid or gas?
   a. When a liquid boils to a vapor
   b. When a vapor remains as a vapor
   c. When a liquid freezes
   d. All of the above
   e. None of the above

4. Heat that is hidden is called:
   a. Absolute heat
   b. Warm heat
   c. Specific heat
   d. Latent heat
   e. All of the above

5. When a vapor is changed back to a liquid, it is called:
   a. Evaporation
   b. Boiling point
   c. Condensation
   d. Accumulation
   e. None of the above

6. As the pressure of a liquid increases, the boiling point of the liquid _____.
   a. Decreases
   b. Increases
   c. Remains the same
   d. Drops by only 2 degrees
   e. None of the above

7. What is the boiling point of R-12 that is not under pressure?
   a. −10 degrees F
   b. −21.7 degrees F
   c. −41.7 degrees F
   d. 30 degrees F
   e. 65 degrees F

8. Heat transfer in an air conditioning system is done in the:
   a. Accumulator
   b. Dehydrator
   c. Compressor
   d. Heat exchangers
   e. Thermostatic switch

9. Which of the following processes is happening in the passenger compartment of an air conditioning system?
   a. The liquid R-12 changes to a vapor.
   b. Large amounts of heat are absorbed in the R-12.
   c. The liquid R-12 boils from the passenger compartment heat.
   d. All of the above
   e. None of the above

10. Condensation of the vapor R-12 back to a liquid takes place at the:
    a. Evaporator
    b. Compressor
    c. Condenser
    d. Accumulator
    e. Receiver

11. Which of the following components is on the high side of the air conditioning circuit?
    a. Evaporator
    b. Condenser
    c. Suction side of the compressor
    d. Low-pressure side of the expansion valve
    e. All of the above

12. Which of the following components is on the low side of the air conditioning circuit?
    a. Evaporator
    b. Low-pressure side of the expansion valve
    c. Suction side of the expansion valve
    d. All of the above
    e. None of the above

13. The _____ is used to store liquid refrigerant.
    a. Evaporator
    b. Condenser
    c. Accumulator
    d. Expansion valve
    e. All of the above

14. The _____ is used to reduce the pressure and temperature of the R-12.
    a. Expansion valve
    b. Accumulator
    c. Compressor
    d. Receiver-dehydrator
    e. Pressure regulator

15. The _____ freezes up if it is operated at the wrong pressures and temperatures.
    a. Compressor
    b. Condenser
    c. Evaporator
    d. Expansion valve
    e. None of the above

16. To control evaporator temperature on the air conditioning system, the _____ is controlled.
    a. Pressure
    b. Compressor speed
    c. Engine speed
    d. Condenser speed
    e. Dc voltage

17. One common type of compressor uses:
    a. A swash plate
    b. A reed valve
    c. Six pistons
    d. All of the above
    e. None of the above

18. What type of device is used to engage and disengage the compressor?
    a. Friction clutch
    b. Electromagnetic clutch
    c. Centrifugal clutch
    d. Roller clutch
    e. None of the above

19. Which two elements are most dangerous to an air conditioning system?
    a.   Dirt and moisture
    b.   Carbon and silicon
    c.   Dirt and dc voltage signals
    d.   Gasoline and oil
    e.   All of the above

20. Which of the following is an easy method used to check for refrigerant in the system?
    a.   Use a sight glass.
    b.   Loosen the system, and watch for fluid to flow out.
    c.   Apply an excess amount of pressure to get more cooling.
    d.   All of the above
    e.   None of the above

21. On an air conditioning system, a propane torch is used:
    a.   To create excess pressure
    b.   To check for pressure
    c.   To check for R-12 leaks
    d.   To solder steel piping
    e.   To heat the evaporator during testing

22. A manifold gauge set is used on an air conditioning system to:
    a.   Discharge the R-12
    b.   Charge the R-12
    c.   Evacuate the R-12
    d.   All of the above
    e.   None of the above

The following questions are similar in format to ASE (Automotive Service Excellence) test questions.

---

23. Technician A says that the most common problems with air compressors are contamination and lack of lubrication. Technician B says that the most common problem with air compressors is engine vibration. Who is right?
    a.   A only
    b.   B only
    c.   Both A and B
    d.   Neither A nor B

24. Technician A says that when the air conditioning system is open to the atmosphere, simply seal the hole and the system can be operated. Technician B says that an opening in the system means moisture will be absorbed into the system. Who is right?
    a.   A only
    b.   B only
    c.   Both A and B
    d.   Neither A nor B

25. A suction throttling valve (STV) cannot keep the pressure in the evaporator to the recommended level. Technician A says the system is OK and can still be run. Technician B says that the evaporator will freeze up. Who is right?
    a.   A only
    b.   B only
    c.   Both A and B
    d.   Neither A nor B

26. Small air bubbles are noticed in the sight glass on the air conditioning system. Technician A says this is normal. Technician B says that the compressor is overcharging the freon. Who is right?
    a.   A only
    b.   B only
    c.   Both A and B
    d.   Neither A nor B

27. An air conditioning system has insufficient cooling. Technician A says the problem is low refrigerant. Technician B says the condenser is clogged. Who is right?
    a.   A only
    b.   B only
    c.   Both A and B
    d.   Neither A nor B

28. An air conditioning system does not cool because the blower does not operate. Technician A says the problem is a blown fuse link. Technician B says the compressor clutch is faulty. Who is right?
    a.   A only
    b.   B only
    c.   Both A and B
    d.   Neither A nor B

29. There are bubbles present in the sight glass. Technician A says there is insufficient refrigerant. Technician B says the system should be checked for refrigerant leaks. Who is right?
    a.   A only
    b.   B only
    c.   Both A and B
    d.   Neither A nor B

30. When checking a malfunctioning air conditioning system, Technician A says to make sure the condenser is not plugged with leaves or other foreign material. Technician B says to check for restrictions or kinks in the refrigerant lines. Who is right?
    a.   A only
    b.   B only
    c.   Both A and B
    d.   Neither A nor B

Essay

31. Describe the process of condensation.

32. What happens to the boiling point of a fluid when the pressure increases or decreases?

33. Describe the purpose and operation of the expansion valve on an air conditioning system.

34. What is the difference between the high and low sides of an air conditioning system?

35. What is the purpose of an accumulator?

36. Describe how pressure is produced in the air conditioning compressor.

Short Answer

37. R-12 refrigerant is known to reduce the _____ above the earth.

38. The major greenhouse gases are: _____, _____, _____, and _____.

39. To protect the environment, a new refrigerant called _____ is being incorporated into the design of A/C systems.

40. To prevent R-12 from getting into the atmosphere during A/C servicing, a machine called _____ is used.

41. On an electronic A/C system, the ACM is used to control the _____.

CHAPTER 33

Heating and Ventilation Systems

INTRODUCTION There are several temperature controls used on the interior of the automobile to maintain a comfortable climate. This chapter discusses the ventilation and heating systems that are used inside the passenger compartment.

OBJECTIVES After reading this chapter, you should be able to:

- Identify the purpose of the heating and ventilation systems used in the automobile.

- Identify common parts used on heating and ventilation systems.

- Analyze how the passenger ventilation system is designed in the automobile.

- Compare vacuum, mechanical, and computer controls on heating and ventilation systems in the automobile.

- Identify various problems, diagnosis, and service steps used on heating and ventilation systems on automobiles.

✔ **SAFETY CHECKLIST** ✔

When working with heating and ventilation systems, keep these important safety precautions in mind.

✔ Be careful not to cut your hands on the edges of the heating and ventilation ductwork parts.

✔ Always use the correct tools when working on heating and ventilation systems to avoid injury.

✔ Make sure the battery is disconnected when working on the fan blower.

✔ Always wear OSHA-approved safety glasses when working with heating and ventilation systems.

✔ Many electrical components are used on heating and ventilation systems. Always use the correct testing tools when diagnosing these systems.

33.1 HEATING AND VENTILATION SYSTEMS

Purpose of Heating and Ventilation Systems

Heating and ventilation systems are used on the automobile to keep the passenger compartment at a comfortable temperature. Several conditions make the passenger compartment either too hot or too cold. During the winter, cold outdoor temperatures may make the compartment too cold.

During the summer, high ambient temperatures may make the compartment too warm. Thus both heating and ventilation are needed to keep the driver comfortable. In addition, as discussed in an earlier chapter, air conditioning may also be used.

Flow-through Ventilation

There are many systems used to heat and vent the passenger compartment. One type is called the flow-through

Some of the information in this chapter can help you prepare for the National Institute for Automotive Service Excellence (ASE) certification tests. The test most directly related to this chapter is entitled

> HEATING AND AIR CONDITIONING
> (TEST A7).

The content areas that closely parallel this chapter are

> HEATING ENGINE COOLING SYSTEM DIAGNOSIS AND REPAIR AND CONTROL UNITS DIAGNOSIS AND REPAIR.

ventilation system. A supply of outside air, which is called *ram air*, flows into the car when it is moving. When the car is not moving, a steady flow of outside air can be produced from the heater fan. *Figure 33–1* shows an example of the flow-through ventilation system. In operation, ram air is forced through an inlet grille. The pressurized air then circulates throughout the passenger and trunk compartment. From there the air is forced outside the vehicle through an exhaust area.

On certain vehicles, air is admitted by opening or closing two vent knobs under the dashboard. The left knob controls air through the left inlet. The right knob controls air through the right inlet. The air is still considered ram air and is circulated through the passenger compartment.

Fan Ventilation

Rather than using ram air (especially if the vehicle is stopped), a ventilation fan can be used. The fan is located in

FIGURE 33–1. A flow-through ventilation system is used on some vehicles. Ram air is forced into the inlet grill and sent throughout the passenger and trunk compartment. The air then flows out of the vehicle through exhaust areas. *(Courtesy of Oldsmobile Division, General Motors Corporation)*

the dashboard. It can be accessible from under the dashboard or from inside the engine compartment. *Figure 33–2* shows a typical ventilator assembly. A blower assembly is attached to the motor shaft. The entire unit is placed inside the blower housing. As the *squirrel cage blower* rotates, it produces a strong suction on the intake. A pressure is also created on the output. When the fan motor is energized by using the temperature controls on the dashboard, air is moved through the passenger compartment.

PROBLEM: Car Heater Doesn't Work

A car doesn't heat up in the passenger compartment, especially when it's very cold outside. When the engine is at operating temperature, heat is available. How could the passenger compartment get warmer, especially on short drives?

SOLUTION:

The heater core is on the bypass circuit around the thermostat when the thermostat is closed. First make sure that the thermostat is operating correctly and is the correct type for the vehicle. Then check to see if the heater core and the hoses to the core are hot before the radiator gets hot. They should be hot before the radiator. Also check to see if there are air bubbles in the coolant. On some vehicles, there may also be a shut-off valve to the heater core. Check the valve for correct operation.

Heater Core

All ventilation and heating systems use a *heater core* to increase the temperature within the passenger compartment. *Figure 33–3* shows an example of a heater core. Hot fluid flowing through the cooling system is tapped off and sent to the heater core. The heater core is much like a small radiator. It is considered a liquid-to-air heat exchanger. As warm or hot water is circulated through the core, air can be heated as it flows through the core fins.

Figure 33–4 shows the flow of coolant from the engine cooling system, through the heater core, and back to the cooling system. Near the top of the engine, just before the thermostat, a coolant line taps off coolant and sends it to the heater core. From the heater core, the coolant is sent back to the suction side of the cooling system. With this system, the thermostat does not have to be open to get heat to the heater core. Different manufacturers may use other circuit connections.

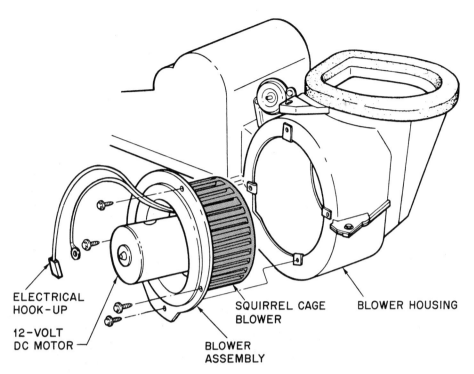

FIGURE 33–2. A fan is used to help move the air throughout the passenger compartment. It is called a squirrel cage fan. *(Courtesy of Motor Publications, Auto Repair Manual)*

Mechanical Duct Controls

One method used to control ventilation and heating systems is by using *air ducts* with small doors that direct the flow of air. The doors can be controlled either mechanically or by vacuum. Mechanical control of the doors is accomplished by moving the controls on the dashboard. As the control is moved, a cable attached to the control moves the duct door. *Figure 33–5* shows an example of two control cables. One is used to operate an air duct door for the temperature control. One is used to operate an air duct door for the *defroster*. The cable is made of a strong steel wire that is wrapped within a flexible tube. As the control assembly knob is moved, the steel wire inside the flexible tube moves, which causes the position of the air duct door to change.

Vacuum Duct Controls

A second method used to operate the air duct doors is to use a vacuum-operated motor. *Figure 33–6* shows an example of how the *vacuum motor* operates. The vacuum motor operates much like a solenoid. Instead of using electricity,

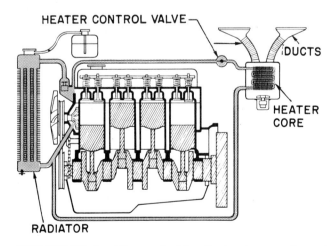

FIGURE 33–4. The coolant for the heater core is sent from the upper portion of the engine, through the heater core, and back to the suction side of the engine coolant system. *(Courtesy of Chevrolet Motor Division, General Motors Corporation)*

FIGURE 33–3. A heater core is used to increase the temperature of the air inside the passenger compartment.

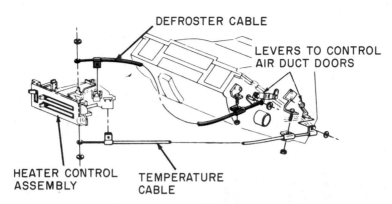

FIGURE 33-5. The ventilation and heating system is controlled by opening and closing air duct doors. These doors can be operated by mechanical cables. Here a temperature and a defroster cable are used to control air flow. As the levers are moved on the control assembly, air duct doors open and close to direct air correctly. *(Courtesy of Oldsmobile Division, General Motors Corporation)*

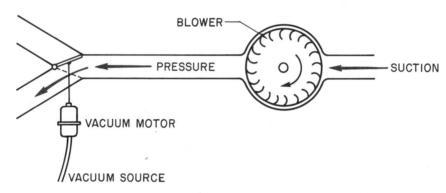

FIGURE 33-6. A vacuum motor can be used to control the operation of air duct doors. When a vacuum is applied to or removed from the vacuum motor, a diaphragm moves. This motion is transmitted by a small rod to the air duct door.

vacuum is used. When vacuum is applied to the motor, it causes a small diaphragm inside the motor to move. This motion is transmitted by a rod to the air duct door. The air duct door is then moved from one position to another. In some vehicles, several vacuum motors may be used to operate air duct doors.

Electrically Controlled Ducts

Another method used to control the air duct doors is to use small electrical motors. On vehicles that use computers to control the heating and ventilation system, electrical motors can be used to completely open and close ducts passages. By using electrical control motors, the exact amount of cool and warm air can also be mixed. Depending on the manufacturer, this motor is referred to by different names. Common names include the function control motor, mode control motor, and blend-air door motor.

Air Outlets in Dashboard

Vehicles today use a variety of ducts and passageways to get the air into the passenger compartment. Each type of vehicle is different. A typical air flow pattern is shown in *Figure 33-7*. Depending on the temperature controls, air can be directed to the feet, front windshield, center of the passenger compartment, or to the side windows. The temperature controls on the dashboard operate to open and close doors, which direct air to the correct location.

Heater Controls

There are numerous types and styles of heater controls. *Figure 33-8* shows an example of a simple dashboard control. Although many controls are much more complex, the functions that can usually be obtained include fan speeds, defrost, heating, venting, and/or air conditioning. The fan control lever is used to control the speed of the fan at different air flow rates. The temperature control lever is used to regulate the temperature of the air sent to the passenger compartment. The *selector control lever* is used to change from heating, to venting, to defrosting.

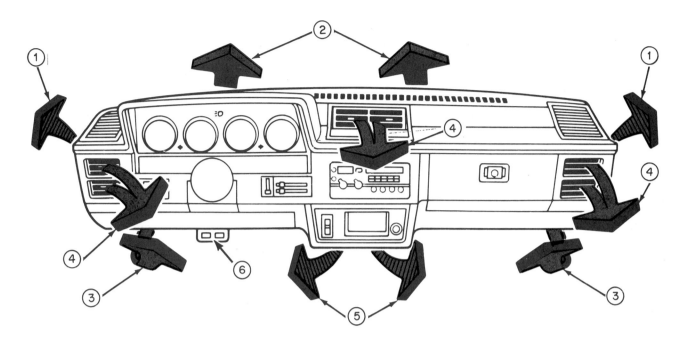

1. SIDE WINDOW DEFOG OUTLETS   4. POWER VENT OUTLETS

2. DEFROST OUTLETS   5. POWER VENT HEAT OUTLETS

3. RAM AIR OUTLETS   6. RAM AIR VENT CONTROLS

FIGURE 33–7. Air can be directed to many locations through the dashboard. Air duct doors, operated both mechanically and by vacuum, open and close to direct air to the correct location. *(Courtesy of Oldsmobile Division, General Motors Corporation)*

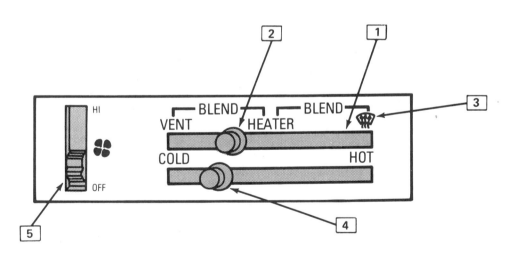

1 THIS POSITION ALLOWS OUTSIDE AIR FLOW TO FLOOR OUTLET. (ADDITIONAL VENTED AIR CAN BE DISTRIBUTED INSIDE CAR BY OPERATING VENT KNOBS.

2 POSITION OF THIS SYSTEM SELECTOR LEVER DETERMINES AIR FLOW FROM FLOOR, INSTRUMENT PANEL OR WINDSHIELD OUTLET—IN "HEATER," FLOW IS ABOUT 80% TO FLOOR AND 20% TO WINDSHIELD OUTLETS (AND SIDE WINDOW DEFOGGERS).

3 THIS POSITION ALLOWS ABOUT 80% AIR FLOW TO WINDSHIELD AND 20% TO FLOOR.

4 TEMPERATURE LEVER POSITION WILL REGULATE OUTLET AIR TEMPERATURE BY BLENDING THE INCOMING OUTSIDE AIR THROUGH/AROUND THE HEATER CORE.

5 THE FAN CONTROL LEVER (OFF - HI) PROVIDES SPEED CONTROL OF THE FAN.

FIGURE 33–8. There are many types of heater controls. There are typically a fan control lever, a temperature control lever, and a selector control lever. *(Courtesy of Oldsmobile Division, General Motors Corporation)*

CAR CLINIC

PROBLEM: Low Volume of Air from Blower

A customer complains that the air volume from the heating and ventilation system is low. The fan motor is running, is able to change speeds, but has low air volume. What could be the problem?

SOLUTION:

This type of problem is usually caused by some type of restriction in the air vents, in the intake of the ventilation system, or in the heater core. Check the suction side of the blower inlet. It may be restricted or blocked by leaves, tissues, or other debris that has been drawn into the system from the outside. Also check the outlet vents, making sure there are no restrictions. Check to make sure the venting ductwork has not become separated under the dashboard. Generally, if these items are checked and repaired, the problem should be eliminated.

Mechanical Control Heating Systems

A mechanical heating system is shown in *Figure 33–9*. Air is first pressurized by the blower. The air is then sent either through the heater core, bypassed, or mixed. The temperature door is positioned so that a mix of air can be obtained. In the uppermost position, air flow through the heater core is blocked. The air is not heated in this mode. When the temperature control knob on the dashboard is adjusted, it moves the temperature door so that more and more air flows through the heater core. The air temperature then increases accordingly. A second air duct door is used to stop all air flow into the passenger compartment. This occurs when the selector control lever is moved to the off position on the dashboard. The defroster door is also moved by the selector control lever. In the defrost position, the door is positioned so that air moves to the upper part of the dashboard against the windshield. Otherwise, the air flow is directed to the heat outlets in the center or lower portion of the dashboard.

Vacuum Control Heating Systems

Another method used to control the heating and ventilation system is to use vacuum. *Figure 33–10* shows a vacuum

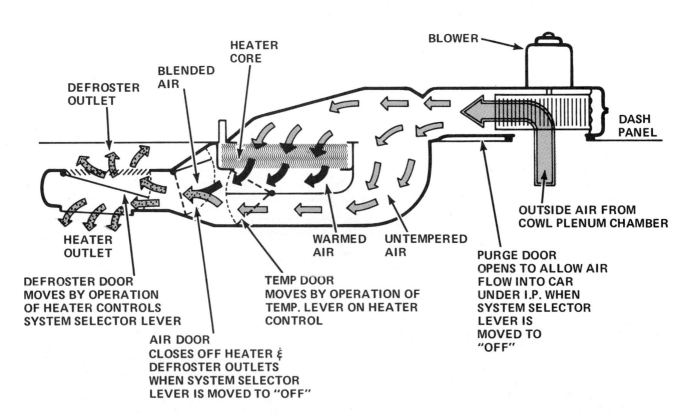

FIGURE 33–9. A typical heating system and air flow. Air from outside is pressurized by the blower. Depending on the position of the air duct doors, different temperatures can be obtained. *(Courtesy of Oldsmobile Division, General Motors Corporation)*

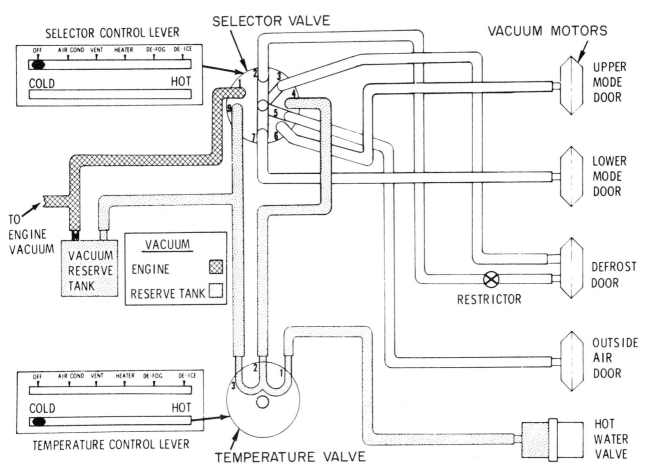

FIGURE 33–10. A vacuum system for controlling air flow is used on some vehicles. The selector control lever controls the selector valve. The temperature control lever controls the temperature valve. Depending on the position of the valve, different doors will be moved to produce the required air flow and venting. *(Courtesy of United Delco, Division of General Motors Corporation)*

system circuit in the heating mode. There are several additional parts included for correct operation. On the right side of the schematic, there are several vacuum motors used to control air duct doors. When vacuum is applied, an air duct door will open or close, depending on the condition required. There are also two valves that direct vacuum to the different vacuum motors. The upper valve is called the selector valve. As the selector lever is moved to different positions on the dashboard, the selector valve directs vacuum to the correct vacuum motor. The temperature valve is controlled by the position of the temperature control lever on the dashboard. A *reserve vacuum tank* also provides extra vacuum when the engine is not running. In addition, there is a hot water valve that opens or closes, allowing engine coolant to circulate through the heater core.

Air Flow with Air Conditioning

If the vehicle has air conditioning, an additional evaporator is placed in the air ducts. See *Figure 33–11*. The evaporator

is used to create cool air. As warm passenger compartment air is passed through the evaporator, heat is absorbed and carried away by the internal freon. Cool air is then sent through the remaining part of the ducting.

Figure 33–12 shows a second air flow system using air conditioning. Here the air flow is recirculating, rather than using fresh air. If the fresh air duct were open, fresh air would be circulated throughout the system. Note the location of the evaporator, heater core, vacuum motors, and fan. The exact design of each air flow system is determined by the vehicle manufacturer, the year, and the model of the vehicle. These two designs show the variation of air flow and supporting controls.

Computerized Automatic Temperature Control

Today many vehicle manufacturers are using computers to accurately control the air temperature in the passenger compartment. This type of system offers more choices on air flow and outlets than previous systems did. It operates using a

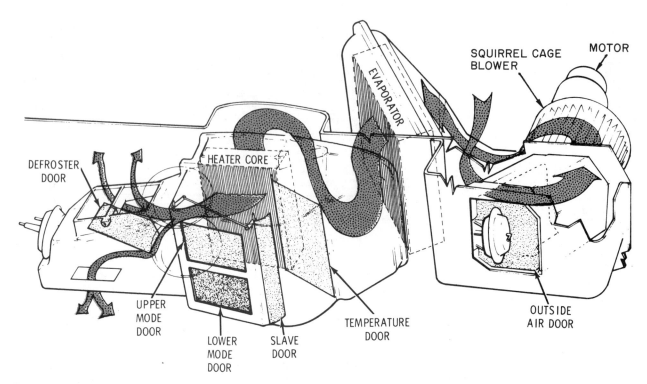

FIGURE 33–11. When an air conditioner is used, an additional evaporator is placed in the air flow. Warm air passing through the evaporator gives up its heat to the internal freon. The cooler air is then sent through the ducting into the passenger compartment. *(Courtesy of United Delco, Division of General Motors Corporation)*

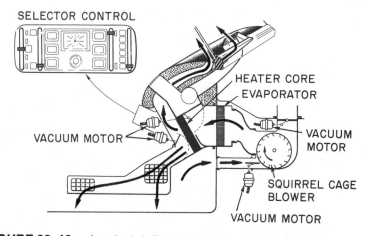

FIGURE 33–12. A typical air flow through a vehicle that has an evaporator used for air conditioning. *(Courtesy of Peugeot Motors of America)*

microprocessor with a memory. The system is designed to regulate the temperature of air in the passenger compartment to the desired temperature level. The microprocessor measures the interior temperature and makes adjustments every few seconds. *Figure 33–13* shows a *computerized automatic temperature control*, including the major parts and their location.

Figure 33–14 shows a typical computerized control system called the EATC (electronic automatic temperature control) system. This system uses the electronic control assembly to control various motors and switches. As with engine com-

puters, not all computers are titled the same. For example, one manufacturer calls this computer the BCM (body control module). The EATC system uses a microcomputer to analyze six major inputs. It then uses this information to determine the correct conditions of six outputs. The inputs include:

1. *Sunload sensor* — Determines if sun is shining inside the vehicle. This sensor is located on the dashboard. The sensor contains an electrical diode that is light-sensitive.

2. *In-car sensor* — Determines the temperature of the air inside the passenger compartment. The sensor is located

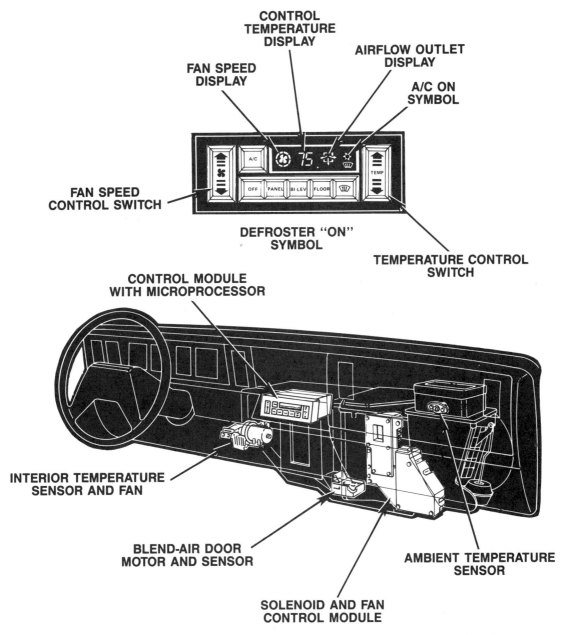

FIGURE 33–13.   Certain vehicles are using computers to control the ventilation and heating system. The computer senses the interior air temperature and adjusts the temperature every few seconds. *(Courtesy of Chrysler Corporation)*

behind the instrument panel. The sensor is able to measure the air temperature inside the passenger compartment.

3. *Ambient sensor* — Determines the temperature of the air outside the vehicle. This sensor is mounted in the front of the condenser or radiator.

4. *Engine temperature sensor* — Determines the coolant temperature of the engine. This sensor is the same as discussed in the cooling system.

5. *Vehicle operator* — Determines the temperature mode selected by the operator.

6. *A/C pressure switch* — Determines the pressure of the air conditioning system.

On the basis of these inputs, the computer is able to make instant adjustments on the heating and ventilation systems. The components that are controlled include:

- The blower speed
- The blend door position
- The floor panel door position
- The defrost door position
- The recirculating outside door position
- The A/C compressor clutch position

EATC (ELECTRONIC AUTOMATIC TEMPERATURE CONTROL)

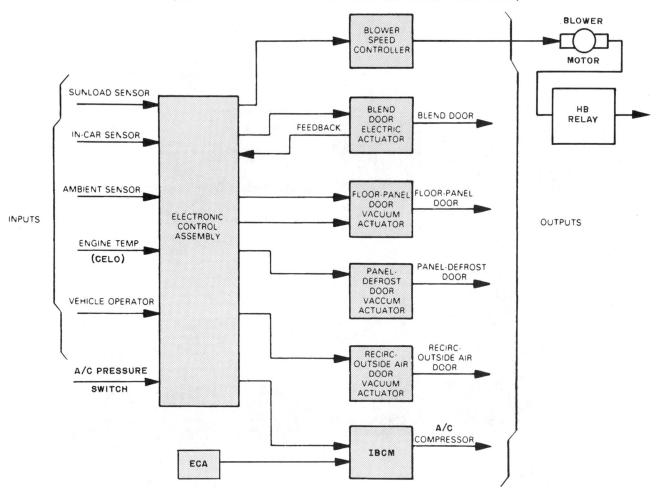

FIGURE 33–14. Many vehicles today use computers to control the heating and ventilation. The electronic control assembly uses six inputs to control various outputs of the heating and ventilation system. *(Courtesy of Motor Publications, Air Conditioning and Heater Manual)*

CAR CLINIC

PROBLEM: Moisture on the Inside Windows

A customer has complained that the windows always have moisture on the inside. It seems that the moisture is coming from the air vents when the blower is used for heating the inside compartment. The heating and ventilation ductwork was recently cleaned. The moisture also has a sweet smell. What could be the problem?

SOLUTION:

When water vapor is found on the inside windows or vapor comes from the vents and the system is not plugged up, the problem is most likely a leaky heater core. Often, the heater core will leak (much like a radiator). If the heater core is leaking into the ductwork, it produces a vapor and moisture in the passenger compartment. The sweet smell comes from the antifreeze in the coolant. The heater core must be removed and either replaced or repaired.

Problems, Diagnosis and Service

PROBLEM: Leaking Heater Core

A car has liquid dripping on the front passenger compartment.

DIAGNOSIS

Water on the front floor mat or passenger compartment may indicate a leaking heater core. Complete the following diagnostic checks:

1. Check the liquid to see if antifreeze is mixed with the liquid. It should be oily because of the antifreeze.

2. If it is oily, check all hose connections for leaks.

3. Check the drain passageways to make sure they are not clogged with foreign material.

4. Use a pressure checker to test the pressure in the cooling system. This procedure may detect a small leak in the heater core.

SERVICE

1. If the heater core is leaking, it must be removed and repaired or replaced. Follow the correct service manual for removal and replacement procedures.

2. During installation, make sure all hose connections are secure and tight.

PROBLEM: Faulty Electronic Control System

A vehicle with a computerized heating and ventilation system is not keeping the interior air temperature at the correct temperature.

DIAGNOSIS

As do engine computers, electronic temperature controls have built-in diagnostics. There are many systems used in vehicles today. One system uses the BCM (body control module) along with the ECM (electronic control module) to continually monitor the operating conditions for possible malfunctions. When a problem is detected, a two-digit numerical trouble code is stored within the computer. *Figure 33–15* shows an example of the BCM diagnostic codes. These codes can be displayed when diagnosing the heating and ventilation system. A "Service Now" warning lamp will illuminate on the dashboard. When this occurs, it will be necessary to follow the manufacturer's procedure to display the trouble codes. Each vehicle and year may be different, so the exact procedure will vary from vehicle to vehicle.

SERVICE

Once the exact trouble is detected, the faulty component will need to be replaced. Follow the manufacturer's procedure for removal and replacement of each item needing repair.

BCM DIAGNOSTIC CODES	
CODE	CIRCUIT AFFECTED
▼F10	OUTSIDE TEMP SENSOR CKT
▼F11	A/C HIGH SIDE TEMP SENSOR CKT
▼F12	A/C LOW SIDE TEMP SENSOR CKT
▼F13	IN-CAR TEMP SENSOR CKT
▼F30	CCP TO BCM DATA CKT
▼F31	FDC TO BCM DATA CKT
▼F32	ECM-BCM DATA CKT'S
▼F40	AIR MIX DOOR PROBLEM
▼F41	COOLING FANS PROBLEM
☑F46	LOW REFRIGERANT WARNING
☑F47	LOW REFRIGERANT CONDITION
☑F48	LOW REFRIGERANT PRESSURE
▼F49	HIGH TEMP CLUTCH DISENGAGE
▼F51	BCM PROM ERROR

☑ TURNS ON "SERVICE AIR COND" LIGHT
▼ DOES NOT TURN ON ANY LIGHT

COMMENTS:
F11 TURNS ON COOLING FANS WHEN
   A/C CLUTCH IS ENGAGED
F12 DISENGAGES A/C CLUTCH
F32 TURNS ON COOLING FANS
F30 TURNS ON FT. DEFOG AT 75° F
F41 TURNS ON "COOLANT TEMP/FANS"
   LIGHT WHEN FANS SHOULD BE ON
F47 & F48 SWITCHES FROM "AUTO"
    TO "ECON"

FIGURE 33–15. These trouble codes are stored in the computer for diagnoses of the heating and ventilation system. *(Courtesy of Motor Publications, Air Conditioning and Heating Manual)*

PROBLEM: Insufficient Heating

A vehicle has insufficient heating in the passenger compartment.

DIAGNOSIS

Many common diagnostic checks can be made to determine the cause of the problem. The following are common checks made on heating and ventilation systems:

1. A gurgle, whine, or "swish" in the heater may indicate that air is mixed with the coolant in the cooling system. Check the engine coolant level in the radiator. Also check for obstructions in the heater core or hoses. Repair as necessary.

2. On some vehicles, the temperature control cable between the dash and the temperature door may need adjustment. This can be done by adjusting the cable length shorter or longer. Follow the manufacturer's recommended procedure for adjusting the cable length. There should be a uniform effort from full cold to full hot. In addition, there should be an audible stop sound when the temperature door reaches the end position.

3. If the fan blower is inoperative, check the blower fuse. If the fuse is not bad, check for an open circuit between the ignition switch and the blower motor. If the circuitry appears to be correct, check the blower fan switch for damage. Also check the blower motor resistance and compare with manufacturer's specifications.

4. Heating and ventilation systems that use vacuum hoses for control should be checked by using a vacuum tester. *Figure 33–16* shows a typical vacuum tester. The vacuum tester is used to place a vacuum on the system to observe sealing and leaks and to see if the components are operating correctly.

5. An engine that has a damaged cooling system with internal rust and other contaminants will usually develop insufficient-heating problems. For example, if silicon and calcium deposits form in the radiator, they will form in the heater core as well. Such deposits cause poor heat transfer into the passenger compartment. The heater core will have to be removed and cleaned before it will operate correctly.

6. For a complete list of diagnostic checks concerning insufficient heating refer to *Figure 33–17* to identify the cause and possible correction.

SERVICE

The service procedure will depend on the damaged or faulty part. Refer to the manufacturer's service manual for the correct procedure.

PROBLEM: Faulty Defrost System

There is an inadequate removal of fog and ice from the front windshield.

DIAGNOSIS

Several malfunctions can cause inadequate removal of fog and ice from the front windshield. *Figure 33–18* shows some of the common causes and corrections. Each of these causes may have a certain procedure for diagnosing its condition.

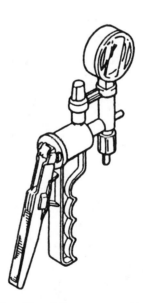

FIGURE 33–16. Use this vacuum pump and gauge to check the condition and operation of vacuum-controlled heating and ventilation systems. *(Courtesy of Honda Motor Company, Ltd.)*

INSUFFICIENT HEATING

Cause	Correction
Slow warming in car.	Incorrect operation of controls. Advise operator of proper operation of heater controls. Explain operation of vents and controls. Low coolant level. Check control cable and blower operation.
Objectionable engine or exhaust fumes in car.	Check for seal between engine compartment and plenum. Check for proper sealing between air inlet duct assembly and cowl. Locate and seal any other air leaks.
Cold drafts on floor.	Check operation and adjustment of vent cables. Advise operator of proper operation of heater system. Advise operator to use blower to force air to rear seat area. Check to be sure front floor mat is under floor mat retainer at cowl.
Insufficient heat to rear seat.	Obstruction on floor, possibly wrinkled or torn insulator material between front seat and floor. Advise operator to use HI blower speed.
Low engine coolant level - drop in heater air temperature at all blower speeds.	Check radiator and cooling system for leaks, correct and fill to proper level. Run engine to clear any air lock.
Failure of engine cooling system to warm up.	Check engine thermostat; replace if required. Check coolant level.
Kinked heater hoses.	Remove kink or replace hose.
Foreign material obstructing water flow through heater core.	Remove foreign material if possible, otherwise, replace core - can usually be heard as squishing noise in core.
Temperature door (valve) improperly adjusted. Air doors do not operate.	Adjust cable. Check installation and/or adjustment of air control or air-defrost cable.

FIGURE 33–17. Insufficient heating can be caused by many damaged or nonoperational parts. *(Courtesy of Oldsmobile Division, General Motors Corporation)*

For example, assume that the blower motor is inoperative. The service manual will give a specific procedure to help diagnose the blower motor. *Figure 33–19* shows one of many charts used to help the service technician diagnose heating and ventilation components.

SERVICE

The exact service procedure will depend upon the problem or malfunction. Refer to the service manual for the correct service procedure to be used.

INADEQUATE REMOVAL OF FOG OR ICE

Cause	Correction
Air door does not open. Defroster door does not open fully.	Check cable operation.
Air door does not open.	Check installation and/or adjustment of air control or air-defrost cable.
Temperature door does not open.	Check and adjust temperature control cable if necessary.
Obstructions in defroster outlets at windshield.	Remove obstruction. Look for and repair loose instrument panel pad cover at defroster outlet.
Damaged defroster outlets.	Reshape outlet flange with pliers. The outlet should have a uniform opening.
Blower motor not connected.	Connect wire. Check ground.
Inoperative blower motor.	Check heater fuse and wiring. Replace motor if necessary. See ETM for blower motor diagnosis.
Inoperative blower motor switch.	Replace switch if necessary.

FIGURE 33–18. Inadequate removal of fog and ice from the windshield can be caused by several malfunctions. *(Courtesy of Oldsmobile Division, General Motors Corporation)*

SERVICE MANUAL CONNECTION

There are many important specifications to keep in mind when working with heating and ventilation systems. To identify the specifications for your vehicle, you will need to know the VIN (vehicle identification number) of the vehicle, the type and year of the vehicle, and the type of engine used. Although they may be titled differently, some of the more common heating and ventilation system specifications (not all) found in service manuals are listed below. Note that these are typical examples. Each vehicle may have different specifications.

Common Specification	Typical Example
Air floor temperature (floor outlet)	150 degrees F at 80 degrees F ambient
Automatic temperature control resistance	2,600 ohms
Blower motor resistance	1.79–2.06 ohms
Water temperature sensor resistance	5,073 ohms at 160 degrees F

In addition, the service manual will give specific directions for various service and testing procedures. Some of the more common procedures include:

- Blend door module replace
- Control display panel replace
- Damper control motor assembly replace
- Diagnosis and testing of automatic temperature controls
- Heater diagnosis
- Heater output performance test

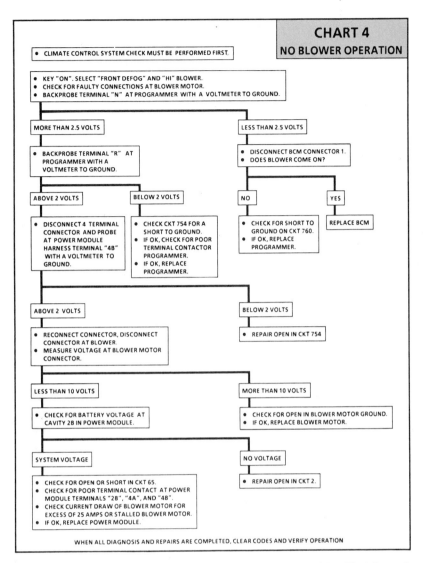

FIGURE 33–19. When a specific component has been identified through the trouble codes various diagnosis charts are available to help the technician further check the component. *(Courtesy of Motor Publications, Air Conditioning and Heater Manual)*

SUMMARY

Heating and ventilation systems are used on automobiles to keep the passenger compartment comfortable during all weather conditions. There are many designs. Most systems are built to heat, cool, ventilate the passenger compartment, and defrost the windows.

Ventilation inside the passenger compartment is done by several methods. The flow-through ventilation system uses ram air from the forward motion of the car to force air into the passenger area. Blower fans are used when the vehicle is not moving. The blower fan used is typically a squirrel cage design. It is driven by a small dc motor and placed inside a housing under the dashboard.

A heater core is used to get heat into the car. Coolant is tapped off of the cooling system and sent through hoses to the heater core. The heater core is a liquid-to-air heat

exchanger. Air passing over the fins picks up the warm air and sends it to the passenger compartment.

Several types of controls are used to direct the air to the proper location. Mechanical duct controls use a steel wire attached to the dashboard controls. As the dashboard controls are moved, a small air duct door is opened or closed to direct air to the proper location. Vacuum duct controls are also used. A vacuum motor (diaphragm inside a housing) is operated by engine vacuum. When vacuum is applied, the diaphragm moves, causing the air duct door to move as well.

Depending on the vehicle manufacturer, style, and year, air outlets are placed in various positions on the dashboard. When air duct doors are opened or closed, air is directed to the proper locations.

(continued)

Linkage to Automotive Manufacturing

HEATING AND VENTILATION SYSTEMS

A great deal of research has gone into heating and ventilation systems. The heating and ventilation system in today's cars is a maze of electronics, control motors, damper doors, and ductwork. To maintain maximum comfort to the passenger, various controls are needed. The conditions to be regulated may include:

■ having the internal air recycled

■ having fresh air come into the passenger compartment

■ heating from the engine coolant

■ air conditioning

■ air flow from the bottom

■ air flow at the top

■ defrosting (removing moisture)

The figure shows an example of a typical heating and ventilation system. Note the fan/blower on the lower right used to move the air through the system. Various types of ducting, vents, control doors, motors, and electrical and mechanical controls are used. *(Courtesy of Volkswagen United States, Inc.)*

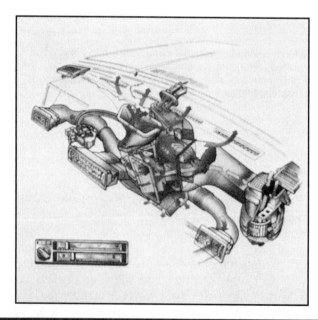

Heater controls are used to create the right temperature of air entering the passenger compartment. Normally an air duct door opens or closes to allow more or less air through the heater core.

Complete systems of heating and ventilation may use a combination of controls. Although each system is different, the basic operational principles remain the same. The selector control lever is used to select the correct mode of operation, defrost, heating, venting, and so on. The temperature control is used to mix the correct amount of heated air with nonheated air. Both mechanical and vacuum controls can be used.

When a heating and ventilation system is used with an air conditioner, an additional evaporator is used in the air flow. As warm passenger compartment air flows through the evaporator, heat is absorbed into the freon and exhausted at the condenser. Cool air (air lacking thermal energy) is then sent into the passenger compartment.

With the increased use of computers on vehicles today, more precise temperature control can be obtained. The computerized automatic temperature control monitors air temperatures inside and outside the vehicle. On the basis of these temperatures and the operator's setting, the air temperature is adjusted every few seconds. An accurate air temperature can thus be easily obtained by using the computer.

There are several diagnosis procedures and service tips that are important for the heating and ventilation system. The most common problems include having a leaky heater core, misadjusted controls, and a faulty cooling system. Check the manufacturer's suggested diagnosis procedure when servicing the heating and ventilation system.

TERMS TO KNOW

Can you explain each of the following terms? Review the chapter until you can use each term correctly.

Ram air	Selector control lever
Squirrel cage blower	Reserve vacuum tank
Heater core	Computerized automatic
Air ducts	temperature control
Defroster	Sunload sensor
Vacuum motor	Ambient sensor

 **REVIEW QUESTIONS**

Multiple Choice

1. Many vehicles are ventilated by using:
   a. The heater core
   b. Flow-through or ram ventilation
   c. The evaporator
   d. Engine coolant
   e. None of the above

2. The fan motor and blower on a typical heating and ventilation system uses a/an:
   a. Squirrel cage blower
   b. Heater core motor
   c. Evaporator to heat the air
   d. Positive displacement cooling pump
   e. Belt-driven pump

3. Heat is put into the air going into the passenger compartment at the:
   a. Evaporator
   b. Vacuum motor
   c. Selector control lever
   d. Heater core
   e. None of the above

4. The actual thermal energy or heat put into the passenger compartment comes from the:
   a. Electrical wires heating up
   b. Evaporator
   c. Coolant from the cooling system
   d. Vacuum motor
   e. Squirrel cage blower

5. To get different temperatures from the temperature control lever on the dashboard:
   a. Cool air is mixed with warm air with through the heater core
   b. The evaporator pressure drops
   c. The electricity on the coils decreases
   d. The selector control lever is put in the off position
   e. All of the above

6. The air duct doors can be operated from/by:
   a. The vacuum motors
   b. Mechanical cables
   c. The control levers on the dashboard
   d. All of the above
   e. None of the above

7. The temperature control lever on the dashboard is used to:
   a. Mix air to the correct temperature
   b. Select venting or heating
   c. Change the temperature of the engine coolant
   d. All of the above
   e. None of the above

8. What type of component(s) is/are used on the vacuum control heating system?
   a. Vacuum motors   d. All of the above
   b. Selector valve   e. None of the above
   c. Vacuum tank

9. When a car has air conditioning, which component is added into the air flow system?
   a. Heater core   d. Computer control
   b. Evaporator   e. Vacuum motor
   c. Heater blower

10. Which type of system monitors air temperature, both inside and outside the vehicle, and makes an adjustment every few seconds to keep the temperature at the correct setting?
    a. Evaporator system
    b. Computerized automatic temperature control
    c. Heater core automatic
    d. Microprocessor control system
    e. None of the above

11. Engine coolant leaking onto the front floor mats could be an indication of a:
    a. Leaky vacuum motor
    b. Poor sealing air duct door
    c. Leaky heater core
    d. Leaky control system
    e. All of the above

12. What would need to be done if the heated air was not hot enough and the temperature control lever didn't seem to work smoothly?
    a. Adjust the temperature control lever
    b. Readjust the position of the evaporator
    c. Readjust the position of the heater core
    d. Replace all vacuum motors
    e. Replace the fan motor and blower assembly

> *The following questions are similar in format to ASE (Automotive Service Excellence) test questions.*

13. There is a gurgle or swishing sound coming from under the dashboard near the heating core. Technician A says that there is air in the cooling system. Technician B says that the dash controls are improperly adjusted. Who is right?
    a. A only
    b. B only
    c. Both A and B
    d. Neither A nor B

14. Antifreeze and water are found on the front seat car mat. Technician A says that the heater core may be leaking and should be repaired. Technician B says that the hose connections to the heater core may be leaking. Who is right?
    a. A only
    b. B only
    c. Both A and B
    d. Neither A nor B

15. There is insufficient heating in the passenger compartment. Technician A says that because the cooling system has silicon and calcium built up in it, this may also damage the heater core. Technician B says that the dash controls may need to be adjusted. Who is right?
    a. A only
    b. B only
    c. Both A and B
    d. Neither A nor B

16. The blower fan is inoperative. Technician A says to check the blower fan fuse. Technician B says to check the heater core for signs of being plugged. Who is right?
    a. A only
    b. B only
    c. Both A and B
    d. Neither A nor B

17. A vehicle with a computerized heating and ventilation system has insufficient heating. Technician A says to check the trouble codes stored in the computer. Technician B says that the light-sensitive diode on the in-car sensor needs replacement. Who is right?
    a. A only
    b. B only
    c. Both A and B
    d. Neither A nor B

18. Technician A says that a vacuum pump and gauge can be used to diagnose heating and ventilation systems. Technician B says that a compression gauge can be used to check the heating and ventilation systems. Who is right?
    a. A only
    b. B only
    c. Both A and B
    d. Neither A nor B

19. Technician A says that air duct doors are controlled by vacuum. Technician B says that air duct doors are controlled by electrical motors. Who is right?
    a. A only
    b. B only
    c. Both A and B
    d. Neither A nor B

20. A car has insufficient heating. Technician A says to check if the cooling system has warmed up. Technician B says to check if foreign material is blocking the water flow through the radiator core. Who is right?
    a. A only
    b. B only
    c. Both A and B
    d. Neither A nor B

Essay

21. Describe the squirrel cage blower design.

22. What is the purpose of the vacuum motor on heating and ventilation systems?

23. What is the purpose of the reserve vacuum tank?

24. Describe the purpose and operation of the heater core.

25. Define the computerized automatic temperature control system.

Short Answer

26. Heating and ventilation ducts can be controlled by vacuum or by _____

27. Name three of the six sensors used to monitor the EATC (electronic automatic temperature control) system.
    _____, _____, _____

28. Name three of the six components controlled by the computer on the EATC system. _____, _____, _____

29. If antifreeze is found on the front passenger compartment it is a sign that the _____ is leaking.

30. If there is air in the coolant, there will be a _____, _____, or _____ sound in the heater core.

CHAPTER 34

Auxiliary and Electrical Systems

INTRODUCTION   This chapter is about various auxiliary and electrical systems that are used on the automobile. These include systems such as cruise controls, windshield washers, energy absorbers, and horn circuits. These systems are designed in a variety of ways. Different vehicle manufacturers may or may not have similar systems. Many of these systems rely on electrical circuits for their operation and analysis. This chapter is designed to analyze several auxiliary systems as well as to understand some of their basic circuitry.

OBJECTIVES   After reading this chapter, you should be able to:

- Identify various wiring circuits, schematics, and their symbols.

- Analyze several electrical circuits, including the headlights, defogger, power seats, and horn.

- Define the parts and operation of windshield wiper systems.

- Describe the operation of energy absorbers used on bumpers.

- Analyze the parts and operation of standard and electronic or computerized cruise control systems.

- Describe the basic operation of passive restraint systems.

- Identify common problems, diagnosis, and service procedures for auxiliary and electrical systems.

✓ SAFETY CHECKLIST ✓

When working with auxiliary and electrical systems, keep these important safety precautions in mind.

✔ Always use the correct tools when working on auxiliary and electrical systems.

✔ Make sure the battery is disconnected when working on electrical circuits to eliminate the possibility of motors accidently starting and electrical shock.

✔ Always wear OSHA-approved safety glasses when working on any auxiliary or electrical system.

✔ Remove all metal jewelry (rings, watches, and so on) when working with electrical components.

Some of the information in this chapter can help you prepare for the National Institute for Automotive Service Excellence (ASE) certification tests. The test most directly related to this chapter is entitled

ELECTRICAL SYSTEMS (TEST A6).

The content areas that closely parallel this chapter are

LIGHTING SYSTEMS DIAGNOSIS AND REPAIR, GAUGES, WARNING DEVICES AND DRIVER INFORMATION SYSTEMS DIAGNOSIS AND REPAIR, HORN AND WIPE/WASHER DIAGNOSIS AND REPAIR, AND ACCESSORIES DIAGNOSIS AND REPAIR.

34.1 READING ELECTRICAL CIRCUITS

Schematics

Electrical schematics are used to troubleshoot the electrical circuits on vehicles. Schematics are used to subdivide the electrical system down into individual parts and circuits. Schematics show only the parts and how electrical current flows. The schematic does not show the actual position or physical appearance of the parts. For example, a four-foot wire is not shown differently than a two-inch wire. All parts are shown as simply as possible, with regard to function only.

Electrical Symbols

The automotive industry uses *electrical symbols* on the schematics to help identify the circuit operation. Not all manufacturers use the same symbols, but they may be similar in nature. *Figure 34–1* shows common symbols that are used by one manufacturer. Many of the symbols are designed to illustrate their meaning by the type of symbol. For example, connector symbols are shaped somewhat like an actual connector. Keep these symbols on hand to be able to read electrical schematics.

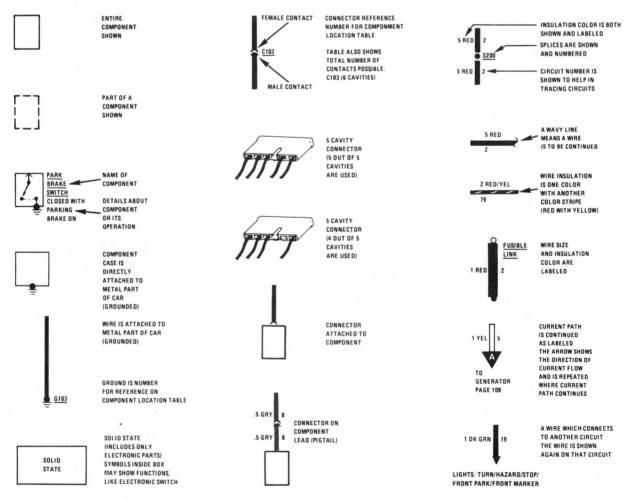

FIGURE 34–1. Various symbols are used to identify electrical circuits. Familiarity with these symbols will help you to identify problems in electrical systems. *(Courtesy of Oldsmobile Division, General Motors Corporation)*

Several numbers and identifying characteristics are also shown on schematics. The color of the wire is represented by letters such as PNK (pink), YEL (yellow), BLU (blue), PPL (purple), ORN (orange), GRY (gray), DK GRN (dark green), and so on. The size of the wire (both metric and AWG, American Wire Gauge, sizes) and the component location (C 103) are also shown. When the technician is ready to match the schematic parts to the actual hardware, this number is referenced to a *component location table*, along with the schematic. The table tells the technician exactly where to find the component. *Figure 34–2* shows an example of a component location table.

Reading a Schematic

Figure 34–3 shows a typical schematic of the heater circuit. This schematic is used here only as an example of how to read it. The schematic is read from top to bottom. With the ignition switch in the "RUN" position, voltage is applied to the fuse block. From the fuse block, electricity flows into the blower switch. The blower switch sets the blower speed by adding resistors in series with the blower motor. In LO

two resistors are connected through the YEL wire. In MED one resistor is connected through the BLU wire. In HI full voltage is applied directly to the blower motor through the ORN wire. When the radio is off, electricity flows directly to the blower motor. When the radio is on, electricity flows first through a radio capacitor. The radio capacitor reduces radio noise that is caused by the blower motor.

Fuse Block

Each circuit that is used on the automobile must be fused. Fuses are used so that if the circuit is overloaded, the fuse will melt and open that particular circuit. All fuses are usually placed on a *fuse block*. The fuse block can be located in several areas. On some older cars, the fuse block is located under the dashboard on the left side of the vehicle. On certain newer cars, the fuse block is located in the glove compartment or under the dashboard on the right side. The location depends on the vehicle manufacturer. There are also several types of fuses that are used. *Figure 34–4* shows an example of several types of fuses used on vehicles. The amperage (20 A) is stamped on the fuse to identify its size.

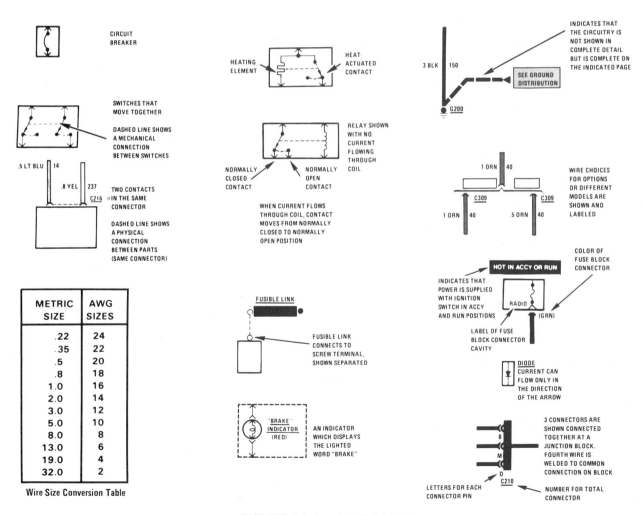

FIGURE 34–1. (CONTINUED)

COMPONENT LOCATION		Page-Figure
COMPONENTS		
Blower Motor	RH rear of engine compartment	201-4-A
Blower Resistors.	On blower housing	201-4-E
Fuse Block	Behind RH side of I/P	201-2-A
Radio Capacitor	Above blower motor.	201-4-E
CONNECTORS		
C118 (1 cavity)	Next to blower motor.	201-8-B
C209 (2 cavities)	Behind center of I/P, near control head	201-10-C
C220 (3 cavities)	Behind center of I/P, near grommet	201-10-C
C241 (2 cavities)	Behind I/P, below control head	201-9-A
GROUNDS		
G104	On EGR solenoid bracket	201-3-A
G106	RH rear of engine compartment	201-4-A
SPLICES		
S106	Engine harness, above water pump	201-18-B

FIGURE 34–2. Component location tables tell the technician the physical location of the actual parts on the schematic. *(Courtesy of Oldsmobile Division, General Motors Corporation)*

CAR CLINIC

PROBLEM: "Check Engine" Light Is Erratic

It is noticed that, on the dashboard of a computer-controlled GM engine, the CHECK ENGINE light goes on intermittently or is erratic. What could be the problem?

SOLUTION:

Most of the time a component fault or light coming on intermittently indicates a faulty electrical connection. The diagnosis should include physical inspection of the wiring and connectors. Check all connections on the electrical circuits on the engine. Also, physically observe the connections for damaged or bent terminals.

Fusible Link

On many electrical circuits, there is a *fusible link*. A fusible link is a type of circuit protector in which a special wire melts to open the circuit when the current is excessive. The fusible link acts like an in-line fuse made of wire with a special non-flammable insulation.

34.2 ELECTRICAL CIRCUITS

As the automobile has been developed over the years, more and more electrical circuits have been added to it. An example of some of the electrical circuits used include the clock, defogger, fog lamps, fuel injectors, gauges, headlights, ignition, cigar lighter, dome lights, power windows, horn, power seats, tachometer, tailgate release, and others. All of these circuits can be identified and analyzed by observing their circuit operation on a schematic. This section looks at several electrical circuits that are commonly used on vehicles.

HEATER

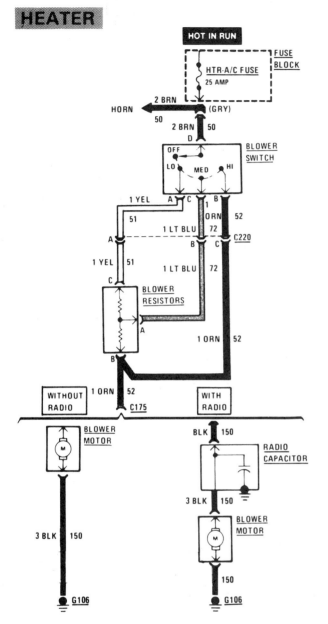

FIGURE 34–3. An example of a simple electrical schematic used to diagnose the heater circuit. Note how the symbols are used to help explain the circuit operation. *(Courtesy of Oldsmobile Division, General Motors Corporation)*

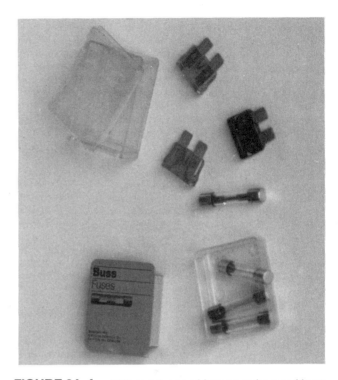

FIGURE 34–4. Different types of fuses can be used in an automobile. The type depends on the manufacturer, the year of the vehicle, and the exact type of circuit.

Headlights

Figure 34–5 shows a headlight circuit. A complete analysis of the headlight circuit can be obtained by tracing the electricity through the schematic. Starting from the top:

1. Electricity is available to the light switch all of the time.

2. The electricity first flows through the circuit breaker.

3. The light switch has three positions. These include OFF, PARK, and HEAD.

4. When the light switch is in the HEAD position, current flows through the switch to the headlight *dimmer switch*.

5. The dimmer switch can be in one of two positions: LO or HI.

6. In the LO position, the current flows through the dimmer switch to terminal D. This wire is identified as 1 TAN.

7. The electricity flows through 1 TAN to each of the dual-beam headlights. One is for the left side, and one is for the right side of the vehicle.

8. There are two electrical circuits inside each dual-beam headlight. One circuit is for the high beam, and one is for the low beam.

9. Electricity flows through the low beam circuit to ground, completing the circuit.

10. When the dimmer switch is positioned to HI, several other circuits also operate.

11. One circuit sends electricity to the instrument panel printed circuit to the HI beam indicator light.

12. From point B on the dimmer switch, electricity can flow through a fog light relay or directly to the HI beam circuit in each headlight.

HEADLIGHT CIRCUIT

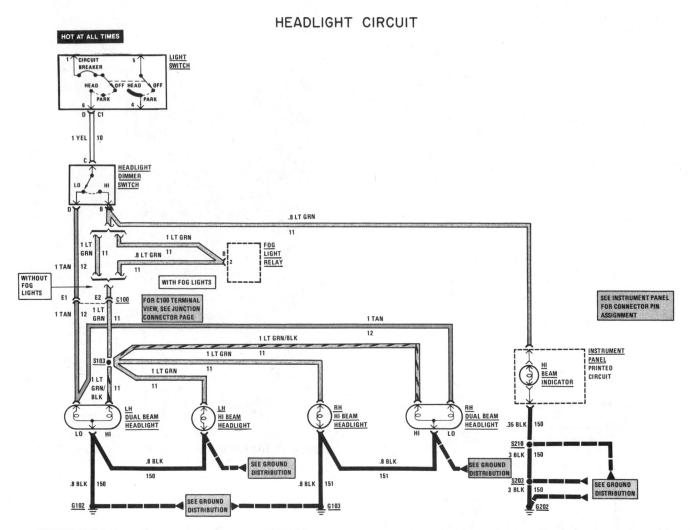

FIGURE 34–5. The headlight circuit for a vehicle. *(Courtesy of Oldsmobile Division, General Motors Corporation)*

13. After passing through the headlight, the electricity then returns to the battery through ground.

14. Electricity also flows from connector (S103) to a second high-beam headlight. Thus when the dimmer switch is on HI beam, both front headlights are on.

Defogger

Figure 34–6 shows an example of a defogger electrical circuit. The defogger operates when voltage is applied to the rear window wires. The wires are on the inside surface of the glass. When current flows through them, the wires heat the window to remove fog and ice from the glass.

When the defogger control ON-OFF switch is moved to ON, the defogger control timer is turned on. The defogger control contacts close, and voltage is applied to the defogger and the ON indicator. When the instrument panel light circuit provides power, voltage is also applied through the GRY wire to the defogger control panel light.

After the defogger control ON-OFF switch is released, the defogger control timer holds the defogger control contacts closed for 10 minutes for the first operation. The timer holds

the contacts closed for 5 minutes for further operation. When the defogger control timer completes its cycle, the contacts open and voltage is removed from the defogger and the defogger control ON indicator.

Power Seats

Many vehicles today use power seats to move the front seats upward, downward, forward, and backward. Many vehicles also use support mats within the seat to fit its shape to the driver. *Figure 34–7* shows an example of the internal parts of a typical power seat. The lumbar (back curvature) supports are also shown. The electrical circuit for a standard power seat system can best be described by referring to *Figure 34–8*. This circuit shows several important parts. The three motors on the bottom are used to move the seat in a specific direction. The motors can run forward or backward, depending on the direction of current through the windings. The switches for the power seats are in the middle of the schematic. The schematic can be traced from the top to the bottom as follows:

1. Current is available at the circuit breaker at all times.

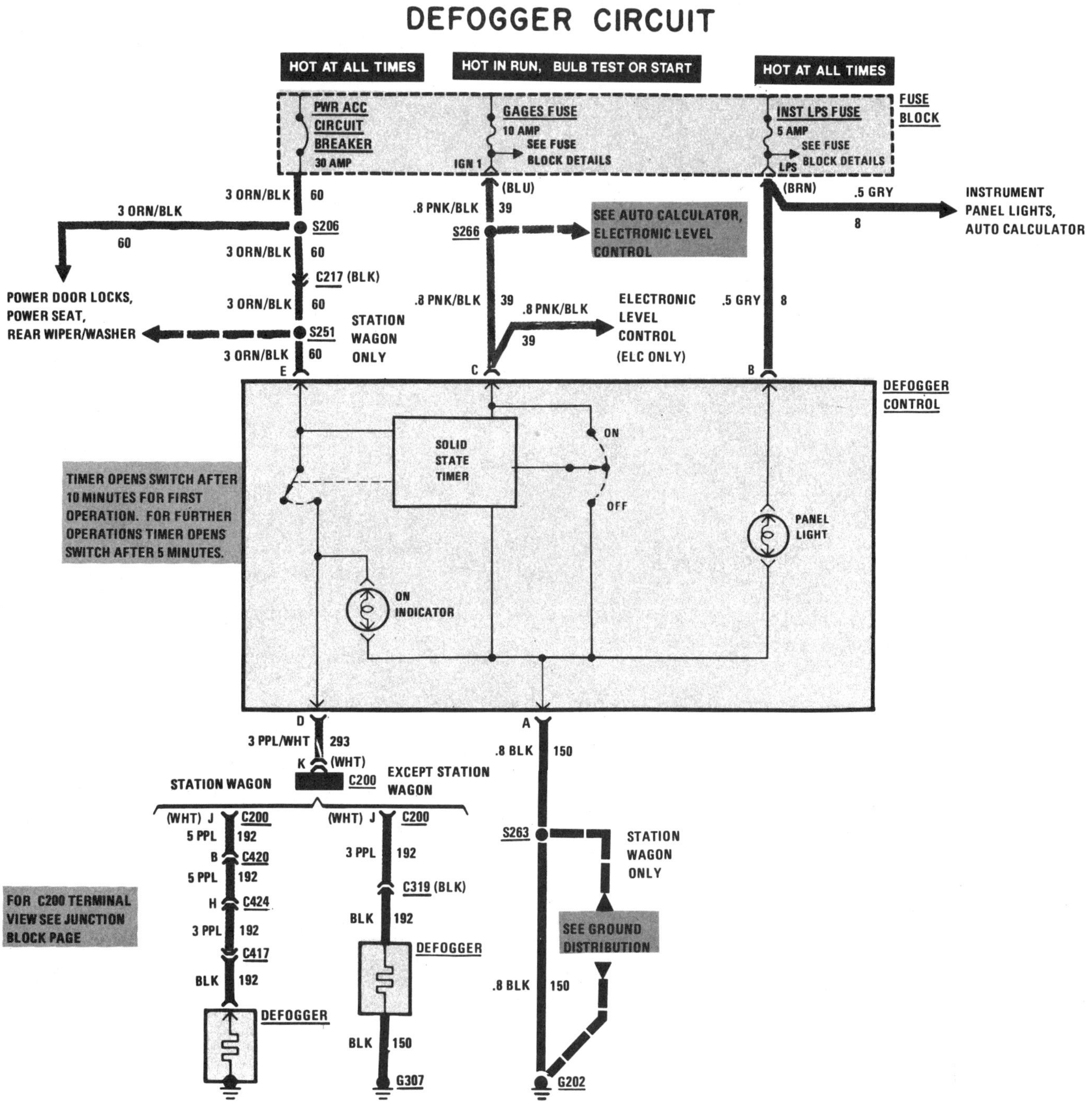

DEFOGGER CIRCUIT

FIGURE 34-6. The defogger is used to remove ice and fog from the rear windows. An electrical wire placed on the inside of the window heats up and removes the ice and fog. *(Courtesy of Oldsmobile Division, General Motors Corporation)*

2. Electricity flows to the upper wire in the LH power seat switch. The current is available at each switch, all of which are normally closed.

3. If the operator pushes the spring-loaded REAR HEIGHT UP switch (far left switch), electricity flows through the switch to the REAR HEIGHT MOTOR.

4. Electricity causes the motor to turn in the correct direction to lift the rear of the seat upward.

5. Electricity then flows through the BLU wire, to the REAR HEIGHT DOWN switch. This switch is open, so the electricity flows directly to ground, through connector A.

6. To get the seat to go down, electricity flows in the opposite direction in the motor. The REAR HEIGHT DOWN switch must be closed and the REAR HEIGHT UP switch must be open. This is done when the operator pushes the switch down.

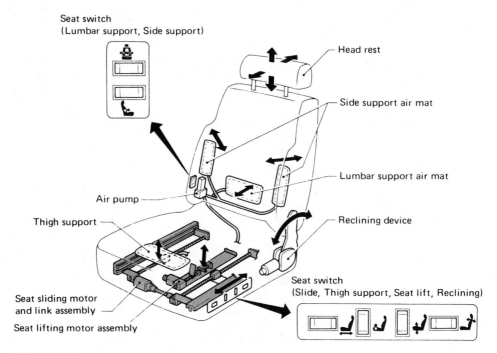

FIGURE 34–7. Power seats are used to adjust the seat and its cushions to best fit the driver. *(Courtesy of Nissan Motor Corporation in USA)*

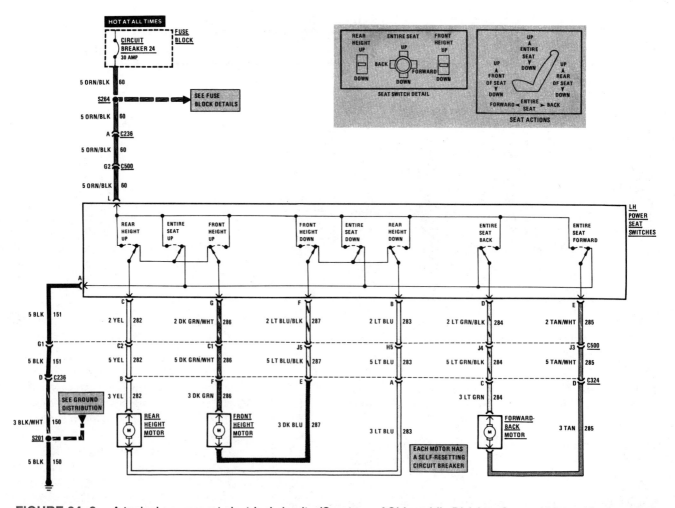

FIGURE 34–8. A typical power seat electrical circuit. *(Courtesy of Oldsmobile Division, General Motors Corporation)*

When the other switches are closed or opened, the electricity flows to the correct motor to adjust the seat accordingly.

Horn

The horn is a simple circuit used by the operator of the vehicle to alarm other drivers of danger. The horn circuit is shown in *Figure 34–9*. It consists of several major components. These include two horns, a horn switch, a *horn brush/slip-ring*, and a horn relay. The circuit operates as follows:

1. Electricity is sent from the battery directly to the fuse block and through the fuse.

2. Electricity now flows through the ORN wire to the horn relay.

3. At this point, current wants to flow through the horn brush/slip-ring assembly. This assembly is used to keep the horn switch in contact with the horn relay when the steering wheel is turned.

4. When the horn switch is pressed, electrical current flows through the left side of the horn relay.

5. As the horn relay (solenoid) is energized, it closes the horn relay switch, causing the horns to operate.

HORN

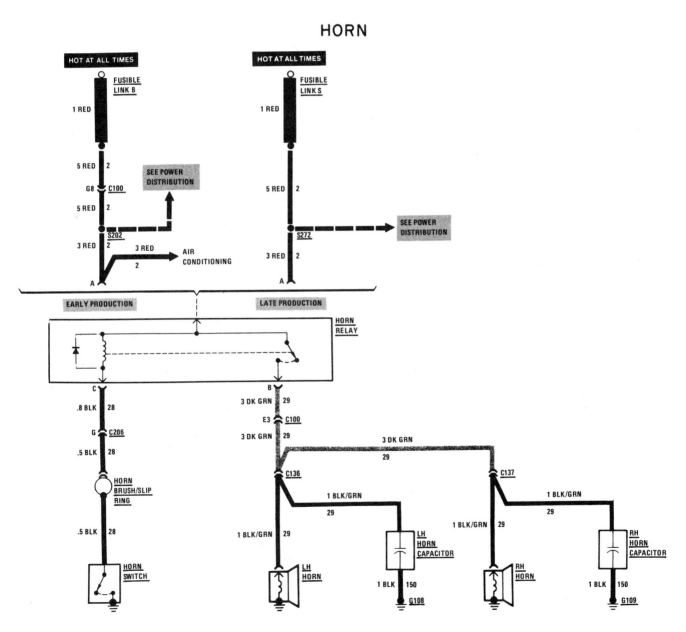

FIGURE 34–9. A horn circuit is used in all automobiles. Two horns, a horn switch, and a horn relay make up the circuit. *(Courtesy of Oldsmobile Division, General Motors Corporation)*

34.3   WINDSHIELD WIPER SYSTEMS

There are several types of windshield wiper systems. Both rear and front window systems are commonly used, Common components usually include the motor, linkage mechanism, switch, electronic logic circuits, and a washer system.

Windshield Wiper Motor

The motor in a windshield wiper system uses a permanent magnet (PM) type motor. Most front wiper motors have two speeds so that the wiper blade speed can be adjusted. In addition, some vehicles use a variable timer and speed control so the operator can control the wipers more precisely. *Figure 34–10* shows a typical motor assembly. It includes several components. The motor produces the rotational motion needed. The washer pump is located in the housing for pumping a water spray onto the windshield. An internal mechanism is used to change the rotational motion of the motor to an oscillation motion, which is needed for the wiper blades. The internal mechanism for changing the motion is shown in *Figure 34–11*. As the center motor rotates, the output is an oscillation motion.

Fluid Washer Nozzle

A fluid washer nozzle is used on some cars for the front

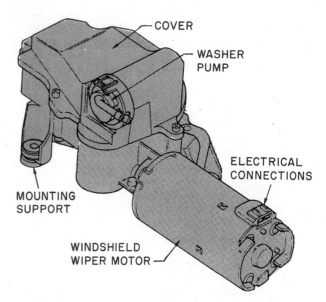

FIGURE 34–10.   A motor for a windshield wiper system. The assembly includes the motor, washer, and oscillating mechanism. *(Courtesy of Oldsmobile Division, General Motors Corporation)*

windshield washer system. The system consists of a fluid container, pump, fluid hoses and pipes, and nozzles or jets. *Figure 34–12* shows a washer system. When the operator

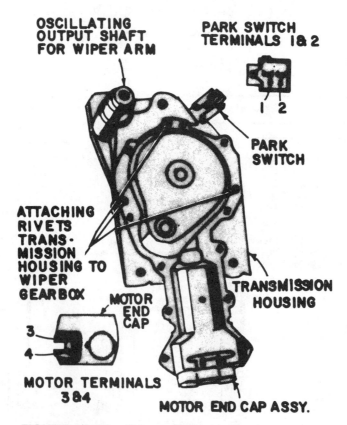

FIGURE 34–11.   This oscillation mechanism is used to change rotational motion to oscillation motion on the windshield wiper motor. *(Courtesy of Motor Publications, Auto Repair Manual)*

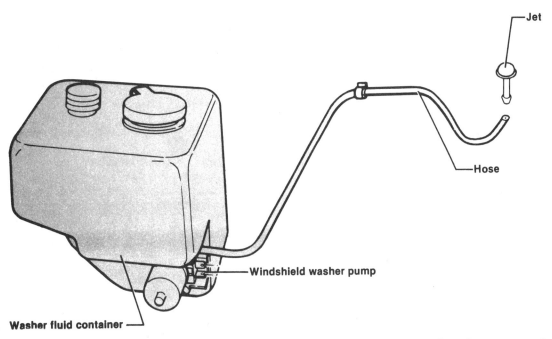

FIGURE 34–12.   The windshield washer system uses a fluid container, a small washer pump, and hose and nozzles (jets) to deliver the wash to the windshield. *(Courtesy of Volkswagen of America, Inc.)*

turns on the washer, the small pump forces fluid through the hoses and pipes to the nozzle or jet by the windshield. The pump can be located either at the fluid container or wiper motor.

Windshield Wiper Linkage

Several arms and pivot shafts make up the linkage used to transmit the oscillation motion at the motor to the windshield wipers. *Figure 34–13* shows an example of the linkage. As the wiper motor oscillates, arm A moves from left to right.

This moves arm B as well. As arm B moves, it causes the two pivot points to oscillate. The windshield wipers are connected to the two pivot points.

Wiper Arm and Blade

The wiper arms and blades are attached directly to the two pivot points operated by the linkage and motor. The wiper arm transmits the oscillation motion to the wiper blade. The wiper blade wipes the windshield clear of water. *Figure 34–14* shows a wiper arm and blade assembly.

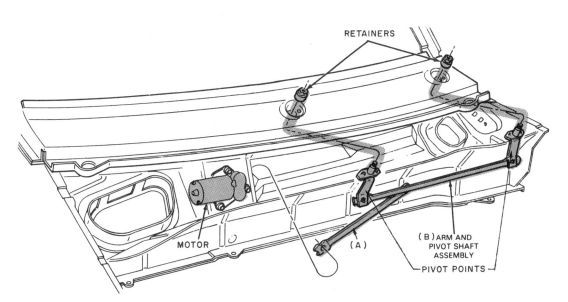

FIGURE 34–13.   The oscillation motion from the wiper motor is transferred by a linkage system to the pivot points for the wipers. *(Courtesy of Ford Motor Company)*

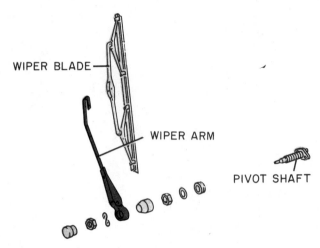

FIGURE 34–14. A wiper arm is used to connect the oscillating motion from the linkage to the wiper blade. *(Courtesy of Volkswagen of America, Inc.)*

Windshield Wiper System Electrical Circuit

It is not practical to show all of the electrical circuits used on windshield wiper systems. *Figure 34–15* shows a complete circuit with a *pulse wiper system*. The operation of the pulse system is as follows:

1. Voltage is available when the ignition switch is on ACCY (accessory) or RUN.

2. When the wiper/washer switch is in the PULSE position, voltage is applied to the PNK and GRY wires on the wiper/washer motor module.

3. Voltage is now applied to the solid state control board. Voltage from the control board is sent out and to the coil inside the park relay. The coil pulls the switch to the left.

4. Another voltage from the control board is sent through the park relay switch, through the YEL wire, to run the wiper motor.

5. The park relay switch is held closed by the mechanical arm until the wipers have completed their sweep. The circuit is then opened, and the wipers remain parked until the control board again applies a pulse voltage to the park relay.

6. The length of delay time between sweeps is controlled by the 1.2 megohm *pulse delay variable resistor* in the

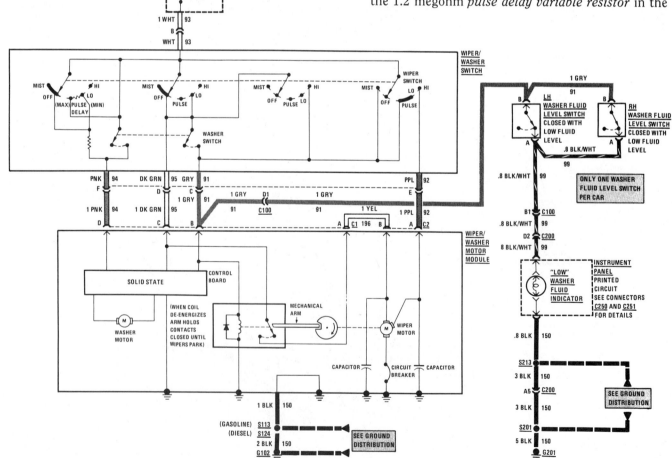

FIGURE 34–15. This circuit shows the complete operation of a pulse wiper system. *(Courtesy of Oldsmobile Division, General Motors Corporation)*

wiper/washer switch. The time delay is adjustable from zero to 25 seconds on this circuit.

The LO speed operates as follows:

1. In the LO position, the wiper switch supplies voltage to the DK GRN wire as well as the PNK and GRY wires.

2. The park relay is again energized.

3. Battery voltage is applied continuously to the relay contacts and to the wiper motor. The wiper motor runs continuously at a low speed.

The HI speed operates as follows:

1. Battery voltage is applied directly to the wiper motor through the PPL wire.

2. Voltage is also applied to the DK GRN and the GRY wires to energize the park relay.

3. When turned OFF, the wipers complete the last sweep and park.

The washer operates as follows:

1. When the washer switch is held on for less than 1 second, voltage is applied to the control board through the PNK and GRY wires.

2. The control board turns on the washer motor for approximately 2 1/2 seconds.

3. The voltage on the GRY wire also operates the park relay.

4. The control board also turns on the wiper motor for about 6 seconds.

34.4 BUMPER ENERGY ABSORBERS

Purpose of Energy Absorbers

Energy absorbers are now being used on the bumper systems of most vehicles. This is primarily a result of safety

PROBLEM: Multiple Electrical Problems

A new car with under 5,000 miles on it has developed unusual electrical problems. For example, certain circuits do not work. These include the automatic door locks, the underhood light, and automatic antenna, and the radio. What could be the problem?

SOLUTION:

The failure of multiple electrical circuits usually indicates the possibility of a burned electrical fusible link. Using the manufacturer's service manual, try to identify which fusible link is common to all of the circuits that are defective. This may take some time. Then check the appropriate fusible link for damage. It should be broken in the center, inside the wire insulation. A fusible link on new cars may be shorted out because the wiring harness rubs against the frame and shorts out. Replace the fusible link, but also identify what caused it to short out; for example, a shorted wiring harness.

standards that were incorporated several years ago. These standards specify that protection for safety-related items be provided for a predetermined series of barrier impacts. Energy absorbers placed in the front bumper system are used to aid in this system. *Figure 34–16* shows a two-stage energy absorber. The absorber uses a hydraulic principle to absorb the impact energy and restore the bumper to its original position after impact.

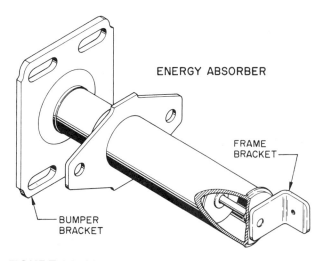

ENERGY ABSORBER

FRAME BRACKET

BUMPER BRACKET

FIGURE 34–16.   An energy absorber is used to absorb the energy from a direct impact, caused by a collision upon the bumper. *(Courtesy of United Delco, Division of General Motors Corporation)*

Operation of Energy Absorbers

Refer to *Figure 34-17*. There is a gas pressure inside the gas-filled piston tube assembly. Hydraulic fluid fills the inside of the cylinder tube assembly. The gas pressure in the piston tube assembly maintains the unit in an extended position. The stop ring is used to limit travel and to provide extra strength during towing.

During low-speed collisions, hydraulic fluid is forced past the orifice into the piston tube. The metering pin determines the size of the orifice by the position of the bumper and piston tube assembly. The metering and flow of fluid provide the energy absorbing action. The floating piston separates the hydraulic fluid from the gas. After impact, the pressure of the gas behind the floating piston pushes the hydraulic fluid back into the cylinder assembly.

During high-speed collisions, the two-stage orifice shears out of the piston cap (see insert). This allows hydraulic fluid to pass faster into the piston tube. After a high-speed impact, the unit must be replaced.

34.5 SAFETY BELTS

Purpose of Retractors and Reels

In the past, safety belts were very cumbersome and binding. Today, retractors and reels rewind and loosen the belt as needed. The reel allows the safety belt wearer to move around inside the vehicle freely during normal conditions. This freedom makes some people skeptical. They feel the belt may not restrain them in a collision. However, the belts lock solidly when needed.

Operation of Safety Belts

The safety belt shown in *Figure 34-18* is called a car-sensitive belt. It uses a *pendulum* located in the car body and a ratchet mechanism. Under normal conditions, the pendulum and bar are in their resting position. The reel, which holds the belt, is free to rotate. As the occupant leans against

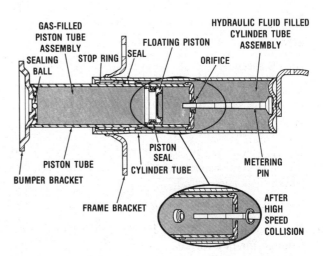

FIGURE 34-17. The parts of an energy absorber. *(Courtesy of United Delco, Division of General Motors Corporation)*

the belt, it "gives" or unreels. Under accident conditions, such as a collision, the pendulum tilts toward the force of the impact. This causes the bar to engage the ratchet. The reel and seat belt now lock, restraining the occupant.

34.6 CRUISE CONTROL

Introduction and Purpose

Because of the constant changes and improvements in technology, each cruise control system may be considerably different. Several types are used, including the nonresume type, the resume type, and the electronic type.

Cruise control systems are designed to allow the driver to maintain a constant speed without having to apply continual foot pressure to the accelerator pedal. Selected cruise speeds are easily maintained. Speed can be easily changed. Several override systems also allow the vehicle to be accelerated, slowed, or stopped.

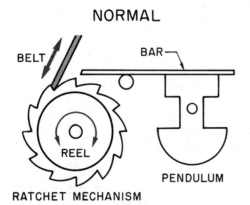
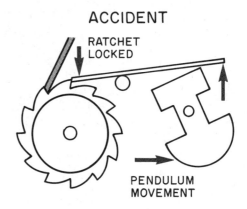

FIGURE 34-18. Some safety belts use a pendulum system to lock up when the vehicle is in a collision.

When engaged, the cruise control components set the throttle position to the desired speed. The speed will be maintained unless heavy loads and steep hills interfere. The cruise control is disengaged whenever the brake pedal is depressed. *Figure 34–19* shows the common components on a cruise control system.

Cruise Control Switch

The cruise control switch is located on the end of the turn signal or near the center or sides of the steering wheel. There are usually several functions on the switch, including off-on, resume, and engage buttons. The switch is different for resume and nonresume systems. *Figure 34–20* shows a cruise control switch.

Transducer

The *transducer* is a device that controls the speed of the vehicle. When the transducer is engaged, it senses vehicle speed and controls a vacuum source. The vacuum source is used to maintain a certain position on a servo. Locate the transducer on Figure 34–19. Note that speed control is sensed from the lower cable and casing assembly attached to the transmission.

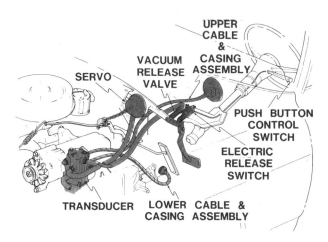

FIGURE 34–19. The parts of a common cruise control system. *(Courtesy of General Motors Product Service Training)*

Servo

The *servo* unit is connected to the carburetor or throttle by a rod or linkage, a bead chain, or a *Bowden cable*. The servo unit maintains the desired car speed by receiving a controlled amount of vacuum from the transducer. The variation

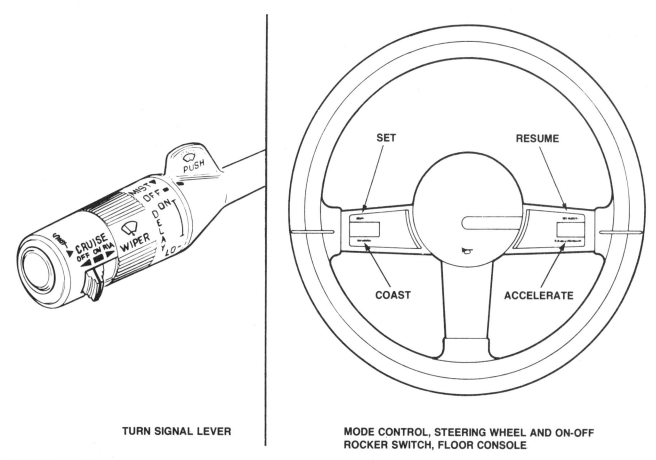

TURN SIGNAL LEVER

MODE CONTROL, STEERING WHEEL AND ON-OFF ROCKER SWITCH, FLOOR CONSOLE

FIGURE 34–20. The cruise control switch is used to set or increase speed, resume speed, or turn the system off and on. *(Courtesy of General Motors Product Service Training)*

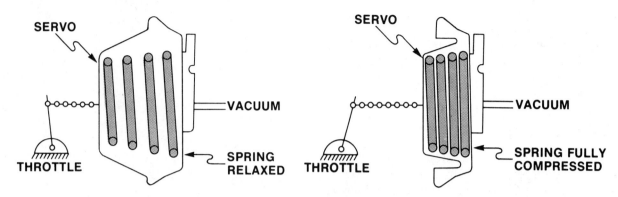

FIGURE 34–21.   Inside the servo, vacuum will compress or relax the spring. When the system is on, the throttle is positioned with the spring compressed. *(Courtesy of General Motors Product Service Training)*

in vacuum changes the position of the throttle. The servo is shown on Figure 34–19.

An inside view of the servo is shown in *Figure 34–21*. When a vacuum is applied, the servo spring is compressed, and the throttle is positioned correctly. When the vacuum is released, the servo spring is relaxed and the system is not operating.

Brake-activated Switches

There are two switches that are operated by the position of the brake. When the brake pedal is depressed, the brake release switch disengages the system. A vacuum release valve is also used to disengage the system when the brake pedal is depressed. *Figure 34–22* shows an example of the location of the two switches.

Electrical and Vacuum Circuits

Figure 34–23 shows an electrical and vacuum circuit diagram. The system operates as follows:

1. The object is to energize the solenoid inside the transducer. If the solenoid is energized, the vacuum valve will shift, allowing vacuum to control the servo.

2. When the system is in the off position, current passes through the ignition switch, fuse, and slider in the switch to the resistance wire.

3. The resistance produces a voltage drop before the current gets to the solenoid coil inside the transducer. There is not enough voltage to energize the solenoid coil.

4. When the cruise control is engaged, current flows through the switch to the engage wire. If the vehicle is above 30 mph, the low-speed switch will be closed. Current can then easily pass through the solenoid coil, which, in turn, will control the vacuum.

5. If the brakes are depressed with the cruise control on, electricity will bypass the solenoid, go through the brake light circuit, and be grounded. This will shut off the cruise control by disengaging the solenoid and closing the vacuum to the servo.

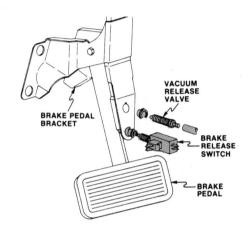

FIGURE 34–22.   Two switches, a vacuum release and a brake release switch, disengage the cruise control when the brake pedal is depressed. *(Courtesy of General Motors Product Service Training)*

6. The object of the vacuum circuit is to get the right amount of vacuum sent to the servo.

7. Vacuum is taken from the manifold and sent through the resume valve. When the cruise control is on, the resume valve is energized and open.

8. Vacuum then flows into the transducer, through the vacuum valve in the transducer, to the servo. Of course, vacuum can only get to the servo if the electrical solenoid is energized.

9. The air control valve inside the transducer acts like a vacuum bleed valve. It is a variable control, depending on the speed of the vehicle. At lower speed settings, the air control valve bleeds off vacuum so less is sent to the servo. At higher speeds, less vacuum is bled off so more vacuum is sent to the servo.

10. When the brake is depressed, disengaging the system, the resume solenoid is closed. When the resume switch is activated, the solenoid is energized to open the vacuum line to the transducer.

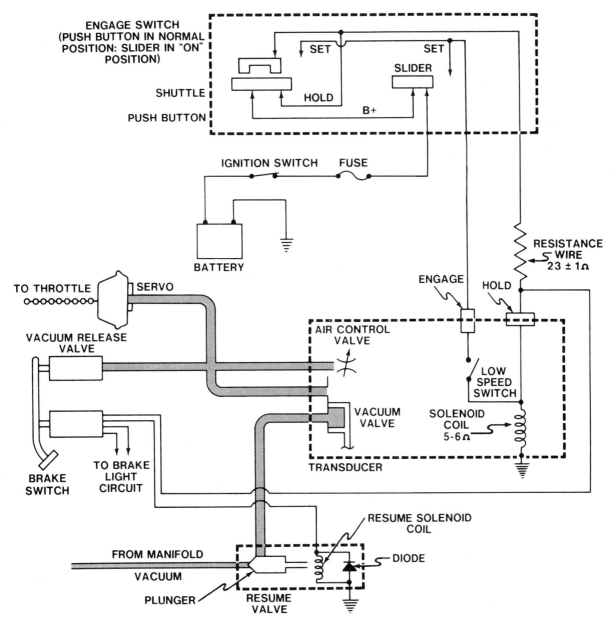

FIGURE 34–23.   A cruise control circuit with vacuum and electrical systems. *(Courtesy of General Motors Product Service Training)*

Electronic Cruise Control Parts

Cruise control can also be obtained by using electronic components rather than mechanical components. Depending on the vehicle manufacturer, several additional components may be used. These include:

1. *Electronic control module*, integrated circuitry — used to control the servo unit. The servo unit is again used to control the vacuum, which in turn controls the throttle.

2. *Vehicle speed sensor (VSS) buffer amplifier* — used to monitor or sense vehicle speed. The signal created is sent to the electronic control module. A generator speed sensor may also be used in conjunction with the VSS.

3. *Clutch switch* — used on vehicles with manual transmissions to disengage the cruise control when the clutch is depressed.

4. *Accumulator* — used as a vacuum storage tank on vehicles that have low vacuum during heavy load and high road speed.

Electronic Cruise Control Operation

Figure 34–24 shows how electronic cruise control components work together. The throttle position is controlled by the servo unit. The servo unit uses vacuum working against a spring pressure to operate an internal diaphragm. The servo unit vacuum circuit is controlled electronically by the con-

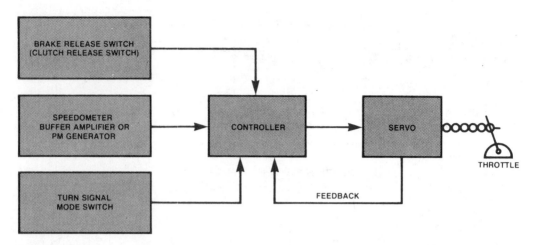

FIGURE 34–24. Electronic cruise control uses an electronic control module (controller) to operate a servo that controls the position of the throttle. *(Courtesy of General Motors Product Service Training)*

troller. The controller has several inputs that help determine how it will affect the servo. These inputs include the:

1. *Brake release switch* (clutch release switch)

2. *Speedometer*, buffer amplifier, or generator speed sensor

3. *Turn signal mode switch* (switch used on the turn signal to control the cruise control)

34.7 AIR BAG (PASSIVE RESTRAINT) SYSTEMS

Description

Air bag systems, also called *passive restraint* systems or SIR (supplemental inflatable restraint) systems, are becoming more popular in vehicles. Their purpose is to supplement the driver's seat belt during an accident. The air bags are designed to inflate through the steering column when the vehicle is involved in a front-end accident of sufficient force. The result is that the driver is protected from serious injury. The restraint system is activated when an accident occurs up to 30% off the centerline of the vehicle. See *Figure 34–25*.

Components

Depending on the vehicle and the year, there are several designs. On one design, there are three sensors on the vehicle:

1. the *forward sensor*,

2. the passenger compartment sensor, and

3. the arming sensor.

These sensors cause the air bags to inflate when there is a rapid change in the vehicle's speed or velocity. Any rapid change means that an accident is occurring. *Figure 34–26* shows the major components and their location for a passive restraint system. Refer to the figure to identify the following components.

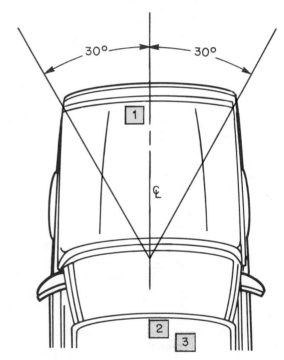

1. FORWARD SENSOR LOCATION

2. PASSENGER COMPARTMENT SENSOR LOCATION

3. ARMING SENSOR LOCATION

FIGURE 34–25. Sensors are located in several positions on the vehicle to sense an impending accident so the air bags can be inflated. *(Courtesy of Motor Publications, Auto Repair Manual)*

1. *Control module* — Acts as the passenger compartment sensor. The control module also contains diagnostics information for the restraint system. It monitors vehicle deceleration and combines this information with the other two sensors. On the basis of the information from these sensors, the control module signals the air bag to be inflated or deployed.

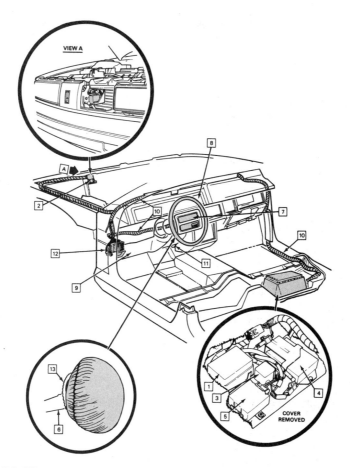

FIGURE 34–26. The major components of a passive restraint (air bag) system and their location. *(Courtesy of Motor Publications, Auto Repair Manual)*

2. *Forward sensor* — Located near the front grill of the vehicle. This sensor is able to detect a rapid drop in vehicle speed. It is normally open electrically. When deceleration occurs, the switch is closed, signaling an impending accident.

3. *Arming sensor* — A normally open mechanical sensor that closes during rapid deceleration. It is considered a backup to the other sensors.

4. *Power supply* — Provides an increased voltage to the air bag during low-voltage conditions to make sure it opens. The power supply also provides power for the diagnostics systems.

5. *Energy reserve module* — Provides extra electrical energy if the vehicle's battery is damaged or disconnected during the accident.

6. *Steering column and coil assembly* — A collapsible steering column and, inside the steering column, a coil. This assembly provides continuous electrical contact between the control module and the steering wheel module (see below) as the steering wheel is turned.

7. *Steering wheel module* — Made of the inflator assembly, which includes the electrical circuit and the inflatable bag. The steering wheel module is located inside the steering wheel hub area and is covered by a vinyl trim cover. When an accident occurs the inflatable bag is blown out by high-pressure gas. The trim cover then opens or ruptures at the seams, allowing the bag to be inflated.

8. *Warning lamp* — Displays the words "Inflatable Restraint." It also helps the service technician diagnose the system.

9. *Knee bolster* — An energy-absorbing pad. It is used to cushion the forward movement of the driver during an accident by restricting leg movement.

10. *SIR wiring harness* — Interconnects all of the system's components electrically.

11. *Test connector* — Used to start or initiate diagnosis of the air bag system.

12. *Fuse panel* — Most vehicles that have an air bag system have a specially designed fuse panel. It is located in the lower instrument panel trim pad and is hinged to swing out for easy access.

13. *Steering wheel* — Used to control the direction of the vehicle during driving conditions.

Problems, Diagnosis and Service

1. Many electrical wires may have very sharp protrusions. When handling wires, be careful not to puncture your hands.
2. Heavy parts are attached to the energy absorbers used on the front of the vehicle. Always be careful to support all parts when working on these absorbers.
3. Always use the correct tools when working on the cruise control. This will eliminate the possibility of injury to the hands.
4. Be careful when handling restraint system sensors. Never strike or jar a sensor in such a way that may cause deployment of the air bag. Before servicing any parts on a restraint system, wait 10 minutes after disconnecting the battery. This prevents accidental deployment and possible injury.
5. Before removal of any auxiliary or electrical system component make sure you understand its operation and how it is hooked into the system. This information will eliminate many possible injuries.

PROBLEM: Electrical and Mechanical Faults

Many problems pertaining to auxiliary and electrical systems can occur. Rather than specify a particular problem, this section will present general diagnostic procedures for both electrical and mechanical problems and give several examples.

DIAGNOSIS

Electrical Problems

When diagnosing problems in electrical circuits use the following general procedures:

1. Check the problem. Make sure you know what the exact problem is. Don't replace a component that is not faulty.

2. Refer to the electrical schematic. Read the schematic to make sure you know exactly how the electrical circuit and its components are to operate.

3. Look for the possible cause. After viewing the schematic, consider possible causes. Check the basic components and those easiest to check such as the fuse and ground, first.

4. Test for correct voltages during operation. Using a voltmeter, check for voltages at various parts of the schematic. On the basis of this information, again try to determine the cause of the problem.

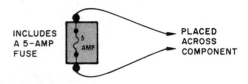

FIGURE 34–27. A jumper wire can be used to bypass a component in an electrical circuit. *(Courtesy of Oldsmobile Division, General Motors Corporation)*

5. Narrow down the problem to one point in the circuit. Make voltage checks and then try to narrow down the problem to only one component. Try to isolate the problem.

6. Find the cause and repair it. Use the component location manuals to help identify where the part is positioned on the vehicle.

7. Check the circuit for correct operation. Make sure the cause has been corrected and replaced.

8. There are many diagnostic tools to help the service technician check electrical circuits and systems.
   a. To check electrical circuits, a *jumper wire* can be used to bypass a particular part of the circuit. *Figure 34–27* shows a jumper wire.
   b. *Short finders* are available to locate hidden shorts to ground.
   c. A *fuse tester* can be used to check for bad fuses.
   d. Testing for voltages can be done as shown in *Figure 34–28*. One lead is grounded, and the other lead is connected to a specific test point.

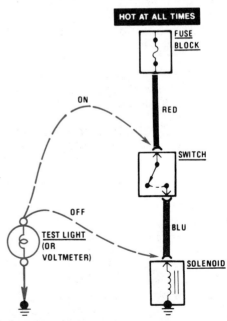

FIGURE 34–28. Voltage can be checked by connecting one lead to ground and the other lead to the test point. *(Courtesy of Oldsmobile Division, General Motors Corporation)*

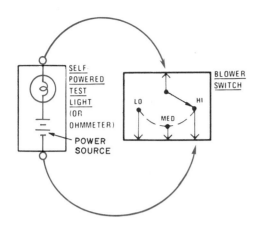

FIGURE 34–29. Continuity can be checked by using a self-powered test light or an ohmmeter. *(Courtesy of Oldsmobile Division, General Motors Corporation)*

e. Test for continuity by using a self-powered test light or ohmmeter. *Figure 34–29* shows an example of testing the continuity of a switch.

Mechanical Problems

Use the following general procedures to help diagnose mechanical problems related to auxiliary and electrical systems:

1. Operate the system especially through all conditions such as low, medium, high, off, and on.

2. Observe the malfunction or operational characteristics. Did the problem occur over a period of time or all at once? Ask the operator to give information about its operation. Know the maintenance record of the system and vehicle.

3. Become completely familiar with how the system should operate. Use the operator's manual, electrical schematics, maintenance manuals, and component locator manual to aid the diagnostic procedure.

4. First check the components that can be easily tested such as fuses, grounds, broken parts, and special noises.

5. Try to isolate the problem to a specific component within the system.

6. Check the suspected component for correct operation (throughout the total range of operation).

7. Replace the cause of the problem.

8. Check the system to make sure the problem has been corrected.

9. If there is still a problem, get a second opinion from another service technician.

Diagnostic Examples

The following are examples of diagnostic procedures used on mechanical or electrical components:

Energy Absorbers

1. Check for oil leakage. If you find a leak or oil, replace the energy absorber.

2. Check for visual distortion or damage to the absorber.

3. Check for a rattling noise as the unit is shaken. This indicates that the metering pin and orifice have been damaged. The orifice has been broken off. Replace if necessary.

4. Check for rotation between the piston tube and the cylinder tube. A good energy absorber should not rotate.

5. The energy absorber can be bench-tested by compressing the unit in an arbor press about 3/8 inch. It should restore to its normal position. If it doesn't, replace the unit.

Cruise Control

1. Always perform a visual inspection of all components.

2. Check the servo for leaks.

3. Check for blown fuses.

4. Bypass the low-speed switch, and check for operation.

5. With the car off and the ignition switch on, engage the cruise control switch. Listen for the solenoid to click or knock. This indicates that the solenoid is operative.

6. Check the brake-activated electric release switch. A small misadjustment can cause the system to be inoperative.

7. Check all electrical connectors for solid contact.

8. Check all electrical components for correct operation.

9. Check the vacuum circuit for correct operation. Check for correct vacuum at the transducer. Observe all vacuum lines for leaks and damaged rubber hoses. Use a vacuum pump if needed to check vacuum operation.

10. Check vacuum hoses that might be pinched.

11. Inspect the mechanical throttle linkage for ease of movement. The bead-chain type should have no slack in it with the engine at the correct idle speed.

12. If no external fault can be found, the transducer may be checked for vacuum leaks or incorrect operation. This is usually done by an authorized transducer repair facility.

13. On computerized speed control systems, a self-diagnostic system may also be used. Trouble codes are stored in the computer and can be accessed by the service technician. When a trouble code is identified, the service technician can then refer to a trouble code diagnostic chart. *Figure 34–30* is one of seven trouble code diagnostic charts available for one type of cruise control.

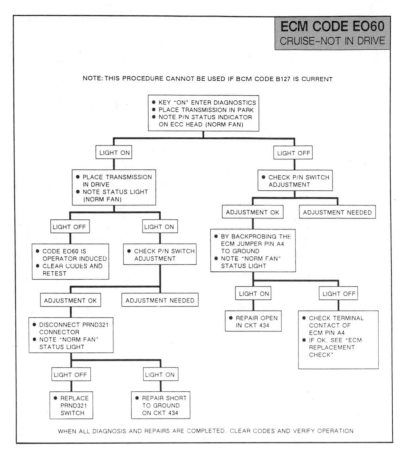

FIGURE 34–30. This type of diagnostic chart will help the service technician troubleshoot a specific component identified as a trouble code on the cruise control system. *(Courtesy of Motor Publications, Auto Repair Manual)*

Passive Restraint Systems

Numerous diagnostic checks can be performed on passive restraint systems. Each will depend on the year and type of vehicle and system. Most passive restraint systems are computer-controlled. Thus, these systems have a built in diagnostic system that monitors the electrical circuits. The diagnostic circuits, through the warning lamp, indicate the condition of the system.

Once it has been determined, by the warning light, that the system is inoperative, a diagnostic check can be made. *Figure 34–31* shows a typical diagnostic procedure to determine the cause of the problem.

Note that most items on a passive restraint system cannot be repaired. The following items are replaced, not repaired:

1. Forward sensor

2. Arming sensor

3. Power supply

4. Energy reserve module

5. SIR control module

6. Coil assembly

7. Steering wheel module

SERVICE

Each service procedure will be different for each component that is faulty. Follow the maintenance or service manuals for the correct procedure to follow.

PROBLEM: Faulty Windshield Wiper System

The windshield wiper system is inoperative.

DIAGNOSIS

Many troubleshooting procedures are used to diagnose windshield wiper systems. The wiper may be inoperative, the motor may not shut off, it may be sluggish as it moves, or, as the problem states, it may be totally inoperative. *Figure 34–32* shows an example of a diagnostic procedure for a specific manufacturer. Always refer to the correct manual to get correct diagnostic procedures.

SERVICE

Refer to the correct service manual, and replace the faulty part as necessary.

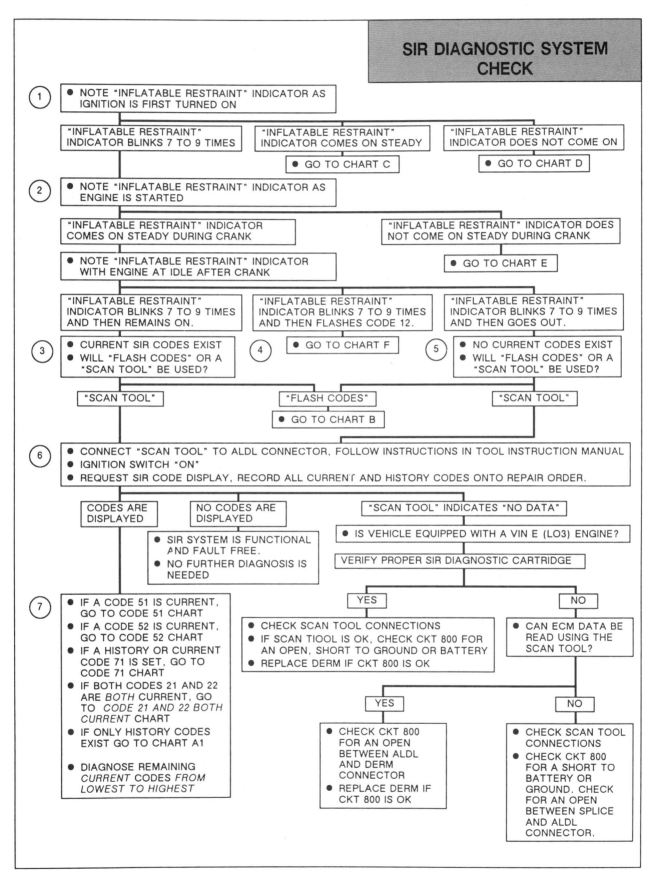

FIGURE 34–31. Passive restraint systems have built-in diagnostic systems to aid the service technician. Specific diagnostic procedures are available to help determine the exact cause of the problem. *(Courtesy of Motor Publications, Auto Repair Manual)*

PROCEDURE I (Wiper Inoperative)

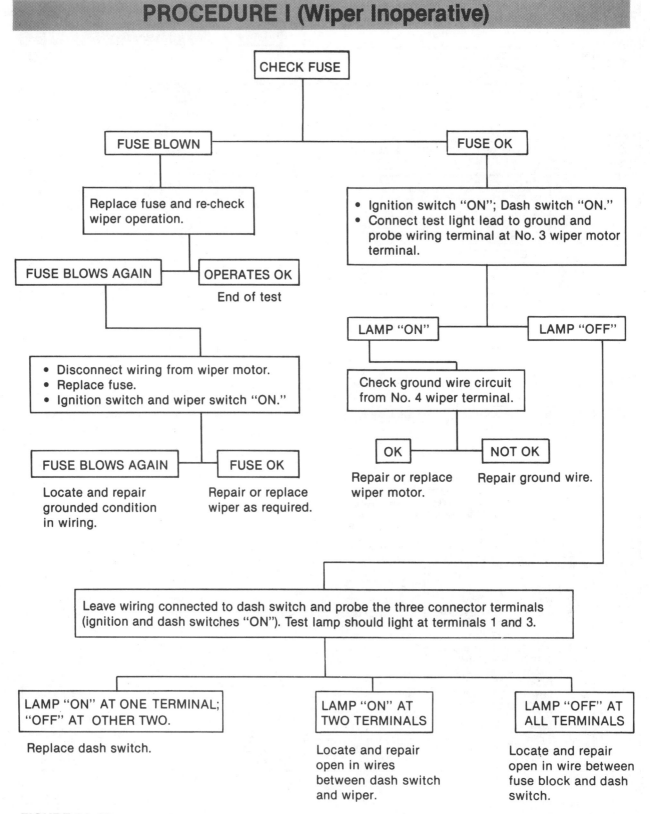

CHECK FUSE

FUSE BLOWN — FUSE OK

Replace fuse and re-check wiper operation.

- Ignition switch "ON"; Dash switch "ON."
- Connect test light lead to ground and probe wiring terminal at No. 3 wiper motor terminal.

FUSE BLOWS AGAIN — OPERATES OK
End of test

LAMP "ON" — LAMP "OFF"

- Disconnect wiring from wiper motor.
- Replace fuse.
- Ignition switch and wiper switch "ON."

Check ground wire circuit from No. 4 wiper terminal.

FUSE BLOWS AGAIN — FUSE OK

OK — NOT OK

Locate and repair grounded condition in wiring.

Repair or replace wiper as required.

Repair or replace wiper motor.

Repair ground wire.

Leave wiring connected to dash switch and probe the three connector terminals (ignition and dash switches "ON"). Test lamp should light at terminals 1 and 3.

LAMP "ON" AT ONE TERMINAL; "OFF" AT OTHER TWO.

LAMP "ON" AT TWO TERMINALS

LAMP "OFF" AT ALL TERMINALS

Replace dash switch.

Locate and repair open in wires between dash switch and wiper.

Locate and repair open in wire between fuse block and dash switch.

FIGURE 34–32. Troubleshooting procedures are available from the manufacturer for a variety of problems encountered in the windshield wiper, as well as other systems. *(Courtesy of United Delco, Division of General Motors Corporation)*

SERVICE MANUAL CONNECTION

There are many important specifications to keep in mind when working with auxiliary and electrical systems. To identify the specifications for your vehicle, you will need to know the VIN (vehicle identification number) of the vehicle, the type and year of the vehicle, and the type of engine used. Although they may be titled differently, some of the more common auxiliary and electrical system specifications (not all) found in service manuals are listed below. Note that these are typical examples. Each vehicle may have different specifications.

Common Specification	Typical Example
Cruise control switch contacts open	1/8–1.2 inches of pedal travel
Disengagement switch brake pedal adjustment (extension from floor)	6.07 inches
Rear wiper motor speed	33–44 RPM
Voltage at cruise switch ON	Battery volts
Wiper washer switch (resistance)	Less than 0.05 ohms
Wiper motor current draw (no load)	3.5–4.0 amps
Wiper motor rated voltage	12 volts

In addition, the service manual will give specific directions for various service and testing procedures. Some of the more common procedures include:

- Air bag restraint system, disable
- Bead chain adjust
- Diagnosing passive restraint systems
- Fuse panel and flasher locations
- Horn sounder replace
- Speed control adjust
- Speed control road test
- Wiper motor replace
- Windshield wiper switch replace

SUMMARY

This chapter discussed various auxiliary systems and electrical circuits used on the automobile. In order to understand these systems, schematics, electrical symbols, and various electrical parts needed to be defined. All electrical circuits are analyzed by using a schematic. Current automotive electrical schematics use symbols that show the parts and how electricity flows through the circuit. Wire size, component location, and wire colors are also shown. With the increased number of electrical circuits used on automobiles, a good understanding of schematics is very important.

The headlight circuit can be analyzed by studying the schematic. Electricity is controlled by the light switch. Additional components in the circuit include the dimmer switch, low and high beam in the headlights, and the fuse panel. The defogger operates by using a defogger switch, a timer to hold the defogger on for a certain period of time, and the fuse panel. The power seats operate by using several motors on the bottom of the seats. The motors can operate in either direction. The switches, which are controlled by the operator, tell the motors which direction to turn. The horn circuit uses electricity from the battery, through the horn button, to the horn solenoid. A solenoid is also used to energize the horn.

The windshield wiper system uses several components. The windshield wiper motor is a permanent magnetic motor used to operate the windshield wipers. There is also a mechanism used to change the rotational motion of the motor to oscillation motion for the wipers. A fluid washer nozzle and pump are used to pump cleaning fluid to the windshield. Each vehicle also uses mechanical linkage to connect the oscillation motion of the motor output to the wiper blades. Windshield wiper systems use an electrical circuit to time the wiper motion as in a pulse mode, to operate on LO and HI operation. In addition, the washer system also uses an electrical circuit to operate.

The purpose of an energy absorber bumper is to guard against vehicle damage in low-speed impacts. A hydraulic absorber is used to cushion the impact. The absorber uses hydraulic fluid and gas inside of a cylinder. During low-speed impacts, hydraulic fluid is forced past small holes and a metering pin inside the cylinder. The metering and flow of the fluid provide the energy absorbing action.

Safety belts are used on all vehicles today. Retractors and reels that rewind and loosen the belt are used for improved passenger comfort. A pendulum located inside the car body and a ratchet mechanism are used to lock the belt during impacts.

Cruise control is used to mechanically or electronically control the position of the throttle during highway operation. These systems help the operator to maintain a constant speed without having to apply foot pressure to the accelerator pedal. A cruise control switch is used to engage or disengage the system. Many types are used.

There are several common parts used on cruise control systems. The servo is connected to the carburetor to control the throttle position. It uses vacuum to move a wire or chain connected to the throttle mechanism. The transducer is used to control the vacuum sent to the servo. A brake-activated

(continued)

Linkage to Automotive Technology

SMART HIGHWAYS

In the future, highways with sophisticated communication systems will be integrated with each driver. These systems, called "smart highways," will feature traffic monitoring, navigational equipment, and computer links to improve safety and reduce travel time. These systems are also identified as intelligent vehicle/highway systems (IVHS).

The figure shows how IVHS might work. As the driver pulls out of the driveway, the car is immediately linked into satellite systems to identify its location and position. This information is read on the instrument panel video display of the car. In addition, the on-board computer would be able to communicate with a traffic information processing center. A citywide network of traffic beacons and sensors would send traffic information (congestion, accidents, road conditions, and so on) to the processing center. A computer voice would then give the driver five possible routes to the destination entered into the on-board computer. The best route would then be outlined in red on the video screen.

Many such systems are being researched and tested. As the technology develops and the systems are placed on automobiles, improved safety, less driving time, and more convenience will be the result.

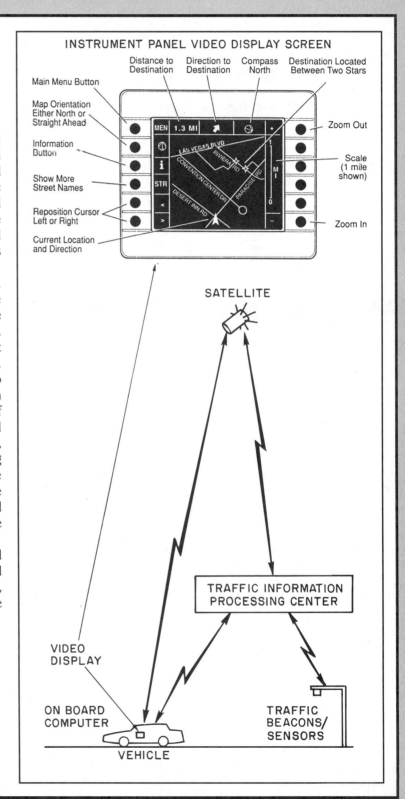

switch is used to disengage the system when the brakes are applied. The electrical circuit is used to control valves, which in turn control the vacuum to the transducer.

Electronic cruise control systems use several additional parts. These include the electronic control module, a vehicle speed sensor (VSS), a clutch switch, and an accumulator used to store vacuum.

Passive restraint systems are now being used on many vehicles. Passive restraint systems use several sensors to determine if a vehicle crash is impending. If the sensors detect an impending crash they send an electrical signal to the computerized control module. The control module then signals the air bag to inflate using a high-pressure gas. The result is additional protection for the driver during violent accidents.

Diagnosis and service of auxiliary and electrical systems are very important. Use a standard troubleshooting procedure to find an electrical problem. For example, always check the problem, don't fix a component that is not faulty, read the schematic, look for possible causes, test for correct voltages, narrow the problem down to one circuit, find the cause, and correct the problem.

Various troubleshooting tools are used on electrical circuits. These include jumper wires, a short finder, and a fuse tester. A volt-ohmmeter can also be used to check for voltages, continuity, and shorts. Always check the easiest components first.

When troubleshooting energy absorber bumpers, check for oil leaking from the absorber, visual distortion, and a rattling noise inside the unit. A rattling noise indicates the orifice and metering pin have been broken due to a high-speed impact.

Common checks that are done on a cruise control system include checking the servo for leaks, checking for blown fuses, checking the brake-activated switch for correct operation, and checking all electrical connectors for solid contact.

TERMS TO KNOW

Can you explain each of the following terms? Review the chapter until you can use each term correctly.

Electrical schematic	Pendulum
Electrical symbol	Transducer
Component location table	Servo
Fuse block	Bowden cable
Fusible link	Amplifier
Dimmer switch	Jumper wire
Horn brush/slip-ring	Short finder
Pulse wiper system	Fuse tester
Pulse delay variable resistor	Passive restraint
Energy absorber	Forward sensor

REVIEW QUESTIONS

Multiple Choice

1. Electrical schematics are used to:
   a. Show the parts of a circuit
   b. Show the direction of electrical flow
   c. Show the color of wire used in the circuits
   d. All of the above
   e. None of the above

2. To find the exact physical location of a part on the schematic:
   a. Look at the position on the schematic
   b. Look at the component location table
   c. Look at the size of the wire
   d. Look at the length of the wire
   e. None of the above

3. To protect electrical circuits from overloaded conditions, _____ are used.
   a. Fuses
   b. Electrical connectors
   c. Motors
   d. ORN wires
   e. PPL wires

4. Which of the following circuits uses a dimmer switch?
   a. Horn
   b. Headlight
   c. Windshield wiper
   d. All of the above
   e. None of the above

5. The defogger system uses an electrical circuit that:
   a. Only operates for a certain period of time
   b. Uses an ON-OFF switch
   c. Uses wires on the inside surface of the window
   d. All of the above
   e. None of the above

6. Electrical seats use motors that:
   a. Have one electromagnet on each motor
   b. Operate in only one direction
   c. Operate in either direction, depending on the current
   d. Are encased in oil
   e. Operate on 1–2 volts

7. The horn circuit uses:
   a. Seven switches to operate correctly
   b. A solenoid and horn relay switch
   c. Motors that operate in either direction
   d. An electronic control module
   e. All of the above

8. The mechanism in a windshield wiper system for changing rotational motion to oscillation motion is located:
   a. On the windshield wipers
   b. In the washer system
   c. Inside the motor assembly
   d. Under the dashboard
   e. In the trunk

9. Which is *not* a part of a common windshield wiper system?
   a. Fluid washer system
   b. Motor
   c. Wiper blades
   d. Servo
   e. Wiper linkage

10. Which component is used in the electrical circuit to adjust the time delay for pulsing the wipers?
    a. Variable motor
    b. Variable washer nozzle
    c. Linkage
    d. Wiper blades
    e. Variable resistor

11. What is used inside the energy absorber to absorb the shock of impact?
    a. Gas
    b. Springs
    c. Hydraulic fluid
    d. Magnetism
    e. All of the above

12. Which of the following is/are used to keep the energy absorber in place and fully extended during normal conditions?
    a. Gas
    b. Springs
    c. Hydraulic fluid
    d. Magnetism
    e. All of the above

13. Safety belts are locked up during a collision by using a _____.
    a. Magnetic circuit
    b. Spur gear
    c. Pendulum
    d. Clutch
    e. Magnetic clutch

14. Which device on a cruise control system is used to control the amount of vacuum?
    a. Servo
    b. Solenoid coil
    c. Brake-activated switch
    d. Transducer
    e. None of the above

15. Which device on a cruise control system is used to adjust and control the position of the throttle?
    a. Servo   d. Transducer
    b. Solenoid   e. Magnetic switch
    c. Brake-activated switch

16. Cruise control circuits operate by using:
    a. Vacuum systems
    b. Electrical systems
    c. Mechanical systems
    d. All of the above
    e. None of the above

17. The servo unit uses vacuum forces working against _____ forces to operate an internal diaphragm.
    a. Gravity
    b. Electrical
    c. Magnetic
    d. Spring
    e. All of the above

18. Which of the following is *not* considered a good trouble-shooting practice on electrical circuits?
    a. Refer to an electrical schematic
    b. Test for correct voltages
    c. Narrow down the problem
    d. Check the easiest and basic components first
    e. Replace items and components until the problem is solved

19. Which of the following is considered a way to check the condition of energy absorbers?
    a. Check for leakage or oil
    b. Check for visual distortion and damage
    c. Check for a rattling noise inside the unit
    d. All of the above
    e. None of the above

20. Which of the following is *not* considered a common check on a cruise control unit?
    a. Check the servo for leaks
    b. Check the brake-activated electric release switch
    c. Check the metering pin and orifice
    d. Check all electrical connections for solid contact
    e. Check for solenoid operation

The following questions are similar in format to ASE (Automotive Service Excellence) test questions.

---

21. An energy absorber on the bumper has a rattling noise when it is shaken. Technician A says that the energy absorber is OK. Technician B says that the absorber simply needs to be readjusted. Who is right?
    a. A only
    b. B only
    c. Both A and B
    d. Neither A nor B

22. Technician A says that a common check on the cruise control is to make sure all vacuum hoses are in good condition. Technician B says that a common check on the cruise control is to make sure that the bead chain on the throttle linkage has no slack in it. Who is right?
    a. A only
    b. B only
    c. Both A and B
    d. Neither A nor B

23. Technician A says that when troubleshooting any electrical circuit, a jumper wire should never be used to bypass a part of the circuit. Technician B says that a voltmeter should be used to test electrical circuits. Who is right?
    a. A only
    b. B only
    c. Both A and B
    d. Neither A nor B

24. When reading an electrical circuit for troubleshooting, Technician A says the flow of electricity normally goes from the left side of the page to the right. Technician B says the flow of electricity normally flows from the top downward through the circuit. Who is right?
    a. A only
    b. B only
    c. Both A and B
    d. Neither A nor B

25. A vehicle has a passive restraint system. Technician A says that the diagnostic process is built into the system. Technician B says that the warning light needs to be off when diagnosing the system. Who is right?
    a. A only
    b. B only
    c. Both A and B
    d. Neither A nor B

26. Technician A says that when diagnosing a mechanical system always make visual checks first. Technician B says that when diagnosing a mechanical system, replace any components that you think might be faulty first. Who is right?
    a. A only
    b. B only
    c. Both A and B
    d. Neither A nor B

27. Technician A says that electronic cruise controls do not have built-in diagnostics. Technician B says the electronic cruise controls keep trouble codes in the computer. Who is right?
    a. A only
    b. B only
    c. Both A and B
    d. Neither A nor B

28. A vehicle has a passive restraint system. Technician A says that the arming sensor can be repaired. Technician B says the forward sensor can be repaired. Who is right?
    a. A only
    b. B only
    c. Both A and B
    d. Neither A nor B

Essay

29. Describe several electrical symbols used on electrical schematics.

30. What is the fuse block used for in an electrical circuit?

31. Describe the electrical operation of the defogger system used on vehicles.

32. What is the purpose of the component location table used along with certain electrical schematics?

33. Describe the purpose and operation of a fusible link.

34. Describe the operation of the energy-absorbing bumpers.

35. Define the purpose and operation of the transducer on a cruise control system.

Short Answer

36. On a passive restraint system the _____ sensor is used to sense if a vehicle is involved with a crash.

37. On a passive restraint system, the _____ sensor is located in the front of the vehicle grill.

38. Three diagnostic tools used to check electrical circuits and systems include a _____, a _____, and a _____.

39. If a service technician finds oil leaking from an energy absorber. It should be _____.

40. On computerized cruise control systems, _____ are used to tell the service technician the possible problem.

MOTOR
P U B L I C A T I O N S

NOBODY DOES IT BETTER

DOMESTIC CARS

*Auto Repair Manual**
Two-volume set:
  Volume I - General Motors
  Volume II - Chrysler/Ford
- Step-by-step repair procedures and specifications for mechanical systems and selected chassis electronic systems
- Multiple-year coverage with shaded areas highlighting new data and manufacturers' changes
- Engine rebuilding specifications

*Auto Engine Tune Up & Electronics Manuals**
Two-volume set:
  Volume I - General Motors
  Volume II - Chrysler/Ford
- Electronic and conventional ignition systems
- Computerized engine controls
- Carburetors and fuel injection
- Emission controls, tune up specs
- Electric fuel pumps, turbochargers, diesels
- On-board diagnosis, troubleshooting

*Parts & Time Guide**
- Comprehensive indexing with tabs for easy reference
- Part numbers and prices, job operational times
- Covers domestic cars and light trucks, including imports with American nameplates
- Transmissions R&R and rear seals

*Including complete coverage of captive imports

LIGHT, MEDIUM, HEAVY DUTY TRUCKS

Light Truck & Van Repair Manual

- Multiple-year coverage for domestic light trucks and vans
- Engines, transmissions, brakes, suspension, steering, air conditioning
- Turbochargers, diesels

Also Available:
Light Truck & Van Repair Manual
- 1st Edition, 1977-84

Truck Engine Tune Up & Electronics Manual

- Electronic and conventional ignition systems
- Carburetors and fuel injection
- Emission controls, application charts, vacuum hose routings
- Computerized engine controls & turbochargers
- Engine compartment reference diagrams and tune up specs

Also Available:
Truck Engine Tune Up & Electronics Manual
- 1st Edition, 1977-84

Heavy Truck Repair Manual

- Multiple-year coverage of medium and heavy duty gasoline and diesel trucks
- Tabbed for easy reference
- Cooling & electrical, clutch & transmissions, truck chassis, steering & suspension, drive axle, fuel & exhaust, brakes, diesel engines

Truck & Van Labor Time Guide

- Multiple-year coverage of light, medium and heavy duty gasoline and diesel trucks
- Domestic and imported vehicles

IMPORTED CARS AND LIGHT TRUCKS

Imported Car Repair Manual — 2 Volume Set

- Mechanical repairs and service for Japanese, British, French and Swedish imports, plus Yugo and Hyundai
- Multiple-year coverage with shaded areas highlighting new data and manufacturers' changes
- Fully illustrated, step-by-step procedures, plus specifications

Also available:
Imported Car Repair Manual,
- 5th Edition, 1975-83
- 10th Edition, 1984-88

Imported Engine Tune Up & Electronics Manual — 2 Volume Set

- Computerized engine controls, electronic fuel injection systems
- Diagnosis and testing of emission controls
- Electronic and conventional ignition systems
- Specifications and step by-step service and repair procedures

Also Available:
- Imported Engine Tune Up & Electronics Manual, 3rd Edition, 1980-86

Imported Car Parts & Time Guide

- Multiple-year coverage for imported cars and light trucks
- Up-to-date part numbers, part prices and labor times
- Comprehensive indexing and tabbed sections for easy reference

WIRING DIAGRAM MANUALS

- Car-specific and factory authentic
- Power and ground distribution diagrams
- Location of connectors, splices and grounds
- Essential information for all types of repair work especially for under-hood repairs

Domestic Vacuum & Wiring Diagram Manuals

- 12th Edition, 1977-78 cars
- 13th Edition, 1979 cars plus 1980 Citation, Omega, Skylark
- 14th Edition, 1980-81 cars, pickups & vans
- 15th Edition, 1982 cars, pickups & vans

- General Motors, 1983-84
- Ford, Chrysler, AMC, 1983-84
- General Motors, 1985
- Ford, Chrysler, AMC, 1985
- General Motors, 1986
- Ford, Chrysler, AMC, 1986
- General Motors, 1987
- Ford, Chrysler, AMC, 1987
- General Motors, 1988

- Ford, Chrysler, AMC, 1988
- General Motors, 1989
- Chrysler, Ford, 1989
- General Motors, 1990
- Chrysler, Ford, 1990

Imported Wiring Diagram Manuals

- 2nd Edition, 1983-84
- 3rd Edition, 1985-86
- 4th Edition, 1987
- 5th Edition, 1988
- 6th Edition, 1989
- 7th Edition, 1990

COMPONENT LOCATOR MANUALS

- Locates under-hood chassis components: electrical, vacuum, emission, relays, switches
- Covers cars, light trucks & vans

Domestic Component Locator Manuals

- Domestic, 1981-85
- Domestic, 1986-87
- Domestic, 1988
- Domestic, 1989-90

Imported Component Locator Manuals

- Imported 1981-86
- Imported, 1987-88
- Imported, 1989-90

TRANSMISSION MANUALS

- Hydraulic oil circuit diagrams
- Oil pan gasket identification
- Transmission identification code charts
- Computer-controlled torque converter clutches
- Troubleshooting & diagnosis
- Step-by-step service & repair procedures

Domestic Cars & Trucks
Includes light truck and Allison medium duty units

- Automatic Transmission Manual, 9th Edition, 1964-82
- Domestic Transmission Manual, (including manual transmissions), 3rd Edition, 1986-90

Imported Cars & Light Trucks

- Imported Transmission Manual, 2nd Edition, 1977-84
- 4th Edition, 1985-89
- 5th Edition, 1986-91

Transmission Parts & Time Guide

- (including manual transmissions), 1st Edition, 1984-91

FRONT END & BRAKE SERVICE MANUALS

- Front & rear wheel alignment specs & procedures
- Front & rear suspension procedures
- Front drive axle service
- Disc & drum brakes procedures
- Anti-lock brakes, power units
- Manual & power steering
- Domestic Cars, 1985-90
- Domestic Cars, 1987-91
- Imported Cars, 1987-90

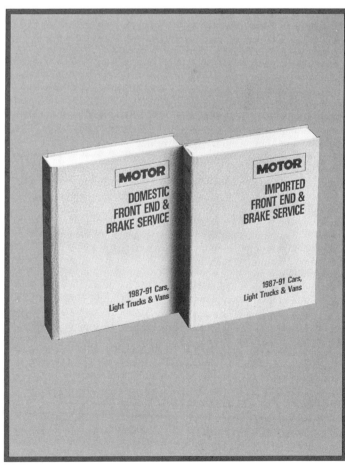

AIR CONDITIONER & HEATER MANUALS

- *Factory-installed units, electronic climate controls for cars, pick-ups, vans and trucks*
- *Leak test, system checks, troubleshooting*
- *Compressor service*
- *Vacuum & wiring diagrams*
- *Specifications and general service procedures*

- 5th Edition, domestic cars & trucks, 1974-80
- 6th Edition, domestic cars & trucks, 1981-83; imports, 1975-82
- 7th Edition, domestic cars & trucks, 1984-85; imports, 1983-84
- 8th Edition, domestic cars & trucks, 1986; imports, 1985
- 9th Edition, domestic cars & trucks, 1987; imports, 1986
- 10th Edition, domestic cars & trucks, 1988; imports, 1987
- 11th Edition, domestic cars & trucks, 1989; imports, 1988
- 12th Edition, domestic cars & trucks, 1990-91; imports, 1989-90

EMISSION CONTROL MANUALS

- *Complete description of emission controls*
- *Application charts, vacuum hose routings*
- *Troubleshooting & diagnosis*
- *Tune up and diesel engine performance specifications*

- 3rd Edition, domestic cars & trucks, 1966-82
- 4th Edition, domestic cars & trucks, 1982-83
- 5th Edition, domestic and imported cars and trucks, 1983-84
- 6th Edition, domestic and imported cars and trucks, 1985-86
- 7th Edition, domestic and imported cars and trucks, 1986-87
- 8th Edition, domestic and imported cars and trucks, 1987-88
- 9th Edition, domestic and imported cars and trucks, 1988-89
- 10th Edition, domestic and imported cars and trucks, 1990
- 11th Edition, domestic and imported cars and trucks, 1991

AUTO REPAIR MANUAL - EARLY MODEL AND VINTAGE EDITIONS

- Vintage Car Edition, Volume I, 1935-53

- Vintage Car Edition, Volume II, 1953-61

- Vintage Car Edition, Volume III, 1962-68

- 5th Early Model Edition, 1968-74

- 8th Early Model Edition, 1974-79

- 49th Auto Repair Manual, 1980-86

- 50th Auto Repair Manual, 1981-87

- 2nd Auto Engine Tune Up & Electronics Manual, 1980-86

- 3rd Auto Engine Tune Up & Electronics Manual, 1982-87

TECHNICAL SERVICE BULLETINS

Domestic Cars

- Manufacturers' bulletins "symptom-indexed" to help diagnosis and troubleshooting
- Updates service procedures and specifications
- Domestic Cars, 1980-83
- Domestic Cars, 1984-85
- Domestic Cars, 1986-89

Imported Cars

- Imported Cars, 1980-83
- Imported Cars, 1984-86
- Imported Cars, 1987-89

SPECIFICATION GUIDE

Complete data for tune ups, wheel alignments, capacities, brakes, engine torque, cylinder head tightening sequence, valve timing marks, piston & rod assembly, wheel nut torque, serpentine drive belt routing, and push & tow.

- Domestic and Imported Cars & Trucks, 1985-91

The magazine for the responsible automotive technician

- 12 monthly issues
- Service Slants-Latest repair bulletins for domestic and imported cars
- Troubleshooter- Answers to professional readers' technical questions and solutions to repair problems
- Eye on Electronics - Monthly diagnostic tips
- Foreign Service - How-to repairs for the growing import segment

- Newsbreak - Latest industry trends that affect shops
- Tools of theTrade - New tools, equipment & supplies
- MOTOR Manual Updates - Repair information to keep manuals current
- Technical and how-to features that keep technicians up-to-date on today's rapidly changing automotive technology

ABCM   Antilock brake computer module
ABS   Antilock braking systems
A/C   Air conditioning
ac   Alternating current
ACM   Air control module
ACR3   Air conditioning refrigerant recovery and recycling
ACT   Air charge temperature
AFL   Altitude fuel limiter
AIR   Air injection reactor
ALCL   Assembly line communication link
ALDL   Assembly line diagnostic link
API   American Petroleum Institute
ARB   Air Resources Board
ASE   Automotive Service Excellence also called NIASE
   (National Institute for Automotive Service Excellence)
ASTM   American Society for Testing and Materials
ATDC   After top dead center
ATF   Automatic transmission fluid
AWG   American Wire Gauge
BAT   Battery
Bbl   Barrels (2Bbl carburetor)
BDC   Bottom dead center
bhp   Brake horsepower
BLU   Blue wire
BMEP   Brake mean effective pressure
BP   Barometric pressure
BSFC   Brake specific fuel consumption
BTDC   Before top dead center
Btu   British thermal unit
Btu/gal   Btus per gallon
Btu/min   Btus per minute
C   Celsius
CAFE   Corporate Average Fuel Economy
cc   Cubic centimeter (cm³)
CCA   Cold-cranking amperes
CCC   Computer command control
CCS   Computer-controlled combustion
CFC   Chlorofluorocarbon
C^3I Computer-controlled coil ignition system
CID   Cubic inch displacement
CIS   Cylinder identification sensor
cm   Centimeter
CO   Carbon monoxide
CO_2 Carbon dioxide

CP   Crankshaft position sensor
CRT   Cathode ray tube
CV   Constant velocity
dB   Decibles
dc   Direct current
DECS   Diesel electronic control system
DIS   Direct ignition system
DIS   Distributorless ignition system
DK GRN   Dark green wire
DOHC   Dual overhead camshaft
DOT   Department of Transportation
E   Voltage (electromotive force)
EBCM   Electronic brake control module
ECC   Electronic engine control
ECCS   Electronic computer control system
ECCS   Electronic constant engine control system
ECM   Electronic control module
ECU   Electronic control unit
EEC   Electronic engine control
EFE   Early fuel evaporation
EGR   Exhaust gas recirculator
ELD   Electric load detector
emf   Electromotive force
EP   Extreme pressure
EPA   Environmental Protection Agency
EPR   Evaporative pressure regulator valve
ESN   Engine sequence number
EST   Electronic spark timing
F   Fahrenheit
fhp   Frictional horsepower
ft-lb   Foot-pound
g   Gram
g/mi   Grams per mile
Gpm   Gallons per minute
GRY   Gray wire
GVW   Gross vehicle weight
H   Hydrogen
HC   Hydrocarbons
HEI   High-energy ignition
HFC   Hydrofluorocarbon
HO   High output
H_2O Water
hp   Horsepower
HPAA   Housing pressure altitude advance

HPCA   Housing pressure cold advance
HSC   High swirl combustion
H_2SO_4 Sulfuric acid
I   Amperage (intensity)
IAC   Idle air control
ICE   Internal combustion engine
IEEGR   Integrated electronic exhaust gas recirculating
ihp   Indicated horsepower
in.-lb   Inch-pound
k   Kilo
KAM   Keep-alive memory
km   Kilometer
kPa   Kiopascals
kW   Kilowatts
L or l   Liter
LOS   Limited operational strategy
LPG   Liquid petroleum gas
M   Motor octane
MA   Mechanical advantage
MAF   Mass air flow
MAP   Manifold absolute pressure
MAT   Manifold air temperature
M/C   Mixture control
MIL   Military
mm   Millimeter
mpg   Miles per gallon
mph   Miles per hour
ms   Milliseconds
MSDS   Material Safety Data Sheets
MVS   Metering valve sensor
N   North pole
N/A   Not applicable
NAPA   National Auto Parts Association
NC   National Coarse threads
NF   National Fine threads
NO_x Nitrogen oxide
O   Oxygen
OASIS   On-line Automotive Service Information System
OD   Overdrive
OHC   Overhead camshaft
OHV   Overhead valves
ORN   Orange wire
OSHA   Occupational Safety and Health Act
P   Power
PbO_2 Lead peroxide
PCM   Power control module
PCV   Positive crankcase ventilation
PFI   Port fuel injection
PIP   Profile ignition pickup

PM   Permanent magnet
PNK   Pink wire
POA   Pilot-operated absolute valve
PPL   Purple wire
ppm   Parts per million
PROM   Programmable read-only memory
psia   Pressure per square inch absolute
psig   Pressure per square inch gauge
R   Research octane
R   Resistance
R_1, R_2, etc.   Resistor one, resistor two, etc.
RAM   Random access memory
ROM   Read-only memory
RPM   Revolutions per minute
RTV   Room temperature vulcanizing
S   South pole
SAE   Society of Automotive Engineers
SEFI   Sequential electronic fuel injection
SFI   Sequential fuel injection
SIR   Supplemental inflatable restraint
SO_4 Sulfate
SOHC   Single overhead camshaft
STV   Suction throttling valve
SUS   Saybolt universal seconds
S/V ratio   Surface to volume ratio
TAMP   Timing, atomizing, metering, pressurizing
TBI   Throttle body injection
TCC   Torque converter clutch
TDC   Top dead center
TEL   Tetraethyl lead
TML   Tetramethyl lead
TPC   Tire performance criteria
TPI   Tuned port injection
TPS   Throttle position sensor
TRS   Transmission regulated spark
TSCV   Throttle solenoid control valve
TV   Throttle valve
U-joint   Universal joint
UNC   Unified National Coarse threads
UNF   Unified National Fine threads
USC   U.S. Customary threads
UTQG   Uniform Tire Quality Grading
VAT   Voltage amperage tester
VECI   Vehicle emission control information
VI   Viscosity index
VIN   Vehicle identification number
VSS   Vehicle speed sensor
W   Watts
YEL   Yellow wire

Glossary

ABCM Antilock brake control module; the computer used to control antilock braking systems. (28)

ABCM Módulo de control de freno de tipo anti-inmovilizador. La computadora (el ordenador) sirve para controlar sistemas de frenos de tipo anti-inmovilizador. (28)

Abrasive Any material used for grinding; e.g., emery cloth or sandpaper. (13)

Abrasivo Cualquier material que sirve para arrancar material por raspado o bruñido; por ejemplo, paño de esmeril o papel de arenilla. (13)

Accumulator A device that cushions the motion of a clutch and servo action in an automatic transmission; a component used to store or hold liquid refrigerant in an air conditioning system. (26) (32)

Acumulador Mecanismo que ablanda (acojina) el movimiento del embrague y servo-acción de una transmisión; un componente que sirve para almacenar o mantener un refrigerante líquido en un sistema de aire acondicionado. (26) (32)

Acidity In lubrication, acidity denotes the presence of acid-type chemicals that are identified by the acid number. Acidity within oil causes corrosion, sludges, and varnish to increase. (11)

Acidez Referente a lubricación, acidez significa la presencia de químicos de tipo ácido que se indentifican según el número del ácido. La acidez dentro del aceite causa un aumento de corrosión, residuos, y barniz. (11)

Acid rain A form of pollution produced when sulfur and nitrogen are emitted into the air. The mixture of these chemicals with water produces an acid solution that is found in rain. (13)

Lluvia ácida Una forma de contaminación producida cuando azufre y nitrógeno se emiten al aire. La mezcla de estos químicos con agua produce una solución líquida que se encuentra en lluvia. (13)

ACM A computer used to control air conditioning system clutches; air control module. (32)

MCA Computadora (ordenador) que sirve para contolar embragues de sistemas de aire acondicionado; módulo de control de aire. (32)

ACR3 A system called an air conditioning refrigerant recovery and recycling system used to recover and recycle the refrigerant R-12 from automobile air conditioning systems. (32)

ACR3 Un sistema llamado "sistema para recuperar y reciclar refrigerantes de aire acondicionado," el cual sirve para recuperar y reciclar el refrigerante R-12 de los sistemas de aire acondicionado de automóviles. (32)

Active suspension system A computerized suspension system able to control body roll, pitch, brake dive, acceleration squat, and ride height. (29)

Sistema de suspensión activa Sistema de suspensión computarizada capaz de controlar tambaleo de carrocería (movimientos angulares), inclinación, caída de pique al frenar, amarre sobre aceleración, y posición de altura correcta. (29)

Actuator A device that causes action or motion on another part. (17)

Activador Aparato que produce acción o movimiento sobre otra parte. (17)

Additives Chemical compounds added to a lubricant for the purpose of imparting new properties or improving those properties that the lubricant already has. (11)

Aditivos elementos químicos añadidos a un lubricante para impartir nuevas propiedades o para mejorar las propiedades que ya tiene el lubricante. (11)

Adjusting sleeve An internally threaded sleeve located between the tie rod ends. The sleeve is rotated to set toe-in/-out. (30)

Manga de ajuste Manga que tiene Rosca interior localizada entre los dos extremos de una barra de acoplamiento de las ruedas directrices. Se gira la manga para ajustar el ángulo de convergencia o divezrgencia de las ruedas delanteras. (30)

Aeration The process of mixing air with a liquid. Aeration occurs in a shock absorber from rapid fluctuations in movement. (29)

Aeración Proceso de mezclar aire con un líquido. Aeración ocurre dentro de un amortiguador cuando hay fluctuaciones rápidas de movimiento. (29)

Aerodynamic The ease with which air can flow over the vehicle during higher speed operation. An aerodynamically sound vehicle has very little wind resistance. (8)

Aerodinámico Facilidad con la que el aire puede fluir sobre un vehículo durante operación de alta velocidad. Un vehículo bien construido aerodinámicamente sufre muy poca resistencia al viento. (8)

Aftermarket Equipment sold to consumers after the vehicle has been manufactured. Aftermarket equipment and parts are sold locally by parts dealers. (17)

Postmercado Equipo vendido al cliente después de que se fabrica el vehículo. Equipo y refacciones de postmercado se venden localmente por medio de comerciantes de partes. (17)

Air injection reactor A type of emission control system that pumps fresh air into the exhaust. (24)

Reactor de inyección de aire Tipo de sistema de control de emisiones que inyecta aire limpio en el escape para gases. (24)

Airborne A term used to describe contaminants floating in air moving through the engine. The contaminants are light enough to be suspended in the air stream. (17)

Aereo Término que sirve para describir contaminates que flotan en el aire que pasa por el motor. Los contaminates son tan ligeros como para estar suspendidos en el chorro de aire. (17)

Air-cooled Removing heat from the engine by circulating air across the cylinder block and heads. (12)

Enfriado por aire El quitarle calor al motor por medio de circular aire a través del bloque de cilindros y las cabezas. (12)

Air ducts Tubes, channels, or other tubular structures used to carry air to a specific location. (33)
Conductos de aire Tubos, canales, u otras estructuras de tubería que sirven para llevar aire a un lugar específico. (33)

Air-fuel ratio The measure of the amount of air and fuel needed for proper combustion. The most correct air-fuel ratio is 14.7 parts of air to 1 part of fuel. (6)
Proporción de aire y combustible Medida de la cantidad de aire y combustible que se requiere para combustión apropiada. La proporción correcta es 14.7 partes de aire por 1 parte de combustible. (6)

Air intake and exhaust system The parts on the automobile engine used to get the air into the engine and the exhaust out of the engine, including air cleaner, muffler, tail pipe, and associated ducting. (1)
Sistema admision y escafe de aire Las partes de un motor automovilístico que sirven para hacer entrar aire en el motor y sacar los gases del motor, incluyendo el filtro de aire, silenciador, tubo de escape, y otra tubería relacionada. (1)

Airtight containers Containers used to hold waste and oily rags, so that spontaneous combustion is eliminated. (2)
Contenedores herméticos Contenedores que sirven para guardar desperdicios y trapos engrasados, para que se elimine la combustión espontánea. (2)

Alignment Fitting the crankshaft to align with holes in the block. Also, the position of vehicle wheels relative to each other and to the car body and frame. Caster, camber, and toe are typically adjusted. (9) (30)
Alineación El ajustarse el cigüeñal para que esté alineado con los agujeros del bloque. También, la posición de las ruedas del vehículo en relacion a si mismas y a la carrocería y la armadura del coche. El caster camber y toe son ajustedos tipicamente. (9) (30)

AllData A computerized information system for service technicians that includes selected service manuals and service bulletins. (5)
Todos datos Sistema de información computarizada para técnicos de servicio, el cual incluye manuales de servicio seleccionados y boletines de servicio. (5)

All-season tire A tire that is designed for all around use in terms of treadwear, ride comfort, snow traction, wet traction, handling, and high speed. (31)
Llantas para todo clima Llanta que está diseñada para todas las ocasiones en el sentido de desgaste de huellas, tracción confortable, tracción sobre nieve, tracción sobre superficies mojadas, manejo, y alta velocidad. (31)

Ambient Surrounding area; e.g., surrounding temperature or circulating air. (13) (32)
Ambiente Area ambiental; por ejemplo, temperatura ambiental o aire circulante. (13) (32)

Ambient sensor A sensor used on computerized automatic temperature control systems that senses the outside air temperature and uses this information as an input to the system. (33)
Sensor ambiental Sensor que se usa en sistemas automaticos de control computarizado automático de temperatura, el cual percibe la temperatura del aire de afuera y emplea esta información como información de entrada al sistema. (33)

Amperage The number of electrons flowing past a given point in one second. (18)
Amperaje Número de electrones que pasan sobre un punto dado dentro de un segundo. (18)

Amperage capacity An indication of the length of time a battery can produce an amperage, or the amount of amperage that a battery can produce before being discharged. (19) (21)

Capacidad de amperaje Indicación de la cantidad de tiempo que una batería puede producir un amperaje, o la cantidad de amperaje que una batería puede producir antes de descargarse. (19) (21)

Anaerobic sealants A chemical sealant placed on a gasket in an engine to aid in sealing and to position the gasket during installation. (3)
Selladores anaerobios Sellador químico puesto en un empaque de un motor para ayudar a sellarlo y colocarlo durante su instalación. (3)

Analog signal A variable signal represented by a voltage within a given range. (18)
Señal análoga Señal variable representada por un voltaje dentro de un rango dado. (18)

Antifreeze A chemical solution added to the liquid coolant to protect against freezing and to increase the boiling point. (12)
Anticongelante Solución química añadida al refrigerante líquido que sirve para proteger contra congelación y para aumentar el punto de ebullición. (12)

Antifriction bearing A type of bearing that uses balls or rollers between the rotating shaft and the stationary part. (3)
Cojinete (Balero) antifricción Tipo de cojinete (balero) que utiliza bolas o rodillos (rolletes) entre un eje rotativo y una parte fija. (3)

Anti-icers Chemicals added to gasoline to eliminate the freezing of gasoline. (13)
Elementos de anti-hielo Químicos añadidos a la gasolina que sirven para eliminar la congelación de gasolina. (13)

Anti-lock brakes A type of braking system that is able to sense the speed of each wheel; in conjunction with a computer, it controls the hydraulic braking pressure to eliminate wheel lockup. (28)
Frenos anti-inmovilizadores Tipo de sistema de frenar que puede percibir la velocidad de cada rueda; en combinación con la computadora (ordenador), controla la presión hidraúlica para evitar la inmovilización de las ruedas. (28)

API American Petroleum Institute. (11)
IPA Instituto de Petróleo Americano (11)

Armature The iron or steel center of an electric motor or solenoid, which is located between two magnets; the movable or rotating part of a generator, which helps to cut the magnetic lines of force; the center moving part or rotational part of the starter. (14) (21) (22)
Armadura El centro férreo o de acero de un motor eléctrico o solenoide, el cual se encuentra entre dos campos magnéticos; la pieza móvil o rotativa de un generador, la cual ayuda a cortar las líneas de fuerza magnéticas; la parte móvil céntrica o parte rotativa del arrancador (Marcha). (14) (21) (22)

Asbestos A fibrous material used to fireproof objects. It may cause cancer. (2) (25)
Asbesto Material fibroso que sirve para hacer objetos anti-inflamables. Puede causar cancer. (2) (25)

ASE Abbreviation for the National Institute for Automotive Service Excellence. This organization is the corporation that certifies automotive service technicians. They also assist in automotive training programs. (1)
ESA Abreviatura para el Instituto Nacional para la Excelencia en Servicio Automotriz. Esta organización es la corporación que certifica a los técnicos de servicio automotriz. La organización ayuda en programas de entrenamiento automotriz. (1)

Aspect ratio The ratio of the height to width of the tire expressed as a percentage. (31)
Proporción de aspecto Proporción de la altura a la anchura de una llanta, expresada como porcentaje. (31)

Aspirator valve   A device used to draw out fluids by suction. In this case, a pollution device is used to draw fresh air by suction into the exhaust flow to reduce emissions. (24)

Válvula aspiradora   Mecanismo que sirve para sacar flúidos por succión. En este caso, se emplea un aparato de (contaminación) polución para sacar aire fresco por succión en un flujo de escape para reducir partículas emitidas. (24)

ATF   Automatic transmission fluid. (26)

LTA   Lubricante (aceite) para transmisión automática. (26)

Atom   Part of a molecule that has protons, neutrons, and electrons. All things are made of atoms. (18)

Atomo   Parte de una molécula que contiene protones, neutrones, y electrones. Todo material consta de átomos. (18)

Atomization   The breaking down of a liquid into small particles (like a mist) by the use of pressure. (13)

Atomatización   La descomposición de un líquido en partículas muy pequeñas (como neblina) por el uso de presión. (13)

Atomized   A liquid is atomized when it is broken into tiny droplets of the liquid, much like a mist or spray form. (15)

Atomizado   Se atomiza un líquido cuando se descompone en forma de gotitas, semejante a una neblina (llovizna) o a un "spray." (15)

Axial load   A type of load placed on a bearing that is parallel to the axis of the rotating shaft. (3)

Carga axial (de eje)   Tipo de carga colocada sobre un cojinete (balero) que se encuentra paralelo a la línea recta del eje rotativo. (3)

Axial motion   Motion that occurs along the axis of a revolving shaft or parallel to the axis of a revolving shaft. (9)

Movimiento axial (de eje)   Movimiento que ocurre a lo largo de la línea recta de un eje rotativo o paralelo a la línea recta de un eje rotativo. (9)

Babbitt   A soft metal material on the inside of a bearing insert to allow for embedability (small dirt particles embedding into the metal). (3) (9)

"Babbitt"   Material blando metálico puesto en el interior de un añadido de cojinete para permitir la empotrabilidad (partículas de mugre o tierra que se pueden empotrar (incrustar) en el metal). (3) (9)

Backing plate   A metal plate that serves as the foundation for the brake shoes and other drum brake hardware. (28)

Placa de respaldo   Placa de respaldo (plato de anclate) metálica que sirve de fundación y soporte para zapatas (patines) de freno y otros elementos relacionados al tambor del freno. (28)

Back injury   Injury to the back usually caused by lifting heavy objects incorrectly. (2)

Daño de espalda   Daño a la espalda causado típicamente por el levantar incorrectamente objetos pesados. (2)

Baffles   A series of thin walls placed in a battery case to allow gases to condense during charging or discharging. (19)

Divisiones (Tabiques)   Una serie de particiones poco densas y colocadas dentro de un contenedor de batería para dejar que los gases se condensen durante el proceso de cargarse o descargarse. (19)

Ball joint   A pivot point for turning a front wheel to right or left. Ball joints can be considered either nonloaded or loaded when carrying the car's weight. (29)

Articulación de rótula (esférica)   Punto giratorio para mover (dirigir) una rueda delatera a la derecha o izquierda. Se pueden considerar las articulaciones cargadas o no cargadas al llevar el peso del automóvil. (29)

Base 10   The base unit in the metric system is 10. All units are increased or decreased in units of 10. One meter has 10 decimeters, 100 centimeters, and 1,000 millimeters. (4)

Base 10   La unidad básica del sistema métrico es 10. Todas las unidades se incrementan o se reducen en módulos de 10. Un metro contiene 10 decímetros, 100 centímetros, y 1,000 milímetros. (4)

Battery cell   That part of a storage battery made from two dissimilar metals and an acid solution. A cell stores chemical energy for use later as electrical energy. (19)

Célda de batería (acumulador)   Esa parte de una batería de carga, hecha de dos metales diferentes y una solución de ácido. Una célda almacena energía química para usarse más tarde como energía eléctrica. (19)

BDC   Position of the piston; bottom dead center. (6)

PCI   Posición del pistón; punto huerio inferior. (6)

Bead   The edge of a tire's sidewall, usually made of steel wires wrapped in rubber, used to hold the tire to the wheel. (31)

Borde   El borde del costado de una llanta, normalmente hecho de alambres de acero envueltos en hule, que sirve para mantener pegada la llanta a la rueda. (31)

Bearing   A device used to eliminate friction between a rotating shaft and a stationary part. (3)

Cojinete   Mecanismo que sirve para eliminar fricción entre un eje rotativo y una parte estática (estacionaria). (3)

Bearing cap   A device that retains the needle bearings that ride on the trunnion of a U-joint and is pressed into the yoke. (27)

Sombrerete de cojinete (Tapa de balero)   Mecanismo que mantiene en posición los cojinetes de agujas que están asentados sobre el muñón de la junta cardán o universal y empotrados en el yugo. (27)

Bellows   A flexible chamber that can be expanded to draw a fluid in and compressed to pressurize the fluid. (14) (29)

Fuelle   Una cámara flexible que puede ser expandida para sorber un flúido y comprimida para presionar el flúido. (14) (29)

Bias   A diagonal line of direction. In relationship to tires, bias means that belts and plies are laid diagonally or crisscrossing each other. (31)

Sentido (Sesgo)   Línea diagonal de direccion. Relacionado a llantas, el sentido (sesgo) quiere decir que las correas y capas están puestas diagonal menté o entrecruzadas. (31)

Bimetallic strip   Two pieces of metal, such as brass and steel, attached together. When heat is applied to the strip, the two metals expand at different rates. This causes the metal to bend. A bimetallic strip senses changes in temperature and causes a mechanical movement. (12) (15)

Franja bimetálica   Dos pedazos de metal, tal como latón y acero, conectados uno al otro. Cuando se les aplica calor, los dos metales se expanden a diferentes coeficientes de expansión. Esta expansión hace que el metal se curve. Una franja bimetálica es sensible a cambios en temperatura produciendo un movimiento mecánico. (12) (15)

Binary codes   A computer code made of combinations of the numbers 1 and 0. (18)

Códigos binarios   Código computarizado hecho de combinaciones de los números 1 y 0. (18)

Bleeding   The act of removing air from the brake hydraulic system. (28)

Purga   El acto de quitarle aire al sistema de frenos hidráulicos. (28)

Blow-by   The gases that escape past the rings and into the crankcase area. These gases from the combustion process produce a positive crankcase pressure. (9) (24)

Compresión negativa   Los gases que escapan alrededor de las anillos y entran en el área del cárter. Los gases del proceso de la combustión producen una presión de cárter positiva. (9) (24)

BMEP Brake mean effective pressure. A measure of pressure on top of the piston during the power stroke. (6)
PMEF Presión media efectiva de freno. Medida de presión arriba del pistón durante el ciclo de potencia. (6)

Body and frame The part of the automobile that supports all other components. The frame supports the engine, drive lines, differential, axles, and so on. The body houses the entire vehicle. (1)
Carrocería y bastidor (armadura) de coche La parte del automóvil que soporta todos los otros componentes. El bastidor soporta el motor, tren propulsor, diferencial, ejes, *etcétera*. La carrocería incorpora todo el vehículo. (1)

Boiling point The temperature of a fluid when it changes from a liquid to a gas or vapor. (12) (13)
Punto de ebullición Temperatura de un flúido cuando cambia de líquido a un gas o vapor. (12) (13)

Bolt hardness Hardness of a bolt is determined by the number of lines on the head of the bolt. More lines mean a stronger bolt. (3)
Dureza de perno (tornillo) La dureza de un perno se determina según el número de líneas en la cabeza del perno. Más líneas significan un perno más fuerte o duro. (3)

Boost The increase in intake manifold pressure produced by a turbocharger. (17)
Aumento de fuerza Incremento en la presión del colector de admisión producido por un turboalimentador. (17)

Bore The diameter of the cylinder. (6)
Calibre Diámetro de un cilindro. (6)

Boss A cast or forged part of a piston that can be machined for accurate balance. (9)
Parte forjada de pistón Pieza fundida o forjada de un pistón, la cual puede ser trabajada (recortada) con máquina herramienta para lograr un balance preciso. (9)

Bourdon tube A curved tube that straightens as the pressure inside it is increased. The tube is attached to a needle on a gauge, which senses the movement of the tube and transmits it as a pressure reading. (12)
Tubo Bourdon Tubo curvado que se endereza mientras se incrementa la presión adentro. El tubo está conectado a una aguja de un indicador, que responde al movimiento del tubo y lo transmite como una indicación de presión. (12)

Bowden cable A small steel cable inside a flexible tube used to transmit mechanical motion from one point to another. (34)
Cable Bowden Pequeño cable de acero dentro de un tubo flexible usado para transmitir un movimiento mecánico de un punto a otro. (34)

Brake horsepower The horsepower available at the rear of the engine. (7)
Potencia de freno La potencia disponible atrás del motor. (7)

Brake shoes The curved metal parts faced with brake lining, that are forced against the brake drum to produce the braking action. (28)
Zapatas (Patines) de freno Las partes metálicas curvadas junto a la guarnición del freno, las cuales están forzadas contra al tambor del freno para producir la acción de frenar. (28)

Breaker points A set of contact points used in the ignition system to open and close the primary circuit. The points act like a switch operated from a distributor cam. (20)
Puntos de ruptura Juego de puntos de contacto usados en el sistema de encendido para abrir y cerrar el circuito principal. Los puntos funcionan como un interruptor puesto en marcha desde la leva distribuidora. (20)

Brinelling The process of producing small dents in a bearing surface due to heat and wear. (3)

Picaduras Proceso de producir abolladuras pequeñitas en la superficie de un cojinete (balero) debido al calor y fricción. (3)

Btu A unit of thermal or heat energy referred to as a British thermal unit. The amount of heat necessary to raise one pound of water 1 degree F. (13)
UTB Unidad de energía termal o calórica que lleva la nomenclatura de Unidad Termal Británica. La cantidad de calor necesaria para elevar una libra de agua un grado de temperatura F. (13)

Buffer Any device used to reduce the shock or motion of opposing forces. (34)
Amortiguador Mecanismo que sirve para reducir el choque o moción de fuerzas opuestas. (34)

Burner The combustion chamber where the continuous combustion of the gas turbine occurs. (8)
Quemador Cámara de combustión en la que ocurre una combustión continua de una turbina de gas. (8)

Bushing A friction-type bearing usually identified as one piece. (3)
Cojinete (Balero) Un balero tipo de fricción usualmente identificado como una pieza. (3)

Bushing installers Tools used to provide correct alignment and applied forces when installing a bushing in a housing. (4)
Instaladores de cojinetes (baleros) Herramientas que sirven para proporcionar correcta alineación y fuerzas aplicadas al instalar un cojinete (balero) dentro de un hueco (Housing) estuche. (4)

Bypass tube A tube directly in front of the thermostat. The coolant bypasses the radiator through this tube when cold. (12)
Tubo de desviación Tubo colocado delante del termóstato. El líquido refrigerante se desvía del radiador por el tubo cuando está frío. (12)

CAFE Corporate Average Fuel Economy. (23)
PCEC Promedio corporativo de economía de combustible. (23)

Calibrate To check or measure any instrument. (14)
Calibrar Revisar o medir cualquier instrumento. (14)

Caliper A C-shaped housing that fits over the rotor, holding the pads and containing the hydraulic components that force the pads against the rotors when braking. (28)
Calibrador Cubierta protectora en forma de una C que se coloca alrededor de un rotor, manteniendo así los cojinetes y conteniendo los componentes hidráulicos que empujan los conjinetes contra los rotores al frenar. (28)

Camber The inward or outward tilt of the wheel at the top. A wheel has a positive camber when the top is tilted out. (30)
Inclinación Inclinación de una rueda hacia dentro o fuera en la parte superior de la rueda. Una rueda muestra una inclinación positiva cuando la parte superior está inclinada hacia fuera. (30)

Cam ground piston Piston ground to a cam shape to aid in controlling expansion from heat. (9)
Pistón recortado por leva Pistón recortado a la forma de leva para ayudar a controlar la expansión debida al calor. (9)

Camshaft A shaft that is used to open and close the valves. (6)
Arbol de levas Arbol o eje que sirve para abrir y cerrar las válvulas. (6)

Capacitor A device for holding and storing a surge of current. (20)
Condensador Aparato que sirve para guardar y almacenar un arranque de ignición eléctrica. (20)

Capacity specifications Specifications used to show quantity or amount of liquid in automobile components. (5)

Especificaciones de capacidad Especificaciones que sirven para indicar la cantidad de líquido encontrada en los componentes automovilísticos. (5)

Carbon canister A canister filled with carbon used to absorb and store fuel vapors that are normally exhausted into the air. (24)

Bote de carbón Bote lleno de carbón que sirve para absorber y almacenar los vapores de combustible que se escapan al aire. (24)

Carbon monoxide A pollutant in automotive exhaust that is produced when there is insufficient oxygen for combustion. It is a deadly, odorless, tasteless gas. (2) (23)

Monóxido de carbono Contaminante en los gases de escape automovilísticos que se produce cuando hay oxígeno insuficiente para hacer combustión. Es un gas (inodoro), (insípido) y mortal. (2) (23)

Carburetor A device used to mix air and fuel in the correct proportions. (6)

Carburador Aparato que sirve para mezclar aire y combustible según proporciones apropiadas. (6)

Carburetor barrel The area within a carburetor where air and fuel are mixed at precise ratios. (15)

Barril carburador El área dentro de un carburador donde aire y combustible se mezclan en proporciones precisas. (15)

Carcass The inner part of the tire that holds the air for supporting the vehicle. (31)

Armadura La parte interior de una llanta que contiene el aire para soportar el vehículo. (31)

Cardan universal joint A universal joint sometimes known as the four-point or cross-and-bearing-type joint. This joint allows the transmission of power at an angle, but causes rhythmic variations in speed at the output yoke of the joint. (27)

Junta (Balero) de Cardán (junta universal) Junta (o balero) de Cardán a veces conocida como una junta de tipo cuatro puntos. Esta junta permite la transmisión de potencia desde un ángulo pero produce variaciones rítmicas de velocidad en el punto de la brida (estribo o yugo) que hace la unión. (27)

Case-hardened The outer surface of a metal that has been hardened to reduce the possibility of excessive wear. (9)

Endurecido por fuera, reforzado Superficie exterior de un metal que ha sido endurecida para reducir la posibilidad de fricción excesiva. (9)

Cast The process of shaping metal by heating to a liquid and pouring the hot metal into a sand mold. (9)

Fundir Proceso de formar metal por medio de calentamiento hasta producir un líquido metálico y vacian el metal super-caliente en un molde de arena. (9)

Caster The backward or forward tilt of the spindle support arm to the top. (30)

Divergencia Inclinación hacia atrás o hacia adelante de un huso de soporte hacia arriba. (30)

Catalyst A chemical that causes or speeds up a chemical reaction without changing its own composition. (11) (24)

Catalizador Químico que causa o produce una velocidad a lo largo de una reacción química sin cambiar su propia composición. (11) (24)

Catalytic converter A type of emission control device used to change the exhaust emission from the vehicle into harmless chemicals. (24)

Convertidor catalítico Aparato para controlar emisiones, el cual sirve para convertir las emisiones de escape del vehículo en químicos inofensivos. (24)

Cavitation A process in a cooling or water system that causes small vacuum bubbles to occur, which, upon implosion, damages the water pump blades. (12)

Cavitación Proceso dentro de un sistema de agua o un sistema refrigerante que hace que ocurran pequeñas burbujas de vacío, las cuales, al hacer implosión, dañan las paletas de una bomba de agua. (12)

Cell density A measure of how many watts can be discharged per hour, per pound of battery. Cell densities are increasing as batteries are being designed better. (19)

Densidad de célda de pila (acumulador, bateria) Medición de cuantos vatios se pueden descargar por hora, por libra de batería. Las densidades de pila incrementan al mejorar el diseño de las baterías. (19)

Center link A steering linkage component connected between the pitman and idler arms. (30)

Conexión central Componente de conexión de manejo entre la barra de conexión y los brazos intermedios (30)

Centrifugal pump A pump that draws coolant into its center and then uses centrifugal force to throw the coolant outward and into the cooling system. (12)

Bomba centrífuga Bomba que atrae el líquido refrigerante hacia su centro y luego emplea una fuerza centrífuga para aventar el refrigerante hace el sistema refrigerante. (12)

Cetane number The ignition quality of a diesel fuel. The time period or delay between injection and explosion of diesel fuel. (13)

Número cetano Calidad de encendido de un combustible diesel. El período o tardanza entre la inyección y la explosión del combustible diesel. (13)

CFC A chlorofluorocarbon or gas such as freon that produces damage to the environment and ozone layer. (32)

CFC Un clorofluorocarburo o gas tal como el freón que produce daño al medio ambiente y la capa de ozono. (32)

Chamfer An angled cut on the end of a tooth of a gear. (22)

Bisel Corte diagonal en el extremo de un diente de una rueda dentada. (22)

Charging When the electrical flow of a battery is reversed, the battery is charged. The metals that are alike are converted to lead peroxide and sponge lead, and the electrolyte is now sulfuric acid and water. (19)

Cargando Cuando se pone al revés el flujo de la corriente eléctrica, se carga la batería. Los metales semejantes se convierten en peróxido de plomo y plomo esponjado, y el electrólito resulta en ácido sulfúrico y agua. (19)

Chassis dynamometer A dynamometer used to measure road horsepower. (7)

Dinamómetro de carrocería Un dinamómetro que sirve para calcular la potencia de caballos en una prueba de camino. (7)

Check ball A ball and spring device in any fluid circuit that allows flow in one direction but stops flow in the other direction. (15)

Balero de retén Mecanismo de una bolita y resorte en un circuito de fluidos que permite el flujo en una dirección pero inhibe el flujo en dirección opuesta. (15)

Chemical hazards Hazards primarily from solvents, gasoline, asbestos, and antifreeze. (2)

Riesgos químicos Peligros provenientes principalmente de solventes, gasolina, asbestos, y anticongelantes. (2)

Closed loop A computer condition in which the air-fuel ratio is being controlled on the basis of various inputs to the computer. (15)

Circuito cerrado Condición de computadora (ordenador) en la que la proporción de aire y combustible se controla a base de un juego de unas condiciones pre-programadas. (15)

Cloud point The temperature at which a diesel fuel begins to produce wax crystals due to cold temperatures. (13)

Punto de cristalización Temperatura en la que un combustible diesel empieza a producir cristales cerosos debido a temperaturas frías. (13)

Clutch The part of a manual transmission that is used to engage and disengage the transmission from the engine. (25)

Embrague Parte de una transmisión manual que sirve para engranar y desengranar la transmisión del motor. (25)

Coefficient of drag A method used to check the air resistance of a moving vehicle. A measure of how much air is moved as the vehicle moves from one point to another. Generally the coefficient of drag ranges between 1.00 and 0.00. (7)

Coeficiente de resistencia Método que sirve para revisar la resistencia de aire de un vehículo en movimiento. Una medida de la cantidad de aire que está desplazado al pasar un vehículo de un punto a otro. En general, el coeficiente de resistencia tiene una distancia de medida de 1.00 a 0.00. (7)

Combustion The process in which air and fuel are burned after being mixed to a correct ratio of 14.7 parts of air to 1 part of fuel. (6)

Combustión Proceso en el que el aire y el combustible queman después de mezclarse en una proporción correcta de 14.7 partes de aire a 1 parte de combustible. (6)

Combustion chamber The location inside the cylinder head or piston in which combustion of the air and fuel occurs. (6)

Cámara de combustión El hueco dentro de la cabeza del cilindro o pistón en el que ocurre la combustión del aire y combustible. (6)

Commutator A device that extracts the electrical energy from the rotating armature. When electrical energy is being extracted from the armature, ac voltage is converted to dc voltage; metal segments that are used on a starter motor to carry electricity to the armature. The commutator also reverses the current flow in the armature at the right time. (21) (22)

Commutador Aparato que extrae la energía eléctrica de un eje rotativo. Cuando la energía eléctrica se extrae de un eje, voltaje CA (corriente alterna) se convierte en un voltaje CC (corriente continua); segmentos metálicos que se usan en un motor de arranque para llevar electricidad al eje. El comutador también pone la marcha de la corriente en dirección opuesta en el eje en el momento apropiado. (21) (22)

Compensating port A passage for excess fluid to return to the reservoir when the brakes are released. (28)

Orificio compensador Pasaje para que el exceso de liquido regrese a un tanque o depósito cuando se sueltan los frenos. (28)

Component location table A table used with an electrical schematic that shows the actual location of the part being investigated. (34)

Tabla de localidad de componentes Una tabla (figura) usada con un esquemá electrico que indica el lugar exacto de la pieza que se investiga. (34)

Compression ratio A measure of how much the air has been compressed in a cylinder of an engine from TDC to BDC. Compression ratio will usually be from 8:1 to 25:1. (6)

Proporción de compresión Medida de la cantidad de aire que se ha comprimido en un cilindro de un motor de TDC a BDC. La proporción de compresión normalmente será de 8:1 a 25:1. (6)

Compression washer A washer used on an engine to reduce oil leakage when the threads of a bolt are in or near oil. (3)

Arandela de presión Arandela que sirve en un motor para reducir el escape o goteo de aceite cuando las roscas de un perno están en o cerca del aceite. (3)

Compressor A device on a gas turbine that compresses the air for combustion. (8) (17)

Compresor Aparato de una turbina de gas que comprime al aire para combustión. (8) (17)

Computer-controlled brakes A system that has a sensor on each wheel feeding electrical impulses into the on-board computer. As the vehicle is stopped, each wheel is stopped or slowed down at the same rate. This condition reduces skidding sideways during rapid braking. (28)

Frenos controlados por computadora (ordenador) Sistema que contiene un sensor en cada rueda, el cual manda impulsos eléctricos a una computadora a bordo. Al pararse el vehículo, cada rueda se detiene o se reduce en la velocidad de rodaje con la misma tasa de velocidad. Esta condición reduce el deslizamiento de movimiento lateral (patinaje) durante el acto de frenar rápidamente. (28)

Computerized automatic temperature control A control system used to monitor and adjust the air temperature inside the passenger compartment. On the basis of several inputs, a small microprocessor adjusts air temperature about every few seconds. (33)

Control de temperatura autómatico computarizado Sistema de control que sirve para vigilar y ajustar la temperatura del aire dentro del compartimiento para pasajeros. A base de varios datos electrónicos enviados, un microprocesador ajusta la temperatura del aire cada rato de unos segundos. (33)

Condensation The process of reducing a gas to a more compact state such as a liquid. This is usually done by cooling the substance below its boiling point. For example, the moisture in the air in a fuel tank condenses to water. (14) (32)

Condensación Proceso de convertir un gas a un estado más condensado como es un líquido. Típicamente se hace el proceso por medio de enfriar la sustancia hasta un punto más bajo que su punto de ebullición. Por ejemplo, la humedad en el aire dentro de un tanque de combustible se condensa en agua. (14) (32)

Condense The process of cooling a vapor to below its boiling point. The vapor changes into a liquid. (13)

Condensar Proceso de enfriar un vapor hasta un punto más bajo que su punto de ebullición. El vapor se convierte en un líquido. (13)

Condenser A capacitor device used to protect the ignition points from corroding; a component in an air conditioning system used to cool a refrigerant below its boiling point. (20) (32)

Condensador Un capacitador que sirve para proteger los puntos de ignición contra corrosión; un componente en un sistema de aire acondicionado que sirve para enfriar un líquido refrigerante bajo de su punto de ebullición. (20) (32)

Conduction Transfer of heat between two solid objects. (12)

Conducción La transferencia de calor entre dos objetos sólidos. (12)

Conductor A substance with three or fewer electrons in the valence ring. (18)

Conductor Sustancia de tres electrones o menos en la banda de valencia. (18)

Configuration The figure, shape, or form of an engine. (8)

Configuración La figura, contorno o forma de un motor. (8)

Conical Having the shape or form of a cone. (16)

Cónico Tener la forma de un cono. (16)

Connecting rod The connecting link between the piston and crankshaft. (6)

Biela El vínculo de conexión entre el pistón y el cigüeñal. (6)

Constant velocity (CV) joint   The CV joint consists of balls or tripods, and yokes designed to allow the angular transfer of power without speed variations common to the Cardan universal joint. (27)

Junta (Balero) de velocidad constante (VC)   La junta VC consiste en bolas o trípodes, y balancines diseñados para permitir la transferencia de potencia angular sin variaciones en velocidad comunes en una flecha universal Cardán. (27)

Contaminants   Various chemicals in the oil that reduce its effectiveness, including water, fuel, carbon, acids, dust, and dirt particles; also impurities in fuel systems, including dirt, rust, water, and other materials; also chemicals that make the air impure, usually produced from the combustion process. (11) (14) (23)

Contaminantes   Varios químicos en el aceite, los cuales reducen la eficacia del aceite, incluyendo agua, combustible, carbón, ácidos, polvo, y partículas de tierra; también impurezas en los sistemas de combustible, como partículas de tierra, orín, agua, y otros materiales; también químicos que resultan en un aire contaminado, típicamente producido por el proceso de combustión. (11) (14) (23)

Continuous combustion   Combustion of air and fuel that continues constantly. (6)

Combustión continua   Combustión del aire y el combustible, la cual sigue constantemente. (6)

Control arm   The main link between the vehicle frame and the wheels. The control arm acts as a hinge to allow the wheels to go up and down independently of the chassis. (29)

Brazo de control   Vínculo principal entre el bastidor de coche y las ruedas. El brazo de control funciona de gozne (bisagra) que permite que las ruedas tengan una acción amortiguadora de altibajos independiente del bastidor. (29)

Convection   Transfer of heat by circulation of heated parts of a liquid or gas. (12)

Convección   La transferencia de calor por circulación de las partículas de un líquido o gas. (12)

Conventional theory   Electrons will flow from a positive to a negative point. (18)

Teoría convencional   Los electrones flotarán de un punto positivo a uno negativo. (18)

Conversion factors   Numbers used to convert between USC and the metric system. (4)

Factores de conversión   Los números que sirven para convertir entre USC y el sistema métrico. (4)

Cooling system   The subsystem on an engine used to keep the engine temperature at maximum efficiency. (1)

Sistema de refrigeración   El subsistema de un motor que sirve para mantener la temperatura del motor a una eficiencia máxima. (1)

Cords   The inner materials running through the plies that produce strength in the tire. Common cord materials are fiberglass and steel. (31)

Cuerdas   Los materiales interiores que pasan por las capas que producen la fuerza de una llanta. El material de dos cuerdas son fibra de vidrio y acero. (31)

Core   The center of the radiator, made of tubes and fins, used to transfer heat from the coolant to the air. (12)

Centro   El centro de un radiador, hecho de tubos y aletas, que sirven para transferir el calor desde el líquido refrigerante hasta el aire. (12)

Core plugs   Plugs inserted into the block that allow the sand core to be removed during casting. Also, at times these plugs will pop out and protect the block if the coolant freezes. (9)

Tapones céntricos   Tapones insertados en el bloque que permiten que se quite la arena durante el proceso de fundición. También, a veces, tales tapones saltan y protegen el bloque si se congela el líquido refrigerante. (9)

Corrosion   Destruction of a metal in an engine because of chemical or electrochemical reactions with acid. (11)

Corrosión   Destrucción de un metal de un motor debido a reacciones químicas o electroquímicas con ácido. (11)

Corrosive   The eating away of metal within the cooling system. (12)

Corrosivo   La carcoma del metal dentro de un sistema refrigerante. (12)

Counterweight   Weight forged or cast into the crankshaft to reduce vibration. (9)

Contrapeso   Un peso fundido en el cigüeñal para reducir vibraciones. (9)

Crank signal   A signal sent to the automotive computer to tell it that the engine is starting. The computer will then enrich the air-fuel ratio for easier starting. (22)

Señal de arranque   Una señal enviada a la computadora del auto para comunicarle que el motor se arranca. La computadora en ese instante enriquece la proporción del aire y combustible para facilitar el encendido. (22)

Crankcase   The area in the engine below the crankshaft. It contains oil and fumes from the combustion process. (9)

Cárter   Area en el motor debajo del cigüeñal.   Contiene aceite y gases que resultan del proceso de combustión. (9)

Crankcase pressure   The pressure produced in the crankcase from blow-by gases. (24)

Presión del cárter   Presión producida en el cárter por los gases que se acumulan en el escape. (24)

Crankshaft   A mechanical device that converts reciprocating motion to rotary motion. (6)

Cigüeñal   Eje que convierte un movimiento recíproco a un movimiento rotativo. (6)

Cross   The central component of the U-joint connecting the input and output yokes. (27)

Cruz   El componente central de una junta universal que conecta las bridas de la entrada de potencia y las del rendimiento (o salida) de potencia. (27)

Crossfire injection   A type of throttle body injection system that uses two injectors mounted on the manifold. Each injector feeds a cylinder on the opposite side by using a crossover port. (16)

Inyección de dos sentidos   Tipo de sistema de inyección a la válvula de admisión, el cual emplea dos inyectores montados en el colector de admisión. Cada inyector suministra al cilindro situado al lado opuesto por medio del uso de un orificio de paso opuesto. (16)

Cubic centimeter   A unit in the metric system to measure volume. There are 100 cubic centimeters in 1 liter. (4)

Centímetro cúbico   Unidad del sistema métrico que sirve para medir volumen. Hay 100 centímetros cúbicos en 1 litro. (4)

Curtain area   An engineering term that relates to the efficiency of the flow of air and fuel entering the combustion chamber. The curtain area represents how evenly the air and fuel are being admitted to the combustion chamber. The greater the curtain area, the more efficient the combustion. (10)

Area de velo   Un término de ingeniería relacionado a la eficiencia del flujo del aire y combustible, los cuales entran en la cámara de combustión. El área de velo representa que tan uniforme se admiten el aire y el combustible en la cámara de combustión. Cuanto más grande sea el área del velo, tanto más eficiente será la combustión. (10)

Cycle   The process of discharging and then recharging a battery. (19)

Ciclo   Proceso de descargar y luego de cargar otra vez una batería. (19)

Cylinder   Internal holes in the cylinder block. (6)

Cilindro   Los huecos dentro del bloque de cilindros. (6)

Cylinder block   Part of the engine that houses all components. The foundation of the engine. (6)

Bloque de cilindros   Una parte del motor donde se encuentran todos los componentes. La fundación del motor. (6)

Cylinder head   The top and cover for the cylinder; it houses the valves. (6)

Cabeza de cilindro   La tapa para los cilindros; contiene las válvulas. (6)

Cylinder sleeve   A round cylindrical tube that fits into the cylinder bore. Both wet and dry sleeves are used. (9)

Funda de cilindro   Un tubo redondo y cilíndrico que cabe dentro de un hueco cilíndrico. Se emplean dos fundas, una mojada y otra seca. (9)

Cylinder taper   The shape of the cylinder after it has been worn by the rings. (9)

Estrechamiento de cilindro   La forma del cilindro después de haberse gastado por los anillos. (9)

Dashpot   A unit using a small cylinder and diaphragm with a small vent hole. It is used to retard, or slow down, movement of some part. (15)

"Dashpot"   Aparato que emplea un cilindro pequeño y diafragma con un pequeño agujero de ventilación. Sirve para retardar el movimiento de alguna parte. (15)

Data link   A device in a computer system to send and receive digital signals. (18)

Vínculo de datos   Aparato en el sistema de computadora que manda y recibe señales digitales. (18)

Dealership   Privately owned service and sales organization that sells and services vehicles for the automobile manufacturer. (1)

Agencia automotriz   Una organización de servicio y ventas con dueño particular que vende autos y servicio para un fabricante automotriz. (1)

Decibel   A unit of sound measurement. Usually 90–100 decibels experienced for a long time can cause hearing damage. (2)

Decibelio   Unidad de medida de sonido. Normalmente una cantidad de 90 a 100 decibelios a que se somete uno durante mucho tiempo puede resultar en un daño al oído. (2)

Deep cycle battery   A battery that is designed to withstand continuous cycling, or discharging and charging. (19)

Batería de ciclo extenso   Batería diseñada para aguantar un ciclismo continuo, o descargar y cargar. (19)

Deep length (well) socket   Socket used when a nut is located on a long stud. (4)

Dado largo extenso (hoyo)   Dado usado cuando se encuentra una tuerca en un montante largo. (4)

Deflection angle   The angle at which the oil is deflected inside the torque converter during operation. The greater the angle of deflection, the greater the torque applied to the output shaft. (26)

Angulo de deflexión   Angulo al cual se desvía el aceite dentro del convertidor de torsión durante la operación. Cuánto más sea la deflexión, tanto más será la torsión aplicada al eje de rendimiento. (26)

Defroster   Part of the ventilation system on an automobile used to remove ice, frost, or moisture from the front windows. (33)

Descongelador   Parte del sistema de ventilación del automóvil que sirve para quitar hielo, escarcha, o humedad de las ventanas delanteras. (33)

Desiccant   A material that absorbs moisture from a gas or liquid. A desiccant substance is used in an air conditioning system to remove moisture from the refrigerant. (32)

Desecante   Material que absorbe humedad de un gas o líquido. Una sustancia desecante se emplea en un sistema de aire acondicionado para quitarle humedad al líquido refrigerante. (32)

Detent springs   Small springs used in conjunction with a small ball. The springs push the ball against an indented part of a shaft, used to hold the shaft from sliding. (25)

Resortes de escape   Resortes pequeños usados en combinación con una bolita. Los resortes empujan la bolita contra una parte dentada de un eje, los cuales sostienen en posición el eje para que no deslice. (25)

Detergent   In a lubrication oil, either an additive or compound having the property of keeping particles suspended so that particles can be filtered. (11) (13)

Detergente   En un aceite lubricante, el detergente es o un aditivo o un compuesto que tiene la propiedad de mantener suspendidas las partículas para que puedan ser filtradas. (11) (13)

Detonation sensor   A sensor used on computerized ignition systems that is able to measure if the engine is producing a "knock." The sensor is able to pick up small, high-frequency vibrations produced from engine knock. (20)

Detector de detonación   Detector usado en sistemas de encendido computarizado, el cual puede percibir si el motor sufre golpes interiores. El detector puede sentir vibraciones pequeñas de alta frecuencia producidas por un golpeteo en un motor. (20)

Diagnosis   The process of finding and determining the cause of problems in the automobile. When the problem is identified, a solution is selected. (5)

Diagnosis   Proceso de encontrar y determinar la causa de problemas de un automóvil. Al identificar un problema, se escoge una solución. (5)

Dial indicator   A measuring tool used to check small clearances up to 0.001 inch. The clearance is read on a dial. (4)

Indicador de caratula   Un instrumento de medición que sirve para verificar las aperturas pequeñas hasta una tolerancia de 0.001 de una pulgada. Se anota la cantidad de apertura en la caratula. (4)

Diaphragm   A partition separating one cavity from another. A fuel pump uses a diaphragm to separate two cavities inside the pump. A diaphragm is usually made of a rubber and fiber material. (14)

Diafragma   Una partición que separa una cavidad de otra. Una bomba de combustible emplea un diafragma para separar dos cavidades dentro de la bomba. Un diafragma normalmente es de un material de hule y fibra. (14)

Diaphragm spring   A type of steel plate spring used in a pressure plate to engage or disengage the friction disc. (25)

Resorte de diafragma   Tipo de resorte revestido de acero y usado en una plancha de presión para embragar o desembragar un disco de fricción. (25)

Die cast   The process of shaping metal by forcing hot metal under pressure into a metal mold. (9)

Fundir a presión (troquelar)   Proceso de formar metal a través de forzar metal super-caliente bajo presión en un molde metálico. (9)

Diesel engine   An intermittent, internal combustion, reciprocating engine that uses the heat of combustion to ignite the fuel. Fuel is supplied by a high-pressure fuel injector instead of a carburetor. (6)

Motor diesel Un motor intermitente, de combustión interna, con reciprocidad que emplea el calor de combustión para encender el combustible. En vez de un carburador, un inyector de alta presión suministra el combustible. (6)

Differential A gear assembly that transmits power from the drive shaft to the wheels. It also allows two opposite wheels to turn at different speeds for cornering and traction. (27)

Diferencial Un montaje de ruedas dentadas, que transmite potencia desde el eje de transmisión hasta las ruedas. También permite que dos ruedas opuestas giren a velocidades diferentes para doblar y tracción. (27)

Differential pressure Difference in pressure on an oil system between the input and the output of a filter. (11)

Presión diferencial Diferencia de presión en un sistema de aceite entre la entrada y la salida de un filtro. (11)

Digital signal A computer signal that has either an on or off condition. (18)

Señal digital Una señal de computadora que tiene una condición de encendida o apagada. (18)

Dilution To make thinner or weaker. Oil is diluted by the addition of fuel and water droplets. (11)

Dilución Hacer un líquido más diluído o menos concentrado (fuerte). Se diluye el aceite por medio de la añadidura de gotitas de combustible y agua. (11)

Dimmer switch A switch in the headlight circuit used to switch electricity between LO and HI positions. (34)

Interruptor de regulador de voltaje Un interruptor en el circuito de los focos delanteros, el cual sirve para cambiar la electricidad entre las posiciones de luces bajas y luces altas. (34)

Diode Semiconductor in an electrical circuit to allow electrical current to flow in only one direction. (18)

Díodo Semiconductor en un circuito eléctrico que permite que una corriente eléctrica fluya en solo una dirección. (18)

Disc brakes Brakes in which the frictional forces act on the faces of a disc. (28)

Frenos de disco Frenos en los que las fuerzas de fricción rozan contra la supericie de un disco. (28)

Discharging When an electrical load is put on a battery, the battery is discharged. The internal parts of the battery are chemically changed to the same metals and water. (19)

Descargar Situación en la que una carga eléctrica se le pone a una batería, ésta descarga. Las partes internas de la batería están cambiadas químicamente a los mismos metales y la misma agua. (19)

Disperse To scatter, spread, or diffuse. (17)
Dispersar Esparcir, disipar, o difundir. (17)

Dispersent A chemical added to motor oil to disperse or keep the particles of dirt from sticking together. (11)

Dispersante Químico añadido al aceite de motor para dispersar o prevenir que partículas de polvo o tierra se peguen. (11)

Displacement The volume the piston displaces from BDC to TDC. (6)

Desplazamiento El volumen que desplaza el pistón de BDC a TDC. (6)

Dissipate To become thinner and less concentrated. (23)
Disipar Llegar a estar más diluído y menos concentrado. (23)

Distillation The process at a refinery that separates the hydrocarbons into many products. Usually boiling a liquid to a vapor and condensing it are involved. (13)

Destilación Proceso de una refinería que separa los hidrocarburos en varios productos. Típicamente el hervir un líquido hasta vapor y el condensarlo son dos procesos. (13)

Distillation endpoint The temperature at which a fuel is completely vaporized. (13)

Punto final de la destilación Temperatura a la que un combustible está completamente vaporizado. (13)

Distributor cam Cams on the distributor shaft used to open and close the breaker points. There is one cam for each cylinder of the engine. (20)

Leva del distribuidor Levas en el eje del distribuidor, las cuales se emplean para abrir y cerrar los puntos de ruptura. Hay una leva para cada uno de los cilindros del motor. (20)

Distributorless ignition An ignition system that uses a computer to distribute the electrical spark, rather than a rotor and distributor cap. (20)

Ignición sin distribuidor Sistema de encendido que emplea una computadora para distribuir una chispa eléctrica, en vez de un rotor (rodete) y una tapa del distribuidor. (20)

Domains Small sections in a metal bar where atoms line up to produce a magnetic field. (18)

Dominios Secciones pequeñas en una barra metal en la que los átomos se congregan para producir un campo magnético. (18)

DOT Department of Transportation. (31)
DT Departamento de Transportación. (31)

Draft The act of drawing or pulling air through a tube. (15)
Succión (tiro) de aire Acto de succionar o aspirar aire por un tubo. (15)

Drive The end of a ratchet or other similar wrench used to hold the socket to the ratchet. (4)

Implemento de acciona (o impulsión) El extremo de una llave de cubo (trinquete, carraca, matraca) u otra llave semejante, que sirve para sostener firme la boquilla (casquilla, adaptador) a la llave de cubo. (4)

Drive lines Components on the vehicle that transmit the power from the engine to the wheels. (1)

Líneas (Flechas) de transmisión Componentes de un vehículo que transmite la potencia desde el motor a las ruedas. (1)

Drive shaft A metal tube with I-joints or CV joints at each end, used to transmit power from a transmission to the wheels on differentials. (27)

Eje impulsor (Arbol de arrastre, Arbol motor, Flecha) Un tubo metálico con juntas I o juntas CV en cada extremo, que sirve para transmitir fuerza desde la transmisión a las ruedas que están en un diferencial. (27)

Drop center wheel A wheel that has its center dropped in with a smaller radius. A drop center wheel is used so that the tire can be easily removed. (31)

Rueda de centro reducido Una rueda que tiene su parte céntrica reducida con un radio más pequeño. Una rueda de centro reducido se emplea para que se le pueda quitar la llanta más fácilmente. (31)

Dual camshaft A type of engine that has two camshafts for opening and closing additional valves. (8)

Arbol de levas doble Tipo de motor que tiene dos árboles de levas para abrir y cerrar válvulas adicionales. (8)

Dwell The length of time in degrees of distributor shaft rotation that the points remain closed. (20)

Duración Cantidad de tiempo en grados de la rotación del eje del distribuidor en que los puntos quedan cerrados. (20)

Dynamic balancing Equal distribution of weight on each side of a centerline of a wheel. Dynamic means moving or action, and dynamic balancing is done with the wheel moving or spinning. (31)

Equilibrio dinámico   Distribución igual de peso a cada lado del centro de un rin. Dinámico significa en movimiento o acción, y equilibrio dinámico se hace con el rin en movimiento o giración. (31)

Dynamometer   A device used to brake or absorb mechanical power produced from an engine for testing purposes in a laboratory situation. (7)

Dinamómetro   Aparato que sirve para frenar o absorber la potencia mecánica producida por un motor con el propósito de hacer pruebas en una situación de laboratorio. (7)

Eccentric   Circles having different center points. (11) (14) (30)

Excéntrico   Círculos que tienen diferentes puntos céntricos. (11) (14) (30)

Eddy current   Small circular currents produced inside a metal core in the armature of a starter motor. Eddy currents produce heat and are reduced by using a laminated core. (22)

Remolino (corriente en remolino)   Pequeñas corrientes circulares producidas dentro del centro de la armadura de un motor de arranque. Los remolinos producen calor y se reducen con un centro o núcleo laminado. (22)

EFE   Early fuel evaporation. (24)

ECA   Evaporación de combustible avanzado (o temprano). (24)

Efficiency   A ratio of the amount of energy put into an engine to the amount of energy coming out of the engine. Gas engines are about 28% efficient. A measure of the quality of how well a particular machine works. (6) (7)

Eficiencia   Proporción de la cantidad de energía que entra a un motor a la cantidad de energía que sale del motor. Los motores de gasolina tienen una eficiencia en el 28%. Es una medida de la calidad de funcionamiento de una máquina en particular. (6) (7)

EGR   Exhaust gas recirculation. (24)

RGE   Recirculación de gas de escape. (24)

Electric load detector   An electric load sensor used to detect the exact amount of electrical load required by various components of an engine. (21)

Detector de carga eléctrica   Un sensor de carga eléctrica que sirve para detectar la cantidad exacta de carga eléctrica requerida por varios componentes de un motor. (21)

Electrical schematic   An electrical system layout, showing the parts, the wires, and the electrical flow of the circuit. (34)

Esquema eléctrico   Una gráfica del sistema eléctrico que demuestra las partes, alambres, y el flujo de corriente del circuito. (34)

Electrical symbol   A symbol used to identify an electrical part in an electrical schematic. (34)

Símbolo eléctrico   Símbolo que sirve para identificar una parte eléctrica en un esquema eléctrico. (34)

Electricity   The flow of electrons from a negative point to a more positive point. (18)

Electricidad   El flujo de electrones desde un punto negativo a un punto más positivo. (18)

Electrochemical   A process (as in a battery) that uses chemical action to produce and store electricity. (19)

Electroquímico   Proceso (como en una batería) que utiliza una acción química para producir y almacenar electricidad. (19)

Electrolyte   A solution of acid and water used as the acid in a battery. Many types of electrolyte are used, but the most common is sulfuric acid and water. (19)

Electrólito   Solución de ácido y agua utilizada como el ácido en una pila. Se utilizan varios tipos de electrólitos, pero el más común es ácido sulfúrico y agua. (19)

Electromagnetic induction   Producing electricity by passing a wire conductor through a magnetic field, causing the wire to cut the lines of force. (18)

Inducción electromagnética   Producción de fuerza electromotriz por medio de pasar un conductor alámbrico por un campo magnético, dejando así que el alambre metálico corte las lineas de fuerza. (18)

Electromagnetism   Producing magnetism by using electricity flowing through a wire. (18)

Electromagnetismo   Producción de magnetismo por medio de electricidad que fluye a lo largo de un alambre metálico. (18)

Electron   The negative (–) part of the atom. (18)

Electrón   Parte negativa (–) de un átomo. (18)

Electronic engine analyzer   A testing instrument capable of measuring many readings such as RPM, spark voltages, timing, dwell, vacuum, and exhaust characteristics. (4)

Analizador electronico para el motor   Instrumento de medición o prueba capaz de medir varias lectures como RPM, voltajes de chispa, tiempo, duración, vacío, y características de gases de escape. (4)

Electron theory   Electrons will flow from a negative to a positive point. (18)

Teoría de electrón   Electrones fluyen de un punto negativo a un punto positivo. (18)

Electronic steering   A steering system in which a small electric motor, in conjunction with a steering effort sensor, is used to move the rack and pinion components of a steering system. (30)

Manejo electrónico   Sistema de manejo o conducción en el que se emplea un pequeño motor eléctrico, en combinación con un sensor del esfuerzo de manejo, para manipular los componentes de piñón y cremallera (barra dentada) del mismo sistema de manejo. (30)

Emission control   Various devices placed on the vehicle and engine to reduce exhaust pollution. (23)

Control de emisión   Varios aparatos montados en el vehículo y motor para reducir los contaminantes del escape. (23)

Emission standards   The federal government has established certain emission and pollutant standards on all automobiles. Because of environmental damage in the past, car manufacturers must now meet strict emission standards. (16)

Estándares de emisión   El gobierno federal ha establicedo ciertas normas de emisión y contaminantes para todo automóvil. Dado el daño medioambiental del pasado, los fabriciantes automotrices ahora tienen que cumplir con estándares de emisión muy estrictos. (16)

Energy   The ability to do work. (6)

Energía   Facultad de producir trabajo. (6)

Energy absorber   A type of shock or impact absorber that absorbs impact energy during a collision on the front or rear bumpers. (34)

Amortiguador de energía   Tipo de amortiguador o absorbedor de impacto que absorbe energía de impacto en el momento de colisión o choque contra las defensas delanteras o traseras. (34)

Engine   The power source that propels the vehicle forward or in reverse. The engine can be of several designs, including the standard gasoline piston engine, diesel engine, and rotary engine. (1) (6)

Motor   Fuente de poder que impulsa a un vehículo para adelante o para atrás. El motor puede ser de varios diseños, incluyendo el típico motor de gasolina y pistón, diesel, y rotativo. (1) (6)

Engine dynamometer   A dynamometer used to measure brake horsepower. (7)

Dinamómetro de motor Dinamómetro que sirve para medir la potencia de caballos frenada. (7)

EPA Environmental Protection Agency. (23)
APM Agencia de Protección del Medioambiente. (23)

Ergonomic hazards Conditions that relate to one's physical body or to motion. (2)
Riesgos ergonómicos Condiciones que se relacionan al cuerpo físico o al movimiento. (2)

Ethanol A hydrocarbon produced from the distillation of corn, wheat, and so on, for use in making gasohol. (13)
Etanol Hidrocarburo producido de la destilación de maíz, trigo, *etcétera,* para producir "gasohol." (13)

Ether A highly volatile and flammable, colorless liquid used for starting diesel engines in cold weather. (13)
Eter Líquido altamente volátil y flamable, incoloro, que sirve para arrancar los motores diesel en condiciones de mucho frío. (13)

Evaporator A component in an air conditioning system used to heat a refrigerant above its boiling point. (32)
Evaporador (Vaporizador) Componente en un sistema de aire acondicionado, que sirve para calentar un refrigerante más arriba de su punto de ebullición. (32)

Expansion valve A component in an air conditioning system used to create a pressure on one side and reduce the pressure on the other side. (32)
Válvula de expansión Componente de un sistema de aire acondicionado, que sirve para crear presión en un lado y reducir la presión del otro. (32)

Explosion-proof cabinet Cabinet used in the automotive shop to store gasoline and other flammable liquids. (2)
Gabinete a prueba de explosiones (antiexplosivo) Gabinete usado en talleres automotrices donde se guardan gasolina y otros líquidos inflamables. (2)

External combustion Combustion of air and fuel externally, or outside of the engine. (6)
Combustión externa Combustión del aire y combustible externamente, o sea, fuera del motor. (6)

Extreme pressure (EP) A term used to represent the consistency number of a particular type of grease. (11)
Presión extrema Término que sirve para representar el número de consistencia de un tipo de grasa en particular. (11)

Eyewash fountains A water fountain that directs water to the eyes for flushing and cleaning. (2)
Fuente lavaojos Fuente de agua que dirige el agua a los ojos para aclarar y lavarlos. (2)

Fastener Objects such as screws, bolts, splines, and so on, which hold together parts of the automobile. (3)
Sujetador Objetos tales como tornillos, pernos, estrías (chaveteros), *etcétera,* los cuales sujetan juntas las partes del automóvil. (3)

Feeler gauge Small, thin metal blades or wires, each having a different thickness, used to measure small clearances such as valve clearances. (4)
Calibre de espesor (lámina calibradora, calibrador de separaciones) Lengüetas o hijas metálicas delgadas, cada una de las cuales tiene un grueso diferente, sirven para medir las separaciones (huecos o distancias) como el espacio de válvulas. (4)

Field circuit An electrical circuit in a generator or alternator that causes the north and south poles to be energized. The field circuit can be either stationary, as in a generator, or rotating, as in an alternator. (21)
Circuito inductor Circuito eléctrico de un generador o alternador, que causa que los polos norte y sur sean energizados con energía. El circuito inductor puede ser fijo, como en un generador, o rotativo, como en un alternador. (21)

Filler neck restrictor A restriction plate located in the inlet of the fuel tank, used to prevent leaded fuel from being put into the gas tank of cars that require unleaded fuel. (14)
Restrictor del cuello de llenado (orificio de entrada) Placa restrictor situada en la boca de entrada de un tanque de combustible, que sirve para impedir que se le pongá combustible con plomo al tanque de autos que requieren un combustible sin plomo. (14)

Fillets Small, rounded corners machined on the crankshaft for strength. (9)
Tira o faja (listón, cinta) Pequeñas esquinas redon deadas de un cigüeñal maquinadas para darle más fuerza. (9)

First-aid box A kit made of various first-aid bandages, creams, and wraps for treating minor injuries. (2)
Caja de primeros auxilios Paquete de vendajes para primeros auxilios, cremas, y otros utensilios para tratar heridas menores. (2)

Fixed caliper A disc brake caliper design where the caliper is rigidly mounted and creates braking force through opposing pistons. (28)
Calibrador fijo Diseño de calibrador para freno de disco, en el que el calibrador está montado rígidamente y produce una fuerza de frenada mediante pistones opuestos. (28)

Flash point A diesel fuel's ignition point when being exposed to an open flame. (13)
Punto de inflamación Punto de encendido del combustible diesel al exponerse a una llama. (13)

Fleet service Service given to a fleet of vehicles owned by a particular company. (1)
Servicio de flotilla Servicio suministrado a una flotilla de vehículos cuyo dueño es una compañía particular. (1)

Floating caliper A moving disc brake caliper with piston(s) on only one side of the rotor. (28)
Calibrador flotante Calibrador de freno de disco flotante con pistón(es) en un solo lado del rotor. (28)

Fluid coupling A fluid connection between the engine and transmission. The greater the speed, the better the fluid coupling between the two. (26)
Acoplamiento fluído Conexión para fluídos (líquidos) entre el motor y la transmisión. Cuanto más rápida la velocidad, tanto mejor sera el acoplamiento fluídico entre los dos. (26)

Fluidity A characteristic of a fluid such as oil, meaning the ease of flow. (11)
Fluidez Característica (atributo) de un fluído como aceite, que significa la facilidad de circulación (paso o movimiento). (11)

Flywheel A heavy circular device placed on the crankshaft. It keeps the crankshaft rotating when there is no power pulse. (6)
Rueda voladora Aparato circular y pesado montado en el cigüeñal. Mantiene al cigüeñal en movimiento rotativo cuando no hay potencia de pulsación. (6)

Foreman A supervisor in a dealership, responsible for organizing work schedules and managing the service technicians. (1)
Capataz Supervisor en una agencia automotriz, responsable para organizar los horarios laborales y supervisar a los técnicos (mecánicos) de servicio. (1)

Forge The process of shaping metal by stamping it into a desired shape. (9)
Forjar Proceso de formar metal por medio de la acción de mazo (máquina de estampar) para estampar la forma deseada. (9)

Forward sensor The sensor used for air bag restraint systems. (34)

Sensor delantero Detector que sirve para sistemas protectores de bolas de aire. (34)

Four-gas analyzer An exhaust gas analyzer able to detect and measure exact amounts of hydrocarbons, carbon monoxide, carbon dioxide, and oxygen. (23)

Analizador de cuatro gases Analizador de gases de escape (emisiones), el cual es capaz de detectar y medir cantidades exactas de hidrocarburos, monóxido de carbono, bióxido de carbono, y oxígeno. (23)

Four-stroke engine An engine that has intake, compression, power, and exhaust strokes within two revolutions of the crankshaft. (6)

Motor de cuatro tiempos Motor que tiene entrada, compresión, encendido, y escape dentro de dos revoluciones del cigüeñal. (6)

Four-valve head A cylinder head on an engine that has four valves. Two are used for intake and two are used for exhaust. (8)

Tapa (Cabeza) para cuatro válvulas Tapa de cilindro de un motor que tiene cuatro válvulas. Se emplean dos para entrada y otras dos para escape. (8)

Four wheel alignment Alignment of both the front and rear wheels together. (30)

Alineación de cuatro ruedas Alineación de las dos ruedas delanteras y las dos traseras juntas. (30)

Franchised dealer A dealership that has a contract with the main car manufacturer to sell and service its automobiles. (1)

Agencia de franquicia Agencia automotriz que tiene contrato con la fabrica automotriz principal para vender y dar servicio a sus automóviles. (1)

Friction The resistance to motion between two bodies in contact with each other. (11) (28)

Fricción Resistencia a moción (movimiento) entre dos cuerpos que tiene contacto entre sí. (11) (28)

Frictional horsepower Horsepower lost to friction caused by bearings, road resistance, tire rolling resistance, and so on. (7)

Potencia en caballos friccional Caballaje perdido a la fricción producida por los cojinetes (baleros), resistencia del camino, resistencia del rodaje de ruedas, *etcétera*. (7)

Friction bearing A type of bearing that uses oil between the rotating shaft and the stationary part. (3)

Cojinete (Balero) de fricción Tipo de cojinete (balero) que utiliza aceite entre el eje rotativo y la parte fija. (3)

Friction disc The part of a clutch system that is clamped between the flywheel and the pressure plate. The friction disc is the output of the clutch system. (25)

Disco de fricción Parte del sistema del embrague que se sujeta entre la rueda voladora y el plato de presión. El disco de fricción es la potencia útil del sistema de embrague. (25)

Friction modifier A chemical added to gear oil to enhance an oil's ability to reduce friction. (27)

Modificador de fricción Químico añadido al aceite para engranes para aumentar la capacidad del aceite de reducir la fricción. (27)

Fuel consumption The amount of fuel that is consumed or used by the vehicle. Four-, six-, and eight-cylinder engines all have different fuel consumption rates. (8)

Consumo de combustible Cantidad de combustible que consume o usa un vehículo. Motores de cuatro, seis, y ocho cilindros tienen diferentes tasas de consumo de combustible. (8)

Fuel injection Injecting fuel into the engine under pressure. (6)

Inyección de combustible El inyectar combustible en un motor bajo una presión. (6)

Fuel injector Normally the carburetor mixes the air and fuel at a ratio of 14.7 to 1. However, today's vehicles are using fuel injectors. These injectors mix the fuel with the air just before the intake valve. The fuel is injected into the port under a low pressure. Computers control the amount of fuel injected. (14)

Inyector de combustible Normalmente un carburador mezcla el aire y el combustible en una proporción de 14.7 a 1. Sin embargo, los vehículos modernos utilizan inyectores de combustible. Estos inyectores mezclan el combustible con el aire justamente antes de la válvula de entrada. El combustible es inyectado en el orificio bajo una presión baja. Computadoras (ordenadores) controlan la cantidad de combustible inyectado. (14)

Fuel system The subsystem on the engine used to mix the air and fuel correctly. (1)

Sistema de combustible El subsistema del motor que sirve para mezclar correctamente el aire y el combustible. (1)

Fuel vapors When gasoline heats up, it gives off vapors. The vapors take space and, at times, stop the fuel from flowing. Fuel vapors should be sent back to the fuel tank. (14)

Vapores de combustible Al calentarse la gasolina, emite vapores. Los vapores ocupan cierto espacio y a veces, impiden que pase el combustible. Los vapores de combustible deben ser enviados de vuelta al tanque de combustible. (14)

Fulcrum The support or point of rest of a lever; also called the pivot point. (25)

Eje fijo (Fulcro) Punto de apoyo sobre el cual descansa una palanca; llamado también punto de pivote. (25)

Full-wave rectification A process of rectifying a voltage from ac to dc by using diodes. The negative half cycle of the voltage is converted to a positive voltage. All cycles are used in full-wave rectification. (21)

Rectificación de onda completa Proceso de rectificar un voltaje de corriente alterna a corriente continua, utilizando díodos. El medio ciclo negativo del voltaje se convierte a un voltaje positivo. Todos los ciclos se emplean en una rectificación de onda completa. (21)

Fuse block A small plastic block in a vehicle where all the electrical fuses are located. On some vehicles, the turn signal flashers and relays are also connected to the fuse block. (34)

Bloque portafusible (Placa de fusibles) Pequeña caja plástica en un vehículo donde se encuentran todos los fusibles. En ciertos vehículos, las luces intermitentes y conmutadores (relés) eléctricos también están conectados al mismo bloque (placa de fusibles). (34)

Fusible link A type of electrical circuit protector made from a special wire that melts when the current is excessive. (34)

Elemento fusible Tipo de protector de circuito eléctrico hecho de un hilo metálico especial que se funde cuando haya una corriente excesiva. (34)

Galling A displacement of metal, usually caused by a lack of lubrication, too loose fit, or capacity overloads on U-joints. (27)

"Galling" Desplazamiento de metal, normalmente producido por falta de lubricación, ajuste demasiado flojo, o sobrecargas más allá de la capacidad de la junta (el balero) universal. (27)

Gasket A rubber, felt, cork, steel, copper, or asbestos material placed between two parts to eliminate leakage of gases, greases, and other fluids. (3)

Empaque (Junta obturadora, Arandela, Guarnición de caucho o de metal) Material de caucho, corcho, acero, cobre, o asbesto colocado entre dos partes para eliminar la salida o escape de gases, lubricantes u otros líquidos. (3)

Gasket sealants A chemical sealant placed on a gasket in an engine to aid in sealing and to position the gasket during installation. (3)

Sellador de empaque Químico sellador puesto en un empaque de un motor para ayudar a sellar y colocarlo durante la instalación. (3)

Gasoline containers   Specially approved OSHA containers used to hold and store gasoline safely. (2)

Contenedores de gasolina   Contenedores (cubos, tinajas) aprobados especialmente por "OSHA," los cuales sirven para guardar y almacenar gasolina con seguridad sin riesgos. (2)

Gas turbine engine   An engine that uses two turbines, continuous combustion, and operates at high speeds to produce power. (8)

Motor de turbina de combustión   Motor que emplea dos turbinas, combustión continua, y funciona a altas velocidades para producir potencia. (8)

Gauge pressure   Pressure read on a gauge, at atmospheric pressure, starting with zero as a reference point. (16)

Presión manométrica   Presión indicada en un manómetro, empezando con cero como punto de referencia. (16)

General engine specifications   Specifications used to identify a style and type of engine. (5)

Especificaciones generales del motor   Especificaciones que sirven para identificar un estilo y clase de motor. (5)

Governor   A device placed on a fuel system to control the amount of fuel being metered into the engine. A governor is only capable of sensing a speed change in the engine. (16)

Regulador (Governador)   Aparato montado en un sistema de combustible para controlar la cantidad de combustible que se mete al motor. Un regulador únicamente es capaz de percibir un cambio en la velocidad del motor. (16)

Gram   A metric unit of measure used to measure mass. (4)

Gramo   Unidad métrica que sirve para medir masas o bultos. (4)

Hall-effect   A device used in electronic and computerized ignition systems that provides a signal for the computer based upon a rotating shaft. (19)

Efecto Hall   Aparato usado en sistemas de encendido electrónicos y computarizados, el cual suministra una señal para la computadora (ordenador) basada en un eje rotativo. (19)

Harmonics   When valve springs are opened and closed rapidly, they may vibrate. Periods of vibration are called harmonics. (10)

Armónicas   Cuando se abren y se cierran rápidamente los resortes de válvula, puede que vibren. Se llaman armónicas a los períodos de vibración. (10)

Hazardous waste   A product used in any system that is considered harmful to people and to the environment. (12)

Desperdicios peligrosos   Producto usado en cualquier sistema que se considera peligroso a la gente y al medioambiente. (12)

Head   The part of a bolt used to tighten it down with a wrench. (3)

Cabeza   Parte de un perno (tornillo) que sirve para apretarlo con llave. (3)

Header   A welded steel pipe used as an exhaust manifold. (17)

Colector (tubo colector)   Tubo de acero soldado y usado como un colector múltiple de escape. (17)

Heat dam   The narrow groove cut into the top of the piston. It restricts the flow of heat down into the piston. (9)

Contenedor de calor   Ranura pequeña cortada en la cabeza de un pistón. Restringe el flujo de calor hacia abajo en el pistón. (9)

Heater core   A small radiator-like heat exchanger. Hot coolant from the engine flows through the heater core. Air flow from a fan passes through the fins on the heater core, picking up heat to warm the passenger compartment. (33)

Tubería del calentador   Intercambiador de calor como un pequeño radiador. Circula refrigerante caliente por los tubos de intercambio térmico. Pasa un flujo de aire por las aletas de los tubos, elevando así su temperatura para calentar el compartimiento de los pasajeros. (33)

Heat exchanger   A device used to transfer heat from one medium to another. The radiator is a liquid-to-air heat exchanger. (12)

Intercambiador de calor   Aparato que sirve para transferir calor de un cuerpo a otro. El radiador es un intercambiador de calor de líquido a aire. (12)

Heat stove   An enclosed area made of thin sheet metal around the exhaust manifold. It preheats air passing over the exhaust manifold before the air enters the air cleaner snorkel. (24)

Estufa térmica   Un área encerrada hecha de hojas delgadas metal de que cubren el colector múltiple de escape antes de que entre el aire al esnórkel de depurador del filtro aire. (24)

Heat transfer   The process of moving heat from a warmer object to a colder object. (12)

Transferencia de calor   Proceso de pasar calor de un objeto más caliente a uno más frío. (12)

Heat treated   A process in which a metal is heated to a high temperature, then is quenched in a cool bath of water, oil, and brine (salt water). This process hardens the metal. (9)

Tratado térmicamente (termotratado)   Proceso en que se calienta un metal a una temperatura alta; luego éste se baña en una solución de agua fresca, aceite, y agua salada. Este proceso endurece al metal. (9)

HEI   High-energy ignition system; a type of ignition system used on vehicles, in which the coil and distributor are physically combined into one unit. (20)

ESE   Sistema de encendido de super-energía; tipo de sistema de encendido usado en vehículos, en el cual la bobina eléctrica y el distribuidor se combinan físicamente en una sola unidad. (20)

Helicoil   A device used to replace a set of damaged threads. (3)

"Helicoil"   Aparato que sirve para reemplazar un juego de roscas dañadas. (3)

Hemispherical combustion chamber   A type of combustion chamber that is shaped like a half of a circle. This combustion chamber has the valves on either side with the spark plug in the center. (10)

Cámara de combustión hemisférica   Tipo de cámara de combustión formada en semicírculo. Esta cámara tiene válvulas en ambos lados con una bujía de encendido en el medio. (10)

HFC-134a   A hydrofluorocarbon gas that is not damaging to the environment and ozone layer that can be used in air conditioning systems. (32)

"HFC-134a"   Un gas de hidroflorocarburo que no daña ni al medioambiente ni a la capa de ozono y puede utilizarse en sistemas de aire acondicionado. (32)

Hi-test   Gasoline that has an octane number near 90–95. (13)

Número alto de octano   Gasolina que tiene un número de octano cercano a 90–95. (13)

Horn brush/slip-ring   An electrical contact ring used in the horn circuit. It is located in the steering wheel and is used to maintain electrical contact when the steering wheel is turned. (34)

Escobilla de bocina/anillo conductor   Anillo de contacto eléctrico usado en el circuito de la bocina. Se sitúa en el volante de manejo y sirve para mantener contacto eléctrico al girarse el volante. (34)

Horsepower   A measure of work being done per time unit. One hp equals the work done when 33,000 pounds have been lifted one foot in one minute. (7)

Potencia en caballos (caballaje)   Una medida de trabajo producido por unidad de tiempo. Un HP (caballo) equivale el trabajo producido cuando 33,000 libras (15,000 kg) se han levantado un pie (aproximadamente 33 centímetos) en un minuto. (7)

Housekeeping The type of safety in the shop that keeps floors, walls, and windows clean, lighting proper, containers correct, and tool storage correct. (2)
Administración interna Tipo de seguridad en un taller, la cual mantiene limpios los suelos, paredes, y ventanas, iluminación apropiada, contenedores apropiados y bien arregladas y guardadas las herramientas. (2)

Hydraulic system A brake system in which brakes are operated and controlled by hydraulic fluid under pressure. (28)
Sistema hidráulico Sistema de frenas en que un líquido bajo presión hidráulica maneja y controla los frenos. (28)

Hydrocarbons A term used to describe the chemical combinations of hydrogen and carbon. A type of automotive pollution produced by incomplete combustion. Hydrocarbons are considered partly burned hydrogen and carbon molecules resulting from combustion. (13) (23)
Hidrocarburos Término que sirve para describir las combinaciones químicas de hidrógeno y carbón. Tipo de contaminación producida por combustión incompleta. Se consideran los hidrocarburos como moléculas de hidrógeno y carbón que resultan de una combustión incompleta. (13) (23)

Hydrometer An instrument used to measure the specific gravity of battery acid. (19)
Hidrómetro Instrumento que mide el peso específico (densidad) del ácido de batería. (19)

Hydrophilic Attraction to water. Some tires have a hydrophilic tread, which means the tread is attracted to water. (31)
Hidrófilo Atracción de agua. Algunas llantas tienen una rodadura (cara) hidrófila, que significa que la llanta se atrae al agua. (31)

Hypoid gear oil A thick oil used in differentials. (27)
Aceite hipoido para ruedas dentadas Aceite espeso usado en diferenciales. (27)

Idler arm A steering linkage component, fastened to the car frame, which supports the right end of the center link. (30)
Eje loco Componente de articulación de manejo, montado en el chasis automotriz, y que soporta el extremo derecho del eslabón central. (30)

Idler gear A third gear placed in a gear train, usually used to reverse the direction of rotation. (25)
Engranaje intermedio (loco) Tercera rueda dentada colocada en el tren de engranajes, usado normalmente para cambiar la rotación en dirección opuesta. (25)

Ignition system The subsystem on the engine used to ignite the air and fuel mixture efficiently. (1)
Sistema de encendido (ignición) Subsistema del motor que sirve para encender eficientemente la mezcla de aire y combustible. (1)

I-head A style of valve arrangement in an engine. I-head refers to the valves being placed directly above the piston in the cylinder head. (8)
Cabeza I Cierto arreglo de válvulas de un motor. Cabeza I se refiere a las válvulas que se encuentran justamente encima de la cabeza de cilindros. (8)

Impact socket Socket used for heavy-duty or high-torque applications. This type of socket is used with an impact wrench. (4)
Cubo (Tintero) de impacto Cubo que sirve para aplicaciones de alta torsión. Se emplea este tipo de cubo con una pistola de impacto. (4)

Impact wrench An air- or electric-operated power wrench that uses impacts during rotation to loosen or tighten bolts and nuts. (4)

Pistola de impacto (de choque, de golpe) Pistola que funciona a base del poder de aire o electricidad y que emplea impactos (golpes) durante la rotación para soltar o ajustar más fuerte los pernos y tuercas. (4)

Inclined surface A slope or slanted surface. An inclined surface is used in valve rotators. (10)
Superifcie inclinada Superficie cuesta arriba o abajo. Se emplea una superficie inclinada en los rotadores de válvulas. (10)

Independent publishers Publishers that provide service information on automobiles. Examples are Motor manuals, Mitchell manuals, Chilton auto repair manual, and so on. (5)
Casa editorial independiente Casa editorial que suministra información de servicio acerca de automóviles. Unos ejemplos son manuales de Motor, manuales Mitchell, manual de reparaciones automovilísticas Chilton, *etcétera*. (5)

Independent rear suspension A rear suspension system composed of trailing arms (like control arms) and MacPherson struts or torsion bars. The system allows the rear wheels to move independently of each other. (29)
Suspensión trasera independiente Sistema de suspensión trasera compuesto de brazos de tracción (como brazos de control) y puntales de poste (codales, postes) MacPherson o barras de torsión. El sistema permite que las ruedas traseras se muevan independientemente, la una de la otra. (29)

Independent service Service provided by independent garages on all types and makes of vehicles. (1)
Servicio independiente Servicio suministrado por talleres independientes para todo tipo y marca de vehículos. (1)

Indicated horsepower Theoretical horsepower calculated by the manufacturer of the engine. (7)
Caballaje indicado Caballaje teórico calculado por el fabricante del motor. (7)

Inertia Objects in motion tend to remain in motion. Objects at rest tend to remain at rest. Inertia is the force keeping these objects in motion or at rest. (22)
Inercia Objetos en movimiento tienden a quedarse en movimiento. Objetos parados tienden a quedarse parados. Inercia es la fuerza que mantienen a los objetos en movimiento o parados. (22)

Inertia drive A drive system on a starter motor using inertia to turn a screw sleeve on a spline. (22)
Impulso inercial Sistema de propulsión de un motor de arranque que utiliza inercia para hacer girar una manguita de tornillo en un chavetero (estría o acanaladura). (22)

Inertia switch A switch used on fuel systems that opens the circuit whenever there is a sudden impact from a vehicle or crash. (14)
Interruptor inercial Interruptor usado en sistemas de combustible, el cual abre el circuito siempre que haya algún impacto de otro vehículo o choque. (14)

Infrared exhaust analyzer An instrument able to detect and measure hydrocarbons, carbon monoxide, carbon dioxide, and oxygen levels. (23)
Analizador infrarrojo de escape Instrumento capaz de detectar y medir los niveles de hidrocarburos, monóxido de carbono, bióxido de carbono, y oxígeno. (23)

Inhibitor Any substance that slows down or prevents chemical reactions such as corrosion or oxidation. (11)
Retardador (Inhibidor) Cualquier sustancia que retarde o impida reacciones químicas tales como corrosión u oxidación. (11)

In-line Cylinders in an engine that are in one line or row, such as an in-line four- or six-cylinder engine. The cylinders are generally vertical as well. (8)

En línea (Alineado, En serie) Cilindros de un motor que se encuentran en una fila, tal como un motor de cuatro en línea o seis en línea. Los cilindros generalmente son verticales también son verticales. (8)

Insert guides Valve guides that are small cast cylinders pressed into the cylinder head. (10)

Guías intertadas Guías de las válvulas son pequeños cilindros fundidos que son metidos a presion en la cabeza de los cilindros. (10)

Insulator A material with five or more electrons in the valence ring. (18)

Aislador Material con cinco electrones o más en la banda de valencia. (18)

Intake manifold vacuum The vacuum produced inside the intake manifold between the valve and the throttle plate. When the throttle plate is closed, there is high intake manifold vacuum. When it is open, there is low intake manifold vacuum. (15) (16)

Vacío del colector múltiple de admisión Vacío producido dentro del colector de admisión entre la válvula y la mariposa (placa) de aceleración. Cuando está cerrada la mariposa, hay mucho alto vacío en el colector de admisión. Cuando está abierta la mariposa, hay poco vacío en el colector. (15) (16)

Integral guides Valve guides that are manufactured and machined as part of the cylinder head. (10)

Guias integrales Guías de la válvula que se fabrican y maquilan como parte de la cabeza del cilindro. (10)

Integrated circuit A circuit board with many semiconductors forming a complex circuit. (18)

Circuito integrado (sólido) Microestructura integrada con muchos semiconductores que forman un circuito complejo. (18)

Intercooler A heat exchanger used on turbocharged engines; used to cool the intake air charge. (17)

Interenfriador (Radiador intermedio) Cambiador de calor usado en motores turbocargados; utilizado para enfriar la carga de aire que entra. (17)

Interference angle When the valve is ground at 45 degrees and the seat is ground at 44 degrees, the two angles will interfere with each other. Interference angles help valves seat faster. (10)

Angulo de interferencia Cuando se recorta (tornear) por máquina una válvula a 45 grados de ángulo y se recorta (tornear) el asiento a un ángulo de 44 grados, los dos ángulos se interfieren uno al otro. Los ángulos de interferencia ayudan a que las válvulas se asienten más rápidamente. (10)

Interference fit A fit between two parts that must be pressed together. Some piston pins have an interference fit with the piston. (9)

Conformidad (Ajuste) de interferencia El ajuste entre dos partes (o cuerpos) que tienen que presionar una contra la otra. Algunos ejes de pie de biela tienen una conformidad interferente con el pistón. (9)

Intermittent combustion Combustion of air and fuel that is starting and stopping. (6)

Combustion intermitente Combustión del aire y del combustible que comienza y se para. (6)

Internal combustion Combustion of air and fuel inside the engine. (6)

Combustión interna Combustión del aire y del combustible dentro del motor. (6)

Jack stand A stand used to support the vehicle when working under the car. Always support the car with such stands before working on the underside of the vehicle. (2)

Soporte de gato Soporte que sirve para sostener un vehículo al trabajar uno debajo de él. Siempre se debe soportar al vehículo con tales soportes antes de meterse debajo del vehículo. (2)

Jet valve A specially designed valve placed in the cylinder head and contacting the combustion chamber to direct the air and fuel into the combustion chamber for maximum efficiency. (8)

Surtidor Válvula diseñada especialmente colocada en la cabeza del cilindro y conectada a la cámara de combustión para dirigir al aire y al combustible en la cámara de combustión para máxima eficiencia. (8)

Jounce The action of a car going over bumps in the road. Jounce is similar to bounce. (29)

Brincar Acción o movimiento de un automóvil al pasar encima de topes o perturbaciones en la superficie del camino. El brinco es similar a movimientos altibajos. (29)

Jumper wire A wire used when troubleshooting an electrical circuit for bypassing or shorting out a specific component. (34)

Cables para diagnostico Alambre usado en la investigación de fallas o averías en un circuito eléctrico al desviar o cortar un componente específico. (34)

Keeper A small, circular, tapered metal piece that keeps the valve retainer attached to the valve. (10)

Retenedor (Fijador) Pequeña pieza metálica circular de forma cónica que mantiene conectado el retén de válvula a la válvula. (10)

Keyway A machined slot on a shaft that holds a metal piece called the key. A slot and key used together attach a pulley or hub to a rotating shaft. (3) (10)

Ranura (cuña) de posición Ranura recortada en el eje que mantiene fija una pieza metálica llamada la clavija. Una ranura y clavija en combinación sirven para juntar una polea o núcleo de rodete a un eje rotativo (3) (10)

Kinetic energy Energy in motion. (28)

Energía dinámica Energía en movimiento. (28)

Knee bolster An energy-absorbing pad used on a passive restraint system used to cushion the forward motion of the driver during an accident by restricting leg movement. (34)

Apoyo de rodilla Zapatilla que absorbe energía y es usada en un sistema de impedimento pasivo, el cual se emplea como cojín para acojinar el movimiento hacia adelante del conductor durante un accidente por medio de restringir el movimiento de las piernas. (34)

Labyrinth seal A type of seal that uses centrifugal forces to eliminate leakage from a rotating shaft. The seal does not touch the rotating part. (3)

Sello de laberinto Tipo de sello que emplea fuerzas centrífugas para eliminar escapes o fugas de un eje rotativo. El sello no toca a la parte rotativa. (3)

Lag The time it takes for a turbocharger to increase the engine power after the throttle has been depressed. (17)

Retraso Tiempo que toma un turboalimentador para aumentar la potencia del motor después de deprimirse el pedal que opera el obturador de la gasolina. (17)

Laminated Describes a series of plates of metal placed together and used as a core in a magnetic circuit. (21)

Laminado Esto describe una serie de placas metálicos juntas y usadas como núcleo en un circuito magnético. (21)

Laminations Thin layers of soft metal used as the core for a magnetic field. (22)

Laminaciones Capas delgadas de metal blando, usados como núcleo en un campo magnético. (22)

Latent heat Heat that is hidden or not readily observable. (32)

Calor latente   Calor que está escondido o no se observa fácilmente. (32)

Lean mixture   Too much air and not enough fuel for combustion. (6)

Mezcla pobre   Demasiado aire e insuficiente combustible para hacer combustión. (6)

Lever   A bar supported by a pivot point with a force applied to one end used to move a force exerted on the other. Force times distance moved on one side will always equal the force times distance moved on the other. Typically a lever is used to gain a force with a loss in distance. (25)

Palanca   Barra sostenida por un punto de pivote con una fuerza aplicada en un extremo, la cual mueve una fuerza ejercida en el otro extremo. La fuerza por distancia movida por el otro lado. Típicamente se utiliza una palanca para ganar una fuerza a costo (expendas) de una distancia. (25)

L-head   A valve arrangement that has the valves located in the block and not in the head. Engines that have L-head designs are commonly called flat-head engines. (8)

Cabeza L   Arreglo de válvulas que coloca las válvulas en el bloque y no en la cabeza. Los motores que tienen un diseño de cabeza L se llaman comúnmente motores de cabeza plana. (8)

Lifter   The small component that rides on the camshaft. The camshaft lobe lifts the lifter to aid in opening and closing the valves. (8)

Levantadores de válvulas   Pequeño componente que se monta en el arbol de levas. El lóbulo del arbol de levas eleva el levantador para ayudar a abrir y cerrar las válvulas. (8)

Limited slip differential   A differential that uses clutches or cones to lock up the side gears to the differential case. These components eliminate having one wheel spin faster, as on ice. (27)

Diferencial de desliz limitado   Diferencial que utiliza embragues o conos para detener el engranaje lateral conectado a la caja del diferencial. Estos componentes eliminan que una rueda gire más rápido, como sobre hielo. (27)

Line contact   The contact made between the cylinder and the torsional rings, usually on one side of the ring. The contact made between the valve and the valve seat. When an interference angle is used, only a small line contact is produced. (9) (10)

Contacto lineal   Contacto hecho entre el cilindro y los anillos de torsión, normalmente en un lado del anillo. Contacto hecho entre la válvula y el asiento de la válvula. Al utilizarse un ángulo interferente, sólo se produce un contacto lineal pequeño. (9) (10)

Lines of force   Invisible forces around a magnet. (18)

Líneas de fuerza   Fuerza imaginaria o invisible alrededor de un campo magnético. (18)

Liquid-cooled   Removing heat from the engine by circulating liquid coolant throughout the internal parts of the engine. (12)

Enfriado por líquido   Reducción o eliminación de calor de un motor por un refrigerante circulante por todas las partes internas de un motor. (12)

Liter   A unit in the metric system to measure volume. Equals 100 cubic centimeters. (4)

Litro   Unidad en el sistema métrico que mide volúmen. Equivale a 100 centímetros cúbicos. (4)

Load   The actual slowing down of the engine output shaft because of a brake applied to the shaft. The load could be that of driving up a hill. The load to the engine is increased in this case. (7)

Elemento disipador de potencia (carga)   La reducción en velocidad del eje de salida de potencia del motor debido a la aplicación de un freno al eje. La carga podría ser la de ir cuesta arriba. En tal caso se aumenta la carga al motor. (7)

Load range   The amount of load the tire is capable of supporting safely. The value is molded into the tire sidewall and is stated in pounds and/or kilograms. (31)

Margen de carga   Cantidad de carga que la llanta puede soportar con seguridad. La cifra está estampada en el costado de la llanta y está expresada en libras o en kilogramos. (31)

Lobe   The part of the camshaft that raises the lifter. (10)

Lóbulo   Parte de un arbol de levas que eleva el levantador. (10)

Lockup clutch   A type of clutch in which a lockup system is able to lock up the torque converter turbine with the engine, eliminating slippage between the two. (26)

Embrague inmovilizador   Tipo de embrague en el que un sistema de inmovilización puede inmovilizar la turbina del convertidor de torsión con el motor, eliminando así cualquier patinaje entre los dos. (26)

Loop scavenging   A method used to remove the exhaust gases from the cylinder in a two-stroke engine. (6)

Vuelta de gases   Método que sirve para eliminar los gases de escape del cilindro en un motor de dos tiempos. (6)

Lubricating system   The subsystem on the engine that is used to keep all moving components lubricated. (1)

Sistema de lubricación   Subsistema de un motor que sirve para mantener lubricado todo componente movible. (1)

MacPherson strut suspension   An independent suspension system consisting of a coil spring, shock absorber, and upper bearing. (29)

Sistema de postes (codales, soportes) MacPherson   Sistema independiente de suspensión que consiste en un resorte espiral, amortiguador contra choques, y cojinete (balero) superior. (29)

Mag wheel   A type of wheel that uses magnesium metal for the rim. (31)

Rin de magnesio   Tipo de rin que utiliza metal de magnesio en el borde. (31)

Magnetic pickup   A sensor that is able to induce a charge of electricity as a magnet passes by. This sensor is usually used to measure crankshaft rotation or position. (16)

Detector magnético   Sensor que puede producir una carga de electricidad al pasarse lateralmente un imán. Normalmente se utiliza este sensor para medir la rotación o posición de un cigüeñal. (16)

Main bearing clearance   The clearance between the main bearing journal and the main bearings. (9)

Margen (holgura) del cojinete (balero) principal   Espacio entre la manga del cojinete (balero) principal y el cojinete (balero) principal. (9)

Major and minor thrust   The thrust forces applied to the piston on the compression and power strokes. (9)

Empuje mayor y menor   Las fuerzas de empuje aplicadas al pistón durante los ciclos de compresión y potencia. (9)

Manual shift valve   A valve in the automatic transmission that is controlled by the position of the gearshift lever. (26)

Válvula de cambio manual   Válvula de una transmisión automática que es controlada por la posición de la palanca de cambio de velocidad. (26)

Manufacturer's service manual   Service information and technical data supplied by the automotive manufacturer. (5)

Manual de servicio de la fabrica   Información de servicio y datos técnicos suministrados por la fabrica automotriz. (5)

Master cylinder   The main unit for displacing brake fluid under pressure in a hydraulic brake system. The master cylinder can be either single or dual design. (28)

Cilindro maestro Unidad principal que desplaza al liquido de freno bajo presión en un sistema hidráulico de freno. El cilindro maestro puede ser de un diseño sencillo o doble. (28)

Mechanical advantage A linkage or lever able to gain either distance or force. The rocker arm uses a mechanical advantage to gain distance to open the valve farther. (10)

Ventaja mecánica Articulación (sistema de enlace) o palanca que puede ganar distancia o fuerza. El balancín (palanca oscilante) utiliza una ventaja mecánica para ganar distancia para abrir una válvula aún más. (10)

Mechanical efficiency A measure of the mechanical operation of a machine. (7)

Eficiencia mecánica Medida de la operación mecánica de una máquina. (7)

Medium Usually referred to as a certain type of material acting as the environment. In this case, the area where dirt is captured in the fuel filter. (14)

Medio Normalmente se le refiere al medio como cierto tipo de material en calidad del medioambiente. En este caso, el área donde se capturan partículas de tierra en el filtro para combustible. (14)

Meter A device used to measure or control the flow of a liquid such as fuel. To control the amount of fuel passing into an injector; fuel is metered to obtain the correct measured quantity. (15) (16)

Instrumento indicador Instrumento de medición que sirve para medir o controlar el flujo de un líquido tal como combustible. Para controlar la cantidad de combustible que entra al inyector; se mide el combustible para obtener la correcta cantidad medida. (15) (16)

Metric system A system of measurement based on the meter. All other units of length and volume are derived from the meter. These include centimeter, kilometer, millimeter, liter, cubic centimeter, and so on. (4)

Sistema métrico Sistema de medición basado en el metro. Todas las demás unidades de longitud y volumen se derivan del metro. Estos incluyen el centímetro, kilómetro, milímetro, litro, centímetro cúbico, *etcétera.* (4)

Metric thread A metric thread is measured by indicating the number of millimeters between each thread. (3)

Rosca métrica Se mide un rosca métrica indicando el número de milímetros entre cada rosca saliente. (3)

Micrometer A measuring tool used to accurately measure length to 0.001 of an inch. A distance measurement used to indicate the size of holes in a filter; 1 micrometer = 0.000039 inch; sometimes called a micron. (4) (14)

Micrómetro Instrumento de medición que sirve para medir con precisión hasta 0.001 de una pulgada de largo. Una medida de distancia utilizada para indicar el tamaño de agujeros en un filtro; 1 micrómetro = 0.000039 de pulgada; a veces se llama un micrón (micra). (4) (14)

Microorganism A small living organism. (14)

Microorganismo Pequeñísimo organismo viviente. (14)

Microprocessor A series of circuits using semiconductors and integrated circuits for computer applications. Microprocessors are also capable of input, storage, and feeding out information to other circuits and systems on the automobile. (18)

Microprocesador Serie de circuitos que utilizan semi-conductores y circuitos integrados para aplicaciones de computadoras (ordenadores). Los microprocesadores también son capaces de recibir información, almacenaje y envío de información a otros circuitos y sistemas en automóviles. (18)

Molecule The smallest physical unit of a chemical compound. (13)

Molécula Unidad física más pequeña de un compuesto químico. (13)

Monolith A single body shaped like a pillar or long tubular structure used as a catalyst in a catalytic converter. (24)

Monolito Cuerpo sencillo en forma de una columna o estructura larga y tubular, usado como catalizador en un convertidor catalítico. (24)

MSDS An abbreviation for Material Safety Data Sheet, which contains hazardous ingredients, physical and chemical properties, fire and explosion data, reactivity data, health hazards, control measures and precautions for using various chemicals in the automotive shop. (2)

HDSM Abreviadura de una Hoja de Datos sobre la Seguridad de Materiales, la cual contiene los ingredientes peligrosos, propiedades físicas y químicas, datos sobre incendios y explosiones, datos sobre reactividad, riesgos contra la salud, y medidas de control y precauciones para manipular varios químicos en un taller automotriz. (2)

Multiple-disc clutch A hydraulic clutch used in the automatic transmission. The clutch uses a series of discs, both friction and smooth metal, to lock up to rotating shafts. (26)

Embrague de discos múltiples Embrague hidráulico usado en una transmisión automática. El embrague utiliza una serie de discos, de ambos tipos: fricción y liso, para inmovilizar los ejes rotativos. (26)

National Lubricating Grease Institute (NLGI) One of several organizations that rate the consistency of greases. (11)

Instituto de Grasa Lubricante Nacional (IGLN) Una de varias organizaciones que evalúan la constancia (o consistencia) de grasas. (11)

Naturally aspirated An engine that uses the atmospheric pressure to force the air into the cylinders. (17)

Aspirado naturalmente Motor que utiliza la presión atmosférica para forzar el aire en los cilindros. (17)

NC National Coarse, or an indicator of the number of threads per inch on a bolt. (3)

Grueso nacional Indicador del número de roscas por pulgada en un perno o tornillo. (3)

Needle valve A small valve used in the center of the fuel injector nozzle. The valve is shaped much like a thick needle and controls the opening and closing of ports for fuel injection. (16)

Válvula de aguja Pequeña válvula usada en el centro de la boquilla (pico o tober) del inyector del combustible. La forma de la válvula se parece a una aguja gruesa y controla la apertura y el cierre de los orificios de inyección del combustible. (16)

NF National Fine, or an indicator of the number of threads per inch on a bolt. (3)

FN Fina Nacional, o indicador del número de roscas por pulgada de un perno o tornillo. (3)

Nitrogen oxide A type of automotive pollution produced when internal combustion temperatures reach 2,200-2,500°F. (13) (23)

Oxido de nitrógeno Tipo de contaminante automotriz producido cuando las temperaturas de combustión interna alcanzan a 2.200–2.500 grados F. (13) (23)

Nonsynchronized mode A mode of operation on a throttle body fuel injection system in which the injector is pulsed every 12.6 milliseconds. The pulses are independent of a distributor reference pulse. (16)

Modo asíncrono (no sincronizado) Modo de operación de un sistema de aceleración por inyección de combustible, en el cual el inyector de la placa de aceleración es pulsado cada 12.6 milisegundos. Los impulsos no dependen de ningún impulso de referencia del distribuidor. (16)

OASIS   A computerized information system for service technicians; stands for "On-Line Automotive Service Information System." (5)

"OASIS"   Sistema de información computarizado para técnicos de servicio; significa "Sistema de Información de Servicio en Línea Automotriz." (5)

Octane number   A number used to identify the resistance to burning of gasoline. (13)

Número de octano   Número que sirve para identificar la resistencia de combustión de gasolina. (13)

Ohm's law   Voltage equals amperage times resistance (E = I × R). (18)

Ley de Ohm   Voltaje equivale a amperaje multiplicado por la resistencia (E = I × R) (18)

Oil relief   A small machined area on the side of the lifter that allows oil to circle around the body of the lifter. (10)

Relieve de aceite   Pequeña área en la parte lateral del (levantador de válvulas) alzaválvulas que permite que el aceite circule alrededor del cuerpo del alzaválvulas. (10)

Open loop   A computer condition in which the air-fuel ratio is being controlled on the basis of a set of preprogrammed conditions. (15)

Circuito abierto   Condición en una computadora (ordenador) en la que la proporción del aire al combustible está controlada a base de unas condiciones pre-programadas. (15)

Open, shorted, grounded circuits   Conditions in an electrical circuit to render the system inoperative. (18)

Circuitos abiertos, cortados, conectados a tierra   Condiciones de un circuito eléctrico para dejar al sistema inoperativo. (18)

Operational specifications   Specifications used to show how the vehicle operates, such as acceleration, tire inflations, and other general information. (5)

Especificaciones operacionales   Especificaciones que sirven para indicar como funciona un vehículo, tal como aceleración, presión de llantas, y otra información en general. (5)

Opposed cylinder   An engine that has two rows of pistons that are 180 degrees from each other. (8)

Cilindros opuestos   Motor que tiene dos filas de pistones que están a 180 grados uno del otro. (8)

Organic   Pertaining to chemicals that are derived from living things. (11)

Orgánico   Relacionado a químicos que se derivan de elementos vivientes. (11)

Organic material   Another term for hydrocarbon pollution. (23)

Material orgánico   Otro término que sirve para indicar contaminantes de hidrocarburos. (23)

O ring   A type of static seal used to eliminate leakage between two stationary parts as fluid passes through them. (3)

Empaque O-ring   Tipo de sello estático que sirve para eliminar escapes o goteras (fugas) entre dos partes fijas al pasar por ellas cualquier líquido. (3)

Oscillation   Fluctuation or variation in motion or in electrical current. When the vehicle hits a bump in the road, the body oscillates up and down. Shocks are used to reduce oscillations. (29)

Oscilación   Fluctuación o variación en movimiento o de corrientes eléctricas. Cuando el vehículo pasa por un bache o tope en el camino, el armazón del coche oscila en brincos. Se emplean amortiguadores para reducir los brincos. (29)

OSHA   Occupational Safety and Health Act of 1970. This act provides safety regulations and rules for industry. (2)

"OSHA"   Acta de Seguridad Industrial y Salud (ASIS) de 1970. Esta acta suministra los reglamentos y reglas de seguridad para toda la industria. (2)

Overdrive   A gear system used on a transmission to reduce the speed of the input. Normally, the highest gear ratio in a standard transmission is 1:1. Overdrive systems have a higher gear ratio of approximately 0.8:1. (25) (26)

Sobremarcha   Sistema de engranaje usado en una transmisión para reducir la velocidad de la entrada de potencia. Normalmente la proporción de engranaje más alta en una transmisión estandard es 1 a 1. Sistemas de sobremarcha tienen una proporción de engranaje más alta de aproximadamente 0.8 a 1. (25) (26)

Overhaul and maintenance specifications   Specifications used to service vehicle components such as pistons, crankshafts, rings, bearings, and so on. (5)

Especificaciones de reparaciones y mantenimiento   Especificaciones que sirven para dar servicio a los componentes de vehículo tales como pistones, cigüeñales, anillos, cojinetes (baleros), *etcétera*. (5)

Overhead camshaft   A camshaft located directly on top of the valves, used on I-head designs. (8)

Eje de leva superior (arriba)   Eje de leva colocado directamente encima de las válvulas, el cual se emplea en motores con diseño de cabeza I. (8)

Overrunning clutch drive   A type of drive on a starter motor that uses a series of rollers that lock up to cause the pinion gear to rotate. (22)

Sistema de mando de un embrague de rueda libre (de sobremarcha)   Tipo de mando de un motor de arranque que emplea una serie de aparatos enrolladores que se inmovilizan para que gire la rueda dentada de piñón. (22)

Oxidation   The process of combining oil molecules with oxygen. (11)

Oxidación   Proceso de combinar moléculas de aceite y oxígeno. (11)

Oxidation inhibitors   Additives to gasoline to reduce the chemicals in gasoline that react with oxygen. (13)

Inhibidores de oxidación   Aditivos que se le agregan a la gasolina para reducir los químicos en la gasolina que reaccionan con oxígeno. (13)

Oxides   Chemicals that form when certain pollutants combine with oxygen. (23)

Oxidos   Químicos que se forman cuando ciertos contaminantes se combinan con oxígeno. (23)

Ozone layer   A transparent shield of gases surrounding the earth. (32)

Capa de ozono   Escudo protector de gases alrededor de la Tierra. (32)

Parallel circuit   In this type of circuit, there is more than one path for the current to follow. (18)

Circuito paralelo   En este tipo de circuito, hay más de un solo camino en el que la corriente puede circular. (18)

Particulates   A form of solid air pollution such as microscopic solid or liquid matter that floats in the air. (23)

Partículas   Forma de contaminación de aire sólido tal como material microscópico que sólido o líquido flota en el aire. (23)

Parts distribution   All service shops must have parts available. Parts distribution shops are retail businesses that sell parts for the automobile. (1)

Distribución de partes (piezas o refacciones)   Todo taller de servicio tiene que tener partes disponibles. Tiendas de distribución de partes son negocios de detallista que venden repuestos para el automóvil. (1)

Parts manager   The person responsible for making sure the customer's parts are immediately available to the service technician. (1)

Gerente de partes y refacciones Persona encargada para asegurar de que las partes que pide el cliente estén al acceso inmediato del técnico (mecánico) de servicio. (1)

Parts specialist A person who sells automotive engine and vehicle parts. (1)

Especialista en partes y refacciones Persona que vende partes para el motor de automóvil y del vehículo, en general. (1)

Passive restraint system A supplemental safety system to safety belts, using air bags that inflate immediately upon impact. (34)

Sistema de restricción pasiva Sistema suplemental de seguridad para los cinturones de seguridad, utilizando cojines de aire que se inflan inmediatamente al chocar el auto. (34)

Passive seal A seal that has no extra springs or tension devices to help make the seal. O-ring seals on valves are called passive valve seals. (10)

Junta (Cierre) hermética pasiva Cierre que no tiene resortes extras o aparatos de tensión para ayudar a hacer la junta hermética. Junta tórica (empaquetadura en O) en las válvulas se llaman cierres de válvula pasivos. (10)

PCV Positive crankcase ventilation. (24)

VCP Ventilación Positiva de Cárter. (24)

Pendulum A swinging device with a weight on one end used to control the movement of a mechanism. Pendulums are used to lock safety belts during impact. (34)

Péndulo Aparato oscilante con un peso en un extremo que sirve para controlar el movimiento del aparato. Se utilizan los péndulos para cerrar (o inmovilizar) los cinturones de seguridad al momento de impacto. (34)

Performance chart A chart that has been produced from a dynamometer. It shows the horsepower, torque, and fuel consumption of an engine at various RPM. (7)

Esquema de funcionamiento (ejecución) Esquema que se ha hecho de una dinamométrico. Indica el caballaje (potencia en caballos), el torque, y consumo de combustible de un motor a varias RPM. (7)

Periphery The external boundary of the torque converter. (26)

Periferia (Circunferencia) Borde externo de un convertidor de torque. (26)

Photochemical smog A type of smog produced when hydrocarbons and nitrogen oxides combine with sunlight. (23)

Contaminación de aire fotoquímico Tipo de contaminante de aire producido cuando se combinan los hidrocarburos y los óxidos de nitrógeno. (23)

Physical hazards Excessive levels of noise from vibration, temperature, and pressure factors. Also crushing hazards. (2)

Riesgos físicos Ruido de niveles excesivos que provienen de vibración, temperatura, y factores de presión. También riesgos aplastantes. (2)

Pinging A sound heard in the automobile engine that is caused by two combustion fronts hitting each other inside the combustion chamber. (13)

Silbido (Zumbido) Sonido que se oye en un motor de automóvil, producido cuando se pegan dos frentes combustidos dentro de la cámara de combustión. (13)

Pinion gear The small gear attached to the armature shaft used to crank the flywheel ring gear. The pinion gear is also the smaller of two gears. (22)

Piñón diferencial Pequeño engrane conectado al eje que sirve para girar la corona dentada (engranaje) de la rueda voladora. (22)

Pintle The center pin used to control a fluid passing through a hole; a small pin or pointed shaft used to open or close a passageway. (16) (24)

Pivote central (Perno pinzote) Aguja central que sirve para controlar al flúido que pasa por un agujero; pequeña aguja (o perno afilado) que sirve para abrir o cerrar un pasadizo. (16) (24)

Piston A cylindrical object that slides in the cylinder. (6)

Pistón Objeto cilíndrico que se desliza dentro del cilindro. (6)

Piston slap The movement of the piston back and forth in the cylinder in a slapping motion. (9)

Golpe de pistón El movimiento del pistón de un lado a otro en el cilindro. (9)

Pitch The angle of the valve spring twist. A variable pitch valve spring has unevenly spaced coils. (10)

Declive (Inclinación) Angulo de contorsión del resorte de válvula. Un resorte de un declive variable tiene espacios no uniformes entre las espirales. (10)

Pitman arm A steering linkage component that connects the steering gear to the linkage at the left end of the center link. (30)

Palanca (Brazo, Eslabón) Pitman Componente de articulación del manejo, el cual conecta el engranaje del volante a la articulación al extremo izquierdo del eslabón céntral. (30)

Pivot point The center point on the rocker arm. (10)

Punto de pivote Punto céntrico de un balancín (brazo oscilante). (10)

Planet carrier The part of a planetary gear system that connects the axis of the planet gears together. (26)

Portador planeta La parte del sistema del engranaje planetario, que conecta el eje del engranaje planetario. (26)

Planetary gear system A gear assembly that includes a sun gear, planet gears, and a ring gear. By locking up one gear, various gear ratios and speeds can be produced. (26)

Sistema de engranaje planetario Montaje de engranaje que incluye una rueda dentada de sol, ruedas dentadas de planeta, y una corona dentada. Cuando se inmoviliza una engrane, se producen varias proporciones de engranaje y velocidades. (26)

Plastigage A small, thin, plastic strip that is used to help determine the clearance between main and/or connection rod bearings and the crankshaft journals. (9)

Indicador plástico Pequeña y delgada cinta de plástico que sirve para ayudar a determinar el espacio entre los cojinetes principales y/o de la varilla de conexión y los muñones del cigüeñal. (9)

Pliers A tool used to grip or cut various objects when working on the automobile. (4)

Alicates (Pinzas) Herramienta que sirve para agarrar o cortar varios objetos al trabajar con un automóvil. (4)

Plies Layers of material that wrap around a tire. (31)

Envolturas Capas de material que envuelven a una llanta. (31)

Pole shoes Soft iron pieces that wire is wrapped around inside the starter motor. (22)

Expansión polar Piezas de metal blando alrededor de las cuales se envuelve un alambre metálico dentro del motor de arranque. (22)

Pollution Addition of harmful products to the environment. Types of pollution include air, water, noise, chemical, thermal, and nuclear. (23)

Contaminación Añadidura de productos peligrosos al medioambiente. Tipos de contaminación incluyen aire, agua, ruido, químico, térmico, y nuclear. (23)

Pollution control system The parts on an automobile engine used to reduce various emissions such as carbon monoxide, nitrogen oxide, and hydrocarbons. (1)

Sistema de control de contaminación Las partes de un motor de automóvil que sirven para reducir varias emisiones tales como monóxido de carbón, óxido de nitrógeno, e hidrocarburos. (1)

Poppet-type valve Mechanical equipment uses many types of valves. One valve is called the poppet valve. Poppet valves are those that operate from a camshaft and open and close a port. Automobile intake and exhaust valves are poppet valves. (10)

Válvula de elevación Equipo mecánico que emplea muchos tipos de válvulas. Una válvula se llama "Poppet." Válvulas Poppet son las que funcionan en un arbol de levas y abren y cierran una abertura. Válvulas automovilísticas de entrada y de escape son válvulas Poppet. (10)

Ported vacuum Vacuum taken from the carburetor slightly above the throttle plate. (15) (20)

Vacío enunorificio (Puerto) Vacío tomado desde el carburador un poco arriba de la mariposa (placa de aceleración). (15) (20)

Positive displacement pump A type of pressure pump that pumps an exact amount of fluid for each revolution. (24)

Bomba volumétrica (de desplazamiento) positiva Tipo de bomba de presión que bombea una cantidad exacta de líquido por cada revolución. (24)

Postignition Ignition that occurs after the engine ignition system is shut off due to carbon buildup in the combustion chamber. (13)

Post-ignición Encendido que ocurre después de que se apaga (cierra) el sistema de encendido, debido a depositos de carbón dentro de la cámara de combustión. (13)

Pour point The temperature at which an oil ceases to flow because of being too cold. (11)

Punto de fluidez Temperatura a la que un aceite deja de fluir debido al frío y la congelación. (11)

Power A measure of work being done. (6)

Potencia Medición del trabajo que se produce. (6)

Power control module A module or computer used in an electronic transmission to aid in control of the shift solenoids. (26)

Módulo de control de potencia Módulo o computadora (ordenador) usado en una transmisión electrónica para ayudar a controlar los solenoides de cambio de velocidades. (26)

Precombustion chamber A second combustion chamber placed directly off the main combustion chamber. The precombustion chamber is used to ignite a rich mixture of air and fuel. This mixture then ignites a lean mixture in the main combustion chamber. (10)

Cámara de pre-combustión Una segunda cámara de combustión montada justamente cerca de la cámara de combustión principal. Se utiliza la cámara de pre-combustión para encender una mezcla rica de aire y combustible. Esta mezcla luego enciende una mezcla pobre en la cámara de combustión principal. (10)

Prefix A term used to indicate how many units the meter is increased or decreased. One thousand meters is equal to one kilometer. Kilo is the prefix. (4)

Prefijo Término que sirve para indicar cuantas unidades se aumenta o reduce el metro. Mil metros equivalen un kilómetro. Kilo- es el prefijo. (4)

Preignition The process of a glowing spark or deposit igniting the air-fuel mixture before the spark plug. (13)

Pre-ignición Proceso de usar una chispa u otro material ardiente para encender una mezcla de aire y combustible antes que la bujía. (13)

Premature Occurring too soon. (14)

Prematuro Lo que ocurre demasiado pronto. (14)

Pressure The exertion of force on a body in contact with it. Pressure is developed within the cooling system and is measured in pounds per square inch on a gauge. (12)

Presión Aplicación de fuerza a un cuerpo, el cual tiene contacto con aquélla. Se aumenta la presión dentro del sistema refrigerante y se mide por libras por pulgada cuadrada en un aparato de medición. (12)

Pressure drop One condition in an antilock brake control module in which the hydraulic braking pressure is reduced to the locked-up brake caliper. (28)

Reducción de presión Una condición en un módulo de control de frenos anti-inmovilizador, dentro del cual la presión de los frenos hidráulicos está reducida al calibrador de freno inmovilizador. (28)

Pressure gauge A gauge used to read various pressures such as fuel pump, transmission oil, and fuel injection pressures. (4)

Manómetro (Indicador de presión) Instrumento de medición que sirve para medir (leer) varias presiones tales como bomba de combustible, aceite de transmisión, e inyección de combustible. (4)

Pressure hold One condition in an antilock brake control module in which no more braking pressure can be produced in the master cylinder. (28)

Retención de presión Una condición en un módulo de control de frenos anti-inmovilizador, en el que no se puede producir más presión de frenos en el cilindro maestro. (28)

Pressure modulator The assembly on an antilock braking system used to control the hydraulic pressure to the brake calipers. (28)

Modulador de presión Agrupación de piezas de un sistema de frenos anti-inmovilizador, la cual sirve para controlar la presión hidráulica a los calibradores de freno. (28)

Pressure plate The part in a clutch system used to squeeze or clamp the clutch disc between it and the flywheel. (25)

Platillo de presión La parte del sistema del embrague que sirve para agarrar o fijar al disco del embrague entre el embrague y la rueda voladora. (25)

Pressure regulator valve A valve used in an automatic transmission to regulate the pressure of the oil inside the valve body. (14) (26)

Válvula del regulador de presión Válvula que sirve en una transmisión automática para arreglar la presión del aceite dentro del cuerpo de la válvula. (14) (26)

Prevailing torque nuts Nuts designed to develop an interference fit between the nut and bolt threads. (3)

Tuercas de torque prevaleciente Tuercas diseñadas para desarrollar un ajuste interferente entre la tuerca y las roscas del perno. (3)

Preventive maintenance Maintenance performed on an engine to prevent potential repairs. (1)

Mantenimiento preventivo Mantenimiento dado al motor para prevenir algunas reparaciones potenciales. (1)

Primary battery A type of battery that cannot be recharged after use. (19)

Batería primaria Tipo de batería que no puede recargarse después de usarse. (19)

Primary circuit A circuit in the ignition system that uses 12 volts to operate. It includes the ignition switch, ballast resistor or resistive wire, primary coil wires, condenser, and contact points. (20)

Circuito primario Circuito del sistema de encendido que utiliza 12 voltios para operarse. Se incluye el switch de encendido, resistencia reguladora o hilo resistor, sistema de bobinas primarias, condensador, y puntos de contacto. (20)

Primary shoe   The forward shoe on a two-shoe drum brake system, often having shorter linings than the other. (28)
Zapata primaria   Zapata delantera de un sistema de tambor de freno de dos zapatas. (28)

Profile ratio   A number used when identifying tires that represents the ratio of the height to width of the tire; generally identified as a percentage. (31)
Perfil de proporción   Número usado al identificar llantas, el cual representa la proporción de altura a anchura de la llanta; generalmente identificado como porcentaje. (31)

PROM   Programmable read-only memory, or permanent storage in an automotive computer that can be easily accessed, removed and/or replaced by installing a new chip. (18)
"PROM"   Memoria programable de lectura solamente, o almacenaje permanente en una computadora (ordenador) automotriz, la cual puede ser accesible fácilmente, eliminada y/o reemplazada con un nuevo (chip). (18)

Propane   One of four gases found in natural gas. Methane, ethane, propane, and butane are in natural gas. Propane and butane have the highest amount of energy and can be made into a liquid by being put into a pressurized container. (13)
Propano   Uno de cuatro gases encontrados en gas natural. Metano, etano, propano, y butano se encuentran en gas natural. Propano y butano tienen la cantidad de energía más alta y pueden convertirse en líquido al ponerse en un recipiente bajo presión. (13)

Property class   A number stamped on the end of a metric bolt to indicate the hardness of the bolt. (3)
Clase de propiedad   Número sellado (cuñado) en el cabo de un perno métrico para indicar la dureza del perno. (3)

Proportioning valve   A valve in the brake hydraulic system that reduces pressure to the rear wheels to achieve better brake balance. (28)
Válvula proporcionadora   Válvula de un sistema de freno hidráulico, la cual reduce la presión a las ruedas traseras para lograr un mejor balance de freno. (28)

Proton   The positive (+) part of the atom. (18)
Protón   Parte positiva (+) de un átomo. (18)

Psig   A type of pressure scale read as pounds per square inch on a gauge. (12)
"Psig"   Tipo de escala de presión expresada como libras por pulgada cuadrada en un indicador. (12)

Puller   A tool attached to a shaft and gear, used to remove the gear from the shaft by applying certain pressures. (4)
Tirador   Herramienta pegada a un eje y engrane, que sirve para quitar el engrane del eje por medio de aplicar ciertas presiones. (4)

Pulse delay variable resistor   A resistor in the wiper system used to time delay the wiper motion from 0 to 25 seconds time delay. (34)
Resistencia variable de retardador de impulsos   Resistencia en el sistema del limpiabrisas, el cual se emplea para retardar el movimiento del limpiabrisas desde cero a 25 segundos de retardo. (34)

Pulse width   A term used to identify the length of time an injector will inject fuel. Large pulse width means more fuel being metered into the engine. (16)
Duración de impulso   Término que sirve para identificar la duración del tiempo que tomará un inyector para inyectar combustible. Una duración de impulso grande significa más combustible que entra medido en el motor. (16)

Pulse wiper system   A wiper system using electronic circuits that cause the wipers to pulse or turn on one time, then off for a certain number of seconds. (34)

Sistema de limpiabrisas de pulso   Sistema de limpiabrisas que utiliza circuitos electrónicos que hacen que los limpiabrisas pulsen u oscilen un rato, luego paren cierto número de segundos. (34)

Purge   To separate or clean by carrying off gasoline fumes. The carbon canister has a purge line to remove impurities. (24)
Purga   Separar o limpiar llevándose los gases de gasolina. El bote de carbón tiene una línea de purgas para eliminar impurezas. (24)

Pushrod   Connector between the lifter and the rocker arm. (8)
Varilla de empuje   Conector entre el levantaválvulas y el balancín. (8)

Quenching   The cooling of the gases by pressing the gas volume out into a thin area. Quenching occurs inside the wedge-type combustion chamber in the quench area. (10)
Enfriamiento repentino   Enfriamiento de gases por medio de apresionar el volumen de gas en una área reducida (angosta). El enfriamiento repentino ocurre dentro de la cámara de combustión de tipo cuña en el área de extincion. (10)

Rack and pinion steering   A steering system consisting of a flat gear (rack) and a mating gear (pinion). The pinion meshes with teeth on the rack causing the rack to move left or right. This motion moves tie rods and the spindle arm to steer the front wheels. (30)
Dirección por piñón y cremallera   Sistema de dirección consistente en un engrane plano (cremallera) y otra rueda dentada (piñón). El piñón se enlaca con dos dientes de la cremallera haciendo que la cremallera se mueva a la izquierda o a la derecha. Este movimiento hace que se muevan las barras tirantes (varillas de tensión) y el huso (mandril) para dirigir las ruedas delanteras. (30)

Radial   Something that radiates from a center point. Radial tires have cord materials running in a direction from the center point of the tire, usually from bead to bead. (31)
Radial   Algo que irradia de un punto central. Las llantas radiales contienen materiales de cuerda pasando en dirección desde el punto central de la llanta, normalmente de borde a borde. (31)

Radial cylinder   An engine configuration in which the pistons are placed in a radial (around the center) fashion about the crankshaft. (8)
Cilindro radial   Configuración de motor en la que los pistones están colocados en forma radial (alrededor de un centro) en relacion al cigüeñal. (8)

Radiation   Transfer of heat by converting heat energy to radiant energy. (12)
Radiación   Transferencia de calor por convirtiendo la energía calórifica a energía radiante. (12)

RAM   Random access memory, or temporary storage of information in a computer. (18)
"RAM"   Memoria de acceso al azar o almacenaje temporal de información en una computadora (ordenador). (18)

Ram air   Air that is forced into the engine or passenger compartment by the force of the vehicle moving forward. (33)
Aire bajo presión dinámica   Aire forzado en un motor o cabina de pasajero por la fuerza producida por el vehículo en movimiento hacia adelante. (33)

Reciprocating engine   An engine in which the fuel energy moves parts up and down or back and forth. (6)
Motor de movimiento alternativo (de émbolos)   Motor en el que la energía de combustible hace que se muevan las partes en movimiento altibajo o para atrás y hacia adelante. (6)

Rectify   To change one type of voltage to another. Usually ac voltage is rectified to dc voltage. (21)

Rectificar Cambiar un tipo de voltaje a otro tipo. Típicamente voltaje de corriente alterna se rectifica a voltaje de corriente directa. (21)

Refrigerant A liquid capable of vaporizing at low temperatures, such as ammonia or freon. (32)

Refrigerante Líquido capaz de vaporizar a temperaturas bajas, tal como amoníaco o freón. (32)

Regenerator A device placed on a gas turbine to take the heat of exhaust and put it into the intake of the engine. (8)

Regenerador Aparato montado en un motor de turbina de gas para sacar el calor de escape y ponerlo en la entrada del motor. (8)

Regional offices and distributorships Offices owned and operated by the automobile company. They are considered to be the link between the automobile manufacturer and the dealerships. (1)

Oficinas regionales y distribuidoras Oficinas que pertenecen a los dueños y operadores de la compañía automotriz. Se consideran el vínculo entre la fabrica automotriz y las agencias. (1)

Regular gasoline Gasoline that has an octane number near 85–90. (13)

Gasolina regular Gasolina que tiene un número de octano cerca de 85–90. (13)

Relay An electromagnetic device by which the opening or closing of one circuit operates another device. A relay in a voltage regulator uses a set of points that are opened and closed by magnetic forces. The opening or closing of the points controls another circuit, commonly the field circuit. (21)

Relé (Conmutador) Aparato electromagnético por medio del cual el abrir y cerrar de un circuito opera a otro aparato. Un relé en un regulador de voltaje emplea un juego de puntos de encendido que se abren y cierran mediante fuerzas magnéticas. El abrir y cerrar de los platinos controla a otro circuito, comúnmente el circuito inductor. (21)

Reluctor In an electronic ignition system, a metal wheel with a series of tips used to produce the signal for the transistor. (20)

Reluctor En un sistema de encendido electrónico, una rueda metálica con una serie de puntas que sirven para producir la señal para el transistor. (20)

Reserve vacuum tank A small vacuum storage tank used on vacuum-operated ventilation and heating controls. (33)

Tanque de vacío de reserva Pequeño tanque de vacío para almacenar, usado para los controles de ventilación y calefacción operados por vacío. (33)

Residual pressure Remaining or leftover pressure. (28)

Presión residual Presión que sobra. (28)

Resistance The part in an electrical circuit that holds back the electrons; also called the load. (18)

Resistencia Parte del circuito eléctrico que retiene los electrones; también llamada la carga. (18)

Resonator A device used in an exhaust system to reduce noise, usually used in conjunction with a muffler. (17)

Resonador Aparato utilizado en el sistema de escape para reducir el ruido, normalmente usado en combinación con un silenciador (mofle). (17)

Rich mixture Too much fuel and not enough air for combustion. (6)

Mezcla rica Demasiado combustible e insuficiente aire para combustión. (6)

Road horsepower Horsepower available at the drive wheels of the vehicle. (7)

Caballaje de camino Caballaje disponible a las ruedas de transmisión del vehículo. (7)

Rocker arm An arm that has a pivot point in the center. One side is lifted by the camshaft movement and the other side moves down, opening the valves. (8)

Balancín Brazo que tiene un punto de pivote en el medio. El movimiento del arbol de levas levanta un extremo del balancín y el otro extremo va para abajo, abriendo así las válvulas. (8)

Rolling resistance A term used to describe the amount of resistance a tire has to rolling on the road. Tires that have a lower rolling resistance usually get better gas mileage. Typically, radial tires have lower rolling resistance. (31)

Resistencia al rodado Término que sirve para describir la cantidad de resistencia que una llanta tiene a la acción de rodar sobre la superficie de un camino. Llantas que tienen una resistencia más baja al rodamiento normalmente resultan en mejor economía de kilometraje. Típicamente las llantas radiales tienen una resistencia más baja al rodamiento. (31)

ROM Read-only memory, or permanent storage of information in a computer. (18)

"ROM" Memoria de lectura solamente, o almacenaje de información permanente de una computadora (ordenador). (18)

Rope seals A type of seal used on crankshafts shaped much like a small, thin rope. (3)

Cierres de cable Tipo de cierre (obturador) usado en los cigüeñales, el cual está formado como una pequeña soga (cuerda) delgada. (3)

Rotary engine An engine that uses a rotor rather than pistons to produce power. It is an intermittent, internal combustion engine, and motion is rotary (circular), not reciprocating. (6)

Motor rotativo Motor que emplea un rotor (rodete) en vez de pistones para producir poder. Tiene un motor de combustión interna intermitente, y el movimiento es rotativo (circular), no recíproco. (6)

Rotor The rotating component in a generator or alternator. (21)

Rotor (Rodete) Componente rotativo de un generador o alternador. (21)

RPM Revolutions per minute on any rotating shaft. (7)

RPM Revoluciones por minuto de cualquier eje rotativo. (7)

RTV sealants A type of sealant that is able to cure in the presence of moisture and oxygen. (3)

Sellador "RTV" Tipo de sellador (empaque) capaz de curarse (enderezarse) en la presencia de humedad y oxígeno. (3)

Runner A cast tube on an intake or exhaust manifold used to carry air in or out of the engine. (17)

Burlete (Corredor) Tubo fundido de un colector de admisión o de escape, el cual se emplea para llevarse el aire para adentro o afuera del motor. (17)

Running gear Component on the automobile that is used to control the vehicle. This includes braking systems, wheels, and tires. (1)

Engrane (de funcionamiento) Componente de un automóvil que sirve para controlar al vehículo. Esto incluye el sistema de frenos, ruedas, y llantas. (1)

Rust inhibitors A type of chemical put into cooling and fuel systems to prevent rust from developing in the liquid. (13)

Inhibidores de óxido (oxidación) Tipo de químico agregado a sistemas de aire acondicionado o de combustible para prevenir oxidación en el líquido. (13)

SAE Society of Automotive Engineers. (11)

"SAE" Sociedad de Ingenieros Automotriz (SIA). (11)

Safety glasses Glasses to be worn at all times when in the automotive shop. They should be designed with safety glass and side protectors, and they should be comfortable. (2)

Lentes protectores Lentes que se deben de usar todo el tiempo cuando uno está presente en un taller automotriz. Deben de ser diseñados con cristal de seguridad y protectores laterales, y deben de ser cómodos. (2)

Safety rims A rim on a wheel that has inside ridges so that when a tire deflates, it stays on the rim. (31)

Aros (Rebordes protectores) de seguridad Aro de la rueda que tiene un borde interior para que, cuando se desinfla la llanta, ésta se quede en posición. (31)

Sales representative A person who sells new and used automobiles. (1)

Representante de ventas (Vendedor) Persona que vende automóviles nuevos y usados. (1)

Saybolt Universal Viscosimeter A meter used to measure the time in seconds required for 60 cubic centimeters of a fluid to flow through a hole on the meter at a given temperature under specified conditions. (11)

Viscosímetro Universal de Saybolt Medidor que sirve para medir el tiempo en segundos requerido para que 60 centímetros cúbicos de un líquido pasen por un agujero del medidor a cierta temperatura bajo condiciones especificadas. (11)

Scanners Electronic analyzers used to analyze and diagnose engine performance. (4)

Exploradores Analizadores electrónicos que sirven para analizar y diagnosticar la eficiencia del motor. (4)

Schrader valve A spring-loaded valve or directional valve used to admit pressure into a sealed system, used on both air conditioning units and tires. (32)

Válvula Schrader Válvula accionada por resorte o válvula direccional que sirve para admitir presión en un sistema sellado, usada en unidades de aire acondicionado y llantas. (32)

Screw-pitch gauge A gauge used to measure the number of threads per inch on a bolt. (3)

Calibre para determinar el paso de tornillo Calibre que sirve para medir el número de roscas por pulgada de un perno. (3)

Scrub radius The distance between the centerline of the ball joints and the centerline of the tire at the point when the tire contacts the road surface. (30)

Radio "scrub" Distancia entre la línea central de las juntas esféricas (o de rótulas) y la línea central de la llanta al punto donde haya contacto entre la llanta y la superficie del camino. (30)

Scuffing Scraping and heavy wear from the piston on the cylinder walls. (9)

Desgaste abrasivo Frotamiento y desgaste fuerte debido al movimiento de pistones contra las paredes interiores de los cilindros. (9)

Seal A device used on rotating shafts to keep oil or other fluid on one side of the seal, thus eliminating leakage. (3)

Cierre (Retenedor) Aparato usado en los ejes rotativos para impedir que el aceite u otro líquido pase de un lado al otro del cierre, y así eliminar la fuga o gotera del líquido. (3)

Sealant A thick liquid placed in engine parts to seal the parts from leakage. (3)

Sellador (Tapador) Líquido espeso puesto en partes del motor para ayudar a sellar y colocar con precisión el empaque durante el proceso de instalación. (3)

Seating When two metals must seal gases and liquids, they must be worked together to make a good seal. This process of getting two metal surfaces to seal is called seating. (10)

Asentamiento Cuando dos metales tienen que sellar gases y líquidos, tienen que ajustarse juntos para que haya un cierre preciso. El proceso de juntar las superficies de los dos metales para que ocluyan se llama asentamiento. (10)

Secondary circuit A circuit in the ignition system that uses 20,000 or more volts to operate. It includes the secondary coil windings, the rotor, distributor cap, coil and spark plug wires, and spark plugs. (20)

Circuito secundario Circuito del sistema de encendido que utiliza 20,000 voltios o más para operar. Incluye enrollados de bobina secundarios, rotor, tapa del distribuidor, bobina, cables de bujía, y bujías. (20)

Secondary shoe The rear shoe on a two-shoe drum brake system, often having a longer lining than the primary shoe. (28)

Zapata secundaria Zapata trasera de un sistema de tambor de freno de dos zapatas, el cual tiene, a veces, un forro más largo que el de la zapata primaria. (28)

Selector control lever A lever located on the dashboard used to select one of several heating and ventilation modes. (33)

Palanca de control del selector Palanca colocada en el panel de controles, que sirve para seleccionar uno de los varios modos de calefacción o ventilación. (33)

Self-energizing A drum brake arrangement where the braking action pulls the shoe lining tighter against the drum. (28)

Auto-activación (Auto-excitación) Sistema de tambor de freno en el que la acción de frenar aprieta al forro de zapata contra el tambor. (28)

Semiconductor A material with four electrons in the valence ring. (18)

Semiconductor Material de cuatro electrones en la banda de valencia. (18)

Series circuit A circuit in which there is only one path for the current to follow. (18)

Circuito en serie Circuito en que hay sólo una vía en la que circula la corriente. (18)

Service Bay Diagnosis System A computerized information network system that is connected to the manufacturer in Detroit, Michigan, used to answer service and diagnostic questions. (5)

Sistema de diagnóstico del área de servicio Red de información computarizada que está conectada con el fabricante en Detroit, Michigan, la cual sirve para contestar preguntas acerca de servicio y diagnósticos. (5)

Service bulletin Technical service information provided by the manufacturer, used as updates for the service manuals. (5)

Boletín de servicio Información de servicio técnico suministrada por la fabrica, que se usa para mantener los manuales con información corriente. (5)

Service manager The person responsible for the entire service operation of the dealership. (1)

Gerente de servicio Persona responsable de toda la operación de servicio de una agencia automotriz. (1)

Service manual A manual provided by the manufacturer or other publisher that describes service procedures, troubleshooting and diagnosis, and specifications. (5)

Manual de servicio Manual suministrado por la fabrica u otra casa editorial que explica procedimientos de servicio, investigación diagnóstica de averías, y especificaciones. (5)

Service procedures A set of listed steps used to disassemble, assemble, or repair an automotive component. (5)

Procedimientos de servicio Juego de pasos específicos que sirve para desmontar, montar, o reparar un componente automovilístico. (5)

Service representative A person who works in the area of providing service to the dealership from the car manufacturer. (1)

Representante de servicio Persona que trabaja en el área de proveer servicio de una fabrica a una agencia automotriz. (1)

Service technician A person who is actively involved in repair and maintenance of the total vehicle. (1)
Técnico de servicio Persona que está involucrada activamente en reparaciones y mantenimiento del vehículo entero. (1)

Servo A hydraulically operated component that operates or controls the operation of the transmission band on the automatic transmission; a device used on a cruise control system to maintain the speed of the vehicle. (26) (34)
Sistema servo Componente operado hidráulicamente, el cual controla la operación de la banda de transmisión que se encuentra en una transmisión automática; aparato usado en el sistema de control de crucero para mantener constante la velocidad del vehículo. (26) (34)

Servo brake A drum brake arrangement where the action of one shoe reinforces the action of the other shoe. (28)
Freno de servo Conjunto del tambor de freno en el que la acción de una zapata refuerza la acción de la otra. (28)

Shackle The small arm between the frame and one end of the leaf spring. It is used to allow the spring to shorten and lengthen during normal driving conditions. (29)
Enganche Parte del enganche entre la armadura (armazón) del coche y un extremo del muelle (resorte de hojas o láminas flexibles). Sirve para dejar que el muelle se acorte o se alargue (se estire) durante las condiciones de conducción normales. (29)

Shank The diameter of the bolt, usually measured in fractions of an inch or in millimeters. (3)
Fuste Diámetro de un perno o tornillo, normalmente medido en fracciones de una pulgada o milímetros. (3)

Shift valve A valve used in an automatic transmission that controls the oil flow to the clutches and transmission bands. (26)
Válvula de cambio Válvula usada en las transmisiones automáticas que controlan el pasaje de aceite al embrague y banda de transmisión. (26)

Shims Metal or plastic spacers of various thicknesses used to adjust caster and/or camber. (30)
Placas de relleno (cuñas) Espaciador de metal o plástico de varios gruesos, el cual sirve para ajustar la inclinación del eje delantero y/o el ángulo de comba (inclinación de la rueda). (30)

Shock absorber A device used on a suspension system to dampen the oscillations or jounce of the springs when the car goes over bumps. (29)
Amortiguador Aparato usado en un sistema de suspensión para absorber (disminuir) las oscilaciones o sacudidas de los resortes o muelles cuando pasa el vehículo sobre los topes y baches. (29)

Shroud An object that covers the area between the fan and the radiator. (12)
Tolva Objeto que cubre el área entre el ventilador y el radiador. (12)

Shrouding When a valve is placed close to the side of the combustion chamber, the air and fuel may be restricted by the side of the chamber. This restriction is referred to as shrouding. (10)
Tolvera (Restricción) Cuando se coloca una válvula cerca del lado de la cámara de combustión, el aire y el combustible pueden estar restringidos al lado de la cámara. Se refiere a esta restricción como tolvera. (10)

Shunt More than one path for current to flow, such as a parallel part of a circuit. (22)
Desvío Más de un camino que la corriente puede seguir, tal como una parte paralela de un circuito. (22)

Siamese ports Intake or exhaust ports inside the cylinder head where two cylinders are feeding through the one port. (10)
Orificio de vaciado (Siamés) Orificio de entrada y escape dentro de la cabeza de cilindros donde dos cilindros utilizan el mismo orificio. (10)

Slant An in-line cylinder arrangement that has been placed at a slant. This arrangement makes the engine have a lower profile for aerodynamic design. (8)
Sesgo (Oblicuidad) Conjunto de cilindros en línea, los cuales están montados en un plano inclinado. Este arreglo hace que el motor tenga un perfil más bajo para un meson diseño aerodinámico. (8)

Slave cylinder A type of hydraulic cylinder used as a means to actuate the clutch mechanism. As the clutch pedal is pushed down, the hydraulic pressure produced in the slave cylinder is used to move the clutch mechanism. (25)
Cilindro esclavo Tipo de cilindro hidráulico usado como un medio de activar el mecanismo del embrague. Al deprimir el pedal para embrague, la presión hidráulica producida en el cilindro esclavo sirve para mover el mecanismo del embrague. (25)

Slip A term used to represent the amount of slippage between the tire and the road during a braking condition. When the tire locks up completely, 100% slip occurs. (28)
Resbalamiento (derrapar, patinar) Vocablo que sirve para representar la cantidad de deslizamiento entre la llanta y el camino durante una condición de frenar (perdida de agarre). Al inmovilizarse la rueda por completo, se ocurre un 100% de resbalamiento. (28)

Slip joint A splined shaft that can slide in a mating shaft to allow changes in drive shaft length. (27)
Junta corrediza Eje ranurado que se puede deslizar en otro eje compañero para permitir cambios en el largo del eje impulsor (flecha o eje motor). (27)

Slipper skirt A piston that has a cutaway skirt so that the piston can come closer to the counterweights. This makes the overall size of the engine smaller. (9)
"Slipper Skirt" Pistón que tiene una falda o borde en corte para que el pistón pueda acercarse a los contrapesos. Esto hace que el tamaño, en general, del motor sea más pequeño. (9)

Slip-ring A type of commutator used on an alternator made of two copper rings that are split in half. (21)
Anillo rozante Tipo de conmutador usado en un alternador y hecho de dos anillos de cobre que están divididos en dos mitades. (21)

Slotted frame Slotted holes on the frame used to reposition parts for camber/caster adjustment. (30)
Armadura ranurada Agujeros ranurados en la armadura (armazón), que sirven para recolocar partes para el ajuste de camber/caster. (30)

Sludges Material formed as a result of oil in the presence of various acids. (11)
Fangos Material formado como resultado del aceite en la presencia de varios ácidos. (11)

Smog The combined effect of various chemicals put into the air by various forms of combustion. (23)
Esmog (Contaminación del aire) Efecto combinado de varios químicos puestos en el aire por varios modos de combustión. (23)

Smoking rules Only smoke in designated "smoking" areas. Dangerous explosive fuels in the shop may be ignited if this rule is not followed. (2)
Reglamentos de fumar Se permite fumar en áreas designadas para fumar. Combustibles explosivos en el taller pueden encenderse si no se obedece esta regla. (2)

Snap rings   Small rings, either external or internal, that are used to prevent gears and pulleys from sliding off the shaft. (3)

Anillos de seguridad (Snap rings)   Pequeños anillos sujetadores, externos o internos, que sirven para prevenir que el engranaje y las poleas se deslicen afuera del eje. (3)

Snorkel tube   A long, narrow tube attached to the air cleaner, used to direct air into the air filter. (24)

Esnórquel   Tubo largo y angosto conectado al limpiador de aire, que sirve para dirigir aire en el filtro para aire. (24)

Socket points   The number of points inside the socket head. Six, 8, and 12 points are most common. In applications where only a small amount of rotation of the ratchet is possible, use a 12-point socket. (4)

Puntos de dado   Número de puntos dentro del dado. Seis, 8, y 12 puntos son los números más comunes. Para aplicaciones en las que es posible una pequeña cantidad de rotación de llave de trinquete (matraca), use un dado de cubo de 12 puntos. (4)

Solenoid   A coil of wire wound around a movable core. When voltage is applied to the coil, the magnetic field causes the metal core to move. A solenoid converts electrical energy into mechanical energy using magnetism. Used in a starter system and other electrical circuits. (15) (22)

Solenoide   Bobina de alambre enrollado en un eje movible. Cuando se le aplica voltaje a la bobina, el campo magnético hace que se mueva el eje metálico. Un solenoide convierte la energía eléctrica en energía mecánica. Aparato que convierte la energía eléctrica en energía mecánica usando magnetismo. Sirve en un sistema de arranque y otros circuitos eléctricos. (15) (22)

Specialty shops   Service shops that specialize in certain components of the automobile. Some include carburetor shops, body shops, transmission shops, muffler shops, and so on. (1)

Tiendas de especialidades   Tiendas de servicio que se especializan en ciertos componentes de automóvil. Incluyen tiendas para carburadores, hojalaterías, transmisiones, silenciadores, etcétera. (1)

Specifications   Any technical data, numbers, clearances, and measurements used to diagnose and adjust automobile components. They are also called specs. (5)

Especificaciones   Cualquier dato técnico, números, distancias, y medidas, que sirven para diagnosticar y ajustar componentes automotrices. También se llaman "specs." (5)

Specific gravity   The weight of a solution as related to water. Water has a specific gravity of 1.000. Sulfuric acid, being heavier than water, has a specific gravity of 1.835. (19)

Peso específico (Gravedad específica)   Peso de una solución con referencia al agua. El agua tiene un peso específico de 1.000. El ácido sulfúrico, al ser más pesado que el agua, tiene un peso específico de 1.835. (19)

Splines   External or internal teeth cut into a shaft, used to keep a pulley or hub secured on a rotating shaft. (3)

Ranuras   Estrías o acanaladuras, externas o internas cortadas en un eje, que sirven para mantener fija una polea o parte central en un eje rotativo. (3)

Spool valve   A cylindrical rod with different-sized diameters. Usually the cylindrical valve is placed inside a bore inside the transmission valve body. As the valve is moved in and out, different hydraulic circuits are operated. (26)

Válvula bobinada   Cilíndrica con diferentes tamaños de diámetros. Normalmente la válvula cilíndrica se coloca dentro del hueco que está dentro del cuerpo de la válvula de transmisión. Al moverse la válvula, hacia adentro o afuera se operan diferentes circuitos hidráulicos. (26)

Sprag   A pointed steel piece inside an overrunning clutch mechanism that allows rotation in one direction but locks up rotation in the opposite direction. (22)

"Sprag"   Pieza de metal apuntada dentro del mecanismo del embrague de rueda libre (de sobremarcha), la cual permite la rotación en una dirección pero inmoviliza la rotación en la dirección opuesta. (22)

Squirm   To wiggle or twist about a body. When applied to tires, squirm is the wiggle or movement of the tread against the road surface. Squirm increases tire wear. (31)

Retorcimiento   Retorcerse alrededor de un cuerpo. Al referirse a las llantas, retorcimiento es un movimiento de las huellas contra la superficie del camino. Retorcimiento aumenta el desgaste de la llanta. (31)

Squirrel cage blower   A type of air pressure fan shaped like a squirrel cage, used to move air throughout a system. The squirrel cage fan is run by a motor and placed inside a housing to improve its efficiency of operation. (33)

Ventilador de jaula de ardilla   Tipo de ventilador de presión de aire formada como una jaula de ardilla, que sirve para mover el aire en el sistema. La jaula de ardilla funciona a base de un motor y está colocada dentro de una cubierta protectora para mejorar su eficiencia de operación. (33)

Stabilizer bar   A reinforcement component on a suspension system that prevents the body from diving or leaning on turns. (29)

Barra estabilizadora   Componente de reforzamiento de un sistema de suspensión que impide que el chasis se incline al dar vueltas. (29)

Stance   The manner of standing or being placed. A vehicle's stance refers to the level or evenness of its position. (29)

Postura   Una postura de estacionarse o de estar estacionado. La postura de un vehículo se refiere a la nivelación de su postura. (29)

Standard bolt and nut torque specifications   A chart showing the standard torque for common sizes of bolts. (3)

Especificaciones de torque de perno (tornillos) y tuerca estándar   Esquema que indica el torque estándar para los tamaños de pernos (tornillos) comunes. (3)

Starting and charging system   The subsystem on the engine used to start the engine and charge the battery. (1)

Sistema de encendido (arranque) y carga   Subsistema de un motor, que sirve para arrancar el motor y cargar la batería. (1)

Static balance   Equal distribution of weight around a center point. Static means stationary, and static balancing is done with the wheels stationary. (31)

Balanceo estático   Distribución de peso igual alrededor de un punto central. Estático significa estacionario o fijo, y se logra hacer balanceo estático con las ruedas estacionarias. (31)

Stator   The stationary part in an alternator that cuts the magnetic lines of force; the part of a torque converter that is stationary, used to direct the flow of fluid back to the rotary pump at the correct angle. (21) (26)

Estator   Parte estacionaria (fija) en un alternador, la cual interrumpe las líneas de fuerza magnéticas; la parte de un convertidor torque, que está estacionaria, que sirve para dirigir el flujo de líquido hacia la bomba rotativa a un ángulo correcto. (21) (26)

Steering axis inclination   The inward tilt of the spindle support arm ball joints at the top. (30)

Inclinación del eje de la dirección   Inclinación hacia el interior de la pieza del extremo del eje delantero que soporta en lo más alto de la palanca de las juntas esféricas. (30)

Steering knuckle   A part of the front suspension that connects the wheel to the suspension system and the tie rod ends for steering. The wheel spindle is also attached to the steering knuckle. (29)

Nudo de dirección (de mando) Parte de la suspensión delantera que conecta la rueda con el sistema de suspensión y con las barras de acoplamiento que sirven para dirigir. (29)

Stellite A very hard metal made from cobalt, chromium, and tungsten, used for insert-type valve seats. (10)

Estelita Un metal muy duro hecho de cobalto, cromo, y tungsteno (volframio), usado en los asientos de tipo-insertado de las válvulas. (10)

Stirling engine An external combustion, continuous combustion engine, having four cylinders that operate in a particular sequence. (8)

Motor Stirling Motor de combustión externa, de combustión continua, con cuatro cilindros que funcionan según una sucesión particular. (8)

Stoichiometric ratio A 14.7 to 1 air-fuel ratio. This is the best ratio to operate an internal combustion engine. (6) (16)

Relación estoiquiometricia (Óptima) Proporción de 14.7 a 1 de aire y combustible. Esta es la mejor proporción para operar un motor de combustión interna. (6) (16)

Stratified To layer or have in layers. (8)

Estratificado (en capas o láminas) Laminar o poner en capas. (8)

Stratified charged engine An engine that has an additional small combustion chamber. The air-fuel mixture in this chamber is very rich. The air-fuel in the regular chamber is leaner. The small chamber ignites the larger chamber mixture, reducing emissions. (8)

Motor de cargo estratificado Motor que tiene un pequeña cámara de combustión adicional. La mezcla de aire y combustible en es cámara es muy rica. La mezcla de aire y combustible en la cámara normal es más pobre. La cámara más pequeña enciende la mezcla de la cámara normal, reduciendo así emisiones. (8)

Stroke The distance from TDC to BDC of piston travel. (6)

Ciclo Distancia de "TDC" a "BDC" del movimiento del pistón. (6)

Strut rod A rod on the suspension system located ahead of or behind a lower control arm to retain the arm in its intended position. (29)

Puntal Barra del sistema de suspensión situada delante de o detrás de un brazo de control más bajo para mantener al brazo en su posición normal. (29)

Sulfur A chemical in diesel fuel that produces pollution. When mixed with oxygen and water, sulfur produces a strong acid. (13)

Azufre Un químico en combustible diesel que produce contaminación. Al mezclarse con oxígeno y agua, el azufre produce un ácido fuerte. (13)

Sump A pit or well where a fluid is collected. Oil is collected in the oil sump. (11)

Sumidero Del carter pozo donde se deposita un fluído. Aceite es depositado en el sumidero (colector) de aceite. (11)

Sunload sensor A sensor placed on the dashboard to determine the amount of sun coming into the vehicle. (33)

Sensor de luz solar Sensor situado en el panel de controles para determinar la cantidad de luz solar que entra en el vehículo. (33)

Supercharger A device placed on a vehicle to increase the amount of air, and therefore the amount of fuel that is sent into the engine. (8)

Supercargador (Sobrealimentador, Turboalimentador) Aparato situado en el vehículo para aumentar la cantidad de aire, y por tanto, la cantidad de combustible que entra en el motor. (8)

Supercharging The process of forcing air into an engine

cylinder with an air pump. The forced air can come from a blower or turbocharger. (17)

Sobrealimentación Proceso de forzar aire en el cilindro del motor con una bomba para aire. El aire forzado puede provenir de soplador o turbocargador. (17)

Supporting career The automotive industry supports careers in the following areas: claims adjusting, vocational teaching, auto body repairing, frame and alignment repair, specialty shops, and others. (1)

Carreras de soporte La industria automotriz soporta carreras en las siguientes áreas; ajustes de reclamos, enseñanza vocacional, reparaciones en hojalatería, reparaciones en armadura y alineación, talleres en especialidades, y otros. (1)

Surging A sudden rushing of water from the water pump. (12)

Oleada (Oleaje o Pulsación) Pulsación repentina de agua desde la bomba de agua. (12)

Suspendability The ability of a fluid to suspend heavier dirt particles within the oil, rather than letting them fall to the bottom. (11)

Suspendibilidad Habilidad de un flúido de suspender las partículas de tierra más pesadas en el aceite, en vez de dejar que se hundan al fondo. (11)

Suspension systems Components that support the total vehicle, including springs, shock absorbers, torsion bars, axles, and connecting linkages. (1)

Sistemas de suspensión Componentes que soportan al vehículo entero, incluyendo los resortes, amortiguadores, barras de torsión, ejes, y palancas de vínculo. (1)

Swash plate An angular plate attached to the bottom of the four pistons on a Stirling engine. As the pistons move downward, the swash plate is turned. A mechanical system that is used for pumping. An angled plate is attached to a center shaft, and pistons are attached to the plate along the axis of the shaft. As the shaft rotates, the pistons move in and out of a cylinder, producing a suction and pressure. (8) (32)

Placa "Swash" Placa angular conectada a la parte inferior de los cuatro pistones de un motor Stirling. Al moverse para abajo los pistones, se gira una placa "Swash." Sistema mecánico que sirve para bombear. Una placa angulada está conectada a un eje central, y se juntan pistones a la placa a lo largo de la línea recta del eje. Al girarse el eje, los pistones se mueven adentro y afuera de un cilindro, produciendo así una succión y presión. (8) (32)

Sway bar A bar on the suspension system that connects the two sides together. It is designed so that during cornering, forces on one wheel are shared by the other. (29)

Barra de balanceo Barra del sistema de suspensión que junta los dos lados. Está diseñada para que al tomar una curva, las fuerzas sobre una rueda están distribuidas en parte sobre la otra. (29)

Synchronized mode A mode of operation on a fuel injection system in which the throttle body injector is pulsed once for each reference pulse from the distributor. (16)

Modo sincronizado Modo de operación de un sistema de inyección de combustible, en el que el inyector de la placa de aceleración (mariposa) está impulsada una vez por cada latido de referencia del distribuidor. (16)

Synchronizer An assembly in a manual transmission used to make both gears rotate at the same speed before meshing. (25)

Sincronizador Conjunto de dispositivos dentro de una transmisión automática, que sirve para hacer que los dos engranajes roten a la misma velocidad antes de o entrelazarse. (25)

Synthetic A product made by combining various chemical elements (a manmade product). (11)

Sintético Producto hecho por la combinación de varios elementos químicos (producto hecho por seres humanos). (11)

Tachometer A meter used to measure speed of any rotating shaft. (4)

Tacómetro Aparato que sirve para medir la velocidad de cualquier eje rotativo. (4)

Tandem Meaning one object behind the other. (28)

Tándem Significa que un objeto está detrás de otro. (28)

Tang A projecting piece of metal placed on the end of the torque converter on automatic transmissions. The tangs are used to rotate the oil pump. (26)

Cola (Rabo) Pieza de metal saliente (proyectante) colocada en el extremo de un convertidor de torque en las transmisiones automáticas. Los rabos sirven para rotar las bombas de aceite. (26)

Tappets Another term for valve lifters. (10)

Botador (Taquete, Levantaválvulas) Otro término para alzaválvulas. (10)

TDC Position of the piston; top dead center. (6)

"TDC" Posición del pistón; punto muerto en la parte superior. (6)

Tensile strength The amount of pressure per square inch the bolt can withstand just before breaking when being pulled apart. (3)

Resistencia a la tracción (a la tensión) Cantidad de presión por pulgada cuadrada que un perno puede aguantar antes de romperse en dos partes. (3)

Test light A small light attached to a wire (inside a sharp, pointed terminal) used to determine if electricity is at a certain point in an electrical circuit. (4)

Luz de prueba Pequeña luz conectada a un alambre metálico (dentro de una terminal puntiaguda) que sirve para determinar si electricidad pasa por un punto determinado en un circuito eléctrico. (4)

Tetraethyl lead A chemical added to gasoline to increase the octane and aid in lubrication of the valves. (13)

Plomo tetraetilo Químico agregado a gasolina para incrementar el octano y ayudar a lubricar las válvulas. (13)

Thermal efficiency A measure of how effectively an engine converts heat energy in fuel into mechanical energy at the rear of the engine. (7)

Eficiencia térmica Medición de la eficacia con que un motor convierte a energía mecánica en un punto detrás del motor. (7)

Thermistor A sensor that is able to change electrical resistance on the basis of a change in temperature. (16)

Termistor Sensor que puede cambiar resistencia eléctrica a base de un cambio en temperatura. (16)

Thermostat The part on a cooling system that controls the engine coolant to its highest operation temperature. (12)

Termostato (Termóstato) Parte del sistema refrigerante que controla al flúido refrigerante hasta su temperatura de operación más alta. (12)

Thermostatic switch A heat-sensitive switch used to turn on and off an air conditioning compressor. (32)

Conmutador (Interruptor) termostático Interruptor sensible al calor que sirve para encender y apagar un compresor de aire acondicionado. (32)

Threaded fasteners A type of fastener such as bolts, studs, setscrews, cap screws, machine screws, and self-tapping screws that has a thread on it. (3)

Sujetadores roscados Tipo de sujetador tales como pernos, espigas, tornillos fijadores de posición, tornillos de capa, tornillos para metales, tornillos autoroscantes que contienen roscas. (3)

Threads per inch A number used to identify bolts, showing the number of threads per inch on the bolt. (3)

Roscas por pulgada Número que sirve para identificar pernos, indicando el número de roscas por pulgada en el perno. (3)

Three-phase Voltages produced from a generator or alternator can be either single-phase or three-phase. Three-phase voltages are electrically 120 degrees apart from each other. (21)

Trifásico (de tres fases) Voltajes producidos en un generador (dínamo) o alternador pueden ser o de fase sencilla o de tres fases. Voltajes trifásicos están separados eléctricamente a 120 grados uno del otro. (21)

Throttle body The part of a fuel system where fuel is injected into the air stream. The throttle body injector is located above the throttle plate. (16)

Cuerpo del regulador Parte del sistema de combustible en la que el combustible es inyectado en el chorro de aire. El cuerpo inyector del regulador está situado sobre la placa del regulador. (16)

Throttle plate The plate or circular disk that controls the amount of air going into an engine. It is usually controlled by the position of the operator's foot. (16)

Placa del regulador (Mariposa) Placa o disco circular que controla la cantidad de aire que entra en el motor. Normalmente es controlada por la posición del pie del conductor. (16)

Throttle valve A valve used in the automatic transmission that changes oil flow on the basis of throttle position of the engine. (26)

Válvula reguladora (de mariposa) Válvula usada en una transmisón automática que controla el flujo del aceite en base a la posición del regulador del motor. (26)

Throw The distance from the center point of the crankshaft to the center point of the connecting rod. (6)

Carrera (Juego) Distancia desde el punto central del cigüeñal hasta el punto central de la barra de conexión. (6)

Thrust bearing An antifriction bearing designed to absorb any thrust along the axis of the rotating shaft. (3)

Cojinete de empuje (Quicionera) Cojinete de antifricción diseñado para absorber cualquier empuje a lo largo de la línea recta de un eje rotativo. (3)

Thrust load Another name for axial load. (3)

Tracción axial Otro término para carga axial. (3)

Thrust plate The plate used to bolt the camshaft to the block, which absorbs camshaft thrust. (10)

Placa de empuje Placa que sirve para sujetar con pernos al arbol de levas al bloque la cual absorbe el empuje del arbol de levas. (10)

Timing The process of identifying when air, fuel, and ignition occur in relation to the crankshaft rotation. (6)

Sincronización Proceso de identificar el momento cuando aire, combustible y encendido ocurren en relación con la rotación del cigüeñal. (6)

Timing diagrams A graphical method used to identify the time in which all of the events of the four-stroke engine operate. (6)

Esquema de reglaje (de puestas a punto) Método gráfico que sirve para identificar el tiempo en que funcionan todos los eventos de un motor de cuatro tiempos. (6)

Timing light A strobe light placed on the number 1 cylinder spark plug wire, which flashes when electricity is available at the spark plug. (4)

Luz de tiempo Luz intermitente montada en el hilo de la bujía del número 1, la cual destella cuando la electricidad llega a la bujía. (4)

Tire placard A permanently located sticker on the vehicle that gives tire information such as load, pressure, and so on. (31)

Anuncio de llanta   Calcomanía situada permanentemente en el vehículo la cual da información sobre las llantas, tal como carga, presión, *etcétera*. (31)

Toe (in, out)   The inward or outward pointing of the front wheels as measured in inches or millimeters. (30)

Convergencia o divergencia de las ruedas delanteras   Dirección hacia adentro o hacia afuera de las ruedas delanteras medida en pulgadas o milímetros. (30)

Torque   A twisting force applied to a shaft or bolt. (3) (7)

Torsión, Torque   Fuerza de torsión aplicada a un eje o perno. (3) (7)

Torque converter   The coupling between the engine and transmission on an automatic transmission. It is also used to multiply torque at lower speeds. (26)

Convertidor de torsión   La union entre el motor y la transmisión de una transmisión automática. Sirve también para multiplicar la torsión a velocidades más bajas. (26)

Torque converter clutch (TCC) valve   A valve used in conjunction with the lockup clutch mechanism on automatic transmission. (26)

Válvula de embrague del convertidor de torsión   Válvula que sirve en conjunto con el mecanismo del embrague de inmovilización de una transmisión automática. (26)

Torque specifications   Specifications used to tell the service technician the exact torque that should be applied to bolts and nuts. (5)

Especificaciones de torsión   Especificaciones que sirven para informar al técnico de servicio la torsión fuerzas exacta que se debe aplicar a pernos y tuercas. (5)

Torque-to-yield bolts   A bolt that has been tightened at the manufacturer to a preset yield or stretch point. (3)

Pernos apretados a torsión antes de ceder (estinanse)   Perno que se ha apretado en la fabrica a un punto de deformación o rendimiento pre-determinado. (3)

Torque wrench   A wrench used to measure the amount of torque or twisting force applied to a bolt or nut. (4)

Llave indicadora de torsión   Llave que sirve para medir la cantidad de fuerza de torsión aplicada a un perno o tuerca. (4)

Torsional rings   Rings that have a slight twist when placed within the cylinder wall. These are made by adding a chamfer or counterbore on the ring. (9)

Anillos (Aros) torsionales   Anillos que tienen una pequeña distorsión cuando se colocan en la pared del cilindro. Estos se hacen con la añadidura de un bisel o contrataladro en el anillo. (9)

Torsional vibration   A vibration produced in a spinning shaft, caused by torque applied to the shaft. (9) (25)

Vibración torsional   Vibración producida en un eje giratorio, que resulta por un par de torsión aplicado al eje. (9) (25)

Torsion bar   A steel shaft that serves the same purpose as a coil spring. It is located between the lower control arm and the frame, and it twists when the vehicle moves up and down. (29)

Barra de torsión   Eje de acero que sirve el mismo propósito que un resorte espiral. Se sitúa entre el brazo del control más bajo y la armadura (armazón), y se distorsiona cuando el vehículo se mueve para arriba y para abajo. (29)

Traction   A tire's ability to hold or grip the road surface. (31)

Tracción   Habilidad que tiene una llanta de pegarse o agarrarse a la superficie del camino. (31)

Transaxle   A type of transmission used on front wheel drive vehicles where the engine is crosswise. The transmission is designed so the differential is built in the transmission and the output goes directly to the front wheels. (25)

Ejetransversal   Tipo de transmisión utilizado en vehículo de tracción delantera en la que el motor está en posición transversal. Se diseña la transmisión para que el diferencial esté construido en la transmisión y la potencia que se produce va directamente a las ruedas delanteras. (25)

Transducer   A device that senses pressure in an exhaust manifold, used to control another circuit. A device that transmits energy from one system to another. A transducer is used in cruise control systems to control vacuum on the basis of vehicle speed. (24) (34)

Transductor   Aparato que percibe presión en el múltiple de escape, que sirve para controlar otro circuito. Aparato que transmite energía de un sistema a otro. Un transductor sirve en un sistema de control de crucero para controlar el vacío a base de la velocidad del vehículo. (24) (34)

Transformer   A set of coils that use magnetism to change one voltage to another. The ignition transformer changes 12 volts to 20,000–60,000 volts. (20)

Transformador   Juego de bobinas que usan el magnetismo para cambiar un voltaje a otro. El transformador de ignición cambia 12 voltios a 20,000–60,000 voltios. (20)

Transistor   A semiconductor used in circuits to turn off or on a second circuit; also used for amplification of signals. (18)

Transistor   Semiconductor empleado en circuitos para apagar o encender un segundo circuito; también sirve para amplificación de señales. (18)

Transmission band   A type of hydraulic clutch that uses a metal band fitted around a clutch housing. As the band is tightened, the housing rotation is stopped. (26)

Banda de transmisión libre   Tipo de embrague hidráulico que emplea una banda metálica ajustada alrededor de la columna del embrague. Al apretarse la banda, se para la rotación de la columna. (26)

Tread   The outer surface of a tire used to produce friction with the road for starting and stopping. (31)

Huella   Superficie exterior de una llanta que sirve para producir fricción con el camino para impulsarse o pararse. (31)

Tread bars   Narrow strips of rubber molded into the tread. When the tread bars show, the tire is worn enough to be replaced. (31)

Bandas de rodadura   Franjas angostas de goma moldeadas en las huellas. Cuando aparecen las bandas de rodadura, se ha desgastado suficiente como para reponerse la llanta. (31)

Tripod   The central part of certain CV joints. It has three arms or trunnions with needle bearings and rollers running in grooves or races in the assembly. (27)

Trípode   Parte central de ciertas juntas CV. Tiene tres muñones (soportes giratorios) con cojinetes de aguja y rodillos colocados en surcos en el montaje. (27)

Troubleshooting   Another term for diagnosis. (5)

Investigación de problemas   Otro término para diagnóstico. (5)

TRS   Transmission-regulated spark. (24)

"TRS"   Chispa controlada por la transmisión (CCT). (24)

Trunnion   The arm or arms of the four-point U-joint, which serves as the inner bearing surface or race. (27)

Muñón (Gorrón, espiga, sorporte giratorio)   Brazo o brazos de una junta universal de cuatro puntos, el cual sirve como la superficie de cojinete interior o anillo-guía. (27)

Tuned ports   Intake ports used on fuel injection engines, designed to produce equal and minimum restriction to the air flow. (16)

Puertos de admisión sintonizados   Orificios de admisión utilizados en motores de inyección de combustible, diseñados para producir restricción igual y mínima en el flujo de aire. (16)

Tune-up specifications Specifications primarily used during a tune-up on an automobile. (5)

Especificaciones de afinación Especificaciones que sirven principalmente cuando se afina el motor. (5)

Turbine A component in a gas turbine engine that changes the energy in the gases into rotary motion for power. A vaned type of wheel being turned by a fluid such as exhaust gases passing over it. The rotary part or vaned wheel inside a torque converter, used to turn the transmission. (8) (17) (26)

Turbina Componente en un motor de turbina de gas, el cual cambia la energía de los gases en movimiento rotativo para crear potencia. Un tipo de rueda o volante con veletas que se deja girar cuando un flúido tal como gases de escape pasan sobre las veletas. La parte rotativa o rueda con veletas dentro de un convertidor de par de torsión, que sirve para hacer girar la transmisión. (8) (17) (26)

Turbocharged An engine that uses the exhaust gases to turn a turbine. The turning turbine forces in extra fresh air for more performance. (17)

Turbocargado Motor que utiliza los gases de escape para propulsar una turbina. La turbina giratoria hace que entre más aire fresco para más rendimiento. (17)

Turbulence A term used to describe combustion chambers. It means rapid movement and mixing of air and fuel inside the combustion chamber. (10)

Turbulencia Término que sirve para describir las cámaras de combustión. Significa movimiento rápido y combinación de aire y combustible dentro de la cámara de combustión. (10)

Turning radius The amount (in degrees) that one front wheel turns more sharply than the other front wheel during a turn. (30)

Radio de giro (vuelta) Cantidad (en grados) que una rueda delantera gira más agudamente que la otra rueda delantera durante el giro. (30)

Two-stroke engine A type of engine that requires only two strokes (or one crankshaft revolution) to produce the intake, compression, power, and exhaust sequence. (6)

Motor de dos tiempos Tipo de motor que requiere sólo dos tiempos (o una revolución del cigüeñal) para producir la sequencia de entrada de aire, compresión, potencia, y escape. (6)

Type A fire A fire resulting from the burning of wood, paper, textiles, and clothing. (2)

Incendio de tipo A Fuego que resulta de la combustión de madera, papel, textiles, y ropa. (2)

Type B fire A fire resulting from the burning of gasoline, greases, oils, and other flammable liquids. (2)

Incendio de tipo B Fuego que resulta de la combustión de gasolina, grasas, aceites, y otros líquidos inflamables. (2)

Type C fire A fire resulting from the burning of electrical equipment, motors, and switches. (2)

Incendio de tipo C Fuego que resulta de la combustión de equipo eléctrico, motores, y conmutadores (interruptores). (2)

USC measurements U.S. Customary (standard English) measurements, including feet, inches, miles, pounds, ounces, and so on. (4)

Medidas de EE.UU acostumbradas (inglés estándar) Medidas, incluyendo pies, pulgadas, millas, libras, onzas, *etcétera*. (4)

Vacuum An enclosed space in which the pressure is below zero psig. (12) (15)

Vacío Espacio encerrado en que la presión está más abajo de cero libras por pulgada cuadrada ("Psig"). (12) (15)

Vacuum diaphragm A device that has a spring on one side of a flexible material and vacuum on the other side sealed in a housing. The position of the flexible material controls the movement of another system. (15)

Diafragma de vacío Aparato que tiene un resorte por un lado de un material flexible y vacío por el otro sellado en una cubierta. La posición del material flexible controla el movimiento de otro sistema. (15)

Vacuum gauge A gauge designed to read various vacuum readings on an engine, the most common being intake manifold vacuum and pollution control equipment. (4)

Vacuómetro (Manómetro de vacío) Indicador que sirve para leer varias indicaciones de vacío de un motor, las más comunes son las del vacío del múltiple de entrada y equipo para control de contaminación. (4)

Vacuum modulator A diaphragm used on automatic transmissions that controls the throttle valve on the basis of engine intake manifold vacuum. (26)

Modulador de vacío Diafragma utilizado en transmisiones automáticas, el cual controla a la válvula de la mariposa a base del vacío del múltiple de entrada del motor. (26)

Vacuum motor A small diaphragm inside a housing operated by vacuum working against a spring pressure. When vacuum is applied, the diaphragm moves. This movement is then used to open or close small air doors or other apparatus. (33)

Motor de vacío Pequeño diafragma dentro de una cubierta protectora, el cual es operado por un vacío que funciona contra una presión de resortes. Al aplicarse el vacío, se mueve el diafragma. Este movimiento sirve para abrir y cerrar pequeños orificios de aire u otros aparatos. (33)

Valence ring The outer orbit of electrons in an atom. (18)

Banda de valencia Orbita exterior de electrones de un átomo. (18)

Valve A device used to open and close a port to let intake and exhaust gases in and out of the engine. (6)

Válvula Aparato que sirve para abrir y cerrar un orificio (puerto) para dejar de los gases de entrada y de escape pasen adentro o afuera del motor. (6)

Valve body The part of an automatic transmission used to direct the oil flow to different parts of the transmission. The valve body also houses most of the valve for control. (26)

Cuerpo de válvula Parte de la transmisión automática que sirve para dirigir el flujo del aceite a diferentes partes de la transmisión. El cuerpo de la válvula también acomoda a la mayoría de la válvula para control. (26)

Valve bounce When a valve is forced to close because of spring pressure, the valve may bounce when it closes. This action can damage the seats or break the valve in two. (10)

Rebote de la válvula Cuando se cierra la válvula a fuerza debido a la presión de resorte, puede que se rebote la válvula al cerrarse. Esta acción puede dañar los asientos o causar que se rompa la válvula. (10)

Valve clearance The clearance or space between the valve and the rocker arm. As the parts heat up, the clearance is reduced because of expansion. This keeps the valves from remaining open when the engine is hot. (8)

Holgura de la válvula Distancia o espacio entre la válvula y el balancín. Al calentarse las partes, se reduce la distancia debido a la expansión. Esto previene que queden abiertas las válvulas cuando esté caliente el motor. (8)

Valve face The part of a poppet valve that actually touches the seat for sealing in the cylinder head. (10)

Cara (Sombrete) de la válvula La parte de una válvula de elevación que realmente toca al asiento para sellar la cabeza del cilindro. (10)

Valve float If a valve spring is not strong enough to close the valve, the valve may float or stay open slightly longer than designed. This condition will limit the maximum RPM an engine can develop. (10)

Válvula flotante Si el resorte de la válvula no tiene suficiente fuerza para cerrar la válvula, ésta puede flotar o quedar abierta un poco más tiempo que lo anticipado por su diseño. Esta condición limitará las rpm máximas que puede producir un motor. (10)

Valve guide The part in the cylinder head that holds the stem of the valve. (10)

Guía de la válvula Parte de la cabeza de la válvula que sostiene el vástago (varilla) de válvula. (10)

Valve train clearance The clearance between the lifters, rocker arms, and valves. This clearance is necessary because as the parts heat up, they will expand. The valve train clearance allows for this expansion. (10)

Holgura del tren de la válvula Distancia o espacio entre los levantaválvulas, balancines y las válvulas. Esta distancia es necesaria porque al calentarse las partes, se expanden. La holgura del tren de la válvula acomoda esta expansión. (10)

Vapor A substance in a gaseous state. Liquids become a vapor when they are brought above their boiling point. (32)

Vapor Substancia en un estado gaseoso. Los líquidos se convierten en vapor cuando superan su punto de ebullición. (32)

Vaporize The process of passing from a liquid to a gas. Fuel is vaporized when it is heated. (13) (15)

Vaporizar Proceso de pasar de un líquido a un gas. Combustible se vaporiza al calentarse. (13) (15)

Vapor lock Vapor buildup that restricts the flow of gasoline through the fuel system. Vapor lock occurs from heating the fuel, causing it to turn to a vapor. (13) (14)

Tapón de vapor Obstrucción por vapores que restringe el flujo de gasolina por el sistema. Tapón de vapor ocurre porque se ha calentado el combustible, produciendo así un vapor. (13) (14)

Variable displacement engine An engine that is able to change its displacement by using either four or eight cylinders. (8)

Motor de desplazamiento (cilindrada) variable Motor que puede cambiar su cilindrada por medio de usar o cuatro u ocho cilindros. (8)

Variable valve timing A mechanical-hydraulic-electrical system able to change the point at which the valve opens and closes. (10)

Reglaje de las válvulas variable Sistema mecánico-hidráulico-eléctrico que puede cambiar el punto al cual la válvula abre y cierra. (10)

Varnish A deposit in an engine lubrication system resulting from oxidation of the motor oil. Varnish is similar to, but softer than, lacquer. (11)

Barniz Depósito en el sistema de lubricación del motor que resulta de la oxidación del aceite de motor. El barniz es similar a, pero más suave que, la laca. (11)

VAT A voltage amperage tester used for checking the output of a charging system. (21)

"VAT" Analizador de amperaje y voltaje (AAV) que sirve para comprobar el rendimiento de un sistema de carga. (21)

V-configuration A style of engine that has two rows of cylinders that are approximately 90 degrees apart and in a V shape. (8)

Configuración V Diseño del motor que tiene dos filas de cilindros que están separados aproximadamente a 90 grados y tienen una forma de V. (8)

Vehicle Emission Control Information (VECI) Emission control information shown directly on a label on each vehicle (23)

Información de control de emisiones de vehículo (ICEV) Información de control de emisiones indicada directamente en la calcomanía de cada vehículo. (23)

Venturi A restriction in a tube where air or liquid is flowing. A venturi always causes a vacuum to be created at the point of greatest restriction. (15)

"Venturi" Restricción en un tubo donde circula aire o líquido. Un venturi siempre causa la producción de un vacío al punto de la restricción más grande. (15)

Venturi vacuum Vacuum tapped off the carburetor at the venturi. (15)

Vacío venturi Vacío derivado del carburador al punto del venturi. (15)

Vernier caliper A measuring tool used to accurately measure length to 0.001 inch. (4)

Calibre de Nonio (de Vernier) Herramienta de medición que sirve para medir con precisión hasta 0.001 de pulgada. (4)

Vernier scale A scale for measuring in which two lines are adjusted to line up vertically with each other. (4)

Escala Vernier (Nonio) Escala que sirve para medir, en la cual dos líneas se ajustan para alinearse verticalmente una con la otra. (4)

VIN The vehicle identification number, located on the left front of the dashboard, which represents various data such as the model of the vehicle, year, body, style, engine type, and serial number. (5)

"VIN" Número de identificación de vehículo (NIV), situado delante y a la izquierda del panel de controles, el cual representa varios datos tales como el modelo del vehículo, año, carrocería, estilo, tipo de motor, y número de serie. (5)

Viscosity A fluid property that causes resistance to flow. The higher the viscosity, the greater the resistance to flow. The lower the viscosity, the easier for the fluid to flow. (11)

Viscosidad Propiedad de flúido que produce resistencia al flujo. Cuanto más alta la viscosidad, tanto más resistencia haya en el flujo. Cuanto menos sea la viscosidad, tanto más fácil es que fluya el fluido. (11)

Viscosity index A common term used to measure a fluid's change of viscosity with a change in temperature. The higher the viscosity index, the smaller the relative change in viscosity with temperature. (11)

Indice de viscosidad Término común que sirve para medir el cambio en la viscosidad de un flúido con un cambio en la temperatura. Cuanto más alto el índice de viscosidad, tanto más pequeño sea el cambio relativo en viscosidad con temperatura. (11)

Volatility The ease with which a fuel is able to ignite. (13)

Volatilidad Facilidad con la que un combustible puede encenderse. (13)

Voltage The push or pressure used to move electrons along a wire. (18)

Voltaje Fuerza o presión que sirve para empujar a los electrones a lo largo de un alambre. (18)

Voltage drop Voltage lost at each resistor, usually defined as $I \times R$ drop. (18)

Perdida de voltaje Voltaje perdido en cada resistencia, normalmente definido como caída $I \times R$. (18)

Volt-ohm-ammeter Also called a multimeter; a testing instrument able to read voltage, resistance, and amperage in an electrical circuit. (4)

Voltiohmímetro-amperímetro Llamado también un multímetro; instrumento de medición para comprobar que haya voltaje, resistencia, y amperaje en un circuito eléctrico. (4)

Volumetric efficiency A measure of how well air flows in and out of an engine. (7)

Rendimiento volumétrico Medición de la eficiencia del flujo del aire hacia adentro y afuera de un motor. (7)

Vulcanized A process of heating rubber under pressure to mold it into a special shape. (31)

Vulcanizado   Proceso de calentar goma bajo presión para moldearla de una forma especial. (31)

Waste spark   A spark occurring during the exhaust stroke on a computerized ignition system. (19)
Chispa de desecho   Chispa que ocurre en el recorrido de escape en un sistema de encendido computarizado. (19)

Wattage   A measure of the total power of an electrical circuit, calculated by multiplying the voltage in the circuit times the amperage in the circuit. (18)
Wataje (Vataje, Vatiaje)   Medición de la potencia total de un circuito eléctrico, calculada al multiplicar el voltaje en el circuito por el amperaje en el circuito. (18)

Watt's law   Power equals voltage times amperage (P = E × I). (18)
Ley de Watt   Potencia equivale al voltaje multiplicado por el amperaje; (P = E × I). (18)

Waveform   A graphical representation of the voltage output on a charging system. (21)
Forma de onda   Representación gráfica del rendimiento (salida o capacidad) de voltaje en un sistema de carga. (21)

Wedge-shaped combustion chamber   A type of combustion chamber that is shaped similar to a wedge or V. This chamber is designed to increase the movement of air and fuel to aid in mixing. (10)
Cámara de combustión cuneiforme   Tipo de cámara de combustión que tiene una forma similar a la de una cuña o V. Esta cámara es diseñada para aumentar el movimiento de aire y combustible para ayudar a mezclarlos. (10)

Wheel cylinder   A device used to convert hydraulic fluid pressure to mechanical force for brake applications. (28)
Cilindro de rueda   Un aparato que sirve para convertir presión de flúido hidráulico en una fuerza mecánica para aplicaciones de frenos. (28)

Wheel runout   A measure of the out-of-roundness of a wheel or tire. (31)

Falta de redondez de llanta o rueda   Medición de la falta de la redondez verdadera de una llanta o una rueda. (31)

Wheel speed sensor   A sensor on each wheel used to monitor speed for antilock braking systems. (28)
Sensor de velocidad de rueda   Sensor montado en cada rueda, el cual sirve para vigilar la velocidad para sistema de frenos anti-inmovilizadores. (28)

Wheel spindle   The short shaft on the front wheel upon which the wheel bearings ride and to which the wheel is attached. (29)
Muñón de rueda   Eje corto en la rueda delantera sobre el cual los cojinetes de rueda se sientan y al cual está conectada la rueda. (29)

Work   Work is defined as the result of a force applied to a mass, moved a certain distance. Work = Force × Distance. (7)
Trabajo   Se define el trabajo como el resultado de una fuerza aplicada a una masa, movida a cierta distancia. Trabajo = Fuerza × Distancia. (7)

Yoke   The Y-shaped metal device that is attached to the drive shaft. (27)
Yugo   Aparato metálico en forma de una Y, el cual está conectado al eje impulsor (motor). (27)

Zener diode   A type of diode that requires a certain amount of voltage before it will conduct electricity. This voltage is used to control transistors in voltage regulators. (21)
Díodo Zener   Tipo de díodo que requiere una cantidad de voltaje determinada antes de que conduzca electricidad. Este voltaje sirve para controlar transistores en reguladores de voltaje. (21)

Zerk   A lubrication fitting through which grease is applied to a steering joint with a grease gun. (29) (30)
"Zerk"   Conector de lubricación por el cual se aplica grasa a una junta de dirección con un pistola (jeringa) para engrasar. (29) (30)

Index